WHO SANG OUR SONGS?

The Official Rhythm & Blues and Doo-Wop Songography

Douglas E. Friedman
and
Anthony J. Gribin

In collaboration with and a Foreword by Ronnie Italiano
Founder and President of the United In Group Harmony Association

Published by HarmonySongs Publications

Special Edition

Copyright ©2003 by Douglas E. Friedman and Anthony J. Gribin
Published by HarmonySongs Publications, West Long Branch, New Jersey

Library of Congress Control Number: 2001095575

ISBN 0-9713979-0-2

Cover Design by Nicole Ruhl Fichera
Layout by Kate Cattani

Printed by Midstates Printing, Aberdeen SD

*To my father, Bill Friedman, from whom I got my love of music,
and to my mother, Rita Friedman, for teaching me to believe in myself.*

Introduction

Tony Gribin and I have both had a lifelong interest in music, an interest that was, no doubt, instilled in us by our families. Tony's mother, Doris Tauber Gribin, was Irving Berlin's musical secretary and wrote many songs including the standard, "Them There Eyes," that were recorded by artists such as Frank Sinatra, Billie Holiday and Ella Fitzgerald and groups such as the Charioteers, Keystoners and Teenchords. My father, Bill Friedman, played bass with the Ted Weems Orchestra, worked with Ray Bloch (the Ed Sullivan Show's orchestra leader) in New York for many years and wrote songs - with co-writers like Ollie Jones of the Ravens and Julius Dixon (who wrote "Lollipop") - that were recorded by artists such as Louis Jordan, Dean Martin, Slim Gaillard and Herb Kenny & The Rockets.

Some years ago, I found my way to Ronnie I.'s Clifton Music in Clifton, New Jersey. At that time, I was a casual fan of the vocal group music of the 1950s. I had a basic collection of CDs by some of the more popular groups, but somehow I knew there had to be more. As I entered the store, I noticed a small television set playing an old movie in which a black group was singing. There were two other people in the store - one standing behind the counter and another who appeared to be more of a friend than a paying customer. The friend pointed to the screen and asked the man behind the counter (who turned out to be Ronnie I.), "Is that Carl Jones?" Ronnie answered, "No, he joined the group in 1944 and this movie was made in 1943." I knew I was in the right place. (By the way, the group was the Delta Rhythm Boys.) I picked out a few CDs I wanted, then described to Ronnie the extent of my collection and said, "Recommend something that's good and that I do not have." Ronnie did, and with that my (music) life was changed. Thanks to Ronnie and others I have discovered a world of incredible music that I had never before explored.

The reason for putting this book together is simple. Tony and I realized that there was no comprehensive book relating to what we call "The Music," that allowed someone to look up virtually any song, by title, and determine which artists recorded that song. This book contains over 30,000 entries, listed by song title. Very few people who write about this topic make any significant money from their efforts - certainly not an amount that would justify the work. The "why" is simple enough for anyone who loves this music; they do it because they enjoy it and want to contribute to the knowledge about it. We believe this book contains one of the most complete lists of early rhythm and blues and doo-wop songs available and is the only book to list the entries alphabetically by song title. Even so, we are sure there are songs that are missing and we invite people to send us this information, as well as any corrections, in the hope that a second edition will be published.

A number of books contain lists of songs that are invaluable for anyone who collects or has a serious interest in vocal group harmony music. Many of these books were used to track down the information for this book. They include, *The Complete Book of Doo-Wop* by Anthony J. Gribin and Matthew M. Schiff, Krause Publications (2000). This contains an exhaustive discography, alphabetized by group, and covers virtually every group. *The Billboard Book of American Singing Groups - A History 1940-1990* by Jay Warner, Billboard Books (1992), includes discographies only for the major groups, arranged by decade and is indispensable because of its unparalleled treatment of the histories of the groups covered. *The Encyclopedia of Rhythm & Blues and Doo-Wop Vocal Groups* by Mitch Rosalsky, Scarecrow Press (2000) has entries for over 1,000 groups with a discography and biographical information for each, as well as an index to group members. *45 RPM Group Collector's Record Label Guide* by Jeff Kreiter (1995), is organized alphabetically by label, while both *A Discography of Rhythm & Blues And Rock 'N' Roll Vocal Groups 1945 to 1965* by Robert D. Ferlingere, Hayward, California, California Trade School (1976), and

Disco-File: The Discographical Catalog of American Rock & Roll and Rhythm & Blues Vocal Groups by Fernando L. Gonzalez (1977) are alphabetized by group. Unlike the books by Warner and Rosalsky, the group entries in these works contain no annotated information about the artists.

What has not been done, and what *Who Sang Our Songs* attempts to do, is provide both collectors and the average fan with a complete listing, alphabetized by song. Entries are in the book the way they were listed in the data from which they were taken. For example, the song "Over The Rainbow" is also found under "Somewhere Over The Rainbow" for those recordings which showed the latter as the title, even though the former title is correct.

Because of the tremendous influence that the United In Group Harmony Association (UGHA), and more particularly, its President and Founder, Ronnie Italiano, have had on the preservation of this music and on us as well, we decided to donate all of the profits from this book to the organization. UGHA is a nonprofit, tax-exempt, member supported organization dedicated to the preservation of, exposure to and education about American pioneer vocal group music. UGHA can be reached at P.O. Box 185, Clifton, New Jersey 07011 or at www.UGHA.org on the web. We encourage you to join and help in the effort to preserve this great music. Ronnie I., as he is universally known, worked with us and contributed significantly to the final product.

We thank our wives, Linda Lashbrook and Gloria Gribin, families (especially my brother Ken) and friends for their encouragement and assistance. Thank you also to two very talented people, Jim Kaplun who did the design for the book, and Kate Cattani, who did the layout.

Douglas E. Friedman
August 2003

Foreword
By Ronnie Italiano

Who Sang Our Songs? is a phenomenal and obviously astronomical undertaking, and the result is an invaluable reference book focused entirely on group recordings, primarily from the 1950s and 1960s. It's an alphabetical song-by-song view of this music, fully loaded with engaging and thought provoking facts, compiled into one book. It's a book that just can't help but create new perspectives in the study of the musical art form of vocal groups—music which is often overlooked, yet vital to the development of popular music, not only of the eras covered in this reference book, but of the popular music styles of today.

Who Sang Our Songs? provides answers and valuable insight to such questions as,

* Who had the earlier up-tempo version of *A Sunday Kind of Love* – the Sentimentals or the Dell Vikings?
* How many recordings had the name Gloria in their titles besides the multiple versions of the Cadillacs classic??
* How many renditions of *Life Is But A Dream* – aside from the Harptones recording – can you name??
* Did you know that the Swallows recorded an R&B version of *I Only Have Eyes For You*—seven years before the Flamingos hit was released?!
* Did you know the Moonglows' first big hit for the Chess Label in 1954, *Sincerely*, was subsequently covered by numerous artists, and then re-recorded by the Moonglows for RCA Victor in 1972 – an effort to capitalize on the beaded string of hits of that song begun by the Moonglows themselves!!?
* Did you know many of the Orioles' recordings on Jubilee during the late 1940s and early 50s were re-recorded for the CP Parker label in the early 60s?? Yep, they were! And listen to this: With Sonny Til on lead, and Gerald Gregory from the Spaniels singing bass on most…who knew???

All this and much more answered in a comprehensive, easy-to-follow, alphabetical, song-by-song reference book! A must-have for the historian, record collector, novice, or anyone else who appreciates vocal group recordings!

This has been a tremendous undertaking by Tony and Doug that has entailed countless hours of research and questioning. The results are evidence of a passion felt by both authors for vocal harmony music. This project is an ongoing effort because as additional information, necessary revisions and updated facts become known, it is hoped that future editions can be issued.

The authors are long-time UGHA members and ardent supporters. The impetus for this project was to provide information and to give something back to the music by having their effort act as a fund raiser to help sustain the nonprofit, tax-exempt organization, UGHA, formed in 1976 to aid in the quest for preservation of and exposure to this great American art form. The entire world-wide organization of over 2000 members extends a heartfelt "thank you" to them.

SONG	GROUP	YEAR	LABEL
A			
A Ballad Of Jed Clampett	Ebb Tides, Nino & the	1962	R&R 303
A Basketful Of Blueberries	Madhattans	1957	Atlantic 1142
A Beggar For Your Kisses	Diamonds (Harold Sonny Wright)	1952	Atlantic 981
A Beggar With A Dream	Five Satins	1960	Cub 9077
A Bench In The Park	Jive Five	1967	United Artists 936
A Big Bite Of The Blues	Captans, Jerry Holland & the	1959	DC 0433
A Bird And A Bee	Colognes	1959	Lummtone 102
A Bird Flies Out Of Sight	Tokens (Brooklyn)	1962	RCA 8114
A Blast From The Past	Farrer, Tony & group	1961	Trans Atlas 001
A Blessing To You	Symphonics, Freddie Scott & the	1959	Enrica 1002
A Bottle Of Pop And A Lollypop	Lollypoppers	1955	Aladdin 3291
A Boy, A Girl And A Dream	Visuals	1963	Poplar 117
A Boy And A Girl	Hollywood Teeners, Jimmy Norman & the	1960	Fun 101
A Boy In Love	Four Graduates	1964	Rust 5084
A Boy Without A Girl	Tokens (Brooklyn)	NA	RCA LP 2631
A Boyfriend's Prayer	Monitors	1958	Circus 219
A Broken Heart	Medallions	1957	Singular 1002
A Broken Promise	Montclairs	1960	Audicon 111
A Castle In The Sky	Royaltones	NA	Old Town (unreleased)
A Casual Kiss	Blue Jays (Venice, Calif.)	1987	Relic LP 5064
A Casual Kiss	Hollywood Saxons	Mid to late 1950s	Early 1980s on EP; originally unreleased
A Casual Kiss	Peels, Leon	1964	Whirlybird 2002
A Casual Look	Darlin, Chris & group	1961	Dore 578
A Casual Look	Six Teens	1956	Flip 315
A Casual Look	Teens, Little Clydie & the	1956	RPM 462
A Certain Kind Of Love	Laddins	1960	Isle (unreleased)
A Certain Smile	Sparks, Milton & group	1958	Vulcan/Hunt 320 (58)
A Cheat's A Cheat	Day, Dawn & Dusk	1955	Kent 519
A Chicken Ain't Nothin' But A Bird	Echoes	1962	Smash 1766
A Christmas Long Ago	Echelons	1987, 1991	BAB 129, 132
A Christmas Prayer	Penguins	1955	Mercury 70762
A Christmas Prayer	Valentines	1955	Rama 186
A Cottage For Sale	Sultans	1961	Knowles 105
A Crowded Room	Montereys (Major)	1959	Major 1009
A Crush On You	Cineemas	1963	Dave 911
A Cuddle And A Kiss	Sparks	1957	Decca 30509
A Dagger In My Chest	Gardner, Don & group	1957	DeLuxe 6133
A Dear John Letter	Four Horsemen	1953	MGM 11566
A Distant Love	Dells	1957	Vee Jay 251
A Door That Is Open	Johnson, Kripp & group	1959	Mercury 71486
A Dream And A Prayer	Melodettes, Norman Dunlap with the	1953	Aladdin 3213
A Dream Can Come True	Elegants	1963	Photo 2662
A Dream Come True	Squires (California)	1954	Kicks 1
A Dream In The Night	Plush Pups, Terrie Parker & the	1961	Queen 24011
A Dream Is But A Dream	Chesterfields	1962	Onyx 40083
A Dream Of Love	Nutmegs	1960	Tel 1014
A Dreamer	Five Keys	1973	Owl 321
A Faded Memory	Chimes (Tennessee)	1957	Arrow 726
A Fallen Tear	El Dorados	1956	Vee Jay 197
A Fallen Tear	Marcels	1975	Monogram 112
A Falling Star	Robins, Maggie Hathaway & the	1951	Recorded In Hollywood 121
A Falling Tear	Knights, Mary Wheeler & the	NA	Atom 701
A Fellow Needs A Girl	Crescendos (Domain)	1963	Domain 1025
A Fellow Needs A Girl	Newports	1961	Kane 008/Guyden 2067
A Fine Fine Boy	Love, Darlene & group	1963	Philles 117
A Fool	Ballads (Klik)	1972	Klik 1021
A Fool	Obsessions	1964	Accent 1182
A Fool	Teardrops	NA	Unreleased
A Fool In Love	Carnations, Ray Allen & the	1959	Ace 130
A Fool In Love	Concords, Sue Kenny & the	1963	Tribute 118
A Fool In Love	Consorts	NA	Clifton EP 501
A Fool In Love	Cordials	1961	Stan 111
A Fool In Love	Keytones	1957	Old Town 1041 (first pressing)

SONG	GROUP	YEAR	LABEL
A Fool In Love	Regents	1961	Gee LP 706
A Fool In Love	Robins	1957	Whippet 206
A Fool In Paradise	Jewels (Los Angeles)	1954	R&B 1303
A Fool No More	Mannish Boys, Eddie Hope & the	1956	Marlin 804
A Fool Such As I	Robins	1952	RCA 5175
A Fool That Was Blind	Jumpers, Jay Nelson & the	1959	Excello 2149
A Fool Was I	Chimes (Royal Roost)	1954	Royal Roost 577
A Fool Was I	Savage, Al & group	1957	Herald 505
A Fool Was I	Vel-Tones	1959	Collectables LP 5037
A Foolish Fool	Zephyrs, Ben Joe Zeppa & the	1956	Specialty 577
A Fool's Fortune	Cuff Links	1958	Dooto 434
A Fools Memory	Shaw, Ricky & group	1962	President 822
A Fool's Prayer	Crowns, Arthur Lee Maye & the	1957	Dig 133
A Friend	Mello-Tones, Nat Williams & the	1959	Aries 1014
A Friend (acappella)	Vibraharps	1975	Relic LP 108
A Funny Feeling	Belmonts, Dion & the	1960	Laurie 3059
A Funny Thing Happened	Stevens, Jimmy (with the Safaris)	1963	Valiant 6033
A G.I. Wish	Ecstasies	1984	Clifton EP 508
A Gal Named Jo	Miracles (Cash)	1955	Cash 1008
A Girl Called Love	Bumble Bees	1963	Joey 6220
A Girl Has To Know	G-Clefs	1962	Terrace 7503
A Girl I Love	Crystal Tones	1959	MZ 007/008/Zebra
A Girl I Marry	Camerons	1961	Cousins 1003/Felsted 8638 (61)
A Girl Like You	Feathers, Johnny Staton & the	1991	Classic Artists 125
A Girl Like You	Ivy League	1965	Cameo 365
A Girl Like You	Robbins, Eddie & group	1958	Power 214/Dot 15702 (58)
A Girl Named Arlene	Del Satins	1965	B.T. Puppy 509
A Girl Named Arlene	Tokens (Brooklyn)	1964, 1969	B.T. Puppy 500/Music Makers 110
A Girl Named Joe	Esquires	1956	Meteor 5022
A Girl Named Marie	Three Dolls, Larry Stevens & the	1960	Epic 9358
A Girl To Call My Own	Avons	1963	Hull 754
A Girl To Love	Chordcats	1954	Cat 112
A Girl Without A Fella	Bon Bons	1956	Columbia 40800
A Golden Tear	Vocaleers	1962	Twistime 11
A Good Woman	Blue Notes, Harold Melvin & the	1960	Val-Ue 213/Red Top 135 (63)
A Guy Is A Guy	Girlfriends, Erlene & the	1963	Old Town 1150
A Happier Time	Wizards	1982	C&J 22650
A Happy Guy	Ebb Tides, Nino & the	1961	Mr. Peacock 102
A Hard Day's Night	Jalopy Five	1966	Hit 134
A Heart Is A Toy	Stevens, Carol Ann & group	1961	Carol 4111
A Henpecked Guy	Reflections	1964	Golden World 16
A Hug and A Kiss	Moonlighters, Bobby Lester & the	1955	Checker 813
A Hum Diddily Dee Do	Capris (New York)	NA	Collectables LP 5016
A Hundred Million Lies	Dynamics	1957	Warner 1016
A Hundred Pounds Of Clay	Laddins	1974	Relic LP 5018
A Hundred Pounds Of Clay	Rubber Biscuits	1986	Starlight 35
A Hundred Wailin' Cats	Accents (Brooklyn)	1962	Jive 888/Vee Jay 484 (62)
A In Love	Adrian, Lee (with the Chaperones)	1962	SMC 1386
A Junior At The Senior Prom	Verity, Lady Jane &	1959	Palette 5031
A Kid In His Teens	Collegiates	1960	RD Globe 009
A Killer Comes To Town	Vibes	1961	Rayna 103
A King For Tonight	Darvell, Barry & group	1962	Atlantic 2138
A King Without A Crown	Neptunes	1964	Marlo 1534
A Kiss And A Rose	Admirations (featuring Joseph Lorello)	NA	N/A
A Kiss And A Rose	Orioles, Sonny Til & the	1949	Jubilee 5009
A Kiss And A Vow	Nitecaps	1955	Groove 0134
A Kiss From Your Lips	Five Boroughs	1990	Classic Artists 122
A Kiss From Your Lips	Flamingos	1956	Checker 837
A Kiss From Your Lips	Originals	1960	Brunswick 55171
A Kiss From Your Lips	Storm, Billy (with the Drifters)	1961	Atlantic 2112
A Kiss From Your Lips	Valentinos	1960	Brunswick 55171
A Kiss Goodbye	Click-Clacks	1958	Algonquin 714
A Kiss Is A Kiss	Rockin' Chairs	1959	Recorte 402
A Kiss Is Not A Kiss	Classmates	1955	King 1487
A Kissin' Friend	Masters, Rick & the	1962	Haral 778

SONG	GROUP	YEAR	LABEL
A Letter From Anne	Videls	1961	Kapp 405
A Letter From Vietnam	Elegants	1965	Laurie 3283
A Letter Full Of Tears	Maddox, Walt and the Marcels	1982	Super M 203073
A Letter To A School Girl	Delacardos	1959, 1963	Elgey 1001
A Letter To My Girl	Dreams	1954	Savoy 1130
A Lifetime From Today	Jackaels, J. J. Jackson & the	1959	Storm 501
A Little Bird	Hollywood Flames	1958	Ebb 131
A Little Bird Told Me	Robins	1958	Knight 2008
A Little Bit	New Yorkers (Fred Parris)	1961	Wall 548
A Little Bit Now	Majors (Philadelphia)	1962	Imperial 5879
A Little Bit Of Blue	Companions	1962	Columbia 42279
A Little Bit Of Everything	Lavenders, Ernie Morales & the	1977	Crystal Ball 100
A Little Bit Of Love	Quails, Bill Robinson & the	1954	DeLuxe 6057
A Little Bit Of Soap	Four Locks	NA	Uptown 761
A Little Bit Of Soap	Jarmels	1961	Laurie 3098
A Little Bit Of Soap	Legacy	1988	Crystal Ball 153
A Little Less Talk	Glens	1961	Laitini 6666
A Little Lie	Dominoes	1954	King 1342
A Little Love From You Will Do	Fallen Angels	1966	Laurie 3343
A Little Lovin'	Larson, Key & group	1961	Lawn 106
A Little More Love	Chordells, Little Chips & the	1961	Hull 746
A Little More Wine, My Dear	Hawks	1958	Del-Fi 4108
A Little Prayer	Six Teens	1960	Flip 351
A Little Rain Must Fall	Del Satins (with Carl Parker)	1967	Diamond 216
A Little Romance	Laurels	1982	Alexis 6873
A Little Tear	Anglos, Linda Martell & the	1962	Fire 512
A Little Too Long	Debonaires (Golden World)	1964	Golden World 17
A Little Too Long	Wanderers	1961	Cub 9094
A Little White Gardenia	Demensions	1963	Coral 62392
A Little Wiser Now	Teenagers	1960	End 1076
A Lonely Boy	Four Eldorados	1958	Academy 8138
A Lonely Fool	Clovers	1956	Atlantic 1118
A Lonely Heart	Dovers	1962	Valentine 1000
A Lonely Island	Lovers, Pete Peter & the	1960	Derby 1030
A Lonely Man's Prayer	Bleu Lights	1968	Bay Sound 67007
A Long Long Time	Four Horsemen	1958	United Artists 134
A Long Time Ago	Candles, Rochell & the	1961	Swingin' 652
A Long Time Ago	Impressions, Jerry Butler & the	1976	Vee Jay LP 1075
A Looka Here	Cadillacs	1958	Josie 836
A Love For Only You	Stereos	1959	Gibraltar 105
A Love I Had	Kingtones	1962	Kitoco/Drummond 105 (65)
A Love In My Heart	Royals	1952	Federal 12098
A Love Like Ours	Lovenotes	1957	Premium 411
A Love Like You	Griffin, Jimmy & female group	1954	Dot 15223
A Love Like Yours	True Loves	1957	Premium 611
A Love Of My Own	Capris (New York)	1982	Ambient Sound LP FZ-37714
A Love Of My Own	Jay Birds, Vinnie Monte & the	1958	Decanter 101
A Love Of My Own	Kings (Baltimore)	NA	Georgie 101
A Love Only You Can Give	Universals (Shepherd)	1962	Shepherd 2200
A Love So Fine	Chiffons	1963	Laurie 3159
A Love So Fine	Delighters, Little ìDî & the	1958	Little D Records 1010
A Love So True	Nutmegs	1956	Herald 492
A Love So True	Shy Guys	1966	Palmer 5008
A Love Such As You	Tones	1962	Elmar 6001
A Love That Can Never Be	Satintones	1960, 1961	Motown 1006
(versions with and without strings)			
A Love That's True	Four Fellows, Bette McLaurin & the	1955	Glory 237
A Love To Last A Lifetime	Crests	1964	Coral 62403
A Lovely One	Speidels	1960	Monte Carlo 101
A Lovely Relationship	Fulton, Sonny & group	1959	Lash 1127
(A Lovely) Summer Night	Tiffanys, Cindy Gibson & the	NA	General 700
A Lovely Way To Spend An Evening	Angels (with Sonny Gordon)	1955	Grand 121
A Lovely Way To Spend An Evening	Caprisians	1960	Indigo 109
A Lovely Way To Spend An Evening	Clouds	NA	Vons 1000
A Lovely Way To Spend An Evening	Four-Evers	1966	Columbia 43886

SONG	GROUP	YEAR	LABEL
A Lovely Way To Spend An Evening	Imperials, Little Anthony & the	1961	End 1104
A Lovely Way To Spend An Evening	Masters	1960	Bingo 1008
A Lovely Way To Spend An Evening	Roommates	1962	Cameo 233
A Lovely Way To Spend An Evening	Run-A-Rounds	NA	Unreleased
A Lovely Way To Spend An Evening (acappella)	Nacks, Nicky & the	1975	Relic LP 103
A Lover	Jeanettes, Gene & the	1963	Fortune 565
A Lover Is A Fool	Coralairs, T. Renaldi & the	1958	Bee 1543
A Lover Of The Time	Leaders	1955	Glory 235
A Lover's Answer	Dreamtones	1959	Astra 551
A Lovers Call (acappella)	Heartaches, Jo Ann & the	1966	Catamount 114
A Lover's Chant	Miracles (Baton)	1955	Baton 210
A Lover's Plea	Doug & Freddy (with the Pyramids)	1959	Rendezvous 111
A Lover's Plea	Moon Beams	1959	Grate 100
A Lover's Poem (To Her)	Angels (Safaris)	1959	Tawny 101
A Lover's Poem (To Him)	Angels (Safaris)	1959	Tawny 101
A Lovers Prayer	Belmonts, Dion & the	1959, 1961	Laurie 3035/LP 2006
A Lover's Prayer	Belmonts, Dion & the	1959	Laurie 3035
A Lover's Prayer	Carvettes	1959	Copa 200-1/200-2
A Lover's Prayer	Delteens	1958	Vee Jay 303
A Lover's Prayer	Galaxys	1959	Carthay 103
A Lover's Prayer	Medallions, Vernon Green & the	1957	Dooto 425
A Lover's Quarrel	Shy-Tones	1960	1 Goodspin 401/Bruce
A Lover's Question	McPhatter, Clyde (with the Cookies & the Cues)	1958	Atlantic 1199
A Magic Island	Blue Jays (Venice, Calif.)	1987	Relic LP 5064
A Magic Island	Hi Tensions, Leon Peels & the	1964	Whirlybird 2008
A Man	Co-Eds	1959	Dwain 802
A Man And A Woman	Four Students, Big John Greer & the	1955	Groove 0131
A Man Goin' Crazy	Love Bugs	1955	Federal 12216
A Man Is Not Supposed To Cry	Masters	1961	End 1100
A Man Should Never Cry	Pretenders, James Moore & the	1964	Tishman 905
A Mans Confusion	Technics	1962	Chex 1012
A Man's Glory	Drivers	1960	Lin 1002
A Meeting Of The Eyes	Del Vikings	1958	B.T. Puppy 507/Mercury LP 3053
A Message To The World	Tokens (Brooklyn)	1965, 1966	B.T. Puppy 516
A Million And One Dreams	Bel-Larks	1963	Hammer 6313/Ransom 5001
A Million Heartaches Ago	Mann, Billy & group	1956	Dig 120
A Million Miles From Nowhere	Echoes	1963	Smash 1807
A Million Miles To Paradise	Superbs	1966	Dore 755
A Million Reasons	Emotions	1963	Kapp 513
A Million Teardrops	Bachelors (National)	1957	National 104
A Million Teardrops	Beasley, Billy & group	NA	Dee Cal 500
A Million Tears	Five Sparks	1959	Jimbo 1
A Million Tears	McCleese, James & group	1961	Marco 106
A Million To One	Five Satins	1957	Ember 1028
A Million To One	Portraits	1967	Sidewalk 928
A Million To One	Revelletts, Jimmy Charles & the	1960	Promo 1002
A Million Years	Visions, Connie McGill & the	1963	Toy 107/Sugar 502
A Million Years Ago	Mello-Maids	1957	Baton 238
A Moment Ago	Angels (New Jersey)	1961, 1962	Caprice 107/121
A Most Unusual Boy	Shirelles, Shirley & the	1969	Bell 760
A Moth Around A Flame	Soft Tones	1955	Samson 103
A Mother's Love	Consorts	NA	Clifton EP 501
A Mother's Love	Five Swans	1956	Music City (unreleased)
A New Dancin' Partner	Olympics	1963	Tri Disc 110
A New Feeling	Rookies, Joe Perkins & the	1957	King 5030
A New World	Do-Reys	1956	Joy 2401
A Night At Daddy Gee's	Lee, Curtis (with the Halos)	1962	Dunes 2012
A Night Like This	Five Satins	1960	Ember 1061
A Night Like Tonight	Hearts, Lee Andrews & the (as Lee Andrews)	1961	Swan 4076
A Night To Remember	Five Satins	1958	Ember 1038
A Night To Remember	Rivieras	1958	Algonquin 718 (first pressing, second is by the Ravenaires)
A 1950s Love Song	Autumns, Joel & the	1979	BAB 128

SONG	GROUP	YEAR	LABEL
A Part Of Me	Spellbounds, Johnny Adams & the	1963	Watch 6333
A Penny For Your Thoughts	Q's, Bruce Clark & the	1964	Hull 762
A Penny For Your Thoughts	Three Pennies	1964	B.T. Puppy 501
A Picture Of You	Danleers	1959	Mercury 71401
A Picture Of You	Elgins	1958	MGM 12670
A Place Called Happiness	Blue Belles	1961	20th Fox 249
A Place Called Love	Roomates	NA	Ban 691
A Place For You (In My Heart)	Preludes	1962	Octavia 8008
A Place In My Heart	Milner, Jimmy & group	1959	Ember 1052
A Place In My Heart	Peppers	1961	Ensign 1076
A Place In My Heart	Videls	1959	Rhody 2000/Medieval 203 (61)
A Place In Your Heart	Encounters	1965	Swan 4205
A Place In Your Heart	Joey & group	1962	Taurus 353
A Plan For Love	Sierras	1963	Cham 101/Dot 16569 (63)
A Pledge Of A Fool	Bears	NA	N/A
A Possibility	Twilighters	1960	Spin 0001
A Prayer	Teardrops	NA	Unreleased
A Prayer And A Juke Box	Imperials, Little Anthony & the	1959	End 1047
A Prayer At Gettysburg	Velvitones	1959	Milmart 113
A Prayer Of Love	Bridges, Curley & group	1960	DC 0436
A Prisoner's Prayer	Prisonaires	1953	Sun 191
A Prom And A Promise	Buddies	1957	Decca 30355
A Prom And A Promise	Velairs	1958	MGM 12667
A Real Sensation	Angels (Hi Tensions)	1960	Audio 203/Milestone
A Ring Around A Chain	Cruisers	1958	Era 1052
A Ring Around A Chain	Scooters	1958	Era 1065
A River Flows	Colognes	1959	Lummtone 102
A Rockin' Good Way	Bowman, Priscilla (with the Spaniels)	1958	Abner 1018
A Rose And A Baby Ruth	Crests	1960	Coed LP 901
A Rose By Any Other Name	Drifters (1959-forward)	1971	Atlantic 2786
A Rose For My Darling	El Dorados	1957	Vee Jay 250
A Rose Growing In The Ruins	Rivingtons	1966	Columbia 43581
A Sad Goodbye	Four Exceptions	1966	Parkway
A Sad Guitar	Bell Notes	1959	Time EP 100
A Sad Sad Story	Vanangos	1975	Monogram 110
A Scandal	Orioles, Sonny Til & the	1952	Jubilee (unreleased)
A School Girl In Love	Sharmeers	1958, 1974	Red Top 109
A Short Prayer	Imperials, Little Anthony & the	1962	Newtime 503
A Shot Of Love	Viriations	1968	Amy 11006
A Simple Prayer	Ravens	1956	Argo 5261
A Sinner In Love	Serenades	1957	Chief 7002
A Slow Dance	Hi-Lites, Ronnie & the	1963	Win 250/Reo
A Small Silver Ring	Vandells	1964	USA 758
A Smile On My Face, A Tear In Your Eye	Hammel Jr., Karl & group	1961	Arliss 1011
A Smile Upside Down	Secrets	1966	Red Bird 10-076
A Soldier's Prayer	Marshalls, Bill Cook & the	1951	Savoy 828
A Spark Met A Flame	Dimples, Eddie Cooley & the	1957, 1960	Royal Roost 626/Roulette 4272
A Special Love	Upstarts, Don Dell & the	1962	East Coast 105/106
A Spoken Letter	Lonely Boys	1959	NuWay 555
A Star	Avalons	1987	Relic LP 5072
A Star	Five Crowns	1952	Rainbow 179
A Star	Keynotes	1955	Apollo 484
A Star	Taylortones	1961	Star Maker 1926
A Star	Tones, W. Williams & the	NA	Kennedy 5146
A Star Fell	Hollywood Flames	1958	Ebb 149
A Story Of Love	Starlighters	1960	End 1072
A Story Of Love (acappella)	Horizons	1975	Relic LP 104
A Story Untold	Emotions	1963	20th Fox 430
A Story Untold	Madara, Johnny & group	1961	Bamboo 511
A Stranger In Love	Spaniels	1958	Charly LP 1114 (86)
A Summer Place	Classmates	1963	Felsted 8673
A Sunday Kind Of Love	Blue Moons	NA	Jaguar 1001
A Sunday Kind Of Love	Dell Vikings	1957	Mercury 30112
A Sunday Kind Of Love	Devotions	1964	Roulette 4556
A Sunday Kind Of Love	Earls	1975	Harvey 100

SONG	GROUP	YEAR	LABEL
A Sunday Kind Of Love	Harptones	1953, 1962	Bruce 101/Relic 1022 (73)/ Raven 8001
A Sunday Kind Of Love	Heard, Lonnie (with the Halos)	1961	Arliss 1008
A Sunday Kind Of Love	Mystics	1961	Laurie 3104
A Sunday Morning Love	Chariots	1959	Time 1006/Brent
A Sunday School Romance	Keynotes	1959	Bell-O-Tonic 001
A Sure Thing	Poets	NA	Symbol 216
A Surprise From Outer Space	Five Crowns	1959	De'Besth 1122
A Talk To Mother	Desires	NA	Hull (unreleased)
A Tear And A Smile	Romeos	NA	Mark II 103
A Tear Fell	Colleagues	1961	Glodus 1651
A Tear Fell	Demensions	1960	Mohawk 123
A Tear Fell From My Eyes	Daylights	1963	Propulsion 601
A Tear In My Eye	Blair, Ronnie & group	1961	Crest 1084
A Teardrop (acappella)	Chessmen	1975	Relic LP 102
A Teardrop And A Lollipop	Shirelles	1959	Scepter 1205
A Teardrop Falls	Mello-Chords	NA	Palm 5000
A Teardrop Fell From My Eyes (acappella)	Chessmen	1975	Relic LP 106
A Teardrop From Heaven	Diablos, Nolan Strong & the	1956	Fortune 522
A Teenage Love Affair	Walker, Wayne & group	1957	Columbia 40905
A Teenage Memory	Leisure Lads	1959	Delco 801
A Teenage Quarrel	Wanderers	1958	Orbit 9003/Cub 9003 (58)
A Teenager In Love	Belmonts, Dion & the	1959	Laurie 3027
A Teenager In Love	Tags, Johnny Newton & the	1959	Bell 114
A Teenager's First Love	Click-Ettes	1958	Dice 83/84
A Thief	Juniors, Danny & the	1958	ABC 9953
A Thief In The Night	Tempos	1964	U.S.A. 810
A Thing Of The Past	Shirelles	1961	Scepter 1220
A Thing Worth Remembering	Dardenelles	1960	Pennington 108
A Thousand Dreams	Hendricks, Bobby (with the Coasters)	1958	Sue 706
A Thousand Miles Away	Arrows, Big Bo & the	1964	Checker 1068
A Thousand Miles Away	Blends	1960	Casa Grande 5000
A Thousand Miles Away	Channels, Earl Lewis & the	1974	Channel 1006
A Thousand Miles Away	Cheques	1969	Sur-Speed 214
A Thousand Miles Away	Day Brothers	1960	Chancellor 1059
A Thousand Miles Away	Diamonds	1956	Mercury 71021
A Thousand Miles Away	Dymensions, Joel & the	1991	Classic Artists 130
A Thousand Miles Away	Four Crickets	1956	Tops 702
A Thousand Miles Away	Heartbeats	1956	Hull 720/Rama 216 (57)
A Thousand Miles Away	Heartspinners, Dino & the	NA	Robin Hood 142
A Thousand Miles Away	Juniors, Danny & the	1960	Swan 4060
A Thousand Miles Away	Reed, Johnny & group	1958	Major 100
A Thousand Miles Away	Tokens (Brooklyn)	NA	RCA LP 3685
A Thousand Stars	Chants	1959	Big Moment 102
A Thousand Stars	Innocents, Kathy Young & the	1960	Indigo 108/Port 3025 (60)
A Thousand Stars	Rivileers, Gene Pearson & the	1954, 1957	Baton 200/Baton 241/Dark 241
A Thousand Times Every Day	Aladdins	NA	Duplex 9012
A Thousand Years From Today	Hearts (Bronx, N.Y.)	1956	J&S 995/Zells 3377 (63)
A Thrill	Rubies, Jewell & the	1963	La Louisianne 8041/ABC 10485 (63)
A Tiger In Your Tank	Chariots	1964	RSVP 1105
A Time And A Place	Empires (Jay Black)	1962	Epic 9527
A Time For Love	Ecstasies	1962	Amy 853
A Time For Us	Fireflies	1967	Taurus 380
A Time To Love	Markeys	1958	RCA 7412
A Time To Love And A Time To Lie	Blendaires, Bobby Carle & the	1958	Decca 30699
A Toast To Your Birthday	Shells	1962	Johnson 120
A Token Of Love	Tokens (Brooklyn)	1962	RCA 8052
A Tribute To The Beach Boys '76	Sands Of Time (Tokens)	1976	Kirshner 4263
A Very Precious Love	Pretenders	1976	Power-Martin 1006/1007
A Very Special Birthday	Cashmeres (Brooklyn)	1961	Laurie 3078
A Victim Of Her Charms	Corvairs	NA	Sylvia 5003
A Vision	Equadors	1958	RCA EP 4286
A Walkin' Miracle	Essex	1963	Roulette 4515
A Way To Love You	Volumes	1967	Inferno 2001
A Way To Tell Her	Nobles, Nicky & the	1958	End 1021

SONG	GROUP	YEAR	LABEL
A Week From Sunday	Ebb Tides, Nino & the	1963	Mr. Peeke 123
A Week From Sunday	Nolan, Miss Frankie (with Nino & the Ebbtides)	1961	Madison 151
A Whole Lot Of Lovin'	Higgins, Ben (with the Five Satins)	1962	Jamie 1217
A Wing And A Prayer	Carnations	1960	University 606
A Wink And A Grin	Incas	1977	Monogram 126
A Winner Never Quits	Elgins (California)	1963	Lummtone 109
A Winner Never Quits	Midnighters, Hank Ballard & the	1964	King 5954
A Wise Man Said	Hearts, Lee Andrews & the, as Lee Andrews)	1960	Jordan 121
A Woman, A Man	Valdoros	1957	Silhouette 517
A Woman Like You	La Rays	1963	Arlen 517
A Woman's Love	Royal Dukes, Don Ellis & the	1960	Bee 201
A Wonderful Day	Dee Cals	1959	Co-Ed 1960/Mayhams 1960 (61)
A Wonderful Dream	Majors (Philadelphia)	1962	Imperial 5855
A Wonderful Thing	Rockmasters	1963	One-Derful 4820
A World Without Love	Angels (New Jersey)	1964	Smash 1931
A Year Ago Tonight	Crests	1959	Coed 521
A Year And A Day	Barons (New York)	1954	Decca 48323
A You're Adorable	Tokens (Brooklyn)	NA	RCA LP 3685
A-1 In My Heart	Spiders	1956	Imperial 5393
ABC-1-2-3	Tokens (Brooklyn)	1963	RCA 8210
ABC's Of Love	Friends, Junior & His	1960	ABC 10089
ABC's Of Love	Reality	1979	U.G.H.A. 13
ABC's Of Love	Saints	1984	Angela 104
ABC's Of Love	Teenagers, Frankie Lymon & the	1956	Gee 1022
ABC's Of Love, The	Nacks, Nicky & the	1977	Crystal Ball 103
ABC's Of Love, The	Persuasions	1978	King Tut 171
Abide (By The Golden Rule)	Hearts, Lee Andrews & the	NA	Collectables LP 5003
Abigail	Embers	1961	Empress 107
About A Quarter To Nine	Jumping Jacks	1956	Capitol 3415
About That Girl Named Lou	Cadillacs	1957	Josie 812
Above Jacob's Ladder	Dominoes	1954	Federal 12193
Absent Minded	Celebritys	1956	Caroline 2302
Absolutely Right	Jaytones	1960	Cub 9057
Academy Award	Blue Belles, Patti LaBelle & the	1962	Newtown 5019
Acapulco Run	Ascots	1963	Dual-Tone 1120
Accentuate The Positive	Belmonts	1963	Sabina 509
Accept Me For What I Am	Medallions, Vernon Green & the	1988	Classic Artists 103
Ace Of Hearts	Matadors	1963	Colpix 698
Aces Up	Dynamics	1959	Guaranteed 201
Aching For You	Carmelettes	1960	Alpine 61
Across The Street From Your House	Clinton, Buddy & group	1959	Time 1016
Actor, The	Crests	1962	Trans Atlas 696
Actor, The	Dovells	1962	Parkway 838
Actor, The	Essentials, Billy & the	1965	Cameo 344
Acts Of Love	Raiders, Joey Vel & the	1962	Promo Rel 102
Adam And Eve	Darvell, Barry & group	1962	Atlantic 2138
Adam And Eve	Mystics	1959	Laurie 3028
Addio Maria	Romancers	1961	Medieval 202/Palette 5075 (61)
Adios	Five Discs	1961	Calo 202
Adios (acappella)	Holidays	1975	Relic LP 102
Adios, Adios	Blue Chips	1961	RCA 7935
Adios My Desert Love	Diablos (featuring Nolan Strong)	1954	Fortune 509/510
Adios My Desert Love	Magnatones	1963	Fortune 555
Adios My Love	Locomotions	1962	Gone 5142
Adios, My Love	Serenaders (New Jersey)	1963	Riverside 4549
Adios, My Love (acappella)	Spirals	1975	Relic LP 108
Adios, My Pretty Baby	Four Wheels, Nick Therry & the	1956	Spin-It 108
Adios My Secret Love	Delighters, Donald & the	1963	Cortland 112
Adorable	Colts	1955	Vita 112/Mambo 112 (55)
Adorable	Drifters (Pre-1959)	1955	Atlantic 1078
Adorable	Ecstasies	1986	Clifton 78
Adreann	Sparks	1957	Hull 724
Adventure	McQuinn, Kevin & group	1962	Diamond 109
Advertising For Love	Voice Masters	1959	Anna 103

SONG	GROUP	YEAR	LABEL
Afar Into The Night	Six Teens	1956	Flip 317
Afraid	Four Sounds	1957	Celeste 3010
Afraid	Pictures, C.L. & the	1962	Dunes 2017
Afraid Of Love	Crests	1965	Scepter 12112
Afraid Of Love	Statues, Gary Miles & the	1960	Liberty 55261
African Cha Cha	Five Notes, Sammy & the	1960	Lucky Four 1010
African Twist	Elads	NA	Unreleased
After	Bachelors (Washington, D.C.)	1957	Poplar 101
After All	Lamp Lighters	1955	Decca 29669
After All	Sophomores (Massachusetts)	1955	Decca 29669
After Everybody's Gone	Heart Beats Quintet	1955	Network 71200/Candlelite 437 (72)/ Candlelite 1135 (76)
After Five	De-Icers	1957	De-Icer 100
After Graduation	Four Fifths	1963	Hudson 8101
After He Breaks Your Heart	Wanderers	1962	United Artists 570
After Hour Blues	Whalers, Hal Paige & the	1959	Fury 1024
After I Propose	Keystoners	1956	Epic 9187/Okeh 7210 (64)
After I Told You	Little Linda & group	1961	Coral 62286
After Last Night	Chiffons	1962	Reprise 20103
After Love	Bowties, Cirino & the	1956	Royal Roost 622
After Midnight	Shirelles	1966	Scepter 12162
After New Year's Eve	Heartbeats	1957	Gee 1047
After School	Teardrops	1957	King 5037
After School Rock	Baritones	1958	Dore 501
After School Rock 'N' Roll	Capri Sisters	1956	Jubilee 5244
After The Dance	Cleftones	1959	Roulette LP 25059
After The Dance	DiMucci, Dion (with the Del Satins)	1963	Laurie 3225
After The Hop	Perks, Bill Pinky & the	1958	Phillips International 3524
After The Lights Go Down	Fidels	1957	Music City 806
After The Lights Go Down Low	Jerome, Patti & group	1955	Josie 774
After The Party	Pixies 3	1964	Mercury 72250
After The Party	Whirlwinds	1963	Philips 40139
After Today	Laine, Linda & group	1964	Tower 108
After Tonight	Frontera, Tommy & group	1960	Rem 103
After You	Dells	1963	Argo 5456
After You	Sweeties	1961	End 1110
After You Walk Me Home	Charmers	1964	Pip 8000
After You've Gone	Dreamers, Sidney Ester & the	1958	Dangold 2001/Goldband 1087 (59)
Aftereffect Of Love	Three Dolls, La Ronda Succeed & the	1961	Magnificent 111
Aftermath	Cyclones, Bob Williams & the	1958	Trophy 503
Again	Bowties, Cirino & the	1956	Royal Roost 619
Again	Classics (Brooklyn)	NA	Bed-Stuy 222
Again	Cleftones	1961	Gee 1077
Again	Concords (Brooklyn)	1961	RCA 7911
Again	Demensions	1961	Coral 62277
Again	Dialtones	1959	Dandy Dan 1
Again	Down Beats	1961	Entente 001
Again	Five Crowns	1952	Old Town 777 (unreleased)/ Relic LP 5030
Again	Five Satins	1957	Ember LP 100
Again	Four Cal-Quettes	1962	Capitol 4725
Again	Four Epics	1963	Laurie 3155
Again	Graydon, Joe & group	1959	Hamilton 50027
Again	Hollywood Saxons	1981	
Again	Mystics	NA	Collectables LP 5043
Again	Symbols	1968	Laurie 3435
Again	Universals (Philadelphia)	1957	Mark-X 7004
Again Again And Again	Philettes	1964	Hudson 8105
Again And Again	Van Dykes	1965	Green Sea 101
Age For Love, The	Charles, Jimmy (with the Reveletts)	1960	Promo 1003
Aggravation	Rob-Roys, Norman Fox & the	19??	
Agnes, The Teenage Russian Spy	Sweet Sick Teens	1961	RCA 7940
Ah Do Me Kitchie	Terrytones, Claire Charles & the	1961	Wye 1002
Ah Ha Crazy	James Boys	1960	Edsel 780
Ah So	Gaylads	1961	Audan 120

SONG	GROUP	YEAR	LABEL
Ah So	Highlights	NA	Play
Ah Sweet Mystery Of Love	Seniors	1960	ESV 1016
Ah-La-La	Debonairs	1961	B&F 1353
Ah-OOO-Ga	Mark IV	1959	Mercury 71403
Aimez-Moi	Four Flickers	1959	Lee 1003
Ain't Cha Ever Coming Home	Starlites	1961	Fury 1045
Ain't Giving Up Nothing	Hi-Lighters	1956	Celeste 3005
Ain't Goin' To Cry No More	Serenaders (Detroit)	1954	Swing Time 347
Ain't Gonna Cry	Five Satins	1964	Roulette 4563
Ain't Gonna Cry No More	Satellites, Bobby Day & the	1959	Class 255
Ain't Gonna Do It	Pelicans	1954	Imperial 5307
Ain't Gonna Kiss Ya	Ribbons	1962	Marsh 202
Ain't Gonna Let You (Break My Heart)	Teenangels	1963	Sun 388
Ain't Gonna Let You Go	Corduroys	1961	Hale 100
Ain't Gonna Tell It Right	Imperials (Detroit)	1953	Gem 212/Great Lakes 1212 (54)
Ain't Gonna Walk Your Dog No More	Charms, Otis Williams & the	1966	Okeh 7261
Ain't Gonna Waste No Tears On You	Middletones	1955	Cadillac 156
Ain't Gonna Worry	Ravens	NA	Mercury (unreleased)
Ain't Got The Money	Mello-Harps	1955	Tin Pan Alley 145/146
Ain't He Sweet	Sensations	1956	Atco 6067
Ain't I Cried Enough	Key, Troyce & group	1959	Warner Bros. 5035
Ain't It Baby	Romeos, Kenny Gamble & the	NA	Arctic 114
Ain't It Funny	Admirations	1964	Hull 1202
Ain't It Good (Mmm, Baby I Love You So)	Topps	NA	Red Robin (unreleased)
Ain't It the Truth	Drifters (1959-forward)	1967	Atlantic 2426
(Ain't Like That) No More	Swans (St. Louis)	1953	Rainbow 233
Ain't Love Grand	Crew, Ron & Joe & the	1959	Strand 25001
Ain't Love Grand	Denton, Mickey & group	1965	Impact 1002
Ain't No Big Thing	Royal Five	1968	Arctic 160
Ain't No Big Thing	Wans, Larry Burns & the	NA	Voom 17
Ain't No Place Like The U.S.A.	Dell Vikings	1991	BVM
Ain't No Soles In These Old Shoes	Corvairs	1966	DC 0433
Ain't No Such Thing	Utopians	1962	Imperial 5861
Ain't No Sunshine	New Emage	1987	Starlight 57
Ain't No Sunshine	Yesterday's News	NA	
Ain't Nobody's Business	Starlights, Jimmy Witherspoon & the	1957	RCA 6977
Ain't Nothin' Shakin	Robins, Little Esther & the (with Johnny Otis)	1950	Savoy 731
Ain't Nothin' Shakin'	Heartbreakers (Washington, D.C.)	1974	Roadhouse 1011 (rec. 1952)
Ain't Nothin' Wrong With That	Shufflers	1954	Okeh 7040
Ain't She Got Nerve (acappella)	Mellows, Lillian Leach & the	1974	Celeste 3008
Ain't She Sweet	Fiestas	1965	Old Town 1189
Ain't That Funny	Tren-Dells	1963	Sound Stage 7 2508
Ain't That Just Like A Boy	Honeybirds	1964	Coral 62414
Ain't That Just Like Me	Coasters	1961	Atco 6210
Ain't That Just Like Me	Counts, Bobby Comstock & the	1964	Lawn 232
Ain't That Love	Bouquets	1965	Blue Cat 115
Ain't That Love	Four Tops	1960	Columbia 41755/Columbia 43356 (65)
Ain't That Lovin' You	Volumes	1968	Inferno 5001
Ain't That Peculiar	Tokens (Brooklyn)	1967	Warner Bros. 7099
Ain't That So	Dubs	1960	ABC 10150
Ain't That The Way Life Is	Impacs	1964	King 5910
Ain't You Glad Nature Did It	Rookies, Joe Perkins & the	1957	King 5005
Ain't You Gonna	Caddy's, Jesse Powell & the	1958	Josie 834
Aisle Of Love	Famous Hearts	1962	Guyden 2073
Al Chiar Di Luna (Porto Fortuna)	Teardrops	1958	Josie 856
Ala Vevo	Diadems	1961	Lavere 187
Aladdin's Lamp	Flairs, Cornel Gunter & the	1956	ABC 9740
Ala-Men-Sa-Aye	Quotations	1961, 1973	Verve 10245
Ala-Men-Sa-Aye (acappella)	Quotations	1973, 1975	Relic 1025
Alaska	Serenaders (Hanover)	1958	Relic LP 109
Alaska, U.S.A.	Huskies	1958	Imperial 5544
Alene, Sweet Little Texas Queen	Souvenirs	1957	Dooto 412
Alexander Graham Bull	Jesters	1962	Amy 859
Ali Baba	Hi-Tones, Bob Jaxon & the	1955	Cadence 1264

SONG	GROUP	YEAR	LABEL
Ali Baba	Sandpipers	1966	Kismet 394
Alibi Baby	Three Beaus And A Peep	1954	Columbia 40344
Alice From Above	Bluejays, Leon Peels & the	1989	Classic Artists 111
Alice My Love	Dovers	1962	Valentine 1000
Alimony	Del Roys	1964	Moon LP AB1
All About You	Clovers	1958	Atlantic 1175
All About You	Goldenaires	1959	Ron 325
All Alone	Channels, Earl Lewis & the	1958	Gone 5019
All Alone	Charmers	1956	Aladdin 3337
All Alone	Climatics	1959	Request 3007/3008
All Alone	Ebonettes	1958	Ebb 147
All Alone	Five Embers	1955	Gem 247 (unreleased)
All Alone	Impalas, Speedo & the	1960	Cub 9066
All Alone	Northern Lights	1959	Patt 058
All Alone	Pharoads	1952	RPM 355 (unreleased)
All Alone	Serenaders, Larry Lee & the	1990	Relic LP 5085
All Alone	Trentons	1962	Shepherd 2204
All Alone	Voices Five, Bud Johnson & the	1959	Craft 116
All Alone (acappella)	Del-Lourds	1963	Solar 1001
All Alone And Lonely	Prisonaires	1976	Sun 511
All Alone In My Lonely Room	Clark, Dee (with the Kool Gents)	1963	Atco 6266
All Around	Toppers (Stacy)	1962	Stacy 927
All Around The Bush	Versatones	1957	RCA LPM-1538/RCA EP 1538
All At Once	Cezannes (featuring Cerressa)	1963	Markay 108
All At Once	Uniques	1962	Tee Kay 112
All Because	Varnells	1961	Arnold 1006
All Because Of Love	Charts	1957	Everlast 5008
All But The Memory	Impalas (Brooklyn)	1958	Cub EP CX5000
All Cried Out	Ross, Ted & group	1959	Arwin 121
All Dressed Up	Starlets	1964	Siana 717
All Grown Up	Crystals (Brooklyn)	1964	Philles 122
All I Ask Is Love	Hearts, Lee Andrews & the	1958	United Artists 151
All I Could Do Was Cry	Combo Kings	NA	Flo-Jo 4095
All I Did Was Cry	Del-Vons	1963	Wells 1001
All I Do Is Cry	Blue Notes, Joe Weaver & his	1960	Fortune 852
All I Do Is Dream Of You	Houston, David & group	1958	NRC 005
All I Do Is Dream Of You	Swinging Earls	1959	Vega 1001
All I Do Is Rock	Robbins	1954	Crown 120
All I Do Is Worry	Clouds	1961	Skylark 116
All I Gotta Do Is Think Of You	Blenders (New York)	1951	Decca 27587
All I Hear	Checker Dots	1959	Peacock 1688
All I Need Is You	Darvell, Barry & group	1959	Colt 45 301
All I Need Is You	Five Keys	1957	Capitol LP 828/Capitol EP 2-828 (57)
All I Need Is You	Knickerbockers, Buddy Randell & the	1965	Challenge 59268
All I Need Is You	Primettes, Al Garner & the	1986	Relic LP 8008
All I Want	Fashions	1961	Warwick 646
All I Want	Five Chances	1955	Blue Lake 115
All I Want	Five Thrills	1990	Relic LP 5087
All I Want	Ivys	1959	Coed 518
All I Want	Starlings	1959	World Pacific 809
All I Want For Christmas	Larks (North Carolina)	1988	Relic LP 8014
All I Want For Christmas Is You	C-Quents	1968	Captown 4027
All I Want Is Love	Montclairs	1956	Sonic 104
All I Want Is Someone To Love	Crowns, Arthur Lee Maye & the	1958	Cash 1065
All I Want Is To Love You	Classmates	1962	Radar 3962
All I Want Is You	Accents (Brooklyn)	1963	Spokane 4007
All I Want Is You	English, Scott (with the Accents)	1964	Spokane 4007
All I Want Is You	Futuretones, Jim Holiday & the	1958	4 Star 1720
All I Want Is You	Gayles	1956	Media 1021
All I Want Is You	Miracles (Detroit)	1960	Chess 1768
All I Want This Christmas	Crosstones	1981	United Artists 594
All I Want To Do Is Run	Elektras	1963	United Artists 594
All In My Mind	Anders, Terri & group	1960	Chief 7027
All In The Game	New Emage	1987	N/A
All In Your Mind	Bobbettes	1971	Mayhew 712297/712298

SONG	GROUP	YEAR	LABEL
All In Your Mind	Harptones	1961	Companion 102
All Is Forgiven	Bee, Richie	1961	Gone 5060
	(Richard Barrett with the Chantels)		
All Is Forgiven	Chantels, Richard Barrett & the	1959	Gone 5060
All Is Forgiven	Dominoes, Lil Greenwood & the	1954	Federal 12165
All Is Forgiven	Lamplighters	1955	Federal (unreleased)
All Is Well	Five Pennies, Big Miller & the	1955	Savoy 1181
All Is Well, All Is Well	Gales	1955	J.V.B. 35/J.O.B. 3001
All Is Well And Fine	Concertones	1961	Legrand 1011
All Kinds Of Dancin' Going On	Spotlites	1959	Catalina 1001
All Kinds Of Twistin'	Dials	1960	Norgolde 105
All Messed Up	Chesterfields	1953	Chess 1559
All Mine	Five Satins	1956, 1973	Standord 100
All Mine	Image	1982	Clifton 68
All My Heart	Marveleers	1953	Derby 842
All My Life	Antones, Joey Pfarr & the	1957	Black Crest 107
All My Life	Metros	1959	Just 1502
All My Love	Arondies	NA	Sherry 69
All My Love	Contrasts, Billy Vera & the	1962	Rust 5051
All My Love	Frazier, Ray (with the Moonrays)	1956	Excel 112
All My Love	Rockets, Little Freddy & the	1957	Chlef 33
All My Love	Scott Brothers	196?	
All My Love	Sharps	1958	Combo 146/Dot 15806 (58)
All My Love	Stevens, Randy & group	1959	Loma 301
All My Love, All My Life	Emjays	1959	Greenwich 412
All My Love Belongs To You	Gadabouts	1956	Mercury 70823/Wing 90062 (56)
All My Love Belongs To You	Hearts (Bronx, N.Y.)	1955	Baton 211
All My Love Belongs To You	Joytones	1956	Rama 191
All My Love Belongs To You	Vibrations	1961	Checker 987
All My Lovin' Baby	Cupcakes, Cookie & the	1963	Lyric 1008
All My Loving	Bennetts	1964	Amcan 401
All My Trials	G-Clefs	1963	Terrace 7514
All My Troubles Are Gone	Emblems, Patty & the	1967	Kapp 850
All Night	Incidentals	1964	Ford 134
All Night Baby	Robins	1953	RCA 5271
All Night Boogie	Clovers	1951	Atlantic (unreleased)
All Night Jump	Redtoppers	NA	Dan 3214
All Night Long	Du Mauriers	1957	Fury 1011
All Night Long	Edwards, Jack & group	1963	Michelle 508
All Night Long	Five Willows	1953	Allen 1002
All Night Long	Orchids	1953	King 4661
All Night Long	Relations	1963	Michelle 506
All Night Long	Royals (with Wynonie Harris)	1952	Federal 12064
All Night Long	Trojans	1960	Triangle 51317
All Night Mambo	Cookies	1954	Lamp 8008
All Nite Long (acappella)	Chessmen	1975	Relic LP 101/Relic LP 106 (75)
All Of A Sudden My Heart Sings	Robins	1957	Whippet 206
All Of Me	Blue Diamonds	1960	London 1954
All Of Me	Executives, Margie Mills & the	1963	Vee Jay 549
All Of Me	Jive Bombers	NA	
All Of My Darling	Ambers	1960	Todd 1042
All Of My Life	Aladdins	1956	Aladdin 3314
All Of My Love	Turbans (Philadelphia)	1956	Herald 486
All On Me	Jaguars	1989	Classic Artists 113
All Or Nothing	Blue Belles, Patti LaBelle & the	1965	Atlantic 2311
All Or Nothing At All	Imperials, Little Anthony & the	1961	End LP 311
All Over Again	Bluenotes, Vince Anthony & the	1963	Viking 1018
All Over Again	Four Bars, Betty Wilson & the	1962	Dayco 1631
All Over But The Crying	Blazers, Rodney Lay & the	1956	Chan 110
All Over Nothing	Satisfiers	1955	Jubilee 5205
All Over You	Royal Ravens	1963	Mah's 0015
All Right	Grandisons	1962	RCA 8159
All Righty!	Five Royales	1953	Apollo 449/Todd 1088
All Roads Lead To Heartbreak	Symphonics	1964	Dee Jon 001
All That Glitters	Rivingtons	1964	Vee Jay 634/A.R.E. American 100 (64)

SONG	GROUP	YEAR	LABEL
All That Good	Kuf-Linx	1958	Challenge 59015
All That Heaven Sent	Hobbs, Louis & group	1964	Buddy Buddy 460
All That I Need	Sandelles	1964	Debonair 309
All That Wine Is Gone	Belvin, Jesse & group	1951	Imperial 5115
All That Wine Is Gone	Echoes	1953	Rockin' 523
All That's Good	Crescendos, Johnny Woodson & the	1958	Spry 108
All That's Good	Fiestas	1964	Old Town 1166
All That's Good	Four Jewels	1964	Start 641
All The Love I Got	Noblemen	NA	Clarity 103
All The Tears Is Gone	El Torros	1958	Fraternity 811
All The Things I Love	Midnighters, Hank Ballard & the	1962	King 5713
All The Things You Are	Belmonts, Dion & the	1960	Laurie LP 2006
All The Time	Emeralds (St. Louis)	1959	Rex 1004
All The Way	Boyd, Eddie (with His Chess Men)	1959	Keyhole 114
All The Way	Danderliers	1967	Midas 9004
All The Way From Heaven	Chancellors	1959	Capacity 61023
All The Way Home	Heart-Throbs	1957	Aladdin 3394/Lamp 2010 (57)
All This Can't Be True	Powell Quintet	1951	Decca 48206
All Through Our Teens	Earls	1976	Rome 114
All Through The Night	Impressions	1960	20th Fox 172
All Through The Night	Mystics	1960	Laurie 3047
All Through The Night	Visions	1961	Big Top 3092
All Through The Night	Williams, Mel & group	1956	Dig 128
All Time Fool	Classmen	1964	Limelight 3016
All With You	Callender, Bob & group	1964	Gold 102
All Women Are The Same	Hawks	1954	Imperial 5317
All Work, No Play	Angels, Gabriel & the	1963	Swan 4133
All You Can Do	Hearts, Lee Andrews & the	1968	Lost Nite 1001
All You Gotta Do	Blue Dots	1958	NRC 504
All You Gotta Do	Charmaines	1961	Fraternity 880
All You Had To Do (Was Tell Me)	Innocents, Kathy Young & the	1962	Monogram 517
All Your Lovin'	Novas, Little Ted & the	NA	Kay-Gee 440/Kay-Gee 1068
All'A Your Love	Nighthawks	1958	Hamilton 50006
Al-Lee-O! Al-Lee-Ay!	Plaids	1956	Darl 1003
Allentown Jail	Trailblazers, Shirlee Hunter & the	1959	Tip Top 720
Alley Oop	Hollywood Argyles	1960	Lute 5905
Alley Oop '66	New Hollywood Argyles	1966	Kammy 105
Alley Oop Cha-Cha-Cha	Pre-Historics	1960	Edsel 779
Alley-Oop	Dyna-Sores	1960	Rendezvous 120
Alley-Oop	Evergreens, Dante & the	1960	Madison 130
Alligator In The Elevator	Corvets	1960	Laurel 1012
Allright Already	Four Buddies	1959	Willett 100
Allright Okay You Win	Uniques	1963	Demand 2940
All-Right-OK You Win	Marcels	1962	Colpix 665
Almost Eighteen	Bees, Honey & the	1959	Pentagon 500
Almost Paradise	Roses	1958	Dot 15816
Alone	Arcs, J. Lambert & the	1958	K&C 100
Alone	Celestrals	1963	Don-El 125
Alone	Del-Lourds	1963	Solar 1001
Alone	Grand Prees	1962	Haral 780
Alone	Ivories	1956	Jaguar 3019/Jaguar 3023 (57)
Alone	Shepherd Sisters	1957, 1965	Lance 125
Alone	Tymes	1964	Parkway LP 7032/Rainbow 206
Alone Again	Five Crowns	1953	York 50002
Alone At The Harbor	Gays	1959	Decca 30988
Alone In The Chapel	Ivy Three	1960	Shell 723
Alone In The Night	Jones Boys	1973	Baron 103
Alone In The Night	Pleasers, Little Wilbur & the	1957	Aladdin 3402
Alone In The Night	Valentines	1964	United Artists 764
Alone In The Night	Ventrills	1967	Ivanhoe 5000/Parkway 141 (67)
Alone In This World	Trojans	1958	Tender 516
Alone On A Rainy Nite	Del Rios	1956	Meteor 5038
Alone Too Long	Satellites, Bobby Day & the	1958	Class 241
Alone Without Love	Fi-Dells, Dean Purkiss & the	1964	United Southern Artists 5-110
Along About Sundown	Orioles, Sonny Til & the	1983	Murray Hill LP M61277

SONG	GROUP	YEAR	LABEL
Along Came Jones	Coasters	1959	Atco 6141
Along Came Love	Markeys	1958	Gone 5028
Along Came Susie	Marchand, Donny & group	1960	Craft 3000
Along My Lonely Way	Utopians	1962	Imperial 5876
A-Loo, A-Loo	Starlings	1955	Dawn 213
Alpha Omega	Checker Dots	1959	Peacock 1688
Alphabet Of Love	Suburbans	1959	Port 70011
Alright	Coastliners	1960	Back Beat 554
Alrightee	Teenos	1958	Dub 2839/Relic 506 (64)
Alrighty, Oh Sweetie	Clovers	1954	Atlantic 1046
Altar Of Dreams	Gino (with the Dells)	1961	Golden Crest 567
Altar Of Love	Channels, Earl Lewis & the	1958	Gone 5019
Always	Distants	1960	Northern 3732/Warwick 546/577
Always	Jay Birds, Vinnie Monte & the	1958	Decanter 101
Always	Ravens	1948	National 9064
Always	Zodiacs, Maurice Williams & the	1961	Herald 556
Always Alone	Rockets, Lois Lee & the	NA	Cool 712
Always And Always	Meadowlarks, Don Julian & the	1955	Dootone 367
Always And Ever	Del-Hearts, Dale & the	1961	Herald 564
Always Be Faithful	Monarchs	1956	Neil 103/Melba 103 (56)
Always Be Good	Decoys	1964	Velvet 1001
Always Be Mine	Shufflers, Jay & the	1962	Crackerjack 4010
Always Be Mine	Star Marks, Sammy Vaughn & the	NA	Stardom 0012
Always Be True	Instants	1962	Rendezvous 193
Always Be True	Tri-Lads	1958	Bullseye 1003
Always Forever	Sabers	1955	Cal-West 847
Always, I Have Loved You	Dynamics	1959	Capri 104
Always It's You	Blackwells	1960	Jamie 1150
Always Late (Why Lead Me On)	Top Notes	1961	Atlantic 2115
Always My Darling	Cadillacs	1959	Josie 866
Always My Love	El Dorados	1957	
Always Naggin'	Del Royals	1961	Minit 637
Always Remember (Not To Forget)	Cues	1960	Festival
Always Stay In Love With Me	Three J's	1957	Glory 253
Always Waitin'	Delrons, Reperata & the	1967	RCA 9185
Always You	Crests	1960	Coed 531
Always You	Teardrops	1959	Josie 873
Always Yours	Ideals	1959	Stars Of Hollywood 1001
Am I Blue	Dominoes	1957	N/A
Am I Blue	Washington, Dinah (with the Dells)	1962	Mercury 72015
Am I Ever Gonna See My Baby Again	Medallions, Vernon Green & the	1964	Minit 30234
Am I Fooling Myself Again?	Teenagers, Frankie Lymon & the	1957	Gee 1035
Am I Gonna Lose You	Perfections	1964	SVR 1005
Am I In Love	Keys	1952	MGM 11168
Am I In Love	Ware, Curtis (with the Four-Do-Matics)	1961	Kaybee 101
Am I Just Your Clown	Dee, Larry & female group	1961	Lagree 703
Am I Reaching For The Moon	Knight, Marie & group	1957	Mercury 71055
Am I The Man?	Lester, Bobby (actually the Moonglows)	1959	Checker 921
Am I The One	Spiders	1955	Imperial 5344
Am I The One	Temptations, Cody Brennan & the	1961	Swan 4089
Am I To Be The One	Harmony Grits	1959	End 1051
Am I Wasting My Time	Five Stars (Detroit)	1959	Note 10031
Amazon Basin Pop	Crowns	1962	Chordette 1001
Amazon Beauty	Hollywood Arist-O-Kats	1953	Recorded In Hollywood 406
Amazon Girl	Chordells, Little Chips & the	1961	Hull 746
Amazons And Coyotes	Dreamlovers	1963	Swan 4167/Casino 1308 (63)/ Swan 5619
Ambassador Blues	Ambassadors	1963	Bay 210
Ambush	Murals	1959	Climax 110
Ambush	Parisians	1961	Felsted 8627
American Teens, The	Monterays (Brooklyn)	1958	East West 124
Amor	Down Beats	1960	Conn 201
Amor	Earls	1965	Old Town 1181/1182
An Angel Cried	Castells	1965	Decca 31834
An Angel Cried	Rays, Hal Miller & the	1961	Topix 6003

SONG	GROUP	YEAR	LABEL
An Angel Cried	Star Dusters	1954	Flair 1047
An Angel Like You	Velvet Satins	1964	General American 716
An Angel Never Cries	Downes, Vinnie & group	1959	Transcontinental 1011
An Angel Up In Heaven	Dell Vikings	1963	ABC 10385
An Angel Up In Heaven	Powers, Roni & group	1961	LT Productions 1022
An Eye For An Eye	Star Drifts	1962	Goldisc G3
An Innocent Kiss	Tops	1957	Singular 712
An Invitation	Dream-Timers	1961	Flippin' 107
	(with the Flippin' Teens Orchestra)		
An Invitation To Cry	Magicians	1965	Columbia 43435
An Island Unknown	Shells	1961	Johnson 107
An Understanding	Rollettes	1960	Melker 103
And I Need You	Pyramids (California)	1955	Federal 12233
And Mine	Corvettes, Irving Fuller & the	1960	Emery 121
And Now You're Gone	Mark, Ronald & group	1964	Gateway Custom 102
And She'll Cry	Celtics	NA	Linjo 106
And So Tomorrow	Candy Makers	NA	Urban 124
And Take My Love	Charms, Otis Williams & the	1960	King 5421
And That's A Natural Fact	Dynamics	1964	Big Top 516
And That's All I Need	Lewis, Little Junior & group	1960	Fury 1039
And The Angels Sang	Del Tones	1961	USA 711
And The Angels Sing	Three Chuckles	1956	X 0194/Vik 0194 (56)
And The Moon Came Down	F. J. Babies	1961	Apt 25068
And Then It Happened	Jiv-A-Tones	NA	Fraternity 823
And We Danced	Emblems, Patty & the	1964	Herald 595
And When I'm Near You	Royals, Richie & the	1961	Rello 1
And You Just Can't Go Through Life Alone	Mello-Moods	1952	Red Robin 104
Angalie	El Reyes	1965	Ideal 95388
Angel	Acorns	1958	Unart 2006
Angel	Blenders (Wanger)	1959	Wanger 189
Angel	Cyclones	NA	Cyclone 500
Angel	Dedications	1989	Clifton 86
Angel	Dukes, Skip Arne & the	1964	Little Fort 8688/Dot 16627 (64)
Angel	Fables	1962	Elgo 3001
Angel	Gay Knights	1958	Pet 801
Angel	Grogan, Toby & group	1963	Vee Jay 560
Angel	Kings (Baltimore)	1958	Jalo 203
Angel	Lavenders	1961	C.R. 103
Angel	Melvetts, Joyce Spivey & the	1965	Olimpic 254
Angel	Montereys, Dean Barlow & the	1957	Onyx 517
Angel	Neanderthals, Dave Meadows & the	1960	Magnum 41160
Angel	Orioles, Sonny Til & the	1956	Jubilee 5231
Angel	Satintones	1961	N/A
Angel	Shalons	1977	Ronnie 203
Angel	Tanno, Marc & group	1961	Whale 501
Angel	Volumes	NA	Chex
Angel Adorable	Velvet Satins	1965	General American 720
Angel And A Rose	Rockin' Dukes	1957	O.J. 1007
Angel, Angel	Cosmos	1962	Big L 502
Angel Angela	Classics (Brooklyn)	1960	Dart 1032
Angel Baby	Brown, Charles & group	1961	King 5439
Angel Baby	Hearts, Billy Austin & the	1953	Apollo 444
Angel Baby	Originals, Rosie & the	1960	Highland 1011
Angel Baby	Swallows (Maryland)	1958	Federal 12319
Angel Child	Chimes (Limelight)	1957	Limelight 3000
Angel Child	Rockers, Paul Winley & the	1955	Premium 401
Angel Child	Toppers, Bobby Mitchell & the	1954	Imperial 5282
Angel Darling	Chanters (New York)	1958	DeLuxe 6172
Angel Darling	Vilons	1972	Bim Bam Boom 104
Angel Dear	Four Dukes	1976	Sun (unreleased)
Angel Eyes	Shells	1957	Johnson 104
Angel Face	Barrons	NA	Guest Star LP 1481
Angel Face	Crescendos (Scarlet)	1961	Scarlet 4009
Angel Face	Neons	1956, 1960	Gone 5090

SONG	GROUP	YEAR	LABEL
Angel Face	Rainbows, Randy & the	1977	Crystal Ball 106/Tetra 4444
Angel Face	Vocaleers	1954	Red Robin 132
Angel From Above	Originals, Rosie & the	1961	Highland 1025
Angel From Heaven	Coyne, Ricky & group	1959	Event 4294
Angel From Nowhere	Four Lords	1978	Crystal Ball 124
Angel Girl	McElroy, Sollie & female group	NA	Ja-Wes 101
Angel In Disguise	Inspirations (Al-Brite)	1960	Al-Brite 1650/1651/Sparkle 102 (60)/ Gone 5097 (60)
Angel In My Eyes	Royal Lancers, Paul Stefan & the	1963	Citation 5004
Angel In My Life	Jewels (Los Angeles)	1955	Imperial 5351
Angel In My Life	Roberts, Allen & group	1959	Knight 2009
Angel, Listen To Me	G-Clefs	1964	Regina 1319
Angel Love	Candletts	1958	Vita 179
Angel Love	Premiers, Julie Stevens & the	1962	Best 1004
Angel Love	Whirlwinds	1961	Guyden 2052
Angel Maureen	Crestones, Jimmy & the	1964, 1985	Maria 101
Angel Mine	Dubs	1955	Unreleased
Angel Mine	Five Playboys	1959	Fee Bee 232
Angel Of Angels	Roaches	1964	Crossway 447
Angel Of Happiness	Spinners, Claudine Clark & the	1958	Herald 521
Angel Of Love	Capitols	1958	Pet 807
Angel Of Love	Crestwoods	1961	Impact 6
Angel Of Love	Devlin, Johnny & group	1962	Coral 62335
Angel Of Love	Echoes	1961	Hi Tide 106/Felsted 8614 (61)
Angel Of Love	Harbor Lites (with Jay Black)	1960	Mala 422
Angel Of Love	Majestics (Detroit)	1961	Pixie 6901/Jordan 123 (61)/ Nu-Tone 123 (61)
Angel Of Love	Schoolboys	1958, 1972	Juanita 103
Angel Of Mine	Bluenotes, James Easterling & the	NA	Reno 133
Angel Of Mine	Boys	1964	SVR 1001
Angel Of Mine	Johnson, Dave & group	1960	Apt 25054
Angel Of Mine	Storm, Billy & group	1958	Barbary Coast 1001
Angel Of My Dreams	Sonnets	1958	Lane 501
Angel Of My Heart	Echoes	1961	Seg-Way 1002
Angel Of Romance	Clairmonts	1957, 1963	Apollo 517
Angel On 4th Avenue, The	Infernos	1980	BAB 127
Angel On The Dance Floor	Nuggets	1961	RCA 7930
Angel Or Not	Adams, Link & group	1961	A Okay 111
Angel Please	Joyjumpers	1962	Zynn 1014
Angela	Bell Hops	1958	Barb 100
Angela	Dell Mates	1964	Fontana 1934/Smash 1934 (64)
Angels Cried	Isley Brothers	1956	Teenage 1004
Angels Cried	Landi, Tony & group	1957	Safari 1001
Angels In Heaven	Angelenos, Camille Brown & the	1961	Peepers 2825
Angels In Heaven	Larados	1957	Unreleased
Angels In Heaven Know I Love You	Climbers	1957	J&S 1652
Angels In The Sky	Monarchs	1955	Wing 90040
Angels In The Sky	Premiers, John McKinney & the	1958	Mad 1009
Angels In The Sky (acappella)	Timetones	1963	Times Square 26/Relic 543 (66)
Angels Like You	Lexons	1958	Lexington 100
Angels Listened In, The	Coasters	NA	Coast 187
Angels Listened In, The	Crests	1959	Coed 515
Angels Listened In, The	Scavengers	1963	Mobile Fidelity 1005
Angels Of Mercy	Compliments, Michael Zara & the	1963	Shell 313
Angels Sang, The	Bon-Aires	1977	Flamingo 1002
Angels Sang, The	Irridescents	1960	Ultrasonic 104/Ultrasonic 109
Angels Sang, The	Solitaires	1956	Old Town 1026 (second pressing)
Angels Say	Four Fellows (Brooklyn - Glory)	1955	Glory 236
Angels Sent You, The	Danleers	1964	Smash 1895
Angels Sent You To Me, The	Carnations	1955	Savoy 1172
Angie	Niptones, Nippy Hawkins & the	1965	Lorraine 1001
Angie Lee	Fantastics	1990	Park Ave. 2
Angry	Pizani, Frank (with the Highlights)	1957	Bally 1040
Angry Angel	Caravelles	1961	Star Maker 1925
Animal	Tokens (Brooklyn)	1968	Warner Bros. 7202

SONG	GROUP	YEAR	LABEL
Ankle Bracelet	Pyramids (Detroit)	1958, 1961	Shell 304
Ann Marie	Cook, Gene & group	NA	Lu Pine 003/Shell 711
Anna	Falcons (Detroit)	1965	Lu Pine 003
Anna	Fiestas	1964	Old Town 1178
Anna	Joey, Guy & group	1961	Coed 563
Anna	Originals	1959	Jackpot 48012
Anna Bell	Heptones	1956	
Anna Macora	Calvaes, Oscar Boyd & the	1959	Checker 928
Anna, My Love	Showcases	1964	Galaxy 732
Annabelle	Sugar Tones	1951	Onyx 2007
Annabelle Lee	Co-Eds	1961	Cha Cha 715/Checker 996 (61)
Annabelle Lee	Dreamlovers	1960	V-Tone 211
Annabelle Lee	Echoes	1963	Smash 1850
Annabelle-Lee	Dolphins, Davey Jones & the	1961	Sinclair 1005
Anne Marie	Davis, Billy & group	1960	R-Dell 118
Annette	Blue Jeans, Bob B. Soxx & the	1963	Philles 113
Annette	Idylls	1960	Spinning 6012
Annette	Shy-Tones	1961	Spot 15
Annie	Dwellers	1963	Howard 503
Annie	Four Dukes	1976	Sun (unreleased)
Annie Do The Dog	Underbeats	1964	Bangar 00632
Annie Don't Love Me Anymore	Hollywood Flames	1965	Symbol 211
Annie Had A Baby	Midnighters, Hank Ballard & the	1954, 1966	Federal 12195
Annie Had A Baby	Romans, Little Caesar & the	1961	King 6055/Del-Fi LP 1218
Annie Kicked The Bucket	Nutones	1955	Hollywood Star 798
Annie Laurie	Ervin, Frankie & group	1959	Contender 1316
Annie Mae	Arrows	1958	Flash 132
Annie Met Henry	Cadets	1956	Modern 969
Annie Met Henry	Champions	1954	Scott/Chart 602
Annie Penguin	Cap-Tans, Wailing Bethea & the	1962	Hawkeye 0430
Annie Pulled A Hum-Bug	Midnights	1954	Music City 746
Annie Was A Stroller	Ideals	1958	Decca 30720
Annie's Answer	El Dorados (with Hazel McCollum)	1954	Vee Jay 118
Annie's Aunt Fanny	Midnighters	1954	Federal 12200
Annie's Back	Five Satins	1974	Relic LP 5024
Annie's Not An Orphan Anymore	Candles, Rochell & the	1962	Challenge 9191
Annie's Place	Knight Riders	1961	United Artists 366
Anniversary Of Love	Caslons	1961	Seeco 6078
Anniversary Of Love	Pussycats	1963	Keyman 600
Ann-Marie	Belmonts	1963	Sabina 509
Another Bachelor	Adventurers	NA	Columbia LP 8547
Another Boy Like Mine	Raindrops	1964	Jubilee 5487
Another Chance	Bitter Sweets	1967	Original Sound 70
Another Chance	Goodfellows	1958	Sun-Nel 0535
Another Chance To Love	Supremes (Ruby Nash & the Romantics)	1961	Apt 25055
Another Day	Ascots	1965	Mir-A-Don 1004
Another Day	Zodiacs, Johnny Ballad & the	1959	Wildcat 0016
Another Fella	Furys	1963	Mach IV 114
Another Girl Like You	Five Sequins, Gary Haines & the	1961	Kapp 383
Another Little Darling	Zodiacs, Maurice Williams & the	1960	Soma 1410
Another Lonely New Year's Eve	Skyliners, Jimmy Beaumont & the	1989	Classic Artists 123
Another Lonely Night	Cruisers	1961	Pharaoh 128
Another Love	Aristocrats, Jackie Leonard & the	1963	Lesley 1926
Another Mile To Go	Joseph, Dave & group	1958	Vanguard 35004
Another Miracle Of Love	Latars	1975	Monogram 100
Another Mr. Blue	Loye Jr., Bobby & group	1963	Wilshire 202
Another Night Alone	Deane, Janet (with the Skyliners)	1958	Gateway 719
Another Night With The Boys	Attributes	1979	U.G.H.A. 12
Another Night With The Boys	Drifters (1959-forward)	1962	Atlantic 2162
Another Rainy Day	Pitt, Eugene & group	1966	Veep 1229
Another Sleepless Night	Baby Dolls, Bill Baker & the	1965	Parnaso 110
Another Sleepless Night	Larks (Don Julian)	1964	Arock 1010
Another Soldier Gone	Question Marks	1954	Swing Time 346
Another Soldier Gone	Violinaires	1954	Drummond 4000
Another Tear Must Fall	Chevelles	1963	Butane 777

24

SONG	GROUP	YEAR	LABEL
Another Train Pulled Out	Renaults	1962	Wand 114
Answer Came Too Late, The	Larks (Don Julian)	1965	Money 119
Answer In Your Heart, The	Countdowns	1962	Rori 706
Answer Is Always You, The	Tangerines	1961	Wildcat 603
Answer Me	Distants, Richard Street & the	1961	Thelma/Harmon 1002 (62)
Answer Me	Sharmettes	1962	King 5648
Answer Me, My Love	Belmonts	1969	Dot 17257
Answer Me My Love	Doo Drops, Misty & the	1963	Imperial 5975
Answer Me, My Love	Harptones	1960	Coed 540
Answer Me My Love	Little Ellen & group	1961	Smash 1724
Answer Me, My Love	Roomates	1963	Philips 40105
Answer Soon	Whirlwinds, Joe Welden & the	1959	Khoury's 714
Answer The Call	Paul, Bunny (with the Harptones)	1954	Essex 359
Answer the Phone	Drifters (1959-forward)	1965	Atlantic 2268
Answer To Love, The	Gallahads, Jimmy Pipkin & the	1962	Donna 1361
Answer To My Dreams	Vocaltones	1957	N/A
Answer To My Prayer, The	Aztecs	1962	Zin-A-Spin 002
Answer To Your Prayer, The	Cupids	1957	Decca 30279
Anticipation	Royal Jacks	1962	Amy 865
Anxious Love	Nuggets	1955	Capitol 3052
Any Old Way	Derbys	1963	KC 111
Anymore	Expressions, Billy Harner & the	1964	Lawn 239
Anything	Zodiacs, Maurice Williams & the	1960	Soma 1418
Anything For You	Furys	1963	World Pacific 386
Anything For You	Sounds	1956	Modern 981
Anything To Please My Man	Four Bars, Betty Wilson & the	1962	DAyco
Anything To Say You're Mine	Reed, Lula (with the Pastels)	1958	Argo 5298
Anything You Can Do	Majors (Philadelphia)	1963	Imperial 5914
Anything You Do	Channels	1964	Groove 0046
Anything You Want Me To Be	Accents (featuring Robert Draper Jr.)	1959	Brunswick 55151/Coral 62151 (59)
Anytime	Ascots	1965	Mir-A-Don 1001
Anytime	Bel-Aires, Eddy Bell & the	1960	Mercury 71677
Anytime	Jive Bombers	1964	Middle-Tone 020
Anytime	Ocapellos	1965	General 107/Checker 1144 (66)
Anytime	Vibrations	1962	Checker 1011
Anytime, Any Place, Anywhere	Blendaires, Bobby Carle & the	1958	Decca 30605
Anytime, Anyplace, Anywhere	Day, Dawn & Dusk	1956	Josie 794
Anytime, Anyplace, Anywhere	Falcons (Detroit)	1985	Relic LP 8005
Anytime Anyplace Anywhere	Smith, Savannah & group	1960	End 1077
Anytime, Anyplace, Anywhere	Taylor, Ted & group	1961	Suncraft 400
Anytime Is Lovin' Time	Stylers, Dick Thomas & the	1955	Jubilee 5208
Anyway	Three Chuckles	1955	X 0186/Vik 0186 (56)
Apart	Five Boroughs	1990	Classic Artists 119
Ape Shape	Monterays (Brooklyn)	1958	Rose 109
Aphrodite	Passions	1961	Octavia 8005
Apple Cider	Nite Riders, Doc Starkes & the	1958	Swan 4003
Apple Of My Heart	Acquinets (Carl Green's)	1961	Teen 114/Lilly 5008
Applesauce	Jades	1959	Christy 111
Appointment With Love	Blue Chips, Carlron Lankford & the	1956	DeLuxe 6100
April	Riptides	1966	Sidewalk 904
A-Rab	Titans	1961	Nolta 351
Arabia	Delcos	1962	Ebony 01/02/Showcase 2501 (63)/ Sound Stage 7 2501 (63)
Are You A Boy Or Are You A Girl	Barbarians (with Vito Piccone & the Elegants)	1965	Laurie 3308
Are You An Angel	El Venos	1990	
Are You Changing	Adams, Richie & group	1964	Congress 226
Are You Comin' To The Party	Jewels (Los Angleles)	1959	Shasta 115
Are You Ever Coming Home	Pageants	1965	RCA 8601
Are You For Me	Bell Boys	1960	Era 3026
Are You For Me	Young, Billy & group	1963	Original Sound 29
Are You For Real?	Casanovas	1955	Apollo 471
Are You Forgetting	Royals	1952	Federal 12113
Are You Forgetting Me	Kidds	1955	Imperial 5335
Are You Going My Way	Essex, Anita Humes & the	1963, 1967	Roulette 4494

SONG	GROUP	YEAR	LABEL
Are You Gonna Do	Diablos, Nolan Strong & the	1960	Roulette 4750/Fortune 536
Are You Happy Now	Rays (Frankie Valli)	1962	Perri 1004
Are You Just My Friend	Friends, Dante & his	1961	Imperial 5798
Are You Lonely	Mastertones	1957	Future 1001
Are You Looking For A Sweetheart	Crickets, Dean Barlow & the	1954	Jay-Dee 789
Are You Looking For A Sweetheart	Run-A-Rounds	1963	Tarheel 065
Are You Making A Fool Out Of Me	Diablos, Nolan Strong & the	1963	Fortune 564
Are You My Girl	Bel-Aires, Little D & the	1962	Raft 604
Are You My Girlfriend	Kidds, Morry Williams & the	1958	Tee Vee 301/Carlton 477 (58)
Are You Ready	Thomas, Randy & group	1966	Faro 622
Are You Ready	Valiants (KC)	1962	KC 108
Are You Ready To Say I Do	El Domingos	1964	Karmin 1001
Are You Real?	Emotions	NA	Johnson 746
Are You Satisfied	Cole, Ann (with the Suburbans)	1955	Baton 218
Are You Satisfied (With Your Love)?	Bobbettes	1961	King 5551
Are You Sincere	Platters	1973	Owl 320
Are You Sorry (acappella)	Five Jades (Bronx, N.Y.)	1975	Relic LP 107
Are You Sorry?	Whispers	1955	Gotham 312
Are You Still My Baby	Shirelles	1964	Scepter 1292
Are You Telling Me Goodbye	Broadways	1966	MGM 13486
Are You The One	Gleems	1963	Parkway 893
Are You Trying To Get Rid Of Me Baby	Crystals (Brooklyn)	1966	United Artists 994
Are You With That	Dreams, Johnny & the	1961	Richie 457
Aretha	Drifters (1959-forward)	1966	Atlantic 2366
Aritha	Corvets, Arthur & the	1964	NRC 2871
Arlene	Cardell, Nick & group	1963	Liberty 55556
Arlene	Del-Airs	1964	Coral 62419
Arlene	Four Winds	1978	Crystal Ball 105
Arlene	Titans	1958	Specialty 632
Arlinda	Margilators	1959	Blue Moon 409
Arline	Starliters	1955	Combo 73
Arms Around You	Candies, Ace Kennedy & the	1960	XYZ 609
Around About Midnight	Robins	1949	Score 4010
Around And Around We Go	Jaynes, Lonnie Jay & the	1963	Arlen 724
Around Midnight	Rays, Doug Warren & the	1960	Image 1011
Around The Clock With You	Gales	1963	Debra 1002
Around The Corner	Del Rays	1959	Moon 110
Around The Corner	Dreams, Frank Rossi & the	1957	Mark 7001
Around The Corner	Duprees	1965	Columbia 43336
Around The Corner (From My House)	Plaids	1959	Era 3002
Around The World	Billboards	1961	Vistone 2023
Arrow Of Love	Six Teens	1957	Flip 322
Arrow Two Hearts	Escorts (O.J.)	1957	O.J. 1010
Art Of Love	Artis, Ray & group	1961	A 111
As I Live From Day To Day	Brentwoods	1960	Dore 559
As I Live On	Sonics (New York - Groove)	1955	Groove 0112
As I Love You	Escorts (Brooklyn)	1962	Coral 62317
As I Remember You	Teasers, Sammy & the	1958	Airport 101
As I Walk Alone	Norvells	1963	Checker 1037
As Long As	Neptunes	1957	Glory 269
As Long As I (Can Dream)	Sands, Jeri Lynn & group	1959	Arcade 153
As Long As I Have You	Angelenos	1961	Peepers 2824
As Long As I Have You	Trojans	1955	RPM 466
As Long As I Live	Four Blues	1950	Apollo 1160
As Long As I Love	Knight, Marie & group	1956	Wing 90069
As Long As She Needs Me	Drifters (1959-forward)	1965	Atlantic LP 8113
As Long As You Love Me	Butler, B. B. & group	1964	Barry 111
As Long As You Love Me	Roleaks	NA	Hope 557
As Long As You're In Love With Me	Clark, Dee (with the Kool Gents)	1963	Atco 6266
As My Tears Fall	Blends, Glenn Wells & the	1960	Jin 139
As Other Lovers Do	Debonairs	1957	Combo 129
As Sure As I Live	Five Keys	1959	King 5285
As The Years Go By	Maye, Hartsy & group	NA	Zell 4397
As Time Goes By	Candies, Ace Kennedy & the	1963	Philips 40111
As Time Goes By	Demensions	1961,1966	Coral 62293/Coral 65611 (67)

SONG	GROUP	YEAR	LABEL
As Time Goes By	Duprees	1962	Coed LP 905
As Time Goes By	Flamingos	1959	End LP 304
As Time Goes By	Three Chuckles	1956	Vik LP 1067
As Time Goes By	Wanderers	1962	Cub 9109/MGM 13082 (62)
As You Can See	Chips	1960	Satellite 105
As You Know	Phaetons	1959	Vin 1015
Ashamed	Nichol, Joey & group	1958	ABC 9951
Ashamed	Ravens	NA	Federal 12210
Ashamed Of Myself	Midnighters	1955	Federal 12210
Asiatic Flu	Uptowns	1963	Laurie 3204
Ask Anybody	Ad Libs	1965	Blue Cat 114
Ask Anybody	Earls	1964	Old Town 1169
Ask Me	Martin, Kenny & group	1959	Federal 12354
Ask Me No Questions	Williams, Billy & group	1957	Mercury 71187
Ask Me To Go Steady	Teen-Timers, Lyn Andrews & the	1964	
Ask Me To Move A Mountain	Royal Jesters	1961	Cobra 611025
Ask The Robin	Press, Don (with the Mystics)	1959	Laurie 3036
Ask The Stars	Twinkle Tones, Jimmie Hombs & the	1959	Jack Bee 1004
Asking	Cap-Tans	1951	Coral 65071
At A Dance	Five Glow Tones	1959	Jax 101
At A School Dance	Arvettes	1961	Hac 104
At Any Cost	Pyramids (Connecticut)	1956	Davis 453
At Christmas Time	Castelles, George Grant & the	1989	Classic Artists 114
At Last	Chordells	1959	Jaro 77005
At Last	Dreamers, Richard Berry & the	1954	Flair 1052
At Last	Harper, Thelma & group	1962	Jell 191
At Last	Majors (Brooklyn)	1951	Derby 779
At Last	Mello-Queens, John Lester & the	1959	C&M 500
At Last	Velvets (New York)	1953	Red Robin 122/Pilgrim 706 (55)/ Event 4285 (55)
At Last You Understand	Three Chuckles	1954	Boulevard 100/X 0066 (54)
At Midnight	Nutones	1956	Combo 127
At My Door	Chanters (New York)	1961	DeLuxe 6194
At My Front Door	Academics	1956	Ancho 100/Relic 509 (64)
At My Front Door	Crowns, Arthur Lee Maye & the	1957	Dig 151
At My Front Door	El Dorados	1955	Vee Jay 147
At My Front Door	Exquisites	1985	Avenue D 13
At My Front Door	Jayos, Johnny Otis & the	1957	Dig LP 104
At My Front Door	Rockets, Bill Marine & the	NA	Prom 1132
At Night	Flamingos	1960	End 1073
At Night	Holmes, Eddie & group	1958	Eagle 1000
At Night	Orioles, Sonny Til & the	1950, 1959	Jubilee 5025/Jubilee 5363
At Night	Reality	1980	Bey 130
At Night	Solitaires	1979	King Tut 178
At Night (acappella)	Bon-Aires	1976	Flamingo 1000
At Night (acappella)	Five Delights	1960	A Cappella - Best of the Bronx (98)
At Seventeen	Vocal Lords	1959	Able (no #)/Taurus (no #)
At Sunrise	Ricks, Jimmy & group	1959	Signature 12013
At The Altar	Feathers, Johnny Staton & the	1991	Classic Artists 125
At The Ball	Unique Teens	1958	Ivy 112/Hanover 4510 (58)
At The Bandstand (The Springer)	Dells	1983	Charly LP 1056
At The Club	Drifters (1959-forward)	1965	Atlantic 2268
At The Country Fair	Impressions	1958, 1963	Abner 1023/Vee Jay 574
At The Dance	Casualairs	1959	Mona Lee 136
At The End Of A Sunset	Jaynells	1984	Angela 101
At The End Of Each Day	Dynamics	1960	Decca 31129
At The Fair	Blue Counts, Mike Lanzo & the	1964	Debra 2006
At The Fair	Shadows, Dave & the	1962	Checkmate 1016
At The Hippety Hop	Highlighters, Jimmy Hall & the	1959	Cannon 369/370
At The Hop	Del-Chords	1960	Cool 5816
At The Hop	Juniors, Danny & the	1957, 1973	Singular 711 (57)/ABC 9871 (57)/ Crunch 18001
At The Hot Dog Stand	Castle-Tones	1960, 1974	Fire Fly 321/Rift 504
At The Party	Domains, Jerry Wright & the	1960	Lanjo 2394
At The Party	Lyrics, Ike Perry & the	1963	Naurline 100/Courier 828

SONG	GROUP	YEAR	LABEL
At The Prom	Flamingos	1959	End 1044/End 1046
At The Start Of A New Romance	Dials	1962	Philips 40040
At The Stroke Of Midnight	Corsairs	1962	Tuff 1840/Chess 1840 (62)
At The Teen Center	Cool Gents, Deroy Green & the	1961	Cee Jay 584
At Times Like This	Originals	1961	Diamond 102
A-Ting-A-Ling	Metrotones	1955	Columbia 40420
Atlanta	Tiffanys (male)	1962	Swan 4104
Atom Bomb Baby	Five Stars (Detroit)	1957	Kernel 319574/Dot 15579 (57)
Audie	Inadequates	1959	Capitol 4232
Audrey	Penn Men, Billy Lehman & the	1959	ARP 014
Audrey	Rob-Roys, Norman Fox & the	1957	Back Beat 501
Aunt Jenny	Five Hearts (Philadelphia)	1959	Arcade 107
Aurelia	Pelicans	1954	Parrot 793
Aut-a-mation	Lefemmes, Cole & the	NA	Varbee 5001
Autograph Book	Four Pages	1962	Plateau 101
Automatic Reaction	Ebb Tides, Nino & the	1964	Mala 480
Automobiles	Spaniels	1959	Charly LP 1021 (81)
Autumn Breeze	Midnighters, Hank Ballard & the	1962	King 5601
Autumn Heart	Efics (with Harvey Connell)	1961	Fraternity 891
Autumn Leaves	Imaginations	1985	Relic LP 5058
Autumn Leaves	Regents	1961	Gee LP 706
Autumn Leaves	Romaines, Romaine Brown & His	1956	Decca 30054
Autumn Leaves	Tymes	1964	Parkway LP 7032
Autumn Leaves (acappella)	Apparitions	1975	Relic LP 105
Autumn Leaves (Les Feuilles Mortes)	Accents (featuring Robert Draper Jr.)	1959	Brunswick 55151/Coral 62151 (59)
Autumn Mood	Five Teenbeats	1960	Big Top 3062
Avalon	Bards	1955	Dawn 209
Ave Maria (acappella)	Majestics (Relic)	1975	Relic LP 104
Ave Maria (Schubert)	Demensions	1960	Mohawk 121
Avenue Of Tears	Tabs	1959	Dot 15887
Aw! Shucks Baby	Topsy, Tiny (with the Five Chances)	1957	Federal 12303
Awake Or Asleep	Five Whispers	1962	Dolton 69
Aw-Aw Baby	Holidays	1954	Specialty 533
Away	Concords (Brooklyn)	1962	Rust 5048
Away	Jacks	1974	Relic LP 5023
Away Over There	Sparks	1975	Broadcast 1121
Ay! Ay!	Quin-Tones (Pennsylvania)	NA	Courtney 134
Ay Ay Ay	Three Vales	1957	Cindy 3007
Ay La Ba	Cadets	1955	Modern 965
Ay La Bah	Cooper, Dolly & group	1955	Modern 965
Ay, Si, Si	Dootones	1955	Dootone 366
Ay Yai Yai	Inspirations (Bim Bam Boom)	1972	Bim Bam Boom 109
Aye Senorita	Echoes	1956	Combo 128
Ayuh, Ayuh	Thunderbirds	1955	Era 1000
B. B. Bug, The	Mercurys	1959	Madison 119

B

SONG	GROUP	YEAR	LABEL
B.I. Moore	Headliners	1962	Beltone 2020
B.I.N.G.O. (Bingo)	Turbans (Philadelphia)	1956	Herald 478
Ba Ba Doo	Lexingtons	1963	International 500
Babalonian	Invictors	1963	TPE 8219
Babalu	Twilights, Phyllis Branch & the	1957	Tuxedo 919
Babalu's Wedding Day	Essentials, Billy & the	1966	Smash 2045
Babalu's Wedding Day	Eternals	1959	Hollywood 70/71/Musictone 1110 (59)
Babalu's Wedding Day	Yesterday's News	1980	Clifton 44
Babba Diddy Baby	Heart-Attacks	NA	Remus 5000
Ba-Bee Da Boat Is Leaving	Gum Drops	1957	King 5051
Baby	Avons	1957,1963	Hull 722/Astra 1023
Baby	Bachelors (Bronx)	1956	Earl 102
Baby	Bachelors (Washington, D.C.)	1956	Royal Roost (unreleased)
Baby	Bop Chords	1957	Holiday 2608
Baby	Boy Friends, Jeanie & the	1959	Warwick 508
Baby	Carribians	1961, 1974	Brooks 2000/2001/Johnson
Baby	Continentals, Joey & the	1965	Laurie 3294
Baby	Crests	1963	Times Square 6/Times Square 97 (64)

SONG	GROUP	YEAR	LABEL
Baby	Crows	1954	Rama 29
Baby	Dynamics	1959	Guaranteed 201
Baby	Ebb-Tones	1956	Crest 1024
Baby	Fabulous Idols	1961	Kenco 5011
Baby	Fabutones	1972	Bim Bam Boom 100
Baby	Flaming Hearts	1958	Vulco V1
Baby	Forevers	1958	Apt 25022
Baby	Links	1958	Teenage 1009
Baby	Majestics (Detroit)	1962	Chex 1009
Baby	Monograms	1975	Monogram 105
Baby	Payne, Chuck & group	1957	Atlas 1072
Baby	Premiers (Los Angeles)	1956	Dig 106
Baby	Quarternotes	1962	Little Star 112
Baby	Sensations	1963	Junior 1006
Baby	Serenaders (Detroit)	1954	DeLuxe 6022
Baby	Sevilles	1964	Galaxy 727
Baby	Spades	1957	Domino 200/100/Liberty 55118 (58)
Baby	Sugar Tones	1960	Cannon 392
Baby	Volcanos	NA	Arctic 106
Baby Baby	Aztecs, Jose & the	1976	Monogram 122
Baby Baby	Dreamers, Richard Berry & the	1963	Crown LP 5371
Baby Baby	Fairlanes	1964	Radiant 101
Baby, Baby	Five Stars (Detroit)	1958	End 1028/Columbia 42056 (61)
Baby Baby	Jackson Brothers	1959	Candy 002
Baby Baby	Penn Boys	1959	Bobby 502
Baby Baby	Royal-Aires	1957	Gallo 108
Baby, Baby	Teenagers, Frankie Lymon & the	1956	Gee 1026
Baby Baby	Velveteens	1961	Stark 101
Baby Baby All The Time	Superbs	1964	Dore 715
Baby, Baby, Baby	Alleycats, Joe Allen & the	1958	Jalo 201
Baby, Baby, Baby	Flames	1953	7-11 2106
Baby Baby Baby	Jaguars	1959,1961	R-Dell 11/Baronet 1
Baby Baby Baby	Novas, Little Ted & the	NA	Kay-Gee 440/Kay-Gee 1068
Baby Baby Baby	Tokays	1967	Brute 001
Baby, Baby, Baby, Baby	Jaguars	1966	Original Sound 59
Baby Baby Every Night	Flairs, Etta James & the	1959	Kent 304
Baby Baby (I Love You)	Hootenaires	1963	Enjoy 2003
Baby, Baby (I Still Love You)	Cinderellas	1964	Dimension 1026
Baby, Baby, My Heart	Adventurers	1966	Reading 602
Baby Baby, Oh My Darling	Clovers	1956	Atlantic 1118
Baby Be Mine	Charts	1957	Everlast 5010
Baby Be Mine	Diablos (featuring Nolan Strong)	1954	Fortune 511
Baby Be Mine	Jelly Beans	1964	Red Bird 10-011
Baby Be Mine	Melo Gents	1959	Warner Bros. 5056
Baby, Be There	Kings, Bobby Hall & the	1953	Jax 316
Baby Blue	Accents (California)	1955	Blue Mill 111
Baby Blue	Echoes	1961	SRG 101/Seg-Way 103 (61)
Baby Blue Eyes	Coralairs, T. Renaldi & the	1958	Bee 1543
Baby Blue Eyes	Monograms	1961	Rust 5036
Baby Blues	Bees	1954	Imperial (unreleased)
Baby Boy	Bossmen	1966	Lucky Eleven 231
Baby Boy And Girl From Home	Grady, Paul & group	1963	Glaze 109
Baby Bye Bye	Gees, Dickie & the	1958	Argo 5288
Baby Bye-O	Fleetwoods	1963	Dolton 86
Baby Can I Take You Home	Gee-Chords, Dino & the	1977	Robin Hood 152
Baby Can't You See	Castelles	1954	Grand 109
Baby Child	Don Juans, Joe Weaver & the	1956	Fortune 832
Baby, Come A Little Closer	Five Willows	1954	Herald 433
Baby Come Along With Me	Spaniels	1956	Vee Jay 202
Baby, Come Back	Hearts, Lee Andrews & the	1954	Rainbow 252/Riviera 965 (54)
Baby Come Back	Hearts, Lee Andrews & the (as Lee Andrews)	1959	Casino 110
Baby Come Back	Prophets	1956	Atco 6078
Baby, Come Back To Me	Five Echoes	1953	Sabre 102
Baby Come Back To Me	Manhattan Transfer	1984	Atlantic 89594
Baby Come Home	English, Anna & group	1958	Felsted 8524

SONG	GROUP	YEAR	LABEL
Baby Come Home	Gunter, Cornel (with the Ermines)	1957	Eagle 301
Baby Come On	Del-Larks, Sammy & the	1961,1978	Ea-Jay 100
Baby Come On	Gliders	1962	Southern Sound 103
Baby Come On Home	Calvanes	NA	Unreleased
Baby Come On Home	Cashmeres (Brooklyn)	1961	Laurie 3105
Baby Come To Me	Shamrocks, Little Henry & the	1961	Kent 398
Baby Daddy-O	Blossoms	1958	Capitol 4072
Baby Darling	Dreamers, Richard Berry & the	1955	Flair 1058
Baby Dee	Harps, Little David & the	NA	Savoy (unreleased)
Baby Do	Dells	1983	Charly LP 1056
Baby Do	Jays, Johnny & the	1961	Fairbanks 2001
Baby Do That Thing	Bees, Honey & the	1968	Arctic 158
Baby Do The Philly Dog	Olympics	1966	Mirwood 5523
Baby Doll	Barlow, Dean & group	1961	Lescay 3004
Baby Doll	Carlo (Carlo Mastrangelo) (with the Tremonts)	1963	Laurie 3151
Baby Doll	Clouds, Little Sunny Daye & the	1961	Tandem 7001
Baby Doll	Crescendos (Robin Hood)	1976	Robin Hood 144
Baby Doll	Crows	1955	Rama 50
Baby Doll	De Vaurs	1956	D-Tone A-3
Baby Doll	Dupries	1960	Thunderbird 106
Baby Doll	Escorts, Del & the	1961	Rome 103
Baby Doll	Excels	1957,1965	Central 2601/Relic 1007
Baby Doll	Four Dukes	1976	Sun (unreleased)
Baby Doll	Highlites, Little Angie & the	NA	Essay
Baby Doll	Lyrics, Leo Valentine & the	1962	Skylight 201
Baby Doll	Three D's	1958	Paris 511
Baby Doll	Vanguards	1958	Dot 15791
Baby Don't	Madison Brothers	1961	Sure 1002
Baby Don't	Royal Demons	1958	Rhythm 5004
Baby Don't Cry	Girlfriends	1964	Colpix 744
Baby Don't Do It	Casinos	1961	Alto 2002
Baby Don't Do It	Five Royales	1952,1963,1964	Apollo 443
Baby Don't Go	Belvin, Jesse & group	1952	Specialty 435
Baby Don't Go	Bennett, Buddy (with the Margilators)	1959	Blue Moon 412
Baby Don't Go	Blue Kings, Andy Charles & the	1959	D 1061
Baby Don't Go	Gentlemen	1954	Apollo 470
Baby Don't Go	Margilators, Buddy Bennett & the	1959	Blue Moon 412
Baby Don't Go Now	Gino (with the Dells)	1961	Golden Crest 567
Baby Don't Leave	Leverett, Chico (with the Satintones)	1963	Bethlehem 3062
Baby Don't Leave Me	Chavis Brothers	1961	Coral 62270
Baby Don't Leave Me	McDowall, Chester & group	1959	Duke 302
Baby Don't Leave Me In This Mood	Du Droppers	1953	Unreleased
Baby Don't Play Around	Dunn, Leona & group	1965	Hallmark 500
Baby, Don't Put Me Down	Sultans	1954	Duke 133
Baby Don't Treat Me This Way	Hi-Liters	1955	Wen-Dee 1927
Baby Don't Want Me	Knight, Sonny & group	1955	Specialty 547/Specialty 594 (57)
Baby Don't Want Me No More	Quails, Bill Robinson & the	1954	DeLuxe 6047
Baby Don't You Cry	Sheiks	1955	Ef-N-De 1000
Baby Don't You Know	Camerons	1960	Cousins (unreleased)
Baby Don't You Know?	Counts	1954	Dot 1199
Baby Dumplin'	De Havilons, Eddie & the	1962	Peacock 1920
Baby Eyes	Strollers	1957	Zebra 22
Baby Face	Five Satins	1987	Standord 7107 (rec. 1956)
Baby, For Your Love	Upfronts	1961,1962	Lummtone 107/108
Baby Girl Of Mine	Sharp, Bobby & group	1958	Wing 90056
Baby, Give Me A Chance	Rockin' Dukes (with Joe Hudson)	1957	Excello 2112
Baby, Go Away	Essentials, Billy & the	1966	Smash 2071
(Baby) Hully Gully	Olympics	1959	Arvee 562
Baby I Do	Passions	1966	Back Beat 573
Baby I Do Love You	Galens	1963	Challenge 59212
Baby I Don't Care	Don Juans	1956	Jaguar 3020
Baby I Don't Care	Guytones	1958	DeLuxe 6163
Baby I Don't Care	Royal Lancers, Paul Stefan & the	1963	Citation 5004
Baby I Don't Need You Now	Q Tones, Don Q & the	NA	Bullet 330

SONG	GROUP	YEAR	LABEL
Baby I Gotta Know	Crests	1961	Coed 561
Baby (I Love You)	Blue Jeans, Bob B. Soxx & the	1963	Philles LP 4002
Baby I Love You	Dawn	1968	Rust 5128
Baby I Love You	Daylighters	1962	Tip Top 2002
Baby, I Love You	Du Mauriers	1957	Fury 1011
Baby I Love You	Endings	1980	Clifton 41
Baby I Love You So	Don Juans, Joe Weaver & the	1956	Fortune 825
Baby, I Love You So	Orioles, Sonny Til & the	1952	Jubilee (unreleased)
Baby, I Love You So	Queens, Shirley Gunter & the	1955	Flair 1065
Baby I Love You So	Romancers	1958	Bay-Tone 101
Baby I Love You So	Tri-Dells	1960	Eldo 104
Baby I Miss You	Big 5	1958	Junior 5000
Baby I Miss You	Popsicles	1965	GNP Crescendo 336
Baby, I Need (Ting-A-Ling)	Zephyrs, Ben Joe Zeppa & the	1956	Specialty 577
Baby I Need You	El Dorados	1954	Vee Jay 115
Baby I Need Your Loving	Emotions	1965	Calla 122
Baby I Wanna Know (acappella)	Velvet Angels	1964,1965	Medieval 207/Co-Op M102
Baby I Want To Marry You	Jackson, Chuck & group	1961	Atco 6197
Baby I Want You	Counts	1954	Dot 1226
Baby I'll Cry	Three Friends	1956	Lido 500/Relic 1021 (73)
Baby, I'm All Alone	Leisure Lads	1959	Delco 801
Baby I'm Gone	Four Shades Of Rhythm	1949	Old Swingmaster 13
Baby I'm In Love With You	Blue Notes, Joe Weaver & his	1953	DeLuxe 6021
Baby I'm Ready	Callender, Bob & group	1964	Gold 102
Baby I'm Serious About You	Crescents	NA	Joyce (unreleased)
Baby, I'm Sorry	Strikes	1956	Lin 5006/Imperial 5433 (57)
Baby, I'm Tired	Four Buddies, Bobbie James & the	1956	Club 51 104
Baby I'm Yours	Olympics	1965	Loma 2017
Baby It's All Right	Cadillacs	1964	Lana 118
Baby It's Gotta Be Love	Saber, Johnny & group	1962	Hitsville 1137
Baby It's Hot	Olympics	1962	Arvee 5056
Baby It's Me	Clouds	1961	Skylark 116
Baby It's You	Four Jewels	1964	Tec 3007
Baby It's You	Shirelles	1961	Scepter 1227
Baby It's You	Spaniels	1953,1958	Vee Jay 101/Chance 1141 (53)/l Vee Jay 301
Baby I've Got It	Popular Five	1970	Mister Chand 8001
Baby Let Me Bang Your Box	Majestics (Detroit)	1991	Boardwalk 121
Baby Let Me Bang Your Box	Toppers (Brooklyn)	1954	Jubilee 5136
Baby, Let Me Be	Dell Vikings	1956	Fee Bee 902
Baby, Let Me Be Your Girl	Monday, Julie & group	1966	Rainbow 500/501
Baby Let's Make Love	Flairs, James Stallcup & the	1961	Le Cam 724
Baby, Let's Make Some Love	Penguins	1955	Dootone 362
Baby Let's Play House	Thunderbirds	1955	DeLuxe 6075
Baby Let's Wait	Romans, Caesar & the	NA	GJM 9000
Baby Looka Here	Avalons	1988	Relic LP 5075
Baby Love	Robins	1961	Gone 5101
Baby Mine	Dynamics, Mickey Farrell & the	1963	Bethlehem 3080
Baby Not Now	Pictures, C.L. & the	1966	Monument 958
Baby Oh Baby	Brown, Charles & group	1961	King 5439
Baby Oh Baby	Hargro, Charles & group	1959	DAB 101
Baby Oh Baby	Innocents, Kathy Young & the	1961	Indigo 137
Baby Oh Baby	Low Notes	NA	N/A
Baby Oh Baby	Shells	1957,1960	Johnson 104
Baby Oh Baby (acappella)	Shells	1966	Candlelite LP 1000
Baby, Only You	Earthquakes, Armando King with the	1962	Fortune 549
Baby Open Up Your Heart	Dells	1959	Vee Jay 324
Baby Please	Chanteclairs	1954	Dot 1227
Baby Please	Dukes (California)	NA	Imperial (unreleased)
Baby Please	Hollywood Four Flames	1952	Recorded In Hollywood 165 (first pressing)
Baby Please	Markeets	1957	Melatone 1005
Baby Please	Midnighters	1958	Federal 12339
Baby Please	Moonglows	1964	Times Square 30
Baby, Please	Moonglows	1953,1964	Chance 1147

SONG	GROUP	YEAR	LABEL
Baby Please	Prisonaires	1953	Sun 186
Baby Please	Thomas, Jerry & group	1958	Khoury's 708
Baby Please Be True	Hi-Liters	1958	Hico 2433/Zircon 1006
Baby Please Come Back Home	Robbins, Billy & group	1957	Dig 127
Baby Please Come Home	Catalina 6	1962	Flagship 127/Candlelite 413 (74)
Baby Please Come Home	Ricky & group	1956	Empire 106
Baby Please Don't go	Key, Troyce & group	1958	Warner Bros. 5007
Baby, Please Don't Go	Orioles, Sonny Til & the	1951	Jubilee 5065
Baby Please Don't Go	Pipes	1958	Jacy 001
Baby Please Don't Go	Rhythm Five	1962	Tifco 829
Baby Please Don't Stop	Castelles, George Grant & the	1991	Classic Artists 126
Baby, Please Let Me Love You	Lincolns	1959	Mercury 71553
(Baby) Please Tell Me	Five Candlelights (actually the Five Roses)	NA	Candlelight 431
Baby, Pretty Baby	Flames	1953	7-11 2107
Baby, Say The Word	Seniors	1961	Decca 31244
Baby Say You Love Me	Delltones	1955	Baton 212
Baby Say You Love Me	Four Tops, Carolyn Hayes & the	1956	Chateau 2001
Baby, Send A Letter	Ivories	1956	Jaguar 3019/Jaguar 3023 (57)
Baby Sitter I Love You	Del Victors	1963	Hi-Q 5028
Baby Sittin' With You	Knick-Knacks	1959	Cub 9030
Baby Sitting	Corvells	1962	Lu Pine 104/Lu Pine 1004 (62)
Baby Stop	Ebb Tones, Don Grissom & the	1956	Million $ 2012
Baby Stop Your Crying	Lovenotes	1954	Unreleased
Baby Sue	Mon-Clairs	1962	Joey 6101
Baby Sweet	Strollers	1955	Chess (unreleased)
Baby Sweets	Spaniels	1960,1979	Vee Jay LP 1024/Skylark 582/ Charly LP 1114 (86)
Baby Take Me Back	Three Pals, Roc La Rue & the	1957	Rama 226
Baby, Take My Hand	Paragons	1963	Music Clef 3001/3002
Baby Talk	Laurels	1960	Spring 1112
Baby Tell Me	Willows	1956	Melba 102 (first pressing)
Baby Tell Me (Why, Why, Why)	Mello-Kings	1958	Herald 511
Baby That's It	Falcons (Detroit)	1956	Mercury 70940
Baby That's No	Echoes, Tommy Vann & the	1966	Hollywood 101
Baby That's What Love Is	Shalimars	NA	Mr. Maestro 778
Baby, The Magic Is Gone	Velvets (Texas)	1966	Monument 961
Baby, Think It Over	Martinels	1963	Success 110
Baby Tonight	Falcons, Candy Rivers & the	1954	Flip 302
Baby Toys	Victorians	NA	Reprise 0434
Baby, Walk On In	Shells	1961	Johnson 112
Baby, Walk On In (acappella)	Shells	1963	Josie LP 4001/Candlelite LP 1000 (66)
Baby Wanna Rock	Wig Twisters	1957	A-Ron 1001
Baby Wants	Flairs	1954	Flair 1041
Baby Wants To Rock	Clouds	1955	Chess (unreleased)
Baby We Two	Rhythm Masters	1956	Flip 314
Baby, What A Fool I've Been	Cruisers	1957	Finch 353
Baby What Am I Gonna Do	Schooners, Smokey Armen & the	1958	Peek-A-Boo 102
Baby What Do You Say	Dimensions	1967	Panorama 41
Baby What I Mean	Drifters (1959-forward)	1966	Atlantic 2366
Baby What You Want Me To Do	Dynamics, Ray Murray & the	1960	Arbo 222
Baby What You Want Me To Do	Halos	1965	Congress 253
Baby What's On Your Mind	Spirits, Doug Sahm & the	1959	Personality 3504
Baby, Where Are You?	Four Escorts, Dave Passecallo & the	1961	Bi-Mi 101
Baby Where Y'Been	Marcels	1962	Colpix (unreleased)
Baby Without You	Legends, Lonnie & the	1966	Impression 109
Baby Won't You Please Come Home	Four Dukes	1960	Imperial 5653
Baby Won't You Please Come Home	Mastertones, Elaine Taylor & the	1960	Band Box 233
Baby Won't You Please Come Home	Mel-O-Dots	1989	Relic LP 5077
Baby Work Out	Dovells	1983	Abkco 4029
Baby Ya Know	Cadets	1957	Modern 1026
Baby You (Baby-O)	Johnson, Marv & group	1958	Kudo 663
Baby You Belong To Me	Four Ekkos, Bernie Campbell & the	1961	Fine 26571
Baby, You Belong To Me	Magic Touch	1973	Roulette 7143
Baby You Belong To Me	Nu Luvs	1961	Clock 2003
Baby (You Got To Change)	Mastertones	1961	Le Cam 717

SONG	GROUP	YEAR	LABEL
Baby You Hurt Me	Pitter Pats	1967	Instant 3284
Baby You Know You're Wrong	Dappers (Boston)	1960	Epic 9423
Baby, You Turn Me On	Charms, Otis Williams & the	1965	Okeh 7225
Baby Your Baby	Miller Sisters	1963	Roulette 4491
Baby You're Alive	Styles	NA	Modern 1048
Baby You're Dynamite	Six Teens	1957	Flip 326
Baby, You're My Love	Impax	1960	Warner Bros. 5153
Baby, You're My Only Love	Marquees, Billy Stewart & the	1957	Okeh 7095
Baby, You're Rich	Maytones, Percy Mayfield & the	1954	Specialty 544
Baby, You're The One	Ebonaires (with the Maxwell Davis Orch.)	1953	Aladdin 3211
Baby You're Wrong	Fabulous Blends, Big John & the	1964	Casa Grande 5001
Baby You've Got It	Danleers	1964	Lemans 004
Baby You've Got It Made	Hart, Rocky (with the Passions)	1961	Big Top 3069
Baby-O	Charms, Otis Williams & his	1958	DeLuxe 6160
Baby-O	Hillsiders, Bobby Angel & the	1961	Rhum 101
Baby-O	Six Teens	1958	Flip 338
Baby-O-Mine	Macs, Terry & the	1956	ABC 9668
Baby's Coming Home	Chimes (Brooklyn)	1963	Metro 1/Laurie 3211 (63)
Baby's Coming Home	Coronets	1953	Chess 1553
Baby's Coming Home To Me	Cadillacs	1959	Jubilee LP 1089
Baby's Gone	Toppers, Bobby Mitchell & the	1954	Imperial 5270
Baby's Gone Away	Superbs	1965	Dore 731
Bachelor Mambo	Bachelors, Dean Barlow & the	1955	Excel 105
Bachelor's Club	Bachelors (Epic)	1960	Epic 9369
Back Door Blues	Metronomes	1962	Riverside 4523
Back Door, The	Allen, Tony & group	1988	Classic Artists 102
Back Home Again	Combinations, Artie Morris & the	1959	Combo 167/Coco 163
Back Home Again	Escorts (Brooklyn)	1963	Coral 62372
Back Home Again	Five Birds, Willie Headen & the	1956	Authentic 703/Dooto 703
Back In My Arms	Catalinas	1973	Jayne 719
Back Mountain Rock	Turbo Jets, Cliff Davis & the	1959	Federal 12366
Back On The Beach Again	Skipper, Buddy & group	1961	Fury 1051
Back On The Road Again	Dovells	1974	Event 216
Back Room	El-Derocks	1958	Sapphire 1004
Back To '55	Brian, Eddie	1988	BAB 130
Back To School	Crystalaires	1990	Crystal Ball 158
Back To School	Schoolboys, Professor Hamilton & the	1961	Contour 0001
Back To School	Tornados	1958	Chess (unreleased)
Back To School	Twiliters	1961	Nix 103
Back To School	Wans, Larry Burns & the	NA	Voom 17
Back To School Again	Deltars, Pearl & the	NA	Unreleased
Back To School, Back To You	Teenettes, Bobby Grabeau & the	1959	Crest 1064
Back To The Beach	Relations	NA	Demand 501/Davy Jones 664
Back To The Chapel Again	Orioles, Sonny Til & the	1962	Charlie Parker 213
Back To The Hop	Juniors, Danny & the	1961	Swan 4082
Backyard Rock	Carallons, Lonnie & the	1960	Mohawk 112
Bacon Fat	Don Juans, Andre Williams & the	1956	Fortune 831/Epic 9196 (56)
Bacon Fat	Viceroys	1963	Bolo 750
Bacon Fat	Williams, Andre & group	1957	Fortune 831/Epic 9196
Bad Baboon	Madisons	1964	Limelight 3018
Bad Bad Guitar Man	Larados	1957	Fox 963
Bad Blood	Coasters	1961	Atco 6210
Bad Boy	Big Daddy & His Boys	1957	King 5013
Bad Boy	Donays	1962	Brent 7033
Bad Boy	Escorts (RCA)	1957	RCA 6834
Bad Boy	Gleams	1960	J-V 101
Bad Boy	Jive Bombers	1957	Savoy 1508
Bad Boy	Rhythm Boys, Hank Farell & the	1960	Solar 1013
Bad Boy	Three Naturals	NA	Sin 725
Bad Buc	Jumpin' Jay & group	1961	Turban 101
Bad Bulldog	Minor Chords, Charles Henderson & the	1959	Flick 005
Bad Credit	Upstarts, Jerry McCain & the	1957	Excello 2111
Bad Dan McGoon	Cadillacs	1959	Josie 870
Bad Detective	Coasters	1964	Atco 6300
Bad Girl	Fabulous Denos	1964	King 5908

SONG	GROUP	YEAR	LABEL
Bad Girl	Miracles (Detroit)	1959	Motown G1/G2/Chess 1734 (59)
Bad Girl	Ramblers (Baltimore)	1955	MGM 55006
Bad Girl	Royal Teens	1965	TCF 117
Bad Girl (acappella)	Shells	1966	Candlelite LP 1000
Bad Habit	Discords, Eddie Corner & the	1960	Smoke 101
Bad Habit	Jewels (Los Angleles)	1953	Imperial 5230
Bad Little Girl	Griffins	1955	Mercury 70650
Bad Little Girl	Orioles, Sonny Til & the	1953	Jubilee 5115
Bad Luck	Lapels	1961	Fortune 862
Bad Luck Blues	Dukes (California)	1956	Imperial (unreleased)
Bad Man	Elements	1960	Titan 1708
Bad Man	Turbans (Philadelphia)	1960	Roulette 4281
Bad Man Brown	Pagans	1960	Music City 832
Bad Man Of Missouri	Suburbans, Jimmy Ricks & the	1957	Baton 236
Bad Motorcycle	Storey Sisters	1958	Cameo 126/Peak 5001
Bad Times Make The Good Times	Dreamlovers	1966	Mercury 72595
Bad Weather	Trells	NA	Port City 1112
Bad Woman	Fallen Angels	NA	Eceip 1004
Bag Of Bones	Buddies	1957	Decca 29953
Bagdad Beat	Triplets	1960	Dore 574
Bagoo	Ivy Three	1961	Shell 306
Bail Out	Catalinas	1963	Dee Jay 1010/Sims 134 (63)
Baion Rhythms	Skyliners	1961	Colpix 607
Baja	Turks	NA	P.B.D. 112
Bake That Chicken Pie	Four Blades	1963	Alert 422
Balabam	Du Droppers	1953	RCA (unreleasedʃ
Balboa Memories	Breakers	1963	Marsh 206
Bald Headed Baby	Shakers, Buddy Sharpe & the	1958	Fee Bee 230
Bald Headed Daddy	River Rovers, Lydia Larsen & the	1951	Apollo 432
Ball And Chain	Hollywood Flames	1960	Atco 6164
Ball N' Chain	Viceroys	1961	Original Sound 15
Ballad Of A Badman	Count Downs, Chuck Hix & the	1959	Verve 10190
Ballad Of A Boy And A Girl	Marks	NA	First
Ballad Of A Boy And A Girl	Question Marks	1959	First 102
Ballad Of A Boy And Girl	Graduates, Johnny Holliday & the	1963	Lawn 208
Ballad Of A D. J.	Del Satins	1962	Laurie 3149
Ballad Of A Girl And Boy	Graduates	1959	Shan-Todd 0055
Ballad Of A Girl And Boy	Question Marks	1959	First 102
Ballad Of A Happy Heart	Perri's	1958	Madison 105
Ballad Of Barbara Allen	Mystics	1959	Lee 1004
Ballad Of Betsy Ross, The	Batchelors	1955	Rama 176
Ballad Of Cassius Clay, The	Alcoves	1964	Carlton 602
Ballad Of Freddie And Rich	Fat Boys, Freddie & the	NA	Fat Man 101
Ballad Of Love	Temptations, Neil Stevens & the	1961	Goldisc 3019
Ballad Of Robert E. Lee	Minor Bops, Dave Atkins & the	NA	Contour 503
Ballad Of Seymour, The	Citizens	1961	Laurie 3107
Ballad Of Stagger Lee, The	Senders	1959	Kent 320
Ballad Of Take Me Back To Baltimore	Montereys Quartet	1964	JC Records 9317
Ballad Of The Unloved	English, Scott (with the Accents)	1972	Janus 192
Ballerina	Jo-Vals	1964	Alwil 101/102
Baltimore	Catalinas, Billy Huhn & the	1962	Lesley 1923
Baltimore	Drifters (1959-forward)	1960	Atlantic 2050
Bam, Jingle, Jingle	Spotlighters	1955	Imperial 5342
Bambinella	Four Barons	1957	Roman 400
Bamboo Rock & Roll	Nitecaps	1956	Groove 0158
Bamboo Tree	Regents	1957	Argo 5268
Banana Boat Song	Tides	1962	Mercury 72045
Banana Boat Song	Tokens (Brooklyn)	1968	Warner Bros. 7233
Band Of Angels	Pearls	1959	On The Square 320
Band Of Gold	Hi-Fi Four	1955	King 4856
Band Of Gold	Roomates	1961	Valmor 010
Bandido	Ambertones	1964	GNP Crescendo 329
Bandit Of My Dreams	Hodges, Eddie (with Sue Wright & group)	1961	Cadence 1410
Bandit, The	Barons (Bellaire)	1963	Bellaire 103
Bandstand Baby	Apollos	1959	Harvard 803

SONG	GROUP	YEAR	LABEL
Bandstand Dance	Orbits, Bobby & the	1959	Seeco 6005/Seeco 6067 (61)
Bandstand March	Rhythm Stars	1959	Corsican 0057
Bandstand Rock	Shy-Tones	1961	Spot 14
Bandstand Sound	Originals	1960	Poor Boy 110
Bang A Lang	Cardinals	1955	Atlantic (unreleased)
Bang Bang	Boyfriends, Janis & Her	1958	RCA 7318
Bang Bang, Shoot 'Em Up Daddy	Emblems	1962	Bay Front 108
Bang Goes My Heart!	Moroccos	1956	United 204/B&F 1347
Banners	Fortune Tellers	1960	
Banzai Washout	Catalinas	1963	Ric 113
Baraboo	Rainbows	NA	Red Robin (unreleased)
Barbara	Blue Jays (Roulette)	1959	Roulette 4169
Barbara	Del Royals	1960	Warwick 111
Barbara	Encores	1957	Bow 302
Barbara	Essents	1966	Laurie 3335
Barbara	Incidentals	1961	Gar-Lo 1000
Barbara	Keys	1965	Jam 501
Barbara	Knight, Sonny & group	1959	Eastman 791
Barbara	Laurels	1986	Ram EP 509049
Barbara	Temptations (Goldisc)	1960	Goldisc 3001
Barbara	Three G's	1959	Columbia 41513
Barbara Ann	Chellows	NA	Hit 237
Barbara Ann	Consorts	NA	Clifton EP 501
Barbara Ann	Desires	NA	Unreleased
Barbara Ann	Earthboys	1958	Capitol 4067
Barbara Ann	Street Corner Society	1979	Clifton 35
Barbara Ann (acappella)	Valids	1966	Amber 855
Barbara, Beware	Elegants	1965	Laurie 3283
Barbara (I Love You)	Ramblers (Almont)	1964	Almont 311
Barbara Jean	El Torros	1958	Duke 194
Barbara, Let's Go Steady	Adrian, Lee (with the Chaperones)	1959	Richcraft 5006/SMC 1385 (62)
Barbara-Ann	Regents	1961	Cousins 1002/Gee 1065 (61)
Barbary Coast	Carnations	1960	Terry Tone 199
Barbie	Cadets, Kenny & the	1960	Randy 422
Barbra Lee	Orioles, Sonny Til & the	1948	It's A Natural 5000/Jubilee 5000 (48)
Barefoot Days	Keys	1952	MGM 11168
Barefootin'	Cheaters	1964	Raynard 1056
Barfly	Orioles, Sonny Til & the	1952	Jubilee 5084
Bargain Love	Angels, Lonny & the	1961	Pledge 102
Bark, Battle And Ball	Platters	1955	Mercury 70633
Barnyard Dance	Shields	1961	Continental 4072
Barnyard Hop	Harmonaires, Bonnie Lou & the	1955	King 1506
Barracuda	Gallahads	1958	Vik 0332
Bars' Boogie	Five Bars	1963	Bullet 1010
Baseball Baby	Darling, Johnny & group	1958	DeLuxe 6167
Bashful Boy	Five Chances	1956	States (unreleased)
Bashful Boy	Original Charmers	1960	Angle Tone 550
Bashful Guy	Earthquakes	1959	Fortune 534
Basic Surf	Basics	NA	Lavender 1851
Basic Things, The	Top Notes	1961	Atlantic 2097
Basin Street Blues	Bay City 5, Luigi Martini & the	1954	Jaguar 3001
Bathroom Wall	Tokens (Brooklyn)	1968	Warner Bros. 7202
Bathsheba	Silvertones	1963	Goliath 1355/Valiant 6045 (64)
Batman And Robin	Thor-Ables	1962	Titanic 1002
Batman, Wolfman, Frankenstein Or Dracula	Diamonds	1959	Mercury 71534
Battle Axe	Charmers	1954	Timely 1011
Battle Of Bull Run	Stardusters	1958	Edison International 404
Battle Of Jericho, The	Mellotones, Doug Williams & the	1959	Hy-Tone 122
Battle Of Love	Ripples	1960	Bond 1479
Bayou Baby Blues	Robins, Maggie Hathaway & the	1950	Recorded In Hollywood 112
Bayou Bayou Baby	Imperials, Little Anthony & the	1960	End 1067
Bazoom (I Need Your Lovin')	Charms, Otis Williams & the	1955	DeLuxe 6076
B-Bomb Baby	Jewels (Los Angeles)	1956	RPM 474
Be A Slave	Vocal-Teens	1972	Downstairs 1000

SONG	GROUP	YEAR	LABEL
Be Anything, Be Mine	Boyfriends, Wini Brown & the	1952	Mercury 8270
Be Anything But Be Mine	Five Keys	1952	Aladdin 3127
Be Anything But Be Mine	Tamaneers	NA	Bramley 102
Be Baba Leba	Harris, Thurston (with the Sharps)	1958	Aladdin 3415
Be Bop A Lula	Expressions	1965	Guyden 2122
Be Bop A Lula	Jesters, Junior Chard & the	1959	Madison 127
Be Bop Baby	Peacheroos	1954	Excello 2044
Be Bop Baby Sitter	Three Jays, Vera & the	1957	El-Bee 162
Be Bop Girl	Gladiolas	1995	Excello (unreleased)
Be Bop Wino	Lamplighters	1953	Federal 12152
Be Careful How You Drive Young Joey	Keller, Jerry & group	1961	Capitol 4630
Be Careful Of Stones That You Throw	DiMucci, Dion (with the Del Satins)	1963	Columbia 42810
Be Careful With My Love	Gibralters, Jimmy Barnes & the	1959	Gibraltar 102
Be Cool, My Heart	Flairs, Fatso Theus & the	1956	Aladdin 3324
Be Ever Wonderful	Taylor, Ted & group	1959	Duke 304
Be Ever Wonderful (acappella)	Velvet Angels	1972	Relic LP 5004/Relic LP 108 (75)
Be Fair	Gallahads	1960	Del-Fi 4148
Be Fair	Little Dixie & group	1959	Las Vegas 101/Strip 101
Be Fair	Pipes	1956	Dootone 388
Be Faithful	Crickets, Dean Barlow & the	1953,1963	Beacon 104/555
Be Good, Be Good, Be Good	Roommates, Dick Dixon & the	1959	Kapp 292
Be Good To Me	Matadors	1958	Sue 701
Be Good To Yourself	Wanderers, Dolly Cooper & the	1954	Savoy 1121
Be I Bumble Bee Or Not	Ravens	1947	National 9039
Be Kind	Hi-Lites, Ronnie & the	1962	Joy 265
Be Kind To Love	Interpreters	1967	A-Bet 9425
Be Lovey Dovey	Four Lovers	1956	RCA 6646
Be Lovey Dovey	Rockets	1956	Modern 992
Be Mine	Bell Notes	1959	Time 1004
Be Mine	Crescents	1985	Relic LP 5053
Be Mine	Dell Vikings	1963	Crown LP 5368
Be Mine	Embers, Jerry Bright & the	1959	Yucca 143
Be Mine	Four Of Us	NA	Modern 222
Be Mine	Heartbeats	1957	Rama (unreleased)
Be Mine	Innocents, Kathy Young & the	1962	Reprise 20112
Be Mine	Mellows	1989	Relic LP 5080
Be Mine	Penguins	1963	Original Sound 27
Be Mine	Rhythm Aces, Preston Jackson & the	1961	Vee Jay 417
Be Mine	Rondels	1981	Clifton 58
Be Mine	Uptones	1962	Lute 6229
Be Mine	Williams, Curley & group	1956	Modern 1004
Be Mine Again	Montalvo, Lenny (with the Crystal Chords)	1958	3-D 373
Be Mine Or Be A Fool	Penguins	1955	Mercury 70610
Be Mine Or Be A Fool	Styles, Chuck Mile & the	1962	Dore 630
Be My Baby	Chellows	1961	Poncello 713
Be My Baby	Fabulous Clovers	1961	Winley 265
Be My Baby	Gayten, Paul & group	1956	Argo 5257
Be My Dancing Partner	Vibraharps	1959	Fury 1022
Be My Girl	Dovells	1963	Parkway 901
Be My Girl	Ervin, Frankie (with the Shields)	1960	Hart 1691-52
Be My Girl	Four-Evers	1964	Smash 1887 (second pressing)
Be My Girl	Madara, Johnny & group	1957	Prep 110
Be My Girl	Nitecaps	1955	Groove 0134
Be My Girl	Royals, Richie & the	1962	Rello 3
Be My Girl	Twilighters, Tony & the	1960	Jalynne 106/Red Top
Be My Girl	Videls	1959	Rhody 2000/Medieval 203 (61)
Be My Lady	Drifters (1959-forward)	1971	Atlantic 2786
Be My Love	Duprees	1967	Columbia 44078
Be My Love	Night Owls, Tony Allen & the	1960	Crown LP 5231
Be My Love	Spandells	1977	Robin Hood 146
Be My Love	Supremes, Billy the Kid & the	1958	Bernice 202
Be My Love, Be My Love	Allen, Tony (with the Wonders)	1961	Kent 364
Be My Lovin' Baby	Diamonds	1955	Coral 61577
Be My Lovin' Baby	Penguins	1957	Dooto 428
Be My Own	Bailey, Don & group	1962	USA 723

SONG	GROUP	YEAR	LABEL
Be My Pussy Cat	Boptones	1958	Ember 1043
Be My Steady	Dimples, Eddie Cooley & the	1959	Triumph 609
Be My Steady Date	Four Dates	1958	Chancellor 1024
Be My Sweetie	Jaguars	1955	Aardell 0006
Be My Wife	Cues	1988	Capitol (unreleased) (recorded 1956)
Be Nice, Don't Fight	Four J's	1958	United Artists 125
Be Nice To Me	Cousins	1958	Decca 30609
Be No Fool No More	Walker, Charles (with the Daffodils)	1959	Champion 1014
Be On The Lookout For My Love	Chex, Tex & the	1963	Newtown 5010
Be On The Lookout For The Woman	Crescents, Dick Watson & the	1962	Gone 5144
Be On Your Merry Way	Ravens	1948	National 9053
Be On Your Way	Valiants, Phil DeMarco & the	1964	Debby 065
Be Only You	Buckeyes	1957	DeLuxe 6110
Be Sincere	Little Dippers	1960	University 6053/6054
Be Sure	Magic Chords	1950	Domino 311
Be Sure	Planets	1957,1962	Era 1049/Aljon 1244
Be Sure My Love	Dubs	1958	Gone 5034/Mark-X 8008 (60)
Be Sure My Love (acappella)	Shells	1966	Candlelite LP 1000
Be There	Shadettes	NA	Romantic 101/102
Be True	Vocaleers	1952	Red Robin 113
Be With You	Del-Chords, Donnie & the	1963	Taurus 363
Be Yourself	Antennas	NA	Clay 201
Be Yourself	Companions	1962	General American 711
Beach Baby	Hi-Lites (Wonder)	1958	Wonder 102
Beach Party	Chex, Tex & the	1963	20th Fox 411
Beach Time	Three Reasons	NA	JRE 223/224
Beach Umbrella	Double Daters	1958	Dot 15780
Beach Walkin'	Catalinas	1963	Ric 113
Beachcomber Song, The	Rocky Fellers	1964	Donna 1383
Beachcomber, The	Flips, Joey & the	1964	Cameo 327
Beale St. Shuffle	Four Cruisers, Joseph Dobbin & the	1953	Chess 1547
Beams Of Heaven	Mighty Mellotones	NA	Honey-B 1017
Beanie	Clippers	1960	Beacon 210
Beans	Superbs	1964	Melmar 121
Beans 'N' Greens	Nutones	1956	Combo 127
Bear Mash Stomp	Daylighters	1961	Nike 1011/Astra 1001 (65)
Beard, The	Trends	1960	RCA 7733
Beat In My Heart, The	Juveniles	1958	Mode 1
Beat Of My Heart, The	Cordells	1961	Bargain 5004
Beat Of Our Hearts, The	Five Blue Notes	1954	Sabre 108
Beatin' On A Rug	Wildcats	1955	RCA 6386
Beating Of My Heart, The	Charmers	1954	Central 1002
Beating Of My Heart, The	Dorells	1963	Gei 4401/Atlantic 2244 (64)
Beating Of My Heart, The	Jesters	1986	Starlight 41
Beating Of My Heart, The	Lyrics (Texas)	1959	Harlem 104
Beating Of My Heart, The	Moonglows	1957	Chess 1669
Beating Of My Heart, The	Petites	1961	Elmor 304
Beatle Bounce, The	Counts, Bobby Comstock & the	1964	Lawn 229
Beatle, The	Buddies	1964	Swan 4170
Beatlemania Blues	Roaches	1964	Crossway 447
Beatnik	Moonglows	1960	Chess 1770
Beatnik	Rock-A-Bouts	1959	Chancellor 1030
Beatnik Baby	Bee Hives	1961	Fleetwood 215
Beatnik Girl	Bi-Tones	1960	Bluejay 1000
Beatrice My Darling	Blackhawks	1972	Roadhouse 1000
Beautiful	Valentines	1963	Lee 5465
Beautiful Brown Eyes	Sonics	1962	Jamie 1235
Beautiful Dreamer	Nutmegs	1964	Lana
Beautiful Dreamer	Passions	1960	Audicon 108
Beautiful Dreamer	Sophomores, Anthony & the	1963	Grand 163
Beautiful Friendship	Casuals	NA	Kern 2755
Beautiful Love	Marvel, Tina & male group	1963	Lu Pine 121
Beautiful Love	Mellomoods, Chuck Higgins & the	1956	Money 214
Beautiful Romance	Sounds, Lee & the	1959	Lido 600
Beautiful Woman	Dolphins	1965	Fraternity 940

SONG	GROUP	YEAR	LABEL
Beautiful Woman	Starr Brothers	1963	Cortland 106
Beautiful, Wonderful, Heavenly You	Interludes	1961	ABC 10213
Beauty And The Beast	Tune Drops, Malcolm Dodds & the	1957	End 1000
Beauty Is Just Skin Deep	Sweethearts	1965	Kent 428
Beaver Shot	Atlantics	1965	Rampart 643
Be-Bop Baby	Confessions	1961	Epic 9474
Be-Bop Mouse, The	Cellos	1957	Apollo 516
Be-Bop Way Marie	Casual Three	1957	Mark-X 7009
Because I Got You	Madisons	1964	Limelight 3018
Because I Love Her	Valadiers	1962	Gordy 7003
Because I Love You	Corvairs	NA	Relic LP 5028
Because I Love You	Innocents	1961	Indigo 124
Because I Love You	Mandells	1961	Smart 325
Because I Really Love You	Technics	1962	Chex 1012
Because Of Love	Customs	1963	Arlen 511
Because Of My Best Friend	Click-Ettes	1960	Dice 92/93
Because Of My Pride	Fireflies	1960	Ribbon 6906
Because Of You	Dreamers (Yonkers, N.Y.)	1961	Cousins 1005/May 133 (61)
Because Of You	Girlfriends, Erlene & the	1963	Old Town 1152
Because Of You	Reflections	1962	Crossroads 402
Because They Tell Me	Horizons, Sunny & the	1962	Luxor 1015
Because We're Very Young	Parlettes	1963	Jubilee 5467
Becky Ann	Four Jacks	1958	Rebel 1313
Bed Bug	Cherokees (Connecticut)	1961	United Artists 367
Bedside Of A Neighbor	Royal Sons Quintet	1952	Apollo 253
Bee Side	Tokens (Brooklyn)	1962	RCA 8064
Been A Long Time	Five Quails	1962	Harvey 114/Harvey 4818
Been Lookin' Your Way	Emotions, Lena Calhoun & the	1961,1962	Flip 356/358
Been So Long	Belltones, Kirk Taylor & the	1958	Tek 2634
Been So Long	Keymasters	NA	Quality Sound 001
Been So Long	Lord, Emmett & group	NA	Antel 520
Been So Long	Pastels (Washington, D.C.)	1957	Mascot 123/Argo 5287 (57)
Beep Beep Beep	Satellites, Bobby Day & the	1957	Class 215
Beer Barrel Boogie	Platters	1954	Federal 12181
Before And After (Losing You)	Fleetwoods	1964	Dolton 302
Before I Go	Connotations	1962,1978	Technichord 1000/1001
Before I Loved her	Crests	1962	United Artists 474
Before I Met You	Four Chimes	1954	States (unreleased)
Before I Saw You Smile	Angels, Lonny & the	1961	Pledge 102
Before I Walk Out The Door	Fiats	1964	Universal 5003
Before It's Too Late	Pyramids (Connecticut)	1957	Davis 457
Before This Time Another Year	Sensationals, Jimmy Jones & the	1959	Savoy 4126
Before We Say Goodnight	Nuggets	1961	RCA 7930
Before We Say Goodnight	Poni-Tails	1959	ABC 10077
Before You	Challengers	NA	GNP Crescendo 400
Before You Change Your Mind	Confessions	1961	Epic 9474
Before You Fall In Love	Ballads (Connecticut)	1956	Franwil 5028
Before You Go	Stories, Smitty & the	1961	Elf 102
Before You Say Goodbye	Caryl, Naomi & group	1956	Ember 1006
Beg And Steal	Highlanders	1957	Ray's 36
Beg And Steal	Strangers	1954	King 4709
Beggar Of Love	Lord, Emmett & group	NA	Antel 520
Beggar That Became King, The	Jack, Johnny & group	1962	Gone 5132
Beggar To A Queen	Cool Gents, Deroy Green & the	1961	Cee Jay 584
Beggin' For Love	Wrens	1955	Rama 53/65/Rama 157 (55)
Beggin' For Your Love	Scott Brothers	1962	Parkway 841
Beggin' You Please	Jive Five	1962	Beltone 2024/Relic 1028 (76)
Begging	King, Sleepy & group	1959	Symbol 904
Begging You, Please	Buckeyes	1957	DeLuxe 6126
Begin The Beguine	Avalons	1963	Olimpic 240/NPC 302 (64)
Begin The Beguine	Flamingos	1959	End LP 304
Begin The Beguine	Paragons	1961	Tap 503
Begin The Beguine	Ravens	1952	Mercury 5764
Begin The Beguine	Teenagers, Frankie Lymon & the	1986	Murray Hill LP 000148
Begin The Beguine (acappella)	Five Delights	1960	A Cappella - Best of the Bronx (98)

SONG	GROUP	YEAR	LABEL
Begin The Beguine (acappella)	Five Jades (Bronx, N.Y.)	1975	Relic LP 107
Beginners At Love	Cleftones	1958	Gee 1048
Beginning Of Love, The	Cameos, Ty Taylor & the	1959	Design 834
Beginning Of Love, The	Twilighters (Bronx, N.Y.)	1961	Fraternity 889
Beginning To Miss You	Orchids	1953	King 4663
Beguino	Thunderbirds	1955	Era 1004
Behave, Hula Girl	Dominoes	1959	Liberty 55181
Behave Yourself	Five Royales	1954	King 4740
Behind The Door	Medallions, Vernon Green & the	1959	Dooto 454
Behind The Make Up	Lee, Shirley & group	1961	Seven Arts 711
Behold	Blues Busters	1962	Capitol 4895
Behold	Dragonaires, Byron Lee & the	NA	Bra 503
Behold	Rivieras, Bobby Meyer & the	1964	Lawn 238/Casino 103
Bei Mir Bist Du Schoen	Sedates	1962	Trans Atlas 692
Being In Love	Florescents	1963	Bethlehem 3079
Believe	Five Moneys	NA	Charlie
Believe	Nutones	1955	Hollywood Star 798
Believe A Traveler	Henry, Earl & group	1958	Dot 15875
Believe In Me	Barons, Marvin Phillips & the	1951	Modern 20-818
Believe In Me	Copasetics	1956	Premium 409
Believe In Me	Cordells	1958	Bullseye 1017
Believe In Me	Del Satins	1964	Mala 475
Believe In Me	Fantastics	1990	Park Ave. 3
Believe In Me	Fortunes	1955	Checker 818
Believe In Me	Hollywood Flames	1962	Coronet 7025/Goldie 1101
Believe In Me	Impressions, Jerry Butler & the	1976	Vee Jay LP 1075
Believe In Me	Lamplighters	1954	Federal 12206
Believe In Me	Lollypops	1958	Universal International 7420/ Holland 7420 (58)
Believe In Me	Meter-Tones	1959	Jax 1002
Believe In Me	Swans (St. Louis)	1956	Steamboat 101
Believe In Tomorrow	Moroccans	1957	Salem 1014
Believe It	Delltones	1956	Baton 223
Believe It Or Not	Elbert, Donnie & group	1957	DeLuxe 6143
Believe It Or Not	Playboys	1959	Souvenir 1001
Believe It Or Not	Twilights, Helen Simon & the	1963	Felice 713
Believe Me	Aristocrats	1954	Essex 366
Believe Me	Champ, Billy & group	1964	ABC 10518
Believe Me	Chromatics, Bob Williams & the	1955	Blend 1005
Believe Me	Ervin, Frankie & female group	1959	Guyden 2010
Believe Me	Gunter, Shirley & group	1957	Tender 503
Believe Me	Ivy, Sheron & group	1961	Heritage 106/Coed 572 (62)
Believe Me	Penguins	1962	Sun State 101
Believe Me	Peppermints	1959	House Of Beauty 1
Believe Me	Pretenders, Linda & the	1963	Assault 1879/1880
Believe Me	Roomates, Cathy Jean & the	1962	Philips 40143
Believe Me	Royal Teens	1959	Capitol 4261
Believe Me	Skyliners	1960	Calico 120
Believe Me	Sparrows Quartette	NA	Broadcast 944
Believe Me	Adapters	NA	Richie 65
Believe Me (My Angel)	Chantels (actually the Veneers)	1960	Princeton 102/End 1103 (61)
Believe Me My Beloved	Chanteclairs	1955	Dot 15404
Believe Me My Darling	Belmonts, Bob Thomas & the	1959	Abel 232
Believe Me, My Love	Earls	1954	Gem 221/Crystal 100
Believe My Heart	Top Hands, Joe Dee & His (with the Tremonts)	1962	Pat Riccio 101
Believe My Heart	Tremonts (with Joey Dee & the Top Hands)	1961	Brunswick 55217/Pat Riccio 101 (62)
Believing In You	Four Sensations	1951	Rainbow 157
Belinda	Cupcakes, Cookie & the	1964	Lyric 1020/Paula 230 (65)
Belinda	Elegants, Vito & the	1965	Laurie 3324
Belinda	Spindrifts	1958	ABC 9904
Belinda Marie	Parker, Little Junior & group	1959	Duke 315
Bell Bottom Slacks	Coasters	1966	Atco 6379
Bell, The	Volumes	1962	Chex 1005
Bella-Marie	Clippers, Johnny Blake & the	1957	Gee 1027
Bells	Belairs	NA	Relic LP 5029

SONG	GROUP	YEAR	LABEL
Bells	Edsels	1958,1961	Dub 2843/Twin 700/Winley 700(64)/ Musictone1144 (64)
Bells	Five Discs	1979	Crystal Ball 136
Bells	Little Boys Blue, Bonnie & the	1960	Nikko 611
Bells	Marcels	1988	Want List 1
Bells	Playgirls	1962	Galaxy 713
Bells Are Ringing	Deltas, Jay & the	1964	Warner Bros. 5404
Bells Are Ringing	Golden Bells	1959	Sure 1002
Bells Are Ringing, The	Epics	1964	Mercury 72283
Bells Are Ringing, The	Overons	1958	Unreleased
Bells Are Ringing, The	Van Dykes	1958	King 5158/DeLuxe 6193 (61)
Bells Are Ringing, The	Pretenders	NA	Rama (unreleased)
Bells Bells	Chessmen	1959	Golden Crest 2661
Bells In My Heart	Pyramids, Little Richard Moreland & the	NA	Picture 7722
Bells In My Heart	Spiders	1955	Imperial 5354
Bells In The Chapel	Crisis, Lonnie & the	1961	Universal 103/Times Square 25 (63)/ Relic 532 (65)
Bells Of Joy	Initials, Angelo & the	1959	Dee 1001/Sherry 667
Bells Of Love	Mint Juleps	1956	Herald 481
Bells Of Love	Velveteens, Terri & the	1962	Kerwood 711
Bells Of Love (acappella)	Count Five	1975	Relic LP 103
Bells Of Love, The	Heartspinners, Dino & the	1981	Starlight 13
Bells Of Love, The	Pearls	1956	Atco 6066
Bells Of My Heart, The	Fascinators (Detroit)	1959	Your Copy 1135
Bells Of Rosa Rita, The	Admirations (featuring Joseph Lorello)	1958	Mercury 71521
Bells Of Rosa Rita, The	Ovations (Starlight)	1988	Starlight 59
Bells Of San Raquel, The	Ravens	1955	Jubilee 5184
Bells Of St. Mary, The	Tokens (Brooklyn)	1965	B.T. Puppy 513
Bells Of St. Mary's, The	Blue Jeans, Bob B. Soxx & the	1963	Philles EP X-EP/Philles LP 4005 (63)
Bells Of St. Mary's, The	Drifters (Pre-1959)	1954	Atlantic 1048
Bells Of St. Mary's, The	Hearts, Lee Andrews & the	1954	Rainbow 259
Bells Of St. Mary's, The	Peachettes, Lynn Taylor & the	1960	Clock 1033/Hawk 2001
Bell's Of St. Mary's, The	Baysiders	1960	Everest 19393
Bell's Of St. Mary's, The	Mellos, Terry & the	1960	Amy 812
Bells Ring	Night Owls	1964	Bethlehem 3087
Bells Ring	Paradons	1960	Milestone 2005
Bells Ring Out, The	L'Cap-Tans	1958	Hollywood 1092
Bells Ring Out, The	Spaniels	1953,1959	Vee Jay 103/Vee Jay 342
Bells, The	Berets	1973	Night Train 904
Bells, The	Chrystalights	1953	Sunset 1141
Bells, The	Corvells	1961	Blast 203
Bells, The	Creations	1961	Jamie 1197
Bells, The	Del Vikings	1958	Mercury LP
Bells, The	Dominoes	1952	Federal 12114
Bells, The	Extremes	1962	Paro 733
Bells, The	Five Dollars	1979,1979	Fortune LP 8016/Skylark 561
Bells, The	Jaytones	1958	Timely 1003/1004
Bells, The	Lavenders	1961	Lake 706
Bells, The	Marquees	1956	Grand 141
Bells, The	Montclairs	1957	
Bells, The	Washington, Baby & group	1959	Neptune 104
Bells Will Ring	Nicholls, Dave (with the Coins)	1961	Sparton 1062
Beloved	Scholars	1957	Imperial 5449
Beloved Stranger	Daarts	1961	Dyna 109
Ben Ben Quaker Ben	Five Encores	1955	Rama 185
Bend Of The River	Four Fellows (Brooklyn - Derby)	1954	Derby 862
Beneath The Moon	Sharpsters	1959	Bella 2208/2209
Beneath The Sun	Equallos	1955	M&M/Romantic Rhythm (55)
Beneath The Sun	Gods	1975	Romantic Rhythm 102
Beneath The Willow	Carousels	1965	Autumn 13
Benji's Cincinnati	Sands Of Time (Tokens)	1976	Kirshner 4263
Berimbau	Belmonts, Dion & the	1966	ABC 10868
Bermuda	Bon-Aires	1956	King 4975
Bermuda	Lassiter, Art & group	1956	Ballad 1020
Bermuda Shorts	Delroys	1957	Apollo 514

SONG	GROUP	YEAR	LABEL
Bermuda Wonderful	Imperials, Little Anthony & the	1963	Capitol 4924
Bertha	Three Notes	1958	Tee Gee 106
Besame Baby	Maestro, Johnny & group	1961	Coed 562
Besame Mucho	Berry, Richard (with the Dreamers)	1958	Flip 339
Besame Mucho	Coasters	1960	Atco 6163
Besame Mucho	Drifters	1953	Rama 22
Besame Mucho	Flamingos	1960	End 1068/1070
Besame Mucho	Pharaohs, Richard Berry & the	1958	Flip 339
Beside My Love	Dubs	1958	Gone 5020
Beside My Love	Dubs, Richard Blandon & the	1987	Starlight 53
Beside You	Crests	1958	Coed 506
Beside You	Diablos, Nolan Strong & the	1962	Fortune 546
Beside You	Flamingos	1960	End 1079
Beside You	Swallows (Maryland)	1952,1958	King 4525/Federal 12329
Bessie's House	Class-Notes	1958	Hamilton 50011
Best Friend Worst Enemy	Popular Five	1970	Mister Chand 8001
Best Girl Of Summer	Hansen Brothers	1979	Crystal Ball 137
Best I Feel Is Sad, The	Blue Emotions	1982	Ambient Sound 03409
Best Love	Debonaires (New York)	NA	Gee (unreleased)
Best Love	Drapers	1960	Vest 831
Best Of The Can Can	Cameos (Philadelphia)	1959	Cameo 176
Best Part Of Breaking Up, The	Symbols	1968	Laurie 3435
Best Thing There Is, The	Shepherd Sisters	1957	Mercury 71244
Best Thing To Be Is A Person, The	Stereos	1964	Val 2
Best Wishes	Del-Tones	1959	Ro-Ann 1001
Best Wishes	Gallahads	1958	Vik 0316
Best Wishes, Good Luck, Goodbye	Del Satins	1962	Laurie 3132
Best You Can, The	Davis Brothers	1965	Guyden 2120
Betcha Didn't Know	Melody Masters & the Sportsmen, Wayne Hardy with the	1957	Renown 104
Better Come Back To Me	Crystals (Metro)	1959	Metro 20026
Better Come Back To Me	Van Dykes	1960	Decca 31036
Better Forget Him	Shells	1961	Johnson 109
Better Get Your Own One Buddy	Superbs	1964	Dore 704
Better Get Your Own One Buddy	Symbols	1963	Dore 666
Better Him Than Me	Pictures, C.L. & the	1963	Dunes 2020
Better Late Than Never	Sophomores, Anthony & the	1963	Mercury 72168
Better Let Her Go	Rocky Fellers	1964	Warner Bros. 5469
Better Luck Next Time	Crowns (Philip Harris)	1963	Vee Jay 546
Better Stop	Ryder, Junior (with the Peacocks)	1954	Duke
Better Tell Him No	Starlets	1961	Pam 1003
Better Than Gold	Shadows	1954	Decca 48322
Better Watch Out Boy	Accents (featuring Sandi)	1964	Commerce 5012/Challenge 1112 (64)/ Challenge 59254 (64)
Betty	Centuries	1963	Klik/Times Square 15
Betty	Gents, Little Freddie & the	1965	Showcase 402
Betty Ann	Cruisers	1959	Coda 3005
Betty Ann	Fabulous Four	1961	Chancellor 1085
Betty Blue Moon	Fabulous Dudes	1994	Presence 4503
Betty Brown	Jayhawks	1958,1974	Eastman 798
Betty Dear	Bell Notes	1959	Time 1013
Betty In Bermudas	Dovells	1963	Parkway 882
Betty Jane	Starlighters	1960	Minit 605
Betty Jean	Boptones	NA	Ember (unreleased)
Betty Jean	Halo, Johnny (with the Four Seasons)	1962	Topix 6004
Betty Jean	Pledges	1957	Revere 3517
Betty Jean	Travelers	1957	Atlas 1086
Betty Jean	Wrens	1955	Rama 175
Betty Jo	Carnations, Ray Allen & the	1959	Ace 130
Betty Jo	Matadors, Hank Ayala & the	1959	Back Beat 530
Betty Lou	Marcels	1973	Baron 109
Betty Lou	Marcels, Bob Jeffries & the	1958	Jody 123
Betty Lou	Nutmegs	1955	Herald 466
Betty Lou And The Lion	Upfronts	1960	Lummtone 103
Betty Morretti	Honeycones, Ernie Cast & the	1968	Ember 1033

SONG	GROUP	YEAR	LABEL
Betty My Angel	Fuller, Jerry & group	1959	Challenge 59052
Betty My Darling	Belvin, Jesse & group	1956	Hollywood 1059
Betty My Love	Cadillacs	1956	Josie 798
Betty, My Love	Joylarks	1959	Snag 107/Candlelite 426
Betty My Own	Dynamics, Tony Maresco & the	1961	Herald 569
Betty-Jo	Carthays	1961	Tag 446
Between Hello And Goodbye	Vibrations	1963	Atlantic 2204
Beulah Lee	Storms, Jody Reynolds & the	1959	Demon 1515
Beverly	El Reyes	1965	Ideal 95388
Beverly	Five Dreamers	1957	Port 5001
Beverly	Jades	1958	Dot 15822
Beverly	Tune Tailors	1958	Century 4158
Beverly	Watkins, Billy & group	1964	Kent 411
Beverly Jean	Lee, Curtis (with the Halos)	1961	Dunes 2008
Beverly My Darling	Individuals, Joe Blackwell & the	1961	Music City 838
Beware	Belvin, Jesse & group	1956	Cash 1056
Beware	Capris (Jesse Belvin & studio group)	1959	Tender 518
Beware	Innocents	1961	Indigo 124
Beware	Showmen, Toni & the	1965	Ten Star 103
Beware Beware	Compliments	1965	Midas 304
Beware Of Love	Ivy Leaguers	1957	Flip 325
Beware Song, The	Trains	1964	Swan 4203
Beware You're Falling In Love	Winchell, Danny (with Nino & the Ebbtides)	1959	Recorte 406
Bewildered	Enchanters (JJ&M)	1962,1963	JJ&M 1562/Candlelite 432
Bewitched	Crescents	1985	Relic LP 5053
Bewitched Bothered And Bewildered	Masters, Rick & the	1962	Haral 778
Bewitched (Bothered And Bewildered)	Mohawks	1960	Val-Ue 211
Bewitched (Bothered And Bewildered)	Rockin R's	1960	Stepheny 1842
Beyond Belief	Carlton, Chick & group	1962	Imperial 5925
Beyond The Clouds	Marigolds, Johnny Bragg & the	1956	Excello 2078
Beyond The Heartbreak	Innocents, Ral Donner & the	1963	Reprise 20192
Beyond The Sea	Reveres	1963	Jubilee 5463
Beyond The Stars	Ran-Dells	1964	RSVP 1104
Beyond Your Wildest Dreams	Indigos	1963	Cadette 8003
Bible Tells Me So, The	Coronets	1955	Groove 0116
Bicycle Hop	Anastasia & group	1962	Stasi 1002
Bicycle Hop	Chandeliers	1962	Du-Well 102
Bicycle Tillie	Swallows (Maryland)	1953	King 4632
Biddy Leg, The	Memos	1959	Memo 34891
Big Axe	Lovers	1958	Casino 103
Big Bad Beulah	Champions	1956	Chart 631
Big Bad Mollie	Lapels	1960	Melker 104
Big Band Polka	Teen Notes	1961	Deb 127
Big Beach Bully	Chappies	NA	Chelton 750
Big Beach Party	Jades	1959	Christy 110
Big Bear, The	Jaguars (with Patti Ross)	1955	Aardell 107
Big Beat, The	Del Vikings	1958	Mercury LP 30353
Big Ben	Ping Pongs	1960	Cub 9062
Big Bill	Snappers	1959	20th Century Fox 148
Big Boat, The	Tokens (Brooklyn)	1962	RCA 8018
Big Bobo's Party	Penguins	1965	Original Sound 54
Big Bounce, The	Caddell, Shirley & group	1963	Lesley 1927
Big Boy Pete	Candles, Rochell & the	1961	Swingin' 652
Big Boy Pete	Olympics	1960,1967	Arvee 595/Mirwood 5533
Big Boy Pete '65	Olympics	1961	Arvee 6501/Everest
Big Break, The	Berry, Richard (with the Flairs)	1955	Flair 1055
Big Break, The	Dreamers, Richard Berry & the	1963	Crown LP 5371
Big Brown Eyes	Holidays	1962	Track 101
Big Brown Eyes	Overons	1958	Unreleased
Big Brown Eyes	Redjacks	1958	Apt 25006/Oklahoma 5005 (58)
Big Chief	Christmas, Connie & group	1962	Checker 1015
Big Chief	Co-Eds	1958	Cameo 129
Big City	Daniels	1963	Lantam 01
Big City Bounce	Hornets	1981	P-Vine Special LP 9036
Big City Boy	Thornton Sisters	1964	Bobsan 1000

SONG	GROUP	YEAR	LABEL
Big Daddy And The Cat	Blackwells	1961	Jamie 1179
Big Dom	Ordells	NA	Dionn 505
Big Eyed Baby	Linnettes	1960	Palette 5112
Big Eyes	Majors (Philadelphia)	1954	Original 1003
Big Fat Lips	Smith Quartet, Ben	1953	Rama 17
Big Feet	Starlighters	1960	Hi-Q 5016
Big Feet Mary	Four Checks	1961	Tri Disc 101
Big Frog	Midnighters (Henry Moore)	1961	King 5513
Big Game Hunter	Night-Riders	1961	Dore 613
Big John	Shirelles	1961	Scepter 1223
Big Joke	Lamp Lighters	1955	Decca 29669
Big Joke	Sophomores (Massachusetts)	1955	Decca 29669
Big Knock, The	Stereos	1961	Cub 9103
Big Leg Mama	Rockets	1953	Atlantic 988
Big Lie, The	Dukays	1961,1975	Nat 4001
Big Lie, The	Duke Of Earl & group	1962	Vee Jay 450
Big Lies	Scooters	1958	Era 1072
Big Lulu	Saints, Danny & the	NA	Fanelle 101
Big Man	Fugitives	1957	Fabor 141
Big Man	Utmosts	1962	Pan Or 1123
Big Mary	Cyclones	1959	Forward 313
Big Mary's House	Solitaires	1958	Old Town 1059
Big McGoon	Spydells	1960	Addit 1220
Big Mo	Dodgers	1958	Skyway 119
Big Momma Wants To Rock	Meadowlarks, Don Julian & the	1957	Dooto 424
Big Mouth Mama	Shadows	1954	Decca 48322
Big Name Button	Royal Teens	1958	ABC 9918
Big Night, The	Serenadetts	1961	Enrica 1008
Big Noise	Jaguars	1959	Janet 201
Big Party	Browns, Barbara & the	1964	Stax 150
Big Pearl	Cameos, Ty Taylor & the	1959	Design 834
Big Rain, The	G-Clefs	1963	Terrace 7514
Big Red	Numbers	1962	Bonneville 101/Dore 641 (62)
Big Red Sunset	Midnighters, Hank Ballard & the	1961	King 5550
Big Ring, The	Royal Jacks	1958	20th Fox 100
Big Rock Inn	Cooper, Dolly & group	1956	Dot 15495
Big Sandy	Ravons, Bobby Roberts & the	NA	Syy 101
Big Shoe, The	Thunderbirds, Ron Holden & the	1961	Donna 1335
Big Shot	Five Superiors	1962	Garpax 44170
Big Silence, The	Dell Vikings	1962	ABC 10304
Big Sound, The	Delmiros	1961	Dade 1821
Big Talkin' Jim	Blossoms	1962	Challenge 9138
Big Time Charlie	Exotics	1964	Coral 62439
Big Town	Fraternity Brothers	1960	Date 1528
Big Town Boy	Big Town Girls, Shirley Matthews & the	1963	Atlantic 2210
Big Triangle, The	Galaxies	1960	Capitol 4427
Big Wheel	Royaltones, Ruth McFadden & the	1960	Goldisc 3004
Big Wheel Rolling	Wilson, Jimmy & group	1959	Goldband 1074
Big Wig Walk	Marbles	1954	Lucky 002
Bigger And Better	Hy-Tones	1966	A-Bet 9415
Bikini Baby	Versatones	1957	RCA 6976
Bila	Versatones	1958	All Star 501/Fenway 7001 (60)/ Atlantic 2211 (63)
Bill Bailey	Hootenaires	1963	Enjoy 2003
Bill Bailey	Orbits, J. Lyndon & the	NA	Whiteley 4282
Bill Collector, The	Debonairs	1957	Combo 129
Bill's Place	Adventurers	NA	Columbia LP 8547
Billy	Bobbettes	1960	Triple-X 104
Billy Boy	Hi-Boys	1959	Mala 400
Billy Boy, Billy Boy	School Belles	1958	Dot 15746
Billy Boy Blow	Thunderbirds, Billy Ford & the	1957	Vik 0263
Billy Boy's Tune	Three Graces	1959	Golden Crest 528
Billy Budd	Monterays (Brooklyn)	1960	Prince 5060
Billy Is My Boyfriend	Conquerors	1962	Lu Pine 108
Billy Is The Boy	Daylights	1963	Propulsion 601

SONG	GROUP	YEAR	LABEL
Billy, My Billy	Crystalettes	1963	Crystalette 753
Billy, My Billy	Four Cal-Quettes	1961	Capitol 4574
Billy Old Buddy	Fleetwoods	1961	Dolton 49
Billy The Continental Kid	Short Stories, Lenny O'Henry & the	1961	ABC 10222
Billy The Kid	Falcons (Detroit)	1986	Relic LP 8006
Billy The Kid	Raves	1959	Swade 104
Billy The Kidder	Continettes	1963	Ritchie 4300
Billy's Blues	Starfires	1961	Pama 117
Billy's Heartache	Marquees, Billy Stewart & the	1957	Okeh 7095
Bim Bam Boom	Cardinals	NA	Atlantic EP only
Bim Bam Boom	El Dorados	1956	Vee Jay 211
Bimbo	Five Keys	1960	King 5398
Bimini Bimbo	Twilights, Teddy & the	1962	Swan 4126
Bing Bong	Silhouettes	1958	Ember 1037
Bip Bam	Drifters (Pre-1959)	1954	Atlantic 1043
Bippin' & Boppin' (Over You)	Birdies, Robert Byrd & His	1956	Spark 501/Jamie 1039 (57)
Bird Brain	Dapper Dans	1960	Ember 1065
Bird Dog	Halos	1962	Warwick LP 2046
Bird Watchin'	Spinners (California)	1959	End 1045
Birdland Baby	Ramblers (Almont)	1964	Almont 313
Birdland, The	Starlighters	1958	End 1031
Birds 'N Bees	Temptations (Parkway)	1959	Parkway 803
Bird's The Word, The	Rivingtons	1963	Liberty 55553
Birth Of An Angel	Three D's	1957	Paris 508
Birth Of Love, The	Four Marksmen	1958	Radio 107
Birth Of The Beat	Novairs, Carl Bell & the	1958	Laurie 3014
Birthday Party	Pixies 3	1963	Mercury 72130
Bite Bite Barracuda	Knickerbockers, Buddy Randell & the	1965	Challenge 59268
Bitter Dreams	Strollers	1957	States (unreleased)
Bitter Tears	Rogues	NA	Beckingham 1083
Blabber Mouth	Five Stars (Detroit)	1958	End 1028/Columbia 42056 (61)
Blabbermouth	Rookies	1959	Donna 1313
Black And Blue	Gigolos	NA	Broadway 1000
Black And Blue	Hi Liters, Buddy Roberts & the	1960	Bonanza 689/690
Black And White Thunderbird	Delicates	1959	Unart 2017
Black Bermudas And Knee Socks	Revlons, Tino & the	1960	Mark 154
Black Bottom	Dreamlovers	1963	Columbia 42752
Black Bread	Griffin Brothers	1954	Dot 1145
Black Cat	Crescendos (Domain)	1963	Domain 1025
Black Denim Trousers And Motorcycle Boots	Diamonds	1955	Coral 61502
Black Jack	Alcons	1959	Brunswick 55128
Black Magic (acappella)	El Caminos	1965	Fellatio 101
Black Magic And Witchcraft	Comic Books	1961	New Phoenix 6199/Citations 5001 (62)
Black Sax	Larados, Danny Zella & the	1959	Fox 10056
Black Sax	Zell Rocks, Danny Zella & His	1959	Fox 10057
Black Silk	Drifters (1959-forward)	1970	Atlantic 2746
Black Stockings	Rockin' Kids	1958	Dot 15749
Blackboard Of My Heart	Golden Tones	1961	Lodestar 22
Blackmail	Arcades	1959	Guyden 2015
Blacksmith Blues	Fireflies	1963	Hamilton 50036
Blah Blah Blah	Etiquettes, Little Nat & the	1961	Clock 2001
Blame It On Another Rainy Day	Fashions, Frankie & the	1994	Avenue D 21
Blame It On Yourself	Orioles, Sonny Til & the	1983	Murray Hill LP M61277
Blame My Heart	Meridians	NA	Parnaso 120
Blanche	Delmar, Eddie (with the Bob Knight Four)	1961	Madison 168
Blanche	Original Three Friends, Joey & the	1963	Chevron 500
Blanche	Platinums	1980	J & M 649
Blanche	Three Friends	1956	Lido 500/Relic 1021 (73)
Blast Off	Monterays (Planet)	1957	Planet 57
Blast Off	Satellites	1961	Chess 1789
Blast Off	Tyrones	1958	Decca 30643
Bleeding Hearts	Baby Dolls	NA	Parnaso 227
Blending	Thunderbolts	1961	Rondak
Bless My Love	Daytones	1963	Jubilee 5452

SONG	GROUP	YEAR	LABEL
Bless You	Capris (Philadelphia)	NA	Collectables LP 5000
Bless You	Carter Rays	1961	Mala 433
Bless You	Fawns	1965	Tec 3015
Bless You	Ravens	Between 1947 & 1950	National (unreleased)
Bless You	Red Caps, Steve Gibson & the	1959	Hunt 326
Bless You (For Being An Angel)	Chordcats	1954	Cat 109
Bless You My Love	Tempos	1959	Climax 102
Bless Your Heart	Harris, Thurston (with the Sharps)	1959	Aladdin 3452
Bless Your Heart	Tiaras, Roy Milton & the	1960	Lou Wa 1002/Warwick 549 (60)
Bless Your Soul	Dreamlovers	1966	Mercury 72595
Blessed Are These Tears	X Classmates, Joe Tex & His	1959	Ace 559
Blessed Are They	Petites	1958	Spinning 6003
Blessing After All	Voxpoppers	1959	Versailles 200
Blessing In Disguise	Ervin, Frankie & group	1959	Rendezvous 112
Blessing Of Love	Eager, Johnny & group	1959	End 1061
Blessings Of Love	Rivieras	1960	Coed 529
Blind Date	Crystals (Felsted)	1959	Felsted 8566
Blind Date	Dynamics	1962	Liban 1006
Blind Date	Eternals	1961	Warwick 611
Blind Date	Foreign Intrigue	1972	E.M. 1001
Blind Date	Mosquitos	1964	Herald 587
Blind Date	Startones	NA	Web 1116
Blind Date	Tretones	1960	B-W 604
Blind Date Fate	Korman, Jerry & group	1959	Meadow 1001/ABC 10024 (59)
Blind Heart	Top Hands, Joe Dee & His	1962	Pat Riccio 105
Blind In Love	Bowties, Cirino & the	NA	Royal Roost (unreleased)
Blond Hair, Blue Eyes, Ruby Lips	Bye Byes	1959	Mercury 71530
Blonde Hair, Blue Eyes And Ruby Lips	Buccaneers	1958	Crystalette 718
Blondie Baby	Double Daters	1958	Carlton 457
Bloop, Bloop	Allie Oop's Group (Gerry Granahan)	1960	Caprice 102
Blossoms	Peppers	1958	Jane 105
Blossoms In The Snow	Skyliners	1961	Unreleased
Blow, Joe	Angels (New Jersey)	1962	Caprice 116
Blow The Whistle	Sugar Tones	1954	Benida 5021
Blow Winds Blow	Videls	1960	Dusty Disc 473/Early 702 (60)
Blowin' The Rock	Jades, Emmett & the	1961	Rustone 1405
Blue	Dovells	1969	Jamie 1369
Blue	Metronomes	1975	Broadcast 1131
B-L-U-E	Superphonics, Dave Kennedy & the	1961	Lindy 101
Blue And Lonely	Pretenders	1958	Central 2605/Apt 25026 (59)/ ABC 10094 (60)
Blue Angel	Beatnicks	1960	Key-Lock 913
Blue Beat	Bon-Aires	1962	Rust TR3
Blue, Can't Get No Place With You	Coins	1954	Gee 10
Blue Day	Raiders	1958	Mercury 71395
Blue Denim	Caruso, Dick & group	1959	MGM 12811
Blue Diamond	King Cobras	1959	Irvanne 117
Blue Diamonds	Royal Dukes, Don Ellis & the	1958	Bee 1110
Blue Dreamer	Bermudas	1964	Era 3133
Blue Dreams	Hot Shots	1954	Savoy 1136
Blue (Enough To Cry)	Visuals	1963, 1981	Poplar 121
Blue Eyes	Big Five	1960	Shad 5019
Blue Eyes	Four Counts	1960	Ace 597
Blue Feeling	Versatiles	1977	Ramco 3717/Marie 101
Blue Fire	Redcoats, Steve Alaimo & the	1959, 1960	Marlin 6064/Imperial 5699 (60)/ Dickson 6445
Blue Flowers	Strangers	1954	King 4709
Blue Heartaches	Marcels	1986	Murray Hill LP 000229
Blue Holiday	Shirelles	1961	Scepter 1217
Blue Hours	Hot Shots	1954	Savoy 1128
Blue Island	Rannels	1963	Boss 2122
Blue Jean	Celestials, Bobby Gee & the	1959	Stacy 922
Blue Jean Cinderella	Pee Wees	1958	Josie 838
Blue Jeans And A Pony-Tail	Valiants (Los Angeles)	1961	Fairlane 21007
Blue Lights Down Low	Three Vales	1957	Cindy 3007

SONG	GROUP	YEAR	LABEL
Blue Little Girl	Four Trumpets, Susie & the	1962	United Artists 471
Blue Lover	Three Chuckles	1955	X 0150
Blue Memories	Jades	1959	Christy 114
Blue Mood	Marie, Elena & group	1962	Gee Bee 01
Blue Mood	Meadowlarks, Don Julian & the	1959	Original Sound 12
Blue Mood	Premiers, Julie Stevens & the	1956	Dig 115
Blue Moon	Classics, Herb Lance & the	1961	Promo 1010
Blue Moon	Diablos, Nolan Strong & the	1962	Fortune 544
Blue Moon	Drivers	1957	RCA 7023
Blue Moon	Dynamics	1959	Delta 1002
Blue Moon	Emanons (New York)	1956	Josie 801
Blue Moon	Five Shadows	1960	N/A
Blue Moon	Four Bel-Aires	1976	King Tut 169
Blue Moon	Four Naturals	1958	Red Top 113
Blue Moon	Janssen, Danny & group	1960	Stepheny 1841
Blue Moon	Maddox, Walt and the Marcels	1983	Super M 304027
Blue Moon	Marcels	1961	Colpix 186
Blue Moon	Meadowlarks, Don Julian & the	1957	Dooto 424
Blue Moon	Naturals	1958	Red Top 113/Hunt 325 (58)
Blue Moon	Satelites, Ronny & the	1960	Dolly 22254
Blue Moon	Sh-Booms	1960	Atlantic 2074
Blue Moon	Surprise	NA	Kape 102
Blue Moon	Teasers, Jimmy Brinkley & the	1957	Note 10002
Blue Moon	Velvet Angels	1975	Relic LP 101
Blue Moon (acappella)	Valids	1966	Amber 853
Blue Mountain Waltz	Sunbeams	1955	Dot 1271
Blue Nights	Hot Shots	1954	Savoy 1136
Blue Ribbon Baby	Three Friends	1961	Cal Gold 169
Blue Sea	Concepts	1964	ABC 10526
Blue Skies	Cleftones	1963	Unreleased
Blue Skies	Harvey (Harvey Fuqua with the Moonglows)	1959	Chess 1749
Blue Skies	Uniques	1963	Capitol 4949
Blue Solitude	Collegians	1956	Groove 0163
Blue Star	Blue Notes, Harold Melvin & the	1961, 1975	20th Century 1213
Blue Star	Mystics	1960	Laurie 3058
Blue Sunset	Majors (Felsted)	1957	Felsted 8501
Blue Valentine	Solitaires	1954	Old Town 1000
Blue Velvet	Catalinas	1973	Jayne 504
Blue Velvet	Clovers	1955	Atlantic 1052
Blue Velvet	Dubs	1962, 1964	Lana 115/Josie LP 4001
Blue Velvet	Moonglows	1964	Lana 132
Blue Velvet	Moonglows, Bobby Lester & the	1962	Chess 1811
Blue Velvet	Page, Joey & group	1961	Roulette 4373
Blue Velvet	Paragons	1960, 1984	Musicraft 1102/Musictone 1102 (62)/ Starlight 23
Blue Velvet	Statues	1960	Liberty 55245
Blue Velvet	Tymes	1964	Parkway LP 7038
Blue Velvet	Velours	1959	Cub 9029
Blue Victory	Meridians	NA	Parnaso 107
Blueberries	Thunderbirds	1955	Era 1000
Blueberry Hill	Premiers, Artie & Linda & the	1964	Chancellor 1147
Blueberry Hill	Sharks	1975	Clifton 10
Blueberry Hill	Three G's	1961	Columbia 41955
Blueberry Sweet	Chandeliers	1958	Angle Tone 521
Blueberry Sweet	Chaperones	1963	Josie 891
Bluebird Of Happiness	Escorts (Essex)	1954	Essex 383
Bluebird Of Happiness	Hearts, Lee Andrews & the	1956	Gotham 318
Bluebird Of Happiness	Overtones, Tony Rice & the	1961	Rae-Cox 106
Bluebird Of Happiness	Street Dreams	1986	Starlight 44
Bluebird, The Buzzard And The Oriole, The	Satellites, Bobby Day & the	1958	Class 241
Bluebirds Over The Mountain	Echoes	1962	Smash 1766
Bluebirds Over The Mountain	Mascots	1962	Mermaid 107
Blue-Eyed Mermaid	Jaybirds, Bobby Darin & the	1956	Decca 29922
Blues	Upsetters	1960	Gee 1055

SONG	GROUP	YEAR	LABEL
Blues Around My Door	Flames, Carol Pegues & the	NA	GM 101
Blues At Dawn	Sultans	1952	Jubilee 5077
Blues At Three	Morris, Count	1955	Vee Jay 134
Blues Came Tumbling Down, The	Capri Sisters	1961	Warwick 673
Blues Don't Care, The	Five Keys	1957	Capitol 3738
Blues Don't Mean A Thing, The	Jive Bombers	1957	Savoy 1513
Blues For Monday	Emanon Four	1956	Flash 106
Blues In A Letter	Flamingos	1954	Chance 1162
Blues In The Closet	Tritones	1955	Grand 126/Jamie 1035 (57)
Blues In The Clouds	Three Clouds	1948	
Blues In The Night	Cleftones	1961	Gee 1074
Blues In The Night	Robins	1956	
Blues In The Night	Stylers	1957	Golden Crest 1181/1182
Blues No More	Paramounts, Eddie Saxon &	1962	Empress 106
Blues No More	Saxon, Eddie & group	1962	Empress 106
Blues Stay Away From Me	Charms, Otis Williams & the	1959	DeLuxe 6187
Blues, The	Elites	1961	Chief 7040
Blues Train	Gadabouts	1956	Mercury 70898
Bluesy Me	Scrubs, Dave Collins & the	1954	Imperial 5294
Bluffin'	Elegants	1960	United Artists (unreleased)
Blushing Bride	Restless Hearts, Fred Parris & the	1966	Green Sea 106
Blushing Bride	Truetones	1961	Felsted 8625
Bo Peep	Lamplighters	1956	Federal 12255
Boat Of Love	Esquires	1963	Argo 5435
Bobbi Ann	Majestics	NA	Fox 5014
Bobbie	Lexingtons, Joey & the	1963	Dunes 2029
Bobbie	Songspinners	1958	Leila 1601
Bobbie Ann	Ze Majestics	1959	Fox 5014
Bobby	Concords (Neal Scott)	1961	Portrait 102
Bobby	Sparkles, Lorelei Lynn & the	1959	Award 128
Bobby Baby	Zee, Ginny & group	1961	Atco 6218
Bobby Jean	Don Juans, Andre Williams & the	1956	Fortune 828
Bobby Layne	Catalinas, Phil & the	1960	Olimpic/Triodex 106
Bobby, My Love	Buddies, Carl Ell & the	1959	Combo 154
Bobby My Love	Kinney, Mary & group	1959	Andex 4031
Bobby Sox Baby	Dominoes	1956	Federal 12263
Bobby Sox Baby	High Liters	1956	Vee Jay 184
Bobby Sox Squaw	Impacts	1959	RCA 7583
Bobby You	Desires	1958	Herald 532
Bobby You	Passionettes	1958	Herald (unreleased)
Bob-O-Link	Jacks	1955	RPM 439
Bob-O-Link	Smart Tones	1958	Herald 529
Bodacious Twist	Echoes, Billy & the	1962	Gala 121
Body Surf	Nobles, Aki Aleong & the	1963	Vee Jay 520
Bohemia Night	Lifesavers, Lucien Farrar & the	1957	Jupiter 2
Bohemian	Twilights	1963	6 Star 1001/1002
Bohemian Daddy	Marquis	1956	Onyx 505/Relic 505 (64)
Bohemian Love	Chauntes	NA	Tonix 15
Boil And Bubble	Heartbeats (Three Friends)	1955	Jubilee 5202
Boll Weevil Is Back	Spy-Dels	1962	Crackerjack 4001
Boll Weevil On The Mountain Top	Cardigans	1958	Mercury 71251
Bom Do Wa	Margilators, Toby & Ray & the	1959	Blue Moon 411
Bon Bon	Powell, Sandy & group	1960	Herald 557/Impala 211
Bon Bon Baby	Jades, Jerry Coulston & the	1959, 1960	Christy 112/131
Bon Voyage	Owens, Buddy & group	1964	Tec 3003
Bone Shaker Joe	Edsels	1962	Capitol 4588
Bong Bong (I Love You Madly)	Castro, Vince (with the Tonettes)	1958	Doe 102/Apt 25007 (58)
Bongo Bongo	Chanters (New York)	1967	MGM 13750
Bongo Gully	Flips, Little Joey & the	1962	Joy 268
Bongo Love	Volchords	1961	Regatta 2004
Bongo Stomp	Flips, Little Joey & the	1962	Joy 262
Bongo Stomp	Inquisitors, Little Isadore & the	1995	Early Bird 5001
Bongo Twist	Castro, Vince (with the Tonettes)	1960	Apt 25047
Bongo Washie Wado	King Trotters, Gene Morris & His	NA	Cal-West 108
Boni Maroni	Rubber Biscuits	1986	Starlight 37

SONG	GROUP	YEAR	LABEL
Bonie Maronie	Customs, Dave &	1965	Dac 502
Bonneville	Rollers	1961	Liberty 55303
Bonnie	Avons	1957	Hull 722
Bonnie	Rockabeats, Jimmy Kelly & the	1958	Cobra 5028/Astra 101 (58)
Bonnie Bonnie	Wilde, Jimmy & group	1962	Chelsea 1006
Bonnie's Part Of Town	Rainbows, Randy & the	1966	Mike 4008
Bony Maronie	Bleu Lights	1968	Bay Sound 67007
Bony Maronie	Counts, Bobby Comstock & the	1960	Jubilee 5392
Bony Maronie	Down Beats	1965	Down Beat 1030
Bony Moronie	Twisters, Joey & the	1962	Dual 505
Boo Babe	Electras	1962	Infinity 016
Boo Baby	Electras	1962, 1963	Lola 100/Challenge 59245/ Infinity 016
Boo Hoo Hoo	Sa-Shays	1961	Alfi 1/Zen 101
Boo Wacka Boo	Velveteers	1956	Spitfire 15
Boo-Dee Green	Olympics	1960	Arvee LP A-423
Boodlya Botten Baby	Top Kicks	1954	Guyden 706
Booga Bear	Creators (with the Alamos)	1957	Hi-Q 5021
Boogie Man	Dodgers	1957	Skyway 117
Boogie Man, The	Cadillacs	1960	Josie 883
Boogie Woogie	Ebb Tones	1961	Bee 301
Boogie Woogie Bugle Boy	Fourteen Karat Soul	1979	Catamount 120
Boogie Woogie Mama	Rockets	NA	Atlantic (unreleased)
Boogie Woogie Pony	Quin-Tones (Pennsylvania)	NA	Courtney 135
Boogie Woogie Teenage	Meadowlarks, Don Julian & the	1956	Dootone 405
Booglay, The	Meadowlarks	1964	Magnum 716
Boogler Pt., The	Olympics	1962	Duo Disc 104
Boo-Hoo-Hoo	Atlantics	1961	Linda 103
Book Of Dance	Monotones	1962, 1974	Hull LP 1002
Book Of Love	Monotones	1957	Mascot 124/Argo 5290 (58)
Book Of Love	Raindrops	1964	Jubilee 5469
Book Of Love	Underbeats	1966	Soma 1449
Book Of Songs	Ly-Dells	1962, 1981	SCA 18001
Boom	Hearts, Lee Andrews & the (as Lee Andrews)	1959, 1981	United Artists 162/Gotham 325
Boom, Baby	Rannels	1963	Boss 2122
Boom Bada Boom	Fascinations	1960	Sure 106
Boom Boom	Barons (New Orleans)	1955	Imperial 5343
Boom Boom	Five Keys	1957	Capitol 3786
Boom Boom Boomerang	Shepherd, Johnnie (with the Belmonts)	1961	Tilden 3001
Boom Chica Boom	Starlites, Kenny Esquire & the	1957	Ember 1021
Boom Chic-A-Boom	Jiveleers	1960	Cousins 1/2
Boom Chip-A-Boom	Creslyns	1963	Beltone 2036
Boom Da Da Boom	Majestics (Florida)	1960	Knight 105
Boom De De Boom	Pastels (Chicago)	1956	United 196
Boom Diddle Boom	El Dorados	1957	Vee Jay 263
Boom Diddy Boom Boom	Charms	1956	Chart 623
Boom Diddy Wawa Baby	Love Bugs	1955	Federal 12216
Boom Mag-Azeno Vip Vay	Cashmeres (Philadelphia)	1955	Mercury 70617
Booma Shooma Rock	Tidal Waves	1961	Tide 0020
Boom-A-Lay	Astro Jets	1961	Imperial 5760
Boomerang	Echoes	1961	SRG 101/Seg-Way 103 (61)
Boomerang	Emotions	1964	20th Fox 478
Boot 'Em Up	Du Droppers	1954	Groove 0036
Bootie Green, The	Clovers	1961	Atlantic 2129
Boots And Saddles	Ravens	1956	Jubilee 5237
Bop Bop Bop	Anthony, Paul & group	1958	Roulette 4099
Bop! Bop! Bop!	Capris (Sabre)	1959	Sabre 201/202
Bop Bop Bu	Dappers (New York)	1956	Rainbow 373
Bop De Do Be Oo Be	Vowels	NA	Lebam 157
Bop Diddlie In The Jungle	Starlites	NA	Claremont 959
Bop Me Baby	Accents, Jackie Allen & the	1955	Accent 1027
Bop-Alena	Shadows	1958	Delta 1509
Bop-A-Lena	Legends	1962	Ermine 43
Bop-A-Loop	Arrows, Joe Lyons & the	1959	Hit Maker 600

SONG	GROUP	YEAR	LABEL
Boppin' (acappella)	Spaniels	NA	Unreleased
Boppin' Around	Dedications	1962	Card 335/336/Card 2001 (62)
Boppin' On The Beach	Valiants, Sandy Vale & the	1959	Decca 30941
Boppin' Sloppin' Baby	Rhythm Aces	1960	Mark-X 8004
Boppin' With The Mambo	Sultans	1954	Duke 135
Bops-A-Bops Love	Wright, Leo & group	1965	Perico 1257
Born To Be A Loser	Velvettones, Lee Martin & the	1962	Jin 159
Born To Be Mine	Melodeers	1962	Shelley 161
Born To Be With You	Echoes	1960	Dolton 18
Born To Love	Echotones, Skip & the	1959	DR 1001/Warwick 634 (60)
Born Too Late	Poni-Tails	1958	ABC 9934
Born Too Late	Shannons	1958	L&M 1003
Born With Rhythm	Calvaes	1957	Cobra 5014
Born With Rhythm	Vows	1963	Ran-Dee 112
Borrow Til Morning	Compliments	1965	Midas 304
Borrowed Time	Ladelles	NA	Debonair 1218
Boss	Rumblers	1963	Downey 103/Dot 16421 (63)
Boss Barracuda	Catalinas	1966	Ric 164
Bossa Nova Baby	Clovers, Tippie & the	1963	Tiger 201
(Bossa Nova) Bird, The	Dells	1962	Argo 5428
Bossa Nova Cha Cha	Uniques	1960	Mr. Cee 100
Bossa Nova (My Heart Said)	Clovers, Tippie & the	1963	Tiger 201
Bossa Nova Stomp	Fabulous Dials	1963	Joy 276/DnB 1000
Bossa Nova Twist	Casualairs	1961	Craig 5001
Bossy Nover	Hollywood Argyles	1963	Felsted 8674
Boston Hop	Playboys	1961	Chancellor 1074
Both Sides Now	Tokens (Brooklyn)	1970	Buddah 174
Bottle Up And Go	Enchanters (Detroit)	1957	Coral 61916
Bottom Of The Top	Wyatt, Johnny & group	1965	Magnum 736
Bottomless Pit	Daylighters, Chuck & the	1963	Tip Top 2006
Bottomless Pit	Mitchell, Billy & group	1957	Poplar 105
Bounce	Rollers	1961	Liberty 55357
Bounce	Spaniels	1953	Vee Jay 101/Chance 1141 (53)
Bounce Again	Olympics	1963	Tri Disc 110
Bounce, The	Del-Rays	1961	Planet 52
Bounce, The	Johnny (with the Kids)	1962	Luck 101
Bounce, The	Olympics	1963, 1966	Tri Disc 106/Mirwood 5525
Bouncin' The Boogie	Royal Kings	1952	Specialty 444
Bouncing Ball	Arabians	1964	Teek 4824-1/4824-2
Bounty Hunter	Nomads	1961	Rust 5028
Bouquet Of Roses	Peacocks, Nunnie Moore & the	1957, 1974	L&M 1002/Firefly 322 (60)
Bow Legged Annie	Deltones	1959	Jubilee 5374
Bow Legged Baby	Rhythmeres	1958	Brunswick 55083
Bow-Legged Boy	Toppers (Avalon)	1954	Avalon 63707
Bow-Wow	Pyramids (California)	1955	Hollywood 1047/C Note 1206 (56)
Boy	Nortones	1959	Warner Bros. 5115
Boy Crazy	Four Del-Aires, Lucy Ann Grassi & the	1964	Volcanic 1002
Boy For Me, The	Tassels	1959	Madison 117/Amy 946 (66)
Boy Friend	Baby Dolls	1959	Elgin 021
Boy Friend	Dynels	1962	Dot 16382
Boy Friends	Percells	1963	ABC 10449
Boy From 'Cross Town, The	Angels (New Jersey)	1964	Smash 1931
Boy From New York City, The	Ad Libs	1965	Blue Cat 102
Boy, He's Got It!	Creators	1962, 1963	T-Kay 110/Philips 40058
Boy I Love, The	Delrons, Reperata & the	1965	World Artists 1062
Boy In Mexico	De Vaurs	1959	Moon 105/Red Fox 104
Boy In My Life	Dovers	1959	Davis 465
Boy Meets Girl	Capris (New York)	1982	Ambient Sound LP FZ-37714
Boy Meets Girl	Heartspinners	1953	Universal
Boy Most Likely, The	Concords (Brooklyn)	1961	RCA 7911
Boy Next Door	Blue Notes, Little Bill & the	1961	Topaz 1305
Boy Next Door	Joyettes	1956	Onyx 502
Boy Of My Dreams	Dungaree Darlings	1956	Rego 1003/Karen 1005 (59)
Boy Of My Heart	Contessas	1963	Witch 113
Boy Trouble	Rev-Lons	1962	Garpax 44168

SONG	GROUP	YEAR	LABEL
Boy Who's Sixteen, The	Dematrons	1963	Southern Sound 202
Boy With The Beatle Hair, The	Swans (Cameo)	1964	Cameo 302
Boy With The Green Eyes, The	Angels (New Jersey)	1968	RCA 9612
Boyee Yoing	Marvellos	1958	Stepheny 1818/Cha Cha 756
Boyfriend	Serenadetts	1961	Enrica 1008
Boys	Shirelles	1960	Scepter 1211 (first pressing)
Boys And Girls	Delrons, Reperata & the	1967	RCA 9123
Boys And Girls Together	Expressions, Johnny & the	1966	Josie 959
Boys Think (Every Girl's The Same)	Blenders (Chicago)	1963	Witch 117
Boys Who Don't Understand	Continettes	1963	Ritchie 4300
Brahm's Lullabye	Holidays, Buddy Sheppard & the	1962	Sabina 506
Brain, The	Ross, Ted & group	1959	Arwin 121
Brand New Automobile	Payments	NA	Kit 101
Branded	Robin, Richie	1960	Gone 5083
Brandy	English, Scott (with the Accents)	1971	Janus 171
Brazil	Coasters	1956	Atco 6073
Brazil	Velaires	1961	Jamie 1198
Bread	Fortunes	1981, 1990	Relic LP 5088/Relic CD
Bread And Butter	Newbeats	1964	
Bread Fred	Sallycats, Sally & the	1959	Rendezvous 105
Break Down And Love Me	Classmates	1956	Dot 15464
Break My Bones	Four Fellows (Brooklyn - Tri-Boro)	1953	Tri-Boro 101
Break The Glass	Donnybrooks	1959	Calico 108
Breaker Of Dreams	Tornados, Johnny Mann & the	1958	Donnie 27746
Breaker Of Hearts	Ravens	NA	Argo (unreleased)
Breaker Of Hearts	Stylers	1957	Jubilee 5279
Breakin' Up Is Hard To Do	Jokers, Jivin' Gene & the	1959	Mercury 71485
Breaking Hearts	Thomases, Varetta & the	1963	Brent 7040
Breaking Hearts To Him Is Just A Game	Delights	1964	Arlen 753
Breaking My Heart	Pharaohs, Al Epp & the	1959	Wildcat 0018
Breaking The Ice	Twiggs, Hugh Bell & the	1954	Blaze 109
Breaking Up Again	Climates	1967	Sun 404
Breaking Up Is Hard To Do	Channels, Earl Lewis & the	1971	Rare Bird 5017
Breaking Up Is Hard To Do	Cupcakes, Cookie & the	1963	Lyric 1009/Paula 312 (68)
Breaking Up Is Hard To Do	Jokers, Jivin' Gene & the	1959	Jin 116
Breaks Of Life	Crowns, Arthur Lee Maye & the	1964	Jamie 1284
Breakthrough	Sunsets, Adrian & the	1963	Sunset 602
Breakup	Dories	1962	Dore 629
Breath Of Air	Squires (California)	1956	Vita 128
Breeze And I, The	Flamingos	1959	End LP 304
Breeze And I, The	Four Most	1959	Milo 107/Relic 501 (63)
Breezy	Tokens (Brooklyn)	1966	B.T. Puppy 519
Brenda	Cherokees (Philadelphia)	1954	Grand (unreleased)
Brenda	Cupids	1962	KC 115/AAnko 1002 (63)
Brenda	Precisions	NA	Rayna 1001
Bride	Hollywood Teeners, Jimmy Norman & the	1960	Fun 101
Bridge Of Love	Baker, Roy Boy & group	1963	Dess 7011
Bridge Of Love	Teardrops	1957	Dot 15669
Bridge Of Tears	Flamingos	1960	End LP 307
Bridgitte	Barons (Whitehall)	1959	Whitehall 30008
Brief Romance	Collegiates	1959	Capo 001
Bright And Early	Nelson, Vikki (with the Wheels)	1956	Premium 402
Bright Brown Eyes	Rays (Frankie Valli)	1962	Perri 1004
Bright Red Skinny Pants	Charades	1959	United Artists 183
Brightest Star In The Sky	Beau-Jives	NA	Lord Bingo 102
Bring Back	Van Dellos	1961	Card 558
Bring Back My Baby	Bel-Airs Five	1964	USA 764
Bring Back My Baby To Me	Morse, Ella Mae & group	1954	Capitol 2992
Bring Back My Life	Van Dyke Five	1967	Corner Closet 101
Bring Back Wendy	Elegants	1965	Laurie 3298
Bring Back Yesterday	Salutations, Vito & the	1966	Boom 60020
Bring Back Your Heart	Darchaes, Nicky Addeo & the	1963	Savoy 200/Earls 1533
Bring Back Your Heart	Dell Vikings	1961	ABC 10208
Bring Back Your Heart	Hines, William A. & group	1960	Ball 508
Bring Back Your Love (To Me)	Smoothtones	1955	Jem 412

SONG	GROUP	YEAR	LABEL
Bring Her Back To Me	Robbins, Billy & group	1957	Dig 127
Bring It Home To Me	Tides	1961	620 1007
Bring It On Home	Dawn	1968	Rust 5128
Bring It On Home To Daddy	Restless Hearts, Fred Parris & the	1966	Atco 6439
Bring It On Home To Me	Bee Jays, Buddy Johnson & the (Ella Johnson with)	1956	Mercury 70912
Bring Me A Bluebird	Ebonaires	1988	Relic LP 5076
Bring Me Happiness (Rosie & Ron)	Thunderbirds, Ron Holden & the (Rosie & Ron)	1961	Donna 1338
Bring Me Love	Clovers	1956	Atlantic 1107
Bring Me Your Love	Midnighters, Hank Ballard & the	1962	King 5703
Bring My Baby Back	Colonials, Bill Bass Gordon & the	1954	Gee 12
Bring My Daddy Home	Entrees, Chuck Corley & the	1966	Sonic 118
Bring The Money Home	Orioles, Sonny Til & the	1983	Murray Hill LP M61277
Bring Yourself Back Here	Mint, Little Eddie & group	1959	Memo 17921
Bristol Stomp	Attractions, J.R. & the	1965	Hunch 928
Bristol Stomp	Dovells	1961	Parkway 827 (first pressing)
Bristol Twistin' Annie	Dovells	1962	Parkway 838
Broadway	Midnighters, Hank Ballard & the	1962	King 5593
Broke	Ballads (Connecticut)	1956	Franwil 5028
Broke	Five Echoes	1954	Sabre 105
Broke	Joy Boys, Chuck Higgins & the	1954	Specialty 532
Broke Down, Baby	Tyrones	1958	Decca 30559
Broke Up	Blue Crystals	1959	Mercury 71455
Broke Up	Moods	1959	Sarg 179
Broken	Bonnie Sisters	1956	Rainbow 328
Broken Date	Hubbcaps, Frank Hubbell & the	1963	Topix 6005
Broken Down Merry-Go-Round	G-Notes	1959	Guyden 2012
Broken Dream	Three Cheers	1959	Glory 291
Broken Dreams	Kittens	1960	Alpine 67
Broken Dreams	Three D's	1956	Pilgrim 719
Broken Heart	Barin, Pete (with the Belmonts)	1962	Sabina 504
Broken Heart	Cadillacs	1957	Josie 820
Broken Heart	Fiestas (not the Fiestas; actually an unknown group)	1962, 1971	Old Town 1122/ Cotillion 44117
Broken Heart	Four Checkers	1959	Ace 129
Broken Heart	Moonlighters	1958	Tara 100/Josie 843 (58)
Broken Heart	Shaw, Joan & group	1956	ABC 9724
Broken Heart	Vel-Tones	1960	Vel 9178
Broken Heart (live)	Bon-Aires	1982	50th U.G.H.A. Show Commemoration 45
Broken Heart Prayer	Montereys, Sandra Patrick & the	1964	Dominion 1008
Broken Heart, The	Bobbettes	1962	Jubilee 5442
Broken Hearted	Three D's	1961	Dean 521
Broken Hearted Baby	Five Notes	1955	Jen D 4185/Josie 784 (55)
Broken Hearted Me	Martineques	1962	Danceland 779
Broken Hip Party	Clean Cut Clan, Dan & the	1962	Accent 1116
Broken Hip, The	Olympics	1963	Tri Disc 112
Broken Love	Fidelitys	1960	Sir 277
Broken Love	Lyrics (Dan-Tone)	1962	Dan-Tone 1002
Brokenest Heart In Town	Mar, Jerry & group	1957	Amp-3 131
Brooklyn	Passions	1990	Crystal Ball 157
Brother Ben	Chestnuts	1956	Davis 452
Brother Bill	Five Blind Boys	1972	Vintage 1000
Brother Bill	Meadowlarks	1951	Imperial 5146
Brown Boy	Jive Bombers	1952	Citation 1161
Brown Eyes	Chateaus	1958	Warner Bros. 5023
Bubbily Bubbily	Landi, Tony & group	1957	Safari 1001
Bubble Gum	Del-Larks	1992	Park Ave. 8
Bubble Gum	Morrocos, Little Joe & the	1959	Bumble Bee 500
Bubble Gum	Vacels, Ricky & the	1962	Express 711
Bubble Gum Bop	Dual Tones	1960	Sabre 204
Buck Dancin'	Kennedy, Ace & group	1961	Swan 4080
Bucket Head	Hightones, Claude & the	1959	Baytone 113
Buena Sera	Belvederes	1959	Jopz 1771

SONG	GROUP	YEAR	LABEL
Buffalo Bill	Cellos	1988	Relic LP 5074 (88)
Buffalo, The	Jesters	1962	Amy 859
Bug Eye	Hollywood Argyles	1960	Lute 5908
Bug Out	Seventeens	1958	Golden Crest 503
Bug, The	Rainbows	NA	Red Robin (unreleased)
Buick '59	Medallions	1954	Dootone 347
Build Me A Cabin	Southwinds	1958	Fury 1017
Bull Fight	Dolphins, Davey Jones & the	1961	Audicon 117
Bull Fight Cha Cha Cha	Mark V	1960	Milo 110
Bull Frog	Silhouettes	1961	20th Fox 240
Bull Moose Stomp	Four Winds	1961	Warwick 633
Bull, The	Highlighters	1958	New Song 116
Bull Tick Waltz	Coasters	1963	Atco 6251
Bulletin	Catalinas	1963	Dee Jay 1010/Sims 134 (63)
Bullseye	Fairlanes	1959	Dart 109
Bully, The	Passions	1963	ABC 10436
Bumble Bee	Rollins, Bird & group	1960	Harvard 805
Bumble Bee	Sonics (New York - Groove)	1955	Groove 0112
Bumble Bee	Vandells	1964	USA 758
Bump, The	Cardinals	1952	Atlantic 972
Bump Ti Dee Ump Bump	Terrifics	1959	Demon 1516
Bump-I-Dy Bump	Kings (Baltimore)	1960	Lookie 18/Epic 9370 (60)
Bumpity Road To Love	Twintones	1960	Banner 60203
Bunny Hill	Rip Chords	1965	Columbia 43221
Bunny Lee	Satelites, Ronny & the	1960	Dolly 22254
Bunny Tale, The	Privateers, Joyce & the	1962	Agon 1003
Buoys And Gulls	Cruisers	1958	Era 1052
Burgers, Fries And Shakes	Januarys, Little June & his	1957	Salem 188
Burgers From Heaven	Rhoades, Darryl & group	1976	Wonder 1976-1
Burn That Candle	Cues	1955	Capitol 3245
Burnin' Lips	Charms, Otis Williams & his	1958	DeLuxe 6165
Burnin' The Torch	Diplomats, Debbie & the	1958	Stepheny 1826
Burning Desire	Tempo-Mentals	1957	Ebb 112
Burning Fire	Clovers	1960	United Artists 263
Burning Love	Classics (Brooklyn)	1960	Top Rank 2061
Burning Love	Love-Lords	1962	Al-King 11021
Bury The Hatchet	Chuckles, Chuck & the	1959	Shad 5015
Burying Ground	Relations	NA	Club
Bus Fare Home	Spaniels	1960	Vee Jay 350
Buscando (Searchin')	Belairs, Mike & the	1963	Cobra 6666
Busiest Corner In My Hometown, The	Blenders (New York)	1951	Decca 27587
Busy As A Bumble Bee	Stanton, Johnny & Louis	1954	Show Time 1105
Busy Bee	Four Jacks, Janet Shay & the	1960	Alcar 1502
Busy Body Rock	Gadabouts	1956	Mercury 70823/Wing 90062 (56)
Busy Body Rock	Mints	1956	Lin 5001
But Always Your Friend	Rockets, Herb Kenny & the	1953	MGM 11487
But Beautiful	Four Embers	1963	Smash 1846
But For Love	Angels (New Jersey)	1968	RCA 9612
But I Do	Jewels (female)	1964	Dimension 1048
But I Forgive You	Serenaders (Detroit)	1952	Coral 65093
But I Know	Blenders (Paradise)	1959	Paradise 111
But I Love You	Beau-Jives	NA	Lord Bingo 102
But It's Too Late	Capitols, Johnny Houston & the	1957	East West 100
But Not For Me	Click-Ettes	1960	Dice 100
But Not For Me	Flamingos	1959	End 1040
But Not For Me	Zodiacs, Maurice Williams & the	1974	Relic LP 5017
But Only With You	Dumonts	1961	King 5552
But That Was Long Ago	Wood, Lori (with the Belmonts)	1962	Amy 842
But Who Will Pay	Show Stoppers	1963	Amber 212
But Yesterday	Gigolos, Jamie Coe & the	1962	Big Top 3107
But You Lied	Mello-Kings	1962	Lescay 3009
But Your Mother She Said No	Oxfords, Darrell & the	1960	Roulette 4230
But You're My Baby	Tabs	1962	Vee Jay 446
Butterball	Butterballs	1963	Times Square 24
Butterball	Penguins	1959	Dooto LP 242/Dooto EP 241

SONG	GROUP	YEAR	LABEL
Buttered Popcorn	Supremes (Detroit)	1961	Tamla 54045
Buttered Popcorn	Vows	1965	V.I.P. 25016
Butterfly	Crests	1960	Coed LP 901
Butterfly	Keynotes, Bill Allen & the	1957	Eldorado 505
Butterfly, The	Challengers	1962	Tri-Phi 1015/Challenge 1105 (62)
Buttermilk	Hitmakers	1965	Dore 738
Butterscotch	Royaltones, Ruth McFadden & the	1960	Goldisc 3016
Buttin' In	Midnighters, Hank Ballard & the	1963	King 5821
Buy A Van	Dreamaires, L. Flaytus & the	1985	Antrell 101
Buy Now, Pay Later	Vails	1960	Belmont 4002
Buy This Record For Me	Metronomes, Leon & the	1965	Carnival 515
Buzz Buzz	Emanons (Brooklyn)	NA	Connie (unreleased)
Buzz Buzz	Satellites	1960	Palace 102
Buzz Buzz Buzz	Aire-Dales, Rocky Roberts & the	1965	Brunswick 55357
Buzz Buzz Buzz	Cadillacs	1961	Jubilee LP 1117/Jubilee LP 5009 (62)
Buzz Buzz Buzz	Decades	1980	Avenue D 1
Buzz-Buzz-Buzz	Hollywood Flames	1957	Ebb 119/Mona Lee 135
Buzz-Buzz-Buzz	Original Cadillacs, Earl Carroll & the	1958	Josie 829
Buzzin'	King Bees	1958	Checker 909
B'wa Nina	Tokens (Brooklyn)	1962	RCA 7991
Bwana	Uniques, Sabby Lewis & the	1959	Gone 5074
By And By My Love	Hi Toppers, V. James & the	1961	Kent 354
By Bye For Just A While	Four Guys	1955	Wing 90036
By Golly Gee	Deuces Wild	1960	Sheen 108
By Love Possessed	Four J's	1964	Jamie 1274
By My Love, Be My Love	Wonders, Tony Allen & the	1958	Forward 601/Tampa 157 (58)
By My Side	Belvin, Jesse & group	1957	Modern 1015
By My Side	Long, Bobby & his Cherrios	1958	Arrow 727
By My Side	Nelson, Vikki (with the Wheels)	1956	Premium 402
By My Side	Tiny Tim & group	1959	DeLuxe 6184
By Nellie's	Aristocrats, Tony Smith & His	NA	Mad 1006
By Now	Dukes, Billy Duke & the	1956	Sound 130
By The Candle Glow	Lance, Herb (with the Classics)	1957	DeLuxe 6150
By The Candleglow	Cherokees (Philadelphia)	NA	Lost Nite 379/Grand 111 (78)
By The Candleglow	Youngtones (with the Dolls)	1958	X-Tra 110/Times Square 13 (63)
By The Candlelight	Cherokees (Philadelphia)	1954	Grand (unreleased)
By The Candlelite	Egyptians, King Pharaoh & the	1961	Federal 12413
By The Fire	Four Escorts, Dave Passecallo & the	1961	Bi-Mi 101
By The Light Of The Silvery Moon	Blazers, Little Bernie & the	1962	Josie 884
(By The Light Of The) Silvery Moon	Emotions	1962, 1981	Card 600/Jason Scott 12
By The River Sainte Marie	Platters	1960	Mercury LP 20481/Mercury 60160 (60)
By The Riverside	Empires	1955	Wing 90050
By The Waters Of Minnetonka	Gadabouts	1954	Mercury 70495
By You By You	Belairs, Lee Bantell & the	NA	Coral 61735
By You, By You	Zane, Herb & group	1956	DeLuxe 6099
Bye And Bye	Dominoes	1959	Liberty LP 3056
Bye And Bye	Turbans (Philadelphia)	1957	Herald 495
Bye, Bay Baby	Juliettes	1980	Catamount 779
Bye Bye	Bon-Aires	1964	Rust 5077
Bye Bye	Cosmic Rays	1960	Saturn 222
Bye, Bye	Dreamers, Richard Berry & the	1954	Flair 1052
Bye Bye	Duals	1959	Arc 4446
Bye Bye	Pastels (Chicago)	1955	States (unreleased)
Bye Bye	Symbols	1973	Vintage 1007
Bye Bye	Winters, David & group	1962	Rori 703
Bye Bye	Wright, Rubin & group	1959	Lancer 101
Bye Bye Baby	Blue Notes, Little Bill & the	1959	Dolton 4
Bye Bye Baby	Channels, Earl Lewis & the	1958	Fury 1021/Fury 1071 (58)
Bye Bye Baby	Charms, Otis Williams & the	1954	DeLuxe 6034
Bye, Bye, Baby	Keynotes	1956	Apollo 493
Bye, Bye Baby	Revlons	NA	VRC 112
Bye Bye Baby	Rocky Fellers	1963	Scepter 1263
Bye Bye Baby	Spices, Sugar & the	1963	Stacy 968
Bye Bye Baby	Symbols	1967	Laurie 3401
Bye Bye Baby	Teenettes	1963	Sandy 250

SONG	GROUP	YEAR	LABEL
Bye Bye Baby Blues	Ravens	1946, 1948, 1949, 1955	Hub 3032/National 9040/ King/Mercury 70413
Bye Bye Bye	Ramblers (Cora)	1964	Cora 101
Bye, Bye, Bye	Tokens (Brooklyn)	1967	Warner Bros. 7099
Bye Bye Love	Count Victors	1961	Rust 5034
Bye Bye Love	Fireflies	1962	Taurus LP 1002
Bye, Bye, My Baby	Eastmen	1959	Mercury 71434
Bye Bye My Love	Chips	1961	Ember 1077
Bye Bye Pretty Baby	Mello-Tone 3, Little E & the	1961	Falco 302
Bye Bye Truly	Students (Philadelphia)	1958	Red Top
Bye Everybody	Impalas (Brooklyn)	1959	Cub 9053
Bye-Bye My Baby	Echoes	1960	Columbia 41549
Bye-Bye-Baby	Travis, Danny & group	1962	Benn-X 54

C

SONG	GROUP	YEAR	LABEL
C. C. Rider	Romans, Little Caesar & the	1961	Del-Fi 4170
C. Percy Mercy (Of Scotland)	Ding-A-Lings	1960	Capitol 4467
C. Percy Mercy Of Scotland Yard	Marathons	1961	Arvee 5038
C.C. Rider	Hollywood Flames	19??	Unreleased
Cabin Hideaway	Limelighters	1956	Josie 795
Caddy Bo	Magnificents	1956	Vee Jay 208
Cadillac Jack	Williams, Andre & group	1968	Checker 1205
Cadillac Man	Jesters	1966	Sun 400
Cadillac Song, The	Ravens	Between 1947 & 1950	National (unreleased)
Cadillac Song, The	Smith Quartet, Ben	1953	Rama 17
Cadwallader	Travelers	1961	Decca 31215
Caesar Haircut	James, Tammy & group	1963	Janlene 776
Cafe Bohemian	Enchanters (Orbit)	1959	Orbit 532/Bamboo 513 (61)
Caissons Go Rolling Along, The	Castle Kings	1962	Atlantic 2158
Calcutta	Valiants (Columbia)	1961	Columbia 41931
Caldonia's Mambo	Street Singers	1956	Tuxedo 899
Calendar Of Love	Team Mates	1964	Le Mans 003
California	Five Chances	1977	Atomic 2494
California Baby	Hearts, Eugene Ball with the	1957	Melatone 1001
California GL-903	Lee, Curtis (with the Halos)	1960	Dunes 801
California On My Mind	Coastliners	1967	Dear 1300
Call A Doctor	Jewels (New York)	1953	Rama 10
Call Baby Call	Diamonds (Harold Sonny Wright)	1952	Atlantic 981
Call Me	Chord Spinners	1961	Liberty 55368
Call Me	Fifes, Edward Hamilton & the	NA	Jameco 1630
Call Me	Steinways	1966	Oliver 2007
Call Me A Coward	Miamians	1958	Amp-3 1006
Call Me A Fool	Gunter, Cornel (with the Ermines)	1957	Dot 15654
Call Me, Call Me, Call Me	Gibson, Dolores & group	1954	Aladdin 3255
Call Me Darling	Caston, Bobby & group	1957	Atlas 1103
Call My Name	Crescents, Clara Hardy & the	NA	Astra 3010
Call My Name	Keystoners	1992	Starbound 515
Call Off The Wedding	Du Droppers, Sunny Gale with the	1954	RCA 5746
Call On Me	Blend-Aires	1977	Arcade 104
Call On Me	Blue Sky Boys	1971	Blue Sky 100
Call On Me	Harper, Chuck & group	1962	Felsted 8658
Call On Me	Mello-Moods (with Teacho Wiltshire Band)	1952	Prestige 799
Call Somebody Please	First Ward Dukes	1977	Clifton 20
Call Somebody Please	Manhattans	1972	Rim LP 101
Call The Doctor	L'Cap-Tans	1958	Hollywood 1092
Call The Police	Monclairs	NA	Fortune LP 8017
Callin' Joann	Dreamlovers	1966	Mercury 72630
Callin' My Love	De-Icers	1957	De-Icer 100
Calling	Long, Bobby & his Cherrios	1959	Unart 2023
Calling All Cows	Blue Rockers	1955	Excello 2062
Calling For Love	Ambassadors	1987	Relic LP 5071
Calling You	Rockets, Herb Kenny & the	1952	MGM 11360
Cal's Tune	Veltones	1959	Coy 101/Kapp 268 (59)
Calypso	Litterbugs	1963	Okeh 7164
Calypso Baby	Sabres	1955	Bullseye 101

SONG	GROUP	YEAR	LABEL
Calypso Beat	Don Juans, Little Eddie & the	1955	Fortune 836
Calypso Fever	Twilights, Phyllis Branch & the	1957	Tuxedo 919
Calypso Jump	Five J's	1958	Fulton 2454
Calypso Mama	Marvellos	1955	Theron 117
Calypso Peacock	Bussy, Terry & group	1956	Jazzmar 103
Calypso Rock 'N' Roll	Deeps	1957	Que 1000
Calypso Song	Ravens	1952	Mercury 8291
Came, Saw, Conquered	Angels, Little Bobby Bell & the	1957	Demon 1501
Camel Caravan	Classicals	1962	Kent 379
Camel Train	Fortune Tellers	1961	Music Makers 105
Camel Walk	Saxons	1960	Sho-Biz 1003
Camel Walk	Starfires	1959	Apt 25030
Camera	Beaumont, Jimmy & group	1961	May 112
Campus Girl	Doug & Freddy (with the Pyramids)	1961	K&G 100
Campus Rock, The	Tyrones	1956	Wing 90072
Can Can Rock & Roll	La Fets & Kitty	1957	Apollo 520
Can I Be In Love	Four Bel-Aires, Larry Lee & the	1959	M-Z 006
Can I Be Sure	Poni-Tails	1957	Marc 1001
Can I Be Your Lover Boy	Contours, Mike Hanks & the	1960	Brax 221/222
Can I Come Over Tonight?	Five Satins	1961	Cub 9090
Can I Come Over Tonight?	Velours	1957	Onyx 512/Gone 5092 (60)/Relic 504 (64)
Can I Come Over?	Youngtones	1959, 1963	X-Tra 120/121
Can I Depend On You	Salutations, Vito & the	1964, 1966	Wells 1008/Rust 5106
Can I Get Him	Pearlettes	1961	Vee Jay 422/Go 712
Can I Have Someone	Quotations	1968	Imperial 66368
Can I Run To You	Hodges, Charles (with the Fi-Tones)	1965	Alto 2016
Can I Take You Home Little Girl	Drifters (1959-forward)	1975	Bell (UK) 1462
Can I Walk You Home?	Velours	1958	Onyx 520/Orbit 9001 (58)/ Cub 9001 (58)
Can It Be	Four Brothers And A Cousin	1954	Jaguar 3005
Can It Be Wrong	Marquees	1960	Do-Ra-Mi 1407
Can It Be?	Rainbows, Randy & the	1966	Mike 4008
Can It Be?	Titans	1958	Specialty 625
Can This Be Christmas?	Falcons (Detroit)	1957	Silhouette 521
Can This Be Love	Pearlettes	1962	Vault 100
Can This Be Love?	Winners	1956	Rainbow 331
Can You Do The Duck	Larks (Don Julian)	1965	Money 115
Can You Find It In Your Heart	Four Blades	1956	Gateway 1170
Can You Go	Roulettes	1964	United Artists 718
Can You Help Me	Knickerbockers	1966	Challenge 59348
Can You Imagine	Madisons	1964	Lawn 240
Can You Love Me	Little Sammy & group	1956	Shade 1002
Can You Please Crawl Out Your Window	Vacels	1965	Kama Sutra 204
Can You Remember	Celtics	1957	Al Jacks 2
Can You Remember?	Cameos (Pittsburgh)	1963	Gigi 100
Can You Talk	Medallions, Vernon Green & the	1973	Dootone 479
Can You Tell Me Why	McNeil, Angele & group	1957	Felsted 8503
Can You Tell Me?	Teenagers (Johnny Houston)	1960	End 1076
Canadian Sunset	Adelphis	1973	Merry-Go-Round 103
Canadian Sunset	Adorations	1972	Dreamtone 202
Canadian Sunset	Arrogants	1963	Lute 6226/Candlelite 425
Canadian Sunset	Cameos (Pittsburgh)	1960	Matador 1813
Canadian Sunset	Dee Jays	1962	Sonata 1100
Canadian Sunset	Dreamers (Yonkers, N.Y.)	1960	Guaranteed 219
Canadian Sunset	Exzels	1963	Crossfire 228
Canadian Sunset	Fabulous Splendors	1960	O-Gee 105
Canadian Sunset	Impacts	1959	Watts 5600/RCA 7609 (59)
Canadian Sunset	Quarter Notes	1960	Imperial 5647
Canadian Sunset	Ribitones	1980	U.G.H.A. 14
Canadian Sunset	Silvertones	1962	Joey 302
Canadian Sunset	Symbols	1966	President 102
Canadian Sunset	Windsong	NA	
Cancel The Call	Blue Belles	1953	Atlantic 987
Cancel The Reservation	Skipper, Buddy & group	1968	Smash 2173
Candle In The Wind	Mitchell, Tony & group	1963	Canadian American 157

SONG	GROUP	YEAR	LABEL
Candlelight	Concords (Brooklyn)	1954	Harlem 2328
Candlelight	Emotions	1958	Fury 1010
Candlelight	Five Satins	1960	Ember 1066
Candlestick Cafe	Sheiks	1959	Jamie 1147
Candy	Astors	1965	Stax 170
Candy	Casual-Aires	1958	Brunswick 55064
Candy	Fabulous Echoes	1965	Liberty 55801
Candy And Gum	Douglas, Ronnie & group	1961	Everest 19425
Candy Apple Red Impala	Mello-Tone 3, Little E & the	1961	Falco 302
Candy Bar Boogie	Parakeets	1973	Roadhouse 1005
Candy Cane Sugary Plum	Juniors, Danny & the	1960	Swan 4064
Candy Coated Kisses	Monitors	1955	Aladdin 3309
Candy Coated Lies	Decaro Brothers	1964	Liberty 55700
Candy Doll	Macree, Vincent & group	1957	Gametime 103
Candy From A Baby	McDonald, Ken & group	1957	DeLuxe 6121
Candy Girl	Chellows	1964	Hit 77
Candy Girl	Hawks	1954	Imperial 5266
Candy Queen	Four Graduates	1964	Rust 5084
Candy Stick Twist	R-Dells	1962	Gone 5128
Candy Store Blues	Capers	1959	Vee Jay 315
Candy Store Blues	Casual Three	1957	Mark-X 7009
Candy Store Love	Val-Chords	1957	Gametime 104
Candy Store Lullabye	Blades, Carol (with the Harptones)	1956	Gee (unreleased)
Can't Believe That You've Grown Up	Squires (Congress)	1964	Congress 223
Can't Do Sixty No More	Dominoes	1955	Federal 12209
Can't Do Sixty No More	Du Droppers	1952	Red Robin 108
Can't Do Without You	Hearts, Lee Andrews & the	1968	Lost Nite 1004
Can't Find A Girl	Newports, Cal Linley & the	1960	DC 0431
Can't Find My Sadie	Checkers	1955	King 4764
Can't Find The Time To Tell You	Pastimes	1986	Starlight 36
Can't Get Enough Of Your Love	Dantes	1966	Jamie 1314
Can't Get Over You	Capris (Fable)	1959	Fable 665
Can't Get You Off My Mind	Dreamers (New York - Jubilee)	1951	
Can't Go For That	Tra-Velles	NA	Debonair 101
Can't Go On	Offitt, Lillian & group	1958	Excello 2139
Can't Help But Sing The Blues	Bluebirds	1952	Rainbow 199
Can't Help Falling In Love	Four Esquires	1962	Terrace 7502
Can't Help Lovin' That Girl Of Mine	Excels	1961	R.S.V.P. 111
Can't Help Lovin' That Girl Of Mine	Leaders	1956	Glory 243
Can't Help Lovin' That Girl Of Mine	Memories, Danny & the	1964	Valiant 6049
Can't Help Loving That Girl Of Mine	Endings	1974	Barrier 101
Can't Help Loving That Girl Of Mine	Hideaways	1956	Ronni 1000
Can't Help Loving You	Bachelors (Washington, D.C.)	1953	Aladdin 3210
Can't It Be True	Counts, Bobby Comstock & the	1964	Lawn 232
Can't Keep From Crying	Five Keys	1953, 1971 (1951)	Aladdin 3113A (unreleased)/ Aladdin 3167
Can't Let Your Lovin' Go	Satellites, Joe Potito & the	1957	Safari 1003
Can't Make It Without You	Superiors	1966	MGM 13503
Can't Play A Playgirl	Jillettes	1963	Philips 40140
Can't See For Lookin'	Hawks	1955	Imperial 5332
Can't See Why	Starfires, Wayne Hammond & the	1959	Gala 105
Can't Seem To Laugh Anymore	Orioles, Sonny Til & the	1950	Jubilee 5040
Can't Stand It Any Longer	Barlow, Dean	1956	
Can't Stand It Any Longer	Four Pals	1956	Royal Roost 616
Can't Stand To Lose You	Colonairs	1957	Ember 1017
Can't Stop	Fascinators (Detroit)	1955	Blue Lake 112
Can't Tag Along	Idols	1961	E-Z 1214
Can't Take It	Del-Rays, Detroit Jr. & the	1964	C.J. 637
Can't Take It	Shells	1961	Johnson 109
Can't Tell You	Ford, Ann & group	1959	Apollo 532
Can't Understand It	Voxpoppers	1959	Versailles 200
Can't Wait	Dell Vikings	1958	Mercury 71266
Can't Wait For Tomorrow	Five Bills	1953	Brunswick 84002
Can't We Be Sweethearts	Armpits, Snake & the	NA	Explo 013
Can't We Be Sweethearts	Blue Stars	1977	Arcade 103

SONG	GROUP	YEAR	LABEL
Can't We Be Sweethearts	Cleftones	1956	Gee 1016
Can't We Be Sweethearts	Taffys	1963	Pageant 608
Can't We Fall In Love	Illusions	1961	Ember 1071
Can't We Just Be Friends	Little Cheryl & group	1963	Cameo 270
Can't We Talk This Over?	Diablos, Nolan Strong & the	1957	Fortune 525
Can't You Come Out	Fidelitys	1958	Baton 256
Can't You Go For Me?	Lincolns	1959	Mercury 71553
Can't You See	Dell Vikings	NA	D.R.C. 101
Can't You See	Keys, Ricky & the	1958	Savoy 1529
Can't You See	Newtones	1965	Relic 1009
Can't You See	Tune Drops, Malcolm Dodds & the	1957	End 1004
Can't You See I Love You	Rainbows	1954, 1973	Gem 214/Baron 105
Can't You See, I Need A Friend	Midnighters, Hank Ballard & the	1961	King 5550
Can't You See I'm Lonely	Fascinators (Burn)	1965	Burn 845
Can't You See It In My Eyes	Electras	1964	Challenge 59245
Can't You See It In My Eyes	Rhythm Rockers, Jimmy Reagan & the	1959	G&G 128/129/Mona-Lee
Can't You See (Oo-Wee)	Clouds, Donna Dee & the	1961	Ramada 501
Can't You Stay A Little Longer	Twiliters	1961	Sara
Can't You Tell	Gents, Larry & the	1964	Delaware 1700
Can't You Tell By The Look In My Eyes	Reflections	1964	Golden World 8/9
Can't You Tell?	Oxfords, Darrell & the	1960	Roulette 4230
Can't You Understand?	King Bees	1957	KRC 302
Cantina	Payments	NA	Kit 101
Captain Of My Ship	Fidelitys	1959	Baton 261
Captain Of Your Ship	Delrons, Reperata & the	1968	Mala 589
Car Crash	Cadets	1960, 1974	Jan-Lar 102
Cara Mia	Chapters, Reuben & the	1979	Surfside 3
Carachi	Medallions (Medalions)	1959	Sultan 1004
Caravan Of Lonely Men	Lafayettes	1962	RCA 8082
Caravan Of Lonely Men	Lovers	1965	Agon 1011
Cards Of Love	Reminiscents	1962	Marcel 1000
Cards Of Love	Triumphs, Tico & the	1963	Amy 876
Cards On The Table	Diplomats	1964	Arock 1000
Care	Graduates	1959	Shan-Todd 0055
Care	Marveltones	1952	Regent 196
Careful With My Heart	Playboys	1962	Cotton 1008
Careless	Gallahads	1955	Capitol 3060
Careless Love	De Marco, Lou & group	1956	Ferris 903
Careless Love	Kennedy, Tom & group	NA	Golden Crest 103
Careless Love	Pilgrims	1956	Baton 235
Careless Love	Ravens	1949	National 9073
Careless Love	Tradewinds, Rudy & the	1962	Angle Tone 543
Careless Lover	Clippers, Big Mike Gordon & the	1956	Baton 233
Careless With Love	Originals	1960	Lo-Lon 101
Carelessly	Cadillacs	1959	Jubilee LP 1089
Carelessly	Keynotes	1957	Pop 111
Caring	Coachmen	1954	X 0044
Caring	Four Jokers	1954	MGM 11815
Carioca	Aqua-Nites	1965	Astra 1000/Astra 2003 (65)
Carmelita	Fabulous Valients	1962	Holiday 61005
Carmella	Bell Hops	1958	Barb 101/102
Carmen, I Wish You Were Here	Matadors	NA	Chavis 103
Carmen My Love	Blue Diamonds	1962	London 10006
Carol	Belltones (Philadelphia)	1953	Grand 100
Carol	Darchaes, Ray & the	1962	Aljon 1249/1250
Carol	Schoolboys	1957	Okeh 7090
Carol Ann	Mon-Vales	1958	Pen Joy 501
Carol Ann	Windsors	1959	Wig Wag 203
Carol Lee	Martels, Eulis Mason & the	1959	Bella 20
Carole	Dreamers, Donnie & the	1961	Decca 31312
Carolina Moon	Melodymakers	1957	Hollis 1001
Carol's Theme	Juliettes	1980	Catamount 779
Carolyn	Five Kids	1955	Maxwell 101
Carolyn	Rivileers	1954	Baton 205
Carolyn	Starfires, Wayne Hammond & the	1959	Gala 105

SONG	GROUP	YEAR	LABEL
Carolyn	Tornados, Aaron McNeil & the	1960	C.J. 615
Carrie	Consorts	1977	Crystal Ball 111
Carrie Lou	Termites	1964	Bee 1825
Carrie (You're An Angel)	Runarounds	1964	Felsted 8704
Carried Away	Flamingos	1953	Chance 1145/Vee Jay 384 (61)
Carrot Top	Donettes, Don Eddy & the	1960	Rona 1002
Cartoon Song, The	Olympics	1969	Jubilee 5674
Cartoons	Ebbs	1959	Dore 521
Ca-Sandra	Mello-Tones	1957	Gee 1040
Casanova	Caronators	1960	Clock 1049
Casanova	Girlfriends, Erlene & the	1963	Old Town 1152
Casanova	Mixers	1959	Bold 102
Casanova	Portee, Robin & group	1963	Diamond 151
Casanova Brown	Young Sisters	1960	Twirl 2001
Casey Cop	Elgins (California)	1961	Flip 353
Cash	Champagnes	1963	Skymac 1002/Laurie 3189 (63)
Cash	Prells	1964	Skyline 1004
Cassius Clay	Accents (California)	1962	Joker 200
Cast Your Vote	Hendricks, Bowithy (with the Coasters)	1959	Sue 710
Casting My Spell	Johnson Brothers	1959	Valor 2006
Castle In The Sky	Bop Chords	1957	Holiday 2601
Castle In The Sky	Honorables	1961	Honor Records 100
Castle In The Sky (acappella)	Citadels	1975	Relic LP 105
Castle Of Dreams	Feathers, June Moy & the	1955	Show Time 1103
Castle Of Love	Buddies	1959	Okeh 7123
Castle Of Love	Catalinas	1958, 1973	Little 811/812/Jayne 502
Castle Of Love, The	Raiders	1958	Atco 6125
Casual	Carnations	1960	Fraternity 863
Casually	Tunesters	1959	Tiara 6129
Cat Hop	Dodgers	1955	Aladdin 3271
Cat 'N' Mouse	Furys	1963	World Pacific 386
Cat Scratching	Williams, Marie & group	1961	Smart 324
Cat Snapper	Nuggets	1962	RCA 8031
Catch A Little Moonbeam	Rinky-Dinks (with Bobby Darin)	1959	Capitol 4146
Catch Me, I'm Falling Again	Teardrops	1958	Rendezvous 102
Catch That Teardrop	Five Royales	1962	ABC 10348
Caterpillar Crawl	Roommates, Dick Dixon & the	1959	Kapp 292
Cathy	Four Temptations	1958	ABC 9920
Cathy Darling	Holidays	NA	Mark IV 725
Catrina	Victorians	NA	Hercules 101
Cat's Meow, The	Romans	1958	Juno 013/014
Cattle Call	Tokens (Brooklyn)	1965	B.T. Puppy 512
Caught In A Lie	Four Graduates	1978	Crystal Ball 116
Caught Raped And Tied	Charmers, Jim Beasley & the	1957	Silhouette 519
Cause I Love You	Capitols	1958	Pet 807
'Cause I Love You	Castro, Vince (with the Tonettes)	1958	Apt 25025
Cause I Love You So	Kooltoppers	1955	Beverly 702
Cause I'm In Love	Baby Dolls	1958	RCA 7296
'Cause I'm Loving You	Marvells	1962	Finer Arts 2024
'Cause I'm Your Friend	Plush Pups, Terrie Parker & the	1961	Queen 24011
Cause Of A Bad Romance	Debonaires (New York)	1958, 1987	Combo 149/Relic LP 5069
'Cause We're In Love	Beau-Marks	1960	Shad 5021
'Cause You're Mine	G-Clefs	1956	Pilgrim 720
Cause You're Mine Alone	Crowns, Arthur Lee Maye & the	1957	Flip 330
Cause You're My Lover	Five Keys	1955	Capitol 3267
Caused By You	Twiliters	1961	Nix 102
Cave Man	Dominoes	1955	Federal 12218
Cave Man	Royal Teens	1959	Mighty 112
Cave Man	Vibrations	1960	Checker 961
Cave Man Hop	Jades, Jerry Coulston & the	1959	Christy 112
Cave Man Love	Blue Jays (Roulette)	1960	Roulette 4264
Cave Man Rock	Majestics (Florida)	1956	Marlin 802
Caveman	Satins, Tommy Roe & the	1960	Judd 1018
Celebrity Party	Scott Brothers	1959	Skyline 501
Cell Block #9	Individuals, Chuck Rio & the	1961	Tequila 103

SONG	GROUP	YEAR	LABEL
Cellar Stomp	Counts, Bobby & the	NA	Count 6985
Centennial March	Con-Dons	1962	Carlton 587
C'est La Vie	Blue Belles, Patti LaBelle & the	1963	Newtown 5777/King 5777 (63)
C'est La Vie	Five Keys	1957	Capitol LP 828/Capitol EP 2-828 (57)
C'est La Vie	Velours	1985, 1992	Clifton 75/100
C'est La Vie	Wrens	1956	Rama 194
C'est Si Bon	Chantels	1958	End EP 202/End LP 312 (61)
Cha Cha Baby	Cardigans, Dave & the	1963	Bay 216
Cha Cha Baby	New Yorkers 5	1955	Danice 801
Cha Cha Boom	Storey Sisters	1958	Baton 255
Cha Cha Boots	Happy Teens	1960	Paradise 114
Cha Cha Doo	Spindrifts	1958	ABC 9904
Cha Cha Go Go (Chicago Cha Cha)	Juniors, Danny & the	1961	Swan 4072
Cha Cha Henry	Imperials, Little Anthony & the	1958	End 1038
Cha Cha Minnie	Royal Aces, Jesse James & the	1962	Shirley 103
Cha Cha Of Love	Don Juans, Don Lake & the	1956	Fortune 520
Cha Cha Rock	Hi-Lighters	1958	Mercury 71342
Cha Cha Rock	Premiers, Ronnie & the	1961	Highland 1014
Cha Jezebel	Notes	1956	Capitol 3332
Cha-Cha Bop	Gray, Carol & group	1958	Rhythm 126
Cha-Cha-Toni	Re-Vels	1956	Sound 135
Cha-Cho Hop	McVea, Jack	1957	Tag 2200/Chess 1690 (58)
Cha-Hua-Hua	Pets	1958	Arwin 109
Chain Me, Baby (Blues Of Desire)	Du Droppers	1952	Red Robin 108
Chain Of Broken Hearts	Camelots	1965	Relic 530
Chain Of Broken Hearts	Street Vocal Band	1980	Starlight 44
Chain Reaction	Ultratones	1960	San Tana 101
Chains	Cookies	1962	Dimension 1002
Chains Around My Heart	Avalons	1956	Groove 0141
Chains Of Love	Drifters (1959-forward)	1965	Atlantic 2285
Chains Of Love	Hollywood Flames	1958	Ebb 146
Cha-Kow-Ski	Pets	1958	Arwin 109
Chalypso	Dukes, Billy Duke & the	1957	Peak
Chalypso Baby	Five Sounds	1958	Deb 1006
Cha-Lyp-So Baby	Nobletones	1958, 1973	C&M 182/Times Square 18 (63)
Chalypso Rock	Satellites, Dick & Slim & the	1959	Cool 113
Chalypso Train	Chancellors	1958	XYZ 105
Champagne	High Type Five, Billy Carr & the	1959	C&P 105
Chance	Four Sierras (Sierras)	1963	Mail Call 2333/2334
Chances Are	Tymes	1964	Parkway LP 7038
Chances I've Taken	Solitaires	1954	Old Town 1008
Chang Chang A-Lang	Royale Cita Chorus	1956	Gee 1021
Change In You, The	Corsairs, Landy McNeil & the	1964	Tuff 402
Change In You, The	Four Sounds	1961	Tuff
Change Of Heart	Vikings, Lee Martin & the	1960	Jin 149
Change Of Heart (acappella)	Nutmegs	NA	Unreleased
Change Of Love	Laurels, Kenny Loran & the	1958	Challenge 59010
Change Of Time	Emanons (New York)	1956	Gee 1005
Change Your Mind	Five Rovers	1956	Music City 798
Change Your Mind	Jones, Davey & group	1959	Marlin 6062
Change Your Mind	Spydels	1962	Assault 1860
Changed	Belgians	1964	Teek 4824-3/4824-4
Changing My Life For You	Z-Debs	1964	Roulette 4544
Changing My Love	Cuff Links	1963	Dooto 474
Changing Partners	Crickets, Dean Barlow & the	1954	Jay-Dee 785
Channel Fever	Phantoms	1957	Baton 244
Chant Of The Isles (acappella)	Holidays	1975	Relic LP 102
Chantel Rock	Chantels	1959	Unreleased
Chapel	Owens, Freddy & group	1961	Wall 550
Chapel Bells	Destinaires	1965	Old Timer 610
Chapel Bells	Fascinators (Brooklyn)	1958	Capitol 4053/Capitol 4544 (61)
Chapel Bells	Imaginations	1985	Relic LP 5058
Chapel Bells	Impossibles	1963	Blanche 029
Chapel Bells	Magics	1963	Debra 1003
Chapel Bells	Mistakes	1959	Lo-Fi 2311/2312/Tip Top

SONG	GROUP	YEAR	LABEL
Chapel Bells	Palisades	1963	Debra 1003
Chapel Bells	Sunny Boys	1959	Mr. Maestro 806/Take 3 2001
Chapel Bells Are Ringing	Keynotes	1989	Relic LP 5080
Chapel By The Sea, The	Four Stars	1958	Kay-Y 66781
Chapel Doors	Notations	1958, 1980	Wonder 100
Chapel In My Memory	Candy Makers	NA	Urban 125
Chapel In The Moonlight	Ecstasies	1979	Clifton 31
Chapel In The Moonlight	Five Chestnuts, Marvin Baskerville & the	1958	Drum 001
Chapel Of Cream Cheese	Four Skins, Eddie Gee & the	1974	Lost Cause 200
Chapel Of Dreams	Dubs	1958	Gone 5046/Gone 5069 (59)
Chapel Of Dreams	Exquisites	1985	Avenue D 13
Chapel Of Dreams	Infernos	NA	Clifton EP 502
Chapel Of Dreams	Time Spinners, Nick & the	1974	Kelway 109
Chapel Of Hearts	Gum Drops	1956	King 4963
Chapel Of Love	Birds, Don Mikkelsen & the	1961	Deck 600
Chapel Of Love	Hitmakers	1958	Original Sound 1
Chapel Of Love	Styles, Donnie & the	1964	Times Square 106
Chapel Of Love	Sundials	1962	Guyden 2065
Chapel Of Love	T-Birds, Don Mikkelsen & the	1959	Deck 600
Chapel Of Love	Williams, Bobby & group	1958	Deck 142
Chapel Of Memories	Twigs, Sonny Woods & the	1954	Hollywood 1015
Chapel Of St. Clair	Solitaires	1978 (1954)	Old Town (unreleased)
Chapel Of Tears	Carallons, Lonnie & the	1959, 1963, 1973	Mohawk 108/902/ Streetcorner 101 (73)
Chapel On A Hill	Dynamics	1963	Liberty 55628
Chapel On The Hill	Mello-Kings	1957	Herald 507
Charades	Sophomores (Massachusetts)	1957	Chord 1302/Epic 9259 (57)
Charge	Camelots	1962	Comet 930
Charged With Cheating	Cupcakes, Cookie & the	1964	Lyric 1015
Charlena	Ambertones	1964	GNP Crescendo 329
Charlena	Cognacs	1961	Roulette 4340
Charlena	Mid-Knighters	NA	Paragon 814/Arc 1028
Charlena	Savoys (Raynard)	NA	Raynard RS 10019
Charlena	Sevilles	1961	JC 116/Galaxy 721 (64)
Charlena	Trippers	1967	Ruby-Doo 5
Charlene	Feathers, Johnny Staton & the	1989	Classic Artists 109
Charlene	Quarter Notes, Neil Darrow & the	1959	Whizz 717
Charles My Darling	Dreamers, Eloise Brooks & the	1955	Aladdin 3303
Charleston	Lynn, Bobby & group	1961	CR 1002
Charleston Fish	Juniors, Danny & the	1961	Swan 4082
Charlie Brown	Coasters	1959	Atco 6132
Charlie Brown	Cues	1956	Capitol 3310
Charlie Brown	Runners	1953	Bell 107
Charlie Brown Got Expelled	X Classmates, Joe Tex & His	1959	Ace 559
Charlie Chan	Eventuals	1961	Okeh 7142
Charlie Chan	Sounds	1959	Sarg 172
Charlotte Amalie	Blue Notes, Todd Randall & the	1955	Tico 1083
Charm Bracelet	Capri, Bobby & group	1961	Artiste 101
Charm Bracelet	Rays, Bob Crewe & the	1957	Vik 0307
Charm Bracelet	Velvet Satins, Bobby Capri & the	1960, 1982	Ariste 101/Jason Scott 17447
Charock	Melodears	1958	Gone 5033
Chartreuse Caboose	Starfires	1961	Pama 117
Chase, The	Blue Denims, Wild Bill & the	1960	Gone 5082
Chasin' The Blues	Arist-O-Kats	1957	Vita 168
Chasin' The Blues	V-8s	NA	Aura 101
Cheap Skate	Five Masters	1959, 1986	Bumble Bee 502/Relic LP 8008
Cheated	Pearlettes	1962	Vault 100
Cheated Heart	Short Stories, Lenny O'Henry & the	1961	ABC 10222
Cheater	Avalons	NA	Unreleased
Cheater Sam	Dukes, Keith Alexander & the	1962	Gemini 901
Cheater Stomp	Playboys	NA	Catalina 1069
Cheatin' Baby	Coins	1954	Gee 10
Cheatin' On Me	Sparks, Curtis Irvin & the	1954	RPM 417
Cheatin' Traces	Sunliners, Sunny & the	1964	Tear Drop 3123
Cheating Game	Starfires	1960	Pama 115

SONG	GROUP	YEAR	LABEL
Cheating Heart	Seminoles	1960	Hi-Lite 109
Cheating On Me	Armen, Mickey & group	1958	Peek-A-Boo 1001
Cheating On Me	Midnights	1954	Music City 762
Check Yourself	Italian Asphalt And Pavement Company	1970	Colossus 110
Check Yourself, Baby	Chimes, Tony Allen & the	1956	Specialty 570
Checkerboard Love	Celestrals	1963	Don-El 125
Checkers	Sophomores (Massachusetts)	1957	Dawn 237
Checking On You Baby	Clair-tones	NA	Announcing 1000
Chee Koo Baby	Dukes, Lloyd Price & the	1954	Specialty 535
Cheek To Cheek	Belmonts	1976	Strawberry 106
Cheek To Cheek	Percells	1963	ABC 10401
Cheer Up	Five Fleets	1961	Seville 112
Cheery	Thrillers, Little Joe & the	1959	Okeh 7116
Cheese Cake	Nite Sounds	1962	Fortune 548
Cheree	Castelles	NA	Atco (unreleased)
Cherie	Blue Sky Boys	1972	Blue Sky 101
Cherie	Gay Notes	1959	Vim 501
Cherie	Hide-A-Ways	1955	MGM 55004
Cherie	Jivers	1956	Aladdin 3329
Cherie	Richie & group	1961	Kip 240
Cherish My Love	Glens	1960	Sudden 104
Cherokee Dance	Landers, Bob & group	1956	Specialty 576
Cherrlyn	Native Boys	1956	Combo 113
Cherry	Barnes, Big Syl & group	1960	Corvair 900
Cherry	Bon-Aires	1976	Flamingo 1000
Cherry	Diamonds (Harold Sonny Wright)	1953	Atlantic 1017
Cherry	Jive Bombers	1957	Savoy 1515
Cherry	Rivingtons	1963	Liberty 55610
Cherry	Velvet Satins	1964	General American 716
Cherry Baby	Millionaires	1965	Bunny 506
Cherry Bee	Dells	1983	Charly LP 1056
Cherry Blossom	Four Students, Varetta Dillard & the	1956	Groove 0152
Cherry Lips	Mar-Vels	1958	Love 5011/5012
Cherry Lips	Robins	1955	Whippet 200
Cherry Pie	Bel-Aires (Crown)	1954	Crown 126
Cherry Pie	Carmen, Jerry & group	1962	Barrish 500
Cherry Pie	Dialtones	1959	Dandy Dan 1
Cherry Pie	Sunsets, Adrian & the	1963	Sunset 602
Cherry Pie	Tri-Lads	1958	Bullseye 1003
Cheryl	Camerons	1960	Cousins 1/2
Cheryl	Elgins (Bronx)	1963	Dot 16563
Cheryl	Reno, Al & group	1961	Kapp 432
Cheryl	Vine, Marty & group	1961	Mastermade 101
Cheryl Ann	Peppermints	1965	Peppermint 1001
Cheryl Ann	Turn Ons, Tim Tam & the	1966	Palmer 5003
Cheryl Anne	Madisons	1965	MGM 13312
Cheryl Lee	Red Caps, Steve Gibson & the	1959	Hunt 326
Chewing Gum	Mystics, Ed Gates & the	1962	Robins Nest 2
Chi Chi	Blazers, John Buck & His	1958	Cadence 1359
Chi Chi	Five Chestnuts	1959	Elgin 003
Chi Chi	Five Chestnuts, Marvin Baskerville & the	1958	Drum 001
(Chica Boom)That's My Baby	Flamingos	1955	Checker 815
Chic-A-Boomer	Del-Rhythmetts	1958	J-V-B 5000
Chicago	Citations	1964	Mercury 72286
Chicago Bird	Dialtones	1963	Lawn 203
Chicago Blues	DiMucci, Dion (with the Del Satins)	1964	Columbia 43096
Chick-A-Dee	Escos	1959	Esta 100
Chick-A-Lou	Tornados, Johnny Mann & the	1958	Donnie 27746
Chicka-Rocka-Chee-Che-Cho	Hi-Lites (Brunswick)	1958	Brunswick 55102
Chicken	Moroccos	1955	United 188
Chicken	Olympics	1959, 1961	Demon 1514/Titan 1718
Chicken Back	Counts, Bobby Comstock & the	1963	Lawn 217
Chicken Backs	Carpets	1956	Federal 12269
Chicken Blues	Dominoes	1950	Federal 12001
Chicken Feed	Jumpin' Jacks, Danny Lamego & the	1956	Andrea 101

SONG	GROUP	YEAR	LABEL
Chicken Hop	Roosters	1959	Shar-Dee 704
Chicken Little Boo Boo	Thrillers, Little Joe & the	1964	Enjoy 2011
Chicken 'N Gravy	Chants	1968	Checker 1209
Chicken Spaceman	Marathons	1962	Arvee 5048
Chicken Spaceman	Tides	1961	Dore 618
Chicken Switch	Wigs	1964	Golden Crest 592
Chicken Twist	Dappers (Foxie)	1961	Foxie 7005
Chicken (Yeah)	Euniques	1961	620 1006
Chickie Chop Chop	Flints	1958	Petite 101
Chickie Um Bah	Flamingos	1959	Checker LP 3005/Chess LP 1433 (59)
Chickie Um Bah	Moonglows	1956	Chess 1619
Chickie-Goo, The	Metronomes	1962	Maureen 1000
Chick-Lets (Don't Let Me Down)	Diamonds	1958	Mercury 71291
Chick's Too Young To Fry, The	Prisonaires	1976	Sun 513
Chicky Chop Chop	Newports (Falcons)	1959	Contour 301
Chico	Rockbusters	1959	Cadence 1371
Chico	Sessions	1964	Guyden 2105
Chief Turn The Hose On Me	Cap-Tans	1950	Dot 1018
Chief Um	Charms, Otis Williams & the	1960	King 5323
Childish Ways	Suddens	1961	Sudden 103
Chil-E Baby	Highlights, Barry & the	1960	Baye 511/Airmaster 700 (60)
Chili Charlie	Astronauts	1960	Trial 3521
Chills	Knight, Alan & group	1960	Tide 007
Chills, Chills, Chills	Deans	1963	Star Maker 1931
Chilly Willy	Saxons, Mary Edwards & the	1956	Meteor 5031
Chimes	Pelicans	1954	Imperial 5307
Chimes Ring Out, The	Chimes (Los Angeles - Specialty)	1955	Specialty 549 (unreleased)
Chimes, The	Shades	1963	Times Square 16/Times Square 93 (64)
China Doll	Downbeats	1956	Gee 1019
China Doll	Premiers (New York)	1958	Cindy 3008
China Girl	Columbus Pharaohs	1958	Esta 290/Ransom 101 (58)/ Paradise 109 (59)/Nanc 1120 (59)
Chinese Boogie	Hy-Tones	1958	Hy-Tone 120
Chinese Lanterns	Galens	1964	Challenge 59253
Chinese Tea Room	Three Friends	1957	Brunswick 55032/Lido 504
Ching A Ling	Accents (featuring Robert Draper Jr.)	1959	Brunswick 55123
Ching Bam Bah	Velveteens	1965	Golden Artist 614
Ching Ching	Afterbeats, Gloria Wood & the	1960	Buena Vista 361
Ching Chong	Pips	1958	Brunswick 55048
Ching-A-Ling Baby	Rocky Fellers	1963	Scepter 1258
Chip Chip	Mello-Kings	1959	Herald 536
Chiquita	Innocents	1961	Indigo LP 503
Chit Chat	Chestnuts, Bill Baker & the	1959	Elgin 013/014
Chit-Chat	Plaids	1958	Liberty 55167
Chittlin Switch	Vocaleers	1951	Savoy 824
Chloe-e	Ravens	1952	Mercury 5800
Chocolate Bar	Uniques	1962	Lucky Four 1024
Chocolate Covered Ants	Ambertones	1965	Dottie 1129
Chocolate Ice Cream	Bobolinks	1958	Key 575
Cholley-Oop (parody)	Hong Kong White Sox	1960	Trans-World 6906
Choo Choo Boogie	Quin-Tones (Pennsylvania)	NA	Courtney 135
Choo Choo Cha Cha	Rinky-Dinks (with Bobby Darin)	1959	Capitol 4146
Choo Choo Train	Valcounts, Tommy Sena & the	1961	Adore 903
Choo-Choo	Cardinals	1956	Atlantic 1090
Choo-Choo	Chants	1961	Verve 10244
Choo-Choo-Choo-Choo Cha-Cha-Cha	Chris-Tones, Tommy Christy & the	1958	Scot 19999
Chop Chop	Chimes (Los Angeles - Specialty)	1956	Specialty 574
Chop Chop	Wheels, Ferris & the	1961	Bambi 801
Chop Chop Boom	Danderliers	1955	States 147/B&F 1344 (61)
Chop Chop Boom	Savoys (Combo)	1955	Combo 90
Chop, Chop, Ching-A-Ling	Roamers	1955	Savoy 1156
Chop Chop Chop	Candy Makers	NA	Urban 124
Chop Chop Hole In The Wall	Boulevards	1959	Everest 19316
Chop Ling Soon	El Dorados	1956	Vee Jay 197

SONG	GROUP	YEAR	LABEL
Chopper, The	Crestones	1964	Markie 127
Chopsticks	La Salles	1958	Back Beat 515
Chosen Few, The	Belmonts, Dion & the	1957	Mohawk 105
Chosen Few, The	Timberlanes, Dino & the	1957	Mohawk 105/Jubilee 5294 (58)
Christen	Contours, Mike Hanks & the	1960	Brax 221/222
Christina	Charades	1964	Impact 2
Christina	Sultans	1963	Guyden 2079
Christine	El Rays	1954	Checker 794
Christine	Tones, Little Sammy & the	1962	Pelham 722/Jaclyn 1161 (62)
Christmas	Faces	1965	Iguana 601
Christmas	Love, Darlene & group	1965	Philles 125X
Christmas (Baby, Please Come Home)	Love, Darlene & group	1963, 1964, 1974	Philles 119/125/Warner-Spector 0401
Christmas Bell Rock	Highlights, Barry & the	1960	Baye 511/Airmaster 700 (60)
Christmas Chimes	Bluenotes	1958	Colonial 7779
Christmas Day	Detroit Jr. & group	1961	Foxy 002
Christmas Each Day Of The Year	Tots, Barry & the	1961	Fury 1058
Christmas Eve Baby	Blazers (Johnny Moore's)	1955	Hollywood 1045
Christmas Every Day	Blazers (Johnny Moore's)	1955	Hollywood 1045
Christmas Holiday	Blackwells	1960	Jamie 1173
Christmas In Heaven	Dominoes	1953	King 1281
Christmas In Jail	Youngsters	1956	Empire 109
Christmas In The Congo	Marquees	1959	Warner Bros. 5127
Christmas Is Coming At Last	Highlighters	1950	Apollo 1141
Christmas Is Coming At Last	Rhythm Kings	1951	Apollo 1171
Christmas Is Here	Classics (MV)	1960	MV 1000
Christmas Letters	La Fets & Kitty	1957	Apollo 520
Christmas Lullabye	Day Dreams, Tony & the	1958	Planet 1054
Christmas Peace	Hansen Brothers	1981	Crystal Ball 146
Christmas Plea	Dynamics	1962	Dynamic Sound 578/9
Christmas Shopping	Brian, Eddie	1988	BAB 130
Christmas Song	Mello-Moods	1977	Ronnie 202
Christmas Song, The	Drifters (1959-forward)	1964	Atlantic 2261
Christmas Song, The	Jackson, Lee & group	1957	Bea & Baby 121
Christmas Song, The	Shantons, Skip Jackson & the	1960	Jay-Mar 181/Dot-Mar (69)
Christmas Song, The	Sparrows Quartette	1974	Jet 3020
Christmas Time For Everyone But Me	Midnighters, Hank Ballard & the	1963	King 5729
Christmas To New Year's	Larks (North Carolina)	1988	Relic LP 8013
Christmas Tree, The	Episodes	1965	Four Seasons 1014
Christmas Won't Be Christmas Without You	Bostick, Calvin & group	1953	Chess 1530
Christopher Columbus	Paramounts	1960	Fleetwood 1014
Christy	Aqua-Nites	1965	Astra 2001
Chu Sen Ling	Bermudas	1964	Era 3125
Chubby	Gaynels	1959	Okeh 7114
Chubby Ain't Chubby No More	Moreland, Prentice & group	1962	Challenge 9154
Chubby Isn't Chubby Anymore	Itels	1961	Magnifico 101
Chuck-A-Luck	Chuck-A-Lucks	1957, 1963	Bow 305/Candlelite 424
Chug-A-Lug	Trends	1960	RCA 7733
Chum	Impalas (Brooklyn)	1958	Cub EP CX5000
Chumba	Angels, Gabriel & the	1960	Amy 802
Chunchin' Song	Conservatives	1968	Ebonic Sound 6569
Church Bells	Philadelphians	1961	Campus 103
Church Bells Are Ringing	Willows	1956	Melba 102 (first pressing)
Church Bells May Ring	Cadets	1956	Modern 985
Church Bells May Ring	Clientells	1961	M.B.S. 7
Church Bells May Ring	Diamonds	1956	Mercury 70835
Church Bells May Ring	Four Blades	1956	Gateway 1174
Church Bells May Ring	Gale, Sunny & group	1960	Warwick 540
Church Bells May Ring	Willows	1956	Melba 102 (second pressing)
Church Bells My Ring	Sultans, Bob Oakes & the	1956	Regent 7502
Church Bells Played The Blues	Five Satins	1974	Relic LP 5024
Church Bells Ring, The	Harris, Sterling & group	NA	VVVV
Church Key	Deltas, Jim Waller & the	1962	Arvee 5072
Church Key	Fabulous Pharaohs	NA	Three Star 2668
Church On The Hill	Gaylarks	1957	Music City 809

SONG	GROUP	YEAR	LABEL
Church On The Hill, The	Charmers	1954	Timely 1011
Cigareetos	Orioles, Sonny Til & the	1983	Murray Hill LP M61277
Cigarette	Visions	1963	Original Sound 32
Cigarettes And Matches	Faulkner, Freddy & group	1963	Swan 4134
Cimarron	Four Lovers	1957	RCA LP 1317
Cin Cin (Che Bell)	Four Buddies	1962	Coral 62325
Cinderella	Bravadoes, Little Mac & the	1961	Little Mac 101
Cinderella	Classics (Brooklyn)	1959	Dart 1015/Musictone 1114 (63)
Cinderella	Dealers, Floyd White & the	1960	Criterion 1
Cinderella	Passions, Gary Kay & the	1981	Jason Scott 20
Cinderella Baby	Crystalaires	1998	Sweet Beat 101
Cinderella, Cinderella	Downbeats, Gene Terry & the	1959	Goldband 1088
Cinderella It's Midnight	Sherry Sisters	1957	Cindy 3000
Cindy Lou	Ambassadors, Vern Young & the	1960	Chords 101
Cindy Lou	Boogie Ramblers	1957	Goldband 1030
Cindy Lou	Downbeats, Gene Terry & the	1958	Goldband 1066
Cindy Lou	Jac-O-Lacs	1955	Tampa 103
Cindy Oh Cindy	Scott Brothers	1960	FTP
Cindy (or Sindy)	Cobras (Ohio)	1955	Modern 964
Cinnamon Cinder	Cinders	1963	Warner Bros. 5326
City Lights (Thank Her For Me)	Gentones	1961	Casino 52261
City Of Angels	Highlights	1956	Bally 1016
City Of People	Illusions	NA	Michelle 1
City Of Strangers	Entrees, Chuck Corley & the	1966	Sonic 118
City Sleeps, The	Sensationals	1961	Candix 319
City, The	Four Fellows (Brooklyn - Ad Lib)	1962	Ad Lib 0208
(City Zoo) Baby Baby Baby	Jaguars	1957	R-Dell 16
Claire	Belltones, Tony Morra & the	1959	Arcade 152
Claire	Morra, Tony & group	1958	Arcade 152
Clap Happy	Escorts (Judd)	1959	Judd 1014
Clap Your Hands	Beau-Marks	1960	Shad 5017/Mainstream 688 (68)
Clap Your Hands	Marcels, Walt Maddox & the	1983	Super M 4027
Clap Your Hands	Sophomores, Anthony & the	1963	Mercury 72103
Clap Your Hands	Wheels	1959	Folly 800
Clap Your Hands And Skate	Tornados	NA	Winley 2017
Clap Your Hands (When I Clap My Hands)	Maddox, Walt and the Marcels	1983	Super M 304027
Clarabel	Bluenotes, Vince Anthony & the	1963	Viking 1018
Class Ring	Four Jays	1958	MGM 12687
Class Ring	Trends	1959	Argo 5341/Clover 1002
Classmate	Beau-Marks	1961	Rust 5035
Claudine	Carlo (Carlo Mastrangelo) (with the Tremonts)	1970	Raftis 110
Clementine	Catalinas, Phil & the	1960	Olimpic
Cleopatra	Capri, Bobby & group	1963	Johnson 124
Cleopatra	Gigolos, Jamie Coe & the	1962	Big Top 3107
Cleopatra	Performers, Bobby Sanders & the	1963	Sound-O-Rama 117
Cleopatra	Precisions	1962	Golden Crest 571
Cleopatra	Velvet Satins, Bobby Capri & the	1963	Johnson 124
Cleopatra 30 B.C.	Fables	1962	Elgo 3001
Cleopatra Brown	Day Brothers	1962	Firebird 103
Cleo's Theme (Vince Mon Tanta)	Philadelphians, Big John & the	1963	Guyden 2093
Click, The	Socialites	1963	Arrawak 1004
Clickety Clack, I'm Leaving	Hollywood Flames	1954	Money 202
Clicky Clicky Clack	Turbans (Philadelphia)	1962	Imperial 5828
Climb Every Mountain	New Silhouettes	1967	Jamie 1333
Climb Every Mountain	Victorians	1963	Liberty 55574
Climb Love's Mountain	Kuf-Linx	1958	Challenge 59015
Climb, The	Coasters	1962	Atco 6234
Climb Upon Your Rockin' Chair	Impaks	1962	Express 716
Cling, The	Bing Bongs, Dicky Dell & the	1958	Dragon 10205
Cling, The	Troys	1959	Okeh 7120
Clipper, The	Clippers, Big Mike Gordon & the	1956	Baton 233
Clock In Lovers Lane, The	Humdingers	1957	Dale 106
Clock (Is Ticking My Life Away), The	Tidal Waves	1961	Tide 0020
Clock Says, The	Blair, Sandy & group	1963	Bobby 111

SONG	GROUP	YEAR	LABEL
Clock, The	Contenders	1963, 1966	Java 101
Clock, The	Hearts, Lee Andrews & the	1957	Grand 157/Main Line 102 (57)/ Chess 1665 (57)
Clock, The	Hi Tensions, Leon Peels & the	1960	Audio 201/K&G 101
Clock, The	Jaytones	1958	Brunswick 55087
Close Friends	Chants	1958	Capitol 3949
Close Friends	Poni-Tails	1958	ABC 9969
Close The Door	Tunes	1959	Swade 102
Close To Me	Blue Flames	1962	Spry 115
Close To Me	Charades	1964	Original Sound 47
Close To Me	Lamarr, Gene (with the Blue Flames)	1958	Spry 115
Close To Me	Marquees	1958	Day-Sel 1001
Close To Me	Penn, Dan & group	1964	Fame 6402
Close To Me	Wilson, Robin & group	1960	Monument 426
Close To My Heart	Commodores	1955	Dot 15425
Close To My Heart	Diamond, Ronnie & group	1958	Imperial 5554
Close To You	Del Royals	1961	Minit 620
Close To You	Four Buddies	NA	Savoy 959 (unreleased)
Close To You	Portraits	1959	Capitol 4181
Close To You	Spades	1959	Major 1007
Close Up The Back Door	Cupcakes, Cookie & the	1959, 1963	Judd 1015/Lyric 1004/1012 (63)
Close Your Eyes	Admirals	1955	King 4782
Close Your Eyes	Bobbettes	1963	Diamond 142
Close Your Eyes	Channels, Earl Lewis & the	1973	Channel 1003
Close Your Eyes	Classics (Lou Christie)	1961	Starr 508/Alcar 207 (63)
Close Your Eyes	Delmonicos	1990	Clifton 88
Close Your Eyes	Five Keys	1955	Capitol 3032
Close Your Eyes	Jones, Jimmy (with the Pretenders)	1961	Port 70040
Close Your Eyes	Jordan, Lou (with the Chaperones)	1962	Josie 888
Close Your Eyes	Palisades	1960	Calico 113
Close Your Eyes	Pretenders	1955	Whirlin' Disc 106/Port 70040 (61)
Close Your Eyes	Skyliners	1961	Colpix 613
Close Your Eyes	Tindley, George & group	1961	Herald 558
Close Your Eyes (acappella)	Five Keys	1973	Bim Bam Boom 116
Closer To Heaven	Monitors	1957	Specialty 622
Closer To Me	Sonics, Vance Charles & the	1963	Lori 9553
Closer To My Heart	Fuller, Walter & group	1954	Kicks 4
Closer You Are, The	Channels, Earl Lewis & the	1956, 1987	Whirlin' Disc 100/Port 70014 (59)/ Soul Jam 712
Closer You Are, The	Illusions	1962, 1974	Kape 1001
Closer You Are, The	Magnificent Four	1961	Whale 506/Blast 210 (63)
Closer You Are (acappella), The	Savoys (New Jersey)	1965	Catamount 105
Closer You Are, The (acappella)	Shells	1966	Candlelite LP 1000
Cloud Full Of Tears	Accents, Gary Trexler & the	1957	Rev 3507
Cloudburst	Orlandos	1957	Cindy 3006
Cloudy And Raining	Five Hollywood Blue Jays	1951	Recorded In Hollywood 185
Cloudy Weather	Eagleaires	1954	J.O.B. 1104
Clown Of The Masquerade	Carnations	1952	Derby 789
Clown Prince	Castells	1962	Era 3098
Club For Broken Hearts	El-Deens	1959	Federal 12356
C'Mere Baby Doll	Friends, Gary Cane & His	1960	Shell 717
C'Mon Back	Thunderbirds, Bert Convy & the	1955	Era 1001
C'Mon Dream	Victorians	NA	Hercules 101
C'Mon Everybody	Belmonts	1964	Sabina 519
C'Mon Everybody	Delicates	1964	Challenge 59232
C'Mon Home	Lee, Addie & group	1958	End 1018
C'mon Home Baby	Cadillacs	1961	Jubilee LP 1117
C'mon, Let Yourself Go	Matadors	1964	Colpix 741
C'Mon Little Darlin'	Dynels	1964	Natural 7001
C'Mon Now Baby	Trevor, Van (with the Four Seasons)	1963	Vivid 1004
C'Mon Sweet Baby	Kruisers	1965	Kiski 2068
C'mon Tiger	Imperials	1958	Liberty 55119
C'mon Wobble	Cinders	1963	Warner Bros. 5326
Coast Of Red	Desires	NA	Hull (unreleased)
Cobra	Boys, Barbara & the	1958	

SONG	GROUP	YEAR	LABEL
Cobra	Versa-Tones	1961	Kenco 5015
Cocksucker's Ball	Clovers, Tippie & the	1975	Jett 3019
Coconut Woman	Sheiks	1961	Le Grand 1016
Coconuts And Palm Trees	Chantones	1959	TNT 167
Code Of Love, The	Tribunes	1962	Derrick 502
Coffee, Cigarettes And Tears	Larks (North Carolina)	1951	Apollo 1177
Coffee Grind	Jives, Charlie & the	1962	Hour 104
Coffee Grind, The	Midnighters, Hank Ballard & the	1960	King 5312
Cold And Frosty Morning	Concords (Brooklyn)	1962, 1963, 1964	Herald 578 (first pressing, second, 597, is by the Snowmen)/Dot 16540
Cold As Ice	Counts, Frankie Brent & the	1958	Vik 0322
Cold Cash	Federals	1957	DeLuxe 6112
Cold Chills	Sounds	1955	Modern 975
Cold, Cold Winter	Pixies 3	1963	Mercury 72208
Cold Feet	Dell Vikings	1972	Bim Bam Boom 111
Cold Feet	Dell Vikings (with Charles Jackson)	1959	Petite 503
Cold Feet	Moonglows	1959	Chess LP 1430
Cold Grey Dawn	Hearts, Lee Andrews & the	1968	Lost Nite 1001
Cold Heart	Penguins	1959	Dooto LP 242/Dooto EP 241
Cold Kisses	Barons (New Orleans)	1955	Imperial 5370
Cold Lonely Heart	Desires	1958	Herald 532
Cold Walls	Kit Kats	1965	Lawn 249
Collecting Girls	Lawrence, Bernie & group	1961	United Artists 388
Collecting Hearts	Wanderers	1958	Cub 9019
Colleen	Rock-A-Ways, Ricky Vac & the	1961	Hilltop 1871
College Girl	Zodiacs, Maurice Williams & the	1959	Selwyn 5121
Collegian	Copasetics	1956	Premium 409
Color Cartoons	Goldenrods	1959	Vee Jay 307
Color My World	Emotions	NA	South Park 1000
Colorado Moon	Four Winds	1956	Vik 0221
Colors	Four-Evers	1964	Chattahoochee 630
Combination	Dukays	1963	Vee Jay 491
Combination, The	Nu Ports, Tyrone & the	1963	Darrow 71/72
Combination, The	Shades	1962	Joey 6206
Come A Little Bit Closer	Ravens	1953	Okeh 6888
Come A Little Bit Closer (acappella)	Ru-Teens	1965	Old Timer 612
Come Along	Zodiacs, Maurice Williams & the	1961	Herald 559
Come Along Baby	Astronauts	1961	Palladium 610
Come Along With Me	Dell Vikings	1957	Mercury 30112/71180
Come Along With Me	Fairlanes, Charles Perrywell & the	1962	Tic Toc 104
Come And Get It	Zodiacs, Maurice Williams & the	1961	Herald 563
Come And Get Me	Lloyd, Jackie (with the Harbor Lights)	1960	Heros 342
Come And Get Your Baby	Bleaters	1963	Guyden 2100
Come Away	Chapman, Grady (with the Suedes)	1959	Imperial 5611
Come Away, Love	Satisfiers	1956	Coral 61727
Come Back	Belles	NA	Tiara 100
Come Back	Blue Chips, Carlron Lankford & the	1956	DeLuxe 6100
Come Back	Castaleers	1958	Felsted 8504
Come Back	Embraceables	1962	Dover 4101
Come Back	Harmonaires	1957	Holiday 2602
Come Back	Lyrics, Leo Valentine & the	1962	Skylight 202
Come Back	Marvells	1961	Winn 1916
Come Back	Med-Tones, Johnny Daril & the	1959	Vita 188
Come Back	Parakeets	1961	Jubilee 5407
Come Back	Rainbows, Randy & the	1963	Rust 5059
Come Back	Velvetones	1959	D 1049/Glad
Come Back And Give Me Your Hand	Supremes (Bronx, N.Y.)	NA	Old Town
Come Back Baby	Crescents	1965	Seven B 7013
Come Back Baby	Deckers	1958	Yeadon 101
Come Back Baby	Echoes, Frankie & the	1958	Savoy 1544
Come Back Baby	Larks (Don Julian)	1965	Money 127
Come Back Baby	Lyrics (San Francisco)	1958	Rhythm 126/127
Come Back Baby	Robins	1950	Aladdin 3031
Come Back, Baby	Sunbeams	1955	Herald 451
Come Back, Baby	Vibes	1957	ABC 9810

SONG	GROUP	YEAR	LABEL
Come Back Baby	Winchell, Danny (with Nino & the Ebbtides)	1959	Recorte 415
Come Back Baby Blues	Blenders (New York)	1949	National 9092
Come Back, Baby, Come Back	Prophets	1955	Go-Lish 101
Come Back Betty	Steel, L.C. & group	NA	K14
Come Back, Cleopatra	Top Notes	1962	Festival 1021
Come Back, Come Back	Emperors	1954	Haven 511
Come Back Home	Mondellos, Alice Jean & the	1957	Rhythm 102
Come Back Into My Heart	Volumes	1962	Chex 1005
Come Back Karen	Expressions	1963	Smash 1848
Come Back Little Girl	Voxpoppers	1958	Poplar 112
Come Back My Love	Anders, Terri & group	1960	Chief 7027
Come Back My Love	Buccaneers	1953	Rama 21
Come Back My Love	Cardinals	1955	Atlantic 1067
Come Back My Love	Darts	1978	Magnet-United Artists LP 850G
Come Back My Love	Dedications	1990	Clifton 92
Come Back My Love	Heartbreakers (Bronx, N.Y.)	1959, 1975	Fordham 109/Vanguard 9093
Come Back My Love	Impressions, Jerry Butler & the	1958	Abner 1017
Come Back My Love	Marvellos	1958	Stepheny 1818/Cha Cha 756
Come Back My Love	Monograms	1975	Monogram 101
Come Back My Love	Serenaders (Clifton)	1976	Clifton 16
Come Back My Love	Solitaires	1956	Murray Hill LP 56
Come Back My Love	Wrens	1955	Rama 65
Come Back To Me	Ambitions	1962	Cross 1005
Come Back To Me	Chordones, Leon Tarver & The	1954	Checker (unreleased)
Come Back To Me	Clicks	1955	Josie 780
Come Back To Me	Copycats, Suzy & the	1961	Brent 7020
Come Back To Me	Dappers (Boston)	1955	Peacock 1651
Come Back To Me	Fi-Dells	1957	Warner 1014
Come Back To Me	Four Students, Zilla Mays & the	1955	Groove 0127
Come Back To Me	Holidays	1961	Brent 7018
Come Back To Me	Pitch Pikes	1957	Mercury 71147
Come Back To Me	Sparrows	1956	Davis 456/Jay Dee
Come Back To Me	Staffords	1956	Decca 29828
Come Back To Me	Talents, Julian Barnett & the	1958	Herald 519
Come Back To Me	Teardrops	1952	Sampson 634
Come Back To Me	Tune Weavers, Margo Sylvia & the	1988	Classic Artists 104
Come Back To Me	Williams, Marie & group	1961	Smart 324
Come Back To Me Darling	Lyrics, Ike Perry & the	1963	Courier 828
Come Back To Me Darling	Rockets, Joe Therrien Jr. & his	1957	Lido 505/Brunswick 55005
Come Back To Me Tomorrow	Striders	1954	Derby 857
Come Back To My Heart	Charmers, Mark Stevens & the	1962	Allison 921
Come Back To Sorrento	Belairs, Barry Petricoin & the	1958	Al-Stan 103
Come Back To These Arms	Marcel, Vic & group	1963	Don-But 17349
Come Back To These Arms	Spaniels	1970	North American 3114
Come Be My Love	Poni-Tails	1959	ABC 10077
Come Dance Baby	Emotions	1962	Kapp 490
Come Dance With Me	Tokens (Gary)	1957, 1984	Gary 1006/Musictone 1113 (59)
Come Dance With Me	Vocaltones	1989	N/A
Come De Nite	Quarter Notes	1957	DeLuxe 6116
Come Down To Earth	Nutmegs	NA	Herald (unreleased)
Come Go My Bail, Louise	Five Keys	1953	Aladdin 3167
Come Go With Me	Chants	1963	Cameo 268/277/Pye 15557
Come Go With Me	Chevrons	1960	Time 1
Come Go With Me	Dell Vikings	1956, 1960, 1972, 1980	Fee Bee 205/Dot 15538 (57)/Dot 16092 (60)/Scepter 12367/ Lightning 9013/Collectables 1251
Come Go With Me	DiMucci, Dion (with the Del Satins)	1963	Laurie 3171
Come Go With Me	Eternals	1968	Quality 1884
Come Go With Me	Federals	1957	DeLuxe 6112
Come Go With Me	Four Jacks	1956	Gateway 1213
Come Go With Me	Majors (Felsted)	1959	Felsted 8576
Come Go With Me	Roomates	1961	Valmor LP 78/Valmor LP 789 (62)/ Relic LP 5041
Come Go With Me	Studebaker 7	NA	Coulee 142
Come Go With Me	Twisters	1960	Apt 25045

SONG	GROUP	YEAR	LABEL
Come Go With Me	Zeu Review, Ziggy & the	NA	Zeu 5011
Come Here	Four Shades Of Rhythm	1958	Mad 1206
Come Here My Darling	Genies	1961	King 5568
Come Home	Gondoliers, Johnny Adams & the	1960	Ric 963
Come Home	Holiday, Bobby & group	1961	Port 70027
Come Home	Hurricanes (Bubber Johnson)	1955	King
Come Home	Knight, Gloria & group	1964	Emerson 2101
Come Home	Rainbeaus, Vinnie Rome & the	1959	Apt 25035
Come Home	Ryan, Cathy (with the Admirals)	1955	King 4848
Come Home	Vestelles	1958	Decca 30733
Come Home, Come Home	Sheppards (Chicago - Apex)	1960	Apex 7760
Come Home Girl	Empires	1962	Chavis 1026/Candi 1026 (62)
Come Home, Little Girl	Diablos	1958	Fortune 841
Come Home My Love	Ferros	1958	Hi-Q 5008
Come Home Right Away	Dwellers	1958	Conrose 101
Come Home Soon	Four Intruders	1961	Gowen 1401
Come Home With Me	Diablos	1984	Fortune LP 8020
Come Home With Me	Miracles (Baton)	1955	Baton 210
Come In World	Royal Dukes, Don Ellis & the	1959	Bee 1111
Come Into My Heart	Tempo-Tones	1957	Acme 718
Come Into My Palace	Leopards, Lee & the	1962	Gordy 7002/Laurie 3197 (63)
Come Into My Parlor	Rogers, Pauline & group	1956	Atco 6071
Come Let Me Show You	Jesters	1961	Winley 252
Come Marry Me	Uniques	1959	Flippin' 202
Come, My Little Baby	Chantels	1957	End 1005
Come My Little Baby	Dewdrops, Honey & the	1959	MMC 005
Come My Little Baby	Lawrence, Bob & group	1957	Mark-X 7005
Come Next Spring	Extremes	1958	Everlast 5013
Come On	Champions	1956	Chart 631
Come On	Clefts	1960	V-Tone 212
Come On	Distants	1960	Northern 3732/Warwick 546 (60)
Come On	Fawns	1958	Apt 15035/Apt 25015 (58)
Come On	Halos	1961	7 Arts 720
Come On	Ivies	1958	Ivy 110/Brunswick 55112 (58)
Come On	Laddins	1960	Isle 801
Come On	Nutones	1965	Relic 1010
Come On	Sharps	1957	Jamie 1040/Vik 0264 (57)/VDJ 6
Come On A Get It	Midnighters	1956	Federal 12285
Come On And Cry	Ebbtides	1962	Monument 520
Come On And Dance	Ambassadors	1963	Playbox 202
Come On And Dance	Elites	1961	Chief 7040
Come On And Dance	Gray, Maureen & group	1961	Chancellor 1091
Come On And Dance With Me	Jewels, Billy Abbott & the	1963	Parkway 874
Come On And Go With Me	Sensationals, Jimmy Jones & the	1959	Savoy 4116
Come On And Let Me Love You	Destinations	1961	Fortune 864
Come On And Love Me	Chevies, Wayne Johnson & the	1959	Dove 1033
Come On And Love Me	Jones, Davey & group	1958	Apt 25013
Come On And Love Me Baby	Du Droppers	1953	Red Robin 116
Come On And Love Me Too	Ran-Dells	1963	Chairman 4407
Come On And Marry Me	Ambrose, Kenny & group	1958	Hamilton 50019
Come On And Rock	Dukes (California)	1955	Imperial 5344 (unreleased)
Come On And Rock	Little Angel	1959	Award 126
Come On And Save Me	Five Royales	1956	King 4952
Come On And Tell Me	Tranells	1956	Chelten 090
Come On Baby	Angelenos	1961	Peepers 2827
Come On Baby	Blue Rays	1964	Philips 40186
Come On Baby	Bon-Bons	1964	Coral 62402
Come On Baby	Challengers	1963	Explosive 3621-10
Come On Baby	Cordovans	1960	Johnson 731
Come On Baby	Danes	1961	Le Cam 718
Come On Baby	Dells	1983	Charly LP 1056
Come On Baby	Don Juans, Andre Williams & the	1956	Fortune 839
Come On Baby	Executives	1963	Revenge 5003/Explosive 3621 (63)
Come On Baby	Five Classics	1960	Arc 4454/A 317 (61)
Come On Baby	Five Discs	1961	Yale 243/244

SONG	GROUP	YEAR	LABEL
Come On Baby	Four Wheels	1992	Park Ave. 6 (rec. 1961)
Come On Baby	Pharaohs	1957	Fascination 001/Skylor 101
Come On Baby	Remarkables, Reggie & the	1962	Musicor 1030
Come On Baby	Rockin' Chairs	1959	Recorte 404
Come On, Baby	Roulettes	1958	Champ 102
Come On Baby	Team Mates	1960	Le Cam 707
Come On, Baby	Van Dykes	1958	Decca 30762
Come On Baby	Youngtones	1958	Brunswick 55089
(Come On Baby) Let The Good Times Roll	Crenshaws	1961	Warner Bros. EP 5505
Come On Baby, Let's Do The Stroll	Enchanters (Bald Eagle)	1958	Bald Eagle 3001
Come On Back	Barnes, Big Syl & group	1960	Corvair 900
Come On Back	Foote, Chuck & group	1961	Soncraft 401
Come On Back	Manhattans, Ronnie & the	1963	Enjoy 2008
Come On Back	Metaphors	NA	Rad (no #)
Come On Back	Ramblers (Trumpet)	1963	Trumpet 102
Come On Back To Me	Sheiks	1960	Amy 807
Come On Back Where You Belong	Lewis, Little Junior & group	1960	Fury 1039
Come On Be Nice	Sandmen (Brook Benton)	1957	Vik 0285
Come On Come On	Majors (Philadelphia)	1964	Imperial LP 9222
Come On, Come On, Come On	Charms, Tiny Topsy & the	1957	Federal 12309
Come On, Dance With Me	T-Birds (Jesse Belvin)	1961	Chess 1778
Come On Everybody	Fiestas	1961	Strand 25046
Come On Everybody	Little Kings, Phil Orsi & the	1963	Lucky 1009
Come On Girl	Jarmels	1963	Laurie 3174
Come On Girl (Be Mine)	Four Fifths	1963	Hudson 8101
Come On Home	Blendtones	1963	Success 105
Come On Home	Darnells	1963	Gordy 7024
Come On Home	Daylighters	1959	Key Hole 107
Come On Home	Enchantments	1962	Gone 5130
Come On Home	Five Bell Aires, John Hall & the	1990	Relic LP 5085
Come On Home	Jumpin' Jay & group	1961	Turban 101
Come On Home	Jumpin' Tones	NA	Unreleased
Come On Home	Little Cheryl & group	1964	Cameo 292
Come On Home	Lollipops, Becky & the	1964	Troy 6493/Epic 9736 (64)
Come On Home	Lyrics (San Francisco)	1958	Vee Jay 285
Come On Home	Orioles, Sonny Til & the (with the Helen Way Singers)	1959	Jubilee 5384
Come On Home	Pearls	1956	Atco 6066
Come On Home	Spears, Calvin & group	1960	Vin 1020
Come On Home	Starlites, Eddie & the	1963	Aljon 1260/1261
Come On Home	Boyd, Eddie (with His Chess Men)	1959	Keyhole 107
Come On Honey	Symphonics, Freddie Scott & the	1959	Enrica 1002
Come On, Joey, Dance With Me	Poni-Tails	1958	ABC 9934
Come On, Let Me Try	Del Rios, Linda & the	1962	Crackerjack 4005
Come On, Let's Dance	Carlos Brothers	1959	Del-Fi 4112
Come On Let's Dance	Filets Of Sole	1968	Savoy 1630
Come On Let's Go	Valiants (New York)	1964	Cortland 114
Come On Little Angel	Belmonts	1962	Sabina 505
Come On, Little Baby	Kings (Baltimore)	1958	Jalo 203
Come On Liza	Keys, Ricky & the	1958	Savoy 1529
Come On Lover	Innocents	1963	Decca 31519
Come On, Make Love To Me	Sweethearts	1968	Como 451
Come On Mama	Wil-Sons	1961	Highland 1020
Come On 'N Rock	Sparkles, Little Angel & the	1959	Award 126
Come On Now	Executives	1963	Explosive 3821/Mink 5004
Come On Over	Strollers	1961	Carlton 546
Come On Over (Baby)	Downbeats	1956	Sarg 168
Come On Over To My Place	Drifters (1959-forward)	1965	Atlantic 2285
Come On, Snake, Let's Crawl	Dominoes	1956	Decca 30043
Come On Strong	Dittos	1961	Warner Bros. 5247
Come On Strong	J's (with Jamie)	1962	Columbia 42635
Come On Tiger	Imperials, Little Anthony & the	1958	Liberty 55119
Come On To My Love House	Five Bell Aires, Henry Hall & the	1990	Relic LP 5085
Come On To My Party	Flamingos	1962	End 1124

SONG	GROUP	YEAR	LABEL
Come On To My Room	Majors (Brooklyn)	1951	Derby 763
Come One	Five Blacks	1961	B&C 100
Come Out Tonight	La Mar, Tony & group	1960	Duco 5001
Come Over Here	Royal Sons Quintet	1952	Apollo 266
Come See Me	Crests	1966	Parkway 999
Come Seven	Satellites, Bobby Day & the	1957	Class 207
Come Shake Hands With A Fool	Doo Drops, Misty & the	1963	Imperial 5975
Come Share The Good Times With Me	Monday, Julie & group	1966	Rainbow 500/501
Come Si Bella	Romans, Frankie Valle & the	1959	Cindy 3012
Come Sit By Me	Constellations	1956	Groove 0140
Come Softly	Echoes, Billy & the	1962	Gala 121
Come Softly To Me	Chantels, Richard Barrett & the	1959	Gone 5056
Come Softly To Me	Fleetwoods	1959, 1964	Dolton 1/Liberty 55188 (59)/ Liberty 77188 (59)/Dolton 307
Come Softly To Me	Four Winds	1978	Crystal Ball 102
Come Take A Walk With Me	Belmonts, Dion & the	1962	Laurie LP 2016/Ace LP 155
Come To Me	Barons (Blue Jay)	NA	Blue Jay 154
Come To Me	George, Othea (with the Volumes)	1963	Volume 1100
Come To Me	Kool Gents	1963	Bethlehem 3061
Come To Me	Levons	1962	Columbia 42506
Come To Me	Pharaohs	1961	Pharaoh 1
Come To Me	Quadrells	1956	Whirlin' Disc 103
Come To Me	Rayber Voices, Marv Johnson & the	1959	United Artists 160/Tamla 101 (59)
Come To Me	Reeves, Harriet & group	1961	Eon 103
Come To Me	Rivals (Junior)	1963	Junior 990
Come To Me	Shantones	1956	Trilyte 5001
Come To Me	Sheppards (Chicago - Vee Jay)	1962	Vee Jay 441
Come To Me	Treys	1959	Bella 16
Come To Me Baby	Belvederes	1955	Baton 214
Come To Me Baby	Charms, Otis Williams & the	1954	DeLuxe 6056
Come To Me Baby	Dominoes	1954	Jubilee 5163
Come To Me Darling	Crystals (New York)	1954	Luna 100/101/Luna 5001 (54)
Come To Me Darling	Monorails	1961, 1973	Lute 6017/Sold 506
Come To Me, Darling	Opals	1954	Luna 100/101/Luna 5001 (54)
Come To Me My Little Darling	Strickland, Jan & gorup	1955	X 0080
Come To Paradise	Fascinators (Brooklyn)	1959	Capitol 4137
Come Up In The World	Four-Evers	1964	Chattahoochee 630
Come What May	Flashes, Jess Davis & the	1959	Bob-O-Link 100/101
Come What May	Hi Tensions	NA	Milestone
Come What May	Thrillers, Little Joe & the	1965	Uptown 715
Come With Me	Belmonts	1966	United Artists 5007
Come With Me	Hart, Rocky (with the Mystics)	1959	Cub 9052
Come With Me	Ivoleers	1959	Buzz 101
Come With Me To The Sea	Tymes	1963	Parkway 884
Come-A Come-A	Bobbettes	1957	Atlantic 1159
Come-A, Come-A, Baby	Twilighters, Tony Allen & the	1961	Bethlehem 3002
Comes Love	Marcels	1964	Kyra
Comes Love	Skyliners	1962	Viscount 104
Comes The Day	Lane, Rusty (with the Mystics)	1959	Laurie 3031
Comic Book Crazy	Ivies, Ezra & the	1959	United Artists 165
Comin' After You	Fairlanes	1960	Argo 5357
Comin' At You	Reflections	1965	Golden World 20
Comin' Back Home	Ravens	Between 1947 & 1950	National (unreleased)
Comin' Down With Love	Delicates	1965	Challenge 59304
Comin Down With The Blues	Bowman, Jane & group	1961	Sapien 1002
Comin' Home	Contours, Texas Red & the	1957	Bullseye 1009
Comin' Home	Nutmegs	1956	Herald 492
Comin' Home To You	Gladiolas	1957	Excello 2110
Comin' On	Clovers	1953	Atlantic 1010
Comin' On Down	Cameos (Relic)	NA	Relic LP 5028
Comin' On Down With Love	Headliners	1962	Beltone 2020
Comin' On Home	Four Bars	1962	Dayco 101/Shelley 180
Comin' Through The Rye	Candy Makers	NA	Urban 125
Comin' Through The Rye	Baysiders	1960	Everest 19393
Coming Back To You	Chimes (Storm)	1959	Storm 501

SONG	GROUP	YEAR	LABEL
Coming Generation, The	Knickerbockers, Buddy Randell & the	1965	Challenge 59321
Coming Home	Monarchs	1961	Liban 1002
Coming Home From School	Donnybrooks	1959	Calico 112
Coming Home To You	Philadelphians	1961	Campus 103
Command My Heart	Gays	1959	Decca 30988
Commandments Of Love, The	Statues	1961	Liberty 55363
Com'n Home	Showmen	1962	Minit 647
Compensation	Del-Knights	1959	Unart 2008
Compensation Blues	Vals	1962	Unique Laboratories (no #)
Completely Lost My Mind	Bay-Tones	1976	Monogram 116
Completely Yours	Four Chaps	1956	Rama 195
Concerto Rock	Question Marks	1959	First 102
Condition Your Heart	Arabians	1964	Teek 4824-1/4824-2
Coney Island Baby	Excellents	1962	Blast 205
Confess	Chelmars	1962	Select 712
Confess	Emeralds (Pittsburgh)	1958	ABC 9948
Confess It To Your Heart	Moonglows	1957	Chess 1669
Confession Is Good For The Soul	Serenaders (Detroit)	1952	Coral 60720
Confession Of A Sinner	Stylers	1956	Jubilee 5253
Confession Of Love	Dell Vikings	1962	ABC 10341
Confession Of Love	Hall, Betty & group	1996	
Confession Of Love	Harlequins	1958	Juanita 102
Confessions Of Love	Carusos	1974	Roadhouse 1020
Confidential	Fleetwoods	1960	Dolton 30
Confucius Say	Dewdrops, Honey & the	1959	MMC 005
Confusin' Blues	Belvin, Jesse & group	1952	Specialty 435
Confusion	Clintonian Cubs (Jimmy Castor)	1960	My Brother's 508
Confusion	Ventrills	1967	Ivanhoe 5000/Parkway 141 (67)
Congratulations	Chantels	1958	End 1030
Congratulations	Crosstones (with the Chriss Chross Orchestra)	1955	Jaguar 3014
Congratulations	Fortunes, Larry Darnell & the	1960	Argo 5364
Congratulations	Hallmarks	1962	Dot 16418
Congratulations	James, Artamer & group	1958	Code 711
Congratulations	James, Tammy & group	1963	Janlene 776
Congratulations	Paramounts	1961	Dot 16175
Congratulations	Reno, Al & group	1961	Kapp 432
Congratulations	Stephens, Jimmy (with the Safaris)	1961	Eldo 112
Congratulations	Street Corner Memories	1981	Clifton 64
Congratulations	Turbans (Philadelphia)	1957	Herald 510
Congratulations (acappella)	Valids	1966	Amber 855
Congratulations Baby	Keynotes	1957	Pop 111
Congratulations Baby	Rendezvous	1962	Reprise 20089
Congratulations, Baby	Welch, Lenny & group	1962	Cadence 1422
Congratulations On Your Birthday	Tune Weavers	1962	Checker 1007
Congratulations To Someone	Shepherd Sisters	1957	Lance 125
Connie	Dubs	1973	Johnson 097 (recorded in 1957)
Connie	Emanons (Brooklyn)	NA	Connie (unreleased)
Connie	Fabulons	1963	Benson Ritco 100/Benson 100 (63)
Connie	Offbeats, Harold L & the	1961	Happy Hearts 124
Conqueror, The	Bouquets, Tootie & the	1963	Parkway 887
Conquistador	Dynamics	1963	Liberty 55628
Consideration	Four Palms	1957	Aladdin 3411
Constantly	Bailey, Jimmy & group	1958	Wynne 103
Constantly	Sugartones, Jimmy Lane & the	1958	Time 6602
Contest, The	Blue Chips	1961	RCA 7923
Continental Walk, The	Midnighters, Hank Ballard & the	1961	King 5491
Continental Walk, The	Rollers	1961	Liberty 55320
Continental With Me Baby	Vibrations	1960	Checker 974
Convention, The	Delegates	1956	Vee Jay 212
Conversation	Rob Roys	1960	Columbia 41650
Coo Coo Cuddle Coo	Admirations	1963	Times Square 19
Coo Coo Over You	Hueys	1968	Instant 3289
Coo-Coo Jug-Jug	Cap-Tans	1950	DC 8054
Cook, Cook, Cookie	Five Cookies	1962	Everest 19429

SONG	GROUP	YEAR	LABEL
Cookie Duster	Count Downs, Chuck Hix & the	1961	Flair 101
Cookie Jar	Emjays	1959	Paris 538
Cookie Man	Nortones	1960	Stack 502
Cookie Rockin' In Her Stockings	Blisters	1963	Liberty 55577
Cookin'	Collegians	1961	Hilltop 1868
Cool And Crazy	Jaguars, Nick & the	1960	Tamla 5501
Cool Baby	Tretones	1960	B-W 604
Cool, Baby, Cool	Flairs	1984	Cadet
Cool Breeze	Daylighters	1962	Tip Top 2002
Cool Breeze	Impax	1960	Warner Bros. 5153
Cool Capri	Stags	1958	M&S 502
Cool Change	Reunion	1987	Clifton 79
Cool, Cool Baby	Magic Tones	1954	King 4681
Cool Cool Baby	Penguins	1957	Mercury 71033
Cool, Cool Baby	Sophomores (Massachusetts)	1956	Dawn 216
Cool, Cool Christmas	Sabers	1955	Cal-West 847
Cool, Cool Daddy	Chords	1973	Baron 107
Cool It	Dorsets	1961	Asnes 101
Cool It	Kays	NA	Choice 3757
Cool It	Sparks	1967	Cub 9151
Cool It Baby	Honeycones, Ernie Cast & the	1958	Ember 1033
Cool It Baby	School Belles	1958	Dot 15801
Cool It Fool	Cadillacs	1959	Josie 861
Cool It, Fool	Cleftones	1959	Unreleased
Cool Lovin'	Crowns, Arthur Lee Maye & the	1955	RPM 420 (unreleased)
Cool Mambo	Sheppards (Chicago - Theron)	1955	Theron 112
Cool School	Hitmakers	1958	Original Sound 1
Cool Sea Breeze	Windsors, Lee Scott & the	1958	Back Beat 506
Cool Shake	Dell Vikings	1957	Mercury 71132
Cool Short	Olympics	1961	Titan 1718
Cool Summer Night	Intentions	1965	Uptown 710
Cool Wailin' Papa	Carter Rays, Eddie Carter & the	1954	Grand 107 (second pressing)
Cool Water	Actors	1962	Laurie 3135
Cool Water	Blue Belles	1962	Newtown 5009
Cool Wool	Unknowns	1958	Felsted 8535
Cool-A-Roo	Accents, Jackie Allen & the	1955	Accent 1025
Coolation	Dusters	1957	ABC 9886
Cooncha	Miller Sisters	1964	Stardust 3001
Cootie Snap	Vocaleers	1962	Twistime 11
Copper Kettle	Honey Dreamers	1959	Dot 15925
Copy Cat	Cadillacs	1959	Josie 857
Copy Cat	Halos	1961	7 Arts 709
Copy Cat	Wheels, Rudy & the	1959	Curtis 751
Coralee	Hemlocks, Little Bobby Rivera & the	1957	Fury 1004
Corn Whiskey	Cadillacs	1954	Unreleased
Corn Whiskey	Empires	1954	Harlem 2325
Corrida Mash	Heartbreakers (Bronx, N.Y.)	1962	Brent 7037
Cosy With Rosy	Vibraharps	1956	Beech 713
Cottage By The Sea	Incas	1976	Monogram 125
Cottage In The Country	Blue Angels	1961	Palette 5077
Cotton	Duvals (Illinois)	1963	Boss 2117/Red Rocket 471 (63)
Cotton Candy	Dots, Lenny Capello & the	1960	Ric 960
Cotton Fields	Angels (New Jersey)	1962, 1963	Caprice 121/Ascot 2139
Cotton Fields	Chantels	1961	Unreleased
Cotton Fields	Dazzlers, Teddy Randazzo & the	1962	ABC 10350
Cotton Pickin' Hands	Dukes (California)	1956	Imperial 5415
Cotton Pickin' Love	Chuck-A-Lucks	1961	Warner Bros. 5234
Cottonhead Joe	Blue Jays (Venice, Calif.)	1987	Relic LP 5064
Cottonhead Joe	Peels, Leon (with the Blue Jays)	1964	Whirlybird 2002
Could Be You	Mar-Vels	1958	Love 5011/5012
Could I Adore You	Blue Jays (Venice, Calif.)	1972	Roadhouse 113472
Could It Be	Edsels	1962	Dot 16311
Could It Be You?	Four Tops	1956	Chess 1623
Could It Be?	Sh-Booms	1955	Cat 117

SONG	GROUP	YEAR	LABEL
Could Somebody Take My Place Tonight?	DiMucci, Dion (with the Del Satins)	1961	Laurie 3101
Could This Be Love	Carmen, Jerry & group	1962	Barrish 500
Could This Be Love	Sinners	1962	Eden 1
Could This Be Magic	Charms, Otis Williams & his	1958	DeLuxe 6158
Could This Be Magic	Dubs	1957, 1964	Gone 5011/Musictone 1141 (61)/ Lana 115
Could This Be Magic	Dubs, The Cleveland Still	1986	Clifton 77
Could This Be Magic	Pictures, C.L. & the	1965	Monument 888
Could This Be Magic	Pretenders	1976	Rome 111/Power-Martin 1005
Could This Be You	Castells	1964	Warner Bros. 5445
Could This Be You?	Supremes (Massachusetts)	1956	Kitten 6969
Could You Mean More	Fireflies	1966	Taurus 376
Couldn't Wait Any Longer	Embers	1960	Dot 16101
Count Down	School Belles	1959	Hanover 4526
Count Down 1-2-3	Twisters	1959	Felco 103
Count Every Star	Blenders (New York)	1950	Decca 48158
Count Every Star	Dreamers, Donnie & the	1961	Whale 500
Count Every Star	Kittens	1963	Chestnut 203
Count Every Star	Metronomes	19??	
Count Every Star	Ravens	1950, 1972	National 9111
Count Every Star	Rivieras	1958	Coed 503
Count Every Star	Rockers	1956	Carter 3029
Count Every Star	Subway Serenade	NA	Clifton EP 504
Count Off Blues	Starlights, Bill Perry & the	NA	Premium 101
Count Ten	Lee, Jerry & group	1961	Rendezvous 147
Count The Tears	Edsels	1961	Tammy 1027
Count The Tears	Parakeets, Vic Donna & the	1957	Atlas 1075/Angletone 1075
Count To Ten	Spindles, Frankie & the	1968	Roc-Ker 100
Count Your Blessings	Kings, Little Hooks & the	1963	Century 1300/Little Rick 909 (63)/ Chess 1867 (63)
Count Your Blessings	Middleton, Tony & group	1959	Triumph 600
Count Your Blessings Instead Of Sheep	Demensions	1961	Coral 62277
Count Your Blessings (Instead Of Sheep)	Orioles, Sonny Til & the	1954	Jubilee 5172
Countdown To Love	/Yesterday's News	1982	Crystal Ball 148
Counted Out	Counts, Tommy Burk & the	1962	Nat 100
Counterfeit Heart	Youngsters	1956	Empire 107
Counterfeiter, The	Chargers (Jesse Belvin)	1958	RCA 7417
Countin' The Days	Rock-A-Fellas, Eddie Bell & the	1959	Coed 512
Counting My Teardrops	Del Satins	1961	Win 702
Counting My Teardrops	Jayhawks	1956	Flash 105
Counting Stars	Gentones	1961	Casino 52261
Counting The Stars	Ladders	1957	Holiday 2611
Counting Wishes	Capri, Tony & group	1961	Liban 1005
Country Fool	Showmen	1961	Minit 632/Imperial 66033 (64)/ Liberty 56166 (67)
Country Fool, The	Royal Robins	1963	ABC 10504
Country Shack	Falcons (Detroit)	1959	Unart 2022
County Jail	Volumes	NA	Chex
Coupe De Ville Baby	Medallions	1955	Dootone 357
Courage To Love	Five Royales	1952	Apollo 441
Court Room Blues	Four Bluebirds (Johnny Otis & Orchestra)	1949	Excelsior 540
Courtin' In A Cadillac	Upstarts, Jerry McCain & the	1956	Excello 2068
Cover Girl	Spencer, Carl & group	1965	Rust 5104
Cow Cow Dulywah	Emanons (Brooklyn)	NA	GGS 443
Cow Jumped Over The Moon, The	Isley Brothers	1956	Teenage 1004
Cow, The	Quails	1963	American 1023
Cowboy Joe	Duds, Dougie & the	1963	Amy 869
Cowboy, The	Fabulous Egyptians	1965	Cindy 96750
Crackerjack	Cues	1956	Capitol 3483
Cracker-Jack Daddy	De Bonairs	1956	Ping 1001
Cradle Love	Francettes	1963	Besche 100
Cradle Rock	Heartbreakers (Donna)	1963	Donna 1381
Cradle Rock	Rhythm Heirs	1959	Yucca 105
Crashing The Party	Feathers	1954	Show Time 1106

SONG	GROUP	YEAR	LABEL
Crave Me	Goofers	1956	Coral 61593
Craving	Cameos (Los Angeles)	1955	Dootone 365
Craving Your Love	Blenders (Wonder)	1959	Wonder 722
Crawl, The	Fireflies	1958	Roulette 4098
Crawlin'	Blue Beards	1958	Guide 1002
Crawlin'	Clovers	1953	Atlantic 989
Crawling	Love Notes (Family Library of Music)	1953	Family Library Of Music EP 1040
Crazee Baby	Spaniels	1957	Vee Jay 264
Crazy	Champagnes	1963	Skymac 1002/Laurie 3189 (63)
Crazy	Expressions	1956	Teen 101
Crazy	Flames	1959	Bertram 203
Crazy	Hollywood Flames	1957	Ebb 119/Mona Lee 135
Crazy	Savoys (New Jersey)	1965	Catamount 104
Crazy About A Woman	Cap-Tans	1962	Loop 100/International Award LP AK222
Crazy Baby	Coasters	1966	Atco 6379
Crazy Baby	Corlettes	1962	Kansoma 02
Crazy Baby	Jets, Buck Rogers & the	1959	Montel 2002
Crazy Baby	Latinaires, Little Joe & the	1970	White Whale 304
Crazy Baby	Sinceres, Johnny H & the	1963	El Zarape 122
Crazy Baby	Smooth Tones	1956	Ember 1001
Crazy Baby	Team Mates	1960	Le Cam 709
Crazy Bells	Halos	1962	Warwick LP 2046
Crazy Bells	Marcels (as the Fabulous Marcels)	1974	Owl 324
Crazy Bells	Premiers, Julie Stevens & the	1956	Dig 115/Eldo 107 (60)
Crazy Bells In My Heart	Marcels	NA	Cycle 2001 (unreleased)/ Colpix LP 416
Crazy Billboard Song	Miller Sisters	1957	Acme 717
Crazy Bones	Omegas	1959	Chord 1305
Crazy Bop	Earthquakes & Rhythm Kings	1960	Fortune 538
Crazy 'Bout My Honey Dip	Cap-Tans	1950	Dot 1009
Crazy 'Bout You	Nutmegs	1962	Herald 574
Crazy Cave	Juniors, Danny & the	1958	ABC 9953
Crazy Chicken	Five Jets	1954	DeLuxe 6064
Crazy Chicken	Gems (Mercury)	1961	Mercury 71819
Crazy Crazy 'Bout You	Lovejoy, Lovey & group	NA	
Crazy Crazy Crazy	Five Royales	1953	Apollo 446
Crazy, Crazy, Crazy	Flamingos	1960	End LP 307
Crazy Crazy Crazy	Vocaltones, Bobby Harris & the	1955	Wen-Dee 1933
Crazy, Crazy Feeling	Spirits, Doug Sahm & the	1959	Personality 3504
Crazy, Crazy Love	Charms, Otis Williams & the	1955	DeLuxe 6082
Crazy Crazy Party	Cues	1957	Prep 104
Crazy Daisy	Playboys	1959	Imperial 5586
Crazy Dance	Von Gayels	1960	Dore 544
Crazy Discharge	Holidays	1959	Pam 111
Crazy Doctor	Revelaires	1954	Burgundy 105
Crazy Dream	Crayons	1963	Counsel 121
Crazy Dream	Sabians	1961	Yale 241
Crazy Eyes For You	Wilde, Jimmy & group	1962	Chelsea 1006
Crazy Feeling	Five Sounds, Russ Riley & the	1957, 1977	Aljon 115/Arcade 1005
Crazy Feeling	Genies	1961	Warwick 643
Crazy For You	Aquatones	1960	Fargo 1016
Crazy For You	Dedications	1983	Avenue D 9
Crazy For You	Heartbeats	1955	Hull 711/Roulette 4194
Crazy For You	Newports	1981	Crystal Ball 143
Crazy For You	Rose, Andy (with the Thorns)	1961	Coral 62271
Crazy For You	Saints, Lola & the	1984	N/A
Crazy Girl	Rays	1958	Cameo 127
Crazy Hop	Crescendos (Nasco)	1958	Nasco 6009
Crazy Jealous	Rhythm Aces	1960	Mark-X 8004
Crazy Kind Of Love	Debonairs	1960	Winter 502
Crazy Little Baby	Gunter, Shirley & group	1957	Tender 503
Crazy Little Fever	Arabians	1960	Magnificent 102/Magnificant 102 (60)
Crazy Little Mama	Ribitones	1979	Off The Wall 69
Crazy Little Mama	Van-Dells, Myron & the	1963	Flo-Roe 15

SONG	GROUP	YEAR	LABEL
Crazy Little Woman	Three D's	1958	Paris 511
Crazy Love	Creators	1963	Epic 9605
Crazy Love	Genies	1960	Warwick 573
Crazy Love	Knight, Bob	1963	Jubilee 5451
Crazy Love	Royaltones	1956	Old Town 1018
Crazy Love	Run-A-Rounds	NA	Unreleased
Crazy Love	Starlighters, Joey Dee & the	1962	N/A
Crazy Love	Stormy Weather	1976, 1988	Catamount 133/Starlight 63
Crazy Love	Velours	1958	Cub 9014
Crazy Lovin'	Louisiana Jemms, Sugar Pie DeSantos & the	1963	Checker 1056
Crazy Loving (Stay With Me)	Midnighters	1954	Federal 12200
Crazy Maisie	Rainbeaus, Vinnie Rome & the	1959	Apt 25035
Crazy Memories	Aldenaires, Paul Alden & the	NA	Glolite 106
Crazy Mixed Up World	Channels, Earl Lewis & the	1972	Channel 1002
Crazy Over You	Calvanes	1955	Dootone 371
Crazy Over You	Gray, Maureen & group	1961	Chancellor 1082
Crazy Over You	Kool Gents	NA	Charly LP 1115/Solid Smoke LP 8026
Crazy Rock	Cupids, Carlo & the	1959	Parker 501/Judd 1007 (59)
Crazy Song, The	Mellow Drops	1954	Imperial 5324
Crazy Times	Lamplighters	1955	Federal (unreleased)
Crazy Yogi	Swingin' Bears, Bernadette & the	1961	Beach 1001
Cream Puff	Commodores	1955	Dot 15425
Creation	Kings (Baltimore)	NA	Collectables LP 5037/ Collectables LP 7003
Creation	Sevilles	1964	Galaxy 727
Creation Of Love	Catamounts, Calvin & the	1976	Catamount 131
Creation Of Love	Charms, Otis Williams & his	1974	Owl 329
Creation Of Love	Teenagers, Frankie Lymon & the	1957	Gee 1039
Creator Of Love	Five Trojans, Nicky St. Clair & the	1959	Edison International 410
Creature, The	Jayhawks	1957	Aladdin 3393
Credit Man	Persians, Paris & the	1961	AKU 921
Creep, The	Legends, Larry & the (with the Four Seasons)	1964	Atlantic 2220
Creepin'	Drew-Vels, Patti Drew & the	1965	Capitol 5244
Creepin'	Starlighters	1960	Wheel 1004
Crew Cuts (We Like)	Escorts, Debs & the	1958	Josie 833
Crewnecks And Khakis	Crewnecks	1959	Rhapsody 71960
Cricket, The	Ryan, Cathy (with the Admirals)	1955	King 4848
Crime Doesn't Pay	Coronets	1955	Groove 0114
Crime Don't Pay	Nobles, Nicky & the	1962	Times Square 12
Croc-O-Doll	Impacts	1959	RCA 7583
Cross Every Mountain	Fabulous Three, Gorgeous George & the	1962	Hale
Cross Fire	Creators	1963	Epic 9605
Cross My Heart	Concords (Brooklyn)	1961	Gramercy 304
Cross My Heart	Earls	1961, 1979	Rome 102/Clifton 39 (74)
Cross My Heart	Emeralds (with Little Milton)	1960	Bobbin 128
Cross My Heart	Emjays	1959	Greenwich 412
Cross My Heart	Lovenotes (Wallace Rose)	1953	
Cross My Heart	Parker, Leroy & group	1962	
Cross My Heart	Playboys	1961	Nite Owl 30
Cross My Heart	Softwinds	1961	Hac 105
Cross My Heart	Themes, Alvin Gaines & the	1959	Fidelity 420592
Cross My Heart And Hope To Die	Dell Mates	1964	Fontana 1934/Smash 1934 (64)
Cross Over The Bridge	Chords	1954	Cat 104 (first pressing)
Cross Over The Bridge	Flamingos	1954	Chance 1154
Crossfire With Me Baby	Continentals, Teddy & the	1961	Richie 453
Crossroads	Gay Notes	1955	Post 2006
Crossroads Of Love	Tempos	1959	Climax 105
Crowd With The Phony Tattoo	Relations	1963	Zells 712
Crowded Classroom	Strollers	1958	Warner 1018
Cruise To The Moon	Chaperones	1960	Josie 880 (second pressing, first is by the Cahperones)
Cruisin'	Cruisers	1959	Winston 1033
Cruising	Casualairs	1961	Craig 5001
Crumble, The	Diamonds	1960	Mercury 71734

SONG	GROUP	YEAR	LABEL
Crush On You	Crosstones	NA	Clifton EP 510
Cry	Concepts (with the Emanons)	NA	J&J 3000
Cry	Flamingos	1956	Checker (unreleased)
Cry	Malibus	1963	Planet 58
Cry All Night	Cool Tones	NA	Dice 750
Cry And Be On Your Way	Demilles	1964	Laurie 3247
Cry Angel Cry	Apollos, Paul Stefen & the	1962	Cite 5008
Cry Baby	Bonnie Sisters	1956	Rainbow 328
Cry Baby	Co-Hearts	1958	Vee Jay 289
Cry Baby	Hurley, John & group	1958	AKA 103
Cry Baby	London, Lloyd (with the Yachtsmen)	1959	Destiny 530
Cry Baby	Mark V	1960	Milo 110
Cry Baby	Scarlets	1955	Red Robin 135
Cry Baby	Walker, Mel & the Bluenotes	1950	Regent 1016
Cry Baby Cry	Angels (New Jersey)	1962	Caprice 112
Cry Baby Cry	Bop Shop	NA	Larric 7301
Cry Baby Cry	Chryslers, Little Nate & the	1959	Johnson 318
Cry Baby Cry	Denhams	1957	Note 10009
Cry, Baby, Cry	Sensations	1956	Atco 6075
Cry Baby Cry	Staffords	1956	Decca 29828
Cry, Cry Baby	Aladdins	1955	Aladdin 3275
Cry Cry Baby	Chimes (Limelight)	1957	Limelight 3000
Cry Cry Cry	Earls	1963	Old Town 1145
Cry Cry Cry	Euniques	1961, 1980	620 1006/Jason Scott 6
Cry Cry Cry	Hawks, Little Tony & the	1966	Original Sound 63
Cry Cry Cry	Lyndon, Frank (with the Regents)	NA	Jab 1004
Cry Cry Cry	Upsets, Eddy & the	NA	Dektr 41668
Cry Fool	Cherlos	NA	Relic LP 5022
Cry For My Baby	Four Duchesses	1957	Chief 7014
Cry For My Baby	Hollywood Four Flames	1951	Unique 009
Cry I Do	Fabulous Echoes	1965	Liberty 55801
Cry Like A Baby	Pixies	1962	AMC 102/Don-Dee 102 (63)
Cry Like A Baby	Versatiles	NA	Staff 210
Cry Like I Cried	Ecstasies	1986	Clifton 78
Cry Like I Cried	Harptones	1957	Gee 1045
Cry Like I Cried	Heartspinners, Dino & the	1972, 1976	Bim Bam Boom 108/Barrier 103
Cry, Little Boy, Cry	Triumphs, Tico & the	1962	Amy 860
Cry No More	Teardrops	1959	Josie 862
Cry On My Shoulder	Kings, Vicki France & the	1959	Sparkette 1002
Cry On My Shoulder	Sparks Of Rhythm	1989	Relic LP 5080
Cry (Only You Cry Alone)	Concepts (with the Emanons)	NA	J&J 3000
Cry Over You	Robins (Nobells)	1964	Musicor 1050
Cry Some More	Five Royales	1954	Apollo 454
Cry Wind Cry	Heartbreakers (Washington, D.C.)	1952	Roadhouse 1007
Cry Your Heart Out	Bluenotes, Donnie Williams & the	1959	Viking 1005
Cryin'	Pyramids (Detroit)	1962	Cub 9112
Cryin' All Night	Nightbeats	1958	Zoom 002
Cryin' For My Baby	Flames	1952	Spin 101
Cryin' For You Baby	Barons (New Orleans)	1954	Imperial 5283
Cryin' My Heart Out	Fountain, Morris & group	1954	Savoy 1139
Cryin' The Blues	Lyrics	NA	N/A
Cryin' The Blues	Moonbeams	1955	Sapphire 1052/Sapphire 1003 (58)/Checker 912 (59)
Crying	Endorsers	1959	Moon 109
Crying	Hart, Rocky (with the Passions)	1961	Big Top 3069
Crying	Teenagers (Joe Negroni/Kenny Bobo)	1960	End 1071
Crying	Versatiles	1958	Atlantic 2004
Crying All Alone	Ray-O-Vacs	1956	Kaiser 384
Crying Alone	Ray-O-Vacs	1957	Atco 6085
Crying Blues	Premiers, Herb Johnson & the	1959	Palm
Crying Cause I Lost	Gibralters, Jimmy Barnes & the	1960	Savoy 1581
Crying For My Baby	Burrage, Harold & group	1959	Vee Jay 318
Crying For My Baby	Dawn Quartet	1952	Decatur 3001
Crying For You	Centuries	1963	Times Square 5/Klik

SONG	GROUP	YEAR	LABEL
Crying For You	Cineramas	1960, 1973	Rhapsody 71963/71964/ Candlelite 433/Clifton 4
Crying In The Chapel	Baker's Satins	1984	Clifton 74
Crying In The Chapel	Four Dukes	1953	Duke 116
Crying In The Chapel	Laurels	1986	Ram EP 509049
Crying In The Chapel	Orioles, Sonny Til & the	1953, 1959, 1964	Jubilee 5122/6001/Lana 109 (64)
Crying In The Chapel	Shields, Johnny & group	1963	Armour 4466
Crying In The Chapel	Superior Angels	1964	Skylark 0023
Crying In The Chapel	Velvets (Texas)	1963	Monument 810
Crying In The Chapel	Vocalaires	1962	Herald (unreleased)
Crying In The Night	Dream Girls, Bobbie Smith & the	1959	Metro 20029
Crying Inside	Thomas, Gene & group	1961	Venus 1444
Crying Like A Baby Over You	Maresca, Ernie (with the Del Satins)	1962	Seville 117
Crying My Heart Out	Masters	1958	Le Sage 713/714
Crying Over You	Broken Hearts	NA	Rosina 147
Crying Over You	Carter, Sonny & group	1959	Dot 15921
Crying Over You	Continentals, Teddy & the	1961	Richie 453
Crying Over You	Cruisers	1960	V-Tone 213/Guyden 2069 (62)
Crying Over You	Hornets	1957	Flash 125
Crying Over You	Lyrics (San Francisco)	1959	Mid South 1500
Crying Over You	Nobells	1962	Mar 101
Crying The Blues	Golden Tones	1955	Samson 107/108
Crying The Blues	Moonbeams	1958	Sapphire 2250
Crying The Blues Over You	Criterions	1959	Cecelia 1010
Cuando Caliente El Sol	Platters	1963	Mercury 72194
Cuca Monga	Honey Bears	1955	Cash 1004
Cuckoo	Four Counts	1958	Josie 840/Go 103
Cuckoo	Teen Tones	1960	Deb 132
Cuddle Up With Carolyn	Fascinators (King)	1958	King 5119
Cuddly Baby	Deb-Tones	1958	RCA 7242
Cumberland And The Merrimac, The	Inspirations (Rondak)	1961	Rondak 9787
Cupid	Impalas (Brooklyn)	19??	Unreleased
Cupid's Poison Dart	Oberle, Scott & group	1964	Lawn 216
Cure For Love	Lasabers, Lafayette & the	1960	Port 70036
Curfew	Jags, Steve Carl with the	1958	Meteor 5046
Curfew Lover	Essex, Anita Humes & the	1964	Roulette 4542
Curfew Time	Turbans (Philadelphia)	1959	Red Top 115
Curiosity Killed The Cat	Neptunes	1961	RCA 7931
Curl Up In My Arms	Nuggets	1954	Capitol 2989
Custer's Last Man	Mohawks, Popcorn & the	1960	Motown 1002
Custer's Last Stand	Emeralds (St. Louis)	1960	Rex 1013
Cut It Out	Cameos, Little Willie Brown & the	1961	Do-Ra-Mi 1404
Cut Me Up	Daarts	1961	Dyna 109
Cute	Counts, Tommy Burk & the	1964	Rich Rose 1001
Cute Chick	Echomores	NA	Rocket 1042
Cute Collegiate	Brooktones	1958	Coed 502
Cute Little Baby	Champions	1958	Ace 541
Cute Little Girl	Johnson, Jesse & group	1958	Symbol 901
Cute Little Ways	Midnighters, Hank Ballard & the	1959	King 5245
Cute Little Wiggle	Lemon Drops	1959	Coral 62145
Cute Thing	Night Owls, Tony Allen & the	1960	Crown LP 5231
Cutie Cutie	Paramours	1961	Smash 1718
Cuttin' Out	Wonders	1957	Reserve 122
Cutting Silhouettes	Sandetts	1960	Smokey 109
Cutups	Cutups	1962	Music Makers 301
Cuzin' Casanova	Cleftones	1959	Roulette 4161
Cynthia	Show Stoppers	1963	Amber 212

D

SONG	GROUP	YEAR	LABEL
D.W. Washburn	Coasters	1968, 1971	Date 1617/King 6385
Da Da Goo Goo	Harvey (Harvey Fuqua with the Moonglows)	1958	Chess 1713
Da Dee Ya Da	Roamers, Wilbert Harrison & the	1954	Savoy 1149
Da Doo	Evergreens, Dante & the	1961	Madison 154
Da Doo Ron Ron	Aztecs	1964	World Artists 1029
Da Doo Ron Ron	Chiffons	NA	Collectables LP 5042

SONG	GROUP	YEAR	LABEL
Da Doo Ron Ron (acappella)	Belmonts	1972	Buddah LP 5123
Da Doo Ron Ron (When He Walked Me Home)	Crystals (Brooklyn)	1963	Philles 112
Da Doo Run Run	Zeu Review, Ziggy & the	NA	Zeu 5011
Da Kind	Royal Drifters	1959	Teen 508
Dad Is Home	Comets, Lynn Tiatt & the	NA	Pussycat 1
Daddy	Darnels, Debbie & the	1962	Columbia 42530
Daddy	Ray-O-Vacs, Flap McQueen & the (with Babe Hutton)	1955	Josie 781
Daddy Cool	Cal-Cons	1962	Allrite 621
Daddy Cool	Diamonds	1957	Mercury 71197
Daddy Cool	Rays	1957	XYZ 102/Cameo 117 (57)
Daddy, Daddy	Dreamers, Richard Berry & the	1955	Flair 1058
Daddy Daddy	Kids, Herman & the	1959	Columbia 41411
Daddy, Daddy	Lavenders	1964	Dot 16584
Daddy Daddy	Melodees	1960	Nu Kat 124
Daddy Do	Jillettes	1962	Amazon 711
Daddy Loves Mommy	Chords	1953	Gem 211
Daddy Must Be	Chanticleers	1958	Lyric 103
Daddy Must Be A Man	Unforgettables	1961	Pamela 204
Daddy Needs Baby	Pretenders	1958	Central 2605/Apt 25026 (59)/ ABC 10094 (60)
Daddy Nolan Strong	Diablos	1984	Fortune LP 8020
Daddy Please	Adorables	1964	Golden World 4
Daddy Rock And Roll	Dukes, Billy Duke & the	1956	Teen 112
Daddy Rockin' Strong	Diablos (featuring Nolan Strong)	1955	Fortune 516
Daddy Rocks Off	Daddy Cool & group	1972	Reprise 1090
Daddy Rollin' Stone	Raves, Jimmy Ricks & the	1962	Atco 6220/Festival 25004
Daddy Rolling Stone	Midnighters, Hank Ballard & the	1964	King 5931
Daddy Said	Beau-Marks	1960	Shad 5017/Mainstream 688 (68)
Daddy Warbucks	Velours	1960	Goldisc 3012
Daddy Woo-Woo	Vibrations	1964	Atlantic 2221
Daddy-O	Harmonaires, Bonnie Lou & the	1955	King 4864
Daddy's Comin' Home	El Sierros	1963	Yussels 7702
Daddy's Going Away	Camelots	NA	Clifton EP 507
Daddy's Going Away Again	Harps	1964	Laurie 3239
Daddy's Gone Away	Misters, Mike Malone & the	1964	Token 1002
Daddy's Gonna Tell You No Lies	Cosmic Rays	1960	Saturn 401
Daddy's Home	Addictions	1972	Kelway 102
Daddy's Home	Duke Of Earl & group	1962	Vee Jay 450
Daddy's Home	Four Winds	1961	Warwick 633
Daddy's Home	Lee, Jimmy (with the Earls)	1978	Bo-P-C 100
Daddy's Home	Limelites, Shep & the	1961	Hull 740
Daddy's Home	Memory	1981	Avenue D 6
Daddy's Home But Mama's Gone	Monotones	1961	Hull 741
Daddy's Little Baby	Midnighters	1958	Federal 12317
Daddy's Little Girl	Teardrops	1959	Josie 873
Dagwood, The	Fairlanes	1962	Minaret 103
Daisy	Corvells	1962	ABC 10324
Daisy	Sultans Five	1964	Raynard 843
Dallas	Dingoes	1957	Dallas 2001
Damage Is Done, The	Turbans (Philadelphia)	1962	Imperial 5847
Dame Tu Corazon	Van Dykes	1959	Felsted 8565
Dan	Mystics	1963	Nolta 353
Dance	Coasters	1958	Atco 6111
Dance	Dolphins	1962	Tip Top 2003/Gemini 501 (62)
Dance	Melson, Joe & group	1962	Hickory 1175
Dance A Little Closer	Lover Boy & group	1963	Crystalette 758
Dance (acappella)	Chessmen	1965	Relic 1015
Dance (acappella)	Uniques	1975	Relic LP 109
Dance All By Myself	Tabs	1961	Vee Jay 418
Dance And Swing	Medallions	1956	Dootone 393
Dance Baby (With Me)	Bravadoes, Little Mac & the	1961	Little Mac 101
Dance Between The Stars	Chordliners	1989	Blue Sky 111
Dance By The Light Of The Moon	Olympics	1960	Arvee 5020

SONG	GROUP	YEAR	LABEL
Dance Close	Miller Sisters	1963	Riverside 4535
Dance Dance	Vocalaires	1962	Herald 573
Dance, Dance, Dance	Cavaliers	1958	Apt 25004
Dance, Dance, Dance	Dells	1957	Vee Jay 236
Dance, Dance, Dance	Deltars, Pearl & the	1961	Fury 1048
Dance Dance Dance	Kodaks	1990	Relic LP 5083
Dance, Dance, Dance	Zodiacs, Maurice Williams & the	1967	Dee-Su 318
Dance Dance, Little Girl Dance	Dolphins, Davey Jones & the	1961	Sinclair 1005
Dance, Darling, Dance	Serenaders (New Jersey)	1957	MGM 12666
Dance D-D-Dance	Gay Charmers	1958	Savoy 1549
Dance Everyone, Dance	Hi-Lighters	1958	Hanover 4506
Dance Forever	Decades	1963	Daytone 1306
Dance Girl	Camelots	1964	Times Square 32/Relic 541 (65)
Dance Girl	Charts	1957	Everlast 5002/Lost Nite 180 (81)
Dance Girl	Teenchords, Lewis Lymon & the	1958, 1984	Juanita 101
Dance Girl, Dance	Granahan, Gerry (with the Wildwoods)	1961, 1995	Caprice 108/X-Bat 1000
Dance, Girl, Dance	Rob-Roys, Norman Fox & the	1958	Back Beat 508
Dance Gypsy (acappella)	Chessmen	1975	Relic LP 106
Dance Her By Me	Citations, Angie & the	NA	Angela 102
Dance Honey Dance	Velvets (New York)	1957	Fury 1012
Dance In The Night	Blenders (Chicago)	1957	Vision 1000
Dance Is Over, The	Essentials, Little Billy & the	1962	Landa 691/Jamie 1229 (62)
Dance Is Over, The	Shirelles	1960	Scepter 1208
Dance Is Over, The	Splendors	1982	Clifton 69
Dance Joanne	Four Epics	1963	Laurie 3183
Dance Little Sister	Miller Sisters	1962	Rayna 5001
Dance Me To Death	Hi-Lighters	1958	Mercury 71342
Dance Now	Persians	1962	RSVP 114
Dance Of Love	Lanham, Richard (with the Tempo-Tones)	1955	Acme 712
Dance Of Love	Superiors	1961	Federal 12436
Dance Of The Land	Fourmosts, Bobby Moore & the	1964	Fantasy 585
Dance On	Tate, Paul & group	1958	Falcon 1012
Dance Party	Tabs	1961	Vee Jay 418
Dance Party Rock	Knights, Frankie Daye & the	1959	Studio 9904
Dance Romeo Dance	King-Pins	1963	Vee Jay 494
Dance Romeo Dance	Winners	1962	Vee Jay 494
Dance Senorita	Hollywood Flames	1965	Symbol 211
Dance The Boomerang	Coanjos	1961	Dapt 208
Dance The Froog	Dovells	1963	Parkway 882
Dance The Last Dance	Continentals, Lenny & the	1963	Tribute 125
Dance The Magoo	Triangles	1962	Fargo 1023
Dance The Rhythm And Blues	Balladiers, Billy Matthews & the	1956	Wrimus
Dance The Slossin	Hollywood Allstars	1963	Admiral 501
Dance They Did, The	Big Tops	1958	Warner 1017
Dance To The Locomotion	Dazzlers, Teddy Randazzo & the	1962	ABC 10350
Dance To The Rhythm Of Love	Blue Belles, Patti LaBelle & the	1969	Atlantic 2610
Dance With Me	Cahperones	1960	Josie 880 (second pressing, first is by the Cahperones)
Dance With Me	Castroes	1959	Grand 2002
Dance With Me	Drifters (1959-forward)	1959	Atlantic 2040
Dance With Me	El Torros	1957, 1960	Duke 175/321
Dance With Me	Majorettes	1963	Troy 1004
Dance With Me	Fabulous Desires	1964	Era 3138
Dance With Me Georgie	Bobbettes	1960, 1961	Triple-X 106/King 5490
Dance With The Rock	Five Encores	1955	Rama 187
Dance With The Teacher	Olympics	1958	Demon 1512
Dancer	Autumns	1981	BAB 128
Dances, The	Starfires	1961	Bargain 5003/Atomic 1912 (61)
Dancin' And Cryin'	Corals	1962	Kram 1001/Rayna 5010 (62)
Dancin' And Romancin'	Catalinas	1980	Catalinas 16560
Dancin' Dan (Sixty Minute Man)	Cadets	1956	Modern 1000
Dancin' Holiday	Olympics	1963	Tri Disc 107
Dancin' In The Congo	Chandeliers	1958	Angle Tone 529
Dancin' Lady, The	Dream-Timers (with the Flippin' Teens Orchestra)	1961	Flippin' 107

SONG	GROUP	YEAR	LABEL
Dancin' Little Girl	Shuffles	1963	Rayco 508
Dancin' The Strand	Gray, Maureen & group	1962	Landa 689
Dancing Alone	Emeralds (Jubilee)	1964	Jubilee 5474
Dancing By Myself	Pals, Gerry Patt & his	1965	Ascot 2129
Dancing Cheek To Cheek	Shadows, Dave & the	1962	Checkmate 1016
Dancing Danny	Vibrations	1963	Checker 1061
Dancing Doll	Fantastics	1961, 1990	United Artists 309/Park Ave. 4
Dancing Fast, Dancing Slow	Intentions	1967	Kent 455
Dancing Girl	Ex-Cels Five	1964	Enith 722
Dancing Girl	Playboys, Gary Gillespie & the	1962	Delta 520
Dancing In A Dream World	Hearts (Bronx, N.Y.)	1957, 1964	J&S 1466/1657
Dancing In The Street	Dovells	1974	Event 216
Dancing Little Clown	Twisters	1960	Capitol 4451
Dancing On Moonbeams	Diadems	NA	Goldie 207
Dancing On The Sand	Initials, Angelo & the	1964	Congress 219
Dancing Senorita	Five Keys	1959	King 5273
Dancing Shadows	Corsairs	1962	Tuff 1830/Chess 1830 (62)
Dancing Shoes	Williams, Eddie & group	1963	Alcor 2013
Dancing The Scratch	Ragmops, Little B. Cook & the	1961	CBM 314
Dancing With Tears In My Eyes	Owens, Garland & group	NA	Lemonade 1502
Dancing With You	Classics (Brooklyn)	1965, 1966	Stork 2/Josie 939
Dancing With You	Computones	1978	U.G.H.A. 3
Dandelion	Chargers (Jesse Belvin)	1958	RCA 7301
Danger Ahead	Debs	1963	Double L 727
Dangerous Lips	Drivers	1957	DeLuxe 6117
Dangerous Lover	Del Rios	1962	Bet-T 7001
Dangling With My Heart	Squires (California)	1957	Aladdin 3360
Danny	Six Teens	1958	Flip 333
Danny Boy	Blue Belles, Patti LaBelle & the	1964	Parkway 935
Danny Boy	Continentals, Bill Harris & the	1958	Eagle 1002
Danny Boy	Darchaes	1983	Nobell 7001
Danny Boy	Duvells	1962	Rust 5045
Danny Boy	Encores	1959	Checker (unreleased)
Danny Boy	Entertainers	1963	Demand 2932
Danny Boy	Flamingos	1962	End LP 316
Danny Boy	Larks (North Carolina)	1971	Dreamtone 201 (unreleased)
Danny Boy	Notations	1965	Relic 1019
Danny Boy	Orioles (featuring Bobby Thomas)	1992	Clifton 105
Danny Boy	Paragons	1977, 1986	Robin Hood 145
Danny Boy	Plazas, Nicky Addeo & the	1962	Revelation 7-101
Danny Boy	Sentimentals	1958	Mint 805
Danny Boy	Spaniels	1954, 1974	Vee Jay (unreleased)/ Canterbury EP101
Danny Boy	Sparks	1957	Hull 723
Danny Boy (acappella)	Chessmen	1975	Relic LP 105
Danny's Blues	Ebbtones	1957	Ebb 100
Dante's Inferno	Mark IV	1959	Mercury 71445
Dapper Dan	Elites	1960	Chief 7028
Dapper Dan	Four Jewels	1963	Checker 1039
Dapper Dan	Tabs, Joanie Taylor & the	1961	Herald 568
Darbytown	Clovers, Tippie & the	1975	Jett 3019
Dare To Dream	Orioles, Sonny Til & the	1948	Jubilee 5001
Dark At The Top Of My Heart	Five Satins	1971	RCA 74-0478
Dark, Dark Sunglasses	Kittens	1960	Alpine 64
Dark Was The Night	Five Knights	1963	Bumps 1504
Darkest Night, The	Gems (Illinois)	1956	Drexel 909
Darkness	Embers, Gene Pitney & the	1990	Relic LP 5085
Darkness	Nobles, Nicky & the	1962	Times Square 12
Darktown Strutters Ball	Satellites	1960	D-M-G 4001
Darktown Strutter's Ball	Platters	NA	Mercury EP 3353
Darla	Keens, Rick & the	1964	Le Cam 113/Tollie 9016 (64)
Darla My Darlin'	G-Clefs	1956	Pilgrim 715
Darla, My Darling	Academics	1956	Ancho 100/Relic 509 (64)
Darlene	Blue Jays (Venice, Calif.)	1987	Relic LP 5064
Darlene	Blue Sky Boys	1974	Blue Sky 109

SONG	GROUP	YEAR	LABEL
Darlene	Dreams	1954	Savoy 1130
Darlene	Earls	1990	Relic LP 5087
Darlene	Hi Tensions, Leon Peels & the	1964	Whirlybird 2008
Darlene	Parliaments, Freddie & the	1959	Twirl 1003
Darlene Darling	Celtics	1960	War Conn 2216
Darlin'	Corvairs	1961	Crown 004
Darlin'	Five Debonaires	1957	Herald 509
Darlin'	Gainors	1961	Tally-Ho 105
Darlin'	Larks (North Carolina)	1952	Apollo 437
Darlin'	Nightcaps	1961	Vandan 7066
Darlin'	Strangers	1962	Checker 1010
Darlin' Come Home	Fireside Singers	1963	Herald 582
Darlin' I Do	Sebastian & group	1959	Mr. Maestro 801/Take 2 2002 (59)
Darlin' In The Moonlight	Emperors	1964	Olimpic 245
Darlin' (Love You So)	Montereys (Trans American)	NA	Trans American 1000/1001
Darlin' Send Me A Letter	Montereys (Trans American)	NA	Trans American 1000/1001
Darlin' Why	Knightsmen	1961	Bocaldun 1006
Darline	Blenders, Earl Curry & the	1987	Relic LP 5069
Darling	Angletones	1985	Relic LP 5051
Darling	Blenders, Ray Frazier & the	1960	Combo 161/Relic LP 5069 (87)
Darling	Creations	NA	Tan
Darling	Dark, Mel & the Giants	1974	Blue Sky
Darling	Debonaires (Atlanta)	1957	Herald 509
Darling	Deb-Teens	1959	Boss 403
Darling	Downs, Bobbie & group	1960	Correc-Tone 3807
Darling	Dubs	1957	Johnson 102/Gone 5002 (57)/ Musictone 1142 (61)
Darling	Dynamos	1964	Azuza 1002
Darling	Falcons (Detroit)	1962	Atlantic 2153
Darling	Five Emeralds	1954	S-R-C 107
Darling	Five Keys	1971 (1952)	Aladdin 3119
Darling	Four Sevilles	NA	Starlight 12
Darling	Gee-Chords, Dino & the	1977	Robin Hood 152
Darling	Giants, Mel Dark & the (Sparrows Quartette)	1974	Blue Sky 108
Darling	Lyrics, William Wigfall & the	1963	(Russel's) Gold Wax 101/ Goldwax 910 (63)
Darling	Magichords	1950	Regal 3238
Darling	Nash, Marvin & group	1961	Pharoah 115
Darling	Pips	1962	Fury 1067
Darling	Ray-O-Vacs (with Herb Milliner)	1954	Josie 763
Darling	Sinceres	1960	Sigma 1003/1004
Darling	Veltones	1966	Goldwax 301
Darling	Vibes	1957	ABC 9810
Darling Angel	Royal Boys	1960	Tropelco 1007
Darling Baby	Elgins (V.I.P)	1965	V.I.P. 25029
Darling Barbara	Del-Brooks	1958	Kid 101
Darling, Be Mine	Earthquakes	1959	Fortune 534
Darling Can't We Talk (acappella)	El Caminos	1965	Fellatio 101
Darling Can't You Tell	Clusters	1958	Tee Gee 102/End 1115 (62)
Darling Come Back	Crescents, Pat Cordel & the	1956	Club 1011/Michele M 503 (59)/ Victory 1001 (63)
Darling Darlin'	Scott, Ricky & group	1960	X-Clusive/Cub 9079 (60)
Darling Dear	Counts	1954	Dot 1188/Dot 16105 (61)
Darling Dear	Visions	1959	Warwick 108
Darling Do You Love Me	Casuals, Harold & the	1959	Scotty 628
Darling Don't Hurt Me	Cole, Ann (with the Suburbans)	1955	Baton 218
Darling Don't Leave Me Now	Bobby-Pins	1959	Okeh 7110
Darling Don't Make Me Cry	Halos, Ernie & the	1963	Guyden 2085
Darling, Farewell	Rivileers	1954	Baton 201
Darling Forever	Darchaes, Ray & the	1962	Buzzy 202
Darling, Forever	Four Chevelles	1957	Band Box 357/Delft 357 (64)
Darling Goodbye	Martin, Benny & group	1960	Astro 109
Darling Hear My Plea	Dymnestics, Evonne Robinson & the	NA	Spacey
Darling Here' My Heart	Paramours	1986	Ronnie 205
Darling How Long	Heartbeats	1956	Hull 713/Gee 1062 (61)

SONG	GROUP	YEAR	LABEL
Darling How Long	Laurels	1989	
Darling, I Fell For You	Castros	1959	Lasso 501
Darling I Know	El Rays	1954	Checker 794
Darling I Know Now	Mystics	1961	Laurie 3104
Darling I Love You	Clouds	1959	Round 1008
Darling I Love You	Corvets, Arthur & the	1964	Na-R-Co 203
Darling, I Love You	Paragons, Tommy Collins & the	1959	Winley 236
Darling I Love You	Teen Five	1963	Times Square 2/Times Square 99 (64)
Darling I Love You	Teen Tones	1959	Dandy Dan 2
Darling I Need You	Roman, Nip & group	1957	Flash 121
Darling I Need Your Love	Chips	1961	Venice 101/Strand 25027 (61)
Darling I Pray	Dell-Rays	1958	Boptown 102
Darling I Really Love You	Markells	1958	R&M 407/408
Darling I Understand	Grady, Paul & group	1963	Glaze 109
Darling I Want To Get Married	Exotics	1961	Coral 62268
Darling, I Want To Get Married	Heartbeats	1959	Guyden 2011
Darling I Want Your Love	Tibbs, Kenneth & group	1958	Federal 12335
Darling I Will	Mello-Tones, Marga Benitez & the	NA	Sampson 102
Darling If I Had You	Caliphs	1958	Scatt 111
Darling I'll Be True	Interludes	1962	King 5633
Darling I'll Love Only You	Ebb Tides	1957	Acme 720
(Darling I'll See You) Tonight	Ascots	1962	King 5679
Darling, I'm Home	Mandells	1961	Smart 323/Chess 1794 (61)
Darling I'm Lonesome For You	Four Jacks	1952	MGM 11179-A
Darling I'm Sorry	Tru Tones	NA	Tree
Darling I'm Sorry (I Made You Cry)	Ambassadors	1954	Timely 1001
Darling I'm Yours	Scarlets	1955	Red Robin 133
Darling, Is It True?	Oliver, Johnny & group	1955	MGM 55012
Darling, Is It True?	Sycamores	1955	Groove 0121
Darling It's Wonderful	Lovers	1957, 1962	Lamp 2005/Imperial 5845/Post 10007 (63)
Darling It's You	Adelphis	1958	Rim 2020
Darling It's You, You, You	Gardenias	1962	Fairlane 21019
Darling Jane	Flames, Carol Pegues & the	NA	GM 101
Darling Je Vous Aime Beaucoup	Chateaus	1956	Epic 9163
Darling Let's Fall In Love	Twylights	1961	Rockin 102
Darling, Listen To The Words Of This Song	Four Students, Varetta Dillard & the	1956	Groove 0139
Darling, Listen To The Words Of This Song	Supremes, Ruth McFadden & the	1956	Old Town 1017
Darling Little Angel	Interiors	1961	Worthy 1008
Darling Lorraine	Knockouts	1959	Shad 5013
Darling Lorraine	Underbeats	1966	Soma 1449
Darling Love	Dusters	1958	Glory 287
Darling My Love	Lovelarks, Steve Kass & the	1957	Class 10
Darling, Now You're Mine	Impacts	1961	Carlton 548
Darling Of Mine	Blue Notes	1958	TNT 150/Dot 15720 (58)
Darling Of Mine	Downbeats	1956	Sarg 168
Darling Oh Darling	Dinos	1962	Fox 101
Darling Patricia	Gales	1955	J.V.B. 35/J.O.B. 3001
Darling Patricia	Palms, Artie Wilkins & the	1956	States 157
Darling Please	Bees	1974 (1954)	Imperial (unreleased)
Darling Please	Reed, John & group	NA	Fore 611
Darling Please Don't Change	Offitt, Lillian & group	1958	Excello 2139
Darling, Please Don't Love Me	Starlarks	1964	Astra 100
Darling Remember	Heartbreakers, TV Slim & His	1957	Cliff 103/Checker 870 (57)
Darling Stay With Me	Savoys (Combo)	1955	Combo 75
Darling What About You	Elites	1960	Chief 7028
Darling You	Four Fellows (Brooklyn - Glory)	1956	Glory 242
Darling You Know	Four Gems	1972	Broadcast 4/Broadcast 1001
Darling (You Know I Love You)	Vocaltones	1956	Apollo 492
Darling You Send Me	Cashmeres (Rubbertown)	NA	Rubbertown 103
Darling You're My Angel (acappella)	Memories	1964	Times Square 11/Times Square 95 (64)
Darling You've Changed	Fiestas	1974	Vigor 712
Darn Your Love	Torches	1965	Ring-O 302
Date With My Man	Relations, Gloria & the	NA	Bonnie 101/102
Date With The Rain	Gee, Frankie & group	1975	Claridge 410

SONG	GROUP	YEAR	LABEL
Dateless Night	Deltones	NA	Moon 302
Datin' With You	Richards, Norm & group	1959	Imperial 5567
Daughter	Blenders (Chicago)	1963	Witch 114
Davilee	Fabulous Dudes	1989	Presence 4502
Davy You Upset My Life	Hi-Fi Four	1955	King 4856
Dawn	Velvets (Texas)	1963	Monument 810
Dawn Is Almost Here	Cordials	1961	7 Arts 707
Day After Forever	Chevrons	1959	Brent 7007
Day And Night	Bobby & Jimmy & group	1963	King 5757
Day Before Yesterday, The	Dreams, Darnell & the	1964	West Side 1020/Cousins
Day By Day	Capitols, Mickey Toliver & the	1958	Gateway 721
Day Dreaming	Creations	NA	Tan
Day Has Come, The	Inspirations, Maurice Williams & the	1963	Candi 1031
Day I Die, The	Petty, Daryl & group	1959	Hornet 502
Day I Met You, The	Bachelors (Smash)	1961	Smash 1723
Day I Met You, The	Lanham, Richard (with the Tempo-Tones)	1956	Acme 722
Day In Court	Varnells	1961	Arnold 1006
Day, The	Enchanters (Detroit)	1963	Coral 62373
Day The Clown Cried, The	Skyliners, Jimmy Beaumont & the	1976	Drive 6520
Day The Rains Came, The	Littlefield, Little Willie & female group	1958	Rhythm 124
Day Train	Blasters	1964	Times Square 31
Day We Fell In Love, The	Ovations (New Jersey)	1961	Barry 101
Day Will Come	Chippendales	1960	Rust 5023
Day You Are Mine, The	Pretenders	1962	Bethlehem 3050
Day You Left Me, The	Statics	1958	Event 4279
Day You Said Goodbye, The	Dootones	1962	Dooto 470
Daybreak	Christopher, Rod & group	1962	Tru-Lite 111
Daydream	Delltones, Dino & the	1965	Cobra 1117
Daydreamer	Juniors, Danny & the	1961	Swan 4068
Daydreamin' Of You	Dreamers (Fairmount)	1963	Fairmount 612
Daydreamin' Of You	Fashionettes	1964	GNP Crescendo 322
Daydreamin' Of You	Swans (Parkway)	1963	Parkway 881
Daylight In Dixie	Cool-Tones	1962	Radiant 1510
Daylight Saving Time	Mondellos	1957	Rhythm 106
Day-O (Banana Boat Song)	Salutations, Vito & the	1964	Wells 1010
Days	Moonrays, Ray Frazier & the	1956	Excel 111
Days Go By	Rubies, Jewell & the	1963	La Louisianne 8055
Days Of Wine And Roses, The	Jive Bombers	1964	Middle-Tone 020
De Obeah Man	Versatones	1957	RCA 6917
De Plu De Pinto De Blue	Terrifics	1958	Bell 88
Deacon Brown	Holidays	1963	Galaxy 714
Deacon Dan Tucker	Belvin, Jesse & group	1958	Knight 2012
Deacon Jones	Orioles, Sonny Til & the	1949	Jubilee 5005
Deacon Moves In, The	Dominoes	1951	Federal 12016
Dead	Poets	1958	Pull 129/Flash 129 (58)
Dead Broke	Du Droppers	1954	Groove 0001
Dead Man's Stroll	Revels	1959	Norgolde 103 (first pressing)
Dead Pigeon	Performers, Bobby Sanders & the	1963	Sound-O-Rama 117
Dead Wrong	Five Stars (Detroit)	1957	Mark-X 7006
Dealer Of Dreams	Penguins	1956	Wing 90076
Dear	Philadelphians	1961	Chesapeake/Campus 101 (61)
Dear Abby	Con-Dons	1962	Carlton 587
Dear Abby	DeNoia, Paul & group	1962	Kenco 5020
Dear Abby	Hearts (Bronx, N.Y.)	1963	Tuff 370
Dear Angels Above	Morris, Jimmy	1955	Baton 214
Dear Ann	Medallions, Vernon Green & the	1962	Pan World 71/10000
Dear Baby	Tanno, Marc & group	1961	Whale 501
Dear Cindy	Valiants (Los Angeles)	1959	Shar-Dee 703
Dear Darling	Medallions	1955	Dootone 379
Dear Diary	Blendtones	1963	Success 101
Dear Diary	Chantones	1959	TNT 167
Dear Diary	Smooth Tones	1956	Ember 1001
Dear Don	Metronomes (Harold Sonny Wright)	1957	Cadence 1339
Dear Donnie	Calendars, Roberta Watson & the	1963	Corsican 111
Dear 53310769 (Elvis' U.S. Army Serial #)	Threeteens	1959	Rev 3516

SONG	GROUP	YEAR	LABEL
Dear Heart	Belvin, Jesse & group	1956	Hollywood 1059
Dear Heart	Spaniels	1956	Vee Jay 189
Dear (Here Comes My Baby)	Blue Jeans, Bob B. Soxx & the	1963	Philles LP 4002
Dear (Here Comes My Baby)	Jones, Toni & group	1963	Smash 1814
Dear I	Dreamers (Tri-Dec)	NA	Tri-Dec 8757
Dear I Swear	Plants	1957	J&S 1602
Dear Joan	Palisades	1960	Leader 806
Dear Joan	Spiedels	1958	Crosley 201
Dear Joanne	Bruno, Bruce & group	1962	Roulette 4427
Dear John	Chancellors	1966	Fenton 2072
Dear Judy	Four Winds	1978	Crystal Ball 102
Dear Lady	Admirations	NA	Atomic 12871
Dear Little Boy	Sparkletones	1963	Pageant 604
Dear Little One	Jivers	1956	Aladdin 3347
Dear Lord	Channels, Earl Lewis & the	1978	King Tut 174
Dear Lord	Continentals (Brooklyn)	1956	Whirlin' Disc 101/Port 70018 (59)
Dear Lord	Fascinators (Brooklyn)	NA	Capitol LP 1008/Relic LP
Dear Lord (acappella)	Universals (Philadelphia)	1973	Relic LP 5006
Dear Lori	Shades	1959	Aladdin 3453/Imperial 5358 (59)
Dear Lorraine	Federals	1957	Fury 1009
Dear Mary	Spiders	1956	Imperial 5393
Dear Mom And Dad	Kids	NA	Hurd 80
Dear Mom And Dad	Tilman, Mickey & group	1958	Vee Jay 296
Dear Mother	Hurricanes	1956	King 4947
Dear Mother	Morning Echoes	1951	Premium 877
Dear Mr. Clock	Chantiers	1964	DJB 112
Dear Mr. Jock	Mello-Kings	1960	Herald 548
Dear Mr. President	Tides	1961	Dore 611
Dear One	Corridors	1963	Zone 4323/Wildcat 0057 (63)
Dear One	Emanons (Brooklyn)	1958	Winley 226/ABC 9913 (58)
Dear One	Feathers	1955	Hollywood 1051
Dear One	Individuals	1959	Show Time 598/Red Fox 105
Dear One	Monograms	1975	Monogram 106
Dear One	Mr. Lee (with the Cherokees)	NA	Terry 220
Dear One	Ravens	1957	Argo 5276/Checker 871
Dear One	Scarlets	1954	Red Robin 128/Event 4287 (55)
Dear One	Shells	1965	Genie 100/101
Dear One	Storm, Billy (with the Storms)	1961	Atlantic 2098
Dear Parents	Robbins, Eddie & group	1958	Power 214/Dot 15702 (58)
Dear Ruth	Buccaneers	1953	Southern 101/Rainbow 211 (53)
Dear Ruth	Raytones, Rudy Rae Moore & the	1957	Ball 0500
Dear Ruth	Universals (Philadelphia)	1960	Southern 102
Dear Ruth	Universals, Sis Watkins & the	1963	Ascot 2124
Dear Someone	Galaxies	1961	Richie 458
Dear Someone	Rockafellers	1963	Southern Sound 112
Dearest	Swallows (Maryland)	1951	King 4458
Dearest	Tempo-Mentals	1957	Ebb 112
Dearest Baby	Zodiacs, Maurice Williams & the	19??	
Dearest, Beloved Darling	Leaders	1956	Glory 239
Dearest Darling	Castroes	1959	Grand 2002
Dearest Darling	Chimes (Royal Roost)	1954	Royal Roost 577
Dearest Darling	Five Chimes	1954	Royal Roost 577/Betta 2017 (55)
Dearest Darling	Fraternity Brothers	1960	Verve 10195
Dearest Darling	Jiving Juniors	1961	Blue Beat 4
Dearest Darling	Jokers, Johnny Williams & the	1961	Pic 1 105
Dearest Darling	Rosebuds	1957	Gee 1033
Dearest Darling (You're The One)	Smith, Huey & group	1959	Ace 571
Dearest Doryce	Rhythm Cadets	1957	Vesta 501/502
Dearest Dream	Lee, Mabel & group	1956	Hull 712
Dearest Little Angel	Angels (Joel Katz)	1964	N/A
Dearest Little Angel	Autumns	1962, 1979	Medieval 208
Dearest Little Angel	Bowman, Jane & group	1961	Sapien 1002
Dearest One	C-Quents	1968	Essica 004
Dearest One	Fashions	1961	Warwick 646
Dearest One	Mellomen, Scatman Crothers & the	1955	Century 710

SONG	GROUP	YEAR	LABEL
Dearest One	Montereys, Dean Barlow & the	1957	Onyx 513/Relic 511 (64)
Dearest To Me	White, Charlie Group	1958	Winley 229
Dearly Beloved	Carroll Brothers	1958	Cameo 145
Death Of An Angel	Hi-Lites (King)	1963	King 5730
Death Of An Angel	Viceroys	1964	Imperial 66058
Death Of An Angel (My Baby's Gone)	Vel-Aires, Donald Woods & the	1955	Flip 306/Happy Tiger Era 5065
Debbie	Lonely Ones	1960	Rendezvous 125
Debbie	Rainbows, Randy & the	1982	Ambient Sound 02872
Debbie Jean	Cavaliers, Jerry Cox & the	1959	Frantic 751
Deborah Ann	Reflections	1965	Golden World 22
Debra-Lee	Crystal Tones	1959	MZ 007/008/Zebra
Decatur Street	Blue Belles, Patti LaBelle & the	1962, 1963	Newtown 5019/Nicetown 5020/ Parkway 896 (63)
Deceived	Three Pals, Johnny Cardell & the	1957	Rama 227
Deceivin' Blues	Robins, Little Esther & the	1950	Savoy 759
Decided By The Angels	Dawson, Ronnie & group	1960	Swan 4054
Decision, The	Enchanters (Sharp)	1960	Sharp 105
Decision, The	Mr. Lee (with the Cherokees)	1960	Winter 501
Declaration Of Love	Envoys	1977	Crystal Ball 110
Dedicated To Love	Kartunes	1958	MGM 12680
Dedicated To The One I Love	Down Beats	1965	Down Beat 1029
Dedicated To The One I Love	Exquisites	1985	Avenue D 12
Dedicated To The One I Love	Five Royales	1957, 1961, 1963	King 5098/5453/5756
Dedicated To The One I Love	Shirelles	1959	Scepter 1203
Dedicated (To The Songs I Love)	Three Friends	1961	Imperial 5763
Dedicated To You	Four Of A Kind	1956	Melba 110
Dedicated To You	Mason, Barbara (with the Larks)	1964	Crusader 114/Arctic (65)
Dee Dee Brown	Strollers	1960	Cub 9060
Dee Dee Di Oh	Innocents	1959	Andex 22012/Indigo 141 (62)
Dee Dee Dum	Caruso, Dick & group	1960	MGM 12852
Dee I	Rocketones	1957	Melba 113
Dee Jay's Dilemma	Incognitos	1961	Zee 001
Deed I Do	Cleftones	1961	Gee 1067
Deed I Do	Swallows (Maryland)	1952	King (unreleased)
'Deed I Do	Gems (Illinois)	1954	Drexel 901
Dee-Dee-Di-Oh	Echoes	1959	Andex 22102
Dee-Do Dee-Do	Goofers	1955	Coral 61480
Deeds To My Heart	Charmettes	1960	Mona 553
Deep Blue Sea	Midnighters, Hank Ballard & the	1961	King 5459
Deep Blue Sea, The	Goodies	1959	Chess 1731
Deep Down In My Heart	Sentimentals	1960	Coral 62172
Deep Down Inside	Rivileers	19??	
Deep Freeze	Adorables	1964	Golden World 4
Deep Freeze	Blue Chips	1962	Sparta 001
Deep Freeze	Five Ivories (Ivories)	1962	Sparta 001/Darla (no number)
Deep Freeze	Roamers	1954	Savoy 1147
Deep In A Young Boy's Heart	Carroll, Cathy (with the Earls)	1961	Triodex 11
Deep In Love	Darwin, Ricky & group	1959	Buzz 103
Deep In My Heart	Belvin, Jesse & group	1959	Class 267
Deep In My Heart	Fi-Tones	1959	Angle Tone 536
Deep In My Heart	Five Bars	1963	Bullet 1010
Deep In My Heart	Five Keys	1954	Aladdin 3245
Deep In My Heart	Muskateers	1953	Swingtime 331
Deep In My Heart	Shells	1962, 1963	Johnson 119/Josie 912
Deep In My Heart	Smith, Kenny & group	1964	Fraternity 934
Deep In My Heart	Sparrows Quartette	1969	Jet 3000
Deep In My Heart For You	Pyramids (California)	1955	Federal 12233
Deep In The Heart Of A Woman	Harlems, Little D & the	1963	Josie 914
Deep In The Heart Of The Ghetto Pt. 1	Cadillacs	1972	Polydor 14031
Deep In The Heart Of The Jungle	Casanovas	1962	Planet 1027
Deep Purple	Dominoes	1957, !959	Liberty 55099
Deep Purple	Ravens	1949	King 4293
Deep Sea Ball	Drifters	1960	Atlantic 2060
Deep Sea Ball	McPhatter, Clyde (with the Cookies & the Cues)	1960	Atlantic 2060

SONG	GROUP	YEAR	LABEL
Deep Sea Blues	Dominoes	1952	Federal 12068
Deep, So Deep	Medallions, Vernon Green & the	1962	Pan World 10000
Deep Water	Rivingtons	1962	Liberty 55427/Wand 11253 (63)
Deep Within	Whipoorwills	1961	Josie 892
Deep Within My Heart	Monterays (Dominion)	1964	Dominion 1019/Ultima 704
Deeper	Rubies	1964	Vee Jay 596
Deeply	Shepherd Sisters	1961	United Artists 350
Deeply In Love With You	New Invictas	1962	Hale 500
Defense Rests, The	Chev-Rons	1962	Gait 100
Defense Rests, The	Ward, Lee (with the Cymbals)	1961	Gait 407
Definition Of Love	Empires	1961	Calico 121
Delicious	Duprees	1975	RCA 10407
Delicious Are Your Kisses	Byrd, Bobby & group	1955	Sage & Sand 203
Delores	Bachelors, Dean Barlow & the	1955	Earl 101
Delores	Boulevards	1959	Everest 19316
Delores	Fascinations	1990	Magic Carpet EP 509
Delores	Fi-Tones	1973	Relic LP 5010
Delores	Four Buddies	1956	Club 51 105
Delores	Thorne, Roscoe (with the Caverliers)	1953	Atlas 1033
Delsinia	Dynamics	1963	Dynamic 1002/Reprise 20183 (63)
Delta Drag	River Rovers, Lydia Larsen & the	1951	Apollo 432
Dem Days (Are Gone Forever)	Orioles, Sonny Til & the	1953	Jubilee 5115
Denise	Newports	1979	Crystal Ball 134
Denise	Rainbows, Randy & the	1963	Rust 5059
Denise	Surprise	NA	Kape 102
Departed	Maria & group	1980	BAB 125
Depending On You	Sallycats, Sally & the	1959	Rendezvous 105
Deposit Your Love In The Bank Of My Heart	Ivy Leaguers	1957	Flip 325
Depot	Blackwells	1959	Jamie 1141
Deserie	Charts	1957	Everlast 5001/Everlast 5026 (63)/ Lost Nite 173 (81)
Deserie	Dovells	1962	Parkway LP 7006
Desert Boots	Vi-Kings	1960	Del-Mann 545
Desert Sands	Blanders	1965	Smash 2005
Desert Tramp	Nomads	1961	Rust 5028
Desert Winds	Feathers, June Moy & the	1955	Show Time 1103
Deserted	Vistones	1959	(Originally recorded on acetate)
Desifinado	Drifters (1959-forward)	1965	Atlantic LP 8113
Desire	Big Edsel Band	1978	Clifton 27
Desire	Essentials, Johnny Lloyd & the	1965	Reading 16000
Desire	Infatuators, Larry Lee & the	1961	Destiny 503
Desire	Trophies	1961	Challenge 9133
Desiree	Charts	1966	Wand 1112
Desirie	Blue Angels	1961	Edsel 781
Desirie	Good Guys, Doug Robertson & the	1964	Jerden 703/Uptown 703 (64)
Desperado	Mello-Chords	1961	Lyco 1001
Desperately	Holidays	1957	Melba 112
Destination Twenty-One Hundred And Sixty-Five	Cues	1956	Capitol 3400
Destiny	Embraceables	1962	Dover 4101
Destiny	Tamblyn, Larry & group	1960, 1965	Faro 612
Destruction	Catalinas	1959	Fortune 535
Detour	Ervin, Frankie & group	1962	Indigo 138
Detroit, Michigan	Love, Ronnie & group	1965	D-Town 1047
Deutsche Rock And Roll	Cupcakes	1959	Time 1011
Devel With The Rest	Five Royales	1954	King 4744
Devil And The Stocker	Velvet Sounds	NA	Cosmopolitan 100/101
Devil Blues	Chromatics	1956	Crest 1011
Devil Darling	Olenn, Johnny (with the Blockbusters)	1959	Personality 1002
Devil Eyes	Collegians, Jackie Roy & the	1953	Okeh 6987
Devil In His Eyes	Adorables	1965	Golden World 25
Devil In His Heart, The	Donays	1962	Brent 7033
Devil In Velvet	Harptones	1961	Cub 9097
Devil Or Angel	Clovers	1956	Atlantic 1083

SONG	GROUP	YEAR	LABEL
Devil Or Angel	Hollywood Flames	1960	Atco 6171
Devil Or Angel	Meadowlarks, Don Julian & the	1994	Unreleased
Devil That I See	Penguins	1955	Mercury 70703
Devil Train	Ramblers (Addit)	1960	Addit 1257
Devil You May Be	Dovers	1961	New Horizon 501
Devil's Angel	Colonairs	1957	Ember (unreleased)
Devil's Cousin, The	Jayhawks	1956	Flash 105
Devil's Train, The	Chuck-A-Lucks	1958	Lin 5010
Devoted To You	Blue Notes	19??	
Devoted To You	Butler, Cliff & group	1958	Nasco 6010
Dew Drop Inn	Maye, Jean & group	1964	Diamond 170
Di Di	Spades, Dell Rays & the	1958	Dice 479
Diamond Pins And Broken Beads	Amorettes, Armond Adams & the	1964	Fortune 572
Diamonds	Hollywood Saxons, Stan Beverly & the	1958, 1963	Entra 711/1214
Diamonds & Pearls	Trojans	1966	Air Town 003/Air Town 70971
Diamonds And Pearls	Destinaires	1965	Old Timer 613
Diamonds And Pearls	El Reyes	1965	Ideal 94706
Diamonds And Pearls	Escos	1960	Federal 12380
Diamonds And Pearls	Laddins	1974	Relic LP 5018
Diamonds And Pearls	Paradons	1960	Milestone 2003
Diamonds And Pearls	Turbans (Philadelphia)	1960	Roulette 4281
Diamonds And Pearls (acappella)	Young Ones	1963	Yussels 7704
Dianne	Palms	1956	States (unreleased)
Dianne	Turks	NA	P.B.D. 112
Diary Of Our Love	Premeers	1962	Herald 577
Diary, The	Imperials, Little Anthony & the	1958	End 1038
Dick Tracy	Chants	1961	Verve 10244
Dickie	Quin-Teens	1963	Pike 5922
Dickie Went And Did It	Delicates	1961	Roulette 4360
Did Anybody Lose A Tear	Bentleys	1965	Smash 1988
Did Anybody Lose A Tear?	Vampires	1964	Carroll 104
Did He Know	Sharpettes, King & the	1964	Aldo 503
Did I Cry	Hi-Fi-Dels	1961	Atlantic 2121
Did I Do Wrong	Cuff Links	NA	
Did I Hear You Right	Channels, Edie & the	1963	Ember 584/Herald 584 (63)
Did I Make A Mistake	Revlons	1962	Toy 101
Did I Remember	Crests	1963	Selma 4000
Did I Remember	Mello-Larks, Vince Massey & the	1953	Herald 414
Did It	Laddins	1957	Central 2602/Times Square 3 (61)
Did She Leave You	Lyrics (San Francisco)	1958	Marvels 1005
Did She Leave You	Marvells	1959	Magnet 1005
Did We Go Steady Too Soon	Madison Brothers, Farris Hill & the	1962	V-Tone 231
Did You Ever	Classmates	1962	Stacy 935
Did You Ever Dream Lucky	Long, Bobby & his Cherrios	1959	Unart 2023
Did You Ever Go Steady?	Chiffons	1965, 1966	Laurie 3340
Did You Ever Love A Guy	Emeralds (Jubilee)	1964	Jubilee 5489
Did You Ever See A Monkey	Flames, Tommy Mary Jo Braden & his	1955	United 177
Did You Have Fun?	Medallions, Vernon Green & the	1956	Dootone 407
Did You Make Up Your Mind	Twilighters, Tony & the	1960	Jalynne 106/Red Top
Diddle-De-Dum	Belmonts	1962	Sabina 507
Diddle-Le-Bom	Lovelarks	1961	Masons 3-070/Fellatio 301
Diddy Bop	Valaquons	1964	Rayco 516
Diddy-Wah-Diddy	Divots	1961	Savoy 1596
Didn't I Say	Orioles, Sonny Til & the	1957	Abner 1016/Vee Jay 244 (57)
Didn't It	Drifters (1959-forward)	1964	Atlantic 2225
Didn't It Rain	Tormentors	1962	Kerwood 712
Didn't Mean To Fall In Love	Statens	1978	Crystal Ball 127
Didn't Want Your Love No More	Vacels, Ricky & the	1963	Fargo 1050
Didn't We Fool Them?	Poor Boys, King Richard & the	1961	Apollo 1201
Didn't We Have A Good Time	Mystics	1965	Dot 16862
Didn't We Have A Nice Time	Hi-Tones, Charles Andrea & the	1961	Tori Ltd. T-2X
Didn't You Get The Letter	Moon Mists	NA	Modern 201
Didn't You Know	Lifesavers, Lucien Farrar & the	1957	Jupiter 1
Difference In Our Ages, The	Hitmakers, Linda Lou & the	1965	Lama 7786
Diggin' The Moonglow	Mayfield, Percy & group	1957	Specialty 607

SONG	GROUP	YEAR	LABEL
Dilly Up, The	Hep Cats	1961	Del-Fi 4159
Dillyn Bop	Gordon, Roscoe & group	1960	Duke 320
Dim Those Lights	Raindrops	1958	Vega 105
Dimples	Del Rays	NA	R&H 1005
Dimples	Fabulous Silver Tones	NA	West Coast 452
D-In Love	Lee, Curtis (with the Halos)	1960	Dunes 2001
Dina	Chevelles, Marvin Nash & the	1963	Courier 111
Dina	Nash, Marvin & group (with the Chevelles)	1961	Pharoah 115
Ding A Ling	Crescendos (Robin Hood)	1976	Robin Hood 144
Ding A Ling	Dreamers, A.L. Maye & the (Crescendos)	1973	
Ding A Ling Coo Coo Mop	Schoolboys	1990	Magic Carpet EP 511
Ding Dang Doo	Johnson, Bubber (with the Wheels)	1955	King 4793
Ding Ding Dong	Jivetones	1958	Rhythm 5000
Ding Dong	Champlains (Fred Parris)	1961	United Artists 346
Ding Dong	Ding Dongs	1960	Eldo 109
Ding Dong	Echoes	1957	Gee 1028
Ding Dong	Four Chickadees	1956	Checker 849
Ding Dong	Hi Liters, Buddy Roberts & the	1960	Bonanza 689/690
Ding Dong	Hometowners	1959	Fraternity 842
Ding Dong	Monarchs, Chuck Mills & the	1959	Band Box 227
Ding Dong	Orlando, Tony & group	1959	Milo 101
Ding Dong	Packards	1956	Paradise 105
Ding Dong	Quin-Tones (Pennsylvania)	1958	Chess 1685
Ding Dong	Rip Chords	1962	Columbia 42641
Ding Dong Bells	Pretenders	1962	Bethlehem 3050
Ding Dong Daddy	Carter Rays	1957	Lyric 2001/Gone 5006 (57)
Ding Dong Darling	Fabulous Dudes	1994	Presence 4503
Ding Dong Doo	Frontiers	1961	King 5481
Ding Dong Honeymoon	Cheerios	1961	Infinity 11/Golden Oldies 1 (61)
Ding Dong, School Is Out	Hollywood Playboys	1960	Sure 105
Ding Dong Teenage Bells	Crystalaires	1990	Crystal Ball 159
Dinga-Ling	Counts, Tommy Burk & the	1964	Rich Rose 1001
Ding-A-Ling-A-Ling	Troys	1959	Okeh 7120
Ding-A-Ling-A-Ling Ding Dong	Bing Bongs, Dicky Dell & the	1958	Dragon 10205
Dingbats	Goldenaires	1960	Ron 332
Dingle Dangle Doll	Bennet, Ron & group	1961	Ta-Rah 1
Dingle Dangle Doll	Jays, Mike & the	1960	Doyl 1001
Dinosaur	Allie Oop's Group (Gerry Granahan)	1960	Caprice 102
Dip Dip	Beau Jives	1961	Vision 111/Lord Bingo 111
Dip, The	Vitells	1962	Decca 31362
Dirty Bird	Flips	1956	Chess (unreleased)
Dirty Tricks	Carousels	1962	Gone 5131
Disappointed	Spinners, Claudine Clark & the	1962	Chancellor 1113
Disappointed Bride	Hearts (Bronx, N.Y.)	1956	Baton 222
Disc Jockey Fever	Chuck-A-Lucks	1958	Lin 5014
Disciples	Disciples	1964	Fortune 573
Disco Hully Gully	Romans, Little Caesar & the	1977	Essar 7803
Disco Mama, Disco Man	Elements Of Life	1981	Starlight 14
Discover A Lover	Jaguars	1964	Faro 618
Disillusioned	Tams	1962	Arlen 711
Disillusioned Love	Newports	1964	Guyden 2116
Ditta-Wa-Do	Vestelles	1958	Decca 30733
Ditty Bop Walk	James, Artamer & group	1958	Code 711
Divided Heart	Majestics (Detroit)	1958	NRC 502
Dividend Blues	Hollywood Four Flames	1951	Unique 003
Dixie Blues, The	Cool-Tones	1962	Radiant 1510
Dixie Cup	Royaltones, Ruth McFadden & the	1960	Goldisc 3016
Dixie Rock	Royaltones, Ruth McFadden & the	1960	Goldisc 3017
Dixie Women	Newports	1961	Kent 380
Dizzy Jones Birdland	Laddins	1963	Butane 779
Dizzy Over You	Georgettes	1959	Jackpot 48001
Dizzy Spell	Loungers	1958	Herald 534
Do Anything	Five Keys	1957	Capitol 3830
Do Baby Do (first pressing)	Mellotones	1957	Herald 502 (first pressing, second is by Mello-Kings)

SONG	GROUP	YEAR	LABEL
Do Baby Do (second pressing)	Mello-Kings	1957	Herald 502 (second pressing, first is by Mellotones)
Do Be Do Be Do	Rays, Bob Crewe & the	1957	Vik 0307
Do Be True	Echoes, Jerry Starr & the	1959	Ron 321
Do Be You	Charms, Otis Williams & his	1956	DeLuxe 6092
Do Dee Do Dee Do Wah	Doo Rays, Davey & the	1958	Guyden 2002
Do Do Baby	Four Towns	NA	A1 1001
Do I	Halos	1965	Congress 244
Do I	Zodiacs, Maurice Williams & the	1961	Herald 559
Do I Do I	Berry, Richard (with the Dreamers)	1958	Flip 339
Do I Do I	Pharaohs, Richard Berry & the	1958	Flip 339
Do I Have A Chance	Note Makers	1958	Sotoplay 007
Do I Have A Chance	Webs	1958	Sotoplay 006
Do I Have The Right	Ideals	1958	Cool 108
Do I Have To Tell You I'm Sorry	Rockets, Herb Kenny & the	1953	MGM 11648
Do I Love You	Echoes	1960	Columbia 41549
Do I Love You	Quails, Bill Robinson & the	1968	Date 1620
Do I Need You	Five Keys	1971 (1951)	Aladdin 3113A (unreleased)
Do I Upset You?	Cashmeres (Philadelphia)	1956	Herald 474
Do It	Four Hits & A Miss	1962	Flamingo 540
Do It	Premieres & the Invictas	1959	F-M 677
Do It Again	Dominoes	1957	Liberty 55099
Do It If You Wanna	Flares	1961	Press 2810
Do It Now	Ballards	NA	Veltone 1738
Do It Right The First Time	Hollywood Saxons	Mid to late 1950s	(Early 1980s on EP; originally unreleased)
Do It With Me	Flares	1961	Press 2807
Do Let That Dream Come True	Jumpin' Jacks	1953	Lloyds 101
Do Lord	Chief-Tones	NA	Cuca 1287
Do Me A Favor	Watts, Bette & male group	1960	Wand 104
Do Not Forget	Dreamers, Richard Berry & the	1956	Flip 319/Flip 354 (61)
Do Not Forsake Me	Young Hearts	1961	Infinity 006
Do Not Pretend	Penguins	1958	Dooto 435
Do Something For Me	Avalons	1988	Relic LP 5075
Do Something For Me	Dominoes	1950	Federal 12001
Do Something For Me	Five Keys	1961	King 5496
Do That Little Thing	Counts, Bobby Comstock & the	1960	Jubilee 5392
Do The Beatle	Upfronts	1964	Lummtone 114
Do The Bop	Crowns, Arthur Lee Maye & the	1955	RPM 438
Do The Bug	Shallows	1962	Forlin 503
Do The Cha Cha Cherry	Five Royales	1958	King 5131
Do The Crank	Belgianetts	1963	USA 731
Do The Dipper	Spaceriders, Mai Casselle & the	NA	Half Peach 500
Do The Do	Flames, Tommy Mary Jo Braden & his	1955	United 177
Do The Dog	Spices, Sugar & the	1963	Stacy 968
Do The Early Bird	Royaltones, Ruth McFadden & the	1961	Goldisc 3028
Do The Funky Foot	New Hollywood Argyles	1966	Kammy 105
Do The Groove	Ineligibles	1960	Capella 501
Do The Hully Gully	Hamber, Kenny & group	1963	Spar 101
Do The Jerk	Original Drifters, Bill Pinkney & the	1964	Fontana 1956
Do The Kangaroo	McHugh, Jimmy & group	1963	Success 106
Do The Madison	Bachelors (Epic)	1960	Epic 9369
(Do The) Mashed Potato	Juniors, Danny & the	1962	Swan 4100
Do The Montoona	Royal Teens	1965	TCF 117
Do The New Continental	Dovells	1962	Parkway 833
Do The Slauson Shuffle	Olympics	1963	Tri Disc 107
Do The Walk	Vels	1963	Amy 881
Do The Whip	Superiors, Tony LaMar & the	1965	Go Go 1000
Do The Wiggle	Mascots	1960	King 5377
Do The Zombie	Tigers, Al Tigro & the	NA	Cuppy 112
Do This Do That	Little Nat (with the Shells)	1961	Pik 242
Do This For Me	Emotions	1965	Vardan 201
Do This For Me	Lovers	1966	Gate 501/Philips 40353 (66)
Do Unto Others	Four Guys	1956	Mercury 70908
Do Unto You	Five Royales	1955	King 4819

SONG	GROUP	YEAR	LABEL
Do Wah	Spaniels	1955	Vee Jay 131
Do What Lovers Do	Channels, Earl Lewis & the	1990	Classic Artists 124
Do What You Did	Delusions, W. Kelley & the	1975	Kelway 115
Do What You Did	Harris, Thurston (with the Sharps)	1957	Aladdin 3399
Do What You Did	Hawks, Little Tony & the	1966	Original Sound 63
Do What You Did	Lullabyes	1961	Embassy 204
Do What You Wanna	Criterions, Tygh & the	1963	Flite 101
Do What You Want	Statens	1978	Crystal Ball 115
Do What You Want To	Superlatives	NA	Dynamics 1011
Do What You Want To Do	Cincinnatians	NA	Roosevelt Lee 16115/Emerald 16116
Do What You're Gonna Do	Syndicates	1965	Mello 552
Do Whop-A-Do	Five Daps	1958	Brax 207/208
Do Wop	De Villes	1958	Aladdin 3423
Do Ya Do?	Kool Gents	1956	Vee Jay 173
Do You	Bye Byes	1959	Mercury 71530
Do You	Cleftones	1961	Gee 1077
Do You	Continentals, Teddy & the	1961	Richie 445
Do You Believe	Twilighters (Bronx, N.Y.)	1961	Eldo 115
Do You Believe	Zodiacs, Maurice Williams & the	NA	Sphere Sound LP 7007
Do You Believe Me	Gallahads	1955	Capitol 3175
Do You Cry	Romancers	1965	Linda 120
Do You Ever Think Of Me	Hollywood Flames	1960	Atco 6171
Do You Ever Think Of Me	Pastels (Pastel)	1964	Pastel 506
Do You Have The Right	Scotchtones	1960	Rustone 1402
Do You Hear Wedding Bells	Jive Five	1962	Beltone 2029/Relic 1029 (77)
Do You Know	Bonnie Sisters	1956	Rainbow 336
Do You Know	Lakettes	1960	Thunderbird 102
Do You Know	Slades, Joyce Harris & the	1961	Domino 903
Do You Know How To Twist	Midnighters, Hank Ballard & the	1962	King 5593
Do You Know?	Chiffons	1960	Big Deal 6003/Zircon 1012
Do You Love Her	Impressors	1958	Cub 9010
Do You Love Me	Cyclones	1957	Flip 324
Do You Love Me	Emotions	1962, 1981	Card 600/Jason Scott 12
Do You Love Me	Idols, Little Joe Bonner & the	1955	B&S 1570
Do You Love Me	Juniors, Danny & the	1959	ABC 10004
Do You Love Me	King, Sonny & group	NA	Marida 101
Do You Love Me	Nobles (Chicago)	1958	Sapphire 1051
Do You Love Me	Stereos	1962	Cub 9106
Do You Love Me	Vann, Teddy & group	1960	Roulette 4300
Do You Love Me?	Edsels	1959	Roulette 4151
Do You Love Me?	Four Winds, Sonny Woods & the	1956	Middle-Tone 008
Do You Love Me?	Willows	1956	Melba 106
Do You Mean It	Four Winds, Sonny Woods & the	1956	Middle-Tone 013
Do You Mind	Chicks, Kell Osborne & the	1962	Class 302
Do You Mind?	Magnificents	1962	Kansoma 03/Checker 1016 (62)
Do You Miss Me	Allen, Mimi & group	1961	Three Speed 711
Do You Miss Me	Everglades	1963	BPV 112577
Do You Promise	Honkers	1959	Okeh 7124
Do You Promise	Ricks, Jimmy & group	1957	Paris 504
Do You Really Wanna Dance	Parlay Brothers	1965	Valjay 2725
Do You Really?	Spaniels	1956	Vee Jay 178
Do You Recall	Casinos	1963	Itzy 404/Olimpic 251 (65)
Do You Remember	Castelles	1954	Grand 105
Do You Remember	Chanters (California)	1988	Relic LP 5076
Do You Remember	Dell Vikings	1991	BVM
Do You Remember	Domains, Jerry Wright & the	1960	Lanjo 2394
Do You Remember	Five Crowns	1956	Gee 1001
Do You Remember	Five Satins	1962	Chancellor 1121
Do You Remember	Hearts (Bronx, N.Y.)	1963	Zells 3378
Do You Remember	Royaltones	NA	Old Town (unreleased)
Do You Remember	Sinceres	1960	Sigma 1003/1004
Do You Remember	Skarlettones	1959	Ember 1053
Do You Remember	Toreadors	NA	Midas 1001
Do You Remember	Uniques	1959	Flippin' 202
Do You Remember	Zodiacs, Maurice Williams & the	1960	Herald 552

SONG	GROUP	YEAR	LABEL
Do You Remember My Darling	Shuffles	1963	Rayco 508
Do You Remember What You Did?	Diablos (featuring Nolan Strong)	1955	Fortune 516
Do You Remember?	Creators	1961	Time 1038
Do You Remember?	Fabulous Flames	1961	Bay-Tone 102
Do You Remember?	Midnighters, Hank Ballard & the	1961	King 5578
Do You Wanna Dance	Classmen	1964	Limelight 3016
Do You Wanna Dance	Teen Tones	1965	T&T 2488
Do You Wanna Go	Miller Sisters	1956	Hull 718
Do You Wanna Jump	Creels	1959	Judd 1005
Do You Wanna Jump Children	Ospreys	1957	East West 110
Do You Wanna Ride	Hamilton Sisters	1954	Columbia 40319
Do You Wanna Rock (Hey Little Girl)	Cadets	1956	Modern 971
Do You Wanna Rock (Hey Little Girl)	Jacks	1957	RPM LP 3006/Crown LP 5372 (58)
Do You Wanna Work Now	Blue Notes, Joe Weaver & the	1955	Jaguar 3011
Do You Want My Love	Scott Brothers	1959	Skyline 501
Do You Want To Dance	Twisters, Joey & the	1962	Dual 509
Do You Want To Go Steady	Dahills	1976	Clifton 13/14
Do You Want To Rock?	Kings (Baltimore)	1954	Jax 323
Do You Want To See My Baby	Mello-Dees, Herman Griffin & the	1960	Anna 1115/Stepp 237
Do Your Best	Untouchables	1961	Madison 147
Do-Ba-Ba-Do	Escorts (Wells)	1959	Wells 102
Do-Be-Do	Gari, Frank & group	1961	Ritco 555
Do-Be-Do-Be-Wop-Wop	Squires (California)	1955	Mambo 105/Vita 105 (60)
Do-Bop-Slam-Boy	Spencer Sisters	1955	Aladdin 3285
Doctor Baby	Five Dollars	1955	Fortune 821/Fraternity 821 (58)
Doctor Of Hearts	Chiffons	1962	Reprise 20103
Doctor Velvet	Romeos	1954	Apollo 466
Dodge City	Olympics	1960	Arvee 5020
Dody Mighty	Gassers	1957	Encino 1011
Doe Doe	Drivers & the Spacemen	1959	Alton 252
Does He Mean That Much To You	Lee, Curtis (with the Halos)	1962	Dunes 2015
Does It Really Matter	Flamingos	1964	Checker 1091
Does My Heart Stand A Chance	Del Satins	1962	Laurie 3149
Does She Know	Aztecs, Jose & the	1955	Roadhouse LP
Does She Know	Magic-Tones	1974	Broadcast 1101
Does She Love Me	Huff, Chauncey & group	1964	Fantasy 587
Does Someone Care (For Me)	Continentals, Billy John & the	1962	N-Joy 1012
Does Your Mama Know About Me	Professionals, Tommy Vann & the	1969	Congress 6001
Doesn't Make Sense To Me	Deep River Boys	1951	Beacon 9143
Dog Eat Dog	Barons (Soul)	1961	Soul 837
Dog Gone Baby	Five Keys	1957	Capitol (unreleased)
Dog Gone It	Hightower, Donna (with the Jacks)	1955	RPM 432
Dog Time	White, Ruth & group	1963	Candi 1029
Doggie In The Window	Idets	NA	Shiptown 007
Doggie In The Window	Kookie Beavers	1960	Gone 5086
Doggone It	Trophies	1961	Challenge 9133
Doggone It, You Did It	Five Keys	1955	Capitol 3032
Doggonit	Gassers	1957	Encino 1011
Doin' Everything	Five Royales	1963	Todd 1086
Doin' Everything	Midnighters (Henry Moore)	1961	King 5513
(Doin' The) Arthur	Four Directions	1965	Coral 68456
Doin' The Bird	Rivingtons	1963	Liberty LP 3282/Liberty LP 7282 (63)
Doin' The Cha Cha Cha	Meadowlarks, Don Julian & the	1958	Original Sound 03
Doin' The Cha Cha In Havana	Night-Riders	1961	Dore 613
Doin' The Continental Walk	Juniors, Danny & the	1962	Swan 4100
Doin' The Look	Mandells	1966	Jubilee 5519
Doin' The Ronde	Shirelles	1959	Scepter 1205
Doin' The Shimmy	Googles, Barney & the	1960	Shimmy 1055
Doin' The Stroll	Four Winds	NA	Explorer 713
Doin' The Stroll	Saints	1958	Prescott 1570
Doin' The Thing	Mondo, Joe & group	1963	EPI 1003
Doin' Things Together With You	Dreamlovers	1965	Warner Bros. 5619
Doing All Right	Cashiers, Eddie Cash & the	1958	Peak 1001
Doing The Cha Cha Cha	Twilighters	NA	
Doing The Hully Gully	Flares	1961	Press 2802

SONG	GROUP	YEAR	LABEL
Doing The Popeye	Robins	1962	Sweet Taffy 400/New Hit 3010
Doing The Rock And Roll	Spears, Calvin & group	1960	Vin 1020
Doing The Slop	Vibrations	1960	Checker 967
Doing The Watusi	Flares	NA	London (England) LP 8034
Doing The Wiggle Wobble	Ly-Dells	1963	Roulette 4493
Do-Ko-Icki-No	Starfires	1958	Bernice 201
Doll Baby	Hits, Tiny Tim & the	1958	Roulette 4123
Doll Baby	Paragons	1960	Winley 240
Doll Baby	Paragons, Tommy Collins & the	1959	Winley 236
Doll Face	Vibranaires	1954	After Hours 103/Chariot 103 (54)
Dollar Bill	Fiestas	1960	Old Town 1080
Dolly	Chandeliers	1958	Angle Tone 529
Dolly	Fabulous Falcons	1966	White Cliffs 249
Dolly In A Toy Shop	Saber, Johnny (with the Passions)	1960	Adonis 103
Dolores	Crescents	NA	Joyce (unreleased)
Dolores	Don Juans	1959	Onezy 101
Dolores	Five Willows	1953	Allen 1002
Dolores	Mood Makers	1961	Bambi 800
Dolores Darlin'	Berry Cups, Terry Clinton & the	1959	Khoury's 710
Dom-De-Dom	Good Guys	1964	San-Dee 1007
Don' Ever Leave Me	Superlatives	NA	Dynamics 1012
Don Juan	Montclairs	1957	Hi-Q 5001
Don Juan	Starr Brothers	1963	Cortland 104
Don Juan In Town	Versalettes	1963	Witch 120
Donald Duck	Kac-Ties	1963	Kape 702
Don'Cha Go	Spaniels	1955	Vee Jay 131
Done Being Lonely	Modern Red Caps, George Tindley & the	1962	Smash 1768
Done Got Over	Blasers	1956	United 191
Donkey Serenade	Orioles, Sonny Til & the	1949	Jubilee 5008
Donkey Step, The	Rebels	1961	Peacock 1909
Donkey Walk	Alamos	1957	Hi-Q 5030
Donna	Channels, Earl Lewis & the	1987	Soul Jam 712
Donna	Innocents	1961	Indigo 128
Donna	Rome, Billy & group	1961	Sultan 5501
Donna Alone	Dragons, St. George & the	NA	Dragon
Donna Lee	Demilles	1964	Laurie 3230
Donna Marie	Pages	1958	Eagle 1005/Don Tan 0001
Donna My Dear	Plurals	1958	Wanger 186/187/Bergen 186/187 (59)
Donna The Prima Donna	DiMucci, Dion (with the Del Satins)	1963	Columbia 42852
Donna The Primadonna	Hall, Ronnie & group	NA	
Donnie	Bermudas	1964	Era 3125
Donnie	Charmettes	1962	Markay 101
Donnie	Playgirls	1962	Galaxy 713
Don't	Cadets	1960, 1974	Jan-Lar 102
Don't	Spiders	1974	Owl 334
Don't Accuse Me	Squires (Gee)	1962	Gee 1082
Don't Act That Way	Tempos	1966	Riley's 5
Don't Ask Me	Dubs, Richard Blandon & the	1987	Starlight 51
Don't Ask Me	Fabulons (with the Tikis)	1966	Tower 259
Don't Ask Me	Lee, James Washington & group	1962	L&M 1003
Don't Ask Me	Shannons	1958	L&M 1003
Don't Ask Me (To Be Lonely)	Dubs	1957, 1964	Johnson 102/Gone 5002 (57)/ Musictone 1142 (61)/Lana 116
Don't Ask Me To Be Lonely	Exotics, Andy Rose & the	1961	Coral 62284
Don't Ask Me To Be Lonely	Five Trojans (Trojans)	1958	Tender 516
Don't Ask Me To Be Lonely	Rose, Andy (with the Thorns)	1961	Coral
Don't Ask Me Why	Bell Notes	1959	Time 1015
Don't Be A Baby, Baby	Ideals	1959	Decca 30800
Don't Be A Fool	Dell Vikings	1957, 1980	Fee Bee 214/Dot 15592 (57)/ Collectables 1252
Don't Be A Fool	Explorers	1960	Coral 62175/Coral 65575 (63)
Don't Be A Fool	Jades	1959	Christy 113
Don't Be A Fool	Regents	1961	Gee 1073
Don't Be A Fool For Love	Ambrose, Kenny & group	1958	Hamilton 50019
Don't Be A Jumpin' Jack	Chords	1958	Casino 451

SONG	GROUP	YEAR	LABEL
Don't Be A Litter Bug	Ly-Dells	NA	Clifton LP 2002
(Don't Be A) Litterbug	Len-Dells	1964	Reach 2
Don't Be Afraid	Starlites	1965	Sphere Sound 705
Don't Be Afraid To Love	Eldees	1963	Dynamics 1013
Don't Be Afraid To Love	Harvey (Harvey Fuqua with the Moonglows)	1959	Chess 1725
Don't Be Afraid To Love	Teardrops	1957	King 5037
Don't Be Angry	Cadets	1955	Modern 956
Don't Be Angry	Four Jacks	1956	Gateway 1121
Don't Be Angry	Sultans	1952	Jubilee 5077
Don't Be Ashamed	Five Royales	1957	King 5098
Don't Be Ashamed	Legends	1964	Warner Bros. 5457
Don't Be Bashful	Shadows	1953	Decca 48307
Don't Be Gone Long	Ragamuffins	1964	Tollie 9027
Don't Be Half Safe	Zodiacs, Maurice Williams & the	1966	Dee-Su 311
Don't Be Heartless	Chevrons	1959	Brent 7000
Don't Be Jealous	Isley Brothers	1958	Cindy 3009
Don't Be Long	Delltones	1955	Baton 212
Don't Be Mad	Cole, Freddy & group	1963	Titantic 100
Don't Be Mad At My Heart	Chords (Sh-Booms)	1957	RCA (unreleased)
Don't Be Mad With My Heart	Cadillacs	1959	Jubilee LP 1089
Don't Be Mean Be Mine	Ravens	NA	Mercury (unreleased)
Don't Be Mean, Geraldine	Marquees	1960	Warner Bros. 5139
Don't Be No Fool	Love Notes (Massachusetts)	1954	Riviera 975
Don't Be No Square	Royal Playboys	1961	Imperial 5782
Don't Be Scared	Rip Chords	1965	Columbia 43221
Don't Be Shy	Suedes	1959	Dart 117
Don't Be Unfair	Melody Masters & the Sportsmen, Wayne Hardy with the	1957	Renown 104
Don't Believe A Word	Tiaras	1963	Valiant 6030
Don't Believe Him	Lanham, Richard (with the Tempo-Tones)	1965	Josie 985
Don't Believe Him	School Belles	1962	Crest 1104
Don't Believe Him Donna	Jive Five	1982	Ambient Sound 03053
Don't Believe What They Say	Cap-Tans	1975	Gotham 261
Don't Blame Me	Metronomes (Harold Sonny Wright)	1960	Wynne LP 706
Don't Blame Me	Platters	NA	Mercury EP
Don't Blooper	Chapman, Grady (with the Suedes)	1955	Money 204
Don't Break My Heart	Dream Girls, Bobbie Smith & the	1959, 1960	Cameo 165/Big Top 3059
Don't Break The Heart That Loves You	Top Kicks	1954	Guyden 706
Don't Break-A My Heart	Scrubs, Dave Collins & the	1954	Imperial 5294
Don't Bug Me Baby	Raves	1956	Liberty 55013
Don't Call For Me	Embraceables	1962	Cy 1004
Don't Call For Me	Implaceables	1960	Kain 1004
Don't Call For Me	Williams, Johnny & group	1961	Cy 001
Don't Call Me	Original Drifters, Bill Pinkney & the	1964	Fontana 1956
Don't Call Me Baby, I'll Call You	Teen Tones	1959	Decca 30895
Don't Call Me Lonely Any More	Innocents	1964	Warner Bros. 5450
Don't Cha Go	Flairs, Richard Berry & the	1955	Flair 1068
Don't Cha Know	Lockets	1963	Argo 5455
Don't Change Your Pretty Ways	Midnighters	1955	Federal 12243
Don't Close The Door	Belvin, Jesse & group	1957	Modern 1015
Don't Come Back	Fabulous Twilights, Nathaniel Mayer & the	1963	Fortune 562
Don't Come Crying	Frontiers	1963	Philips 40113
Don't Come Too Late	Jeeters, Ron Willis & the	1960	Ace 588
Don't Count On Me	Salutations, Vito & the	1964	Wells 1010
Don't Cry	Ciufo, Jerry & group	1965	Jeree 65
Don't Cry	Crystaliers, Cleo & the	1957, 1976	Johnson 103/Cindy 3003 (57)
Don't Cry	Curtis, Eddie Tex & group	1956	Dot 15505
Don't Cry	Dreamers (Nugget)	1959	Nugget 1000
Don't Cry	Innocents	1963	Decca 31519
Don't Cry	Inspirations (Philadelphia)	1958	Lamp 2019
Don't Cry	Larks, Irma & the	NA	Priority 322
Don't Cry	Orioles, Sonny Til & the	1955	Jubilee (unreleased)
Don't Cry	Viscounts, Sammy Hagen & the	1957	Capitol 3818
Don't Cry Baby	Angelenos	1961	Peepers 2824
Don't Cry Baby	Belvin, Jesse & group	1951	Imperial 5115

SONG	GROUP	YEAR	LABEL
Don't Cry Baby	Impacs	1964	King 5910
Don't Cry Baby	Jayos, Mel Williams & the	1956	Dig 123
Don't Cry, Baby	Orioles, Sonny Til & the	1952	Jubilee 5092
Don't Cry, Baby	Paragons	1958	Winley 228/Times Square 9 (63)
Don't Cry Baby	Williams, Mel & group	1956	Dig 123
Don't Cry Darling	Stereos	1962	Robins Nest 1588
Don't Cry, Della	Five Roses	1959, 1975	Nu Kat 100/101/Clifton 11
Don't Cry For Me This Christmas	Marcels	1961	Colpix 617
Don't Cry Katy	Three G's	1959	Columbia 41513
Don't Cry Little Boy Sad	Butlers, Frankie Beverly & the	1967	Fairmount 1012
Don't Cry My Soldier Boy	Shondelles	1962	King 5597
Don't Cry No More	Offbeats with the Montclairs, Jimmy Dee & the	1957	TNT 148/Dot 15664 (57)
Don't Cry No More	Weekenders, Alan & the	1963	Mohawk 140
Don't Cry Pretty Baby	Demensions	1963	Coral 62392
Don't Cry (Sing Along With The Music)	Essentials, Billy & the	1966	Smash 2071
Don't Cry, Sing Along With The Music	Tokens (Brooklyn)	1966	B.T. Puppy 518
Don't Cry, Sure It Hurts	Informers	1960	Dore 562
Don't Cry (Tomorrow's Tears Tonight)	Rockaways	1964	Red Bird 10-005
Don't Darken My Door	Jamies	1959	United Artists 193
Don't Deceive Me	Derringers	1961	Capitol 4572
Don't Deceive Me	Spaceriders, Mai Casselle & the	NA	Half Peach 500
Don't Deny Me	Charms, Otis Williams & his	1957	DeLuxe 6138
Don't Deprive Me	Coronets	1955	Sterling 903
Don't Do It	Penguins	1955	Mercury 70610
Don't Do It Baby	Continentals (Davis)	1959	Davis 466
Don't Do It Baby	Vocaltones, Bobby Harris & the	1955	Wen-Dee 1933
Don't Do Me Wrong	Playboys	1957	Mercury 71228
Don't Do Nothing I Wouldn't Do	Wanderers	1975	Savoy 1098 (unreleased)
Don't Do That	Fentones, Shane Fenton & the	1963	Laurie 3287/20th Fox 439 (63)
Don't Do That!	Five Tinos	1955	Sun 222
Don't Do That, Baby	Blue Dots	1954	DeLuxe 6052
Don't Do That To Me	Reflections	1964	Golden World 16
Don't Do This To Me	Blake, Cicero & group	1963	Success 107
Don't Dog Me	McPhatter, Clyde (with the Drifters)	1960	Atlantic 2049
Don't Don't Don't (Drop Out)	Schoolmates, Ronnie & the	1964	Coed 605
Don't Drive Me Away	Impressions, Jerry Butler & the	1976	Vee Jay LP 1075
Don't Drop It	Blue Jays (Los Angeles)	1956	Dig EP 780
Don't Drop It	Singing Wanderers	1954	Decca 29230
Don't Even Know Your Name	Cobras (Philadelphia)	1964	Monogram 519
Don't Ever Get Married	Meloaires	1958	Unreleased
Don't Ever Leave Me	Paragons	NA	Winley LP 6003
Don't Ever Leave Me	Pyramiders	1958	Scott 1505
Don't Ever Leave Me	Rivileers	1955	Baton 209
Don't Ever Leave Me	Zodiacs, Maurice Williams & the	1966	Dee-Su 309
Don't Ever Let Me Go	Teenettes, Bobby Grabeau & the	1959	Crest 1064
Don't Expect A Miracle	Accents (California)	1955	Blue Mill 111
Don't Fall In Love	Sequins	1956	Red Robin 140
Don't Fall In Love	Solitaires	1955	Old Town 1014
Don't Fall In Love Too Soon	Preludes	1956	Empire 103
Don't Fall In Love Too Soon	Tonettes	1956	Modern 997
Don't Fall In Love With Me	Midnighters, Hank Ballard & the	1964	King 5860
Don't Feel Like The Lone Ranger	Sensations, Sonya & the	1963	Gend
Don't Feel That Way	Dialtones, Johnny Bersin & the	1959	Jin 117
Don't Fight	Ledo, Les & group	1960	Shell 721
Don't Fool With Lizzie	Whispers	1954	Gotham 309
Don't Forget	Cameron, Ken & group	1961	Zynn 500
Don't Forget	Corvells	1961	Blast 203
Don't Forget	Earls	1964	Old Town 1149/Barry 1021
Don't Forget	Platters	NA	Mercury EP 3355
Don't Forget I Love You	Butanes	1961	Enrica 1007
Don't Forget That I Love You	Intentions	1967	Philips 40428
Don't Forget To Be True	Little Four Quartet	NA	Southern 122
Don't Forget To Write	Embers, Joe D'Ambra & the	1960	Mercury 71725
Don't Forget To Write	Rialtos, Chano & the	1960	Jin 154

SONG	GROUP	YEAR	LABEL
Don't Forsake Me	Cypress, Buddy & group	1957	Flash 118
Don't Fuck Around With Love (alternate take of Jay Dee 780)	Blenders (New York)	1971	Kelway 101 (unreleased)
Don't Gamble With My Heart	Marksmen	1957	Starday 320/Mercury 71139
Don't Get Around Much Anymore	Belmonts	1961	Sabrina 501
Don't Get Around Much Anymore	Imperials, Little Anthony & the	1961	End LP 311
Don't Get Mad	Larand, Johnny & group	1965	Octavia 0005
Don't Get Slick On Me	Dell Vikings	1961	ABC 10248
Don't Give It Away	Fascinators (Detroit)	1959	Your Copy 1136
Don't Give My Love Away	Fascinators (Detroit)	1955	Blue Lake 112
Don't Give No More Than You Can Take	Five Royales	1960	King 5329
Don't Go	Accents, Jackie Allen & the	1955	Accent 1025
Don't Go	Aristocrats	1962	Home Of The Blues 237
Don't Go	Chestnuts	1954	Mercury 70489
Don't Go	Gay Tunes	1958	Dome 502
Don't Go	Kings (Baltimore)	1957	Gone 5013
Don't Go	Laurels	1989	
Don't Go	Love Notes (New York)	1957	Holiday 2607
Don't Go	Memories, Danny & the	1964	Valiant 6049
Don't Go	Pennants	1961	World 102
Don't Go	Versitiles	1962	Amaker 417
Don't Go Away	Moon Beams	1959	Grate 100
Don't Go Away	Teddy Bears	1959	Imperial 5594
Don't Go Away (Pretty Little Girl)	Barons (Epic)	1963	Epic 9586/Epic 10093 (66)
Don't Go Baby	Cubans	1958	Flash
Don't Go Home	Jaguars	1960	R-Dell 117
Don't Go Home (My Little Darlin')	Shirelles	1967	Scepter 12185
Don't Go I Love You	Midnighters	1960	King LP 700
Don't Go Now	Concords (Brooklyn)	1962	Herald 578 (first pressing, second is by the Snowmen)
Don't Go Now	Lisi, Ricky (with the Concords)	1963	Roulette 4511
Don't Go To Strangers	Orioles, Sonny Til & the	1954, 1956	Jubilee 5137/5231
Don't Go To Strangers	Sheiks	1975	Monogram 109
Don't Goof On Me	Chic-Lets	1964	Josie 919
Don't Grieve, Don't Sorrow, Don't Cry	Striders, Savannah Churchill & the	1951	RCA 4448
Don't Hafta Shop Around	Counts	1964	Rich Rose 711
Don't Hang Up The Phone	Nite Riders	1958	Teen 118
Don't Have To Cry No More	Whalers, Hal Paige & the	1957	Fury 1002/Checker 873 (57)
Don't Have To Hunt No More	Five Crowns	1953	Rainbow 206
Don't Have To Shop Around	Prime	NA	Clifton EP 506
Don't Have To Shop Around (acappella)	Chessmen	1965	Relic 1020
Don't Hold It	Blue Dots	1954	DeLuxe 6055
Don't Hurt A Good Thing	Caddell, Shirley & group	1963	Lesley 1927
Don't Hurt Me, Baby	Skyliners	1966	Jubilee 5520
Don't Hurt Me No More	Meteors, Jimmy Dee & the	1961	Pixie 7411
Don't Jump	Dories	1960	Dore 556
Don't Just Stand There	Five Chords, Johnny Jones & the	1958	Jamie 1110
Don't Just Stand There	Laurels	1985	Nobletown 821
Don't Just Stand There	Teen Kings	1959	Willett 118
Don't Keep It To Yourself	Four Chanels, Virgil & the	1959	Deb 508
Don't Keep It To Yourself	Orioles, Sonny Til & the	1983	Murray Hill LP M61277
Don't Keep Our Love Hidden In The Dark	Smoothtones	1957	Okeh 7078
Don't Knock	Pastels (Washington, D.C.)	1958	Argo 5314
Don't Knock	Spiders	1961	Imperial LP 9140
Don't Know What To Do	Chordliners, Mike & the	1989	Crystal Ball 154
Don't Know What To Do	Edsels	1960	Tammy 1010
Don't Know What You've Got	Mandells	1963	York 202
Don't Know Where I'm Going	Versatiles, Dee Thomas & the	1960	Coaster 800
Don't Know Why	Marathons	1959	Sabrina 334/JC 101 (59)
Don't Know Why I Cry	Chromatics	1956	Million 2014
Don't Know Why I Love You	Four Buddies	1959	Willett 100
Don't Laugh At Me	Dubs	1960	ABC 10100
Don't Lead Me On	Up-Tunes	1966	Genie 103
Don't Leave Me	Bachelors, T. La Mar & the	1963	Five-Four 5440

SONG	GROUP	YEAR	LABEL
Don't Leave Me	Blend-Aires	1982	Story Untold 503
Don't Leave Me	Continentals	1959	
Don't Leave Me	Dynamics	1959	Dynamic 1001
Don't Leave Me	Gordon, Sonny & group	1962	Bethlehem 3017
Don't Leave Me	Impressions	1962	Swirl 107
Don't Leave Me	Intervals	1959	Ad 103
Don't Leave Me	Magnificents	1958	Vee Jay 281
Don't Leave Me	Sweet & Sassy	1959	Del Pat 207
Don't Leave Me	Tempos	1966	Riley's 8781
Don't Leave Me Alone	Mints	1956	Lin 5001
Don't Leave Me Alone	Thrillers, Little Joe & the	1958	Okeh 7099
Don't Leave Me, Baby	Arabian Knights, Ray Gant & the	1971	Jay Walking 014
Don't Leave Me Baby	Barlow, Dean	1955	
Don't Leave Me Baby	Camelots	1963	AAnko 1001
Don't Leave Me Baby	Gentlemen	1954	Apollo 470
Don't Leave Me Baby (acappella)	Apparitions	1975	Relic LP 105
Don't Leave Me Baby (acappella)	Camelots	1961, 1964	Crimson 1001/Cameo 334/1001
Don't Leave Me Baby, Don't	Maroons	1962	Queen 24012
Don't Leave Me, Fanny	Royal Jokers	1956	Atco 6062
Don't Leave Me Here To Cry	Allen, Sue & group	1954	Groove 0037
Don't Leave Me Here To Cry	Deejays	NA	SRC 101
Don't Leave Me Here To Cry	Supremes (Ohio)	1957	Ace 534
Don't Leave Me No Choice	Hi-Tones	1961	Eon 101
Don't Leave Me Now	Four Buddies	1951	Savoy 779
Don't Leave Me Now	Notes	1956	Capitol 3332
Don't Leave Me Poor	Dikes	1955	Federal 12249
Don't Leave Me This Way	Dominoes	1953	Federal 12129
Don't Leave Me This Way	Royal Masters	1962	Guyden 2078
Don't Leave Me This Way (acappella)	Universals (Philadelphia)	1973	Relic LP 5006
Don't Leave Me To Cry	Belvaderes	1956	Hudson 4
Don't Leave Me Today	Dusters	1956	Hudson 4
Don't Leave My Broken Heart	Earls (Road House)	1974	Road House (recorded 1954)
Don't Let Go	Cookies	1954	Lamp 8008
Don't Let Go	Hamilton, Roy (with the Cues)	1957	Epic 9257
Don't Let Go	Raindrops	1964	Jubilee 5497
Don't Let Her Be Your Baby	Del-Rays	1968	Stax 162
Don't Let Her Cry Tonight	Deans	NA	Crystal Ball LP 126
Don't Let Her Go	Romancers	1964	Linda 117
Don't Let Her Have Her Way	Citations, Buddy & the	1964	IRC 6918
Don't Let Him Go	Savoys, Marva & the	1963	Coed 582
Don't Let Him Take My Baby	Velvets (Texas)	1962	Monument 458
Don't Let It Be In Vain	Five Royales	1958	King 5153
Don't Let It Die	Jennings, Vee & group	1957	
Don't Let It Fade Away	Centuries	NA	Rich 112
Don't Let It Get You Down	Lyrics, Ike Perry & the	1963, 1964	Mama 3614/Courier 828/ Naurline 100
Don't Let It Get Your Girl	Rollins, Debbie & group	1964	Ascot 2159
Don't Let It Happen Again	Cashmeres (Philadelphia)	1955	Mercury 70617
Don't Let It Happen Again	Kittens Five	1964	Herald 588
Don't Let It Happen Again	Vanguards	1954	Derby 854
Don't Let It Happen To Us	Shirelles	1963	Scepter 1259
Don't Let It Happen To You	Stereos	1964	Val 2
Don't Let Me Down	Minor Chords, Sunnie Elmo & the	1960	Flick 006
Don't Let Me Down	Persians	1963	Sir Rah 501
Don't Let Me Down This Weekend	Relations	1971	Lebby 7966
Don't Let Me Dream Tonight	Warner, Merrill & group	NA	Travel 505
Don't Let Me Love You	Fi-Dells	1961	Imperial 5780
Don't Let Me Shed Any More Tears	Amaker, Donald & group	1959	Raines 418
Don't Let Me Shed Any More Tears	Lincolns	1957	Atlas 1100
Don't Let Nobody	Fairfield Four	1960	Old Town 1081
Don't Let Nothing Stand In Your Way	Gibralters, Jimmy Barnes & the	1959	Gibraltar 106
Don't Let Temptation	Midnighters, Hank Ballard & the	1964	King 5835
Don't Let The Green Grass Fool You	Channels, Earl Lewis & the	1974	Channel 1006
Don't Let The Sun Catch You Crying	Gales	1955	J.V.B. 34
Don't Lie	Taylor, Sammy & group	1964	Enjoy 2028

SONG	GROUP	YEAR	LABEL
Don't Like The Way You're Doin'	Robins	1950	Aladdin 3031
Don't Listen To What Others Say	Creations	1964	Radiant 103
Don't Look Around	Ebb Tides, Nino & the	1959	Recorte 413
Don't Look At Me	Belmonts, Frank Lyndon with the	1964	Sabina 520
Don't Look Back	Lords	1988	Starlight 62
Don't Look Back	Revelations	NA	Starlight 16
Don't Look Now	Ravens	1950	National 9101
Don't Look Now, But	Honeytones	1958	Big Top 3002
Don't Lose Your Cool	Majors (Philadelphia)	1964	Imperial LP 9222
Don't Love You Anymore	Sparks Of Rhythm	1955	Apollo 479
Don't Make Believe	Cues	1956	Capitol 3400
Don't Make It A Sad Holiday	Orioles (featuring Bobby Thomas)	1992	Clifton 105
Don't Make It So Good	Lamplighters	1955	Federal 12242
Don't Make Me A Lonely Boy	Lancers (with Larry Smith)	NA	Central 6001
Don't Make Me Cry	Classmates	1960	Marquee 101
Don't Make My Cry	Musketeers, Debbie Andrews & the	1952	United 144
Don't Mention My Name	Ravens	1952	Mercury 5853
Don't Mention My Name	Shepherd Sisters	1963	Atlantic 2176
Don't Mess Around With My Love	Orioles, Sonny Til & the	1962	Charlie Parker 214
Don't Mind Dyin'	Jayhawks	1956	Flash 111
Don't Monkey With A Donkey	Vol-Tones	1957	Dynamic 108
Don't Monkey With Another Monkey's Monkey	Tropics, Eddie & the	1965	Josie 930
Don't Need You Anymore	Parliaments	1958	Len 101
Don't Open That Door	Chantones	1960	Top Rank 2066
Don't Open That Door	Friday Knights	1960	Strand 25019
Don't Open The Grave	Valdoros	1957	Silhouette 517
Don't Pass Me By	Du Droppers	1953	RCA 5504
Don't Pass Me By	Original Casuals	1958	Back Beat 510
Don't Pick On Me Baby	Legends, Larry & the (with the Four Seasons)	1964	Atlantic 2220
Don't Pity Me	Belmonts, Dion & the	1958	Laurie 3021
Don't Pity Me	Hunter, Herbert & group	1961	Poncello 711
Don't Pity Me	Spiders, Chuck Carbo & the	1956	Imperial 5376
Don't Pity Me	Velours	1967	MGM 13780
Don't Play Around With Love	Blenders (New York)	1953	Jay-Dee 780
Don't Play That Song	Sophomores, Anthony & the	NA	
Don't Press Your Luck	Leopards, Lee & the	1964	Fortune 867
Don't Pull, Don't Push, Don't Shove	Willows	1956	Club 1014/Michelle 501
Don't Put All Your Onions In One Basket	Beau Jives	1961	Vision 111/Lord Bingo 111
Don't Put Me Down Baby	Arabian Knights, Haji Baba & the	1956	Gotham 313
Don't Put Off For Tomorrow	Zircons	1967	Heigh Ho 607
Don't Put Onions On Your Hamburger	Dell Woods	1963	Big Top 3137
Don't Read The Letter	Pacettes	1963	Regina 1306
Don't Restrain Me Joe	Corvettes	1958	ABC 9891
Don't Run Away	Ebb Tides, Nino & the	1961	Madison 162
Don't Run Away	Thorpe, Lionel (Chords)	1960	Roulette
Don't Run To Me	Spitfires, Tony Carmen & the	1959	Abel 224
Don't Say Goodbye	Capri, Johnny & group	1961	Master 13
Don't Say Goodbye	Criterions	1959	Cecelia 1010
Don't Say Goodbye	Diamonds	1957	Mercury 71128
Don't Say Goodbye	Kents	1965	Relic 1013
Don't Say Goodbye	Knockouts	1965	Tribute 1039
Don't Say Goodbye	Moonglows	1956	Chess 1651
Don't Say Goodbye	Shells	1958	Johnson 106/Juanita 106 (58)
Don't Say Goodbye	Superiors	1957	Atco 6106/Main Line 104 (58)
Don't Say Goodbye	Trinidads	1959	Formal 1005
Don't Say Goodbye	Vibrations	1960	Checker 982
Don't Say Goodnight	Bobbettes	1959	Atlantic 2027
Don't Say Goodnight	Bop Shop	1972	Kelway 105
Don't Say Goodnight	Shades Of Brown	1982	Clifton EP 505
Don't Say Goodnight	Valentines	1957	Rama 228
Don't Say Goodnight (acappella)	Five Shadows	1965	Mellomood 011/012
Don't Say Goodnight And Mean Goodbye	Shirelles	1963	Scepter 1255
Don't Say He's Gone	Shortcuts	1959	Carlton 513

SONG	GROUP	YEAR	LABEL
Don't Say Hi	Turn Ons, Tim Tam & the	1967	Palmer 5014
Don't Say Nothin'	Roecker, Sherrill & group	1964	Swan 4173
Don't Say Nothin' Bad (About My Baby)	Cookies	1963	Dimension 1008
Don't Say Tomorrow	Hollyhocks	1957	Nasco 6001
Don't Say Tomorrow	Prisonaires	1976	Sun 512
Don't Say We're Through (acappella)	Durhams	1975	Relic LP 103
Don't Say You Love Me	Hearties, Kip Hale & the	1954	Jubilee 5166
Don't Say Your Last Goodbye	Midnighters	1954	Federal 12185
Don't Say You're Sorry	Kings Men	1957	Club 51 108
Don't Say You're Sorry	Rivals (New Jersey)	1950	Apollo 1166
Don't Say You're Sorry	Winchell, Danny (with Nino & the Ebbtides)	1959	Recorte 410
Don't Send Me Away	Five Kings	1964	Columbia 43060
Don't Send Me Away	Naturals	1959	Era 1089
Don't Shake The Tree	Doodlers	1955	RCA 6074
Don't Shoot Baby	Medallions	1955	Dootone 379
Don't Sit Down	Rocky Fellers	1964	Donna 1383
Don't Stop	Encounters	1965	Swan 4205
Don't Stop	Orioles, Sonny Til & the	1983	Murray Hill LP M61277
Don't Stop Baby	Twilighters (Roadhouse)	1974	Roadhouse 1014
Don't Stop Dan	Checkers	1954	King 4710
Don't Stop Loving Me	Cliques	1956	Modern 967 (unreleased)
Don't Stop Now	Kiddieos, Jay Bryant & the	NA	Alfa 201
Don't Stop Now	Robins	1954	RCA 5564
Don't Stop The Music	Tangiers (Strand)	1961	Strand 25039
Don't Take A Chance	Slip & Dell & group	1960	
Don't Take Away The Girl I Love	Rainbows	19??	
Don't Take It So Hard	Gum Drops	1955	King 8853/King 1499 (55)
Don't Take It So Heard	Gum Drops	1955	King 1496
Don't Take My Love	Invictors	1963	TPE 8219
Don't Take My Picture, Take Me	Velvet Keys	1958	King 5109
Don't Take My Word	Majors, Otis Blackwell & the	1957	Gale 102
Don't Take My Word (Take My Heart)	Rockets, Herb Kenny & the	1953	MGM 11648
Don't Take The Stars	Mystics	1959	Laurie 3038
Don't Take Your Love	Sensations	1962	River 228
Don't Take Your Love From Me	Cadillacs	1956	Unreleased
Don't Take Your Love From Me	Calvanes	1955	Dootone 371
Don't Take Your Love From Me	Demensions	1960	Mohawk 120
Don't Talk Back	Hi-Tones, Willie Mae Thornton & the	NA	Irma 13
Don't Tarry Little Mary	Magnets	1958	RCA 7391
Don't Tease Me	Cruisers	1960	V-Tone 213/Guyden 2069 (62)
Don't Tease Me	Williams, Bernie & group	1955	Imperial 5360
Don't Tell Her What Happened To Me	Orioles, Sonny Til & the	1963	Charlie Parker 216
Don't Tell Her What's Happened To Me	Orioles, Sonny Til & the	1951	Jubilee 5065
Don't Tell Me	Five Techniques	1961	Imperial 5742
Don't Tell Me	Marsh, Billy & group	1956	Arrow 716
Don't Tell Me	Surgeons	1963	Cee-Jam 100
Don't Tell Me Your Troubles	Checkmates, Emil Ford & the	1959	Andie 5018/Cub 9063 (60)
Don't Tell Nobody	Dells	1984, 1985	Solid Smoke LP 8029/ Charly LP 1055 (85)
Don't Tell Tales Out Of School	Velairs	1958	MGM 12667
Don't Tell William	Keytones	1961	Chelsea 1002
Don't Thank Me	Dominoes	1953	King 1280
Don't Think I Will	Young Jessie (with the Jacks)	1955	Modern 961
Don't Throw My Toys Away	Rocky Fellers	1965	Warner Bros. 5497
Don't Throw Stones	Moniques	1963	Centaur 104
Don't Torment Me	Rock-A-Fellas	1958	ABC 9923
Don't Touch	Williams, Andre & group	1957	Fortune 839X
Don't Touch Me	Lovers	1956	Decca 29862
Don't Touch My Gal	Empires	1956	Wing 90080
Don't Touch The Moon	Blakely, Cornel & group	1957	Fulton 2543
Don't Try	Tangiers (Los Angeles)	1958	Class 224
Don't Turn Away From Me	Doves	1960	Big Top 3046
Don't Turn Your Back On Me	Carter Quartet, Eddie	1953	MGM 11405
Don't Turn Your Back On Me	Marcels	1963	Colpix 683
Don't Turn Your Back On Me	Park Avenue Jesters	NA	N/A

SONG	GROUP	YEAR	LABEL
Don't Twist	Cole, Clay (with the Capris)	1961	Imperial 5804
Don't Vote For Luke McCabe	Dovells	1972	MGM 14568
Don't Wait	Cellos, Dolly Lyon & the	NA	N/A
Don't Wake Me Up	Gray, Wilhemina & group	1957	MGM 12500
Don't Wake Me Up	Velaires	1962	Jamie 1223
Don't Wake Up The Kids	Charms, Otis Williams & his	1958	DeLuxe 6174
Don't Wake Up The Kids	Four Dots, Jerry Stone & the (with Eddie Cochran & Jewel Akens)	1959	Freedom 44005
Don't Walk Away	Davis, Jan & group	1963	Rendezvous 214
Don't Walk Away	Superlatives	NA	Dynamics 1016/Westbound 144
Don't Walk Away	Talents, Julian Barnett & the	1958	Herald 519
Don't Walk Out	Barons (New Orleans)	1956	Imperial 5397
Don't Wanna Leave The Congo	Valiants, Norman Sands & the	1960	Warwick 598
Don't Wanna Say Goodbye	Stites, Gary & group	1960	Carlton 525
Don't Wanna Twist No More	Angels, Gabriel & the	1959, 1962	Casino 107/Swan 4118 (62)/Itzy 7 (62)
Don't Want No Teasing!	Kodaks	1960	J&S 1683/1684
Don't Want No Woman	Jokers	NA	Teen 1006
Don't Want To	Day, Bobby & the Blossoms	1959	Class 263
Don't Want To Be Your Fool	New Yorkers	1964	Tac-Ful 101
Don't Want To Have To Do It	Duprees	1966	Columbia 43802
Don't Want Your Love No More	Vacels, Ricky & the	1963	Fargo 1050
Don't Wonder Why	Steinways	1966	Oliver 2007
Don't Worry About A Thing	Sweet Teens	1956	Flip 311
Don't Worry About Bobby	Demensions	1963	Coral 62382
Don't Worry Baby	Tokens (Brooklyn)	1970	Buddah 159
Don't Worry 'Bout Me	Hope, Lynn & group	1959	Aladdin 3155
Don't You Care	Hearties, Kip Hale & the	1954	Jubilee 5166
Don't You Do Me Like That	Marquees, Terry Brown & the	1961	Jo-Ann 130
Don't You Feel	Edsels	1962	Capitol 4836
Don't You Forget	Miller Sisters, Jeannie & the	1962	Hull 750
Don't You Go	Crystals (New York)	1953	Rockin' 518
Don't You Hear Me Calling, Baby	Tren-Dells	1961	Tilt 779
Don't You Hear Them Laughing	Modern Red Caps	1963	Rowax 801
Don't You Just Know It?	Titans	1958	Specialty 625
Don't You Know	Ravens, Rico & the	1965	Rally 1601/Autumn 6 (65)
Don't You Know	Temptations (New Jersey)	1958	Savoy 1550
Don't You Know	West Siders	1963	Leopard 5004/United Artists 600 (63)
Don't You Know I Care	Sevilles	1962	Cal Gold 172
Don't You Know I Love You	Clovers	1951	Atlantic 934
Don't You Know I Love You	Five Keys	1955	Capitol 3185
Don't You Know (I Love You)	Pleasures	1964	RSVP 1102
Don't You Know (I Love You So)	Crowns, Arthur Lee Maye & the	1985	Relic LP 5054
Don't You Know Love	Preludes Five	1961	Pik 231
(Don't You Know) Love You, Baby	Fi-Tones	1956	Atlas 1052
Don't You Know What I Believe	Show Stoppers	1961	Brent 7021
Don't You Know?	Ramblers (Federal)	1956	Federal 12286
Don't You Remember	Four Escorts	1961	Skyla 1113
Don't You Run	Long, Bobby & his Cherrios	1959	Glow-Hill 503
Don't You Think I Ought To Know	Orioles, Sonny Til & the	1953	Jubilee 5122/Lana 109 (64)
Don't You Worry My Pretty Pet	Teddy Bears	1958	Dore 503
Don'tcha Back Track	Runarounds, Ritchie & the	1963	Ascot 2136
Don'tcha Go	Berry, Richard (with the Flairs)	1955	Flair 1068
Dontcha Keep Me Wanting	Capri, Mike & group	NA	Cecil 4450
Doo Be Dum	Four-Evers	1964	Smash 1921
Doo Dee Doo Doop	Afterbeats, Gloria Wood & the	1960	Buena Vista 361
Doo Doo Dah	Demons	1958	Unart 2002
Doo Doo Wah	Cellos	1988	Relic LP 5074 (88)
Doo Wop Jingle Bells	Hansen Brothers	1981	Crystal Ball 146
Doodle Bug	Hightones, Claude & the	1959	Baytone 113
Doodle Bug Twist	Five Notes, Sammy & the	1962	Lucky Four 1019
Doodle Doo Doo	Ebonaires	1988	Relic LP 5076
Doodle-Doo, The	Gaylarks	1958	Music City 819
Doodlum	Off Beats	1964	Guyden 2101
Dooley	Olympics	1961	Arvee 5031
Doo-Li-Op	Four Kings	1955	Fortune 517

SONG	GROUP	YEAR	LABEL
Dooly Bump	Newports	1977	Crystal Ball 108
Doom-A-Rocka	Debs	1957	Keen 34003
Doom-Lang	Tokens (Gary)	1957, 1984	Gary 1006/Musictone 1113 (59)
Doom's Day	Shirelles	1964	Scepter 1278
Doop Doop A Walla Walla	El Torros	1962	Duke 353
Door Is Always Open, The	Belvin, Jesse & group	1960	RCA 7675
Door Is Still Open, The	Cardinals	1955	Atlantic 1054
Door Is Still Open, The	Skyliners	1961	Colpix 188
Doowaddie	Threeteens	1959	Rev 3516
Doo-Wopp Disco	Fourteen Karat Soul	1979	Catamount 737
Do-Pop-Si	Colonairs	1963	Tru-Lite 127
Dora	Donato, Mike & group	NA	PM 0101
Dora, He Told Me To Tell You It Hurts	Informers	1960	Dore 562
Doreen	Discounts, Bobby & the	NA	Generation 100
Doreetha	Golden Tones	1959	Hush 101
Do-Re-Mi	Rob-Roys, Norman Fox & the	1990	Back Beat 499
Do-Re-Mi Rock	Jokers, Johnny & the	1959	Harvard 804
Dore's Blues	Masters	1960	Bingo 1008
Dori Anne	Winters, David & group	1962	Rori 703
Doris	Big Dog & group	1962	N/A
Dormilona	Fleetwoods	1960	Dolton 27
Dorothy	Dreamers, Donnie & the	1961	Whale 500
Dorothy	Hi-Fives	1958	Decca 30657
Dorothy Jane	Midnite Raiders, Mills Allen & the	NA	Black Gold 304
Dorothy, My Monster	Campanions	NA	Dee-Dee 1047
Dot, My Love	Aladdins	1958	Frankie 6
Dottie	Computones	1981	Clifton 61
Dottie	Juniors, Danny & the	1958	ABC 9926
Dottie	Vows	1963	Tamara 760 (same # used twice)
Dottie Baby	Buckeyes	1957	DeLuxe 6126
Double Clutch	Sharps	1960	Star-Hi 10406
Double Crossin' Baby	Robbins	1954	Crown 106
Double Crossin' Blues	Robins, Little Esther & the	1950	Savoy 731
Double Date	Cutups	1962	Jim 852
Double Date	Dolphins, Dougie & the	1959	Angle Tone 542
Double Date	Five Encores	1955	Rama 180
Double Date	Premiers (Clock)	1961	Clock 1042
Double Dealing Baby	Souvenirs	1957	Dooto LP 224
Double Dutch Twist	Blue Chips	1961	Laurel 1026
Double Eye Whammie	Ridgley, Tommy & group	1961	Ric 978
Double Love	Chandeliers	1964	Loadstone 1601
Double Or Nothing	Five Royales	1958	King 5141
Double Rock	Bengals, Bobby & the	1960	B&W 1
Double Shot Of My Baby's Love	Holidays, Dick Holler & the	1962	Comet 2152
Double Talk	Playboys	1958	Martinique 101/Cameo 142 (58)
Double Trouble	Renegades, Patty McCoy & the	1962	Counsel 119
Double Trouble	Roomates, Cathy Jean & the	1962	Philips 40143
Double Trouble	Tattletales	1959	Warner Bros. 5066
Doubt	Angel, Johnny & group	1960	Imperial 5673
Doubt In Your Mind	Magic Chords	NA	Domino 360
Doubtful	Moonglows	1955	Chess (unreleased)
Down	Marveliers	1960	Cougar 1868
Down And Out	Daps	1956	Marterry 5249
Down And Out	Four Winds	1964	Chattahoochee 655
Down At Hayden's	Hunters	1953	Flair 1017
Down At Mary's House	Curios, Bobby Brown & the	1959	Vaden 100
Down At The Beach	Pentagons	1960	Fleet Int'l 100/Donna 1337 (61)
Down At The Corner	Raging Storms	1962	Trans Atlas 691
Down At The Go Go	Modernistics	1965	Pioneer 7315
Down Be The Stream	Embers, Frankie Joe & the	1957	Fee Bee 224
Down By The Ocean	Exceptions	1963	Pro 1/Cameo 378 (65)
Down By The River	Cookies	1956	Atlantic 1110
Down By The River	Georgettes	1960	Fleet 1111/United Artists 237 (60)
Down By The Riverside	Uptowners	1989	Starlight 67
Down By The Shore	Holidays	NA	Mark IV 725

SONG	GROUP	YEAR	LABEL
Down By The Stream	Dell Vikings	1956	Fee Bee 210/Dot 15571 (56)
Down By The Well	Revelaires	1954	Burgundy 1001
Down, Down, Down I Go	Dubs	1961	ABC 10269
Down Home	Jaynells	1963	Cameo 286/Diamond 153
Down Home Girl	Coasters	1967	Date 1552
Down In Bermuda	Dell Vikings	1956	Fee Bee 206
Down In Cuba	Royal Holidays	1959	Herald 536
Down In Mexico	Coasters	1956	Atco 6064
Down In Mexico	Kappaliers	NA	Shadow 1229
Down In Mexico	Kidds	NA	Post (unreleased)
Down In Mexico	Nutmegs	1963	Times Square 27/Relic 528 (65)
Down In Mexico	Pelicans	NA	Imperial (unreleased)
Down In My Heart	Visions	1965	Co-Ed 598
Down In New Orleans	El Tempos, Big Mike Gordon & the	1955	Savoy 1152
Down In New Orleans	Marathons	1961	Chess 1790/Argo 5389 (61)
Down In The Alley	Gents	NA	Midnight 102
Down In The Alley	Gibralters, Nappy Brown & the	1960	Savoy 1582
Down In The Alley	Lyrics (San Francisco)	1959	Mid South 1500
Down In The Bottom	Rockers	1956	Federal 12273
Down In The Valley	Clovers	1957	Atlantic 1152
Down In The Valley	Emersons	1961	United Artists 379
Down In The Valley	Storytellers	1963	Capitol 5042
Down It Went	Four Deuces	1956	Music City 796
Down On My Knees	Heartbeats	1958, 1959	Roulette 4054/4194
Down On My Knees	Starr Brothers	1963, 1964	Cortland 104/Nike 1016
Down On My Knees (acappella)	Enchantments	1966	Relic LP 103
Down On The Beach	Maresca, Ernie (with the Del Satins)	1962	Seville 119
Down On The Beach Tonight	Drifters (1959-forward)	1974	Bell (UK) 1381
Down On The Farm	Devilles	1961	Acclaim 1002
Down On The Farm	Poe Rats, Al Downing & the	1958	Challenge 59006
Down Our Street	Raindrops, Jackie & the	1964	Colpix 738
Down Slow	Five Jets	1954	DeLuxe 6071
Down That Lonely Road	Cousins	1960	Versatile 105
Down The Aisle	Blue Belles, Patti LaBelle & the	1963	Newtown 5777/King 5777 (63)
Down The Aisle	Duets, Leo & the	NA	Co-Op 514
Down The Aisle Of Love	Concords (Brooklyn)	1966	Boom 60021/Polydor 14036 (70)
Down The Aisle Of Love	Quin-Tones (Pennsylvania)	1958	Red Top 108/Hunt 321 (58)
Down The Block And Up To Heaven	Lornettes	1965	Gallico 110
Down The River Of Dreams	Platters	1960	Mercury 71697
Down The Road	Cadillacs	1955	Josie 778
Down The Road	Dootones	1962	Dooto 471
Down The Road	Halos	1962	Warwick LP 2046
Down The Road	Legacy	1988	Crystal Ball 153
Down The Road	Thomas, Gene & group	1961	Venus 1444
Down The Road And Over The Hill	Bobby & Jimmy & group	1963	King 5757
Down The Road I Go	Five Echoes	1956	Vee Jay 190
Down The Stream To The River	Thomas, Vic (with the Four-Evers)	1964	Philips 40228
Down To Earth	Nutmegs	1963	Times Square 19
Down To The Sea	Five Rovers	1956	Music City 798
Down Went The Curtain	Citations	1965	MGM 13373
Downtown	Five Satins	1962	Chancellor 1121
Dr. Geek	Alexander, Jeff	1955	Aardell 0001
Dr. Jekyll And Mr. Hyde	Emersons	1959	Cub 9027
Drafted, Volunteered And Enlisted	Creators (Los Angeles)	1961	Dooto 463
Drag	Delaires, Ronnie & the	1964	Coral 62404
Drag City	Tokens (Brooklyn)	NA	RCA LP 2886
Drag It	Knights, Frankie Daye & the	1959	Studio 9904
Drag It Home, Baby	Jets (Washington, D.C.)	1953	Rainbow 201
Drag, The	Isley Brothers	1959	Gone 5048/Mark-X 8000
Drag, The	Mar-Villes	1962	Infinity 027
Dragon Walk	Dantes	1964	Courtney 713
Dragster On The Prowl	Dovells	1963	Parkway 901
Draw	Hi-Boys	1959	Mala 400
Draw, The	Teenagers, Joey & the (with Sherman)	1961	Columbia 42054
Drawbridge	Barons (Tender)	1958	Tender 511

SONG	GROUP	YEAR	LABEL
Dream	Admirations, Keith & the	1965	Columbia 43268
Dream	Cliches	NA	N/A
Dream	Five Keys	1957	Capitol LP 828/Capitol EP 2-828 (57)
Dream	Hamilton, Judd & group	1963	Dolton 80
Dream	Imperials, Little Anthony & the	1961	End 1104
Dream	Monotones	1960	Hull 735
Dream	Rogues	1958	Old Town 1056
Dream	Velaires	1961	Jamie 1203
Dream	Young Ideas	1959	Swan 4044
Dream A Dream	Mood Makers	1961	Bambi 800
Dream A Little Dream	New Yorkers (Fred Parris)	1961	Wall 547
Dream A Little Longer	Jacks	1956	RPM 467
Dream Angel	Royal Flairs	NA	Sam 119
Dream Angel Goodnight	Tokens (Brooklyn)	1962	RCA 8089
Dream Around You	Leen Teens	1959	Imperial 5593
Dream Awhile	Innocents, Kathy Young & the	1962	Indigo 147
Dream Baby	Laddins	1963	Butane 779
Dream Boat	Debs	1962	Infinity 035
Dream Boy	Angels (New Jersey)	1964	Smash 1915
Dream Boy	Collegiates, Dicky Lee & the	1957	Tampa 131
Dream Boy	Dreams, Frank Rossi & the	1957	Mark 7001
Dream Boy	Innocents, Kathy Young & the	1962	Monogram 506
Dream Boy	Marie Ann & group	1960	Warwick 605
Dream Boy (Oh, Oh, Oh)	Dean, Terry & group	1957	Poplar 102
Dream Come True	Earls	1975	Harvey 100
Dream Date	Boy Friends, Terry Corin & the	1960	Colony 110
Dream Date	Curios, Bucky Brown & the	1960	XYZ 610
Dream Dream	Blenders, Earl Curry & the	1956	R&B 1313
Dream Dream Dream	Chiffons	1976	Laurie 3648
Dream, Dream, Dream	Four Bells	1954	Bell 1039
Dream Girl	Belvin, Jesse & group	1951	Hollywood 120
Dream Girl	Chimes (Brooklyn)	1961	Tag 447
Dream Girl	Chordliners	1989	Blue Sky 111
Dream Girl	Crosstones	NA	Clifton EP 510
Dream Girl	Delacardos	1961	Shell 308
Dream Girl	Dons	NA	Heartbeat 1
Dream Girl	Dynamics	1961, 1962	Dynamic 1008/Dynamic Sound 578/9
Dream Girl	Flamingos	1961	End 1092
Dream Girl	Lovenotes	NA	Joyce (unreleased)
Dream Girl	Rob-Roys, Norman Fox & the	1958	Hammer 544/Capitol 4128 (59)
Dream Girl	Spiedells	1966	Providence 418
Dream Girl	Statues, Gary Miles & the	1960	Liberty 55279
Dream Girl	Suddens	NA	N/A
Dream Land	Evergreens, Dante & the	1960	Madison 135
Dream Land	Four Evers	1978	Crystal Ball 121
Dream Lover	Darin, Bobby & group	1959	Atco 6140
Dream Lover	Nitebeaters	NA	Carib 1010
Dream Lover	Richie & group	1961	Kip 240
Dream Lover	School Boys	1960	Studio 1
Dream Lover	Showvenistics	1993	Clifton 106
Dream Maker	Crests	1961	Coed (unreleased)
Dream Man	Dee, Fern & group	1958	Ember 1035
Dream, My Darling, Dream	Re-Vels	1956	Sound 135
Dream Of A Lifetime	Ecstasies	1979	Clifton 31
Dream Of A Lifetime	Flamingos	1954, 1959	Parrot 808/Checker 915
Dream Of Love	Packards	1956	Paradise 105
Dream Of Romance	Lincoln's Quintett	1958	Angle Tone 522
Dream Of You	Satellites, Ronny & the	1959	Rose 1001
Dream On	Five Keys	1959	King 5273
Dream On	Precisions	1960	Strand 25038
Dream On	Sevilles, Richard Barrett & the	1960	Seville 104
Dream On Little Fool	Amato, Jerry & group	NA	Tacit 109
Dream (or Two People In The World)	Imperials, Little Anthony & the	1960	End 1083
Dream Ship	Vocalaires	1976	Ronnie 200
Dream Street	Bell Notes	1959	Time EP 100

SONG	GROUP	YEAR	LABEL
Dream Street	Lollypops	1960	Kandee 6001
Dream, The	Bobbettes	1958	Atlantic 1194
Dream (When You're Feeling Blue) (acappella)	Shells	1966	Candlelite LP 1000
Dream World (acappella)	Citadels	1975	Relic LP 103
Dreamer	Blue Belles, Patti LaBelle & the	1966	Atlantic 2408
Dreamer	Brown, Bobby & group	1962	Pak 1313
Dreamer	Dapps, Johnnie Mae Matthews & the	1960	Northern 3727
Dreamer From My Heart	Crescendos, Johnny Woodson & the	1958	Spry 108
Dreamin'	Allen, Tony (with the Wonders)	1961	Kent 364
Dreamin'	Four J's	1969	Congress 6003
Dreamin'	Night Owls, Tony Allen & the	1960	Crown LP 5231
Dreamin'	Uptones	1962	Lute 6229
Dreamin' And Dreamin'	Scale-Tones	1956	Jay-Dee 810
Dreamin' And Schemin'	Accents (featuring Robert Draper Jr.)	1958	Brunswick 55100
Dreaming	Clefts	1960	V-Tone 212
Dreaming	Cosmic Rays	1960	Saturn 401
Dreaming	Five Stars (Detroit)	1958	Note 10011/Hunt 318 (58)/ ABC 9911 (58)
Dreaming	Melvetts, Joyce Spivey & the	1965	Olimpic 254
Dreaming	Page, Priscilla & group	1961	Rose 500
Dreaming	Sportsmen	1959	A 104
Dreaming	Universals (Amityville, N.Y.)	1961	Festival 1601
Dreaming	Uptones	1963	Watts 1080/Magnum 714 (63)
Dreaming In The Meadow	Bees	1974	Firefly 325
Dreaming Of An Angel	Crystal, Lou & group	1962	SFAZ 1001
Dreaming Of You	Dimples	1964	Cameo 325
Dreaming Of You	Five Shits	1973	Lost Cause 100
Dreaming Of You	Identicals	1963	Firebird 101
Dreaming Of You	Kaptions	NA	Ham-Mil 1520
Dreaming Of You	Prisonaires	1976	Sun 519
Dreamland	Four-Evers	NA	Magic Carpet LP 1004
Dreamland	Jones, Dee & group	1961	Brent 7023
Dreamland Last Night	Doyle, Dicky & group	1961	Wye 1009
Dreamlover	Treytones	NA	Sunliner
Dreams (first pressing)	Valumes	1962	Chex 1002 (first pressing, second is by Volumes)
Dreams (second pressing)	Volumes	1962	Chex 1002 (second pressing, first is by Valumes)
Dreams And Memories	Flames, Farrell & the	1961	Fransil 14
Dreams And Wishes	Crickets, Dean Barlow & the	1953	Jay-Dee 777
Dreams And Wishes	Crystals (Brooklyn)	1961	Indigo 114
Dreams Are A Dime A Dozen	Four J's	1958	Herald 528
Dreams Are For Fools	Revalons	1958	Pet 802
Dreams Can Come True	Originals	1988	Starlight 64
Dreams Come True	Earls	1973	Clifton 47
Dreams Come True	Gee-Chords	1974	Romantic Rhythm 101
Dreams Come True	Strangers	1955	King 4766
Dreams Never Hurt Nobody	James, Jesse (with the Royal Aces)	1961	Musicor 1008
Dreams Of Contentment	Dells	1955	Vee Jay 166
Dreams Of Heaven	Legacy	1987	Crystal Ball 151
Dreams Of Heaven	Serenaders, Larry Lee & the	1990	Relic LP 5085
Dreams Of You	Royals, Chuck Willis & the	1951	Okeh 6832
Dreamtime	Rosebuds, Rosemary & the	1963	Larkwood 1101
Dreamworld	Calvanes	1958	Deck 579
Dreamworld	Midnighters, Hank Ballard & the	1962	King 5677
Dreamy	Rondells	1958	Carlton 467
Dreamy Eyes	Four Of A Kind	1957	Melba 117
Dreamy Eyes	Hendricks, Bobby (with the Coasters)	1958	Sue 708
Dreamy Eyes	Squires (California)	1957	Aladdin 3360
Dreamy Eyes	Terry, George & group	1965	Sphere Sound 711
Dreamy Eyes	Till, Johnny & group	1960	San Leon
Dreamy Eyes	Viceroys	1961	Original Sound 15
Dreamy Eyes	Youngsters	1956	Empire 109
Dreamy Nights	Collegiates, Dicky Lee & the	1958	Sun 297

SONG	GROUP	YEAR	LABEL
Dressin' Up	Elegants	1963	Photo 2662
Dressin' Up	Originals	1988	Starlight 64
Dressin' Up	Rays	1958	Cameo 127
Dribble Twist	Raging Storms	1962	Warwick 677
Dribble Twist, The	Magnificents	1962	Kansoma 03/Checker 1016 (62)
Drift Away	Reunion	NA	Starlight 17
Driftin' Away From You	Drifters (Pre-1959)	1957	Atlantic 1141
Drifting And Dreaming	Dinning Sisters	1955	Essex 392
Drifting Apart	Mellows, Mack Starr & the	1962	Cub 9117
Driftwood	Dimples, Eddie Cooley & the	1957	Royal Roost 626
Drink Up	Du Droppers	1954	Unreleased
Drinkin' Pop Sodee Odee	Dimensionals, Donnie Baker with the	1953	Rainbow 219
Drinkin' Wine	Medallions, Vernon Green & the	1991	Classic Artists 129
Drinking Wine, Spodee-Odee	Stereos, Little Benny & the	1959	Spot 106
Drip, Drip, The Coffee Grinder	Cherokees (Philadelphia)	1955	Peacock 1656
Drip Drop	Chippendales	1959	Andie 5013
Drip Drop	Deb-Teens	1959	Boss 403
Drip Drop	DiMucci, Dion (with the Del Satins)	1963	Columbia 42917
Drip Drop	Dodgers	1955	Aladdin 3271
Drip Drop	Drifters (Pre-1959)	1958	Atlantic 1187
Drip Drop	Squires, Shirley & the	1963	Constellation 107
Drip Drop	Stuart, Glen & chorus	1960	Abel 235
Drive Away Blues	Cincos, Ben Harper & the	1960	Talent 106
Drive In	Jaguars	1959	Epic 9325
Drive It Home	Clovers	1961	Atlantic 2129
Drive Me Crazy	Court Jesters	NA	Jester 2034
Drive, The	Shells	1962	Johnson 120
Drive-In	Delmars (with the Modern Trenaire Band)	NA	RST 135
Drive-In Movie	Academics	1958	Elmont 1001/1002
Drive-In Movie	Carousels	1959	Jaguar 3029/Spry 121 (59)
Drive-In Rock	Four Guys	1956	Mercury 70908
Drive-In, The	Aquatones	1958	Fargo 1003
Driving Along	Bon-Aires	1962	Rust TR3
Driving Down The Highway	Blue Flamers	1954	Excello 2026
Driving Guitars	Incidentals	1964	Ford 134
Driving Home	Good Guys, Doug Robertson & the	1964	Jerden 739
Driving Wheel	Wheels, Midge Olinde & the	1962	Viking 1011
Drop By	Metallics	1962	Baronet 14
Drop Down To My Place	Strangers	1954	King 4745
Drop Me A Line	Harmonaires, Bonnie Lou & the	1955	King 1476
Drop Me A Line	Hollywood Flames	1963	Vee Jay 515
Drop Me A Line	Johnson, Bubber (with the Wheels)	1955	King 4793
Drown In My Tears	Key, Troyce & group	1958	Warner Bros. 5007
Drowning Every Hope I Ever Had	Orioles, Sonny Til & the	1954	Jubilee 5143
Drum Beat	Fantastics	1990	Park Ave. 2
Drunk, Drunk, Drunk	Kidds	1955	Imperial 5335
Drunkard, The	Thrillers (Detroit)	1953	Big Town 109
Dry Bones Twist	Drivers	1962	King 5645
Dry Cereal	Divots	NA	Mark 3516
Dry Tears	Ginger & group	1962	Titan 1717
Dry Tears	Ginger (with the Safaris)	1961	Titan 1717
Dry Your Eyes	Belvin, Jesse & group	1956	Cash 1056
Dry Your Eyes	Chiffons	NA	Collectables LP 5042
Dry Your Eyes	Dells	1959	Vee Jay 324
Dry Your Eyes	Delmiros	1961	Dade 1821
Dry Your Eyes	Four Pennies	1963	Rust 5071
Dry Your Eyes	Imperials, Little Anthony & the	1959	End (unreleased)
Dry Your Eyes	Inspirations (Jamie)	1956	Jamie 1034/Jamie 1212 (62)
Dry Your Eyes	Rainbows, Randy & the	1964	Rust 5080
Dry Your Eyes	Reality	1978	U.G.H.A. 02
Dry Your Eyes	Revlons	1962	Capitol 4739
Dry Your Eyes	Tokens (Brooklyn)	1961	RCA 7896
Du Du'nt Du	Innocents, Kathy Young & the	1961	Indigo 125
Du Wap	Chimes (Limelight)	1957	Limelight 3002
Du-Bi-A-Do	Falcons (Flip)	1954	Flip 301

SONG	GROUP	YEAR	LABEL
Dubio	Four Feathers, Gene Forrest & the	1954	Aladdin 3224
Duchess Conquers Duke	Conquerors	1962	Lu Pine 108
Duchess Of Earl	Pearlettes	1962	Vee Jay 435
Duchess, The	Ideals	1962	Fargo 1024
Duck, The	Olympics	1966	Mirwood 5525
Duck Walk	Moods	1960	Sarg 176
Duck Walk	Playboys	1962	Chancellor 1106
Duffy	Songspinners	1958	Leila 1601
Duke Of Earl	Chandler, Gene (with the Dukays)	1961	Vee Jay 416/Nat 4003 (62)
Duke, The	Syndicates	1965	Mello 552
Duke's Cookies	Jiving Juniors	1961	Blue Beat 24
Duke's Place	Furness Brothers	1960	Rae-Cox 104
Dum De Dum Dum	Cadillacs	1962	Jubilee LP 5009
Dum Doodee Dum Dum	Keynotes	NA	Index
Dum Dum	Dynamics, Johnny Christmas & the	1959	P.D.Q. 5002
Dum Dum De Dip	Affections, Judy & the	NA	Dode
Dum Dum Song	Red Coats	1965	Laurie 3319
Dumb Dora	Realtones	NA	Famous LP 501
Dumbell	Cadillacs	1959	Josie 870
Dune Buggy, The	Contenders	1964	Chattahoochee 644
Dunkin' Boy	Hi-Liters	1975	Monogram 101
Dust Off The Bible	Ebb-Tones	1957	Crest 1032
Dusty Roads	Lapels	1961	Fortune 862
Dutch Treat	Utopians	1962	Imperial 5861
Dutchess Of Earl	Dream Girls, Bobbie Smith & the	1962	Big Top 3100
Du-Whop	Chessmen	1958	Mirasonic 1002/Mirasonic 1868 (58)
Dynaflow	Caverliers Quartet	1954, 1955	Atlas 1031
Dynamite Darling	Charms, Otis Williams & his	1957	DeLuxe 6149

E

SONG	GROUP	YEAR	LABEL
E Basta Cosi	Midnighters	1957	Federal 12293
Each Day	Suburbans, Ann Cole & the	1956	Baton 232
Each Night	Candles, Rochell & the	1962	Challenge 9158
Each Night	Five Dots	1954	Dot 1204
Each Night	Satellites	1960	D-M-G 4001
Each Night At Night	Star Fires	1962	Haral 7777/7778
Each Night I Pray	Frontiers	1962	King 5609
Each Passing Day	Hi-Fis	1960	Mark 148/Devere 006
Each Passing Day	Singleton, Jimmy (Royal Satins)	1958	
Each Time	Bon-Bons	1964	Coral 62435
Each Time	Ivy-Tones	1958	Red Top 105
Each Time I Hold You	Sophomores (Massachusetts)	1957	Dawn 237
Eagle, The	Essex	1966	Bang 537
Early Christmas	Classic IV	1962	Algonquin 1650
Early In The Morning	Ding Dongs (featuring Bobby Darin)	1958	Brunswick 55073
Early In The Morning	Dubs	1959	ABC 10056
Early In The Morning	Four Kings	1963	M.O.C. 655
Early In The Morning	Rinky-Dinks (Ding Dongs) (featuring Bobby Darin)	1958	Atco 6121
Early In The Morning	Tiaras, Roy Milton & the	1960	Lou Wa 1002/Warwick 549 (60)
Early Morning Blues	Robins	1950	Recorded In Hollywood 150
Early Morning Rock	Deltones	1958	Vee Jay 288
Early One Morning	Arabian Knights, Haji Baba & the	1956	Gotham 313
Early One Morning	Capers	1958	Vee Jay 297
Early One Morning	Keynotes	1989	Relic LP 5080
Early One Morning	Midnighters	1956	Federal 12270
Early Sunday Morning	Sha-Weez	1953	Aladdin 3170
Early To Bed	Poni-Tails	1959	ABC 9995
Earth Angel	Belmonts, Frank Lyndon with the	1964	Sabina 520
Earth Angel	Blue Jays (Los Angeles)	1956	Dig EP 777
Earth Angel	Carroll, Yvonne & group	1963	Domain 1020
Earth Angel	Cleftones	1961	Gee 1074
Earth Angel	Crests	1978	King Tut 172
Earth Angel	Crowns, Arthur Lee Maye & the	1956	Dig 100 (unreleased)
Earth Angel	Dreamers, Joy Anthony & the	1958	Sinclair 1001

SONG	GROUP	YEAR	LABEL
Earth Angel	Freese, Harrison & group	NA	Freshman 302
Earth Angel	Jayos, Johnny Otis & the	1957	Dig LP 104
Earth Angel	Penguins	1954, 1956	Dootone 348/Power 7023 (54)/ Mercury 70943
Earth Angel	Rhythmaires (with Gayle Lark)	NA	Tops EP 252
Earth Angel	Street Corner Symphony	1975	Bang 719
Earth Angel	Tokens (Brooklyn)	NA	RCA LP 3685
Earth Angel	Viceroys	1964	Imperial 66058
Earth Angel (acappella)	Citadels	1975	Relic LP 109
Earthquake	Channels (Chester, Pa.)	1959	Mercury 71501
Earthquake	Customs	1963	Arlen 511
Ease The Pain	Fabulous El Dorados	1987	Delano 1099
Ease The Pain	Gomez, Yvonne & group	1967	Hawaii 128
Easier Said Than Done	Ascots	1959	Arrow 736
Easier Said Than Done	Essex	1963	Roulette 4494
East Is East	Dematrons	1963	Southern Sound 202
East L.A.	Arlin, Bob & group	1960	Olympia 823/824
East Of The Sun	Scarlets	1960	Fury 1036
Easy	Altecs	1961	Felsted 8618
Easy Baby	Scaletones	1956	
Easy Cash	Portraits	1959	Capitol 4181
Easy Come, Easy Go	Emblems, Patty & the	1966	Congress 263
Easy Easy Baby	Cole, Ann (with the Suburbans)	1956	Baton 224
Easy Easy Baby	Moore, Rudy May (with the Raytones)	1960	World Pacific 821
Easy Going	Moods	1960	Sarg 176
Easy Going Baby	Bards	1954	Dawn 208
Easy Lovin'	Clovers	1960	United Artists 227
Easy To Fall In Love	Valentinos	1982	Clifton 70
Easy To Love	Chiffons	1963	Laurie 3224
Easy To Remember	Heartbeats	1981	Collectables 1021
Easy To Remember	Rivieras	1960	Coed 542
Easy To Remember (When You Want To Forget)	Limelites, Shep & the	1963	Hull 761
Easy To Say	Versatiles	1967	Richtone 186
Eat 'Em Up	Carter Quartet, Eddie	1953	MGM 11405
Eat Your Mush And Hush	Cleeshays, Sonny Knight & the	1958	Eastman 787
Eatin' And Sleepin'	Dominoes	1958	Liberty LP 3083
Ebb Tide	Avalons	1958	Unart 2007
Ebb Tide	Blue Belles, Patti LaBelle & the	1966	Atlantic 2333
Ebb Tide	Platters	1960	Mercury 71624
Ebb Tide	Welch, Lenny & group	1962	Cadence 1422
Ebb Tide (acappella)	Five Delights	1960	A Cappella - Best of the Bronx (98)
Ebb Tide (acappella)	Five Jades (Bronx, N.Y.)	1975	Relic LP 107
Ebb Tide (acappella)	Universals (Philadelphia)	1973	Relic LP 5006
Ebbing Of The Tide	Hi Tensions	1963	Milestone 2018
Ebony Eyes	Harmonaires, Elaine Gay & the	1955	DeLuxe 2029
Echo	Emotions	1962	Kapp 490
Echo	Four Persuasions	1972	Pay-4-Play 100
Echo	Holloway, Brenda (with the Carrolls)	1962	Donna 1358
Echo '90	Emotions	1990	Crystal Ball 155
Echo Boogie	Bumble Bees	1963	Joey 6220
Echo From The Blue	Ivyliers	1957	Donna A-3
Echo In My Heart	Stereos	1962	Columbia 42626
Echo In My Heart	Stevens, Kenny & group	1964	Old Town 1158
Echo Tells Me, The	Splendors	1959	Taurus 101
Echo, The	Epsilons	1969	Stax 0021
Echoes	Interiors	1961	Worthy 1009
Echoes In The Night	Castells	1962	Era 3089
Echoes Keep Calling Me, The	Thrillers, Little Joe & the	1957	Okeh 7094
Echoes Of November	Allen, Rich (with the Ebonistics)	1968	Groovey Grooves 160
Echoes On My Mind	Richards, Jay & group	1959	Hollywood 1100
Ecstasy	Echoes	1960	Columbia 41709
Ecstasy	Marquees	1958	Day-Sel 1001
Ecuador	Knockouts	1965	Tribute 1039
Eda Weda Bug	Coolbreezers	1958	Bale 100/101

SONG	GROUP	YEAR	LABEL
Eddie My Darling	Innocents, Kathy Young & the	1960	Indigo 108/Port 3025 (60)
Eddie My Love	Sweethearts	1965	Kent 428
Edna	Medallions	1955	Dootone 364
Edna	Palms	1957	United 208
Eefenanny	Ardells (Johnny Maestro)	1963	Epic 9621
Eek	Cordials	1961	Stan 111
Eenie Meenie	Salutations, Vito & the	1963	Herald 586
Eenie Meenie Gypsaleenie	Debonaires (Golden World)	NA	Golden World 26
Eenie, Meenie, Minie And Mo	Classics (Brooklyn)	1960, 1963	Dart 1032/Musicnote 1116
Eeny Meeny	Storms, Wally Lee & the	1959	Sundown 123
Eeny-Meeny-Miny-Moe	Three G's	1960	Columbia 41584
Effigy, The	Collegiates	1961	Campus 123
Egyptian Lover	Metros	NA	RCA LP 3776
Eight O'Clock Scene	Casals	1961	Seville 105
Eight Reasons Why (I Love You)	Precisions	1962	Highland 300
Eighteen Year Old Blues	Jags, Steve Carl with the	1958	Meteor 5046
18th Floor Girl	Runaways	NA	Alamo 105
80-96	Dantes	1966	Jamie 1314
Eileen	Altones	1961	Gardena 121
El Dorado	Rivieras	1961	Coed 551
El Merengue	Charters	1962	Tarx 1003
Elaine	Del-Airs	1963	Coral 62370
Elaine	Glenwoods	1960	Jubilee 5402
Elaine	Klixs	1958	Music City 823
Elaine	Rhythmeres	1958	Brunswick 55083
Eleanor	Rhythm Cadets, Little Willie & the	1988	Crystal Ball 152
Elephant Drag	Composers	1963	Ampen 221
Elephant Walk	Chords	1959	Metro 20015
Elephant Walk	Kings (Baltimore)	1958	RCA 7419
Elephant Walk, The	Five Splendors	1960	Stroll 106
Elevator Of Love	Crystalaires	1995	Crystal Ball 163
Elevator Operator	Rays	1958	XYZ 2001
Elevator Operator	Sheppards (Chicago - Abner)	1962	Abner 7006
Eleven Roses (And The Twelfth Is You)	Wrens	1955	Rama 65/110
11th Hour Melody	Balladeers	1990	Clifton 89
Eleventh Hour Melody	Rivieras	1959	Coed 522
Elizabeth	Hollywood Flames, Dave Ford & the	1962	Goldie 1101
Ellen	Merry Men, Robin Hood & his	1962	Mohawk 130
Eloise	Four Dates	1957	Chancellor 1014
Eloise	Hypnotics	1959	Warkee 905
Elvira	Lords	1987	Starlight 52
Elvis Leaves Sorrento	Twisters	1961	Campus 125
Elvis Presley Blues	Bluenotes, Ivan Gregory & the	1956	G&G 110
Elvis Presley's Sergeant	Bobolinks	1958	Key 573
Emanons Rock	Emanons	1960	Delbert 5290
Embarrassing Moments	Meadowlarks, Don Julian & the	1955	Dootone 359
Embraceable You	Heartbreakers (Washington, D.C.)	1952	Roadhouse 1010
Embraceable You	Jumpin' Jacks, Danny Lamego & the	1954	Bruce 115
Embraceable You	Metronomes (Harold Sonny Wright)	1960	Wynne EP/Wynne LP 706 (60)
Embraceable You	Solitaires	1959, 1993	Old Town 1066
Embraceable You	Sophomores, Anthony & the	1963	Grand 163
Emily	Turks	1955, 1960	Money 211/Ball 101
Emily Please	Five Keys	1958	Capitol 4009
Emmitt Lee	Frank, Carol & group	1957	Excello 2118
Emperor Of My Baby's Heart	Harris, Kurt & group	1963	Diamond 158
Empty Bottles	Robins	1953	RCA 5489
Empty Halls	Dodd, Cally & group	1959	Calico 110
Empty Heart	McCallister, Lon & group	1961	Apt 25061
Empty Mailbox, The	Singing Belles	1960	Madison 126
Empty Seat	Passions	1963	ABC 10436
Empty World	Modern Red Caps	1965	Lawn 254
EMT, The	Desires, Rosko & the	1963	Domain 1021
Enchanted	Platters	1959	Mercury 71427
Enchanted Garden	Accents (California)	1963	Mercury 72154
Enchanted Love	Dynamics	1959	Arc 4450

SONG	GROUP	YEAR	LABEL
Enchanted Summer	Bachelor Three	1961	Vi-Way 288
Enchantment	Melody Mates	1961	Nix 100
End Of A Dream	Knight, Sonny & group	1957	Dot 15542
End Of A Story, The	Skyliners	1961	Colpix 607
End Of The Fair, The	Five Crowns	1952	Old Town 778 (unreleased)/ Relic LP 5030
End Of The Story, The	Cardinals	1956	Atlantic 1103
End Of The World	Tokens (Brooklyn)	1969	Warner Bros. 7323
End Of The World For Me, The	Wood, Lori (with the Belmonts)	1962	Amy 842
End Of Time	Escapades, Georgie Salo & the	1960	Hi-Q 5014
End Of Time	Fabulous Egyptians	1965	Cindy 96750
Endless	Honey Bees	1956	Imperial 5400
Endless Love	Capris (Jesse Belvin & studio group)	1959	Impact 34/Tender 518
Endless Love	Chestnuts	1960	Coral 62176
Endless Love	Hollywood Saxons	1959	Tender 518
Endless Night (acappella)	Five Jades (Bronx, N.Y.)	1975	Relic LP 107
Endless Nights	Mar-Vels	1964	IN 102
Endlessly	Four Uniques	1964	USA 753
Endlessly	Reality	1979	U.G.H.A. 13
Enfold Me	Mel-O-Aires, Rudy Jackson & the	1954, 1955	R&B 1310
Erlene	Blue Stars	1977	Arcade 101
Erlene	Devotions	1994	Avenue D 22
Erlene	Utopians, Mike & the	1958	Cee Jay 574 (first pressing)
Errand Boy	Vondells	1964	Marvello 5003
Escortin' or Courtin'	Ravens	1954	Mercury 70240
Especially	Chimes, Tony Allen & the	1956	Specialty 570
Especially For You	Five Whispers	1962	Dolton 69
Espresso	Crystals (Brooklyn)	1961	Regalia 17
Estelle	Belltones (Philadelphia)	1954	Grand 102
Esther	Parisians	1961	Argyle 1006
Eternal Dream	Superiors	1963	Real Fine 837
Eternal Love	Cordials	1962	Reveille 106
Eternal Love	Heralds	1954	Herald 435
Eternal Love	Lampkin, Tommy (with the Kidds)	1955	Imperial 5361
Eternal Love	Markeys	1956	20th Century 1210
Eternal Love	Rivileers	1954	Baton 205
Eternal Love	Romancers	1973	Vintage 1013
Eternal Love	Williams, Mel (with the Montclairs)	1955	Decca 29499
Eternal Love, Eternal Spring	Castells	1962	Era 3098
Eternal Lovers	Diamonds	1958	Mercury 71366
Eternal Triangle	Valiants (New York)	1963	Roulette 4510/Roulette 4551 (64)
Eternally	Chantels	1963	Ludix 101
Eternally	Dells	1962	Argo 5428
Eternally	Laddins	1959	Grey Cliff (unreleased)
Eternally	Swallows (Maryland)	1951	King 4501
Eternally	Twilighters (Bronx, N.Y.)	1956, 1958	Caddy 103/Dot 15526 (56)/ Pla-Bac 1113
Eternally	Wright, Little Cholly & Group	1956	Cholly 7093
Eternally Yours	Barons (New Orleans)	1955	Imperial 5343
Eternally Yours	Dreamers, Joy Anthony & the	1958	Sinclair 1001
Eternity	Chimes, Leigh Bell & the	1961	Rust 5031
Eternity Of Love	Caraman, Art (Turk) & group	1962	Dasa 101
Etta Mae	Sliders, Slick Gipson & the	1956	Specialty 587
Evelyn	Silhouettes, Billy Horton & the	1959	Ace 563/Junior 400 (59)
Even Now	Jumpin' Tones	1989	Unreleased
Even Now	Tennyson, Bill & group	1958	Pet 805
Even Then	Metrotones	1955	Columbia 40486
Even Though	Cupcakes, Cookie & the	1964	Lyric 1016/Jewel 744 (65)
Even Though	Cupcakes, Little Alfred with the	1965	Jewel 744
Even Though You Can't Dance	Raindrops	1963	Jubilee 5455
Evening	Rainbows	1955	Red Robin 134/Pilgrim 703 (56)/ Fire 1012 (60)
Evening Bells	El Domingoes	1958	Kappa Rex 206/Candlelite 418 (74)
Evening Shadows Falling (I Think Of You)	Seniors	1956	Tetra 4446
Evening Star	Premiers, Julie Stevens & the	1961	Dore 603

SONG	GROUP	YEAR	LABEL
Evening Star, The	Jamies	1959	United Artists 193
Ever Lovin' Slick	Whispers	1950	Apollo 1156
Ever Since	Travis, Danny & group	1962	Benn-X 54
Ever Since I Can Remember	Bowties, Cirino & the	1956	Royal Roost 624
Ever Since I Met Lucy	Flamingos	1959	Decca 30880
Ever Since My Baby's Been Gone	Jacks	1955	RPM 433
Ever Since We Met	Belvin, Jesse & group	1958	RCA 7310
Ever Since You Been Gone	Hawks	1956	Modern 990
Ever Since You Kissed Me	Strollers	1963	Jubilee 5449
Evergood	Keynoters	1959	Pepper 896
Evergreen	Bonaires	1960	Shasta 126
Everlasting	Four-Evers	1964	Smash 1921
Everlasting Love	Scale-Tones	1956	Jay-Dee 810
Everlasting Love	Vibrations	1961	Checker (unreleased)
Everlovin'	Chimes, Dave Burgess & the	1959	Challenge 59045
Everlovin' (Baby Mine)	Cousins	1960	Versatile 105
Evermore	Dominoes	1956	Era 1072
Every Beat Of My Heart	Drakes, Little Duck & the	1961	Pee Wee
Every Beat Of My Heart	Laddins	1974	Relic LP 5018
Every Beat Of My Heart	Midnighters, Henry Booth & the	1960	DeLuxe 6190
Every Beat Of My Heart	Pips	1961	Huntom 2510/Vee Jay 386 (61)/ Fury 1050 (61)
Every Beat Of My Heart	Royals	1952	Federal 12064/12064AA
Every Boy In Town	Duchesses	1960	Chief 7023
Every Breath I Take	Pitney, Gene & group	1961	Musicor 1011
Every Day	Challengers III	1962	Tri-Phi 1020
Every Day	Hart, Rocky (with the Mystics)	1959	Cub 9052
Every Day, Every Way	Hollywood Flames	1959	Atco 6155
Every Day My Love Is True	Peacheroos	1954	Excello 2044
Every Day Of The Week	Ardells (Johnny Maestro)	1961	Marco 102
Every Day Of The Week	Students (Ohio)	1958	Note 10012/Argo 5386 (61)/ Checker 902 (61)
Every Day Of The Week (acappella)	Majestics, Little Joe & the	1975	Relic LP 104
Every Dog Has His Day	Five Royales	1955	King 4770
Every Dog-Gone Time	Orioles, Sonny Til & the	1950	Jubilee 5025
Every Heart Is Home At Christmas	Five Keys	1990	Capitol CDP 7-94701-2
Every Little Dream Comes True	Emblems, Eddie Carl & the	1962	Oh My 1000
Every Little Movement	Platters	1962	Mercury 71986
Every Little Thing I Do	Belmonts, Dion & the	1959	Laurie 3035
Every Minute Of The Day	Laurels	1982	Bishop 1016
Every Night	Brooklyn Boys	1956	Ferris 902
Every Night	Drifters (1959-forward)	1972	Bell 1269
Every Night	Essex	1963	Roulette LP 25234
Every Night	Lyrics (San Francisco)	1958	Rhythm 126/127
Every Night	Robins	1957	Whippet 208
Every Night About This Time	Sophomores (Massachusetts)	1956	Dawn 216
Every Night (I Pray)	Chantels	1958	End 1015
Every Night I Pray	Creations	1956	Tip Top 400
Every Now And Then	Sheppards (Chicago - Wes)	1961	Wes 7750/Vee Jay 406 (61)
Every Once In A While	Debonaires (New York)	1959, 1961, 1963	Dore 526/592/702
Every Other Day	Debonaires (New York)	1959	Maske 804
Every Road	Explorers, Dennis & the	1961	Coral 62295
Every Road I Walk Along	Anastasia & group	1962	Stasi 1002
Every Star Was Out That Night	Sharps, T. Phillips & the	1960	Firefly 332
Every Step	Dukays	1963	Vee Jay 491
Every Step Of The Way	McQuinn, Kevin & group	1961	Diamond 101
Every Time	Aquatones	1959	Fargo 1015
Every Time	Emotions	1966	20th Fox 623
Every Time	Pizani, Frank (with the Highlights)	1957	Bally 1040
Every Time I Think Of You	Flamingos	1960	End LP 308
Every Time The Phone Rings	Buddies	1957	Decca 29953
Every Time We Kiss	Donnybrooks	1959	Calico 108
Every Week Every Month Every Year	Sunglows, Sunny & the	1963	Tear Drop 3014/Sunglow 110
Every Word	De Ville Sisters, Rueben Grundy & the	1958	Spry 110
Every Word Of The Song	Fortune, Billy & group	1958	Dice 478

SONG	GROUP	YEAR	LABEL
Every Word Of The Song	Squires, Billy Jones & the	1958	Deck 478
Every Year About This Time	Four Graduates	1978	Crystal Ball 119
Everybody	Islanders, Rick & the	NA	H&G 185
Everybody	Pearlettes	1962	Vee Jay 435
Everybody But Me	Tate, Paul & group	1958	Falcon 1012
Everybody Do The Chicken	Five Jets	1954	DeLuxe 6064
Everybody Had A Dream	Curios, Bucky Brown & the	1960	XYZ 610
Everybody Happy	Titans	1960	Fidelity 3016
Everybody I Know	Sweethearts	1963	Brunswick 55255
Everybody Jump	Cardell, Nick & group	1964	Amcan 405
Everybody Knew	La Rells	1961	Robbee 109
Everybody Knew But Me	Crescents	1957	Joyce 102
Everybody Knew But Me	Empires	1962	Colpix 680
Everybody's Knows	Drew-Vels, Patti Drew & the	1964	Capitol 5145
Everybody Knows	Fabulous Four	1961	Chancellor 1090/1098
Everybody Knows	Four Tops, Delores Carroll & the	1956	Chateau 2002
Everybody Knows	Royaltones, El Pauling & the	1960	Federal 12396
Everybody Knows	Sharell, Jerry & group	1961	Alanna 560
Everybody Knows	Standards	1963	Magna 1315/Glenden 1315 (64)
Everybody Knows	Velvets (Texas)	1959	Plaid 101
Everybody Let's Dance	Denims	1965	Columbia 43367
Everybody Likes To Cha Cha Cha	Olympics	1962	Arvee 5051
Everybody Loves A Lover	Angels (New Jersey)	1962	Caprice 116
Everybody Loves A Lover	Shirelles	1962	Scepter 1243
Everybody Loves Me	Sophomores (Massachusetts)	1957	Dawn 225
Everybody Loves To Rock And Roll	Candletts	1958	Vita 179
Everybody Needs A Friend	Scott, Chyvonne & group	1963	Alto 2010
Everybody Needs Somebody	Lovers, Cliff Butler & the	NA	Frantic 801
Everybody Needs To Know	Senders	1959	Kent 324
Everybody Pony	Continentals, Teddy & the	1961	Richie 1001/Pik 235 (61)
Everybody Rock And Go	Sparks Of Rhythm	1960	Apollo 541
Everybody Seems To Know	Hollywood Saxons	Mid to late 1950s	(Early 1980s on EP; originally unreleased)
Everybody South Street	Four-Evers	1963	Jamie 1247
Everybody South Street	Taffys	1963	Fairmount 610
Everybody Wants My Boyfriend	Bon-Bons	1964	Coral 62435
Everybody's Cryin'	Beaumont, Jimmy & group	1961	May 112
Everybody's Doin' It Now	Mariners	1955	Cadence 1278
Everybody's Doing The Pony	Logics	1960	Everlast 5015
Everybody's Goin' Mad	Shirelles	1965	Scepter 12101
Everybody's Gonna Rock & Roll	Isley Brothers	1958	Gone 5022
Everybody's Got A Girl	Scooters	1958	Era 1065
Everybody's Got A Home	Flamingos	1960	End LP 308
Everybody's Got A Home	Street Dreams	1986	Starlight 38
Everybody's Got A Home But Me	Kraftones	1962	Medieval 206
Everybody's Got A Little Something	Allen, Bob & group	1966	Diamond 197
Everybody's Got A Right	Blenders (Chicago)	1962, 1963	Cortland 103/Witch 114
Everybody's Got Somebody	Skylarks	1962	Everlast 5022
Everybody's Got You	Essex, Anita Humes & the	1967	Roulette 4750
Everybody's Gotta Lose Someday	Del-Cords	1960	Impala 215/Genius 401 (63)
Everybody's Laughing	Untouchables	1960	Madison 139
Everybody's Laughing At Me	Ravons	1962	Yucca 142
Everybody's Movin'	Debonaires (New York)	1964	Dore 712
Everybody's Singing The Blues	Five Dukes Of Rhythm	1954	Rendezvous 812/Fortune 812 (54)
Everybody's Somebody's Fool	Decades	1980	Avenue D 3
Everybody's Somebody's Fool	Heartbeats	1957	Rama 231
Everybody's Somebody's Fool	Hi-Lites (Connecticut)	1962, 1976	Dandee LP 206/Monogram 119
Everybody's Somebody's Fool	Wanderers, Tony Allen & the	1961	Kent 356
Everybody's Talking	Baker, Joan	1964	Diamond 164
Everybody's Trying To Be My Baby	Suedes, Rosie Stevens & the	1960	Spinning 6011
Everybody's Woman	Coasters	1968	Date 1607/1617
Everyday	Secrets	1966	Red Bird 10-076
Everyday	Tren-Dells	1964	Southtown 22001
Everyday Blues	Counts, Bobby Comstock & the	1960	Mohawk 124
Everyday Blues	Williams, Kae & group	1956	Kaiser 385

SONG	GROUP	YEAR	LABEL
Everyday, Everyday	Belles	1962	Choice 29
Everyday Holiday	Saxons	1961	Hareco 102
Everyday Of The Week	Monels	1989	Starlight 66
Everyday's A Holiday	Hollywood Saxons	1961	Hareco 102/Swingin' 631 (61)/ Elf 101 (61)/20th Century 312 (63)
Everyone But You	Skyliners	1962	Cameo 215
Everyone Has Someone	Killers, Hank Blackman & the	1962	Brent 7030
Everyone Knows	Sapphires	1958	RCA 7357
Everyone Should Know	Jayhawks	1957	Aladdin 3393
Everyone Was There	Michels, Ginny & group	1962	Mala 446
Everyone's Laughing	Chips	1980	Clifton 54
Everyone's Laughing	Drifters (Pre-1959)	1954	Atlantic 1070
Everyone's Laughing	Spaniels	1957	Vee Jay 246
Everything	Chantels	1963	Spectorious 150
Everything	Del-Knights	1959	Unart 2008
Everything About You	Voice Masters, Ty Hunter & the	1960	Anna 1114
Everything But You	Ravens	1951	Okeh 6825
Everything Has Its Place	Chancellors	1956	Unique 341
Everything Is Fine	Skyliners	1965	Jubilee 5506
Everything Is Gonna Be All Right	Atlantics	1961	Linda 103
Everything Is Gonna Be All Right	Majestics (Detroit)	1963	Linda 111
Everything Is Gonna Be Alright	Limelites, Shep & the	1963	Hull 753
Everything Is Wrong	Ramblers (Flash)	1956	Flash 101
Everything Plus	Indigos	1958	Cornel 515
Everything That You Said	V-Eights	1961	Vibro 4006
Everything They Said Came True	Orioles, Sonny Til & the	1950	Jubilee 5028
Everything To Me	Teenagers (Billy Lobrano)	1957	Gee 1046
Everything Will Be All Right	Ascots	1956	J&S 1628/1629
Everything Will Be Alright	Martineques	1962	Danceland 779
Everything's All Right	Lamplighters	1956	Federal 12261
Everything's All Right	Rogers, Pauline & group	1956	Flair-X 5001
Everything's Cool	Pork Chops	1956	Herald 493
Everything's Fine	Clark, Jimmy & group	1964	Diamond 157
Everything's Gonna Be All Right	Blue Jeans, Bob B. Soxx & the	1963	Philles LP 4002
Everything's Gonna Be Alright	Cashmeres (Brooklyn)	1960	Lake 703
Everything's Gonna Be Alright	Eldorays	1961	Bud 114
Everything's Gonna Be Alright	Giant, Jimmy & group	1960	Vee Jay 345
Everything's Gonna Be Alright	Thunderbirds, Ron Holden & the	1960	Donna 1328
Everything's That Way	Delchords, David Campanella & the	1959, 1962	Kane 25593
Everytime	Levons	1962	Columbia 42506
Everytime	Meadowlarks, Don Julian & the	NA	Chance
Everytime	Noblemen	NA	Clarity 103
Everytime	Springer, Walter & group	1959	Kaiser 401
Everytime	Stone, Lawrence & group	1957	Dig 130
Everytime	Voice Masters, Ty Hunter & the	1960	Anna 1123
Everytime I Fall In Love	Fallen Angels	1966	Laurie 3343
Everytime I See You	Heartbreakers (Donna)	1963	Donna 1381
Everytime I Think Of You	Tri-Tones	1964	Miss Julie 6501
Everytime It Rains	Skylarks, Chet Barnes & the (Starlarks)	1961	Embassy 201
Everytime You Smile	Argyles	1957	Bally 1030
Everytime (You're Mine)	Page, Ricky & female group	1961	Coin 711/Dot 16261
Everywhere	Continental Gems	1963	Guyden 2091
Everywhere I Go	Impossibles	1960	RMP 501
Evie My Darling	House, Herman & group	NA	Call 106
Evil	Ru-Bee-Els	1962	Flip 359
Evil	Interludes	1960	Valley 107
Evil Eye	Sonics	1959	Nocturne 110/RKO Unique 411 (59)
Evil One	Dundees, Carlyle Dundee & the	1954	Space 201
Evil Ways	Savoys (Combo)	1955	Combo 81
Ev'ry Day	Bell, Johnny & group	1959	Fleetwood 1001
Ev'ry Day	Belltones, Johnny & the	1957	Cecil 5050
Ev'ry Minute Of The Day	Diamonds	1956	Mercury 71021
Ev'ry Night About This Time	Diamonds	1956	Mercury 70889
Ev'ry Now And Then	Thrillers, Little Joe & the	1959	Okeh 7134
Ev'ry Time	Crewe, Bob & group	1960	Warwick 601

SONG	GROUP	YEAR	LABEL
Ev'rybody Needs Love	Olympics	1958	Demon 1512
Exactly Like You	Barons (New York)	1954	Decca 29293
Exactly Like You	Four Riffs, Julie Lang & the	1955	Campus 104
Exactly Like You	Orioles, Sonny Til & the	1948	Jubilee (unreleased)
Excelsior	Adventurers	1959	Jerden 105
Excuse Me	Midnighters, Hank Ballard & the	1962	King 5655
Exit 6	Jaguars	1959	Epic 9325
Exodus	Rand, Johnny & group	1965	Keno 928
Exodus (acappella)	Autumns	1966	Amber 856/Power
Exodus (acappella)	Foretells	1965	Catamount 109
Exodus Song	Duprees	1966	Columbia 43577
Explain It To Me	Shells	1961, 1972	Johnson 099 (unreleased)/107
Express Train	Triumphs, Tico & the	1962	Amy 845
Express Yourself Back Home	Keys, Rudy West & the	1989	Classic Artists 115
Exterminator Man	Star-Tels	NA	Lamarr 1000
Extra, Extra	Elgins (California)	1961	Titan 1724 (first pressing)
Extraordinary Girl	Salutations, Vito & the	1963	Herald 586
Eyeballin'	Kuf-Linx	1958	Challenge 59004
Eyes	Earls	1963	Old Town 1141
Eyes	Sensations, Yvonne Baker & the	1962	Argo 5412
Eyes For You Only	Bees	1974	Firefly 325
Eyes Of An Angel, The	Legends	1957	Melba 109
Eyesight To The Blind	Larks (North Carolina)	1951	Apollo 427

F

SONG	GROUP	YEAR	LABEL
F.B.I. Story	Thunderbirds, Rudy Grayzell & the	1959	Award 130
Fabulous 50's	Klein, Robert & group	1973	Brut 802
Fabulous 50's	KOs, Little Robert & the	NA	
Fabulous Cars And Diamond Rings	Larks (Philadelphia)	1961	Cross Fire 74-49/74-50/ Guyden 2103 (61)
Face In The Crowd	Delconte, David & group	NA	Delcon 1
Face In The Crowd	Monterays (Brooklyn)	1963	Astra 1018/Blast 219
Face Of An Angel, The	Dee, Joey & group	1960	Scepter 1210
Face Of An Angel, The	Five Keys	1957	Capitol 3786
Face Of An Angel, The	Starliters, Joey Dee & the	1960	Scepter 1210
Face The Music	Dell Vikings	1961	ABC 10278
Face To Face	Tiny Tim & group	1959	DeLuxe 6184
Facing This World Without You	Gents	NA	Midnight 102
Fact Of The Matter, The	Hi-Lites, Ronnie & the	1962, 1963	Raven 8000/Win 251
Facts Of Love, The	Fluorescents	1959, 1963	Hanover 4520/Candelite 420 (59)
Faded Letter	Satintones	1961	Motown 1020
Faded Love	Teen Tones	1959	Nu-Clear 1/Wynne 107
Faded Pictures	Citrones, Freddy Powell & the	1962	Sheraton 105
Fading Away	Carousels	1960	G&C 201
Fair Exchange	Orioles, Sonny Til & the	1955	Jubilee 5177
Fair Exchange	Satisfiers	1960	Vegas 626
Fair Weather Friend	Dominoes	1961	Ro-Zan 10001
Fair Weather Lover	Solitaires	1964	MGM 13221
Fairest, The	Hearts, Lee Andrews & the	1954, 1965	Rainbow 259/Lost Nite 104
Fairy Tale	Cinderellas	1965	Mercury 72394
Fairy Tales	Avons	1960, 1977	Hull LP 1000
Fairy Tales	Capri Sisters	1962	Newtown 5002
Fairy Tales	Caronators	1960	Clock 1047
Fairy Tales	Fashions	1962	Elmor 301
Fairy Tales	Rivingtons	1964	Liberty 55671
Fairy Tales	Spaniels	1970	North American 001/Calla 172 (70)
Fairy Tales	Twinkles	1963	Musicor 1031
Faith	Commodores	1957	Challenge 1007
Faith	DiMucci, Dion (with the Del Satins)	1963	Laurie 3153
Faith	Five Royales	1965	Smash 1963
Faith Can Move Mountains	Counts, Freddy Davis & the	1958	Count 405
Faith, Hope And Charity	Spartans	1954	Capri 7201
Faithful And True	Diamonds	1957	Mercury 71060
Faithful To Me	Fabulous Chimes (Arlene Smith)	1964	Invincible Arts 1177
Faithfully	Rendezvous	1962	Reprise 20089

SONG	GROUP	YEAR	LABEL
Faithfully Yours	Imperials, Little Anthony & the	1961	Carlton 566
Fake It	Delshays	1964	Charger 102
Falabalon	Ping Pongs	1962	Marco 107
Faleroo	Rockaways, Ken Darrell & the	1957	Epic 9226
Fall Guy	V.I.P.s	1963	Carmel 44
Fall In Love	Vitones	1989	Relic LP 5079
Fall In Love (acappella)	Vi-Tones	1964	Times Square 105
Fall Is Here	Googles, Barney & the	1960	Shimmy 1055
Fallen Angel	Four Fellows (Brooklyn - Glory)	1956	Glory 238
Fallen Angel	Hurricanes	1957	King 5018
Fallen Out Of Love	Three Chuckles	1956	Vik 0232
Falling	Companions	1958	Dove 240
Falling For You	Caraman, Art (Turk) & group	1962	Dasa 101
Falling For You	Caravelles	1962	Joey 301
Falling For You	Embertones	1962	Bay 203
Falling For You	Valentines	1955	Rama 171
Falling From Paradise	Brown, Bobby & group	1962	Pak 1313
Falling In Love	Five Jades (Bronx, N.Y.)	1984	Clifton 73
Falling In Love	New Emage	1985	Starlight 29
Falling In Love	Omegas	1960	Decca 31138
Falling In Love	Teenchords, Lewis Lymon & the	1957	Fury 1006
Falling In Love Again	Paul, Clarence & group	1959	Roulette 4196
Falling Like The Rain	Tempests	1959	Williamette 103
Falling Rain	Emeralds, Bobby Woods & the	1960	Dot 16053
Falling Star	Premiers (Connecticut)	1961	Rust 5032
Falling Star	Valquins	1959	Gaity 161/162
Falling Star	Vogues	1958	Dot 15859
Falling Stars	Downbeats, O. S. Grant & the	1956	Sarg 197
Falling Teardrops	Angel, Johnny & group	1960	Imperial 5673
Falling Teardrops	Deckers, Jigger & the	NA	GWS 3105
Falling Tears	Five Lords	1960	D.S. 2078
Falling Water	Zebulons	1960	Cub 9069
False Alarm	Blue Stars	1991	Clifton 95
False Alarm	Darts	1981	Kat Family LP JW37356
False Alarm	Honeytones	1955	Wing 90013
False Alarm	Infernos	1981	Clifton 59
False Alarm	Re-Vels	1958	Chess 1708
False Face	Jackals, J. J. Jackson & the	1963	Everest 2012
False Love	Premiers, Julie Stevens & the	1962	Best 1004
False Love	Randolph, Dean & group	1963	Chancellor 1138
False Love	Spaniels	1955, 1956	Vee Jay (unreleased)/178
False Love	Strollers	1955	Chess (unreleased)
Fame And Fortune	Coachmen	1954	X 0044
Family Man	Blue Belles, Patti LaBelle & the	1966	Atlantic 2347
Family Monkey	Rainbows	1963	Dave 909
Family Rules	Famous Flames (with Johnny Spain)	1958	Back Beat 516
Fan Me, Baby	Enchanters (Detroit)	1957	Coral 61832
Fanarri	Allen, Rich (with the Ebonistics)	1968	Groovey Grooves 160
Fancy Talk	Roberts, Dave & group	1958	PL 14
Fanessa	Masquerades	1961	Boyd 1027
Fannie Mae	Del-Reys	1960	Delreco 500
Fannie Mae	Imaginations	1985	Relic LP 5058
Fannie Mae	Mastertones	1959	Band Box 226
Fanny Mae	Four Counts	1962	Fine 2562
Far Away	Dovells	1972	Verve 10701
Far From The Maddening Crowd	Drifters (1959-forward)	1965	Atlantic 2298
Faraway Places	Diante, Denny & group	1964	Holiday 1210
Fare Thee Well	Hollywood Flames	1954	Money 202
Fare Thee Well My Love	Shields	1958	Tender 521/Dot 15940 (58)
Farewell	Astronauts	1960	Trial 3521
Farewell	Belmonts	1962	Sabina 507
Farewell	Five Willows	NA	
Farewell	Laurels, Bobby Relf & the	1955	Flair 1063
Farewell	Voyagers	1960	Titan 1712
Farewell, Farewell	Mellows, Carl Spencer & the	1956	Candlelight 1012

SONG	GROUP	YEAR	LABEL
Farewell To Arms	Turbans (Philadelphia)	1956	Herald (unreleased)
Farewell To You My Love	Mellow Larks	1957	Argo 5285
Farmer's Daughter	Seegrams, Basil Swift & the	1965	Mercury 72386
Fast Way Of Living	Uniques	1965	Paula 219
Fat Girls	Neons	1962	Challenge 9147
Fat Lady	Spidels	1963	Minaret 112
Fat Mama Twist	Shakers	1961	Fee Bee 901
Fat Man	Del Mates, John Steele & the	1965	Wand 194
Fat Mouth	Frazier, Ray (with the Moonrays)	1956	Excel 112
Fat Sally	Nite-Liters	1960	Sudden 101
Fat Sally	Sevilles	1961	JC 120
Fatal Charms Of Love	Four Cheers	1958	End 1034
Fate Of Rock And Roll	Lyrics, Kenneth Churchill & the	1958	Joyce 304
Fate Planned It This Way	Showmen	1962	Minit 632
Fat-Fat-Fat! Mom-Mi O	Chalets	1961	Tru-Lite 1001/Dart 1026 (61)/ Musicnote 1115 (61)
Father Dear	Sensations, Yvonne Baker & the	1963	Argo 5446
Father Sebastian	Ramblers (Almont)	1964	Almont 311
Father Time	Melotones	1962	Lee Tone 700
Father Time	Poni-Tails	1959	ABC 9995
Fathertime	Turks	1958	Keen 4016
Fatso	Chellos	1961	Columbia 42044
Fatty Patty	Ox-Tones	1958	Phonograph 1024
Fatty-Boom Bi Laddy	Tokays	1952	Bonnie 102
Favors	Strollers	1960	Cub 9060
Feast Of The Beast	Lions	1960	Rendezvous 116
Feed Me Baby	Upstarts	1954	Apollo 468
Feel All Right	Chell-Mars	1963	Jamie 1266
Feel Allright	Dardenelles	1953	Entre 102
Feel Good	Miller Sisters	1964	Stardust 3001
Feel In Love For The Very First Time	Nu-Tones	1961	Cha Cha 716
Feel Like A Million	Mystery Men	1963	Pow 1001
Feel Like A Million	Nu Ports, Tyrone & the	1963	Darrow 5-20
Feel Like Balling Some More	Cap-Tans	1974	Roadhouse 1023
Feel Like Lovin'	Sheppards (Chicago - Apex)	1960	Apex 7752
Feel Like Riding On	Bluebirds	1952	Rainbow 199
Feel So Bad	Vibrations	1960	Checker 961
Feel So Bad	Wade, Earl & group	1961	Seville 111
Feel So Fine	Contrails	1967	Millage 104
Feel So Good	Alley Cats	1962	Philles 108
Feel So Good	Five Thrills	1953	Parrot 796
Feelin' No Pain	Del Satins	1963	Columbia 42802
Feelin' Right Saturday Night	Velvetiers	1958	Ric 958
Feeling Alright	Hi-Liters	NA	Charly LP 1115 (Vee Jay unreleased - 1956)
Feeling Blue	Confidentials, Billy Joe & the	1965	BJ 64
Feeling Is Mutual, The	Manhattans	1963	Big Mack 3911
Feeling Is Real	Fingerpoppers, Ronny Williams & the	1960	Ultra Sonic 111
Feeling Is Real, The	Five Royales	1958	King 5131
Feeling Is So Good, The	Clovers	1953	Atlantic 1010
Feeling Kinda Lonely	Velvatones	1957	Meteor 5042
Feeling Low	Orioles, Sonny Til & the	1983	Murray Hill LP M61277
Feeling Of Her Kiss	Inspirations (Sultan)	1959	Sultan 1
Feeling Sad	Sha-Weez	1953	Aladdin (unreleased)
Feels Good	Falcons (Detroit)	1986	Relic LP 8006
Feeny Jones	Singleton, Bebo (with the Notes)	1959	Stentor 101
Felicia	Hi-Fives	1960	Bingo 1006
Felicia	Orbits, Bobby & the	1959	Seeco 6005/Seeco 6067 (61)
Felicia	Trophies	1962	Challenge 9170
Fell In Love With You Baby	Charts	1966	Wand 1112
Fender Bender	Starfires	1959	Apt 25030
Ferny Roast	Duvals (Prelude)	1963	Prelude 110
Festival Of Love	Dukays	1962	Nat 4002/Vee Jay 430 (62)
Fever	Carlo (Carlo Mastrangelo) (with the Tremonts)	1970	Raftis 110
Fever	Embers, Pete Bennett & the	1961	Sunset 1002

SONG	GROUP	YEAR	LABEL
Fever	Knockouts	1961	MGM 13010
Fever	Romans, Little Caesar & the	1961	Del-Fi 4158
Fever	Saints, Dave & the	1963	Band Box 341
Fever Of Love	Bossmen	1964	Busy Bee 1001
Fickle Little Girl	Temptations (Goldisc)	1960	Goldisc 3007
Fidgety	Supremes (Ruby Nash & the Romantics)	1961	Apt 25055
Fifi's Place	Parisians	1961	Felsted 8627
15-40 Special	Blue Notes, Joe Weaver & his	1953	DeLuxe 6006
15th Row Down	Twains, Tommy Sawyer & the	1962	Diamond 112
Fifth St. Blues	Royals	1952	Federal 12088
Fifty Million Heartbeats	Crests	1962	United Artists 474
Fifty Million Women	Carols	1953	Savoy 896
50-50 Love	Ramblers (Baltimore)	1953	Jax 319
Fifty-Five Seconds	Charms, Otis Williams & the	1954	DeLuxe 6050
'59 Volvo	Medallions, Vernon Green & the	1959	Dooto 446
Fight, The	Barons (Demon)	1959	Demon 1520
Fight, The	Friends, Gary Cane & His	1960	Shell 717
Fight's Not Over, The	Charlettes	1963	Angie 1002
Finally	Elgins (California)	1963	Lummtone 112/Lantam 01
Finally	Heartbeats (Three Friends)	1955	Jubilee 5202
Find Another Fool	Marcels	1961	Colpix 606
Find Another Love	Tams	1962	General American 714
Find Another Way	Hollywood Argyles	1963	Felsted 8674
Find Me A Dream	Elder, Nelvin & group	1961	Brent 7027
Find Someone New	Four Winds	1956	Vik 0221
Find Yourself Another Guy	Mann, Billy & group	1956	Dig 111
Find Yourself Another Job	Blenders (Wonder)	1959	Wonder 722
Finders Keepers	Crescendos (Los Angeles)	1956	Atlantic 1109
Finders Keepers	Miller Sisters	1956	Sun 255
Finding A Sweetheart	Elgins (California)	1964	Lummtone 113
Fine As Wine	Crickets, Dean Barlow & the	1953	Jay-Dee 781
Fine As Wine	Five Barons	1985	Krazy Kat LP 797
Fine Brown Frame	Buccaneers	1953	Southern 101/Rainbow 211 (53)
Fine, Fine	Downbeats, Gene Terry & the (with Ronnie Dee)	1959	Savoy 1559
Fine Fine Baby	Laurels, Jake Porter & the	1955	Combo 66
Fine, Fine Baby	Romeos	1957	Fox 845/846/Atco 6107 (57)
Fine, Fine, Fine	Atlantics	1965	Rampart 643
Fine, Fine, Fine	Jaguars	1961	Rendezvous 159/ Rendezvous 216 (63)
Fine Fine Frame	Continentals (Brooklyn)	1956	Whirlin' Disc 101/Port 70018 (59)
Fine, Fine Frame	Grand Central Echoes	1985	Clifton 76
Fine Fine Girl	Falcons (Detroit)	1963	Atlantic 2207
Fine Fine Girl	Moonglows	1954	Chance 1166 (unreleased)
Fine Foxy Frame	Dippers, Georgie Torrence & the	1965	Duo-Disc 117
Fine Girl	Calvaes	1956	Cobra 5003
Fine Little Girl	Arcades (with King Curtis)	1959	Johnson 116/Johnson 320 (62)
Fine Little Girl	Solitaires	1956	Old Town 1019
Fine Little Girl (acappella)	Shells	1966	Candlelite LP 1000
Fine Lookin' Baby	Cadets	1955	Modern 960
Fine Momma's Daughter	Capitols	1962	Portrait 109
Fine One, The	Five Hearts (Los Angeles)	1954	Flair 1026
Fing Fang Foy	Darnell, Larry & group	1957	DeLuxe 6136
Finger Poppin' Time	Midnight Lighters	1972	Polydor 14128
Finger Poppin' Time	Midnighters, Hank Ballard & the	1960	King 5341
Finger Poppin' Woman	Dell Vikings	1957	Fee Bee 227
Finger, The	Sparks	1957	Hull 724
Fingerprints	Mixmasters, Sonny Fulton & the	1959	Sunbeam 125
Fink	Starfires	1965	Triumph 61
Fire	Four Jewels	1963	Start 638 (same # used twice)
Fire	Fulton, Sonny & group	1959	Chelsea 533
Fire	Love-Tones, Gino Parks & the	1962	Tamla 54066
Fire	Minor Chords, Charles Henderson & the	1959	Flick 005
Fire Engine Baby	Jiv-A-Tones	1957	Fox 1/Felsted 8506 (58)
Fire In My Heart	Kings (Baltimore)	1954	Harlem 2322

SONG	GROUP	YEAR	LABEL
Fire In Your Heart	Three Jays, Vera & the	1957	El-Bee 162
Fire Of Romance	Heartspinners	1953	Universal
Fireball Mail	Carnations, Cosmo & the	1961	Tilt 780
Fires Burn No More, The	Chesters	1958	Apollo 521
Fires Burn No More, The	Imperials, Little Anthony & the	1961	Apollo 755
Fireside	Incidentals	1964	Ford 138
Firewater	Premiers (Nu-Phi)	1959	Nu-Phi 429/Nu-Phi 701
Fireworks	Olympics	1963	Tri Disc 106
First Date	Ebon-Knights	1958	Stepheny 1822
First Date	Impalas (Brooklyn)	1959	Hamilton 50026
First Day Of School, The	Ko Kos	1957	Combo 141
First Kiss	El Vireos	1959	Revello 1002
First Kiss	Monterays (Brooklyn)	1964	Dominion 1019
First Love	Ebbtides	1964	Duane 1022
First Love Baby	Emotions, Lena Calhoun & the	1961	Flip 357
First Man To The Moon	Delteens	1958	Vee Jay 303
First Of Summer, The	Orioles, Sonny Til & the	1959	Jubilee 5384
First One, The	Shirelles	1962	Scepter LP 502
First Sign Of Love	Charms, Otis Williams & the	1960	King 5389
First Sign Of Love	Penn Men, Billy Lehman & the	1959	ARP 014
First Signs Of Love, The	Star Steppers	1960	Amy 801
First Star	Love, Frankie	1962	La Rosa 101
First Star	Tabs	1959	Dot 15887
First Taste Of Love, The	Willows, Tony Middleton & the	1957	Eldorado 508
First Teenager, The	Moontars, Don Deal & the	1958	Era 1070
First Time	Genies	1959	Shad 5002
First Time	Madisons, Billy Kidd & the	1961	Madison 153
First Time In My Life, The	Comic Books	1967	Dynamic Sound
First Time Romance	Crystalaires	1990	Crystal Ball 156
First Time, The	Moonglows	1961	Chess 1781
First Time We Met, The	Charms, Otis Williams & the	1954	DeLuxe 6065
Fish And Twist	Flares	NA	London (England) LP 8034
Fish, The	Superbs	1961	Heritage 103
Fisherman	Blenders, Goldie Coates & the	1962	Cortland 102
Fisherman	Trinkets	1963	Cortland 111
Fishing Chant, The	Dell Vikings	1963	ABC 10385
Five Hundred Miles	Endings	1976	Barrier 104
Five Hundred Miles	Tokens (Brooklyn)	NA	RCA LP 2631
Five Hundred Miles To Go	Heartbeats	1957	Gee 1047
Five Hundred Years	Little, Horace & group	1962	Ascot 2102
Five Little Kisses	Chanters (New York)	1958	DeLuxe 6172
Five Little Numbers	Chantones	1958	Carlton 485
5 Minus 3	Chancellors	1966	Fenton 2072
Five Minutes Longer	Lamplighters	1954	Federal 12192
Five Minutes More	Campbell, Jo Ann (with the Dubs)	1962	Rori 711
Five Minutes More	Carlo (Carlo Mastrangelo) (with the Tremonts)	1963	Laurie 3175
Five Minutes More	Covinas	NA	Hilton 3751
Five Minutes More	Four Winds	1957	Decor 175
Five Minutes To Love You	Monorays (with Tony March)	1959	Tammy Records 1005 (first pressing)/ Tammy 1005 (59) (second pressing)/Red Rocket 476 (60)
5, 7 Or 9	Calvanes	1958	Deck 579
535	Dreamers (Philadelphia)	1955	Grand 131
Fixer, The	Van Dykes	1958	Decca 30654
Flame In My Heart	Checkers	1952	King 4558
Flame In My Heart	Lexing, Bobby & group	1961	Good Sound 107
Flame In My Heart	Ware, Curtis (with the Four-Do-Matics)	1961	Kaybee 101
Flame Mambo	Flames	1956	Aladdin 3349
Flame Of Love	Atlantics	1962, 1963	Linda 107/Faro 613
Flame Of Love	Flamingos	1962	End 1121
Flame Of Love	Leggeriors	1963	Goliath 1351
Flame Of Love	Masters, Rick & the	1962	Taba 101/Cameo 226 (62)
Flame Out	La Chords	1962	Gay 629
Flame Remains, The	Steelers	NA	Crash 428

SONG	GROUP	YEAR	LABEL
Flames	Heartspinners, Dino & the	NA	Pyramid 164
Flames	Reminiscents	1962	Marcel 1000
Flames (acappella)	Five Sharks	1964, 1965	Old Timer 604/Siamese 404 (65)
Flames In My Heart	Channels, Earl Lewis & the	1957	Whirlin' Disc 109/Port 70022 (61)
Flaming Love	Gardenias	1956	Federal 12284
Flaming Love	Petty, Daryl & group	1959	Hornet 502
Flamingo	Charades	1964	Skylark 502
Flang Dang Do	Highlighters	1958	New Song 116
Flat Foot Charlie	Desideros	1963	Renee 1040
Flat Tire	Dell Vikings	1958	Mercury 71390
Flavor Craver	Cravers	1958	Chock Full Of Hits 109
Flee The Scene	Superiors	1961	Fal 301
Fleeoowee	Calvanes	NA	Dootone LP 855/
			Collectables LP 5048
Fling	Phaetons	1959	Hi-Q 5012
Flip, Flip	Delicates	1960	United Artists 210
Flip Flip Zoo-Wah	Computones	1978	N/A
Flip Flop	Cheerios, Bobby Long & the	1963	Cub 9120
Flip Flop	Preludes	NA	Imperial
Flip Flop	Teenagers (Billy Lobrano)	1957	Gee 1046
Flip, Flop And Fly	Dukes, Billy Duke & the	1955	Casino 138
Flip Flop And Fly	Goofers	1955	Coral 61383
Flip Skip, The	Miller Sisters	1957	Acme 111/Acme 721 (58)
Flip, The	Royaltones, Ruth McFadden & the	1960	Goldisc 3011
Flip To The Twist	Citrones, Freddy Powell & the	1962	Sheraton 105
Flip Your Daddy	Cocoas	1955	Chesterfield 364
Flippin' Their Top	Egyptians	1962	Danae 1002
Flip-Skip, The	Twin Tones	1958	RCA 7148
Flirting With Florence	Larks	1959	Chess (unreleased)
Flirty Gertie	Jiv-A-Tones	1957	Fox 1/Felsted 8506 (58)
Float, The	Midnighters, Hank Ballard & the	1961	King 5510
Florabelle	Calvanes	1956	Dootone 380
Florence	Paragons	1957, 1984	Winley 215
Florence Don't Leave Me	Paragons	1977	Robin Hood 145
Flossie Mae	Corvets, Arthur & the	1964	NRC 2871
Flossie Mae	Saucers	1964	Kick 100
Flossie Mae	Zeroes	1963	Ty-Tex 105
Flower Blossom	Texas Matadors	NA	IMA 101
Flower Of Love	Crests	1959	Coed 511
Flower Of Love	Dedications	1989	Clifton 86
Flower Of Love	Mid-Knighters	NA	Paragon 814
Flowerpot	Marcels	1962	Colpix 640
Flowers Mr. Florist, Please	Sharp, Bobby & group	1958	Wing 90056
Flowers On The Wall (acappella)	Chessmen	1975	Relic LP 106
Fly Away	Toy Dolls	1962	Era 3093
Fly By Night	Thomases, Varetta & the	1963	Brent 7040
Fly Me To The Moon	Demensions	1963	Coral 62359
Fly Swatter, The	Tokens (Brooklyn)	1962	RCA 8064
Flying Formation With You	Catalinas	1958	Back Beat 513
Flying Twist	Legs, Stick & group	1962	Hard Times 3002
Flying Twist	Stick Legs & The Butchering Persians	NA	Hard Times 3002
Focused On You	Blue Notes, Bernard Williams & the	1964	Harthon 136
Follow Me	Drifters (1959-forward)	1965	Atlantic 2292
Follow Me	Four Bars, Shane Hunter & the	1959	IPS 101
Follow Me	Four Esquires	1956, 1958	Pilgrim 717/Paris 526
Follow Me	Gainors	1958	Red Top 110/Cameo 156 (59)
Follow Me	Tides	1961	Dore 579
Follow The Leader	Masterettes	1958	Le Sage 716
Follow The Rock	Bay Bops	1958	Coral 61975
Follow The Swallow	Charles, Jimmy (with the Reveletts)	1960	Promo 1003
Following You	Farrer, Tony & group	1961	Trans Atlas 001
Fontella	Peacocks, Nunnie Moore & the	1957, 1974	L&M 1002/Firefly 322 (60)
Foo Man Choo	Revels	1959	Norgolde 104
Fool	Cadillacs, Ray Brewster & the	1963	Arctic 101
Fool #2	Darchaes, Nicky Addeo & the	1964	Selsom 104

SONG	GROUP	YEAR	LABEL
Fool, Fool, Fool	Clovers	1951	Atlantic 944
Fool, Fool, Fool	Collegiates, Dicky Lee & the	1958	Sun 297
Fool, Fool, Fool	Flips, Joey & the	1964	Cameo 327
Fool, Fool, Fool	Hi-Tones	1960	King 5414
Fool Fool Fool	Impalas (Brooklyn)	1959	Cub 9022
Fool Heart	Whispers	1954	Gotham 309
Fool In Love	Casuals (Sue Kenny)	1963	Tribute 118
Fool In Love	Veltones	1959	Satellite 100/Mercury 71526 (59)
Fool No More	Four Persuasions	1972	Pay-4-Play 100
Fool That I Am	Pagans, Lynn Dee & the	1960	Music City 835
Fool That I Am	Quin-Tones (Pennsylvania)	NA	Vo 5172
Fool That I Am	Ravens	1947	National 9039
Fool That I Am	Solitaires	1964	MGM 13221
Fool, The	Ford, Ann & group	1959	Apollo 532
Fool, The	Gallahads	1956	Jubilee 5252
Fooled By Her Kisses	Willows	NA	Mercury
Foolin' Me	Cameos, Londie & the	1963	ABC 10508
Foolish	Danleers	1961	Everest 19412
Foolish Dreamer	Fiestas	1963	Old Town 1148
Foolish Dreams	Fi-Tones	1955	Atlas 1050
Foolish Dreams	Porto, Billy & group	1957	Mercury 71205
Foolish Little Butterfly	Four Chaps	1956	Rama 195
Foolish Little Fool	Pedal Pushers, B. Dale & the	NA	Ko Ko 8803
Foolish Little Girl	Shirelles	1963	Scepter 1248
Foolish Little Girl	Six Teens	19??	
Foolish Love	Parker, Bobby & group	1960	Amanda 1001
Foolish Lover	Rounders, Jimmy Tig & the	1963	Spar 779
Foolish Me	Cruisers	1958, 1981	Zebra 119
Foolish Me	Evans, Donna & group	1962	Cheer 1003
Foolish Me	Harptones	1961	Companion 103
Foolish Me	Marigolds, Johnny Bragg & the	1956	Excello 2078
Foolish Me	Moonglows	1955	Chess 1598
Foolish One	Rocketeers	1953	Herald 415
Foolish One	Stompers	1962	Landa 684
Foolish Pride	Downes, Vinnie & group	1959	Transcontinental 1011
Foolish Tears	Gees, Dickie & the	1958	Argo 5288
Foolish Tears	Three G's	1961	Columbia 41955
Foolishly	Three Chuckles	1955	X 0095
Fools Fall In Love	Capris (Mel Williams & the Montclairs)	1955	Rage 101
Fools Fall In Love	Ciufo, Jerry & group	1965	Jeree 65
Fools Fall In Love	Drifters (Pre-1959)	1957	Atlantic 1123
Fools Fall In Love	Four Of A Kind	1957	Melba 117
Fools Fall In Love	Montclairs, Mel Williams & the	1955	Rage 101
Fools Fall In Love	Starfires	1962	Duel 518
Fools Hall Of Fame	Richardson, Rudi & group	1957	Sun 271
Fools Love	Debonairs	1961	B&F 1353
Fool's Paradise	Emotions	1963	Laurie 3167
Fool's Paradise	Goode, Ray & group	1959	Vel-Tone 25
Fool's Prayer	Five Echoes	1955	Vee Jay 156
Fools Rush In	Cadets	1956	Modern 1006
Fools Rush In	Diablos	1984	Fortune LP 8016
Fools Rush In	Metronomes (Harold Sonny Wright)	1960	Wynne LP 706
Fools Rush In	Original Charmers	1972	Blue Sky 102
Fools Rush In	Tom Cats, Tom Riley & the	NA	Time 6603
Fools Rush In	Tune Drops, Malcolm Dodds & the	1957	End 1004
Fools Rush In	Velvet Angels	1975	Relic LP 101
Fools Will Be Fools	Monotones	1959	Argo 5339
Fools Will Be Fools	Tucker, Frankie & group	1958	Decca 30707
Fools Will Take Chances	Nighthawks, Johnny Gosey & the	NA	MOA 1001
Foot Stompin'	Dovells	1962	Parkway LP 7006
Foot Stompin'	Underbeats	1964	Garret 4004
Foot Stomping	Flares	1961	Felsted 8624
Footloose And Fancy-Free	Sliders, Slick Gipson & the	1956	Specialty 587
Footprints In The Sand	Marcels	1962	Colpix 629
Footsteps	Coronets, Sammy Griggs & the	1960	J.O.B. 100

SONG	GROUP	YEAR	LABEL
Footsteps To The Sea	Robin, Ruth & group	1962	Titan 1725
For A Lifetime	Five Pennies	1978	King Tut 176
For A Lifetime	Jaxon Sisters	1957	Big 605
For A Love That Is Mine	Pentagons	1961	Donna 1344
For A Thrill	Spiders	1955	Imperial 5354
For A While	Cardinals	1953	Atlantic (unreleased)
For All We Know	Caslons	1962	Amy 836
For All We Know	Flamingos	1962	End 1116
For All We Know	Orioles, Sonny Til & the	1956	Vee Jay 228
For All We Know	Starlites, Jackie & the	1962	Mascot 128
For All We Know (acappella)	Chessmen	1975	Relic LP 101/Relic LP 106 (75)
For Better Or For Worse	Medallions, Vernon Green & the	1957	Dooto 419
For Bobby	Belmonts, Dion & the	1967	ABC 10896
For Days	Clovers	1968	Josie 992
For Dreams Come True	Swans (St. Louis)	1955	Ballad 1000/1001
For Eternity	Cutouts, Brian Brent & the	1963	Penny 2201
For Eternity	Diaz, Vickie & group	1960	Del-Fi 4149
For Ever And Ever	Duals	1957	Fury 1013
For Everybody There's A Girl	Neville, Aaron & group	1967	Instant 3282
For Her (acappella)	Sessions	1976	Arcade 100
For Just A Little While Tonight	Little Dippers	1964	Dot 16602
For Love	Three Beaux And A Peep	1957	Aladdin 3382
For Lovers	Hi-Lites, Ronnie & the	1982 (1962)	UGHA 16 (previously unreleased - Joy)
For Lovers Only	Crystalaires	1990	Crystal Ball 156
For Lovin' Me	Fleetwoods	1964	Dolton 315
For My Baby	Daylighters	1964	Tip Top 2010
For My Baby	Shakers, Pepper & the	1966	Chetwyd 45002
For My Sake	Girlfriends	1963	Colpix 712
For My Very Own	Cates, Ronnie (with the Travelers)	1962	Terrace 7508
For Old Time's Sake	Diablos, Nolan Strong & the	1959	Fortune 529
For Only A Moment	Gay Notes	1955	Drexel 905
For Only You	Moroccos, Lillian Brooks & the	1956	King 4934
For Pete's Sake	Apollos, Paul Stefen & the	1962	Cite 5006
For Sale	Electrons	1964	Laguna 103
For Sale	Knight, Bob	1961	Laurel 1023
For Sentimental Reasons	Charmers	NA	Angletone/Relic LP 5051 (85)
For Sentimental Reasons	Chocolateers	1974	Owl 334
For Sentimental Reasons	Clovers	1978	
For Sentimental Reasons	Fireflies	1962	Taurus LP 1002
For Sentimental Reasons	Four Lovers	1957	RCA LP 1317
For Sentimental Reasons	Hi-Lites (Connecticut)	1962	Record Fair 501
For Sentimental Reasons	Illusions	1962, 1974	Kape 1001
For Sentimental Reasons	Marvells	1961	Winn 1916
For Sentimental Reasons	Monterays (Brooklyn)	1964	GNP Crescendo 314
For Sentimental Reasons	Original Charmers	1960	Angle Tone 550
For Sentimental Reasons	Rivileers	1955	Baton 207
For Sentimental Reasons	Simms, Lloyd & female group	1961	Atlantic 2078
For Sentimental Reasons	Spaniels	1964	Double L 720
For Sentimental Reasons	Voices Five, Bud Johnson & the	1959	Craft 116
For Sentimental Reasons (acappella)	Velvet Angels	1972	Relic LP 5004
For That Great Day	Visions, Connie McGill & the	1963	Toy 107
For The Birds	Charts	1959	Guyden 2021
For The First Time	Dreamlovers	1960, 1980	Len 1006/Collectables LP 5005/ Relic LP 5066
For The First Time	Dubs	1960	ABC 10150
For The First Time	Platters	1958	Mercury 30075
For The First Time	Twilights	1964, 1967	Harthon 135/Parkway 128
For The Longest Time	Marveleers	1953	Derby 829
For The Love Of Mike	Impalas (Washington, D.C.)	1961	Checker 999
For The Love Of Mike	Threeteens	1958	Rev 3522/Todd 1021 (59)
For The Love Of Money	Dawn	1967	Laurie 3417
For The Love Of Money	Larks (Don Julian)	1964	Arock 1010
For The Love Of You	Larks (North Carolina)	1988	Relic LP 8014
For The Rest Of My Life	Fellows, Eugene Church & the	1958	Class 235

SONG	GROUP	YEAR	LABEL
For The Rest Of My Life	Mastertones, Scotty & Bobo & the	1960	Band Box 238
For The Rest Of My Life	Sunny Boys	1959	Mr. Maestro 805/Take 3 2001
For The Woman I Love	Debonairs	1958	Combo 149
For This I Thank You	Love-Tones, Gino Parks & the	1962	Tamla 54066
For You	Charades	1962	Northridge 1002
For You	Charles, Nick & group	1961	Guyden 2049
For You	Cupids	1962	KC 115/AAnko 1002 (63)
For You	Decoys	1963	Aanko 1005
For You	Four Pips, Pop & the	1959	Mercedes 5001
For You	Pioneers	1961	Golden Crest 565
For You	Ravens	1947	Hub 3030/National 9038
For You And You Alone	Casanovas	1957	Apollo 519
For You, For You	Aquatones	1960	Fargo 1111
For You I Have Eyes	Crickets, Dean Barlow & the	1953	MGM 11507
For You My Darling	Showmen	NA	Unreleased
For You My Love	Limelites, Shep & the	1963	Hull 759
For Your Love	Bell Hops, Buddy White & the	NA	The Wheeler Dealers 501
For Your Love	Chevrons	1961	Cuca 6381
For Your Love	Dedications	1990	Clifton 92
For Your Love	Fideltones	1960	Poop Deck 101
For Your Love	Inconquerables	1964	Flodavieur 803
For Your Love	Lovetones	1974	Barrier 100
For Your Love	Persuasions, Donna & the	1973	Blue Sky 103
For Your Love	Reminiscents	1963	Cleopatra 104
For Your Love	Spindles, Frankie & the	1968	Roc-Ker 13314
For Your Love	Wanderers	1961	Cub 9089
For Your Love (acappella)	Delstars	1964	Mellomood 1001
For Your Precious Love	Five Boroughs	1988	Avenue D 15
For Your Precious Love	Hi-Lites (Connecticut)	1962	Record Fair 501/Julia 1105
For Your Precious Love	Impressions, Jerry Butler & the	1958	Vee Jay 280/Falcon 1013 (58)/ Abner 1013 (58)/Vee Jay 396 (61)
For Your Precious Love	Medallions, Vernon Green & the	1991	Classic Artists 129
For Your Precious Love	Sinclairs	1979	UGHA 7
For Your Precious Love (acappella)	Notations	1975	Relic LP 104
Forbidden City	Blazers, John Buck & His	1958	Cadence 1359
Forbidden Love	Sequins & Rhythm Kings, (Jimmy Burke with the)	1960	Fortune 537
Forbidden Love	Sinceres	1960	Jordan 117
Forecast Of Our Love	Clusters	1959	Epic 9330
Foreign Affair	Manhattan Transfer	1980	Atlantic 3772
Foreign Girl	Gallant Men	1962	Ford 117
Forever	Barons, Marvin Phillips & the	1951	Modern 20-818
Forever	Blen-Dells	1962	Bella 608
Forever	Bleu Lights	1969	Bay Sound
Forever	Cooke, Sam & group	1957	Specialty 619
Forever	Fabulous Four	1962	Chancellor 1102
Forever	Little Dippers	1959	University 210
Forever	Marvelettes	1963	Tamla 54077
Forever	Rivileers	1954	Baton 201
Forever	Seminoles	1962	Mid Town 101
Forever	Teenangels, Buzz Clifford & the	1962	Columbia 42290
Forever	Trilons	1961	Tag 449
Forever	Vidaltones	1961	Josie 900
Forever And A Day	Five Masks	1958	Jan 101
Forever And A Day	Impacs	1963	Arlen 741
Forever (And A Day)	Jack, Johnny & group	1964	Lawn 230
Forever And A Day	Spirals	1961	Smash 1719
Forever And Always	Traditions	1996	Savoy 2004
Forever And Ever	C-Notes, Frankie & the	1961, 1963	Richie 2/Times Square 10 (63)
Forever Darling	Minor Tones, Robbie Meldano & the	1958	Music City 816
Forever Dear	Swingin' Kools, Royal Earls & the	1959	Harlem 103
Forever For You	Sonnets	1964	Guyden 2112
Forever I Vow	Chestnuts	1956	Davis 452
Forever In Love	Dreamaires, L. Flaytus & the	1985	Antrell 101
Forever In Love	Five Blacks	1961	B&C 100

SONG	GROUP	YEAR	LABEL
Forever In Love	Five Blacks, Willis, Herman & the	1958	B&C
Forever Is A Long Long Time	Jaycees, Chuck Jackson & the	1964	Gateway 738
Forever Love	Dynamics, Tony Maresco & the	1961	Herald 569
Forever Mine	Four Kings, Ben & the	1961	Revival 635
Forever Mine	Harptones	1954	Bruce 109
Forever More	Griffins	1956	Wing 90067
Forever More	Magnificent 6	NA	L-Brown 01659
Forever More	Six Teens	19??	
Forever More	Sweet Teens	1956	Flip 311
Forever My Love	Del Capris	1967	Ronjerdon 39/Kama Sutra 235 (67)
Forever My Love	Startones	1956	Rainbow 341
Forever, My Love	Thrashers	1957, 1963	Masons 0-1
Forever On My Mind	Blue Notes	1960	Brooke 116
Forever Yours	Accents, Jackie Allen & the	1955	Accent 1031
Forever Yours	Corduroys	1961	Hale 100
Forever Yours	Monotones	1986	Murray Hill LP 000180
Forever Yours	Pentagons	1961	Sutter 100
Forget	Apollos, Bobby Charles & the	1962	Tide 1084/1085
Forget About Him	Trueleers	1963	Checker 1026
Forget About Me	Barons (New York)	1954	Decca 29293
Forget About Tomorrow	Superlatives	NA	Dynamics 1011
Forget Her	Five G's	1959	Washingtonian (no number)
Forget It	Incognitos	1961	Zee 001
Forget It	Larks (North Carolina)	1954	Lloyds 114
Forget Me	Larks (Don Julian)	1964	Money 106
Forget Me Not	Balladiers	1952	Aladdin 3123
Forget Me Not	Fabulous Dials	1963	Joy 276/DnB 1000
Forget Me Not	Georgettes	1960	Goldisc 3006
Forget The Past	Fabulous Playboys	1960	Daco 1001/Apollo 758 (60)
Forgive And Forget	Orioles, Sonny Til & the	1949	Jubilee 5016
Forgive And Forget	Orioles, Sonny Til & the (with chorus)	1959	Jubilee 6001
Forgive And Forget	Travellers, Frankie Valley & the (featuring Frankie Valli)	1954	Mercury 70381
Forgive Me	Dreamers, Danny & the	1960	Dream 7
Forgive Me	Knights	1965	USA 800
Forgive Me	Stompers	1961	Gone 5120
Forgive Me Darling	Ohio Untouchables	1962	Lu Pine 110/Lu Pine 1010 (62)
Forgive Me Darling	Ran-Dells	1964	Chairman 4403
Forgive Me My Darling	Fascinators (Brooklyn)	1972	Bim Bam Boom 110
Forgive Me, My Darling	Two Jays, Jimmy Allen &	1959	Al-Brite 1200
Forgive Me, My Love	Vibra-Tones, Sabby Lewis & the	1956	ABC 9687
Forgive This Fool	Royals, Fay Simmons & the	1960	Jordan 122
Forgotten	Sheppards (Chicago - Constellation)	1964	Constellation LP 4/ Collectables LP 5078
Forgotten Love	Clippers	1961	Tri 211
Forgotten Spring	Bellatones	1959	Bella 21
Forgotten Spring	Martells	1961	Cessna 477/Bella 45 (61)/ Relic 517 (64)
Forgotten Spring (acappella)	Apparitions	1975	Relic LP 105
Formula Of Love	Imperials, Little Anthony & the	1960	End 1083
Fort Lauderdale	Interludes	1960	Valley 106
Fortunate Fellow	Teenagers, Frankie Lymon & the	1977	Murray Hill LP 000148
Fortune Hunter	Exotics	1962	Coral 62310
Fortune In Love	Flairs, Shirley Gunter & the	1956	Modern 1001
Fortune Teller	Del Rays	NA	R&H 1005
Fortune Teller	King, Freddy & group	NA	Roulette 7003
Fortune Tellers	Banners	1960	MGM 12862
Forty 'Leven Dozen Ways	Cues	1954	Lamp 8007
48 Hours	Pioneers	1961	Golden Crest 565
45 R.P.M.	Mark IV	1958	Cosmic 704
Found A New Baby	Sentimentals	1968	Mint 807
Found Me A Sugar Daddy	Nic Nacs, Mickey Champion & the	1950, 1961	RPM 313/316/342
Fountain Of Love	Darvell, Barry & group	1961	Cub 9088
Fountain Of Love	Metronomes	NA	Milestone
Fountain Of Love	Starlarks	1957	Elm 001/Ember 1013 (57)

SONG	GROUP	YEAR	LABEL
4 X 11 = 44	Toppers, Bobby Mitchell & the	1953, 1973	Imperial 5250
Four Corners, The	Zodiacs, Maurice Williams & the	1968	Veep 1294
442 Glenwood Avenue	Pixies 3	1963	Mercury 72208
Four In Love	Stagg, Tommy & group	1961	Bambi 802
Four Leaf Clover	Ardees, Phil Alan & the	NA	Ko Co Bo 1010
Four Lonely Nights	Cashmeres (Brooklyn)	1960	Lake 703
Four Nights	Originells 4	1965	Apt 25074
Four O'Clock In The Morning	Tornados, Stanley Mitchell & the	1956	Chess 1649
Four Seasons	Coleman, Lenny (with Nino & the Ebbtides)	1965	Laurie 3290
Four Seasons 1960s Medley	Playground	1983	Clifton 72
Four Shy Girls (In Their Itsy Bitsy Teenie Weenie Yellow Polka-Dot Bikinis)	Girlfriends	1960	Pioneer 71833
Four Steps To Love	Safaris	1960	Eldo 101
4000 Miles Away	English, Scott (with the Accents)	1960	Dot 16099
4000 Miles Away	Hi-Lites (Jet)	1961	Jet 502
Four Walls	Five Keys	1957	Capitol 3710
Four Women	Crystals (New York)	1953	DeLuxe 6013
Fourteen And Getting Older	Trains	1964	Swan 4203
Fox	Mystics	1963	Nolta 353
Foxy Devil	Pharaohs, Artie & the	1964	Cuca 1162
Fraidy Cat	Neptunes	1957	Glory 269
Framed	Deltones	1960	20th Century Fox 175
Framed	Robins	1955	Spark 107
Frankenstein	Cadillacs	1959	Unreleased
Frankenstein's Den	Hollywood Flames	1958	Ebb 144
Frankenstein's Party	Swinging Phillies	1958	DeLuxe 6171
Frankie	Jokers, Darlene & the	1960	Danco 115
Frankie And Johnny	New Emage	1987	Starlight 55
Frankie And Johnny	Romans, Little Caesar & the	1961	Del-Fi 4164
Frankie And Johnny	Velaires	1961	Jamie 1198
Frankie, My Eyes Are On You	Culmer, Little Iris (with the Majestics)	1956	Marlin 803
Frankie's Angel	Valiants (KC)	1962	KC 108
Franklin Delano Brown	Four Sportsmen	1960	Sunnybrook 1
Frankochinese Cha Cha Cha	Cupcakes, Shelton Dunaway & the	1961	Khoury's 727
Frannie, Come Back To Me	Buzz-Off Boys Quintet	1978	Clifton 28
Franny Franny	Ebb Tides	1957	Acme 720
Frantic Antic	Jumpin' Jaguars	1956	Decca 29973
Frantic Flip	Quarter Notes	1960	Imperial 5647
Fraternity, U.S.A.	Lady Bugs	1962	Legrand 1033
Freckle Face	Freckles	1961	Madison 158
Freckle Face	Limelites, Shep & the	1959	Apt (unreleased)
Freddie	Boleros, Carmen Taylor & the	1954	Atlantic 1041
Freddie	Daddy-O's	NA	Shell
Freddie, Freddie	Little Miss Peggy & group	1960	Goldband 1109
Free	Modern Red Caps, George Tindley & the	1965	Penntowne 101
Free	Voice Masters, Ty Hunter & the	1960	Anna 1123
Free And Easy	Titans	1957	Specialty 614
Free As A Bird	Chanters (New York)	1967	MGM 13750
Freeze	Heralds	1954	Herald (unreleased)
French Blues	Tune Tones	1961	Zynn 1007
French Riviera	Holidays	1958	Brunswick 55084
Freshman Queen	Catalinas, Billy Huhn & the	1962	Lesley 1923
Friction	Five Stars (Detroit)	1958	Note 10016
Friday Better Come	Daytons	1959	Norgolde 101
Friday Night Go Go	Hi-Lites (Brunswick)	1958	Brunswick 55102
Friday Night With My Baby	Jades	1959	Christy 113
Friday The 13th	Young Champions	1985	Nobletown 822
Fried Chicken	Marylanders	1953	Jubilee 5114
Fried Chicken And Macaroni	Fascinators (Brooklyn)	1959	Capitol 4247
Frieda, Frieda	Valiants (Los Angeles)	1958	Keen 4026/Andex 4026 (59)
Friendly Loans	Marcels	1962	Colpix 651
Friendly Moon	Del Vikings	1958	Mercury LP 30353
Friendly Mr. Hendley	Emeralds, Bobby Woods & the	1960	Dot 16053
Friendly People	Barlow, Dean & group	1961	Warwick 618
Friendly Star	Bell Notes	1960	Madison 141

SONG	GROUP	YEAR	LABEL
Friendly Stranger	Accents (featuring Sandi)	NA	Gazzari 90391
Friends	Classmates	1956	Dot 15504
Friends Call Me A Fool	Prisonaires	1990	Sun LP 1062
Friendship Ring	Royal-Aires	1957	Gallo 108
Frisco Sands	Millionaires, Rocky & the	1963	Orchestra 102
From Me	Plants	1958	J&S 1617/1618
From Me To You	Five Keys	1957	Capitol 3861
From Me To You	Sweethearts, Gene & Wendell with the	1961	Ray Star 777
From My Heart	Overtones	1966	Ajax 174
From Now On	C-Notes	1957	Everlast 5005
From Now On	Fabulous Twilights, Nathaniel Mayer & the	1963	Fortune 567
From Out Of Nowhere	Belvederes	NA	Count
From Out Of This World	Majestics, Kirk Taylor & the	1959	Bandera 2507
From Rags To Riches	Pemberton, Jimmy (with the Chantels)	1959	End 1059/Mark-X 8002 (59)
From Somebody Who Loves You	Embraceables	1959	Sandy 1025
From The Bottom Of My Heart	Clovers	1956	Atlantic 1107
From The Bottom Of My Heart	Diamonds	1959	Mercury 71404
From The Bottom Of My Heart	Fantastic Five Keys	1962	Capitol 4828
From The Bottom Of My Heart	Five Keys	1956	Capitol LP 828/Capitol EP 1-828 (57)
From The Bottom Of My Heart	Harris, Thurston (with the Sharps)	1959	Aladdin 3448
From The Chapel	Velons	1963	Blast 216
From The Love Side	Midnight Lighters	1972	Polydor 14128
From The Vine Came The Grape	Capris (New York)	1962	Mr. Peacock 118/Mr. Peeke 118 (63)
From The Word Go	Teenettes	1959	Brunswick 55125
From This Day Forward	Cute-Teens	1959	Aladdin 3458
From This Day On	Counts	1955	Dot 1243
From This Moment On	Chantels	1966	Unreleased
From Twelve To Seven	Young, Donny & group	1964	Amcan 407
From You, Only You	Dawns	1964	Atco 6296
From Your Heart	Bachelors (National)	1957	National 104
Front Page Blues	Solotones	1955	Excello 2060
Froze	Omegas	1959	Decca 31008
Fugi Womma	Masquins, Tony & the	1961	Ruthie 1000
Fuji Yama Mama	Allen, Anisteen (with the Cues)	1955	Capitol 3048
Fuji-Yama Mama	Antennas	NA	Clay 201
Full Moon Above	Fretts	1959	Blue Moon 414
Full Moon And Empty Arms	Platters	1963	Mercury LP 20759/ Mercury LP 60759 (63)
Full Race Cam	Classics, Jimmy Ringo & the	1959	Dart
Full Racing Cam	Ringo, Eddie & group	1960	Twin Star 1016
Fun	Peels	1966	Karate 522
Fun House	Roosters	1959	Shar-Dee 704
Fun Lovin' Mama	Dukes, Billy Duke & the	1955	Casino 138
Fun We Had, The	Ragamuffins	1964	Tollie 9027
Funky Monkey	Premiers (Odex)	NA	Odex 1711
Funky Soul Train	Midnighters, Hank Ballard & the	1967	King 6131
Funky Wunky Piano	Castanets	1963	TCF 1
Funny	Belvin, Jesse & group	1958	RCA 7387
Funny	Contours	1961	Motown 1012
Funny	Juniors, Danny & the	1962	Swan 4113
Funny	Sonics	1962	Armonia 102
Funny	Zodiacs, Maurice Williams & the	1963	Atlantic 2199
Funny Feelin'	Guys	1965	Original Sound 56
Funny, Funny, Funny	Orbits (Lani Zee)	1961	Seeco 6074
Funny How Love Can Be	Ivy League	1965	Cameo 356
Funny How Time Goes By	Intervals	1962	Class
Funny Little Things We Used To Do, The	Three Chuckles	1955	X 0186/Vik 0186 (56)
Funny Papers	Ramblers (Impact)	1961	Impact 10
Funny Thing	Classics (Lou Christie)	1961	Starr 508/Alcar 207 (63)
Funny Time	Carnations, Cosmo & the	1963	Laurie 3163
Funny What A Little Kiss Can Do	Unforgettables, Little John & the	1962	Alan-K 6901
Funny What A Little Kiss Can Do	Untouchables	1962	Alan K 6901
Funny What True Love Can Do	Charms, Otis Williams & the	1959	DeLuxe 6187
Fussy	Hawks	1958	Del-Fi 4108

SONG	GROUP	YEAR	LABEL
G			
G.I. Blues	Notes	1959	Sarg 177
Gail	Legends	NA	Key 1002
Gambler's Prayer	Four Students, Tommy Brown & the	1956	Groove 0143
Gamblin' Man	Five Stars (Detroit)	1959	Note 10031
Game Of Love	Fidelitones	1958	Aladdin 3442
Game Of Love, The	Browne, Doris (with the Capris)	1953	Gotham 298
Game Of Romance, The	Four Bars	1961	Len 1014
Gang All Knows, The	Carallons, Lonnie & the	1960	Mohawk 113
Gang That Sang Heart Of My Heart, The	Exotics	1961	Coral 62289
Gang's All Back, The	Sherwoods	1961	Johnson 111
Garbage Man	Impossibles, Linda Carr & the	1961	Ray Star 779
Garden In The Rain	Delmar, Eddie (with the Bob Knight Four)	1965	Vegas 628
Garden In The Rain	Four Young Men	1961	Dore 621
Garden Of Eden	Hamilton Sisters	1954	Columbia 40368
Garden Of Eden, The	Counts, Bobby Comstock & the	1961	Festival 25000
Garden Of Love	Safaris	1961	Eldo 113
Garden Of Love	Suddens	1961	Sudden 103
Garlens Mambo	Ze Majestics	1959	Fox 5014
Gasoline	Jaytones	1958	Brunswick 55087
Gates Of Gold	Serenaders (Teen Life)	1958	Teen Life 9
Gaucho Serenade	New Silhouettes	1968	Goodway 101
Gaucho Serenade	Silhouettes	NA	Goodway LP 100
Gaudamaus	Escorts (Brooklyn)	1962	Coral 62317
Gee	Aladdins	1962	Prism 6001
Gee	Crowns, Arthur Lee Maye & the	1957	Dig 146 (unreleased)
Gee	Crows	1953	Rama 5
Gee	Exotics	1963	Springboard 101
Gee	Harmony Grits	1959	End 1063
Gee	Heartspinners, Dino & the	1980	Starlight 9
Gee	Hollywood Flames	1961	Chess 1787
Gee	Jayos, Johnny Otis & the	1957	Dig LP 104
Gee	Marathons	NA	Collectables LP 5081
Gee	Moonglows	1961	Crimson 1003
Gee	Pixies 3	1964	Mercury 72250
Gee	Roomates	1963	Philips 40105
Gee	Sophomores, Anthony & the	1965	ABC 10737
Gee	Tokens (Brooklyn)	NA	RCA LP 3685
Gee Baby	Montells	1963	Golden Crest 585
Gee Baby Gee	Butterflys	1964	Red Bird 10-016
Gee Baby What About You	Limelites, Shep & the	1963	Hull 753
Gee But I Like Your Smile	Storytellers	1990	Classic Artists 118
Gee, But I Miss Him	Brentwoods	1963	Talent 1003
Gee But I Wish	Spi-Dells	1966	Little Town 575
Gee (But I'd Give The World)	Ecstasies	1984	Clifton EP 508
Gee (But I'd Give The World)	Crests	1960	Coed 525
Gee (But I'd Give The World)	Sophomores, Anthony & the	1959	ABC 10073
Gee, But I'd Give The World	Twilighters, Tony & the	NA	Red Top
Gee But I'm Lonesome	Hearts, Lee Andrews & the (as Lee Andrews)	1962	Parkway 860/Parkway 5213/5214 (63)
Gee, But I'm Lonesome	Playgirls	1960	RCA 7719
Gee But I'm Lonesome	Thunderbirds, Ron Holden & the	1960	Donna 1324
Gee But It's Great To Be In Love	Jills, Jacqueline & the	1961	Goldisc 3023
Gee Golly	Coasters	1958	Atco 6111
Gee (How I Love You)	Premiers, John McKinney & the	1958	Mad 1009
Gee How I Wish	Lee, Curtis (with the Halos)	1961	Dunes 2007
Gee! I Love You Baby	Harmonaires, Eddie Elders & the	1957	Vita 176
Gee, I'm In Love	Elchords, Butchie Saunders & the	1957	Good 544/Musictone 1107 (59)
Gee I'm Sorry	Curtin, Lee & group	1961	Gizmo 003
Gee Oh Gee	Echoes	1961	Seg-Way 1002
Gee Oh Gee	Premeers	1962	Herald 577
Gee Oh Gosh	Jarmels	1961	Laurie 3116
Gee, That's Bad	Sparks	1959	Carlton 522
Gee What A Boy	Fantastic Vontastics	1965	Tuff 406
Gee! What A Boy	Joytones	1956	Rama 202
Gee What A Girl	Persians	1962	Gold Eagle 1813

SONG	GROUP	YEAR	LABEL
Gee What A Guy	Carroll, Yvonne & group	1963	Domain 1018
Gee Whittakers	Five Keys	1955	Capitol 3267
Gee Whiz	Casinos	1964	Terry 115
Gee Whiz	Corvairs	1962	Twin 1001
Gee Whiz	Dazzlers	1958	Lee 100
Gee Whiz	Hollywood Saxons	1975	Action Pac 2023 EP
Gee Whiz	Honeycones	1958	Ember 1042
Gee Whiz	Innocents	1961	Indigo 111
Gee Whiz	Street Vocal Band	1980	Starlight 44
Gee Whiz	Blend-Aires	1978	Story Untold 501
Gee-Ver-Men-Nee-Vers	Darts	1958	Dot 15752
Geisha Girl	Pixies	1965	Autumn 12
Genevieve	Dots, Lenny Capello & the	1962	Ric 991
Genevieve	Rockets, Randy & the	1959	Viking 1000
Genevieve Jump, The	Collegiates, Harold Teen & the	1960	Goldisc 3014
Genie	Delatones	1968	N/A
Genie In The Jug	Tornados	1959	Bumble Bee 503
Genie Of The Lamp	Ly-Dells	1961	Master 111
Genie, The	Inspirations (Sultan)	1959	Sultan 1
Genie, The	Sparks	1959	Carlton 522
Gentle Art Of Loving	Symbols	1966	President 102
Gentle As A Teardrop	Stylers	1954	Kicks 2
Gently My Love	Triplets	1960	Dore 574
George Washington	Toppers (ABC)	1956	ABC 9667
(Georgia May Is) Movin'	Diablos (Andre Williams & Gino Parks)	1960	Fortune 851
Georgie Porgie	La Donna, Marie & group	1960	Gateway 730
Geraldine	Chants, Casanova & the	NA	Sapphire 2254
Geraldine	El Venos	1956	Groove 0170
Geraldine	Hamilton, Bob & group	1980	Lu Pine (unreleased)/Relic LP
Geraldine	Jivetones	1958	Rhythm 5000
Geraldine	Lee, Warren & group	1963	Jin 173
Geraldine	Pastel Keys, Ronnie Gill & the	1958	Rip 108/Rio 129/Expiditus 500
Geraldine	Swingtones	1958	Rhythm 1
Gerald's Blues	Spaniels	1953	Vee Jay (unreleased)
Gert's Skirts	Debonaires (New York)	1961	Dore 592/Dore 702 (63)
Get A Baby Like Mine	V-Notes	1958	Volk 102
Get A Hold Of Yourself	Persians	1963	Pageant 601
Get A Hold Of Yourself (acappella)	Timetones	1963	Times Square 34/Relic 526 (65)
Get A Job	Corvairs	1966	Columbia 43861
Get A Job	Mystics	NA	Jenny Lynn 101
Get a Job	Salutations, Vito & the	1964	Regina 1320
Get A Job	Silhouettes	1957	Junior 391/Junior 593 (57)/ Ember 1029 (57)
Get A Job	Tokens (Brooklyn)	1966	B.T. Puppy 525
Get A Load Of Crazy	Gordon, Phil & group	1953	Hub Of Hollywood 1105
Get A Mule	Gay-Tunes	1974	Broadcast 1100
Get Aboard	Valrays	1963	Parkway 880
Get Away Baby	Bees	1954	Imperial 5420
Get Back To You	Sophomores, Anthony & the	1966	ABC 10770
Get Clean	Nite Sounds	1962	Seafair 112
Get Hep Little Girl	Twilights, James Carter & the	1959	Tuxedo 932
Get In And Shut The Door	Gay Charmers	1959	Grand 2001/Swan 4032 (59)
Get It	Parkays	1961	ABC 10242
Get It	Royals (with Alonzo Tucker)	1953	Federal 12133
Get It	Silvertones	1963	Goliath 1355/Valiant 6045 (64)
Get It In A Minute	Saratogas	1961	Imperial 5738
Get It Off Your Mind	Robins	1954	RCA 5564
Get It One More Time	Strangers	1954	King 4745
Get It Together	Upstarts	NA	Top Ten 7000
Get Lost	Du Droppers	1953	RCA 5504
Get Lost	Metallics	1962	Baronet 14
Get Lost Baby	Electras	NA	Dauphin
Get Mad Baby	Gaylords	1952	Savoy 852
Get Me To The Church On Time	Rock-A-Byes, Baby Jane & the	1963	Spokane 4004
Get Off My Back	Melo Gents	1959	Warner Bros. 5056

SONG	GROUP	YEAR	LABEL
Get Off My Feet	Aladdins	1955	Aladdin 3298
Get Off My Train	Love Notes (Massachusetts)	1953	Imperial 5254
Get Off The Fence Hortence	Four Shots	1955	Cadillac 154
Get Offa The Telephone	Caltones	1960	Verve 10205
Get On The Right Track	Elegants, Vito Piccone with the	1963	IPG 1016
Get On Up And Dance The Continental	Earls	1976	Woodbury 1000
Get Out	Blue Notes, Harold Melvin & the	1962	Landa 703
Get Out	Troopers	1957	Lamp 2009
Get Out Of My Life	Adolescents, Little Willie & the	NA	Tener 1009
Get Out Of My Life	Imperials, Little Anthony & the	1965	DCP 1149/Veep 1244 (66)
Get Out Of My Life Woman	Noblemen 4	NA	Recap 291
Get Out Of The House	Legends	1961	Magenta 02
Get Ready Baby	Go Boys, Dudley Callicutt & the	1959	DC 0412
Get Ready, Get Right	Phantones	1958	Code 707
Get Something Out Of It	Five Royales	1956	King 4952
Get That Bread	Thor-Ables	1962	Titanic 1001
Get To School On Time	Quails (Harvey Fuqua)	1961	Harvey 114
Get To Stepping	Fabulous Flames	1961	Bay-Tone 102
Get Together Blues	Little Esther	1951	Savoy 824
Get Up And Do The Wonder	Triumphs, Tico & the	1962	Amy 860
Get Up And Go To School	Zircons	1962	Federal 12478
Get Up Now	Majors (Philadelphia)	1963	Imperial 5968
Get Well Soon	Elegants	1959	Hull 732
Get Wise Baby	Ravens	1949	National 9089
Get With It	Flamingos	1955, 1956	Parrot 811/Checker 837
Get With It	Riley, Pat & group	1957	Tin Pan Alley 175
Get You Daddy's Car Tonight	Petites	1960	Columbia 41662
Get Your Enjoys	Davis, Eunice & Blue Dots	1954	DeLuxe 6068
Get Yourself A Baby	Skyliners	1966	Jubilee 5512
Get Yourself Another Fool	Tempo-Tones	1957	Acme 713
Get Yourself To School	Orientals	1958	Kayo 927
Get Yourself Together	Caesars	NA	Lanie 2001
Gettin' High	Flairs	1954	Flair 1028
Gettin' Mellow	Debuts	NA	Scudder 101
Gettin' Old	Fabulous Five	1959	King 5220
Gettin' Ready For Freddy	Lalarettes, La La & the	1963	Elpeco 2922
Gettin' Ready For Freddy	Shepherd Sisters	1957	Mercury 71244
Getting Dizzy	Elegants	1958	Apt 25005
Getting Even	Jeromes	1961	Dar 300
Getting Married In June	Bel-Larks	1963	Hammer 6313
Getting Nearer	Mello-Queens, John Lester & the	1959	C&M 500
Getting Tired, Tired, Tired	Orioles, Sonny Til & the	1952	Jubilee 5084
Ghaly Ghaly Man, The	Revelers	NA	Masquerade 22458
Ghost Of A Chance	Five Keys	1971 (1951)	Aladdin 3099A (unreleased)
Ghost Of A Chance	Satisfiers	1960	Vegas 626
Ghost Of Mary Meade, The	Ark Angels, Little Caesar & the	1960	Jack Bee 1008
Ghost Of My Baby	Checkers	1953	King 4626
Ghost Town	Blue Counts, Mike Lanzo & the	1964	Debra 2006
Ghoul In School, The	Fortunes	1963	Cub 9123
Ghoul Love	Denny & Lenny (with the Hollywood Ghouls)	1963	Chance (N.Y.) 569
Giddy-Up And Ding-Dong	Continentals (New York - Rama)	1956	Rama 190
Giddyup Horsey (acappella)	Nutmegs	NA	Unreleased
Giddy-Up-A-Ding-Dong	Playmates	1957	Savoy 1523
Gift From Heaven	Peebles, Robert & group	1959	Jax 132
Gift O' Gabbin' Women	Nutmegs	1956	Herald 475
Gift Of Love	Van Dykes	1960	Spring 1113/Donna 1333 (60)
Gift Of Love	Whirlwinds, Kenny Beau & the	1959	PL 1015
Gift Of Love, The	Impressions	1958	Abner 1023
Gift Of Love, The	Impressions, Jerry Butler & the	1963	Vee Jay 574
Gig-A-Lene	Sharps	1958	Jamie 1114
Giggle Goo	Saucers	1964	Lynne 101
Giggles	Lions	1960	Everest 19388/Mark IV 1
Giggles	Tyrones	1958	Decca 30559
Gimme A Little Kiss, Will Ya Huh	Originals	1961	Diamond 102
Gimme, Gimme, Gimme	Carnations	1959	Enrica 1001

SONG	GROUP	YEAR	LABEL
Gimme Gimme Gimme	Dominoes	1954	Jubilee 5163
Gimme, Gimme, Gimme	Queens, Shirley Gunter & the	1955	Flair 1070
Gimme Jimmy	Dimples	1958	Era 1079/Era 3079 (62)
Gimme Some	Harptones	1956	Andrea 100
Gimme What You Got	Eko's, Penny & the	1958	Argo 5295
Gimmie	Rand, Rose Marie & group	1956	Vik 0206
Gimmie Some	Dontells	NA	Ambassador 3346
Gina Baby	Mellow Jacks	1962	Marquee/Ascot 2115 (62)
Ginchy	Cool-Tones	1959	Warwick 505
Ginger	Chase, Eddie & group	1959	Viscount 529
Gingerbread	Four Dates	1958	Chancellor 1021
Gingerbread	Gingersnaps	1958	Kapp 226
Ginny	Duprees	1962	Coed 571
Ginny	Smart Tones	1958	Herald 529
Ginza	Angels, Gabriel & the	1961	Norman 506
Girl	Magistrates	1968	MGM 13946
Girl	Tejuns	NA	100 Proof 144
Girl Around The Corner, The	Hearts, Lee Andrews & the	1957	Grand 156/Main Line 105 (57)/ Argo 1000 (57)/Chess 1675 (57)
Girl Around The Corner, The	Shields	1960	Falcon 100/ Transcontinental 1013 (60)
Girl, Break Away	Pastel Keys, Ronnie King & the	NA	Gateway 786
Girl By My Side, The	Inspirations (Beltone)	1963	Beltone 2037
Girl By The Gate, The	Dynamics	1960	Decca 31129
Girl By The Wayside	Epics	1961	Lynn 510
Girl By The Wayside	Indigos	1961	Image 5001
Girl Don't Cry	Natural Facts	NA	Lucky Lou 813
Girl Down The Street	Dreamers (ABC)	1956	ABC 9746
Girl For Me, The	Desires	1962	Dasa 102
Girl Friend	Paramounts	1960	Carlton 524
Girl From Across The Sea (Angel Marie)	Halos, Ernie & the	1963	Guyden 2085
Girl From The Land Of 1000 Dances	Curtiss, Jimmy (with the Regents)	1965	Laurie 3315
Girl Girl	Delacardos	1962	Shell 311
Girl Girl	Dell Vikings	1958, 1973	Luniverse 114/Bim Bam Boom 115
Girl I Left Behind, The	Beck, Carlton & group	1963	Troy 100
Girl I Left Behind, The	Three Emotions	1959	Fury 1026
Girl I Love, The	Cadillacs	1956	Josie 805
Girl I Love, The	Cues	1956	Capitol 3483
Girl I Love, The	Edsels	1961	Tammy 1023
Girl I Love, The	Glowtones	1957	East West 101/Atlantic 1156 (57)
Girl I Love, The	Lexingtons, Joey & the	1962	Comet 2154
Girl I Love, The	Lyrics (Texas)	1959	Harlem 101/Wildcat 0028 (59)/ Coral 62322 (62)
Girl I Love, The	Retrospect	1980	Clifton 42
Girl I Love, The	Tyson, Roy & group	1963	Double L 733
Girl, I Love You	Temptones (Daryl Hall)	1966	Arctic 130
Girl I Met Last Night, The	Dynamics	1959	Dynamic Sound 504
Girl I Used To Know, The	Belltones, J. Brothers with the	1958	Mermaid 3360
Girl I Walk To School, The	Dee, Joey & group	1958	Little 813/814/Bonus 7009
Girl I Wanna Bring Home, The	Four-Evers	1966	Columbia 43886
Girl I'm Searching For, The	Dynatones	1959	Bomarc 303
Girl In Chinatown, The	Esquirers	1963	Internationale 263
Girl In My Dreams	Capris (New York)	1961	Old Town 1107
Girl In My Dreams	Cliques	1956	Modern 987
Girl In My Dreams, The	Four Lovers	1956	RCA 6518
Girl In My Dreams, The	Statics	1958	Event 4279
Girl In My Dreams, The	Topics (Frankie Valli & the Four Seasons)	1962	Perri 1007
Girl In My Heart	Del-Rays, Dave T. & the	1959	Carousel 213
Girl In My Heart	Kac-Ties	1963	Kape 501
Girl In My Heart, The	Tamblyn, Larry (with the Standells)	1964	Linda 112
Girl In Red	Vows	1963	Ran-Dee 112
Girl In The Bikini	Travelers	1959	MGM 928
Girl In The Candy Store	Reflections	1965	Golden World 29
Girl In The Chapel	Keynotes	NA	Apollo LP 1000/Relic LP 5072 (1000)
Girl In The Drugstore	Sevilles, Bobby Mathis & the	1960	Sioux 51860

SONG	GROUP	YEAR	LABEL
Girl In The White Convertible	Randolph, Dean & group	1963	Chancellor 1138
Girl In Trouble	Fawns	1965	Tec 3015
Girl In Zanzibar	Rituals	1959	Arwin 120
Girl Next Door, The	Channels, Earl Lewis & the	1959	Fire 1001
Girl Next Door, The	Citations	1963	Vangee 301/Fraternity 910 (63)/ Fraternity 992 (67)
Girl Next Door, The	Holidays, Dick Holler & the	1961	Herald 566
Girl Of Mine	El Capris	1958	Hi-Q 5006
Girl Of Mine	Rockin' Chairs, Lenny Dean & the	1959	Recorte 412
Girl Of Mine	Sedates	1962	Trans Atlas 692
Girl Of Mine	Solitaires	1955	Old Town 1010
Girl Of Mine	Vocal Lords	1959	Able (no #)/Taurus (no #)
Girl Of My Best Friend	Starfires, Ral Donner & the	1961	Gone 5102
Girl Of My Dreams	Darrow, Jay & group	1961	Keen 82124
Girl Of My Dreams	Falcons (Detroit)	1985	Relic LP 8005
Girl Of My Dreams	Five Thrills	1981	Parrot 803
Girl Of My Dreams	Granahan, Gerry & group	1958	Sunbeam 102
Girl Of My Dreams	Innocents	1961	Indigo LP 503
Girl Of My Dreams	Jaguars	1960	R-Dell 117
Girl Of My Dreams	Majestics (Detroit)	1965, 1991	Linda 121
Girl Of My Dreams	Playboys	1962	Cotton 1008
Girl Of My Dreams	Synthetics	NA	Armour 5577
Girl Of My Dreams, The	Don Juans	1959	Onezy 101
Girl Of My Heart	Gladiators	1957	Dig 135
Girl That I Love	Academics	1958	Ancho 104 (unreleased)
Girl That I Love, The	Matthews, Dino & group	1962	Dot 16365
Girl That I Marry, The	Starlings	NA	Unreleased
Girl, That's An Awful Thing To Say	Neptunes	1963	Gem 100
Girl, The	Hound Dogs	1964	Dee Dee 773
Girl With The Bells, The	Hi-Lites (Mercury)	1956	Mercury 70987
Girl With The Story In Her Eyes	Safaris	1960	Eldo 105
Girl With The Wind In Her Hair, The	Corvairs	1963	Leopard 5005
Girl With The Wind In Her Hair, The	Jive Five	1962	Beltone 3002
Girl You Better Stop It	Five Keys	1960	King LP 692
Girl You Do Something	Fourmost	1966	Red Bird 10-071/D.W. 105
Girl, You Do Something To Me	Fourmosts, Bobby Moore & the	1966	D.W. 106/Redbird 10071
Girl, You're My Kind Of People	Olympics	1969	Warner Bros. 7369
Girlfriend	Five Scalders	1956	Drummond 3001
Girlfriend (Please Be My)	J's, Jimmy J. & the	1961	Salco 647
Girlie Girlie Girlie	Stylers	1958	Golden Crest 1291
Girlie That I Love	Cellos	1957	Apollo 516
Girls	Carians	1961	Magenta 04
Girls	Hi-Tones	1961	Seg-Way 105
Girls	Squires (Boss)	1964	Boss 2120
Girl's A Devil, The	Dukays	1961	Nat 4001
Girls Back Home, The	Four Speeds	1954	DeLuxe 6070
Girls, Girls, Girls	Coasters	1961	Atco 6204
Girls, Girls, Girls	Fourmost	1966	Capitol 5591
Girls Girls Girls	Targets	1961	King 5538
Girls Go For Guys	Sessions	1964	Guyden 2105
Girls Grow Up Faster Than Boys	Cookies	1963	Dimension 1020
Girls I Know	Salutations, Vito & the	1964	Regina 1320
Girls Were Made For Boys	Chord-A-Roys, Bobby Roy & the	1960	Roys 5001/JDS 5001 (60)
Git Up Paint	Four Sportsmen	1961	Sunnybrook 4
Giuseppe Mandolino	Gadabouts	1954	Mercury 70495
Give A Hug To Me	Sheppards (Chicago - Pam)	1961, 1964	Pam 1001/Constellation 123
Give A Little Bit	Echoes, Tommy Vann & the	1966	Academy 118
Give A Little Try	Scarfs	NA	Arc 7452
Give All Your Love To Me	Fireflies	1960	Canadian American 117
Give Her Back	Casher, Billy & group	1961	Epic 9478
Give In	Acquinets (Carl Green's)	1961	Lilly 5008
Give In	Five Jets	1954	DeLuxe 6058
Give It A Chance To Grow	Toppiks	NA	Larsam
Give It Up	Deb-Tones	1958	RCA 7384
Give It Up	Hawks	1954	Imperial 5306

SONG	GROUP	YEAR	LABEL
Give It Up	Midnighters	1955	Federal 12230
Give It Up	Royals	1953	Federal 12177
Give Me	Lamplighters	1953	Federal 12152
Give Me A Chance	Chanells	1963	Times Square 24
Give Me A Chance	Epiks	1965	Process 146
Give Me A Chance	Gleams	1960	J-V 101
Give Me A Chance	Montclairs	1956	Premium 404
Give Me A Chance	Night Owls, Tony Allen & the	1960	Crown LP 5231
Give Me A Cigarette	Majestics (Florida)	1962	Chex 1000
Give Me A Girl	Randolph, Lil & group	1958	Chock Full Of Hits 103
Give Me A Girl	Serenaders (New Jersey)	1957	MGM 12666
Give Me A Kiss	Hornets	1964	V.I.P. 25004
Give Me A Kiss	Starlites (New York - Peak)	1957	Peak 5000
(Give Me) A Little Something	Cardinals	1951	Atlantic (unreleased)
Give Me A Second Chance	Revelers	NA	Masquerade 22458
Give Me All Your Love	Thrillers, Little Joe & the	1959	Okeh 7127
Give Me Another Chance	Cardinals	1951	Atlantic (unreleased)
Give Me Another Chance	Sheiks	1955	Ef-N-De 1000
Give Me Back My Broken Heart	Four Fellows (Brooklyn - Derby)	1957	Glory 250
Give Me Back My Heart	Hollywood Flames	1958	Ebb 131
Give Me Back My Ring	Fabulons	1960	Ember 1069
Give Me Back Your Love	Marcels	1963	Colpix 687
Give Me Courage	Carlton, Chick & group	1962	Imperial 5873
Give Me Love	Belvin, Jesse & group	1959	RCA 7596
Give Me Love	Cyclones	1961	Festival 25003
Give Me Love	Knights, Eddie Shaw & the	NA	Rand 2
Give Me Love	Originals, Rosie & the	1960	Highland 1011
Give Me Love	Paragons	1957	Winley 223
Give Me One More Chance	Expressions, Johnny & the	1966	Josie 959
Give Me One More Chance	Five Royales	1951	Apollo 434
Give Me One More Chance	Four Imperials	1958	Fox 102
Give Me One More Chance	Rev-Lons	1962	Garpax 44168
Give Me One More Chance	Royalls	1952	Apollo 434
Give Me One More Chance	Sheiks	1975	Monogram 109
Give Me One More Chance	Solitaires	1956	Old Town 1032
Give Me Some Consideration	Du Droppers	1955	Groove 0104
Give Me Some Old Fashioned Love	Miller Sisters	1960	Miller 1141
Give Me The Power	Five Chums	1958	Excello 2123
Give Me The Right	Medallions	1960	Dooto 456 EP
Give Me The Right	Reed, Lula (with the Teeners)	1958	Argo 5298
Give Me Time	Dusters	1956	Arc 3000
Give Me Time	Earls	1978	
Give Me Time	Parakeets	1954, 1973	Gem 218
Give Me Tomorrow	Escorts (Brooklyn)	1963	Coral 62385
Give Me You	Balladeers	1992	Clifton 96
Give Me You	Dominoes	1955	King 1502
Give Me Your Hand	Mel-O-Aires, Rudy Jackson & the	1957	Imperial 5425
Give Me Your Hand	Roberts, Allen & group	1959	Knight 2009
Give Me Your Heart	Madison Brothers	1961	Sure 1002
Give Me Your Heart	Misfits	1961	Hush 105
Give Me Your Heart	Performers	1956	All Star 714/Tip Top 402 (57)
Give Me Your Heart	Termites	1964	Bee 1825
Give Me Your Love	Admirals	1955	King 4782
Give Me Your Love	Bonnevilles	1959	Capri 102
Give Me Your Love	Buddies	1959	Okeh 7123
Give Me Your Love	Catalinas	1958, 1973	Little 811/812/Jayne 502/813
Give Me Your Love	Chandeliers	1962	Sue 761
Give Me Your Love	Columbus Pharaohs	1957	Esta 290/Ransom 101 (58)/ Paradise 109 (59)/Nanc 1120 (59)
Give Me Your Love	Cool Cats, Robin & the	NA	Pussy Cat 501
Give Me Your Love	Egyptian Kings	1961	Nanc 1120
Give Me Your Love	Fascinations, Jordan & the	1961	Carol 4116
Give Me Your Love	Four Pharaohs	1958	Ransom 101/Paradise 109 (58)
Give Me Your Love	Johnson, Delores & female group	1960	Bobbin 132
Give Me Your Love	Patterns	1980	Clifton 55

SONG	GROUP	YEAR	LABEL
Give Me Your Love	Satisfactions	1964	Smash
Give Me Your Number	King Bees	1957	Flip 323
Give My Love A Chance	Deltas, Jim Waller & the	1964	Cambridge 124/125
Give Thanks	Platters	1953, 1956	Federal 12153/12271
Give Up	Indelgents	NA	Jenges
Give Us Your Blessings	White, Ruth & group	1963	Candi 1029
Give Your Love To Me	Devilles	1961	Acclaim 1002
Give Your Love To Me	Honey Bees	1964	Bee 1101
Give Your Love To Me	Three Playmates	1958	Savoy 1537
Givin' Up Love	Norman, Zack & group	1957	Poplar 111
Givin' Up On Love	Fabulous Fanatics	1961	T-Bird 201
Giving My Love To You	Restless Hearts, Fred Parris & the	1966	Green Sea 106
Glad Glad Glad	Four Bits	1958	Coin 1501
Glad To Be Back	Chantels	1961	Carlton 555
Glad To Be Here	Hearts, Lee Andrews & the	1958	United Artists 136
Gladiator, The	Ascots	1963	Dual-Tone 1120
Gladly	Honeydreamers, Kirk Stuart & the	1958	Josie 832
Glamour Girl	Lake, Tony & group	1959	Herald 543
Glass Heart	Gadabouts	1955	Wing 90008
Gleam In Your Eyes, The	Channels, Earl Lewis & the	1956	Whirlin' Disc 102/Port 70017 (60)
Gleep, The	Gleepers, Coke Willis & the	NA	Daco 101
Glenda	Pagents	1964	Era 3124
Glendora	Young, Billy & group	1963	Original Sound 29
Glitter In Your Eyes	Sheppards (Chicago - Wes)	1961	Wes 7750/Vee Jay 406 (61)/ Sharp 6039
Gloria	Blue Knights, Steve Colt & the	1962	Fleetwood 4550
Gloria	Cadillacs	1954, 1964	Josie 765/Lana 119
Gloria	Channels, Earl Lewis & the	1971 (1956)	Channel 1000
Gloria	Chapelaires	1961	Hac 102
Gloria	Chariots	1959	Time 1006/Brent
Gloria	Clark, Dee (with the Kool Gents)	1957	Falcon 1002/Vee Jay 355 (60)
Gloria	Clefftones	1955	Old Town/Murray Hill LP 000083
Gloria	Crowns, Arthur Lee Maye & the	1956	Specialty 573
Gloria	Darchaes, Nicky Addeo & the	1963	Savoy 200/Earls 1533
Gloria	Del-Lourds	1963	Solar 1003
Gloria	DiMucci, Dion	1969	Warner Bros.
Gloria	Escorts (Brooklyn)	1962	Coral 62302
Gloria	Five Chances	1956	States 156
Gloria	Five Thrills	1954	Parrot 800
Gloria	Four Gabriels	1948	World 2505
Gloria	Good Guys, Doug Robertson & the	1965	Jerden 767
Gloria	Love Notes (Wilshire)	1964	Wilshire 203
Gloria	Newports	1981	Crystal Ball 143
Gloria	Parrish, Troy (with the Metallics)	1962	Baronet 10
Gloria	Passions	1960	Audicon 106
Gloria	Rubber Biscuits	1986	Starlight 37
Gloria	Salutations, Vito & the	1962	Rayna 5009/Red Boy 5009 (66)
Gloria	Sultans	1965	Ascot 2228
Gloria	Ubans	1964	Radiant 102
Gloria	Vandells, Johnny Greco & the	1963	Far-Mel 1
Gloria	Wallace, Jerry & group	1956	Mercury 70812
Gloria (acappella)	Five Sharks	1964, 1965	Old Timer 604/Siamese 404 (65)
Gloria (acappella)	Lanterns	1973	Baron 110
Gloria (acappella)	Savoys (New Jersey)	1965	Catamount 105
Gloria (acappella)	Youngones	1962	Times Square 28/Relic 540 (65)
Gloria My Darling	Hi-Lites (Connecticut)	1962	Julia 1105
Gloria, My Darling	New Yorkers 5	1955	Danice 801
Glory Be	Belltones, Ronnie Baker & the	1963	Jell 200
Glory Of Love	Angels	1956	Gee 1024
Glory Of Love	Hollywood Four Flames	1952	Recorded In Hollywood 165 (second pressing)
Glory Of Love	Platters	1955	Federal LP 395-549/King LP 549 (56)/ Mercury LP 20146 (56)
Glory Of Love	Roomates	1961	Valmor 008
Glory Of Love	Street-Tones, Patty & the	1981	Clifton 63

SONG	GROUP	YEAR	LABEL
Glory Of Love	Velvetones	1957	Aladdin 3372/Imperial 5878 (62)
Glory Of Love, The	Cleftones	1961	Gee LP 705
Glory Of Love, The	Cytations, Chris & the	1963	Catamount 100
Glory Of Love, The	Five Keys	1951, 1971	Aladdin 3099
Glory Of Love, The	Imperials	1958	Liberty 55119
Glory Of Love, The	Sharks	1976	Broadcast 1132
Glory Of Love, The	Skylarks	1951	Decca 48241
Glory Of Love, The	Velvetones	1964	Imperial 66020
Glow	Supremes (Ohio)	NA	Grog 500
Glow Of Love	Moonlighters	1958	Tara 100/Josie 843 (58)
Go Ahead	Contenders	1964	Chattahoochee 644
Go Ahead	Miranda, Billy & group	1960	Checker 957
Go And Get Some More	Hollywood Flames	1954	Swing Time 346
Go And Get Your Heart Broken	Imperials, Little Anthony & the	1962	Newtime 505
Go Ask Your Mama	Jades, Jerry Coulston & the	1959, 1960	Christy 119/131
Go Away	Bluenotes, Harold Melvin & the	1966	Arctic 135
Go Away	Travelers	1953	Okeh 6959
Go Away And Find Yourself	Shirelles, Shirley & the	1969	Bell 815
Go Away Baby	Baby Dolls	1961	Maske 103
Go Away (Far Away)	Dippers, Georgie Torrence & the	1960	King 5376
Go Away Little Girl-Young Girl	Tokens (Brooklyn)	1969	Warner Bros. 7280
Go Away With Me	Legends	1962	Caldwell 410
Go Back	Du Droppers	1953	Red Robin 116
Go Back Baby	Convincers	1962	Movin' 100
Go Back Where You Came From	Summits	1961	Times Square 422
Go Bohemian	Scott, Neil (with the Concords)	1960	Clown 3011
Go Boom Boom	Gadabouts	1955	Mercury 70581
Go, Charley, Go	Davi (with the Spidels)	1962	Stark 110
Go Chattanooga	Starfires	1962	Chip 1010
Go Go Baby	Cardinals	1962	Cha Cha 741
Go, Go Daddy Go	Stylists (Maryland)	1955	Crown 145
Go, Go, Go Right Into Town	Berry Kids	1956	MGM 12379
Go Go With Ringo	Whippets	1964	Josie 921
Go Little Go Cart	Four Teens	1958	Challenge 59021
Go! Little Susie	Four Eldorados	1958	Academy 8138
Go On	Fabulous Dudes	1989	Presence 4502
Go On And Cry, Cry	Zircons	1967	Heigh Ho 645/646
Go On And Have Yourself A Ball	Mar-Vells	1963	Butane 778
Go On Baby	Gaylords	1952	Savoy 852
Go On, Girl	Cheques	1969	Sur-Speed 214
Go On, Go On	Jokers, Jivin' Gene & the	1960	Mercury 71561
Go On (This Is Goodbye)	Blue Belles, Patti LaBelle & the	1962	Newtown 5007
Go On To School	Three Friends	1961	Imperial 5773
Go Out And Buy Yourself A Hat	Huskies	1958	Imperial 5544
Go Out And Play	Angels (New Jersey)	1967	RCA 9246
Go Right Ahead	Hume, Don & group	1963	Felsted 8679
Go To School	Five Reasons	1958	Cub 9006
Go To Sleep My Little Girl	Newports	1977	Crystal Ball 108
Go Way	Majors (Philadelphia)	1954	Original 1003
Go 'Way And Leave Me	Dahlias	1957	Big H 612
Go Where Baby Lives	Strollers	1957	States 163
Go With Me	Majors (Felsted)	1965	Felsted 8707
Go! Yes Go!	McPhatter, Clyde (with the Cookies & the Cues)	1960	Atlantic 2082
God Bless The Child	Dells	1962	Argo 5415
God Bless The Child	Sensation-Ivies	1961	Willow 23003
God Bless This Moment	Ragmops, Little B. Cook & the	1961	CBM 314
God Bless You	Five Crowns	1956	Gee 1001
God Gave Me You	Flairs, Richard Berry & the	1955	Flair 1068
God Gave Me You	Williams, Mel (with the Montclairs)	1955	Decca 29554
God Gave Me You	Wonders, Tony Allen & the	1959	Jamie 1143
God Loves You, Child	Blue Dots	1954	DeLuxe 6061
God Loves You Child	Constellations	1956	Groove 0140
God Made You Mine	Kings (Baltimore)	1956	Gotham 316
God Must Have Sent You To Me	Lyrics, Ike Perry & the	1979	King Tut 181

SONG	GROUP	YEAR	LABEL
God Only Knows	Capris (Philadelphia)	1954	Gotham 7304/20th Century 7304 (57)
God Only Knows	Crystals (New York)	1955	DeLuxe 6077
Goddess	Arc-Angels	1961	Lan-Cet 142
Goddess Of Angels	Devilles	1960	Talent 103
Goddess Of Angels	Falcons (Detroit)	1959	Flick 001/Unart 2013 (59)/United Artists 2013X (59)/United Artists 420 (62)
Goddess Of Love	Enchanters (Epsom)	1962	Epsom 103
Goddess Of Love	Five Keys	1973	Landmark 101
Goddess Of Love	Lee (with the Regents)	1961	Scepter 1222
Goddess Of Love	Mareno, Lee (with the Regents)	1961	New Art 103/Scepter 1222 (61)
Goddess Of Love	Nutones	1955	Hollywood Star 797
God's Christmas	Demensions	1960	Mohawk 121
Go-Go	Five Discs	1961	Yale 240
Goin' Cruisin'	Infernos	1963	Hawk 101
Goin' Down To Birdland	Moniques	1962	Benn-X 55
Goin' Downtown	Five Keys	1971 (1952)	Aladdin 3119
Goin', Goin', Gone	Broadways	1966	MGM 13486
Goin', Goin', Gone	Jewels (Los Angeles)	1956	Imperial 5387
Goin' Home	Satelites, Baby Boy Jennings & the	1960	Savoy 1589
Goin' Home To Stay	Hearts (Bronx, N.Y.)	1956	Baton 222
Goin' Out Of My Head	Imperials, Little Anthony & the	1964	DCP 1119/Veep 1241 (66)
Goin' Round In Circles	Toppers, Bobby Mitchell & the	1956	Imperial 5392
Goin' Steady	Griffins, Jean Simms & the	1954	Dot
Goin' Steady	Groovers, Joe Dodo & the	1958	RCA 7207
Goin' To A Party	Internationals	1958	ABC 9964
Goin' To A Party	O'Henry, Lenny (with the Four Seasons)	1961	ABC 10272
Goin' Uptown	Earls	1976	Columbia 10225
Going Away	Manderins	1960	Band Box 236
Going Back Home	Turks	1960	Ball 101
Going Back To My Hometown	Whalers, Hal Paige & the	1959	Fury 1024
Going Back To The Village Of Love	Fabulous Twilights, Nathaniel Mayer & the	1963	Fortune 557
Going Down To Tia Juana	Don Juans, Andre Williams & the	1956	Fortune 824
Going Home	Ravens	1954	Mercury 70307
Going My Way	Five C's	1981	P-Vine Special LP 9036
Going Out With The Tide	Jokers, Jivin' Gene & the	1959	Jin 109/Jin 7331
Going Places	Zircons	1963	Bagdad 1007
Going Steady	Debutantes	1958	Kayo 928
Going Steady	Newtones	1959	Baton 260
Going Steady Anniversary	Stylers	1963	Gordy 7018
Going To A Party	Whipoorwills	1961	Josie 892
Going To The City	Sevilles, Bobby Mathis & the	1960	Sioux 51860
Going To The Hop	Satintones	1960	Tamla 54026
Going To The Moon	Quills	1959	Casino 106
Going To The River	Jaye Sisters	1958	Atlantic 1171
Gold	Four Mints	1957	Decca 30465
Gold Will Never Do	Emeralds, Luther Bond & the	1959	Showboat 1501
Golden Angel	Montclairs	1957	Hi-Q 5001
Golden Apple	Chanters (California)	1955	Kem 2740
Golden Dreams	Neons	1960, 1974	Gone 5090/Vintage 1016
Golden Earrings	Five Satins	1961	Cub 9090
Golden Girl	Marbles	1954	Lucky 002
Golden Rings	Turbans (Philadelphia)	1961	Parkway 820
Golden Rule Of Love	Escos	1961	Federal 12430
Golden Sunset	Wildwoods	1961	May 106
Golden Teardrops	Flamingos	1953	Chance 1145/Vee Jay 384 (61)
Golden Teardrops	Modern Red Caps	1966	Swan 4243
Golden Vanity	Mello-Chords	1961	Lyco 1001
Golden Years, The	Splendors	1959	Taurus 101
Golly Boo	Swensons	1956	X-Tra 100
Golly Gee	Bua, Gene & group	1958	Safari 1007/ABC 9928 (58)
Golly Gee	Crystals, Howie & the	NA	Fleetwood 4521
Golly Gee	Sunglows, Sunny & the	1959	Sunglow 104/Okeh 7143 (62)
Golly Gee	Zodiacs, Maurice Williams & the	1959	Cole 100
Golly Golly	Gents	1961	All Boy 8501

SONG	GROUP	YEAR	LABEL
Golly Gosh Oh Gee	Playboys	1958	United Artists 124
Gomen Nasai	Jets (7-11)	1953	7-11 2101/2102
Gone	Belvin, Jesse (with the Feathers)	1955	Specialty 550
Gone	Blenders (New York)	1950	Decca 48156
Gone	Darvels	1963	Eddies 69
Gone	Drifters (Pre-1959)	1955	Atlantic 1055
Gone	Fleetwoods	1963	Dolton (unreleased)
Gone	Gallahads	1961	Nite Owl 20/Rendezvous 153
Gone	Mello-Harps	1956	Tin Pan Alley 157/158
Gone	Rip Chords	1963	Columbia 42812
Gone	Rituals	1959	Arwin 127
Gone	Statlers	1962	Little Star 108
Gone Away	Flips	1959	Mercury 71426
Gone Forever	Del-Vons	1963	Wells 1001
Gone From Me	Carrol, Eddie & group	1961	Guyden 2046
Gone, Gone, Get Away	Romeos	1957	Fox 748/749
Gone Gone Gone	Flaming Embers	1961	Fortune 869
Gone, Gone, Gone	Hearts (Bronx, N.Y.)	1955	Baton 215
Gone In The Night	Furys	1962	Fleetwood 4569
Gone Is My Love	Dynamics	1957	Cindy 3005
Gone So Long	Invictas	1959, 1962	Jack Bee 1003/Vault 903
Gone Too Long	Darts, Herb Price & the	1959	Tempus 1506
Gone With The Wind	Duprees	1963	Coed 576
Gone With The Wind	Shepherd Sisters	1954	Capitol 2706/Melba 101 (56)
Gonna Be Lonely	Moonglows	NA	
Gonna Be Loved	Epics, Linda & the	1959	Blue Moon 415
Gonna Be Too Late	Five Keys	1960	King 5330
Gonna Build Myself A Castle	Matches	NA	Jaguar 712
Gonna Catch You Nappin'	Avons	1958	Hull 726
Gonna Feed My Baby Poison	Rocketeers	1953	Herald 415
Gonna Find A New Love	Yo Yo's	NA	Goldwax 310
Gonna Find My Pretty Baby	Admirations, Norveen Baskerville & the	1960, 1974	X-Tra 100/Candlelite 414 (74)
Gonna Fix You Good	Ithacas	1957	Fee Bee 220
Gonna Get Right Tonight	Crowns	1964	Limelight 3031
Gonna Get Together Again	Youngtones	1959, 1963	X-Tra 120/121
Gonna Go Down	Rainbows	NA	Mercury
Gonna Keep Lovin' You	Royals Five	NA	Tyler 200
Gonna Let You Go	Five Tinos	1976	Sun (unreleased)
Gonna Love You Every Day	Heralds	1954	Herald 435
Gonna Make A Change	Dubs	1958	Gone 5020
Gonna Make It Alone	Prophets, Ronnie Dio & the	1963	Lawn 218
Gonna Make It On Back	Cameos, Little Willie Brown & the	1961	Do-Ra-Mi 1404
Gonna Make That Little Boy Mine	Dreamettes	1965	United Artists 921
Gonna Rock Tonite	Gainors	1958	Cameo 151
Gonna Take A Chance	Real McCoys	NA	Pico
Gonna Tell	Catalinas	1964	Original Sound 48
Gonna Tell 'Em	Stylers	1956	Jubilee 5253
Gonna Wait For You	Pentagons	1961	Sutter 100
Goo Goo (Sounds)	Melodeers	1961	Studio 9909
Good Book, The	Kings (Baltimore)	1956	Gotham 316
Good Earth, The	Wheels, Arthur Lake & the	1956	Premium 406
Good For A Laugh	Apollos, Paul Stefen & the	1962	Cite 5006
Good For Me	Spinner, Alice & group	NA	Hugo 11722
Good Friends	Fireflies	1964	Taurus 366
Good Friends Forever	Utopias	NA	Fortune 102X
Good Girls	Chantels	1963	Spectorious 150
Good Golly Miss Molly	Crests	1961	Coed 543
Good Golly Miss Molly	Masquerades	NA	Unreleased
Good Golly, Miss Molly	Playboys, Charles White & the	1955	Cat 115
Good Golly, Miss Molly	Valiants (Los Angeles)	1957	Keen 34004
Good Good	Rondells	1958	Carlton 467
Good Good Feeling	Falcons (Big Wheel)	1967	Big Wheel 1972
Good Good Lovin'	Chevrons	1961	Cuca 6381
Good Good Lovin'	Embers	1964	JCP 1008
Good, Good Lovin'	Royal Lancers, Paul Stefan & the	1963	Hi Mar HM-501

SONG	GROUP	YEAR	LABEL
Good Goodbye	Knight, Bob	1961	Laurel 1020
Good Goodbye	Magic Moments	1990	Clifton 90
Good Goodbye	Tears, Linda & the	1965	Challenge 59317
Good Good-Bye (acappella)	Nacks, Nicky & the	1975	Relic LP 105
Good Goodnight	Cyclones	1959	Forward 313
Good Googa Mooga	Magic Tones	1953	King 4665
Good Googley Woo	Tucker, Frankie & group	1958	Decca 30707
Good Gravy	Crackerjacks, O. Jay Oliver & the	1958	Coed 500
Good Grief	Revels	1959	Swingin' 620
Good Gully	Orchids	1961	Wall 549
Good Life, The	Drifters (1959-forward)	1965	Atlantic LP 8113
Good Lookin' Woman	Bossmen	1964	Busy Bee 1001
Good Looking Baby	Orioles, Sonny Til & the	1983	Murray Hill LP M61277
Good Looking Out	Five Crystals	1959	Kane 25592/Relic 1003 (65)
Good Love	Berry, Richard (with the Dreamers)	1956	RPM 477
Good Love	Dreamers, Richard Berry & the	1963	Crown LP 5371
Good Lovin'	Clovers	1953	Atlantic 1000
Good Lovin'	Collegiates, Dicky Lee & the	1957	Sun 280
Good Lovin'	Olympics	1965	Loma 2013
Good Lovin'	Teenagers (Billy Lobrano)	1986	Murray Hill LP 000148
Good Lovin'	Universals (Philadelphia)	1960	Southern 102
Good Lovin'	Velours	1985	Clifton 75
Good Lovin'	Velvet Tones	1965	Velvet Tone 104
Good Lovin' Daddy	Esquires	1959	
Good Lovin' Man	Earls	1974	
Good Loving	Kids	NA	Gaylord 2203
Good Loving (acappella)	Universals (Philadelphia)	1973	Relic LP 5006
Good Lovin's Hard To Find	Cinders	1965	Ric 156
Good Luck Charm	Charmers, Prince Charles & the	1962	Class 301
Good Luck Charm	Four Uniques	1961	Deer 3002
Good Luck Darlin'	Five Crowns	1952	Old Town 777 (unreleased)/790/ Relic LP 5030
Good Luck To You	Dots (Jeanette Baker)	1957	Caddy 111
Good Luck To You	Shakers	NA	Star
Good Man	Bobbettes	1974	Mayhew 712861
Good Morning Judge	Gordon, Phil & group	1953	Hub Of Hollywood 1105
Good News	Fiestas	1959	Old Town 1074
Good News	Hawks	1954	Imperial 5281
Good News	Stereos	1963	World Artists 1012
Good Night Kiss	Coronados	1958	United Artists 135
Good Old 99	Marylanders	1953	Jubilee 5114
Good Old Acappella	Emery's	1977	Clifton 17
Good Old Acappella	Enchantments	1975	Rogue (no #)
Good Old Acappella	Persuasions	1973	Reprise 0977
Good Old Rock & Roll Music	Fabulous Fortunes, Norm N. Nite & the	1971	Globe 107
Good Old Summertime, The	Clovers	1958	Poplar 111
Good Poppin' Daddy	Ramsey, Gloria & group	1960	Hap 1894
Good Rockin' Daddy	King Bees	1974	Outhouse 101
Good Rockin' Tonight	King Bees	1958	Checker 909
Good Thing, Baby	Sultans	1954	Duke 125
Good Thing Goin'	Rainbows	1968	Instant 3291
Good Things	Five Royales	1954	Apollo 452
Good Things	Olympics	1968	Parkway 6003
Good Time Baby	Five Sounds	1960	Baritone 940/941
Good Time Girls	Swallows (Maryland)	1954	After Hours 104/Chariot 104 (54)
Good To The Last Drop	Randolph, Leroy & group	1971	Spring 121
Good Twistin' Tonight	Midnighters, Hank Ballard & the	1962	King 5635
Goodbye	Carnegies, Alphonso Jones & the	1963	Brunswick 55230
Goodbye	Carousels	1973	Vintage 1012
Goodbye	Continentals (Owl)	1974	Owl 331
Goodbye	Five Speeds	1959	Wiggie 131
Goodbye	Hustlers	1965	Fascination 6570
Goodbye	Inspirations (Jamie)	1956	Jamie 1034/Jamie 1212 (62)
Goodbye	Pastels (Chicago)	1955	States (unreleased)
Goodbye	Raiders, Joey Vel & the	1962	Promo Rel 102

SONG	GROUP	YEAR	LABEL
Goodbye	Renegades, Patty McCoy & the	1962	Counsel 116
Goodbye	Spiders	1956	Imperial 5405
Good-Bye	Temptones (Daryl Hall)	1966	Arctic 130
Goodbye	Four Students, Piano Red with the	1955	Groove 0118
Goodbye Angel Baby	Maria & group	1980	BAB 125
Goodbye Baby	Cheryl Ann & group	NA	Patty 52
Goodbye Baby	Con Chords, Bob Brady & the	1966	Chariot 100
Goodbye Baby	Four Jacks	1952	Federal 12075
Goodbye Baby	Heartbreakers (Washington, D.C.)	1952	Roadhouse 1012
Goodbye Baby	Hearts (Bronx, N.Y.)	1957	J&S 4571/4572
Goodbye Baby	Kappaliers	NA	Shadow 1229
Goodbye Cindy Goodbye	Concords, Tony Colton & the	1963	Roulette 4475
Goodbye Dad	Castle Sisters	1962	Terrace 7506
Goodbye Darling	Corsairs	1957	Hy-Tone 110
Goodbye, Goodbye	Envoys, Bill Tally & the	1959	Canadian American 105
Goodbye Jesse	Legends, Billy Davis & the	1960	Peacock 1694
Goodbye Linda	C-Notes, Ron Jones & the	1962	Mobie 3419
Goodbye Little Girl	Balladeers	1952	RCA 4612
Goodbye Mary Ann	Dells	1963	Argo 5456
Goodbye Matilda	Diablos, Nolan Strong & the	1959	Fortune 531
Goodbye, Maureen	Four Winds	1978	Crystal Ball 105
Goodbye Mister Blues	Renditions, Billy De Marco & the	1960	Up 113
Goodbye Molly	Cobras (Philadelphia)	1964	Casino 1309
Goodbye Mr. Blues	Mystics	1961	Laurie 3086
Goodbye My Love	Chapters	1953	Republic 7038
Goodbye My Love	Graduates	1963	Lawn 208
Goodbye My Love	Monterays (Brooklyn)	1956, 1959	Saturn 1005/Arwin 130
Goodbye My Love	Muskateers	1953	Roxy 801
Goodbye My Love	Serenaders (Detroit)	1974 (1952)	Roxy 801
Goodbye My Love	Wheeletts, Sammy & the	NA	Rip Cor 6001
Goodbye She's Gone	Sprouts	1957	RCA 7080/Spangle 2002 (57)
Goodbye To Love	Chantels	1959	End 1048
Goodbye To Love	Fantastics	1964	DMD 103
Goodbye To Love	Marcels	1961	Colpix 186
Goodbye To Love	Streetcorner Serenade	1988	Starlight 65
Goodbye To Love	Twilights, Teddy & the	1962	Swan 4102
Goodness Gracious	Class-Notes	1958	Dot 15786
Goodnight	Candles, Rochell & the	1961	Swingin'
Goodnight	Castle-Tones	1959	Rift 502
Goodnight	Celebrities	1959	Boss 502
Goodnight	Elegants	1958	Apt 25017
Goodnight	Fascinations	1978	Crystal Ball 123
Goodnight	Four Intruders	1979	King Tut 179
Goodnight	Plurals	1959	Wanger 188
Goodnight	Wyatt, Johnny (with the Candles)	1961	Swingin' 643
Goodnight Baby	Butterflys	1964	Red Bird 10-009
Goodnight Baby	Imaginations	1961	Music Makers 103
Goodnight, Irene	Clippers	1960	Beacon 210
Goodnight Irene	Diadems	1961, 1964	Goldie 715
Goodnight Irene	Jaycees, Chuck Jackson & the	1964	Gateway 738
Goodnight Irene	Orioles, Sonny Til & the	1950	Jubilee 5037
Goodnight Kiss	Sapphires	1964	Swan LP 513
Goodnight, Little Girl	Thrillers, Little Joe & the	1959	Okeh 7134
Goodnight Mother	Cap-Tans	1959	DC 8064
Goodnight My Love	Belvin, Jesse & group	1956, 1959	Modern 1005/Jamie 1145
Goodnight My Love	Cupids, Darwin & the	1960	Jerden 9
Goodnight My Love	Del-Mingos	1963	Lomar 702
Goodnight My Love	Deltas, Jim Waller & the	1964	Cambridge 124/125
Goodnight My Love	Duprees	1968	Heritage 805
Goodnight My Love	Fleetwoods	1963	Dolton 75
Goodnight My Love	Ricks, Jimmy & group	1959	Signature 12013
Goodnight My Love	Shufflers, Benny Williams & the	NA	Champion 103
Goodnight My Love	Tymes	1964	Parkway LP 7032
Goodnight Sweetheart	Duets, Leo & the	NA	Co-Op 514
Goodnight Sweetheart	Flamingos	1959, 1964	End 1046/Checker 1091

SONG	GROUP	YEAR	LABEL
Goodnight Sweetheart	Kingsmen	NA	Arnold 2106
Goodnight Sweetheart	Serenaders (Clifton)	1976	Clifton 16
Goodnight Sweetheart	Spaniels	1969	Buddah 153
Goodnight, Sweetheart, Goodnight	Carter Rays, Eddie Carter & the	1954	SLS 102/Jubilee 5142 (54)
Goodnight, Sweetheart, Goodnight	Du Droppers, Sunny Gale with the	1954	RCA 5746
Goodnight Sweetheart Goodnight	Morse, Ella Mae & group	1954	Capitol 2800
Goodnight, Sweetheart, Goodnight	Spaniels	1954	Vee Jay 107
Goodnight Sweetheart, Goodnight	Untouchables	1960	Madison 134
Goodnight, Sweetheart, It's Time To Go	Platters	1957	Wing LP MGW 12112
Goodnight, Well It's Time To Go	Montclairs	1960	Audicon 111
Goody Good Things	Lamplighters	1954	Federal 12197
Goody, Goody	Five C's	1955	United 180
Goody Goody	Royals, Richie & the	1961	Rello 1
Goody Goody	Teenagers, Frankie Lymon & the	1957	Gee 1039
Goody Goody Girl	Teenagers, Frankie Lymon & the	1959	Gee 1052
Goody Goody Gum Drop	Newmarks	1963	Chattahoochee 627
Goody Gumdrop	Mellowlarks	1957	
Goof Ball	Five Royales	1962	Home Of The Blues 257/ABC 10348
Goofin'	Spinners (California)	1958	Capitol 3955
Goofy Dry Bone	Goofers	1955	Coral 61431
Goon	Harris, Kurt & group	1963	Diamond 158
Goose Is Gone	Four Deuces	1956	Music City 796
Goose Is Gone, The	Turbans (Oakland)	1955	Money 209
Gosh But This Is Love	Classics (Los Angeles)	1957	Class 219
Gosh Golly Gee	Paramounts	1976	Broadcast 1138
Gossip	Keystoners	1992	Starbound 515
Gossip	Tiffanys	1964	MRS 777/Atlantic 2240 (64)
Gossip, The	Ozells	1963	Cub 9126
Gossip Wheel, The	Clovers	1958	Poplar 110/Poplar 139 (59)
Got A Good Feeling	Hi Tensions	1963	Milestone 2018
Got A Job	Miracles (Detroit)	1958	End 1016
Got A Little Shadow	Flames	1953	7-11 2110 (unreleased)
Got A Little Shadow	Jets (Aladdin)	1954	Aladdin 3247
Got A Little Woman	Dimples, Eddie Cooley & the	1956	Royal Roost 621
Got A Lot I Want To Say	Emperors, Ernie & the	1965	Reprise 0414
Got Everything But You	Four Buddies	NA	Savoy 955 (unreleased)
Got Me A Six Button Benny	Nite Riders	1958	Teen 118
Got Me A Sweetheart	Consorts, Les Levo & the	1959	Nina 1601
Got My Eye On You	Rollers	1961	Liberty 55303
Got My Mo-Jo Working (But It Won't Work On You)	Suburbans, Ann Cole & the	1957	Baton 237
Got The Water Boiling	Regals	1955	Atlantic 1062
Got To Find Out About Love	Edsels	1961	Tammy 1023
Got To Get Along	Lyrics, Leo Valentine & the	1962	Skylight 202
Got To Get Her Back	Fabulous Four	1964	Brass 311/Coral 62479 (64)
Got To Get Used To You	Avons	1967	A-Bet 9419
Got To Get You In My Life	Baby Dolls	1961	Hollywood 1111
Got To Go Back Again	Four Barons	1950	Regent 1026
Got To Have You Baby	Combo-Nettes, Jane Porter & the	1988	Relic LP 5076
Got To Keep Her Down On The Farm	Chromatics	1960	Ducky 716
Got To Tell Them	Maestro, Johnny & group	1961	Coed 545
Got You On My Mind	Confidentials, Billy Joe & the	1965	BJ 64
Got You On My Mind	Cupcakes, Cookie & the	1963	Chess 1848
Got You On My Mind	Del Royals	1961	Minit 620
Got You On My Mind	Dillard, Varetta (with the Four Students)	1956	Groove 0159
Got You On My Mind	Gay Tunes	1958	Dome 502
Got You Where I Want	Intimates	1964	Amcan 402
Got Your Letter	Holidays	1961	Lyons 107
Gotta Be A False Alarm	Volcanos	1964	Harthon 138
Gotta Be On Time	Emeralds (St. Louis)	1959	Rex 1004
Gotta Feed The Ol' Horse Lotta Hay	Volumes	1954	Jaguar 3004
Gotta Find A Way	Jewels (female)	1964	Dimension 1034
Gotta Find Me A Love	Globeliters	1964	Guyden 2119
Gotta Find My Baby	Ravens	1951	Columbia 39194
Gotta Get Moving	Townsmen (New York - Columbia)	1964	Columbia 43207

SONG	GROUP	YEAR	LABEL
Gotta Get Myself Together	Charms, Otis Williams & the	1966	Okeh 7235
Gotta Get On The Train	Twilighters (Bronx, N.Y.)	1955	MGM 55011
Gotta Girl	Impalas, Bobby Byrd & the	1958	Corvet 1017
Gotta Give Her Love	Volumes	1964	American Arts 6
Gotta Go And See My Baby	Classmates	1956	Silhouette 509/510
Gotta Go, Go, Go	Styles	1961	Serene 1501
Gotta Go To School	Serenaders (New Jersey)	1959	Rae-Cox 101
Gotta Have All Your Lovin'	Flamingos	1974	Ronze 111
Gotta Have Some Fun	Revels	1963	Diamond 143
Gotta Have You	Lee, Curtis (with the Halos)	1960	Hot 7
Gotta Help Me	Agents	NA	Rally 504
Gotta Keep On Walking	Little Herman & group	1964	Arlen 751
Gotta Little Baby	Chancellors	1957	XYZ 104/XYZ 601 (59)
Gotta Little Girl	Universals, Sis Watkins & the	1963	Ascot 2124
Gotta Make A Hit Record	Montgomerys	1963	Amy 883
Gotta New Girl	Satellites, Bobby Day & the	1959	Class 252
Gotta Pay The Price	One-O-Two's, Skip & the	1963	KayBee 106
Gotta Pretty Little Baby	Embraceables	1959	Sandy 1025
Gotta Quit You	Clovers	1961	Winley 265
Gotta Travel On	Gino & group	1963	Golden Crest 588
Gotta Whole Lot Of Lovin' To Do	Lovers	1957	Lamp 2005
Grabitis	Royal Jokers	1960	Metro 20032
Graduation	Chantiers, Rodney Baker & the	1961	Jan Ell 8
Graduation	Classmates	1963	Radar 2624
Graduation	Four Counts	1962	Fine 2562
Graduation Day	Crowns, Stark Whiteman & the	1960	Sho-Biz 1004
Graduation Day	Ivy League	1965	Cameo 377
Graduation Kiss	Young Lads	1963	Felice 909/Felice 712 (63)
Graduation Souvenirs	Garrett, Scott (with the Mystics)	1959	Laurie 3029
Graduation's Here	Fleetwoods	1959	Dolton 3/Dolton S-3 (59)
Grand, Nice, Swell	Ebony Moods	1955	Theron 108
Grand Spanish Lady	Royal Ravens	NA	Mah's 0015
Grandfather	Tokens (Brooklyn)	1968	Warner Bros. 7233
Grandma Bird	Four Hollidays	1963	Markie 109
Grandma Gave A Party	Fiestas	1959	Old Town 1067
Grandma Told Me So	Collegians	1962	Post 10002
Grandma's Hearing Aid	Jumpin' Tones	1964	Raven 8005
Grandpa Can Boogie Too	Four Jacks, Lil Greenwood & the	1952	Federal 12093
Grandpa's Gully Rock	Montclairs, Floyd Smith with the	1961	Fortune 540
Granny Baby	Deli-Cados	1960	PMP
Granny Rock	Hunters, Little Moose & the	1959	SMC 1373
Grass In Your Own Backyard	Four Kings And A Queen	1952	United (unreleased)
Grass Is Greener On The Other Side, The	Avons	1963	Hull 754
Grasshopper Baby	Knight, Marie & group	1956	Mercury 70969
Grasshopper Dance, The	Crestones	1964	Markie 117
Grateful	Cap-Tans	1975	Gotham 261
Grateful	Click-Ettes	1960	Dice 96/97
Grateful	Four Wheels, Nick Therry & the	1956	Spin-It 108
Gravel Gert	Barons (Demon)	1959	Demon 1520
Graveyard	Blenders (Afo)	1962	Afo 305
Graveyard Cha-Cha	Three D's	NA	Square 502
Graveyard Is Waiting, The	Four Kings	NA	Gotham 763
Gravy	Bards	1955	Dawn 209
Gravy Train	Instants	1962	Rendezvous 193
Greasy Kid Stuff	Norvells	1963	Checker 1037
Great Big Eyes	Rivieras	1960	Coed 538
Great Big Heart	Buddies, Little Butchie Saunders & his	1956	Herald 491
Great Big World	Rocky Fellers	1962, 1963	Scepter 1245/1254
Great Day	Magic Tones	NA	Ram-Brock 2001
Great Googley Moo	Spaniels	1958	Vee Jay 278
Great Googly Moo	Cadillacs	1958	Unreleased
Great, Great Pumpkin, The	Bel-Aires, Eddy Bell & the	1961	Lucky Four 1012
Great Jumping Catfish	Wanderers	1957	Onyx 518
Great Mistake	Tiger Lilies	1959	Gone 5047

SONG	GROUP	YEAR	LABEL
Great Physician, The	Masters, Johnny (Johnny Maestro) (with the Crests)	1960	Coed 527
Great Pretender, The	Dusters	NA	4 Hits EP only
Great Pretender, The	Four Jacks	1956	Gateway 1151
Great Pretender, The	Innocents, Kathy Young & the	1961	Indigo 137
Great Pretender, The	Newports	1994	Avenue D 20
Great Pretender, The	Platters	1955	Mercury 70753
Great Red Rat	Pery Mates	1961	CaJo 210
Great Somewhere	Vails	1960	Belmont 4002
Great Thinker, The	Darwin, Ricky & group	1959	Buzz 103
Greatest Gift Of All, The	Five Sounds	1958	Deb 1006
Greatest Love Of All, The	Coolbreezers	1958	Bale 100/101
Greatest Moments Of A Girl's Life, The	Tokens (Brooklyn)	1966	B.T. Puppy 519
Greatest Of Them All, The	Demens	1957	Toenage 1008
Greatest Of Them All, The	Demons, Eddie Jones & the	NA	Kairay 1003
Greatest, The	Percells	1963	ABC 10516
Green Door, The	Four Blades	1956	Big 4 Hits EP 203
Green Eyes	Elegants	1960	United Artists (unreleased)
Green Eyes	Ravens	1955	Jubilee 5184
Green Plant	Tokens (Brooklyn)	1967	B.T. Puppy 552
Green Satin	Chanticleers	1963	Old Town 1137
Green Stamps	T-Birds (Jesse Belvin)	1961	Chess 1778
Green Town Girl	Travelers	1958	Andex 4012
Greenfields	Good Guys, Doug Robertson & the	1964	Jerden 729
Greetings (This Is Uncle Sam)	Valadiers	1961	Miracle 6
Gretchen	Diamonds	1959	Mercury 71449
Grief By Day, Grief By Night	Four Bars	1954	Josie 762
Grizzly Bear, The	Chanteurs	1963	Vee Jay 519 (63)
Groceries, Sir	Dukes (California)	1959	Flip 343
Groove	Higgins, Chuck & group	1954	Kicks 6
Groove Juice	Love Bugs, Preston Love & the	1955	Ultra 101
Groover	Crescents, Dick Watson & the	1962	Gone 5144
Groovey Shoes	Gay Charmers	1958	Savoy 1549
Groovie Time	Altairs	1960	Amy 803
Groovin' To The Music-Sesame Street	Tokens (Brooklyn)	1970	Buddah 187
Groovin' With My Thing	Devons	1969	Mr. G 825
Groovy	Griffins, Jean Simms & the	1954	Dot
Groovy	Groovers, Joe Dodo & the	1958	RCA 7207
Groovy	Hi-Lites (Wassel)	1965	Wassel 701
Groovy Baby	Jewels, Billy Abbott & the	1963	Parkway 874
Groovy Groovy Love	Cadillacs	1962	Capitol 4825
Groovy Kind Of Love	Blue Belles, Patti LaBelle & the	1965	Atlantic 2318
Grounded	Epics	1962	Eric 7001
Grow Old Along With Me	Four Fellows, Bette McLaurin & the	1955	Glory 233
Grow Up Romeo	Upnilons	1964	Lummtone 115
Growing Love	Downbeats	NA	Hampshire 1002
Growing Up	Collegiates	1961	Heritage 105
Growing Up Is Hard To Do	Snaps, Ginger Davis & the	1965	MGM 13413
Grubble, The	Hollywood Argyles	1961	Paxley 752
Guaranteed	Blendaires	1959	Decca 30938
Guaranteed	Four Cousins, Bill Murray & the	1955	20th Century 75020
Guard Your Heart	Sad Sacks	1958	Imperial 5517
Guardian Angel	Camerons	1961	Cousins 1003/Felsted 8638 (61)
Guardian Angel	Capris (New York)	1982	Ambient Sound LP FZ-37714
Guardian Angel	Del-Chords, Donnie & the	1963	Taurus LP 1000
Guardian Angel	Fashions, Frankie & the	1994	Crystal Ball 162
Guardian Angel	Imaginations	1961	Music Makers 108/Duel 507 (61)/ Bo Marc 301 (61)
Guardian Angel	Kingsmen	1957	Allstar 500/East West 115 (58)/ East West 120 (58)
Guardian Angel	Kodaks	1960	Fury 1020
Guardian Angel	Rialtos, Chano & the	1960	Jin 154
Guardian Angel	Selections	1958	Antone 101/Mona Lee 129
Guardian Angel	Van Dykes	1960	Spring 1113/Donna 1333 (60)
Guardian Angel	Wizards	1982	C&J 22651

SONG	GROUP	YEAR	LABEL
Guess I'm Still The Lonely One	Caldwell, Joe & group	NA	M-C-I
Guess I'm Through With Love	Debonaires, Bob & the	1961	Debonair 2251
Guess We're Not In Love	School Girls	1962	Express 712
Guess What	V-Eights	1961	Vibro 4006
Guess Who	Belvin, Jesse & group	1959	RCA 7469
Guess Who	Clefftones	1955	Old Town/Murray Hill LP 000083
Guess Who	Four Kings	1960	Cee Jay 580
Guess Who	Miller Sisters	1956	Ember 1004
Guess Who	Monarchs	1962	Reegal 512
Guide Me	Duvals (Gee)	1956	Gee 1003
Guided Missiles	Cuff Links	1957	Dootone 409
Guiding Angel	Colts	1959	Antler 4007
Guiding Angel	Gales	1958	Mel-O 111/113
Guiding Angel	Marvels (Pyramid)	1962, 1982	Pyramid 6211/Jason Scott 42021
Guiding Angel	Squires (California)	1956	Vita 117
Guiding Light	Three Wishes	1963	Dolton 72
Guilty	Crests	1962	Selma 311
Guilty	Harmony	1980	Starlight 7
Guilty	Johnson, Herb (with the Cruisers)	1960	Len 1007
Guilty Of Love	Vance, Sammy & group	1958	Ebb 134
Guitar Player	Evergreens	1955	Chart 605
Guitar Rock	Joe, Willie	1956	Specialty 576
Guitar Shuffle	Nu-Tones	1959	Spin Time 1001
Guitarro	Rituals	1959	Arwin 120
Gum Drop	Four Jacks	1956	Gateway 1136
Gum Drop	Gum Drops	1955	King 1496
Gum Drop Shoes And Bells In Her Hair	Gum Drops	1958	Decca 30584
Gumdrop	New Group, Otis Williams & his	1956	DeLuxe 6090
Gumma Gumma	Mello-Harps	1959	Casino 104
Gun Totin' Critter Named Jack	Hollywood Argyles	1960	Lute 5908
Gunga Din	Contenders	NA	Whitney Sound 1929
Guy, The	Varcels, Fannie & the	1963	Lash
Guy With A Million Dollars	Downbeats, Gene Terry & the	1959	Goldband 1088
G'Wan Home Calypso	Titans	1957	Vita 158
Gwendolyn	Majestics (Detroit)	1962	Chex 1006
Gwendolyn	Super Heroes	NA	Dice 100
Gypsy Boogie	Teen Tones	1959	Wynne 107/Nu-Clear 1
Gypsy In My Soul	Three Chuckles	1956	X 0216/Vik 0216 (56)
Gypsy Lady	Alston, Walter & group	1961	Gamut 101
Gypsy Lady	Charms, Otis Williams & his	1956	DeLuxe 6098
Gypsy Ribbon	Crystals (Brent)	1960	Brent 7011
Gypsy Said, The	Fiestas	1963	Old Town 1134
Gypsy, The	Dominoes	1960	ABC 10156
Gypsy, The	Five Keys	1957	Capitol T-828 (D.J. copy)
Gypsy, The	Four Chymes	1963	Musicnote 121
Gypsy Woman	Five Discs	1972	Laurie 3601
Gypsy Woman	Things To Come	1993	Clifton 107

H

SONG	GROUP	YEAR	LABEL
Ha Ha He Told On You	Technics, Tony & the	1962	Chex 1010
Ha-Chi-Bi-Ri-Bi-Ri	Encores	1954	Look 105/Ronnex 1003 (54)/ Hollywood 1034 (55)
Had To Play My Number	Du Droppers	1954	Unreleased
Ha-Ha-Ha-Ha, Ha	Desires	1962	Dee Impulse/Moneytown 602 (62)
Haircut	Dreamers, Leon & the	1962	Parkway 843
Hair-Net	Five Peaks	1987	Jay-R 100
Half A Heart	Moonglows	1964	Lana 135
Half A Love (Is Better Than None)	Dominoes	1956	Decca 30149
Half Angel	Twilighters (Bronx, N.Y.)	1955	MGM 55014
Half Breed	Cardigans	1959	Spann 431
Half Deserted Street	Rock-A-Byes, Baby Jane & the	1962, 1963	Spokane 4001/4004
Half Moon	Versatiles, Sonny Day & the	1958	Checker 886
Half Of Me	Royal Dukes, Don Ellis & the	1959	Bee 1114
Half Past Nothing	Duponts	1958	Roulette 4060
Half Ton Tillie	McCall, Little J. & group	1961	Wow 1000/Donna 1334 (61)

SONG	GROUP	YEAR	LABEL
Halfway To Heaven	Plaids	1956	Darl 1003
Hallelujah	Four Kings	NA	Gotham 763
Hallelulu-la	Marvels (Pyramid)	1962	Pyramid 6211/Jason Scott 42021
Halo	Moniques	1963	Centaur 104
Ham The Space Monkey	Embers, Ray Allen & the	1961	Sinclair 1002
Hambone	Uptowners	1989	Starlight 67
Hamburgers On A Bun	Vibrations	1962	Checker 1022
Hand Clappin'	Flares	1961	Press 2808
Hand Full Of Blood	Starfires	1963	Sonic 7163
Hand Holdin' Baby	Shaw, Joan & group	1956	ABC 9724
Hand In Hand	Day Dreams, Tony & the	1958, 1961	Planet 1054/1055
Hand In Hand	Eboniers	1959	Port 70013
Hand In Hand	Four Ekkos	1959	Label 2022
Hand In Hand	Laurels	1959	ABC 10048
Hand Jivin' Baby	Velvets (Texas)	1959	Plaid 101
Hand Me Down Love	Valentines	1955	Rama 181
Hands	Newports	1978	Image 501
Hands Across The Table	Cadets, Will Jones & the	1957	Modern 1024
Hands Across The Table	Velours	1957	Onyx 515/Relic 516 (64)
Hands Off	Azaleas	1963	Romulus 3001
Hands Off Baby	Heartbeats	1957	Gee 1043
Handsome	Matadors, Hank Ayala & the	1959	Back Beat 530
Handwriting On The Wall	Dominoes	1954	Federal 12184
Handwriting On The Wall	Spindles, Frankie & the	1968	Roc-Ker 101
Handy Andy	Five Keys	1958	Capitol 4009
Handy Man	Jones, Jimmy (with the Cues)	1959	Cub 9049
Handy Man	Sparks Of Rhythm	1960	Apollo 541
Hang Around	Del Satins	1965	B.T. Puppy 506
Hang It In Your Ear	Noblemen 4	NA	Recap 292
Hang On	Dolphins	1963	Laurie 3202
Hang On	Travelers	1965	Yellow Sand 452
Hang On Baby	Three Naturals	NA	Sin 725
Hang On Sloopy (acappella)	Notations	1975	Relic LP 105
Hang Your Tears Out To Dry	Belvin, Jesse & group	1951	Hollywood 120
Hangin' Around	Hamilton, Willie & group	1960	Contour 500
Hangin' Around	Royal Teens	1958	ABC 9945
Hanky Panky	Raindrops	1963	Jubilee 5466
Hanky Panky	Rip Tides, Johnny Hudson & the	1959	Challenge 59062
Hanky Panky	Summits	1963	Harmon 1017/Rust 5072 (63)
Happening After School	Gants	1957	Aladdin 3387
Happiest Boy And Girl	Three D's	1959	Brunswick 55152
Happiest Girl In The World	Tiffanys	1964	Arctic 101
Happiest Years, The	Deans, Dolly & the	NA	Thornett 1008
Happiness	Chevelles, Marvin Nash & the	1963	Courier 111
Happiness	Dreamlovers	1964	
Happiness	Duvals (Gee)	1956	Gee 1003
Happiness	Elegants	1961	United Artists 295
Happiness	Pips	1963	Everlast 5025
Happiness And Love	Dynamics	1959	Arc 4450
Happiness Street	Mondellos	1957	Rhythm 109
Happy	Dovells	1965	Swan 4231
Happy	Escorts, Del & the	1961	Taurus 350
Happy	Fabulous Four	1964	Brass 314
Happy	Swans (St. Louis)	1955	Ballad 1000/1001/1007
Happy Am I	Five Keys	1951	Aladdin (unreleased)
Happy Am I	Four Lovers	1956	RCA 6768
Happy And Gay	Castelles	1956	Atco 6069
Happy Are We	Charms, Otis Williams & the	1953	DeLuxe 6014
Happy As A Man Can Be	Three Friends	1961	Imperial 5763
Happy Beat	Kents	1958	Dome 501
Happy Birthday	Kac-Ties	1963	Kape 501
Happy Birthday Blue	Victorians	1964	Liberty 55693
Happy Birthday Blues	Innocents, Kathy Young & the	1961	Indigo 115
Happy Birthday Elise	Flamingos	1960	End LP 308
Happy Birthday Just The Same	Dovells	1964	Parkway 911

SONG	GROUP	YEAR	LABEL
Happy Birthday To Julie	Dynamics, Susan & the	1963	Dot 16476
Happy Blues	Tears, Linda & the	1965	Challenge 59317
Happy Boy	Nornetts	1964	Wand 153
Happy Days Are Here Again	Superiors	1963	Real Fine 837
Happy Days Are Here Again	Velvets (Texas)	1959	20th Century Fox 165
Happy Feet Time	Montclairs	1965	Sunburst 106
Happy Fool	Dinos	1962	Fox 105
Happy Go Lucky	Chances, Chuck Corby & the	NA	Sound 717
Happy Go Lucky Baby	Ravens	1955	Mercury 70413
Happy Go Lucky Local Blues	Orioles, Sonny Til & the	1951	Jubilee 5055
Happy Habit	Morse, Ella Mae & group	1954	Capitol 2800
Happy Happy Birthday	Allures	1987	Starlight 50
Happy Happy Birthday Baby	Tune Weavers	1957	Casa Grande 4037/Checker 872 (57)
Happy Holiday	Jaguars	1989	Classic Artists 113
Happy Holiday	Sherwoods	1964	Magnifico 105
Happy Holiday (acappella)	Shells	1966	Candlelite LP 1000
Happy Honeymoon	Four Fellows (Brooklyn - Aljon)	1963	Aljon 1261
Happy Life	Del Roys	NA	Carol unreleased
Happy Memories	Chapelaires, Joni Kay & the	1964	Gateway 744
Happy Memories	Cleftones	1956	Gee 1025
Happy Over You	Pearls	1962	Warner Bros. 5300
Happy Parakeet	Collegians	1961	Hilltop 1868
Happy Rock & Rollers	Five Johnson Brothers	1958	Fulton 2455
Happy Summer Days	Dovells	1966	Diamond 198
Happy Teen-Age Times	Melodeers	1961	Studio 9909
Happy Teenager	Impossibles, Linda Carr & the	1961	Skyla 1111
Happy Teenager	Rainbows, Randy & the	1964, 1982	Rust 5080
Happy Teenager (acappella)	Ru-Teens	1965	Old Timer 612
Happy Till The Letter	Orioles, Sonny Til & the	1956	Vee Jay 196
Happy Time	Cordells	1964	Ador 6402
Happy Time	Skyliners	1960	Calico 120
Happy Together	Aladdin, Johnny (with the Passions)	1960	Chip 1001
Happy Together	Pageants	1960	Goldisc 3013
Happy Years	Diamonds	1958	Mercury 71330
Happy-Go-Lucky Me	Bobbettes	1966	RCA 8983
Hapsburg Serenade	Shepherd Sisters	1961	Big Top 3066
Harbor Lights	Dominoes	1951	Federal 12010
Harbor Lights	Platters	1960	Mercury 71563
Harbor Lights	Vintage	1966	Catamount 117
Hard Guy To Please	Contessas	1963	Witch 113
Hard Head	Romancers	1961	Palette 5085
Hard Headed Girl	Daylighters	1964	Tip Top 2008
Hard Rockin' Daddy	Down Beats	1958	Dee-Cee 714
Hard Times	Majestics (Detroit)	1960	Contour 501
Hard Times	Royal Jokers	1961	Big Top 3064
Hard To Get	Blossoms	1961	Challenge 9122
Hard To Get	Charmers	1961	Jaf 2021
Hard To Hold Back Tears	Fabulous Denos	1965	King 5971
Hard To Please	Marcels	1984	Rhythm 118
Hard To Please	Mondellos	1957	Rhythm 109
Hard Way, The	Orchids, Dick Bardi & the	NA	Maestro 409/410
Hard Way To Go	Informers	1965	J-Rude 1400
Hard Workin' Woman	Imperials (Detroit)	1953	Derby 858
Hard-Working Mama	Five Dollars	1956	Fortune 830
Harem	Dynamos	1961	Press 101
Harem Girl	Nite Sounds	1962	Fortune 552
Harlem Tango, The	Orchids	1964	Columbia 42913
Harmony Of Love	Five Dollars	1955	Fortune 821/Fraternity 821 (58)
Harriet	Diablos	1958	Fortune 841
Harry Goody	Imaginations	1985	Relic LP 5058
Harry On A Safari	Teasers, Bobby & the	1960	Fleetwood 1012
Harvey's Got A Girl Friend	Royal Teens	1958	ABC 9945
Has Anybody Seen My Boyfriend	Christain, Diane & group	1963	Smash 1862
Has It Happened To You	Falcons (Detroit)	1964	Lu Pine 124/Lu Pine 1020 (64)
Has Somebody Taken My Place	Bees, Honey & the	NA	Bell 217

SONG	GROUP	YEAR	LABEL
Hash, The	Jewels (female)	1964	Olimpic 244
Hasten Jason	Roulettes	1959	Scepter 1204
Hatchet Man, The	Robins	1955	Spark 116
Haunting Memories	Carusos	1974	Roadhouse 1020
Haunting Memories	Halliquins	1959	Juanita 102
Haunting Memories	Harlequins	1958	Juanita 102
Have A Ball	Rainbows	19??	
Have A Good Time	Reflections, Howie Butler & the	1960	Gaity 6017
Have A Heart	Del Rays	1959	Moon 110
Have A Heart	Echoes	1987	Relic LP 5069
Have A Heart	Premiers (Los Angeles)	1956	Dig 113
Have A Heart	Williams, Eddie & group	1963	Alcor 2013
Have A Little Faith	Lanham, Richard (with the Tempo-Tones)	1965	Josie 985
Have A Merry Christmas	Robins	1950	Savoy (unreleased)
Have A Party	Penn Boys	1959	Bobby 502
Have Faith In Me	Blossoms	1958	Capitol 3878
Have Faith In Me	Crystals (New York)	1954	DeLuxe 6037
Have Faith In Me	Night Owls, Tony Allen & the	1960	Crown LP 5231
Have Fun Baby	Loreleis	1955	Dot 15268
Have Good Faith	Kingtones	1964	Derry 101
Have Gun	Clovers	1961	United Artists 307
Have I Been Gone Too Long	Cardinals	1974	Atlantic EP/Bim Bam Boom EP 1000 (74)
Have I Lost Your Love	Dandies	1959	Peach 726
Have I The Right	Mohawks, Popcorn & the	1962	Motown 1019
Have Love, Will Travel	Gallahads	1964	Sea Crest 6005
Have Love Will Travel	Gallahads (with the Counts)	1964	Sea Crest 6005
Have Love Will Travel	Imperialites	1964	Imperial 66015
Have Love Will Travel	Off Beats	1964	Guyden 2101
Have Love Will Travel	Pharaohs, Richard Berry & the	1959	Flip 349
Have Love Will Travel	Sharps	1958	Jamie 1108
Have Mercy	Empires	1964	DCP 1116
Have Mercy	Midnighters, Hank Ballard & the	1964	King 5835
Have Mercy Baby	Bobbettes	1960	Triple-X 106
Have Mercy Baby	Dominoes	1952, 1957, 1960	Federal 12068/12308
Have Mercy Baby	Matadors	1958	Sue 701
Have Mercy Baby	Swallows (Maryland)	1986	Starbound 506
Have Mercy Baby	Universals (Philadelphia)	1960	Southern 101
Have Mercy Baby (acappella)	Universals (Philadelphia)	1973	Relic LP 5006
Have No Fear	Answers	1957	United 212
Have Rock, Will Roll	Heartbeats	1960	Roulette LP 25107
Have You Changed Your Mind?	Champlains (Fred Parris)	1961	United Artists 346
Have You Ever	Enchanted Five	1961	CVS 1002
Have You Ever Been In Love	T-Birds	1967	Vegas 720
Have You Ever Fell In Love	Sweethearts	1963	Brunswick 55265
Have You Ever Loved A Girl	Four Fifths	1966	Columbia 43913
Have You Ever Loved Someone?	Vocaleers	1959	Paradise 113
Have You Ever Met An Angel?	Valtones	1956	Gee 1004
Have You Ever Watched A Teardrop	Royals, Ronnie Bennett & the	1960	Jin 143
Have You Forgotten	Meridians	NA	Parnaso 107
Have You Found Someone New	Emberglows	1961	Dore 591
Have You Heard	Belmonts	1969	Dot 17257
Have You Heard	Chellos	1961	Columbia 42044
Have You Heard	Johnson, Herb (with the Cruisers)	1960	Len 1007
Have You Heard	Royal Knights	NA	Rendezvous 01
Have You Heard	Vows	1962	Markay 103
Have You Heard?	Duprees	1963	Coed 585/Heritage 826 (69)
Have You No Heart	Calvanes	1991	Classic Artists 127
Havertown Doo Doo Hoe Down	Four Skins, Eddie Gee & the	1974	Lost Cause 200
Havin' A Good Time (With My Baby)	Quotations	1968	Imperial 66368
Havin' Fun	DiMucci, Dion (with the Del Satins)	1961	Laurie 3081
Havin' Fun	Tokens (Brooklyn)	1964	B.T. Puppy 504
Having Fun	Bobbettes	1966	RCA 8832
Hawaiian Dream	Hollywood Flames	1959	Ebb 162
Hawaiian Rock 'N Roll	Vocaltones	1957	Cindy 3004

SONG	GROUP	YEAR	LABEL
Hawaiian Sway	Capri Sisters	1958	Dot 15851
Hawaiian War Chant	Playboys	1959	Souvenir 1001
Hay Bob E Re Bob	Cadillacs	1964	Lana 119
He	Cameos (Pittsburgh)	1963	Gigi 100
He Ain't Heavy, He's My Brother	Kelway Quintet	1972	Kelway 104
He Ain't No Angel	Ad Libs	1965	Blue Cat 114
He Ain't No Angel	Lovejoys, Leola & the	1964	Tiger 101
He Broke A Young Girl's Heart	Superbs	1966	Dore 755
He Came Along	Midnighters, Hank Ballard & the	1966	King 6055
He Can't Dance	Meridians	NA	Parnaso 120
He Created You For Me	Visions, Connie McGill & the	1963	United International 1009
He Cries Like A Baby	Dovells	1970	Decca 32919
He Doesn't Love Me	Breakaways	1964	Cameo 323
He Don't Want You	Delrons, Reperata & the	1966	RCA 8921
He Fell For Me	Upnilons	1964	Lummtone 115
He Follows She	Five Cats	1954	RCA 5885
He Got It	Starlets	1960	Lute 5909
He Hit Me (And It Felt Like A Kiss)	Crystals (Brooklyn)	1962	Philles 105
He Is My Friend	Sparrows Quartette	1974	Jet 3020
He Is The Boy	Little Eva & group	1962	Dimension 1000
He Knows I Love Him Too Much	Chantels	1961	Big Top 3073
He Knows I Love Him Too Much	Smith, Arlene & female group	1961	Big Top 3073
He Left Me Crying	Alston, Jo Ann & group	1963	Vest 8001
He Lied	Moonglows	1954	Unreleased
He Loves Me He Loves Me Not	Jills, Jacqueline & the	1961	Goldisc 3023
He Loves Me, He Loves Me Not	Tonettes	1958	Doe 103
He Loves You, Baby	Emeralds, Luther Bond & the	1956	Federal 12279
He Makes Me Feel So Crazy	Maye, Jean & group	1964	Diamond 170
He Man Looking For A She Girl	Four Dots (Pittsburgh)	1956	Bullseye 103
He Played 1, 2, 3, 4	Darlings	1963	Dore 677
He Pretty Girl	Twin Tones	1955	Atlantic 1064
He Promised Me	Blossoms	1957	Capitol 3822
He Said	Depippo Sisters	1964	Magnifico 104
He Still Loves Me	Capris (Philadelphia)	NA	Collectables LP 5000
He Stole Flo	Plaids	1959	Era 3002
He Sure Could Hypnotize	Clovers	1965	Port 3004
He Was A Fortune Teller	Wheels, Ferris & the	1962	United Artists 458
He Was Mine	Rubies	1961	Empress 103
He Wasn't On The Air	Swans (Roulette)	1959	Roulette 4213
He Will Break Your Heart	Collegians	NA	N/A
He Won't Tell	Noblemen	1963	USA 1215
Head Bo Thread Bo	Bachelor Three	1961	Vi-Way 289
Head Strong Baby	Teen Tones	1959	Swan 4040
Headache	Citations, Angie & the	NA	Angela 102
Headin' Home	Flairs, Shirley Gunter & the	1956	Modern 989
Heading For The Poor House	Silhouettes	1958	Ember 1032
Heading For The Rooftop	Velvet Satins	1965	General American 720
Heads Up, High Hopes Over You	Pharaos	1960	Donna 1327
Hear My Plea	Gay Notes	1955	Post 2006
Hear My Plea	Midnights	1954	Music City 746
Hear My Plea	Vocaleers	1960	Vest 832
Hear My Prayer	Choraletters	1957	Duke 214
Hear That Train	Ly-Dells	1962	SCA 18001
Hear The Bells	Tokens (Brooklyn)	1963	RCA 8210
Hear The Word	Belles	1961	Choice 18
Heart	Chandler, Lenny & group	1963	Laurie 3158
Heart And Soul	Cleftones	1961	Gee 1064
Heart And Soul	Dell Vikings	1957	Mercury EP 3362
Heart And Soul	Four Buddies	1951	Savoy 817
Heart And Soul	Radiants, Little Jan & the	1960	Vim 507
Heart And Soul	Shepherd Sisters	1959	MGM 12766
Heart And Soul	Spaniels	1958	Vee Jay 301
Heart And Soul	Whooping Cranes	NA	El Rey 1000
Heart Attack	Nomads	1959	Northern 503
Heart Breaker	Christie, Dean & group	1962	Select 715

SONG	GROUP	YEAR	LABEL
Heart Breaking Train	Crowns	1959	Wheel 1001
Heart Breaking World	Craftys	1961	Lois 5000/Seven Arts 5708 (61)
Heart Darling Angel	Orlons	1961	Cameo 198
Heart 'n' Soul	Four Sevilles	1985	Starlight 30
Heart Of A Fool	Penguins	1959	Dooto LP 242/Dooto EP 241
Heart Of A Rose	Charms	1956	Chart 613
Heart Of Gold	Tindley, George & group	1961	Herald 558
Heart Of Mine	Wildwoods	1960	Caprice 101/102
Heart Of My Heart	Happy Jesters	1957	Dot 15566
Heart Of Saturday Night	Reunion	NA	Starlight 18
Heart Of Stone	Platters	1956	Mercury LP 20216/Mercury EP 3343
Heart Repair Shop	Arnells	1963	Roulette 4519
Heart Strings	Emotions	1966	20th Fox 623
Heart That's True, The	Aqualads, Anthony & the	NA	Gold Bee 1650
Heart To Heart	Bell Tones	1955	Rama 170
Heart To Heart	Dominoes	1951	Federal 12036
Heart To Heart	Little Esther (with the Dominoes)	1951	Federal 12036
Heart To Heart	Pleasers, Little Wilbur & the	1957	Aladdin 3402
Heart Trouble	Go Boys, Dudley Callicutt & the	1959	DC 0412
Heart You Break May Be Your Own, The	Blue Jays (Venice, Calif.)	1987	Relic LP 5064
Heartache Heartbreak	Elgins (California)	1961	Titan 1724 (second pressing)
Heartache Street	Pleasers, Bobbie Please & the	1961	Era 3044
Heartache To Me	Dubs, Richard Blandon & the	1987	Starlight 53
Heartaches	Dream Girls, Bobbie Smith & the	1960	Metro 20034
Heartaches	Marcels	1961	Colpix 612
Heartaches	McPhatter, Clyde (with the Cookies & the Cues)	1957	Atlantic 1149
Heartaches	Panics	1959	ABC 10072
Heartaches	Van-Dells, Myron & the	1963	Flo-Roe 15
Heartaches Don't Care	Collegiates	1961	Campus 123
Heartbeat	Echoes	1960	Edco 100
Heartbeat	Four Sevilles	1980	Starlight 6
Heartbeat	Sh-Booms (Chords)	1955	
Heartbeat	Whirlwinds	1963	Philips 40139/Times Square 112
Heartbreak	Platters	1963	Mercury 72060
Heartbreak	Sophomores, Anthony & the	1966	ABC 10844
Heartbreak Hotel	Cadets	1956	Modern 985
Heartbreak Hotel	Grand Prees	NA	Go Go 101
Heartbreak Hotel	Hillsiders, Bobby Angel & the	1962	Astra 300
Heartbreak Melody	Carr, Wynonie & group	1957	Specialty 600
Heartbreak Of Love	Poore, Bobby & group	1958	Beta 1003
Heartbreaker	Counts	1955	Dot 1275
Heartbreaker	Crows	1954	Rama 10
Heartbreaker	Four Sevilles	1980	Starlight 8
Heartbreaker	Heartbreakers (Washington, D.C.)	1951, 1974	RCA 4327
Heartbreaker	Interludes	1959	Valley 1005
Heartbreaking Moon	Victorians	1956	Saxony 103
Heartbreaking World	Halos	1962	Warwick LP 2046
Heartburn	Crests	1966	Parkway 987
Heartless	Buddies	1959	Tiara 6121
Hearts Can Be Broken	Jewels (Los Angeles)	1955	Imperial 5351
Hearts Of Stone	Blue Jays (Los Angeles)	1956	Dig EP 777
Hearts Of Stone	Charms, Otis Williams & the	1954	DeLuxe 6062
Hearts Of Stone	Goofers	1954	Coral 61305
Hearts Of Stone	Jewels (Los Angeles)	1954, 1964	R&B 1301/Original Sound 38
Hearts Of Stone	Top Notes	1961	Atlantic 2097
Heartsick And Lonely	Dots (Jeanette Baker)	1957	Caddy 111
Heartthrob	Co-Eds	1962	USA 724
Heaven	Alcoves	1964	Carlton 602
Heaven	Lexingtons, Joey & the	1962	Comet 2154
Heaven Above	Five Techniques	1961	Imperial 5742
Heaven Above Me	Jets (New York)	1956	Gee 1020
Heaven And Cindy	Five Boroughs	1990	Classic Artists 122
Heaven And Earth, The	Ramblers (Federal)	1956	Federal 12286
Heaven And Paradise	Chants	1960	Nite Owl 40

SONG	GROUP	YEAR	LABEL
Heaven And Paradise	Dell Vikings	1973	Luniverse 110
Heaven And Paradise	Meadowlarks, Don Julian & the	1955	Dootone 359
Heaven And Paradise	Vikings, Erik & the	1965	Karate 503
Heaven Have Mercy	Saunders, Jay & group	1956	Club 1012
Heaven Help Me	Cadets	1957	Modern 1012
Heaven Help Me	DiMucci, Dion (with the Del Satins)	1961	Laurie 3090
Heaven Help Me	Metronomes (Harold Sonny Wright)	NA	Cadence (unreleased)
Heaven In My Arms	Vel-Aires, Donald Woods & the	1956	Flip 312
Heaven In Your Eyes	Jones Boys, Jimmy Jones & the	1957	Arrow 717
Heaven Is The Place	Quails, Bill Robinson & the	1954	DeLuxe 6059
Heaven Knows	Chuck-A-Lucks	1957, 1963	Bow 305/Candlelite 424
Heaven Knows	Four Sensations	1951	Rainbow 157
Heaven Knows I Love You	Six Teens	1959	Flip 346
Heaven Knows Why	Boyfriends, Wini Brown & the	1952	Mercury 8270
Heaven Must Have Run Out Of Angels	Chaps	1959	Matador 1814
Heaven On Earth	Del Vikings	1973	Broadcast 1123
Heaven On Earth	Delmonicos	1990	Clifton 88
Heaven On Earth	Platters	1956	Mercury 70893
Heaven On Earth	Tiffanys	1966	Josie 952
Heaven On Fire	Four Tones, Dusty Brooks & the	1953	Sun 182
Heaven On Wheels	Lockettes, Richard Berry & the	1958	Flip 336
Heaven Only Knows	Charms, Otis Williams & the	1953	Rockin' 516/DeLuxe 6000 (53)
Heaven Only Knows	Checkers	1958	King 5156
Heaven Only Knows	Cleopatra & group	1961	Sheryl 335
Heaven Only Knows	Cognacs	1961	Roulette 4340
Heaven Only Knows	Kashmirs	1958	Wonder 104
Heaven Only Knows	Larks (Don Julian)	1965	Money 122
Heaven Only Knows	Leeds	1959	Wand 102
Heaven Only Knows	Little Cheryl & group	1963	Cameo 270
Heaven Only Knows	Meadowlarks, Don Julian & the	1962	Dynamite 1112
Heaven Sent You	Arabians	1960	Jam 3738/Twin Star 1018 (60)
Heaven To Me	Larand, Johnny & group	1965	Octavia 0005
Heaven Was Mine	Gemtones, Eddie Woods & the	1953	Gem 204
Heavenly	Four Counts	1960	Ace 597
Heavenly	Madara, Johnny & group	1962	Landa 687
Heavenly	Tremaines	1959	Kane 007/008/V-Tone 507 (60)
Heavenly Angel	Cupids	NA	Unreleased
Heavenly Angel	Dandevilles	1959	Forte 314
Heavenly Angel	Del Rios	1962	Bet-T 7001
Heavenly Angel	Flamingos	1959	End 1062
Heavenly Angel	Penguins	1965	Original Sound 54
Heavenly Angel	Satellites	1958	Class 234/Malynn 234 (58)
Heavenly Angel	Squires (California)	1956	Vita 116
Heavenly Angel	Superiors	1969	Sue 12
Heavenly Angel	Viscaynes	1961	VPM 1006
Heavenly Bliss	Classic IV	1962	Twist 1003/1004
Heavenly Father	Algers, Skip & Fruit & the	1960	Northern 3730
Heavenly Father	Castelles	1955	Grand 122
Heavenly Father	Cleftones	1976	Robin Hood 132
Heavenly Father	Cleftones (featuring Pat Spann)	1961	Gee LP 705
Heavenly Father	Larks (Don Julian)	1964	Money 112
Heavenly Father	Reunited	1980	Clifton 50
Heavenly Father	Starlarks, Wes Forbes & the	1957	Ancho 102/Relic 508 (64)
Heavenly Father (acappella)	Chessmen	1965	Relic 1016
Heavenly Love	Academics	1957	Ancho 101/Relic 510 (64)
Heavenly Night	Collegians	1958	X-Tra 108/Times Square 11 (63)
Heavenly One	Owens, Freddy & group	1961	Wall 550
Heavenly Place	Chiffons	1965	Laurie 3318
Heavenly Road	Harmonaires, Lula Reed & the	1953	King 4590
Heavenly Ruby	Californians	1955	Federal 12231
Heavenly You	Chanters (New York)	NA	SSP
Heaven's For Real	Storytellers	1991	Classic Artists 128
Heaven's Not So Far	Moonrays, Ray Frazier & the	1962	Dynamite 1009
Heaven's One Desire	Five Arcades (Dave Antrell overdubbed)	1973, 1985	Sacto 103 (phony label; rec. 1973)/ Antrell 103

SONG	GROUP	YEAR	LABEL
Heaven's Own Choir	Five Crystals	1958	Music City 821/Delcro 827
Heavy Hips	Flamingos	1975	Ronze 115
He'd Better Go	Hong Kong White Sox	1960	Trans-World 6906
Hee Hee Ha Ha	Flamettes	1961	Laurie 3109
Heel And Toe	Versatiles	1975	Monogram 114
Heidi	Revlons, Tino & the	1963	Pip 4000
Helen	Cardells	1956	Middle-Tone 011
Helen Isn't Tellin'	Voxpoppers, Freddie & the	1960	Warwick 589
Helene	Twilighters (Bronx, N.Y.)	1960	Spin-It 202
Helene (Your Wish Came True)	Excellents	1964	Bobby 601/Old Timer 601 (64)
He'll Be Back	Memory	1981	Avenue D 5
He'll Be Sorry	Unforgettables	1963	Titanic 5012
Hell Cats	Dolphins, Davey Jones & the	1968	Tower 4527
He'll Come Back	Sham-Ettes	1967	MGM 13798
He'll Only Hurt You	DiMucci, Dion (with the Del Satins)	1963	Columbia 42662
He'll Only Hurt You	Pictures, C.L. & the	1964	Kirk 639/Monument 854 (64)
Hello	Januarys, Little June & his	1957	Salem 188
Hello	Nutmegs	1963	Times Square 6/Relic 531 (65)
Hello	Subway Serenade	NA	Clifton EP 504
Hello And Good-Bye	Jades, Chris Newton & the	1961	Mikesell 134
Hello Baby	Commodores, Darrell Glenn & the	1957	RPM 488
Hello Baby	Young Sisters	1961	Twirl 2008
Hello, Darling	Saucers	1964	Lynne 101
Hello, Dear	High Liters	1956	Vee Jay 184
Hello Dolly	Salutations, Vito & the	1966	Rust 5106
Hello Dolly	Stagehands	1964	T.A. 101
Hello Is The You?	Red Tops	NA	Sky 703/RCA 7144
Hello Little Girl	Fourmost	1963	Atco 6280
Hello Love	Casuals	1957	Dot 15671
Hello Love	Standards	1963	Magna 1314/Chess 1869 (63)
Hello Lover	Nu Luvs	1961	Clock 2003
Hello Mama	Cool Tones	NA	Dice 750
Hello Miss Fine	Royals	1953	Federal 12150
Hello, Mr. New Year	Coolbreezers	1958	Bale 102/103
Hello Muddah, Hello Faddah	Martin, Dick	1964	Hit 77
Hello My Lover	K-Doe, Ernie & group	1960	Minit 614
Hello Operator	Richards, Donald (with the Volumes)	1962	Chex 1003
Hello, Schoolteacher!	Four After Fives	1961	All Time 9076
Hello There Mister Grave Digger	Creators	1962	Dore 635/Lummtone
Hello Young Lovers	Tymes	1964	Parkway LP 7038
Help	Lifesavers, Lucien Farrar & the	1957	Jupiter 1
Help	Premiers, Herb Johnson & the	1959	Palm
Help A Lonely Guy	Companions	1962	General American 711
Help Me	Aladdins	1957	Aladdin 3358
Help Me	Del-Chords	1960	Jin 126
Help Me	Nutmegs	1971	Relic LP 5002
Help Me	Twilighters (Bronx, N.Y.)	1961	Ricki 907
Help Me Baby	Dovells	1963	Parkway 861
Help Me Baby	Little Angel	1959	Award 126
Help Me Somebody	Five Royales	1953, 1962	Apollo 446/Vee Jay 431
Help Me Somebody	Impacts	1961	Carlton 548
Help Me With My Heart	Stewart, Sylvester & group	1962	G&P 901
Help! Murder! Police!	Hi-Fidelities	1957	Hi-Q 5000
Help, There Is A Burglar	Climatics	1959	Request 3007/3008
Helpless	Flamingos	1957	Decca 30454
Helpless	Platters	1958	Mercury 71246
Helpless	Reflections	1981	Old Town 1071
Helpless	Solitaires	1959	Old Town 1071
Henry And Henrietta	Illusions	1960	Coral 62173
Henry, Henry, Henry	Dreamers (United Artists)	1965	United Artists 841
Henry Said Goodbye	Crystalaires	1963	Sound Souvenir 1/2
Henry's Got Flat Feet (Can't Dance No More)	Midnighters	1955	Federal 12224
Hep, 2, 3, 4	Manis, Georgie & group	1958	Eclaire 105
Hep Teenager	Harptones	1959	Warwick 512

SONG	GROUP	YEAR	LABEL
Her Bermuda Shorts	Pledges	1957	Revere 3517
Her Diary	Accents, Danny & the	1965	Valli 307
Her Final Letter	Members, Wayne Marshall & the	1965	
Her Moustache	Dell Woods	1963	Big Top 3137
Here	Four Bells	1954	Bell 1039
Here	Downbeats	1958	Safari 1010
Here Alone	Daylighters	1964	Tollie 9028
Here Am I	Four Sounds, Lois Blaine & the	1963	Open-G 00
Here Am I	Jokers, Ty Stewart & the	1961	Amy 828
Here Am I	Perkins, Roy & group	1955	Meladee 112
Here At My Phone	Williams, Mel & group	1956	Dig 107
Here Come The Ho-Dads	Denels	1962	Union 502/Bamboo 517
Here Comes Baby	Dream Girls, Bobbie Smith & the	1962	Big Top 3111
Here Comes Big Ed	Wildwoods	1961	May 106
Here Comes Heaven Again	Platters	1963	Mercury 72129
Here Comes Heaven Again	Shepherd Sisters	1959	Warwick 511
Here Comes Marsha	Pyramids (Best)	1963	Best 102/Best 13002 (64)
Here Comes My Baby	Five Kings	1966	Yvette 101
Here Comes Nancy	Masters, Rick & the	1962	Taba 101/Cameo 226 (62)
Here Comes Night	Nighthawks, B. Guitar & the	1958	Decca 30634
Here Comes Romance	Clovers	1957	Atlantic 1129
Here Comes Sally	Lopez, Trini & group	1959	King 5198
Here Comes Santa Claus	Blue Jeans, Bob B. Soxx & the	1963	Philles LP 4005
Here Comes Summer	Whispers	1966	Laurie 3344
Here Comes Suzy	Classmates	1961	Seg-Way 104
Here Comes That Song Again	Velvets (Texas)	1964	Monument 836
Here Comes The Bride	Donnels	1963	Alpha 001
Here Comes The Fool	Lakettes	1960	Thunderbird 102
Here Comes The Heartaches	Lovells	1967	Brent 7073
Here Comes The Judge	Dovells	1968	MGM 13946
Here Comes The Pain	Accents (Brooklyn)	1963	Spokane 4007
Here Comes The Pain	English, Scott (with the Accents)	1964	Spokane 4007
Here Comes The Pain	Legends	1964	Warner Bros. 5457
Here Goes A Fool	Allures	1986	Starlight 32
Here Goes A Fool	Clovers	1953	Atlantic 1000
Here Goes A Fool	Prinder, Shad	1962	Infinity 009
Here Goes My Girl	Cincos, Ben Harper & the	1960	Talent 106
Here I Am	Individuals	1959	Delwood
Here I Am	Moonglows	1957	Chess 1681
Here I Am	Savoys, Sonny Brooks & the	1956	Tip Top 1007
Here I Am Broken Hearted	Four J's	1964	Jamie 1267
Here I Come	Offbeats, Jimmy Dee & the	1958	Dot 15721
Here I Go Again	Tillman, Lee	1962	Sonora 211
Here I Stand	Dee, Sonny & group	1961	Kapp 421
Here I Stand	Newcomers, Wade Flemons & the	1958	Vee Jay 295
Here I Stand	Rip Chords	1963	Columbia 42687
Here I Stand	Teenbeats, Gene & the	NA	Raven 2011
Here I Stand	Watkins, Sis & group	1964	Diplomacy 9
Here I Stand	Williams, Maurice & female group	1961	Herald 572
Here I Stand	Zodiacs, Maurice Williams & the	1962	Herald 572
Here In My Arms	Tigers, Little Julian Herrera & the	1957	Dig 137
Here In My Heart	Boyfriends, Wini Brown & the	1952	Mercury 5870
Here In My Heart	Chargers (Jesse Belvin)	1958	RCA 7417
Here In My Heart	Time-Tones	1961	Times Square 421 (first pressing)/ Relic 538 (65)
Here In The Darkness	Chromatics	1956	Million 2014
Here In The Darkness	Chromatics, Sherry Washington & the	1955	Million 2010
Here In Your Arms	Elgins (Congress)	1964	Congress 225
Here Is My Heart	Ravens	1957	Argo 5284
Here Is Why I Love You	Spaniels	1958	Vee Jay 290
Here It Comes Again	Chantels	1961	Carlton 569
Here Lies My Love	Mr. Undertaker	1955	Music City 790
Here She Comes	Darlettes, Diane & the	1962	Dunes 2026
Here She Comes	Tymes	1964	Parkway 924
Here She Comes Again	Uptowns	1963	Laurie 3204

SONG	GROUP	YEAR	LABEL
Here She Comes Now	Fulton, Sonny & group	1959	Lash 1127
Here There And Everywhere	Fourmost	1966	Capitol 5738
Here With Me	Knight, Alan & group	1960	Tide 016
Here You Come	Fayettes, Hattie Littles & the	1962	Gordy 7007
Here You Come Again	Crescents	1965	Watch 1902
Here's A Heart	Belvin, Jesse & group	1959	RCA 7543
Here's A Heart For You	Chordells	1956	Onyx 504/Relic 523 (64)
Here's A Letter From Home	Rouzan, Wanda & group	1963	Frisco 115
Here's My Heart	Sharps	1958	Jamie 1114
Here's That Rainy Day	Automations	1974	Clifton 6
Here's That Rainy Day	Intervals	1962	Class 304
Here's The Question	Blackwells	1959	G&G 126
Here's Why I Love You	Patterns	1980	Clifton 55
He's A Braggin'	Tip Tops	1963	Parkway 868
He's A Fugitive	Rainbows, Randy & the	1966	Mike 4004
He's A Lover	Taylor, Mike & group	1963	Dream
(He's A) Quiet Guy	Love, Darlene & group	1964	Philles 123
He's A Rebel	Crystals (Brooklyn)	1962	Philles 106
He's A Square	Belvederes	1961	Lucky Four 1003
He's A Wise Guy	Charmettes	1964	Kapp 570
He's A Yankee	Sweethearts	1963	Brunswick 55240
He's An Angel	Summits	1963	Harmon 1017/Rust 5072 (63)
He's Coming Home	Indigos	1965	Cor 6581/Verve Folkways 5002
He's Crying Inside	Janettes	1962	Goldie 1102
He's Gone	Blend-Aires	1978	Story Untold 500
He's Gone	Blue Belles, Patti LaBelle & the	1969	Atlantic 2610
He's Gone	Chantels	1957, 1969	End 1001/Roulette 7064
He's Gone	Charmers	1956	Aladdin 3341
He's Gone	Mareno, Lee (with the Regents)	1961	New Art 103/Scepter 1222 (61)
He's Gone	Now & Then	1981	Clifton 65
He's Gone	Pearlettes	1961	Craig 501/502
He's Gone (acappella)	Adorables, Ginger & the	1975	Relic LP 104
He's Gone For Good	Vidletts	1963	Herald 594
He's Gonna Get It	Dar-Letts	1964	Shell 101
He's Good For Me	Tiffanys	1967	KR 120/RKO 120
He's Got The Nerve	True Tones	1965	Soulville/Josie 950 (65)/ Josie 1003 (69)
He's Got The Whole World In His Hands	Crenshaws	1961	Warner Bros. 5254
He's Got The Whole World In His Hands	Travelers	1958	Andex 4012
He's Got You	Pixies	1965	Autumn 12
He's Got Your Number	Demures	1963	Brunswick 55284
He's In Town	Tokens (Brooklyn)	1964	B.T. Puppy 502
He's Just A Playboy	Drifters (1959-forward)	1964	Atlantic 2253
He's Lazy	Deberons	1960	Bond 1480
He's Mine	Platters	1957	Mercury 71032
He's Mine	Swans (Swan)	1963	Swan 4151
He's My Baby	Hightower, Donna (with the Jacks)	1956	RPM 481
He's My Boy	Motor Scooter, Beverly & the	1964	Epic 9654
He's My Guy	Delrons, Reperata & the	1964	World Artists 1036
He's My Guy	Jades	1964	Port 70042
He's My Guy	Kittens	1985	Relic LP 8004
He's My Guy	Lee, Mabel & group	1956	Hull 712
He's My Hero	Curls	1960	Everest 19350
He's My Man	Blue Belles, Patti LaBelle & the	1968	Atlantic 2548
He's My Man	Queen City Ramblers, Laura Gunter & the	1958	Excellent 807
(He's My) Superman	Sweethearts	1963	Brunswick 55237
He's No Lover	Teenagers (Sherman Garnes)	1981	Crystal Ball LP 142
He's No Lover	Teenagers, Joey & the	NA	Columbia
He's Not There	Revellons, Ria & the	1964	RSVP 1110
He's Not Your Boyfriend	Charades	1964	Warner Bros. 5415
He's So Fine	Chiffons	1963	Laurie 3152
He's So Fine	Corvells	1962	Lu Pine 104/Lu Pine 1004 (62)
He's So Good	Lullabies, Lisa & the	1964	Coed 589
He's So Right	Universals (Philadelphia)	1958	Cora-Lee 501
He's So Sweet	Francettes	1963	Wolfie 104

SONG	GROUP	YEAR	LABEL
He's Sure The Boy I Love	Crystals (Brooklyn)	1962	Philles 109
He's The Fatman	Hawks	1970	Imperial LP 94003 (rec. 1955)
He's The Greatest	Delrons, Reperata & the	1965	World Artists 1075
He's The One	Accents (featuring Sandi)	1964	Karate 529
(He's The) The Great Impostor	Fleetwoods	1961	Dolton 45
Hesitating Fool	Striders	1955	Apollo 480
Hetta Hetta	Contenders	1966	Java 104
Hex, The	Moroccos	1957	United 207
Hey	Angels, Gabriel & the	1960	Amy 802
Hey!	Sparrows	1954	Jay-Dee 790
Hey Babe Let's Go Downtown	Rockets, Joe Therrien Jr. & his	1957	Lido 505/Brunswick 55005
Hey Baby	Alston, Walter & group	1961	Gamut 101
Hey Baby	Arketts, Argie & the	1961	Ronnie (no number)
Hey Baby!	Arribins, Duke Savage & the	1959	Argo 5346
Hey Baby	Baby Dolls	1959	Warner Bros. 5086
Hey Baby	Banlons	1959	Fidelity 4051/Baron 108 (73)
Hey Baby	Cleftones	1957	Gee 1041
Hey Baby	Emotions	1964	Karate 506
Hey, Baby	Five Campbells	1956	Music City 794
Hey Baby	Five Emprees	1965	Freeport 1002
Hey Baby	Four Bars	1954	Josie 762
Hey Baby	Heartbreakers (Washington, D.C.)	1952	Roadhouse 1008
Hey Baby	Hi-Lites (Wassel)	1965	Wassel 701
Hey Baby	Intentions	NA	Black Pearl 100
Hey Baby	Lawrence Brothers, Bill Lawrence & the	1959	Bertram International 207
Hey Baby	Paragons	1961	Tap 500
Hey Baby	Storytellers (with Timmy Lymon)	1959	Stack 500
Hey Baby	Telegrams	1978	Creole 163
Hey Baby	Vel-Tones	NA	Del Norte 725
Hey, Baby, Baby	Castelles	1956	Atco 6069
Hey, Baby, Hey	Sentimentals, James Carter & the	1957	Tuxedo 922/Tuxedo 943
Hey, Baby, Stop	Ebonaires	1956	Money 220
Hey Boy	Illusions	1962	Mali 104/Sheraton 104 (62)/ Northeast 801 (62)/Relic 512 (64)
Hey Boy	London, Paul & group	1963	Limelight 3015
Hey Boy	Street Dreams	1986	Starlight 38
Hey! (Bring My Baby Back)	Moonglows	NA	
Hey! Chickie Baby	Randell, Denny & group	1963	Cameo 255
Hey, Chiquita	Rivileers, Gene Pearson & the	1954	Baton 200
Hey, Clarice	Jades, Freddy Koenig & the	1963	Lori 9548/Valerie 225 (63)
Hey Cleopatra	Crane, Lor & group	1961	Radiant 1512
Hey! Country Girl	Don Juans, Andre Williams & the	1958	Fortune 842
Hey Doc	Blue Notes	19??	
Hey Doc	Timbers, Ronnie Martin & the	1956	Pilgrim 721
Hey Doll	Norman, Zack & group	1957	Poplar 111
Hey, Doll Baby	Clovers	1956	Atlantic 1083
Hey Dreamboat	Four Bits	1958	Coin 1501
Hey Everybody	Royal Lancers	1963	Lawn 215
Hey Fine Mama	Five Notes, Henry Pierce & the	1952	Specialty 461
Hey Fool	Holloway, Brenda (with the Carrolls)	1962	Donna 1358
Hey Girl	Dennis, Bradford & group	NA	Canadian 1600
Hey Girl	Five Keys	1965	Inferno 4500
Hey Girl	Hollywood Saxons	1975	Action Pac 2023 EP
Hey Girl	Knightbeats	1962	Planet 55
Hey Girl	Moniques	1962	Benn-X 55
Hey Girl	Perfections	1962	Lost Nite 111
Hey, Girl	Wrens	1955	Rama 174
Hey Girl Don't Leave Me	Technics	1962	Chex 1013
Hey Girl, I'm In Love With You	Channels, Earl Lewis & the	1972	Channel 1001
Hey Girl, Stop Leading Me On	Vacels	1965	Kama Sutra 200
Hey, Girlee	Marktones	1958	Ember 1030
Hey Good Lookin'	Ban Lons	1962	Fidelity 4056
Hey Good Lookin'	Ravens (with Dinah Washington)	1951	Columbia 39408
Hey Good Looking	Silvertones	1960	Elgin 005/006
Hey Hester	Tucker, Frank & group	1956	Baton 234

SONG	GROUP	YEAR	LABEL
Hey, Hey Baby	Salutations, Vito & the	1962, 1963	Kram 1202/Kram 5002/Herald 583
Hey, Hey Baby (acappella)	Islanders	1975	Relic LP 103
Hey, Hey, Girl	Zip, Danny & group	1964	MGM 13254
Hey Hey Gypsy Woman	Mackinteers, Teddy Mack & the	NA	Monroe 1
Hey Hey Hey	Sevilles	1964	Galaxy 717
(Hey Hey Hey) Alright	Dovells	1965	Swan 4231
Hey, Hey, I Love You	Allison, Gene & group	1957	Vee Jay 256
(Hey Hey) Juanita	Tokens (Date)	1961	Date 2737
Hey Hey Love Me	Halos	1965	Congress 253
Hey Hey Pretty Baby	Admiral Tones	1959	Felsted 8563
Hey, Hey, Pretty Baby	Colts	1962	Plaza 505
Hey Honey	Belvederes	1958	Dot 15852
Hey It's Love	Commands	1964	Dynamic 104
Hey Jean, Hey Dean	Dean & Jean (with the Del Satins)	1964	Rust 5075
Hey, Juanita	Five Stars (Detroit)	1957	Blue Boys Kingdom 106
Hey Jude	Royal Teens	1969	Musicor 139
Hey Jude	Velvet Five	1973	Nostalgia 102
Hey Junior	Four Guys	1963	Stride 5001
Hey, Landlord	Five Crystals	1959	Kane 25592/Relic 1003 (65)
Hey, Lena	Desires	1959	Hull 730
Hey Little Angel	Mascots	1962	Blast 206
Hey Little Baby	Codas, Charles Gully & the	1963	C.J. 641
Hey Little Boy	Gibson, Dolores & group	1954	Aladdin 3255
Hey Little Cobra	Rip Chords	1963	Columbia 42921
Hey, Little Cupid	Uniques	1958	End 1012
Hey Little Donkey	Rocky Fellers	1963	Scepter 1258
Hey Little Fool	Fabulous Blends, Big John & the	1964	Casa Grande 5001
Hey Little Fool	Holidays, Dick Holler & the	1962	Comet 2146
Hey Little Girl	Bachelors (Smash)	1961	Smash 1723
Hey, Little Girl	Buzzards, Big John & the	1954	Columbia 40345
Hey Little Girl	Catalinas	1961, 1980	Zebra 101
Hey Little Girl	Del Capris	1967	Ronjerdon 39/Kama Sutra 235 (67)
Hey, Little Girl	Deltones	1961	Dayhill 1002
Hey! Little Girl	Gladiolas	1957	Excello 2120
Hey Little Girl	Harris, Thurston (with the Sharps)	1959	Aladdin 3450
Hey Little Girl	Jades	1959	Nau-Voo 807
Hey! Little Girl	Larks (North Carolina)	1951	Apollo 429
Hey Little Girl	Quarter Notes	1966	Boom 60018
Hey! Little Girl	Techniques	1957	Stars 551/Roulette 4030 (57)
Hey, Little Girl Of Mine	Crestones	1964	Markie 123
Hey Little Lola	Rhythm Steppers	1959	Spinning 6010
Hey, Little Neil	Four Mints	1958	NRC 003
Hey Little One	Royal Lancers	1963	Lawn 215
Hey Little Rosie	Demolyrs	1964	U.W.R. 900/Jason 45-7
Hey Little School Girl	Imaginations	1991	Collectables CD 5726
Hey, Little School Girl	Marquees	1957	Okeh 7096
Hey, Little School Girl	Paragons	1957, 1986	Winley 215
Hey, Little School Girl	Winstons	1957	Cinemascope 8705
Hey, Little Schoolgirl	Cupcakes, Cookie & the	1964	Lyric 1015
Hey Little Willie	X-Cellents, Little Willie & the	1965	Smash 1996
Hey! Little Woman	Orioles, Sonny Til & the	1962	Charlie Parker 212
Hey Lonely One	Apollos, Paul Stefen & the	1963	Citation 5007
Hey Lover	Five Empressions	1965	Freeport 1001 (first pressing)
Hey, Mae Ethel	Wanderers	1953	Savoy 1109
Hey, Man	Mad Lads	1962	Mark Fi 1934
Hey Marvin	C & C Boys	1962	Duke 358
Hey, Maryann	Sputniks	1957	Pam Mar 602/Class 217
Hey Miss Fancy	Premiers (New York)	1957	RCA 6958
Hey, Miss Fannie	Clovers	1952	Atlantic 977
Hey Miss Fine	Spencer, Sonny & group	NA	Music Hall 2400
Hey Moon	Spindletoppers, Carl & the	1962	ABC 10346
Hey Mr. Banjo	Dell-Coeds	1962	Enith 712/Dot 16314 (62)
Hey Mrs. Jones	Check Mates	1961	Arvee 5030
Hey Mrs. Jones	Mr. Lee (with the Frank Andrade 5)	1964	Skylark 503
Hey Nita	Four Bells	1954	Bell 5047

SONG	GROUP	YEAR	LABEL
Hey, Norman!	Royaltones	1956	Old Town 1028
Hey Now	Flamingos	1959	Decca 30948
Hey Now	Pedestrians, Jaywalker & the (featuring Pete Antell)	1962	Amy 848
Hey Now	Platters	1953	Federal 12153
Hey, Now	Voices	1955	Cash 1014
Hey Now Baby	Horizons	1964	Regina 1321
Hey Now Baby	Page Boys	1959	Tel 1007
Hey, Operator	Charades	1964	Warner Bros. 5415
Hey, Pappa	Blue Jays (Checker)	1953	Checker 782
Hey Patty	Leerics	NA	Un-Released Gold 799
Hey, Peanuts	Inventions	1960	Up 111
Hey Phoebe, Get Off The Phone	Jet Streams	1958	Decca 30743
Hey Pretty Baby	Blue Stars	1977	Arcade 102
Hey, Pretty Baby	Candles, Rochell & the	1961	Swingin' 634
Hey, Pretty Baby	Ladders	1959	Vest 826
Hey Pretty Girl	Crowns, Arthur Lee Maye & the	1957	Flip 330
Hey Roly Poly	Four Dates	1958	Chancellor 1019
Hey Rube	Flannels	1956	Tampa 121
Hey Rube	Rocketeers	1956	Modern 999
Hey Ruby	Valentines	1960	King 5433
Hey Sally Mae	Corvairs	1962	Comet 2145
Hey Sam	Jive Five	1982	Ambient Sound 03053
Hey! Santa Claus	Moonglows	1953	Chance 1150
Hey Senor	Tiaras	1963	Valiant 6030
Hey Senorita	Admirations (featuring Joseph Lorello)	1962	Mercury 71883
Hey Senorita	Catalinas	1961	Zebra 101
Hey Senorita	Dell Vikings	1973	Blue Sky 104
Hey, Senorita	Dell Vikings	1957, 1973	Luniverse 106
Hey Senorita	Drifters (1959-forward)	1960	Atlantic 2062
Hey Senorita	Exquisites	1985	Avenue D 12
Hey Senorita	Heartspinners, Dino & the	1973	Bim Bam Boom 119
Hey Senorita	Jades	1962	Adona 1445
Hey Senorita	Penguins	1954	Dootone 348/Power 7023 (54)
Hey Senorita	Street Corner Society	1979	U.G.H.A. 8
Hey Senorita	Swallows (Maryland)	1991	Starbound 510
Hey Senorita	Tokays	1967	Brute 001
Hey Senorita	Wonders	1959	Ember 1051
Hey Senorita (acappella)	Valids	1966	Amber 853
Hey, Sister Lizzie	Spaniels	1955	Vee Jay 154 (first pressing)
Hey Sister Lizzie	Spaniels	1955	Vee Jay 154 (second pressing)
Hey Sport	Playgirls	1959	RCA 7546
Hey Sugar (Don't Get Serious)	Dells	1965	Vee Jay 712
Hey Swamper	Alamos, Sammy Houston & the	1960	Cleveland 104
Hey There	Castaways	1962	Assault 1869
Hey There	Crescents	1963	Hamilton 50033
Hey There	Iridescents	1963	Hudson 8107
Hey There	Possessions	1964	Britton
Hey There	Twiliters	1961	Nix 102
Hey There Sexy Lady	Midnighters, Hank Ballard & the	1974	Stang 5058
Hey Theresa	White, Floyd & group	1958	Tee Vee 302
Hey You	Contels	1959	Warwick 103
Hey You	Dimples, Eddie Cooley & the	1957	Royal Roost 628
Hey You	Imaginations	1961	Music Makers 108/Duel 507 (61)/ Bo Marc 301 (61)
Hey You	Microgrooves	1990	Crystal Ball 160
Hey You	Miller Sisters	NA	Capri
Hey You	Murphy, Bob & group	1963	Lawn 221
Hey You (acappella)	Reminiscents	1975	Relic LP 109
Hey You, Shoobeoohbee	Colts	1956	Vita 130
Hey, Young Girl	Demens	1957	Teenage 1008
Hey-Da-Da-Dow	Dolphins	1964	Fraternity 937
Hi Diddley Dee Dum Dum	Dells	1963	Argo 5442
Hi Fi Baby	Castaleers	1958	Felsted 8504
Hi Ho Merry O	Maye, Hartsy & group	NA	Zell 4397

SONG	GROUP	YEAR	LABEL
Hi Lily, Hi Lo	Raiders, Tony Castle & the	1961	Gone 5099
Hi Ya Honey!	Barlow, Dean	1956	Davis 444
Hiccup	Magnificents	1956	Vee Jay 208
Hickory Dickory	Lions	1960	Imperial 5678
Hickory Dickory Dock	Rock-A-Byes, Baby Jane & the	1962	Spokane 4001
Hickory Dickory Dock	Sha-Weez, Big Boy Myles & the	1956	Specialty 590
Hickory Dickory Rock	Jumpin' Jacks, Danny Lamego & the	1956	Andrea 101
Hide And Seek	Astro Jets	1961	Imperial 5760
Hideaway	Sequins	1963	Terrace 7515
Hideaway Heaven	Jones, Dee & group	1961	Brent 7023
Hi-Diddle-Diddle	Combo-Nettes, Jane Porter & the	1955	Combo 74
Hiding My Tears With A Smile	Atomics, Dennis Brown & the	1957	Atomic 57-101
Hi-Fi Sweetie	Teen Notes	1961	Deb 127
High And The Mighty, The	Dukes, Billy Duke & the	1954	Coral 61203
High Blood Pressure	Marathons	NA	Collectables LP 5081
High Blood Pressure	Zodiacs, Maurice Williams & the	1961	Herald 565
High Falutin' Honey	Ryan, Cathy (with the Admirals)	1956	King 4890
High Flyin' Baby	Harptones	1954, 1956	Bruce 123/Tip Top 401
High Heel Shoes	Marie Ann & group	1960	Warwick 605
High Heel Sneakers	Playboys, John Fred & the	1962	Montel 998
High Noon	Salutations, Vito & the	1965	Apt 25079
High Noon	Singing Belles	1960	Madison 132
High On A Hill	Accents, Scott English & the	1963	Sultan 4003/Spokane 4003 (63)
High On a Hill	Marcels	1973	Queen Bee 47001
High Sailing	Hightones, Claude & the	1958	Pam Mar 614
High School	Classmates	1960	Marquee 101
High School Affair	Five Chums	1958	Excello 2123
High School Dance	Davies, Johnny Greco & the	1959	Sonic 813
High School Dance	El Pollos	1958	Studio 999
High School Diploma	Capers	1959	Vee Jay 315
High School Dreams	Damons, Carl Lawrence & the	1958	Jean 0001
High School Flame	Freelancers, Dan Williams & the	NA	Beth 20/Freelance 20
High School Girl	Rock-A-Fellas, Eddie Bell & the	1958	Coed 505
High School Lovers	Rhythmettes	1960	Coral 62186
High School Queen	Johnson 3 Plus 1	1969	Tangerine 1013
High School Romance	Hi-Lites, Ronnie & the	1963, 1965	Win 252/ABC 10685
High School Social	Indigos	1958	Cornel 515
High Sign	Diamonds	1958	Mercury 71291
Higher And Higher	Revelations	NA	Starlight 15
Highest Mountain	Banlons	1959	Fidelity 4051/Baron 108 (73)
Hi-Heel Sneakers	Aztecs	1964	World Artists 1029
Hillum Boy	Five Crowns	1959	De'Besth 1123
Hindu Baby	Emanons (New York)	1956	Gee 1005
Hindu Lullaby	Tokens (Brooklyn)	1963	RCA 8148
Hi-Oom	Saucers	1964	Kick 100
Hip Enough	Marvellos	1962	Exodus 6216
Hip Talk	Ascots	1962	Bethlehem 3046
Hip Talk	Exzels	1963	Crossfire 228
Hippity Ha	Miller Sisters	1955	Herald 455/Herald 527 (58)
Hippity Hop	Sharptones, Billy Sharp & the	1958	Kudo 668
Hippity Hop	Sugar Tones	1960	Cannon 391
Hippy Dippy	Gems (Mercury)	1961	Mercury 71819
Hippy-Dippy-Daddy	Cookies	1957	Josie 822
His Girl	Vacels, Ricky & the	1963	Fargo 1050
His Greatest Creation	Sunglows, Sunny & the	1964	Tear Drop 3040
His Hand In Mine	Belltones, Lacille Watkins & the	1956	Kapp 145
His Lips Get In The Way	Shirelles	1964	Scepter 1267
His Way With The Girls	Lornettes	1965	Gallico 110
History Of Love	Payne, Little Leon & group	NA	Daco 701
Hit And Runaway Love	Voice Masters	1959	Anna 103
Hit 'N Run Lover	Sandelles	1964	Debonair 309
Hitch Hiken	Romeos	1962	Amy 840
Hitchhiker, The	Five Cashmeres	1962	Golden Leaf 108
(H-mmm, Andre Williams Is) Movin'	Diablos (Andre Williams & Gino Parks)	1960	Fortune 851
Ho Ho	Drivers & the Spacemen	1959	Alton 252

SONG	GROUP	YEAR	LABEL
Hobo	Curry, Earl (with the Blenders)	1951	Post 2011
Hobo's Prayer, The	Fiestas	1961	Old Town 1111
Hockaday Pt. 1	Four Pennies	1963	Rust 5070
Hogwalk	Davies, Johnny Greco & the	1959	Sonic 813
Ho-Hum Deedle-Dum	Indigos	1961	Image 5001
Ho-Hum-Deedle-Dum	Epics	1961	Lynn 510
Hokey Pokey	Emersons	1959	Cub 9027
Hokey Pokey	Spydells	1963	Beltone 2032
Hokey-Smokey Mama	Starlings	1955	Dawn 212
Hold Back The Dawn	Debonaires (New York)	1962	Dore 654
Hold Back The Dawn	Jades	1963	Dore 687
Hold Back The Tears	Delacardos	1961	United Artists 310
Hold 'Em, Joe	Four Fellows (Brooklyn - Glory)	1956	Glory 238
Hold Me	Five Jades (Bronx, N.Y.)	1972	Kelway 103
Hold Me	Five Keys	1952	Aladdin 3136
Hold Me	Frank, Carol & group	1959	Excello 2175
Hold Me	Kent, Al & group	1959	Wizzard 100
Hold Me	Kings (Baltimore)	1959	Jay-Wing 5805
Hold Me	Larks (North Carolina)	1952	Apollo 1194
Hold Me	Long, Bobby & his Cherrios	1959	Glow-Hill 504
Hold Me Baby	Barons (New Orleans)	NA	Imperial (unreleased)
Hold Me, Baby	Chordcats	1954	Cat 112
Hold Me Close	Carallons, Lonnie & the	1959	Mohawk 111
Hold Me Close	Jay, Lori & group	1956	
Hold Me Close	Lovers, Billy Love & the	1964	Dragon 4403
Hold Me Close	Marktones	1957	Ember 1022
Hold Me Close	Sparks, Nathan Ray & the	1958	Rocko 510
Hold Me Darling	Quarternotes	1962	Little Star 112
Hold Me Lover	Versatones	1963	Richie 4081
Hold Me, Squeeze Me (Hold Me Tight)	Orioles, Sonny Til & the	1951	Jubilee 5061
Hold Me, Thrill Me, Chill Me	Flairs	1955	Flair 1056
Hold Me, Thrill Me, Kiss Me	Deltas	1962	Philips 40023
Hold Me, Thrill Me, Kiss Me	Orioles, Sonny Til & the	1953	Jubilee 5108
Hold Me Tight	Blue Dots	1954	DeLuxe 6067
Hold Me Tight	Jaguars	1958	Ebb 129
Hold Me Tight	Treasures, Pete Anders & the	1964	Shirley 500
Hold Me Tight	Videls	NA	Magic Carpet LP 1005
Hold Me Until Eternity	Diablos (featuring Nolan Strong)	1955	Fortune 514
Hold My Baby	Five Letters	1958	Ivy 102
Hold My Hand	Clusters, Gus Coletti & the	1957	Tin Pan Alley 206
Hold My Hand	Endorsers	1959	Moon 109
Hold My Hand	Sequins, Jessie & the	1959	Boxer 201/Profile 4008 (59)
Hold My Hand	Spencer, Sonny & group	NA	Music Hall 2400
Hold On	Marcels	1962	Colpix 640
Hold On	Peppers	1954	Chess 1577
Hold On Baby	Magnificent 6	NA	L-Brown 01659
Hold On To What Cha Got (And Get One More)	Fidelitys	1958	Baton 252
Hold On To What You've Got	Dells	1961	Vee Jay 376
Holding On To A Memory	Beard, Dean & group	1959	Challenge 59048
Holding Your Hand	Diamonds	1959	Mercury 71468
Hold-Out	Impacs	1963	Arlen 741
Hole 'Em Joe	Romaines, Romaine Brown & His	1956	Decca 30122
Hole In The Bucket	Rhythm Jesters	1956	Rama 213
Hole In The Middle Of The Moon	Ravens	1959	Top Rank 2003
Holey Money	Sharp Cats, Verna Williams & the	NA	Versailles 865
Holly Golly Reel	Miller Sisters	1962	Hull 752
Hollywood Actor	Jaynells	1984	N/A
Hollywood And Vine	Dell Vikings	1977	Fee Bee 173
Holy One	Fender, Freddy & group	1958	Duncan 1000/Imperial 5659 (60)
Holy Smoke Baby	Cadillacs	1958	Josie 842
Holy Sombrero	Blackwells	1959	G&G 131/Guyden 2020 (59)
Hombre	Belmonts	1962	Sabina 503
Home	Commodores	NA	4-S
Home	Scott, Jimmy & group	1958	King 5104

SONG	GROUP	YEAR	LABEL
Home By Eleven	Redcoats, Steve Alaimo & the	1959	Dade 1800
Home In Pasadena	Skylarks	1953	RCA 5257
Home Is Where The Heart Is	Dreamlovers	1960	V-Tone 211
Home Is Where You Come From	Little David & group	1963	Savoy 1617
Home Is Where You Hang Your Heart	Dominoes	1956	Decca 29933
Home Of The Brave	Treasures, Bonnie & the	1965	Phi-Dan 5005
Home On The Range	Atlantics	1965	Rampart 614
Home On The Range	Saxons	1957	Our
Home Town	Medallions	1961	Sarg 194
Home Type Girl	Overtones	1967	Ajax 175
Home Under My Hat	Dubs	1973	Johnson 097 (recorded in 1957)
Home Work	L'Cap-Tans	1959	Savoy 1567/D.C. 0416 (59)
Home Wrecker	Night Owls, Tony Allen & the	1960	Crown LP 5231
Homemade	Phaetons	1959	Hi-Q 5012
Homesick	Raves, Jimmy Ricks & the	1962	Atco 6220
Hometown Girl	Palisades	1961	Dore 609
Homework	Classmates	1961	Seg-Way 104
Homework	Diplomats, Dino & the	1961	Vida 0100/0101
Honest	Gazelles	1956	Gotham 315
Honest I Do	Audios, Cell Foster & the	1956	Ultra 105
Honest I Do	Cooper, Babs & group	1962	Indigo 144
Honest I Do	Fulton, Sonny & group	1959	Chelsea 533
Honest I Do	Innocents	1960	Indigo 105
Honest I Do	Playboys, Gary Gillespie & the	1962	Delta 520
Honest I Will	Chateaus	1963	Coral 62364
Honestly Sincere	Marcels	1963	Colpix LP 454
Honey	Honey Boys	1974	Owl 333
Honey	Ravens	1946, 1949	King 310
Honey Babe	Solitaires	1963	Old Town 1139
Honey Baby	Blue Diamonds (Ernie K-Doe Kador)	1954	Savoy 1134
Honey Bee	Drifters (1959-forward)	1961	Atlantic 2096
Honey Bee	Knightcaps	1958	Punch 6000
Honey Bee	Spiders	1957	Imperial 5423
Honey Bee	Stevedores, Steve & the	1958	Rebel 1314
Honey Bug	Chromatics, Sherry Washington & the	1956	Million 2016
Honey Bun	Cleftones	1957	Unreleased
Honey Bun	Colts	1956	Vita 121
Honey Bun	Fabulous Embers, Willis Sanders & the	1958	Millionaire 775
Honey Bun	Neons	1974	Vintage 1016
Honey Bun	Playboys, Charles White & the	1955	Cat 115
Honey Chile	Arrows, Joe Lyons & the	1956	Hollywood 1065
Honey Chile	Echoes, Sonny Roberts & the	1958	Impala 1001
Honey Chile	Poets	1960	Spot 107/Imperial 5664 (60)
Honey Dew	Lawrence, Bob & group	1957	Mark-X 7005
Honey Dew	Sliders, Byron Gipson & the	1955	Specialty 566
Honey Doll	Hi-Lites, Randy Hard & the	1958	NRC 013
Honey Doll	Randells, Rick & the	1959	ABC 10055
Honey Drop	Velours	1956	Onyx 501/Relic 503 (64)
Honey For Sale	Nelson, Chip & group	1960	Edsel 783
Honey From The Bee	Larks (North Carolina)	1955	Apollo 475
Honey Gee	Saigons	1955	Dootone 375
Honey, Honey	Blackwells	1960	Jamie 1150
Honey, Honey	Capitols	1973	Baron 103
Honey, Honey	Crowns, Arthur Lee Maye & the	1956, 1958	Cash 1063/Imperial 5790 (61)/ Dig 124
Honey Honey	Supremes (Ohio)	1957	Ace 530 (unreleased)
Honey Honey	Teenchords, Lewis Lymon & the	1957, 1984	Fury 1003
Honey, Honey	Toppers (ABC)	1956	ABC 9667
Honey, Honey	Truetones	1958	Monument 4501
Honey, Honey, Honey	Challengers	1962	Tri-Phi 1012
Honey Hush	Rainbows	NA	Red Robin (unreleased)
Honey, I Could Fall In Love	Four Stars	1954	King 1382
Honey I Don't Want You	Ravens	1951	Columbia 39198
Honey, I Love You	Laurels	1985	R.A.M. 501012
Honey In The Rock	Larks (North Carolina)	1952	Apollo 1189

SONG	GROUP	YEAR	LABEL
Honey Let Me Stay	Entrees, Chuck Corley & the	1957	Fee Bee 219
Honey Love	Honey Boys	1974	Boogie Music 1
Honey Love	Crowns, Arthur Lee Maye & the	1957	Dig 100 (unreleased)/151
Honey Love	Drifters (Pre-1959)	1954	Atlantic 1029
Honey Love	Four Lovers	1956	RCA 6519
Honey Love	Harptones (with Bunny Paul)	1954	Essex 364
Honey Love	Jayos, Johnny Otis & the	1957	Dig LP 104
Honey Love	Romans	NA	Haven
Honey Love	Storm, Billy (with the Storms)	1961	Atlantic 2112
Honey Please Believe Me	Johnson, Arthur & group	1959	Wanger 190
Honey, Take Me Home With You	Parliaments	1958	Len 101
Honey-Bun	Embers, Willis Sanders & the	1958	Millionaire 775/Unart 2004 (58)
Honeybun Cha Cha	Honeytones	1955	Wing 90013
Honeybunch	Du Droppers	1955	Groove EP EGA-2
Honey-Dew	Honey-Do's	1961	Sue 746
Honeydripper, The	Clovers	1961	United Artists 307
Honeydrop	Three Honeydrops	1957	Music City 813
Honeymoon, The	Solitaires	1956	Old Town 1019
Honeysuckle Baby	Satellites, Bobby Day & the	1958	Class 220
Honeysuckle Rose	Blenders (New York)	1950	Decca 48156
Honeysuckle Rose	Platters	1960	Mercury LP 20589/ Mercury LP 60254 (60)
Hong Kong	Hi Fives (with Rex Middleton)	1956	Flair-X 3000
Hong Kong	Quinns	1958	Cyclone 111
Hong Kong	Ray-O-Vacs	1956	Kaiser 389
Hong Kong Baby	Tabbys	1963	Metro 2
Hong Kong Jelly Wong	Royaltones	NA	Murray Hill LP 000083
Hongry	Coasters	1965	Atco 6341
Honk	Honkers	1959	Okeh 7124
Honkey Tonk Woman	Fabulous Playboys	1960	Apollo 760
Honky Tonk	Drifters (1959-forward)	1960	Atlantic LP 8041
Honky Tonk	Valrays	1964	Parkway 904
Honky Tonk Hardwood Floor	Nitecaps, Clyde Stacy & the	1958	Bullseye 1008
Honky Tonk Hop	Beau Belles	1958	Arrow 729
Honky Tonk Joe	Valiants (Columbia)	1961	Columbia 41931
Honky-Tonk Guitar	Top Hands, Joe Dee & His	1962	Pat Riccio 105
Honolulu	Serenaders (Hanover)	1958	Hanover 4507
Honor Bright	Cavaliers	1955	Decca 29556
Honor Role Of Love	Privateers, Joyce & the	1962	Agon 1003
Hoo Bop De Bow	Thunderbirds, Bert Convy & the	1955	Era 1001
Hoochi Coochi Coo, The	Midnighters, Hank Ballard & the	1960	King 5430
Hoodoo The Voodoo	Highschool Chanters	1959	Fashion 001
Hook, Line And Sinker	Relations, Gloria & the	NA	Bonnie 101/102
Hoopla	Dumonts	1961	King 5552
Hooray For Love	Run-A-Rounds	1963	KC 116
Hootch, The	Pixies 3	1964	Mercury 72288
Hootin' In The Kitchen	Boyle, Billy	1963	Lawn 221
Hooty Sapperticker	Boys, Barbara & the	1958	
Hop And Skip	Premiers (Bond)	1958	Bond 5803/5804
Hop Scotch	Monitors	1958	Specialty 636
Hop Scotch Hop	Revelletts, Jimmy Charles & the	1960	Promo 1002
Hop Scotch Rock	Five Quails	1957	Mercury 71154
Hop, Skip And Jump	Opals	1962	Beltone 2025
Hope	Duprees	1969	Heritage 811
Hope And Pray	Bel-Aires (Arc)	1959	Arc 4451
Hope And Pray	Voice Masters	1959	Anna 101
Hope, Faith And Dreams	Rays, Hal Miller & the	1961	Topix 6003
Hope He's True	Marquis	1956	Onyx 505/Relic 505 (64)
Hope, Prayer And A Dream	Delfis 117	1978	Crystal Ball 117
Hopefully Yours	Larks (North Carolina)	1951	Apollo 1180
Hopeless Love	Creoles, Lil Millet & His	1956	Specialty 565
Hopeless Love	Geoles, Lil Millet & the	1955	Specialty 565
Hopin' For Your Return	Savoys (Sold)	1973	Sold 505
Hoping You'll Fall In Love	Five Arcades (Dave Antrell overdubbed)	1973. 1985	Sacto 103 (phony label; rec. 1973)/ Antrell 103

SONG	GROUP	YEAR	LABEL
Hoping You'll Understand	Strangers	1954	King 4728
Hoppin' & Boppin'	Belairs	1955	GG 521
Hoppy Hop, The	Mystics	1962	King 5678
Horizontal Lieutenant, The	Diamonds	1962	Mercury 71956
Horror Pictures	Calvanes	1958	Deck 580
Horse's Neck	Hot Shots	1954	Savoy 1128
Hot Biscuits	Pheasants	1963	Throne 802
Hot Blood	Trailblazers, Shirlee Hunter & the	1959	Tip Top 720
Hot Dog	Curtin, Lee & group	1961	Gizmo 003
Hot Dog Dooly Wah	Original Pyramids	1961	Shell 304
Hot Dog Dooly Wah	Pyramids (Detroit)	1958	Shell 711
Hot Fudge Sundae	Romeo, Al & group	1963	Laurie 3177
Hot Licks	Starlighters	1960	Wheel 1004
Hot Love	Wailers	1954	Columbia 40288
Hot Mamma	Chanters, Gene Ford & the	1955	Combo 92
Hot Rod	Bel Raves, Lou Berry & the	1959	Dreem 1001
Hot Rod	Flips, Little Joey & the	1975	Monogram 111 (bootleg)
Hot Rod	Markeys	1958	RCA 7256
Hot Rod Hop	Sportsmen	1955	Key 503
Hot Rod USA	Rip Chords	1964	Columbia 43035
Hot Rotten Soda Pop	Cues	1955	Groove
Hot Rotten Soda Pop (Oh, My Toe)	Four Students	1955	Groove 0110
Hot Tamale	Hatfield, Bobby & group	1963	Moonglow 220
Hot Tamales	Counts	1954	Dot 1199
Hot Time	Metronomes	1962	Challenge 9157
Hot Water	V-Eights, Stoney Jackson & the	1961	Vibro 4007
Hot Ziggety	Drifters	1954	Atlantic 1070
Hotcha Cha-Cha Brown	Flares	1960	Felsted 8604
Hotcha Mighty Knows	Exotics	1961	Coral 62289
Houdini	Gardenias	1958	Hi-Q 5005
Hound Dog	Raging Storms	1962	Warwick 677
Hound Dog Blues	El-Derocks	1958	Sapphire 1004
House Cat	Romancers	1956	Dootone 381
House Cleaning	Spaniels	1953	Vee Jay 103
House I Live In, The	Ravens	1949	National 9065
House Of Blue Lights	El-Rich Trio	1966	Elco SK-1
House Of Cards	Grant, Jason & group	1959	20th Fox 151
House Of Cards	Wrens	1986	Rama (unreleased)
House Of Heartache	Neptunes	1963	Instant 3255
House Of Love	Five Bell Aires, Henry Hall & the	1990	Relic LP 5085
House Of Tears	Fabulons, Bobby Winslow & the	NA	Fabulous 1001
House On The Hill	Midnighters, Hank Ballard & the	1963	King 5719
House Where Lovers Dream (acappella)	Timetones	1963	Times Square 34/Relic 526 (65)
House With No Windows	Checkers	1954	King 4710
House With No Windows	Midnighters, Hank Ballard & the	1959	King 5245
Housewife Blues	Enchanters (Queens, N.Y.)	1952	Jubilee 5080
How	Jewels (Los Angeles)	1956	Imperial 5377
How	Medallions	1954, 1972	Dootone 344 (unreleased)
How	Phantoms, Vernon Green & the	1956	Specialty unreleased
How A Woman Does Her Man	Lyrics, William Wigfall & the	1963	(Russel's) Gold Wax 101/ Goldwax 910 (63)
How About A Date	Honorables	1961	Honor Records 100
How About It	Sunbeams	1956	Dot 1280
How About Me?	Belmonts	1962	Sabina 505
How About That	Blue Diamonds, Don & the	1961	Skylark 113
How Am I Doing	Thrillers, Little Joe & the	1963	Rose 835
How Am I To Know	Miller Sisters	1956	Ember 1004
How Are You	Foxettes, Lady Fox & the	1962	Don-El 118
How Are You?	Monarchs	1956	Neil 103/Melba 103 (56)
How Blind Can You Be	Falcons (Regent)	1952	Regent 1041
How Blind Can You Be	Orioles, Sonny Til & the	1952	Jubilee 5071
How Blue My Heart	Shepherd, Johnnie (with the Belmonts)	1961	Tilden 3001
How Can I Be Sure	Thunderbirds, Billy Ford & the	1957	Vik 0263
How Can I Find True Love	Dell Vikings	1956, 1980	Fee Bee 205/Dot 15538 (57)/ Dot 16092 (60)/Collectables 1251

SONG	GROUP	YEAR	LABEL
How Can I Forget	Holiday, Jimmy & group	1963	Everest 2022
How Can I Forget Her	Van Dykes	1966	Green Sea 108
How Can I Forget You?	Five Keys	1960	King 5302
How Can I Get Along Without You	Wanderers	1975	Savoy 1098 (unreleased)
How Can I Help It	Cardell, Nick & group	1963	Liberty 55556
How Can I Let You Know	La Donna, Marie & group	1960	Gateway 730
How Can I Love You	Swinging Hearts	1961	620 1002/NRM 1002 (61)
How Can I Make Her Mine	Ravons, Bobby Roberts & the	1964	Cameo 339
How Can I Pretend	Sugar Tones	1960	Cannon 391
How Can I Tell Her	Fourmost	1964	Atco 6317
How Can I Tell Him	Lords, Yvette & the	1964	Yvette 103
How Can I Tell You?	Flairs, Shirley Gunter & the	1955	Flair 1076
How Can I Thank You	Pastels	NA	Unreleased
How Can I Win	Hi-Fives	1958	Decca 30576
How Can I Win Your Love	Twin Tones	1955	Atlantic 1064
How Can You Be	Young Lions	1958	Tampa 158
How Can You Be So Foul	Meadowlarks, Don Julian & the	1965	Jerk 100
How Can You Forget So Soon	Sugar Tones	1960	Cannon 392
How Can You Treat Me This Way?	Magic Tones	1954	King 4681
How Clever Of You	Fortunes	1958	Decca 30688
How Come	Duvells	1962	Rust 5045
How Come	Green, Birdie & group	1962	End 1117
How Could I Ever Leave You?	Wheels	1957	Premium 410
How Could I Know	Ravens	1948	National 9056
How Could You	Bussy, Terry & group	1956	Jazzmar 103
How Could You	Companions	1962	Amy 852
How Could You	Dell Vikings	1958	Mercury 71390
How Could You	Mello-Moods	1951	Red Robin 105
How Could You (Break My Heart)	Enchanters (Queens, N.Y.)	1952	Onyx 2007/Jubilee 5072 (52)
How Could You Call It Off	Chantels	1958, 1960	End 1020/1069
How Could You (different version from the one in 1951)	Mello-Moods	1964	Oldies 45 167
How Could You Do This To Me	Five Keys	1953	Audio-Video (unreleased)
How Could You Hurt Me So	Marvells	1962	Finer Arts 2024
How Could You Hurt Me So?	Teasers	1954	Checker 800
How Could You Know	Arlington, Bruce & group	1964	King 5918
How Could You Leave	Midnighters, Hank Ballard & the	1963	King 5746
How Deep Is The Ocean	Cleftones	1961	Gee 1080
How Deep Is The Ocean	Dawns	1959	Climax 104
How Deep Is The Ocean	Marcels	1963	888 101
How Deep Is The Ocean	Three Chuckles	1956	Vik LP 1067
How Deep Is The Ocean	Twains, Tommy Sawyer & the	1962	Diamond 112
How Deep Is The Ocean?	Sultans	1954	Duke 125
How Do I Keep The Girls Away	Mar-Vells	1963	Butane 778
How Do I Know	Georgettes	1960	Goldisc 3006
How Do I Say I'm Sorry	Manhattans	1958	Warner 1015
How Do I Stand Today	Sharpettes, King & the	1964	Aldo 503
How Do You Break An Angels Heart	Aldenaires, Paul Alden & the	NA	Glolite 106
How Do You Do With Me	Boys	1964	SVR 1002
How Do You Expect Me To Get It	Five Keys	1954	Aladdin 3245
How Do You Feel	Cleftones	1961	Gee 1064
How Do You Feel	Corlettes	NA	Pace/Nita 711
How Do You Like It	Sheppards (Chicago - Mirwood)	1966	Mirwood 5534
How Do You Like It (acappella)	Dell Vikings	1975	Relic LP 109
How Do You Mend A Broken Heart	Serenaders (New Jersey)	1959	Cross Country
How Do You Speak To An Angel	Marcels, Walt Maddox & the	1982	Super M 3073
How Do You Speak To An Angel	Sonotones	1954	Bruce 105
How Do You Speak To An Angel?	Devotions	1972	Kape 701
How Do You Think I Feel	Rock-A-Ways, Ricky Vac & the	1961	Hilltop 1871
How Does It Feel To Be Lonely	Echomores	NA	Rocket 1048
How Far Does A Friendship Go	Sultans	1962	Jam 107
How Foolish Am I	Skylighters	NA	Emjay 6152
How High Is The Mountain	Illusions	1961	Ember 1071
How High The Moon	Royal Robins	1964	ABC 10542
How Hurt I Am	Dockett, Jimmy & group	NA	Camille 3002

SONG	GROUP	YEAR	LABEL
How I Feel	Spiders, Chuck Carbo & the	1956	Imperial 5376
How I Love You	Alaimo, Chuck	1957	MGM 12508
How I Love You	Catalinas	1979	Crystal Ball 132
How I Need You, Baby!	Dappers (New York)	1956	Rainbow 373
How I Wish I Was Single Again	Four Epics	1963	Laurie 3183
How It Feels	Pyramiders	1958	Scott 1505
How Long	Capris (Philadelphia)	NA	Collectables LP 5000
How Long	Cupids, Darwin & the	1960	Jerden 1
How Long	Five Keys	1952	Aladdin 3131
How Long	Robins	1957	Whippet 212
How Long	Solitaires	1956	Murray Hill LP 56
How Long	Versa-Tones	1961	Kenco 5015
How Long Has She Been Gone	Marsmen, Marvin & Johnny & the	1954	Specialty 488
How Long, How Long Blues	Dominoes	1956	Federal 12263
How Long Must A Fool Go On (Second Pressing)	Guides	1959	Guyden 2023 (second pressing, first is by the Swallows)
How Long Must A Fool Go On? (First Pressing)	Swallows (California)	1959	Guyden 2023 (first pressing, second is by the Guides)
How Long Must I Wait For You?	Larks (North Carolina)	1952	Apollo 435
How Long Must I Wait?	Rays	1957	Argo 1074/Chess 1678 (57)
How Long Must I Wait?	Strangers	1955	King 4766
How Lucky I Am	Shallows	1961	Rae-Cox 108
How Many More Times?	Robins	1961	Lavender 001
How Many Souls	Mellotones, Doug Williams & the	1958	Hy-Tone 103
How Many Times	Dantes	1964	Rotate 5008
How Many Times?	Twilighters (Bronx, N.Y.)	1957	J.V.B. 83
How Much	Skyliners	1960	Calico 114
How Much Do You Love Me	Entertainers	1963	Demand 2932
How Much I Love You	Metronomes (Harold Sonny Wright)	1957	Cadence 1339
How Much I Love You (acappella)	Five Jades (Bronx, N.Y.)	1965	Your Choice 1012
How Much Is That Doggie In The Window	Rock-A-Byes, Baby Jane & the	1962	United Artists 560
How Much Longer?	Du Droppers	1954	Groove 0013
How Much Love Can One Heart Hold	Rookies, Joe Perkins & the	1957	King 5030
How My Prayers Have Changed	Clinton, Buddy & group	1959	Time 1016
How Nice	Tokens (Brooklyn)	1967	Warner Bros. 7056
How Old Must I Be	Knight, Bob	1961	Laurel 1020
How Sentimental Can I Be	Subway Serenade	NA	Clifton EP 504
How Sentimental Can I Be	Swans (St. Louis)	1955	Ballad 1004/1005
How Sentimental Can I Be?	Mellows	1954	Jay-Dee 793
How Should I Feel	Dynamics	1960	Decca 31046/Decca 31450 (62)
How Soon	Wonderlettes	NA	Baja 4506
How Soon?	Jacks	1956	RPM 454
How Soon?	Vocaleers	1953	Red Robin 119
How Still The Night	Chord'R Notes	1964	Fargo 1061
How Strange	Naturals	1958	Red Top 113/Hunt 325 (58)
How Sweet	Pacers	1961, 1980	Guyden 2064
How The Time Flies	Wallace, Jerry (with the Jewels)	1958	Challenge 59013
How To Do The Bacon Fat	Five Dollars	1957	Fortune 833
How To Love A Woman	Mandells	NA	Trans World 711
How To Love Him	Frontera, Tommy & group	1960	Rem 103
How To Make A Hit Record	Hitmakers	1965	Dore 738
How To Pick A Winner	Zodiacs, Maurice Williams & the	1966	Dee-Su 311
How To Start A Romance	Kings, Little Hooks & the	1963	Century 1300/Little Rick 909 (63)/ Chess 1867 (63)
How To Win Your Love	Martin, Sonny & group	1959	Rocko 518
How Was Your Weekend	Mac, Bobby & group	1962	Vended 104
How Will I Know	Pitch Pikes	1957	Mercury 71147
How Will I Know	Strands	1960	Firefly 331
How Will I Know My Love	Strays, Ray & the	1962	Larric 101
How Will I Remember?	Sunsets	1959	Rae-Cox 102
How Would You Know	Robins	1953	RCA 5434
How Would You Like Me To Love You	Shevelles	1964	World Artists 1025
How You Lied	Cuff Links	1957	Dootone 413
How You Move Me	Four Bars	NA	
Howie	Tonettes	1958	Doe 101/ABC 9905 (58)

SONG	GROUP	YEAR	LABEL
How's Your Bird	Ferns, Baby Ray & the	1963	Donna 1378
How's Your New Love Treating You	Debonaires (Golden World)	NA	Golden World 38
Hoy Hoy	Nitecaps, Clyde Stacy & the	1957	Candlelight 1015
Huckle-Buck	Flares	NA	London (England) LP 8034
Hucklebuck With Jimmy	Five Keys	1971 (1951)	Aladdin 3099
Huckster Man, The	Derbys	1963	KC 111
Huddle, The	Elgins (California)	1962	Joed 716
Huffin' And Puffin'	Stylers	1956	Jubilee 5246
Hug A Little, Kiss A Little	Lamplighters	1955	Federal 12242
Hug Me Baby	Five Crowns	1954	Rainbow 251
Hug-A-Bee	Hearts, Lee Andrews & the (as Lee Andrews)	1965	V.I.P. 1601
Huggie's Bunnies	Blendells	1964	Rampart 641/Reprise 0291 (64)
Hula Hands	Capitols, Johnny Houston & the	1957	East West 100
Hula Hop	Platters	1958	Unreleased
Hully Gully	Hollywood Argyles	1960	Lute 6002
Hully Gully	Olympics	1967	Mirwood 5533
Hully Gully	Seniors	1960	Kent 342
Hully Gully	Solitaires	1979	King Tut 178
Hully Gully	Turks	1959	Class 256
Hully Gully Again	Romans, Little Caesar & the	1961	Del-Fi 4164
Hully Gully All Nite Long	Peridots	1961	Deauville 100
Hully Gully Baby	Dovells	1962, 1983	Abkco 4029/Parkway 845
Hully Gully Baby	Fireflies	1962	Taurus LP 1002
Hully Gully Callin' Time	Jive Five	1962	Beltone 2019/Relic 1027 (75)
Hully Gully Fever	Angelenos	1961	Peepers 2827
Hully Gully Guitar	Percells	1963	ABC 10476
Hully Gully Jones	Tren-Dells	1962	Jam 1100/Capitol 4852 (62)
Hully Gully Lamb	Renaults	1962	Wand 120
Hully Gully Mama	Buddies	1961	Comet 2143
Hully Gully Papa	Woods, Jasper & group	1962	VPM 1009
Hully Gully Twist	Sunliners	1962	Hercules 182
Hum	Ebb-Tones	1957	Crest 1032
Hum De Dum	Gassers	1956	Cash 1035
Hum Gully Gully	Dellrays	NA	Lavette 1007
Hum, The	Neevets	1964	Reon 1303
Hum-Dibby-Do-Wah	East-Men, Hal Jaxon & Watsie Lumbard & the	NA	Glow 100
Hummingbird	One, Bobby & group	1959	NRC 021
Humpty Dumpty	Deans	1960	Mohawk 119
Humpty Dumpty	Fenways	1964	Bevmar 401
Humpty Dumpty	Five Stars (Detroit)	1956	Atco 6065
Humpty Dumpty	Kingsmen	NA	Arnold 2106
Humpty Dumpty	Selectones, Jay Jay & the	1962	Guest 6201/6202
Humpty Dumpty	Virgos	1965	Pioneer 6621
Humpty Dumpty Rock	Errico, Ray (with the Honeytones)	1956	Masquerade 56003
Hungry	Emersons	1958	Newport 7004
Hungry For Your Love	Embers, Willis Sanders & the	1959	Coral 62146
Hungry For Your Love	Plaids	1958	Liberty 55167
Hungry, I'm Hungry	Annuals	1962	Marconn CR1
Hunky Dory	Guytones	1958	DeLuxe 6159
Hunt, The	Five Echoes	1971	Sabre 106
Hurry, Arthur Murray	Newports (Falcons)	1959	Contour 301
Hurry Back	Jive Five	1962	Beltone 3001/Relic LP 5020
Hurry Back	Korman, Jerry & group	1959	Meadow 1001/ABC 10024 (59)
Hurry Back Home	Four Kings	1952	Fortune 807
Hurry Back, Please Come Home	Little, Lee Roy & group	1960	Cee Jay 579
Hurry Home	Cadillacs	1957, 1961	Josie 821/Jubilee LP 1117
Hurry Home	Ellingtons	1964	G-Clef 708
Hurry Home	Sparks Of Rhythm	1955	Apollo 481
Hurry Home	Vocaleers	1952	Red Robin 114
Hurry Home Baby	Flamingos	1953	Chance 1140
Hurry Home Baby	Heartbeats	1956	Hull 713/Gee 1062 (61)
Hurry Hurry Baby	Ramblers (Flash)	1956	Flash 101
Hurry, Hurry Home	Lynn, Sandy (with the Corvets)	1961	Laurel 1024
Hurry To Your Date	Utopians	1962	Imperial 5876
Hurry Up And Ding Dong	Pilgrims	NA	

SONG	GROUP	YEAR	LABEL
Hurry Up And Marry Me	Mello-Dees, Herman Griffin & the	1960	Anna 1115/Stepp 237
Hurry Up Honey	Dubs	1955	Unreleased
Hurry Up Honey	Five Wings, Billy Nelson & the	NA	Savoy 999 (unreleased)
Hurry Up Honey	Rollins, Bird & group	1958	Vanguard 35003
Hurt	Four Buddies	1961	Coral 62217
Hurt	Imperials, Little Anthony & the	1966	DCP 1154/Veep 1245 (66)
Hurt	Tears	1961	Astronaut 501
Hurt By A Letter	Berry Cups, Terry Clinton & the	1959	Khoury's 710
Hurt Me	Robins	1956	Whippet 201X
Hurt So Bad	Imperials, Little Anthony & the	1965	DCP 1128/Veep 1242 (66)
Hurtin' All Over	Sugar Tones, Candy & the	1958	Jackpot 48008
Hurtin' Love	Fabulous Twilights, Nathaniel Mayer & the	1962	Fortune 547
Hurts Me To Work	Leaping Flames	1963	MRC 1201
Hurts My Soul	Modernistics, Little E & Al & the	1961	Falco 304
Hush	Coronets	1955	Groove 0116
Hush Little Baby	Charlie & Don & group	1962	Duel 513
Hush Little Baby	Ivy Three	1960	Shell 723
Hush Of Love	Carousels	1961	ABC 10233
Hush Your Mouth	Marchan, Bobby (with the Clowns)	1960	Ace 595
Hushabye	Grasshoppers	NA	
Hushabye	Lancers	1965	Vee Jay 654
Hushabye	Mystics	1959	Laurie 3028
Hush-A-Bye	Champ, Billy & group	1964	ABC 10518
Hushabye My Love	Diplomats, Dino & the	1961	Vida 0100/0101
Hush-A-Meca	Casanovas	1955	Apollo 474
Hustler, The	Rumblers	1964	Downey 119
Hy Wocky Toomba	Mighty Jupiters	1958	Warner 1020
Hydrogen Bomb	Laurels	1986	Ram EP 509049
Hypnotized	Drifters (Pre-1959)	1957	Atlantic 1141

I

SONG	GROUP	YEAR	LABEL
I	Bi-Langos, Donny & the	NA	Colton 101
I	Blackwells	1961	Jamie 1199
I	Champs, Tony Allen & the	1955	Specialty 560
I	Chantels (actually the Veneers)	1960	Princeton 102/End 1103 (61)
I	Flamingo, Johnny & group	1957	Canton 1785
I	Velvets (New York)	1953	Red Robin 122/Pilgrim 706 (55)/ Event 4285 (55)
I	Veneers	1960	Princeton 102
I + Love + You	Falcons (Detroit)	1960	United Artists 255
I Adore Him	Angels (New Jersey)	1963	Smash 1854
I Adore You	Regan, Tommy & female group	1965	World Artists 1049
I Ain't Comin' Back Anymore	Four Jacks (with Cora Williams & Shirley Haven)	1952	Federal 12079
I Ain't Fattenin' Frogs For Snakes	Larks (North Carolina)	1951	Apollo 427
I Ain't Getting' Caught	Five Royales	1955	King 4830
I Ain't Givin' Up Nothin'	Bowman, Priscilla (with the Spaniels)	1958	Abner 1018
I Ain't Gonna Cry No More	Penguins	1955	Dooto EP 101 (55)/Dooto LP 224 (57)/ Authentic LP 224 (57)
I Ain't Gonna Cry (No More)	Sequins	1963	Terrace 7515
I Ain't Gonna Dance	Five Satins	19??	
I Ain't Gonna Give Nobody	Vocaltones	1989	Relic LP 5082
I Ain't Gonna Love You	Derbys	1953	
I Ain't Gonna Tell	Hightower, Donna (with the Jacks)	1956	RPM 481
I Ain't Got The Money To Pay For This Drink	Thrills, George Zimmerman & the	1956	Jab 103
I Ain't Got Time	Combo-Nettes, Jane Porter & the	1956	Combo 118
I Almost Lost My Mind	Harptones	1955	Bruce 128
I Am A Believer	Meadowlarks, Don Julian & the	1956	Dootone 405
I Am All Alone	Topics, Billy Dixon & the	1960	Topix 6002
I Am Bewildered	Dreamers, Richard Berry & the	1963	Crown LP 5371
I Am Climbing A Mountain	Bobbettes	1964	Diamond 166
I Am In Love	Five Jets	1953	DeLuxe 6018
I Am Just A Lonely Girl	El Venos	1958	Amp 3 (unreleased)

SONG	GROUP	YEAR	LABEL
I Am Lonely	Silhouettes	1957	Junior 391/Junior 593 (57)/ Ember 1029 (57)
I Am Looking Too	Strategics	NA	Lyndell 773
I Am Old Enough	Schoolboys	1957, 1990	Okeh 7085
I Am So Proud	Portee, Robin & group	1963	Diamond 151
I Am The Japanese Sandman	Masked Marauders	NA	Deity LP 6378
I Am With You	Diablos, Nolan Strong & the	1959	Fortune 531
I Am With You	Dominoes	1951	Federal 12039
I Am Yours	Sevilles, Richard Barrett & the	1960	Seville 104
I Apologize	Classics (Brooklyn)	1967	Piccollo 500
I Apologize (acappella)	Chessmen	1965	Relic 1015
I Ask Myself	Valrays	1964	Parkway 904
I Ask Of You	Marvellos	1962	Exodus 6216
I Ask You	Desires	1962	Seville 118
I Asked For Your Hand	Blenders (Chicago)	1957	Vision 1000
I Be Good To You	Four Riffs, Julie Lang & the	1955	Campus 104
I Been Crying	Five Fleets	1958	Felsted 8513
I Been Thinkin'	Riffs	1964	Jamie 1296
I Beeped When I Shoulda Bopped	Magichords	1950	Regal 3238
I Beg For Your Love	Blend-Aires	1982	Story Untold 503
I Beg For Your Love	Cellos	1958	Apollo 524
I Beg You Please	Romeos	1954	Apollo 461
I Beg Your Forgiveness	Co-Eds	1956	Old Town 1027
I Beg Your Pardon	Terrytones	1961	Wye 1010
	(with Claire Charles & Gayle Fortune)		
I Began To Realize	El Dorados	1955	Vee Jay 165
I Begin To Think Again Of You	Mystics	1960	Laurie 3047
I Believe	Battery Park	1973	Vintage 1001
I Believe	Blue Belles, Patti LaBelle & the	1964	Parkway 935
I Believe	Chessmen	1961	Pac 100
I Believe	Coronados	1960	Columbia 41550
I Believe	Corvets, Arthur & the	1964	NRC 2781
I Believe	Dee-Vines	1960	Lano 2001/Relic 514 (64)
I Believe	Delrons, Reperata & the	1967	Mala 573
I Believe	Earls	1964, 1971	Old Town 1149/Barry 1021
I Believe	Revivals	1987	DCA 100/Clifton 84 (89)
I Believe	Twilighters (Bronx, N.Y.)	1956, 1958	Caddy 103/Dot 15526/Pla-Bac 1113
I Believe (acappella)	Five Delights	1960	A Cappella - Best of the Bronx (98)
I Believe I Love You	Watts, Jimmy Mack & the	1960	Gee 1056
I Believe In All I Feel (Je Croix En Tout A Que Je Resent)	G-Clefs	1964	Regina 1314
I Believe In Love	Doug & Freddy (with the Pyramids)	1959	Rendezvous 111
I Believe In St. Nick	Cashmeres (Brooklyn)	1961	Laurie 3078
I Believe In You	Glens, Billy & the	1959	Jaro 77006
I Believe In You	Heartspinners, Dino & the	1980	Starlight 9
I Believe In You	Innocents	1961	Indigo LP 503
I Believe In You	Soothers	1965	Port 70041
I Believe (In Your Love)	Montclairs	1963	ABC 10463
(I Believe) Something Funny Is Going On	Tillman, Bertha & group	1962	Brent 7032
I Belong To You	Fi-Tones	1956	Atlas 1055
I Blew Out The Flame	Four Wheels	1959	Laurel 1003
I Bow To You	Pelicans, Earl Nelson & the	1957	Class 209
I Burned Your Letter	Five Keys	1960	King 5302
I Call To You	Fi-Tones	1956	Atlas 1052
I Call To You	Mellows, Lillian Leach & the	1974	Relic LP 5014
I Came Back To Say I'm Sorry	Coronados	1956	Vik 0217
I Can Dream	Four Shades Of Rhythm	1949	Old Swingmaster 23
I Can Dream	Starlites, Eddie & the	1973	Vintage 1004
I Can Dream, Can't I	Blenders (New York)	1949	National 9092
I Can Dream Can't I	Skyliners	1959	Calico LP 3000
I Can Hear Raindrops	Noblemen 4	NA	Recap 292
I Can Hear The Rain	Delrons, Reperata & the	1967	RCA 9185
I Can Learn	Chains	1963	Peacock 1922
I Can Live	Cobanas, Roy Hines & the	NA	Solitaire 1001

SONG	GROUP	YEAR	LABEL
I Can Make It If I Try	Royal Premiers	1965	M.B.S. 105
I Can Make You Mine	Originells 4	1965	Apt 25074
I Can Really Satisfy	Restless Hearts, Fred Parris & the	1966	Green Sea 107
I Can Remember	Celtics	1957	Al Jacks 1
I Can See	Couplings	1958	Josie 831
I Can See An Angel	Original Four Aces	1954	Big Town 112/Big Town 118 (55)
I Can See You Dancing With Me	Tokens (Brooklyn)	1970	Buddah 174
I Can Tell	Calhoun, Lena (with the Emotions)	1962	Flip 358
I Can Tell	Challengers, Walter Ward & the	1957	Melatone 1002
I Can Tell	Delrons, Reperata & the	1965	RCA 8721
I Can Tell	Emotions	1961	Flip 358
I Can Tell	Sandmen, Chuck Willis & the	1955	Okeh 7055
I Can Tell You Love Me Too	Ultimates	1961	Envoy 2302
I Can't Be Free	Escorts, Goldie & the	1963	Coral 62349
I Can't Begin To Tell You	Sensationals, Jimmy Jones & the	1962	Savoy 4174
I Can't Believe	Beacham, Rufus & group	1956	Chart 627
I Can't Believe	Diplomats, Dino & the	1961	Laurie 3103
I Can't Believe	Do-Wells, Tony Morra & the	1960	Du-Well 1005
I Can't Believe	Four Chevelles	1957	Band Box 358
I Can't Believe	Gems (Drexel)	1975	Drexel 900 (unreleased)
I Can't Believe	Lovers, Cliff Butler & the	NA	Frantic 801
I Can't Believe	Ravens	1956	Argo 5255
I Can't Believe It	Apollos	1961	Galaxy 707
I Can't Believe It	Larks (Philadelphia)	1961	Sheryl 334/Uptown (65)
I Can't Believe (That You Don't Love Me Anymore)	DiMucci, Dion (with the Del Satins)	1963	Columbia 42810
I Can't Believe That You're In Love With Me	Hornets	1953	States 127
I Can't Change	Sensations	1964	Junior 1010
I Can't Dance	Impossibles	1961	RMP 508
I Can't Dream	Dells	1983	Charly LP 1056
I Can't Escape From You	Dominoes	1951	Federal 12022
I Can't Escape From You	Five Keys	1964	King 5877
I Can't Fall In Love	Overtones	1961	N/A
I Can't Find The Girl On My Mind	Satins Four (with the Cinnamon Angels)	1965	B.T. Puppy 515
I Can't Forget	Four Jacks	1958	Rebel 1313
I Can't Forget	Jacks & Jills	1958	MGM 12671
I Can't Forget	Rockettes	1954	Parrot 789
I Can't Forget	Wheels	1957	Premium 410
I Can't Forget About You	Rev-Lons	1963	Reprise 20200/Starburst 123
I Can't Get A Hit Record	Hollywood Flames	1962	Coronet 7025
I Can't Get Along Without You	Lyrics (Dan-Tone)	1962	Dan-Tone 1002
I Can't Get Enough Of Your Stuff	Mandells	NA	Trans World 711
I Can't Get Sentimental	Sonnets	1964	Guyden 2112
I Can't Get Started With You	Humphries, Fatman (with the Four Notes)	1952	Jubilee 5085
I Can't Get Up	Valcounts, Tommy Sena & the	1961	Adore 903
I Can't Give You Anything But Love	Dynamics	1961	Lavere 186
I Can't Go	Townsmen (Louie Lymon)	1963	PJ 1340/1341
I Can't Go On Like This	Ladds, George Dee & the	NA	Kon-Ti-Ki 230
I Can't Go On (Rosalie)	Belmonts, Dion & the	1958	Laurie 3015
I Can't Go On Without You	Wheels	NA	Premium
I Can't Hear You No More	Down Beats	1965	Down Beat
I Can't Help But Wonder Where I'm Bound	DiMucci, Dion (with the Del Satins)	1969	Columbia 44719
I Can't Help It	Falcons (Big Wheel)	1966	Big Wheel 1967
I Can't Help It	Irwin, Big Dee (with the Pastels)	NA	Astra 1024
I Can't Help Myself	Counts, Bobby Comstock & the	1963	Lawn 224
I Can't Help Myself	Dells	1979, 1984	Solid Smoke LP 8029/ Charly LP 1056 (85)
I Can't Leave You	Destinations	NA	Ando 114
I Can't Let Him	Cheryl Ann & group	NA	Patty 52
I Can't Live Alone	Tangents	1960	Fresh 1
I Can't Live Without You	Volumes	1964	American Arts 6
I Can't Love No One But You	Marvel, Tina & male group	1963	Lu Pine 121
I Can't Love You Anymore	Knight Lites, Gary & the	1959	Prima 1016

SONG	GROUP	YEAR	LABEL
I Can't Pretend	Five Crowns	1955	Caravan 15609/Trans-World 717 (56)
I Can't Quit	Palisades	1960	Calico 113
I Can't Refuse	Orchids	1955	Parrot 819
I Can't Say Goodbye	Fireflies	1959	Ribbon 6904
I Can't Say I Love You	Themes, Lanny Hunt & the	1964	Sure Star 5001
I Can't See Him Again	Twans	NA	N/A
I Can't See Me Without You	Impalas (Five Discs)	1966	Rite-On 101/Red Boy 113/ Steady 044
I Can't See Nobody	Juniors, Danny & the	1968	Ronn 24
I Can't Sleep	Danleers	1959	Mercury 71441
I Can't Sleep	Skyliners	NA	Doc 496
I Can't Stand Another Broken Heart	Whirlwinds, James Loyd & the	1963	Empala 117
I Can't Stand It	G-Clefs	1953, 1966	Veep 2048/Loma 2048
I Can't Stand It	Lamplighters	1953	Federal 12166
I Can't Stand It	Seminoles	1962	Check Mate 1012
I Can't Stand It	Sophisticates	NA	Mutt 27318
I Can't Stand It	Underbeats	1966	Soma 1458
I Can't Stand Up Alone	McPhatter, Clyde (with the Cookies & the Cues)	1958	Atlantic 1199
I Can't Stop	Corvettes, Irving Fuller & the	1960	Emery 121
I Can't Stop Crying	Daylighters, Chuck & the	1963, 1964, 1968	Tip Top 2006/2007/2009
I Can't Stop These Tears	Stereos	1968	Cadet 5626
I Can't Take It Anymore	Hitmakers	1959	Angletone 1104
I Can't Take It (There's Our Song Again)	Chantels	1958	End 1037
I Can't Tell You Now	Falcons (Regent)	1952	Regent 1041
I Can't Wait	Dontells	NA	Ambassador 3346
I Can't Wait	Wanderers, Pearl Woods & the	NA	UGHA LP 001
I Can't Wait Till Tomorrow	Junior Five	1963	Laurie 3213
I Can't Waste My Tears	Lynn, Gloria (with the Wheels)	1957	Premium 412
I Care About You	Crests	1966	Parkway 999
I Care For You	Four Of A Kind	1958	Chancellor 1012/Bomarc 302 (59)
I Care So Much	Fleetwoods	1959	Dolton 1/Liberty 55188 (59)/ Liberty 77188 (59)
I Challenge Your Kiss	Orioles, Sonny Til & the	1949	Jubilee 5008
I Cheated	Slades, Joyce Harris & the	1961	Domino 903
I Confess	Belmonts	1962	Sabina 503
I Confess	Clovers	1954	Atlantic 1046
I Confess	Dots (Jeanette Baker)	1956	Caddy 101
I Confess	Four-Evers	1961	Josie 901
I Confess	Jacks	1956	RPM 472
I Could Be	Tokens (Brooklyn)	1969	Warner Bros. 7323
I Could Conquer The World	Shevelles	1964	World Artists 1025
I Could Cry	Foster Brothers	1958	Hi Mi 3005
I Could Have Cried	Velaires	1965	Hi-Mar 9173
I Could Have Danced All Night	Souvenirs	1967	Inferno 2001
I Could Have Loved You So Well	Skyliners, Jimmy Beaumont & the	1974	Capitol 3979
I Could Have Told You	Harmony Grits	1959	End 1051
I Could If I Would	Jaguars	1959	Janet 201
I Could Love You	Five Royales	1956	King 4901
I Could Love You	Midnighters, Hank Ballard & the	1959	King 5275
I Could Never Love Another	Enchantments	1975	Rogue (no #)
I Could Never Love Another	Persuasions	1970	Catamount 1957
I Could Never Stop Crying	Persianettes, Timmy Carr & the	1964	Guyden 2104
I Could Try	Echoes, Mitch & the	1963	Bethlehem 3077
I Could Write A Book	Chants	1964	Cameo 297/Pye 15591
I Could Write A Book	Dream Girls, Bobbie Smith & the	1960	Big Top 3059
I Couldn't Believe	Mello-Harps	1956	Tin Pan Alley 159
I Couldn't Care Less	Modern Red Caps, George Tindley & the	1962	Smash 1768
I Couldn't Let You Down	Midnight Riders, Kasandrea & the	1959	Imperial 5638
I Couldn't Let You See Me Crying	Hearts (Bronx, N.Y.)	1956	J&S 1180/1181
I Couldn't See	Downbeats	1956	Sarg 186
I Couldn't Sleep A Wink Last Night	Imperials, Little Anthony & the	1961	End LP 311
I Couldn't Sleep A Wink Last Night	Mello-Moods	1952	Red Robin 104
I Couldn't Stand It	Blendaires, Bobby Carle & the	1958	Decca 30699
I Couldn't Stop Crying	Zircons	1967	Heigh Ho 608/609

SONG	GROUP	YEAR	LABEL
I Count The Tears	Drifters (1959-forward)	1960	Atlantic 2087
I Cover The Waterfront	Imperials, Little Anthony & the	1958	End (unreleased)
I Cover The Waterfront	Orioles, Sonny Til & the	1953	Jubilee 5120
I Cried	Bobbettes	1960	Galliant 1006
I Cried	Charmers	1963	Laurie 3173
I Cried	Churchill, Savannah & group	1954	Decca 29194
I Cried	Cupcakes, Cookie & the	1963	Lyric 1009/Paula 312 (68)
I Cried	Dukes, Billy Duke & the	1954	Coral 61203
I Cried	Four Cal-Quettes	1963	Liberty 55549
I Cried	Hearts, Lee Andrews & the (as Lee Andrews)	1961	Swan 4087
I Cried	Legends, Lonnie & the	1966	Impression 109
I Cried	Lincolns	1957, 1972	Aljon 113/114
I Cried	Pearls	1961	Amber 2003
I Cried	Starlighters	1959	End 1049
I Cried	Toppers, Bobby Mitchell & the	1955	Imperial 5346
I Cried	Velvets (New York)	1954	Red Robin 127/Pilgrim 710 (55)
I Cried A Tear Over You	Swinging Rocks, Ruby & her	1985	Relic LP 8004
I Cried All Night	Miller Sisters	1962	Hull 752
I Cried All Night	Silks, Charles McCullough & the	1962	Dooto 467
I Cried And Cried	Five Diamonds	1955	Treat 501
I Cried Enough	Alleycats, Joe Allen & the	1958	Jalo 201
I Cried For You	Five Keys	1952	Aladdin 3158
I Cried For Your Love	Richards, Donald (with the Volumes)	1962	Chex 1003
I Cried Last Night	Lewis, James & group	1958	Arrow 730
I Cried My Heart Out	Starlites, Jackie & the	1964	Hull 760
I Cried My Heart Out	Sultans	1954	Duke 133
I Cried Oh, Oh	Valentines	1957	Rama 228
I Cross My Fingers	Five Dukes, Bennie Woods & the	1955	Atlas 1040
I Cross My Fingers	Uniques	1959	World Pacific 808
I Crossed My Fingers	Orioles, Sonny Til & the	1950	Jubilee 5040
I Cry	Cadets	1955	Modern 963
I Cry	Delights	1964	Arlen 753
I Cry	Emeralds, Luther Bond & the	1956	Federal 12279
I Cry	Miracles (Detroit)	1958	End 1029/End 1084 (60)
I Cry	Voices, Frankie Bearse & the	1964	Olimpic 247
I Cry All The Time	Hollyhawks	1963	Jubilee 5441
I Cry My Heart Out	Four Jacks	1950	Gotham 219
I Cry The Blues	Terrytones	1960	Wye 1003
	(with Claire Charles & Gayle Fortune)		
I Dare You Baby	Alston, Henry & group	1959	Skyline 500
I Dare You Baby	Hurricanes	1958	
I Declared My Love	Lake, Tony & group	1959	Herald 543
I Dedicate My Heart	Allen, Sue & group	1954	Groove 0037
I Depended On You	Harptones	1954	Bruce 104
I Destroyed Your Letters	Choralettes	1964	Fargo 1063
I Did The Wrong Thing	Romancers	1964	Linda 117
I Didn't Know	Companions	1959	Brook's 100/Federal 12397 (60)
I Didn't Know	Five Keys	1960	King 5358
I Didn't Know	Five Satins	1960	Cub 9071
I Didn't Know	Marshall Brothers	NA	Savoy (unreleased)
I Didn't Know Him	Cupids, Sandy & the	1963	Charter 2
I Didn't Lie	Classmates, Marc Cavell & the	1961	Candix 329
I Didn't Lose A Doggone Thing	Flares	NA	Press 2814
I Didn't Lose A Doggone Thing	Flares, Cookie Jackson & the	1961	Press 2814
I Didn't Mean It	Scott, Ricky & group	1960	X-Clusive/Cub 9079 (60)
I Didn't Mean To Hurt You	Shalimars	NA	Mr. Maestro 778
I Didn't Mean To Hurt You	Shirelles	1963	Scepter 1255
I Didn't Want Her	Faces	1965	Regina 1328
I Didn't Want To Do It	Scholars	1957	Imperial 5459
I Didn't Want To Do It	Spiders	1954	Imperial 5265/Imperial 5618 (59)
I Do	Bonnevilles	1959	Whitehall 30002
I Do	Castells (with Brian Wilson)	1964	Warner Bros. 5421
I Do	Champions	1958	Ace 541
I Do	Clouds	1956	Cobra 5001
I Do	Crests	1959	Coed 509

SONG	GROUP	YEAR	LABEL
I Do	Delusions, W. Kelley & the	1975	Kelway 115
I Do	Five Royales	1954	Apollo 452
I Do	Jokers	1960	Danco 117
I Do	Marvelows	1965	ABC 10629
I Do	Miflin Triplets	1958	Ember 1045
I Do	Royal Debs	1962	Tifco 826
I Do	Veltones	1966	Goldwax 301
I Do	Youngtones	1964	Times Square 31
I Do All Right	Skyliners	NA	Double AA 1045
I Do Believe	Crystals (Aladdin)	1957	Aladdin 3355
I Do Believe	Devilles	1962	Arrawak 1001
I Do Believe	Maharajahs	1958	Flip 332
I Do Believe (acappella)	Count Five	1975	Relic LP 103
I Do, I Do	Winchell, Danny & group	1957	MGM 12577
I Do Love You	Chex, Tex & the	1961	Atlantic 2116
I Don' Know (If You Really Love Me)	Master, Ronnie & group	1961	Landa 669
I Done Done It	Four Dukes	1953	Duke 116
I Done Got Over It	Arrows, Big Bo & the	1964	Checker 1068
I Don't Believe In Tomorrow	Larks (North Carolina)	1951	Apollo 430
I Don't Believe In You	Girlfriends	1964	Colpix 744
I Don't Believe Them	Triumphs, Tico & the	1961	Madison 169/Amy 835 (61)
I Don't Care	Centuries, Ronnie & the	1962	Luna 3076
I Don't Care	Chants	1963	Cameo 268/277/Pye 15557
I Don't Care	Del Satins	1995	Park Ave. 11
I Don't Care	Del-Chords, Donnie & the	1963	Taurus 357
I Don't Care	Diablos, Nolan Strong & the	1962	Fortune 544
I Don't Care	Exciting Invictas	1960	Kingston 427
I Don't Care	Keytones	1962	Chelsea 101
I Don't Care	Lollipops, Becky & the	1964	Troy 6493/Epic 9736 (64)
I Don't Care	Martinels	1963	Success 110
I Don't Care	Pleasers, Wilbur Whitfield & the	1957	Aladdin 3396
I Don't Care	Rockets, Herb Kenny & the	1952	MGM 11360
I Don't Care Anymore	Intensions	NA	Bluelight 1214
I Don't Care How You Do It	Terrifics	1959	Demon 1516
I Don't Care If The Sun Don't Shine	Williams, Mel & group	1957	Dig 140
I Don't Care One Bit	Ascots	1962	King 5679
I Don't Cry Anymore	Neptunes	1964	Victoria 102
I Don't Cry Over Girls	Rue-Teens	1964	Louis 6805
I Don't Dig (Western Movies)	Tiffanys (male)	1963	Rockin Robin 1
I Don't Have To Ride No More	Ravens	1949	National 9098
I Don't Have To Worry	Quotations	1968	DeVenus 107
I Don't Have You	Mandells	1961	Smart 325
I Don't Know	Avalons	1987	Relic LP 5072
I Don't Know	Cupids	1956	Chan 107
I Don't Know	Davis, Hal Sonny & group	1963	G.S.P. 2
I Don't Know	Fantastics	1964	DMD 103
I Don't Know	Misfits	1961	Aries 7-10-3
I Don't Know	Upbeats	1957	Prep 119
I Don't Know But One	Midnighters, Hank Ballard & the	1964	King 5884
I Don't Know What I'll Do	Five Discs	1961	Yale 243/244
I Don't Know What It Is	Blue Notes	1959	Brooke 111 (first pressing)
I Don't Know What To Do	Van Dykes	1960	Decca 31036
I Don't Know Why	Allison, Gene & group	1958	Vee Jay 286
I Don't Know Why	Belmonts	1965	United Artists 809
I Don't Know Why	Delicates	1961	Roulette 4387
I Don't Know Why	Desires	1960	20th Fox 195
I Don't Know Why	Ecstasies	1979	U.G.H.A. 05
I Don't Know Why	Hi-Tones	1961	Fonsca 202
I Don't Know Why	Keystoners	1984	Starbound 501
I Don't Know Why	Platters	NA	Mercury EP 3345
I Don't Know (Why I Love You Like I Do)	Keynotes	1955	Apollo 484
I Don't Know Why I Love You Like I Do	Ravens	1948	National 9056
I Don't Know Why You Sent For Me	Gleams	1962	Kip 236/237
I Don't Like It	Penn, Tony & group	1959	P.R.I. 101
I Don't Like It Like That	Bobbettes	1961	Gone 5112/End 1095

SONG	GROUP	YEAR	LABEL
I Don't Like You That Much	Royal Jokers	1958	Fortune 840
I Don't Love Him	Sweet Nuthins	1964	Swan 4195
I Don't Mind	Adventurers	1962	Ran-Dee 106
I Don't Mind	Creschendos	1960	Music City 839
I Don't Mind	Flaming Hearts	1958	Vulco V1
I Don't Miss You Anymore	Blenders (New York)	1953	MGM 11488
I Don't Need No One	Four Of Us	1963	Brunswick 55288
I Don't Need You	Blazers	1963	Brass 306
I Don't Need You	Hamiltons, Alexander & the	1966	Warner Bros. 5844
I Don't Need You Anymore	Rumblers	1963	Downey 103/Dot 16421 (63)
I Don't Need You Anymore	Teddy Bears	1959	Imperial 5562
I Don't See Me In Your Eyes Anymore	Arist-O-Kats	1957	Vita 168
I Don't See Stars In Your Eyes	Neanderthals, Dave Meadows & the	1960	Magnum 41160
I Don't Seem To Care Anymore	Talkabouts	1959	Poplar 117
I Don't Stand A Chance	Orbits, Bobby & the	1962	Gone 5126
I Don't Stand A Ghost Of A Chance	Concords (Neal Scott)	1967	Cameo 476
I Don't Stand A Ghost Of A Chance	Four Shades Of Rhythm	1958	Mad 1206
I Don't Stand A Ghost Of A Chance	Metro-Liners	1976	Catamount 132
I Don't Stand A Ghost Of A Chance	Solitaires	1955	Old Town 1010
I Don't Stand A Ghost Of A Chance With You	Dominoes	1957	Decca 30420
I Don't Think So	Shirelles	1962	Scepter 1243
I Don't Think You Missed Me	Orchids	1962	Harlow 101
I Don't Understand You No More	Zel, Rita & group	1960	J&S 1685
I Don't Wanna Be Without You Baby	Corvairs	1963	Leopard 5005
I Don't Wanna Cry	Ovations (Capitol)	1963	Capitol 5082
I Don't Wanna Cry	Smith, Richard & group	1958	Hi-Q 5042
I Don't Wanna Go	Invictors	1959	Bee 1117
I Don't Wanna Go To School	Four Holidays	1960	Verve 10204/Verve 740
I Don't Wanna Make You Cry	Fun-Atics	1967	Select 571
I Don't Want A New Baby	Rivingtons	1967, 1973	Wand 11253/Quan 1379
I Don't Want An Angel	Storytellers	1963	Capitol 5042
I Don't Want Everything	McHugh, Jimmy & group	1963	Success 106
I Don't Want Nobody	Cuff Links	1963	Dooto 474
I Don't Want Nobody	Heartbreakers (Bronx, N.Y.)	1971	Broadcast 99
I Don't Want Nobody But You	Four Kings	1960	Cee Jay 580
I Don't Want To	Satellites, Bobby Day & the	1959	Class 232/Class 263 (59)
I Don't Want To Be Loved	Del Rios, Linda & the	1962	Crackerjack 4005
I Don't Want To Be Without You	Jive Five	NA	Beltone (unreleased)
I Don't Want To Be Without You Baby	Jive Five	1962	Beltone 3002
I Don't Want To Be Your Baby Anymore	Popsicles	1965	GNP Crescendo 336
I Don't Want To Cry	Cooke, Sam & group	1958	Specialty 627
I Don't Want To Cry	Del Pris	NA	Varbee (unreleased)
I Don't Want To Cry	Gray, Maureen & group	1961	Chancellor 1091
I Don't Want To Cry	Shirelles	1962	Scepter LP 502
I Don't Want To Cry	Woods, Cora & group	1955	Federal 12223
I Don't Want To Cry (acappella)	Quotations	1975	Relic LP 105
I Don't Want To Cry Over You	Strikes	1957	Imperial 5446
I Don't Want To Do A Thing But Love You	Temples	1958	Date 1004
I Don't Want To Go Home	Gardner, Don & group	1957	DeLuxe 6155
I Don't Want To Go Home	Quarter Notes	1963	Guyden 2083
I Don't Want To Go On Without You	Blue Belles, Patti LaBelle & the	1966	Atlantic 2373
I Don't Want To Go On Without You	Dolphins	1964	Fraternity 937
I Don't Want To Go On Without You	Drifters (1959-forward)	1964	Atlantic 2237
I Don't Want To Know	Chimes, Dave Burgess & the	1959	Challenge 59037
I Don't Want To Know	Premiers, Julie Stevens & the	1957	Dig 129
I Don't Want To See Tomorrow	Creations	NA	Tan
I Don't Want To Set The World On Fire	Pyramids, Ruby Whitaker & the	1957	Mark-X 7007
I Don't Want To Set The World On Fire	Sh-Booms	1957	Vik 0295
I Don't Want To Take A Chance	Orioles, Sonny Til & the	1952	Jubilee 5102
I Don't Want To Wait	Deans	1961, 1964	Laurie 3114/Mohawk 126
I Don't Want To Wait	Ping Pongs	1964	G-Note
I Don't Want To Walk Without You Baby	Startime Kids	1959	Okeh 7111
I Don't Want To Wind Up In Love	Darling, Johnny & group	1958	DeLuxe 6167
I Don't Want You To Go	Casanovas	1955	Apollo 477

SONG	GROUP	YEAR	LABEL
I Don't Want Your Love	Marquis	1956	Rainbow 358
I Don't Want Your Love	Masters, Rick & the	1963	Cameo 247
I Double Dare You	Accents, Ted Newman & the	1957	Rev 3511
I Dream	Elder, Nelvin & group	1961	Brent 7027
I Dream Of You	Senders	1959	Kent 320
I Dreamed	Three Playmates	1958	Savoy 1537
I Dreamed I Dwelt In Heaven	Five Keys	1956	Capitol 3392
(I Dreamed Of A) Star Spangled Banner	Rockets, Herb Kenny & the	1953	MGM 11487
I Dreamed Of You	Hornets, Don Ray & the	1959	Hornet 501
I Dreamt I Dwelt In Heaven	Newports	1993	Avenue D 18
I Dunno	Vandells, Johnny Greco & the	1963	Far-Mel 1
I F I C	Rivera, Lucy & group	1959	End 1041
I Fall To Pieces	Charms, Otis Williams & the	1966	Okeh 7235
I Feel A Heartache Comin' On	Fortune, Jimmy & group	1961	Chancellor 1097
I Feel A Love Comin' On	Concords (Brooklyn)	1966	Boom 60021/Polydor 14036 (70)
I Feel Good	Four Dates	1958	Chancellor 1027
I Feel Good All Over	Drifters (1959-forward)	1963	Atlantic 2201
I Feel Good All Over	Dukays	1962	Vee Jay 460
I Feel Good All Over	Fiestas	1962	Old Town 1127
I Feel In My Heart	Knights, Mary Wheeler & the	NA	Atom 701
I Feel Like A Million	Bradley, Mamie & group	1958	Sue 702
I Feel Like A Million	Newports, Tyrone & the	1963	Darrow 5-20
I Feel Like Rockin'	Offbeats, Jimmy Dee & the	1959	TNT 161
I Feel So Blue	Chestnuts	1957	Eldorado 511
I Feel So Blue	Glens	1962	Ro-Nan 1002
I Feel So Blue	Royals	1953	Federal 12121
I Feel So Funny	Themes	NA	Ideal 21
I Feel So Good	Hearts (Bronx, N.Y.)	1956	J&S 995/Zells 3377 (63)
I Feel So Lonely	Juniors, Danny & the	1958	ABC 9978
I Feel So Low	Songettes	1959	Decca 30945
I Feel Sorry For You Baby	Velveteens	1965	Golden Artist 614
I Feel Soul A'Coming	Stereos	1968	Cadet 5626
I Feel That-A-Way	Royals	1953	Federal 12150
I Feel The Same Way Too	Tiffanys	1965	Josie 942
(I Feel) You're Torturing My Heart	Cosmos	1962	Big L 502
I Fell For You	Nocturnes	NA	Sensation 22
I Fell For Your Loving	Cues	1955	Jubilee 5201
I Fell In Love	Rajahs	1957	Klik 7805
I Fell In Love With You	Del Royals	1961	Minit 637
I Finally Found You	Baxter, Ronnie (with the Chantels)	1959	Gone 5050
I Flipped	Four Pals	1955	Royal Roost 610
I Follow The Stars	Avalons	NA	Groove (unreleased)
I Fooled You	Fabulous Playboys	1959	Contour 004
I Found	Sedates	1958	MRB 171/20th Century 1011 (59)/ Port 70004 (59)/ 20th Century 1212 (61)
I Found A Boy	Hollywood Flames	1960	Atco 6164
I Found A Dream	Pacers	1958	Calico 101
I Found A Girl	Satellites	1958	United Artists 141
I Found A Girl	Valadiers	1963	Gordy 7013
I Found A Job	Heartbeats	1958	Roulette 4054
I Found A Love	Don-Tels	1963	Witch 119
I Found A Love	Dukes (California)	1955	Imperial 5344 (unreleased)
I Found A Love	Fabutones	1972	Bim Bam Boom 100
I Found A Love	Falcons (Detroit)	1962	Lu Pine 103/Lu Pine 1003
I Found A Love	Hi-Lites (Okeh)	1954	Okeh 7046
I Found A Love	Velaires, Danny & the	1967	Ramco 1983
I Found A Love	Velvetones	1957	Aladdin 3391
I Found A New Baby	Flamingos	1964, 1990	Relic LP 5088/Constellation LP 3/ Chess LP 702 (76)
I Found A New Love	Blue Belles	1962	Newtown 5006 (1st printing)
I Found A Penny (And I Made A Wish)	Utopians, Mike & the	1958	Cee Jay 574 (first pressing)
I Found An Angel	Chimes (Los Angeles - Dig)	1957	Dig 148 (unreleased)
I Found An Angel	Night Owls, Tony Allen & the	1956	Dig 109
I Found Heaven	Del-Chords, Donnie & the	1963	Taurus 363

SONG	GROUP	YEAR	LABEL
(I Found) Heaven In Love	Raindrops	1956	Spin-It 104
I Found Her	Texas Matadors	NA	IMA 101
I Found Love	Bachelors (Washington, D.C.)	1956	Royal Roost 620
I Found Me A Lover	Lovelites	1961	Bandera 2515
I Found My Baby	Corvairs, Billy Martin & the	NA	Monitor 1402
I Found My Baby	Fabulous Fabuliers	1959	Angle Tone 539
I Found My Baby	Fi-Tones	1959	Angle Tone 539
I Found My Baby	Lexingtons	1960	Everest 19369
I Found My Girl	Kents	1958	Argo 5299
I Found My Love	Infatuators	1961	Destiny 504/Vee Jay 395 (61)
I Found My Love	Majors (Felsted)	1965	Felsted 8707
I Found My Love	Panthers, Charles Gray Watson & the	NA	Village 103
I Found My Love	Peanuts, M&M & the	1964	Money 107
I Found My Love	Tip Tops, Tiny Tip & the	1962	Scarlet 4129
I Found My Love	Velvetones	1964	Imperial 66020
I Found My Place	Delrons, Reperata & the	1965	World Artists 1062
I Found Myself A Brand New Baby	Modifiers, Mike & the	1962	Gordy 7006
I Found Out	Astors	1965	Stax 170
I Found Out	Disciples	1964	Fortune 573
I Found Out	Robins	1950	Savoy (unreleased)
I Found Out My Troubles	Robins	1987	Savoy Jazz LP 1188
I Found Out Too Late	Starlites, Jackie & the	1961	Fury 1057
I Found Out (What You Do When You Go Around There)	Du Droppers	1953	RCA 5321
I Found Out Why	Teenchords, Lewis Lymon & the	1957, 1962, 1994	End 10071113//Fury 1007 (57)
I Found Some Lovin'	Original Drifters	1963, 1967	Veep 1264
I Found Someone	Crusaders	1963	Dooto 472
I Found Someone	Rogers, Menard & group	NA	Drum Boy 45104
I Found Someone New	Prizes	1964	Parkway 917
I Found True Love	Dolphins	1960	Shad 5020
I Found You	Castaways	1962	Assault 1869
I Found You	Iridescents	1963	Hudson 8107
I Found You	Metrics	1964	Chadwick 101
I Gave Up Everything	Detroit Harmonettes	1954	DeLuxe 6039
I Get A Feeling, My Love	Dream Girls, Bobbie Smith & the	1962	Big Top 3111
I Get A Thrill	Sophomores (Massachusetts)	1956	Dawn 218
I Get All My Lovin' On A Saturday Night	Ravens	1951	National 9148
I Get Blue	Nite-Lites	1962	Sequoia 502
I Get Dreamy	Castells	1961	Era 3048
I Get So Happy	Gayles	1955	King 4846
I Get That Feeling	Sonics	1962	Armonia 102
I Get That Feeling	Victorials	1956	Imperial 5398
I Get The Feeling	Pyramids, Ruby Whitaker & the	1957	Mark-X 7007
I Get Weak	Drivers	1957	RCA 7023
I Give My Heart To You	Accents (featuring Robert Draper Jr.)	1959	Brunswick 55123
I Give You My Word	Platters	1956	Mercury EP 3344
I Give You My Word	Royaltones	NA	Old Town (unreleased)
I Go Ape	Tyler, Frankie	NA	Seasons 4 Ever
I Go For You	Calhoun, Millie & group	1965	Lo Lace 708
I Go For You	Travelers	1959	Andex 4033
I Go Plenty O Nuttin'	Chiffons	1963	Laurie 3364
I Go To Pieces	Showvenistics	1993	Clifton 106
I Got A Feeling	Belmonts	1965	United Artists 966
I Got A Feeling	Carols	1953	Savoy 896
I Got A Fine Little Girl	Harptones	1956	Rama (unfinished)
I Got A Gal	Mohawks	1960	Val-Ue 211
I Got A Girl	Satins, Tommy Roe & the	1960	Judd 1018
I Got A Girl	Sinceres	1978	Crystal Ball 126
(I Got A) Good Lookin' Baby	Casanovas	1958	Apollo 523
I Got A Good Thing Going And I Ain't Gonna Blow It	Executive Four	1966	Lumar 202
I Got A Job	Tempos	1958	Kapp 213
I Got A Man	Crystals (Brooklyn)	1966	United Artists 994
I Got A Wife	Mark IV	1959	Mercury 71403
I Got A Woman	Zodiacs, Maurice Williams & the	1974	Relic LP 5017

SONG	GROUP	YEAR	LABEL
I Got A Woman's Love	Varieteers	1954	Hickory
I Got A Zero	Fantastics	1960	RCA 7664
I Got Feelings	Joey & group	1962	Taurus 353
I Got Fired	Chesterfields	1958	Cub 9008
I Got Fired	Mistakes	1959	Lo-Fi 2311/2312/Tip Top
I Got It	Delacardos	1960	United Artists 276
I Got It Bad And That Ain't Good	Blendaires	1959	Decca 30938
I Got Loaded	Cadets	1956	Modern 1000
I Got Loving	Charms, Otis Williams & the	1966	Okeh 7248
I Got My Mind Make Up	Caine, Gladys & group	1963	Togo 602
I Got News	Upsets, Eddy & the	NA	Dektr 41668
I Got News For You	Angloes, Julie Gibson & the	1962	Herald 575
I Got News For You	Holidays	NA	Dixie 1145
I Got That Feeling	Rivals (Anna)	1960	Anna 1113
I Got The Blues	Belmonts, Dion & the	1959	Laurie LP 1002/Laurie LP 2002 (60)/ Collectables LP 5025
I Got The Blues	Curios, Bobby Brown & the	1959	Vaden 100
I Got The Blues	DiMucci, Dion (with the Del Satins)	1965	Laurie 3303
I Got The Blues	Mulrays	1957	Trans World 719
I Got The Blues	Van Delles	1962	Bolo 731
I Got The Message	Shirelles	1958	Decca 30761
I Got To Know	Five Royales	1960	Home Of The Blues 112
I Got Tore Up	Meadowlarks, Don Julian & the	1955	Dootone 367
I Gotta	Trebelaires	1955	Nestor 16
I Gotta Get Myself A Woman	Drifters (Pre-1959)	1956	Atlantic 1101
I Gotta Go	Cashmeres (Brooklyn)	1961	Laurie 3088
I Gotta Go	Ditalians	1996	Saxony 2004
I Gotta Go Now	Rhythm Kings	1951	Apollo 1181
I Gotta Go Now	Starlings	1955	Dawn 213
I Gotta Have Love	Colos, David Dayton & the	1955	Lomar 704
I Gotta Have Somebody (Lonely Boy)	Four After Fives	1961	All Time 9076
I Gotta Have Your Love	Harptones	1963	KT 201
I Gotta Have Your Lovin'	Fiestas	1965	Old Town 1189
I Gotta Know	Originals (Lonnie Nye)	1960	Lo-Lon 101
I Gotta Know	Passions	1961	Octavia 8005
I Gotta Leave This Town	Kellum, Murry & group	1964	MOC 653
I Gotta Make A Move	Tempos	1966	Montel 955
I Gotta Sing The Blues	Hepsters	1956	Ronel 110
I Gotta Tell Her Now	Duprees	1963	Coed 580
I Gotta Tell It	Sharmettes	1962	King 5656
I Guess I Brought It All On Myself	Counts	1956	Note 20000
I Guess I'll Be	Viscaynes	1961	Tropo 101
I Guess I'll Miss The Prom	Gordan, Joni & group	1964	Musicnote 125
I Guess I'll Never Stop Loving You	La Rells	1962	Liberty 55430
I Guess It's All Over Now	Five Budds	1953	Rama 2
I Guess You Don't Love Me (No More)	Dynamics	1963	Do-Kay-Lo 101
I Had A Dream	Collegiates	1961	Heritage 105
I Had A Dream	Composers	1963	Era 3118
I Had A Dream	Computones	1979	Clifton 32
I Had A Dream	Fabulous Twilights, Nathaniel Mayer & the	1963	Fortune 554
I Had A Dream	Hayes, Linda (with the Flairs)	1956	Antler 4000
I Had A Dream	Jewels (Monogram)	1976	Monogram 117
I Had A Dream	Jumpin' Tones	1964	Raven 8004
I Had A Dream	Paradons	1962	Milestone 2015
I Had A Dream	Reno, Nicky & group	1959	Ges 100
I Had A Dream I Lost You	Angels (New Jersey)	1967	RCA 9129
I Had A Dream Last Night	Pips	1963	Everlast 5025
I Had A Dream Last Nite	Aladdins	1955	Aladdin 3298
I Had A Feeling This Morning	Fabuleers	1960	Kenco 5002
I Had A Guy	Hearts (Bronx, N.Y.)	1956	Baton 228
I Had A Little Too Much	Ensenators	1962, 1997	Tarx 1001/Reissue (97)
I Had A Love	Boptones	1958	Ember 1043
I Had A Love	Dreams, Darnell & the	1964	West Side 1020/Cousins
I Had A Love	Five Hollywood Blue Jays	1952	Recorded In Hollywood 396
I Had A Love	Flairs	1953	Flair 1012

SONG	GROUP	YEAR	LABEL
I Had A Love	Hollywood Bluejays	1953	Recorded In Hollywood 396
I Had A Love	Vibrations	1961	Checker LP 2978
I Had A Thrill	Cherokees (Philadelphia)	1954	Grand 106
I Had Fifty Cents	Cadets	1963	Crown LP 5370
I Had My Moment	Serenaders (Colony)	1952	Colony 100
I Had The Blues	Cupcakes, Shelton Dunaway & the	1959	Khoury's 715
I Had The Craziest Dream	Skylarks	1953	RCA 5257
I Had To Leave Town	Orioles, Sonny Til & the	1983	Murray Hill LP M61277
I Had To Let You Go	Hepsters	1955	Ronel 107
I Had To Lose You	Gayles	1955	King 4860
I Had To Walk Home Myself	Motor Scooter, Beverly & the	1964	Epic 9654
I Hadn't Anyone Till You	Five Keys	1952	Aladdin 3136
I Hate To Cry	Essex	1963	Roulette LP 25234
I Hate To See A Little Girl Crying	Imaginations	1961	Music Makers (unreleased)
I Hate To See You Go	Washington, Baby (with the Hearts)	1959	J&S 1632/1633
I Have	G-Clefs	1965	Veep 1218
I Have A Boyfriend	Chiffons	1963	Laurie 3212
I Have A Father Who Cares	Baronaires	1960	Carrie
I Have A Love	Parakeets Quintet (New Jersey)	1956	Atlas 1068/Angletone 1068
I Have Chosen You	Tilman, Mickey & group	1958	Vee Jay 296
I Have Love	Pageboys	1963	Seville 135
I Have News For You	Rockin' Bradley & group	1959	Fire 1007
I Have Problems	McKinnon, Preston & group	1960	Sharp 104
I Have Sinned	Elbert, Donnie & group	1957	DeLuxe 6148
I Have Someone	Starfires	1958	Decca 30730
I Have The Right	Twilights	NA	Select 742
I Have Two Loves	Valentines	1963	King 5830
I Haven't Found It With Another	Concords (Neal Scott)	1961	Portrait 102
I Haven't The Heart	Beau Brummels	1956	Vik 0208
I Hear A Melody	Jacks & Jills	1956	Empire 101
I Hear A Rhapsody	Excellents	1963	Blast 207
I Hear A Rhapsody	Four Naturals	1959	Red Top 119
I Hear A Rhapsody	Masters, Thurston Harris & the	1958	Aladdin 3440
I Hear A Rhapsody	Sonotones	1955	Bruce 127
I Hear An Echo	Challengers III	1962	Tri-Phi 1020
I Hear Bells (acappella)	Vibraharps	1975	Relic LP 108
I Hear Bells Ding Dong	Belles, Glorius Wilson & the	1956	Fairbanks 2002
I Hear Bells (Wedding Bells)	Dell Vikings	1961	ABC 10248
I Hear Mission Bells	Tune Weavers	NA	Casa Grande (unreleased)
(I Hear) Silver Bells	Zircons	1964	Cool Sound 1030
I Hear The Angels Cry	Teenagers (Joe Negroni)	1981	Crystal Ball LP 142
I Hear The Rain	Kings Five	1959	Trophy 9
I Hear The Trumpets Blow	Tokens (Brooklyn)	1966	B.T. Puppy 518
I Hear The Wind (acappella)	Tremonts	1975	Relic LP 104
I Hear Those Bells	Five Trojans, Nicky St. Clair & the	1959	Edison International 410
I Hear Wedding Bells	Cubs	1956	Savoy 1502
I Heard That Story Before	Cupcakes, Cookie & the	1963	Lyric 1008
I Heard Those Bells	Ekhoes, Con Pierson & the	1964	LeMans 007
I Heard You	Starlites, Jackie & the	1962	Mascot 128
I Heard You Call Me Dear	Dudads	1955	DeLuxe 6083
I Hope I Don't Cry	Butler, B. B. & group	1964	Barry 111
I Hope I Never Fall In Love	Ballards	NA	Veltone 1738
I Hope You Won't Hold It Against Me	Harris, Thurston (with the Sharps)	1957	Aladdin 3398
I Hope You're Happy	Counts, Freddy Davis & the	1958	Count 405
I Hurt So	Quin-Teens	1963	Pike 5922
I Just Can't	Bee Hives	1961	Fleetwood 215
I Just Can't Help It	Click-Ettes	1963	Checker 1060
I Just Can't Help Myself	Kool Gents	1956	Vee Jay 207/Vee Jay LP 1019/ Charly LP 1113
I Just Can't Help Myself	Sheiks, Eddie Williams & the	NA	Coronado 112
I Just Can't Help Myself	Volumes	1965	American Arts 18
I Just Can't Keep The Tears From Tumblin' Down	Four Tops, Delores Carroll & the	1956	Chateau 2002
I Just Can't Keep The Tears From Tumblin' Down	Sophomores (Massachusetts)	1957	Dawn 228

SONG	GROUP	YEAR	LABEL
I Just Can't Stand It	Pearls	NA	Astor 1005
I Just Can't Tell No Lie	Moonglows	1952	Champagne 7500
I Just Can't Understand	Downbeats, O. S. Grant & the	1956	Sarg 197
I Just Can't Understand	Essents	1966	Laurie 3335
I Just Can't Understand	La Rells	1961	Robbee 114
I Just Cry	Flamingo, Johnny & group	1959	Malynn 101
I Just Don't Know	Roulettes, Adam Faith & the	1964	Amy 913
(I Just Go) Wild Inside	Barons (Imperial)	1964	Imperial 66057
I Just Got A Letter	Fashions	1961	Ember 1084
I Just Got Kissed	Duotones	NA	Harlequin 611026
I Just Got Lucky	Orioles, Sonny Til & the	1956	Vee Jay 196
I Just Got Rid Of A Heartache	Flairs, Shirley Gunter & the	1956	Modern 1001
I Just Love The Things She Do	Five Dots	1955	Note 10003
I Just Might	Team Mates	1959	Le Cam 701
I Just Might Fall In Love	Foxes	1963	ABC 10446
I Just Wanna Boy Or Girl	Tiffanys	1965	Josie 942
I Just Want Somebody	Middleton, Tony & group	1959	Triumph 600
I Just Want To Dream	Sugar Tones	1953	Okeh 6992
I Just Want To Know	Delacardos	1961	Shell 308
I Just Want To Know	Noblemen	NA	Clarity 106
I Just Want To Love You	McPhatter, Clyde & group	1960	Mercury 71692
I Just Want You	Frontiers	1963	Philips 40148
I Keep Crying	Hurricanes, Bob Gaye & the	1954	Audivox 109
I Keep Forgettin'	Hi Fi's	1965	Cameo 349
I Keep On Walking	Embers, Billy Scandlin & the	1959	Viking 1002
I Kissed An Angel	Roses	1958	Dot 15816
I Kneel At Your Throne	Emeralds (St. Louis)	1960	Rex 1013
I Knew	Caribbeans	1958	20th Fox 112
I Knew	Williams, Jimmy & group	1956	Neil 104
I Knew From The Start	Moonglows	1956	Chess 1646
I Knew I'd Fall In Love	Penguins	1957	Atlantic 1132
I Knew It All The Time	Charms, Otis Williams & his	1959	DeLuxe 6185
I Knew It Was You All The Time	Lawson Boys, Teddy Lawson & the	1957	Mansfield 611/612
I Know	Drifters (Pre-1959)	1957	Atlantic 1161
I Know	Four Chevelles	1957	Band Box 358
I Know	Futuretones	1959	Tress 1/2
I Know	Hinton, Joe & group	1958	Back Beat 519
I Know	Hollywood Flames	1953	Swing Time 345/Lucky 009 (55)/ Decca 48331 (55)
I Know	Illusions	1966	Columbia 43700
I Know	Irridescents	1960	Ultrasonic 104/Ultrasonic 109
I Know	Jokers, Johnny & the	1962	Beltone 2028
I Know	Medallions	1955	Essex 901
I Know	Prisonaires	1953	Sun 191
I Know	Rainbows	1963	Dave 908
I Know	Sentimentals, James Carter & the	1957	Tuxedo 922/Tuxedo 943
I Know	Spaniels	1960	Vee Jay 350
I Know	Teardrops	NA	Col-Vin 777
I Know	Zodiacs, Maurice Williams & the	1965	Scepter 12113
I Know A Valley	Velvetones, Bingo Miller & the	NA	Young Artists 103
I Know About The Boy Next Door	Whirlwinds, James Loyd & the	1963	Empala 117
I Know Better	Flamingos	1962	End 1121
I Know Better	Goldtones, Bill Bryan & the	1962	Pike 5915
I Know By Baby Cares	Catamounts, Calvin & the	1976	Catamount 131
I Know How It Feels	Satintones	1961	Motown 1010
I Know I Know	Honeytones	1958	Big Top 3002
I Know I Know	Hudson, Pookie (with the Imperials)	1963	Double L 711
I Know, I Know	Spaniels	1963	Double L 711
I Know I Love You So	Royals	1952	Federal 12077
I Know I Was Wrong	Barons (New Orleans)	1955	Imperial 5359
I Know I Was Wrong	Dukes, Billy Duke & the	1956	Teen 110
I Know I'm In Love	Viceroys, Jimmy Norman & the	1963	Little Star 121
I Know It's Hard But It's Fair	Five Royales	1959	King 5191
I Know It's True	Starr, Andy & group	NA	Arcade 115
I Know (Lift Up Your Head)	Imperials, Little Anthony & the	1961	Apollo 755

SONG	GROUP	YEAR	LABEL
I Know Love	Four Fellows (Brooklyn - Glory)	1955	Glory 231
I Know My Baby Loves Me So	Springers	1965	Way Out 2699
I Know She Loves Me	Tuggle, Bobby & group	1956	Checker 840
I Know She's Gone	Quails, Bill Robinson & the	1954	DeLuxe 6047
I Know Somewhere	Contenders	1966	Java 104
I Know Somewhere	Kaptions	NA	Ham-Mil 1520
I Know The Feelin'	Jades	NA	Poncello 7703
I Know The Meaning Of Love	Juniors, Jimmy Castor & the	1956	Wing 90078
I Know What I Want	Charms, Tommy G & the	1961	Hollywood 1109
I Know Why	New Yorkers	1963	Park Ave 100
I Know Why	Spectors Three	1960	Trey 3001
I Know Why	Springers	1965	Way Out 2699
I Know Why Dreamers Cry	Hamptons	1961	Legrand 1007
I Know You	Chants, Casanova & the	NA	Sapphire 2254
I Know You Gotta Go	Sugar Tones	1953	Okeh 6992
I Know You Know That I Know	Styles	NA	Modern 1048
I Know You'll Be My Love	Paramounts	1960	Fleetwood 1014
I Know Your Lyin' (But Say It Again)	Pyramids, Doug & Freddy & the	1961	Finer Arts 1001
I Know You're In There	Nite Riders	1958	Teen 116
I Laughed	Highlands	1961	N/A
I Laughed	Jesters	1958	Cyclone 5011
I Laughed So Hard	Defenders	1964	Parkway 926
I Laughed So Hard	Rip Chords	1958	MMI 1236
I Laughed So Hard I Cried	Trophies	1962	Challenge 9149
I Leave You In Tears	Turn Ons, Tim Tam & the	1966	Palmer 5006
I Left My Sugar Standing In The Rain	Sophomores (Massachusetts)	1957	Dawn 223
I Let Her Go	Capitols	1958	Carlton 461
I Lie	Delconte, David & group	NA	Delcon 1
I Lied To My Heart	Duvals, Phil Johnson & the	1958	Kelit 7033
I Lied To My Heart	Enchanters (Musitron)	1961	Musitron 1072
I Like Girls	Bradford, Sylvester & group	1958	Atco 6130
I Like It	Ban Lons	1962	Fidelity 4056
I Like It Like That	Casinos	1961	Alto 2002
I Like It Like That	Clovermen, Tippie & the	1962	Stenton 7001
I Like It Like That	Contenders	1966	Java 103
I Like It Like That	Five Royales	1954, 1964	Apollo 454/Smash 1936
I Like It Like That	Spaniels	1959	Vee Jay 310
I Like Moonshine	Five Owls	1955	Vulcan 1025
I Like The Way You Look At Me	Pentagons	1961	Donna 1344
I Like To Cha Cha	Nutmegs	1971	Relic LP 5002
I Like To Throw My Head Back And Sing	Tokens (Brooklyn)	1972	Bell 190
I Like Your Style Of Making Love	Cleftones	1957	Gee 1031
I Live For You	Chessmen	1958	Mirasonic 1002/Mirasonic 1868 (58)
I Live For Your Love	Do-Reys	1956	Joy 2401
(I Live) Half A Block From An Angel	Danleers	1960	Epic 9367
I Live True To You	Larks (North Carolina)	1952	Apollo 1194
I Long For You	Five C's	1981	P-Vine Special LP 9036
I Lost Again	Vikings, Lee Martin & the	1960	Jin 149
I Lost My Baby	Darvels	1963	Eddies 69
I Lost My Baby	Furys	1963	Mach IV 118
I Lost My Baby	Nighthawks, Johnny Gosey & the	NA	MOA 1001
I Lost My Heart	Populaires	1957	Marvello 5001
I Lost My Job	Don Clairs, Harold Perkins & the	1958	Amp-3 1001/1002
I Lost My Job	Supremes Four	1961	Sara 1032
I Lost My Love	Royals	NA	Liban
I Lost My Love In The Big City	Elgins (California)	1963	Lummtone 112
I Lost The Love	Rivingtons	1968	AGC 5
I Lost You	Charters	1963	Alva 1001
I Lost You	Dots (Jeanette Baker)	1957	Caddy 107
I Lost You	Spaniels	1957	Vee Jay 264
I Love	Dolls	1958	Teenage 1010
I Love An Angel	Blue Notes, Little Bill & the	1959	Dolton 4
I Love An Angel	Co-Eds	1957	Old Town 1033
I Love And Care For You	Midnighters, Hank Ballard & the	1962	King 5693
I Love Brooklyn	Honey Bears	1955	Cash 1004

SONG	GROUP	YEAR	LABEL
I Love Candy	Echoes	1965, 1981	Ascot 2188/ Crystal Ball 150
I Love Girls	Ebb Tides, Nino & the	1959	Recorte 413
I Love Her So	Blue Notes	1958	TNT 150/Dot 15720 (58)
I Love Her So	Velvetones	1957	Aladdin 3372/Imperial 5878 (62)
I Love Him	Castanets	1963	TCF 1
I Love Him So	Renegades, Patty McCoy & the	1962	Counsel 119
I Love L.A.	Crowns, Henry Strogin & the	1962	Amazon 1001
I Love Marie	Floridians	1961	ABC 10185
I Love Me And You	Four Jewels	1964	Start 641
I Love My Baby	Crystals (Aladdin)	1957	Aladdin 3355
I Love My Baby	Enchantments	1963	Ritz 17003
I Love My Baby	Good Guys	1964	San-Dee 1007
I Love My Baby	Mason, Little Billy (with the Rhythm Jesters)	1956	Rama 212
I Love My Baby	Phaetons	1959	Vin 1015
I Love My Baby	Savoys (Bella)	1959	Bella 18
I Love My Baby	Sweet Marquees	1961	Apache 1516
I Love My Baby	Tokens (with Neil Sedaka)	1958	Melba 104
I Love My Darling	Original Casuals	1958	Back Beat 503 (second pressing, first is by Casuals)
I Love My Girl	Metronomes (Harold Sonny Wright)	1957	Cadence 1310
I Love My Teddy Bear	Cones, Connie & the	1960	Roulette 4223
I Love Nadine	Lovetones, Raymond Pope & the	1962	Squalor 1313
I Love Only You	Crescents, Billy Wells & the	1956	Reserve 105
I Love Only You	Mello-Harps	1955	Tin Pan Alley 145/146
I Love Only You	Nickels & the Three Pennies, Ed Henry with the	NA	Nu Sound 180
I Love Paris	Desires	NA	Hull (unreleased)
I Love Paris	Robins	1955	Spark 113
I Love That Girl	Darrow, Jay & group	1961	Keen 82124
I Love That Girl So	Chevies, Wayne Johnson & the	1959	Dove 1033
I Love The Life I Live	Delighters, Rose Morris & the	1962	
I Love The Life I Live	Pipes	1956	Dootone 401
I Love The Way You Walk	Castaways, Tony Rivers & the	1964	Constellation 128
I Love Thee	Bell Boys	1960	Era 3026
I Love To Be Loved	Dynamics	1961	Douglas 200
I Love You	Belvaderes	1956	Hudson 4
I Love You	Blue Flames, Buddy Love & the	1958	Thunder 1A
I Love You	Boyd, Eddie (with His Chess Men)	1957	J.O.B. 1114
I Love You	BQE	1988	Starlight 61
I Love You	Brothers, Little Toni & the	1960	Top Rank 2090
I Love You	Caesars	NA	Lanie 2001
I Love You	Castaways, Tony Rivers & the	1964	Constellation 128
I Love You	Catalinas	1973	Jayne 813
I Love You	Chanters, Gene Ford & the	1955	Combo 92
I Love You	Chavis Brothers	1962	Clock 1025
I Love You	Climbers	1957	J&S 1658
I Love You	Corlettes	1962	Kansoma 02
I Love You	Dreams	1963	Talent 1004
I Love You	Dukes (California)	1959	Flip 345
I Love You	Fabulous Tears, Little Dooley & the	1965	Baylor 101
I Love You	Flairs	1963	Crown LP 5356
I Love You	Four Most	1959	Milo 107/Relic 501 (63)
I Love You	Gales	1960	Winn 916
I Love You	Gaytunes	1957	Joyce 101
I Love You	Idols	NA	Collectables LP 5039
I Love You	Kokonuts	1962	Bertram International 215
I Love You	Larks (Don Julian)	1971	Money 601
I Love You	Motivations	1973	Eastbound 604
I Love You	Nobletones	1958	C&M 183/Times Square 17 (63)/ Relic 529 (65)
I Love You	Shadows	1959	El-Gee-Bee 101
I Love You	Symbols	1973	Vintage 1007
I Love You	Valumes	1962	Chex 1002 (correct!) (first pressing, second is by Volumes)

SONG	GROUP	YEAR	LABEL
I Love You	Volumes	1962	Chex 1002 (second pressing, first is by Valumes)
I Love You (acappella)	Bon-Aires	1976	Flamingo 1001
I Love You Always	Rivingtons	1964	Vee Jay 649
I Love You Baby	Barons (New Orleans)	NA	Imperial (unreleased)
I Love You Baby	Con Chords, Bob Brady & the	1966	Chariot 525
I Love You Baby	Jaguars	1957	R-Dell 16
I Love You, Baby	Kings, Bobby Hall & the	1953, 1973	Jax 314
I Love You Baby	Miracles (Detroit)	1959	Motown G1/G2/Chess 1734 (59)
I Love You Baby	Moovers	1967	Brent 7065
I Love You Baby	Starr, Andy & group	NA	Arcade 115
I Love You Baby	Volumes	1968	Inferno 5001
I Love You Baby	Wrens	NA	Casa Grande
I Love You Baby	Zodiacs, Maurice Williams & the	1974	Relic LP 5017
I Love You, Can't You See	Showmen	1962	Minit 647
I Love You Conrad	Little Cheryl & group	1964	Cameo 292
I Love You Darling	Apollos	1959	Harvard 803
I Love You, Darling	Belltones (Yonkers)	1956	Scatt 1609/1610/J&S 1609/1610 (58)
I Love You Darling	Lovenotes, Sybil Love & the	1959	Valex 505
I Love You, Darling	Sweet Teens, Faith Taylor & the	1960	Bea & Baby 105
I Love You, Darling	Valentines	1955	Rama 181
I Love You Darling	Vanguards	NA	Regency 743
I Love You Diane	Four Epics	1963	Laurie 3155
I Love You Eddie	Crystals (Brooklyn)	1962	Philles 106
I Love You For Sentimental Reasons	Cleftones	1961	Gee 1067
I Love You For Sentimental Reasons	Devotions	1961	Delta 1001/Roulette 4406 (61)/ Roulette 4541 (64)
I Love You For Sentimental Reasons	Sharks	1975	Clifton 10
(I Love You) For Sentimental Reasons	Spaniels, Pookie Hudson & the	1961	Neptune 124
I Love You For Sentimental Reasons	Styles	1964	Josie 920
I Love You For Sentimental Reasons	Thrillers, Little Joe & the	1961	20th Century 1214
I Love You Girl	Double Dates	1959	Luck 103
I Love You, I Love You	Toppers (Avalon)	1954	Avalon 63707
I Love You, I Love You So-o-o	Midnighters, Hank Ballard & the	1960	King 5341
I Love You I Swear	Click-Ettes	1960	Dice 100
I Love You (Inka Doo)	Fortune Tellers	1963	Atlantic 2197
I Love You Judy	Fi-Tones, Carl Thomas & the	1959	Stroll 101/O Gee 1004 (59)
I Love You Like I Do	Parakeets	1962	Big Top 3130
I Love You Madly	Emotions	1964	20th Fox 478
I Love You More	Coronets	1955	Groove 0114
I Love You More (Than Anyone)	Imaginations	1961	Bacon Fat 101
I Love You More Than You Know	Galens	1966	Challenge 59402
I Love You Mostly	Orioles, Sonny Til & the	1955	Jubilee 5177
I Love You, My Love	Perfections	1964	SVR 1005
I Love You, Oh Darling	Warner, Little Sonny & group	1960	Swingin' 627
I Love You, Patricia	Supremes Four	1961	Sara 1032
I Love You, Really I Do	Tantones	1957	Lamp 2002
(I Love You) Sherry	Enchantments	1962	Gone 5130
I Love You So	Arabians	1960	Lanrod 1605
I Love You So	Bonnevilles	NA	N/A
I Love You So	Cap-Tans	1974	Roadhouse 1016
I Love You So	Carvels	1985	Relic LP 5050
I Love You So	Chantels	1958	End 1020
I Love You So	Crows	1953	Rama 5
I Love You So	Day, Darlene (with the Imaginations)	1961	Music Makers 106
I Love You So	Fashions	1959	V-Tone 202
I Love You So	Five Satins	1973	Klik 1020
I Love You So	Fleetwoods	1960	Dolton 30
I Love You So	Heartspinners, Dino & the	1972	Bim Bam Boom 112
I Love You So	Imaginations, Darlene Day & the	1961	Music Makers 106
I Love You So	Internationals	1958	ABC 9964
I Love You So	Kents	1958	Dome 501
I Love You So	Kittens	1985	Relic LP 8004
I Love You So	Master, Ronnie & group	1961	Landa 669
I Love You So	McCleese, James & group	1961	Marco 106

SONG	GROUP	YEAR	LABEL
I Love You So	Miracles, Carl Hogan & the	1957	Fury 1001
I Love You So	Pretenders	1957	Holiday 2610
I Love You So	Reno, Frank & group	1962	Diamond 118
I Love You So	Sir Nites, T.L. Clemons & the	1960	Combo 168
I Love You So	Suedes	1954	Money 204
I Love You So	Swans (Parrot)	1981	Parrot (unreleased)/Relic LP 5088 (90)
I Love You So	Tendertones	1959	Ducky 713
I Love You So	Three D's	1961	Dean 521
I Love You So (acappella)	Crests	1963	Times Square 6/Times Square 97 (64)
I Love You So Dearly	Startones	1956	Rainbow 341
I Love You So Much	Top Notes	1963	ABC 10399
I Love You So Much I Could Die	Sparrows Quartette	1973	Del Tone 3001
I Love You Tenderly	Edwards, Sonny & group	1963	Cavetone 516
I Love You The Most	Rip-Chords	1956	Abco 105
I Love You, This I Know	Temptations (New Jersey)	1958	Savoy 1550
I Love You To The Nth Degree	Charmettes	1960	Mona 553
I Love You True	Medallions	1961	Sarg 191
I Love You With All My Heart	Four Counts	1958	Cham 003
I Love You With Tender Passion	Magnatones	1963	Fortune 555
I Love You With Tender Passion	Nite Sounds	1962	Fortune 548
I Love You Yes I Do	Four Buddies	NA	Savoy 951 (unreleased)
I Love You, Yes I Do	Vikings, Barry & the	1964	Jamie 1281
I Love You, You Love Me	Slicks, Jimmy Sommers & the	NA	Space
I Loved Him So	Dories	1959	Dore 528
I Loved Only You	Piccadilly Pipers	1956	Chart 615
I Loved You	Popcorns	1963	Vee Jay 537
I Made A Boo Boo	Mastertones	1957	Future 1001
I Made A Mistake	Kennedy, Ace & group	1961	Swan 4080
I Made A Vow	Robbins	1954	Crown 106
I Made A Wish	Drakes	1965	Olimpic 252
I Make Believe	McPhatter, Clyde (with the Cues)	1956	Atlantic 1117
I Make This Pledge (To You)	Chanters (New York)	1961	DeLuxe 6191
I May Be Small	Five Chances	1954	Chance 1157
I May Be Wrong	Angels, Little Betty & the	1961	Savoy 1603
I May Be Wrong	Emperors	1954	Haven 511
I May Be Wrong	Orioles, Sonny Til & the	1983	Murray Hill LP M61277
I Mean Really	Bartell, Eddie	1958	Star-X 501
I Mean Really	Ricardos	1958	Star-X 512
I Met Her On The First Of September	Technics	1962	Chex 1013
I Met Him At A Dance	Invictas	1963	Mavis 221
I Met Him On A Sunday	Shirelles	1958	Decca 25506/Decca 30588 (58)/ Tiara 6112 (59)
I Met Him On A Sunday '66	Shirelles	1965	Scepter 12132
I Met My Lost Love	Revels	1961	Palette 5074
I Met You	Neptunes	1964	Marlo 1534
I Miei Giorni Felici	Airdales, Wess & the	1967	Durium 9259
I Miei Giorni Felici	Valentinos	1992	Clifton 101
I Might Like It	Deltairs	1958	Ivy 105
I Miss My Baby	Hearts, Lee Andrews & the	1981	Gotham 325
I Miss You	Avalons	1956	Aladdin (unreleased)
I Miss You	Carbo, Chuck (with the Spiders)	1957	Imperial 5479
I Miss You	Dreamlovers	1962	Down/End 1114 (62)
I Miss You Baby	Mandells	NA	Trans World 821
I Miss You, Darling	Falcons (Cash)	1955	Cash 1002
I Miss You Most Of All	Marveleers	1953	Derby 844
I Miss You So	Andrews, Lee (with the Hearts)	1960	Swan 4065
I Miss You So	Barons (Spartan)	1961	Spartan 402
I Miss You So	Delcos	NA	Monument
I Miss You So	Excels	1955	X 0108
I Miss You So	Hearts, Lee Andrews & the (as Lee Andrews)	1961	Swan 4065
I Miss You So	Imperials, Little Anthony & the	1965	DCP 1149/Veep 1244 (66)
I Miss You So	Miller Sisters	1962	Rayna 5001
I Miss You So	Notes, Reed Harper & the	1958	Vik 0328/Smart 1001 (58)
I Miss You So	Orioles, Sonny Til & the	1951, 1953, 1962	Jubilee 5051/5107/ Charlie Parker 215

SONG	GROUP	YEAR	LABEL
I Miss You So	Rockets, Herb Kenny & the	1953	MGM 11397
I Miss You So	Tren-Dells	1962	Tilt 788
I Miss You So	Wilson, Faye & group	1957	Hip 401
I Miss You So Much	Lanterns	1973	Baron 110
I Miss Your Love	Capris (Philadelphia)	NA	Collectables LP 5000
I Missed Her	Philadelphians	1962	Cameo 216
I Must Be Crazy	Allen, George & group	1961	Sotoplay 0031
I Must Be Dreamin'	Robins	1955	Spark 116
I Must Be Dreaming	Coasters	1964	Atco 6321
I Must Forget About You	Real McCoys	NA	Pico 523
I Must Forget You	Maples	1954	Blue Lake 111
I Must Have Love	Oliver, Johnny & group	1954	MGM 55001
I Must See You Again	Rivals (Darryl)	1957, 1963	Darryl 722/Junior 990
I Must See You Again	Vines	1961	Cee Jay 582
I Need A Change	Miracles (Detroit)	1960	Chess 1768
I Need A Girl	Feathers	1955	Aladdin 3277
I Need A Girl	Hatfield, Bobby & group	1963	Moonglow 220
I Need A Girl	Marvellos	1958	Marvello 5005
I Need A Helping Hand	Marquees, Terry Brown & the	1961	Jo-Ann 130
I Need A Helping Hand	Servicemen	1967	Pathway 102
I Need A Shoulder To Cry On	Buddies, Billy Bunn & the	1951	RCA 4483
I Need A True Love	Arabian Knights, Ray Gant & the	1971	Jay Walking 014
I Need An Angel	Victors, Little Man & the	1963	Tarheel 064
I Need Her	Dominions	NA	Graves 1091
I Need Her	Taylor, Adam & group	NA	N/A
I Need Him To Love Me	Sweet Teens, Faith Taylor & the	1960	Bea & Baby 104
I Need It	Zircons	1957	Winston 1020/Dot 15724 (58)
I Need Love	Blasers, Eddie Foster & the	1961	Lyons 108
I Need Love	Calveys	1961	Comma 84349/Comma 445
I Need Love	Cyclones	NA	Cyclone 500
I Need Some	Ambertones	1965	Dottie 1130
I Need Some Money	Starlites, Eddie & the	1963	Aljon 1260/1261
I Need Somebody	Evans Sister with male group	1956	Dot 15449
I Need Somebody	Lee, James Washington & group	1962	L&M 1003
I Need Somebody	Thrillers, Little Joe & the	1959	Okeh 7121
I Need Someone	Belmonts	1961	Sabina 502
I Need Someone	Ray-Dots	1960	Vibro 1651
I Need Someone	Valets	1958	Jon 4025
I Need Someone	Victors, Jimmy Vick & the	1963	Cherry 7888
I Need Thee	Detroit Harmonettes	1954	DeLuxe 6039
I Need You	Agee, Ray & female group	1955	R&B 1311
I Need You	Caliphs	1973	Vintage 1008
I Need You	Columbo, Joe & group	1963	Taurus 359
I Need You	Dreamlovers	1961	
I Need You	Gladiators	1958	Donnie 701
I Need You	Griffin, Herman & group	1959	House Of Beauty 112
I Need You	Haff-Tones	1961	Twilight 001
I Need You	Ivy, Sheron & group	1961	Heritage 106/Coed 572 (62)
I Need You	Little People, Mike Lynam & the	NA	Emanon 101
I Need You	Magnatones	1960	Cedargrove 313/Time 108 (60)
I Need You	Orbits	NA	Don-J 48798
I Need You	Prodigals	NA	Acadian 1000
I Need You	Puzzles	1968	Fatback 216
I Need You	Rayber Voices, Herman Griffin & the	NA	H.O.B. 112
I Need You	Rivals (Anna)	1960	Anna 1113
I Need You	Snap Shots	1963	Federal 12496
I Need You	Sophisticates	NA	Mutt 27318
I Need You	Tartans	1966	Impact 1010
I Need You	Tempos	1966	Riley's 8781
I Need You	Utmosts	1962	Pan Or 1123
I Need You	Van Dellos	1961	Card 558
I Need You	Weston, Billy & group	1962	Ep-Som 1002
I Need You All The Time	Platters	1953, 1955, 1956	Federal 12164/12250/12271
I Need You Always	Counts	1954	Dot 1188/Dot 16105 (61)
I Need You, Baby	Enchords	1961	Laurie 3089

SONG	GROUP	YEAR	LABEL
I Need You, Baby	Four Speeds	1954	DeLuxe 6070
I Need You Baby	Minor Tones, Robbie Meldano & the	1958	Music City 816
I Need You Baby	Orioles, Sonny Til & the	1955	Jubilee 5189
I Need You Darling	Debonaires (Elmont)	1958	Elmont 1004
I Need You More	Wanderers	1960	Cub 9075
I Need You Now	Clovers	1961	Winley 265
I Need You Now	Drifters (1959-forward)	1968	Atlantic 2471
I Need You So	Belvin, Jesse & group	1957	Modern 1013
I Need You So	Chapman, Grady (with the Suedes)	1955	Money 204
I Need You So	Corvairs	1962	Twin 19671
I Need You So	Four Buddies, Bobbie James & the	1956	Club 51 104
I Need You So	Four Sounds, Lois Blaine & the	1963	Open-G 00
I Need You So	McLain, Tommy & group	NA	MSL 197
I Need You So	Oliver, Johnny & group	1956	MGM 12319
I Need You So	Orioles, Sonny Til & the	1950	Jubilee 5037
I Need You So	Pipes, Rudy Harvey & the	1959	Capri 103
I Need You So	Planets	1959	Nu-Clear 7422
I Need You So	Ramblers (Larkwood)	1963	Larkwood 1104
I Need You So	Romans, Little Caesar & the	1961	Del-Fi LP 1218
I Need You So	Sheppards (Chicago - Robin Hood)	1976	Robin Hood 135
I Need You So	Vel-Tones	1960, 1961	Zara 901/Lost Nite 103 (65)
I Need You So	Victones	NA	Front Page 1001
I Need You So Much	Gibralters, Jimmy Barnes & the	1959	Gibraltar 102
I Need You So Much	Impalas (Washington, D.C.)	1961	Checker 999
I Need You Tonight	Counts	1955	Dot 1265
I Need Your Kisses	A Moment's Pleasure	1986	Starlight 39
I Need Your Kisses	Spaniels	1957	Vee Jay 257
I Need Your Love	Blue Belles, Patti LaBelle & the	1967	Atlantic 2446
I Need Your Love	Del-Rhythmetts	1958	J-V-B 5000
I Need Your Love	Downbeats	1956	Sarg 173
I Need Your Love	Egyptian Kings	1961	Nanc 1120
I Need Your Love	Emeralds, Bobby Woods & the	1961	Rumble 348
I Need Your Love	Enchanters (Epsom)	1962	Epsom 103
I Need Your Love	Entrees, Chuck Corley & the	1957	Fee Bee 219
I Need Your Love	Gay Poppers	1959	Savoy 1573
I Need Your Love	Impressions	1962	Swirl 107
I Need Your Love	Reflections	NA	Went 001
I Need Your Love	Rhythm Cadets, Little Willie & the	1988	Crystal Ball 152
I Need Your Love	Sultans, Wardell & the	1962	Imperial 5886
I Need Your Love So Bad	Viceroys	1962	Ramco 3715
I Need Your Love So Bad	Vocaleers	1959	Paradise 113
I Need Your Love Tonight	Kittens	1963	Don-El 205
I Need Your Lovin'	Paul, Clarence & group	1959	Hanover 4519
I Need Your Lovin'	Perenials	NA	Ruby-Ray 2
I Need Your Lovin'	Twilighters (Bronx, N.Y.)	1968	Vanco 204
I Need Your Lovin' Again	Coronas	1965	Corona 520
I Need Your Lovin' Baby	Five Royales	1955, 1964	King 4806/King 5892
I Need Your Loving	McCracklin, Jimmy & group	1958	Peacock 1683
I Need Your Tenderness (I Love You Darling)	Chanters (New York)	1958	DeLuxe 6162
I Never Dreamed	Cookies	1964	Dimension 1032
I Never Dreamed	Gems (20th Century)	1955	20th Century 5037
I Never Dreamed	Nu-Tones	1958	20th Century 75030
I Never Felt This Way	Storms, Wally Lee & the	1959	Sundown 123
I Never Had A Girl Like You	Redtoppers	NA	Dan 3214
I Never Knew	Colts	1959	Del-Co 4002
I Never Knew	Deltones	1960	20th Century Fox 175
I Never Knew	Dukays	1962	Vee Jay 460
I Never Knew	Dynamics, Ray Murray & the	1963	Fleetwood 7005
I Never Knew	Fabulous Echoes	1964	Liberty 55769
I Never Knew	Orioles, Sonny Til & the	1951	Jubilee 5060
I Never Knew	Victory Five	1958	Terp 101
I Never Knew What Love Could Do	Lee, Curtis (with the Halos)	1960	Hot 7
I Never Loved Anyone	Voyagers	1960	Titan 1712
I Never Loved Like This	Desires	1962	Smash 1763
I Never See My Baby Alone	Three D's	1958	Paris 514

SONG	GROUP	YEAR	LABEL
I Never Told You	Five Gents	1958	Crest 516
I Never Will Forget	Del-Larks, Sammy & the	1961, 1978	Ea-Jay 100
I Never Will Forget	Royal Jesters	1962	Cobra 7777
I Offer You	Charms	1956	Chart 613
I Often Wonder	Academics	1958	Ancho 104 (unreleased)
I Only Cry Once A Day Now	Puffs	NA	Dore 757
I Only Had A Little	Du Droppers	1955	Groove EP EGA-2
I Only Have Eyes For You	Ambertones	NA	Rayjack 1002
I Only Have Eyes For You	Blue Stars	1977	Arcade 102
I Only Have Eyes For You	Dubs	1972	Clifton 2
I Only Have Eyes For You	Fabulous Royals	NA	Aegis 1006
I Only Have Eyes For You	Flamingos	1959	End 1046
I Only Have Eyes For You	Frontiers	1963	Philips 40113
I Only Have Eyes For You	Swallows (Maryland)	1952	King 4533
I Only Have Eyes For You	Three Chuckles	1956	Vik LP 1067
I Only Want To Be Your Guy	Heartbreakers (Washington, D.C.)	1952	Roadhouse 1008
I Only Want You	Decoys	1963, 1964	Aanko 1005/Times Square 9/96 (64)
I Only Want You	Passions	1960	Audicon 105
I Only Want You	Roomates, Cathy Jean & the	1961, 1963	Valmor 011/Philips 40106
I Only Want You (acappella)	Young Ones	1965	Times Square 104
I Play The Part Of A Fool	Hart, Rocky (with the Passions)	1961	Glo 216
I Played 1, 2, 3, 4	Delicates	1961	Celeste 676/Dee Dee 677 (61)
I Played The Fool	Clovers	1952	Atlantic 977
I Played The Fool	Four B's	1958	D 1013
I Played The Fool	Galleons	1959	Vita 184
I Played The Fool	Mann, Gloria & group	1955	Sound 114
I Pledge My Love	Desideros	1963	Renee 1040
I Pray	Premiers (Connecticut)	1960	Fury 1029
I Pray For Love	Moonglows	1973	Relic 1024
I Pray For You	Inquisitors, Little Isadore & the	1995	Early Bird 5000
I Prayed For Gold	Raindrops	1956	Spin-It 104
I Prayed For love	Teardrops	1957	King 5004
I Prayed For You	Audios, Cell Foster & the	1956	Ultra 105
I Pretend	Cues	1957	Prep 104
I Pretend And Cry	Wright, Leo & group	1965	Perico 1257
I Promise	Bob-O-Links	1962	Hi-Ho 101
I Promise	Fay, Flo & group	1963	Lawn 206
I Promise	Four Winds, Sonny Woods & the	1956	Middle-Tone 008
I Promise	Jokers, Willie & the	1962	Viking 1007
I Promise	Juniors, Jimmy Castor & the	1956	Wing 90078
I Promise	Mello-Kings	1960	Herald 554
I Promise	Memories	1962	Way-Lin 101
I Promise	Velours	1959	Studio 9902
I Promise	Velvets, Bobby & the	1959	Rason 501
I Promise Love	Revlons	1961	Rae-Cox 105
I Promise To Remember	Teenagers, Frankie Lymon & the	1956	Gee 1018
I Promise To Remember	Twilighters, Tony & the	NA	Red Top
I Promise You	Checkers	1954	King 4673
I Promise You	Orioles, Sonny Til & the	1983	Murray Hill LP M61277
I Promise You Love	Turbans (Philadelphia)	1959	Red Top 115
I Ran Around	Dialtones, Johnny & the	1960	Jin 134
I Ran To You	Emotions	1961	Flip 356
I Ran To You	Emotions, Lena Calhoun & the	1961	Flip 357
I Really Do	Five Echoes	1955	Vee Jay 129
I Really Do	Orbits	1956	Flair-X 5000
I Really Do	Spectors Three	1960	Trey 3001
I Really Don't Care	Marylanders	1974 (1954)	Roadhouse 1015
I Really Don't Want To Know	Dominoes	1954	King 1368
I Really Don't Want To Know	Flamingos	1955	Parrot 811
I Really Don't Want To Know	Royal Jesters	1962	Jester 106
I Really Feel Good	Furys	1963	Mach IV 115
I Really Had A Ball	Ontarios	1973	Baron 104
I Really Love Her So	Bop Chords	1957	Holiday 2603
I Really Love You	Blue Jays (Los Angeles)	1961	Blujay 1002
I Really Love You	Channels, Earl Lewis & the	1956	Whirlin' Disc 107/Port 70023 (60)

SONG	GROUP	YEAR	LABEL
I Really Love You	Danleers	1958	Mercury 71356
I Really Love You	Diablos, Nolan Strong & the	1963	Fortune 553
I Really Love You	Dovells	1962	Parkway LP 7006
I Really Love You	Dreamers (Blue Star)	1960	Blue Star 8001
I Really Love You	Mystics	1964	Teako 370
I Really Love You	Shepherd, Johnnie & group	1964	ABC 10548
I Really Love You	Stereos	1961	Cub 9095
I Really Love You So	Sweet & Sassy	1959	Del Pat 207
I Really Love You So (Honey Babe)	Solitaires	1957	Old Town 1044
I Really Must Know	Reflections	1961	Crossroads 401
I Really Really Do	Chancellors	1959	Storm 503
I Really Really Love You	Crows	1954	Rama 30
I Really Want To Know	Ivies	1959	Roulette 4183
I Refuse To Pay	Four Gents	1963	Vida 0123
I Remain Truly Yours	Criterions	1959	Cecelia 1208/Laurie 3305 (65)
I Remember	Aqualads, Anthony & the	NA	Gold Bee 1650
I Remember	Embertones	1962	Bay 203
I Remember	Five Discs	1958	Emge 1004/Vik 0327 (58)/ Rust 5027 (63)
I Remember	Harptones	1959	Warwick 500
I Remember	Marshans	1964	Etiquette
I Remember	Suburbans	1956	Baton 227
I Remember	Wayne, Wee Willie (with the Kidds)	1955	Imperial 5355
I Remember	Zodiacs, Maurice Williams & the	1961	Herald 556
I Remember (acappella)	Durhams	1975	Relic LP 104
I Remember Christmas	Drifters (1959-forward)	1964	Atlantic 2261
I Remember, Dear	Mello-Maids	1957	Baton 238
I Remember Dear	Tune Weavers	1957	Casa Grande 4038
I Remember (In The Still Of The Night)	Crests	1961	Coed 543
I Remember In The Still Of The Night	Raindrops	1961	Imperial 5785
I Remember Linda	Tigers, Little Julian Herrera & the	1957	Starla 6
I Remember The Night	Del Satins	1961	End 1096
I Remember The Nite	Nutones	1965	Relic 1009
I Remember When	Cameos (Pittsburgh)	1960, 1985	Matador 1808
I Rocked When I Should Have Rolled	Saints	1957	Cue 7934
I Run To You	Skyliners	1966	Jubilee 5520
I Said A Prayer	Tip Tops, Tiny Tip & the	1962	Scarlet 4129
I Said Hear	Cruisers	1959	Arch 1611
I Said I Wouldn't Beg You	Midnighters, Hank Ballard & the	1959	King 5289
I Said Look	Lavenders	1961	Lake 706
I Said, She Said	Four Tees	1964	Vee Jay 627
I Said She Wouldn't Do	Foster Brothers	1957	El-Bee 161
I Saw A Cottage In My Dreams	Volumes, Jimmie Lewis & the	1958	Ivy 104
I Saw A Tear	Shirelles	1960, 1964	Scepter 1207/1292
I Saw Mommy Cha Cha Cha With You Know Who	Bonnie Sisters	1956	Rainbow 328
I Saw You	Cadillacs, Bobby Ray & the	1963	Capitol 4935
I Saw You	Crayons	1963	Counsel 122
I Say Babe	Four Dates	1958	Chancellor 1019
I Say Goodbye	Team Mates	1964	Le Mans 003
I Searched The Seven Seas	Plants	1958	J&S 248/249/J&S 1604 (58)
I See A Girl	Ballards, Billy Brown & the	1963	El Tone 439
I See A Star	Jumpin' Tones	NA	Unreleased
I See A Star	Little Stevie & group	1961	Guyden 2060
I See A Star	Roulettes	1958	Champ 102
I See It	Classmates, Marc Cavell & the	1961	Candix 329
I See Me	Coastliners	1967	Dear 1300
I See The Image Of You	Cones, Connie & the	1959	NRC 5006
I Send My Love	Blazers (Johnny Moore's)	1956	Hollywood 1056
I Set A Trap For You	Fashions	1963	Amy 884
I Shall Not Fail	Honey Bears	1955	Spark 111
I Shall Return	Hollywoood Flames	1954	
I Shed A Million Tears	Interludes	1958	RCA 7281
I Shed A Tear At Your Wedding	Flamingos	1959	End 1040
I Shed So Many Tears	Marvels (Washington, D.C.)	1958	Laurie 3016

SONG	GROUP	YEAR	LABEL
I Sho Lawd Will	Diamonds	1961	Mercury 71782
I Shook The World	Blue Jeans, Bob B. Soxx & the	1963	Philles LP 4002
I Shot Mr. Lee	Bobbettes	1960	Atlantic 2069/Triple-X 104
I Should Be Loving You	Enchanters (Delta)	NA	Delta Ltd. 156
I Should Have Done Right	Drifters (1959-forward)	1971	Atco LP 375
I Should Have Known	Baby Dolls (Rosie's)	1961	Fargo 1017
I Should Have Listened	Initials, Angelo & the	1964	Congress 229
I Should Have Loved You	Sierras	1962	Goldisc G4
I Should Have Stayed	Dolphins	1966	Yorkshire 125
I Should Have Stayed At Home Tonight	Alley Cats	1965	Epic 9778
I Should Have Treated You Right	Green, Barbara & group	1964	Vivid 105/Hamilton 50027
I Should'A Listened To Mama	Octobers	1963	Chairman 4402
I Shouldn't Care	Senators	1962	Winn 1917
I Shouldn't Have Passed Your House	Rhythm Kings	1949	Ivory 751
I Shouldn't Love You But I Do	Hawkins, Buddy (Keynotes)	19??	
I Simply Crack Up	Petty, Eddie îPrinceî & group	1957	Guest 1003
I Sing For You	Plaids	1956	Darl 1001
I Sing This Song (That's Why)	Dreamers (Yonkers, N.Y.)	1960	Apt 25053
I Sit In My Window	Four Fellows (Brooklyn - Glory)	1956	Glory 244
I Slipped-Tripped	Long, Bobby & his Cherrios	1959	Glow-Hill 503
I Smell A Rat	Young Jessie (with the Flairs)	1954	Modern 921
I Sold My Heart To The Junkman	Basin St. Boys	1948	Exclusive 39/Cash 1052 (56)
I Sold My Heart To The Junkman	Basin St. Boys, Charles Brown & the	1956	Exclusive 39/Cash 1052 (56)
I Sold My Heart To The Junkman	Blue Belles	1962	Newtown 5000
I Sold My Heart To The Junkman	Silhouettes	1958	Ace 552/Junior 396 (58)
I Spoke Too Soon	Gum Drops	1959	Coral 62102
I Stand Alone	Cardell, Nick & group	1964	Amcan 405
I Stand Alone	Percells	1963	ABC 10516
I Started Out	Chordells	1956	Onyx 504/Relic 523 (64)
I Stayed Home	Ad Libs	1988	Johnnie Boy 1
I Stayed Home (New Year's Eve)	Creators	1963	Philips 40060
I Still	Chantels	1961	Carlton 564
I Still Care	Mellows, Lillian Leach & the	1955	Jay-Dee 801
I Still Care	Nolan, Miss Frankie (with the Four Seasons)	1961	ABC 10231
I Still Care	Rays, Hal Miller & the	1964	Amy 909
I Still Do	Lafayettes	1962	RCA 8082
I Still Like Rock And Roll	Darlenes	1963	Stacy 965
I Still Love Her	Reveliers	1962	Soma 1180
I Still Love Him	Joys	1964	Valiant 6042
I Still Love That Man	Intervals	1958	Ad 104/Apt 25019 (58)
I Still Love You	Flares, Paul Ballenger & the	1958	Reed 711
I Still Love You	Impalas (Bunky)	1969	Bunky 7762
I Still Love You	Inspirations, Andre Bacon Fat Williams & the	1960	Fortune 856
I Still Love You	Monterays (Brooklyn)	1964	GNP Crescendo 314
I Still Love You	Nobletones	1973	Vintage 1014
I Still Love You	Originals, Tony Allen & the	1960	Original Sound 13
I Still Love You	Ovations (Hawk)	1964	Hawk 153
I Still Love You	Profiles	NA	Bamboo 108
I Still Love You	Prophets	NA	Shell
I Still Love You	Raindrops	1964	Sotoplay 0028
I Still Love You	Vibrations	1961	Checker (unreleased)
I Still Love You So	Ray-O-Vacs, Flap McQueen & the (with Herb Milliner)	1955	Josie 781
I Still Remember	Endings	1975	Barrier 102
I Still Remember	Romancers	1956	Dootone 381
I Still Remember	Starlites, Jackie & the	1964	Hull 760
I Stole Your Heart	Buddies	1955	Glory 230
I Stopped The Duke Of Earl	Upfronts	1962	Lummtone 107
I Sure Do Love You Baby	Nitecaps, Clyde Stacy & the	1958	Bullseye 1008
I Sure Need You	Pearls	1957	Onyx 510/Relic 520 (64)
I Swear By All The Stars Above	Griffins	1955	Mercury 70558
I Swear By All The Stars Above	Heartbreakers (Washington, D.C.)	1952	Roadhouse 1007
I Talk To My Echo	Beltones	1957	Hull 721
I Thank Heaven	Tuneblenders	1958	Play 1002
I Thank My Lucky Star	Austin, Little Augie (with the Chromatics)	1960	Pontiac 101

SONG	GROUP	YEAR	LABEL
I Thank My Lucky Star	Yo Yo's, Delma Goggins & the	1961	Vibro 4008
I Thank The Moon	Crests	1958, 1959	Coed 501/515
I Thank The Moon	Streetcorner Serenade	1989	Starlight 70
I Thank You	Velveteens	1962	Laurie 3126 (62)
I Thank You, Baby	Overtones, Tony Rice & the	1961	Action 100
I Think I Know	Five G's	1959	Washingtonian (no number)
I Think I Know Her	Sweet Tymes	1967	Epic 10227
I Think I Love You	Premiers (Mink)	1959	Mink 021/Parkway 807 (60)
I Think I'm Going To Fall In Love With You	Twilights	NA	Select 742
I Think It's Time	Shepherd Sisters	1959	Warwick 511
I Think Of You	Dunham, Jackie & group	1961	Imperial 5768
I Think Of You	Foxettes, Lady Fox & the	1962	Don-El 114
I Thought	Quails (Harvey Fuqua)	1962	Harvey 120
I Thought About You	Millionaires	1965	Bunny 506
I Thought I Could Forget You	Cap-Tans	1974	Roadhouse 1016
I Thought I Heard You Call My Name	Baker, Roy Boy & group	1963	Dess 7011
I Thought I Heard You Calling My Name	Top Hands, Joe Dee & His	1962	Pat Riccio 1107
I Thought You Knew	Outcasts, Mac Boswell & the	1960	Wonder 117
I Thought You'd Care	Gems (Illinois)	1954	Drexel 903
I Thought You'd Like That	Castells	1966	Decca 31967
I Told Myself	Eagles	1955	Mercury 70524
I Told You Baby	Watesians	1962	Donna 1371
I Told You Once	Fantastics	1961, 1990	United Artists 309/Park Ave. 4
I Told You So	Archiads	NA	Ro-Cal
I Told You So	Charts	1957	Everlast 5008
I Took A Chance	Invictors	1963	TPE 8223
I Took A Trip Way Over The Sea	Plants	1958	J&S 248/249/J&S 1604 (58)
I Took Your Love For A Toy	Five Keys	1959	King 5251
I Tried	Elegants	NA	Elegants 101
I Tried	Four Fellows (Brooklyn - Glory)	1954	Derby 862
I Tried	Rhythm Five	1962	Tifco 829
I Tried	Rivingtons	1964	Reprise 0293
I Tried And Tried And Tried	Mello-Moods (with Teacho Wiltshire Band)	1952	Prestige 799
I Tried So Hard	Toppers, Bobby Mitchell & the	1956	Imperial 5392
I Try So Hard	Quin-Tones (Pennsylvania)	1958	Chess 1685
I Understand	Duprees	1967	Columbia 44078
I Understand	Eager, Johnny & group	1959	End 1061
I Understand	Page, Ricky & female group	1961	Coin 711/Dot 16261
I Understand	Royale Cita Chorus	1956	Gee 1021
I Understand Him	Click-Ettes	1963	Tuff 373
I Understand (Just How You Feel)	G-Clefs	1961	Terrace 7500
I Used To Cry Mercy, Mercy	Lamplighters	1953	Federal 12176
I Waited	Blue Notes	1958	Colonial 9999
I Waited	Buddies	1955	Glory 230
I Waited	Chanteers	1962	Mercury 72037
I Walk Alone	Vocaleers	1953	Red Robin 119
I Walk In Circles	Four Rivers, Little Lynn & the	1962	Music City 845
I Walk On	Elgins, Little Tommy & the	1962	Elmar 1084/ABC 10358 (62)
I Walk With An Angel	Treasurers	1961	Crown 005
I Walked Beside The Sea	Shepherd Sisters	1957	Melba 108
I Walked Through A Forest	Wanderers	1959	Cub 9054
I Wanna	Platters	1957	Mercury 71093
I Wanna Be A Millionaire Hobo	Fantastics	1959	RCA 7572
I Wanna Be Free	Duvals (La Salle)	1961	La Salle 502
I Wanna Be Lonely	Sorrows, Nicky De Matteo & the	1966	Cameo 407
I Wanna Be Loved	Lovers	1957	Lamp 2013
I Wanna Be That Way	Taylortops	1959	Alton 2000
I Wanna Be The Leader	Marcels	1963	Colpix 687
I Wanna Be With You	Fabulous Falcons	1966	White Cliffs 249
I Wanna Be Your Man	Volumes	NA	Chex
I Wanna Be Yours	Visions, Connie McGill & the	1963	Triode 115
I Wanna Boogie	Joyjumpers	1962	Zynn 1014
I Wanna Chance	Vows	1962	Markay 103
I Wanna Come Home	Chestnuts	1954	Mercury 70489

SONG	GROUP	YEAR	LABEL
I Wanna Dance	Avantis	1963	Argo 5436
I Wanna Dance	Cavaliers	1959	Tel 1006
I Wanna Dance With You	Pacers	1958	Calico 101
I Wanna Do Everything For You	Sandmen (Brook Benton)	1957	Vik 0285
I Wanna Fly	Carousels	1964	Guyden 2102
I Wanna Go Home	Dells	1956, 1959	Vee Jay 230/338
I Wanna Go Home	Hometowners	1959	Fraternity 842
I Wanna Go Home	Omegas	1961	Groove G-4
I Wanna Go Steady	Oliver, Big Danny & group	1958	Trend 012X/Kapp 941
I Wanna Holler	Buddies, Little Butchie Saunders & his	1956	Herald 491
I Wanna Know	Baker, Bill (with the Del Satins)	1961	Audicon 115
I Wanna Know	Blue Dots	1958	Zynn 511
I Wanna Know	Boys	1964	SVR 1001
I Wanna Know	Cavaliers	1962	Gum 1002
I Wanna Know	Checkers	1953	King 4626
I Wanna Know	Dawns, Billy Horton & the	1970	KayDen 403
I Wanna Know	Diablos, Nolan Strong & the	1959	Fortune 532
I Wanna Know	Du Droppers	1953	RCA 5229
I Wanna Know	Dynamics	1964	Big Top 516
I Wanna Know	Emmy Lou & group	1961	Lute 6018
I Wanna Know	Five Birds, Willie Headen & the	1956	Authentic 703/Dooto 703
I Wanna Know	Gladiolas	1957	Excello 2120
I Wanna Know	Isley Brothers	1958	Gone 5022
I Wanna Know	Jones, Vivian & group	1962	Twirl 1017
I Wanna Know	Lamplighters	1954	Federal 12206
I Wanna Know	Sultans	1965	Ascot 2228
I Wanna Know	Watkins, Billy & group	1961	Chess 1786
I Wanna Know How To Twist	Fun-Atics	1962	Versailles 100
I Wanna Know Why	Cliques	1956	Modern 987
I Wanna Love	Bobby-Pins	1963	Mercury 72193
I Wanna Love	Crowns, Arthur Lee Maye & the	1954	Modern 944
I Wanna Love	Crowns, Henry Strogin & the	1963	Ball 1012
I Wanna Love	Jiving Juniors	1961	Blue Beat 24
I Wanna Love	Strogin, Henry & group	1962	Ball 1012
I Wanna Love Him So Bad	Jelly Beans	1964	Red Bird 10-003
I Wanna Love Just You	Up-Tunes	1966	Genie 103
I Wanna Love Love Love	Royal Premiers	1962	Toy 103
I Wanna Love You	Du Droppers	1955	Groove 0120
I Wanna Make Love	Cap-Tans	1963	Sabu 501
I Wanna Make Love To You	Trojans	1955	RPM 466
I Wanna Party Some More	Joy-Tones	1964	Coed 600
I Wanna Rendezvous With You	Desires	1960	Hull 733
I Wanna Run To You	Tellers	1960	Fire 1038
I Wanna See My Lovin' Baby	Pork Chops	1956	Herald 493
I Wanna Swim With Him	Daisies	1964	Roulette 4571
I Wanna Talk To You	Kelly, Karol & group	1962	Joy 272
I Wanna Woman	Valaquons	1965	Tangerine 951
I Want	Jupitors	1958	Planet X 9621
I Want A Boy	Relatives	1961	Colpix 481/Colpix 601 (61)
I Want A Boy For Christmas	Delvets	1961	End 1106
I Want A Boy For My Birthday	Cookies	1963	Dimension 1012
I Want A Boy With A Hi-Fi Supersonic Stereophonic Bloop Bleep	Teenettes	1959	Brunswick 55125
I Want A Date	Furness Brothers	1960	Future 1002
I Want A Girl	Bachelors (National)	1958	National 115
I Want A Girl	Fabulons	NA	Ember (unreleased)
I Want A Girl	Imaginations	1961	Bacon Fat 101
I Want A Girl Just Like The Girl That Married Dear Old Dad	Four Lovers	1957	RCA LP 1317
I Want A Guy	Supremes (Detroit)	1961	Tamla 54038
I Want A Little Girl	Roomates	1960	Promo 2211
I Want A Love	Medallions	1956	Dootone 393
I Want A True Friend	Lapels	1960	Melker 104
I Want A Woman	Fabulous Twilights, Nathaniel Mayer & the	1962	Fortune 545/United Artists 449 (62)/ Fortune 563 (63)

SONG	GROUP	YEAR	LABEL
I Want A Woman	Five Jets	1954	DeLuxe 6053
I Want A Yul Brenner Haircut	Campanions	NA	Dee-Dee 1047
(I Want) An Old Fashioned Girl	Diablos	1954	Fortune 509/510
I Want 'Cha Baby	Sliders, Byron Slick Gipson & the	1956	Specialty
I Want Her Back	Five Budds	1953	Rama 2
I Want Her To Love Me	Larks (Philadelphia)	1961, 1963	Guyden 2098/Violet 1050/1051 (63)
I Want Him So Bad	Velvetones	1962	Ascot 2117
I Want It Like That	Five Royales	1962	ABC 10368
I Want Love	Mascots	1974	Rumble 4197
I Want Love	Paradons	1960	Milestone 2003
I Want Love And Affection	Fabulous Twilights, Nathaniel Mayer & the	1963	Fortune 567
I Want My Girl	Lonely Ones	1959	Baton 270/Sir 270 (59)
I Want My Love	Reno, Frank & group	1962	Diamond 118
I Want My Love	Whipoorwills	1953	Dooto 1201
I Want My Love Close By	Classmates	1956	Dot 15504
I Want My Loving Now	Hawks	1970	Imperial LP 94003 (rec. 1955)
I Want My Woman	Emperors	NA	Sabra 5555
I Want Somebody	Five Knights, Tommy Taylor & the	1961	Minit 636
I Want Somebody	Harvey (Harvey Fuqua with the Moonglows)	1958	Chess 1713
I Want To Be A Part Of You	Chellows	1961	Poncello 713
I Want To Be Free	Visions, Connie McGill & the	NA	Sugar 502
I Want To Be Happy	Girlfriends	1963	Melic 4125
I Want To Be Loved	Bees	1954	Imperial 5420
I Want To Be Loved	Belltones, Ronnie Baker & the	1962	Jell 188
I Want To Be Loved	Cadillacs	1959	Unreleased
I Want To Be Loved	Deltones, Ronnie Baker & the	1962	Laurie 3128
I Want To Be Loved	Golden Arrow Quartet	NA	Continental 6048
I Want To Be Loved	Lovers	1962	Imperial 5845/Post 10007 (63)
I Want To Be Loved	Royal Jesters	1962	Cobra 7777
I Want To Be Loved	Sharmettes	1962	King 5686
I Want To Be Ready	Voices	1955	Cash 1015
I Want To Be The Boy You Love	Four Buddies	1964	Imperial 66018
I Want To Be There	Four Kings	1963	M.O.C. 655
I Want To Be With You	Blenders, Earl Curry & the	1954	R&B 1304
I Want To Be With You Baby	Melodymacks, George Mack & the	NA	Mac
I Want To Be Your Boyfriend	Tyson, Roy & group	1963	Double L 733
I Want To Be Your Girl	Betty Jean & group	1963	JR 5001
I Want To Be Your Girl	Epics	1960	Dante 3004
I Want To Be Your Happiness	Strong, Nolan (with the Diablos and Tony Valla & the Alamos)	1963	Fortune 564
I Want To Cry	Teenage Moonlighters	1960	Mark 134
I Want To Dance (acappella)	Chessmen	1975	Relic LP 102/Relic LP 106 (75)
I Want To Dance (Every Night)	Wheels, Ferris & the	1961	Bambi 801
I Want To Dance With You	Arvettes	1966	Ideal 100A
I Want To Do It	Counts, Bobby Comstock & the	1962	Lawn 202
I Want To Do It	Del-Rays	1968	Stax 162
I Want To Get Married	Delicates	1965	Challenge 59267
I Want To Hear It From You	Ashley, John & group	1960	Silver 1002
I Want To Kiss You	Hy-Tones, Georgia Harris & the	1958	Hy-Tone 121
I Want To Know	Bluffs	1960	
I Want To Know	Cadillacs	1958	Josie 842
I Want To Know	Diablos	1984	Fortune LP 8020
I Want To Know	El Domingos	1964	Karmin 1001
I Want To Know	Empires	1955	Wing 90023
I Want To Know	Extensions	1963	Success 109
I Want To Know	Gay Poppers	1960	Fire 1026
I Want To Know	Heartbeats	1957	Rama 231
I Want To Know	Kings (Baltimore)	1960	Lookie 18/Epic 9370 (60)
I Want To Know	Ladders	1957	Holiday 2611
I Want To Know	Lyrics (Texas)	1959	Harlem 104
I Want To Know	Mastertones	1961	Le Cam 717
I Want To Know	Pretenders	19??	
I Want To Know	Simms, Lloyd & female group	1961	Atlantic 2078
I Want To Know	Turner, Bennie & group	NA	Skyline 1005
I Want To Know	Vel-Tones	1964	Wedge 1013

SONG	GROUP	YEAR	LABEL
I Want To Know About Love	Bachelors, Dean Barlow & the	1955	Earl 101
I Want To Know About Love	Cadillacs	1954	Josie 769
I Want To Know Baby (acappella)	Velvet Angels	1972	Relic LP 5004
I Want To Live	Wizards	1965	Era 3161
I Want To Love You	Flamingos	1955, 1961	Checker 821/End 1099
I Want To Love You	Sentimentals	1957, 1972	Mint 801/Checker 875 (57)/Mint 808
I Want To Love You	Tokens (Brooklyn)	1969	Warner Bros. 7280
I Want To Love You	Tuxedo Sleepers, James Carter & the	1960	Tuxedo 938
I Want To Love You, Baby	Serenaders (Detroit)	1953	Red Robin 115
I Want To Marry You	Corridors	1963	Zone 4323/Wildcat 0057 (63)
I Want To Marry You	Dell Vikings	1957, 1972	Fee Bee 221/Bim Bam Boom 111
I Want To Party	Halos	1962	Warwick LP 2046
I Want To See My Baby	Rivileers	1955	Baton 207
I Want To Talk About It (World)	Debonaires (New York)	1967	Galaxy 787
I Want To Talk With You	Whippets	1964	Josie 921
I Want To Thank You	Five Royales	1953	Apollo 449
I Want To Thank You	Midnighters, Hank Ballard & the	1962	King 5655
I Want To Thrill You	Alleycats, Joe Allen & the	1958	Jalo 202
I Want You	Bobby-Pins	1959	Okeh 7110
I Want You	Cadets	1956	Modern 994
I Want You	Cardinals	NA	Cha Cha 740
I Want You	Celebrities	1961	Music Makers 101
I Want You	Five Crowns	1959	De'Besth 1123
I Want You	Flairs, Shirley Gunter & the	1956	Modern 989
I Want You	Heartbeats, Richie Hart & the	1960	MCI 1025
I Want You	Metronomes	1953	Specialty 462 (unreleased)
I Want You	Newports	1965	Laurie 3327
I Want You Back	Larks (Don Julian)	1971	Money 601
I Want You Back	Webs	1968	Verve 10610
I Want You Back Again	Playboys, Gene Vito & the	1964	Blast 214
I Want You For Christmas	Keys, Rudy West & the	1989	Classic Artists 115
I Want You For My Own	Minorbops	1957	Lamp 2012
I Want You I Need You	Colleagues	1961	Glodus 1651
I Want You, I Need You, I Love You	Montereys, Don Dell & the	1964	Roman 2963
I Want You Madly	Gunter, Cornel (with the Ermines)	1957	Eagle 301
I Want You Now	Lovetones	1961	Marlo 1515
I Want You Only	Ebb-Tones	1956	Crest 1016
I Want You Right Now	Parakeets	1962	Big Top 3130
I Want You Round	Royal Jesters	1962	Jester 104
I Want You So	Rollers	1961	Liberty 55320
I Want You So Bad	Charms, Tommy G & the	1961	Hollywood 1109
I Want You So Bad	Five Flames	1959	Federal 12348
I Want You To Be Mine	Flairs	1963	Crown LP 5356
I Want You To Be My Baby	Salutations, Vito & the	1966	Boom 60020
I Want You To Be My Baby	Sound Masters	NA	Julet 102
I Want You To Be My Boy	Capri Sisters	1962	Newtown 5002
I Want You To Be My Boy	Essex	1964	Roulette 4591
I Want You To Be My Boyfriend	Chic-Lets	1964	Josie 919
I Want You To Be My Boyfriend	Shirelles	1958	Decca 25506/Decca 30588 (58)/ Tiara 6112 (59)
I Want You To Be My Girl	Four Blades	1956	Gateway 1170
I Want You To Be My Girl	Four Fellows, Scatman Cruthers & the	1956	Tops EP 285
I Want You To Be My Girl	Jo-Vals	1964	Alwil 101/102
I Want You To Be My Girl	Silvertones, Ronnie Rice & the	1964	Limelight 3029
I Want You To Be My Girl	Teenagers, Frankie Lymon & the	1956	Gee 1012
I Want You To Be My Girl	Teenchords, Lewis Lymon & the	1984	Starlight 21
I Want You To Be My Mambo Baby	Royals (Muskateers)	1954	Venus 103
I Want You To Know	Coronets	1953	Chess (unreleased)
I Want You To Know	Coyne, Ricky & group	1959	Event 4294
I Want You To Know	Five Ramblers	1963	Lummtone 111
I Want You To Know	Interludes	1959	Star-Hi 103
I Want You To Know	Peacocks	1958	Noble 711
I Want You To Love Me	Holidays	1964	Coral 62430
I Want You To Love Me	Redcoats, Steve Alaimo & the	1959	Marlin 6064/Imperial 5699 (60)
I Want You To Love Me Too	Gay Tunes	1987	Relic LP 5071

SONG	GROUP	YEAR	LABEL
I Want You With Me Christmas	Belvin, Jesse & group	1956	Modern 1005
I Want Your Arms Around Me (All The Time)	Preludes	1956	Empire 103
I Want Your Love	Cruisers	1959	Arch 1611
I Want Your Love	Delongs	NA	Art Flow 3906
I Want Your Love	Everett, Bracey & group	1959	Atlantic 2013
I Want Your Love	Mellow Drops	NA	Imperial (unreleased)
I Want Your Love	Montereys, Sandra Patrick & the	1964	Dominion 1008
I Want Your Love Tonite	Hearts (Bronx, N.Y.)	1955	J&S 1626/1627
I Wanted You	Jaguars	1956, 1958	Aardell 0003/R-Dell 45
I Wanted You So Long	Trojans	1960	Triangle 51317
I Was A Fool	Dukes (California)	1956	Imperial 5399 (unreleased)
I Was A Fool	Golden Nuggets	1959	Futura 2-1691
I Was A Fool	Impalas (Brooklyn)	1959	Hamilton 50026
I Was A Fool	Night Riders, Johnny Fairchild & the	1959	Ace 565
I Was A Fool	Wright, Mary & group	1960	Kim 101
I Was A Fool To Let You Go	Mellows, Lillian Leach & the	1955	Jay-Dee 801
I Was A Fool To Love You	Teasers	1954	Checker 800
I Was Alone	Teenagers, Frankie Lymon & the	1957	Gee (unreleased)
(I Was) Born To Cry	DiMucci, Dion (with the Del Satins)	1962	Laurie 3123
I Was Dreaming	Cleftones	1956	Gee 1000
I Was Dreaming	Street Singers	1955	Dawn 211
I Was Gone	Clearwater, Eddie & group	1962	Federal 12446
I Was Made To Love	Strong, Karen & group	NA	N/A
I Was Only Fifteen	Cinderellas	1959	Decca 30925
I Was So Wrong	Five Cats	1955	RCA 6181
I Was Such A Fool	Flamingos	1959	End 1062
I Was Such A Fool	Originals	1990	Starlight 72
I Was Such A Fool (acappella)	Five Jades (Bronx, N.Y.)	1975	Relic LP 107
I Was Such A Fool (To Fall In Love With You)	Five Budds	1953	Rama 1
I Was The Third On A Match	Rhythmasters	NA	Bennett 401
I Was Too Careful	Embers	1961	Empress 104
I Was Wrong	Charmers	1954	Timely 1009
I Was Wrong	Five Crowns	1954	Rainbow 251
I Was Wrong	Moonglows	1954, 1972	Chance 1156/RCA 74-0759
I Was Wrong	Yellow Jackets, Walter & the	1957	Goldband 1033
I Wasn't Thinkin', I Was Drinkin'	Checkers	1954	King 4751
I Watch The Stars	Quin-Tones (Pennsylvania)	1958	Red Top 116
I Went To A Party	Craftys	1962	Elmor 310
I Went To The S&S	Everglades	NA	Brenne 502
I Went To Your House	Bennett, Chuck & group	1962	Bonnie 101
I Whisper Your Name	McKay, Johnny & group	1960	United Artists 21
I Who Love You	Dahills	1978	Crystal Ball 107
I Will Be Home Again	Escorts (Scarlet)	1960	Scarlet 4005
I Will Do It (Cause He Wants Me To)	Baby Dolls	1966	Boom 60002
I Will Go	Royal Aces, Jesse James & the	1962	Shirley 103
I Will Return	Cobras (Ohio)	1955	Modern 964
I Will Stand By You	Citations	1967	Ballad 101
I Will Wait	Five Dollars	1956	Fortune 830
I Will Wait	Four Buds	1950, 1951	Savoy 769
I Wish	Castaways	1954	Excello 2038
I Wish	Platters	1958	Mercury 71353
I Wish	Plazas, Eric & the	1963	Production 612
I Wish	Powers, Roni & group	1961	LT Productions 1022
I Wish	Prisonaires	1976	Sun 511
I Wish	Tillman, Bertha & group	1962	Brent 7032
I Wish	Utopians, Mike & the	1958	Cee Jay 574 (second pressing)
I Wish	Videls	1960	Dusty Disc 473/Early 702 (60)
I Wish For Someone	Richards, Ricky & group	1961	Wye 1011
I Wish I Could Believe You	Duprees	1963	Coed 574
I Wish I Could Meet You	Dots (Jeanette Baker)	1956	Caddy 101
I Wish I Could Shimmy Like My Sister Kate	Olympics	1960	Arvee 5006
I Wish I Didn't Know You	Four Fellows (Brooklyn - Glory)	1955	Glory 231

SONG	GROUP	YEAR	LABEL
I Wish I Didn't Love You So	Embers	NA	Valmor
I Wish I Knew	Legends	1962	Ermine 43
I Wish I Knew	Toppers, Bobby Mitchell & the	1955	Imperial 5326
I Wish I Was Single Again	Balladeers	1952	RCA 4612
I Wish I Weren't In Love	Landis, Jerry & group	1961	Canadian American 130
I Wish I'd Never Learned To Read	Five Keys	1955	Capitol 3185
I Wish It Were Summer	Chordials	1964	Big Top 513
I Wish It Were Summer	Tempos	1965	Ascot 2173
(I Wish It Were) Summer All Year Round	Nolan, Miss Frankie (with the Four Seasons)	1961	ABC 10231
I Wish That We Were Married	Hi-Lites, Ronnie & the	1962	Joy 260
I Wish The World Owed Me A Living	Jayhawks	1957	Eastman 792
I Wish You Love	Velours	1988	Clifton 82
I Wish You Love (acappella)	Five Jades (Bronx, N.Y.)	1975	Relic LP 107
I Wish Your Love	Drifters (1959-forward)	1965	Atlantic LP 8113
I Wonder	Butterflys	1964	Red Bird 10-016
I Wonder	Camelots	1973	Dream 1001
I Wonder	Charles, Nick & group	1961	Guyden 2049
I Wonder	Eljays, Leo Wright & the	1964, 1965	CB 5008/Red Fox 103 (65)
I Wonder	Emotions	1964	Karate 506
I Wonder	Falcons (Detroit)	1985	Relic LP 8005
I Wonder	Five Discs	1978	Crystal Ball 114
I Wonder	Hearts, Lee Andrews & the (as Lee Andrews)	1959	Casino 110
I Wonder	Jumpin' Tones	1964	Raven 8004
I Wonder	Laurels	1982	Bishop 1016
I Wonder	Millionaires, Benny Curtis & the	1961	Bridges 1102
I Wonder	Shallows	1962	Forlin 503
I Wonder	Striders	1955	Apollo 480
I Wonder	Stylists (New York)	1960, 1974	Rose 16/17
I Wonder	Three Coquettes	1960	Hope 1002
I Wonder	Tuggle, Bobby & group	1956	Checker 840
I Wonder	Turbans (Philadelphia)	1962	Imperial 5847
I Wonder	Wonders	1961	Chesapeake 604
I Wonder And Wonder	Gum Drops	1956	King 4913
I Wonder (Can It Be True)	Lee, Jimmy & group	1961	Canadian American 122
I Wonder, I Wonder, I Wonder	Little Dippers	1960	University 608
I Wonder, I Wonder, I Wonder	Medallions, Vernon Green & the	1957	Dooto 419
I Wonder If I Care As Much	Columbo, Joe & group	1963	Taurus 359
I Wonder If You Know	Jivers	1959	RCA 7478
I Wonder (If Your Love Will Ever Belong To Me)	Pentagons	1961	Jamie 1201
I Wonder When?	Orioles, Sonny Til & the	1950	Jubilee 5026
I Wonder Who	Fascinators (Brooklyn)	1958	Capitol 4053/Capitol 4544 (61)
I Wonder Who's Calling	Twilighters (Roadhouse)	1974	Roadhouse 1014
I Wonder Who's Dancing With Her Now	Majors (Philadelphia)	1964	Imperial LP 9222
I Wonder Why	Ambassadors	1962	Bon 001/Reel 117 (62)
I Wonder Why	Belmonts, Dion & the	1958	Laurie 3013
I Wonder Why	Cadillacs	1954	Josie 765
I Wonder Why	Embers	1965	Ara 210
I Wonder Why	Gents	1967	Normandy 91067
I Wonder Why	Legends, Rick & the	1963	JD 162/United Artists 50093 (66)
I Wonder Why	McDowall, Chester & group	1959	Duke 302
I Wonder Why	Poppies	NA	Epic 9893
I Wonder Why	Rainbows, Randy & the	1977	Crystal Ball 106
I Wonder Why	Shadows	1961	Dottie 1006
I Wonder Why	Sheps	1996	Early Bird 5002
I Wonder Why (acappella)	Quotations	1975	Relic LP 103
I Wonder Why (You Make Me Blue)	Crowns (Philip Harris)	1963	Vee Jay 546
I Wonder Why?	Daybreakers	1958	Lamp 2016/Aladdin 3434 (58)
I Wonder Why?	Largos	1961	Starmaker/Dot 16292 (62)
I Wonder, Wonder	Waters, Larry & group	1956	Dig 121
I Won't Be Around	Tangiers (Los Angeles)	1955	Decca 29603
I Won't Be Back	Kidds	1955	Post 2003
I Won't Be Lonely	Invaders	1964	Calendar 223-66
I Won't Be The Fool Anymore	Heartbeats	1957	Rama 222
I Won't Be The Fool Anymore	Students	1998	Clifton CD

SONG	GROUP	YEAR	LABEL
I Won't Be Your Fool	Diablos	1963	Fortune 551
I Won't Be Your Fool	El Tones, Jo Ann Boswell & the	1955	Chief 800
I Won't Be Your Fool	Nite Sounds, Melvin Davis with the Diablos & the	1962	Fortune 551
I Won't Believe You Anymore	Emeralds, Luther Bond & the	1955	Savoy 1159
I Won't Come To Your Wedding	Wrens	1955	Rama 184
I Won't Cry	Classmen	1963	CM 8464
I Won't Cry	Harps, Little David (Baughan) & the	1955	Savoy 1178
I Won't Cry	Raindrops	1964	Jubilee 5469
I Won't Cry Any More	Embers	1961	Empress 104
I Won't Have You Breaking My Heart	Dubs	1973	Johnson 098 (recorded in 1957)
I Won't Have You Breaking My Heart	Marvels (New York)	1956	ABC 9771
I Won't Love Nobody	Wilco, Roger & group	1961	Milestone 2007
I Won't Make You Cry	Washington, Roger & group	1964	Beacon 563
I Won't Make You Cry Anymore	Cardinals	1956	Atlantic 1103
I Won't Need You	Four Hollidays	1963	Markie 115
I Won't Stand In The Way	Scott, Chyvonne & group (with Chick Willis)	1963	Alto 2010
I Won't Tell A Soul	Butterballs	19??	
I Won't Tell A Soul	Lewis, Billy & group	1956	Flo-Lou 101
I Won't Tell A Soul	Volumes	1954	Jaguar 3004
I Won't Tell A Soul I Love You	Striders, Betty McLaurin & the	1952	Derby 804
I Won't Tell The World	Blenders (Paradise)	1959	Paradise 111
I Worry 'Bout You	Jewels (Los Angeles)	1959	Shasta 115
I Would	G-Notes	1958	Tender 510/Jackpot 48000 (59)
I Would If I Could	Z-Debs	1964	Roulette 4544
I Would Never Dare	Teenettes, Betty Jayne & the	1961	Net 101
I Wrote A Letter	Serenaders (New Jersey)	1957	Chock Full O' Hits 101/102/ MGM 12623 (58)
I Wrote A Poem	Monte, Vinnie & group	1958	Fargo 1000
I Wrote A Song	Essentials, Billy & the	1967	SSS International 706
I Wrote You A Letter	Daniels, Dotty & group	1963	Amy 885
I.O.U.	Maestro, Johnny & group	1961	Coed 557
I.O.U.	Spaniels	1957	Vee Jay 246
I-Ay-Ou-Lay-Oo-Ya	Sugar Tones, Candy & the	1958	Jackpot 48008
Ice	Penguins	1956	Mercury 70943
Ice Cream Baby	Pearls	1957	Onyx 511/Relic 521 (64)
Ichi Bon, Volume I	Jaguars, Nick & the	1960	Tamla 5501
Ichi-Bon Tami Dachi	Rovers	1954	Music City 750/Capitol 3078 (55)
Icy Fingers	Playboys	1959	Dolton 8
I'd Be A Fool Again	Blenders (New York)	1952	Decca 28092
I'd Be A Fool To Let You Go	Thunderbirds	1955	Era 1004
I'd Be Good For You	Angels (New Jersey)	1962	Caprice 118
I'd Be Lost Without You	Rogers, Dan & group	1964	Era 3131
I'd Best Be Going	Salutations, Vito & the	1966	Red Boy 1001/Sandbag 103
I'd Better Make A Move	Five Royales	1957	King 5053
I'd Climb The Highest Mountain	Debonaires (New York)	NA	Gee (unreleased)
I'd Climb The Highest Mountain	Four Buddies, Dolly Cooper & the	1953	Savoy 891
I'd Climb The Highest Mountain	Platters	NA	Mercury EP 3343
I'd Climb The Hills And Mountains	Flairs	1959	Antler 4005
I'd Cry For You	Centuries	NA	Rich 102
I'd Die	Skyliners	1963	Atco 6270/Motown 1046 (63)
I'd Give A Million Yesterdays	Mello-Men	1953	MGM 11607
I'd Like To Know	Castells	1968	Laurie 3444
I'd Like To Thank You Mr. D.J.	Charms, Otis Williams & his	1956	DeLuxe 6097
I'd Love To Take You Walking	Torkays, Little Denny & the	NA	Perri 2
I'd Never Forgive Myself	Bell-Aires	1955	Ruby 103
I'd Rather Be Here In Your Arms	Duprees	1963	Coed 574
I'd Rather Be Hurt All At Once	Destinations	1966	Cameo 422
I'd Rather Be Wrong Than Blue	Shadows	1950	Lee 202
I'd Rather Die	Superiors	1969	Sue 12
I'd Rather Have A Memory Than A Dream	Zodiacs, Maurice Williams & the	NA	Plus 4401
I'd Rather Have You Under The Moon	Orioles, Sonny Til & the	1950	Jubilee 5031
I'd Wait Forever	Del Royals	1960	Warwick 111
I'd Wait Forever	Three G's	1958	Columbia 41256

SONG	GROUP	YEAR	LABEL
I'd Want You	Belles, Terry & the	1959	Ducky 711
I'd Write About The Blues	Keystoners	1956	G&M 102
Idaho	Clovers	1958	Poplar 111
Iddy Biddy Baby	Mello-Fellows	1954	Lamp 8006
Idle Gossip	Reed, Lula (with the Teeners)	1959	Argo 5355
Idol With The Golden Head	Coasters	1957	Atco 6098
If	Danleers	1964	Smash 1872
If	Love, Darlene & group	1966	Reprise 534
If	Paragons	1961	Tap 500
If	Velvets (Texas)	1964	Monument 861
If And When	Four Jacks, Janet Shay & the	1960	Alcar 1502
If He Don't	Vibrations	1962	Checker 1022
If I	Caruso, Dick & group	1960	MGM 12852
If I	Four Sevilles	1980	Starlight 3
If I Can't Have The One I Love	Four Pals	1955	Royal Roost 610
If I Can't Have You	Flamingos	1953, 1973	Chance 1133
If I Could Be Loved By You	Clovers	1955	Atlantic 1073
If I Could Be With You	Velvets (Texas)	1959	20th Century Fox 165
If I Could Be With You Tonight	Diablos, Nolan Strong & the	1959	Fortune 532
If I Could Do It Once Again	Lee, Jimmy (with the Earls)	1978	Bo-P-C 100
If I Could Do It Over Again	Earls	1966	Mr. G. 801
If I Could Forget	Gales	1958	Mel-O 111/113
If I Could Hold Your Hand	Calendars	1974	Relic LP 5019
If I Could Hold Your Hand	Callenders	1959	Cyclone 5012
If I Could Love You	Flamingos	1964, 1990	Constellation LP 3/Chess LP 702 (76)/ Relic LP 5088
If I Could Make You Mine	Love Notes (New York)	1957	Holiday 2607
If I Could Make You Mine	Wanderers	1960	Cub 9075
If I Could Stop Every Clock	Swans (Roulette)	1959	Roulette 4213
If I Could Tell	Sultans	1957	Duke 178
If I Could Tonight	Newports	1961	Kane 008/Guyden 2067
If I Didn't Care	Chateaus	1959	Warner Bros. 5043
If I Didn't Care	Mellows, Lillian Leach & the	NA	100th UGHA Show Commemoration 45
If I Didn't Care	Platters	1961	Mercury 71749
If I Didn't Have You	Magics	NA	RFA 100
If I Didn't Love You	Angels (New Jersey)	1968	RCA 9541
If I Didn't Love You	Ravens	NA	Mercury (unreleased)
If I Didn't Love You Like	McPhatter, Clyde (with the Drifters)	1960	Atlantic 2082
If I Didn't Love You So	Robins	1949	Savoy 726
If I Do	Ambertones	1965	Dottie 1130
If I Give My Heart To You	Chymes	1964	Musictone 6125
If I Give My Heart To You	Dynamics	1962	Liban 1006
If I Give My Heart To You	Four Bars	1954	Josie 768
If I Give My Heart To You	Quantrils, Freddie & the	1964	Karem
If I Give You My Word	Gallahads	1956	Jubilee 5259
If I Had A Car	Miller Brothers	1958	Mercury 71293
If I Had A Choice	Pearls	1962	Warner Bros. 5300
If I Had A Hammer	Coasters Two Plus Two	1976	American International 1122
If I Had A Talking Picture	Jive Bombers	1957	Savoy 1513
If I Had Aladdin's Lamp	Night Owls, Tony Allen & the	1960	Crown LP 5231
If I Had Another Chance	Fabuleers	1960	Kenco 5002
If I Had Another Chance	Matadors	1961	Duchess 1005
If I Had It To Do All Over Again	Four Bars, Betty Wilson & the	1962	DAyco
If I Had Known	Halos	1962	Warwick LP 2046
If I Had Known	Hearts (Bronx, N.Y.)	1956	J&S 1002/1003
If I Had My Chance	Big Boys	1964	Melmar 113
If I Had My Life To Live Over	Royal Reveros	NA	Jump Up 114
If I Had My Way	Playboys	1962	Chancellor 1106
If I Had My Wish	Combo-Nettes, Jane Porter & the	1955	Combo 74
If I Had The Power	Pharaohs	1961	Pharaoh 1
If I Had Your Love	Fascinations	1961	Paxley 750/Dore 593 (61)
If I Just (Had My Way)	Avons (with the Miller Sisters)	1961	Hull 744
If I Knew	Cruisers	1960	V-Tone 207
If I Knew The Way	Raves	1956	Liberty 55013

SONG	GROUP	YEAR	LABEL
If I Knew Then	Chiffons	1967	Laurie 3377
If I Love Again	Ravens	1950	Columbia (unreleased)
If I Love You	Victorians	1964	Liberty 55728
If I Loved Only You	Short Stops, Short & the	NA	Fortune LP 8017
If I Loved You	Skyliners	1959	Calico LP 3000
If I Loved You	Solitaires	1978 (1954)	Old Town (unreleased)
If I Never Get To Heaven	Dominoes	1955	Federal 12209
If I, Oh I	Diablos, Nolan Strong & the	1963	Fortune 532
If I Only Had Magic	Dubs	1961	ABC 10198
If I Only Knew	Rhythmaires, Curt Jensen & the	1958	Pet 806
If I Should Lose You	Dreamlovers	1962	Down/End 1114 (62)
If I Should Lose You (acappella)	Del-Capris	1966	Amber 854
If I Should Lose Your Love	Sophomores (Massachusetts)	1957	Dawn 228
If I Thought You Needed Me	Hollywood Flames	1959	Atco 6155
If I Were A Countryside	4 Most, Lincoln Chase & the	1956	Dawn 217
If I Were A Magician	Dreamlovers	1963	Columbia 42698
If I Were A Magician	Four-Evers	1964	Smash 1887 (first pressing)
If I Were King	Five Crowns, Chuck Edwards & the	1959	Alanna 557/558
If I Were King	Inspirations, Benny Bunn & the	1959	Eastmen 790
If I Were King	Prisonaires	1976	Sun 513
If I Were To Lose You (acappella)	Five Jades (Bronx, N.Y.)	1975	Relic LP 107
If I'm A Fool	Empires	1957	Amp-3 132
If It Ain't One Thing It's Another	Dells	1963	Argo 5442
If It Hadn't Been For You	Dreamers, Leon & the	1962	Parkway 843
If It Is Wrong	Cadets	1956	Modern 971
If It Isn't For You	Sentimentals	1959	Vanity 589
If It Wasn't For My Baby	Upstarts, Jerry McCain & the	1956	Excello 2079
If It Wasn't For You	Gallahads	1955	Capitol 3175
If It's A Crime	Larks (North Carolina)	1954	Lloyds 110
If It's Meant To Be	Paramounts, Eddie Saxon &	1962	Empress 106
If It's Our Destiny	Blue Notes	1957	Josie (unreleased)
If It's So Baby	Robins	1949	Savoy 726
If It's To Be	Orioles, Sonny Til & the	1950	Jubilee (unreleased)
If It's Tonight	Gatorvettes	1958	Thunder 1001/Bocaldun 1001 (59)
If Love Is	Echoes	1963	Smash 1850
If Love Is What You Want	Sharps	1960	Star-Hi 10406
If Love Was Money	Night Owls, Tony Allen & the	1960	Crown LP 5231
If Love Was Money	Wanderers, Tony Allen & the	1961	Kent 356
If Love Were Like Rivers	Tams	1961	Heritage 101
If Loving You Is Wrong	Inspirators	1955	Treat 502
If My Heart Could Write A Letter	Crests	1960	Coed 535
If My Teardrops Could Talk	Del-Sharps, Sonny Ace & the	1958	TNT 153
If Only I Had Known	Kilts, Charlie Jester & the	1961	Le Cam 722
If Only I Had Known	Team Mates	1959, 1966	Le Cam 706/ABC 10760
If Only The Sky Was A Mirror	Classics (Los Angeles)	1957	Class 219
If Only You Cared	Madisons, Billy Kidd & the	1961	Madison 153
If Only You Were Mine	Five Scalders	1956	Drummond 3000/Sugarhill 3000 (56)
If She Should Call	Brooklyn Boys	1956	Ferris 902
If She Should Call	Dynamics	1961	Dynamic 1008
If She Should Call	Vol-Tones	1957	Dynamic 108
If Someone Would Care (acappella)	Five Jades (Bronx, N.Y.)	1975	Relic LP 107
If Teardrops Were Kisses	Robins	1955	Spark 110
If Tears Could Speak	Page Boys	1963	Decca 3105
If That Would Bring You Back To Me	Three Beaus And A Peep, Rick Vallo & the	1953	MGM 11473
If That's The Way You Want It, Baby	Blenders (New York)	1953	MGM 11488
If The Sun Isn't Shining	Reed, Lula (with the Teeners)	1954	King 4714
If The World Doesn't End Tomorrow (I'm Comin' After You)	Rays, Doug Warren & the	1960	Image 1011
If The World Don't End Tomorrow	Fairlanes	1960	Argo 5357
If There Wasn't Any You	Perry, Charles & group	1962	Melic 4119
If There Were	Snappers	1959	20th Century Fox 148
If There's A Next Time	Furys	1963	Mach IV 114
If They Ask Me	Bluenotes, Phil Cay & the	1959	Hart 1001
If They Only Knew	G-Notes	1959	Form 102
If This Is Goodbye	Keyavas, Harry & the	1963	IPG 1011

SONG	GROUP	YEAR	LABEL
If This World Were Mine	Celtics, Bobby Lanz & the	1973	Bridges 5003
If We Should Meet Again	Byrd, Bobby & group	1957	Zephyr 70-018
If We Should Meet Again	Ervin, Frankie & group	1960	Rendezvous 126
If Wishes Were Kisses	Debs	1961	Echo 1008
If You Are But A Dream	Imperials, Little Anthony & the	1961	End LP 311
If You Are Meant To Be	Dales	1957	Onyx 509
If You Believe	Four Coachmen	1959	Castle 507
If You Believe	Orioles, Sonny Til & the (with the Sid Bass Orchestra)	1954	Jubilee 5161
If You Believe, If You Believe	Howard, Vince & group	1961	Era 3056
If You Can't Give Me All	Monotones	1965	Hickory 1306
If You Can't Rock Me	Strikes	1956	Lin 5006/Imperial 5433 (57)
If You Care	Metronomes	NA	Milestone
If You Care	Neptunes	1958	Payson 101/102
If You Care	Tyler, Frankie	NA	Seasons 4 Ever
If You Cry	Fourmost	1964	Atco 6307
(If You Cry) True Love, True Love	Drifters (1959-forward)	1959	Atlantic 2040
If You Didn't Mean It	Four Sevilles	1980	Starlight 5
If You Didn't Mean It	Ravens	1949	National 9085
If You Don't Care	Danleers	1960	Epic 9367
If You Don't Care	Whispers	1966	Laurie 3344
If You Don't Come Back	Drifters (1959-forward)	1963	Atlantic 2191
If You Don't Come Back	Gents	1966	Duane
If You Don't Love Me	Five Echoes	1971	Sabre 106
If You Don't Need Me	Five Royales	1961	Home Of The Blues 218
If You Don't Want Me	Emperors	NA	Graham
If You Don't Want My Love	Sunglows	NA	Carrib 1025
If You Ever Get Lonesome	Love Bugs, Preston Love & the	1955	Ultra
If You Ever Need A Friend	Thrillers (Detroit)	NA	Herald (unreleased)
If You Ever Need Me	Markays, Doug Sahm & the	1961	Harlem 107/Swingin' 625 (61)
If You Give A Party	Incredables	NA	Kelrich 850/851
If You Give Me A Chance	Dons, Gene Kennedy & the	1959	Paradise 112
If You Go	Darnell, Larry & group	1957	DeLuxe 6136
If You Have Faith	Gee, Billy & group	1959	Coronet 1303
If You Just Don't Leave	Du Droppers	1954	Unreleased
If You Leave Me	Starlets, Ella Thomas & the	1962	Gedinson's 101
If You Left Me Today	Matadors	1963	Keith 6502
If You Listen With Your Heart	Scholars	1956	Dot 15519
If You Love Me	Altairs	1960	Amy 803
If You Love Me	Blue Notes, Todd Randall & the	1956	Josie 800/Port 70021 (61)
If You Love Me	Clovers	1955	Atlantic 1052
If You Love Me	Fascinations, Jordan & the	1990	Magic Carpet EP 509
If You Love Me	Five Sharks	1964	Times Square 35/Relic 525 (65)
If You Love Me	Informers	1965	J-Rude 1400
If You Love Me	Paragons	1961	Tap 504
If You Love Me	Radiants, Little Jan & the	1960, 1961	Vim 507/Goldisc G15/Queen 24007
If You Love Me	Rogues	1956	Old Town 300
If You Love Me	Royals, Chuck Willis & the	1951	Okeh 6832
If You Love Me	Stacy, Clarence & group	1961	Carol 4114
If You Love Me, Pretty Baby	Valentines	1986	Murray Hill LP 000202
If You Love Me Really Love Me	Fascinations, Jordan & the	1962	Josie 895
If You Loved Me	Stardusters, Bobby Chandler & His	1956	O.J. 1000
If You Need Me, I'll Be There	Laddins	1962	Angie 1790
If You Only Cared	Hearts, Lee Andrews & the (as Lee Andrews)	1960	Jordan 121
If You Only Had A Heart	Gadabouts	1955	Wing 90043
If You Only Knew	Chase, Eddie & group	1959	Viscount 529
If You Only Knew	Five Keys	1971 (1953), 1991	Aladdin 3167A (unreleased)/ EMI CDP7-92709
If You Only Knew	Teddy Bears	1959	Imperial 5581
If You Only Knew What A Three Cent Stamp Could Do	Esquires	1954	Epic 9024
If You Only Take The Time	Mellomen, Kitty White & the	1955	Century 711
If You Really Care	Rockets, Randy & the	1959	Viking 1000
If You Really Want Me To, I'll Go	Ron-Dels (Delbert McClinton)	1965	Brownfield 18/Smash 1986 (65)
If You See Mary Lee	Raindrops	1974	Firefly 313

SONG	GROUP	YEAR	LABEL
If You See My Baby	Cardinals	1952	Atlantic (unreleased)
If You See My Baby	Pirouettes	1964	Diamond 165
If You Should Leave Me	Sinceres	1961	Richie 545
If You Should Love Again	Three Chuckles	1955	X 0095
If You Still Want Me	Four Fifths	1966	Columbia 43913
If You Still Want Me	Sunshine Boys	1959	Scottie 1307
If You Try	Chantels	1958	End 1030
If You Wanna Do A Smart Thing	Candies	1963	Fleetwood 7003
If You Want A Little Lovin'	Barons (Key)	1959	Key 1001
If You Want Me	Sandmen	1965	Blue Jay 5002
If You Want My Heart	Foster Brothers	1958	Mercury 71360
If You Want My Love	Ithacas	1957	Fee Bee 220
If You Want To	Carousels	1961	Gone 5118 (second pressing)
If You Want To	Ovations (Starlight)	1988	Starlight 59
If You Want To Be A Woman Of Mine	Cadillacs	1957	Unreleased
If You Want To Be My Baby	Caryl, Naomi & group	1956	Ember 1006
If You Want To Call Me	Martineques	1965	Me O 1002
If You Were Gone For Me	Shells	1976	Candlelite LP 1000
If You Were Gone From Me (acappella)	Savoys (New Jersey)	1963	Catamount 101
If You Were Gone From Me (acappella)	Shells	1966	Candlelite LP 1000
If You Were Here Tonight	Chansonaires	1958	Hamilton 50012
If You Were Here Tonight	Debs	1955	Crown 153
If You Were Mine	Charmaines	1961	Fraternity 873
If You Were Mine	Clantones	1959	Emony 1021
If You Were My Darling	Dootones	NA	
If You Were The Only Girl	Castelles	1954	Grand 105
If You Were The Only Girl In The World	Individuals, Chuck Rio & the	1961	Tequila 103
If You Were The Only Girl In The World	Larks (North Carolina)	1988	Relic LP 8013
If You'd Forgive Me	Midnighters, Hank Ballard & the	1960	King 5400
If You'd Only Be My Love	Gallant, Billy (with the Roulettes)	1962	Goldisc G6
If You'll Be Mine	Blue Notes (with Joe Loco & Quintette)	1953	Rama 25
If You'll Be True	Harris, Dimples & group	1956	Crest 1013
If Your Heart Aches	Vocaleers	NA	Relic LP 5094
If Your Heart Can Take It	Four Sportsmen	1962	Sunnybrook 6
If Your Heart Says Yes	Serenaders (New Jersey)	1964	V.I.P. 25002
If Your Pillow Could Talk	Edsels	1962	Capitol 4675
If You're Mine	Penguins	1958	Dooto 435
If You've Never Been In Love	Rock-Its	1958	Spangle 2010
Ific	Chantels	1961	End LP 312/
			Murray Hill LP 000385 (87)
Iga Diga Doo	Four Of Us	1963	Brunswick 55288
I-I-I	Velvets (New York)	1957	Fury 1012
I-I-I Could Love You	Sugarmints	1957	Brunswick 55042
I-I-I Love You	Clovers	1957	Atlantic 1139
Ike Hammer	Carallons, Lonnie & the	1960	Mohawk 113
Ik-Heb-Je-Lief	Delatones	1960	TNT 9028
I'll Always Be	Embers, Jerry Bright & the	1959	Yucca 143
I'll Always Be A Fool	Hollywood Four Flames	1952	Recorded In Hollywood 164
I'll Always Be By Your Side	X-Cellents, Little Willie & the	1965	Smash 1996
I'll Always Be In Love With You	Danleers	1960	Epic 9421
I'll Always Be In Love With You	Five Keys	1971 (1953)	Aladdin 3182
I'll Always Be In Love With You	Hurricanes	1957	King 5018
I'll Always Be In Love With You	Ravens	1956	Jubilee 5237
I'll Always Be In Love With You	Ray-O-Vacs	1960	Sharp 103
I'll Always Be In Love With You	Skyliners	NA	
I'll Always Be In Love With You	Travelers	1959	Andex 4033
I'll Always Be Nearby	Belles, Terry & the	1959	Ducky 711
I'll Always Be There	En-Solids, Drake & the	NA	Alteen 8652
I'll Always Care For You	Invictors	1959	Bee 1117
I'll Always Have You	Thunderbirds, Ron Holden & the	1961	Eldo 117
I'll Always Love	Cardinals	1951	Atlantic 952
I'll Always Love You	Cardinals	1977	Robin Hood 154
I'll Always Love You	Companions	1962	Columbia 42279
I'll Always Love You	Festivals	1966	Smash 2056
I'll Always Love You	Gay Tunes	1987	Relic LP 5071

SONG	GROUP	YEAR	LABEL
I'll Always Love You	Tiffanys, Cindy Gibson & the	NA	General 700
I'll Always Love You	Tokens (Brooklyn)	1961, 1963	Warwick 615/Laurie 3180
I'll Always Remember	Devotions, Little Marcus & the	1964	Gordie 1001
I'll Always Remember	Keystoners	1984	Starbound 501
I'll Always Remember	Originals, Rachael & the	1962	Night Star 010
I'll Always Remember	Sharptones	1959	Ace 133
(I'll Always Remember) The Chapel On The Hill	Little Jerry & group	1960	Aldo 502
I'll Always Say Please	Concords (Brooklyn)	1956	Ember 1007
I'll Always Watch Over You	Turbans (Philadelphia)	1956	Herald 469
I'll Be	Vel-Tones	NA	Del Norte 725
I'll Be A Cry Baby	Gems, Pearl Woods & the	1962	Wall 551
I'll Be A Little Angel	Little Angels	1961	Warwick 672
I'll Be Around	Castaleers	1959	Folsted 8585
I'll Be Around	Four Checks	1961	Tri Disc 101
I'll Be Around	Mohawks	1961	Motown 1009
I'll Be Around	Monterays (Twin Hit)	1965	Twin Hit 2865
I'll Be Around	Phantoms, Lynn Roberts & the	1956	Oriole 101
I'll Be Back	La Dolls	1985	Relic LP 8004
I'll Be Back	Ravens	1952	Mercury 5853
I'll Be Back	Voices, Ravon Darnell & the	1956	Million 2015
I'll Be By	Van Dykes	1967	Co-Op 516
I'll Be By Your Side	Paul, Clarence & group	1959	Hanover 4519
I'll Be Faithful	Dreams	1955	Savoy 1157
I'll Be Forever Loving You	El Dorados	1955	Vee Jay 165
I'll Be Forever Loving You	Fascinations, Jordan & the	1961	Dapt 203
I'll Be Forever Loving You	Magic Touch	1990	Starlight 73
I'll Be Forever Loving You	Marcels	1975	Monogram 112
I'll Be Glad	Hurricanes	NA	UGHA LP 001
I'll Be Gone	Fascinators (Burn)	1965	Burn 845
I'll Be Gone	Ron-Dells	1963	Arlen 723
I'll Be Hanging On	Restless Hearts, Fred Parris & the	1966	Green Sea 107
I'll Be Happy	Thunderbirds, Ron Holden & the	1961	Eldo 117
I'll Be Home	Coastliners	1960	Back Beat 566
I'll Be Home	Flamingos	1955, 1973	Checker 830
I'll Be Home	Keens, Rick & the	1961	Austin 313/Le Cam 721 (61)/ Smash 1705 (61)
I'll Be Home	Sharks	1975	Broadcast 1128
I'll Be Home	Sharks Quintet	NA	Broadway
I'll Be Home (acappella)	Quotations	1975	Relic LP 104
I'll Be Home Again	Four Jacks	1952	Federal 12087
I'll Be Home Again	Hollywood Arist-O-Kats	1953	Recorded In Hollywood 406
I'll Be Home For Christmas	Five Fashions	1966	Catamount 116
I'll Be Home For Christmas	Travelers	1958	Andex 2011
I'll Be Home Some Day	Midnighters	1956	Federal 12285
I'll Be Lovin' You	Sparrows	1954	Jay-Dee 790
I'll Be Loving You	Saratogas	1961	Imperial 5738
I'll Be Satisfied	Dominoes	1952	Federal 12105
I'll Be Satisfied (acappella)	Universals (Philadelphia)	1973	Relic LP 5006
I'll Be Seeing You	Crescendos (Los Angeles)	1959	Atlantic 2014
I'll Be Seeing You	Five Satins	1960	Ember 1061
I'll Be Seeing You	Hollywood Flames	1959	Ebb 153
I'll Be Seeing You	Poni-Tails	1959	ABC 10047
I'll Be Seeing You	Rainbows, Randy & the	1967	B.T. Puppy 535
I'll Be Seeing You	Skyliners	1960	Calico 117/Original Sound 36 (63)
I'll Be Singing	Arpeggios	1963	Aries 001
I'll Be Spinning	Cadets	1956	Modern 1006
I'll Be The One	Equadors	1958	RCA EP 4286
I'll Be There	Aladdins	1959	Angie
I'll Be There	Commodores	1957	Challenge 1007
I'll Be There	Conner, Harold & group	NA	Recona 3504
I'll Be There	Joy Boys, Chuck Higgins & the	1954	Specialty 532
I'll Be There	Majors (Philadelphia)	1963	Imperial 66009
I'll Be There	Tren-Dells	1964	Southtown 22001
I'll Be There	Uptones	1962	Lute 6225

SONG	GROUP	YEAR	LABEL
I'll Be True	Charms	1956	Chart 623
I'll Be True	Infernos	NA	Clifton EP 502
I'll Be True	Kilts, Herman Jones & the	1958	Gaynote 105
I'll Be True	Maestro, Johnny & group	1963	Cameo 256
I'll Be True	Orlons	1961	Cameo 198
I'll Be True	Trends	1959	Argo 5341/Clover 1002
I'll Be True	Tymes	1963	
I'll Be Waiting	Clefs	1954	Peacock 1643
I'll Be Waiting	Spaniels	1959	Solid Smoke LP (84)/ Charly LP 1114 (86)
I'll Be Waiting	Swallows (Maryland)	1954	King 4676
I'll Be Waiting	Sycamores	1955	Groove 0121
I'll Be Waiting	Trojans	1961	Zynn 1006
I'll Be With You	Embers	1958	Juno 215
I'll Be With You In Apple Blossom Time	Del-Chords, Donnie & the	1963	Taurus 357
(I'll Be With You In) Apple Blossom Time	Platters	1960	Mercury 71624
I'll Be Your Love Tonight	Cupons, Materlyn & the	1964	Impact 28
I'll Be Yours	Roberts, Penny (with the Paramours)	1962	Moonglow 201
I'll Beg	Five Emeralds	1954	S-R-C 106
I'll Believe It When I See It	Sierras	1962	Goldisc G4
I'll Belong To You	Dual Tones	1960	Sabre 204
I'll Burn Your Letters	Starlites, Jackie & the	1963	Mascot 131
I'll Catch A Rainbow	Spidels	1963	Minaret 112
I'll Catch You On The Rebound	Metronomes, Leon & the	1965	Carnival 515
I'll Cherish You Love	Headliners, George Goodman & the	1965	Val 5
I'll Close My Eyes	Skyliners	1961	Colpix 188
I'll Come Running Back To You	Cooke, Sam & group	1957	Specialty 619
I'll Come To You	Cheertones	1961	ABC 10277
I'll Conquer The World	Metallics	1962	Baronet 18
I'll Cry And Cry Every Night	Smith, Jimmie & group	1959	Flip 347
I'll Cry Later	Emblems, Patty & the	1967	Kapp 870
I'll Cry No More	Crickets, Dean Barlow & the	1953	MGM 11507
I'll Cry Tomorrow	Serenaders (New Jersey)	1964	V.I.P. 25002
I'll Cry When You're Gone	Platters	1953	Federal 12164
I'll Die In Love With You	Rockers	1956	Federal 12267
I'll Do A Little Bit More	Olympics	1967	Mirwood 5529
I'll Do Anything	Diadems	1961, 1964	Goldie 715
I'll Do Anything	Thrillers, Little Joe & the	1963	Rose 835
I'll Do It	Robins	1953	RCA 5486
I'll Do My Crying Tomorrow	Heatwaves	1965	Josie 941
I'll Do My Crying Tomorrow	Tokens (Brooklyn)	1962, 1969	RCA 8089/B.T. Puppy 563
I'll Do The Same Thing Too	Shirelles	1962	Scepter LP 502
I'll Drink A Toast	Capitols	1962	Portrait 109
I'll Drink A Toast	Ontarios	1974	Firefly 323
I'll Find Her	Dukes (California)	1954	Specialty
I'll Find Myself A Guy	Watesians	1962	Donna 1371
I'll Follow You	Cinders	1964	Original Sound 43
I'll Follow You	Five Keys	1951	Groove 0031
I'll Follow You	Four Towns	NA	A1 1001
I'll Follow You	Gum Drops	1956	King 4913
I'll Follow You	Jarmels	1961	Laurie 3116
I'll Follow You	Little Buck & group	1960	Duke 324
I'll Follow You	Orbits, Bobby Grayson & His	1963	Jamco 105
I'll Forever Love You	Swans (St. Louis)	1955	Fortune 822
I'll Forget	Corey, John (with the Four Seasons)	1961	Vee Jay 466
I'll Forget About You	Five Crowns	1958	R&B 6901
I'll Forget Her Tomorrow	Rainbows, Randy & the	1966	Mike 4001
I'll Forget You	Valentines	1962	Bethlehem 3055
I'll Forget You	Videls	1960	JDS 5004
I'll Gamble	Zodiacs, Johnny Ballad & the	1959	Wildcat 0017
I'll Get Along	Five Satins	1957	Ember LP 100/Ember EP 102
I'll Get By	Hollywood Flames	1958	Ebb 149
I'll Get By	Marglows, Andy & the	1963	Liberty 55627
I'll Get By	Platters	NA	Mercury EP 3344
I'll Get You Yet	Parliaments	1963	Symbol 917

SONG	GROUP	YEAR	LABEL
I'll Give You Love	Five Shades	1965	Veep 1208
I'll Go	Greenwood, Lil (with the Dominoes)	1954	Federal 12158
I'll Go	Lamplighters	1955	Federal (unreleased)
I'll Go On	Bee Jay & group	1961	Clock 1743
I'll Go Through Life Loving You	Sophomores, Anthony & the	1966	ABC 10844
I'll Hang My Letters Out To Dry	Innocents, Kathy Young & the	1962	Indigo 146
I'll Have To Decide	Socialites, Kenny & the	1958	Crosstown 001
I'll Hide My Love	Shortcuts	1959	Carlton 513
I'll Hide My Tears	Flames	1953	7-11 2110 (unreleased)
I'll Hide My Tears	Jets (Aladdin)	1954	Aladdin 3247
I'll Just Have To Go On (Dreaming)	Universals (Amityville, N.Y.)	1961	Festival 1601/Festival 25001 (62)
I'll Keep Coming Back	Bobbettes 1981	1981	QIT
I'll Keep On Seeing You	Barbarians (with Vito Piccone & the Elegants)	1965	Laurie 3326
I'll Keep On Waiting	Videls	1960	Kapp 361
I'll Keep Tryin'	Poni-Tails	1959	ABC 10047
I'll Keep You Happy	Midnighters, Hank Ballard & the	1959	King 5195
I'll Kiss Your Teardrops Away	Aladdins	1959	Angie
I'll Kiss Your Teardrops Away	Laddins	1962	Angie 1790
I'll Know	Fentones, Shane Fenton & the	1963	Laurie 3287/20th Fox 439 (63)
I'll Know	Wanderers	1963	United Artists 648
I'll Let You Know	Del-Phis	1961	Checkmate 1005
I'll Live Again	Diamonds (Harold Sonny Wright)	1953	Atlantic 1003
I'll Love That Man	Innocents, Kathy Young & the	1962	Monogram 506
I'll Love You	Deans, Barry & the	1960	Zirkon 1001
I'll Love You Again	Monterays (Brooklyn)	1958	East West 124
I'll Love You Forever	Deans	1960	Mohawk 114
I'll Love You Forever	Delshays	1964	Charger 102
I'll Love You Forever	Escapades, Georgie Salo & the	1960	Hi-Q 5014
I'll Love You Forever	Rollins, Bird & group	1960	Harvard 805
I'll Love You 'Til The Day I Die	Pirates	1962	Mel-O-Dy 105
I'll Love You (Till The End Of Time)	Bluenotes	1965	Bluejay 101
I'll Love You Till The End Of Time, Pt. 1	Royal Teens	1965	Swan 4200/Blue Jay 101
I'll Make A Bet	Ambers	1958	Ebb 142
I'll Make A Vow	Crescents	1965	Seven B 7013
I'll Make Her Mine	Valiant Trio	1965	EV 97500
I'll Make You Mine	Twin Tunes	1955	Sound 115
I'll Make You Understand	Performers	1956	All Star 714/Tip Top 402 (57)
I'll Miss These Things	Sentimentals	1968	Mint 807
I'll Miss You This Christmas	Chirps, Marvin & the	1958	Tip Top 202
I'll Never Ask For More Than This	Dominoes	1958	Liberty LP 3083
I'll Never Be Lonely Again	Belvin, Jesse & group	1959	RCA 7596
I'll Never Be Mean	Radiants	1958	Wizz 713
I'll Never Be The Same	Beau-Jives	1962	Shepherd 2202
I'll Never Be The Same	Beau-Marks	1962	Rust 5050
I'll Never Be The Same	Melody Masters	1957	Renown 107
I'll Never Change	Chromatics, Bob Williams & the	1955	Blend 1006
I'll Never Change	Night Riders, Mel Smith & the	1959	Sue 713
I'll Never Change	Teen Tones	1959	Crest 1057
I'll Never Come Back	Four Cal-Quettes	1962	Capitol 4725
I'll Never Cry	Earls	1961	Rome 5117
I'll Never Ever Love Again	Pharaohs	1960	Flip 352
I'll Never Fall In Love	Olympics	1977	Robin Hood 151
I'll Never Fall In Love Again	Legends	1957	Melba 109
I'll Never Fall In Love Again	Mello-Tones	1957	Fascination 1001/Gee 1037 (57)
I'll Never Find Another Girl Like You	Falcons (Detroit)	1985	Relic LP 8005
I'll Never Fool My Heart	Arrows	1973	Baron 107
I'll Never Forget	Clifford, Buzz (with the Teenagers)	1961	Columbia
I'll Never Forget You	Crewnecks	1959	Rhapsody 71960
I'll Never Get Married	Impossibles, Linda Carr & the	1961	Skyla 1111
I'll Never Get Over You	Pirates, Johnny Kidd & the	1963	Capitol 5065
I'll Never Get Over You	Roamers	1954	Savoy 1147
I'll Never Know	Del Satins	1995	Park Ave. 11
I'll Never Leave You Again	Youngsters, Little Pete & the	1962, 1963	Lesley 1925
I'll Never Leave You Alone	Honeytones, Gene Worth & the	NA	Ace 118
I'll Never Let Her Go	Royals	1952	Federal 12098

SONG	GROUP	YEAR	LABEL
I'll Never Let You Down	Delacardos	1959, 1963	Elgey 1001
I'll Never Let You Go	Cadillacs	NA	Josie (unreleased)
I'll Never Let You Go	Daylighters	1959	Domino 904
I'll Never Let You Go	Dollettes, Jimmy Carter & the	NA	Cayce 2002
I'll Never Let You Go	Echoes, Sonny Roberts & the	1958	Impala 1001
I'll Never Let You Go	Flairs	1955	Flair 1056
I'll Never Let You Go	Flames	1959	Bertram 203
I'll Never Let You Go	Gents	1964	Times Square 2/Times Square 99 (64)
I'll Never Let You Go	Imaginations	1976	Harvey 101
I'll Never Let You Go	Original Cadillacs	1964	Josie 915
I'll Never Let You Go	Thrillers, Little Joe & the	1959	Okeh 7127
I'll Never Let You Go	Valentines	1956	Rama 201
I'll Never Let You Go	Vocaltones	1956	Apollo 497
I'll Never Let You Go (acappella)	Citadels	1975	Relic LP 104
I'll Never Let You Go (acappella)	Five Sharks	1964	Old Timer 605
I'll Never Let You Go (acappella)	Gents	1963	Times Square 2/Times Square 99 (64)
I'll Never Love Again	Medallions, Johnny Twovoice & the	1955	Dootone 373
I'll Never Love Again	Satintones	1960	Tamla 54024
I'll Never Love Again	Three Dots And A Dash	1951	Imperial 5164
I'll Never, Never Do It Again	Creators (New Jersey)	1962	T-Kay 110
I'll Never Smile Again	Daddy Cool & group	1972	Reprise 1090
I'll Never Smile Again	Imperials, Little Anthony & the	1961	End LP 311
I'll Never Smile Again	Platters	1961	Mercury 71847
I'll Never Smile Again	Velours	1958	Cub 9014
I'll Never Smile Again	Wanderers	1961	Cub 9094
I'll Never Smile Again (acappella)	Five Delights	1960	A Cappella - Best of the Bronx (98)
I'll Never Stand In Your Way	Sherwoods, Tony Reno & the	1963	Johnson 123
I'll Never Stop Crying	Dell Vikings	1961	ABC 10208
I'll Never Stop Loving You	Five Keys	1964	King 5877
I'll Never Stop Loving You	Four Students, Big John Greer & the	1955	RCA (unreleased)
I'll Never Stop Loving You	Regan, Tommy (with the Marcels)	1964	Colpix 725
I'll Never Stop Wanting You	Moonglows	1959	Chess 1717
I'll Never Tell	Day Dreams, Tony & the	1958, 1961	Planet 1008/1009/1055
I'll Never Tell	Ecstasies	1979	U.G.H.A. 04
I'll Never Tell	Harptones	1953	Bruce 101/Relic 1022 (73)
I'll Never Tell	Harptones (with Bunny Paul)	1954	Essex 364
I'll Never Tire Of You	Bombers	1955	Orpheus 1101
I'll Never Turn My Back On You	Airdales, Wess & the	1967	Durium 9259
I'll Never Walk Alone	Rivals (Treyco)	1963	Treyco 401
I'll Not Be The One (To Say Goodbye)	Royal Teens	1959	Mighty 111
I'll Pay As I Go	Alexander, Jeff	1955	Aardell 0001
I'll Play Along	Bracelets	1962	Congress 104
I'll Pray For You	Del Satins	1961	End 1096
I'll Remember	Butterball Five, Billy Bowen & the	1957	Xtra
I'll Remember	Four Xs	1960	Lost 103/20
I'll Remember All You Kisses	G-Clefs	1962	Ditto 503
I'll Remember Carol	Boyce, Tommy & group	1962	RCA 8074
(I'll Remember) In The Still Of The Night	Five Satins	1956	Standord 200/Ember 1005
(I'll Remember) In The Still Of The Night	Tokens (Brooklyn)	NA	RCA LP 3685
(I'll Remember) One And All	Firesiders	1961	Swan 4074
I'll Remember You	Charms, Otis Williams & his	1956	DeLuxe 6098
I'll See You In My Dreams	Platters	1963	Mercury 72107
I'll See You Next Fall	Tempters	1956	Empire 105
I'll See You Somewhere	Taylortops	1959	Alton 2000
I'll Show You How To Love	Dedications, Denny & the	1965	Susan 1111
I'll Stay Home	Computones	1981	Clifton 66
I'll Stay Home	Creators	1982	Jason Scott 24
I'll Stay Home	Jaynells	1982	
I'll Stay Home New Year's Eve	Jaynells	1963	Cameo 286/Diamond 153
I'll Still Be Around	Mohawks, Popcorn & the	1961	Motown 1009
I'll Still Be Loving You	Dons, Gene Kennedy & the	1959	Paradise 112
I'll Still Go On Loving You	Salems	1961	Mercury 71754
I'll Stop Crying	Spiders	1954	Imperial 5280
I'll Tag Along	Crowns, Henry Strogin & the	1962, 1963	Amazon 1001/Ball 1015
I'll Take Care Of You	Marland, Cletus & group	1961	Roulette 4388

SONG	GROUP	YEAR	LABEL
I'll Take Care Of You	Pharaohs, Artie & the	1964	Cuca 1162
I'll Take You Home	Corsairs	1962	Tuff 1818/Chess 1818 (62)
I'll Take You Home	Drifters (1959-forward)	1963	Atlantic 2201
I'll Take You Where The Music's Playing	Drifters (1959-forward)	1965	Atlantic 2298
I'll Tell It	Davis, Hal Sonny & group	1960	MJC 104
I'll Tell You In The Morning	Massey, Barbara & group	1961	Imperial 5786
I'll Tell You In This Song	Caruso, Dick & group	1959	MGM 12811
I'll Try	Ru-Bee-Els	1962	Flip 359
I'll Try Harder	Arabians, Lawrence & the	NA	Hem
I'll Wait	Blossoms	1961	Challenge 9109
I'll Wait	Chuckles	1964	West Side 1019
I'll Wait	Co-Eds	1961	Challenge 9109
I'll Wait	Erhardt, Dian & group	1957	RCA 7137
I'll Wait	Hudson, Glinda & group	NA	Smalltown 300
I'll Wait	Revleras	1964	Victoria 103
I'll Wait For One More Train	Gum Drops	1955	King 8853/King 1499 (55)
I'll Wait Forever	Shamans	1959	Kayham 3/4
I'll Walk Alone	Chantels	1958	End EP 202/End LP 312 (61)
I'll Walk Alone	Faces	1965	Regina 1328
I'll Walk In The Shadow	Crescents	NA	Joyce (unreleased)
I'll Walk The Earth	Friends, Gary Cane & His	1960	Shell 719
I'll Whisper In Your Ear	Versatiles	1960	Rocal 1002
I'll Write A Book	Wonders	1959	Ember 1051
Illusion	Con Chords, Bob Brady & the	1966	Chariot 525
I'm A Cool Teenager	Royaltones, El Pauling & the	1960	Federal 12383
I'm A Fool	Hy-Tones	1958	Hy-Tone 120
I'm A Fool	Turks	1956, 1958	Money 215/Knight 2005/ Imperial 5783
I'm A Fool For Losing You	Marvells	1962	Finer Arts 2026
(I'm A Fool) I Must Love You	Falcons (Big Wheel)	1966	Big Wheel 321/322
I'm A Fool To Care	Castelles	1954	Grand 114
I'm A Fool To Care	Star Dusters	1954	Flair 1047
I'm A Fool To Want You	Suburbans, Jimmy Ricks & the	1957	Baton 236
I'm A Fugitive	Ravons	1959	Davis 464
I'm A Happy Little Christmas Tree	Tots, Barry & the	1961	Fury 1058
I'm A Happy Man	Jive Five	1965	United Artists 853
I'm A Happy Man (acappella)	Shells	1966	Candlelite LP 1000
I'm A Hog For You	Coasters	1959	Atco 6146
I'm A Hog For You Baby	El Caminos, Mr. Lee & the	1964	Camelot 107/Nolta
I'm A Hurtin' Inside	Limelites, Shep & the	1965	Hull 772
I'm A Little Mixed Up	Carnations, Cosmo & the	1961	Tilt 787
I'm A Loser	Christie, Dean & group	1962	Select 715
I'm A Love Maker	Popular Five	1968	Minit 32050
I'm A Lover	Thin Men, Dennis Binder & his	1956	United 194
I'm A Sentimental Fool	Marylanders	1952	Jubilee 5079
I'm A Stranger	Starlets, Ella Thomas & the	1962	Gedinson's 101
I'm A Travelin' Man	Combinations, Artie Morris & the	1959	Coco 163
I'm A Victim	Pageants	1965	RCA 8601
I'm A Wine Drinker	Bards	1954	Dawn 208
I'm A Young Man	Toppers, Bobby Mitchell & the	1954	Imperial 5309
I'm A Young Rooster	Chordones, Leon D. Tarver & the	1954	Checker 791
I'm Afraid	Buddies, Billy Bunn & the	1951	RCA 4483
I'm Afraid	Cap-Tans	1960	Anna 1122
I'm Afraid Of You	Ravens	1949	National 9089
I'm Afraid The Masquerade Is Over	Moonglows	1956	Chess 1651
I'm Afraid They're All Talking About Me	Dawn	1967	Laurie 3388
(I'm Afraid) You Hurt Me	Darlenes	1963	Stacy 965
I'm All Alone	Coronets	1953	Chess 1549
I'm All Alone	Earls	1974	
I'm All Alone	Limelites, Shep & the	1964	Hull 767
I'm All Dressed Up With A Broken Heart	Five Bars	1963	Bullet 1009
I'm All Right	Jades	1964	Ector 101
I'm Alone	Cosytones	1957	Willow 1001
I'm Alone	Five Keys	1954	Capitol 2945
I'm Alone Again	Allen, Bob & group	1966	Diamond 197

SONG	GROUP	YEAR	LABEL
I'm Alone Because I Love You	Belles, Terry & the	1958	Hanover 4505
I'm Alone Tonight	Tavares, Ernie Trio	1953	Dootone 325
I'm Alright	Imperials, Little Anthony & the	1959	End 1053
I'm Always Chasing Rainbows	Tymes	1964	Parkway LP 7039
I'm Always Doing Something Wrong	Fabulous Four	1964	Brass 316
I'm Angry Baby	Heart-Attacks	NA	Remus 5000
I'm Anxious	Kinney, Mary & group	1959	Andex 4031
I'm Ashamed	Cordials	1960	Cordial 1001
I'm Ashamed	Velvetones	1963	Ascot 2126
I'm Asking Forgiveness	Harris, Thurston (with the Sharps)	1957	Aladdin 3399
I'm Asking Forgiveness	Lee, Curtis (with the Halos)	1960	Sabra 517
I'm Asking Forgiveness	Pictures, C.L. & the	1961	Dunes 2010/Sabra 517 (60)
I'm Begging You Baby	Vibra-Tones	1962	Candi 1025
I'm Beginning To Think You Care For Me	Orioles, Sonny Til & the	1983	Murray Hill LP M61277
I'm Beginning To Understand Them	Hound Dogs	1964	Dee Dee 773
I'm Betting My Heart	Radiants, Cleve Duncan & the	1959	Dooto 451
I'm Blind	Wizards	1965	Era 3161
I'm Broke	Sultans, Wardell & the	1962	Imperial 5886
I'm Calling	Dells	1958	Vee Jay 292
I'm Calling	Intruders	NA	
I'm Calling On You	Dynamics, Mickey Farrell & the	1963	Bethlehem 3080
I'm Checking On You Baby	Arrows	1964	Hugo 1174
I'm Climbing A Mountain	Bobbettes	1965	Diamond 181
I'm Cold	Tune Weavers	1958	Casa Grande 4040
I'm Comin' Home	De-Lights	1962	Ad Lib 0207/Pop Line
I'm Comin' Home	Del-Knights	1961	Sheryl
I'm Comin' Home	Fabulous Four	1961	Chancellor 1090
I'm Comin' Home	Hollywood Flames	1965	Symbol 215
I'm Comin' Home	Olympics	1964	Loma 2010
I'm Coming Home	Chancellors	1957	XYZ 104/XYZ 601 (59)
I'm Coming Home	Deltones	1958	Vee Jay 288
I'm Coming Home	Flamingos	1963	End LP 316
I'm Coming Home	Hide-A-Ways	1956	Ronni 1000
I'm Coming Home	Neptunes	1964	Victoria 102
I'm Coming Home	Revlons, Tino & the	1966	Dearborn 530
I'm Coming Home	Sequins, Janice Rado & the	1961	Edsel 782
I'm Coming Home	Starlites, Jackie & the	1961	Fury 1057
I'm Coming Home	Woods, Jasper & group	1962	VPM 1009
I'm Confessin'	Belvin, Jesse & group	1959	Class 267
I'm Confessin'	Chantels	1959	End 1048
I'm Confessin'	Ebb Tides, Nino & the	1959	Recorte 409
I'm Confessin'	Jacks	1955	RPM 433
I'm Confessin'	Riff-Tones, Riff Ruffin & the	1957	Ball 0501
I'm Confessin'	Uniques	1960	Bliss 1004/Gone 5113 (61)
I'm Confessin' That I Love You	Clovers	1960	United Artists 227
I'm Confessin' That I Love You	Four Wheels	1959	Laurel 1003
I'm Counting On You	Brewer, Mike & group	1963	Lesley 1929
I'm Crying	Del Rios	1959	Neptune 108
I'm Crying	Greenwood, Lil (with the Dominoes)	1954	Federal 12158
I'm Crying	Lamplighters	1955	Federal (unreleased)
I'm Crying	Mel-O-Aires, Rudy Jackson & the	1954, 1955	R&B 1310
I'm Crying	Toppers, Bobby Mitchell & the	1953	Imperial 5236
I'm Destroyed (Because Of You)	Sheps	1996	Early Bird 5002
I'm Downtown	Dubs, Richard Blandon & the	1971	Vicki 229
I'm Dreamin'	Night Owls, Tony Allen & the	1956	Dig 109
I'm Dreaming	Emeralds (Pittsburgh)	1958	ABC 9948
I'm Dreaming Of You	Fashions	1959	V-Tone 202
I'm Dressed Up To Cry	Swans (St. Louis)	1955	Ballad 1004/1005
I'm Falling	Casinos	1959	Maske 803
I'm Falling	Cooke, L.C. & group	1959	Checker 925
I'm Falling For You	Twilights, James Carter & the	1956	Tuxedo 917
I'm Falling In Love	Hi-Lites (Connecticut)	1961	Record Fair 500
I'm Falling In Love	Jesters	1957	Winley 221
I'm Falling In Love	Laddins	1958	Central (unreleased)/ Isle (unreleased) (60)

SONG	GROUP	YEAR	LABEL
I'm Falling In Love	Poets	1960	Shade 1001
I'm Falling In Love With You	Minor Chords, Sunnie Elmo & the	1960	Flick 006
I'm Fed Up	Delmonicos	1961	Aku 6139
I'm Feelin' Sad	Drifters (1959-forward)	1974	Bell 45,600
I'm Feeling Alright Again	Embers	1961	Empress 101
I'm Feeling Sad	Strangers	1960	Maske 101
I'm Feeling Sad (And Oh So Lonely)	Drifters (1959-forward)	1973	Bell 45,320
I'm Following You	Four Dolls	1958	Capitol 3895
I'm Free	Five Embers	1960, 1995	Royce 0006/X Bat 1006
I'm Free (For The Rest Of Your Life)	Drifters (1959-forward)	1974	Bell 1339
I'm Free To Choose	Four Tiers, Jimmy Kemper & the	1964	Le Mans 2
I'm Free To Choose	Tiers, Jimmy Kemper & the	1964	Le Mans 002
I'm Gabriel	Angels, Gabriel & the	1961	Norman 506
I'm Giving All My Love	Reed, Lula (with the Teeners)	1955	King 4811
I'm Glad I Waited	Deane, Janet (with the Skyliners)	1958	Gateway 719
I'm Goin' Home	Fascinations, Jordan & the	1962	Josie 895
I'm Goin' Home	Jaye, Jerry & group	1963	Carlton 598
I'm Going Home	Dells	1962	Argo 5415
I'm Going Home	Genies	1963	Lennox 5562
I'm Going Home	Memos	1959	Memo 5000/5001
I'm Going To Be Blue	Ramadas	1964	New World 2000
I'm Going To Cry	Corvets, Arthur & the	1959	Moon 100
I'm Going To Live My Life Alone	Crickets, Dean Barlow & the	1954	Jay-Dee 795/Davis 459 (58)
I'm Going To Live My Life Alone	Famous Flames	1960	Harlem 114
I'm Going To Live My Life Alone	Five Jets	1973	Broadcast 999
I'm Going To Live My Life Alone	Thrillers (Detroit)	1953	Thriller 3530
I'm Going To Spend My Money	Poor Boys, King Richard & the	1961	Apollo 1203
I'm Going To Stick To You	Acorns	1958	Unart 2006
I'm Gone	Debonaires (New York)	1956	Gee 1008
I'm Gone	Delairs	1956	Rainbow 348
I'm Gone	Grand Prees	1962	Haral 780
I'm Gone Mama	Accents, Jim Murphy & the	1957	Rev 3508
I'm Gonna Ask That Boy To Dance	Emeralds (Jubilee)	1964	Jubilee 5489
I'm Gonna Be A Wheel Some Day	Bleaters	1963	Guyden 2100
I'm Gonna Be Another Man	Capri, Bobby & group	1963	Johnson 126
I'm Gonna Be Another Man	Velvet Satins, Bobby Capri & the	1963, 1976	Johnson 126
I'm Gonna Be Glad	Delegates	1957	Vee Jay 243
I'm Gonna Build A Mountain	Keynoters	1959	Pepper 896
I'm Gonna Change	Velours	1967	MGM 13780
I'm Gonna Come Home To Mama	Sunbeams	1955	Dot 1271
I'm Gonna Cry	Fascinations	1972	A&G 101
I'm Gonna Do That Woman In	Sparrows	1971	Kelway 101 (unreleased)
I'm Gonna Dry My Eyes	Chiffons	1963	Laurie 3212
I'm Gonna Find Me Another Girl	Del-Rays, Detroit Jr. & the	1964	C.J. 636
I'm Gonna Find Out	Blue Notes	1960	Brooke 116
I'm Gonna Find You	Nortones	1960	Stack 502
I'm Gonna Forget You	Tiaras	1963	Valiant 6027
I'm Gonna Get	Mello-Tones	1954	Decca 48319
I'm Gonna Get Me A Girl Somehow	Metronomes (Harold Sonny Wright)	1957	Cadence 1310
I'm Gonna Get That Gal	Vocaltones	1956	Apollo 488
I'm Gonna Getcha	Josie, Lou & group	1959	Baton 269
I'm Gonna Have Some Fun	Paul, Bunny (with the Harptones)	1954	Essex 352
I'm Gonna Hold My Baby Tight	Sparrows	1985	Krazy Kat LP 797
I'm Gonna Knock On Your Door	Isley Brothers	1959	RCA 7537
I'm Gonna Laugh At You	Calendars	1961	Coed 564
I'm Gonna Leave	Wayne, Scotty & group	1964	Talent 1008
I'm Gonna Leave You Baby	Wright, Willie (with the Sparklers)	1961	Federal 12406
I'm Gonna Love	Lovers, Valentino & the	1960	Donna 1345
I'm Gonna Love Him	Petites	1964	Ascot 2166
I'm Gonna Love Him Anyway	Four Cal-Quettes	1961	Capitol 4657
I'm Gonna Love You	Deans	NA	Tin Pan Alley 316/Crystal Ball LP 126
I'm Gonna Love You	Four Counts	1958	Dart 1014
I'm Gonna Love You A Long Long Time	Emblems, Patty & the	1967	Kapp 897
I'm Gonna Love You So	Cooper, Wade & group	1960	Ember 1059
I'm Gonna Love You So	Dukays	1962	Vee Jay 442

SONG	GROUP	YEAR	LABEL
I'm Gonna Make You Cry	Impacs	1963	Parkway 865
I'm Gonna Marry You	Corvairs	1962	Twin 19671
I'm Gonna Miss You	Midnighters, Hank Ballard & the	1961	King 5578
I'm Gonna Move	Ontarios	1974	Firefly 323
I'm Gonna Move To The Outskirts	Donnells, Jo Baby & the	1965	Ty-Tex 114
I'm Gonna Move To The Outskirts Of Town	Dominoes	1954	Federal 12178
I'm Gonna Paper My Walls With Your Love Letters	Ravens	1950	National 9111
I'm Gonna Pick Your Teeth With An Ice Pick (acappella)	Mellows, Lillian Leach & the	1974	Celeste 3009
I'm Gonna Put The Hurt On You	Little Herman & group	1964	Arlen 751
I'm Gonna Put You Down	Down Beats	1961	Entente 001
I'm Gonna Quit While I'm Ahead	Relatives	1961	May 111
I'm Gonna Rebuild This World	Romeos	1963	Felsted 8672
I'm Gonna Rock And Roll 'Til I Die	Goofers	1956	Coral 61664
I'm Gonna Run It Down	Five Royales	1954	King 4740
I'm Gonna Stand By You	Hollywood Flames	1965	Symbol 215
I'm Gonna Take To The Road	Ravens	1950	National 9131
I'm Gonna Tell My Daddy	Four Students, Varetta Dillard & the	1956	Groove 0152
I'm Gonna Tell On You	Cardinals	NA	Cha Cha 748
(I'm Gonna) Tell On You	Gordon, Sonny & group	1962	Bethlehem 3017
I'm Gonna Tell Them	Five Royales	1961	Home Of The Blues 218
I'm Gonna Tell Your Mother	Four Evers	1978	Crystal Ball 121
I'm Gonna Thank Him	Spaniels	1958	Vee Jay (unreleased)
I'm Gonna Try	Twylights	1961	Rockin 102
I'm Gonna Try	Flames	1960	
I'm Gonna Win Him Back	Chantels	1970	RCA 0347
I'm Gonna Wish For You	Capri Sisters	1960	ABC 10158
I'm Good To You Baby	Gypsies	1955	Groove 0117
I'm Growing Up	Little Dixie & group	1959	Las Vegas 101/Strip 101
I'm Happy	Consuls	1959	Abel 222
I'm Happy	Four Dates	1957	Chancellor 1014
I'm Happy In Love	Maye, Arthur Lee & group	1985	Antrell 102
I'm Hip To You	Jelly Beans	1965	Eskee 001
I'm Home	Orbits	NA	Don-J 48798
I'm Hopin' You'll Be Mine	Echoes, Tommy Vann & the	1966	Hollywood 101
I'm Hospitalized Over You	Chuck-A-Lucks	1961	Warner Bros. 5234
I'm Hurt	Rockers, Rick Randle & the	1958	Arc 4445
I'm Hypnotized	Sheppard, Buddy & group	1959	Play Me 3517
I'm In A Whirl	Deuces Wild	1958	Specialty 654
I'm In A World Of My Own	Valiants (New York)	1963	Imperial 5915
I'm In Heaven	Chesterfields	1953	Chess 1559
I'm In Love	Big Tops	1958	Warner 1017
I'm In Love	Blossoms	1963	Okeh 7162
I'm In Love	Brown, Sammy & group	1964	Bee Bee 701
I'm In Love	Cadillacs	1960	Unreleased
I'm In Love	Co-Eds	1957	Old Town 1033
I'm In Love	Emeralds (with Little Milton)	1960	Bobbin 128
I'm In Love	Ex-Tones, Mr. X & the	NA	H.O.B. 1000
I'm In Love	Flames, Johnny Spain & the	NA	Back Beat 516
I'm In Love	Fourmost	1963	Atco 6285
I'm In Love	Ivories	1957	Mercury 71239
I'm In Love	Lyrics (Hy-Tone)	1958	Hy-Tone 111
I'm In Love	Pentagons	1962	Jamie 1210/Caldwell 411 (62)
I'm In Love	Poets	1960	Spot 107/Imperial 5664 (60)
I'm In Love	Toppers, Bobby Mitchell & the	1955	Imperial 5346
I'm In Love	Universals (Shepherd)	1962	Shepherd 2200
I'm In Love	Wyatt, Don & group	1961	Brent 7026
I'm In Love	Young Lads	1956	Neil 100
I'm In Love (acappella)	Velvet Angels	1964, 1965	Medieval 201/Co-Op M102
I'm In Love Again	Deb-Tones	1959	RCA 7539
I'm In Love Again	Ravons, Bobby Roberts & the	1964	Cameo 339
I'm In Love Again	Raytones, Laverne Ray & the	1957	Okeh 7091
I'm In Love Again	Royal Jacks	1958	20th Fox 100

SONG	GROUP	YEAR	LABEL
I'm In Love Again-All Shook Up	Chevrons	1960	Time 1
(I'm In Love) Real True Love	Diablos, Nolan Strong & the	1964	Fortune 563
I'm In Love With A Gal	Cliques	1956	Modern 995
I'm In Love With A Go-Go Girl	Intentions	1964	Melron 5014
I'm In Love With The Garbage Man	Impossibles, Linda Carr & the	1961	Ray Starr 779
I'm In Love With You	Cousins	1958	Decca 30609
I'm In Love With You	Dream Girls, Bobbie Smith & the	1959	Metro 20029
I'm In Love With You	Gainors	1960	Mercury 71630/Mercury 71632
I'm In Love With You	Tuneblenders	1958	Play 1002
I'm In Love With Your Daughter	Enchantments	1964	Faro 620
I'm In Misery	Marquees	1958	Len 100
I'm In Need	Squires, Shirley & the	1963	Constellation 107
I'm In Pain	Jones, Davey & group	1961	Apt 25064
I'm In The Doghouse	Shells	1975	Monogram 108
I'm In The Mood For Love	Chimes (Brooklyn)	1961	Tag 445
I'm In The Mood For Love	Del-Chords, Donnie & the	1963	Taurus 364
I'm In The Mood For Love	Flamingos	1959	End LP 304/End EP 205 (59)
I'm In The Mood For Love	Furness Brothers	1952	MGM 11356
I'm In The Mood For Love	Townsmen (New York - Joey)	1962	Joey 6202
I'm In The Mood For Love	Tyler, Gladys & group	NA	N/A
I'm In The Mood For Love	Young Ones	1963	Yussels 7703
I'm In The Mood For Love (acappella)	Five Delights	1960	A Cappella - Best of the Bronx (98)
I'm In The Mood For Love (acappella)	Versailles	1965	Old Timer 607
I'm In Your Corner All The Way	Vincente, Vin & group	1962	Swingin' 644
I'm Just A Crying Fool	Starlings	1955	Dawn 212
I'm Just A Dancing Partner	Platters	1955	Mercury 70753
I'm Just A Dreamer	Four Haven Knights	1956	Atlas 1066/Josie 824 (57)/ Angletone 1066 (75)
I'm Just A Fool	Five Keys	1954	Capitol (unreleased)
I'm Just A Fool	Stewart, Danny (Sly Stone)	1961	G&P 901
I'm Just A Fool In Love	Orioles, Sonny Til & the	1951	Jubilee 5061
I'm Just A Loser In Love	Gents, Larry & the	1965	Delaware 1711
I'm Just A Poor Boy	Vacels	1965	Kama Sutra 204
I'm Just Another One In Love With You	Blue Sky Boys	1972	Blue Sky 101
I'm Just Another One In Love With You	Mello-Tones	1954	Decca 48319
I'm Just Looking For Love	Relatives	1963	Almont 306
I'm Just Your Clown	Twilights, Teddy & the	1962	Swan 4126
I'm Knockin' Love	Modernistics, Little E & Al & the	1961	Falco 304
I'm Laughing At You	Gardenias	1958	Hi-Q 5005
I'm Learning	Midnighters, Hank Ballard & the	1963	King 5821
I'm Leaving	Blue Flames, Buddy Love & the	1958	Thunder 1A
I'm Leaving Baby	Chimes (Los Angeles - Specialty)	1955	Specialty 549 (unreleased)
I'm Leaving Home	Velvatones (with Li'l Walter's Band)	1959	Nu Kat 110
I'm Leaving It All Up To You	Heartbreakers (Bronx, N.Y.)	1962	Brent 7037
I'm Leaving It All Up To You	Specials	1963	Marc 103
I'm Leaving You	Francettes	1963	Wolfie 104
I'm Living My Life For You	Carterays, Gloria Mann & the	1954	Sound 102
I'm Living OK	Robins	1950	Savoy 752
I'm Lonely	Baby Dolls	1961	Maske 103
I'm Lonely	Careless Five	1962	Careful 1010
I'm Lonely	Del-Airs	1962	Arrawak 1003
I'm Lonely	Dominoes	1952	Federal 12106
I'm Lonely	Hollywood Playboys	1961	Rita 118
I'm Lonely	Landis, Jerry & group	1961	Canadian American 130
I'm Lonely	Nitelites, Nickie & the	1959	Brunswick 55155
I'm Lonely	Shakers, Buddy Sharpe & the	NA	Rumble
I'm Lonely	Triumphs, Tico & the	1961	
I'm Lonely Tonight	McPhatter, Clyde & female group	1956	Atlantic 1106
I'm Lonesome For You	Escos	1959	Esta 100
I'm Lookin' Around	Danleers	1961	Everest 19412
I'm Looking For A Job	Cadets, Bennie Bunn & the	1960	Sherwood 211
I'm Looking For A Lover	Bell-Aires	1955	Ruby 103
I'm Looking Through Your Window	Cooper, Dolly & group	1956	Dot 15495
I'm Losing My Grip	Rivingtons	1963	Liberty 55553
I'm Losing My Mind	Dreams	1954	Savoy 1140

SONG	GROUP	YEAR	LABEL
I'm Losing My Mind Over You	Motley, Frank	1954	Gem 218
I'm Losing Something I Never had	Orioles, Sonny Til & the	1948	Jubilee (unreleased)
I'm Lost	Bachelors, Dean Barlow & the	1955	Excel 106
I'm Lost	Mello-Moods	1953	Prestige 856/Hamilton 143
I'm Lost Without You	Knight, Sonny & group	1959	Eastman 791
I'm Loving You, You're Leaving Me	Motivations	1973	Eastbound 604
I'm Movin'	Vanguards	1958	Ivy 103
I'm Movin' On	Duprees, Willis Sanders & the	1961	Regatta 2000
I'm My Baby's Sitter	Four Tops	1956	Chess (unreleased)
I'm No Fool Anymore	Flamingos	1962	End 1111
I'm No Longer Jimmy's Girl	Teenettes, Betty Jayne & the	1961	Carellen 107
I'm No Runaround	Snaps, Ginger Davis & the	1962	Swan 4090
I'm Nobody's	Turbans (Philadelphia)	1956	Herald 478
I'm Nobody's Baby Now	Delrons, Reperata & the	1965	RCA 8820
I'm Not A Deceiver	Mellow Keys	1956	Gee 1014
I'm Not A Juvenile Delinquent	Revivals	1987	Avenue D 14
I'm Not A Juvenile Delinquent	Teenagers, Frankie Lymon & the	1956	Gee 1026
I'm Not A Kid Anymore	Beechwoods	1963	Smash 1843
I'm Not A Know It All	Four Sevilles	1980	Starlight 8
I'm Not A Know It All	Heartspinners, Dino & the	1973	Bim Bam Boom 119
I'm Not A Know It All	Pictures, C.L. & the	1964	Kirk 635
I'm Not A Know It All	Teenagers, Frankie Lymon & the	1956	Gee 1012
I'm Not A Know-It-All	Bi-Langos, Donny & the	NA	Colton 101
I'm Not Afraid	Relf, Bobby (with the Laurels)	1956	Dot 15510
I'm Not Ashamed	Concords, Pearl Reeves & the	1955	Harlem 2332
I'm Not Ashamed	Henry, Stacy (with the Dream-Timers)	1961	Flippin' 108
I'm Not Ashamed	Hollidays	1958	Prep 136
I'm Not Ashamed	Imperials, Stacy Henry & the	1961	Flippin' 108
I'm Not Ashamed	Poor Boys, King Richard & the	1961	Apollo 1201
I'm Not Ashamed	Three Pals, Roc La Rue & the	1957	Rama 226
I'm Not Ashamed	Wanderers	1959	Cub 9035
I'm Not Ashamed (Ugly Woman)	Concords, Pearl Reaves & the	1955	Harlem 2332
I'm Not Crying Anymore	Cordials	1962	Bethlehem 3019
I'm Not Falling In Love With You	Robins	1950	Regent 1016
I'm Not Free	Belvin, Jesse & group	1957	Modern 1020
I'm Not Going Steady	Rockaways, Ken Darrell & the	1957	Epic 9226
I'm Not Gonna Cry	Fabulous Twilights, Nathaniel Mayer & the	1963	Fortune 554
I'm Not In Love With You	Delltones (& the Kelly Owens Orchestra)	1954	Rainbow 244
I'm Not In Love With You	Demens	1957	Teenage 1007
I'm Not Jimmy	Fleetwoods	1964	Dolton 307
I'm Not Kidding You	El Domingoes	1958	Kappa Rex 206/Candlelite 418 (74)
I'm Not Like I Used To Be	Dixie-Aires	1954	Harlem
I'm Not Pretending	Hi-Notes, Tommy Frederick & the	1958	Carlton 450
I'm Not Ready	Street Corner Symphony	1975	Bang 719
I'm Not Sure	Debs, Ty Robin & the	1960	Rex 1010
I'm Not The Kind Of Guy	Fairlanes	1962	Minaret 103
I'm Not The Kind Of Guy	Wrens	1991	Classic Artists 131
I'm Not The One For You	Dee, Sonny & group	1961	Kapp 421
I'm Not The Same One You Love	Crickets, Dean Barlow & the	1953, 1963	Jay-Dee 781/Beacon 555
I'm Not Too Young To Dream	Teenagers, Frankie Lymon & the	1959	Gee 1052
I'm Not Too Young Too Fall In Love	Teenchords, Lewis Lymon & the	1957	Fury 1006
I'm Not Wanted	Sheppards (Chicago - Constellation)	1964, 1969	Constellation LP 4/Collectables LP 5078/Bunky 7766
I'm Not Worthy Of You	McPhatter, Clyde & female group	1955	Atlantic 1081
I'm Not You Fool Anymore	Peek, Paul & group	1958	NRC 008
I'm Not Your Fool Anymore	Spriggs, Walter & the Five Echoes	1955	Blue Lake 109
I'm Not Your Fool Anymore	Turbans (Philadelphia)	1961	Roulette 4326
I'm On A Holiday	Hall, Betty & group	1962	Ember 1096
I'm On Fire	Spades	1959	Major 1007
I'm On My Merry Way	Blue Notes, Joe Weaver & his	1955	Fortune 820
I'm On My Merry Way	Don Juans	1956	Fortune 831
I'm On My Way	Boppers, Alonzo & the	1963	Rojac 8127
I'm On My Way	Sanders, Bobby (with the Performers)	1961	Kaybo 618
I'm On My Way	Toughtones, Bobby Sanders & the	1961	Kaybo 60618
I'm On My Way To Love	Four Epics	1962	Heritage 109

SONG	GROUP	YEAR	LABEL
I'm On The Outside	Saints	1988	Clifton 81
I'm On The Outside (Looking In)	Imperials, Little Anthony & the	1964	DCP 1104/Veep 1240 (66)
I'm On The Outside Looking In	Sidewinders, Jim Harris & the	1966	Fabar 15564
I'm On To You Girl	Shantons, Skip Jackson & the	1969	Dot-Mar 324
I'm Only A Boy	Three Friends	1956	Lido 502
I'm Only A Fool	Belvin, Jesse & group	1955	Money 208
I'm Only Fooling My Heart	Heartbreakers (Washington, D.C.)	1951	RCA 4508
I'm Only Making It Easier For You	Candies	1962	Ember 1092
I'm Only Trying	Moonglows	1976	Robin Hood 143
I'm Out To Getcha	Harris, Thurston (with the Sharps)	1958	Aladdin 3415
I'm Past Sixteen	Four Fellows (with Bette McLaurin)	1956	Glory 241
I'm Pleadin'	Corvets	1961	Sure 1003
I'm Reachin'	Little Caesar & group	1958	RCA 7270
I'm Ready	Boss Men	1964	Score 1003
I'm Ready	Collegians	1962	Post 10002
I'm Ready	Midnighters, Hank Ballard & the	1965	King 6031
I'm Ready	Raytones, Rudy Ray Moore & the	1958	Cash 1060
I'm Really Crying	Nobletones	1958	C&M 188/C&M 438
I'm Really In Love	Dee Jays	1954	After Hours 102
I'm Really In Love	Resonics	1964	Lucky Token 108
I'm Really Too Young	Nobletones	1958	C&M 183/Times Square 17 (63)/ Relic 529 (65)
I'm Rollin'	Victorians	1956	Saxony 103
I'm Sad	Ermines	1956	Loma 705
I'm Satisfied With Rock 'N' Roll	Concords (Brooklyn)	1956	Ember 1007
I'm Saying Goodbye	Angels (Hi Tensions)	1960	Audio 203/Milestone
I'm Searchin'·	Generals, Mickey Farrell & the	1960	Tammy 1009
I'm Searching	Masters	1958	Le Sage 713/714
I'm Searching	Spiders	1954	Imperial 5291
I'm Seeking Revenge	Cap-Tans	1974	Roadhouse 1023
I'm Selling My Heart	Knight, Bob	1962	Taurus 356
I'm Sending S.O.S.	Avons	1956	Hull 717
I'm Serious	Stardusters, Bobby Chandler & His	1956	O.J. 1000
I'm Shook	Tyrones	1958	Decca 30643
I'm Sittin' On Top Of The World	Dell Vikings	1957	Mercury EP 3362
I'm Sixteen Years	Sentimentals, Ann Nichols & the	1958	Tuxedo 926
I'm Slippin' In	Spiders	1954	Imperial 5291
I'm So Afraid	Passions	NA	Topaz 1317
I'm So All Alone	Fabulous Flames	1961	Bay-Tone 105
I'm So All Alone	Marylanders	NA	Unreleased
I'm So All Alone	Mello-Chords	NA	Palm 5000
I'm So Alone	Marco & group	1963	Mohawk 135
I'm So Alone	Professionals, Tommy Vann & the	1969	Congress 6001
I'm So Ashamed	Barrons	NA	Guest Star LP 1481
I'm So Ashamed	Crescendos (Scarlet)	1961	Scarlet 4009
I'm So Blue	Champions	1958	Ace 541 (duplicate # IS correct!)
I'm So Blue	Chestnuts	NA	Night Train 906
I'm So Crazy For Love	Blenders (New York)	1950	Decca 48183
I'm So Crazy For Love	Cap-Tans	1950, 1953	Dot 15114
I'm So Crazy For Love	Ravens	1950	Columbia 39050
I'm So Down Hearted	Savoys, Sonny Brooks & the	1956	Tip Top 1008
I'm So Glad	Bell, Johnny & group	1959	Fleetwood 1001
I'm So Glad	Continentals, Bill Harris & the	1958	Eagle 1002
I'm So Glad	Impacts	1966	Brunswick 55393
I'm So Glad	Rayber Voices, Herman Griffin & the	NA	H.O.B. 112
I'm So Glad	Twinettes	1958	Vee Jay 284
I'm So Glad I Learned To Do The Cha Cha Cha	Griffin, Herman & group	1959	House Of Beauty 112
I'm So Glad You Love Me	Five Joys, Juanita Rogers & Lynn Hollings & Mr. J's	1961	Pink Clouds 333
I'm So Glad You're Mine	Hamilton, Willie & group	1960	Contour 500
I'm So Happy	Five Bell Aires, Henry Hall & the	1990	Relic LP 5085
I'm So Happy	Pretenders	1961	Power-Martin 1001/Relic 1004 (65)
I'm So Happy	Teen Tones	1961	Tri Disc 102
I'm So Happy (Tra La La)	Ducanes	1961	Goldisc 3024

SONG	GROUP	YEAR	LABEL
I'm So Happy (Tra-La-La-La)	Teenchords, Lewis Lymon & the	1957	Fury 1000
I'm So Helpless	Four Bars, Shane Hunter & the	1959	IPS 101
I'm So High	Five Keys	1953	Aladdin 3204
I'm So In Love	Daychords, Roxy & the	1962, 1977	Don-El 116/Candlelite 430 (74)
I'm So In Love	Infascinations	1961	Clauwell 003/004
I'm So In Love	Moonrays, Lee Williams & the	1960	King 5409
I'm So In Love	Street-Tones, Patty & the	1979	Clifton 37
I'm So In Love With You	Blue Chips	1959	Wren 302
I'm So In Love With You	Dew Drops, Henry Clement & the	1961	Zynn 503
I'm So In Love With You	Heptones	1956	Abco 105
I'm So In Love With You	Passionettes	1958	Unreleased
I'm So Jealous	Hi Lites	1965	Daran 222
I'm So Lonely	Adrian, Lee (with the Chaperones)	1959	Richcraft 5006/SMC 1385 (62)
I'm So Lonely	Denhams	1957	Note 10009
I'm So Lonely	Fullylove, Leroy & group	1961	Tandem 7002
I'm So Lonely	Goldtones	1961	YRS 1001
I'm So Lonely	Hi-Fis	1959	Montel 1005
I'm So Lonely	Kids From Texas	1958	Hanover 4500
I'm So Lonely	Kings & Queens	1957	Everlast 5003
I'm So Lonely	Lavenders, Ernie Morales & the	1977	Crystal Ball 100
I'm So Lonely	Phaetons	1963	Sahara 102
I'm So Lonely	Regals	1955	Atlantic 1062
I'm So Lonely	Regents	1961	Cousins 1002/Gee 1065 (61)
I'm So Lonely Over You	Beginners	1964	Dot 16629
I'm So Lonely (What Can I Do?)	Limelites, Shep & the	1960	Apt 25046
I'm So Mad	Little Jerry & group	1960	Aldo 502
I'm So Mad	Midnighters, Hank Ballard & the	1964	King 5860
I'm So Proud	Hi-Tides, Mike Harris & the	1963	Krimmie 24
I'm So Satisfied	Hunter, Herbert & group	1961	Poncello 711
I'm So Sorry	Impollos, Johnny Inman & the	1958	Aladdin 3426
I'm So Sorry (It's Ending With You)	Viceroys	1961	Little Star 107/Smash 1716 (61)
I'm So Tired	Catalinas	1973	Jayne 175
I'm So Tired	Headliners, George Goodman & the	1965	Val 6/1000/Warner Bros. 5632 (65)/ A&M 1011 (68)
I'm So Unhappy	Uniques	1960	Bliss 1004/Gone 5113 (61)/ Pride 4/1018
I'm So Used To You Now	Ermines	1956	Loma 703
I'm So Weak	Del Amos	1959	Nikko 703
I'm So Young	Gray, Maureen & group	1961	Chancellor 1100
I'm So Young	Saints	1988	Clifton 81
I'm So Young	Starlets	1960	Lute 5909
I'm So Young	Students (Ohio)	1958	Note 10012/Argo 5386 (61)/ Checker 902 (61)
I'm So Young	Tren-Dells	1961	Tilt 779
I'm So Young (acappella)	Heartaches, Jo Ann & the	1966	Catamount 114
I'm So Young (acappella)	Majestics, Little Joe & the	1975	Relic LP 104
I'm Sold	Four Intruders	1961	Gowen 1401
I'm Sold	Plurals	1959	Wanger 188
I'm Some Kind Of Wonderful	Four Of Us	1961	Adore 902/Bruce
I'm Sorry	Carnations	1959	Checker 914
I'm Sorry	Carroll, Eddie & group	1962	Santo 504
I'm Sorry	Chevelles	1964	Infinity 029
I'm Sorry	Danleers	1964	Lemans 008
I'm Sorry	Love Notes (Massachusetts)	1954	Riviera 970/Rainbow 266 (54)
I'm Sorry	Martin, Kenny & group	1958	Federal 12330
I'm Sorry	Pictures, C.L. & the	1963	Dunes 2023
I'm Sorry	Platters	1957	Mercury 71032
I'm Sorry	Pledges	1959	Hamilton 50028
I'm Sorry	Trells	NA	Port City 1112
I'm Sorry	Five C's	NA	Standord (unreleased)
I'm Sorry (acappella)	Canaries	1964	Dimension 1047
I'm Sorry Baby	Cineramas	1960	Rhapsody 71963/71964/ Candlelite 433
I'm Sorry, Baby			
I'm Sorry Baby (I Didn't Mean To Do You Wrong)	Superiors	1961	Federal 12436

SONG	GROUP	YEAR	LABEL
I'm Sorry (I Did You Wrong)	Royal Holidays	1958	Penthouse 9357/Carlton 472 (58)
I'm Sorry I Made You Cry	Bay City 5, Luigi Martini & the	1954	Jaguar 3002
I'm Sorry Now	Shields	1958	Tender 518/Dot 15856 (58)
I'm Sorry Now	Tempters	1956	Empire 105
I'm Sorry Now	Youngsters	1956	Empire 109
I'm Sorry Pillow	Hearts, Lee Andrews & the (as Lee Andrews)	1962	Parkway 860/Parkway 5213/ 5214 (63)
I'm Sorry You're Gone	Channels, Earl Lewis & the	1978	King Tut 174
I'm Spinning	Dell Vikings	1957, 1973	Fee Bee 218/Dot 15636/Mercury 71198/Bim Bam Boom 115
I'm Standing In The Shadows	Five Royales	1963	Todd 1086
I'm Stepping Out Of The Picture	Crests	1965	Scepter 12112
I'm Stepping Out Tonight	Bobbettes	1962	King 5623
I'm Stepping Out With My Memories	Vals	1964	Ascot 2163
I'm Still Alone	Jokers	1962	Viking 1009
I'm Still Dancin'	Shepherd Sisters	1961	United Artists 350
I'm Still Dancing	Imperials, Little Anthony & the	1963	Capitol 4924
I'm Still In Love With You	Bel-Aires, Eddy Bell & the	1961	Lucky Four 1012
I'm Still In Love With You	Berry, Richard (with the Flairs)	1953	Flair 1016
I'm Still In Love With You	Chapelaires	1961	Hac 101
I'm Still In Love With You	Imperials, Little Anthony & the	1959	End 1060
I'm Still In Love With You	Rockin' R's, Ron Volz & the	1959	Tempus 1515/Vee Jay 334 (59)
I'm Still In Love With You	Saunders, Jay & group	1956	Club 1012
I'm Still In Love With You	Showmen, Carl Frost & the	1963	Lawn 223
I'm Still Lonely	Hall Brothers	1962	Four Star 1760
I'm Still Loving You	Frontiers	1963	Philips 40148
I'm Still Waiting	Blue Belles, Patti LaBelle & the	1966	Atlantic 2347
I'm Stuck	Five Jets	1954	DeLuxe 6053
I'm Stuck On You	Poets	1964	Red Bird 046
I'm Taking A Vacation From Love	Imperials, Little Anthony & the	1960	End 1074
I'm Talking About You	Fortune, Johnny (with the Paramours)	1963	Park Ave. 4905
I'm Talking About You	Paramours, Johnny Fortune & the	1964	Park Ave 4905
I'm Telling It Like It Is	Miller Sisters	1967	GMC 10006
I'm Telling You Baby	Robins	19??	
I'm Thankful	Timbers, Ronnie Martin & the	1956	Pilgrim 721
I'm The Child	Twilighters, Buddy Milton & the	1954	RPM 419
I'm The Girl	Chantels	1961	End 1105
I'm The Guy	Yeomans	1964	Heidi 113
I'm The Jivin' Mr. Lee	Martin, Kenny & group	1958	Federal 12310
I'm The Little Fooler	Knight, Marie & group	1957	Mercury 71055
I'm The Man	Dynamics	1963	Big Top 3161
I'm The One	Deccors, Marie & the	1962	Cub 9115
I'm The One	Trilons	1961	Tag 449
I'm The Playboy	Pyramids (Detroit)	1962	Cub 9112
I'm The Richest One Of All	Fay, Flo & group	1963	Lawn 206
I'm Thinking Of You	Midnighters, Hank Ballard & the	1960	King 5430
I'm Through	Robins	1950	Savoy 762
I'm Through Crying	Carter, Martha & group	1961	Ron 336
I'm Through With Love	Belmonts, Dion & the	1960	Laurie LP 2006
I'm Thru With You	Dreamlovers	1963	Columbia 42842
I'm Tired	Elegant IV	1965	Mercury 72516
I'm Tired	Ohio Untouchables	1962	Lu Pine 1011/Lu Pine 116/117 (64)
I'm Touched	Ascots	1962	Ace 650
I'm Traveling Light	Five Lyrics	1956	Music City 799
I'm Troubled	Four Interns	1955	Federal 12239
I'm Trying (To Make You Love Me)	Rollettes	1960	Melker 103
I'm Twisted	Cupcakes, Cookie & the	1963	Lyric 1003/Paula 221 (65)
I'm Waitin'	Richards, Lee & group	1959	Wanger 193
I'm Waiting For Ships	Aristocrats	1954	Essex 366
I'm Waiting In Green Pastures	Wanderers	1959	Cub 9054
I'm Waiting Just For You	Charms, Otis Williams & his	1957	DeLuxe 6115
I'm Walkin' (Into The Crowd)	Four-Evers	1965	Constellation 151
I'm Walkin' Proud	Valrays	1967	United Artists 50145
I'm Walking Behind You	Dominoes	1965	Ro-Zan 10001
I'm Wanderin'	Five Jets	1957	Fortune 833

SONG	GROUP	YEAR	LABEL
I'm Warning You	Classmen	1963	CM 8464
I'm Watching A Wedding	Gordan, Joni & group	1964	Musicnote 125
I'm Willing	Cadillacs, Bobby Ray & the	1961	Mercury 71738
I'm Willing	Quintones (Gee)	1956	Gee 1009
I'm With You	Five Royales	1960	King 5329
I'm With You	Tabs	1963	Wand 139
I'm With You All The Way	Moniques	1963	Centaur 105
I'm Without A Girl Friend	Gallahads	1960	Del-Fi 4148
I'm Wondering	Clefs	1954	Peacock (unreleased)
I'm Worried	Kittens	1963	Chestnut 203
I'm Wrong	Golden Tones	1955	Samson 107/108
I'm Young	Midnighters, Hank Ballard & the	1962	King 5635
I'm Young	Teardrops, Billy Taylor & the	1959	Felco 101
I'm Your Baby	Del-Airs	1964	Coral 62419
I'm Your Fool	Berry, Richard & group	1961	K&G 1004
I'm Your Fool	Veltones	1959	Jin 115
I'm Your Fool, Always	Sentimentals	1958	Mint 803
I'm Your Fool Always	Sentimentals, Sylvester Jackson & the	NA	Playfare 601
I'm Your Hoochie Coochie Man	DiMucci, Dion	1969	Warner Bros.
I'm Your Hoochie Coochie Man	DiMucci, Dion (with the Del Satins)	1964	Columbia 42977
I'm Your Lover Man	Kingsmen	1957	Allstar 500/East West 115 (58)/ East West 120 (58)
I'm Your Man	Hollywood Saxons	1961	Swingin' 651/Elf 103 (61)
I'm Your Slave	Fiestas	1959	Old Town 1067
I'm Your Soldier Boy	Soldier Boys	1962	Scepter 1230
I'm Yours	Attractions, J.R. & the	1965	Hunch 928
I'm Yours	Clippers, Johnny Blake & the	1957	Gee 1027
I'm Yours	Duprees	1964	Coed 596
I'm Yours	Flamingos	1955	Parrot 812
I'm Yours	Four Bars, Betty Wilson & the	1962	Dayco 1631
I'm Yours	Four Buddies	1951	Savoy 809 (unreleased)
I'm Yours	Mellows, Lillian Leach & the	1956	Celeste 3004
I'm Yours	Playboys, Caleb & the	1963	Olimpic 4575
I'm Yours	Rand, Johnny & group	1965	Keno 928
I'm Yours Anyhow	Tenderfoots	1955	Federal 12225
I'm Yours As Long As I Live	Vice-Roys	1955	Aladdin 3273
I'm Yours Forever	Perry, Tony & group	1957	Ember 1015
I'm Yours 'Til The End	Perennials	1963	Ball 1016
Image Of A Girl	Charms, Otis Williams & the	1960	King 5372
Image Of A Girl	Safaris	1960	Eldo 101
Image Of A Girl (acappella)	Apparitions	1975	Relic LP 108
Image Of Love	Glens	1962	Ro-Nan 1002
Image Of Love	Tridels	1964	San-Dee 1009
Imagination	Quotations	1961, 1973	Verve 10245/Relic 1025
Imagination	Windsong	NA	
Imagine	Capris (New York)	1982	Ambient Sound LP FZ-37714
Imaginez Vous	Curls	1959	Everest 19319
Ima-Lika-You (Pizza Pie)	Holidays	1953	King 1217
Immortal Love	Platters	1961	Mercury 71791
Impala	Jades, Chris Newton & the	1961	Mikesell 134
Imperial Gents Stomp, The	Imperial Gents	1970	Laurie 3540
Impossible	Velvatones	1961	Candlelite 412
Impossible	Velvatones (with Li'l Walter's Band)	1959	Nu Kat 110
Impressions	Starlets, Danetta & the	1962	Okeh 7155
Imprison Me Baby	Four Kings, Ben & the	1961	Revival 635
In A Dream	Paramounts	1963	Ember 1099
In A Fairy Tale	Elements Of Life	1981	Starlight 14
In A Letter To Me	Castells	1967	Solomon 1351
In A Little Inn In Italy	Bachelors, Dean Barlow & the	1955	Excel 105
In A Little Spanish Town	Platters	1963	Mercury LP 20759/ Mercury LP 60759 (63)
In A Real Big Way	Berry, Richard & group	1961	K&G 1004
In A Round About Way	Techniques	1957	Stars 551/Roulette 4030 (57)
In Bermuda	Goodies	1959	Chess 1731
In Between	Capri Sisters	1959	Hanover 4531

SONG	GROUP	YEAR	LABEL
In Between Kisses	Sweethearts	1963	Brunswick 55237
In Between Tears	Equallos	1955	M&M/Romantic Rhythm (55)
In Between Tears	Four Sevilles	1980	Starlight 12
In Between Tears	Gods	1975	Romantic Rhythm 102
In Between (Wishing I Was Sweet Sixteen)	Baby Dolls (Rosie's)	1961	Fargo 1017
In Case I Forget	Limelites, Shep & the	1965	Hull 772
In Desperation	Inspirations, Benny Bunn & the	1959	Eastmen 790
In Each Corner Of My Heart	Nitecaps	1956	Groove 0176
In Everyone's Life	Five Degrees	NA	
In Exchange For Your Love	Tigers, Little Julian Herrera & the	1956	Dig 118
In Love	Dolls	1959	Okeh 7122
In Love	Moonglows	1955	Chess 1605
In Love In Vain	Voicemasters	1960	Frisco 15235
In Memory Of Our Love	Blends, Glenn Wells & the	1960	Jin 139
In My Arms To Stay	Channels	1963, 1973	Hit Record 700/Channel 1004
In My Diary	Infernos	1981	
In My Diary	Maskmen & Agents	1961	
In My Diary	Moonglows	1955, 1964	Chess 1611/Lana132
In My Dream	Chorals	1956	Decca 29914
In My Dreams	Castros	1959	Lasso 502
In My Dreams	Robins	1958	Whippet 211
In My Dreams	Sporttones	1959	Munich 101
In My Dreams	Tempo-Tones	1957	Acme 715
In My Faithful Heart	Mystics	1965	Unreleased
In My Heart	Browns, Barbara & the	1964	Stax 158
In My Heart	Ravens, Rico & the	1965	Rally 1601/Autumn 6 (65)
In My Heart	Rebels	1959	Kings-X 3362
In My Heart	Time-Tones	1961	Times Square 421 (second pressing)
In My Heart	Volumes, Jimmie Lewis & the	1958	Ivy 104
In My Heart You'll Always Remain	Universals (V-Tone)	1962	V-Tone 236
In My Land Of Dreams	Casanovas	1962	Planet 1027
In My Letter To You	Lyrics, Ike Perry & the	1963	Mama 1/2/Mama 1074 (63)
In My Lonely Room	Embers	1964	JCP 1008
In My Lonely Room	Four Haven Knights	1956	Atlas 1066/Josie 824 (57)/ Angletone 1066 (75)
In My Lonely Room	Larks (North Carolina)	1952	Apollo 1190
In My Memories	Satins, Sunny & the	1978	Crystal Ball 122
In My Tenement	Lovers	1965	Agon 1011
In My Thunderbird	Thunderbirds	1957	Holiday 2609
In My Younger Days	Admirations (featuring Joseph Lorello)	1974	Kelway 108
In My Younger Days	Monarchs	1956	Neil 101/Melba 101 (56)
In My Younger Days	Time Spinners, Nick & the	1974	Kelway 109
In Other Words	Belmonts, Dion & the	1960	Laurie LP 2006
In Over My Head	El Dorados	1970	Torrid 100
In Paradise	Bobbettes	1964	Diamond 166
In Paradise	Charms, Otis Williams & his	1956, 1959	DeLuxe 6093/6186
In Paradise	Cookies	1956	Atlantic 1084/Atlantic 2079 (60)
In Self Defense	Beau Brummels	1956	Vik 0208
In Self Defense	Flairs, Cornel Gunter & the	1956	ABC 9698
In Spite Of Everything You Do	Striders, Savannah Churchill & the	1951	RCA 4448
In That Order	Troopers, George Powell & the	1959	Lummtone 101
In The Arms Of A Girl	Christie, Charles (with the Crystals)	1966	HBR 473
In The Beginning	Innocents	1961	Indigo 116
In The Beginning (I May Be Wrong)	Illusions	1964	Laurie 3245
In The Chapel	Corvettes	1961	Sheraton 201
In The Chapel	Suburbans, Ann Cole & the	1956	Baton 232
In The Chapel In The Moonlight	Fabulous Earthquakes	1960	Meridian 1518
In The Chapel In The Moonlight	Fabulous Four	1960	Chancellor 1062
In The Chapel In The Moonlight	Glenns	1960	Rendezvous 118
In The Chapel In The Moonlight	Kestrels	1960	Laurie 3053
In The Chapel In The Moonlight	Orioles, Sonny Til & the	1954, 1962	Jubilee 5154/Charlie Parker 212
In The Chapel In The Moonlight	Ping Pongs	1960	Cub 9062
In The Chapel In The Moonlight	Storm, Billy (with the Storms)	1960	Atlantic 2076
In The Cool Of The Evening	Five Blue Flames, Chris Powell & the	1951	Columbia 39407

SONG	GROUP	YEAR	LABEL
In The Dark	Hollywood Flames	1959	Ebb 163
In The Deep	Crystals (Brooklyn)	1959	Specialty 657
In The Depths Of My Soul	Chevrons	1968	Independence 94
In The Dim Light Of The Dark	Shells	1961	Johnson 110
In The Doorway Crying	Midnighters	1957	Federal 12293
In The Doorway Crying	Quintones, Pat Foster & the	1960	Lee 1114
In The Evening	Darlings	1959	Penguin 0698
In The Evening	Keynotes	1956	Apollo 503
In The Garden Of Love	Versatiles, Dee Thomas & the	1960	Coaster 800
In The Halo Of Your Love	Marquees	1960	Do-Ra-Mi 1407
In The Jungle	Mystics, Ed Gates & the	1962	Robins Nest 2
In The Land Of Make Believe	Drifters (1959-forward)	1964	Atlantic 2216
In The Light Of The Dark	Shells	1977	Clifton 22
In The Little Chapel	Elites	1959	Abel 225
In The Meantime	Juniors, Danny & the	1958	ABC 9926
In The Middle Of Love	Cronies, Herb & the	1960	Personality 700
In The Middle Of The Night	Metallics, J. D. Wright & the	1962	Baronet 16
In The Middle Of The Night	Moonglows	1958	Chess 1689
In The Middle Of The Night	Vibes	1987	Relic LP 8011
In The Midst Of The Night	Paragons	1961	Tap 503
In The Mission Of St. Augustine	Buccaneers	1953	Rama 24
In The Mission Of St. Augustine	Orioles, Sonny Til & the	1953	Jubilee 5127
In The Moonlight	Four Troys	1959	Freedom 44013
In The Morning	Quats	1958	
In The Morning	Swans (St. Louis)	1956	Steamboat 101
In The Morning Time	Clovers	1955	Atlantic 1060
In The Night	Bitter Sweets	1967	Original Sound 70
In The Night	Fortunes	1959	Top Rank 2019
In The Night	Hi-Liters (with King Bassie & the Three Aces)	1958	Hico 2432
In The Night	Quotations	1964	Admiral 753
In The Night	Spydells	1963	Beltone 2032
In The Palm Of My Hand	Swallows (Maryland)	NA	Federal (unreleased)
In The Park	Rebels	1959	Kings-X 3362
In The Pines	Travelers	1963	Gass 1000
In The Rain	Charmers	1954	Central 1006
In The Rain	Debonaires (Tobin)	NA	Tobin 340
In The Rain	Four Fellows (Brooklyn - Glory)	1955	Glory 236
In The Rain	Joylarks	1959	Snag 107/Candlelite 426
In The Still Of The Night	Baker's Satins	1984	Clifton 74
In The Still Of The Night	Belmonts, Dion & the	1960	Laurie 3059
In The Still Of The Night	Dell Vikings	1973	Luniverse 113
In The Still Of The Night	Evergreens, Eddie & the (see Sha Na Na)	1973	Kama Sutra 578
In The Still Of The Night	Flamingos	1960	End LP 308
In The Still Of The Night	Jays, Kelly Troy & the	NA	Harvey
In The Still Of The Night	Marcels	1973	Queen Bee 47001
In The Still Of The Night	Moonglows	1973	Relic 1024
In The Still Of The Night	Persuasions, Donna & the	1973	Blue Sky 103
In The Still Of The Night	Reflections	1962	Tigre 602
In the Still Of The Night	Safaris	1960	Eldo 110
In The Still Of The Night	Teen Kings	NA	Relic LP 5033
In The Still Of The Night	Three Chuckles	1956	Vik LP 1067
In The Still Of The Night 67	Five Satins	1967	Mama Sadie 1001
In The Still Of The Night 67	Restless Hearts, Fred Parris & the	1967	Mama Sadie 1001
In The Still Of The Night, (I'll Remember)	Five Satins	1956	Standord 200/Ember 1005
In The Still Of The Nite	Fender, Freddy & group	1964	Norco 108
In The Still Of The Nite (acappella)	Five Jades (Bronx, N.Y.)	1975	Relic LP 107
In The Storm	Sensationals, Jimmy Jones & the	1962	Savoy 4174
In The Summer	Three Honeydrops	1957	Music City 813
In The Sun	Blue Angels	1959	Palette 5038
In The Valley Of The Roses	Darnels, Gus Gordon & the	1957	Bana 525
In The Wee Small Hours Of The Morning	Explorers	1960	Coral 62175/Coral 65575 (63)
In The Woods	Chords	1953	Gem 211
In This Whole World	Centuries	1961	Life 501
In This Whole World	Velvetones	NA	Vanda 0001

SONG	GROUP	YEAR	LABEL
In This World	Four Couquettes	1961	Capitol 4534
In Time For The Blues	Falcons (Big Wheel)	1967	Big Wheel 1971
In Times Like These	Fantastics	1961	Impresario 124
In Togetherness	Del Chords	1962	Midas 09
In You Baby, In You Baby	Simmons, Little Maxine & group	NA	Varbee 117
In Your Dreams	Strollers	1957	States 163
In Your Heart	Dontells	1965	Vee Jay 666
Incidentally	Lover Boy & group	1963	Crystalette 758
Indebted To You	Melo-Aires	1958	Nasco 6019
Indian Bop Hop	Arrows	1958	Flash 132
Indian Fever	Scarlets	1955	Red Robin 138
Indian Girl	Capris (New York)	1958	Planet 1010/1011/ Old Town 1094 (60)/Lost Nite 101 (60)/Trommers 101 (60)
Indian Giver	Chantels	1966	Verve 10435
Indian Jane	Inspirations (Philadelphia)	1958	Lamp 2019
Indian Joe	Dapps, Johnnie Mae Matthews & the	1960	Northern 3727
Indian Love Call	Minor Chords, Sunnie Elmo & the	1960	Flick 009
Indiana Style	Highlights	1958	Bally 1044
Indiff'rent	Platters	1958	Mercury 71246
Inexperience	Dreams	1962	Smash 1748
Infatuation	Twiliters	1961	Flippin' 106
Initials	Castells	1963	Era 3102
Ink Dries Quicker Than Tears	Volumes	1963	Times Square 22
In-Laws	Vels	1963	Amy 881
Insha Allah	Knight, Sonny & group	1957	Dot 15597
Instant Love	Fabulous Dinos	1964	Saber 1009
Insurance	Leeds, Randy & group	1959	Roulette 4153
Intermission	Lee, Jimmy & group	1958	Apollo 525
International Twist, The	Cordials	1962	Reveille 106
Interview, The	Quarter Notes	1958	RCA 7327
Into The Shadows	Ravens	1959	Top Rank 2003
Invisible Thing, The	Casual Three	1956	Luniverse 109
Invitation, The	Fidelitys	1959	Sir 271
Invitation To A Party	Dimples	1959	Dore 517
Ipsy Opsie Ooh	Flairs, Shirley Gunter & the	1955	Flair 1076
Irene	Holidays	1954	Specialty 533
Irene My Darling	Feathers, Johnny Staton & the	1989	Classic Artists 109
Irresistible	Angels (New Jersey)	1963	Ascot 2139
Irresistible You	Fireflies	1962	Taurus LP 1002
Is A Man Really Worth It	Rubies	1964	Enith International 720
Is Everybody Happy (acappella)	Chessmen	1975	Relic LP 102/Relic LP 106 (75)
Is Everybody Happy (acappella)	Meadowbrooks	1965	Catamount 108
Is It A Dream	Baker, Bill (with the Del Satins)	1961	Audicon 115
Is It A Dream?	Premiers (New York)	1957	Gone 5009
Is It A Dream?	Vocaleers	1952	Red Robin 114
Is It A Sin	Oro, Emmy & group	1962	Chelsea 1005
Is It All Gone?	Magicians	1966	Villa 704
Is It All Over	Townsmen (New York - Herald)	1963	Herald 585
Is It Any Wonder	Dell Vikings	1957	Mercury LP 20314/ Mercury EP 3363 (57)
Is It Because	Baxter, Ronnie (with the Chantels)	1959	Gone 5050
Is It Fair	Milner, Jimmy & group	1959	Ember 1052
Is It Just A Game	Fads, Buddy & the	1958	Morocco 1001
Is It Love	Firestone, Johnny & group	1958, 1985	Elmont 1003/D&M 001
Is It Me	Royal Boys	1961	
Is It Real	Heartbreakers (Washington, D.C.)	1974	Roadhouse 1011 (rec. 1952)
Is It Really Love?	Starlighters	1960	Minit 605
Is It Really You	Ascots	1959	Arrow 736
Is It Right	Monotones	1964	Hickory 1250
Is It Right?	Castros	1959	Lasso 502
Is It The End	Avalons	1964	Roulette 4568
Is It Too Late	Fidelitones	1955	Aladdin (unreleased)/ Imperial LP 94005 (70)
Is It Too Late	Four Pharaohs	1958	Ransom 102

SONG	GROUP	YEAR	LABEL
Is It Too Late	Impressors	1957	Onyx 514
Is It Too Late	Romanaires	NA	D&J 100
Is It Too Soon?	Debutantes	1956	Savoy 1191
Is It True	Orchids	NA	Savoy 964 (unreleased)
Is It True What They Say About Barbara	Regal, Mike & group	1963	Kapp 506
Is It True?	Radiants, Little Jan & the	1960, 1961	Clock 1028/Queen 24007
Is It True?	Saxons	1958, 1965	Contender 1313/Relic 1011
Is It True?	Spiders	1955	Imperial 5366
Is It True?	Click-Clacks	1958	Algonquin 714
Is It Wrong	Crests	1967	Parkway 118
Is It You?	Orioles, Sonny Til & the	1950	Jubilee 5018
Is My Heart Wasting Time	Cherokees (Philadelphia)	1955	Peacock 1656
Is She Real?	Kooltoppers	1955	Beverly 702
Is That Exactly What You Wanna Do	Royal Jesters	1961	Cobra 611025
Is That Good Enough For You	Harbor Lites (with Jay Black)	1960	Jaro 77020
Is That Too Much To Ask	Wynnewoods	1959	Wynne 108
Is That Wrong	Blue Notes	1957	Josie (unreleased)
Is There A Doctor In The House	Dubs	1958, 1962	Gone 5046/Gone 5069 (59)/5138
Is There A Love for Me	Sophomores (Massachusetts)	1957	Dawn 225
Is There A Someone For Me	Four Flickers	1959	Lee 1002
Is There A Way	Mackinteers, Teddy Mack & the	NA	Monroe 1
Is There Any Doubt	Fanatics	1961	Skyway 127
Is There Still A Chance	Carnations (Startones)	1961	Lescay 3002
Is There Such A World	Petites	1964	Ascot 2166
Is Thirteen Too Young To Fall In Love	Cineramas	1973	Clifton 4
Is This All Mine	Bachelors, Dean Barlow & the	1951	International 777
Is This Goodbye	Echoes, Tommy Vann & the	1966	Academy 123
Is This Love	Five Chances	1960	P.S. 1510
Is This Love	Joytones	1956	Rama 202
Is This Really The End?	Jive Bombers	1958	Savoy 1535
Is This The End	Phantones	1959	Bale 105
Is This The End	Baby Dolls	1959	Elgin 021
Is This The End?	Warblers	1973	Baron 101
Is This The Real Thing	G-Clefs	1957	Paris 506
Is This The Way	Count Downs, Chuck Hix & the	1959	Verve 10190
Is You Is	Skylarks, Chet Barnes & the (Starlarks)	1961	Embassy 201
Is You Is	Bluenotes, Donnie Williams & the	1959	Viking 1005
Is Your Love	Midnighters	1957	Federal 12299
Is Your Love For Real	Splendors	1962	Jano 004
Island Called Romance	Flyers	NA	Fabbi
Island Love	Copas	1979	U.G.H.A. 11
Island Of Love	Defenders	1964	Parkway 926
Island Of Love	Four Uniques	1961	Deer 3002
Island Of Love	Gents	1964	Times Square 4/Times Square 98 (64)
Island Of Love	Hearts, Lee Andrews & the	1967, 1968	Crimson 1009/Lost Nite 1005
Island Of Love	Leerics	NA	Un-Released Gold 799
Island Of Love	Sheppards (Chicago - Apex)	1959, 1964, 1969	Apex 7750/Bunky 7764/ Constellation 123
Island Of Love (acappella)	Gents	1963	Times Square 4/Times Square 98 (64)
Island Of Paradise	Classic IV	1962	Twist 1001
Island Of Paradise	Populaires	1957	Marvello 5001
Isle Of Love	Tymes	1964	Parkway LP 7039
Isle Of Trinidad	Regents	1957	Argo 5268
Isn't It A Shame?	Blenders (New York)	1953	MGM 11531
Isn't It Amazing	Crests	1960	Coed 537
Isn't That A Lovely Way To Say Goodnight	Four-Evers	1966	Columbia 42303
Istanbul	Gladiators, Bruno & the	1962	Vault 901
It Ain't As Easy As That	Elektras	1963	United Artists 594
It Ain't Fair	Passions	NA	Topaz 1317
It Ain't Gonna Be Like That	Orioles, Sonny Til & the	1952	Jubilee (unreleased)
It Ain't No Use	Ends	1960	Vin 1029
It Ain't Nothin' But Rock 'N' Roll	Matadors	1963	Keith 6502
It Ain't Right	Lamplighters	1956	Federal 12261
It Ain't That Way	Hawks	1954	Imperial 5292

SONG	GROUP	YEAR	LABEL
It Ain't The Meat	Swallows (Maryland)	1951	King 4501
It Ain't True	Sonics	1958, 1963, 1975	X-Tra 107
It All Comes (Back To Me Now)	Marshall Brothers	NA	Savoy (unreleased)
It All Depends On You	Harptones	1955	Paradise 103
It All Happened So Fast	Admirations (featuring Joseph Lorello)	NA	Mercury (unreleased)
It Breaks My Heart	Rendezvous	1961	Rust 5041
It Can Happen To You	Quotations	1968	DeVenus 107
It Can't Be True	Turks	1957, 1958	Cash 1042/Knight 2005/ Imperial 5783 (61)
It Could Be True	Twilights	1962	Twilight 1028
It Could Happen To You	Revlons	1964	Parkway 107
It Could Have Been Me	Four Buddies	NA	Savoy 951 (unreleased)
It Could've Been Worse	Belvin, Jesse & group	1959	RCA 7543
It Depends On You	Sophomores, Anthony & the	1959, 1965	ABC 10073/10737
It Doesn't Matter	Continentals (Hunter)	1962	Hunter 3503
It Doesn't Matter	Grant, Jason & group	1959	20th Fox 151
It Doesn't Matter	Senators	1959	Abner 1031
It Doesn't Matter	Targets	1961	King 5538
It Doesn't Matter Anymore	Kingtones	NA	Eucalyptus 002/Cotillion 44069
It Doesn't Matter Anymore	Youngsters	1961	Candix 313
It Don't Make Sense	Fiestas	1960	Old Town 1080
It Don't Pay	Blue Notes, Tracy Pendarvis & the	1961	Scott 1202
It Feels So Good	Swallows (Maryland)	1954	King 4676
It Finally Happened	Jaguars	1961	Rendezvous 159/Rendezvous 216 (63)
It Had To Be You	Blue Notes	1960	Brooke 119
It Had To Rain	Catalina 6	1962	Flagship 127/Candlelite 413 (74)
It Happened To Me	Graydon, Joe & group	1959	Hamilton 50027
It Happened To Me	Re-Vels	1956	Teen 122
It Happened Today	Paramounts	1985	Avenue D 10
It Happened Today	Skyliners	1959, 1963	Calico 109/Original Sound 37
It Happened Today (acappella)	Holidays	1975	Relic LP 102
It Happens Every Day	Gum Drops	1959	Coral 62138
It Happens Every Night	Firestone, Johnny & group	1958, 1985	Elmont 1003/D&M 001
It Happens This Way	Chains	1963	Peacock 1922
It Hurts	Rialtos	1962	CB 5009
It Hurts	Unforgettables	1961	Colpix 192
It Hurts, Doesn't It Girl	Valrays	1967	United Artists 50145
It Hurts Inside	Five Royales	1959	King 5266
It Hurts Me	Citations	1961, 1977	Don-El 113
It Hurts Me	Majestics (Detroit)	1965	Linda 121
It Hurts Me	Metallics	1962	Baronet 18
It Hurts Me So	Monterays (Brooklyn)	1959	Arwin 130
It Hurts Me So	Twilighters, Tony Allen & the	1962	Bethlehem 3004
It Hurts So Bad	Treys, Wes Griffin & the	1959	Bella 17
It Hurts So Much	Superbs	1965	Dore 736
It Hurts To Wonder	Note Makers	1958	Sotoplay 007
It Is I	Eljays, Leo Wright & the	1964, 1965	CB 5008/Red Fox 103 (65)
It Isn't Fair	Duprees	1964	Coed 595
It Isn't Fair	Standards	1963	Magna 1315/Glenden 1315 (64)
It Isn't Right	Four Blades	1956	Big 4 Hits EP 203
It Isn't Right	Platters	1956	Mercury 70948
It Just Ain't Fair	Imperials, Little Anthony & the	1963	Roulette 4379
It Just Ain't Right	Williams, Otis & group	1964	King 5816
It Keeps Raining	Arrows, Big Bo & the	1962	Duchess 1016
It Looks Like It's Over	Dells	1985	Charly LP 1055
It Looks Like Love	Dolls, Spongy & the	1966	Bridgeview 7001
It Makes A Difference To Me	Three Belles	1955	Jubilee 5219
It Makes No Difference	Harmony Kings, Clyde Tillis & the	1958	Cash 1064
It Makes No Difference Now	Tillis, Clyde & group	1956	Cash 1054
It May Be Wrong	Four Lovers	1959	Decca 30994
It Might Break Your Heart	Dolphins	1962	Tip Top 2005
It Moves Me	Holland, Eddie & group	1959	Tamla 102/United Artists 172 (59)
It Must Be Love	Cineramas	1959	Champ 103
It Must Be Love	Flamingos	1962	End 1111
It Must Be Love	Foxettes, Lady Fox & the	1962	Don-El 118

SONG	GROUP	YEAR	LABEL
It Must Be Love	Lee, Jimmy & group	1958	Apollo 525
It Must Be Love	Maestro, Johnny & group	1961	Coed 562
It Must Be Love	Pearls	1961	Amber 2003
It Must Be Love	Playmates	1957	Savoy 1523
It Must Be Love	Rosettes	1961	Herald 562
It Must Be Magic	Vibraharps	1959	Atco 6134
It Must Be Raining	Misters, Mike Malone & the	1964	Token 1002
It Must Have Been Love	Del Pris	NA	Varbee (unreleased)
It Only Happens To You	Penguins	1955	Mercury 70654
It Only Happens To You	Romancers	1961	Medieval 202/Palette 5075 (61)
It Only Takes One	Deberons	1960	Bond 1408
It Seems Like Yesterday	Dawns	1964	Atco 6296
It Seems So Long Ago	Orioles, Sonny Til & the	1949	Jubilee 5002
It Shouldn't Happen In A Dream	Baby Dolls, Bill Baker & the	1965	Parnaso 110
It Takes A Lot	Seminoles	1962	Check Mate 1012
It Takes A Lot Of Love	Freeloaders, Bobby Sue & the	1955	Harlem 2335
It Takes More Than A Loan	Chances	1961	Bea & Baby 130
It Takes Time	Argyles	1959	Brent 7004
It Takes Time	Blenders (Afo)	1962	Afo 305
It Takes Two	Del-Phis	1961	Checkmate 1005
It Takes Two	Jupitors	1958	Planet X 9621
(It Takes) Two To Fall In Love	Del Cades	1964	United Sound Associates 175
It Took A Long Time	Del-Airs	1965	Delsey 302
It Took A Long Time	Tune Drops, Malcolm Dodds & the	1957	End 1000
It Took Time (It Took You)	Upfronts	1960, 1962	Lummtone 103/108
It Was A Lie	Fourmost	1966	Red Bird 10-071/D.W. 105
It Was A Lie	Fourmosts, Bobby Moore & the	1966	D.W. 106/Redbird 10071
It Was A Night Like This	Four Pharaohs	1958	Ransom 102
It Was A Night Like This	Turbans (Philadelphia)	1956	Herald 486
It Was A Night Like This	Wade, Morris (with the Four Pharaohs)	1958	Ransom 102
It Was A Tear	Drifters (Pre-1959)	1957	Atlantic 1123
It Was A Tear	Innocents	1961	Indigo LP 503
It Was Fun	Robbins, Eddie & group	NA	David 1001
It Was Just For Laughs	Harptones	1954	Bruce 102/Relic 1023 (73)
It Was Like Heaven	Flips, Little Joey & the	1962	Joy 268
It Was Love At First Sight	Stevens, Kenny & group	1964	Old Town 1158
It Was Moonglow	Capris (Philadelphia)	1955	Gotham 7306
It Was Never Meant To Be	Belmonts, Dion & the	1960	Laurie LP 2016
It Was The Night (acappella)	Uniques	1975	Relic LP 105
It Was You	Pery Mates	1961	CaJo 210
It Was You	Sanders, Bobby (with the Performers)	1961	Kaybo 618
It Was You	Tempos	1966	Montel 955
It Was You	Toughtones, Bobby Sanders & the	1961	Kaybo 60618
It Wasn't A Lie	Allures	1985	Starlight 26
It Wasn't A Lie	Fi-Tones	1955, 1958	Atlas 1051/Angle Tone 530
It Wasn't So Long Before (Graduation Is Here)	Four Townsmen	1963	Artflow 145
It Were You	Flamingo, Johnny & group	1957	Canton 1785
It Will Happen By And By	Victors	1959	Jackpot 48015
It Will Never Be The Same	Flips	1959	Mercury 71426
It Will Stand	Pieces Of Eight	1967	A&M 907
It Will Stand	Showmen	1961	Minit 632/Imperial 66033 (64)/ Liberty 56166 (67)
It Won't Always Be Raining	Murraymen	1955	Arcade 131
It Won't Be A Sin	Corsairs	1961	Smash 1715
It Won't Be A Sin	Four Sounds	1961	Tuff
It Won't Be Easy	Downbeats	1962	Dynamite 243/Diamond 243
It Won't Be Long	Downs, Bobbie & group	1960	Correc-Tone 3807
It Won't Be Long	Resonics	NA	Lil-Larry 1005
It Won't Be Long	Symphonics	1964	Dee Jon 001
It Won't Be This Way	Weston, Billy & group	1962	Ep-Som 1002
It Won't Be Very Long	Four Arcs	1954	Boulevard 102
It Won't Be Very Long	Imperials (Detroit)	1954	Great Lakes 1201
It Won't Take Long	Native Boys	1954	Modern 939
It Won't Work Out	Bobbettes	1974	Mayhew 712861

SONG	GROUP	YEAR	LABEL
It Would Be	Young Lions	1960	Dot 16172
It Would Be Heavenly	Coronets	1953	Chess 1553
It Would Be So Nice	Teenagers, Frankie Lymon & the	1986	Murray Hill LP 000148
It Wouldn't Be Right	Rainbows	1963	Dave 909
It Wouldn't Be The Same	Peppers	1961	Press 2809
Itchy Koo	Killers, Hank Blackman & the	1962	Brent 7030
Itchy Twitchy Feeling	Hendricks, Bobby (with the Coasters)	1958	Sue 706
Itchy Twitchy Feeling	Swallows (Maryland)	1958	Federal 12333
Itchy Twitchy Too	Metallics	1962	Baronet 2
It'll Be Easy	Sultans	1961	Tilt 782
It'll Be Me	Chessmen	1959	Salem 001
It'll Never Happen Again	Williams, Otis & group	1964	King 5816
It's A Cold, Cold, Rainy Day	Twiliters	1956, 1961	Groove 0154
It's A Cold Summer	Orioles, Sonny Til & the	1949	Jubilee 5009
It's A Cryin' Shame	Rays	1959	XYZ 605
It's A Crying Shame	Chadons	1964	Chattahoochee 664
It's A Crying Shame	Five Keys	1957	Capitol 3830
It's A Doggone Shame	Diamonds	1961	Mercury 71831
It's A Funny Way We Met	Charmers	1965	Louis 6806
It's A Good Thought	Chandeliers	1964	Loadstone 1601
It's A Groove	Five Keys	1957	Capitol 3710
It's A Happening World	Tokens (Brooklyn)	1967	Warner Bros. 7056
(It's A) Happy Holiday	Shells	1962	Johnson 119
It's A Mad, Mad, Mad, Mad World	Shirelles	1963	Scepter 1260
It's A Miracle	Capris (Philadelphia)	1956	Gotham 7308
It's A Miracle	Honey Bears	1954	Spark 104
It's A Miracle	Revelaires	1954	Burgundy 105
It's A Must	Swans (St. Louis)	1955	Ballad 1006
It's A Sad, Sad Feeling	Admirals	1955	King 4792
It's A Shame	Metro-Chords	1961	Admiral 300
It's A Sin To Tell A Lie	Sonotones	1955	Bruce 127
It's A Treat	Charms, Otis Williams & the	1960	King 5323
It's A Wig	Prells	1964	Skyline 1004
It's A Wonderful Night	Cinderellas	1964	Tamara 763
It's All In The Game	Clovers, Buddy Bailey & the	1963	Porwin 1004
It's All In Your Mind	Barlow, Dean & group	1961	Warwick 618
It's All In Your Mind	Cook, Johnny & group	1957	Lamp 2006
It's All My Fault	Quardells, Billy Kope & the	1958	Kudo 662
It's All Over	Bobbettes	1966	RCA 8983
It's All Over	Capri Sisters	1959	Hanover 4531
It's All Over	Charms, Otis Williams & his	1956	DeLuxe 6095
It's All Over	Don Juans, Andre Williams & the	1956	Fortune 828
It's All Over	Gees	1966	Port 3011
It's All Over	Hawks	1956	Modern 990
It's All Over	Klixs	1958	Music City 817
It's All Over	Martin, Kenny & group	1959	Federal 12354
It's All Over	Roecker, Sherrill & group	1964	Swan 4173
It's All Over	Tunemasters	1957	Mark-X 7002
It's All Over	Versatiles, Jerry Shelly & the	NA	Star 220
It's All Over	Videls	1963	Musicnote 117
It's All Over Because We're Through	Orioles, Sonny Til & the	1952	Jubilee 5082
It's All Over Now	C & C Boys	1964	Duke 379
It's All Over Now	Kittens	1959	Unart 2010
It's All Over Now	Limelites, Shep & the	1963	Hull 757
It's All Right	Berry, Richard & group	1960	Warner Bros. 5164
It's All Right	Williams, Maurice	1962	Herald 572
It's All Right Now	Four Interns	1955	Federal 12239
It's All Said And Done	Three Wishes	1963	Dolton 72
It's Almost Christmas	Dappers Quintet	1955	Flayr 500
(It's Almost) Sunday Morning	Corsairs	1963	Tuff 1847/Chess 1847 (63)
It's Almost Tomorrow	Four Pearls	1960	Dolton 26
It's Almost Tomorrow	Marshans	1964	Etiquette
It's Almost Tomorrow	Pearls	1960	Dolton 26
It's Almost Tomorrow	Velaires	1962	Jamie 1211
It's Almost Tomorrow	Velvet, Jimmy & group	1965	Velvet Tone 102

SONG	GROUP	YEAR	LABEL
It's Alright	Adventurers	1962	Ran-Dee 106
It's Alright	Top Notes	1963	ABC 10399
It's Alright	Williams, Maurice & female group	1961	Herald 572
It's Alright With Me	Heartbeats	1960	Roulette LP 25107
It's Aw'rite	Corvairs	1962	Twin 1001
It's Been A Long Long Time	Starfires, Ral Donner & the	1961	Gone 5102
It's Been A Long Long Time	Three Chuckles	1956	Vik LP 1067
It's Been A Long Time	Casanovas	1955	Apollo 474
It's Been A Long Time	Empalas	1958	Mark V 501
It's Been A Long Time	Original Casuals	1958	Back Beat 514
It's Been A Long Time	Seniors	1959	Tampa 163
It's Been A Long Time	Swinging Rocks, Ruby & her	1985	Relic LP 8004
It's Been A Long Time	Thrillers, Little Joe & the	1959	Okeh 7121
It's Been A Long Time Coming	Earls	1969	ABC 11109
It's Been A Long Winter	Visions	1963	
It's Been So Long	Leaping Flames	1963	MRC 1201
It's Been So Long	Pageants	1955	Beacon 559
It's Been So Long	Twilights	1964	Harthon 135
It's Better That Way	Four Of A Kind	1958	Chancellor 1012/Bomarc 302 (59)
It's Better That You Love	Cardigans	1959	Mercury 71349
It's Better This Way (acappella)	Destinaires	1965	Old Timer 610
It's Better To Love	Slades	1961	Domino 901
It's Breaking My Heart	Larks (North Carolina)	1988	Relic LP 8013
It's Christmas Time	Bonairs	1953	Dootone 325
It's Christmas Time	Castelles	1954	Grand 118
It's Christmas Time	Five Discs	1980	Crystal Ball LP
It's Christmas Time	Five Keys	1951	Aladdin 3113
It's Cold	Spotlighters	1955	Imperial 5342
It's Crazy	Sheppards (Chicago - Apex)	1960	Apex 7755
It's Easy Child	King, Freddy	1962	Federal 12477
It's Easy To Remember	Melodettes, Norman Dunlap with the	1953	Aladdin 3213
It's Fair To Me	Curtains, Mr. Lee &	1970	Boardwalk 18
It's For Real	Gallaway, Bill & group	NA	Clarke 1605
It's Funny	Serenaders (Detroit)	1952	Coral 60720
It's Funny But It's True	Avalons	1956	Groove 0174
It's Funny To Everyone But Me	Five Crowns (with Jan Andre)	1955	Emerald 2007
(It's Gonna Be A) Lonely Christmas	Orioles, Sonny Til & the	1948	Jubilee 5001
It's Gonna Be Allright	Decoys	1963	Times Square 8
It's Gonna Be Alright	Dreamers (Nugget)	1959	Nugget 1000
It's Gonna Be Too Late	Niptones, Nippy Hawkins & the	1965	Lorraine 1001
Its Gonna Happen Soon	Scott Brothers	1963	Comet
It's Gonna Work Out	Rivals (Detroit)	1964	Puff 1001/Lu Pine 118 (64)
It's Gonna Work Out Fine	Cherokees (Gary)	NA	Gary
It's Good Enough For Me	Sensations	1963, 1964	Junior 1002/1021
It's Good To Me (You Don't Know And I Don't Know)	Ospreys	1957	East West 110
It's Goodbye	Chevelles	1963	Butane 777
It's Got To Be A Great Song	Tiffanys	1967	KR 120/RKO 120
It's Got To Come From Your Heart	Uniques	1960	Pride 1018/Gone 5113 (61)/Pride 4
It's Hard Being A Girl	Heartbreakers (MGM)	1963	MGM 13129
It's Heaven	Four Dots, Jerry Stone & the (with Eddie Cochran & Jewel Akens)	1958	Freedom 44002
It's Heaven Being With You	Palisades	1963	Chairman 4401
It's Hopeless	Boys	1964	SVR 1002
It's Impossible, Why Try	Chapelaires, Joni Kay & the	1965	Gateway 746
It's In Your Mind	Incidentals	NA	Paris Tower 126
It's Just A Matter Of Time	Elegants	1974	Bim Bam Boom 121
It's Just A Summer Love	Chantones	1958	Carlton 485
It's Just Me	Chantels	1966	Verve 10435
It's Just My Luck To Be Fifteen	Poni-Tails	1957	ABC 9846
It's Just Your Kiss	Dean, Terry & group	1957	Poplar 102
It's Love	Cadillacs, Speedo & the	1960, 1961	Josie 876/Jubilee LP 1117/ Jubilee LP 5009 (62)
It's Love	Emotions	1958	Fury 1010
It's Love	Four-Evers	1963	Smash 1853

SONG	GROUP	YEAR	LABEL
It's Love	Hollywood Flames	1957	Ebb 143
It's Love	Midnighters, Hank Ballard & the	1963	King 5798
It's Love	Rock-Its	1958	Spangle 2010
It's Love	Smith, Roy & group	NA	Adaire 90
It's Love And It's Real	Majors, Otis Blackwell & the	1957	Gale 102
It's Love Baby	Midnighters	1955	Federal 12227
It's Love Baby	Monorays	1958	Nasco 6020
It's Love Baby	Runaways	1961	Lavender 003
It's Love Because	Melodears	1959	Gone 5040
It's Love, It's Love	Champions	1956	Scott 1201/Chart 611
It's Love, Love, Love	Pearls	1957	Onyx 516/Relic 522 (64)
It's Love That Really Counts	Shirelles	1962	Scepter 1237
It's Love To Me	Escorts (New Jersey)	1956	Premium 407
It's Magic	Platters	1962	Mercury 71921
It's Me	Hearts, Lee Andrews & the	1956	Gotham 321
It's Me Knocking	Boy Friends, Jeanie & the	1959	Warwick 508
It's Mighty Easy	Lovetones	1961	Marlo 1515
It's Mighty Nice	Lovejoys	1964	Tiger 105/Red Bird 003 (64)
It's Mine	Shirelles	1962	Scepter LP 502
It's Misery	Candletts	1959	Vita 182
It's Misery	Hendricks, Bobby (with the Coasters)	1959	Sue 710
It's More Like Voodoo	Bad Boys	1964	Herald 592
It's My Fault	Chordones, Leon Tarver & The	1954	Checker (unreleased)
It's My Party	Chiffons	NA	Collectables LP 5042
It's My Time	Drew-Vels, Patti Drew & the	1964	Capitol 5145
It's Needless To Say	Blue Notes, Bernard Williams & the	1964	Harthon 136
It's Never Too Late	Blue Sonnets	1963	Columbia 42793
It's Never Too Late	Robins	1958	Knight 2008
It's Never Too Soon	Keystoners	1991	Starbound 512
It's Nice	Don Juans, Marsha Renay & the	1960	Hi-Q 5017
It's No Fun	Pizani, Frank (with the Highlights)	1959	Afton 616
It's No Good	Mandells	1963	York 202
It's No Secret	Delighters, Rose Morris & the	1962	Puff 1002
It's No Sin	Churchill, Savannah (with Four Tunes)	1951	RCA
It's No Sin	Duprees	1964	Coed 587
It's No Sin	Fabulous Four	1962	Chancellor 1102
It's No Sin	Four Buddies	1951	Savoy 817
(It's No) Sin	Shepherd Sisters	1959	MGM 12766
It's No Wonder	El Dorados	1974	Oldies 45 (Rec. 1957)
It's Not For Me	Imperials, Little Anthony & the	NA	Rhino LP 70919
It's Not For Me	Wheels, Rudy & the	1959	Curtis 751
It's Not For Me To Say	Four Lyrics	1964	Phillips 40218
It's Not For Me To Say	Teers, Lancelo & the	NA	Promenade 12
It's Not Like You	Sabers	NA	Prism 1893
It's Not My Will	Pretenders, Linda & the	1963	Assault 1879/1880
It's Not The End	Master Four	NA	Tay-Ster 6012
It's Not The End Of The World	Four Kings	1956	Fraternity 752
It's Not Time Now	Duprees	1966	Columbia 43802
It's Not Unusual	Dells	1965	Vee Jay 674
It's O.K. With Me	Heartbreakers (Washington, D.C.)	1952	RCA 4869
It's Only A Paper Moon	Belmonts, Dion & the	1960	Laurie LP 2006
It's Only A Paper Moon	Mystics	NA	Collectables LP 5043
It's Only You Dear	Deltairs	1957	Ivy 101
It's Our Wedding Day	Concords (Brooklyn)	1964	Epic 9697
It's Over	Exclusives	1958	K&C 102
It's Over	Velaires, Danny & the	1967	Ramco 1983
It's Over Because We're Through	Magic Chords	NA	Domino 360
It's Over Now	Youngtones	1958, 1963	X-Tra 104/Candlelite 417
It's Rainin'	Echoes	1961	Seg-Way 106
It's Raining	Tifanos	1960	Tifco 822
It's Raining Outside	Platters	1958	Mercury 71353
It's Real	Leigh, Linda & group	1959	Rendezvous 103
It's Saturday Night	Chev-Rons	1962	Gait 100
It's So Good	Lovenotes	1954	Unreleased
It's So Hard	Roomates, Cathy Jean & the	1991	Cure 91-02801

SONG	GROUP	YEAR	LABEL
It's So Hard To Be Young	Yachtsmen	1958	Destiny 402
It's So Hard To Laugh, So Easy To Cry	Vitamins	1972	Vita 101
It's So Hard To Say Goodbye To Yesterday	Charm	1992 (1983)	Clifton 98
It's So Hard To Say Goodbye To Yesterday	Echelons	1992	Clifton 102
It's So Nice	Gold Bugs	1965	Coral 62453
It's So Strange	Pals, Gerry Patt & his	1965	Ascot 2129
It's So Strange	Thomas, Jerry & group	1966	Ascot 2212
It's So Wonderful	Raindrops	1963	Jubilee 5444
It's Spring	Cadillacs	1958	Unreleased
It's Spring Again	Jive Bombers	1952	Citation 1160
It's Spring Again	Pentagons	1958	Specialty 644
It's Still Love	Crowns	1964	Limelight 3031
It's Such A Shame	Willows	1964	Heidi 103
It's Summer	New Emage	1985, 1987	Starlight 29/57
It's Summer Time	Pixies 3	1964	Mercury 72288
It's Terrific	Rainbows	1973	Baron 100
It's The Beat	Doo Rays, Davey & the	1958	Guyden 2002
It's The Bomp	Peridots	1961	Deauville 100
It's The Last Kiss	Plazas, Eric & the	1963	Production 612
It's The Last Thing I Do	Flasher Brothers	1953	Aladdin 3186
It's The Little Things	Emblems, Patty & the	1966	Congress 263
It's The Talk Of The Town	Ravens	1972	National 9158
It's The Talk Of The Town	Royal Teens	1960	Capitol 4402
It's The Twist	Crystal Tones, Billy James & the	1959	M-Z 111
It's Time	Squires (Boss)	1964	Boss 2120
It's Time	Townsmen (Vanity)	1960	Vanity 579/580
It's Time To Cry	Russell, Rick & group	1963	Poplar 120
It's Time To Go	Carlos Brothers	1959, 1960	Del-Fi 4118/4145
It's Time To Rock	Hy-Tones, Georgia Harris & the	1958	Hy-Tone 117
It's Too Bad	Modifiers, Mike & the	1962	Gordy 7006
It's Too Bad	Souvenirs	1967	Inferno 2001
It's Too Bad (We Had To Part)	Strangers	NA	King (unreleased)
It's Too Bad We Had To Say Goodbye	Thrillers, Little Joe & the	1958	Okeh 7107/Epic 9293 (58)
It's Too Late	Companions	1963	Arlen 722/Gina 722 (63)
It's Too Late	Dell Vikings, Buddy Carle & the	NA	Eedee 3501/Star 223
It's Too Late	Sunglows, Sunny & the	1964	Tear Drop 3034
It's Too Late Now	Cuff Links	1957	Dootone 422
It's Too Late Now	Four Deals	1950	Capitol 1313
It's Too Late Now	Hawks	1955	Imperial 5332
It's Too Late To Cry	Gents	1961	All Boy 8501
It's Too Soon To Know	Clovers, Tippie & the	1975	Jett 3019
It's Too Soon To Know	Ecstasies	1984	Clifton EP 508
It's Too Soon To Know	Flamingos	19??	
It's Too Soon To Know	Four Lovers	1957	RCA LP 1317
It's Too Soon To Know	Keystones	NA	N/A
It's Too Soon To Know	Lyrics, Ike Perry & the	1979	King Tut 180
It's Too Soon To Know	Moonbeams, Jeanne Sterling & the	1957	Capitol 3802
It's Too Soon To Know	Orioles, Sonny Til & the	1948, 1962	It's A Natural 5000/Jubilee 5000 (48)/ Charlie Parker 215
It's Too Soon To Know	Ravens	1948	National 9053
It's Too Soon To Know	Velours	1998	Clifton CD
It's Too Soon To Know (acappella)	Velvet Angels	1972	Relic LP 5004/Relic LP 108 (75)
It's Tough	Tempos	1959	Hi-Q 100
It's True	Rogues	1956	Old Town 304
It's True	Twilighters (Atlanta)	1955	Specialty 548
It's Twelve O'Clock	Starlighters	1958	End 1031
It's Twistin' Time	Midnighters, Hank Ballard & the	1962	King 5601
It's Unbelievable	Hearts, Lee Andrews & the Hearts	1960	Chancellor 1057
It's Unbelievable	Larks (Philadelphia)	1961	Sheryl 334/Uptown (65)
It's Uncle Willie	Gifts, Little Natalie & Henry & the	1963	Roulette 4540
It's Waiting There For You	Delrons, Reperata & the	1967	Mala 573
It's Willy	Cupcakes	1959	Time 1011

SONG	GROUP	YEAR	LABEL
It's Witchcraft	Blue Echoes	NA	Bon 2112
It's Wonderful	Five Pyramids	1975	Nile 101
It's Worth Remembering	Notes, Reed Harper & the	1960	Luck 105
It's Written	Clocks & Classmen	1958	Mail Call 1011
It's Written In The Stars	Emeralds, Luther Bond & the	1955	Savoy 1159
It's Written In The Stars	Sparrows Quartette	NA	Broadcast 1000
It's Written In Your Eyes	Spindletoppers, Carl & the	1962	ABC 10346
It's Wrong	Ontarios	1973	Baron 101
It's You	Deans	1961	Mohawk 126
It's You	Earls	1961	Rome 101
It's You	Five Bells	1960	Clock 1017
It's You	Giants, Little Guy & the	1961	Lawn 103
It's You	Hollywood Saxons	1961	Swingin' 651/Elf 103 (61)
It's You	Plants	1957	J&S 1602
It's You	Queens, Shirley Gunter & the	1954	Flair 1050
It's You	Sonics	1962	Amco 001
It's You	Wayne, James & female group	1957	Peacock 1672
It's You	Harptones	1982	Ambient Sound 02807
It's You And Me	C-Quents	1968	Essica 004
It's You, Darling, It's You	Marigolds, Johnny Bragg & the	1956	Excello 2091
It's You For Me	Syllables	1959	Imperial 5619
It's You I Love	Chestnuts	1956	Davis 447
It's You I Love	Croom Brothers	1958	Vee Jay 283
It's You I Love	Lancers	1954	Trend 73
It's You I Love Best	Angels	1956	Gee 1024
It's You I Miss	Falcons (Savoy)	1953	Savoy 893
It's You, It's You I Love	Carvels	1985	Relic LP 5050
It's You That I Love	Aztecs	1962	Zin-A-Spin 002
It's You, Yes You	Charms, Otis Williams & the	1955	DeLuxe 6089
It's You, You, You	Fabulous Gardenias	1961, 1962	Liz 1004/Fairlane 21019 (62)
It's Your Turn	Fabulous Blends	1960	Casa Grande 3037
It's Your Turn	Slades	1961	Domino 906
Itsy Bitsy, Teenie Weenie, Yellow Polka Dot Bikini	Kittens	1960	Alpine 64
Itty Bitty Mama	Emanons	NA	
Itty Bitty Twist	Blue Belles	1962	Newtown 5000
I've Always Been A Dreamer	Five Keys	1960	King LP 688
I've Been A Fool	Freeways	1965	Hugo 11723
I've Been A Fool	Ravens	1949	National 9098
I've Been A Fool From The Start	Orchids	1953	King 4663
I've Been Accused	Turks	1956	Money 215
I've Been Blue	Deltas, Jim Waller & the	1961	Trac 502
I've Been Dreaming	Rogues	1958	Old Town 1056
I've Been Good To You (acappella)	Chessmen	1975	Relic LP 106
I've Been Hurt	Barons (Spartan)	1961	Spartan 400
I've Been Hurt	Delicates	1964, 1965	Challenge 59232/59267
I've Been Hurt	Individuals	1959	Sparrow 101
I've Been Jilted	Syllables	1959	Imperial 5619
I've Been Loved	Quarter Notes	1966	Boom 60018
I've Been Mistreated	Courtiers	1959	Case 107
I've Been Pretending	Rogers, Pauline & group	1956	Flair-X 5001
I've Been Searching	Combo-Nettes, Clemons Penix & the	1956	Combo 117
I've Been So Lonely	Cupcakes, Cookie & the	1963	Chess 1848
I've Been There Before You	Overtones	1967	Slate 3072
I've Been Thinking	Escorts (Essex)	1955	Essex 389
I've Been Treated Wrong Too Long	Royals, Chuck Willis & the	1953	Okeh 6985
I've Been Waiting For You	Stylists (Maryland)	1960	Sage 317
I've Been Wondering	Charts	1957	Everlast 5006/Lost Nite 186 (81)
I've Been Your Dog (Ever Since I've Been Your Man)	Moonglows	1952	Champagne 7500
I've Chosen You	Winchell, Danny (with Nino & the Ebbtides)	1959	Recorte 415
I've Cried	Chantels	1958	Unreleased
I've Cried Before	Belmonts, Dion & the	1959	Laurie 3027
I've Cried Enough	Carousels	1959	Spry 116
I've Cried Enough For Two	Ivy Three	1961	Shell 302

SONG	GROUP	YEAR	LABEL
I've Done It Again	Neville, Aaron & group	1967	Instant 3282
I've Enjoyed Being Loved By You	Fabulous Denos	1965	King 5971
(I've Fallen Into) The Tender Trap	Randolph, Leroy & group	1971	Spring 121
I've Got A Crush On You	Imperials, Little Anthony & the	1961	End LP 311
I've Got A Dream	Monitors	1957	Specialty 595
I've Got A Feeling	Creations	1962	Meridian 7550
I've Got A Feeling	Ebbtones	1957	Ebb 100
I've Got A Feeling	Hanks, Mike & group	1962	Al-Jacks 000.1
I've Got A Feeling	Native Boys	1956	Combo 120
I've Got A Feeling	Timetones	1961	Atco 6201 (Times Square Productions)/Relic 539 (65)
I've Got A Feeling	Topps	1954	Red Robin 131
I've Got A Feeling	Versatiles, Tootsie & the	1962	Elmar 6000
I've Got A Girl	Capitols	1958	Carlton 461
I've Got A Girl	Notations, Augie Rios & the	1963	Shelley 181
I've Got A Girl	Tiffanys (male)	1963	Rockin Robin 1
I've Got A Lot To Offer Darling	Imperials, Little Anthony & the	1963	Roulette 4477
I've Got A Notion	Harptones	1955	Paradise 103
I've Got A Notion	Lumpkin, Henry & group	1961	Motown 1005
I've Got A Right To Cry	Andrews, Lee (with the Hearts)	1960, 1961	Swan 4065
I've Got A Secret	Offbeats, Jimmy Dee & the	1963	Cutle 1400
I've Got A Secret	Uniques	1959	C-Way 2676
I've Got A Tiger In My Tank	Intimates	1964	Epic 9743
I've Got A Woman	Del-Chords, Donnie & the	1963	Taurus 364
I've Got An Awful Lot Of Losing To Do	Delrons, Reperata & the	1969, 1970	Kapp 989/2050
I've Got An Invitation To A Dance	Williams, Billy & group	1957	Mercury 71187
I've Got Better Things To Do	Accents (featuring Sandi)	1964	Charter 1017
I've Got Everything	Crystalettes	1963	Crystalette 755
I've Got Eyes	Strangers	1954	King 4697
I've Got It	Gay Poppers	1960	Fire 1026
I've Got It	Swinging Hearts	1964	Magic Touch 2001
I've Got It Bad	Keynotes, Gene Anderson & the	NA	Top Ten 252
I've Got My Baby	Hy-Tones	1966	A-Bet 9415
I've Got My Eyes On You	Channels	1964	Groove 0046
I've Got My Eyes On You	Clovers	1954	Atlantic 1035
I've Got News For You	Ebony Moods	1955	Theron 108
(I've Got) No Regrets	Three Reasons	1963	JRE 223/224
I've Got No Time	Whispers	1950	Apollo 1156
I've Got Plenty Of Love	Seniors	1956	Tetra 4446
I've Got Sand In My Shoes	Drifters (1959-forward)	1964	Atlantic 2253
I've Got That Feeling	Raytones, Laverne Ray & the	1957	Okeh 7091
I've Got The Feeling	Knights	1965	USA 800
I've Got The Right	Moonglows	1964	Times Square 30
I've Got The Right To Be Blue	Magic Chords	1950	Domino 311
I've Got The World On A String	Ravens	NA	National (unreleased)
I've Got Time	Five Satins	1960	Ember LP 401
I've Got To Find Her	Creations	1967	Globe 103
I've Got To Have You, Baby	Pretenders	1956	Rama 198
I've Got To Know	Carmacks	1960	Autograph 205
I've Got To Know	Dell Vikings	1964	Gateway 743
I've Got To Let Him Know	Blue Belles	1962	Newtown 5000
I've Got To Move	Four Bars	1964	Falew 108
I've Got To Run On	Choraletters	1957	Duke 214
I've Got What You Want	Pagans, Lynn Dee & the	1960	Music City 835
I've Got You Covered	Lyrics, Ike Perry & the	1960	Cowtown 801
I've Got You Under My Skin	Ravens	1954	Mercury 70330
I've Gotta Drive	Jan & Dean	1964	Colpix 718
I've Gotta Face The World	Bobbettes	1966	RCA 8832
I've Gotta Know	Passions	1981	Jason Scott 9
I've Gotta Love	Pages, Gene Morris & the	1957	Vik 0287
I've Gotten Over You	Sonnettes	1963	Kayo 0001
I've Had It	Bell Notes	1959	Time 1004
I've Had It	Crestones	1964	Markie 123
I've Had It	Hearts, Lee Andrews & the	1968	Crimson 1015
I've Had It	Starlets	1965	Tower 144

SONG	GROUP	YEAR	LABEL
I've Had You	Creators (Los Angeles)	1961	Dooto 463
I've Heard About You	Montclairs	1956	Sonic 104
I've Known	Drew-Vels, Patti Drew & the	1965	Capitol 5244
I've Learned My Lesson	Bryant, Helen & group	1961	Fury 1042
I've Lied	Juveniles	1958	Mode 1
I've Lied	Tunemasters, Willie Wilson & Arlene Smith & the	1958	End 1011
I've Lived Before	Seniors	1960	Decca 31112
I've Lost	Enchanters (Queens, N.Y.)	1952	Jubilee 5080
I've Lost	Five Satins	1960	Ember LP 401
I've Lost	J's, Jimmy J. & the	1961	Salco 647
I've Lost	Scarlets	1954	Red Robin 128/Event 4287 (55)
I've Never Been There	Chanteclairs	1955	Dot 15404
I've Never Seen A Straight Banana	Hi-Tones	1960	Candix 307
I've Only Myself To Blame	Marveleers	1953	Derby 842
I've Searched	Heartspinners	1958, 1963	X-Tra 109/Times Square 20
I've Seen Everything	Elegants	1961	ABC 10219
I've Seen Everything (acappella)	Quotations	1975	Relic LP 103
I've Settled Down	Delighters, Donald Jenkins & the	1963	Cortland 116
I've Taken All I Can	Ravens, Mike & the	1962	Empire 1
I've Thought It Over	Rich, Dave & group	1959	RCA 7141
I've Tried	Tune Weavers, Margo Sylvia & the	1988	Classic Artists 104
I've Waited	Envoys, Bill Tally & the	1959	Canadian American 105
I've Waited All My Life For You	Four Triumphs	1958	Mira 2050
I've Waited For A Lifetime	Wheels	1960	Roulette 4271
I've Waited Long Enough	Four Jacks, Bill Erwin & the	1960	Pel 601
I've Waited So Long	Del-Hearts, Dale & the	1961	Herald 564
I've Waited So Long	Scharmeers	1974	Vintage 1017
Ivory Tower	Charms, Otis Williams & his	1956	DeLuxe 6093
Ivy League Clean	El Capris	1958	Paris 525
Ivy League Clothes	Gaylarks	1958	Music City 819
Ivy League Lover	Ideals	1959	Decca 30800
Ivy On The Old School Wall	Travelers	1961	Decca 31215
I-Yi	Hawks	1954	Imperial 5292

J

SONG	GROUP	YEAR	LABEL
J. J.'s Blues	Blue Jays (Laurie)	1959	Laurie 3037
J.B. Boogie	Blue Notes, Joe Weaver & his	1953	DeLuxe 6021
Jack The Ripper	Elites	1960	Chief 7032
Jack The Ripper	Stacy, Clarence & group	1961	Carol 4114
Jack The Ripper, Pt. 1	Tip Tops, David Lastie & the	1962	Chess 1800
Jack The Ripper, Pt. 2	Tip Tops, David Lastie & the (with Little Sonny)	1962	Chess 1800
Jackie	Girlfriends	1960	Pioneer 71833
Jackie	Green, Janice & group	1958	Nasco 6013
Jackie Brown	Passions	1958	Era 1063/Capitol 3963 (58)
Jackie Please	Wheeletts, Sammy & the	NA	Rip Cor 6001
Jackpot	Drifters (1959-forward)	1962	Atlantic 2151
Jackpot	Shufflers, Benny Williams & the	NA	Champion 103
Jacqueline	Triangle	1970	Paramount 0055
Jacqueline	Tune Tones	1961	Zynn 1007
Jadda	Rovers	1955	Music City 780
Jaguar	Jaguars	1959	Epic 9308
Jail Bird	Veltones	1959	Jin 115
Jail Wall	Tuxedo Sleepers, James Carter & the	1960	Tuxedo 938
Jailer Bring Me Water	Basics	NA	Lavender 1851
Jailhouse Blues	Inspirations, Andre Bacon Fat Williams & the	1960	Fortune 856
Jam Session	Larks (North Carolina)	1988	Relic LP 8013
Jamaica Farewell	Clovers	1959	United Artists LP 3033
Jamaica Joe	Angels (New Jersey)	1964	Smash 1915
Jambalaya	Beasley, Jimmy & group	1956	Modern 1009
Jambalaya	Counts, Bobby Comstock & the	1960	Atlantic 2051
Jambalaya	Four Lovers	1956	RCA 6646
Jamboree	Four Students, Charles Calhoun & the	1956	Groove 0149

SONG	GROUP	YEAR	LABEL
Jamie	Identicals	1963	Firebird 101
Jane	Corona, Larry & group	1956	Fortune 523
Jane	Reid, Matthew (with the Four Seasons)	1961	ABC 10259
Jane Why Did You Do It	Alamos, Tony Valla & the	1961	Fortune 858
Janet	Holiday, Jimmy & group	1963	Everest 2022
Janice	Aquarians, Marc Haven & the	1961	Villa-Yore
Janice	Corvettes	NA	Duncan 401
Janice	Robbins, Eddie & group	NA	David 1001
Janie	Barrons	NA	Guest Star LP 1481
Janie Girl	Diplomats	1961	May 105
Janie Made A Monster	Fabulous Five	1959	King 5220
January 1st, 1962	Resolutions	1962	Valentine 1001
Japanese Rhumba	Twin Tunes	1955	Sound 115
Japanese Sandman	Jumpin' Tones	NA	Unreleased
Java	Angels (New Jersey)	1964	Smash 1885
Java Java	Things To Come	1993	Clifton 108
Java Jive	Platters	1964	Mercury 72242
Jawbone	Naturals, Yolanda & the	1962	Kimley 923
Jay Walk	Barons (Key)	1959	Key 1001
Jay Walker	Cadillacs	1959	Josie 857
Jay's Rock	Delegates (Big Jay McNeely)	1956	Vee Jay 212
Jealous Fool	Breedlove, Jimmy & group	1963	Diamond 144
Jealous Fool	Counts, Bobby Comstock & the	1959	Triumph 602
Jealous Heart	Hudson, Pookie (with the Imperials)	1963	Double L 711
Jealous Heart	Nite Liters	1962	Verve 10256
Jealous Heart	Spaniels	1970	North American 001/Calla 172 (70)
Jealous Hearted Woman	Doves, Cliff Butler & the	1953	States (unreleased)
Jean Of The Ville	Teenagers (Joe Negroni)	1961	Columbia (unreleased)
Jeanette	Antones	1956	Black Crest 106
Jeanette	Castle Kings	1962	Atlantic 2158
Jeanette, Jeanette	Regents	1961	Gee LP 706
Jeanie	Neat-Teens	NA	N/A
Jeanie Baby	Bon-Aires	1964	Rust 5097
Jeanie, Joanie, Shirley, Toni	Four Palms	1957	Aladdin 3411
Jeanie With The Light Brown Hair	Statues	1960	Liberty 55292
Jeanine	Platters	1960	Mercury LP 20589/ Mercury LP 60254 (60)
Jeannie	Five Chords	1961	Cuca 1031
Jeannie	Grand Central Echoes	1985	Clifton 76
Jeannie	Highlighters, Jimmy Hall & the	1959	Cannon 369/370
Jeannie	Josie, Lou & group	1961	Rendezvous 143
Jeannie	Skylarks	1962	Everlast 5022
Jeannie	Thrashers	1957, 1963	Masons 0-1
Jeannie	Unique Teens	1958	Ivy 112/Hanover 4510 (58)
Jeannie	Winchell, Danny (with Nino & the Ebbtides)	1959	Recorte 406
Jeannie, Joanie, Shirley	Tri-Five, John Lythgoe & the	1961	Varbee 2002
Jeannie Memsah	Rocky Fellers	1964	Warner Bros. 5440
Jeannine	All Americans, Joey Rogers & the	1958	Nu-Clear (no number)
Jeannine	Idols	1961	E-Z 1214
Jeebla Jabla Jingo	Jets, Roy Jordan & the	1956	Orpheus 1102
Jeepers Creepers	Dells	1958	Vee Jay 292
Jelly Bean	Cadillacs	1958	Unreleased
Jelly Bean	Dreamtones	1959	Express 501
Jelly Bean	Galaxys	1959	Carthay 103
Jelly Bean	Rainbows	NA	Red Robin (unreleased)
Jelly Roll	Dreamers, Richard Berry & the	1955	Flair 1075
Jelly Roll Brown	Four Sportsmen	1962	Sunnybrook 5
Jellyfish	Teardrops	1957	Dot 15669
Jennie Lee	Dominoes	1958	Liberty 55136
Jennifer	Four Winds	1964	Dery 1002/Felsted 8703 (64)
Jenny Jenny	Chancellors	1965	USA 783
Jenny Lee	Shantons, Skip Brown & the	1959	Pam 112
Jenny Lee	Students (Ohio)	1956	Fordham 109/Vanguard 9093
Jerk Baby Jerk	Hustlers, Carl Burnett & the	1965	Carmax 102
Jerk, The	Dukays	1964	Jerry-O 105

SONG	GROUP	YEAR	LABEL
Jerk, The	Larks (Don Julian)	1964	Money 106
Jerri Lee	Flamingos	1959	Decca 30948
Jerrilee	Perri's	1958	Madison 105
Jerry	Deltones	1958	Roulette 4081
Jerry	Minors	1957	Celeste 3007/Mello 554
Jerry	Royal Debs	1962	Tifco 826
Jerry Boy	Young Sisters	1963	Mala 467
Jerry (I'm Your Sherry)	Day, Tracey & group	1961	Vee Jay 467
Jerusalem	Castells	1968	United Artists 50324
Jessie Mae	Spaniels	1956	Vee Jay (unreleased)
Jezebel	Counts, Bobby Comstock & the	1963	Jubilee 5396
Jezebel	Illusions	1963	Round 1018
Jigsaw Puzzle	Chelmars	1962	Select 712
Jigsaw Puzzle	Falcons (RCA)	1957	RCA 7076
Jigsaw Puzzle	Pictures, C.L. & the	1966	Monument 958
Jim	Williams, Little Cheryl & group	1962	Kapp 500X
Jim Dandy	Campbell, Jo Ann (with the Dubs)	1962	Rori 711
Jim Jam	I. V. Leaguers	1959	Nau-Voo 803
Jim, That's Him	Tangerines	1964	Fina 7002
Jimbo Jango	Joytones	1956	Rama 215
Jimmy	Socialites	1963	Arrawak 1004
Jimmy Baby	Blue Jeans, Bob B. Soxx & the	1963	Philles LP 4002
Jimmy Beware	Fleetwoods	1963	Dolton 75
Jimmy Joe	Three Graces	1959	Golden Crest 515
Jimmy Lee	Jewels (female)	1964	Olimpic 244
Jimmy Love	Carroll, Cathy (with the Earls)	1961	Triodex 11
Jimmy Went Walkin'	Beau-Marks	1960	Shad 5021
Jingle Bell	Dynamo, Skinny & group	1956	Excello 2097
Jingle Bell Hop	Jackson Trio (with the Ebonaires)	1955	Hollywood 1046
Jingle Bell Stomp	Jumpin' Tones	1989	Unreleased
Jingle Bells	Newports	1978	Crystal Ball 129
Jingle Jangle	Penguins	1955	Mercury 70762
Jingle Jangle Joe	Ravens	1956	Argo (unreleased)
Jingle, Jingle	Tremaines	1958	Cash 100/101/Val 100/101 (58)/ Old Town 1051 (58)
Jingle Jump	Tigers, Danny Peil & the	NA	Raynard 602
Jingles	Catalinas	1979	Crystal Ball 132
Jinx	Three Friends	1956, 1957	Lido 502/Brunswick 55032
Jitterbug	Blanders	1965	Smash 2005
Jitterbug Jamboree	Emeralds, Luther Bond & the	1959	Showboat 1501
Jitterbug Mary	Dell Vikings	1957	Mercury 71132
Jitterbug, The	Dovells	1962	Parkway 855
Jitterbuggin'	Five Bops	1959	Hamilton 50023
Jivarama Hop	Ebbonaires, Jackson Trio & the	1956	Hollywood 1062
Jive Time Turkey	Click-Ettes	1958	Dice 83/84
Jivin' Guy	Debonaires (New York)	1959	Maske 804
Jivin' Jean	Maidens, Sir Joe & the	1962	Lenox 5563
Jo Ann	McHugh, Richie & group	1963	Raewood 587
Jo Baby	Dynamics	1959	Arc 4453
Jo Jo	Dells	1956	Vee Jay 204
Jo Jo	Marsmen, Marvin & Johnny & the	1954	Specialty 488
Jo Jo	Wheeler, Art & group	1962	Swingin' 642
Jo Jo The Big Wheel	Gallahads	1960	Donna 1322/Del-Fi 4137 (60)
Joan Of Love	Devilles	1959	Orbit 540
Joanie	Bay Bops	1958	Coral 61975
Joanie	Smoothies	1960	Decca 31105
Joanie	Starlites	1965	Relic 1001
Joanie Don't You Cry	Hallmarks, Rickie & the	1963	Amy 877
Jo-Ann	Impacs	1964	King 5851
Joanne	Crosstones	NA	Clifton EP 510
Joanne	Martin, Trade & group	1964	Coed 594
Joanne	Tantones, Trade & the	NA	Adam & Eve LP 502
Joanne's Sister	Twin Tones	1958	RCA 7235
Joannie Joannie	Emersons	1958	Newport 7004
Jo-Baby	Accents	1958	Robbins 108

SONG	GROUP	YEAR	LABEL
Jocko Sent Me	Darchaes, Ben White & the	1962	Aljon 1247/1248/Coney Island
Joe Cool	Twinkle Tones, Jimmie Hombs & the	1959	Jack Bee 1001
Joe Smith Theme, The	Valentines	1986	Murray Hill LP 000202
Joe The Grinder	Hawks	1954	Imperial 5266
Joe's Calypso	Baltineers	1956	Teenage 1002
Joey	Rosebuds	1959	Lancer 102
Joey Baby	So-And-Sos, Anita & the	1961	RCA 7974
Joey Or Jim	Betty Jean & group	1963	JR 5001
Joey's Diamond Ring	Secrets, Colleen Kaye & the	1963	Big Top 3151
John Brown	Spaniels, Pookie Hudson & the	1962	Parkway 839
John Henry	Cadets	1963	Crown LP 5370
John Henry	Four Dukes	1960	Imperial 5653
John Law	Heartbreakers (Bronx, N.Y.)	1962	Markay 106
John Smith's Body	Toledos	1961	Down 2003/End 1094 (61)
Johnnie, Darling	Debs	1957	Keen 34003
Johnnie's Coming Home	Jogettes	1962	Mar 102
Johnny	Antwinetts	1958	RCA 7398
Johnny	Charmers	1962	Laurie 3142
Johnny	Crosstones	NA	Clifton EP 511
Johnny	Dialtones	1960	Goldisc 3005/Goldisc 3020 (61)
Johnny	Dots (Jeanette Baker)	1957	Caddy 107
Johnny	Robins	1962	Sweet Taffy 400/New Hit 3010
Johnny Ace's Last Letter	Blazers (Johnny Moore's)	1955	Hollywood 1031
Johnny B. Goode	Contenders	1964	Chattahoochee 656
Johnny B. Goode	DiMucci, Dion (with the Del Satins)	1964	Columbia 43096
Johnny Brown	Medwick, Joe & group	1959	Duke 311
Johnny Clean-Up	Masters	1958	Len 103
Johnny Darlin'	Larks (North Carolina)	1954	Lloyds 115
Johnny Darling	Excels, Sandy Stewart & the	1955	X 0126
Johnny, Darling	Feathers	1954	Aladdin 3267/Show Time 1104
Johnny Has Gone	Five Wings	1955	King 4778
Johnny Has Gone	Jerome, Patti & group	1955	Josie 774
Johnny I'm Sorry	Elgins (California)	1963	Lummtone 109
Johnny Jealousy	Four Jewels	1963	Start 638 (same # used twice)
Johnny, Johnny	Charmettes	1959	Federal 12345
Johnny Johnny (acappella)	Velvet Angels	1972	Relic LP 5004/Relic LP 109 (75)
Johnny, Johnny, Johnny	G-Notes	1959	Guyden 2012
Johnny Lonely	Valiants (New York)	1963	Roulette 4510/Roulette 4551 (64)
Johnny Mae	Blue Rockers	1955	Excello 2062
Johnny My Boy	Ad Libs	1965	Blue Cat 123
Johnny My Dear	Charmers	1956	Aladdin 3337
Johnny Never Knew	Jive Five	1963	Beltone 2030
Johnny Oh	Donnels	1963	Alpha 001
Johnny On My Mind	Shirelles	1961	Scepter LP 501
Johnny One Heart	Valentines	1962	Ludix 102
Johnny Preacher	Teenettes, Betty Jayne & the	1961	Carellen 102
Johnny Rhythm	Fairlanes	1959	Lucky Seven 102
Johnny Run Run	Dew Drops	1963	Jeff 1963
Johnny The Dreamer	Four Fellows, Miss Toni Banks & the	1957	Glory 263
Johnny Won't Run Around	Crescents	1963	Arlen 743
Johnny's Got A Girl Friend	Mixers	1958	Bold 101
Johnny's House Party	Jayhawks, Earl Palmer & the	1957	Aladdin 3379
Johnny's House Party	Rockets	1957	Modern 1021
Johnny's Little Lamb	Sputniks	1958	Class 222
Johnny's Place	Kittens	1963	Don-El 205
Johnny's Still Singing	Five Wings	1955	King 4778
Joker, The	Nutmegs	1956	Herald (unreleased)
Joke's On Me, The	Castelles	NA	Atco (unreleased)
Joke's On Me, The	Corvells	1963	Cub 9122
Jolene	Nic Nacks	1963	Ovation 6201
Jolene	Premiers (Connecticut)	1959	Alert 706
Jolly Green Giant	Valaquons	1964	Rayco 516
Jonelle	Chimes (Los Angeles - Dig)	1957	Dig 148 (unreleased)
Jones Girl, The	Chevrons	1964	Kiski 2065
Jones Girl, The	Five Satins	1956	Standord 200/Ember 1005 (56)

SONG	GROUP	YEAR	LABEL
Joni	Rhythm Aces, Preston Jackson & the	1961	Vee Jay 417
Joogie Boogie	Dubs	1961	ABC 10198
Josephine	Fabulous Flames	1958	Rex 3000
Josephine	Gales	1958	Mel-O 113
Joshua	Dominoes	1959	Liberty LP 3056
Joshua	Tokens (Brooklyn)	NA	RCA LP 2631
Journey	Chancellors	1966	Fenton 2066
Journey Bells	Goldtones	1962	YRS 1002
Journey Of Love	Crests	1959, 1960	Coed 535
Journey's End	Royal Sons Quintet	1952	Apollo 253
Joy In The Beulah Land	Violinaires	1954	Drummond 4000
Joyce	Computones	1981	Clifton 61
Joyce	Jay Birds, Lenny Young & the	1958	Jay Scott 1001/Jackpot 48006 (58)
Joyce	Sinceres	1978	Crystal Ball 126
Joyce	Squires (Congress)	1964	Congress 223
Joyride	Rainbows, Randy & the	1964	Rust 5101
Joys Of Love, The	Hemlocks, Little Bobby Rivera & the	1957	Fury 1004
Juanita	Celebritys	1956	Caroline 2301
Juanita	Dedications	1983	Avenue D 8
Juanita	Dippers, Georgie Torrence & the	1978	King Tut 170
Juanita	Monorails	1976	Broadcast 1136
Juanita Banana	Peels	1966	Karate 522
Juanita Of Mexico	Schoolboys, Professor Hamilton & the	1961	Contour 0001
Judy	Charlettes, Larry & the	1963	Sapien 1004
Judy	Love, Ronnie & group	1965	D-Town 1047
Judy	Prodigals	1958	Falcon 1011/Abner 1011 (58)/ Tollie 9019 (64)
Judy	Ray-Vons	1964	Laurie 3248
Judy	Unitones	1959	Candy 005
Judy	Weber, Lewis & group	1959	Scottie 1304
J-U-D-Y	Strangers	1959	Christy 107/108
Judy, Don't Be Moody	Darin, Bobby & group	1958	Atco 6117
Judy (I Love You So)	Sounds (featuring Frank Williams)	1961	Queen 24008
Judy My Love (Judy Mi Amor)	Astros, Pepe & the	1961	Swami 553/554
Judy Or Jo Ann	Escorts (Soma)	1961	Soma 1144
Juella	Phillips, Phil (with the Twilights)	1959	Khoury's 711/Mercury 71465 (59)
Juicin' And Goofin'	Fountain, Morris & group	1954	Savoy 1139
Juicy Crocodile	Cellos	1957	Apollo 515
Juicy Lucy	Romeos	NA	Mark II 101
Juicy Melon	Boppers, Alonzo & the	1963	Rojac 8127
Ju-Judy	Original Casuals	1958	Back Beat 510
Juke Box	Co-Eds	1958	Cameo 129
Juke Box Rock 'n' Roll	Marigolds, Johnny Bragg & the	1956	Excello 2091
Juke Box Saturday Night	Ebb Tides, Nino & the	1961	Madison 166
Juke Box Saturday Night	Enchantments	1972	Clifton 3
Juke Hop	Falcons (Detroit)	1985	Relic LP 8005
Julie	Crescents, Billy Wells & the	1956	Reserve 105
Julie	Fiestas	1961	Strand 25046
Julie	Hi-Fives	1964	Bell 634
Julie	Romeos	1963	Felsted 8672
Julie	Senators	1959	Abner 1031
Julie Anna	Barrons	NA	Guest Star LP 1481
Julie Is Her Name	Signatures	1957	Whippet 210/Gen Norman 210X (57)
Julie Is Mine	Celestials, Bobby Gee & the	1959	Stacy 922
Julie, Julie (16 & 23)	Cherubs	1960	Dore 545
Julocka Jolly	Jumpin' Jacks	1989	Relic LP 5077
Jump And Bump	Flares	1960	Felsted 8607
Jump And Hop	Romancers	1956	Dootone 404
Jump Back Honey Ride	Four Flares	1958	Edison International 402
Jump Children	Flamingos	1954	Chance 1162
Jump In The Line	Gents	1961	Liberty 55332
Jump Lula	Original Mustangs, Dolores Curry & the	1959	Hi-Q 5040
Jump, Rock And Roll	Marvels (New York)	1956	ABC 9771
Jump, Shake And Move	Diablos (featuring Nolan Strong)	1955	Fortune 518
Jumpin' Bean, The	Mystics	1963	King 5735

SONG	GROUP	YEAR	LABEL
Jumpin' Jack	Three D's	1958	Paris 514
Jumpin' Jungle	Romancers	1960	Palette 5067
Jumpin' Over The Moon	Fullylove, Leroy & group	1961	Tandem 7002
Jumpin' Twist	Alam-Keys	1962, 1980	Kiski 2056
June Bride	Reflections	1965	Golden World 24
June, July, August And September	Travelers	1960	ABC 10119
June 30th	Catalinas, Phil & the	1960	Olimpic/Triodex 106
June Was The End Of August	Arcades	1959	Guyden 2015
Jungle	Concepts	1961	Apache 1515/Musictone 1109 (61)
Jungle Baby	Five Quails	1957	Mercury 71154
Jungle Bunny	Pearls	1959	Dooto 448
Jungle Drums	Passions	1960	Audicon 106
Jungle Fever	Creators	NA	Fortune LP 8017
Jungle Fever	Grand Prees	1963	Candi 1020
Jungle Fever	Playboys	1959	Rik 572
Jungle Fever	Shadows	1958	Del-Fi 4109
Jungle Fever (acappella)	Velvet Angels	1972	Relic LP 5004
Jungle Hop	Flips, Kip Tyler & the	1958	Challenge 59008
Jungle Lights	Channels (Chester, Pa.)	1959	Mercury 71501
Jungle Love	Starlettes	1958	Checker 895
Jungle Lullabye	Legends	1962	Caldwell 410
Jungle Superman	Individuals	1959	Show Time 598/Red Fox 105
Jungle Walk	Dyna-Sores	1960	Rendezvous 120
Junior	Candles	1964	Nike 1016
Junior	Moonglows	1960	Chess 1770
Junior Prom	Escorts, Bobby Chandler & the	1958	O.J. 1012
Junkeroo, The	Vibrations	1960	Checker 974
Jupiter-C	Satellites, Pat & the	1959	Atco 6131
Jury, The	Christie, Lou & group	1963	American Music Makers 006
Jury, The	Lions, Lugee & the	1961	Robbee 112
Just A Bad Thing	Charmers, Janice Christian & Johnny & the	1964	Swan 4174
Just A Boy	Chiffons	1966	Laurie 3350
Just A Down Home Girl	Ad Libs	1965	Blue Cat 123
Just A Dream	Thunderbirds, Chris Farlow & the	1965	General American 718
Just A Face In The Crowd	Dynels	1964	Natural 7001
Just A Fool	Capris (Philadelphia)	NA	Collectables LP 5000
Just A Fool	Four Kings And A Queen	1952	United (unreleased)
Just A Fool	Williams, Bobby & group	1960	Swingin' 619
Just A Friend	Grogan, Toby & group	1963	Vee Jay 560
Just A Friend	Nuggets	1962	RCA 8031
Just A Game	Vanguards, Buddy Gibson & the	1959	Swingin' 615
Just A Little	Prominents	1965	Lummtone 116
Just A Little Bit	Counts	1964	Rich Rose 711
Just A Little Bit	Townsmen (New York - Herald)	1963	Herald 585
Just A Little Bit More	Idols	1961	Reveille 1002/Dot 16210 (61)
Just A Little Bit More	Mad Lads, Frank Deaton & the	1957	Bally 1042
Just A Little Bit O' Lovin'	Chance, Wayne & group	1964	Whirlybird 2006
Just A Little Bit Of Loving	Masters, Scotty Mann & the	1956	Peacock 1665
Just A Little Bit Of Your Love	Fortune Tellers	1961	Sheryl 340
Just A Little Boy	Chanteers	1962	Mercury 72037
Just A Little Love	Reactions	1964	Cool Sound 701/Cloud 10498 (64)
Just A Little Lovin'	Titans, Don & Dewey & the	1957	Specialty 617
Just A Little Loving	Quintones (Chicago)	1954	Jordan 1601
Just A Little Walk With Me	Blenders (New York)	1952	Decca 28092
Just A Little While	Como, Nicky (with the Del Satins)	NA	Tang 1231
Just A Lonely Christmas	Moonglows	1953	Chance 1150
Just A Loser	Mystics	1964	Constellation 138/Safice 333
Just A Matter Of Time	Delltones, J. Jay & the	1963	Cobra 5555
Just A Memory	Paragons, Mack Starr & the	1961	Winley 250
Just A Moment	Sunglows, Sunny & the	1961	Lynn 511
Just A Picture	Largos	1961	Starmaker 1002
Just A Piece Of Paper	Counts, Bobby Comstock & the	1961	Festival 25000
Just A Poor Boy In Love	Marshall Brothers	1952	Savoy 833
Just A Shoulder To Cry On	Demensions	1963	Coral 62382
Just A Shoulder To Cry On	Hi-Fives	1958	Decca 30657

SONG	GROUP	YEAR	LABEL
Just A Stranger	Blue Flames	NA	Flame 1102
Just A Summer Kick	Class Cutters, Herbie & the	1959	RCA 7649
Just About Daybreak	Trojans	1961	Dodge 804
Just Across The Street	Del Rios	1962	Stax 125
Just Another Date	Galaxies	1976	Ronnie 201
Just Another Day In The Life Of A Fool	Lassiter, Art & group	1956	Ballad 1020
Just Another Fool	Debs	1963	Double L 727
Just Another Fool	Fashions, Dolly & the	1965	Ivanhoe 5019
Just Another Fool	Lee, Curtis (with the Halos)	1962	Dunes 2012
Just Another Fool	Marvels (Mun Rab)	1959	Mun Rab 1008
Just Another Lie	Bernard, Rod & group	1966	Arbee 105
Just Another Way To Break A Heart	Bobbinaires	NA	Jen-D
Just Around The Corner	Jive Bombers	1958	Savoy 1535
Just As I Am	Five Royales	1956	King 4973
Just As I Needed You	Fleetwoods	1964	Dolton 310
Just As Though You Were Here	Innocents, Kathy Young & the	1961	Indigo 121
Just Ask	Delcos	1963	Sound Stage 7 2515/Monument
Just Because	Cook, Bill	1951	Savoy 828
Just Because	Dreamlovers	1961	Heritage 102
Just Because	Drew-Vels, Patti Drew & the	1963	Capitol 5055
Just Because	Happy Jesters	1957	Dot 15566
Just Because	Juniors, Danny & the	1961	Swan 4084
Just Because Of A Kiss	Don Juans, Andre Williams & the	1956	Fortune 831/Epic 9196 (56)
Just Before You Leave	Dolls	1958	Teenage 1010
Just Bid Me Farewell	Four Bars	1961	Len 1014
Just Born (To Be Your Baby)	Schoolmates, Ronnie & the	1964	Coed 605
Just Can't Let Her Go	Twi-Lites	NA	Spenada 101
Just Come A Little Bit Closer	Four Fellows, Bette McLaurin & the	1955	Glory 237
Just Couldn't Please You	Cooper, Babs & group	1962	Indigo 144
Just Cry	Regents	1961	Gee LP 706
Just Dance	Performers	1966	ABC 10777
Just Don't Care	Strangers	1954	King 4728
Just Don't Sit There	Stylists (Maryland)	1955	Crown 145
Just Dreaming	Apollos	1960	Mercury 71614
Just Dreaming	Tillis, Clyde & group	1956	Cash 1054
Just Enough Of Your Love	Four Buddies	1964	Imperial 66018
Just Enough To Hurt Me	Astors	1963	Stax 139
Just Fall In Love	Ebb Tones, Don Grissom & the	1956	Million $ 2011
Just For A Little While	Tendertones	1959	Ducky 713
Just For A Thrill	Five Keys	1957	Capitol T-828 (D.J. copy)
Just For Fun	Thorns, Andy Rose & the	1960	Gold Crest 3807
Just For Kicks	Flamingos	1956	Checker 853
Just For Me	Chimes, Dave Burgess & the	1959	Challenge 59045
Just For Me	Fairlanes	1959	Dart 109
Just For Me	Nobles (Timbers)	1959	ABC 10012
Just For Tonight	Chiffons	1967	Laurie 3423
Just For Tonight	Four Young Men	1961	Crest 1083
Just For Tonight	Roommates (Roomates)	1964	Canadian American 166
Just For Tonite	Del-Rios	NA	Fortune LP 8017
Just For You	Citations	1962	Sara 101
Just For You	Cooke, Sam & group	1961	Sar 122
Just For You	Hi-Tones	1961	Fonsca 201
Just For You	Hollywood Flames	1959	Ebb 153
Just For You	Lamplighters	1955	Federal (unreleased)
Just For You	Rhythmaires, Curt Jensen & the	1958	Pet 806
Just For You	Roma, Teena & group	1961	Arteen 1002
Just For You	Shy-Tones	1960	1 Goodspin 401/Bruce
Just For You	Watkins, Billy & group	1964	Kent 411
Just For You And I	Supremes (Ohio)	1957	Ace 534
Just For You (Dance Dance)	Islanders, Rick & the	NA	H&G 185
Just For Your Love	Carousels	1973	Vintage 1012
Just For Your Love	Falcons (Detroit)	1959	Chess 1743/Anna 1110 (60)
Just For Your Love (I Would Do Anything)	Mystics	1963	King 5735
Just Forget About Me	Charms, Otis Williams & the	1961	King 5497

SONG	GROUP	YEAR	LABEL
Just Friends	Reed, Ursula (with Harriet Reeves & group)	1961	Eon 103
Just Give Her My Love	Calendars, Freddy Meade & the	1961	20th Fox 287
Just Give Me A Ring	McPhatter, Clyde (with the Cookies & the Cues)	1960	Atlantic 2049
Just Give Me Your Heart	Rebels	1961	Peacock 1909
Just Go	Hi-Fidelities, Gino Parks & the	1958	Fortune 528
Just Got The Feeling	Sweethearts	1958	Terrific 151
Just Got To Be Mine	Rivingtons	1964	Vee Jay 677
Just Got Up	Trojans	1961	Dodge 804
Just Gotta Be That Way	Travelers, Roger & the	1961	Ember 1079
Just How Long	Mel-O-Dots	1952	Apollo 1192
Just In Case	Fourmost	1963	Atco 6280
Just In Case	Pearlettes	1961	Craig 501/502/562/Seg-Way 1003 (61)
Just In Case You	Antlers	1952	Artists 1260
Just In Case You Change Your Mind	Naturals	1964	Chattahoochee 633
Just In Make Believe	Matadors, Tommy Liss & the	1963, 1997	Saxony 1005
Just In The Nick Of Time	Fun-Atics	1967	Select 571
Just In Your Imagination	Savoys, Marva & the	1963	Coed 582
Just Keep Me In Mind	Devilles	1960	Talent 103
Just Keep On Loving Me	Halos	1965	Congress 244
Just Leave It To Me	Debutantes	1956	Savoy 1191
Just Leave Me Alone	Derbys	1959	Mercury 71437
Just Let Me Love You	Wright, Willie (with the Sparklers)	1961	Federal 12406
Just Like A Baby	Admirations	1961	Apollo 753
Just Like A Fool	Kool Gents	1974	Vee Jay LP 1019/Charly LP 1113/ Solid Smoke LP 8026
Just Like A Fool	Robins	1955	Spark 122/Atco 6059 (56)
Just Like A Little Bitty Baby	Opals	1965	Laurie 3288
Just Like A Tear	Pixies	1962	AMC 102/Don-Dee 102 (63)
Just Like Before	Ensenators	1962, 1997	Tarx 1001/Reissue (97)
Just Like Before	Mann, Billy & group	1956	Dig 120
Just Like Before	Twilighters, Tony Allen & the	1961	Bethlehem 3002
Just Like In The Movies	Upbeats	1958	Swan 4010
Just Like Me (Ain't That)	Coasters	1961	Atco 6210
Just Like Mine	Renaults	1962	Wand 114
(Just Like) Romeo & Juliet	Reflections	1964	Golden World 8/9
Just Like That	Olympics	1961	Arvee LP A-424
Just Like That	Robins	1960	Arvee 5001
Just Like The Bluebird	Genies	1960	Warwick 607
Just Like Two Drops Of Water	Five Keys	1951	Aladdin (unreleased)
Just Like You	Sheppards (Chicago - Apex)	1961	Apex 7762
Just Love You So	River Rovers, Lydia Larsen & the	1989	Relic LP 5077
Just Me And You	Beatniks, Charles Walker & the	1958	Rhythm 116
Just Me And You	Dreamliners	1963	Cobra 013
Just My Imagination	Lords	1988	Starlight 62
Just My Imagination	Shades Of Brown	1982	Clifton EP 505
Just One Chance	Sparkletones	1963	Pageant 604
Just One Look	Marglows, Andy & the	1963	Liberty 55570
Just One Love	Glad Rags	1957	Excello 2121
Just One More	Williams, Eddie & group	1960	R-Dell 114
Just One More Chance	Combinations	NA	Carrie 010
Just One More Chance	Demensions	1963	Coral 62344
Just One More Chance	Modernistics, Al Lewis & the	1959	Music City 829
Just One More Kiss	Monterays (Brooklyn)	1964	Dominion 1019
Just One More Time	Concertones	1961	Legrand 1011
Just One More Time	Muffins	1963	Planet 59
Just One Smile	Tokens (Brooklyn)	1965	B.T. Puppy 513
Just Out Of Reach	Brown, Billy & group	1960	Republic 2007
Just Out Of Reach	Holidays	1954	King 1246
Just Outside Of Love	Pal, Ricki & group	1958	Arwin 115
Just Pretending	Versatiles	1977	Ramco 3717/Marie 101
Just Remember Me	Creations	1967	Globe 102
Just Room For Two	Coolbreezers	1974	Roadhouse 1019
Just Say The Word	Jay Cees	1962	Enjoy 1004

SONG	GROUP	YEAR	LABEL
Just Sittin'	Five Keys	1956	Capitol (unreleased)
Just Suppose	Hearts, Lee Andrews & the	1956, 1959 ,1981	Gotham 321/323/United Artists 162
Just The Boy Next Door	Deuces Wild	1960	Sheen 108
Just The Things That You Do	Eventuals	1961	Okeh 7142
Just The Things That You Do	Ineligibles	1960	Capella 501
Just Think Of Me	Crystalettes	1963	Crystalette 753
Just To Be In Love	Four Haven Knights	1957, 1973	Atlas 1092/Angletone 1092 (73)
Just To Be Near You	Baker, Bill & group	1962	Audicon 118/Musictone 1108 (62)
Just To Be Near You	Five Satins	1961	Musictone 1108
Just To Be With You	Five Keys	1959	King 5276
Just to Be With You	Paramounts	1963	Laurie 3201
Just To Be With You	Passions	1959	Audicon 102
Just To Be With You	West, Rudy & male group	1959	King 5276
Just To Hold My Hand	McPhatter, Clyde (with the Cues)	1957	Atlantic 1133
Just To Hold My Hand	Sha-Weez, Big Boy Myles & the	1956	Specialty 590
Just To Live Again	Honey Bees	1956	Imperial 5416
Just To Say Hello	Belvin, Jesse & group	1957	Modern 1027
Just To See You Smile Again	Four Buddies	1951	Savoy 769
Just To See You Smile Again	Four Buds	1950	Savoy 769
Just Today	Centuries	NA	Rich 112
Just Two Kinds Of People (acappella)	Youngones	1962	Times Square 28/Relic 540 (65)
Just Wait And See	Miller Sisters	1960	Hull 736
Just Wait For Me	Big Dog & group	1962	Joey 501
Just Waiting	Cardinals, Bobby Gregory & the	1959	Kip 403
Just Waiting For You	Margilators, Toby & Ray & the	1959	Blue Moon 411
Just Walk Away	Castells	1965	Decca 31834
Just Walking In The Rain	Prisonaires	1953	Sun 186
Just When I Needed You Most	Sheppards (Chicago - Apex)	1960	Apex 7759
Just Whisper	Du Droppers	1954	Groove 0013
Just Whisper	Reed, Lula (with the Teeners)	1954	King 4714
Just Wigglin' 'N Wobblin'	Del-Airs	1963	Coral 62370
Just Words	Cosmo (with the Carnations)	1962	Tilt 789
Just Words	Versatiles	1962	Peacock 1910
Just Yell	Supremes (Ohio)	1960	Mascot 126
Just You	Belmonts, Dion & the	1958	Laurie 3021
Just You	Crickets, Dean Barlow & the	1954	Jay-Dee 786
Just You	Darlettes, Diane & the	1962	Dunes 2016
Just You	Dubs	1963	Wilshire 201
Just You	Slades	1961	Domino 901
Just You And I	Rubies	1955	Verne 103
Just You And I And Love	Jades, Joe Beilin & the	1960	Christy 122
Just You And I Together	Excels	1960	Gone 5094
Just Young	Rose, Andy (with the Thorns)	1958	Aamco 100
Justine	Hollywood Allstars	1963	Admiral 501
Justine	Leggeriors	1963	Goliath 1351
Juvenile Delinquent	Citations, Buddy & the	1964	IRC 6918

K

SONG	GROUP	YEAR	LABEL
Ka Joom	Dynamics	1957	Warner 1016
Ka-Ding-Dong	Diamonds	1956	Mercury 70934
Ka-Ding-Dong	G-Clefs	1956, 1962	Pilgrim 715/Ditto 503
Kan-Cu-Wa	Scholars	1957	Imperial 5459
Kangaroo	Five Satins	1963	Warner Bros. 5367
Kangaroo Hop	Clark, Dee (with the Kool Gents)	1957	Falcon 1002
Kangaroo Hop	Runaways	NA	Teensound 1924
Kangaroo Twist	Three Reasons	1963	JRE 224
Kansas City	Midnighters, Hank Ballard & the	1959	King 5195
Kansas Kapers	Blenders (New York)	1956	Davis 441
Karen	Illusions, Jimmy & the	1963	Jolynn 36
Karen	Kruisers	1965	Kiski 2068
Karen	Lane, Rusty (with the Mystics)	1959	Laurie 3031
Karen	Ly-Dells	1963	Roulette 4493
Karen	Rip Chords	1962, 1963	Columbia 42641/42687
Karen My Darling	Flores, Teddy & group	NA	Deflor 65729
Karine	Consoles, Bobby & the	1966	Verve 10402

SONG	GROUP	YEAR	LABEL
Karine	Pedrick, Bobby & group	1966	Verve 10402
Kasanutu	Owls	NA	Arden 1000
Kathi, Please Don't Cry	Swordsmen	1961	Semac 2114
Kathleen	Adelphis	1958	Rim 2020
Kathleen	Chordliners	1988	
Kathy	Bluenotes, Ivan Gregory & the	1956	G&G 110
Kathy	Innocents	1961	Indigo 116
Kathy	Romeos, Jimmy & the	1960	Southside 1003
Kathy Jo	Trinities, Kayo & the	1960	Souvenir 1004
Kathy-O	Diamonds	1958	Mercury 71330
Katie Doll	Barrons	NA	Guest Star LP 1481
Katie The Kangaroo	Travelers	1958	Andex 2011
Keep A Light In The Window	Salutations, Vito & the	NA	Unreleased
Keep A Walkin'	Knight, Sonny & group	1955	Specialty 547/Specialty 594 (57)
Keep An Eye	Cordials	1961	7 Arts 707
Keep An Eye On Her	Echoes	1963	Smash 1807
Keep A-Tellin' You	Earls	1963	Old Town 1133
Keep Away From Carol	Crests	1960	Coed (unreleased)
Keep Cool	Jets, Roy Jordan & the	1956	Orpheus 1102
Keep Cool Crazy Heart	Upbeats	1959	Joy 227
Keep Her By My Side	Caribbeans	1958	20th Fox 112
Keep It A Secret	Five Crowns	1953	Rainbow 202
Keep It A Secret	Nite Riders, Doc Starkes & the	1989	Relic LP 5078
Keep It To Yourself	Royal Kings	1961	Forlin 502/Candlelight 410
Keep It Up	Antell, Pete & group	1963	Cameo 264
Keep It Up	Strings	NA	Mellow Town 1006
Keep Laughin'	Alteers	1961	Laurie 3097
Keep Laughin'	Renegades	1961	Dorset 5007
Keep Laughing	Scott Brothers	1960	Ribbon 6905
Keep Listening To Your Heart	Carter Rays	1961	Mala 433
Keep Me	Lands, Liz (with the Temptations)	1963	Gordy 7030
Keep Me Alive	Ermines	1956	Loma 704
Keep Me From Crying	Windsors	1959	Wig Wag 203
Keep Me On Your Mind	McQuinn, Kevin & group	1961	Diamond 101
Keep On Dancing	Avantis	1963	Argo 5436
Keep On Dancing	Midnighters, Hank Ballard & the	1961	King 5535
Keep On Loving You	Roleaks	NA	Hope 557
Keep On Moving	Persians	1955	Capitol 3230
Keep On Rolling	Coasters	1961	Atco 6192
Keep On Smiling	Flames	1953	7-11 2106
Keep On Trying	Ambassadors	1956	Air 5065
Keep On Writin'	George, Othea (with the Volumes)	1963	Volume 1100
Keep Singing And Look Ahead	Rebelaires	1957	B&K 103
Keep Talkin'	Wildcats	1955	RCA 6386
Keep That Beat	Belles, Terry & the	1958	Hanover 4505
Keep That Coffee Hot	Mellomen, Scatman Crothers & the	1955	Century 710
Keep The Boy Happy	Chiffons	1967	Laurie 3377
Keep The Hall Light Burning	Statues	1960	Liberty 55245
Keep The Magic Working	Lee, Shirley & group	1961	Seven Arts 711
Keep Twisting	Five Cookies	1962	Everest 19429
Keep Walking	Swanks	1957	Jaguar 3027
Keep Your Feet On The Floor	Jewels (Los Angeles)	1974	Imperial LP only
Keep Your Hands Off	Magicians	1966	Villa 706
Keep Your Heartaches To Yourself	London, Paul & group	1963	Limelight 3015
Keep Your Love Handy	Barnes, Jimmy & group	1959	Gibraltar 101
Keep Your Love Handy	Gibralters, Jimmy Barnes & the	1958	Gibraltar 101
Keep Your Love Strong	Fabulous Echoes	1964	Liberty 55769
Keep Your Mind On Me	Jarmels	1963	Laurie 3174
Keep Your Mind On Me	Robins	1958	Whippet 211
Keep-A-Rockin'	Champions	1954	Scott/Chart 602
Keeper Of Dreams	Gallahads	1960	Beechwood 3000/Starla 15
Keeper Of My Heart	Plaids	1956	Darl 1001
Keeper Of My Love	Chessmen	1959	Safari 1011
Keeps Me Worried All The Time	Answers	1957	United 212
Kenny	Pin-Ups	1964	Stork 1

SONG	GROUP	YEAR	LABEL
Kentuckian Song, The	Sandmen, Brook Benton & the	1955	Okeh 7058
Kentucky	Infatuators, Larry Lee & the	1961	Destiny 503
Kentucky Babe	Clovers	1959	United Artists LP 3033
Kentucky Babe	Harmonaires	1955	Royale
Kentucky Babe (acappella)	Notations	1975	Relic LP 104
Key, The	Dorn, Jerry (with the Hurricanes)	1957	King 5029
Key To My Heart	Rainbows	1962, 1968	Instant 3291
Key To My Heart	Robbins	1954	Crown 120
Key To My Heart	Taffys	1963	Fairmount 610
Key To My Heart	Twilighters, Tony & the	1960, 1977	Red Top 127
Key To My Heart, The	Four Sparks	1958	Cleff-Tone 152
Key To The Kingdom (Of Your Heart)	Nutmegs	1956	Herald 475
Key To Your Heart	Gunter, Cornel & group	1964	Challenge
Kickapoo Joy Juice	Rivingtons	1962	Liberty 55513
Kickapoo, The	Clovers	1963	Brunswick 55249
Kicked Around	Ad Libs	1965	Blue Cat 102
Kickin' Child	DiMucci, Dion (with the Del Satins)	1965	Columbia 43293
Kicking With My Stallion	Kings Men	1957	Club 51 108
Kid Me Not Baby	Dariens	NA	Carlson International 0027
Kid Stuff	Mello-Kings	1960	Herald 554
Kiddy Car Love	Sensations	1958	Atco 6115
Kidnapper	Rubies, Jewell & the	1963	La Louisianne 8041/ABC 10485 (63)
Kilimanjaro	Dell Vikings	1962	ABC 10341
Kill It	Antwinetts	1958	RCA 7398
Killer Diller	Cues	1988	Capitol (unreleased) (recorded 1956)
Killer Joe	Rocky Fellers	1963	Scepter 1246
Kimberly	Turn Ons, Tim Tam & the	1966	Palmer 5006
Kind Of Boy You Can't Forget, The	Jelly Beans	1964	Red Bird 10-011
Kind Of Boy You Can't Forget, The	Raindrops	1963	Jubilee 5455
Kind Of Trouble I Love, The	Delrons, Reperata & the	1967	RCA 9123
King Cobra	Wildtones	1958	Tee Gee 105
King Kong	Holidays, Dick Holler & the	1961	Herald 566
King Kong	Saints, Orlie & the	1961	Band Box 253
King Love	Allures	1963	Melron 5009
King Of All Fools	Strollers	1960	20th Fox 226
King Of Broken Hearts	Daytons	1959	Norgolde 101
King Of Broken Hearts	Suburbans	1960	Kip 221
King Of Fools	Crystals, Sam Hawkins & the	1959	Gone 5042
King Of Fools	Pastels (Limelight)	1963	Limelight 3007
King Of Fools	Van Dykes	1962	Atlantic 2161
King Of Hearts	Cookies	1957	Josie 822
King Of Hearts	Gee, Billy & group	1959	Coronet 1303
King Of Love	Paramounts	1976	Broadcast 1138
King Of Lovers	Blenders, Ray Frazier & the	1960	Combo 161/Relic LP 5069 (87)
King Of Lovers	Davis, Hal Sonny & group	1959	Alden 1303
King Of Rock And Roll	Continental Five	1959	Nu Kat 104/105
King Of The Blues	Furness Brothers, Al Berry & the	1957, 1964	Prep 107/Melmar 116
King Of The Mountain	Victors, Little Man & the	1963	Tarheel 064
King Of The World	Sherwoods, Johnny Schilling & the	1963	C&A 507
King Of Wealth	Joseph, Mike & group	1962	Lucky Four 1017
King Or A Fool	Penn, Tony & group	1959	P.R.I. 101
King, The	Adams, Richie & group	1964	Congress 226
King Tut Rock, The	Socialites, Kenny & the	1958	Crosstown 001
King Without A Queen	DiMucci, Dion (with the Del Satins)	1963	Laurie 3171
Kingdom Of Love	Preludes	1958	Acme 730/Cub 9005 (58)
Kingdom Of Love	Scott Brothers	1959, 1961	Skyline 502/FTP 415
Kingdom Of Love	Tempos	1957	Kapp 178
Kingless Castle	Kodaks	1958	Fury 1019
Kiss A Fool Goodbye	Penguins	1955	Dootone 362
Kiss A Fool Goodbye	Whipoorwills	1953	Dooto 1201
Kiss And Make Up	Five Crowns	1958	R&B 6901
Kiss And Run Driver	Furys, Ray & the	1961	Coed 558
Kiss And Run Lover	Stylers	1958	Golden Crest 1291
Kiss And Say Goodbye	Choice	1988	Clifton 80
Kiss And Tell	Desires, Julie & the	1964	Laurie 3266

SONG	GROUP	YEAR	LABEL
Kiss Away	Clips	1956	Calvert 105
Kiss In The Night	Citations	1961, 1977	Don-El 113
Kiss In Your Eyes, The	Bon Bons	1957	Columbia 40887
Kiss Kiss	Royal Demons	1961	Pek 8101
Kiss, Kiss, Kiss	Five Fashions	1965	Catamount 107
Kiss, Kiss, Kiss	Jive Five	1965	United Artists 853
Kiss, Kiss, Kiss	Uniques	1981	Clifton 62
Kiss Me	Dell Vikings	1961	ABC 10278
Kiss Me	Five Grands	1958	Brunswick 55059
Kiss Me	Scarlets	1955	Red Robin 138
K-I-S-S Me	Valentines	1955	Rama 186
Kiss Me Again And Again	Devilles	1958	Aladdin 3423
Kiss Me Baby	Cardinals	1952	Atlantic 958
Kiss Me Baby	Four Tops	1956	Chess 1623
Kiss Me Baby	Moonglows	1959	Chess LP 1430/Chess LP 701 (76)
Kiss Me, Benny	Rollettes	1956	Class 203
Kiss Me Goodbye	Chants	1961	Tru Eko 3567/UWR 4243 (61) MGM 13008 (61)
Kiss Me Goodnight	Rosebuds	1959	Lancer 102
Kiss Me My Love	Blue Rays, Joe Hammond & the	1958	Bee 1102
Kiss Me My Love	Honey Bees	1964	Bee 1101
Kiss Me Quickly	Neons	1956	Tetra 4444
Kiss Me, Sugar Plum	Four Dots (Pittsburgh)	1956	Bullseye 104
Kiss Me Tenderly	Dates, Lincoln Fig & the	1958	Worthy 1006
Kiss Of Fire	Harvey Sisters	1962	Newtime 512
Kiss, The	Delicates	1960	United Artists 228
Kiss, The	Mello Kings	1950	Imperial 5105
Kiss The Hurt Away	Dovells	1970	Decca 32919
Kiss Them For Me	Eagles	1957	Prep 118
Kiss You A Thousand Times	Rock-A-Bops, Jeannie Dell, Johnnie B & the	1960	Josie 878
Kiss-A-Kiss	Adelphis	1958	Rim 2022
Kiss-A-Kiss, Hug-A-Hug	Chromatics, Eddie Singleton & the	1958	Amasco 3701
Kiss-A-Me	Flamingos	1959	Decca 30880
Kisses And Roses	Four Thoughts	1964	Womar 103
Kisses Left Unkissed	Duvals, Phil Johnson & the	1958	Kelit 7032
Kissin'	Earls	1963	Old Town 1145
Kissin' At The Drive-In	Four J's	1958	Herald 528
Kissin' Game	DiMucci, Dion (with the Del Satins)	1961	Laurie 3090
Kissin' In The Back Row Of The Movies	Drifters (1959-forward)	1974	Bell 45,600
Kissin' In The Kitchen	Chandler, Gene (with the Dukays)	1961	Vee Jay 416/Nat 4003 (62)
Kissin' In The Kitchen	Dovells	1962	Parkway 855
Kissin' Like Lovers	Specials	1963	Marc 103
Kissing Behind The Moon	Style Kings	1959	Sotoplay 0011
Kissing Bug	Tenderfoots	1955	Federal 12214
Kissing Song (Sweetie Lover), The	Sheiks	1955	Cat 116
Kissy Face	Dupries	1960	Thunderbird 106
Kitty	Drakes	1958	Conquest 1001
Kitty From New York City	Gems (Illinois)	1954	Drexel 903
Knee Bop	Ballads (Connecticut)	1960	Ron-Cris 1003
Knee Socks	Ideals, Johnny Brantley & the	1959	Checker 920/Checker 979 (61)
Kneel And Pray	Paragons, Mack Starr & the	1961	Winley 250
Kneel And Pray	Ravens	1956	Argo 5255
Knew I Had A Chance	Palms	1956	States (unreleased)
Knock Her Down	Orbits	1959	Nu Kat 116/117
Knock, Knock, Knock (Knocking On My Door)	Bel-Aires, Eddy Bell & the	1961	Mercury 71763
Knock, Knock, Who's There	Deb-Tones	1959	RCA 7539
Knock On Any Door	Executives, Margie Mills & the	1963	Vee Jay 549
Knock On Wood	Evans, Jerry (with the Off Keys)	1962	Bubble 1333
Knock You Flat	Dimensions	1967	Panorama 41
Knock Yourself Out	Washington, Baby (with the Hearts)	1959	J&S 1632/1633
Knocked Out	Gondoliers, Johnny Adams & the	1959	Ric 957
Knock-Kneed Nellie From Knox	Jumpin' Jaguars	1956	Decca 29938
Knockout	Ivy Jives	1960	Jaro 77036
Know It All	Enchanters (Spellbound)	1956	Stardust 102

SONG	GROUP	YEAR	LABEL
Knowing It Was Heartbreak	Chase, Bobby & group	1965	Ascot 2195
Knowing You	Roomates	NA	Ban 691
Ko Ko Mo	Flamingos	1955, 1960	Parrot 812/End 1085
Ko Ko Mo (I Love You So)	Charms, Otis Williams & the	1955	DeLuxe 6080
Ko Ko Mo, The	Valtairs	1965	Selsom 106
Kola	Serenaders (Detroit)	1974 (1952)	Roadhouse 1017
Kookie Ookie	Sinceres	1963	Epic 9583
Kool It	Impacs	1964	King 5891
Korea	Velps	1972 (1957)	Roadhouse 1002
Krambuli	Daytones	1963	Jubilee 5452
Kum Ba Yah	Blue Jays (Roulette)	1960	Roulette 4264
Kwela, Kwela	Colts, Jackie Kelso & the	1955	Vita 114

L

SONG	GROUP	YEAR	LABEL
L. A. Lover	Hollywood Saxons	1961	Hareco 102/Swingin' 631 (61)/ Elf 101 (61)/20th Century 312 (63)
L.A. Shuffle, The	Storytellers	1991	Classic Artists 133
La Bamba	Alamos, Tony Valla & the	1961	Fortune 858
La Bamba	Carlos Brothers	1960	Del-Fi 4145
La Bamba	Tokens (Brooklyn)	1962	RCA 8052
La Bamba	Upbeats, Ray Allen & the	1962	Blast 204
La Bomba	Cadillacs, Bobby Ray & the	1963	Capitol 4935
La Corrida	Matadors	1964	Colpix 718
La De Da	Payne, Chuck & group	1957	Atlas 1072
La De Do De Do	Chromatics, Sherry Washington & the	1955	Million 2010
La Do Da Da	Fabulous Futuras	NA	Okon (no #)
La Hora Del Crepusculo (Twilight Time)	Platters	1963	LP SR 60808
La La	Four Knights	1962	Triode 104
La La (Hey Baby)	Cobras (Philadelphia)	1964	Casino 1309/Swan 4176
(La La) I Love You	Caesars	NA	Lanie 2001
La La La	Deltones	1959	Jubilee 5374
La La La La La	Blendells	1964	Rampart 641/Reprise 0291 (64)
La La La (Lessons Of The Cha Cha)	Co-Eds	1958	Cameo 134
La La La Song	Volumes	NA	Chex
La Lala Lala	True Tones	1965	Spot 1121
La Macerena	Jayhawks	1961	Argyle 1005
La Macerena	Sparks	1959	Decca 30974
Lad	G-Clefs	1962	Terrace 7503
Ladder	Cues	1991	Capitol (unreleased) (recorded 1956)
Ladder Of Love	Chateaus	1959	Warner Bros. 5071
Ladder Of Love, The	Flamingos	1957	Decca 30335
Ladder Of Prayer	Hinton, Joe & group	1958	Back Beat 519
Ladies Choice	Kingsmen	1961	Jalynne 108
Ladies In The Sky	Eagles	1957	Prep 118
Ladise	Packards	1956	Pla-Bac 106
La-Do-Da-Da	Keytones	1962	Chelsea 101
Lady Is A Tramp, The	Our Gang	NA	Starlight 4
Lady Like	Coasters	1965	Atco 6341
Lady Love	Del-Larks	1958	East West 116
Lady Luck	Creations	1962	Penny 9022/Take Ten 1501 (63)
Lady Of Spain	Halos, Johnny Angel & the	1961	Felsted 8633
(Lady Of The) Caravan	Deans	1963	Star Maker 1931
Lady Of The Sea	Downbeats	1956	Sarg 162
Lady Of The Sea	Moods	1959	Sarg 162
Lady, Play Your Mandolin	Jumping Jacks	1956	Capitol 3415
Lah-Tee-Lah-Tah	Falcons (Detroit)	1962	Atlantic 2153
Laid Off	Cordells	1961	Bargain 5004
Laki-Lani	Medallions	1955	Essex 901
La-La-La	Manhattans	1962	Capitol 4730
La-La-La-La-La	Overtones	1966	Ajax 173
Lama Rama Ding Dong	Edsels	1958	Dub 2843
Lambie Baby	Van Dykes	1958	Decca 30762
Lament Of Silver Gulch, The	Turbans (Philadelphia)	1961	Imperial 5807
Lamplight	Deltas	1957, 1973	Gone 5010
Lana	Velvets (Texas)	1961	Monument 448

SONG	GROUP	YEAR	LABEL
Land Of 1000 Dances	Fabulous Royals	NA	Aegis 1006
Land Of A 1000 Dances (acappella)	Five Sharks	1966	Amber 852
Land Of Beauty	Diamonds	1957	Mercury 71242
Land Of Broken Hearts	Restless Hearts, Fred Parris & the	1966	Atco 6439
Land Of Love	Foster Brothers, Lefty Guitar Bates & the	1960	Dilly 101
Land Of Love	Tridels	1964	San-Dee 1009
Land Of Love (despite label, not by Five Chances)	Five Chances	1960	Corina 2002
Land Of Promises	Cashiers, Eddie Cash & the	1958	Peak 1001
Land Of Rock And Roll	Echos	1982	Crystal Ball 150
Land Of You And Me	Four Esquires	1958	Paris 526
Language Of Love	El Dorados	1956	Vee Jay (unreleased)
Lanky Linda	De Bonairs	1956	Ping 1000
Large Charge	Chargers	1959	B.E.A.T. 1006
Lariat	Legends	NA	Key 1002
Larry Applebaum	Three Graces	1960	Golden Crest 546
Las Vegas Drive	Highlighters	1959	New Song 133
Lassie Come Home	Ding Dongs	1960	Todd 1043
Last Chance	Satellites, Collay & the	1960	Sho-Biz 1002
Last Dance	Essentials, Billy & the	1963	Mercury 72210
Last Dance	Twisters, Joey & the	1962	Dual 509
Last Dance, The	Harptones	1961	Companion 102
Last Date	Travelers	1963	Yellow Sand 2
Last Drag, The	Voxpoppers	1958	Amp-3 1004/Mercury 71282 (58)
Last Goodbye	Darvels, Frankie & the	1977	Crystal Ball 109
Last Letter, The	Blossoms	1989	Classic Artists 110
Last Minute Miracle	Shirelles	1967	Scepter 12198
Last Night	Alley Cats	1957	Whippet 209
Last Night	Cashmeres, Dale & the	1961	Matt 161
Last Night	Marylanders	1974 (1954)	Roadhouse 1015
Last Night	Starlighters	1956	Irma 101
Last Night	Vikings, Barry & the	1964	Jamie 1281
Last Night I Cried	Hi-Fidelities, Gino Parks & the	1958	Fortune 528
Last Night I Dreamed	Epics	1961	Lynn 516/Sabra 516
Last Night I Dreamed	Fiestas	1958	Old Town 1062
Last Night I Dreamed	Satellites, Ronny & the	1959	Rose 1001
Last Night I Dreamed	Streetcorner Serenade	1989	Starlight 65
Last Night I Saw A Girl	Impalas (20th Fox)	1963	20th Fox 428
Last Nights Dream	Motions, Ron & the	NA	Red Bug
Last Nite I Dreamed (acappella)	Chevieres	1975	Relic LP 109
Last Of The Good Rockin' Men, The	Four Jacks	1952	Federal 12087
Last Of The Real Smart Guys	Premiers, Julie Stevens & the	1961	Dore 603
Last One To Know, The	Fleetwoods	1960	Dolton 27
Last Ride, The	Dukes (California)	1956	Imperial (unreleased)
Last Saturday Night	C-Notes	1959	Arc 4447
Last Summer Love	Grand Prixs	1963	Pancho
Last Summer Love	Mondo, Joe & group	1963	Epi 1003
Last Supper, The	Duvals (Prelude)	1963	Prelude 110
Last Year About This Time	Symbols	1963	Dore 666
Last Years Christmas Tree	Heartstrings, Johnny Jason & the	NA	Romantic 101/102
Late Darlin'	Montereys	NA	Trans American 1000/1001
Late Date	Parkays	1961	ABC 10242
Late In The Evening	Francettes	1963	Besche 100
Late Last Night	Ding Dongs	1960	Todd 1043
Late Rising Moon	Blenders, Earl Curry & the	1954	R&B 1304
Later	Four Flames, Bobby Day & the	1952	Specialty 423
Later Baby	Four Kittens, Fat Man Matthews & the	1952	Imperial 5211
Later Baby	Raiders, Hal Goodson & the	1957	Solo 108
Later For You, Baby	Solitaires	1955	Old Town 1015
Later, Later	Cookies	1955	Atlantic 1061
Later Later Baby	Five Crowns	1952	Old Town 792
Later, Later, Baby	Re-Vels	1956	Sound 129
Latin Love	Royaltones	1956	Old Town 1028
Laugh	Parrish, Troy (with the Metallics)	1962	Baronet 10
Laugh	Velvets (Texas)	1961	Monument 448

SONG	GROUP	YEAR	LABEL
Laugh Of The Town, The	Fortunes	1964	Yucca 168/170
Laugh (Though You Want To Cry)	Swallows (Maryland)	1953	King 4612
Laughin'	Snaps, Ginger Davis & the	1962	Swan 4090
Laughing	Orioles, Sonny Til & the (with the Sid Bass Orchestra)	1954	Jubilee 5161
Laughing At Me	Silver Slippers, Barbara J & the	1961	Lescay 3001
Laughing Blues	Du Droppers	1953	RCA 5229
Laughing Blues	Hollywood Saxons	1962	Action-Pac 111
Laughing Boy	Love-Tones, Mary Wells & the	1963	Motown 1039
Laughing Boy	Swallows (Maryland)	1958	Federal 12329
Laughing Girl	Hollywood Saxons	1968	Swingin' 654
Laughing Love	Native Boys	1956	Combo 119
Laughing On The Outside	Crystals (Iona)	NA	Iona 1009
Laughing On The Outside	Harptones	1959	Warwick 500
Laughing On The Outside	Premiers, Artie & Linda & the	1964	Chancellor 1147
Laughing On The Outside, Crying On The Inside	Majors (Brooklyn)	1951	Derby 763
Laughing With Tears In My Eyes	Commodores	1959	Brunswick 55126
Laughing With Tears In My Heart	Runaways	1978	Crystal Ball 125
Laundromat Blues	Five Royales	1953	Apollo 448
Launie, My Love	Val-Aires	1959	Willette 114/Coral 62119 (59)/ Coral 62177 (59)
Laura	Camerons	1977	Crystal Ball 112
Laura	Ovations (Starlight)	1986	Starlight 43
Laura My Darling	Regents	1961	Gee 1071
Laura My Darling (acappella)	Semesters	1975	Relic LP 104
Lavender Blue	Fleetwoods	1961	Dolton BLP 2007/BST 8007
Lavern	Lamplighters	NA	Unreleased
Laverne	Earls	1990	Relic LP 5087
Laverne	Five Thrills	1981	Parrot 803
Lawd, Lawd, Lawd	Ebonaires (with the Maxwell Davis Orch.)	1953	Aladdin 3212
Lawdy Miss Clawdy	Four Lovers	1957	RCA LP 1317
Lawdy Miss Clawdy	Stites, Gary & group	1960	Carlton 525
Lawdy Miss Mary	Five Keys	1951, 1989	Groove 0031/Detour LP 33-010
Lawdy When She Kissed Me	Aristocats	1958	Sue 714
Lawful Wedding	Cuff Links	1958	Dooto 438
Lawman, The	Fiestas	NA	Ace LP CH173
Lawrence Was His Name	Miller Brothers	1963	Coed 577
Lay It On The Line	Dominoes	1961	King 5463
Lay Your Head On My Shoulder	Five Willows	1954	Herald 433
Lay Your Head On My Shoulder	Quails, Bill Robinson & the	1968	Date 1620
Lazy Bonnie	Four Imperials	1958	Lorelei 4444/Dot 15737 (58)
Lazy Country Side	Four Vagabonds	1953	Lloyds 102
Lazy Daisy	Willows	NA	Mercury
Lazy Love	Demilles	1964	Laurie 3247
Lazy Love	Laurie, Linda & group	1962	Rust 5042
Lazy Mary Memphis	Revlons, Tino & the	1966	Dearborn 530
Lazy Mule	Ravens	1957	Argo 5284
Lazy River	Platters	1960	Mercury LP 20481/ Mercury LP 60160 (60)
Lazy River Rolls By	Orioles, Sonny Til & the	1948	Jubilee (unreleased)
Lazy Susan, The	Blue Notes, Joe Weaver & the	1955	Jaguar 3011
Lazy Walker	Royal Teens	NA	Empire 1001
Lazy Woman	West, Eastin & group	1963	Everest 2028
Le Chaim (Good Luck)	Deans	1960	Mohawk 119
Lead Me Back	English, Scott (with the Accents)	1971	Janus 171
Lead Me On	Derbys	1962	Savoy 1609
Lead Me On	Sensationals, Jimmy Jones & the	1965	Savoy 4234
Leaf, The	Collegians, Jackie Roy & the	1953	Okeh 6970
Leaky Heart And His Red Go-Kart	Escorts (Scarlet)	1960	Scarlet 4005
Lean On Me	Crests	1964	Cameo 305
Lean On Me	Reunion	NA	Starlight 17
Lean On Me When Heartaches Get Rough	Four Bars, Betty Wilson & the	1962	Dayco 4564
Lean Pretty Baby	Four Kings And A Queen	1952	United (unreleased)

SONG	GROUP	YEAR	LABEL
Leap Year	Carnations	1960	University 606
Leap Year Cha Cha	Dukes (California)	1959	Flip 345
Learnin' The Blues	Dominoes	1955	King 1492
Learning About Love	Crests	1960	Coed (unreleased)
Leave Her For Me	Jades	1958	Time 1002
Leave Her To Me	Jades	1958	Dot 15822/Time 1002
Leave It To Me	Griffins	1956	Wing 90067
Leave Me Alone	Fabulous Twilights, Nathaniel Mayer & the	1962	Fortune 547
Leave Me Alone	Malibus	1963	Planet 58
Leave Me Baby	Chalons	1958	Dice 89
Leave Me If You Want to	Yo Yo's, Delma Goggins & the	1961	Vibro 4008
Leave Me Never	Sundowners	1965	Coed 603
Leave My Gal Alone	Ravens	1949	King 4293
Leave My Gal Alone	Suburbans	1957	Baton 240
Leave My Woman Alone	Cox, Herbie (with the Cleftones)	1958	Rama 233
Leave My Woman Alone	Lovenotes	1953	
	(Clarence Johnson & Ed Anderson)		
Leave Those Cats Alone	Roses, Don & His	1958	Dot 15784
Leave Us Alone	Delrons, Reperata & the	1964	Laurie 3252
Leave Us Alone	Vonns	1963	King 5793
Leavin' Surf City	Saints, Dave & the	1963	Band Box 341
Leaving You Baby	Angels (Philadelphia)	1956	Irma 105
Lebone Delada	Buddies	1961	Swan 4073
Left Front Row	Fabulous Cry-Tels	1960	
Left With A Broken Heart	Admirals	1955	King 4772
Leg, The	Continentals, Morris Rogers & the	NA	Delta 601
Legend Of Love	Lovers, Billy Love & the	1964	Dragon 4403
Legend Of Love	Top Hands, Joe Dee & His (with the Tremonts)	1962	Pat Riccio 101
Legend Of Love	Tremonts (with Joey Dee & the Top Hands)	1961	Brunswick 55217/Pat Riccio 101 (62)
Legend Of Love, The	Legends	1958	Hull 727
Legend Of Sleepy Hollow, The	Monotones	1959	Argo 5321
Legion Of The Lost	Safaris	19??	Image LP
Lemon Squeezer	Four Barons	1950	Regent 1026
Lemon Squeezing Daddy	Sultans	1951	Jubilee 5054
Lemonade Baby	Oliver, Johnny & group	1954	MGM 55001
Lend Me Your Ear	Originals	1960	Poor Boy 110
Lenny Lenny	Gingersnaps	1958	Kapp 226
Lenora	Corvets	1958	Way-Out 101
Lenora	Travelers	1957	Atlas 1086
Lenora	Vondells	1964	Marvello 5006
Lenore	Matthews, Dino & group	1962	Dot 16365
Lenore	Po Boys, Edgar Allen & the	1962	Rust 5053
Leona	Dimples, Eddie Cooley & the	1959	Triumph 609
Leona	Elbert, Donnie & group	1957	DeLuxe 6148
Leona	Hearts, Lee Andrews & the	1956	Gotham 320
Leonore	Reveres	1958	Glory 272
Leopard, The	Galaxies	1961	Richie 458
Leotards	Royal Teens	1959	Mighty 111
Les Qua	Majors (Felsted)	1959	Felsted 8576
Lessie Mae	Thrillers (Detroit)	1953	Thriller 3530
Lesson	Blends, Glenn Wells & the	1960	Jin 122
Lesson From The Stars	Charmers	1963	Sure Play 104
Lessons In Love	Allisons	1962	Smash 1749
Lessons In Love	Montclairs, Mel Williams & the	1954	Decca 29370
Lest You Forget	Invictas	1958	Pix 1101
Let A Smile Be Your Umbrella	Four Most	1956	Dawn 220
Let Christmas Ring	Coolbreezers	1958	Bale 102/103
Let 'Em Roll	Midnighters	1957	Federal 12305
Let 'Em Try	Gordon, Roscoe & group	1961	Vee Jay 385
Let Her Feel Your Kiss	Showmen	1963	Airecords 334
Let Her Go	Carpets	1956	Federal 12257
Let Her Go	Techniques	1958	Roulette 4048
Let Her Go Man	Minor Chords	1962	Lu Pine 112
Let Her Know	Bluenotes	1958	Colonial 7779
Let Him Go	Starlites, Jackie & the	1991	Relic LP 5090

SONG	GROUP	YEAR	LABEL
Let Him Go Little Heart	Emblems, Patty & the	1966	Kapp 791
Let It Be	Smith, Savannah & group	1960	End 1077
Let It Be Me	Falcons (Detroit)	1985	Relic LP 8005
Let It Be Me	Jades, McMillin Brothers & the	1959	Christy 120
Let It Be Me	Watts, Bette & male group	1960	Wand 104
Let It Be Now	Little Buck & group	1960	Duke 324
Let It Be You	Randells, Rick & the	1959	ABC 10055
Let It Please Be You	Carolons	1964	Mellomood 1003
Let It Please Be You	Desires	1959	Hull 730
Let It Please Be You	Masters, Rick & the	1963	Cameo 247
Let It Please Be You	Re'Vells	1962	Roman Press 201
Let It Please Be You	Street-Tones, Patty & the	1980	Clifton 49
Let It Rain	Five Pennies	1955	Savoy 1182
Let It Ride	Blue Chips	1961	RCA 7935
Let It Ride	Four Winds	1968	B.T. Puppy 555
Let It Rock	Hearts, Buddy & the	1964	Landa 701
Let Love Come Later	Utopians	1963	Imperial 5921
Let Me	Minor Chords, Sunnie Elmo & the	1960	Flick 009
Let Me Back In There Again	Earls, Paul Crawford & the	1956	DC 0400
Let Me Be Baby	Permanents	1963	Chairman 4405
Let Me Be The First To Know	Lovers	1956	Decca 29862
Let Me Be The One	Crests	1958	Coed (unreleased)
Let Me Be The One	Teenettes	1963	Sandy 250
Let Me Be True To You	Hi-Liters (with King Bassie & the Three Aces)	1958	Hico 2432
Let Me Be Your Girl	Originals	1960	Brunswick 55171
Let Me Be Your Girl	Valentinos	1960	Brunswick 55171
Let Me Be Your Man	Five Hearts	NA	Unreleased
Let Me Call You	Atlantics	1965	Rampart 614
Let Me Come Back	Checkers	1952, 1960	King 4581/Federal 12375
Let Me Come Back (acappella)	Chessmen	1975	Relic LP 102
Let Me Come Back (acappella)	Velvet Angels	1964	Medieval 201
Let Me Come Back Home	Five Royales	1954	Apollo 458
Let Me Cry	Five Birds, Willie Headen & the	1957	Authentic 410/Dootone 410
Let Me Down Easy	Cadillacs	1961	Jubilee LP 1117
Let Me Down Easy	Love, Jimmy & group	1963	Violet 1052
Let Me Dream	Belvin, Jesse (with the Feathers)	1958	Aladdin 3431
Let Me Dream	Classics (Los Angeles)	1959	Crest 1063
Let Me Dream	Matadors	1966	Forbes 230/Chartmaker 404
Let Me Dream	Sharptones, Jesse Belvin & the	1958	Aladdin 3431
Let Me Explain	Cadillacs	1955	Josie 785
Let Me Get Close To You Baby	Clips	1956	Calvert 105
Let Me Get Next To You	Four Jacks, Mac Burney & the	1956	Hollywood 1058
Let Me Give You Money	Pipes	1956	Dootone 388
Let Me Go Home Whiskey	Little, Lee Roy & group	1960	Cee Jay 579
Let Me Go Home Whisky	Lovenotes	1953	Tivoli 1041
Let Me Go Lover	Counts	1955	Dot 1235
Let Me Go Lover	Valiants (New York)	1959	Joy 235
Let Me Hang Around You	Reactions	1964	Cool Sound 701/Cloud 10498 (64)
Let Me Have Your Love	Moods	1959	Sarg 179
Let Me Hear It Again	Pebbles	1955	Middle-Tone 2002
Let Me Hear You Say Yeah	Originals, Tony Allen & the	1960	Original Sound 10
Let Me Help You	Wil-Sons	1961	Highland 1020
Let Me Hold You	Clovers	1961	Winley 255
Let Me Hold Your Hand	Hy-Tones, Georgia Harris & the	1958	Hy-Tone 121
Let Me Hold Your Hand	Midnighters	1957	Federal 12288
Let Me Hold Your Hand	Moonglows	1956	Chess (unreleased)
Let Me In	Five Knights	1961	Minit 626
Let Me In	Rialtos	1962	CB 5009
Let Me In	Sensations	1961	Argo 5405
Let Me In Your Heart	Zane, Herb & group	1956	DeLuxe 6099
Let Me In Your Life	Kac-Ties	1963	Shelley 165/Atco 6299 (64)
Let Me In Your Life	Vilons	1961	Lake 713
Let Me Know	Impressions, Jerry Butler & the	1976	Vee Jay LP 1075
Let Me Know	Kings (Joe Van Loan)	1957	Baton 245
Let Me Know	Miller Brothers	1963	Coed 577

SONG	GROUP	YEAR	LABEL
Let Me Know	Three D's	1957	Paris 503
Let Me Know, Let Me Know, Let Me Know	Embers, Jeff Milner & the	1959	Dale 113
Let Me Know Tonight	Blue Dots	1954	DeLuxe 6067
Let Me Know Tonight	Nitecaps	1956	Groove 0176
Let Me Live	Four Bars	1955	Josie 783
Let Me Love You	Charades	1959	United Artists 183
Let Me Love You	Headliners, George Goodman & the	1964, 1965	Val 1/1000/Warner Bros. 5632 (65)/ A&M 1011 (68)
Let Me Love You	Metallics, J. D. Wright & the	1962	Baronet 16
Let Me Love You	Sheppards (Chicago - United)	1956	United (unreleased)
Let Me Love You Baby	Zephyrs	1965	Rotate 5009
Let Me Love You, Love You	Bells	1955	Rama 166
Let Me Love You Tonight	Belvin, Jesse & group	1956	Modern 1005
Let Me Love You Tonight	Scotties	1959	Scottie 1305
Let Me Make My Own Mistakes	Wayne, Art & group	1961	Xavier 8890
Let Me Make Up Your Mind	Penguins	1958	Dooto 432
Let Me Make You Happy	Superiors	1966	MGM 13503
Let Me Out	Ginos, Jeff & the	1963	Mercury 72138
Let Me Ride	Valiants (New York)	1959	Joy 235
Let Me Share Your Dreams	Deltas	1957, 1973	Gone 5010
Let Me Show You (Around My Heart)	Turbans (Philadelphia)	1955	Herald 458
Let Me Sleep Woman	Ecuadors	1959	Argo 5353
Let Me Steal Your Heart Away	Mystics	NA	Collectables LP 5043
Let Me Take You Home	Webs	1958	Sotoplay 006
Let Me Take You Out Tonight	Five Emeralds	1954	S-R-C 106
Let Me Tell You	Five Shits	1973	Lost Cause 100
Let Me Tell You	Litations	1963	N/A
Let Me Tell You	Mitlo Sisters (with the Dreamtones)	1958	Klik 8405
Let Me Tell You	Nutmegs	1963	Times Square 6/Relic 531 (65)
Let Me Tell You, Baby	Chateaus	1956	Epic 9163
Let Me Think It Over	Concords (Neal Scott)	1967	Cameo 476
Let Me Walk With You	Dreamers, Sidney Ester & the	1958	Dangold 2001/Goldband 1087 (59)
Let Me Weep, Let Me Cry	Uniques	1959	C-Way 2676
Let My Prayers Be With You	Elegants	1960	United Artists 230
Let Nature Take It's Course	Du Droppers	1954	Groove 0036
Let No One Tell You	Thunderbirds, Ron Holden & the	1961	Donna 1335
Let Nothing Separate Me	Royal Sons Quintet	1952	Apollo 266
Let Our Hearts Be Our Guide	Hitchhikers, Chuck Thomas & the	1957	Band Box 360
Let Some Love In Your Heart	Charms, Otis Williams & his	1958	DeLuxe 6160
Let The Bells Ring	Manderins	1960	Band Box 236
Let The Boogie Woogie Roll	Drifters	1960	Atlantic 2060
Let The Boogie Woogie Roll	McPhatter, Clyde (with the Drifters)	1953	Atlantic 2060
Let The Fool Kiss You	Velvets (Texas)	1964, 1966	Monument 861/961
Let The Four Winds Blow	Mr. Lee (with the Frank Andrade 5)	1964	Skylark 503
Let The Four Winds Blow	Romans, Caesar & the	NA	Hi-Note 602
Let The Good Times Roll	Blue Jeans, Bob B. Soxx & the	1963	Philles LP 4002
Let The Good Times Roll	Juniors, Danny & the	1973	Crunch 18001
Let The Good Times Roll	Topsiders	1963	Josie 907
Let The Good Times Roll	Velvets (Texas)	1962	Monument 464
Let The Happening Happen	Charms, Otis Williams & the	1955	DeLuxe 6087
Let The Music Play	Drifters (1959-forward)	1963	Atlantic 2182
Let The Old Folks Talk	Vibes	1959	Allied 10007
Let The People Talk	Twinettes	1958	Vee Jay 284
Let The Show Begin	Jackaels, J. J. Jackson & the	1959	Storm 502/Prelude 502 (59)
Let The Sunshine Shine On You	Cardinals	1956	Atlantic (unreleased)
Let The Tears Fall	Day, Dawn & Dusk	1955	Apollo 476/Kent 519
Let Them Love	Dreamlovers	1961	Heritage 104
Let Them Talk	Celtics, Bobby Lanz & the	1973	Bridges 5003
Let Them Talk	Drakes	1955	States (unreleased)
Let Them Talk	Dreamlovers	1982	Collectables LP 5004
Let Them Talk	Duprees	1966	Columbia 43577
Let Them Talk	Penn, Dan & group	1964	Fame 6402
Let Them Talk	Regents	1962	K-C
Let Them Talk	Run-A-Rounds	1963	Tarheel 065

SONG	GROUP	YEAR	LABEL
Let Them Talk	Stingrays	1964	Crazytown 101/102
Let Them Talk	Upbeats, Ray Allen & the	1961	Sinclair 1004
Let There Be Love	Carlo (Carlo Mastrangelo) (with the Tremonts)	1970	Raftis 112
Let There Be Love	Cavaliers, Tommy Rocco & the	1960	F-M 3264
Let There Be Love	Fireballs, Chuck Tharp & the	1960	Jaro 77029/Lucky 0012
Let There Be Love	Twilighters (Bronx, N.Y.)	1958	Cholly 712
Let There Be Rockin'	Jumpin' Jacks	1956	One-O-One 100
Let There Be You	Five Keys	1957	Capitol 3660
Let There Be You	Royal Jesters	1962	Jester 106
Let This Night Last	Ly-Dells	1962, 1981	Master 251
Let True Love Begin	Crests	1960	Coed (unreleased)
Let Us Part For A Year	Mates, Marci & the	1962	Big Top 3116
Let Us Pretend	Cones, Connie & the	1959	NRC 5006
Let Your Conscience Be Your Guide	Bailey, Jimmy & group	1958	Wynne 103
Let Your Conscience Be Your Guide	Sugartones, Jimmy Lane & the	1958	Time 6602
Let Your Love Light Shine	Kac-Ties	1963	Shelley 163/Kape 503 (63)
Let Yourself Go	Sheppards (Chicago - ABC)	1966	ABC 10758
Let's	Lovers	1958	Casino 103
Let's	Strickland, Jan & group	1955	X 0080
Let's Babalu	Hayes, Linda (with the Platters)	1955	King 4752
Let's Be In Love	Diplomats	1961	May 105
Let's Be Lovers	Starglows	1963	Atco 6272
Let's Be Partners	Romeos	1957	Fox 748/749
Let's Be Sweethearts Again	Lyrics (San Francisco)	1961	Fernwood 129/Fleetwood 233 (61)
Let's Boogaloo	Magics	NA	RFA 100
Let's Call It A Day	Belmonts	1963, 1964	Sabina 513/517
Let's Cuddle Again	Stars	1959	Vega 001
Let's Dance	Epics	1958	Lifetime 1004
Let's Dance	Mad Lads, Little Becky Cook & the	1961	CBM 504
Let's Dance	Teardrops	NA	Col-Vin 777
Let's Dance Close	Curtiss, Jimmy (with the Regents)	1965	Laurie 3315
Let's Dance The Screw Pt. 1	Crystals (Brooklyn)	1963	Philles 111
Let's Do It	Jones, Davey & group	1961	Apt 25064
Let's Do It	Three Dots And A Dash	1951	Imperial 5164
Let's Do It Again	Dynels	1962	Dot 16382
Let's Do It Over	Dells	1984	Solid Smoke LP 8029/ Charly LP 1055 (85)
Let's Do The Cajun Twist	Rockets, Randy & the	1962	Jin 161
Let's Do The Cha Cha	Magnificents	1960	Vee Jay 367
Let's Do The Hunch	De Velles	NA	Emanuel 107
Let's Do The Kangaroo	Majorettes	1963	Troy 1004
Let's Do The Pony	Corvets	1961	Sure 1003
Let's Do The Pony	Starfires	1961	D&H 200
Let's Do The Razzle Dazzle	Rip-Chords	1956	Abco 105
Let's Do The Slop	Thrillers, Little Joe & the	1956	Okeh 7075
Let's Drink A Toast	Larks (Philadelphia)	1961	Sheryl 338
Let's Drink To Happiness	Buccaneers	1954	Tiffany 1308
Let's Elope	Extremes	1958	Everlast 5013
Let's Elope	Lovers	1957, 1963	Lamp 2013/Imperial 5960
Let's Exchange Hearts For Christmas	Lyrics (Hy-Tone)	1958	Hy-Tone 117
Let's Fall In Love	Boyfriends	1964	Kapp 569
Let's Fall In Love	Chimes (Brooklyn)	1961	Tag 447
Let's Fall In Love	Citadels	1962	Monogram 501
Let's Fall In Love	Fi-Tones	1955	Atlas 1050
Let's Fall In Love	Five Discs	NA	Pyramid 166
Let's Fall In Love	Five Stars (New York)	1955	Treat 505
Let's Fall In Love	Sonics, Vance Charles & the	1963	Lori 9553
Let's Fall In Love	Willows, Tony Middleton & the	1958	Gone 5015
Let's Find Out Tonight	Dell, Joey & group	1962	Roulette 4422
Let's Forget The Past	Zippers	1963	Long Fiber 202
Let's Get Acquainted	Coronados	1956	Vik 0217
Let's Get Back Together	Honey Bees	1966	Wand 1141
Let's Get Back Together Now	Bees, Honey & the	NA	Garrison 3005

SONG	GROUP	YEAR	LABEL
Let's Get Married	Belvederes	1958	Trend 2595
Let's Get One	Imperialites	1964	Imperial 66015
Let's Get Show	Midnighters, Hank Ballard & the	1964	King 5954
Let's Get Together	Cadillacs	NA	Roulette 4654
Let's Get Together	Exotics	1964	Coral 62399
Let's Get Together	Raindrops	1964	Jubilee 5475
Let's Get Together Again	Corby, Doug & group	1963	Vault 922
Let's Give Love A Try	Squires (Los Angeles)	1953	Combo 35
Let's Go	Edsels	1961	Tammy 1014/Ember 1078 (61)
Let's Go	James, Bobby & group	NA	Lant 66009
Let's Go	Moonglows	1976	Chess LP 701
Let's Go Again	Midnighters, Hank Ballard & the	1961	King 5459
Let's Go Again	Night Owls	1964	Bethlehem 3087
Let's Go Baby	Fire Balls, Billy Eldridge & His	1959	Vulco 1501/Unart 2011 (59)
Let's Go Back To Yesterday	Heartspinners, Dino & the	NA	Robin Hood 141
Let's Go Fishing	Darlings	1959	Penguin 0698
Let's Go For A Ride	Collegians	1958	X-Tra 108/Times Square 11 (63)
Let's Go Get Stoned	Coasters	1965	Atco 6356
Let's Go, Let's Go, Let's Go	Midnighters, Hank Ballard & the	1960	King 5400
Let's Go Rock 'N Roll	Jackals, Frank Sandy & the	1958	MGM 12678
Let's Go Skiing	Juniors, Danny & the	1964	Mercury 72240
Let's Go Steady	Downbeats	1958	Peacock 1679
Let's Go Steady	Shaynes	1961	Pee Vee 5000
Let's Go Steady For The Summer	Three G's	1958, 1960	Columbia 41175/41678
Let's Go Steady For The Summer	Tren-Dells	1965	Boss 9921
Let's Go To The Dance	Robins	1953	RCA 5434
Let's Go To The Drag Strip	Tokens (Brooklyn)	1964	RCA 8309
Let's Go To The Rock & Roll Ball	Pastels (Washington, D.C.)	1958	Argo 5297
Let's Have A Ball	Gordon, Gary & group	1959	Fleetwood 1002
Let's Have A Ball	Wheels	1956	Premium 405
Let's Have A Good Time	Hi-Tones	1960	King 5414
Let's Have A Good Time Baby	Four Havens	1965	Veep 1214
Let's Have A Party	Jack, Johnny & group	1964	Lawn 226
Let's Jam	Foster Brothers, Lefty Guitar Bates & the	1960	Dilly 101
Let's Jump The Broomstick	Themes, Alvin Gaines & the	1959	Fidelity 420592
Let's Kiss And Make Up	Falcons (Detroit)	1963	Atlantic 2179
Let's Kiss And Make Up	Royal Jesters	1961	Cobra 2222
Let's Kiss Hello Again	Ebbonaires, Jackson Trio & the	1956	Hollywood 1062
Let's Leave It Like It Is	Brown, Sammy & group	1964	Bee Bee 701
Let's Leave It That Way	Marco & group	1963	Mohawk 135
Let's Linger Awhile	Capris (Philadelphia)	1956	Gotham 7308
Let's Live Together As One	Birds, Bobby Byrd & the	1956	Cash 1031
Let's Love In The Moonlight	Washington, Baby & group	1959	Neptune 107
Let's Make A New Start	Gold Coasters	1964	Blue River 206
Let's Make A Scene	Four Imperials	1958	Lorelei 4444/Dot 15737 (58)
Let's Make A Whole Lot Of Love	Dodgers	1955	Aladdin 3259
Let's Make It Real	Coraltones, Dave Bryan & the	1956	Speck 103
Let's Make Love	Blue Jays (Venice, Calif.)	1961	Milestone 2010
Let's Make Love	Jaye, Jerry & group	1963	Carlton 598
Let's Make Love Again	Duprees	1963	Coed 576
Let's Make Love Tonight	Carolons	1964	Mellomood 1003
Let's Make Love Tonight	Ovations (Starlight)	1986	N/A
Let's Make Love Tonight	Tymes	1964	Parkway LP 7032
Let's Make Love Worthwhile	Melodymakers	1957	Hollis 1001
Let's Make Up	Belvin, Jesse & group	NA	Crown LP 5187
Let's Make Up	Doves	1960	Big Top 3046
Let's Make Up	Flamingos	1957	Decca 30335
Let's Make Up	Jacks	1956	RPM 467
Let's Make Up	Palisades, Frank Gonzales & the	1961	FG 1001
Let's Make Up	Spaniels	1954	Vee Jay 116
Let's Make With Some Love	Flairs	1954	Flair 1044
(Let's Monkey) At The Party	Persians	1963	Goldisc G17/Music World 102 (63)
Let's Not Break Up	Five Sharks	1986	Starlight 34
Let's Party Awhile	Vel-Aires, Donald Woods & the	1955	Flip 303 (first pressing, second is by Vel-Aires)

SONG	GROUP	YEAR	LABEL
Let's Pony Again	Vibrations	1961	Checker 990
Let's Put Our Cards On The Table	Cap-Tans	1959	DC 8064
Let's Ride, Ride, Ride	Savoys (Combo)	1954	Combo 55
Let's Rock	Cupids	1964	Times Square 1
Let's Rock	Kodaks	1961	Wink 1004
Let's Rock And Roll	Cadets	NA	Relic LP 5025
Let's Rock Little Girl	Inspirations, Ronnie Vare & the	1959	Dell 5202/5203
Let's Run Away	Rip Tides, Johnny Hudson & the	1959	Challenge 59062
Let's Run Away And Get Married	Candles, Rochell & the	1962	Challenge 9191
Let's Say A Prayer	Larks (North Carolina)	1951	Apollo 1184
Let's See What's Happening	Honey Bees	1956	Imperial 5400
Let's Sit And Talk	Allison, Gene & group	1958	Vee Jay 286
Let's Start All Over Again	Chadons	1964	Chattahoochee 664
Let's Start All Over Again	Four Beats, Donn Bruce & the	1956	Tuxedo 914
Let's Start All Over Again	Paragons	1957	Winley 220
Let's Start Anew	Meteors	1963	Beltone 2041
Let's Start Anew	Miller Sisters	1957	Acme 111/Acme 721 (58)
Let's Stay After School	Velvet Keys	1957	King 5090
Let's Stay Together	Del Reys	1960	Columbia 41784
Let's Stick Together	Tempos	1966	Riley's 5
Let's Stomp	Counts, Bobby Comstock & the	1962	Lawn 202
Let's Take A Chance	V-Eights, Stoney Jackson & the	1961	Vibro 4007
Let's Take A Ride	Lee, Curtis (with the Halos)	1960	Sabra 517
Let's Take A Ride	Pictures, C.L. & the	1961	Dunes 2010/Sabra 517 (60)
Let's Take A Stroll (Down Lover's Lane)	Starlighters	1960	End 1072
Let's Take A Walk	Barrons	NA	Guest Star LP 1481
Let's Take A Walk	Crescendos (Scarlet)	1960	Scarlet 4007
Let's Talk About Jesus	Swallows (Maryland)	1991	Starbound 513
Let's Talk About Us	Chapman, Grady (with the Suedes)	1959	Imperial 5611
Let's Talk It Over	Counts, Bobby Comstock & the	1960	Atlantic 2051
Let's Talk It Over	Hollywood Flames	1953, 1958	Swing Time 345/Lucky 009 (55)/ Decca 48331 (55)/ Ebb146/7-11 2108 (unreleased)
Let's Tell The World	Portraits	1967	Sidewalk 928
Let's Try Again	Fabulous Four	1961	Chancellor 1068
Let's Try Again	Roosters	1962	Epic 9487/Felsted 8642 (62)
Let's Try It Again	Fabulous Fortunes, Norm N. Nite & the	1971	Globe 107
Let's Twist	Cupids	1962	UWR 4241/4242
Let's Twist Again	Dreamlovers	1982	Collectables LP 5004
Let's Untwist The Twist	Salutations, Vito & the	1962	Rayna 5009/Red Boy 5009 (66)
Let's Vote For Tom Berkeley	Goldenkeys	1956	Irma 100
Let's Waddle	Earls	1962	Old Town 1130
Let's Walk	Cleeshays, Danny Tyrell & the	1958	Eastman 784
Let's Workout Baby	Showstoppers, Curtis & the	1964	Travis 039
Let's You And I Go Steady	Pearls	1956	Onyx 503/Relic 513 (64)
Letter	Blue Notes, Harold Melvin & the	1960	Lost 105
Letter Came This Morning, The	Chimes (Tennessee)	1957	Arrow 724
Letter From My Baby	Scott Brothers	1963	Comet 2153
Letter From My Darling	Valentines, Little Tom & the	1961	Mr. Big 222
Letter Full Of Tears	Marcels	1963	Chartbound 009
Letter I Wrote Today, The	Hi-Jacks	1956	ABC 9742
Letter Of Devotion	Temptations (Goldisc)	1960	Goldisc 3007
Letter Of Love, The	Markells	1958	R&M 407/408
Letter On His Sweater	Kittens	1960	Alpine 67
Letter, The	Camelots	1961	Crimson 1001
Letter, The	Charmers	1963	Co-Rec 101
Letter, The	Eternals	1995	Martin/Manor CD (Rec. 1961)
Letter, The	Illusions	1960	Coral 62173
Letter, The	Imperials, Little Anthony & the	1962	Newtime 505
Letter, The	Larktones	1958	ABC 9909
Letter, The	Little Stevie & group	1961	Guyden 2060
Letter, The	Medallions	1954	Dootone 347
Letter, The	Melodeers	1961	Shelley 127
Letter To An Angel	Dynamics, Susan & the	1963	Dot 16476
Letter To An Angel	Five Shillings	1958	Decca 30722

SONG	GROUP	YEAR	LABEL
Letter To Dick Clark	Gates	1959	Peach 628
Letter To Donna	Kittens	1959	Unart 2010
Letter To My Love	Hollywood Flames	1963	Vee Jay 515
Letters	Blue Notes, Todd Randall & the	1957	Josie 814
Letters Don't Have Arms	Charmers	1957	Silhouette 522
Letters Of Love	Chordells, Willie Howard & the	1961	Mascot 127
Letters Of Love	Dovells	1961	Parkway 819
Liar	Regents	1961	Gee 1073
Lie	Meadowlarks	1964	Magnum 716
Lie, The	Tunes	1959	Pel 101/Pel 345 (59)
Lies	Bifield, Lenore & group	1964	Sketch 217
Lies	Crosstones	1955	Jaguar 3014
	(with the Chriss Chross Orchestra)		
Lies	Knickerbockers, Buddy Randell & the	1965	Challenge 59321
Lies	Satisfiers	1955	Jubilee 5205
Lies, Lies, Lies	Rand, Rose Marie & group	1956	Vik 0206
Life	Scott Brothers	196?	
Life	Sounds	1959	Sarg 172
Life	Sterios	1966	Ideal 110
Life Begins At Sixteen	Artistics	1962	S&G 302
Life Can Be Beautiful	Cineramas	1959	Champ 103
Life Goes On	Castells	1966	Decca 31967
Life Is But A Dream	Darchaes	1980	Clifton 56
Life Is But A Dream	Earls	1961	Rome 101
Life Is But A Dream	El Sierros	1964	Times Square 101
Life Is But A Dream	Harptones	1955	Paradise 101
Life Is But A Dream	Platinums	1979	J & M 647
Life Is But A Dream	Tokens (Brooklyn)	NA	RCA LP 3685
Life Is But A Dream	Whalers, Kenny & the	1961	Whale 504
Life Is But A Dream (acappella)	Shells	1966	Candlelite LP 1000
Life Is But A Dream Sweetheart	Classics (Brooklyn)	1961	Dart 1038/Mercury 71829 (61)
Life Is Grand	Premiers (New York)	1958	Cindy 3008
Life Is Groovy	Tokens (Brooklyn)	1966	B.T. Puppy 524
Life Is Like A River	Sultans Five	1964	Raynard 1053
Life Is Sweeter Now	Larks (Philadelphia)	1961	Cross Fire 74-49/74-50/
			Guyden 2103 (61)
Life Of Ease	Four Arcs	1954	Boulevard 102
Life Of Ease	Imperials (Detroit)	1954	Great Lakes 1201
Life To Go	Mystics	1959	Lee 1004
Life-Line	Cashmeres (Brooklyn)	1961	Josie 894/Laurie 3105
Life's But A Dream	Classics (Brooklyn)	1961	Streamline 1028
Life's Too Short	Lafayettes	1962	RCA 8044
Lifetime	Duds, Dougie & the	1963	Amy 869
Lifetime Of Happiness	Four Joes	1957	Darl 1005
Lift Me Up Angel	Gunter, Cornell & group	1962	Warner Bros. 5266
Lift Up Your Head	Chesters	1958	Apollo 521
Light A Candle	Laddins	1959	Grey Cliff 721
Light A Candle In The Chapel	Solitaires	1959	Old Town 1071
Light Bulb	Five Kings	1964	Columbia 43060
Light Finger Willie	Climatics	1962	Re-No 1000
Light Me Up	Dikes	1955	Federal 12249
Light, The	Four Buddies	1962	Coral 62325
Light Up The Sky	Aquatones	NA	Fargo LP 5033X
Lighten-Up Slim	Glitters	NA	Rubaiyat 413
Lights Are Low	El Dorados	1958	Vee Jay 302
Lights Go On, The Lights Go Off, The	Velvets (Texas)	1962	Monument 464
Lights Please	Blend Tones	1961	Chic-Car 100/Don-El 106 (61)/
			Imperial 5758 (61)
Like A Baby	Bowman, Priscilla & group	1959	Abner 1033
Like A Baby	Sounds, Vikki Nelson & the	1957	Vik 0273
Like A Bee	Spidels	1962	Chavis 1035
Like A Kid At Christmas	Five Boroughs	1991	Classic Artists 135
Like A Mad Fool	Kelloggs	1969	Laurie 3476
Like A Waterfall	Curls	1960	Everest 19350
Like Adam And Eve	Reflections	1966	ABC 10794

SONG	GROUP	YEAR	LABEL
Like Columbus Did	Reflections	1964	Golden World 12
Like Heaven	Blue Angels	1961	Edsel 781
Like I Love You	Shevelles	1964	World Artists 1023
Like I Never Felt Before	Marland, Cletus & group	1961	Roulette 4388
Like, Later Baby	Hearts (Bronx, N.Y.)	1955	J&S 1626/1627
Like Man It's Spring	Four Jacks, Bill Erwin & the	1960	Pel 601
Like Mattie	El Tones	1958	Cub 9011
Like My Baby	Four Tees	1964	Vee Jay 627
Like Sister And Brother	Drifters (1959-forward)	1973	Bell 45,387
Like Socks And Shoes	Star Fires	1966	Laurie 3332
Like The Big Guys Do	Rocky Fellers	1963	Scepter 1254
Like Those Ivy Walls	Class Cutters, Herbie & the	1959	RCA 7649
Like To See You In That Mood	Dawns, Billy Horton & the	1964	Lawn 241
Like You Bug Me	Quarter Notes	1957	Dot 15685
Like You Hurt Me	Exotics	1964	Coral 62439
Lil Blue Tears	Up-Tunes	1965	Genie 103
Lil' Dream Girl	Gaylarks	1955	Music City 793
Li'l Girl Of My Dreams	Five Swans	1956	Music City 795
Li'l Li'l Lulu	Bel Mars	1960, 1961, 1974	X-Tra 100/Candlelite 414 (74)
Li'l Ol' Me	Breedlove, Jimmy & group	1963	Diamond 144
Li'l Tipa-Tina	Five Swans	1956	Music City 795
Lil Valley	Peanuts, M&M & the	1964	Money 101
Lilacs In The Rain	Ravens	1951	Mercury 8257
Lili Marlane	Jive Five	1963	Beltone 2030
Lillie Mae	Cupids	1958	Aladdin 3404
Lilly	Blentones	1959	MGM 12782
Lilly Lou	Four Dates	1958	Chancellor 1024
Lily Lou	Thrillers, Little Joe & the	1957	Okeh 7088
Lily Maebelle	Chalets	1984	Starlight 20
Lily Maebelle	Del Rays	1958	Future 2203
Lily Maebelle	Valentines	1955	Rama 171
Lily Marlane	Mulrays	1957	Trans World 719
Lily Of The West	Alley Cats	1965	Epic 9778
Lima Beans	Five Owls	1974	Owl 327
Limbo	Capris (New York)	1962	Mr. Peacock 118/Mr. Peeke 118 (63)
Limbo	Imperials, Little Anthony & the	1960	End 1080
Limbo Rock	Tides	1962	Mercury 71990
Limbo Under The Christmas Tree	Classic IV	1962	Algonquin 1650
Linda	Adorations	1971	Dreamtone 200
Linda	Continentals, Joey & the	1965	Komet 1001
Linda	Empires	1956	Whirlin' Disc 104
Linda	Fashions, Frankie & the	1993	Avenue D 19
Linda	Four Gents	1957	Park 113
Linda	Grand Prixs	1962	Sara 6354
Linda	Hustlers	1965	Rich 113
Linda	Impacts	1964	Anderson 104
Linda	Nacks, Nicky & the	1977	Crystal Ball 103
Linda	Pips	1962	Fury 1067
Linda	Rhythm Gents	1964	Merri 6008
Linda	Sophomores (Massachusetts)	1956	Dawn 218
Linda	Troy, Ricky & group	1963	Cavetone 511
Linda Baby	Moroccans, Sammy Fitzhugh & the	1958	
Linda Jean	Satellites	1959	Cupid 5004/ABC 10038 (59)
Linda Lee	Shakers	1961	Fee Bee 907
Linda Lee	Shakers, Buddy Sharpe & the	1958	Fee Bee 230
Linda Linda	Andrews, Gene & group	1963	Rust 5054
Linda Lou	Accents, Ron Peterson & the	1965	Jerden 728
Linda Lou Garrett (Likes 24 Karat)	Ebb Tides, Nino & the	1964	Mala 480
Linda Loves Me	Hoppers	NA	Valley's Mead 104
Linda Please Wait	Genells	1963	Dewey 101
Lindy Lou	Buddies, Little Butchie Saunders & his	1956	Herald 485
Lindy-Lou	Sparkles, Jerry Diamond & the	1958	RCA 7257
Ling Ting Tong	Blue Jays (Los Angeles)	1956	Dig EP 778
Ling, Ting, Tong	Charms, Otis Williams & the	1955	DeLuxe 6076
Ling Ting Tong	Fabulous Persians	1974	Bobby-O 3123

SONG	GROUP	YEAR	LABEL
Ling Ting Tong	Five Keys	1954	Capitol 2945
Lion Is Awake, The	Five Notes, Sammy & the	1962	Lucky Four 1019
Lion Sleeps Tonight, The	BQE	1988	Starlight 60
Lion Sleeps Tonight, The	Tokens (Brooklyn)	1961	RCA 7954
Lion Sleeps Tonight (acappella), The	Five Sharks	1966	Amber 852
Lions Sleeps Tonight, The	Paramounts	1985	Avenue D 10
Lip Lockin'	George, Sunny & group	1958	MGM 12697
Lips Red As Wine	Colts	1955	Vita 112/Mambo 112 (55)
Lips Were Meant For Kissing	Dreamers (Manhattan)	1956	Manhattan 503
Lipstick	Playthings	1958	Liberty 55147
Lipstick And High-Heel Shoes	Sweethearts, Valentine & the	1963	Big Top 3147
Lipstick Kisses	Cleeshays, Sonny Knight & the	1958	Eastman 787
Lisa	Landis, Jerry & group	1962, 1982	Amy 875
Lisa	Montclairs	1967	United International 1007
Lisa Maree	Notables	1963	Big Top 3141
Listen	Impressions	1958	Bandera 2504/Port 70031 (60)
Listen	Matadors	1962	Jamie 1226
Listen Baby	Five Pastels	1962	Dome 249
Listen, Baby	Mellow Keys	1956	Gee 1014
Listen Baby	Swing Masters, Angel & the	1959	DC 0420
Listen For A Lonely Tambourine	Starlets	1960	Astro 204
Listen My Children And You Shall Hear	Quotations	1963	Liberty 55527
Listen My Heart	Bon-Bons	1964	Sampson 1003
Listen My Love	Highlights	1956	Bally 1016
Listen To Me	Decoys	1964	Velvet 1001
Listen To Me	Mystics, Gene Fisher & the	1962	Plateau 101
Listen To My Heart	Cordials	1962	Whip 276
Listen To My Little Heart	Corsairs	1962	Tuff 1840/Chess 1840 (62)
Listen To My Plea	Flamingos	1954	Chance 1154
Listen To The Bells	Casanovas	NA	Apollo LP 1004/Relic LP 5073 (87)
Listen To The Drums	Caiton, Richard & group	1964	GNP Crescendo 327
Listen To The Rain	Delteens (with the Orbits)	1961	Fortune 541
Listen To The Raindrops	Delverts	NA	Salem 1302
Listen To The Words, Listen To The Music	Tokens (Brooklyn)	1970	Buddah 187
Listen To Your Heart	Fortune, Billy & group	1958	Dice 478
Listen To Your Heart	Squires, Billy Jones & the	1958	Deck 478
Listen To Your Heart (Caroline)	Ambers	1959	Greezie 501
Listen! Young Girls	Upstarts, Jerry McCain & the	1957	Excello 2111
List'nin' To The Green Grass Grow	Holidays	1956	King 1520
Lita	Zodiacs, Maurice Williams & the	1960	Soma 1410
Lite Bulb	Kittens	1963	Don-El 122
Litterbug	Catalinas	1973	Jayne 177
Little Alice	Moods	1959	Sarg 162
Little Angel	Blue Notes, Little Bill & the	1961	Bolo 725
Little Angel	Chords, Phil Moore & the	NA	Time 101
Little Angel	Swanks	1957	Jaguar 3027
Little Angel Lost	Darvell, Barry & group	1961	Cub 9088
Little Baby	Posse, Marshall Laws & the	1961	Forum 702
Little Baby Be Mine	Sounds (featuring Frank Williams)	1961	Queen 24008
Little Bad Wolf	Tra-Velles	NA	Debonair 101
Little Beatle Boy	Angels (New Jersey)	1964	Smash 1885
Little Billy Boy	Dell Vikings	1957	Dot 15571
Little Billy Boy	Three D's	1957	Paris 503
Little Bird	Hearts, Lee Andrews & the	1968	Crimson 1015
Little Bird	Suburbans	1960	Kip 221
Little Bit More	Mello-Tones	1958	Key 5804
Little Bit Of Lovin'	Gigi & group	1961	Seg-Way 1010
Little Bit Of Loving	Fourmost	1964	Atco 6307
Little Bit Square, But Nice	Goofers	1959	Tiara 6123
Little Bitty Bandit	Incredables	NA	Kelrich 850/851
Little Bitty Bed Bug	Twilighters (Bronx, N.Y.)	1962	Bubble 1334
Little Bitty Pretty One	Harris, Thurston (with the Sharps)	1957	Aladdin 3398
Little Bitty Pretty One	Popular Five	1968	Minit 32050
Little Bitty Pretty One	Satellites, Bobby Day & the	1957	Class 211

SONG	GROUP	YEAR	LABEL
Little Black Train	Dominoes	1954	Federal 12193
Little Bo	Royal Tones	1959	Jubilee 5362
Little Bo Peep	Admirations (featuring Joseph Lorello)	1958	Mercury 71521
Little Bo Peep	Bonnie Sisters	1956	Rainbow 336
Little Bo Peep	Five Sparks	1959	Jimbo 1
Little Boy	Classinettes (female)	1962	Markay 107
Little Boy	Cole, Freddy & group	1963	Titantic 100
Little Boy	Coronets	1955	Sterling 903
Little Boy	Crystals (Brooklyn)	1964	Philles 119/Philles 119X (63)
Little Boy	Georgettes	1963	Troy 1001
Little Boy	Lockets	1963	Argo 5455
Little Boy	Ray-O-Vacs	1960	Sharp 103
Little Boy	Trinkets	1958	Imperial 5497
Little Boy	Tune Weavers	1958	Casa Grande 101
Little Boy And Girl	Earls	1976	Rome 112
Little Boy and Girl	Kodaks	1957	Fury 1007
Little Boy Blue	Accents (Brooklyn)	1962	Matt 0001
Little Boy Blue	Bradford Boys	1955	Rainbow 307
Little Boy Blue	Dee, Ronnie & group	1961	Wye 1008
Little Boy Blue (Is Blue No More)	Elegants	1959	Hull 732
Little Boy Lost	Venetians, Nick Marco & the	1960	Dwain 813
Little Boy Of Mine	Delicates	1961	Roulette 4360
Little Bug	Jarmels	1962	Laurie 3141
Little By Little	Impossibles	1963	Blanche 029
Little Carmen	Tides	1959	Dore 546
Little Chick	Echomores	NA	Rocket 1042
Little Chick-A-Dee	Chicks, Kell Osborne & the	1962	Class 302
Little Chickie	Rockabeats, Jimmy Kelly & the	1958	Cobra 5028/Astra 101 (58)
Little Cricket	Royal Teens	1959	Capitol 4261
Little Cupid	Carlos Brothers	1959	Del-Fi 4118
Little Cupid	Smoothtones	1957	Okeh 7078
Little Curly Top	Condors	1962	Hunter 2503/2504
Little Cutie	Avalons	NA	Groove (unreleased)
Little Cutie	Vincente, Vin & group	1962	Swingin' 644
Little Daddy	Jaye Sisters	1958	Atlantic 2000
Little Darlin'	Chevrons	1960	Brent 7015
Little Darlin'	Diamonds	1957	Mercury 71060
Little Darlin'	Four Jacks	1956	Gateway 1211-A/Big 4 Hits EP 213
Little Darlin'	Gladiolas	1957	Excello 2101
Little Darlin'	Imperial Gents	1970	Laurie 3540
Little Darlin'	Keystoners	1991	Starbound 512
Little Darlin'	Willows	1957	Melba 115
Little Darling	Belvin, Jesse & group	1958	Knight 2012
Little Darling	Del-Larks, Sammy & the	1961	Stop 101
Little Darling	Jaxon Playboys, Eddie Bush & the	1953	Jaxon 503
Little Deuce Coupe	Tokens (Brooklyn)	NA	RCA LP 2886
Little Diane	DiMucci, Dion (with the Del Satins)	1962	Laurie 3134
Little Did I Dream	Twilighters (Bronx, N.Y.)	1955	MGM 55011
Little Did I Know	Christie, Lou & group	1963	American Music Makers 006
Little Did I Know	Ducanes	1961	Goldisc 3024
Little Did I Know	Lions, Lugee & the	1961	Robbee 112
Little Do I Know	Tri-Dells	1960	Eldo 104
Little Doll	Five Trojans	1959	Edison International 412
Little Donna	Dolphins	1965	Fraternity 940
Little Dream Girl	Cashmeres (Philadelphia)	1956	Herald 474
Little Drifter Amy	Faulkner, Freddy & group	1963	Swan 4134
Little Egypt	Cliches	1959	Maar C 1530
Little Egypt	Coasters	1961	Atco 6192
Little Eva	Locomotions	1962	Gone 5142
Little Flirt	Cosytones	1957	Willow 1001
Little Fool	Charmers	1961	Jaf 2021
Little Fool	Ivorytones	1960	Norwood 101
Little Fool	Relf, Bobby (with the Laurels)	1956	Dot 15510
Little Fool	Sunbeams, Donna Rae & the	1959	Satellite 103
Little Genie	Adventurers	1959	Jerden 105

SONG	GROUP	YEAR	LABEL
Little Girl	Blazons	NA	Fanfare 5901/Bravura 5001
Little Girl	Capris (New York)	NA	Lost Nite 148
Little Girl	Clefftones	1955	Old Town/Murray Hill LP 000083
Little Girl	Concords (Neal Scott)	1963	Herald 581
Little Girl	Cousins	1960	Swirl 102
Little Girl	DiMucci, Dion (with the Del Satins)	1964	Laurie 3240
Little Girl	Dreamers (Yonkers, N.Y.)	1961	Cousins 1005/May 133 (61)
Little Girl	Imperials, Little Anthony & the	1958	End (unreleased)
Little Girl	Marveliers	NA	Joany 4439
Little Girl	Notes	1959	Sarg 177
Little Girl	Riffs	1964	Sunny 22
Little Girl	Rivileers	1955	Baton 209
Little Girl	Rockets, Bill Bodaford & the	1958	Back Beat 507
Little Girl	Satelites, Baby Boy Jennings & the	1960	Savoy 1589
Little Girl	Scott, Neil (with the Concords)	1963	Herald 581
Little Girl	Shantones	1956	Trilyte 5001
Little Girl	Upfronts	1961	Lummtone 106
Little Girl	Velps	1972	Roadhouse 1002
Little Girl	Young Lions	1960	Dot 16172
Little Girl 5'3	New Yorkers	1963	Park Ave 100
Little Girl Charm	Sunliners	1962	Hercules 184
Little Girl, I Love You	G-Clefs	1961	Terrace 7500
Little Girl I Love You	Velvitones	1959	Milmart 113
Little Girl, I Love You So	Velvetones	1960	Aladdin 3463
Little Girl In Blue	Bell Notes	1960	Autograph 204
Little Girl, Little Girl	Fairlanes	1960	Argo 5357
Little Girl, Little Girl	Revlons, Tino & the	1965	Dearborn 525
Little Girl, Little Girl (You'd Better Stop Talkin' In Your Sleep)	Du Droppers	1953	RCA 5321
Little Girl Lost	Chord-A-Roys, Bobby Roy & the	1960	Roys 5001/JDS 5001 (60)
Little Girl Lost	Sheppards (Chicago - ABC)	1966	ABC 10758
Little Girl Next Door	Classmates, Ronnie Jones & the	1957	End 1002
Little Girl Next Door	Embers	1965	Ara 210
Little Girl Next Door	Satellites, Collay & the	1960	Sho-Biz 1002
Little Girl Of Mine	Cleftones	1956	Gee 1011
Little Girl Of Mine	Cupids	1963	Musicnote 119
Little Girl Of Mine	Diamonds	1956	Mercury 70835
Little Girl Of Mine	Dovells	1962	Parkway LP 7006
Little Girl Of Mine	Electras	1966	Ruby-Doo 2
Little Girl Of Mine	Five Palms (Palms)	1957	States 163
Little Girl Of Mine	Hurricanes	1956	King 4926
Little Girl Of Mine	Zip Codes	1988	Clifton 83
Little Girl Of Mine (acappella)	Versailles	1957	Harlequin 401
Little Girl So Fine	Darchaes, Ray & the	1962	Aljon 1249/1250
Little Girls Dream	Statics, Lynn & the	NA	Mantis 101
Little Green Man	Corondolays, Chico & the	1965	Style 1927
Little Green Man, The	Echoes, Sonny Roberts & the	1958	Swan 4013
Little Heart Attacks	Corvettes	NA	Oak 4429/4430
Little Heart Take Care	Sherwoods	1963	Mercury 72042
Little Hit And Run Darling	True Tones	1964	Spot 1121
Little Hot Rod Susie	Rainbows, Randy & the	1964	Rust 5101
Little Indian Girl	Moonlighters, Billy & the	1978	Crystal Ball 101
Little Island Girl	Golden Tones	1959	Hush 101
Little Jeanie	Townsmen (Vanity)	1960	Vanity 579/580
Little Joe	Carter Quartet, Eddie	1975	Monogram 107
Little Joe	Spaniels	1960, 1974	Vee Jay LP 1024
Little Joe And Linda Lee	Continentals, Lenny & the	1963	Tribute 119
Little Johnny	Lynn, Sandy (with the Corvets)	1961	Laurel 1024
Little Lamb	Elektras	1960	End 1082
Little Latin Lupe Lu	Chancellors	1965	Soma 1421
Little Linda	Anthony, Mike & group	1961	Imperial 5813
Little Linda	Royal Drifters	1959	Teen 506
Little Little	Cherlos	NA	Relic LP 5022
Little Liza Jane	Neville, Art & group	1965	Cinderella 1401
Little Lonely Boy	G-Clefs	1966	Loma 2034

SONG	GROUP	YEAR	LABEL
Little Lonely Girl	Originals, Tony Allen & the	1960	Original Sound 13
Little Lonely One	Jarmels	1961	Laurie 3085
Little Louie	Blossoms	1958	Capitol 3878
Little Louie	Treble Chords	NA	Decca (unreleased)
Little Love	Petites	1961	Columbia 42053
Little Love	Terrigan Brothers	NA	Fortune 207
Little Love Of Mine	Crystals, Claudia & the	1961	Dore 601
Little Lover	Beard, Dean & group	1959	Challenge 59048
Little Lover	Danleers	1960	Epic 9421
Little Lover	Diante, Denny & group	1964	Holiday 1210
Little Lover	Ly-Dells	1978	Clifton LP 2002
Little Maiden	Chords	1954	Cat 104 (second pressing)
Little Maiden	Four Sevilles	1980	Starlight 10
Little Maiden	Sh-Booms	1961	Atco 6213
Little Mama	Clovers	1954	Atlantic 1022
Little Mama	Jivers	1956	Aladdin 3329
Little Mama	Jokers	1961	Grace 510
Little Mama	Zodiacs, Maurice Williams & the	NA	Sphere Sound LP 7007
Little Man	Danderliers	1955	States 152
Little Man	Galaxies	1976	Ronnie 201
Little Mary	Unforgettables, Little John & the	1962	Alan-K 6901
Little Mary	Untouchables	1962	Alan K 6901
Little Match Girl	Blackwells	1960	Jamie 1173
Little Me	J's (with Jamie)	1962	Columbia 42635
Little Miracles	Crests	1961	Coed 561
Little Miss Blue	DiMucci, Dion (with the Del Satins)	1960	Laurie 3070
Little Miss Blue	Ebb Tides, Nino & the	1961	Marco 105
Little Miss Blue	Emotions	1963	20th Fox 452
Little Miss Dreamer	Paris, Bobby & group	1963	Chattahoochee 631
Little Miss Dreamer	Prophets	1963	Jairick 201
Little Miss Fantasy	Celestials, Bobby Gee & the	1960	XYZ 611
Little Miss Love	El Dorados	1955	Vee Jay 127
Little Miss Muffet	Colonairs	1963	Tru-Lite 127
Little Miss Muffet	Fabulons	NA	Ember (unreleased)
Little Miss Pinocchio	Crystalaires	1998	Sweet Beat 101
Little Miss Sad	Five Empressions	1965	Freeport 1001 (first pressing)
Little Miss Sad One	Fleetwoods	1961	Dolton 40
Little Miss Sweetness	Vipers	NA	Duchess 102
Little Miss Twist	Beau-Marks	1962	Quality 1370/Port 70029 (62)
Little Moon	Visions	1960	Elgey 1003/Lost Nite 102 (61)
Little One	Raindrops	1958	Spin-It 106
Little One	Sabers, J. & the	1962	Vavrey 1003
Little Orphan Annie	Blazers, Rodney Lay & the	1956	Chan 110
Little Orphan Doll	Carlo (Carlo Mastrangelo) (with the Tremonts)	1963	Laurie 3157
Little Otis	Spinners (California)	1959	Warner Bros. 5084
Little Pancho	Marathons	1962	Plaza 507
Little Pedro	Olympics	1961	Arvee 5023
Little Piece Of Paper	Peppers	1961	Press 2809
Little Pony	Massi, Nick & group	NA	One Way 244
Little Pony Tail	Lynn, Bill & group	1961	Amy 820
Little Queenie	Gents, Larry & the	1964	Delaware 1700
Little Red Kitten	Sorrows, Nicky De Matteo & the	1966	Cameo 407
Little Richard	Twilights	1963	6 Star 1001/1002
Little Rose	Blenders (Class)	1958	Class 236
Little Sad Eyes	Castells	1961, 1963	Era 3038/3102
Little Sally Walker	Bandits	NA	Jerden 773
Little Sally Walker	Donnells, Jo Baby & the	1965	Ty-Tex 114
Little Sally Walker	Rivingtons	1963	Liberty 55610
Little Sally Walker	Supremes (Ohio)	1960	Mascot 126
Little Sally Walker	Zodiacs, Maurice Williams & the	1960	Soma 1418
Little Sandy	Tune Tones	1958	Herald 524
Little School Girl	Continentals, Michael & the	1965	Audio Fidelity 139
Little School Girl	Overtones, Tony Rice & the	1961	Rae-Cox 106
Little Senorita	Swans, Paul Lewis & the	1955	Fortune 813

SONG	GROUP	YEAR	LABEL
Little Sheryl	Richards, Jay & group	1959	Hollywood 1100
Little Ship	Blue Diamonds	1962	London 10006
Little Ship	Delicates	1961	Roulette 4321
Little Short Daddy	Delltones (& the Kelly Owens Orchestra)	1954	Rainbow 244
Little Side Car	Larks (North Carolina)	1951	Apollo 429
Little Sister	Barlow, Dean & group	1961	Seven Arts 704
Little Sister Nell	Flame Tones, Richard Willans & the	1972	Bell 192
Little Small Town Girl	Blenders (New York)	1951	Decca 27403
Little Star	Chevrons	1960	Brent 7015
Little Star	Corwins	NA	Gilmar 222
Little Star	Elegants	1958	Apt 25005
Little Star	Fraternity Men	1964	Courier 114
Little Star	Freckles	1961	Madison 158
Little Star	Glitters	1958	Promenade A552
Little Star	Limelites, Shep & the	1959	Apt (unreleased)
Little Star	Memory Lane	1982	Crystal Ball 149
Little Star	Rainbows, Randy & the	1964	Rust 5091
Little Star	Rob-Roys, Norman Fox & the	1988	Back Beat 499
Little Star	Romans, Little Caesar & the	1961	Del-Fi LP 1218
Little Star	Terrifics	1958	Bell 88
Little Star	Zeu Review, Ziggy & the	NA	Zeu 5011
Little Suzanne	Del-Fis, Jerry & the	NA	Hound 102
Little Suzie	Monograms	1961	Rust 5036
Little Sweetheart	Velours	1959	Studio 9902
Little Things	Capitols, Mickey Toliver & the	1958	Gateway 721
Little Things	El Venos	1960	Calico (unreleased)
Little Things Mean A Lot	Dominoes	1954	King 1368
Little Things Mean A Lot	Platters	1964	Mercury 72359
Little Tin Soldier	Toy Dolls	1962	Era 3093
Little Trixie	Royal Teens	1961	Mighty 200
Little Turtle Dove	Charms, Otis Williams & the	1961	King 5455
Little Turtle Dove	Satellites, Bobby Day & the	1958	Class 225
Little Wallflower	Dungaree Darlings	1956	Rego 1003/Karen 1005 (59)
Little Wallflower	Sensations	1956	Atco 6083
Little Wanda	Searchers	1961	Mac 351
Little Wheel	Arc-Angels	1961	Lan-Cet 142
Little White Cloud That Cried, The	Soothers	1965	Port 70041
Little White Gardenia	Deans	1961	Laurie 3114
Little White Lies	Kenjolairs	1962	A&M 704
Little White Lies	Teenagers, Frankie Lymon & the	1957	Roulette LP 25021/Forum LP 9006
Little Willie Wampum	Emblems, Eddie Carl & the	1962	Oh My 1000
Little Young Girl	Genies	1961	Warwick 643
Live And Let Live	Lancers	1954	Trend 82
Live It Up	Orioles, Sonny Til & the	1960	Vee Jay LP 1021
Live Just To Love You	Bradford, Sylvester & group	1958	Atco 6130
Live Like A King	Twilighters (Atlanta)	1957	Ebb 117
Live Wire Suzie	Robins	1960	Arvee 5013
Liverlips	Quintones (Chicago)	1961	Lee 1113
Liverpool Baby	Martin, Trade & group	1964	Coed 594
Liverpool Bound	Salutations, Vito & the	1964	Wells 1008
Livin' By The Gun	Rockets, Dick Holler & His	1958	Ace 540
Livin' The Life	Chord'R Notes	1964	Fargo 1061
Livin' The Night Life	Charts	1966	Wand 1124
Living From Day To Day	Jewels, Johnny Torrance with the	1954	R&B 1306
Living In A Dream	Four Winds, Sonny Woods & the	1956	Middle-Tone 013
Living In Paradise	Valiants (Los Angeles)	1963	Imperial 5915
Living Just For You	Rapid Transit	1978	Clifton 26
Living Letter	Twilights, Helen Simon & the	1963	Felice 713
Living One Day At A Time	Edward Sisters	1958	Kaiser 388
Living Truth, The	Sanders, Will & group	1961	Regatta 2003
Living With Vivian	El Dorados (with Hazel McCollum)	1954	Vee Jay 118
'Lizabeth	Thrillers (Detroit)	1954	Herald 432
Lizard Grizzard	Reptiles, Johnny Cole & the	1961	Radiant 1503
Lizzie	Del Rios	1956	Meteor 5038

SONG	GROUP	YEAR	LABEL
Loaded With Goodies	Four Jewels	1963	Checker 1039/Start 638
			(same # used twice)
Loaded With Goodies	Rubies	1961	District 301
Loafin'	Quadrells, Alan & the	1961	Goldisc G14
Loch Lomond	Castle Kings	1961	Atlantic 2107
Lock My Heart	Sharps	1957	Lamp 2007
Locked Out	Jesters, Junior Chard & the	1959	Madison 127
Locking Up My Heart	Marvelettes	1963	Tamla 54077
Loco	Wheels	1956	Premium 408
Loco In The Coco	Teen Notes	1960	Deb 121
Locomotion	Ultratones	1962	Cary 2001
Locomotion, The	Chiffons	NA	Collectables LP 5042
Locomotion, The	Little Eva & group	1962	Dimension 1000
Lola	Chessmen	1961	Pac 100
Lola	Howards	1958	ABC 9897
Lola (acappella)	Velvet Angels	1972	Relic LP 5004/Relic LP 102 (75)
Lola Lee	Five Trojans	1959	Edison International 412
Lolita	Bonaires	1960	Shasta 126
Lolita	Shepherd Sisters	1962	United Artists 456
Lolita Cha Cha	Blaze, Johnny & group	1959	Apon 2142
Lollipop	Zodiacs, Maurice Williams & the	1965, 1966	Vee Jay 678
Lollipop Baby	Marcels	1962	Colpix 665
Lollipop Girl	Jiving Juniors	1961	Blue Beat 4
Lollypops And Shotguns	Romanaires	NA	D&J 100
Lolo Baby	Medallions	1957	Singular 1002
London Bridge	Lee, Warren & group	1963	Jin 173
London Town	Chandler, Gene (with the Dukays)	1962	Vee Jay 440
Londonderry Air	Decals	1975	Monogram 103
Lone Lonely One	Saints, Tom Allen & the	1961	Band Box 249
Lone Lover	Click-Ettes	1960	Guyden 2043
Lone Stranger	Del Counts, Ronald Bobo & the	1976	Rose 23
Lone Stranger	Denotations	1965	Lawn 253
Lone Stranger	Vilons	1963	Aljon 1259/1260/Relic 524 (64)
Lone Stranger, The	Majestics (Detroit)	1959	Sioux 91459/20th Century 171 (59)/
			Foxie 7004 (59)
Lone Stranger (acappella), The	Zircons	1966	Amber 851
Lone Stranger Went Mad, The	Devotions, Little Marcus & the	1964	Gordie 1001
Lone Teen Ranger	Landis, Jerry & group	1962, 1982	Amy 875
Loneliest Girl In Town	Delrons, Reperata & the	1965	RCA 8820
Loneliest Guy In The World, The	Barin, Pete (with the Belmonts)	1963	Sabina 512
Loneliest Man In The World, The	DiMucci, Dion (with the Del Satins)	1963	Columbia 42776
Loneliest Man In Town	Barries	1964	Di-Nan 101
Loneliness	Bobbettes	1962	Jubilee 5427
Loneliness	Emersons	1961	United Artists 379
Loneliness	Impressors	1958	Cub 9010
Loneliness	Jarmels	1962	Laurie 3124
Loneliness	Knick-Knacks	1959	Cub 9030
Loneliness	Quarter Notes	1957	DeLuxe 6116
Loneliness	Von Gayels	1963	USA 1221
Loneliness	Zodiacs, Maurice Williams & the	1963	Atlantic 2199
Loneliness Never Entered My Mind	Ovations (Capitol)	1963	Capitol 5082
Loneliness Or Happiness	Drifters (1959-forward)	1961	Atlantic 2117
Lonely	Astra-Lites	1962	Tribute 101
Lonely	Channels	1959	Mercury
Lonely	Epics	1958	Lifetime 1004
Lonely	Graduates	1959	Corsican 0058
Lonely	Guerillas	1965	Donna 1406
Lonely	Hi-Fives	1958	Decca 30744
Lonely	Little Dippers	1960	University 608
Lonely	Solitaires	1954	Old Town 1008
Lonely	Toppers (ABC)	1956	ABC 9759
Lonely Am I	Chantels	1966	Unreleased
Lonely And Blue	Bobbies	1964	Crusader 115
Lonely Birthday	Mitchum, Jim & group	1960	20th Century 277
Lonely Blue Boy	Aktones, Will Wendel & the	1962	Trans America 10000

SONG	GROUP	YEAR	LABEL
Lonely Blue Nights	Innocents, Kathy Young & the	1962	Indigo 146
Lonely Blue Nights	Originals, Rosie & the	1961	Brunswick 55205/Highland 1031 (61)
Lonely Bluebird	Impossibles	1964	Reprise 0305
Lonely Bluebird	Scott Brothers	1961	FTP 415
Lonely Boy	Castaleers	1958	Felsted 8512
Lonely Boy	Classmates, Ronnie Jones & the	1958, 1963	End 1014/1125
Lonely Boy	Don-Tels	1963	Witch 121
Lonely Boy	Fabulons	1963	Jo-Dee 1001
Lonely Boy	Five Shades	1961	Ember 1074
Lonely Boy	Hurley, John & group	1958	AKA 103
Lonely Boy	Justifiers	1958	Kim 101
Lonely Boy	Laurels, Kenny Loran & the	1958	Challenge 59010
Lonely Boy	Marcels	1963	888 101
Lonely Boy	Rob-Roys, Norman Fox & the	19??	
Lonely Boy	Versatiles	1964	Sea Crest 6001
Lonely Boy And Pretty Girl	Smoothies	1960	Decca 31159
Lonely Boy, Lonely Girl	Swordsmen	1961	Semac 2114
Lonely Broken Heart	Rhythmaires, Jessie Lee with the	1958	Mida 110
Lonely Cabin	Hamilton Sisters	1956	King 4892
Lonely Christmas	Orioles, Sonny Til & the	1962	Charlie Parker 213
Lonely Day	Homesteaders	1958	End 1017
Lonely Days, Lonely Nights	Fabulaires	1963	Chelsea 103
Lonely Drummer	Decades	1964	Daytone 6403
Lonely Drummer Boy	Mason, Peter & group	1960	Lawn 105
Lonely Eyes	Robin, Ruth & group	1962	Titan 1725
Lonely For Kathy	Four Tiers, Jimmy Kemper & the	1964	Le Mans 2
Lonely For Kathy	Tiers, Jimmy Kemper & the	1964	Le Mans 002
Lonely For You	Crowns	1959	Wheel 1001
Lonely For You	Voxpoppers, Freddie & the	1960	Warwick 589
Lonely Friday Night	Blossoms	1989	Classic Artists 110
Lonely Girl	El Venos	1959	Memo 96
Lonely Girl	Knight, Gloria & group	1964	Emerson 2101
Lonely Girl	Reflections	1964	Golden World 12
Lonely Girl Blue	Four Seasons, Gigi Parker & the	1962	Coral 62314
Lonely Girl's Prayer	Cones, Connie & the	1960	Roulette 4223
Lonely Guy	Dwellers	1958	Conrose 101
Lonely Guy	Gallahads	1960	Donna 1322/Del-Fi 4137 (60)
Lonely Guy	Valiants, Phil DeMarco & the	1964	Debby 065
Lonely Heart	Enchantments	1962	Romac 1001
Lonely Heart	Majestics (Detroit)	1962	Chex 1006
Lonely Heart	Williams, Mel & group	1955	Federal 12236
Lonely Hearted	Stevens, Carol Ann & group	1961	Carol 4111
Lonely Hearts	Five Satins	1974	Relic LP 5024
Lonely Hearts	Lester, Bobby (actually the Moonglows)	1959	Checker 921
Lonely Hearts Club	Elements	1960	Titan 1708
Lonely Highway	Jayhawks	1961	Argyle 1005
Lonely Hours	Valiants (New York)	1964	Cortland 114
Lonely Hours, The	Sun-Rays	1958	Sun 293
Lonely In A Crowd	Superlatives	NA	Dynamics 1016/Westbound 144
Lonely Is As Lonely Does	Fleetwoods	1964	Dolton 302
Lonely Island	Parliaments	1960	Flipp 100/101
Lonely Little Girl	Martin, Steve & group	1963	Magnasound 700
Lonely Lonely	Sound Masters	NA	Julet 102
Lonely Lonely Heart	Rhythm Rockers, Jimmy Reagan & the	1959	G&G 128/129/Mona-Lee
Lonely, Lonely Nights	Tigers, Little Julian Herrera & the	1956	Dig 118
Lonely, Lonely Village	Calvaes	1957	Cobra 5014
Lonely Lover	Contenders	1966	Java 103
Lonely Lover	Fabulous Five Flames	1960	Time 1023
Lonely Lover	Four Kings	1964	Canadian American 173
Lonely Lover	Heartbeats	1960	Roulette LP 25107
Lonely Lover's Prayer	Picadilly Pipers	1956	Chart 619
Lonely Man	Escorts (RCA)	1957	RCA 6963
Lonely Man	Spaniels	1970	North American 002
Lonely Man	Versatiles	NA	Staff 210
Lonely Me	Carpets	1956	Federal 12269

SONG	GROUP	YEAR	LABEL
Lonely Mood	Five Echoes	1953	Sabre 102
Lonely Night	Jackson, George (with the Jive Five)	NA	Double R 248
Lonely Night	June Voices, Jimmy Von Carl & the	1959	Flick 002
Lonely Night	Ultimates	1961	Envoy 2302
Lonely Night	Von Carl, Jimmy (with the June Voices)	1959	Flick 002
Lonely Nights	Falcons (Detroit)	1964	Lu Pine 124/Lu Pine 1020 (64)
Lonely Nights	Hearts (Bronx, N.Y.)	1955	Baton 208/Main Line 102 (57)
Lonely Nights	King Crooners	1959	Hart 1002
Lonely Nights	Wilson, Sonny & group	1961	Plaza 1
Lonely One	Dapper Dans	1960	Ember 1065
Lonely One	Impressions	1959	Abner 1025
Lonely One	Mondells, Johnny C & the	1972	Saluda 106
Lonely One	Ravels, Sheriff & the	1959	Vee Jay 306
Lonely One, The	Impalas (Sundown)	1959	Sundown 115
Lonely One, The	Velours	1961	End 1090
Lonely Rain	Mascots	1960	King 5435
Lonely Road	Passions	1962	Jubilee 5406
Lonely Road To Nowhere	Raphael, Johnny & group	1958	Aladdin 3409
Lonely Room	Andrews, Gene & group	1963	Rust 5054
Lonely Room	Hearts, Lee Andrews & the	1956, 1962	Gotham 320/Gowen 1403
Lonely Room	Ivy League	1965	Cameo 356
Lonely Sands	Dunes	1961	Madison 156
Lonely Sea	Mitlo Sisters (with the Dreamtones)	1958	Klik 8405
Lonely Soldier	Cavaliers, Little Bernie & the	1962	Jove 100
Lonely Soldier	Illusions	1962	Mali 104/Sheraton 104 (62)/
			Northeast 801 (62)/Relic 512 (64)
Lonely Soldier's Pledge	Knight Lites, Gary & the	1965	Bell 643
Lonely Star	Chapelaires, Joni Kay & the	1964	Gateway 744
Lonely Star	Quails, Bill Robinson & the	1954	DeLuxe 6030
Lonely Street	Caronators	1960	Clock 1047
Lonely Street	Dappers (Foxie)	1961	Foxie 7005
Lonely Street	Echoes, Benny Barnes & the	1958	Mercury 71284
Lonely Summer	Four Buddies	1965	Philips 40122
Lonely Summer	Four Tops	1960	Columbia 41755/
			Columbia 43356 (65)
Lonely Summer	Holidays	1961	Robbee 107
Lonely Summer	Laurels	1986	Ram EP 509049
Lonely Summer	Lee (with the Regents)	1961	Scepter 1222
Lonely Surfer Boy	Sunsets	1963	Challenge 9198
Lonely Teardrops	Fortunes	NA	Bishop 1005
Lonely Teardrops	Rocky Fellers	1963	Scepter 1246
Lonely Teardrops	Starlight	1989	Clifton 85
Lonely Tears	Ramadas	1963	Philips 40117
Lonely Teen	Adams, Link & group	1961	A Okay 111
Lonely Teenager	Camerons	1960	Cousins (unreleased)
Lonely Teenager	DiMucci, Dion (with the Del Satins)	1960	Laurie 3070
Lonely Teenager	Teenettes, Betty Jayne & the	1961	Mona Lee 139
Lonely Telephone, The	Quintones (Chicago)	1954	Jordan 1601
Lonely Traveller	Chuckles	1961	ABC 10276
Lonely Valley	Ardells (Johnny Maestro)	1963	Epic 9621
Lonely Way	Skyliners	1959	Calico 109
Lonely Way (acappella)	Zircons	1963	Mellomood 1000/Relic 1008 (65)
Lonely Weatherman	Premiers (Mohican)	NA	Mohican
Lonely Weekend	Essentials, Billy & the	1963	Mercury 72127
Lonely Weekends	Fairlanes	1963	Reprise 20213
Lonely Weekends	Pictures, C.L. & the	1963	Dunes 2020
Lonely Winds	Drifters (1959-forward)	1960	Atlantic 2062
Lonely Woman	Metronomes (Harold Sonny Wright)	NA	Cadence (unreleased)
Lonely Women, Lonely Men	Dales	1957	Onyx 509
Lonely World	DiMucci, Dion (with the Del Satins)	1963	Laurie 3187
Lonely Years	Josie, Lou & group	1959	Baton 269
Lonesome	Ebbtides	1959	Jan-Lar 101
Lonesome	Elgins (A-B-S)	1961	A-B-S 113
Lonesome	Five Vultures	1973	Roadhouse 1006
Lonesome	Thrillers, Little Joe & the	1957	Okeh 7094

SONG	GROUP	YEAR	LABEL
Lonesome Again	Warblers	1974	Outhouse 102
Lonesome And Sorry	Three Graces	1959	Golden Crest 528
Lonesome Baby	Hornets	1953	States 127
Lonesome Boy	Regents	1961	Gee 1075
Lonesome Desert	Flairs	1963	Crown LP 5356
Lonesome Desert	Young Jessie (with the Flairs)	1954	Modern 921
Lonesome For You	Grier Quartet	1958	Swan 4019
Lonesome For You	Parkway	1992	Clifton 99
Lonesome Little Lonely Girl	Vibrations	1963	Atlantic 2204
Lonesome Lover	Solitaires	1961	Old Town 1096
Lonesome Me	Chanters (California)	1955	Kem 2740
Lonesome Old Story	Five Keys	1953	Aladdin 3190
Lonesome Old World	King, Freddy & group	NA	Roulette 7003
Lonesome Playgirl	Hepcats, Daisy Mae & the	1956	Gotham 317
Lonesome Rhythm Blues	Swing Teens, Wayne McGinnis & the	1956	Meteor 5035
Lonesome Road	Dominoes	1954	King 1364
Lonesome Road	Fashions	1959	V-Tone 202
Lonesome Road Rock	Nightbeats	1958	Zoom 002
Lonesome Road, The	Ravens	1954	Mercury 70307
Lonesome Romeo	Imperials, Little Anthony & the	1963	Roulette 4477
Lonesome Soul	Tune Tones	1959	Herald 539
Lonesome Teenager	Impressions, Joey & the	NA	Cagg 101
Lonesome Tonight	Feathers	1955	Hollywood 1051
Lonesome Town	Fleetwoods	1964	Dolton 93
Lonesome Walk, The	Curtains, Mr. Lee &	1970	Boardwalk 18
Lonesome Weekend	Elegants	1974	Bim Bam Boom 121
Lonesome Wind	Bobolinks	1961	Tune 226
Long After	Dovells	1966	Diamond 198
Long Ago	Pageants	NA	Vira
Long Black Stockings	Four Pals	1959	Roulette 4127
Long Black Veil	Jokers, Johnny Williams & the	1961	Pic 1 105
Long Cigarette	Reflections	1966	ABC 10822
Long Cold Winter ahead	Teen Tones	1965	T&T 2488
Long Drink Of Water In A Topless Bathing Suit, The	Hustlers, Richard Ward & the	1964	Downey 121
Long For Jean	Kidds, Morry Williams & the	1974	Firefly 319
Long Haired Unsquare Dude Named Jack	Hollywood Argyles	1965	Chattahoochee 691
Long Head Leggy Rascal	Jumpin' Jacks	1989	Relic LP 5077
Long Hot Summer	Caronators	1960	Clock 1045
Long John	Chuck-A-Lucks	1961	Warner Bros. 5198
Long John	V.I.P.s	1963	Carmel 44
Long John Silver	Coronets, Sammy Griggs & the	1960	J.O.B. 100
Long Lasting Love	Thrillers (Detroit)	NA	Herald (unreleased)
Long Legged Linda	Kids From Texas	1958	Hanover 4500
Long Legged Maggie	Clusters	1959	Epic 9330
Long, Lonely Nights	Hearts, Lee Andrews & the	1957	Grand 157/Main Line 102 (57)/ Chess 1665 (57)
Long Lonely Nights	Kings (Joe Van Loan)	1957	Baton 245
Long Lonely Nights	McPhatter, Clyde (with the Cues)	1957	Atlantic 1149
Long Lonely Nights (alternate)	Hearts, Lee Andrews & the	1981	Gotham 324
Long Lonely Winter	Chips	1965	Tollie 9042
Long Long Ago	Four Naturals	1959, 1977	Red Top 125/Arcade 1004
Long Long Ago	Saints, Danny & the	NA	Fanelle 101
Long, Long Ponytail	Fireballs, Chuck Tharp & the	1960	Jaro 77029/Lucky 0012
Long Long Time	Pyramids (RCA)	1959	RCA 7556
Long Man, The	Thin Men, Dennis Binder & his	1956	United 194
Long Tall Girl	Carnations (Startones)	1961	Lescay 3002
Long Tall Sally	Green, Barbara & group	1963	Atco 6250
Long Tall Sally	Rocky Fellers	1962	Parkway 836
Long Tall Texan	Demons, Eddie Jones & the (with Jim Mann)	NA	Kairay 1003
Long Tall Texan	Four Flickers	1959	Lee 1003
Long Tall Texan	Kellum, Murry & group	1964	MOC 653
Long Time	Katz, Ronnie & group	1961	N/A
Long Time	Travellers, Ronnie Cates & the	1962	Terrace 7501/7508

SONG	GROUP	YEAR	LABEL
Long Time Ago	Cupcakes, Cookie & the	1964	Lyric 1017
Long Time Alone	Stewart, Danny (Sly Stone)	1961	G&P 901
Long Time Away	Stewart, Sylvester & group	1962	G&P 901
Long Time Baby	Sonotones, Harry Carlton & the	NA	Jarman
Long Time Dead	Romaines	1954	Groove (unreleased)
Long Time No See	Manhattans, Ronnie & the	1963	Enjoy 2008
Long Time No See	Rouzan, Wanda & group	1963	Frisco 115
Long Walk	Catalinas	1959	Fortune 535
Long Way Home	Breakers	1963	Marsh 206
Long Way To Go	Four Bells	1953	Gem 207/Crystal 102
Longing	Clusters	NA	Unreleased
Longing	Desires	1960	20th Fox 195
Longing	Orioles, Sonny Til & the	1954	Jubilee 5161
Looby Loo	Byrd, Bobby & group	1957	Zephyr 70-018
Look	Casuals (Sue Kenny)	1963	Tribute 118
Look	Concords, Sue Kenny & the	1963	Tribute 118
Look	Mustangs	1965	Vest 8005
Look A Here, Baby	Shirelles	1959	Scepter 1203
Look A Who	A-Tones, Roger & the	1961	Nike 002
Look A Who	Ballin, Roger & group	1960	Nike 002
Look At Her Eyes	Nu Ports, Tyrone & the	1963	Darrow 71/72
Look At Little Sister	Midnighters, Hank Ballard & the	1959	King 5289
Look At Me	Contenders	1966	Java 101
Look At Me	Four Pearls	1960	Dolton 26
Look At Me	Knight, Marie & group	1956	Mercury 70969
Look At Me	Pearls	1960	Dolton 26
Look At Me	Sharps	1958	Jamie 1108
Look At Me	Uniques	1960	Mr. Cee 100
Look At Me	Velvets, Ronnie Price & the	NA	Carousel 1001
Look At Me	Uneeks	1960	Toledo 1501
Look At Me Girl	Coins	1954, 1956	Gee 11/1007
Look At Me, Look At Me	Medallions, Vernon Green & the	1964	Minit 30234
Look At Me, Look At You	Fortunes, Larry Darnell & the	1960	Argo 5364
Look At Me Now	Anthony, Paul & group	NA	Metro International 1003
Look At Me Now	Visions	1963	Original Sound 32
Look At That Girl	Fiestas	1961, 1962	Old Town 1104/1127
Look At That Guy	Percells	1963	ABC 10449
Look At The Stars	Bobbettes	1957	Atlantic 1144
Look Away	Magic Tones	NA	Ram-Brock 2001
Look Away	Shirelles	1967	Scepter 12178
Look Down That Lonesome Road	Tune Weavers	1958	Casa Grande 101
Look For A Job	Mosley, Little Joe	1958	Del-Fi 4107
Look For A Lie	Jades	1959	Christy 114
Look For A Star	Statues, Gary Miles & the	1960	Liberty 55261
Look For Cindy	Barin, Pete (with the Belmonts)	1963	Sabina 512
Look For The Silver Lining	Baysiders	1960	Everest 19386
Look Homeward Angel	Monarchs	1964	Sound Stage 7 2516
Look Homeward Angel	Tempos	1959	Paris 550
Look In My Eyes	Chantels	1961	Carlton 555
Look Into My Eyes	Jaguars	1959	Original Sound 06/ Original Sound 20 (62)
Look Into The Future	Newports	1993	Avenue D 18
Look Into The Sky	Lytations	1964	Times Square 107
Look Me In The Eyes	Five Willows	1954	Herald 442
Look My Way	Idets	NA	Shiptown 007
Look My Way	King Bees	1974	Outhouse 101
Look Out	Four Buddies	1956	Club 51 105
Look Out	Masters	1961	End 1100
Look Out	Rockin' Bradley & group	1959	Fire 1007
Look Over Here Girl	Orbits, Bobby Grayson & His	1963	Jamco 105
Look To The Rainbow (acappella)	Sessions	1976	Arcade 100
Look Up And Live	Four Imperials	1958	Fox 102
Look Up To The Sky	Kodaks	1960	J&S 1683/1684
Look What I've Found	Dappers Quintet	1955	Flayr 500
Look What You're Doin' To Me	Debs	1955	Crown 153

SONG	GROUP	YEAR	LABEL
Look What You're Doing Baby	Titans	1957	Vita 158
Look What You've Done	Earthquakes, Armando King with the	1962	Fortune 549
Look What You've Done To Me	Sharps	1958	Combo 146/Dot 15806 (58)
Look What You've Done To My Heart	Shirelles, Shirley & the	1969	Bell 760
Looka Here	Midnighters	1955	Federal 12227
Looka Here, Mattie Bee	Hobson, Emmett & group	1953	Central 1001
Looka Here, Pretty Baby	Don Juans, Joe Weaver & the	1956	Fortune 832
Look-A-There	Fortuneers	1963	Skytone 1000
Lookie Cookie	Jewels (female)	1966	King 6068
Lookie Lookie Lookie	Shades, K.C. Grand & the	1961	Matt 0003
Lookin'	Four Labels	1958	Gralow 5524
Lookin'	Metros	1959	Just 1502
Lookin' For A Gal	Delltones	NA	Maestro 1919
Lookin' For A Love	Olympics	1968	Parkway 6003
Lookin' For A Man	Little Esther (with the Dominoes)	1951	Federal 12036
Lookin' For Boys	Pin-Ups	1964	Stork 1
Lookin' For Love	Prestos	1955	Mercury 70747
Lookin' For My Baby	Earls	1961, 1979	Rome 102/Clifton 39 (74)
Lookin' For My Baby	Night Riders	1959	Sue 719
Lookin' My Way	Earls	1963	Old Town 1141
Lookin' Out The Window	Furness Brothers	1964	Melmar 114
Looking	Infernos	1980	BAB 126
Looking Ahead	Cap-Tans	1962	Design LP DLP705
Looking Around	Shirelles	1966	Scepter 12162
Looking Back	Hearts, Lee Andrews & the (as Lee Andrews)	1963	Parkway 866
Looking For A Fool	Halos, Johnny Angel & the	1962	Felsted 8659
Looking For A Girl	Hill, Grant & group	1959	Topaz 1300
Looking For A Love	Four Uniques	1961	Adam 9002
Looking For A Lover	Bobbettes	1961	King 5551
Looking For A New Love (Bad Thing To Know)	Bobbettes	1972	Mayhew 712237
Looking For A Summertime Girl	High Tensions	1964	Hitt 6601
Looking For An Echo	Vance, Kenny	1976	Atlantic
Looking For Love	Newports	1978	Crystal Ball 113
Looking For My Baby	Blue Dots	1958	Zynn 511
Looking For My Baby	Do-Wells, Tony Morra & the	1960	Du-Well 1005
Looking For My Baby	Ravens	1952	Mercury 5764
Looking For My Baby	Wonders, Tony Allen & the	1959	Jamie 1119
Looking For Trouble	Charmers	1964	Pip 8000
Looking For True Love	Madisons	1965	MGM 13312
Looking For You	Dukes (California)	1959	Flip 343
Looking Glass	Shirelles, Shirley & the	1969	Bell 787
Looking In From The Outside	El Dorados	1971	Paula 347
Looking Like A Fool	Alston, Jo Ann & group	1963	Vest 8001
Looking Over My Life	Miller Sisters	1965	Yorktown 75
Looly Lou	Shadows	1959	El-Gee-Bee 101
Loomy	Rockers, Rockin' Bradley & the	1958	Hull 729
Loop De Loop De Loop	Crowns, Arthur Lee Maye & the	1955	RPM 429
Loop De Loop Mambo	Four Escorts	1954	RCA 5886
Loop De Loop Mambo	Robins	1955	Spark 107
Loop The Hoop	Night Owls	1957	NRC 015
Loose Bootie	El Dorados	1972	Paula 369
Loose Caboose	Blue Notes, Joe Weaver & his	1955	Fortune 820
Lo-o-ve	Lemon Drops	1959	Coral 62145
Lord Can't Do A Solo, The	Tokens (Brooklyn)	1974	Atco 7009
Lord, If You're A Woman	Love, Darlene & group	1976	Warner-Spector 0410
Lord Knows I Tried	El Dorados	1958	Vee Jay (unreleased)
Lord, Lord, Lord	Apollos	1961	Galaxy 708
Lord Show Me	Aladdins	1957	Aladdin 3358
Lord's Prayer, The	Orioles, Sonny Til & the	1950	Jubilee 5045
Lorelei	Maresca, Ernie (with the Del Satins)	1963	Seville 125
Loretta	Coins	1955	Model 2001
Loretta	Count Downs, Chuck Hix & the	1961	Flair 101
Loretta	Legacy	1987	Crystal Ball 151
Loretta	Midnighters, Lil' Ray & the	1964	Impact 30

SONG	GROUP	YEAR	LABEL
Loretta	Senators	1958	Golden Crest 514
Lorie	Count Victors	1962	Coral 62356
Lorraine	Allures	1986	Starlight 32
Lorraine	Ambassadors	1963	Playbox 202
Lorraine	Bonnevilles	1960	Munich 103/Barry 104 (62)
Lorraine	Cupids	1963	Musicnote 119
Lorraine	Dee, Joey & group	1958	Little 813/814/Bonus 7009
Lorraine	Del-Rays	1961, 1981	Planet 52
Lorraine	Exotics	1963	Springboard 101
Lorraine	Harmonaires	1957	Holiday 2602
Lorraine	Preludes	1961	Arliss 1004
Lorraine	Retrospect	NA	Collage
Lorraine	Vacels, Ricky & the	1962	Express 711
Lorraine (acappella)	Versailles	1965	Old Timer 607
Lorraine From Spain	Skyliners	1960	Calico 114
Loser, The	Skyliners	1965	Jubilee 5506
Loser, The	Vi-Counts	1960	Ace 587
Loser's Advice	Accidentals	NA	Harbor 7593
Losing Game	Beaus, Bobbie & the	1959	Unart 2009
Losing You Baby	Chimes (Jay-Tee)	NA	Jay-Tee 1000
Lost	Darlettes	1965	Mira 203
Lost	Dupree, Nelson & group	1960	Palm 201
Lost	Spartans	1954	Capri 7201
Lost And Bewildered	Spiders	1955	Imperial 5331
Lost And Found	Chants	1958	Capitol 3949
Lost And Found	Phantoms	1957	Baton 244
Lost And Found	Tokays	1952	Bonnie 102
Lost And Lonely Boy	Magic Touch	1973	Roulette 7143
Lost Angel	Mann, Billy & group	1956	Dig 111
Lost Boogie	Impalas (Sundown)	1959	Sundown 115
Lost Caravan	Furys	1963	Manor 51621
Lost Dream Blues	Robins, Little Esther & the	1950	Savoy 759
Lost Dreams	Dukes (California)	1956	Imperial (unreleased)
Lost For Sure	DiMucci, Dion (with the Del Satins)	1962	Laurie 3134
Lost Horizon	Countdowns	1963	Summit 0004
Lost In A City	Majors (Big Three)	NA	Big Three 403
Lost In A Dream	Charters	1963	Merry-Go-Round 103
Lost In A Dream	Clair-tones	NA	Announcing
Lost In Dreams	Wisdoms	1959	Gaity 169
Lost In The Crowd	Runarounds, Ritchie & the	1963	Ascot 2136
Lost In The Night	Basin St. Boys, Charles Brown & the	1948, 1956	Exclusive 39/Cash 1052 (56)
Lost In The Wilderness	Dubs, Richard Blandon & the	1971	Vicki 229
Lost In Your Eyes	Harborside	1991	Clifton 93
Lost John	Stylers	1956	Jubilee 5246
Lost Love	A Moment's Pleasure	1986	Starlight 42
Lost Love	Belvederes	1962	Poplar 114
Lost Love	Cymbals, Lee Williams & the	1965	Carnival 527
Lost Love	Darin, Bobby & group	1958	Atco 6127
Lost Love	Darvell, Barry & group	1961	Atlantic 2128
Lost Love	Dedications, Denny & the	1965	Susan 1111
Lost Love	Earls	1976, 1980	Rome 112
Lost Love	Flips, Little Joey & the	1962	Joy 262
Lost Love	Jesters, Lendon Smith with the	1956	Meteor 5030
Lost Love	Magic Moments	1990	Clifton 90
Lost Love	Scott Brothers	1960	Ribbon 6911
Lost Love	Sensational	1958	Mida 109
Lost Love	Shirelles	1964	Scepter 1284
Lost Love	Storey Sisters	1959	Mercury 71457
Lost Love	Superiors	1957	Atco 6106/Main Line 104 (58)
Lost Love (acappella)	Notations	1975	Relic LP 104
Lost Love Affair	Blue Boys, Mr. Bo & the	NA	Diamond 852
Lost Lover	Cameos (New Jersey)	1960	Dean 504/Johnson 108 (60)
Lost Lover	Magnificents	1957	Vee Jay 235
Lost Lullabye	Topics, Billy Dixon & the	1961	Topix 6008
Lost My Heart	Spirals	1962	Luxor 1012

SONG	GROUP	YEAR	LABEL
Lost My Job	Del-Airs	1960	MBS 001
Lost My Love Yesterday	Larks (Don Julian)	1965	Money 119
Lost Romance	Ultimates	1962	Ford 117
Lost Symphony	Ramblers (Cora)	1964	Cora 101
Lost The Best Thing I Ever Had	Taylor, Ted & group	1961	Suncraft 400
Lost Weekend	Brown, Billy & group	1960	Republic 2007
Lost Weekend	Lovettes	1959	Knight 2010
Lost Without You	Ivys	1959	Coed 518
Lots And Lots Of Love	Fi-Tones	1955	Atlas 1051
Lots Of Luck	Revels	1963	Diamond 143
Lotsa Lotsa Lovin'	Carousels	1959	Spry 116
Lottery	Buddies	1957	Decca 30355
Lou Ann	Clouds, Little Sunny Daye & the	1961	Tandem 7001
Loudness Of My Heart, The	Gay Knights	1958	Pet 801
Louella	Avalons	1958	Dice 90/91
Louella	Sevilles	1961	JC 118
Louie Hoo Hoo	Rays	1961	XYZ 607
Louie, Louie	Blue Notes, Little Bill & the	1961	Topaz 1305
Louie, Louie	Pharaohs, Richard Berry & the	1957	Flip 321
Louise	Cadillacs	1960	Unreleased
Louise	Chordells, Willie Howard & the	1961	Mascot 127
Louise	Swallows (Maryland)	1986	Starbound 508
Louisiana	Tifanos	1960	Tifco 822
Louisiana Rug Roll	Belairs, Lee Bantell & the	1956	Coral 61605
Lovable	Embers, Willis Sanders & the	1958	Millionaire 775/Unart 2004 (58)
Lovable	Jay Birds, Lenny Young & the	1958	Jay Scott 1001/Jackpot 48006 (58)
Lovable Girl	Butlers	1963	Guyden 2081
Lovable Lily	Mellows, Lillian Leach & the	1955	Jay-Dee 807
Lovable You	Fabulous Embers, Willis Sanders & the	1958	Millionaire 775
Love	Ascots	1965	Mir-A-Don 1004
Love	Fortunes	1981, 1990	Relic LP 5088/Relic CD
Love	King, Mabel (with the Harptones)	1963	Amy 874
Love	Monorays	1965	20th Fox 594
Love	No Names	1964	Guyden 2114
Love	Opals	1962	Beltone 2025
Love	Sheppards (Chicago - Theron)	1955	Theron 112
L-O-V-E	Craftys	1961	Lois 5000/Seven Arts 5708 (61)
L-O-V-E	Drivers, Leroy & the	1965	Coral 62515
L-O-V-E	Emotions	1963	Kapp 513
L-O-V-E	Swinging Phillies	1958	DeLuxe 6171
Love A La Mode	Bystanders	1956	Dot 15512
Love All Night	Platters	1954	Federal 12188
Love Always	Obsessions	1964	Accent 1182
Love Always Finds The Way	Chansonaires	1958	Hamilton 50012
Love And Affection	Night Rockers, Freddie Hall & the	1959	CJ 610
Love And Devotion	Vocaleers	1960	Old Town 1089
Love And Happiness	Richettes	1962	Apt 25069
Love And Kisses	Mixers	1959	Bold 102
Love And Learn	Carroll, Cathy (with the Earls)	1962	Warner Bros. 5284
Love And Learn	Holidays	1964	Coral 62430
Love And Understanding	Counts	1955	Dot 1243
Love Angel	Corvans	1959	Cabot 131
Love Another Girl	Rays	1964	Amy 900
Love At First Sight	Crayons	1963	Counsel 122
Love At First Sight	Mello-Kings	1961	Herald 567
Love At First Sight	Statues	1961	Liberty 55363
Love Bandit	Cadets	1957	Modern 1012
Love Bandit	Twiliters	1961	Nix 103
Love Bells	Delmar, Eddie (with the Bob Knight Four)	1961	Madison 168
Love Bells	Five Willows	1953	Pee Dee 290
Love Bells	Galens	1963	Challenge 59212
Love Bells	Memories	1962	Way-Lin 101
Love Bells	Swallows (Maryland)	1986	Starbound 505
Love Birds	Five Embers	1954	Gem 224
Love Boat	Ka-Rillons	1964	Laurie 3244

SONG	GROUP	YEAR	LABEL
Love Bound	Universals (Amityville, N.Y.)	1961	Festival 1601/Festival 25001 (62)
Love, Boy (Made A Fool Out Of You)	Alamos, Tony Valla & the	1961	Fortune 859
Love Bug	Agee, Ray & group	1962	Marjan 001
Love Bug Bit Me	Lovers	1958	Aladdin 3419/Lamp 2018 (58)
Love Bug's Got Me, The	Lyrics, Ike Perry & the	1958	Bridge 110
Love Call	Ebonaires	1959, 1964	Lena 1001/Cameo 334
Love Call	Three G's	1960	Columbia 41678
Love Came To Me	DiMucci, Dion (with the Del Satins)	1962	Laurie 3145
Love Came Tumbling Down	Cardinals	1955	Atlantic (unreleased)
Love Came Tumbling Down	Jackson, Dimples & group	1960	Gardena 114
Love Can Be Blind	Wanderers, Dolly Cooper & the	1954	Savoy 1121
Love Can Do Most Anything	Cadets, Will Jones & the	1957	Modern 1024
Love Can't Be A One Way Deal	Rev-Lons	1963	Reprise 20200/Starburst 123
Love Come Back	Blue Kings, Andy Charles & the	1959	D 1061
Love Comes In Many Ways	Valiants (Los Angeles)	1962	Imperial 5843
Love Comes Tumbling Down (Love Song)	Belvin, Jesse & group	1953	Hollywood 412
Love Cry	Starlighters	1956	Irma 101
Love Doctor	Ebbtides	1959	Jan-Lar 101
Love Doll	Scarlets	1955	Red Robin 133
Love Don't Grow On Trees	Charms, Otis Williams & the	1965	Okeh 7225
Love Dreams	Stephens, Jimmy (with the Safaris)	1961	Eldo 112
Love Drops	Earlington, Lyn & group	NA	Lemonade 1501
Love Epidemic	Earls	1976	Woodbury 1000
Love Eternal	Four B's	1958	D 1013
Love Every Moment	Four Of A Kind	1958	Cameo 154
Love Express	Mellos, Terry & the	1960	Amy 812
Love Express, The	Maresca, Ernie (with the Del Satins)	1963	Seville 125
Love Express, The	Velvets (Texas)	1962	Monument 458
Love Eyes	Duprees	1963	Coed 585/Heritage 826 (69)
Love Finds A Way	Castells	1964	Warner Bros. 5486
Love For A Year	Students, Bill Starr & the	1960	Applause 1235
Love For Christmas	Jackson Trio (with the Ebonaires)	1955	Hollywood 1046
Love For Me	Capri, John (with the Fabulous Four)	1959	Bomarc 306
Love For Today	Classics (Brooklyn)	1967	Piccollo 500
Love From The Far East	Master Four	NA	Tay-Ster 6012
Love Game	Mudlarks	1959	Roulette 4143
Love Game	Valiants, Billy Storm & the	1969	Famous LP 504
Love Gave Me To You	Flasher Brothers	1952	Aladdin 3156
Love Has Forgotten Me	Majestics (MGM)	1966	MGM 13488
Love Has Its Ways	Galaxies (with Eddie Cochran on guitar)	1960	Guaranteed 216
Love, Hate And Revenge	Del Satins	1967	Diamond 216
Love Her In The Mornin' And Love Her In The Night Time	G-Clefs	1957	Paris 502
Love Her So	Corvairs	1961	Clock 1037
Love Him	Dream Girls, Bobbie Smith & the	1960	Metro 20034
Love Him	Manselles	1965	Diamond 172
Love Hit Me And I Hollered	Four Shots	1955	Cadillac 154
Love I Beg Of You	Ensenadas	1963	Tarx 1005
Love (I Found In You), The	Precisions	NA	Wild 903
Love I Found In You, The	Sheppards (Chicago - Robin Hood)	1976	Robin Hood 135
Love I Hold, The	Agents	NA	Liberty Bell 3260
Love I Long For (acappella), The	Universals (Philadelphia)	1973	Relic LP 5006
Love I Wish I Had, The	Drapers	1960	Unical 3001
Love (I'm So Glad) I Found You	Spinners	1961	Tri-Phi 1004
Love In Portofino	Earthquakes, Tino Cairo with the	1957	Hi-Q 5020
Love In Return	Dell-Coeds	1962	Enith 712/Dot 16314 (62)
Love In Return	Nightingales	1961	Ray Star 784
Love In Your Life	Tornados	1959	Bumble Bee 503
Love Is A Beautiful Thing	Gees	1966	Port 3011
Love Is A Beautiful Thing	Macs, Terry & the	1956	ABC 9668
Love Is A Beautiful Thing	Nomads, Ben Atkins & the	NA	Goldwax 336
Love Is A Clown	Teenagers, Frankie Lymon & the	1957	Gee 1035
Love Is A Dangerous Thing	Melson, Joe & group	1962	Hickory 1175
Love Is A Funny Little Game	Vogues	1958	Dot 15798
Love Is A Gamble	Sentimentals	1959	Vanity 589

SONG	GROUP	YEAR	LABEL
Love Is A Game	Alvans	1961	May 102
Love Is A Game	Dame, Freddy & group	1962	Nic Nac 331
Love Is A Good Thing Going	Blenders (Chicago)	1966	Mar-V-Lous 6010
Love Is A Many Splendored Thing	Chord Spinners	1961	Liberty 55368
Love Is A Many Splendored Thing	Imperials, Little Anthony & the	1959	End LP 303/End EP 204 (59)
Love Is A Many Splendored Thing (acappella)	Nacks, Nicky & the	1975	Relic LP 103
Love Is A One Time Affair	Satellites, Bobby Day & the	1959	Class 255
Love Is A Problem	Thunderbirds	1955	G.G. 518
Love Is A River	Moonglows	1959, 1964	Chess 1717/Lana 133
Love Is A River (acappella)	Universals (Philadelphia)	1973	Relic LP 5006
Love Is A Story	Patios, Billy & the	1961	Lite 9002
Love Is A Stranger	Sun-Rays	1958	Sun 293
Love Is A Swingin' Thing	Shirelles	1962	Scepter 1228
Love Is A Treasure	Blenders, Goldie Coates & the	1962	Cortland 102
Love Is A Vow	Mello-Harps	1955	Do-Re-Mi 203
Love Is A Vow	Teentones	1958	Rego 1004
Love Is a Wonderful Thing	Titans	1958	Specialty 632
Love Is All I Crave	Travelers	1973	Relic LP 5012
Love Is Amazing	Ohio Untouchables	1962	Lu Pine 110/Lu Pine 1010 (62)
Love Is Better Than Ever	Levons	1963	Columbia 42798
Love Is Blind	Bobbettes	1965	Diamond 189
Love Is Everywhere	Dovells	1966	MGM 13628
Love Is Funny	Hannibal (with the Angels)	1960	Pan World 517
Love Is Gone	Classmen	1963	Limelight 3012
Love Is Good To Me	Fiestas	1965	Old Town 118
Love Is Here To Stay	Starfires	1959	Decca 30916
Love Is Just For Two	Inspirations, Ronnie Vare & the	1959	Dell 5202/5203
Love Is Like A Mountain	Raindrops	1960	Corsair 104/Dore 561 (60)
Love Is Like A Mountain	Roma, Teena & group	1961	Arteen 1002
Love Is Like A Mountain	Sliders	1961	Chevron 012/Chevron 750
Love Is Like Music	Five Chords, Johnny Jones & the	1958	Jamie 1110
Love Is Love	El Torros	1958	Fraternity 811
Love Is Love	Thorns, Andy Rose & the	1960	Gold Crest 3807
Love Is No Dream	Ravens	1954	Mercury 70330
Love Is No Stranger	Lefemmes, Cole & the	NA	Varbee 5001
Love Is No Thing To Play With	Palms	1957	States (unreleased)
Love Is So Wonderful	Stereophonics	1958	Apt 25003
Love Is Something From Within	Kings (Baltimore)	1957	Gone 5013
Love Is Strange	Dolphins, Davey Jones & the	1961	Audicon 116
Love Is Strange	Empires	1964	DCP 1116
Love Is Strange	Fiestas	1965	Old Town 118
Love Is Strange	Jones, Toni & group	1963	Smash 1814
Love Is Strange	Spartans	1961	Audio International 102
Love Is Such A Beautiful Thing	Five Satins	1974	Kirshner 4252
Love Is Such A Good Thing	Corvairs	NA	Sylvia 5003
Love, Is That You?	Barlow, Dean & group	1961	Seven Arts 704
Love Is The Answer	Majors	1966	ABC 10777
Love Is The Greatest Thing	Delacardos	1962	Shell 311
Love Is The Thing	Blue Stars	1991	Clifton 95
Love Is The Thing	Metronomes	1975	Broadcast 1131
Love Is The Thing	Ravens	1952	HHP 5007
Love Is The Thing	Silver Slippers, Barbara J & the	1961	Lescay 3001
Love Is True	Chestnuts	1956	Davis 447
Love Is True	Little Beats	1957	Mercury 71155
Love Is What The World Is Made Of (acappella)	Chessmen	1965	Relic 1020
Love Is Where You Find It	Manhattans	1958	Warner 1015
Love Is Wonderful	Packards	1956	Decca (unreleased)
Love Keeps The Doctor Away	Flamingos	1976	Ronze 116
Love Leads A Fool	Four Beats, Donn Bruce & the	1956	Tuxedo 914
Love Letters	Goldenaires	1960	Ron 332
Love Letters	Medalions	1960	Card 1
Love Letters	Redcoats, Steve Alaimo & the	1959	Dade 1805
Love Like A Fool	Georgettes	1957	Ebb 125

SONG	GROUP	YEAR	LABEL
Love Look In Her Eyes	Falcons (Big Wheel)	1967	Big Wheel 1971
L-O-V-E, Love	Dovells	NA	Paramount 0134
Love, Love, Baby	Rhythm Casters	1957	Excello 2115
Love, Love, Love	Chantels	1961	Big Top 3073
Love Love Love	Clovers	1963	Brunswick 55249
Love, Love, Love	Clovers	1956, 1963	Atlantic 1094
Love, Love, Love	Diamonds	1956	Mercury 70889
Love, Love, Love	Dominoes	1952, 1957	Federal 12072/12308
Love, Love, Love	Dreamers (United Artists)	1965	United Artists 841
Love, Love, Love	Falcons (Big Wheel)	1966	Big Wheel 321/322
Love Love Love	Genies	1961	King 5568
Love Love Love	Sensations	1963	Junior 1006
Love, Love, Love	Smith, Arlene & female group	1961	Big Top 3073
Love, Love, Love D-R-E-A-M	Genies, Gene Wilson & the	1961	King 5568
Love Love Stick Stov	Charms	1955	Chart 608
Love Machine	Marquees	1959	Warner Bros. 5072
Love Made Me A Fool	Gibralters, Jimmy Barnes & the	1959	Gibraltar 106
Love Makes All The Difference In The World	Chantels	1970	RCA 0347
Love Marches On	Vistas, Little Victor & the	1962	Rendezvous 183
Love Me	Avalons	1956	Aladdin (unreleased)
Love Me	Bob-Wheels	1963	Tarx 1008
Love Me	Cardinals	NA	Atlantic EP/Bim Bam Boom EP 1000 (74)
Love Me	Corrente, Sal & group	1966	Roulette 4673
Love Me	Faithfuls, Philip & the	1964	Goldwax 109
Love Me	Five Classics	1961	Pova 6142
Love Me	Four Escorts	1954	RCA 5886
Love Me	Impressions, Jerry Butler & the	1958	Abner 1017
Love Me	Innocents, Kathy Young & the (with Chris Montez)	1962	Monogram 517
Love Me	Jackson Brothers	1954	Atlantic 1034/Atco 6139 (59)
Love Me	Latons	1962	Port 70030
Love Me	Lee, Jimmy (with Wayne Walker & group)	1955	Chess 4863
Love Me	Little David & group	NA	521 1001
Love Me	Rainbows	1977	Ronnie 202
Love Me	Rivals (Detroit)	1964	Puff 1001/Lu Pine 118 (64)
Love Me	Romeos	1954	Apollo 461
Love Me	Royal Jesters	1961, 1962	Cobra 2222
Love Me	RPMs	1963	Port 70032
Love Me	Suburbans	1961	Gee 1076/Flamingo 539
Love Me	Thrillers, Little Joe & the	NA	Peanuts 85211
Love Me	Tiffanys	1964	Arctic 101
Love Me	Versitiles	1962	Amaker 417
Love Me	Williams, Clarence & group	1962	Chancellor 1118
Love Me Again	Hightower, Donna (with the Jacks)	1955	RPM 432
Love Me Again	Idylls	1960	Spinning 6012
Love Me All The Time	Nutones	1963	Dart 135
Love Me All The Way	Romancers, Rocky Homan & the	1961	Flip 355
Love Me Always	Crowns, Arthur Lee Maye & the	1955	RPM 429
Love Me And Don't Fool Around	Elegants	NA	Elegants 101
Love Me Baby	Bartley, Chris & group	1967	Vando 101
Love Me Baby	Casanovas	NA	Apollo LP 1004/Relic LP 5073 (87)
Love Me Baby	Deejays	NA	SRC 101
Love Me Baby	Ontarios	1973	Baron 106
Love Me Baby	Perkins, Al & group	1966	Jive 1003
Love Me, Baby	Re-Vels	1954	Atlas 1035
Love Me Baby	Shadows, Jan Strickland & the	1954	Hub
Love Me Completely	Harptones	1959	Warwick 512
Love Me Crazy	Mellards	1956	Ballad 1016
Love Me Do	Fireflies	1962	Taurus LP 1002
Love Me Forever	Sequins	1962	Terrace 7511
Love Me Forever More	Four Bars	1960	Cadillac 2006
Love Me Girl	Flairs	1954	Flair 1028
Love Me In The Afternoon	Dreamtones	1958, 1975, 1996	Klik 8505/Sold 501 (75)

SONG	GROUP	YEAR	LABEL
Love Me, Kiss Me, Thrill Me	Dawn, Billy Quartet	1954	Celeste (unreleased)
Love Me, Leave Me	Squires (Robway)	NA	Robway 1
Love Me Like I Know You Can	Legends, Rick & the	1963	JD 162/United Artists 50093 (66)
Love Me Like You Can	Hawks, Ronnie Hawkins & the	1959	Roulette 4209
Love Me Like You Should	Vibrations	1960	Bet 001/Checker 954 (60)
Love Me Like You're Gonna Lose Me	Chiffons	1969	Laurie 3497
Love Me Long	Teenagers (Joe Negroni)	1981	Crystal Ball LP 142
Love Me Long	Teenagers, Joey & the	NA	Columbia
Love Me, Love	Berry Kids	1956	MGM 12379
Love Me Love Me	Altones	1961	Gardena 121
Love Me, Love Me	Jokers, Darlene & the	1960	Danco 115
Love Me, Love Me	Pixies 3	1964	Mercury 72357
Love Me, Love Me, Love Me	Chimes (Los Angeles - Flair)	1954	Flair 1051
Love Me More	Dale, Bobby & group	1961	De Rose 8469
Love Me My Darling	Sharps	1954	Two Mikes 101
(Love Me) Now	Angels (New Jersey)	1963	Smash 1834
Love Me Now	Chex, Tex & the	1963	20th Fox 411
Love Me Now	Serenaders (Teen Life)	1958	Teen Life 9
Love Me Now Or Let Me Go	Dominoes	1955	Federal 12218
Love Me Once Again	Memories	NA	Klik
Love Me Or I'll Die	Bon Bons	1957	Columbia 40887
Love Me Or Let Me Go	Avalons	1988	Relic LP 5075
Love Me, Please Love Me	Musketeers, Debbie Andrews & the	1952	United 144
Love Me Right	Five Playboys	1957	Fee Bee 213
Love Me Right	McCain, Jerry & group	1965	Continental 777
Love Me Right	Skyhawks	NA	Collectables LP 5039
Love Me Sincerely	Billie & Lillie (with the Thunderbirds)	1963	ABC 10421
Love Me Tender	Fidels	1957	Music City 806
Love Me Tender	Platters	1964	Mercury 72359
Love Me Tender	Sparrows	1956	Davis 456/Jay Dee
Love Me Tenderly	Del Roys	1961	Carol 4113
Love Me Tenderly	Scott Brothers	1963	Comet 2153
Love Me The Way I Love You	Snaps, Ginger Davis & the	1961	Tore 1008
Love Me Till My Dying Day	Serenaders (Detroit)	1974 (1952)	Roxy 801
Love Me Tonight	Lopez, Trini & group	1959	King 5198
Love Me Tonight	Louisiana Jemms, Sugar Pie DeSantos & the	1963	Checker 1056
Love Me Tonight	Persians	1962	Gold Eagle 1813
Love Me Too	Vibes	1987	Relic LP 8011
Love Me True	Larks (Philadelphia)	1965	Jett 3001
Love Me True	Moonglows (Moonlighters)	NA	Chess (unreleased)
Love Me, Want Me	Marveleers	1953	Derby 844
Love Me When I'm Old	Blackhawks	1972	Roadhouse 1000
Love Me With All Your Heart	Eternals	1968	Quality 1884
Love Mobile	Romeos	1958	Felsted 8528
Love Music	Regal Dewey	1977	Milennium 603
Love Must Be	Jack, Johnny & group	1964	Lawn 230
Love My Baby	Sparrows Quartette	1969	Jet 3000
Love My Love	Four J's	1969	Congress 6003
Love My Loving	Five Keys	1954	Aladdin 3228
Love Needs A Heart	Harptones	1982	Ambient Sound 02807
Love No One	Kings, Bobby Hall & the	1953, 1973	Jax 320
Love No One	Top Hits	1961	Norman 504
Love No One But You	Excellents	1963	Mermaid 106
Love No One But You	Five Chancells	1965	Fellatio 103/Dawn 302
Love No One But You	Jesters	1957	Winley 218
Love Nobody	Rockettes	1954	Parrot 789
Love Notes	Charlettes, Larry & the	1963	Sapien 1004
Love Of A Girl	Emotions	1965	Vardan 201
Love Of a Lifetime	Platters	1959	Mercury 71467
Love Of My Life	Quails, Bill Robinson & the	1955	DeLuxe 6074
Love Of My Life, The	Belvin, Jesse (with the Feathers)	1955	Specialty 559
Love Of My Own	El Dorados	1984	Solid Smoke LP 8025
Love, Oh Love	Chords	1954	Cat (unreleased)
Love Only Me	Versatiles, Jerry Shelly & the	NA	Star 220
Love Only Me	Williams, Jimmy & group	1956	Neil 104

SONG	GROUP	YEAR	LABEL
Love Only One	Teenos	1958	Dub 2839/Relic 506 (64)
Love Only You	Feathers	1954	Show Time 1106
Love Only You	Meadowlarks, Don Julian & the	1954	RPM 399
Love, Open Up My Heart	Carnations	1959	Enrica 1001
Love Or Infatuation	Videos	1959, 1972	Casino 105
Love Or Money	Blackwells	1961	Jamie 1179
Love Pains	Prophets, Ronnie Dio & the	1962	Atlantic 2145
Love Potion No. 9	Clovers	1959	United Artists 180
Love Potion No. 9	Coasters	1971	King 6385
Love Potion No. 9	Revelations	NA	Starlight 16
Love Put Me Out Of My Head	Teenagers, Frankie Lymon & the	1977	Murray Hill LP 000148
Love Rhythm	Bobbettes 1981	1981	QIT
Love, Rock And Thrill	Lamplighters	1955	Federal 12212
Love Shall Never Return	Hearts, Joan & the	1961	
Love So Sweet	Intervals	1958	Irma 820
Love So Sweet	Vines	1961	Cee Jay 582
Love So True	Lamar, Chris & group	1963	Don-El 121
Love So Wonderful	Moniques	1962	Benn-X 58
Love Somebody	Curry, Earl (with the Blenders)	1951	Post 2011
Love Song	Five Keys, Jesse Belvin & the	NA	Candlelight 427
Love Story	Garrett, Scott (with the Mystics)	1959	Laurie 3029
Love Story	Stardusters	1958	Edison International 404
Love Stranger, The	Majestics (Florida)	1959	20th Fox 171
Love Tears	Earls (Road House)	1974	Road House (recorded 1954)
Love Tears	Five Embers	1955	Gem 247 (unreleased)
Love That Girl	Cellos	1988	Relic LP 5074 (88)
Love That Girl	Medallions	1959	Sultan 1004
Love That I Lost, The	Philadelphians	1961	Chesapeake/Campus 101 (61)
Love That I Needed, The	Blendells	1968	Cotillion 44020
Love That I'm Giving To You, The	Fabulous Four (with Fabian)	1961	Chancellor 1079
Love That Man	Shirelles	1965	Scepter 12114
Love That Melody	Tigre Lilies	1959	Gone 5047
Love That's True	Holidays	NA	Willjer 6002
Love To A Guy	Dynamics	NA	Top Ten 927
Love To Last A Lifetime	Voxpoppers	1958	Poplar 107
Love Train	Jayhawks	1956	Flash 111
Love, True Love	Mann, Barry (with the Edsels)	1961	ABC 10237
Love Unreturned	Red Coats	1965	Laurie 3319
Love Walked In	Flamingos	1959	End 1044
Love Walked In	Pixies 3	1964	Mercury 72231
Love Walked In	Re'Vells	1962	Roman Press 201
Love Walked Out	Newlyweds	1961	Homogenized Soul 601
Love Was A Stranger To Me	Parakeets, Vic Donna & the	1957	Atlas 1075/Angletone 1075
Love Was Here With You	Jackson Brothers	1952	Arrow 1003
Love Wasn't There	Checkers	1953	King 4596
Love Wasn't There	Original Checkers	1962	King 5592
Love Went Away	Objectives	1965	Jewel 751
Love Will Break Your Heart	Starfires	1961	Bargain 5003/Atomic 1912 (61)
Love Will Find A Way	Pictures, C.L. & the	1963	Cadette 8005
Love Will Make You Cry	Darlettes	NA	Taffi 100
Love Will Make Your Mind Go Wild	Fascinations, Jordan & the	1961, 1990	Dapt 207/Magic Carpet EP 509
Love Will Make Your Mind Go Wild	Penguins	1955	Dootone 353
Love With No Love In Return	Five Satins	1957	Ember 1028
Love Wouldn't Mean A Thing	Kodaks	1961	Wink 1006
Love Ya	Four Holidays	1960	Verve 10204/Verve 740
Love Ya, Need Ya	Emmy Lou & group	1961	Lute 6018
Love You	Fireflies	NA	G.M. 1001
Love You	Persuasions	1973	MCA 40118
Love You	Strings	NA	Mellow Town 1006
Love You	Vocaleers	1954	Red Robin 125
Love You As You Love Me	Metronomes	1976	Robin Hood 131
Love You Baby	Three Queens	1960	J.O.B. 1122
Love You Baby All The Time	Co-Eds	1956	Old Town 1027
Love You Like You've Never Been Loved	Falcons (Big Wheel)	1967	Big Wheel 1972
Love You, Love You	Chapters	1953	Republic 7038

SONG	GROUP	YEAR	LABEL
Love You, Love You, Love You	Marigolds	1955	Excello 2061
Love You Lovely Stranger	Pedal Pushers, B. Dale & the	NA	Ko Ko 8803
Love You Madly	Sherwoods	1967	Crimson 104/Ray Star
Love You So	Crystals (Brooklyn)	1959	Specialty 657
Love You So	El Sierros	1964	Times Square 29/Relic 534 (65)
Love You So	Good Guys, Doug Robertson & the	1964	Jerden 703/Uptown 703 (64)
Love You So	Larks (Philadelphia)	1965	Jett 3001
Love You So	Thunderbirds, Ron Holden & the	1959	Donna 1315/Nite Owl 10 (59)
Love You So Bad	Empires	1962	Candi 1026/Chavis 1026
Love You So Much	Hi-Lites, Roy Smith & the	1959, 1961	Nu Tone 1182/Key 1182
Love You So Tonight	Dawns	1959	Catalina 1000
Love You Some More	Interiors	1961	Worthy 1009
Love You Still	Velvets (New York)	1958	Unreleased
Love You That's Why	Monarchs	1961	Liban 1002
Love You 'Til My Dying Day	Muskateers	1953	Roxy 801/Swingtime 331
Love You Till The Day I Die	Heartbreakers (Bronx, N.Y.)	1957	Vik 0299
Love You Too Much	Gothics	1961	Carol 4115
Love Your Way	Jones, Davey & group	1958	Apt 25013
Love-A Love-A Love	Rose, Andy (with the Thorns)	1958	Aamco 100
Loveable	Cooke, Dale (Sam Cooke) & group	1957	Specialty 596
Lovebug	Clovers	1955	Atlantic 1060
Loved And Lost	Note-Torials	1959	Sunbeam 119
Loved Her The Whole Week Through	Marcels	1962	Colpix 651
Lovely Charms	Lyrics (San Francisco)	1958	Marvels 1005
Lovely Charms	Marvells	1959	Magnet 1005
Lovely Dee	Untouchables	1961	Liberty 55335
Lovely Dream	Upstarts	NA	Top Ten 7000
Lovely Emotions	Arvettes	1961	Hac 104
Lovely Girl	Cardells	1956	Middle-Tone 011
Lovely Girl	Cardinals	1955	Atlantic 1079
Lovely Lady	Twilighters (Bronx, N.Y.)	1955	MGM 55014
Lovely Lady Please Be Mine	Jades, Bobby Klint & the	1959	Christy 117
Lovely Lies	Rainbows, Randy & the	1966	Mike 4001
Lovely Lies	Raye, Cal & group	1965	Providence 412
Lovely Little Girl	Videls	NA	
Lovely Little Lady	Beau-Marks	1962	Quality 1370/Port 70029 (62)
Lovely Loretta	Barons (Dart)	1960	Dart 126
Lovely Love	King Bees	1957	KRC 302
Lovely Lovely Girl	London, Ralph & group	1964	Coed 588
Lovely Lover	Contenders	1966	Java 102/103
Lovely One	Casinos	1964	Terry 115
Lovely One	Hunters, Little Moose & the	1959	SMC 1373
Lovely Teenage Girl	Versatones	1957	RCA 6976
Lovely Way To Spend An Evening	Autumns	1980	Clifton 52
Lovely Way To Spend An Evening	Flamingos	1964	Times Square 102
Lovely Way To Spend An Evening	Four Graduates	1963	Rust 5062
Lovely Way To Spend An Evening	Plazas, Nicky Addeo & the	1962	Revelation 7-101
Lovely, Wonderful, Beautiful	Kartels, Wilbert Lombard & the	1957	Deb 1002
Love-Me-Boy	Carter Rays, Eddie Carter & the	1954	SLS 102/Jubilee 5142 (54)
Lover	Aktones, Will Wendel & the	1962	Trans America 10000
Lover	Fabulous Flames	1961	Bay-Tone 105
Lover	Jones, Jimmy (with the Pretenders)	1960	Roulette 4232
Lover	Pretenders, Jimmy Jones & the	1956	Rama 210/Roulette 4322 (60)
Lover Boy	Cleftones	1958	Gee 1048
Lover Boy	Gailtones	1958	Decca 30726
Lover Boy	Twigs, Sonny Woods & the	1954	Hollywood 1026
Lover Boy Blue	Continentals, Billy John & the	1962	N-Joy 1014
Lover Come Back	Flamingos	1961	End (unreleased)
Lover Come Back To Me	Cleftones	1961	Gee 1079
Lover Come Back To Me	Flamingos	1964	Checker 1084
Lover Come Back To Me	Four-Evers	1963	Smash 1853
Lover, Come Back To Me	Velours	1961	End 1090
Lover, Come Home	Eastmen	1959	Mercury 71434
Lover Doll	Adventurers	1966	Reading 602
Lover Doll	Rob-Roys, Norman Fox & the	1990	Back Beat 499

SONG	GROUP	YEAR	LABEL
Lover Doll	Teen Tones, Jules Blattner & the	NA	K-Ark 612
Lover Don't You Weep	Aqua-Nites	1965	Astra 1000/2001/2003 (65)
Lover How I Miss You	Storey Sisters	1959	Mercury 71457
Lover (How Much Longer)	Evans, Kay & group	1961	Whip 274
Lover, I'm Waiting For You	Sentimentals, Ann Nichols & the	1958	Tuxedo 926
Lover, Love Me	Moonglows	1955	Chess 1611
Lover, Lover	Valiants (Los Angeles)	1957	Keen 34007
Lover Lover Lover	Thorpe, Lionel (Chords)	1959	Roulette 4144
Lover Man	Bachelor Three	1961	Vi-Way 288
Lover Of Mine	Keytones	1962	Chess 1821
Lover Or Fool	Penguins	1959	Dooto LP 242/Dooto EP 241
Lover' Question	Swallows (Maryland)	1986	Starbound 504
Lover, The	Emeralds (Venus)	1959	Venus 1002
Lover, The	Precisions, Tommy Genova & the	1962	Bella 606
Lover (Where Are You?)	Zodiacs, Maurice Williams & the	1959	Cole 101
Lovers	Blendtones	1963	Success 101
Lovers	Leaders	1956	Glory 243
Lover's Bells	Royal Boys	1960	Tropelco 1007
Lover's Blues	Veltones	1959	Jin 107
Lovers By Night, Strangers By Day	Fleetwoods	1962	Dolton 62
Lover's Chant	Chantels	1966	Unreleased
Lover's Cry	Emeralds (St. Louis)	1960	Bobbin 121
Lover's Curse, The	Everett, Bracey & group	1959	Atlantic 2013
Lover's Dream	Contels	1959	Warwick 103
Lovers Gotta Cry	Flamingos	1960	End 1081
Lover's Hill	Five Satins	1974	Relic LP 5024
Lover's Holiday	Dinos	1962	Fox 105
Lover's Island	Blue Jays (Venice, Calif.)	1961	Milestone 2008
Lover's Lane	Counts, Frankie Brent & the	1960	Strand 25014
Lover's Lane	Impressions, Jerry Butler & the	1976	Vee Jay LP 1075
Lover's Lane	Runarounds	1961	Pio 107
Lover's Lullabye	Stratfords	NA	Universal Artists 1215
Lovers' Mambo	Ontarios	1965, 1974	Big Town 121
Lover's March	Shantons	1959	Jay-Mar 165
Lovers' Melody	Dawn	1967	Laurie 3388
Lover's Mountain	Night Owls, Tony Allen & the	1960	Crown LP 5231
Lovers Never Say Goodbye	Allures	1989	Starlight 71
Lovers Never Say Goodbye	Flamingos	1958	End 1035
Lovers Never Say Goodbye	Modern Red Caps	1965	Penntown
Lovers Never Say Goodbye	Pirates, Black Beard & the	1958	Ad 101
Lover's Never Say Goodbye	Holden, Ron & group	1959	VMC 748
Lover's Plan	Davis, Hal Sonny & group	1963	G.S.P. 2
Lover's Plea	Lampkin, Tommy (with the Kidds)	1955	Imperial 5361
Lover's Plea	Pagans	1960	Music City 832
Lover's Plea	Velvettones, Lee Martin & the	1962	Jin 159
Lover's Plea, The	Heartspinners, Dino & the	1981	Starlight 11
Lover's Prayer	Click-Ettes	1960	Dice 96/97
Lover's Prayer	Keith, Ann & group	1959	Memo 96
Lover's Prayer (All Through The Night)	G-Clefs	1962	Terrace 7510
Lovers Promise	Martin, Jerry & group	1962	R 507
Lover's Quarrel	Hi-Tones	1961	Fonsca 201
Lover's Quarrel	Ivoleers	1959	Buzz 101
Lover's Quarrel	Starr, Suzy & group	1961	Morgil 711
Lovers Quarrel (acappella)	Meadowbrooks	1965	Catamount 108
Lover's Reunion	Dontells	1963	Beltone 2040
Lovers, The	Jets (Washington, D.C.)	1953	Rainbow 201
Lover's Twist	Nite-Lites	1962	Sequoia 502
Lovers Who Wander	DiMucci, Dion (with the Del Satins)	1962	Laurie 3123
Love's All I'm Putting Down	Spiders	NA	Imperial (unreleased)
Love's Burning Fire	Channels, Edie & the	1963	Ember 584/Herald 584 (63)
Love's Burning Fire	Revlons	NA	VRC 112
Love's Funny That Way	Six Teens	1958	Flip 333
Love's Gamble	Rialtos, Bobby Hollister & the	1961	Pike 5910
Loves Intentions	Hot Tamales	1964	Detroit 101
Love's Our Inspiration	Charms	1955	Chart 608

SONG	GROUP	YEAR	LABEL
Love's Prayer	Spinners (California)	1958	Capitol 3955
Love's Something That's Made For Two	Wrens	1955	Rama 53/110/174/157
Love's The Thing	Romancers	1965	Linda 120
Loves We Share, The	Impalas (Brooklyn)	19??	Unreleased
Love's Young Dream	Granahan, Gerry & group	1958	Mark 121
Lovesick	Madara, Johnny & group	1957	Prep 110
Lovesick Blues	Knight, Sonny & female group	1957	Dot 15597
Lovey	Clovers	1960	United Artists 209
Lovey Dovey	Clovers	1954	Atlantic 1022/United Artists 209
Lovey Dovey	Coasters	1964	Atco 6300
Lovey Dovey	Jacks	1963	Crown LP 5372
Lovey Dovey	Morse, Ella Mae & group	1954	Capitol 2992
Lovey Dovey	Paul, Bunny (with the Harptones)	1954	Essex 359
Lovey Dovey	Royal Jokers	1960	Keldon 322
Lovey Dovey, Baby, Be Mine	Spaniels	1958	Charly LP 1114 (86)
Lovey Dovey Pair	Three Playmates	1958	Savoy 1528
Lovie Darling	Cardinals	1953	Atlantic 995
Lovin'	Reed, Lula (with the Teeners)	1959	Argo 5355
Lovin'	Victorians	1963	Arnold 571
Lovin' At Night	Accents	1958	Robbins 108
Lovin' Baby	Chimes (Tennessee)	1957	Arrow 726
Lovin' Baby	Vocaleers	1954	Red Robin 132
Lovin' Daddy	Styles, Chuck Mile & the	1962	Dore 630
Lovin' From My Baby	True Tones	1964	Spot 1115
Lovin' Hands	Suburbans	1961	Gee 1076
Lovin' Honey	Pages, Gene Morris & the	1957	Vik 0287
Lovin' On My Mind	Shufflers	1954	Okeh 7040
Lovin' Papa	Lyrics, Ike Perry & the	1965	Bee 95/Bee 1875
Lovin' Sickness	Heartbeats	1957	Rama (unreleased)
Lovin' Time	Ebb Tides, Nino & the	1962	Mr. Peacock 117
Lovin' Time	Hideaways	1963	Duel 521
Lovin' Time	Medallions	1961	Sarg 194
Lovin' Time	Tillman, Bertha & group	1962	Brent 7029
Lovin' Up A Storm Tonight	Bon-Bons	1964	Sampson 1003
Lovin' With A Beat	El Tones	1958	Cub 9011
Lovin' You	Dukes (California)	1956	Imperial 5408
Loving A Girl Like You	Four Of Us	1961	Adore 902/Bruce
Loving A Girl Like You	Harptones	1954	Bruce 123
Loving And Losing	Echoes	1960	Columbia 41709
Loving Baby	Charms, Otis Williams & the	1953	Rockin' 516/DeLuxe 6000 (53)
Loving Man	Savoys (Combo)	1955	Combo 81
Loving Rules	Blue Belles, Patti LaBelle & the	1969	Atlantic 2629
Loving Tree	Ambers	1959	Greezie 501
Loving Tree	Loye Jr., Bobby & group	1963	Wilshire 202
Loving You	Five Satins	1982	Elektra 47411
Loving You	Flares	1960	Felsted 8604
Loving You	Hollywood Saxons	1962	Action-Pac 111
Loving You	Sheppards (Chicago - Abner)	1962	Abner 7006
Loving You	Uniques	1963	Capitol 4949
Loving You	Wonders, Tony Allen & the	1959	Jamie 1119
Loving You, Darling	Four Fellows (Brooklyn - Glory)	1957	Glory 250
Loving You (Is My Desire)	Sevilles	1961	JC 116/Galaxy 721 (64)
Loving You Is Sweeter Than Ever (acappella)	Belmonts	1972	Buddah LP 5123
Low As I Can Be	Beavers	1958	Capitol 4015
Low Grades And High Fever	Laine, Linda & group	1964	Tower 108
Low Tide	Ebb Tides, Nino & the	1962	R&R 303
Lowdown Dirty	Flasher Brothers	1953	Aladdin 3186
Lower The Flame	Shirelles	1961	Scepter LP 501
LSMFT Blues	Meadowlarks	1954	RPM 406
Lt. Colonel Bogey's Parade	Merry Men, Steve Douglas & his	1962	Philles 104
Lu La	Ray-Dots	1960	Vibro 1651
Lu Lu	Sh-Booms	1957	Vik 0295
Lubby Lou	Midniters, Al Chase & the	1960	Jin 118
Lucille	Drifters (Pre-1959)	1954	Atlantic 1019

SONG	GROUP	YEAR	LABEL
Lucille	Four Sportsmen	1961	Sunnybrook 2
Lucille	Incidentals	1964	Ford 138
Lucille	Shantons	1959	Jay-Mar 242
Lucille, I Want You	Prisonaires	1976	Sun 517
Lucinda	Dominoes	1957	Liberty 55071
Lucinda	Spaniels	1957	Vee Jay (unreleased)
Lucky Boy	Rue-Teens	1964	Louis 6805
Lucky Guy	Blend-Aires	1978	Story Untold 500
Lucky Guy	Fairmounts	1962	Planet 53
Lucky Guy	King-Pins	1963	Vee Jay 494
Lucky Guy	Mellows, Lillian Leach & the	1956, 1974	Celeste 3002
Lucky Guy	Winners	1962	Vee Jay 494
Lucky In Love	Jays, Kelly Troy & the	NA	Harvey
Lucky Joe	McGee, Al & group	1961	Aries 7-10-2
Lucky Me	Castros	1959	Lasso 501
Lucky Me	Chiffons	1963	Laurie 3166
Lucky Me	Sun-Rays, Cliff & the	1960	Zil 9002
Lucky Me, I'm In Love	El Domingos	1963	Chelsea 1009/Candlelite 418 (62)
Lucky Old Sun	Windsong	NA	
Lucky Sixteen	Youngsters	1959	Checker 917
Lucky Star	Barons (Epic)	1964	Epic 9747
Lucky Star	Crestwoods	1961	Impact 6
Lucky Star	Knights, Eddie Shaw & the	NA	Rand 2
Lucy	Cadillacs	1957, 1961	Josie 821/Jubilee LP 1117
Lucy And Jimmy Got Married	Five Crowns, Chuck Edwards & the	1959	Alanna 557/558
Lucy Brown	Larks (North Carolina)	1952	Apollo 437
Lucy Lou	Squires (California)	1954	Kicks 1
Lucy Lucy	Three Notes	1958	Tee Gee 106
Lucy Watusi	Robins (Nobells)	1964	Musicor 1050
Lugene	Jays, Johnny & the	1961	Fairbanks 2001
Lula	Robinson, Mike & group	1961	Vibro 4000
Lula Mae	Barons (Dart)	1960	Dart 126
Lullaby	Angorians	1964	Tishman 9078
Lullaby	Dubs	1961	ABC 10269
Lullaby Of Love	Poppies	NA	Epic 9893
Lullaby Of The Bells	Deltairs	1957	Ivy 101
Lullaby Of The Bells	Five Crowns	1952	Old Town 792
Lullabye	Chevrons	1959	Brent 7007
Lullabye	Ravens	1946	Hub 3033
Lullabye My Love	Cheerettes	1956	Vita 143/Vita 145 (56)
Lulu	Camelots	1961	Nix 101
Lulu	Chimes, Dave Burgess & the	1959	Challenge 59037
Lulu	Highlighters, Walter Webb & the	1970	Chess 2091
Lulu	Quardells, Billy Kope & the	1958	Kudo 662
Lulu	Sabres	1958	Liberty 55128
Lulubell Blues	Humphries, Fatman (with the Four Notes)	1952	Jubilee 5085
Lulu's Party	Key Brothers	1960	Gardena 102
Lunale	Romeos, Jimmy & the	1960	Southside 1003
Lundee Dundee	Majors (Philadelphia)	1960	Rocal 1002
Lundee Dundee (acappella)	Sintells	1975	Relic LP 105
Lydia	Sunsets	1963	Petal 1040
Lydia	Teenchords, Lewis Lymon & the	1957	Fury 1000
Lydia (acappella)	Gents, Vic & the	1964	Dorana 1170
Lying	Coronados	1961	Ric 979
Lynn	Rhythm Stars	1959	Clock 1007
Lynne	Fraternity Men	1964	Courier 114

M

SONG	GROUP	YEAR	LABEL
M And M	Exodus	1963	Wand 11248
Ma Ma Marie	Del-Airs	1965	Delsey 302
Mad At Love	Temptations (New Jersey)	1958	Savoy 1532
Mad, Baby, Mad	Sky Boys, Thurl Ravenscroft & the	1955	Fabor 4005
Mad Gas	Royal Teens	1957	Astra 1012/Power 113 (59)
Mad House	Flares	1961	Press 2803
Mad House Jump	Daylighters	1959	Bea & Baby 103

SONG	GROUP	YEAR	LABEL
Mad Lover	Teenaires, Harley Davis & the	1961	Wildcat 0064
Made For Lovers	Passions	1960	Audicon 112
Made For Lovers	Shells, Roy Jones & the	1960	Swirl 101
Made For Me	Cooke, Sam & group	1961	Sar 122
Made In Heaven	El Domingos	1963	Chelsea 1009/Candlelite 418 (62)
Made To Love	Sharptones	1955	Post 2009
Madelaine	Valaquons	1964	Laguna 102
Mademoiselle	Cousins	1957	Nar 224
Mademoiselle	Elgins (California)	1958	MGM 12670
Mademoiselle	Emeralds (Venus)	1959	Venus 1002
Madly In Love	Bad Boys, Jessie Perkins & the	1960	Savoy 1584
Madly In Love	Lincolns	1957, 1972	Aljon 113/114
Madness	Original Rhythm Rockers	1959	Gone 5073
Madness	Rhythm Rockers	1960	Square 505
Maggie	Dell Vikings	1956	Fee Bee 206
Maggie	Inspirations (Philadelphia)	1956	Apollo 494
Maggie	Live Wires, Andy & the	1960	Applause 1249
Maggie Doesn't Work Here Anymore	Platters	1954	Federal 12204
Magic	Ideals	1961	Paso 6402/Dusty Disc
Magic	Tru-Tones	1957	Chart 634
Magic Age Of Sixteen, The	Cavaliers	1963	Music World 101
Magic Age Of Sixteen, The	Planetts	1963	Goldisc G7
Magic Carpet	Aladdins	NA	Duplex 9012
Magic Circle	Teenangels, Buzz Clifford & the	1962	Columbia 42290
Magic Eyes	Citations	1962, 1982	Canadian American 136
Magic Genie	Cincinnatians	1962, 1963	Roosevelt Lee 16115/Emerald 16116
Magic Is The Night	Innocents, Kathy Young & the	1961	Indigo 125
Magic Kiss	Epics	1961	Lynn 516/Sabra 516
Magic Kiss, The	Keystoners	1956	Epic 9187/Okeh 7210 (64)/G&M 102
Magic Lamp	Blazons	NA	Fanfare 5901/Bravura 5001
Magic Make, Music Maker	Jive Five	1982	Ambient Sound 02742
Magic Mirror	Empires	1955	Harlem 2333
Magic Mirror	Whirlers	1957	Whirlin' Disc 108/Port 70025 (60)
Magic Moment	Neons	1962	Challenge 9147
Magic Moments With You	Magic Moments	1999	Magic Moments 100
Magic Moon	Allures	1989	Starlight 71
Magic Moon (Claire De Lune)	Rays	1961	XYZ 607
Magic Moonlight	Medallionaires	1958	Mercury 71309
Magic Mountain	Medallions, Vernon Green & the	1959	Dooto 446
Magic Of A Dream	Robins	1961	Lavender 002
Magic Of First Love, The	Chuck-A-Lucks	1958	Lin 5014
Magic Of Love	Mints	1958	Airport 103
Magic Of Love	Premieres & the Invictas	1959	F-M 677
Magic Of Love, The	Sinceres	1966	Taurus 377
Magic Of Our Summer Love, The	Tymes	1964	Parkway 919
Magic Of Summer, The	Hammel Jr., Karl & group	1961	Arliss 1007
Magic Of You, The	Themes	1959	Excello 2152
Magic Of Your Love, The	Co-Eds	1962	USA 724
Magic Rose	Charmers, Mark Stevens & the	1962	Allison 921
Magic Rose	Solitaires	1955	Old Town 1015
Magic Star	Five Classics	1962	Medieval 204/Rode 101
Magic Star	Fleetwoods	1960	Dolton 15
Magic Star	Loran, Kenny & group	1959	Capitol 4276
Magic Touch	Daylighters	1964	Tip Top 2009
Magic Touch, You've Got The	Platters	1956	Mercury 70819
Magic Wand	Dell, Tony & group	1963	King 5766
Magic Wand	Scott Brothers	196?	
Magic Wand	Tattletales	1959	Warner Bros. 5066
Magnolia	Rainsford, Billy & group	NA	Hermitage 803
Mah Mah (Chicken Pot Pie)	Leopards	1963	Leopard 5006
Mahzel	Ravens	1947	Hub 3030
Mailbox	Charmettes	1964	Mala 491
Mailman Blues	Five Bob-O-Links	1952	Okeh
Mailman Blues	Pyramids, Little Richard Moreland & the	NA	Picture 7722
Main Drag	Escorts (Soma)	1961	Soma 1144

SONG	GROUP	YEAR	LABEL
Main Man	Marshans	1965	Johnson 736
Main Nerve	Chiffons	1975	Laurie 3630
Mainliner	Nunn, Bobby (with the Robins)	1952	Federal 12100
Mairzy Doats	Carlo (Carlo Mastrangelo) (with the Tremonts)	1963	Laurie 3157
Mairzy Doats	Schoolmates, Colleen & the	1958	Coral 62024
Majestic, The	DiMucci, Dion (with the Del Satins)	1961	Laurie 3115
Make A Box	Blue Notes, Todd Randall & the	1955	Tico 1083
Make A Chance	Dontells	1963	Beltone 2040
Make A Little Love	Sparks, Curtis Irvin & the	1954	RPM 417
Make A Memory	Neptunes	1963	Instant 3255
Make A Record Man	Markeys	1958	RCA 7412
Make Believe	Young Jessie & group	1957	Atco 6101
Make Believe Baby	Skipper, Buddy & group	1961	Fury 1051
Make Believe Love	Upstarts, Don Dell & the	1964	Roman 2963
Make Believe Lover	Debonaires (New York)	1960	Gee 1054
Make Believe Lovin'	Bonnevilles	1959	Whitehall 30002
Make Believe Wedding	Castells	1961	Era 3057
Make Believe World	Kodaks	1957	Fury 1015
Make Her Mine	Ray, Little Jimmy & group	1959	Galliant 1001
Make It Be Me	Flares	1961	Press 2803
Make It Easy On Yourself	Imperials, Little Anthony & the	1964	DCP 1119/Veep 1241 (66)
Make It Last	Pageants	1965	Groove 0056
Make It Soon	Sonnets	1958	Checker
Make It Up	Trojans	1958	Felsted 8534
Make Love To Me	Five Chances	1977	Atomic 2494
Make Love To Me	Royal Premiers	1965	M.B.S. 105
Make Me A Love	Motions	1961	Laurie 3112
Make Me A Sweetie	El Dorados	1958	Vee Jay (unreleased)
Make Me Happy Baby	Charades	1958	United Artists 132
Make Me Lose My Mind	Nutmegs	1955	Herald 452
Make Me Love You	Contrails	1967	Millage 104
Make Me Or Break Me	Empires (with Johnny Ace, Jr.)	1955	Harlem 2333
Make Me Queen Again	Rivera, Lucy & group	1959	End 1041
Make Me Smile Again	Roomates, Cathy Jean & the	1961	Valmor 009
Make Me Thrill Again	Marylanders	1952	Jubilee 5091
Make Me Your Own	Mason, Little Billy (with the Rhythm Jesters)	1956	Rama 212
Make The Night A Little Longer	Palisades	1963	Chairman 4401
Make Up My Mind	Crests	1964	Cameo 305
Make Up Your Mind	Arrogants	1960	Big A 12184/12185
Make Up Your Mind	Cardigans	1959	Spann 431
Make Up Your Mind	Emberglows	1962	Amazon 1005
Make Up Your Mind	G-Clefs	1962	Terrace 7507
Make Up Your Mind	Impaks	1962	Express 716
Make Up Your Mind	Rivals (Puff)	1962	Puff 3912
Make Up Your Mind	U.S. Four	1962	Heritage 110
(Make With) The Shake	Mark IV	1958	Cosmic 704
Make You My Queen	Pageants	1962	Du-Well 101/Arlen 731 (62)
Making Believe	Roomates	1960	Promo 2211
Making Love Girl	Original Jaguars	NA	Val-Vo 110
Making Miracle	Petites	1961	Columbia 42053
Malanese	Avalons	1963	Olimpic 240/NPC 302 (64)
Malena	Bombers	1955	Orpheus 1101
Malibu	Tymes	1964	Parkway 924
Malibu Sunset	Travelers	1965	Yellow Sand 452
Mama	Moonglows	1961	Chess 1781
Mama Ain't Always Right	Belmonts, Freddy Cannon & the	1981	Mia Sound 1002
Mama Cried	Smith, Richard & group	1958	Hi-Q 5042
Mama Didn't Lie	Fascinations	1963	ABC 10387
Mama Don't Allow	Delrons, Reperata & the	1965	World Artists 1051
Mama Don't Care	Debonaires (New York)	1959, 1962, 1964	Dore 526/654/712
Mama, Here Comes The Bride	Shirelles	1962	Scepter 1234
Mama I Have Come Home	Valentines	1962	Ludix 102
Mama I Think I'm In Love	Del-Capris, Beverly & the	1964	Columbia 43107

SONG	GROUP	YEAR	LABEL
Mama Loocie	Moonglows, Harvey & the	1959	Chess 1738
Mama Look At Me	Elites	1960	Chief 7032
Mama Lucie	Dreamers (Dream)	1958	Dream 101
Mama, Mama, Mama	Hobbs, Louis & group	1964	Buddy Buddy 460
(Mama) My Soldier Boy			
Is Coming Home	Shirelles	1965	Scepter 12123
Mama Papa	Bobbettes	1962	Jubilee 5442
Mama Put The Law Down	Fiestas	1963	Old Town 1134
Mama Said	Shirelles	1961	Scepter 1217
Mama, Take Your Daughter Back	Rainbows	1962	Gramo 5508
Mama Told Me	Precisions	1962	Highland 300
Mama Ubangi Bangi	Four Sounds	1962	Ran-Dee
Mama Wanna Rock	Teenagers (Billy Lobrano)	1958	Roulette 4086
Mama Wants To Drive	Zircons	1962	Federal 12452
Mama What'll I Do	Royal Robins, Patricia Conley & the	1962	Aldo 504
Mama Won't You Turn Me Loose	Sugar Lumps, Sugar Boy & the	1963	Peacock 1925
Mama Worries	Erhardt, Dian & group	1957	RCA 7137
Mama (Your Daughter			
Told A Lie On Me)	Five Keys	1953	Aladdin 3175
Mamacita Mia	Mastertones, Scotty & Bobo & the	1960	Band Box 238
Mama-Oom-Mow-Mow	Rivingtons	1963	Liberty 55528
Mama's Cookin'	El Torros	1962	Duke 353
Mama's Daughter	Checkers	1954	King 4751
Mama's Doin' The Jerk	Attitudes	1967	Times Square 110
Mama's Gone, Good Bye	Du Droppers, Sunny Gale & the	1953	RCA 5543
Mama's House	Posse, Marshall Laws & the	1961	Forum 702
Mama's Little Baby	Imaginations	1962	Ballad 500
Mama's Little Baby	Loran, Kenny & group	1959	Capitol 4276
Mama's Little Baby	Meteors, Junior Thompson with the	1956	Meteor 5029
Mama's Little Baby	Scott Brothers	1960	FTP
Mama's Little Girl	Delrons, Reperata & the	1966	RCA 8921
Mambo Baby	Five Tinos	1976	Sun (unreleased)
Mambo Beat, The	Challengers, Walter Ward & the	1957	Melatone 1002
Mambo Boogie	Harptones	1954, 1962	Bruce 104/Raven 8001
Mambo Boogie	Nobletones	1958	C&M 188/C&M 438
Mambo Carolyn	Octaves	1958	Val 1001
Mambo Daddy	Celebrities	1961	Music Makers 101
Mambo Fiesta	Calvaes	1956	Cobra 5003
Mambo Love	Street Singers	1955	Dawn 211
Mambo Of Love, The	Diablos, Nolan Strong & the	1957	Fortune 525
Mambo Oongh	Dappers (Boston)	1955	Peacock 1651
Mambo Santa Mambo	Enchanters (Detroit)	1957	Coral 61916
Mambo Shevitz	Crows	1955	Tico 1082
Mambo Sh-Mambo	Charms, Otis Williams & the	1954	DeLuxe 6072
Mambo, The	Charmers	1954	Timely 1009
Mambo Train	Miracletones	1958	Jam 5803
Mamie Wong	Williams, Ben E.	1961	Riff
Mamma Linda	Monitors	1958	Specialty 636
Mamma's Boy	Kokomos (with the Four Seasons)	1962	Gone 5134
Mammy Jammy	Five Sharps	1964	Jubilee 5478
Mam'Selle	Ravens	1952	Mercury 8291
Man About Town	Passions	1966	Back Beat 573
Man Above, The	Rays, Hal Miller & the	1958	Cameo 133
Man From The Moon	Crystalaires	1990	Magic Carpet EP 512
Man From The Moon, The	Chaperones	1963	Josie 891
Man From The Moon, The	Crickets, Dean Barlow & the	1954	Jay-Dee 795/Davis 459 (58)
Man From The Moon, The	Five Crowns	1952	Old Town 778 (unreleased)/
			Relic LP 5030
Man From Utopia	Vel-Aires, Donald Woods & the	1955	Flip 306/Happy Tiger Era 5065
Man I'm Gonna Be, The	Trojans	1958	Felsted 8534
Man In Orbit	Satellites	1961	Chess 1789
Man In The Moon	Del-Capris	1966	Catamount 115
Man In The Stained Glass Window	Dominoes	1961	Ro-Zan 10001
Man Love Woman	Mello-Tones, Marga Benitez & the	1954	Decca 48318
Man On The Shelf	Hi-Lights	1963	JR 5003

SONG	GROUP	YEAR	LABEL
Man, The	Mark III	1961	ABC 10280/BRB 100
Man With A Broken Heart	Continentals (M)	NA	M
Man With The Blue Guitar, The	Rocky Fellers	1965	Warner Bros. 5497
Manana	Crenshaws	1961	Warner Bros. EP 5505
Mandolins Of Love	Donnybrooks	1959	Calico 112
Manhunt	Dynamos	1961	Cub 9096
Mannyon	Higgs & Wilson & group	1960	Time 1028
Manpower	Exotics	1962	Coral 62310
Mansion On The Hill	Blackwells	1960	Jamie 1157
Manuel	Comic Books	1961	New Phoenix 6199/Citations 5001 (62)
Many A Day	Minor Chords	1962	Lu Pine 112
Many Things From Your Window	Avalons	1964	Roulette 4568
Marcella	Castelles	1954	Grand 114
Marcelle	Sherwoods, Johnny Schilling & the	1963	C&A 507
March	Chiffons	1966, 1968	Laurie 3357/3460
March On	Kids, Herman & the	1959	Columbia 41411
March (You'll Be Sorry)	Shirelles	1965	Scepter 12101
Marcheta	Dons	NA	Heartbeat 1
Marcheta	Lemon Drops	1960	Aladdin 3465
Mardi Gras Mambo	Hawketts	1955, 1958	Chess 1591/Sapphire 2250
Margaret	Royal Holidays	1958	Penthouse 9357/Carlton 472 (58)
Margaritte	Embers, Frankie Joe & the	1957	Fee Bee 224
Margie	Larks (North Carolina)	1954	Lloyds 108
Margie	Supremes (Massachusetts)	1956	Kitten 6969
Marguerite	Petites	1958	Spinning 6003
Maria	Moonbeems	NA	Sapphire (unreleased)
Maria Christina	Alamos, Tony Valla & the	1961	Fortune 859
Maria Elena	Flamingos	1960	End LP 307
Maria Elena	Sherwoods, Tony Reno & the	1963	Johnson 123
Maria Mia	Johnson Quartet, Bill	1955	Jubilee 5211
Maria My Love	Maldoneers (with the Deltairs)	1973	Vintage 1015
Marianne	Coachmen	1960	Iona 1004
Marianne	Fireflies	1960	Canadian American 117
Marianne	Four-Evers	NA	Magic Carpet LP 1004
Marianne	Thomas, Vic (with the Four-Evers)	1964	Philips 40183
Maria's Cha Cha	Emeralds (St. Louis)	1959	Bobbin 107
Marie	Fidelitys	1959	Sir 271
Marie	Harps	1964	Laurie 3239
Marie	Harptones	1974	Rama (previously unreleased)
Marie	Hollywood Flames	Mid to late 1950s	(Early 1980s on EP; originally unreleased)
Marie	Kentones	1958	Siroc 202
Marie	Ravens	1951	Okeh 6843
Marie	Styles, Donnie & the	1964	Times Square 106
Marie	Young Ones	1963	Yussels 7701
Marie, Give Him Back	Affections, Judy & the	NA	Dode
Marie My Love	Cadets	1963	Crown LP 5370
Marie That's You	Romancers	1962	Palette 5095
Marilyn	Domino, Bobby & group	1961	Donna 1339
Marilyn	Gothics	1959	Dynamic 101
Marilyn	Wonders	1963	Colpix 699
Marina Girl	Harvey Boys	1956	Cadence 1306
Marindy	Techniques	1958	Roulette 4048
Marionette	Legends	1962	Ermine 45
Marjolaine	Candy Canes, Jimmy James & the	1958	Columbia 41192
Mark My Words	Coeds (with the Tokens)	1964	Swing 101
Marlene	Barnette, Billy & group	1961	Parkway 826
Marlene	Catalinas	1958	Glory 285
Marlene	Concords (Brooklyn)	1962	Herald 576
Marlene	Sonics	NA	Gaiety 114
Marlene	Visions	1959	Warwick 108
Marlina, Marlina	Marveleers	1955	Dot 15320
Marnie (I Love You)	Themes	1964	Stork 001
Marquette	Titans	1961	Nolta 351
Married Jive	Upfronts	1960	Lummtone 104

SONG	GROUP	YEAR	LABEL
Married Life	Cupcakes, Cookie & the	1958	Khoury's 703/Judd 1002 (59)
Marry Her Joe	Fortune Tellers	1963	Atlantic 2197
Marry Young	Royal Boys	1961	
Marsha	Emeralds (Venus)	1959	Venus 1003
Marsha	Prodigals	1958	Falcon 1011/Abner 1011 (58)/ Tollie 9019 (64)
Marsha-Mellow	Del-Chords	1960	Cool 5816
Marta	Three Chuckles	1956	Vik LP 1067
Martha Sue	Velvetones, Bingo Miller & the	NA	Young Artists 103
Martian Hop, The	Ran-Dells	1964	Chairman 4403
Marty At The Party	Teens, Barbara Jean & the	1962	Allison 920
Marvel Stomp	Mar-Vels	1961	Tammy 1019
Marvella	Spinners (California)	1958	Rhythm 125
Mary	Arpeggios	1963	Aries 001
Mary	Pastels (Limelight)	1963	Limelight 3007
Mary	Schoolboys	1957, 1990	Okeh 7085
Mary	Students (Philadelphia)	1958	Red Top
Mary	Thunderbirds	1957	Holiday 2609
Mary (acappella)	Velvet Angels	1972	Relic LP 5004/Relic LP 102 (75)
Mary Ann	Love Notes, Honey Love & the	1965	Cameo 380
Mary Ann	Nobles, Aki Aleong & the	1963	Vee Jay 520
Mary Ann (acappella)	Young Ones	1975	Relic LP 102/Relic LP 5079 (89)
Mary Anna	Hansen Brothers	1979	Crystal Ball 137
Mary Ellen	Crystals (Felsted)	1959	Felsted 8566
Mary Go Round	Pictures, C.L. & the	1962	Dunes 2017
Mary Had A Little Lamb	Five Shades	1961	Ember 1074
Mary Had A Little Lamb	Suburbans	1963	Shelley 184
Mary Had A Little Man	Hi Tensions, Leon Peels & the	1964	Whirlybird 2005
Mary Had A Rock N' Roll Lamb	Bluedots	1959	Hurricane 104
Mary, Hear Those Love Bells	Chestnuts	1957	Standord 100
Mary Is Her Name	Del-Rays	1963	Tammy 1020
Mary Jane	Maresca, Ernie (with the Del Satins)	1962	Seville 119
Mary Lee	Rainbows	1955	Red Robin 134/Pilgrim 703 (56)/ Fire 1012 (60)
Mary Lisa	Beltones, L. Farr & the	1964	N-Joy 1001
Mary Lou	Daychords, Roxy & the	1962, 1977	Don-El 116/Candlelite 430 (74)
Mary Lou	Dedications	1963, 1981	C&A 506
Mary Lou	Devilles	1960	Jerden 107
Mary Lou	Freese, Harrison & group	NA	Freshman 302
Mary Lou	Hawks, Ronnie Hawkins & the	1959	Roulette 4177
Mary Lou	Medallions	1955	Dootone EP 202
Mary Lou	Sneakers	NA	Delta 1868
Mary Lou	Williams, Fletcher & group	1957	Bullseye 1001
Mary Lou	Young Jessie (with the Jacks)	1955	Modern 961
Mary Lou Loves To Hootchy Kootchy Koo	Robins	1961	Lavender 002
Mary Lou, Mary Lou	Temps, Bobby & the	1963	ABC 10428
Mary Mary	Bachelor Three	1961	Vi-Way 289
Mary Mary	Dreamers (Yonkers, N.Y.)	1960	Guaranteed 219
Mary, Mary	Electras	1966	Ruby-Doo 2
Mary, Mary	Sultans	1962	Jam 107
Mary, Mary Lou	Sparks	1957	Decca 30378
Mary My Darling	High Type Five, Clarence Green with the	1959	Chess 1732
Maryann	Len-Dells	1964	Reach 2/Clifton LP 2002
Maryann	Merri Men, Robin Hood & his	1961	Delsey 303
Mary-Ann	Barries	1962, 1963	Vernon 102/Ember 1101
Mary's Lamb	Ideals, Johnny Brantley & the	1959	Checker 920/Checker 979 (61)
Mary's Little Lamb	Dischords	1963	Bonneville
Mary's Little Lamb	Dreamers (Yonkers, N.Y.)	1960	Apt 25053
Mary's Little Lamb	Ricardos	1958	Star-X 512
Mary's Magic Show	Dovells	1972	MGM 14568
Mary's Party	Silks, Charles McCullough & the	1962	Dooto 467
Mash Dem Taters	Tabs	1962	Vee Jay 446
Mash Potato Party	Cal-Cons	1962	Allrite 621
Mash Potatoes With Me	Mystics	1962	King 5678

SONG	GROUP	YEAR	LABEL
Mash Them 'Taters	Olympics	1961	Arvee 5044
Mashed Potato Girl	Monte, Vince & group	1962	Jubilee 5428
Mashed Potato Mary	Runarounds	1961	Cousins 1004
Mashed Potato Stomp	Halos, Johnny Angel & the	1962	Felsted 8646
Mashed Potatoes	Kilts, Herman Jones & the	1958	Gaynote 105
Mashed Potatoes One More Time	Marathons	1962	Plaza 507
Mask Off	Wanderers	1957	Gone 5005
Mask, The	Debs	1962	Infinity 035
Masked Man (Hi-Yo Silver), The	Bel-Aires, Eddy Bell & the	1960	Mercury 71677
Masquerade Ball	Bishops	1961	Lute 6010
Masquerade Is Over, The	Blenders (New York)	1951	Decca 27403
Masquerade Is Over, The	Chateaus	1959	Warner Bros. 5043
Masquerade Is Over, The	Clefftones	1955	Old Town 1011
Masquerade Is Over, The	Five Satins	1962	Chancellor 1110
Masquerade Is Over, The	Harptones	1956	Rama 214
Masquerade Is Over, The	Hollywood Four Flames	1951	Unique 015
Masquerade Is Over, The	Original Drifters	1967	Veep 1264
Masquerader	Pendulums	1962	May 109
Master Of Me	Four Shades Of Rhythm	1949	Old Swingmaster 23
Mathematics Of Love	Love Notes (Wilshire)	1964	Wilshire 203
Matilda	Cupcakes, Cookie & the	1958, 1963	Khoury's 703/Judd 1002 (59)/ Lyric 1003/Paula 221 (65)
Matilda	Rondels	1963	Shalimar 104/Dot 17323 (70)
Matilda Has Finally Come Back	Cupcakes, Cookie & the	1961	Mercury 71748
Matrimony	Tip Tops, Tiny Tip & the	1962	Chess 1822
Mattie, Leave Me Alone	Thrillers (Detroit)	1953	Big Town 109
Maureen	Autumns	1962, 1979	Medieval 208
Maureen	DeNoia, Paul & group	1962	Kenco 5020
Maureen (acappella)	Durhams	1975	Relic LP 103
May God Be With You	Danderliers	1955	States 152
May God Bless And Keep You	Regals	1954	Aladdin 3266
May Heaven Bless You	Paul, Clarence & group	1959	Roulette 4196
May I	Ravens	NA	Mercury (unreleased)
May I	Zodiacs, Maurice Williams & the	1965, 1966, 1967	Vee Jay 678/Dee-Su 304
May I Count On You?	Wheels, Arthur Lake & the	1956	Premium 406
May I Have This Dance	Four Graduates	1978	Crystal Ball 116
May I Have This Dance	SeÒors	1962	Sue 756
May I Kiss The Bride	Dreamlovers	1961	V-Tone 229
May I Never Love Again	Clantones	1959	Emony 1021
May I Never Love Again	Dominoes	1955	King 1492
May It Be My Fortune	Hi-Lites, Randy Hard & the	1958	NRC 013
May It Be My Fortune	Upstarts, Don Dell & the	1961	East Coast 101/102
May The Best Man Win	Vibrations	1963	Checker 1038
May We Always	Todds	1961	Todd 1064
May We Be On Better Terms	Debonaires	NA	Dootone (unreleased)
Maybe	Chantels	1957, 1969	End 1005/Roulette 7064
Maybe	Consoles, Bobby & the	1966	Verve 10402
Maybe	Deja-Vu	1984	Starlight 22
Maybe	Elegants	1980	Crystal Ball 139
Maybe	Four Closures	1958	Specialty 643
Maybe	Illusions	1964	Laurie 3245
Maybe	Keens, Rick & the	1961	Smash 1722
Maybe	Pedrick, Bobby & group	1966	Verve 10402
Maybe	Raindrops	1960	Corsair 104/Dore 561 (60)
Maybe	Spaniels	1969	Buddah 153
Maybe	Utopias	NA	Fortune 102X
Maybe Baby	Derringers	1961	Capitol 4572
Maybe Baby	Dorells	1963	Gei 4401/Atlantic 2244 (64)
Maybe It's All For The Best	Hurricanes	1956	King 4867
Maybe It's Wrong	Rainbeaus	1960	World Pacific 810
Maybe Next Christmas	Parkway	1990	BAB 131
Maybe Next Summer	Four Uniques	1964	USA 753
Maybe Someday	Young Lions	1959	United Artists 177
Maybe Tomorrow	Reflections	1961	Crossroads 401
Maybe Tonight	Shirelles	1964	Scepter 1284

SONG	GROUP	YEAR	LABEL
Maybe You	Visuals	1962	Poplar 115
Maybe You'll Be There	Belltones, Lacille Watkins & the	1956	Kapp 145
Maybe You'll Be There	Essentials, Billy & the	1962	Jamie 1239
Maybe You'll Be There	Five Keys	1957	Capitol LP 828/Capitol EP 2-828 (57)
Maybe You'll Be There	Healeys, Tom Austin & his	1963	Old Town 1147
Maybe You'll Be There	Hearts, Lee Andrews & the	1954, 1958	Rainbow 252/Riviera 965 (54)/ United Artists 151
Maybe You'll Be There	Hi-Lites (Connecticut)	1962, 1976	Dandee LP 206/Monogram 121
Maybe You'll Be There	Orioles, Sonny Til & the	1954	Jubilee 5143
Maybe You'll Be There	Three Chuckles	1956	Vik LP 1067
Maybe You'll Be There (acappella)	Quotations	1975	Relic LP 103
M-A-Y-B-E-L-L	Serenaders (Detroit)	1954	Swing Time 347
McCoy, The	Belvederes	NA	Rhapsody 5163
McDonald's Rock	Magnatones	1960	Cedargrove 313/Time 108 (60)
Me And My Deal	Squires (California)	1955	Vita 113
Me And My Imagination	Stardusters, Bobby Chandler & His	1957	O.J. 1005
Me And You	Desires	NA	Hull (unreleased)
Me And You	Ivories	1957	Mercury 71239
Me And You	Regents	1965	Blue Cat 110
Me Heart	Marvelows	1965	ABC 10629
Me Heart	Stereos	1962	Robins Nest 101
Me Heart	Sweethearts	1958	Terrific 151
Me Make Um Pow Wow	Five Keys	1955	Capitol 3127
Me Makem Powwow	Hide-A-Ways	1955	MGM 55004
Me Neither	Superphonics, Dave Kennedy & the	1961	Lindy 101
Me Tarzan Twist	Reid, Matthew (with the Four Seasons)	1962	ABC 10305
Mean Man	Dreamtones	1959	Astra 551
Mean Old Blues	Moonglows, Harvey & the	1958	Chess 1705
Mean Old World	Halos	1962	Trans Atlas 690
Mean Poor Girl	Courtiers	1959	Case 107
Mean To Me	Platters	NA	Mercury EP 3355
Mean Woman	Buzzards, Big John & the	1954	Columbia 40345
Mean Woman	Fender, Freddy & group	1958	Duncan 1000/Imperial 5659 (60)
Meaning Of Love	Deuces Wild	1958	Specialty 654
Meaning Of Love	Van Dykes	1958	King 5158/DeLuxe 6193 (61)
Meaning Of Love, The	Goldentones	1955	Jay-Dee 806/Beacon 560 (55)
Meaning Of Love, The	Towers, Jimmy & the	NA	Debann 102
Meant For Me	Toppers, Bobby Mitchell & the	1954	Imperial 5295
Meant To Be	Hull, Terry (with the Starfires)	NA	Staff 103
Meant To Be	Seminoles	1960	Hi-Lite 109
Meant To Be	Sheppards (Chicago - Apex)	1960	Apex 7755
Meant To Be	Velveteens	1962	Stark 105/Laurie 3126 (62)
Meanwhile Back At The Ranch	Continentals (New York - Key)	1956	Key 517
Meanwhile, Back In My Heart	Impressions	1960	20th Fox 172
Measure Of My Love, The	Five Keys	1959	King 5305
Mechanical Man	Bobolinks	1958	Key 575
Medicine Man	Untouchables	1962	Liberty 55423
Meditation	Earls	1977	Woodbury 101
Mediterranean Moon	Rays	1959	XYZ 605
Medley (Cherry Pie	Trojans	1966	Air Town 003/Air Town 70971
Meek Man	Spaniels, Pookie Hudson & the	1961	Neptune 124
Meet Me After School	Castanets, Yolanda & the	1961	Tandem 7002
Meet Me At The Candy Store	Chesterfields	1958	Cub 9008
Meet Me At The Corner	Emperors, Ernie & the	1965	Reprise 0414
Meet Me At The Crossroads	Tempo-Tones, Nancy Lee & the	1957	Acme 711
Meet Me In The Barnyard	Bluenotes, Phil Cay & the	1959	Hart 1001
Meet Me Tonight	Medallions	1954, 1972	Dootone 344 (unreleased)
Meet Me Tonight	Rollins, Debbie & group	1964	Ascot 2159
Melancholy	Renaults	1959	Warner Bros. 5094
Melba	Dreamers (Philadelphia)	1954	Rollin' 5/Rollin' 1001 (55)
Melba	Four Sevilles	1980	Starlight 5
Mello Mama	Spiders	NA	Imperial (unreleased)
Mello-Jello Pt. 2	Gee-Chords	1974	Romantic Rhythm 101
Mellow As A Man Can Be	Hollywood Flames	Mid to late 1950s	(Early 1980s on EP; originally unreleased)

SONG	GROUP	YEAR	LABEL
Mellow Sunday	Jaguars	1988	Classic Artists 106
Mellow You Down	Mellow Jacks	1962	Marquee/Ascot 2115 (62)
Mellow-Feznecky	Dukays	1964	Jerry-O 106
Melody Of Love	Rhythmaires (with Gayle Lark)	NA	Tops EP 250
Melody Of Love	Velvetones	1957	Aladdin 3391
Melvin	Beaus, Bobbie & the	1959	Unart 2009
Melvin	Belles	NA	Tiara 100
Memoirs	King Krooners (Little Rico)	1960	Excello 2187
Memories	Debutantes	1958	Kayo 928
Memories	Decoys	1963	Aljon 1261
Memories	Knight, Bob	1962	Josie 899
Memories	Kraftones	1962	Medieval 206
Memories	Mistics	1963	Capri 631
Memories	Platters	1963	Mercury 72060
Memories	Playboys	1959	ABC 10070
Memories	Scott Brothers	1962	Parkway 841
Memories Are Here To Stay	Admirations	NA	Atomic 12871
Memories Are Made Of This	Drifters (1959-forward)	1966	Atlantic 2325
Memories Can't Be Broken	Determinations	1959	Space 304
Memories Linger On	Reasons, Ria & the	1964	Amy 888
Memories Never Grow Old	Collegiates, Dicky Lee & the	1957	Sun 280
Memories Of A Summer Day	Angel, Gary (with the Halos)	1961	Kama 501
Memories Of Days Gone By	Five Satins	1982	Elektra 47411
Memories Of El Monte	Penguins	1963	Original Sound 27
Memories Of Love	Epics, Linda & the	1959	Blue Moon 415
Memories of Love	Rockin' Chairs, Lenny Dean & the	1959	Recorte 412
Memories Of Love	Stagg, Tommy & group	1961	Bambi 802
Memories (Of My Mother)	Fairfield Four	1960	Old Town 1081
Memories Of The Past	Fairlanes	1989	Relic LP 5079
Memories Of Those Oldies But Goodies	Romans, Little Caesar & the	1961	Del-Fi 4166
Memories Of Yesterday	Five Crowns	1959	De'Besth 1122
Memories Of You	Blenders (New York)	1952	Decca 28241
Memories Of You	Cadets	NA	Relic LP 5025
Memories Of You	Chantels	1958	End EP 202/End LP 312 (61)
Memories Of You	Fidelitys	1958	Baton 256
Memories Of You	Four Bars	1954	Republic 7101
Memories Of You	Four Lovers	1957	RCA LP 1317
Memories Of You	Fuller, Jerry & group	1959	Challenge 59052
Memories Of You	Ontarios	1965, 1974	Big Town 121
Memories Of You	Rapid-Tones, Willie Winfield & the	1962	Rapid 101
Memories We Share, The	Carole, Nancy & group	1964	Luxor 1029
Memory Lane	Hippies	1963	Parkway 863
Memory Lane	Stereos	1959	Mink 022/Parkway 863
Memory Lingers On, The	Redwoods	1961	Epic 9447
Memory Tree	Velaires	1962	Jamie 1223
Mend The Torn Pieces	Sensations	1964	Junior 1010
Mendelsohn Rock	Wildtones	1958	Tee Gee 105
Mepri Stomp	Calendars, Freddy Meade & the	1961	20th Fox 287
Merchant Of Love	Davis, Hal Sonny & group	1961	Wizard 101/Vee Jay 387 (61)
Merchant St. Blues	Bell Hops	1956	Tin Pan Alley 153
Mercy	Rexettes, Larry & the	NA	Zorro 420
Mercy Me	Dominoes, Lil Greenwood & the	1954	Federal 12165
Mercy Me	Lamplighters	1955	Federal (unreleased)
Merengue, The	Belltones (Yonkers)	1956	Scatt 1609/1610/J&S 1609/1610 (58)
Merry Christmas	Cameos (Philadelphia)	1957	Cameo 123
Merry Christmas Darling	Crosstones	NA	Clifton EP 511
Merry Christmas Baby	C-Quents	1968	Captown 4027
Merry Christmas Baby	Meadowlarks, Don Julian & the	1988	Classic Artists 105
Merry Christmas Baby	Poets	1964	Red Bird 046
Merry Christmas Baby	Sparrows Quartette	1963	Broadcast
Merry Christmas Darling	Uniques	1963	Dot 16533/Demand 2936
Merry Christmas My Love	Cavaliers	NA	Herald (unreleased)
Merry Christmas One And All	Rhythm Kings	1951	Apollo 1171
Merry Christmas Song	Holidays	1960	Monument 431
Merry Christmas Tonight	Starlites	1962	Goldband 1151

SONG	GROUP	YEAR	LABEL
Merry Go Rock	Robins	1956	Whippet 201X
Merry Go Round	Angels (New Jersey)	1968	RCA 9681
Merry Go Round	Drapers	1960	Unical 3001
Merry Go Round	Hollywood Saxons	1968	Swingin' 654
Merry Go Round	Schoolgirls, Wendy & the	1958	Golden Crest 502
Merry Merry Christmas Baby	Tune Weavers, Margo Sylvia & the	1988	Classic Artists 107
Merry Twist-Mas	Marcels	1961	Colpix 617
Merry-Go-Round	Holland, Eddie & group	1959	Tamla 102/United Artists 172 (59)
Merry-Go-Round Love (acappella)	Tremonts	1975	Relic LP 104
Merry-Go-Round Of Home	Four Esquires	1962	Terrace 7502
Mess Around	Newports, Cal Linley & the	1960	DC 0431
Mess Around, The	Lockettes, Richard Berry & the	1958	Flip 336
Message From Me	Bobolinks	1961	Tune 226
Message Of Love	Orbits	1956	Flair-X 5000
Message, The	Four Plaid Throats	1953	Mercury 70143
Message, The	Sandmen, Lincoln Chase & the	1955	Columbia 40475
Message To Pretty	Little People, Mike Lynam & the	NA	Emanon 101
Message With Flowers	Gainors	1959	Mercury 71466
Messed Up	Cavaliers	1959	Tel 1006
Messin' Up	Five Royales	1957	King 5082
Messy Bessy	Jesters	1960	Shimmy 1054
Met A Girl On The Corner	Orchids	NA	Parrot (unreleased)
Met Her At A Dance	Individuals	1959	Show Time 595
Meusurry	Delicates	1959	Unart 2024
Mexicali Moon	Lemon Drops	1960	Aladdin 3465
Mexican Divorce	Drifters (1959-forward)	1962	Atlantic 2134
Mexican Hop, The	Vallandeers	1960	
Mexico	Del Roys	NA	Carol unreleased
Mexico	Fiestas	NA	Ace LP CH173
Mexico	Heartspinners, Dino & the	1981	Starlight 11
Mexico	Rocketones	1957	Melba 113
Mexico Bound	Champions	1956	Scott 1201/Chart 611
Mi Amor	Five Hi Lighters	1959	Cannon 580488
Mi Amor	Victors	1959	Jackpot 48015
Mi Amore	Denton, Mickey & group	1965	Impact 1002
Mi Amore	Quentins	1960	Andie 5014
Mi Mi Girl	Howards	1958	ABC 9897
Mia Bella Donna	Squires (Flair)	1954	Flair 1030
Mi-A-Suri Talk	Taylor, Mike & group	1963	Dream
Michelle	Dahills	1964	Musicor 1041
Mickey Mouse Chant	Yesterday's News	1979	U.G.H.A. 06
Mickey Mouse March	Pussycats	1963	Keyman 600
Mickey's East Coast Jerk	Larks (Don Julian)	1964	Money 110
Middle Of The Night	Clovers	1952	Atlantic 963
Midnight	Five Budds	1953	Rama 1
Midnight	Flames, Patti Anne Mesner & the	1952	Aladdin 3162
Midnight	Gatorvettes	1958	Thunder 1001/Bocaldun 1001 (59)
Midnight Blues	Ravens	1950	Columbia 39070
Midnight Flyer	Rivieras	1959, 1964	Coed 513/592
Midnight Flyer	Tramps	1959	Arvee 570
Midnight Hours	Drivers	1957	DeLuxe 6104
Midnight Journey	Lands, Liz (with the Temptations)	1963	Gordy 7030
Midnight Limbo	Tides	1962	Mercury 71990
Midnight (or It's Midnight)	Fascinations	1960	Sure 106
Midnight Run	Omegas	1961	Groove G-4
Midnight Shuffle	Star Marks, Sammy Vaughn & the	NA	Stardom 0012
Midnight Star	Brentwoods	1960	Dore 559
Midnight Star	Misfits	1961	Aries 7-10-3
Midnight Stomp	Jackals, Frank Sandy & the	1958	MGM 12678
Midnight Stroll	Revels	1959	Norgolde 103 (second pressing)
Midnight Sun	Five Whispers	1962	Dolton 61
Midnight Sun	Funny Bunnies	1960	Dore 542
Midnight Sun	Players, Leroy Lovett & the	1955	Atlantic 1058
Midnight Til Dawn	Three Chuckles	1956	Vik 0232
Midnight Train	Cavaliers, Tommy Rocco & the	1960	F-M 3264

SONG	GROUP	YEAR	LABEL
Midnight Walk	Genotones	NA	WGW 3003
Midsummer Night	Castelles	1953	Grand (unreleased)
Mighty Joe	Vel-Aires, Donald Woods & the	1956	Flip 312
Mighty Like A Rose	Carols	NA	Savoy
Mighty Lou	Bluenotes, Henry Wilson & the	1958	Dot 15692
Mighty Low	Bluenotes	1957	Colonial 434
Mighty Mighty Man	Rinky-Dinks (with Bobby Darin)	1958	Atco 6128
Mike's Riff	Alleycats, Joe Allen & the	1958	Jalo 202
Mildred	Del-Capris, Beverly & the	1964	Columbia 43107
Military Kick	Blentones	1959	MGM 12782
Milk And Gin	Capris (Philadelphia)	NA	Gotham (unreleased)
Milk And Gin	Crickets, Dean Barlow & the	1953	MGM 11428
Milk Shake Mama (acappella)	Dell Vikings	1975	Relic LP 109
Milky White Way (acappella)	Five Delights	1960	A Cappella - Best of the Bronx (98)
Millie	Capitols, Mickey Toliver & the	1957	Cindy 3002
Millie Brown	Jets (New York)	1956	Gee 1020
Million Dollar Girl	Ivy Jives	1960	Jaro 77036
Million Drums	Mitchell, Tony & group	1963	Canadian American 157
Millionaire	Original Drifters	1971	Game 394
Millionaire Hobo	Yesterday's News	1981	Clifton 60
Mind Over Matter (I'm Gonna Make You Mine)	Diablos, Nolan Strong & the	1962	Fortune 546
Mind Over Matter (I'm Gonna Make You Mine)	Pirates	1962	Mel-O-Dy 105
Mind Reader	Rhythmettes	1957	Brunswick 55012
Mind Your Mama	Showmen, Carl Frost & the	1963	Lawn 223
Mind Your Man	Rivingtons	1968	AGC 5
Mine	Hi Larks	1959	Beat 0050
Mine	Thrillers, Little Joe & the	1958	Okeh 7107/Epic 9293 (58)
Mine, All Mine	Centuries	1961	Life 501
Mine All Mine	Dream Girls, Bobbie Smith & the	1962	Big Top 3100
Mine All Mine	Meadowlarks, Don Julian & the	1955	Dootone 372
Mine All Mine	Sharp Cats, Verna Williams & the	NA	Versailles 865
Mine Alone	Capri, Johnny & group	1961	Master 13
Mine Alone	Harrison, Lee & group	1958	Judd 1003
Mine Alone	Kounts, Lee Harrison & the	1958	Pearl 717
Mine And Mine Alone	Angelettes	1957	Josie 813
Mine Exclusively	Olympics	1966	Mirwood 5513/Mirwood LP 7003
Mine Forever More	Chevrons	1968	Indpendence 94
Mine Forever More	Five Royales	1956	King 4973
Mine Forever More	Yellow Jackets, Walter & the	1957	Goldband 1033
Mine Mine Mine	Five Cats	1955	RCA 6012
Mini Movement, The	Blue Chords	NA	Reverb 6745
Mink Coat And Sneakers	Valentines	1964	United Artists 764
Minnie	Fi-Tones	1959	Angle Tone 536
Minnie	Rainbows	1957	Rama 209
Mio Amore	Flamingos	1960	End 1065
Mio Amore	Velours	1984	Starlight 19
Miracle	Five Knights	1959	Specialty 675
Miracle After Miracle	Van Dykes	1966, 1967	Green Sea 108/Co-Op 515
Miracle In Milan	Stylers	1957	Jubilee 5279
Miracle In The Rain	Teenagers, Frankie Lymon & the	1957	Gee 1036
Miracle Maker	Partylights, Shona & the	1963	Chicory 1601
Miracle Moment Of Love	Keys, Rudy West & the	1989	Classic Artists 112
Miracle Of Life	Marvells	1961	Finer Arts 2019
Miracle Of Love	Chantels	1959	Unreleased
Miracle Of Love	Dawn Quartet	1973	Vintage 1010
Miracle Of Love	Five Royales	1959, 1961	King 5191/5453
Miracle Of Love	Tunemasters	NA	
Miracle Of The Bells	Automations	1974	Clifton 6
Miracle, The	Williams, Tony & group	1961	Reprise 20030
Miracles	Corvets, Arthur & the	1964	NRC 2781
Miracles	Spaniels	1964	Double L 720
Mirror Mirror	Arrogants	1963	Lute 6226
Mirror Mirror	Five Discs	1978	Crystal Ball 114

SONG	GROUP	YEAR	LABEL
Mirror Mirror (On The Wall)	Playboy Band, John Fred & His	1962	Montel 2001
Mirror On The Wall	Janssen, Danny & group	1960	Stepheny 1841
Misery	De Velles	NA	Emanuel 107
Misery	Dynamics	1963	Big Top 3161
Misery	Ravenetts	1959	Moon 103
Misery	Robins, Little Esther & the	1950	Savoy 735
Misery	Serenaders (Detroit)	1952	Coral 65093
Mish Mash	Combo Kings	NA	Flo-Jo 4095
Mish Mash Baby	Cleftones	1959	Roulette 4161
Misirlou	Cardinals	1955	Atlantic 1054
Miss America	Friends, Dante & his	1962	Imperial 5827
Miss Annie	Plurals	1958	Wanger 186/187/ Bergen 186/187 (59)
Miss Fine	Cruisers	1960	V-Tone 207
Miss Fine	New Yorkers (Fred Parris)	1961	Wall 547
Miss Frankenstein	Unisons, George Jackson & the	1961	Lescay 3006
Miss Heartbreaker	Ascots	1965	M.B.S. 106
Miss Jones	Corvells	1957	Lido 509/Tip Top 509 (57)
Miss Lonely Hearts	Deb-Tones	1958	RCA 7242
Miss Lucy	Kidds	NA	Imperial (unreleased)
Miss Petunia	Day, Dawn & Dusk	1955	Apollo 476
Miss Selma's Boogie	Lollypoppers	1955	Aladdin 3291
Miss Silhouette	Volumes	NA	Chex
Miss Social Climber	Paramours	1961	Smash 1718
Miss The Love	Harmonaires, Bonnie Lou & the	1955	King 1506
Miss The Love (I've Been Dreaming Of)	New Group, Otis Williams & his	1955	DeLuxe 6088
Miss Thing	Silhouettes	1958	Ember 1032
Miss Wonderful	Moore, Rudy May (with the Raytones)	1960	World Pacific 821
Miss You	Crows	1954	Rama 30
Miss You	Holidays	1961	Robbee 103
Miss You, My Dear	Capers	1958	Vee Jay 297
Miss You So	Topsy, Tiny (with the Five Chances)	1957	Federal 12303
Miss You Tonite	Phantoms, Lynn Roberts & the	1956	Oriole 101
Missed	Three Graces	1960	Golden Crest 534
Missing Someone	Chase, Bobby & group	1965	Ascot 2195
Missing You	Divots	1961	Savoy 1596
Missing You	Four Blues	1950	Apollo 1160
Missing You	Starlites (New York - Peak)	1957	Peak 5000
Mission Bells	Esquires	1962	Meridian 6283
Mission By The Sea	Four Winds	1958	Hide-A-Way 101
Mississippi Mud	Five Classics	1961	Pova 6142
Mississippi Mud	Suburbans	1961	Flamingo 539
Mistakes	Five Keys	1952	Aladdin 3131
Mister Dee-Jay	Cinderellas	1959	Decca 30830
Mister Juke Box	Temptations (New Jersey)	1958	Savoy 1532
Mister Love	Rhythmettes	1957	Brunswick 55012
Mister Magoo	Kodaks	1961	Wink 1006
Mister Man The Guitar Man	Masquerades	1960	Formal 1011/1012
Mister Mirror	Centuries, Ronnie & the	1962	Luna 3076
Mister Moon	Golden Tones	1961	Lodestar 22
Mister Sam	Rommels	1960	Trend 4104
Mister Santa, Bring Me A Doll	Merry Men, Robin Hood & his	1962	Mohawk 130
Mistrustin' Blues	Robins, Little Esther & the	1950	Savoy 735
Misty	Shells	1976	Candlelite LP 1000
Misty	Vibrations	1965	Okeh 7230
Misty (acappella)	Shells	1966	Candlelite LP 1000
Misty Eyes	Escorts (O.J.)	1957	O.J. 1010
Misty Summer Night	Orientals	NA	New Dawn 413
Misunderstood	Vibes	1959	Allied 10007
Mixed Up, Shook Up Girl	Emblems, Patty & the	1964	Herald 590
Mixture Of Love	Admirations	1963	Times Square 20/Relic 537 (65)
Mmm Mmm Baby	Spiders	1954	Imperial 5305
Mo' Jerk	Dukays	1964	Jerry-O 105
Mo Jo	Knockouts	1964	Tribute 199
Moana	Jades, Bobby Klint & the	1959	Christy 109

SONG	GROUP	YEAR	LABEL
Moanin'	Ambassadors	1987	Relic LP 5071
Model Girl	Maestro, Johnny & group	1961	Coed 545
Modley, The	Angels (New Jersey)	1968	RCA 9541
Moe & Joe	Continental Five	1959	Nu Kat 10132
Mohawk Squaw	Five Royales	1955	King 4785
Mojo Hannah	Binders	NA	Sara 7771
Molly	Sherwoods	1964	Magnifico 105
Molly Be Good	Hendricks, Bobby (with the Coasters)	1958	Sue 708
Molly Bee	Cousins	1960	Swirl 102
Molly Mae	Crests	1959, 1960	Coed 511/537
Mom & Dad	Upsets	1961	Harwood 7
Moments Like This	Baltineers	1956	Teenage 1000
Moments Like This	Tren-Dells	1962	Tilt 788
Moments Like This	Wheels, Ferris & the	1962	United Artists 458
Moments To Recall	Burgess, Dewayne & group	NA	Branley 103
Moments To Remember	Candlettes	1963	Rhonda 1001
Moments To Remember You By	Romeos	1957	Fox 845/846/Atco 6107 (57)
Momma	Famous Hearts	1962	Guyden 2073
Momma Llama, Poppa Llama	Bon-Bons	1955	London International 1585
Mommy And Daddy	Creations	1956	Tip Top 400
Mommy And Daddy	Street-Tones, Patty & the	1981	Clifton 63
Mommy And Daddy	Students (Philadelphia)	1958	Red Top 100
Mommy-O	Impalas (Brooklyn)	19??	Unreleased
Mon Cherie Au Revoir	Smith, Arlene & group	1963	End 1120
Mona	Crystalaires	1990	Crystal Ball 159
Mona	Epps, Arthur & group	1961	Spark 900
Mona Lisa	Villa, Joey (with the Original Three Friends)	1962	MF 101
Mona My Love	Blue Denims, Wild Bill & the	1960	Gone 5082
Monday Morning Blues	Four Jacks, Lil Greenwood & the	1952	Federal 12082
Monday To Sunday	Dale, Alan & group	1961	Sinclair 1003
Money	Allisons	1963	Tip 1011
Money	Duvals, Phil Johnson & the	1958	Kelit 7033
Money	Five Pennies	1956	Savoy 1190
Money	Miracles (Detroit)	1958	End 1029/End 1084 (60)
Money	Mohawks	1961	Motown 1009
Money	Rayber Voices, Barrett Strong & the	1960	Tamla
Money Blues	Spaniels	1970	North American 3114
Money Don't Grow On Trees	Barons (Spartan)	1961	Spartan 402/Soul 837
Money, Fortune And Fame	Spices	1958	Carlton 480
Money Honey	Coasters	1965	Atco 6356
Money Honey	Drifters (Pre-1959)	1953	Atlantic 1006
Money Honey	Hollywood Flames	1960	Atco 6180
Money Honey (acappella)	Universals (Philadelphia)	1973	Relic LP 5006
Money Hungry	Starlets	1961	Pam 1004
Money Money Money	Carpenter, Freddie & group	1958	East West 112
Money Talks	Penguins	1959	Dooto LP 242/Dooto EP 241
Money Talks	Smith, Kenny & group	1964	Fraternity 934
Money's Funny	Washington, Baby & group	1961	Neptune 122
Monkey Business	Pharotones	1963	Times Square 21/ Times Square 94 (64)
Monkey Dance, The	Endells	1963	Heigh Ho 604/605
Monkey Do	Tempos	1963	Fairmount 611
Monkey Face Baby	Gems (Illinois)	1957	Drexel 915
Monkey Hips And Rice	Five Royales	1954	King 4744
Monkey Hop	Volumes	1964	Old Town 1154
Monkey Stroll, The	Victorians	1963, 1964	Liberty 55656/55728
Monkey Stuff	Hightones, Claude & the	1958	Pam Mar 614
Monkey, The	Limelites, Shep & the	1963	Hull 756
Monkey Walk	Pets, Jerry Warren & the	1959	Arwin 118
Monkey Walk, The	Flares	1961	Press 2810
Monster, The	Pleasers, Bobbie Please & the	1959	Jamie 1118
Monster's Love	Denny & Lenny (with the Hollywood Ghouls)	1963	Chance (N.Y.) 569
Monticello	Concords (Harlem)	1954	Harlem 2328
Moo Goo Gai Pan	Rays	1955	Chess 1613
Mooba-Grooba	Holidays, Dick Holler & the	1962	Comet 2146

SONG	GROUP	YEAR	LABEL
Moocher, The	Lancers (with Larry Smith)	NA	Central 6001
Mood To Be Wooed	Accents, Jackie Allen & the	1955	Accent 1027
Moody	Poni-Tails	1959	ABC 10027
Moody	Romancers	1960	Palette 5067
Moody Over You	Orioles, Sonny Til & the	1955	Jubilee 5221
Moon 2000	Catalina 6	1962	Flagship 126
Moon Dawg	Versatiles	1964	Sea Crest 6001
Moon Eyes	Lamarr, Gene (with the Blue Flames)	1958	Spry 115
Moon Flight	Lonely Guys	1957	Caddy 117
Moon Guitar	Rangoons	1961	Laurie 3096
Moon In The Afternoon	Five Whispers	1962	Dolton 61
Moon Is Yours, The	Cruisers	1957	Finch 353
Moon Of Silver	Mellows, Lillian Lee & the	1956	Candlelight 1011
Moon Out There	Puffs	NA	Dore 757
Moon Over Miami	Collegiates, Harold Teen & the	1960	Goldisc 3014
Moon Over Miami	Platters	1963	Mercury LP 20759/ Mercury LP 60759 (63)
Moon Over My Shoulder	Echoes, Benny Barnes & the	1958	Mercury 71284
Moon River	Fireflies	1962	Taurus LP 1002
Moon Shining Bright	Tremaines	1958	Cash 100/101/Val 100/101 (58)/ Old Town 1051 (58)
Moon Tan	Techniques	1958	Roulette 4097
Moonbeam	Argyles	1957	Bally 1030
Moonglow	Four Buddies	1961	Coral 62217
Moonglow	Ravens	NA	National (unreleased)
Moonglow	Valentinos	1982	Crystal Ball 147
Moonglow, You Know	Videos	1958	Main Line 106/Casino 102 (58)
Moonlight	Admirations	1964	Hull 1202
Moonlight	Dynamics	1958	Impala 501/Seeco 6008 (59)
Moonlight	Hi-Lites (Connecticut)	1962, 1976	Dandee LP 206/Monogram 119
Moonlight	Maye, Arthur Lee & group	1985	Antrell 102
Moonlight	Orioles, Sonny Til & the	1950	Jubilee 5026
Moonlight	Vanguards	1958	Ivy 103
Moonlight	Young Lads	1956	Neil 100
Moonlight and I	Five Satins	1957	Ember LP 100/Ember EP 102
Moonlight And Music	Starlight	1989	Clifton 85
Moonlight And Roses	Dickson, Richie & group	1962	Class 308
Moonlight And Roses	Fraternity Brothers	1960	Verve 10195
Moonlight And Roses	Notables	1958	Big Top 3001
Moonlight And Roses	Platters	1963	Mercury LP 20759/ Mercury LP 60759 (63)
Moonlight And Roses	Rosebuds, Richie Dixon & the	1963	Class 308
Moonlight And You	Jaguars	1956	Aardell 0011
Moonlight Angel	Revlons	1980	Crystal Ball 138
Moonlight Bay	Drifters (Pre-1959)	1958	Atlantic 1187
Moonlight Becomes You	Romeo, Al & group	1963	Laurie 3177
Moonlight Cocktails	Rivieras	1960, 1964	Coed 529/592
Moonlight In Vermont	Crenshaws	1961	Warner Bros. 5254
Moonlight In Vermont	Flamingos	1962	End LP 316
Moonlight In Vermont	Valtairs	1965	Selsom 106
Moonlight In Your Eyes	Four Buddies	1951	Savoy 809 (unreleased)
Moonlight Lover	Jiving Juniors	1961	Asnes 103
Moonlight Memories	Platters	1963	Mercury LP 20759/ Mercury LP 60759 (63)
Moonlight Mountain	Howard, Vince & group	1961	Era 3056
Moonlight, Music And You	Essex	1966	Bang 537
Moonlight On The Colorado	Platters	1960	Mercury LP 20481/ Mercury LP 60160 (60)
Moonlight (Part 1)	Rendezvous, Annette &	1996	
Moonlight (Part 2)	Rendezvous, Annette &	1997	
Moonlight Rock	Walcoes	1959	Drum 011
Moonlight Serenade	Rivieras	1958	Coed 508
Moonlight Shadows	Fortune, Jimmy & group	1961	Chancellor 1097
Moonlight Sky	Mark, Ronald & group	1964	Gateway Custom 102
Moonlight Was Made For Lovers	Townsmen (New York - Joey)	1962	Joey 6202

SONG	GROUP	YEAR	LABEL
Moonrise	Midnighters	1954	Federal 12205
Moonrise	Royals (with Alonzo Tucker)	1952	Federal 12088
Moonrise	Terrans, Rene Harris & the	1963	Graham 801
Moon's Not Meant For Lovers (Anymore), The	Royal Teens	1960	Capitol 4335
Moonshine	Immortals	1961	Laurie 3099
Mope De Mope	Playboys	1963	Legato 101
Mope-itty Mope	Bosstones	1959	Boss 401/V-Tone 208 (60)
Mope-itty Mope Stomp	Dovells	1962	Parkway 833
Mop-Top	Jumpin' Jacks	1956	One-O-One 100
Mora Dora	Mathews Brothers	1963	ABC 10473
More	Destinaires	1965	Old Timer 613
More	Drifters (1959-forward)	1965	Atlantic LP 8113
More	Ladds, George Dee & the	NA	Kon-Ti-Ki 230
More And More	Dee-Vines	1958	Brunswick 55095
More And More	Glenns	1960	Rendezvous 118
More And More	Lovelarks	1961	Masons 3-070/Fellatio 301
More And More	Metrotones	1957	Reserve 114
More I See Him, The	Clouds, Donna Dee & the	1961	Ramada 501
More Important Things To Do	Belmonts	1964	Sabina 517
More Lovin' Less Talkin'	Halo, Johnny (with the Four Seasons)	1962	Topix 6004
More, More, More	Thorpe, Lionel (Chords)	1959	Roulette 4144
More Than A Notion	Quintones (Chicago)	1957	Park 57-111/57-112
More Than Enough For Me	Feathers, Johnny Staton & the	1989	Classic Artists 117
More Than Ever	Press, Don (with the Mystics)	1959	Laurie 3036
More Than Riches	DeMarco, Ralph (with the Paramounts)	1959	Guaranteed 202
More Than Riches	Sorrows, Nicky De Matteo & the	1960	Guyden 2024
More Than The Day Before	Sapphires, Howie & the	1959	Okeh 7112
More Than Yesterday	Cinderellas	1964	Tamara 763
More Than Yesterday, Less Than Tomorrow	Dream Kings	1957	Checker 858
More Than You Know	Platters	1962	Mercury 71986
More Than You Realize	Rollettes	1956	Class 203
Mo'Reen	Juniors, Danny & the	1968	Ronn 24
Morning After	Hollywood Argyles	1961	Finer Arts 1002
Morning Mail, The	Gallahads	1956	Jubilee 5252
Morocco Chant	Moroccos	1955	United (unreleased)
Morrine	Five Campbells	1956	Music City 794
Morse Code Of Love	Capris (New York)	1982	Ambient Sound 02697
Morse Code Of Love	Charm	1992	Clifton 98
Most Happy Fella	Buddies	1956	Decca 29840
Most Important Thing, The	Brewer, Mike & group	1963	Lesley 1929
Most Of All	Danes	1961	Le Cam 718
Most Of All	Five Discs	1978	Crystal Ball 114
Most Of All	Four Cal-Quettes	1961	Capitol 4657
Most Of All	Jamecos, Diana Tyler & Nat Brown with the	1965	Jameco 2004
Most Of All	Key, Troyce & group	1959	Warner Bros. 5070
Most Of All	Marcels	1975	Monogram 115
Most Of All	Moonglows	1955, 1964	Chess 1589/Lana 131
Most Of All	Persuasions	1973	MCA 40118
Most Of All	Ribitones	1979	Clifton 38
Most Of All	Rovers	1974	Vintage 1018
Most Of All	Sabres	1965	Jameco 2002
Most Of All	Team Mates	1965	Soft 104/Paula 220 (65)
Most Of All	Twintones	1960	Banner 60203
Most Of The Pretty Young Girls	Upfronts	1964	Lummtone 114
Mother	Dreamlovers	1982	Collectables LP 5004
Mother	Swallows (Maryland)	1991	Starbound 513
Mother Dear	Caliphs	1958	Scatt 111
Mother Dear	Marauders, Hayward Lee & the	NA	Jet
Mother In Law	Four Sportsmen	1961	Sunnybrook 2
Mother Nature	Del Counts, Ronald Bobo & the	1976	Rose 23
Mother Nature	Vilons	1963	Aljon 1259/1260/Relic 524 (64)
Mother Said	Ascots	1965	Mir-A-Don 1002

SONG	GROUP	YEAR	LABEL
Mother Was Right	Combinations	NA	Fortune LP 8017
Mother-In-Law	Del-Rays, Detroit Jr. & the	1964	C.J. 637
Mother-In-Law	K-Doe, Ernie	1961	
Mother-In-Law	Laddins	1974	Relic LP 5018
Mother's Love	Diamonds	1959	Mercury 71449
Mother's Son	De Bonairs	1956	Ping 1000
Mother's Son	Delegates	1957	Vee Jay 243
Motor City	Satintones	1960	Tamla 54026
Motorcycle	Triumphs, Tico & the	1961	Madison 169/Amy 835 (61)
Moulty	Barbarians	1965	Laurie 3326
	(with Vito Piccone & the Elegants)		
Mountain Dew	Batchelors	1955	Rama 176
Mountain Dew	Foxes, Johnny Fox & the	1962	Newtime 507
Mountain, The	Whirlwinds	1961	Guyden 2052
Mountains, The	Sequins	1959	Cameo 161
Mourning	Stylists (Maryland)	1959	Jay Wing 5807
Move And Groove	Hamilton, Gil & group	1962	Vee Jay 479
Move Around, The	Egyptian Kings	NA	Nanc (unreleased) (Rec. 1961)
Move Around, The	Four Pharaohs	1957	Ransom 100
Move In A Little Closer	Victorians	1963	Arnold 571
Move It Over	Ivorytones	1960	Unidap 448
Move It Over, Baby	Stylists (Maryland)	1959	Jay Wing 5807
Move Me Baby	Lamplighters, Jimmy Witherspoon & the	1953	Federal 12156
Move On	Blossoms	1957	Capitol 3822
Move On Out	Gunter, Gloria & group	1959	Arch 1610
Move Out	Leigh, Linda & group	1959	Rendezvous 103
Move Over Rover	Mark IV	1959	Mercury 71445
Movements	Spandells	1977	Robin Hood 146
Movie Magazines	Four Cal-Quettes	1963	Liberty 55549
Movies, The	Titones	1959	Scepter 1206
Movin' Along	Accents (Brooklyn)	1962	Matt 0001
Movin' And Groovin'	Volcanos	1964	Harthon 138
Movin' Man	Belmonts, Dion & the	1967	ABC 10896
Movin' On	Dells	1956	Vee Jay 230
Movin' Out	Cool-Tones	1959	Warwick 505
Movin' Out	Squires (Chan)	1961	Chan 102/MGM 13044 (61)
Moving Out	Robins	NA	Push 764
Mozelle	Sheppards (Chicago - United)	1956	United 198/B&F 198 (56)
Mr. & Mrs. Rock 'n' Roll	Satellites, Bobby Day & the	1959	Class 252
Mr. Astronaut	Drivers	1962	King 5645
Mr. Auctioneer	Starr Brothers	1963	Cortland 106
Mr. Bassman	Marcels	NA	Colpix (unreleased)
Mr. Blue	Fleetwoods	1959	Dolton 5
Mr. Blue	Streetcorner Serenade	1988	Starlight 65
Mr. Blues	Hayden Sisters	1961	Tilt 784
Mr. Brush	Crystals (Brooklyn)	1961	Indigo 114
Mr. Butterball	Picadilly Pipers	1956	Chart 619
Mr. Cool	Leeds	1959	Wand 102
Mr. Cool Breeze	Swans (St. Louis)	1955	Fortune 822
Mr. Cupid	Chessmen	1962	AMC 101/Don-Dee 101 (62)/ Mercury 72559 (65)
Mr. Cupid	Four Epics	1963	Swan 4156
Mr. Cupid	Tokens (Brooklyn)	1965	B.T. Puppy 505
Mr. Cupid	Vespers	1963	Swan 4156
Mr. D.J.	McCoy, Van & group	1961	Rock'N 101
Mr. Dee Jay	Contenders	1959	Blue Sky 105
Mr. Dillon	Delacardos	1961	United Artists 310
Mr. Dillon, Mr. Dillon	Fiestas	1961	Old Town 1104
Mr. Doughnut Man	Tren-Dells	1963	Sound Stage 7 2508
Mr. Echo	Five Playboys	1959	Petite 504
Mr. Echo	Four Deans	1992 (1958)	Park Ave. 7
Mr. Echo	Val, Frankie & group	1962	Fee
Mr. Engineer (Bring Her Back To Me)	Moonglows	1957	Chess 1661
Mr. Fine	Dapps, Johnnie Mae Matthews & the	1960	Northern 3729
Mr. Fine	Dream Girls, Bobbie Smith & the	1961	Big Top 3085

SONG	GROUP	YEAR	LABEL
Mr. Fortune Teller	Darvels, Frankie & the	1977	N/A
Mr. Frog	Bob-O-Links	1962	Hi-Ho 101
Mr. Happiness	Coeds, Johnny Maestro with the	1961	Coed 552
Mr. Happy Love Joy	Cinderellas	1965	Mercury 72394
Mr. Hard Luck	Orbits	1957	Argo 5286
Mr. Heartbreak	Ravens, Mike & the	1962	Empire 1
Mr. Johnny Jones	Darnels, Debbie & the	1962	Columbia 42530
Mr. Johnny Q	Bobbettes	1961	End 1093/Gone 5112
Mr. Jones	Chanteurs	1963	Bolo 745
Mr. Jones	Zircons	1962	Federal 12478
Mr. Junkman	Penguins	1960	Dooto EP 456
Mr. Leader Of The Band	Sequins	1963	Ascot 2140
Mr. Lee	Bobbettes	1957	Atlantic 1144
Mr. Lee's Plea	Mr. Lee (with the Cherokees)	NA	Terry 220
Mr. Lonely	Videls	1960	JDS 5004
Mr. Maestro	Impossibles	1959	RMP 1030
Mr. Magic	G-Clefs	1996	Unreleased/Relic CD 7105
Mr. Magic Moon	Gleams	1963	Kapp 565
Mr. Magic Moon	Valentinos	1963	Kapp
Mr. Meadowlands	Chessmen	1964	Jerden 743
Mr. Misery	Intentions	1963, 1980	Jamie 1253
Mr. Mistaker	Pictures, C.L. & the	1963	Dunes 2021
Mr. Moon	Crystalaires	1990	Magic Carpet EP 512
Mr. Moon	Five Pennies	1955	Savoy 1182
Mr. Moon	Honeymoons, Denny Dale & the	1966	Soma 1447
Mr. Moon	Planets	1964	Roulette 4551
Mr. Moon	Skytones	NA	Gaylo 101
Mr. Moon, Mr. Cupid And I	Pitney, Gene & group	1961	Musicor 1011
Mr. Moonglow	El Reyes	1958	Jade 501
Mr. Moonglow	Invincibles	1959	Chess 1727
Mr. Moto	Ebb Tides, Nino & the	1969	R&R
Mr. Night	Motions	1961	Laurie 3112
Mr. Robin	Spectors Three	1960	Trey 3005
Mr. Rock & Roll	Choice	1988	Clifton 80
Mr. Rock 'n' Roll	Gaylarks	1957	Music City 809
Mr. Sandman	Beau-Jives	NA	Lord Bingo 107
Mr. Sandman	Fleetwoods	1964	Dolton 98
Mr. Santa Claus	Fabulous Twilights, Nathaniel Mayer & the	1962	Fortune 550X
Mr. Santas Boogie	Marshall Brothers	1951	Savoy 825
Mr. Snail	Tokens (Warner)	1968	Warner Bros. 7183
Mr. Starlight	Hot Tamales	1964	Detroit 101
Mr. Taxicab Driver	Dedications	1964	Ramarca 602
Mr. Twenty One	Orlons	1962	Cameo 211
Mr. Twist	Fabulous Four	1960, 1961	Chancellor 1062/1098
Mr. Whisper	Juniors, Danny & the	1961	Swan 4072
Mr. Zebra	Chanteers	1962	Mercury 71979
Mrs. Mother U.S.A.	Williams, Andre & group	1968	Checker 1205
Mrs. Women	Earls	1976	Columbia 10225
Much As I Do	Four Pages	1962	Plateau 101
Much In Need	Five Royales	1961	Vee Jay 412/Home Of The Blues 234
Much Obliged	Cues	1988	Capitol (unreleased) (recorded 1955)
Much Too Much	Hearts, Lee Andrews & the	1954, 1965	Rainbow 256/Lost Nite 104
Much Too Much	Hollywood Flames	1959	Ebb 163
Much Too Much Too Soon	Cardinals, Claudia & the	NA	Teltone
Mucha Cha	Debs	1961	Echo 1008
Muchacha, Muchacha	Ermines	1956	Loma 704
Muddy Road	Larks (Philadelphia)	1963	Violet 1050
Mugmates	Hodges, Eddie (with Sue Wright & group)	1961	Cadence 1410
Multiply By Three	Starlets	1965	Tower 115
Mumblin'	Twisters, Joey & the	1962	Dual 505
Mumbling Word	Stereos	1963	World Artists 1012
Mummy, The	Naturals	1959	Era 1089
Mummy Walk	Contrails	1965	Reuben 711/Diamond 213 (66)
Mummy's Ball, The	Verdicts	1961	East Coast 103/104/Relic 507 (64)
Munch	Aladdins	1962	Witch 109

SONG	GROUP	YEAR	LABEL
Munch	Diamonds	1961	Mercury 71818
Muscle Bound	Shondelles	1962	King 5705
Music	Festivals	1966	Smash 2056
Music City	Pleasures	1963	Catch 100
Music Goes Round And Round	Steadies	1959	Tad 0711
Music Goes Round And Round, The	Gayten, Paul & group	1956	Argo 5257
Music, Maestro, Please	Blends	1960	Casa Grande 5000
Music, Maestro, Please	Dominoes	1958	Liberty 55136
Music Maestro Please	Flamingos	1959	End LP 304/End EP 205 (59)
Music, Maestro, Please	Starlings	1954	Josie 760
Music, Music, Music	Sensations	1961	Argo 5391
Music Swayed, The	Tranells	1956	Chelten 090
Music To My Ears	Camelots	NA	Clifton EP 507
Musical Chairs	Five Satins	1963	Sammy 103
Must Be Falling In Love	Duponts	1955	Winley 212/Savoy 1552 (58)
Must Be Falling In Love	Imperials, Little Anthony & the	1958	Savoy 1552
Must Be True Love	Buddies	1961	Comet 2143
Must You Go So Soon	Strands	1960	Firefly 331
Mustang	Chessmen	1964	Jerden 743
Mustard	Dittos	1961	Warner Bros. 5247
My Aching Feet	Crowns, Henry Strogin & the	1960	Dynamic 1002
My Aching Heart	Aztecs, Jose & the	1955, 1976	Roadhouse LP
My Aching Heart	Flippers	1955	Flip 305
My Aching Heart	Passions	1958	Era 1063/Capitol 3963 (58)
My Aloha Sand	Quin-Tones (Pennsylvania)	NA	Courtney 134
My Angel	Californians	1955	Federal 12231
My Angel	Dovers, Miriam Grate & the	1955	Apollo 472
My Angel	Russell, Rick & group	1963	Poplar 120
My Angel	Viscount V	NA	Lavette 5009
My Angel	Willows	1956, 1957	Melba 106/115
My Angel Eyes	Masquins, Tony & the	1961	Ruthie 1000
My Angel Eyes	Ramadas	1963	Philips 40097
My Angel Lover	Cleftones	1990	CAR 121
My Angel Of Love	Royal Jesters	1960	Harlem 105
My Autumn Love	Danderliers	1955	States 147/B&F 1344 (61)
My Autumn Love	Versatiles	1975	Monogram 114
My Babe	Cleftones	1962	Gee LP 707
My Babe	Coasters	1962	Atco LP 135
My Babe	Escorts, Charlie McCoy & the	1964	Monument 842
My Babe	Goofers	1955	Coral 61383
My Babe	Jesters	1966	Sun 400
My Babe	Motifs	NA	Baton 23112
My Babe	Semitones, Ron Ricky & the	NA	Semitone 1
My Babe	Supremes (Bronx, N.Y.)	1956	Old Town 1024 (second pressing)
My Babe	Thunderbirds, Ron Holden & the	1959	Donna 1315/Nite Owl 10 (59)
My Baby	Admirations	1961	Apollo 753
My Baby	Dardenelles	NA	Playgirl 501
My Baby	Four Intruders	1961	Gowen 1404
My Baby	Jewels (Los Angeles)	1956	Imperial 5387
My Baby	Neville, Art & group	1965	Cinderella 1400
My Baby	Perfections	1962	Lost Nite 111
My Baby	Raytones	NA	Ball 0503
My Baby	Royal Monarchs	NA	Star
My Baby	Swallows (Maryland)	1954	After Hours 104/Chariot 104 (54)
My Baby	Sweet Hearts	1961	D&H 500
My Baby Ain't Nothing But Bad	Gross Sisters	1959	Checker 932
My Baby And Me	Chords, Phil Moore & the	NA	Time 101
My Baby And Me	Kodaks	1958	Fury 1019
My Baby Changes	Victones	NA	Front Page 1001
My Baby Cries	Classmates, Ronnie Jones & the	1958	End 1014
My Baby Dearest Darling	Charms, Otis Williams & the	1954	DeLuxe 6056
My Baby Dearest Darling	Monograms	1957	Saga 1000
My Baby Doesn't Smile Anymore	Fascinations, Jordan & the	1961	Dapt 207
My Baby Doll	Echotones	1959	Dart 1009
My Baby Doll	Gladiators	1957	Dig 135

SONG	GROUP	YEAR	LABEL
My Baby Doll	Key Brothers	1960	Gardena 102
My Baby Done Told Me	Four Bluebirds	1949	Excelsior 540
My Baby Done Told Me	Robins	1953	RCA 5486
My Baby Don't Need Chargin'	Kinglets	1959	Bobbin 104
My Baby From Me	El Rays	1963	M.M. 104/Wolf 104
My Baby Hully Gully's	Innocents	1960	Indigo 105
My Baby Is Fine	Fortunes	1955	Checker 818
My Baby Is Gone	Sharpsters	1959	Bella 2208/2209
My Baby Is So Refined	Ravens	1949	National 9064
My Baby Knows	Gibralters, Nappy Brown & the	1960	Savoy 1582
My Baby Left Me	Rockin' Dukes	1957	O.J. 1007
My Baby Left Me Swingin'	Twinkletones, Rocky Storm & the	1958	Josie 847
My Baby Likes To Rock	Newcomers, Wade Flemons & the	1958	Vee Jay 295
My Baby Likes To Rock	Pals	1958	Turf 1000/1001/Guyden 2019 (59)
My Baby Loves Me	Echolettes	1963	Imperial 5934
My Baby Loves Me	Five Discs	1961	Calo 202
My Baby Loves Me	Freeways	1965	Hugo 11723
My Baby Loves Me	Tams	1962	General American 714
My Baby Loves Me (acappella)	Holidays	1975	Relic LP 102
My Baby Misses Me Too	Dudads	1955	DeLuxe 6083
My Baby, My Baby	Empires	1954	Harlem 2325
My Baby Said	Ribbons	1962	Marsh 202
My Baby Scares Me	Belltones, Tony Morra & the	1959	Arcade 152
My Baby Scares Me	Morra, Tony & group	1958	Arcade 152
My Baby (She Loves Me)	Four Dots, Jerry Stone & the (with Eddie Cochran & Jewel Akens)	1958	Freedom 44002
My Baby, She's The Talk Of The Town	Rockafellas	1963	SCA 18003
My Baby-O	Five Dollars	1960	Fortune 854
My Baby's 3-D	Dominoes	1954	Federal 12162
My Baby's All Right	Castaleers	1960	Planet 44/Donna 1349 (61)
My Baby's Done Me Wrong	Griffin Brothers	1954	Dot 1145
My Baby's Gone	Barons (New York)	1954	Decca 48323
My Baby's Gone	Electronaires, Chuck Ranado & the	1959	Count 507
My Baby's Gone	Five Thrills	1953	Parrot 796
My Baby's Gone	Griffins	1956	Mercury 70913
My Baby's Gone	Medallions	1961	Sarg 191
My Baby's Gone	Ravens	1950	Columbia 39050
My Baby's Gone	Tren-Teens	1964	Carnival 501
My Baby's Gone	Velvet Keys	1957	King 5090
My Baby's Gone	Zodiacs, Maurice Williams & the	NA	Sea-Horn 503
My Baby's Gonna Get It	Orioles, Sonny Til & the	1983	Murray Hill LP M61277
My Baby's In Love With Me	Bowties, Cirino & the	1955	Royal Roost 614
My Baby's Left Me	Laddins	1958	Central (unreleased)
My Baby's Love	Casanovas	1955	Apollo 483
My Baby's Tops	Gardenias	1956	Federal 12284
My Barbara Ann	Tempos	1965	Ascot 2167
My Beatle Haircut	Twilighters (Bronx, N.Y.)	1964	Roulette 4546
My Beau Joe	Echolettes	1963	Imperial 5934
My Beautiful Dream	Coronados	1957	Vik 0265
My Beauty, My Own	Fascinators (Detroit)	1959	Your Copy 1136
My Belief	Peanuts, M&M & the	1965	Money 111
My Beloved One	Apollo Brothers	1960	Cleveland 108/Locket 108 (60)
My Beloved (versions with and without strings)	Satintones	1960	Motown 1000
My Bernadette	Four Gents	1963	Vida 0123
My Best Friend	Corals	1962	Kram 1001/Rayna 5010 (62)
My Best Friend's Girl (acappella)	Creations	1975	Relic LP 109
My Best Girl	Cascades	1964	Charter 1018
My Best Girl	Dells	1958	Vee Jay 300
My Big Brother's Friend	Portraits	1961	RCA 7900
My Big Dream	Manhattans, Eli Price & the	1959	Dooto 445
My Big Mistake	Perennials	1963	Ball 1016
My Billy	Five Chestnuts, Hayes Baskerville & the	1958	Drum 003/004
My Birthday Wish	Robinson, Faith & group	1960	Dolphin
My Bleeding Heart	Mello-Harps	1956	Tin Pan Alley 159

SONG	GROUP	YEAR	LABEL
My Block	Four Pennies	1963	Rust 5071
My Block	Chiffons	NA	Collectables LP 5042
My Blue Heaven	Belgianettes	1963	Okeh 7172
My Blue Heaven	Day, Bobby & the Blossoms	1959	Class 232/Class 263 (59)
My Blue Heaven	Galaxies	1961	Dot 16212
My Blue Heaven	Hamilton Sisters	1954	Columbia 40368
My Blue Heaven	Satellites, Bobby Day & the	1959	Class 263
My Blue Heaven (acappella)	Quotations	1975	Relic LP 108
My Blue Tears	Fire Balls, Billy Eldridge & His	1959	Vulco 1501/Unart 2011 (59)
My Blue Walk	Four Shades Of Rhythm	1949	Old Swingmaster 13
My Bonnie	Baysiders	1960	Everest 19366
My Bonnie (Lies Over The Ocean)	Jaywalkers	1962	Pam 210
My Boy	Stylettes	1965	Cameo 353
My Boy Flat Top	Gayles	1955	King 4846
My Boy John	Rock-A-Byes, Baby Jane & the	1962	United Artists 560
My Boy Sleepy Pete	Tempo-Tones	1957	Acme 715
My Boyfriend's Back	Angels (New Jersey)	1963	Smash 1834
My Boyfriend's Back	Chiffons	1963	Laurie 3364
My Broken Heart	Teenagers (Billy Lobrano)	1958	Roulette 4086
My Brother	Coolbreezers	1957	ABC 9865
My Buddie Stole My Chippie	Playboys	1954	
My Bull Fightin' Baby	Castaleers	1958	Felsted 8512
My Candy Apple Vet	Del Satins	1965	B.T. Puppy 506
My Candy Apple Vette	Tokens (Brooklyn)	NA	RCA LP 2886
My Charlene	Aladdins	1958	Frankie 6
My Cherie	Browne, Doris (with the Capris)	1953	Gotham 298
My Cherie	Shells	1972	Johnson 099 (unreleased)
My Chick Is Fine	Backus, Gus & group	1958	Carlton
My Chickadee	Neons	1957	Tetra 4449
My China Doll	Glad Rags	1957	Excello 2121
My Chinese Girl	Five Discs	1959	Dwain 6072/Dwain 803 (59)/Mello Mood 1002 (64)/Downstairs 1001
My Choice For A Mate	Troopers, George Powell & the	1959	Lummtone 101
My Clumsy Heart	Jacks	1955	RPM 444
My College Girl	Collegians, Professor Marcell & the	1967	Mayhams 212
My Confession	Blue Dots	1976	Robin Hood 136
My Confession	Ebbtides, David Ford & the	1956	Specialty 588
My Confession	Rockers, Paul Winley & the	1955	Premium 401
My Confession	Tenderfoots	1955	Federal 12219
My Confession Of Love	Elbert, Donnie & group	1958	DeLuxe 6161
My Confession To You	Dave & Larry & group	1965	B'n Kc 102
My Congratulations, Baby	Tune Weavers	1960	Casa Grande 3038
My Conscience	Chromatics	1960	Ducky 716
My Country Gal	Raytones, Rudy Ray Moore & the	1958	Ball 0504
My Cutie Pie	Five Bells	1971	Stolper 100
My Dada Say	Girlfriends, Erlene & the	1963	Old Town 1150
My Darlin'	Chantels	1961	End LP 312
My Darlin' Dear	Climbers	1957	J&S 1652
My Darlin' Forever	Originals, Rosie & the	1961	Brunswick 55213
My Darling	Aquatones	1960	Fargo 1111
My Darling	Cleopatra & group	1961	Sheryl 335
My Darling	Corvets	1958	Way-Out 101
My Darling	Cymbols, Little Sonny Knight & the	NA	New Teenage 5001
My Darling	Del Rays	1958	Warner Bros. 5022
My Darling	Delfis 117	1978	Crystal Ball 117
My Darling	Five J's	1958	Fulton 2454
My Darling	Imperials (Detroit)	1952	Savoy 1104/Buzzy 1 (62)
My Darling	Jacks	1955	RPM 428 (second pressing)
My Darling	Mellows, Lillian Leach & the	1956, 1974	Celeste 3002
My Darling	Premiers (Los Angeles)	1956	Dig 113
My Darling	Reno, Nicky & group	1959	Ges 100
My Darling	Starlites	1960	Queen 5000
My Darling	Tabbys	1959	Time 1008
My Darling Dear (acappella)	Five C's	NA	Standord (unreleased)
My Darling My Sweet	Bay Bops	1958	Coral 62004

SONG	GROUP	YEAR	LABEL
My Darling, My Sweet	Flairs	1955	Flair 1067
My Darling One	Chatters	1959	Viking 1001
My Darling To You	Bop Chords	1957	Holiday 2601
My Darling Wait For Me	Clusters, Gus Coletti & the	1957	Tin Pan Alley 207
My Darling Y-O-U	Overtones, Tony Rice & the	1961	Action 100
My Day	Belmonts, Bob Thomas & the	1959	Abel 232
My Day	Belmonts, Dion & the	1960	Laurie LP 2006
My Days Are Blue	Five Chances	1957	Federal 12303
My Dear	Constellations	1963	Violet 1053
My Dear	Crystals (New York)	1953	DeLuxe 6013
My Dear	Cyclones	1957	Flip 324
My Dear	Four Dots (Washington, D.C.)	1951, 1956	Dot 1043/Bullseye 104
My Dear	Hi-Fis	1959	Montel 1005
My Dear	Solitaires	1955	Old Town 1012
My Dear	Starlarks, Wes Forbes & the	1957	Ancho 102/Relic 508 (64)
My Dear	Twin Tones	1958	RCA 7148
My Dear	Valquins	1959	Gaity 161/162
My Dear	Vel-Tones	1964	Wedge 1013
My Dear, Dearest Darling	Five Willows	1953	Allen 1000
My Dear Dearest Darling	Neville, Art & group	1965	Cinderella 1400
My Dear, Dearest Darling	Willows (Dotty Martin)	1960	Warwick 524
My Dear Little Doll	Lee, Jimmy & group	1961	Canadian American 122
My Dear My Darling	Cook, Johnny & group	1957	Lamp 2006
My Dear, My Darling	Counts	1954	Dot 1210
My Dear One	Centennials	1961	Dot 16180
My Dearest	Bobbettes	1962	King 5623
My Dearest Darling	Clefftones	1955	Old Town 1011
My Dearest Darling	Embers	1960	Dot 16162
My Dearest Darling	Metronomes	1962	Maureen 1000
My Dearest One	Duprees	1963	Coed 584
My Dearest One	Rob-Roys, Norman Fox & the	1958	Back Beat 508
My Debut To Love	Sensations	1957	Atco 6090
My Definition Of You	Teenaires, Harley Davis & the	1961	Wildcat 0064
My Desire	Belvin, Jesse & group	1959	Jamie 1145
My Desire	Cliques	1956	Modern 995
My Diane	Charts	1957	Everlast 5010
My Doctor Of Love	Packards	1956	Pla-Bac 106
My Dog Likes Your Dog	Cupids	1957	Decca 30279
My Dream	Diplomats, Dino & the	1961	Laurie 3103
My Dream	Gothics	1961	Carol 4115
My Dream	Platters	1957	Mercury 71093
My Dream	Sharmettes	1962	King 5648
My Dream Girl	Indigos	1963	Cadette 8003
My Dream Girl	Pharaohs, Al Epp & the	1959	Wildcat 0018
My Dream Island	El Tempos	1963	Vee Jay 561 (first pressing)
My Dream Island	Tempos	1964	Vee Jay 580
My Dream Love	Dialtones, Johnny & the	1960	Jin 134
My Dream Love	Moonrays, Ray Frazier & the	1962	Dynamite 1009
My Dream, My Love	Barons (New Orleans)	1955	Imperial 5359
My Dreams	Concords (Brooklyn)	1962	Gramercy 305
My Dreams	Dells	NA	Unreleased
My Dreams	Jovations	1963	Taurus 362
My Easy Baby	Four Chimes	1954	States (unreleased)
My Elise	Coronados	1961	Ric 979
My Empty Room	Imperials, Little Anthony & the	1960	End 1067
My Every Dream	Montclairs	1956	Premium 404
My Every Thought	Velvetones	1960	Aladdin 3463
My Eyes Keep Me In Trouble	Gales	1955	J.V.B. 34
My Eyes On The World	Beatniks, Charles Walker & the	1958	Rhythm 116
My Faith	Fi-Tones	1957	Old Town 1042
My Faith In You	Flamingos	1957	Decca 30454
My Falling Star	Cardigans, Dave & the	1963	Bay 216
My Fantasy	Quarter Notes	1957	DeLuxe 6129
My Fault	Passionettes	NA	Path 101
My Favorite Dream	Lourdes	1960	Mercury 71655

SONG	GROUP	YEAR	LABEL
My Favorite Record	English, Anna & group	1958	Felsted 8524
My Favorite Things	Talents	1961	Twink 1215
My First And Last Romance	Suburbans	1957	Baton 240
My First Broken Heart	Rhythm Steppers	1959	Spinning 6010
My First Discovery	Empires	1956	Wing 90080
My First, Last and Only Girl	Wanderers	1975	Savoy 1099 (unreleased)
My First Love	Tune Tailors	1958	Century 4158
My First Love Letter	Flips, Little Joey & the	1960	Joy 243
My First True Love (There She Goes)	Dante's Infernos	1957	Lido 507
My First Year	Escorts (Judd)	1959	Judd 1014
My Flaming Heart	Danleers	1958	Mercury 71356
My Foolish Heart	Belmonts, Dion & the	1960	Ace (UK) LP 251
My Foolish Heart	Carmelettes	1959	Alpine 53
My Foolish Heart	Chalets	1982	L.I.R.R.A. 1000
My Foolish Heart	Dell Vikings	1957	Mercury EP 3362
My Foolish Heart	Demensions	1963, 1966	Coral 62344/65611
My Foolish Heart	Excels	1960	Gone 5094
My Foolish Heart	Five Discs	1976	Robin Hood 137
My Foolish Heart	Flamingos	1960	End LP 307
My Foolish Heart	Gale, Sunny & group	1960	Warwick 540
My Foolish Heart	Joytones	1956	Rama 215
My Foolish Heart	Matadors	1963	Keith 6504
My Foolish Heart	Roomates	1961	Valmor 013
My Foolish Heart	Upbeats	1958	Swan 4010
My Foolish Heart (acappella)	Notations	1975	Relic LP 108
My Foolish Pride	Embraceables	1962	Cy 1004
My Foolish Pride	Implaceables	1960	Kain 1004
My Foolish Pride	Williams, Johnny & group	1961	Cy 001
My Fragile Heart	Five Embers	1960, 1995	Royce 0006/X Bat 1006
My France	Kings, Vicki France & the	1959	Sparkette 1002
My Fraternity Dance	Three D's	NA	Lowell 212
My Friend	Hi-Fives	1958	Decca 30576
My Friend	Rivieras	1960	Coed 538
My Friend Charlie	Mello-Fellows	1954	Lamp 8006
My Friend Mary Ann	Vanguards	1958	Dot 15791
My Friend Sam	Sunny Boys	1959	Mr. Maestro 806
My Friends	Charms, Otis Williams & the	1958	DeLuxe 6178
My Friends	Five Bell Aires, Henry Hall & the	1990	Relic LP 5085
My Friends	Strangers	1954	King 4697
My Friends Call Me	Five Scripts	1965	Script 103
My Friend's Car	Tokens (Brooklyn)	1963	
My Fumbling Heart	Ives, Jimmy & group	1961	Comet 2141
My Funny Valentine	Del-Airs	1964	Coral 62404
My Funny Way Of Looking At You	Victors, Little Man & the	1964	Roulette 4576
My Gal	Five Wings, Billy Nelson & the	NA	Savoy 999 (unreleased)
My Gal	Moonglows	1954	Chance 1161
My Gal Is Gone	Five Blue Notes	1954	Sabre 103
(My Gal Is) Red Hot	Carroll Brothers	1958	Cameo 145
My Gift From Heaven	Climatics	1962	Re-No 1000
My Girl	Bell, Tony & group	NA	N/A
My Girl	Chancellors	1965	USA 783
My Girl	Crystals (New York)	1953, 1955	Rockin' 518/DeLuxe 6077
My Girl	Dell, Tony & group	1963	King 5766
My Girl	Downbeats	1956	Gee 1019
My Girl	Eternals	1959	Hollywood 70/71/ Musictone 1110 (59)
My Girl	Fireflies	1960	Ribbon 6906
My Girl	Five Fashions	1965	Catamount 107
My Girl	Four Imperials	1958	Chant 101
My Girl	Holidays	1961	Nix 537
My Girl	Ideals	1958	Decca 30720
My Girl	Lonely Boys	1959	NuWay 555
My Girl	Midnighters, Lil' Ray & the	1964	Impact 30
My Girl	Monterays (Brooklyn)	1956	Saturn 1002
My Girl	Parlay Brothers	1965	Valjay 2725

SONG	GROUP	YEAR	LABEL
My Girl	Plants	1958	J&S 1617/1618
My Girl	Silks, Charles McCullough & the	1961	Dooto 462
My Girl	Tears Of Joy	1986	Starlight 47
My Girl	Vanangos	1975	Monogram 110
My Girl	Viscounts	1957	Mercury 71073
My Girl	Vocaltones	1956	Apollo 488
My Girl Awaits Me	Castelles	1953	Grand 101
My Girl Babe	Rhythm Stars	1959	Corsican 0057
My Girl Flip-Flop	Serenaders (New Jersey)	1959	Rae-Cox 101
My Girl Friend	Cadillacs	1957	Josie 820
My Girl Friend	Exclusives	1958	K&C 102
My Girl Friend	V.I.P.s	1961	Congress 211
My Girl Friend (acappella)	Five Jades (Bronx, N.Y.)	1965	Your Choice 1012
My Girl Is A Pearl	Two Jays, Jimmy Allen &	1959	Al-Brite 1200
My Girl Is Gone	Tabs	1959	Noble 720
My Girl Is Just Enough Woman For Me	Belvin, Jesse & group	1959	RCA 7469
My Girl Ivy	Quintones, Jimmy Witherspoon & the	1956	Atco 6084
My Girl Josephine	Aztecs, Billy Thorpe & the	1965	GNP Crescendo 359
My Girl, My Girl	Jumping Jacks	1957	ABC 9859
My Girl Pearl	Premonitions	1967	Jade
My Girl Sloopy	Consuls, Little Caesar & the	1965	Mala 512
My Girl Sloopy	Vibrations	1964	Atlantic 2221
My Girl, The Month Of May	Belmonts, Dion & the	1966	ABC 10868
My Girls	Fantastics	1990	Park Ave. 3
My Gloria	Windsors, Lee Scott & the	1958	Back Beat 506
My God Is Real	Prisonaires	1953	Sun 189
My Grandfather's Clock	Mudlarks	1959	Roulette 4143
My Grandmother's Christmas	Swallows (Maryland)	1991	Starbound 510
My Greatest Sin	Gaylarks	1956	Music City 805
My Greatest Sin	Normanaires	1953	MGM 11622
My Greatest Thrill	Excels	1965	Relic 1007
My Greatest Thrill	Fidelitys	1959	Baton 261
My Greatest Thrill	Starlites	1965	Relic 1001
My Greatest Wish	Teen Kings	1959	Willett 118
My Guardian Angel	Mar-Vels	1961	Tammy 1019
My Guardian Angel	Monorays (with Tony March)	1959	Tammy Records 1005 (first pressing)/ Tammy 1005 (59) (second pressing)/Red Rocket 476 (60)
My Guardian Angel	Sams	NA	Ebony 008
My Guiding Angel	Relatives	1961	May 111
My Guiding Light	Echoes	1960	Dolton 18
My Guy	Percells	1963	ABC 10476
My Guy	Schoolgirls, Wendy & the	1958	Golden Crest 502
My Guy	Young Sisters	1960	Twirl 2001
My Guy And I	Tassels	1959	Madison 121
My Happiness	Beasley, Jimmy & group	1956	Modern 1009
My Happiness	Serenaders (Detroit)	1974 (1952)	Roadhouse 1018
My Head Goes Acting Up	Four Kings	1954	Fortune 811
My Heart	Carallons, Lonnie & the	1959	Mohawk 108/Streetcorner 101 (73)
My Heart	Champions	1958	Ace 541 (duplicate # IS correct)
My Heart	Cordovans	1960	Johnson 731
My Heart	Cuff Links	1957	Dootone 409
My Heart	Fi-Tones	1957	Old Town 1042
My Heart	Mondellos, Rudy Lambert & the	1958	Rhythm 114
My Heart	Ontarios	1974	
My Heart	Rays, Rich & the	1956	Richloy 101
My Heart	Roommates (Roomates)	1964	Canadian American 166
My Heart	Teardrops	1954	Josie 771
My Heart	Tunes	1959	Swade 102
My Heart	V-Eights	1960	Vibro 4005/ABC 10201 (61)
My Heart	Viceroys	1962	Ramco 3715
My Heart Beat A Little Faster	Love, Darlene & group	1963	Philles 111
My Heart Beats A Little Faster	Blue Jeans, Bob B. Soxx & the	1963	Philles LP 4002
My Heart Beats Again	Keystoners	1991	Starbound 514
My Heart Beats Faster	El Venos	1957, 1964	Vik 0305/RCA 8303

SONG	GROUP	YEAR	LABEL
My Heart Beats For You	Echoes	1957	Gee 1028
My Heart Beats Over And Over Again	Arabians	1960	Magnificent 102/Magnificant 102 (60)
My Heart Beckons You	Delmar, Eddie (with the Bob Knight Four)	1965	Vegas 628
My Heart Believes	Anders, Bernie & group	1955	King 4833
My Heart Belongs To Only You	Roomates, Cathy Jean & the	1963	Philips 40106
My Heart Belongs To Only You	Standards	1963	Magna 1314/Chess 1869 (63)
My Heart Belongs To Only You	Striders, Betty McLaurin & the	1952	Derby 804
My Heart Belongs To Only You	Twilights	1959	Finesse 1717
My Heart Belongs To You	Shirelles	1965	Scepter 12114
My Heart Cried	Raindrops, Tony & the	1962	Crosley 340
My Heart Cries	Contrasts, Billy Vera & the	1962	Rust 5051
My Heart Cries	Romancers	1965	Linda 119
My Heart Cries	Thomas, Randy & group	1966	Faro 622
My Heart Cries For You	Blue Notes	1961	Gamut 100
My Heart Cries For You	Escorts (Brooklyn)	1963	Coral 62385
My Heart Cries For You	Larks (North Carolina)	1951	Apollo 1177
My Heart Cries For You	Lullabyes	1964	Dimension 1039
My Heart Cries For You	Sensations	1956	Atco 6075
My Heart Is A Ball Of String	Rangoons	1961	Laurie 3096
My Heart Is An Open Door	Students (Philadelphia)	1958	Red Top 100
My Heart Is Calling	Magnificents (released as by the El Dorados)	1966	Dee Gee 3008
My Heart Is Free Again	Flames, Patti Anne Mesner & the	1952	Aladdin 3162
My Heart Is Low	Deans	1960	Mohawk 114
My Heart Is Made Of The Blues	Staffs, Curtis Wilson & the	1960	Cherry 1014
My Heart Is Not	Steinways	1966	Oliver 2002
My Heart Is Not A Toy	Hi Toppers, V. James & the	1961	Kent 354
My Heart Is On A Merry-Go-Round	Schoolmates, Colleen & the	1958	Coral 62024
My Heart Is Sad	Channels, Earl Lewis & the	1959	Fire 1001
My Heart Is So Full Of You	Emblems, Patty & the	1967	Kapp 897
My Heart Is True	Metropolitans	1958	Junior 395
My Heart Is Your Heart	Raindrops, Jackie & the	1964	Colpix 738
My Heart Is Yours	Marveltones	1952	Regent 194
My Heart Is Yours	Rainbows	1954	Gem 214
My Heart Isn't In It	Superbs	1964	Dore 722
My Heart Knows	Collegians, Jackie Roy & the	1953	Okeh 6987
My Heart Let Me Be Free	Chromatics, Augie Austin & the	1958	Brunswick 55080
My Heart Never Knows	Holidays	1959	Wonder 115
My Heart Never Said Goodbye	Redcoats, Steve Alaimo & the	1960	Dickson 6445
My Heart Runneth Over (with Love)	Shells	1963	Johnson 125
My Heart Stood Still	Decaro Brothers	1964	Liberty 55700
My Heart Stood Still	Innocents	1964	Warner Bros. 5450
My Heart Stood Still	Spectors Three	1960	Trey 3005
My Heart Tells Me	Parakeets Quintet, Leroy Williams & the	1956	Atlas 1069
My Heart Trembles	Five Pennies	1956	Savoy 1190
My Heart Went Zing	Taylortones	NA	C&T 0001
My Heart Will Always Belong To You	Diablos, Nolan Strong & the	1959	Fortune 529
My Heart Will Never Forget	Blenders (New York)	1951	Decca 48244
My Heartbeat	Four Horsemen	1958	United Artists 134
My Heart's Been Broken	Osburn, Bobby & group	1964	Arlen 747
My Heart's Crying For You	Chimes (Los Angeles - Flair)	1954	Flair 1051
My Heart's Crying For You	Flairs	1963	Crown LP 5356
My Hearts Desire	Earls	1961, 1974, 1973, 1980	Rome 5117
My Heart's Desire	Avalons	1958	Unart 2007
My Heart's Desire	Blenders (Class)	1958	Class 236
My Heart's Desire	Bon-Aires	1976	Catamount 130
My Heart's Desire	Cordials	1962	Whip 276
My Heart's Desire	Crescendos (Berkeley)	1957, 1960	Music City 831/Gone 5100
My Heart's Desire	Earls	1973	Clifton 47
My Heart's Desire	Fabulous Pearls	1959	Dooto 448
My Heart's Desire	Opals	1954	Apollo 462
My Heart's Desire	Wheels	1956	Premium 405
My Heart's Got The Blues	Five C's	1955	United 180
My Heart's On Fire	Dell Tones	1953	Brunswick 84015
My Heart's On Fire	Hollywood Flames	1960	Atco 6180

SONG	GROUP	YEAR	LABEL
My Heart's The Biggest Fool	Robins	1952	RCA 5175
My Heavenly Angel	Cherokees (Connecticut)	1961	United Artists 367
My Hero	Blue Notes, Harold Melvin & the	1960	Val-Ue 213/Red Top 135 (63)
My Hero	Imaginations	1991	Collectables CD 5726
My Hero	Impalas (Brooklyn)	1982	UGHA 17
My Hero	Three Graces	1960	Golden Crest 546
My Honey	Dots, Tiny Dee & the	1963	Success 104
My Honey Loves Another Girl	Lexingtons	1963	International 500
My Honey, Sweet Pea	Five Lyrics	1956	Music City 799
My Honey Sweet Pea	Lyrics, Ike Perry & the	1963	Mama 1/2/Mama 1074 (63)
My Hula Hula Lulu	Discorders	1957	Stepheny 1806
My Humble Prayer	Spirals	1962	Luxor 1012
My Illness	Elgins (California)	1961	Titan 1724 (first pressing)
My Imagination	Camelots	1963	AAnko 1004
My Imagination	Fascinations, Jordan & the	1961	Dapt 203
My Imagination	Five Classics	1960	Arc 4454/A 317 (61)
My Imagination	Oasis	1978	Arcade 105
My Imagination (acappella)	Sintells	1975	Relic LP 108
My In-Laws Are Outlaws	Brochures	1961	Apollo 757
My Inspiration	Four Plaid Throats	1953	Mercury 70143
My Inspiration	Inspirations (Bim Bam Boom)	1972	Bim Bam Boom 109
My Inspiration	Moonglows	1961	Crimson 1003
My Inspiration	Teardrops	1957	King 5004
My Island In The Sun	Capris (New York)	1961	Old Town 1107
My Islands In The Sun	Drifters (1959-forward)	1966	Atlantic 2325
My Jealous One	Edsels	1962	Capitol 4588
My Jelly Bean	Consoles, Bobby & the	1963	Diamond 141
My Joan	Fabulous Flames	1958	Rex 3000
My Joey	Carole, Nancy & group	1964	Luxor 1029
My Johnny	Little Miss Wanda & group	1961	Aries 1020
My Juanita	Crests	1957	Joyce 103/Musictone 1106 (62)
My Juanita	Dymensions, Joel & the	1991	Classic Artists 130
My Juanita	Kents	1965	Relic 1013
My Juanita	Newports	1978	Crystal Ball 129
My Juanita	Visuals	1963	Poplar 117
My Judge And Jury	Diamonds	1956	Mercury 70983
My Kind Of Baby	Five Chestnuts	1959	Elgin 003
My Kind Of Dream	Royal Teens	1958	ABC 9955
My Kind Of Girl	Volumes	1967	Inferno 2004
My Kind Of Love	Charmers	1962	Laurie 3142
My Kind Of Love	Satintones	1961	Motown 1010
My Kind Of Lovin'	Diablos	1984	Fortune LP 8020
My Kinda Woman	Baum, Allen (with the Larks)	1954	Red Robin 124
My Kisses For Your Thoughts	Roomates	1961	Valmor 013
My Kissin' Cousin	Mandels	1961	Lilly 502
My Lady Chocaonine	Wanderers	1957	Gone 5005
My Lady Fair	De Marco, Lou & group	1956	Ferris 903
My Last Affair	Serenaders (Colony)	1952	Colony 100
My Last Cry	Starlets	1961	Pam 1004
My Last Dance With You	Don Juans, Andre Williams & the	1958	Fortune 842
My Last Dance With You	Fabulous Twilights, Nathaniel Mayer & the	1961, 1963	Fortune 542/557
My Last Frontier	Upbeats	1958	Prep 131
My Last Goodbye To You	Vocaltones	1989	Relic LP 5082
My Last Hour	Four Jacks, Lil Greenwood & the	1952	Federal 12082
My Last Love	Cytones, Johnny Duraine & the	1961	Dore 624
My Last Mile	Barons, Walter Miller & the	1956	Meteor 5037
My Last Phone Call	Earlington, Lyn & group	NA	Lemonade 1501
My Last Song	Royal Kings	1957	Lance 1035
My Letter	Holiday, Bobby & group	1961	Port 70027
My Letter	Page, Priscilla & group	1961	Rose 500
My Letter To Santa	Marshans	1965	Johnson 736
My Letter To You	Spindles, Frankie & the	1968	Roc-Ker 100
My Life	C & C Boys	1964	Duke 379
My Life For Your Love	Four Lovers	1957	Epic 9255
My Life Is My Life	Marshall Brothers	NA	Savoy (unreleased)

SONG	GROUP	YEAR	LABEL
My Life, My Loved One	Incredible Upsetters	1959	Audio Lab EP 2
My Life's Desire	Verdicts	1961	East Coast 103/104/Relic 507 (64)
My Life's Desire, Pt. 2	Exotics	1962	Coral 62343
My Little Angel	Martin, Steve & group	1963	Magnasound 700
My Little Baby	Belltones, Johnny & the	1957	Cecil 5050
My Little Baby	Hot Rods, Little Shy Guy & the	1956	Calvert 107
My Little Baby	Teen Tones	1959	Swan 4040
My Little Baby's Shoes	Crickets, Dean Barlow & the	1954	Jay-Dee 786
My Little Beach Bunny	Sunsets	1963	Challenge 9208
My Little Darlin'	Doyle, Dicky & group	1961	Wye 1009
My Little Darling	Diadems	NA	Goldie 207
My Little Darling	Fabulous Twilights, Nathaniel Mayer & the	1961	Fortune 542
My Little Girl	Charters	1963	Alva 1001
My Little Girl	Crescendos (Tap)	1957	Tap 7027/Nasco 6005 (57)
My Little Girl	Imaginations	1985	Relic LP 5058
My Little Girl	Pharaohs	NA	Specialty
My Little Girl	Pharoads	1952	RPM 355 (unreleased)
My Little Girl	Runarounds	1967	MGM 13763
	(with Tommy Cosgrove & the Elegant Four)		
My Little Girl	Squires (Los Angeles)	1953	Combo 42
My Little Girl	Trebels	1963	Viking 1021
My Little Girl	Treble Chords	1959	Decca 31015
My Little Homin' Pigeon	Darnels, Gus Gordon & the	1957	Bana 525
My Little Honey	Echoes	1956	Combo 128
My Little Honeybun	Dreams	1955	Savoy 1157
My Little Sailor Boy	Hallmarks	1962	Dot 16418
My Little Surfin' Woodie	Sunsets	1963	Challenge 9208
My Little Tree-House	Winchell, Danny & group	1957	MGM 12577
My Lonely Friend	Continental Five	1959	Nu Kat 104/105
My Lonely Friend	Continentals (Candlelite)	1961	Candlelite 412
My Lonely Life	Carter, Sonny & group	1959	Dot 15921
My Lonely Lonely Room	Earls	1969	ABC 11109
My Lonely One	Rockmasters	1963	One-Derful 4820
My Lonely Prayer	Drivers	1957	DeLuxe 6104
My Loss, Your Gain	Jades	NA	Poncello 7703
My Lost Love	Larks (North Carolina)	1952	Apollo 435
My Lost Love	Melloharps	19??	
My Lost Love	Re-Vels	1954	Atlas 1035
My Lost Love	Webtones	1958	MGM 12724
My Love	Arcades	1959	Johnson 116/Johnson 320 (62)
My Love	Bonnevilles	1959	Ka-Hi 121
My Love	Cardinals	1974	Atlantic EP/
			Bim Bam Boom EP 1000 (74)
My Love	Channels	1963	Enjoy 2001
My Love	Charmers	1963	Sure Play 104
My Love	Charmettes	1958	Hi 2003
My Love	Chex, Tex & the	1961	Atlantic 2116
My Love	Chimes, Lenny & the	1962	Tag 450
My Love	Clientells	1961	M.B.S. 7
My Love	Co-Hearts	1958	Vee Jay 289
My Love	Crystals (New York)	1954	DeLuxe 6037
My Love	Dandoliers	1956	States 160/B&F 160
My Love	Dovers, Miriam Grate & the	1988	Relic LP 5075/Relic LP 5078 (89)
My Love	Five Diamonds	1977	Treat 9/10
My Love	Five Keys	1954	Aladdin 3263
My Love	Heartbreakers (Bronx, N.Y.)	1957	Vik 0299
My Love	Isley Brothers	1959	Gone 5048
My Love	Jayos, Mel Williams & the	1956	Dig 123
My Love	Milky Ways	1960	Liberty 55255
My Love	Moonglows	1954	Chance 1166 (unreleased)
My Love	Moroccos	1956	United (unreleased)
My Love	Orbits	1959	Nu Kat 116/117
My Love	Quails (Harvey Fuqua)	1962	Harvey 116
My Love	Ramsey, Gloria & group	1960	Hap 1894
My Love	Revlons	NA	Klik

SONG	GROUP	YEAR	LABEL
My Love	Shondelles	1962	King 5597
My Love	Time-Tones	1961	Times Square 421 (first pressing)/ Relic 538 (65)
My Love	Turner, Ike & group	1959	Sue 722
My Love	Williams, Mel & group	1956	Dig 123
My Love And Your Love	Spinners (California)	1958	Rhythm 125
My Love Bug	Five Shadows	1960	Frosty 1
My Love Came Tumbling Down	Dell-Fi's, Leon Peterson & the	1960	Kable 437
My Love Come Back	Velours	1956	Onyx 501/Relic 503 (64)
My Love Dreamy Eyes	George, Terry & group	1961	Comet 2144
My Love For You	Austin, Little Augie (with the Chromatics)	1960	Pontiac 101
My Love For You	Calvert, Duane & group	1964	D.M.D. 102
My Love For You	Casanovas	NA	Apollo LP 1004/Relic LP 5073 (87)
My Love For You	Casinos	1960	Casino 111
My Love For You	El-Deens	1959	Federal 12347
My Love For You	Fashions, Frankie & the	1993	Avenue D 19
My Love For You	K-Doe, Ernie & group	1961	Ember 1075
My Love For You	Legends	1962	Ermine 39
My Love For You	Mad Lads, Frank Deaton & the	1957	Bally 1042
My Love For You	Marcels	1961	Colpix 612
My Love For You	Rockets	1956	Wrimus
My Love For You	Superbs	1964	Melmar 121
My Love For You	Superphonics	1961	Lindy 102
My Love For You Will Never Change	Funkytones, Vincent MacRee & the	1957	Gametime 110
My Love Goes Deep	Tempos	1964	Vee Jay 580
My Love Grows Deep	El Tempos	1963	Vee Jay 561 (first pressing)
My Love Grows Stronger	Voices	1955	Cash 1014
My Love Has Gone	Five Blue Flames, Chris Powell & the	1951	Columbia 39407
My Love Has Gone	Hearts (Bronx, N.Y.)	1956	J&S 425/426
My Love Has Gone	Justifiers	1958	Kim 101
My Love Has Gone	Keys	NA	Lee 0759
My Love I Can't Hide	McCall, Little J. & group	1961	Wow 1000/Donna 1334 (61)
My Love I Give	Four Ekkos	1958	RIP 12558
My Love, I Have You	Blazers, Little Bernie & the	1962	Josie 884
My Love Is A Charm	Shirelles	1958	Decca 30669
My Love Is Blue	Dukes (California)	1956	Imperial 5399 (unreleased)
My Love Is Gone	Ladders	1959	Vest 826
My Love Is Gone	Minute Men	1964	Argo 5469
My Love Is Gone	Shades, Joey & the	NA	Wild 905
My Love Is Gone	Sputniks	1957	Pam Mar 602/Class 217
My Love Is High	Sultans	1957	Duke 178
My Love Is Just For You	Blendairs	1958	Tin Pan Alley 252
My Love Is Real	Dappers (Boston)	1960	Epic 9423
My Love Is Real	Holidays, Tony & the	1959	ABC 10029/ABC 10295 (62)
My Love Is Real	Lollypops	1958	Universal International 7420/ Holland 7420 (58)
My Love Is True	Parakeets	1973	Baron 105
My Love Is True	Royal Halos	1959	Aladdin 3460
My Love Is True	Saxons	1958	Tampa 139
My Love Is With You	Cuff Links	1958	Dooto 433
My Love Lady	Oliver, Johnny & group	1955	MGM 55012
My Love My Love	Bon-Aires	1964	Rust 5077
My Love, My Love	Duprees	1969	Heritage 808
My Love, My Love	Expressions	1961	Arliss 1012
My Love, My Love	Four J's	1964	Jamie 1274
My Love, My Love	Philadelphians, Big John & the	1963	Guyden 2093
My Love, My Love	Vann, Joey & group	1965	Coed 606
My Love, My Love, My Love	Sunshine Boys	1959	Scottie 1307
My Love She's Gone	Intentions	1967	Kent 455
My Love Song	Calvanes	1958	Deck 580
My Love Song	Powers, Wayne & group	1958	Phillips International 3523
My Love Song For You	Casuals	1957	Nu-Sound 801/Dot 15557 (57)
My Love, The Blues, And Me	Mello-Men	1953	MGM 11607
My Love Will Follow You	Continental Gems	1963	Guyden 2091
My Love Will Last	Harris, Thurston (with the Sharps)	1959	Aladdin 3450

SONG	GROUP	YEAR	LABEL
My Love Will Never Change	Visions, Connie McGill & the	1964	Edge 502
My Love Will Never Die	Blue Stars	1977	Arcade 101
My Love Will Never Die	Channels, Earl Lewis & the	1958	Fury 1021/Fury 1071 (58)
My Love Will Never Die	Excitements, Elroy & the	1961	Alanna 188/Alanna 565 (63)
My Love Will Never Die	Retrospect	1980	Clifton 42
My Loved One	Orioles, Sonny Til & the	1983	Murray Hill LP M61277
My Lovely One	Deputees, Peter Marshall & the	1956	Melba 103
My Lovely One	Flamingos	1963	End LP 316
My Lover	Cookies	1956	Atlantic 1110
My Lover	Neons	1961	Waldon 1001
My Lover Is A Boy Scout	Charmettes	1964	Mala 491
My Lover Waits For Me	Scavengers	1963	Mobile Fidelity 1005
My Lovin' Baby	El Dorados	1954	Vee Jay 115
My Loving Baby	Channels, Earl Lewis & the	1957	Whirlin' Disc 109/Port 70022 (61)
My Loving Partner	Danderliers	1955	States 150/B&F 150 (61)
My Lucky Night	Standards, Larry & the	1962	Laurie 3119
My Lucky Star	Teenettes	1958	Josie 830
My Lucy Lou	Chevelles, Art Barron & the	1964	Golden 101
My Lullabye	Ovations (New Jersey)	1960, 1961	Andie 5017/Barry 101
My Mama Done Told Me	Miracles (Detroit)	1958	End 1016
My Mama Done Tole Me	Adventurers	1961	Columbia 42227
My Mama Don't Like Him	Raindrops	1964	Jubilee 5497
My Mama Said	Bobbettes	1964	Diamond 156
My Mama Said It's Alright	Starbells, Terry Star & the	1963	New-Art 1008
My Man	Cadets (Dolly Cooper)	1955	Modern 965
My Man	Golden Tones, Marie Reynaud & the	1958	Goldband 1049
My Man A-Go-Go	Gomez, Yvonne & group	1967	Hawaii 128
My Marie	Earls	1975 (1954)	Gem 227
My Mary Lou	Cruisers	1959	Winston 1033
My Mary Lou	Medallions, Vernon Green & the	1956	Dootone 407
My May	Blue Angels	1961	Palette 5077
My Melancholy Baby	Marcels	1961, 1988	Colpix 624
My Memories Of You	Churchill, Savannah & group	1954	Decca 29194
My Memories Of You	Dreamers, Donnie & the	1961	Whale 505
My Memories Of You	Flamingos	1961	End 1099
My Memories Of You	Harptones	1954, 1957, 1973	Bruce 102/Tip Top 401/Relic 1023
My Memories Of You	Naturals, Yolanda & the	1962	Kimley 923
My Memories Of You	Royal Teens	1961	Mighty 200
My Mind's Made Up	Renowns	1961	Everest 19396
My Miracle	Castells	1961	Era 3057
My Momma Said	Dollars, Little Eddie & the	1959	Fortune 845
My Most Precious Possession	Memos	1959	Memo 5000/5001
My Mother-In-Law	Misfits	1961	Hush 105
My Mother's Eyes	Clovers	1959	United Artists LP 3033
My Mother's Eyes	Four Buddies	1953	Savoy 888
My Mother's Eyes	Soft Tones	1955	Samson 103
My Mother's Eyes	Uniques	NA	Dapper 4401
My Mother's Prayers	Five Keys	1959	King 5285
My Mother's Prayers	Harmonaires, Lula Reed & the	1953	King 4590
My Movie Queen	Newports	1994	Avenue D 20
My Movie Queen (The Movies)	Titones	1960	Wand 105
My Mummy	Kokonuts	1962	Bertram International 215
My, My, Ain't She Pretty	Cap-Tans	1951	Gotham 233
My My Darling	Chanters (New York)	1958, 1961	DeLuxe 6162/6194
My Name Ain't Annie	Hayes, Linda (with the Platters)	1955	King 4752
My Need	Extensions	1963	Success 109
My Need For Love	Jokers, Jivin' Gene & the	1959	Mercury 71485/Jin 116
My New Hi-Fi	Peacocks	1958	4 Star 1718
My Next Door Neighbor	Upstarts, Jerry McCain & the	1957	Excello 2103
My Offering	Gallahads (with the Counts)	1964	Sea Crest 6005
My Oh My	Leeds, Randy & group	1959	Roulette 4153
My, Oh My	Pearls	1956	Onyx 506/Relic 519 (64)
My Oh My	Triangles	1964	Fifo 107
My Ol' Lady	Synthetics	NA	Armour 5577
My Old Flame	Platters	1958	Mercury 71320

SONG	GROUP	YEAR	LABEL
My Old Girl Friend	Demensions	1964	Coral 62432
My One	Chancers	1958	Dot 15870
My One And Only Dream	Pastels (Washington, D.C.)	1957	Mascot 123/Argo 5287 (57)
My One And Only Dream	Sinclairs	1979	UGHA 7
My One And Only, Jimmy Boy	Girlfriends	1963	Colpix 712
My One And Only Love	Five Chestnuts, Hayes Baskerville & the	1958	Drum 003/004
My One And Only One	Randle, Johnny & female group	1961	Jayree 2205
My One Desire	Aquatones	1959	Fargo 1005
My One Desire	Casuals, Gary & the	1962	Vandan 609
My One Desire	Delights	1961	Nite 1034
My One Desire	Orbits, J. Lyndon & the	NA	Whiteley 4282
My One Desire	Terrell, Clyde & group	1959	Excello 2151
My One Desire	Tricks	1959	Jane 108
My One Possession	Arabians	1961	Carrie 1516
My One Sincere	Storks, Lenny & the	1982	Jason Scott 25
My One Sincere	Welch, Lenny & group	1958	Decca 30637
My Only Darling	Jayhawks	1956	Flash 109
My Only Desire	Flyers	1957	Atco 6088
My Only Friend	Buddies	1964	Swing 102
My Only Girl	Bennet, Ron & group	1961	Ta-Rah 1
My Only Girl	Goldenaires	1959	Ron 325
My Only Girl	Jays, Mike & the	1960	Doyl 1001
My Only Girl	Skylites	1961	Ta-Rah 101
My Only Love	Candletts	1959	Vita 182
My Only Love	C-Quins	1962	Ditto 501/Chess 1815 (62)
My Only Love	Falcons (Quality)	1957	Quality 1721/Falcon 1006 (57)/ Abner 1006 (57)
My Only Love	Jaytones	1960	Cub 9057
My Only Love	Parliaments	1961	U.S.A. 719
My Only Love	Silvertones	1960	Elgin 005/006
My Only You	Sweet Hearts	1961	D&H 500
My Own	Miller Sisters	1957	Onyx 507
My Own True Love	Deltas	1962	Philips 40023
My Own True Love	Duprees	1962	Coed 571
My Own True Love	Gum Drops	1958	Coral 62003
My Own True Love	Rapid Transit	1978	Clifton 26
My Paradise	Five Stars (Detroit)	1958	Note 10016
My Perfection	Perfections	NA	Pam-O 101
My Picture Of You	Enchantones	1962	Poplar 116
My Pigeon's Gone	Five Keys	1956	Capitol 3455
My Pigeon's Gone	Four Students, Charles Calhoun & the	1956	Groove 0149
My Piggie's Gotta Dance	Satellites	1958	United Artists 141
My Pillow	Darlings	1963	Dore 677
My Pillow	Delicates	1961	Celeste 676/Dee Dee 677 (61)
My Pillow	Numbers	1962	Bonneville 101/Dore 641 (62)
My Pillow Of Dreams	Sounds	1959	Sarg 181
My Place	Crystals (Brooklyn)	1965	United Artists 927
My Plea	Dreamers, Eloise Brooks & the	1955	Aladdin 3303
My Plea	Passionettes	NA	Path 101
My Plea For Love	Starlings	1954	Josie 760
My Pledge To You	Bell Tones	1959	Clock 71889/Mercury 71889 (61)
My Pledge To You	Belltones (Mercury)	1961	Mercury 71889
My Pledge To You	Five Bells	1960	Clock 1017
My Prayer	Deeptones	1954	Music City 736/Musicon 736
My Prayer	Four Jacks	1956	Gateway 1183-B
My Prayer	Orioles, Sonny Til & the	1951	Jubilee 5060
My Prayer	Platters	1956	Mercury 70893
My Prayer	Rocky Fellers	1963	Scepter 1271
My Prayer	Stenotones, Billy James & the	1961	Rust 5038
My Prayer	Williams, Tony & group	1961	Reprise 20030
My Prayer (acappella)	Rondells	1975	Relic LP 104
My Prayer For You	Fireflies	1964	Taurus 366
My Prayer To Heaven	Revivals	1984	Memory Lane 100
My Prayer Tonight	Charms, Otis Williams & his	1959	DeLuxe 6183
My Prayer Tonight	Five Hearts (Ransom)	1959	Ransom

SONG	GROUP	YEAR	LABEL
My Prayer Tonite	Checkers	1953	King 4596
My Precious Jewel	Teen Notes	1960	Deb 121
My Precious Love	Romancers, Rocky Homan & the	1961	Flip 355
My Precious Love	Salems	1961	Mercury 71754
My Present Love	Five Satins	1974	Relic LP 5024
My Pretty Baby	Medallions, Johnny Twovoice & the	1955	Dootone 373
My Pretty Baby	Plaids	1958	Nasco 6011
My Pretty Little Girl	Five Shits	1970	Chance 1163
My Prince Will Come	Montells	1963	Golden Crest 585
My Private Joy	Belmonts, Dion & the	1960	Laurie LP 2006
My Promise	Curry, James (with the Jayhawks)	1956	Flash 110
My Promise To You	Anthony, Paul & group	1958	Roulette 4099
My Promise To You	Capris (Sabre)	1959	Sabre 201/202
My Promise To You	Roberts, Lou & group	1966	Genie 102
My Proudest Possession	Dominoes	1957	Liberty 55111
My Reason For Livin'	Zodiacs, Maurice Williams & the	1968	Veep 1294
My Reckless Heart	Rocketeers	1958	M.J.C. 501
My Reckless Heart	Thor-Ables	1962	Titanic 1002
My Resolution	Troopers	1957	Lamp 2009
My Reverie	Larks (North Carolina)	1951	Apollo 1184
My Reverie	Platters	1963	Mercury LP 20759/
			Mercury LP 60759 (63)
My Reverie	Ryan, Allen & group	1957	Sonic 1600
My Reverie (acappella)	Five Jades (Bronx, N.Y.)	1965	Your Choice 1011
My Reward	Rivingtons	1962	Liberty 55513
My Road Is The Right Road	Volumes	1967	Inferno 2004
My Rock 'N' Roll Baby	Tyrones	1956	Mercury 70939
My Rosa-Lee	Orbits	NA	Friddell 102
My Rose	Charters	1962	Tarx 1003
My Rosemarie	Belltones, Kirk Taylor & the	1958	Tek 2634
My Rosemarie	Bowties, Cirino & the	1955	Royal Roost 614
My Royal Love	Shells	1963	Johnson 127
My Sad Love	Carroll, Yvonne & group	1963	Domain 1020
My Saddest Hour	Five Keys	1953	Aladdin 3214
My Satellite	Belvin, Jesse & group	1957	Modern 1027
My Secret	Barons (New Orleans)	1974	Imperial (unreleased)
My Secret	Nightbeats, Elray & the	NA	Revive 103
My Secret	Platters	1959	Mercury 71538
My Secret	Six Teens	1957	Flip 329
My Secret Heartache	Anthony, Mike & group	1961	Imperial 5813
My Secret Love	Carter Rays	1957	Lyric 2001/Gone 5006 (57)
My Secret Love	Chiffons	1968	B.T. Puppy 558
My Sentimental Heart	Cashmeres (Philadelphia)	1954	Mercury 70501
My Sentimental Heart	Four Stars	1958	Kay-Y 66781
My Shadow And Me	Chaperones	1962	Josie 885
My Shining Hour	Wanderers	1958	Orbit 9003/Cub 9003 (58)
My Ship	Hummingbirds	1962	Cannon 4600
My Silent Love	Rivieras	NA	Coed LP only
My Silent Prayer	Twilighters (Bronx, N.Y.)	1962	Bubble 1334
My Sin	Winners	1952	Derby 802
My Singing Idol And Poor Little Fool	Petite Teens	1959	Brunswick 55119
My Sister's Beau	Dimples	1959	Dore 517
My Son	Armpits, Snake & the	NA	Explo 013
My Song	Jewels (Federal)	1963	Federal 12541
My Song	Rockets, Herb Kenny & the	1952	MGM 11332
My Song	Zodiacs, Johnny Ballad & the	1959	Wildcat 0016
My Soul	Seniors	1959, 1960	Ball 001
My Special Angel	Classmen	1963	Limelight 3012
My Special Angel	Crests	1960	Coed LP 901
My Special Angel	Duprees	1968	Heritage 804
My Special Angel	Saints, Ricky & the	1962	7 Teen 101
My Special Girl	Four Escorts	1961	Skyla 1113
My Special Guy	Six Teens	1957	Flip 320
My Special Love	Delltones	1956	Baton 223
My Special Lover	Fleetwoods	1962	Dolton BLP 2020/BST 8020

SONG	GROUP	YEAR	LABEL
My Special Prayer	Five Blue Notes	1964	Onda 888
My Special Prayer	Jammers	1959	Onda 108
My Star All Alone	Prince, Rod & group	1961	Comet 2140
My Steady Girl	Bluenotes, Henry Wilson & the	1958	Dot 15692
My Steady Girl	Raiders	1958	Brunswick 55090
My Steady Girl	Rays	1957	XYZ 100
My Story	Deltones, Ronnie Baker & the	1962	Laurie 3128
My Story	Nutmegs	1959	Herald 538
My Story	Orchids	NA	Savoy 964 (unreleased)
My Story Of Love	Valentines	1956	Rama 208
My Success (It All Depends On You)	Harptones	1955	Paradise 103
My Sugar Is So Refined	Ravens	1946, 1949	King 4272
My Sugar Sugar	Five Royales	1959	King 5266
My Summer's Gone	Four Buddies	1951	Savoy 789
My Sun Is Going Down	Midnighters, Hank Ballard & the	1965	King 6018
My Surprise	Six Teens	1957	Flip 326
My Suzanne	Henry, Earl & group	1958	Dot 15875
My Sweet	Teen Tones	1959	Dandy Dan 2
My Sweet Baby	Puzzles	1968	Fatback 216
My Sweet Dreams	Nutmegs	1963	Times Square 27/Relic 528 (65)
My Sweet Juanita	Four Sparks	1958	ABC 9906
My Sweet Lord	Chiffons	1975	Laurie 3630
My Sweet Lord (acappella)	Belmonts	1972	Buddah LP 5123
My Sweet Norma Lee	Limelighters	1956	Josie 795
My Sweetest Dream	Nutmegs	1959	Herald 538
My Sweetheart	Errico, Ray (with the Honeytones)	1956	Masquerade 56003
My Sweetheart	Mellards, Fred Green & the	1955	Ballad 1012
My Sweetheart	Stereos, Little Benny & the	1959	Spot 106
My Sweetie Pie	Wanderers	NA	UGHA LP 001
My Tattle Tale	Galaxies (with Eddie Cochran on guitar)	1960	Guaranteed 216
My Tears	Crescents, Pat Cordel & the	1956	Club 1011/Michele M 503 (59)/ Victory 1001 (63)
My Tears	Don Juans, Andre Williams & the (with Gino Purifoy)	1956	Fortune 837
My Tears Start To Fall	Class-Aires	NA, 1982	Honey Bee 1
My Tears Start To Fall	Raye, Cal & group	1966	Super 101
My Tears Will Go Away	Clouds (Bill Medley)	1964	Medley 1001
My Thanks	Hollywood Teeners, Jimmy Norman & the	1960	Fun 102
My Thoughts To You	Chancellors	1959	Storm 503
My Thrill Girl	Du Droppers	1953	Unreleased
My Time	Crests	1967	Parkway 118
My Time Ain't Long	King, Sleepy & group	1959	Symbol 904
My Time To Cry	Lovells	1967	Brent 7073
My Tired Feet	Fi-Tones	1956	Atlas 1056
My Treasure	Aquatones	1959, 1962	Fargo 1005/1022
My Tree	Four Bells	1954	Gem 220/Crystal 101
My Troubles Are Not At An End	Penguins	1956	Mercury 70799
My True Love	Brothers	1961	Checker 995
My True Love	Swans (St. Louis)	1953	Rainbow 233
My True Love And I	Moore, Sonny & group	1958	Old Town 1063
My True Story	Jive Five	1961	Beltone 1006/Relic 1026 (75)
My True Story	Platinums	1979	J & M 647
My True Story	Tempests	NA	Top 6 Hits EP 4
My True Story (acappella)	Islanders	1975	Relic LP 103
My Truest Love	Satellites, Dick & Slim & the	1959	Cool 113
My Turn	Servicemen	1967	Pathway 102
My Type Of Girl	Memos	1959	Memo 34891
My Unfaithful Love	Gants	1957	Aladdin 3387
My Usual Self	Casuals	NA	Kern 2755
My Valentine	Sweet Teens	1957	Gee 1030
My Valerie	Note-Torials	1959	Sunbeam 119
My Version Of Love	Vocaltones	1956	Apollo 497
My Very Own	Bluedots	1959	Hurricane 104
My Very Own	Vel-Aires, Donald Woods & the	1955	Flip 309
My Vow	Williams, Colly & group	1963	Poplar 118

SONG	GROUP	YEAR	LABEL
My Vow To You	Blue Sky Boys	1974	Blue Sky 109
My Vow To You	Embers, Jeff Milner & the	1959	Dale 114
My Vow To You	Students (Ohio)	1958	Note 10019/Checker 1004 (62)
My Wandering Love	Fortune, Johnny (with the Paramours)	1963	Park Ave. 4905
My Wandering Love	Paramours, Johnny Fortune & the	1964	Park Ave 4905
My Wants For Love	Five Royales	1956	King 4901
My Way Of Saying	Essentials, Billy & the	1966	Smash 2045
My Weakness	Capris (Philadelphia)	1956	20th Century 1201
My Wedding Day	Castelles	1955	Grand 122
My Whispering Heart	Edsels	1962	Dot 16311
My White Convertible	Hall Brothers	1958	Arc 4444
My Wife Can't Cook	Russ, Lonnie & group	1962	4-J 501
My Willow Tree	Shirelles	1962	Scepter LP 502
My Wish	Lonely Ones	1959	Baton 270/Sir 270 (59)
My Wishes	Corondolays, Chico & the	1965	Style 1927
My Woman	El Caminos, Mr. Lee & the	1964	Camelot 107/Nolta
My Yearbook	Bel-Aires (Chicago)	1958	Decca 30631
My Young And Foolish Heart	Four Friends	1957	Fee Bee 225
My Young Heart	Davis, Hal Sonny & group	1959	Alden 1301
Mysterious	Uniques	1960	Peacock 1695
Mysterious Teenage	Vels	1957	Trebco 16/Trebco 702 (57)
Mystery	Del Rios	1963	Rust 5066
Mystery	Echelons	1987	BAB 129
Mystery Man, The	Masters, Scotty Mann & the	1956	Peacock 1665
Mystery Of Love	Citations	1962, 1982	Canadian American 136
Mystery Of Love, The	Imaginations	1976, 1985	Harvey 101/Relic LP 505
Mystery Of The Night, The	Flips, Little Joey & the	1975	Monogram 111 (bootleg)
Mystery Of You, The	Platters	1957	Mercury 71184
Mystery Train	Nightcaps	1961	Vandan 7066

N

Na Na Hey Hey (Kiss Him Goodbye) (acappella)	Belmonts	1972	Buddah LP 5123
Nadine	Coronets	1953	Chess 1549
Nag	Halos	1961	7 Arts 709
Nagasaki	Five Chances	1954	Chance 1157
Naggity Nag	Pearls, Speedo & the	1959	Josie 865
Nag-Nag (Pack Your Bag)	Cashmeres (Brooklyn)	1959	ACA 1216/1217
Nails And Snails	Sugar Buns	1959	Warner Bros. 5046
Nairna Nairna	Melodeers	1961	Shelley 127
Name Song, The	Accents (California)	1956	Accent 1037
Nameless	Goofers	1959	Tiara 6127
Na-Na-Na	Friends, Morningside Drive &	1973	Laurie 3615
Nancy	Love Notes (Wilshire)	1963	Wilshire 200
Napoleon Bonaparte	Thomas, Vic (with the Four-Evers)	1964	Philips 40183
Nare	Goofers	1955	Coral 61431
Nashville, Tennessee	Sweet Nuthins	1964	Swan 4195
Nasty Breaks	Dandevilles	1959	Guyden 2014
Natalie	Dreamers (Yonkers, N.Y.)	1960	Goldisc 3015
Nationwide Stamps	Darchaes, Ben White & the	1962	Aljon 1247/1248/Coney Island
Native Girl	Native Boys	1954	Modern 939
(Native Girl) Elephant Walk	Delighters, Donald Jenkins & the	1963	Cortland 109
Natural Born Lover	Gum Drops	1956	King 4963
Natural Born Lover	Vets	1961	Swami 551/552
Natural, Natural Ditty	Jewels (Los Angeles)	1955	Imperial 5362
Natural Thing To Do, The	Golden Tones, Sticks Herman & the	1958	Goldband 1056
Nature Boy	Shields	1958	Tender 518/Dot 15856 (58)
Nature Of My Love, The	Coronados	1960	Columbia 41550
Nature's Beauty	Five Masqueraders, Seaphus Scott & the	1958	Joyce 303
Nature's Creation	Horizons, Sunny & the	1962	Luxor 1015
Nature's Creation	Valentines	1956	Rama 208
Naughty Naughty Baby	Monte, Vinnie & group	1958	Fargo 1000
Near You	Cardinals	1957	Atlantic 1126
Near You	Flamingos	1962	End 1116
Nearer My Heart	Sierras (Four Sierras)	1962	Knox 102

SONG	GROUP	YEAR	LABEL
Nearest Thing To Heaven	Frontiers	1961	King 5534
Nearest Thing To Heaven, The	Runarounds	1961	Pio 107
Nearest To My Heart	Duals	1959	Arc 4446
Nearness Of You, The	Lovenotes	1954	Unreleased
Nearness Of You, The	Roomates	1963	Philips 40153/Philips 40161 (63)
Nearness Of You, The	Zodiacs, Maurice Williams & the	1974	Relic LP 5017
Neckin'	Inspirations (Beltone)	1963	Beltone 2037
Necklace Of Roses	Chanticleers	1963	Old Town 1137
Necklace Of Tear Drops	Humdingers	1957	Dale 106
Need Someone	Desires	1962	Dee Impulse/Moneytown 602 (62)
Need You So	Casual Teens	1958	Felsted 8529
Need You To Help Me	Zel, Rita & group	1960	J&S 1685
Need You Tonight	Minorbops	1957	Lamp 2012
Need Your Love	Doug & Freddy (with the Pyramids)	1961	K&G 100
Need Your Love	El Reyes	1958	Jade 501
Need Your Love	Five Chances	1960	Corina 2002/P.S. 1510
Need Your Love	Flamingos	1955	Checker 830
Need Your Love	Metallics	1962	Baronet 2
Need Your Love	Shakers, Pepper & the	1966	Chetwyd 45002
Need Your Lovin'	Hawks, Ronnie Hawkins & the	1959	Roulette 4177
Needed (For Lovers Only)	Voice Masters	1959	Anna 102
Needles Of Evergreen	Tokens (Warner)	1968	Warner Bros. 7183
Needless	Clovers	1951	Atlantic 944
Neil's Twist	Marvels, Neil Sedaka & the	1962	Pyramid 623
Neither Rain Nor Snow	Rivieras	1958	Coed 508
Nek I Hok I	Cardinals	1956	Atlantic (unreleased)
Neki-Hokey	Cleftones	1956	Gee 1016
Nelda Jane	Cyclones, Bill Taylor & the	1958	Trophy 500
Nellie	Fabulous Idols	1961	Kenco 5011
Nellie	Invictas	1959	Jack Bee 1003
Nena	Denotations	1965	Lawn 253
Nervous	Fabulous Playboys	1960	Daco 1001/Apollo 758 (60)
Nervous	Nite Liters	1962	Verve 10256
Nervous About Love	Passions	1958	Dore 505
Nervous Auctioneer	Wilson, Robin & group	1960	Monument 426
Nervous Heart	Chimes (Reserve)	1957	Reserve 120
Nest Is Warm, The	Turbans (Philadelphia)	1955	Money 209
Never	Autumns	1966	Amber 856/Power
Never	Dedications	1983	Avenue D 9
Never	Dundees, Carlyle Dundee & the	1954	Space 201
Never	Earls	1963	Old Town 1133
Never	Guardians, Kempy & the	NA	Romunda 1/Lucky Sound 1006
Never	Nightriders	1956	Sound 128
Never	Oasis	1979	Story Untold 502
Never	Profiles	1965	Gait 1444
Never	Saints, Tom Allen & the	1961	Band Box 249
Never	Silhouettes	1961	20th Fox 240
Never	Strands	1962	Triode 101
Never A Moment	Chums, Mary Eustace & the	NA	Apt 25009
Never Again	Brooktones	1958	Coed 507
Never Again	Foster Brothers	1958	Hi Mi 3005
Never Again	Four Jacks, Lil Greenwood & the	1952	Federal 12093
Never Again	Imperials, Little Anthony & the	1966	DCP 1154/Veep 1245 (66)
Never Again	Magic Notes	1957	Era 1035
Never Again	Paradons	1960	Tuffest 102
Never Again	Planets	1957	Era 1038
Never Again	Supremes (Detroit)	1961	Tamla 54038
Never Again	Three Moods	1955	Sarg 124
Never Again	Trend-Tones	1959	Superb 100
Never Anymore	Rhythm Jesters, Bob Davis & the	1957	Rama 224
Never Be Another Boy Like You	Pearlettes	1961	Vee Jay 422/Go 712
Never Be Lonely	Cap-Tans	1951	Gotham 233
Never Been In Love Before	Camelots	1961	Nix 101
Never Before	Cameos (Pittsburgh)	1960	Matador 1813

SONG	GROUP	YEAR	LABEL
Never Bite Off More Than You Can Chew	Taylor, Andrew & group	1961	Gone 5109
Never Coming Back	Rockaways, Alicia & the	1956	Epic 9191
Never Doubt My Love	Sky Boys, Thurl Ravenscroft & the	1955	Fabor 4005
Never Ever	Spi-Dells	1966	Little Town 575
Never Felt Like This Before	Eskridge, Murrie & group	1961	Apex 7764
Never Felt Like This Before	Five Quails	1962	Harvey 116
Never Felt Like This Before	Sheppards (Chicago - Apex)	1959	Apex 7750
Never Fo'get	Tabs	1959	Noble 719/Gardena 110 (60)
Never For Me	Crystal Tones, Billy James & the	1959	M-Z 111
Never Give Up	Shirelles, Shirley & the	1969	Bell 815
Never Give Up Hope	Crickets, Dean Barlow & the	1954	Jay-Dee 789
Never Go To Mexico	Holidays	1958	Music City 818
Never Gonna Cry	Cinemas	1963	Dave 911
Never Gonna Leave Me	Carvettes	1959	Copa 200-1/200-2
Never Had A Chance	True Tones	1964	Spot 1115
Never Happen	Pedestrians, Jaywalker & the (featuring Pete Antell)	1962	Amy 848
Never In A Hundred Years	Royal, Billy Joe & group	1961	Fairlane 21009
Never In A Million Years	Blenders (New York)	1952	Decca 28241
Never In A Million Years	Honey Bees	1966	Wand 1141
Never In My Life	Upbeats	1957	Prep 119
Never In This World	Flamingos	1960	End LP 307
Never Kiss A Good Man Goodbye	Modern Red Caps, George Tindley & the	1965	Penntowne 101
Never Knew	Midnighters, Hank Ballard & the	1959	King 5275
Never Knew	Roomates	1961	Valmor 008
Never Leave Again	Tangents	1960	Fresh 2274
Never Leave Me	Carver, Bobby & group	1962	Coral 62337
Never Leave Me	Stratfords	1964	O'Dell 100
Never Leave Me Alone	Mondellos, Yul McClay & the	1957	Rhythm 105
Never Leave Me Baby	Orioles, Sonny Til & the	1956	Vee Jay 228
Never Leave The One You Love	Dee, Ronnie & group	1961	Wye 1008
Never Leave You Again	Inspirations, Maurice Williams & the	1963	Candi 1031
Never Let Her Go	Downbeats, Gene Terry & the	1959	Goldband 1081
Never Let Him Go	Carousels	1962	Gone 5131
Never Let Me Go	Bandmasters, Lou Rall & the	1964	Way Out (no number)
Never Let Me Go	Chantels	1958	End 1037
Never Let Me Go	Chordliners	1988	
Never Let Me Go	Dominoes, Joe Taylor & the	NA	HMF 2002
Never Let Me Go	Duprells	1960	
Never Let Me Go	Holman, Eddie & group	1966	Parkway 157
Never Let Me Go	Jackson, Chuck & group	1961	Atco 6197
Never Let Me Go	Jeffries, Bob (with the Mondellos)	1957	Rhythm 110
Never Let Me Go	Poets	1956, 1960	Shade 1001
Never Let Me Go	Roamers	1955	Savoy 1156
Never Let Me Go	Royaltones	1956	Old Town 1018
Never Let Me Go	Serenaders (New Jersey)	1957	Chock Full O' Hits 101/102/ MGM 12623 (58)
Never Let Me Go	Sheppards (Chicago - Pam)	1961	Pam 1001
Never Let Me Go	Sundowners, Big Jim & the	1962	Chip 1008
Never Let Me Go	Tempos (Four Eldorados)	1958	Rhythm 121
Never Let Me Go	Verdicts	1973	Vintage 1009
Never Let You Go	Ambers	1958	Ebb 142
Never Let You Go	Five Discs	1962	Cheer 1000
Never Let You Go	Imaginations	1985	Relic LP 5058
Never Let You Go	Street Corner Memories	1981	Clifton 64
Never Let You Go	Teenchords, Lewis Lymon & the	1994	Park Ave. 9
Never Let You Go	Tempests	1959	Williamette 103
Never Let You Go	Three D's	1957	Paris 508
Never Like This	Kapers, Paul London & the	1962	Check Mate 1006
Never Look Behind	Lovenotes	1957	Premium 411
Never Look Behind	True Loves	1957	Premium 611
Never Lose Faith In Me	Honey Boys	1956	Modern 980
Never Love Again	Elgins, Little Tommy & the	1962	Elmar 1084/ABC 10358 (62)
Never Love Another	Five Chimes	1955	Betta 2011

SONG	GROUP	YEAR	LABEL
Never More	Furys	1963	Mach IV 112
Never Never	Chiffons	1961	Wildcat 601
Never Never	Four Lovers	1956	RCA 6768
Never, Never	Jive Five	1961	Beltone 1014/Relic 1030 (78)
Never Never	Masterettes	1958	Le Sage 716
Never, Never	Paradons	1962	Milestone 2015
Never Never	Taylor, Johnny & group	1962	Sar 131
Never Never Land	Blue Notes	1958	Colonial 9999
Never Never Land	Pitch Pikes	1957	Mercury 71099
Never, Never, Never	Candies, Ace Kennedy & the	1963	Philips 40111
Never, Never, Never	Moonlighters	1958	Tara 102
Never No More	Colts	1956, 1959	Vita 130/Antler 4003
Never Take It Away	Redwoods	1961	Epic 9473
Never Till Now	Kings, Johnny & the	1961	Warwick 658
Never Too Late	Generals, Mickey Farrell & the	1960	Tammy 1009
Never Too Late	Williams, Eddie & group	1960	R-Dell 114
Never Too Young	Modern Red Caps	1966	Swan 4243
Never Too Young	TR 4	1966	Velvet Tone
Never Trust A Friend	McCoy, Van & group	1961	Rock'N 101
Never Turn Your Back	Five Royales	1965	Smash 1963
Never Wake Up	Keller, Jerry & group	1961	Capitol 4630
Never Was A Girl	Universals	1963	Kerwood
Never Will I Love You Again	Relatives	1963	Almont 306
Never Will Part	Silhouettes, Billy Horton & the	1959	Ace 563/Junior 400 (59)
Never You Mind	Tempos	1957	Kapp 199
Nevertheless	Hearts, Lee Andrews & the	1967	Crimson 1009
New Beat (acappella), The	Uniques	1975	Relic LP 108
New Fad	Untouchables	1960	Madison 128
New Gal	Moonlighters, Bobby Lester & the	1955	Checker 813
New Girl On My Block	Crestones, Jimmy & the	1964, 1985	Maria 101
New Hully Gully, The	Miller Sisters	NA	
New Hully Gully, The	Vibrations	1962	Checker 1011
New Kind Of Gold	Revelaires	1960	Crystalette 737
New Kind Of Gold	Talents	1961	Skylark 106
New Love	Baltineers	1956	Teenage 1000
New Love	Cole, Ann (with the Suburbans)	1956	Baton 224
New Love	Impressions	1960	Abner 1034
New Love	Jayhawks	1958, 1974	Eastman 798
New Love I Have Found	Fabulous Uptones	1962	Tulip 100
New Love Tomorrow (acappella)	Citadels	1975	Relic LP 102
New Me	Bon-Aires	1976	Catamount 130
New Moon	Premiers (Los Angeles)	1956	Dig 106
New Rockin' Baby	Chanteurs	1961	La Salle 501
New Trucking, The	Holidays	1961	Lyons 107
New Way (Shu-Wop), The	Danderliers	1955	States 150/B&F 150 (61)
New Year's Eve	Cameos (Philadelphia)	1957	Cameo 123
New Year's In, The	Blue Chips	1961	Laurel 1026
New Year's Resolution	Faces	1965	Iguana 601
New York City Lady	Chimes (Brooklyn)	1986	Freedom 223
New York Honky Tonk	Shades, Joey & the	NA	Wild 905
New York Sound, Pt. 1, The	Fairlanes	1964	Radiant 104
Newly Wed	Orchids	1955	Parrot 815
Next Fall	Four Of A Kind	1961	Rex 104
Next Four Years, The	Hi-Lites (Mercury)	1956	Mercury 70987
Next Spring	Desires	1958	Herald (unreleased)
Next Time	Dreamers, Richard Berry & the	1963	Crown LP 5371
Next Time We Meet	Blazers (Johnny Moore's)	1956	Hollywood 1056
Next Time You See Me	Nitecaps	1966	Vandan 4280
Next Time You See Me, The	Blue Notes, Little Bill & the	1961	Bolo 725
Next To You	Cufflinks	1962	Gait 543
Next Year	Gliders, Glen Pace & the	1960	ABC 10091
Nice And Cozy	Deputees, Peter Marshall & the	1956	Melba 103
Nice Guy	Partylights, Shona & the	1963	Chicory 1601
Nice Guys	Street Corner Symphony	1975	Bang 722
Nickel, Three Dimes and Five Quarters	Royal Jokers	1960	Keldon 322

SONG	GROUP	YEAR	LABEL
Nickelodian Tango	Triads	1956	Encino 1002
Nicotine	Emeralds, Paul Chaplain & His	1960	Harper 100
Night	Quotations	1974	Downstairs 1003
Night After Night	Blendells	1968	Cotillion 44020
Night After Night	Derbys	1959	Mercury 71437
Night After Night	Rhythm Kings	1949	Ivory 751
Night After Night	Royal Jacks	1959	Studio 9903
Night After Night	Young Lads	1963	Felice 909/Felice 712 (63)
Night Air	Four Mints	1956	Choctaw 8002/Imperial 5432 (57)
Night Air	Mints	1956	Lin 5007/Imperial 5432 (57)
Night And Day	Cabot, Johnny & group	1962	Columbia 42283
Night Angel	Teenettes, Betty Jayne & the	1961	Carellen 102
Night Before Christmas, The	Playboys	1963	Legato 101
Night Before Last	Tone Deafs, Dean Barlow & the	NA	Beltone
Night Curtains	Checkers	1952	King 4581
Night Has Come	Hearts, Billy Austin & the	1953	Apollo 444
Night Is Over, The	Gems (Win)	1958	Win 701
Night Is Quiet, The	Vocaleers	1960	Vest 832
Night Is Young, The	Deeps	1957	Que 1000
Night Moon	Crowns, Danny & the	1963	Mercury 72096
Night Owl	Clarendons, Lee & the	NA	H.S.
Night Owl	Clouds (Bill Medley)	1964	Medley 1001
Night Owl	Dukays	1975	Monogram 102
Night Owl	Paris, Bobby & group	1966	Cameo 396
Night Party	Rock-A-Fellas, Eddie Bell & the	1959	Coed 512
Night Rider	Casanovas	NA	Apollo LP 1004/Relic LP 5073 (87)/ Relic LP 5075 (88)
Night Rider	Intentions	1967	Philips 40428
Night Ridin'	Night Riders	1960	Sue 731
Night, The	Capri, Bobby & group	1963	Johnson 126
Night, The	Five Diamonds	1977	Treat 9/10
Night, The	Memory Lane	1982	Crystal Ball 149
Night, The	Nacks, Nicky & the	1962	Barry 108
Night, The	Velvet Satins, Bobby Capri & the	1963, 1976	Johnson 126
Night Time Is The Right Time	Carnations	1955	Savoy 1172
Night Time Is The Time	Smith, Jimmie & group	1959	Flip 347
Night Train	Kids From Cleveland	1957	Whippet 204
Night Train	Stars	1959	Vega 002
Night Train	Swans (St. Louis)	1955	Ballad 1006
Night We Both Said Goodbye, The	Upbeats	1958	Joy 223
Night We First Met, The	Newports	1978	Crystal Ball 113
Night We Met, The	Three Emotions	1959	Fury 1026
Night Winds	Strangers	1964	Warner Bros. 5438
Nightcap Rock	Nitecaps	1960	Vandan 7491
Nightlite	Del-Tinos	1964	Sonic 1451
Nightmare	Sinners	1962	Eden 1
Nightmare	Velvets (Texas)	1964	Monument 836
Nights Are So Lonely	Mar-Villes	1962	Infinity 027
Nights Of Ecstasy	Eldorays	1961	Bud 114
Nightspot	Teenbeats	1961	Myrl 407
Niki Niki Mambo	Nutones	1955	Hollywood Star 797
Nina	Consorts, Les Levo & the	1959	Nina 1601
Nina	Rocky Fellers	1964	Warner Bros. 5469
900 Quetzals	Hushabyes, Hale & the	1964	Apogee 104/Reprise 0299
Nine More Miles	Checkers	1958	King 5156
Nine Out Of Ten	Ivy Three	1961	Shell 302
Nine To Five	Regan, Tommy & female group	1965	World Artists 1049
$19.50 Bus	Five Crowns	1952	Rainbow 184
90 Pound Weakling	Dots, Lenny Capello & the	1962	Ric 991
99 Guys	Maples	1954	Blue Lake 111
Nip Sip	Clovers	1955	Atlantic 1073
Nip Sip	Diamonds	1955	Coral 61502
Nita	Monitors	1958	Circus 219
Nita, I Need You So	Consoles, Bobby & the	1963	Diamond 141
Nite Owl	Champs, Tony Allen & the	1955	Specialty 560

SONG	GROUP	YEAR	LABEL
Nite Owl	Dukays	1962	Nat 4002/Vee Jay 430 (62)
Nite Owl	Tren-Dells	1962	Jam 1100/Capitol 4852 (62)
Nitey Nite	Majestics (Florida)	1956	Marlin 802
No	Ladelles	NA	Debonair 1218
No	Spiedels	1958	Crosley 201
No Baby	Montclairs	1963	ABC 10463
No Chance	Cadillacs	1955	Josie 773
No Changes	Sensations, Yvonne Baker & the	1962	Argo 5420
No Chemise Please	Granahan, Gerry & group	1958	Sunbeam 102
No Darlin' No	Delltones	NA	Maestro 1919
No Dice	Bell Notes	1959	Time 1017
No Doubt About It	Chanteurs	1963	Bolo 745
No Doubt About It	Shirelles	1967	Scepter 12198
No Doubt About It	Smoothtones	1955	Jem 412
No End	Alteers	1964	G-Clef 705
No End To Love	Voices, Frankie Bearse & the	1964	Olimpic 247
No End To True Love	Arrows, Joe Lyons & the	1956	Hollywood 1071
No Evil	Combo-Nettes, Clemons Penix & the	1956	Combo 117
No Fool Am I	Companions	1962	Amy 852
No Girl For Me	Rogers, Dan & group	1964	Era 3131
No Good	Mello-Harps	1959	Casino 104
No Got De Woman	Charms, Otis Williams & his	1957	DeLuxe 6130
No Greater Love	Belltones, Ronnie Dove & the	1962	Jalo 1406
No Greater Love	Embers, Jeff Milner & the	1959	Dale 113
No Greater Love	Romancers	1961	Celebrity 701/Beacon 701
No Greater Miracle	Harptones	1960	Warwick 551
No Guy	Honey Bees	1964	Vee Jay 611
No Hard Feelings	Dials	1961	Hilltop 219
No Hard Feelings	Five Spenders	1960	Versatile 113/Kayo 101
No Hard Feelings	Parliaments, Sammy & the	1960	Arnold 1001
No Help Wanted	Crows	1953	Rama 3
No I Won't	Torches	1965	Ring-O 302
No I Won't Believe It	Visions, Connie McGill & the	1963	United International 1009
(No) I Won't Cry Any More	Moonrays, Lee Williams & the	1960	King 5409
No It Ain't	Royals	1953	Federal 12133
No Kissin' And A Huggin'	Pharaohs, Richard Berry & the	1956	Flip 318
No Letter From You	Stars	1959	Vega 002
No Lies	Kokomos (with the Four Seasons)	1962	Josie 906
No Love	Mondells, Johnny C & the	1972	Saluda 106
No Love Like Her Love	McPhatter, Clyde (with the Cookies & the Cues)	1958	Atlantic 1170
No Mail Today	Downbeats, Gene Terry & the	1959	Goldband 1081
No, Mama, No	Larks (North Carolina)	1955	Apollo 475
No Man Is An Island	Dreamers (Philadelphia)	1954	Rollin' 5/Rollin' 1001 (55)
No Matter	Blazers, Jimmy Feagans & the	1961	Howard 501
No Matter	Five Keys	1965	Inferno 4500
No Matter	Tantones	1957	Lamp 2002
No Matter What	McPhatter, Clyde (with the Cookies & the Cues)	1957	Atlantic 1133
No Matter What I Do	Casher, Billy & group	1961	Epic 9478
No Matter What Shape	Upsetters	NA	Hit 237
No Matter What You Are	Platters	1958	Mercury 71383/Mercury 10001 (58)
No Mistakin' It	Adams, Richie & group	1961	Beltone 1001
No Money	Apollos, Bobby Charles & the	1962	Tide 1084/1085
No Money	Blue Diamonds (Ernie K-Doe Kador)	1954	Savoy 1134
No Money	Devilles	1962	Arrawak 1001
No Money No Luck Blues	Continentals (Vandan)	NA	Vandan 8067
No More	Uptones	1962	Lute 6225
No More	Vistas, Little Victor & the	1962	Rendezvous 183
No More Doggin'	Starlites	1961	Fury 1045
No More Heart	Starlites, Jackie & the	1991	Relic LP 5090
No More Heartaches	Stereophonics	1958	Apt 25003
No More Kisses For Baby	Ravens	NA	National (unreleased)
No More Knockin'	Genies	1959	Hollywood 69
No More Loneliness	Mellows, Carl Spencer & the	1956	Candlelight 1012

SONG	GROUP	YEAR	LABEL
No More Love	Possessions	1964	Britton 1003/Parkway 930 (64)
No More Love For You	Perfections	NA	Pam-O 101
No More Pain	Hi-Tones	1961	Fonsca 202
No More Sorrows	Solitaires	1957	Old Town 1049
No More Tears	Fabulous Five Flames	1960	Time 1023
No More Tears	Girlfriends	1963	Melic 4125
No More Tears	Jones, Davey & group	1959	Glades 601
No More Tears	Lovenotes, Sybil Love & the	1959	Valex 505
No More Tears	Prisonaires	1976	Sun 512
No More Tears	Sweethearts	1966	Kent 442
No More Tears	Tibbs, Kenneth & group	1958	Federal 12335
No More Teasing	Spydels	1961	MZ 103/MZ 009
No More Tomorrows	Chiffons	1961	Wildcat 601
No More Will I Cry	Olympics	1965	Loma 2017
No Need For Crying	Pal, Ricki & group	1958	Arwin 115
No, No	Fabulaires	1957	East West 103/Main Line 103 (58)
No No	Sweethearts	1963	Brunswick 55265
No No Blues	Coronados	1957	Vik 0265
No No Cherry	Turbans (Oakland)	1955	Money 209
No No Don't Cry	Young Ones	1963	Yussels 7703
No, No, I Can't Stop	Thrillers, Little Joe & the	1963	Reprise 20142
No, No More	Strays, Ray & the	1962	Larric 101
No, No, Never Again	Opals	1965	Laurie 3288
No, No, No	Chanters (New York)	1961, 1963	DeLuxe 6191/6200
No, No, No	Chanters, Bud Johnson & the	1958	DeLuxe 6177
No No No	Dovells	1961, 1963	Parkway 819/889
No No No	Impressors	1957	Onyx 514
No No No	Revivals	1991	N/A
No No No	Standards	1963	Debro 3178/Roulette 4487 (63)
No, No, No	Street-Tones, Patty & the	1980	Clifton 49
No Not Again	Jive Five	1962	Beltone 2019/Relic 1027 (75)
No Not Much	Four Jacks, Ben Joe Zeppa & the	1956	Gilmar 278
No Not Now	Mixmasters, Sonny Fulton & the	1959	Sunbeam 125
No Obligation	Dreamers (Manhattan)	1956	Manhattan 503
No One	Allen, Tony & group	1988	Classic Artists 102
No One	Dubs	1959	ABC 10056
No One	Emmets	1959	Addison 15002
No One	Gordon, Gary & group	1959	Fleetwood 1002
No One	Jades, Emmett & the	1961	Rustone 1405
No One	Rios, Augie & group	1964	Shelley 186
No One But You	Dynamics	1959	Capri 104
No One But You	Dynamos	1964	Azuza 1002
No One But You	Fantasys	1960	Guyden 2029
No One But You	Wheels	1960	Roulette 4271
No One But You	Medlin, Joe & group	1957	King 5054
No One Can Take Your Place	Dawns, Billy Horton & the	1970	KayDen 403
No One Cares	Gunga Dins	NA	Busy-B 2
No One Cares For Me	Firesiders	1961	Swan 4074
No One Else Will Do	Sunliners, Sunny & the	1964	Tear Drop 3027/3123
No One Ever Loved Me	Four Pals	1956	Royal Roost 616
No One Ever Tells You	Crystals (Brooklyn)	1962	Philles 105
No One For Me	Interludes	1960	Valley 106
No One Has Eyes For Me	Saints, Danny & the	1959	Warner Bros. 5134
No One Knows	Belmonts, Dion & the	1958	Laurie 3015
No One Knows	Excitements, Elroy & the	1961	Alanna 188/Alanna 565 (63)
No One Knows	Five Satins	1963	Sammy 103
No One (No One But You)	Lions	1960	Everest 19388/Mark IV 1
No One To Love	Crests (with Johnny Maestro)	1957	Joyce 105/Times Square 2 (62)
No One To Love Me	Sha-Weez	1953	Aladdin 3170
No One To Tell Her	Highlites	1965	Pit 403
No One Will Ever Know	Omegas	1960	Decca 31138
No One's Gonna Help You	Daylighters	1963	Checker 1051
No One's Waiting For Me	DiMucci, Dion (with the Del Satins)	1963	Columbia 42917
No Other Arms	Arrows	1964	Hugo 1174
No Other Girl	Larks (North Carolina)	1954	Lloyds 112

SONG	GROUP	YEAR	LABEL
No Other Guy	Dew Drops	1963	Jeff 1963
No Other Love	Blossoms	1958	Capitol 4072
No Other Love	Fi-Dells	1957	Warner 1014
No Other Love	Holidays	1961	Brent 7018
No Other Love (Like Yours)	Copycats, Suzy & the	1961	Brent 7020
No Other One	Lamplighters	NA	Unreleased
No Parking	Bengals, Bobby & the	1960	B&W 1
No Parking	Moroccos, Lillian Brooks & the	1956	King 4956
No Parking	Nitecaps	1961	Vandan 3587
No Pork In The Beans	Castle-Tones	1959	Rift 502
No Power On Earth	Platters	NA	Mercury EP 3353
No Reason	Accidentals	1962	Beau Monde 1633
No Regrets	Barnes, Jimmy & group	1959	Gibraltar 101
No Regrets	Emperors	1958	3-J 121
No Regrets	Gibralters, Jimmy Barnes & the	1958	Gibraltar 101
No Rock And Rollin' Here	Counts, Frankie Brent & the	1960	Strand 25014
No Room	Dominoes	1952	Federal 12105
No Room	Pharaohs, Richard Berry & the	1959	Flip 349
No! Says My Heart	Dominoes	1951	Federal 12010
No Says My Heart	Five Keys	1960	King 5358
No Secret Now	Hood, Darla (with the Rocketeers)	1957	Encino 1007/Acama 122 (60)
No Shoulder To Cry On	Jewels (Los Angeles)	1974	Imperial LP only
No Stone Unturned	Bystanders	1956	Dot 15512
No Stoppin' This Boppin'	Tunerockers	1958	Pet 804
No Story Unturned	Four Horsemen	1953	MGM 11566
No Sweet Lovin'	Drifters (1959-forward)	1961	Atlantic 2105
No Tears	Tonettes	1962	Volt 101
No Tears Left For Crying	West Siders	1963	Leopard 5004/United Artists 600 (63)
No There Ain't No News Today	Penguins	1954	Dootone 345
No Time	Slades	1958	Domino 800
No Time	Titans	1959	Class 244
No Time For Fun	Falcons (Detroit)	1985	Relic LP 8005
No Time For Love	Commands	NA	Back Beat 570
No Time For Lovin'	Four Nuggets	1963	Songbird 204
No Time For Tears	Cones, Connie & the	1960	Roulette 4313
No Time For Tears	Startones	NA	N/A
No Time For You	Commands	1964	Dynamic 104
No Time To Lose	Grand Prees	NA	Scotty 825
No Treason In My Heart	Sun-Rays, Cliff & the	1960	Zil 9002
No Twistin' On Sunday	Zircons	1962	Federal 12452
No Use	Shadows	1953	Decca 28765
No Use In Crying	Restless Hearts, Fred Parris & the	1965	Checker 1108
No Wonder	Pacers	1961, 1980	Guyden 2064
No You For Me	Climates	1967	Sun 404
Noah's Ark	Classics (Karen)	NA	Karen 316
Nobody But Betty	G-Clefs	1964	Regina 1319
Nobody But Me	Drifters (1959-forward)	1960	Atlantic 2071
Nobody But Me	Epitomes, Buford Busbee & the	1959	Dee Dee 101
Nobody But Me	Tucker, Frank & group	1956	Baton 234
Nobody But Me And My Girl	Royal Halos	1959	Aladdin 3460
Nobody But The Lord	Sensationals, Jimmy Jones & the	1959	Savoy 4126
Nobody But You	Clark, Dee (with the Kool Gents)	1958	Abner 1019
Nobody But You	Hawks	1954	Imperial 5306
Nobody But You	Lafayettes	1962	RCA 8044
Nobody But You	Petites	1961	Elmor 304
Nobody But You	Strollers	1960	Dart 1017
Nobody But You	T-Birds	1967	Vegas 720
Nobody But You	Tokens (Brooklyn)	1965	B.T. Puppy 505
Nobody But You	Trinkets	1963	Cortland 111
Nobody But You	Versatiles, Tootsie & the	1962	Elmar 6000
Nobody But You And Me	Starlites, Eddie & the	1972	Bim Bam Boom 102
Nobody Can Love You	Supremes (Ohio)	1958	Mark 129
Nobody Cares (About Me)	Washington, Baby & group	1961	Neptune 122
Nobody Heard About Me	Corsells	1964	Hudson 8104
Nobody In Mind	McVea, Jack	1955	Combo 90

SONG	GROUP	YEAR	LABEL
Nobody Knows	Carter, Martha & group	1961	Ron 336
Nobody Knows	Compliments, Michael Zara & the	1963	Shell 313
Nobody Knows	Crystalaires	1963	Sound Souvenir 1/2
Nobody Knows	Escapades	1964	Glow 87896
Nobody Knows	Tejuns	NA	100 Proof 144
Nobody Knows	Zodiacs, Maurice Williams & the	1965	Scepter 12113
Nobody Knows What's Going On	Chiffons	1965	Laurie 3301
Nobody Loves Me	Creations, Bobby Richardson & the	1961	Ember 1076
Nobody Loves Me	Leaders	1956	Glory 239
Nobody Loves Me Like You	Flamingos	1960	End 1068
Nobody Loves You Like I Do	Rays	1957	XYZ 100
Nobody Loves You Like-A Me	Four Holidays	1959	United Artists 163 (unreleased)
Nobody Made You Love Me	Charts	1966	Wand 1124
Nobody Nowhere	Crystalaires	1963	
Nobody Wants Me	Four Sounds	1962	Ran-Dee
Nobody Wants You Anymore	Classics Four, Bob Gerardi & the	1960	Recorte 441
Nobody's Baby After You	Shirelles	1967	Scepter 12185
Nobody's Business If I Do	Cavaliers	1958	Gilt-Edge 3935
Nobody's Fault	Nite Riders, Melvin Smith & the	1962	Chime 101
Nobody's Fault But Mine	White, Charlie Group	1958	Winley 229
Nobody's Going Out With Me	Dynamics	1959	Dynamic Sound 504
Nobody's Here	Cap-Tans	NA	International Award LP AK222
Nobody's Home	Hearts, Lee Andrews & the	1958	Casino 452/United Artists 123 (58)
Nobody's Kisses But Yours	Del Vikings	1958	Mercury LP 30353
Nobody's Love	Flamingos	1959	Checker LP 3005/Chess LP 1433 (59)
Nobody's Loving Me	Swallows (Maryland)	1953	King 4632
Nobody's Sweetheart	Flips, Mario & the	1959	Cross Country 100
Noise	Crowns, Stark Whiteman & the	1960	Sho-Biz 1004
Noise	Triumphs, Tico & the	1963	Amy 876
Noisy Clock	Four Sounds	1957	Celeste 3013
Noisy Clock	Mellows, Lillian Leach & the	1974	Celeste 3011
Nona	Feathers	1954	Show Time 1104
None Of Your Tears	Accents, Ted Newman & the	1957	Rev 3511
Nonsense	Matadors	1961	Duchess 1005
Non-Support	Troupers	1959	Red Top 118
Norma Jean	Duprees	1965	Columbia 43464
Norman	Lollypops	1960	Kandee 6001
North By Northeast	Five Notes, Sammy & the	1960	Lucky Four 1010
Northeast End Of The Corner	DiMucci, Dion (with the Del Satins)	1961	Laurie 3081
Northern Star	Elites	1959	Abel 225
Nosey Neighbors	Vibraharps	1959	Atco 6134
Nosy Neighbor	Larktones	1960	Riki 140
Nosy Rosy	Henderson, Floyd & group	1959	Triangle 51315
Not A Day Goes By	Commodores	1957	Challenge 1004
Not A Hand To Shake	Five Jets	1953	DeLuxe 6018
Not A Letter	Passionettes	1958	Unreleased
Not Again	Exciting Invictas	1960	Kingston 427
Not Even Judgment Day	Sunliners, Sunny & the	1963	Tear Drop 3022/Sunglow 111
Not For All The Money In The World	Shirelles	1963	Scepter 1248
Not Going To Cry	Five Royales	1961	Home Of The Blues 232
Not Good Enough	Chapelaires	1961	Hac 101
Not Me	Individuals (with the Merceedees)	1962	Gold Seal 1000
Not Me Baby	New Silhouettes	1968	Goodway 101/Goodway LP 100
Not Other Love	Mighty Dukes	1952	Duke 104
Not Tomorrow	Delicates	1961	Roulette 4321
Not Too Long Ago	Uniques	1965	Paula 219
Not Too Much Twist	Viceroys	1964	Bethlehem 3088
Not Too Young	Four Starlings	1972	Dreamtone 202
Not Too Young To Get Married	Blue Jeans, Bob B. Soxx & the	1963	Philles 113
Not Too Young To Sing The Blues	Tyson, Roy & group	1963	Double L 723
Not Wanted	Guytones	1957	DeLuxe 6152
Note In The Bottle, The	Du Droppers, Sunny Gale & the	1953	RCA 5543
Note That I Wrote, The	Saber, Johnny & group	1962	Hitsville 1137
Nothin'	Kittens Five	1964	Herald 588
Nothin'	Twilighters (Bronx, N.Y.)	1961	Eldo 115

SONG	GROUP	YEAR	LABEL
Nothin' Shakin' Baby	Four Buddies	1952	Unreleased
Nothin' To Do	Mellows	1954	Jay-Dee 793
Nothin' To Wear	Three D's	1959	Brunswick 55152
Nothing Beats My Girl	Anastasia & group	1961	Stasi 1001
Nothing But Good	Midnighters, Hank Ballard & the	1961	King 5535
Nothing But Love	Tartans	1966	Impact 1010
Nothing But Love	Tears	1956	Dig 112
Nothing But Love Can Save Me	Fawns	1967	Capacity 105
Nothing But Love, Love, Love	Four Coachmen	1959	Castle 507
Nothing But Nothing	Dontells	1965	Vee Jay 666
Nothing But The Two-Step	Lovers, Little Louie & the	1962	Viscount 102
Nothing Can Change My Love For You	Bandits	1963	Emjay 1928/1935
Nothing Can Compare To You	Velvet Satins	1965	General American 006
Nothing Can Go Wrong	Domineers	1960	Roulette 4245
Nothing Else Matters	Discorders	1957	Stepheny 1806
Nothing In Return	Belmonts	1964	Sabina 521
Nothing Is Too Good For You	Harvey Boys	1956	Cadence 1306
Nothing Like a Little Love	Solitaires	1956	Old Town 1032
Nothing Matters Anymore	Fortunes	1961	Queen 24010
Nothing Means More To Me	Gainors	1960	Mercury 71630/Mercury 71632
Nothing Sweet As You	Toppers, Bobby Mitchell & the	1955	Imperial 5326
Nothing Sweeter	Flames, Alton & the	NA	Duchess
Nothing To Offer You	Fenways	1964	Bevmar 401/Ricky L 10
Now	Vel-Tones	1960, 1961	Zara 901/Lost Nite 103 (65)
Now	Yachtsmen	1958	Destiny 402
Now Ain't That A Shame	Astros, Pepe & the	1961	Swami 553/554
Now And Always	Clippers	1961	Tri 211
Now And For Always	Mystics	1965	Dot 16862
Now And Then	Juniors, Danny & the	1962	Guyden 2076
Now Baby Don't Do It	Royaltones, El Pauling & the	1960	Federal 12396
Now Darling	Capistranos, John Littleton & the (with James Brown)	1958	Duke 179
Now Don't That Prove I Love You	Five Keys	1956	Capitol 3597
Now He's Gone	Dream Girls, Bobbie Smith & the	1962	Big Top 3129
Now I Cry	Peppermints	1965	Peppermint 1001
Now I Know	Keynotes	1956, 1957	Apollo 498/513
Now I Know	Mandells	NA	Trans World 695
Now I Know	Martin, Kenny & group	1959	Federal 12350
Now I Know I Love You	Five Keys	1960	King LP 692
Now I Pray	Dells	1979, 1984, 1985	Solid Smoke LP 8029/ Charly LP 1055 (85)
Now I Wonder	Five Royales	1955	King 4785
Now I'm Broken Hearted	Loreleis	1955	Dot 15268
Now I'm Telling You	Legends	1958	Hull 727
Now Is The Hour	Radiants, Little Jan & the	1960, 1961	Clock 1028/Goldisc G15
Now Is The Hour	Secrets	1960	Columbia 41861
Now Is The Time	Impacts	1959	Watts 5599
Now It's All Over	Holidays, Buddy Sheppard & the	1963	Sabina 510
Now It's Your Turn	Blends	1960	Casa Grande 5037
Now I've Confessed	Deli-Cados	1960	PMP
Now I've Got You	Friends, Dante & his	1962	Imperial 5827
Now Look At Who's Crying	Four Chymes	1963	Musicnote 121
Now, Now, Now	Esquires	1954	Epic 9024
Now, Only Me	Rob Roys	1960	Columbia 41650
Now That I Have You	Willows	1961	Four Star 1753
Now That I Need You	Hurricanes	1957	King 5042
Now That It's Over	Falcons (Quality)	1957	Quality 1721/Falcon 1006 (57)/ Abner 1006 (57)
Now That I've Found You	Robins, Mike Robin & the	NA	Clarity 105
Now That I've Lost You	Baby Dolls	1966	Boom 60002
Now That She's Gone	King Crooners	1959	Excello 2168
Now That Summer Is Here	Mystics	1982	Ambient Sound 02871
Now That Summer Is Here	Videls	1960	Tic Tac Toe 5005/JDS 5005 (60)
Now That We Broke Up	Dubs	1961	End 1108
Now That You're Gone	Expressions	1956	Teen 101

SONG	GROUP	YEAR	LABEL
Now That You're Gone	George, Othea (with the Volumes)	1962	Chex 1008
Now That You're Gone	Hollywood Flames	1959	Ebb 162
Now That You're Gone	Jesters	1958	Cyclone 5011
Now That You're Gone	Three Friends	1957	Lido 504
Now That You're Gone	Tribunes	1962	Derrick 502
Now That You're Mine	Expressions, Johnny & the	1966	Josie 955
Now That You've Gone	El Dorados	1956	Vee Jay 180
Now The Parting Begins	Larados	1957	Fox 963
Now We Know	Velvets, Bobby & the	1959	Rason 501
Now We're One	Rinky-Dinks (with Bobby Darin)	1958	Atco 6121/Brunswick 55073
Now We're Together	El Venos	1956	Groove 0170
Now You Cry	Fabulous Four	1964	Brass 311/Coral 62479 (64)
Now You Did It	Verdicts	1973	Vintage 1009
Now You Have To Cry Alone	Arabians	1960	Lanrod 1605
Now You Know (I Love You So)	Channels, Earl Lewis & the	1956	Whirlin' Disc 100/Port 70014 (59)
Now You Say We Are Through	Hall Brothers	1958	Arc 4444
Now You Tell Me	Cupids	1958	Aladdin 3404
Now You're Gone	Dardenelles	1953	Entre 102
Now You're Gone	Laddins	1957	Central 2602/Times Square 3 (61)
Now You're Talking Baby	Boys Next Door	1956	Rainbow 349
Nowhere On Earth	Charms, Otis Williams & his	1957	DeLuxe 6130
Nowhere To Go	Gondoliers, Johnny Adams & the	1960	Ric 963
Nowhere To Go	Heatwaves	1965	Josie 941
Number One Baby	Eagleaires		J.O.B. 1104
Number One In The Nation	Interludes	1961	ABC 10213
Number One Song In The Country	Fenways	1964	Ricky L 106
Number One With Me	Crests	1962	Selma 311
Nunca (Never)	Latin Lads, Julito & the	1963	Rico-Vox 27
Nursery Love	Freeloaders, Little Prince & the	1973	M&M 1263
Nursery Rhyme	Emperors	1958	3-J 121
Nursery Rhyme Rock	Demensions	1960	Mohawk 116
Nursery Rhymes	Ebb Tides, Nino & the	1961	Madison 151
Nursery Rhymes	Gems (Win)	1958	Win 701
Nursery, The	Four J's	1963	4-J 506
Nutmegs Medley	Masters, Rick & the	1992	Clifton 104
Nuts 'N' Sprinkles	Bop Shop	NA	Larric 7301
Nuttin' In The Noggin'	Classics (Brooklyn)	1961	Streamline 1028
Nylon Stockings	Drifters (1959-forward)	1965	Atlantic 2310

O

SONG	GROUP	YEAR	LABEL
O Holy Night	Dominoes	1965	King 6016
O Holy Night	Juniors, Danny & the	1960	Swan 4064
O, Tell Me	Youngtones	1958	Brunswick 55089
Oasis	Majestics (Florida)	1962	Chess 1802
Oasis	Murraymen	1955	Arcade 131
O-Bop, She-Bop	Dells	1957	Vee Jay 251
Occarina Roll, The	Capri Sisters	1956	Jubilee 5244
Ocean Blue	Sophomores (Massachusetts)	1957	Dawn 223
Ocean Of Tears	Golden Tones	1960	Hush 102
Octopus' Garden	Delrons, Reperata & the	1971	Laurie 3589
Of Love	Juniors, Danny & the	1959	ABC 10052
Off Shore	Cardinals	1956	Atlantic 1090
Off Shore	Crenshaws	1961	Warner Bros. EP 5505
Off The Mountain	Magnificents	1957	Vee Jay 235
Off-Day Blues	Cuff Links	1957	Dootone 414
Oh! Babe!	Five Keys	1953	Aladdin 3214
Oh Babe	Jaywalkers	1962	Pam 210
Oh Babe	Poe Rats, Al Downing & the	1958	Challenge 59006
Oh Babe!	Ravens (Nancy Reed)	1950	
Oh Baby	Algers, Skip & Fruit & the	1960	Northern 3730
Oh Baby	Belairs	1963	Times Square 8
Oh Baby	Browne, Doris (with the Capris)	1953	Gotham 290
Oh Baby	Chrystalights	1953	Sunset 1141
Oh Baby	Creations	1967	Globe 1000
Oh Baby	Del Vikings	1958	Mercury LP 30353

SONG	GROUP	YEAR	LABEL
Oh, Baby	Del-Prados	1962	Lucky Four 1021
Oh Baby	Falcons (Detroit)	1963	Atlantic 2207
Oh Baby	Five Kids	1955	Maxwell 101
Oh Baby	Jesters	1958	Winley 225
Oh Baby	Jive Five	1982	Ambient Sound 02742
Oh Baby	Majors, Jesse Powell & the	1958	Josie 845
Oh Baby	Nobles, Nicky & the	1976	Klik
Oh Baby	Original Mustangs, Dolores Curry & the	1959	Hi-Q 5040
Oh Baby	Regents	1961	Gee 1075
Oh Baby	Rondels	1981	Clifton 58
Oh Baby	Satellites, Joe Nettles & the	NA	Circle 1174
Oh Baby	Softwinds	1961	Hac 105
Oh Baby	Speidels	1960	Monte Carlo 101
Oh, Baby!	Tangiers (Los Angeles)	1956	Decca 29971
Oh Baby	Tri-Five, John Lythgoe & the	1961	Varbee 2002
Oh, Baby	Velvetiers	1958	Ric 958
Oh, Baby, Come Dance With Me	Diatones	1960	Bandera 2509
Oh Baby Don't	Four Sevilles	1980	Starlight 10
Oh Baby Don't	Heartbeats	1956	Hull 720/Rama 216 (57)
Oh Baby (Don't Keep Chasing Me)	Lullabies, Tommy Tucker & the	1975	Kelway 111
Oh Baby Love	Roomates	1961	Valmor 010
Oh Baby Love	Twilights	1959	Finesse 1717
Oh Baby Mine	Dreamlovers	1964	Cameo 326
Oh Baby Oh	Romeos	1989	Relic LP 5078
Oh Baby Please	Telegrams	1978	Creole 163
Oh Baby You	Funkytones, Vincent MacRee & the	1957	Gametime 110
Oh Boy	Adorables	1965	Golden World 25
Oh Boy	Glens, Billy & the	1959	Jaro 77006
Oh Boy	Rainbows, Sonny Spencer & the	1959	Memo
Oh Boy	Rhythm Rockers	1960	Satin 921
Oh Boy	Spencer, Sonny & group	1959	Memo 17984
Oh Boy, What A Girl	Visions	1962	Mercury 72188
Oh, But She Did	El Capris	1956	Bullseye 102/Argyle 1010 (61)
Oh, But She Did	Opals	1954	Apollo 462
Oh Cathy	Satins Four (with the Cinnamon Angels)	1965	B.T. Puppy 515
Oh Cindy	Vibrations	1962	Checker 1002
Oh, Dale	Demons, Bobby & the	1960	MCI 1028
Oh Darlin'	Trebels	1963	Viking 1021
Oh Darling	Jaytones	1958, 1963	Timely 1003/1004/Times Square 5
Oh, Darling	Squires (Los Angeles)	1953	Combo 42
Oh, Dear, What Can The Matter Be	Brentwoods	1963	Talent 1003
Oh Dear, What Can The Matter Be	Permanents	1963	Chairman 4405
Oh Delilah	Marvels, Neil Sedaka & the	1962	Pyramid 623
Oh Devil	Seniors, Danny & the	1966	Panorama 26
Oh Dolly	Young Lions	1958	Tampa 158
Oh, Gee Baby	Avons	1963	Groove 0022
Oh Gee, Oh Golly	Pelicans, Earl Nelson & the	1957	Class 209
Oh Gee Oh Gosh	Kodaks	1957	Fury 1015
Oh Gee Oh Gosh	Savoys (New Jersey)	1980	Catamount 778
Oh Gee, Oh Gosh	Valentinos	1998	Clifton CD
Oh Genie	Scott, Neil (with the Concords)	1960	Clown 3011
Oh Gloria	Grier Quartet	1958	Swan 4019
Oh Happy Day	Five Satins	1957	Ember 1014
Oh Happy Day	Gothics, Stephanie & the	1961	Shelley 126
Oh Happy Day	Singing Belles	1960	Madison 132
Oh Happy Day	Skylites	1961	Ta-Rah 101
Oh Happy Day (Tra-La-La)	Fantastic Vontastics	1965	Tuff 406
Oh, Heavenly Father	Quin-Tones (Pennsylvania)	1958	Red Top 116
Oh Holy Night	Blue Notes, Harold Melvin & the	1960	Val-Ue 215/Valve 115
Oh Holy Night	Orioles, Sonny Til & the	1950	Jubilee 5045
Oh Honey	Escorts (Essex)	1954	Essex 372
Oh How Happy	Skyliners	1978	Tortoise Int'l 11343
Oh How I Hate To Go Home	Laddins	1961	Theatre 111
Oh How I Love Her	Cordials	1965	Liberty 55784
Oh How I Love You	Revels	1961	Palette 5074

SONG	GROUP	YEAR	LABEL
Oh How I Love You	Valleyites, Nathan McKinney & the	1964	Rayco 526
Oh How I Love You So	Bi-Tones	1960	Bluejay 1000/Tag 444
Oh How I Miss My Baby	Innocents, Kathy Young & the	1962, 1963	Reprise 20112/20125
Oh How I Miss You Tonight	Crewe, Bob & group	1960	Warwick 601
Oh How I Miss You Tonight	Goofers	1956	Coral 61593
Oh How I Miss You Tonight	Platters	1963	Mercury LP 20759/ Mercury LP 60759 (63)
Oh, How I Wish	Diamonds	1957	Mercury 71165
Oh I	Dell Vikings	NA	D.R.C. 101
Oh I Need Your Love	Collegians	1961	Winley 261
Oh It Feels So Good	Larks (North Carolina)	1951	Apollo 430
Oh, It's Crazy	Six Teens	1958	Flip 338
Oh Joan	Beau-Marks	1961	Time 1032
Oh Joan	Coachmen Five	NA	Janson 100
Oh Joe, Joe	Centurys	1959	Fortune 533
Oh Judy	Angel, Gary (with the Halos)	1961	Kama 501
Oh Judy	Sonnets	1958	Lane 501
Oh Julie	Barrons	NA	Guest Star LP 1481
Oh Julie	Charms, Otis Williams & his	1958	DeLuxe 6158
Oh Julie	Crescendos (Tap)	1957	Tap 7027/Nasco 6005 (57)
Oh Kathy	Tokens (Brooklyn)	1964	B.T. Puppy 502
Oh, Lady Be Good	Dominoes	1957	Decca LP 7885 /Decca LP 8621 (57)
Oh Lana	Boyfriends	1964	Kapp 569
Oh, Let Me Dream	Native Boys	1956	Combo 120
Oh Let Me Dream	Reminiscents	1963	Day 1000
Oh Let Me Dream (acappella)	Reminiscents	1975	Relic LP 109
Oh Little Girl	Lancers	1963	Lawn 205
Oh Little Girl	Off Keys, Jerry Evans & the	1962	Rowe 002
Oh Little One	Dodgers	1958	Skyway 118
Oh Little Star	Deans	1963	Dean 1928/Star Maker 1928 (63)
Oh, Little Star	Twinkles	1963	Musicor 1031
Oh Lonely Me	Basics	NA	Lavender 2002
Oh Lonesome Me	Swallows (Maryland)	1958, 1986	Federal 12319/Starbound 504
Oh Lord, Let It Be	Fleetwoods	1959	Dolton 3/Dolton S-3 (59)
Oh Louise	Kidds, Morry Williams & the	1958	Tee Vee 301/Carlton 477 (58)
Oh Love	Magnetics	NA	JV 2501
Oh Lover	Del Victors	1963	Hi-Q 5028
Oh Lover	Miller Sisters	1960	Miller 1140
Oh Lover Of Mine	Hi-Lights	1963	JR 5003
Oh Lovin' Baby	Blaze, Johnny & group	1959	Apon 2142
Oh Mama	Invictas	1963	Mavis 221
Oh Maria	Cubans, Joe Alexander & the	1955	Ballad 1008
Oh Marie	Bay City 5, Luigi Martini & the	1954	Jaguar 3002
Oh Mary	Constellations	1963	Violet 1053
Oh Me	Teens, Little Clydie & the	1956	RPM 462
Oh Me Oh My	Cooper, Wade & group	1960	Ember 1059
Oh Me Oh My	Pastels (Owl)	1974	Owl 332
Oh Mein Papa	Bobbettes	1961	King 5490
Oh Melancholy Me	Passions	1959	Audicon 102
Oh Miss Dolly	Cubans	1958	Flash
Oh, Miss Nellie	Drivers	1957	DeLuxe 6117
Oh Mom	Daylighters	1964	Tip Top 2008
Oh Moon	Rhythm Stars	1959	Clock 1007
Oh My	Electronaires, Chuck Ranado & the	1959	Count 505
Oh My	Gray, Maureen & group	1962	Landa 689
Oh My	Raindrops	1959	Hamilton 50021
Oh My Angel	Street-Tones, Patty & the	1979	U.G.H.A. 09
Oh My Angel	Tillman, Bertha & group	1962	Brent 7029
Oh, My Darlin'	Chips	1956	Josie 803/Jozie 803 (56)
Oh, My Darlin'	Cues	1955	Capitol 3245
Oh My Darling	Bay-Tones	1976	Monogram 116
Oh, My Darling	Capris (Philadelphia)	1958, 1963	Lifetime 610/Candlelite 422
Oh My Darling	Delighters, Little iDi & the	1958	Little D Records 1010
Oh My Darling	Little Kings, Phil Orsi & the	1963	Lucky 1009
Oh My Darling	Nightwinds, Frank & Jack & the	1958	Felsted 8539

SONG	GROUP	YEAR	LABEL
Oh, My Darling	Rhythm Casters	1957	Excello 2115
Oh, My Love	Allisons	1962	Smash 1749
Oh My Love	Blackwells	1959	G&G 131/Guyden 2020 (59)
Oh My Love	Blue Belles, Patti LaBelle & the	1967	Atlantic 2446
Oh My Love	Caribbeans	1963	Amy 871
Oh My Love	Creshendals	1963	Fortune 566
Oh My Love	Drifters (1959-forward)	1959	Atlantic 2025
Oh, My Love	Hearts, Lee Andrews & the	1968	Lost Nite 1004
Oh, My Love	Januarys, Little June & his	1959	Profile 4009
Oh My Love	Mellows, Mack Starr & the	1962	Cub 9117
Oh My Love	Objectives	1965	Jewel 751
Oh My Love	Palisades	1961	Dore 609
Oh My Love	Quin-Tones (Pennsylvania)	1958	Red Top
Oh My Love (Love Me)	Travelers	1961	Decca 31282
Oh My Lover	Chiffons	1963, 1976	Laurie 3152/3648
Oh, My Mother-In-Law	Volumes	1963	Jubilee 5454
Oh My Papa	Bobbettes	1960	Galliant 1006
Oh, My, You	Crystals (Bronx)	1959	Cub 9064
Oh, My, You	Poni-Tails	1960	ABC 10114
Oh Nancy	Ambassadors	1963	Bay 210
Oh Night Of Nights	Dynamics	1963	Do-Kay-Lo 101
Oh No	Robins	1960	Arvee 5013
Oh No, I Still Love Her	Quotations	1964	Admiral 753
Oh No You Won't	Pyramids (RCA)	1959	RCA 7556
Oh Nurse	Frontiers	1961	King 5534
Oh, Oh, Baby	Raindrops	1958	Vega 105
Oh! Oh! Darlin'	Satellites, Pat & the	1959	Atco 6131
Oh! Oh! Get Out Of The Car	Berry, Richard (with the Flairs)	1955	Flair 1064
(Oh Oh) Get Out Of The Car	Flairs, Richard Berry & the	1955	Flair 1064
Oh Oh Henry	Rhythm Rockers	1960	Square 505
Oh! Oh! Honey	Original Rhythm Rockers	1959	Gone 5073
Oh, Oh, Lolita	Cadillacs	1958	Jo-Z 846 (first pressing)/Josie 846 (58) (second pressing)
Oh Oh Mama	Saxons, Mary Edwards & the	1956	Meteor 5031
Oh Oh Oh Baby	Checkers	1952	King 4558
0021-0021-Ooh	Charmettes	1964	Kapp 570
Oh, Oh Yes	Georgettes	1959	Jackpot 48001
Oh Pattie	Sportsmen	1959	A 103
Oh Play That Thing	Tempos	1963	Fairmount 611
Oh Please	Boleros, Carmen Taylor & the	1956	Apollo 489
Oh, Please	Downbeats	1956	Sarg 186
Oh Please	Revivals	1984	Memory Lane 100
Oh, Please, Genie	Preludes	1961	Arliss 1004
Oh, Please Love Me	Lyrics (Texas)	1959	Harlem 101/Wildcat 0028 (59)/ Coral 62322 (62)
Oh Pretty Baby	Moreland, Prentice & group	1959	Edsel 778
Oh Promise Me	Platters	NA	Mercury EP 3355
Oh Rose Marie	Fascinators (Brooklyn)	1959, 1972	Capitol 4247/Bim Bam Boom 110
Oh Rosemarie	Enchanters (JJ&M)	1962, 1963	JJ&M 1562/Candlelite 432
Oh Rosemarie	Enchantments	1972	Clifton 3
Oh, Shirley	Maharajahs	1958	Flip 335
Oh So Happy	Midnighters	1957	Federal 12299
Oh So Much	Heartspinners	1958	X-Tra 109
Oh Starlite	Quinns	1958	Cyclone 111
Oh Stop It	Du Woppers	1970	Kelway 100
Oh, Stop It!	Teardrops	1954	Josie 766/Port 70019 (60)
Oh, Sugar	Quails, Bill Robinson & the	1955	DeLuxe 6074
Oh Summer Love	Unknowns	1958	Felsted 8535
Oh, Suzette	Three G's	1959	Columbia 41383
Oh, Sweetie	Dwellers	1959	Oasis 101
Oh! That Girl	Emanon Four	1956	Flash 106
Oh, That'll Be Joyful	Savoys (Combo)	1954	Combo 55
Oh There He Goes	Unforgettables	1963	Titanic 5012
Oh There She Goes	Three J's	1957	Glory 253
Oh Theresa	Premiers (Connecticut)	1959	Alert 706

SONG	GROUP	YEAR	LABEL
Oh, This Is Why	Dream Girls, Bobbie Smith & the	1959	Cameo 165
Oh, To Get Away	Rainbows, Randy & the	1967	B.T. Puppy 535
Oh To Get Away	Tokens (Brooklyn)	1969	Buddah 151
Oh Tonight	Del Vikings	1958	Mercury LP 30353
Oh Tonight	Georgettes	1957	Ebb 125
Oh Wailey Routa	Saucers	1959	Felco 104
Oh Well-A-Watcha Gonna Do	Granahan, Gerry & group	1958	Mark 121
Oh, What A Baby	Dream Kings	1957	Checker 858
Oh What A Baby	Tonettes	1958	Doe 101/ABC 9905
Oh What A Beautiful Dream	Pebbles	1965	Eiffel 2085
Oh What A Day (same song as Day We Fell In Love)	Ovations (New Jersey)	1961	Epic 9470
Oh, What A Dream	Shells	1966	Candlelite LP 1000
Oh What A Dream (acappella)	Savoys (New Jersey)	1963	Catamount 101
Oh, What A Dream I Had Last Night	Brown, Ruth & Rhythmakers	1955	Atlantic 1036
Oh, What A Feeling!	Companions	1958	Dove 240
Oh What A Feeling	Del Rios, Jimmy Hurt & the	1959	Do-Re-Mi 1401
Oh What A Feeling	Del-Rios	1958	
Oh, What A Feeling	Essentials, Billy & the	1967	SSS International 706
Oh, What A Feeling	Five Fleets	1958	Felsted 8513
Oh What A Feeling!	Inspirators	1958	Old Town 1053
Oh, What A Feeling	Januarys, June & the	1958	Profile 4009
Oh, What A Feeling	Januarys, Little June & his	1959	Profile 4009
Oh What A Feeling	Limelites, Shep & the	1961	Hull 747
Oh What A Fool	Impalas (Brooklyn)	1959	Cub 9033
Oh What A Fool	Warner, Little Sonny & group	1960	Swingin' 627
Oh What A Girl	El Dorados	1958	Vee Jay 302
Oh What A Good Night	Dells	1964	Vee Jay 615
Oh What A Night	Caprisians	1961	Lavender 004
Oh What A Night	Dells	1956, 1959	Vee Jay 204/338
Oh What A Night	Halos	1962	Warwick LP 2046
Oh What A Night	Kac-Ties	1963	Shelley 165/Atco 6299 (64)
Oh What A Night	Shells	1970	Boardwalk 17
Oh What A Night	Tokens (Date)	1961	Date 2737
Oh What A Night For Love	Tyson, Roy & group	1963	Double L 723
Oh What A Night For Love	Victorians	1964	Liberty 55693
Oh What A Time	Earls	1964	Old Town 1169
Oh, What A Waste Of Love	Shirelles	1961	Scepter LP 501
Oh What A Way To Be Loved	Daylighters	1961	Nike 10011/Dot 16326 (62)/ Tip Top 2001 (62)
Oh, What A Wonderful Feeling	Mitchum, Jim & group	1960	20th Century 277
Oh What It Seemed To Be	Castells	1962	Era 3083
Oh What It Seemed To Be	Upbeats	1958	Joy 223
Oh What Love Is	Naturals, Jack Bailey & the	1959	Ford 105
Oh! Whatcha Do	Cadillacs	1956	Unreleased
Oh, When You Touch Me	Red Coats	1959	Del-Co 4002
Oh! Where	Vocaleers	1952, 1964	Red Robin 113
Oh Where Did You Go	Deckers, Lynn Christie & the	1957	Nar 225
Oh Why	Jades	1959	Christy 110
Oh Why	Miller Sisters	1962	Rayna 5004
Oh Why	Satisfactions	1962	Chesapeake 610
Oh Why	Softones	1957	Cee Bee 1062
Oh Why	Teddy Bears	1959	Imperial 5562
Oh Why?	Orchids	1953	King 4661
Oh Why?	Robins	1953	RCA 5271
Oh Wishing Well	Unforgettables	1961	Pamela 204
Oh, Woh, Baby	Fortuneers	1963	Skytone 1000
Oh Yeah	Baron, Nancy & group	1962	Chelsea 102
Oh Yeah!	Blue Tones	1957	King 5088
Oh Yeah	Carnations	1959	Checker 914
Oh Yeah	Dreamers (Bullseye)	1958	Bullseye 1013
Oh Yeah	Imperials, Little Anthony & the	1958	End 1036
Oh Yeah	Squeaks, Bobby Knotts & the	1961	Gee Clef 077
Oh Yeah Hm-m-m	Keynotes	1956	Apollo 485
Oh, Yeah, Hm-m-m	Keynotes	1956	Apollo 503

SONG	GROUP	YEAR	LABEL
Oh Yeah Maybe Baby	Crystals (Brooklyn)	1961	Philles 100
Oh Yes	Admirals	1955	King 4772
Oh! Yes	Charmers	1956	Aladdin 3341
Oh Yes I Know	Jewels (Los Angeles)	1954, 1964	R&B 1303/Original Sound 38
Oh, Yes, I Know	Tune Blenders	1954	Federal 12201
Oh Yes, I Love You	Lewis, Bobby & female group	1961	Beltone 1002
Oh Yes, I'll Be True	Sensations	1961	Argo 5405
Oh Yes, Indeed I Do	Locos	1958	20th Fox 102
Oh Yes My Darling	Midniters, Al Chase & the	1960	Jin 118
Oh You	Chalons	1958	Dice 89
Oh, You Sweet Girl	Nitecaps	NA	Detour LP 33-010
Oh-Be-Dum	Wilson, Steve & group	1961	Pamela 205
Oh-h-h	Mello-Maids	1956	Baton 231
Oh-Kay	Dukes (California)	1954	Specialty 543
Oh-Rooba-Lee	Crowns, Arthur Lee Maye & the	1956	Specialty 573
Oink Jones	Ding-A-Lings	1960	Capitol 4467
Oink Jones	Marathons	NA	Collectables LP 5081
Okay	Turks	1958	Keen 4016
Okay, Baby!	Pyramids (Connecticut)	1956	Davis 453
Okey Dokey, Mama	Five Delights	1958	Newport 7002/Unart 2003 (58)
Ol' Man River	Emanons	1960	Delbert 5290
Ol' Man River	Flamingos	1962, 1963	Roulette 4524/End LP 316
Ol' Man River	Gems (Illinois)	1954	Drexel 904
Ol' Man River	Ravens	1947, 1955	National 9034/Jubilee 5217
Ol' Man River	Skylarks	1957	Verve 10082
Ol' Man River	Tune Weavers	1957	Checker 872/880/ Casa Grande 4037
Old Black Magic	Clovers	1959	United Artists 174
Old Buttermilk Sky	Page Boys	1963	Decca 3105
Old Cape Cod	Five Classics	1962	Medieval 204/Rode 101
Old Chinatown	Channels	1965	Groove 0061
Old Crowd, The	Cookies	1964	Dimension 1032
Old Devil Moon	Rays	1960	XYZ 608
Old Enough To Break A Heart	Originals	NA	Van 04166
Old Enough To Know	Four Barons	1957	Roman 400
Old, Faithful And True Love	Harmonaires, Bonnie Lou & the	1955	King 1476
Old Fashioned Christmas	Velours	1988	Clifton 82
Old Fashioned Christmas	Williams, Kenny & group	1973	Ben Mor 100
Old Folks Boogie While The Young Ones Twist	Crowns, Henry Strogin & the	1963	Ball 1012
Old Folks Boogie While The Young Ones Twist	Strogin, Henry & group	1962	Ball 1012
Old Grandpa	High Type Five, Clarence Green with the	1959	Chess 1732
Old Love	Love-Tones, Mary Wells & the	1962	Motown 1032
Old MacDonald	Blenders (Wanger)	1959	Wanger 189
Old MacDonald	Chargers (Jesse Belvin)	1958	RCA 7301
Old MacDonald	Orlandos	1957	Cindy 3006
Old MacDonald (acappella)	Velvet Angels	1972	Relic LP 5004
Old Man Mose	Impalas (Five Discs)	NA	Rite-On 101
Old Man Mose	Williams, Kae & group	1956	Kaiser 385
Old Man River	Cues	1960	Festival
Old Man River	Earls	NA	Woodbury LP 104
Old Man River	Fireflies	NA	G.M. 1001
Old Man River	Four Winds	1965	Sherluck 1027
Old Man River	Hi-Lites, Skippy & the	1962	Elmor/Stream-Lite 1027
Old Man River	Original Drifters	1971	Game 394
Old Man River	Strands	1962	Triode 101
Old Man River	Travellers, Ronnie Cates & the	1962	Terrace 7501
Old Man River	Yesterday's News	1980	Clifton 44
Old Man, The	Don-Tels	1963	Witch 121
Old Man's Blues	Men From Mars, Marvin Phillips & the	NA	Specialty 445
Old Master Painter, The	Hines, William A. & group	1960	Ball 508
Old McDonald	Diablos	1984	Fortune LP 8016
Old McDonald (Had A Farm)	Five Keys	1951, 1952	Aladdin 3113/3118
Old Mother Nature	Emeralds, Luther Bond & the	1959	Federal 12368

SONG	GROUP	YEAR	LABEL
Old Shep	DeMarco, Ralph (with the Paramounts)	1959	Guaranteed 202
Old Spanish Town	Bell Notes	1959	Time 1010
Old Time Rock And Roll	Chavis Brothers	1961	Coral 62270
Old Times	Hi Tensions	NA	Milestone
Old Willow Tree, The	Phantoms, Vernon Green & the	1956	Specialty 581
Oldies But Goodies	Flame Tones, Richard Willans & the	1972	Bell 192
Oldies But Goodies Show	McGee, Al & group	1961	Donna 1348
Oldies In The Nineties	Imaginations	1991	Collectables CD 5726
Oldsmo William	Peek, Paul & group	1958	NRC 008
Ole	Hollywood Argyles	1965	Chattahoochee 691
Ole King Cole	Drakes	1965	Olimpic 252
O-Mi Yum-Mi Yum-Mi	Shells	1961	Johnson 110
On A Clear Night	Explorers	1960	Coral 62147
On A Day When It's Raining	Superbs	1966	Dore 753
On A Little Island	Enchanters (Tee Pee)	1963	Tee Pee 65
On A Lover's Island	Five Satins	1961	United Artists 368
On A Night Like Tonight	Charmettes	1962	Tri Disc 103
On A Night When Flowers Were Dancing	Wallace, Jerry & group	1956	Mercury 70812
On A Saturday Night	Mystery Men	1963	Pow 1001
On A Saturday Night	Newports, Tyrone & the	1963	Darrow 5-20
On A Slow Boat To China	Platters	1960	Mercury LP 20481/ Mercury LP 60160 (60)
On Account Of You	Four Cruisers, Joseph Dobbin & the	1953	Chess 1547
On An Island	Angelenos	1961	Peepers 2824
On And On	Ensenadas	1963	Tarx 1005
On Bended Knee	Excels	1955	X 0108
On Bended Knee	Flyers	1957	Atco 6088
On Bended Knee	Four Gents	1957	Park 113
On Broadway	Drifters (1959-forward)	1963	Atlantic 2182
On Broadway	Nite Sounds	1962	Seafair 112
On Chapel Hill	Ravens	1955	Jubilee 5203
On Fire	Stylettes	1964	Cameo 337
On Main Street	Magnificents (released as by the El Dorados)	1966	Dee Gee 3008
On My Birthday	Junior Five	1963	Laurie 3213
On My Happy Way	Trinidads	1959	Formal 1005
On My Honor	Hearts, Lee Andrews & the Hearts	1960	Chancellor 1057
On My Honor	Shells	1963, 1977	Johnson 127
On My Knees	Dreamers, Hal Hedges & the	1963	ABC 10406
On My Merry Way	Flamingos	1954	Parrot 808
On My Mind	Darts	1958	Apt 25023
On My Mind Again	Four Pals, Dean Beard & the	1957	Atlantic 1137
On My Own Again	Cabot, Johnny & group	1962	Columbia 42283
On My Own Two Feet	Rays, Hal Miller & the	1964	Amy 909
On My Word Of Honor	Platters	1956	Mercury 71011
On Our Way From School	Hot Rods, Doug Connell & the	1959	Alton 600
On Our Wedding Day	Essentials, Johnny Lloyd & the	1965	Reading 16000
On Sunday Afternoon	Balladeers	1990	Clifton 89
On Sunday Afternoon	Harptones	1956	Rama 214
On Sunday Afternoon	Valentinos	1992	Clifton 101
On That Beautiful Day	Sa-Shays	1961	Zen 110
On The Alamo	Voices Five, Budd Johnson & the	1959	Stereo Craft 111A
On The Bridge	Ubans	1964	Radiant 102
On The Corner	Ad Libs	1965	Blue Cat 119
On The Corner	Expressions	1963	Parkway 892
On The Edge Of Town	Genies	1959	Hollywood 69
On The Go	Buddies	1964	Swing 102
On The Island	Avons	1959	Hull 731
On The Move	Moods	1960	Sarg 185
On The Other Side Of The World	Noblemen	NA	Clarity 106
On The Other Side Of Town	G-Clefs	1965, 1966	Veep 1218/1226
On The Outside Looking In (acappella)	Shells	1966	Candlelite LP 1000
On The Run	Accents (featuring Sandi)	1964	Karate 529
On The Spanish Side	Corsairs, Landy McNeil & the	1964	Tuff 402
On The Street Of Tears	Castells	1962	Era 3073
On The Street Where You Live	Chuckles	1964	West Side 1019

SONG	GROUP	YEAR	LABEL
On The Street Where You Live	Chymes	1964	Musictone 6125
On The Street Where You Live	Drifters (1959-forward)	1965	Atlantic LP 8113
On The Sunny Side Of The Street	Parisians	1962	Pova 1003/1004
On The Wagon	Charmaines	1962	Dot 16351
On The Wings Of The Wind	Gum Drops	1958	Coral 62003
On Your Mark	C-Tones	1957	Everlast 5005
On Your Merry Way	Collegians	1957	Winley 224
On Your Radio	Lanham, Richard (with the Tempo-Tones)	1955	Acme 712
Once A Day	Demensions, Lenny Dell & the	1964	Coral 62444
Once A Day	Russell, Bobby & group	1965	Monument 899
Once A Heart	Millionaires	NA	N/A
Once Again	Trends	1959	Scope 102
Once And For All	Ravens	1946, 1948	Hub 3032/National 9040
Once He Loved Me	Gaynotes	1958	Aladdin 3424
Once I Had A Girl	Wheelers	1960	Cenco 107
Once I Had A Love	Fabulous Denos	1964	King 5908
Once In A Beautiful Lifetime	Alston, Henry & group	1959	Skyline 500
Once In A Blue Moon	Day, Tracey & group	1961, 1962	Vee Jay 467
Once In A Lifetime	Annuals	1962	Marconn CR1
Once In A Lifetime	Barons (New Orleans)	1956	Imperial 5397
Once In A Lifetime	Cordials	1962	Felsted 8653
Once In A Lifetime	Hamptons	1961	Legrand 1007
Once In A Lifetime	Planets	1962	Aljon 1244
Once In A Lifetime	Sonics	1958, 1963, 1975	X-Tra 107
Once In A Lifetime	Waymates	NA	Skyland
Once In A Million	Chancellors	1966	Fenton 2066
Once In A While	Chimes (Brooklyn)	1960	Tag 444/Music Note 1101 (61)
Once In A While	Flips, Mario & the	1959	Cross Country 100
Once In A While	Platters	1963	Mercury 72107
Once In A While	Ravens	1948	National 9045
Once In A While	Sensationals	1960	Candix 306
Once In A While (acappella)	Traditions	1965	Fellatio 102
Once In Awhile	Big Edsel Band	1980	Clifton 48
Once In Love	Premonitions	1979	Crystal Ball 133
Once More	Chandeliers	1962	Du-Well 102
Once There Lived A Fool	Striders, Savannah Churchill & the	1951	Regal 3309/Derby 468
Once There Was A Time	Team Mates	1960, 1962	Le Cam 707/Philips 40029
Once Upon A Dream	Van Dykes	1959	Felsted 8565
Once Upon A Love	Bluejays, Leon Peels & the	1989	Classic Artists 111
Once Upon A Love	Mascots	1962	Blast 206
Once Upon A Time	Avons	1960, 1977	Hull LP 1000
Once Upon A Time	Candles, Rochell & the	1960	Swingin' 623
Once Upon A Time	Elgins (California)	1962	Joed 716
Once Upon A Time	Fascinations, Jordan & the	1961, 1990	Carol 4116/Magic Carpet EP 509
Once Upon A Time	Johnson, Marv & group	1958	Kudo 663
Once Upon A Time	Orioles, Sonny Til & the	1983	Murray Hill LP M61277
Once Upon A Time	Shades, Royal & the	NA	Band Box 358
Once Upon A Time	Wyatt, Johnny & group	1965	Magnum 736
Once We Loved	Rebelaires	1957	B&K 103
One And Two	Poore, Bobby & group	1958	Beta 1003
One At A Time	Downbeats	1960	Wilco 16
One Bad Stud	Honey Bears	1954	Spark 104
One By One	Jarmels	1962	Laurie 3141
One Chance	Echoes, Mitch & the	1963	Bethlehem 3077
One Chance	Infascinations	1961	Clauwell 003/004
One Dab Man	Dabettes, Karen Caple & the	1962	Advance 3933
One Day	Starr, Suzy & group	1961	Morgil 711
One Day	Vectors	1958	Standord 700
One Day	Velvetones	1946	Coronet 1
One Day (acappella)	Spaniels	NA	Unreleased
One Day At A Time	Wonders	1961	Manco 1024
One Day Next Year	Heartbeats	1958	Roulette 4091
One Day, One Day	King Krooners	NA	Unreleased
One Desire	McCallister, Lon & group	1961	Apt 25061
One Face In The Crowd	Four Winds	1968	B.T. Puppy 555

SONG	GROUP	YEAR	LABEL
One Fine Day	Charms, Otis Williams & the	1955	DeLuxe 6089
One Fine Day	Chiffons	1963	Laurie 3179
One Fine Day	Studebaker 7	NA	Coulee 142
One Foolish Mistake	Kingsmen	1956	Neil 102
One Friday Morning	Toppers, Bobby Mitchell & the	1953, 1973	Imperial 5250
One Girl, One Girl	Honey Bees	1964	Vee Jay 611
One Great Love	Five Keys	1958	Capitol 4092
One Guy	Wright, Mary & group	1960	Kim 101
One Hand, One Heart	Escorts, Goldie & the	1963	Coral 62349
One Happy Ending	Majors (Philadelphia)	1963	Imperial 5968
One Heart	Students, Bill Starr & the	1960	Applause 1235
One Hen	Blue Chips	1962	Groove 0006
One Hot Dog	Five Shades	1961	MGM 13035
One Hundred Baby	Chuckles, Chuck & the	1959	Shad 5015
One Hundred Pounds Of Clay	Cleftones	1961	Gee LP 705
100 Pounds Of Potatoes	Secrets, Carlo & the	1962	Throne 801
100 Years From Today	Mondellos, Alice Jean & the	1957	Rhythm 102
One Hundred Years From Today	Spaniels	1959	Vee Jay 328
One I Adore, The	Del Rays	1958	Warner Bros. 5022
One I Adore, The	Emeralds (Pittsburgh)	1957	ABC 9889
One I Love, The	Fanados	1957	Carter 2050
One I Love, The	Pleasers, Wilbur Whitfield & the	1957	Aladdin 3381
One I Love, The	Secrets, Colleen Kaye & the	1963	Big Top 3151
One I Love, The	Sliders, Byron Gipson & the	1955	Specialty 566
One In A Million	Platters	1956	Mercury 71011
One (Is Such A Lonely Number)	Corvells	1963	Cub 9122
One Kind Word From You	Charms, Otis Williams & his	1957	DeLuxe 6137
One Kiss	Chevelles, Art Barron & the	1964	Golden 101
One Kiss	Robins	1955	Spark 113
One Kiss And That's All	Steadies	1958	Josie 837
One Kiss Led To Another	Coasters	1956	Atco 6073
One Kiss, One Smile And A Dream	Del Rays	1958	Cord 101
One Last Kiss	Marcels	1963, 1988	Colpix 694
One Last Look At My Darling	Ambassadors, Vern Young & the	1960	Chords 101
One Last Teardrop	Jades, Freddy Koenig & the	1963	Lori 9548/Valerie 225 (63)
One Life, One Love, One You	Emotions	1963	20th Fox 430
One Little Blessing	Belvin, Jesse (with the Feathers)	1955	Specialty 550
One Little Dance	Moovers	1967	Brent 7065
One Little Kiss	Caravelles	1962	Joey 6208
One Little Kiss	Holidays	1961	Nix 537
One Little Kiss	Keynotes	1957	Apollo 513
One Little Moment With You	Furness Brothers	1960	Rae-Cox 104
One Little Prayer	Berry, Richard (with the Flairs)	1953	Flair 1016
One Little Star	Fleetwoods	1961	Dolton BLP 2007/BST 8007
One Little Teardrop	Castelles, George Grant & the	1989	Classic Artists 114
One Lonely Heart	Brothers	1961	Checker 995
One Lonely Night	Electronaires, Chuck Ranado & the	1959	Count 505
One Lonely Night	Trinidads	1959	Formal 1006
One Look	Wanderers	1960	Panama 3900
One Look At You	Frank, Carol & group	1957	Excello 2118
One Look At You Is All It Took	Passions	1960	Audicon 108
One Look Is All It Took	Passions	1962	Jubilee 5406
One Love	Bennetts	1964	Amcan 401
One Love	Cardinals	1957	Atlantic 1126
One Love	Dissonaires, Mike L. & the	1959	Altair 101
One Love	Four Marksmen	1958	Radio 107
One Love	Logics	1960	Everlast 5015
One Love	Mayfield, Percy & group	1959	Imperial 5577
One Love	Roomates, Cathy Jean & the	1961	Valmor 011
One Love Alone	Gallahads	1957	Vik 0291
One Love Alone	McDonald, Ken & group	1958	Prep 128
One Love For Me	Hi-Lites (Wonder)	1958	Wonder 102
One Love Forgot (acappella), The	Chessmen	1975	Relic LP 106
One Love Is Lost	Wil-Ettes	1962	Jamie 1234
One Lovely Yesterday	Chaps	1960	Brent 7016

SONG	GROUP	YEAR	LABEL
One Man Woman	Emblems, Patty & the	1967	Kapp 870
One Mile	Redtops, Eddie Dugosh & the	1958	Award 116
One Million Miles Away	Uniques	1962	Tee Kay 112
One Million Years	Heartbeats	1959	Guyden 2011
One Mint Julep	Clovers	1952, 1960	Atlantic 963/United Artists 209
One Mint Julep	Crowns, Arthur Lee Maye & the	NA	Dig (unreleased)
One Mint Julep	Jayos, Johnny Otis & the	1957	Dig LP 104
One Mint Julep	Yesterday's Today	NA	Starlight 1
One Minute More	Marx	1959	Chante 1002
One Mistake	Five Royales	1954	King 4762
One Moment With You	Dominoes	1954, 1957	Federal 12184
One Monkey	Rivingtons	1964	Reprise 0293
One Monkey Don't Stop The Show	Midnighters, Hank Ballard & the	1964	King 5963
One More Break	Sandmen, Chuck Willis & the	1955	Okeh 7055
One More Chance	Cadets, Bennle Bunn & the	1960	Sherwood 211
One More Chance	Chances	1961	Bea & Baby 130
One More Chance	Davis, Hal Sonny & group	1962	Gardena 125
One More Chance	El Dorados	1955	Vee Jay 127
One More Chance	Frank, Carol & group	1959	Excello 2175
One More Chance	Peppers	1961	Ensign 1076
One More Chance	Spartans	1961	Audio International 102
One More Chance	Springer, Walter & group	1959	Kaiser 401
One More Chance	Towers, Jimmy & the	NA	Debann 102
One More Chance	Unknowns	1957	Shield 7101/X-Tra 102 (57)
One More Fool Than I	Monterays (Brooklyn)	NA	Saturn
One More For The Road	Dolphins	1961	Empress 102
One More For The Road	Paramounts	1963	Laurie 3201
One More Kiss	Bad Boys, Jessie Perkins & the	1960	Savoy 1584
One More Kiss	Calvanes	1956	Dootone 380
One More Kiss	Happy Teens	1960	Paradise 114
One More Kiss	Senders	1959	Kent 324
One More Kiss	Triads	1956	Encino 1002
One More Kiss Goodnight	Escorts (Wells)	1959	Wells 102
One More Once	Lavenders	1963	Mercury 72126
One More River	Classicals	1962	Kent 379
One More River To Cross	Dell Vikings	1962	ABC 10304
One More Step	Chandeliers	1958	Angle Tone 521
One More Tear	Raindrops	1964	Jubilee 5487
One More Time	Charmettes	1962	Marlin 16001
One More Time	Clovers, Buddy Bailey & the	1963	Porwin 1001
One More Time	Daychords, Roxy & the	1962	Don-El 120
One More Time	Drapers	1960	Vest 831
One More Time	Four-Evers	1963	Jamie 1247
One More Time	Gems, Pearl Woods & the	1962	Wall 552
One More Time	Lavenders	1963	Mercury 72126
One More Time	Mel-O-Dots	1952	Apollo 1192
One More Time	Notes	1956	MGM 12421
One More Time	Orioles, Sonny Til & the	1953	Jubilee 5120
One More Time	Palms	1957	States (unreleased)
One More Time	Satellites	NA	Arc 149
One More Time	Thrillers, Little Joe & the	1961	20th Century 1214
One More Tomorrow	Halos, Johnny Angel & the	1962	Felsted 8646
One Night	Four Kings	1964	Canadian American 173
One Night	Jewels (Los Angeles)	NA	Imperial (unreleased)
One Night, One Night	Skyliners	1959	Calico 103/104/Original Sound 35 (63)
One Night Only	Charms, Otis Williams & his	1956	DeLuxe 6095
One Night With A Fool	Hollywood Flames	1954	Lucky 001
One Night With You	Candles, Rochell & the	1985	Relic LP 5060
One Night With You	Wyatt, Johnny (with the Candles)	1961	Swingin' 643
One Note Samba	Alcons	1959	Brunswick 55128
One O'Clock Twist	Fireflies	1962	Taurus 355
One Of These Days	Cotillions	1963	ABC 10413
One Of These Mornings	Voices, Ravon Darnell & the	1956	Million 2015
One Phone Call	Blue Belles, Patti LaBelle & the	1964	Parkway 913
One Piece Bathing Suit	Concords (Neal Scott)	1963	Herald 581

SONG	GROUP	YEAR	LABEL
One Piece Topless Bathing Suit	Rip Chords	1964	Columbia 43093
One Plus One	Expressions	1965	Reprise 0360
One Potato, Two Potato	Dovells	1964	Parkway 911
One Question	Playboys	1956	Tetra 4447
One Room	Stylists (New York)	1960, 1974	Rose 16/17
One Scotch, One Bourbon, One Beer	Five Encores	1955	Rama 187
One Sided Love	Velvet Satins, Bobby Capri & the	1960, 1982	Ariste 101/Jason Scott 17447
One Step From Heaven	Concords (Brooklyn)	1962	Rust 5048
One Step Too Far	Cymbals	1962	Amazon 709
One Step Too Far	Hughes, Fred & group	1965	Minasa 709
One Stop	Fortune Bravos, Spider Turner & the	1963	Fortune 570
One Summer In A Million	Ginos, Jeff & the	1963	Mercury 72138
One Summer Night	Ambertones	1965	Dottie 1129
One Summer Night	Diamonds	1961	Mercury 71831
One Summer Night	Platinums	1979	J&M 122648
One Summer Night	Roomates	1961	Valmor LP 78/Valmor LP 789 (62)/ Relic LP 5041
One Summer Night	Sophomores, Anthony & the	1967	Jamie 1340
One Summer Night	Spina, Vic & group	NA	VM
One Summer Night (acappella)	Zircons	1966	Amber 851
One Summer Night (first pressing, second is by the Danleers)	Dandleers	1958	Amp-3 2115 (first pressing, second is by the Danleers)
One Summer Night (second pressing, first is by the Dandleers)	Danleers	1958	Amp-3 2115 (second pressing, first is by the Dandleers)/Mercury 71322 (58)/Amp 3 1005 (58)
One Teardrop Too Late	Lovers, Valentino & the	1960	Donna 1345
One Thing For Me	Ermines	1956	Loma 705
One Time	Blenders (Chicago)	1963	Witch 122
One Too Many Lies	Five Boroughs	1990	Classic Artists 119
One Too Many Times	Arrows, Joe Lyons & the	1956	Hollywood 1071
One Touch Of Heaven	Shades	1959	Aladdin 3453/Imperial 5358 (59)
One, Two, Button My Shoe	De-Lights	1962	Ad Lib 0207/Pop Line
One Two Button My Shoe	Del-Knights	1961	Sheryl
1, 2, I Love You	Heartbreakers (Bronx, N.Y.)	1957	Vik 0261
One, Two, Three	Keytones	1963	Chelsea 1013
One, Two, Three, Go	Gypsies	1955	Groove 0117
One Way	Artistics	1962	S&G 302
One Way Love	Drifters (1959-forward)	1964	Atlantic 2225
One Way Lover	Volumes	1965	American Arts 18
One Week From Today	Limelites, Shep & the	1960	Apt 25046
One Week Romance	Calendars	1961	Swingin' 649
One Winter Love	Dovells	1969	Jamie 1369
One Woman Man	Gems (Illinois)	1956	Drexel 909
One Wonderful Night	Honey Bees	1964	Smash 1939
One Word For This	Esquires	1957	Hi-Po 1003
One Year Today	Fugitives	1957	Fabor 141
One-Sided Love	Capri, Bobby & group	1961	Artiste 101
One-Sided Love Affair	Marveleers	1953	Derby 829
1-2-3	Downbeats	NA	Kanwic 137
1-2-3	Fascinations	1978	Crystal Ball 123
Onions (Remind Me Of You)	Onions, Tommy Sena & the	NA	Valmont 905
Onions (Remind Me Of You)	Val-Monts, Tommy Sena & the	1962	Valmont 905
Only A Dream	Carians	1961	Magenta 04
Only A Dream	Chimes, Gene Moore & the	1955	Combo 63
Only A Dream	Crowns, Arthur Lee Maye & the	1964	Jamie 1284
Only A Dream	Dave & Larry & group	1965	B'n Kc 102
Only A Dream	Ryan, Cathy (with the Admirals)	1956	King 4890
Only A Fool	Madisons	1965	Jomada 601/Jumaca 601
Only A Miracle	Four Bells	1954	Gem 220/Crystal 101
Only A Picture	Rainbows	1963	Dave 908
Only A Tear	Jokers, J.W. & the	1959	Simpson 1130
Only At Christmas	Five Boroughs	1991	Classic Artists 135
Only Be Mine	Ebb Tides	1957	Teen 121

SONG	GROUP	YEAR	LABEL
Only Because	Platters	1957	Mercury 71184
Only By You (I Want To Be Loved)	Five C's	1981	P-Vine Special LP 9036
Only Fate	Furness Brothers	1964	Melmar 114
Only For You	Cameos (Los Angeles)	1955	Dootone 365
Only Forever	Chimes, Lenny & the	1964	Vee Jay 605
Only Girl For Me	Intimates	1964	Amcan 402
Only Girl For Me	Young, Bobby (with Rick & the Masters)	1968	Guyden 2087
Only Girl For Me, The	Roomates	NA	Relic LP 5041
Only Girl (I'll Ever Love), The	Mello-Kings	1958	Herald 511
Only Girl, The	Chevells, Don & the	1964	Speedway 1000
Only Girl, The	Dialtones, Johnny Bersin & the	1959	Jin 117
Only Heaven Knows	Donna Lou & group	1963	Lomar 703
Only Heaven Knows (acappella)	Dovers	1988	Relic LP 5075
Only If I Had Your Love	Van Dyke Five	1967	Corner Closet 101
Only In A Dream	Keynotes	1959	Bell-O-Tonic 001
Only In America	Drifters (1959-forward)	1963	Atlantic (unreleased)
Only In My Dreams	Empires	1961	Calico 121
Only Jim	Six Teens	1957	Flip 320
Only Last Night	Dell, Joey & group	1962	Roulette 4422
Only Last Night (In A Garden)	Corvets	1960	20th Fox 223
Only Love	Chimes (Brooklyn)	1961	Tag 445
Only Love	Fashionettes	1964	GNP Crescendo 322
Only Love Of Mine, The	Vibraharps	1959	Fury 1022
Only Love, Sweet Love	Determinations	1959	Space 304
Only Memories	Marlettes	19??	
Only My Friend	Chiffons	1963	Laurie 3159
Only My Friend	Tokens (Brooklyn)	1965	B.T. Puppy 512
Only My Heart	Willows, Tony Middleton & the	1957	Eldorado 508
Only Now And Then	Persianettes, Timmy Carr & the	1964	Guyden 2104
Only One	Castells	1962	Era 3089
Only One	Wayne, Scotty & group	1964	Talent 1008
Only One For Me	Lynn, Bill & group	1961	Amy 820
Only One Love	Cufflinks	1962	Gait 543
Only One Love	Zircons	1957	Winston 1020/Dot 15724 (58)
Only One Love Is Blessed	Harris, Thurston (with the Sharps)	1958	Aladdin 3428
Only Only You	Ebon-Knights	1958	Stepheny 1822
Only Reason, The	Chessmen, Barbara McBride & the	NA	Mari 451
Only Sympathy	Imperials, Little Anthony & the	1960	End 1074
Only The Angels Know	Esquires	1957	Hi-Po 1003
Only The Angels Know	Revelaires	1954	Burgundy 1001
Only The Lonely	Celtics	1960	War Conn 2216
Only The Stars	Teenbeats	1961	Myrl 407
Only Then	Scott Brothers	1960	Ribbon 6911
Only Time	Dreamers (Tri-Dec)	NA	Tri-Dec 8757
Only Time Will Tell	Tunes	1959	Pel 101/Pel 345 (59)
Only To Other People	Cookies	1963	Dimension 1020
Only To You	Fidelitys	1959	Sir 274
Only Way, The	Roberts, Penny (with the Paramours)	1962	Moonglow 201
Only Way To Fly, The	Dolphins, Davey Jones & the	1968	Tower 4527
Only When You're Lonely	Wanderers	1959	Cub 9035
Only You	Comets, Herb Kenny & the	1952	Federal 12083
Only You	Crowns, Arthur Lee Maye & the	1957	Dig 146 (unreleased)
Only You	Cues	1955	Jubilee 5201
Only You	Four Jacks	1956	Gateway 1147
Only You	Havens	1963	Poplar 123
Only You	Jayos, Johnny Otis & the	1957	Dig LP 104
Only You	Renaults	1962	Wand 120
Only You (And You Alone)	Platters	1955	Federal 12244/Mercury 70633/ Power 7012
Only You Can Give	Watkins, Sis & group	1964	Diplomacy 9
Only You, Only Me	Sunsets	1963	Petal 1040
Only Young Once	Charms, Otis Williams & the	1961	King 5682
Only Your Love	Dreamers (Bullseye)	1958	Bullseye 1013
Oo La La	Joseph, Dave & group	1958	Vanguard 35004
Oo Wee	Hearts (Bronx, N.Y.)	1955	Baton 208/Main Line 102 (57)

SONG	GROUP	YEAR	LABEL
Oo Wee Baby	Jacks	1957	RPM LP 3006
Oo Wee So Good	Drakes	1958	Conquest 1001
Ooba-Gooba	Charts	1959	Guyden 2021
Oobidee-Oobidee-Oo	Harptones	1954	Bruce 113
Oochi Pachi	Gadabouts	1955	Mercury 70581
Oochi Pachi	Platters, Linda Hayes & the	1955	King 4773
Oochie Pachie	Crowns, Arthur Lee Maye & the	1955	RPM 424
Oo-Ee What's Wrong With Me	Chordones, Leon D. Tarver & the	1954	Checker 791
Oo-Ee-Baby	Dukes, Lloyd Price & the	1954	Specialty 535
Oof Goof	Beltones	1957	Hull 721
Oogly Googly Eyes	Fanatics	1961	Skyway 127
Ooh	Sandmen, Brook Benton & the	1955	Okeh 7058
Ooh Ah	Gallahads	1955	Capitol 3060
Ooh Baby	Carterays, Eddie Carter & the	1954	Sound 105
Ooh Baby	Five Blue Notes	1954	Sabre 103
Ooh, Baby	Teardrops	1954	Josie 771
Ooh Baby Baby	Prime	NA	Clifton EP 506
Ooh Baby Baby (acappella)	Chessmen	1975	Relic LP 105
Ooh, Baby Baby (acappella)	Shells	1966	Candlelite LP 1000
Ooh! Baby It Scares Me	Four Most	1956	Dawn 220
Ooh Baby Ooh	Hollywood Flames	1988	Specialty LP 2166
Ooh Bah Baby	Midnighters	1957	Federal 12288
Ooh Bop Sha Boo (Give All Your Love To Me)	Guytones	1957	DeLuxe 6144
Ooh Bop She Bop	Dukes (California)	1954	Specialty 543
Ooh, But You're Nice To Hold	Gleepers, Coke Willis & the	NA	Daco 101
Ooh How I Love Ya	Aristocrats, Murray Schaff & the	1955	Josie 788
Ooh I	Boleros, Carmen Taylor & the	1954	Atlantic 1041
Ooh, I Feel So Good	Vibranaires	1954	After Hours 103/Chariot 103
Ooh La La	Long, Bobby & his Cherrios	1959	Glow-Hill 504
Ooh La La	Woods, Cora & group	1955	Federal 12229
Ooh Looka There, Ain't She Pretty	Imperials, Little Anthony & the	1961	End LP 311
Ooh Lovin' Baby	Carter Quartet, Eddie	1975	Monogram 107
Ooh My Soul	Raindrops	1974	Firefly 313
Ooh, Ooh, Those Eyes	Don Juans, Don Lake & the	1956	Fortune 520
Ooh! Ooh! Those Eyes	Sequins & Rhythm Kings, Jimmy Burke with the	1960	Fortune 537
Ooh Poo Pah Doo	Mystics	1966	Black Cat 501
Ooh Poo Pah Doo	Shevelles	1964	World Artists 1023
Ooh Pooh Pah Doo	Continentals, Billy John & the	1962	N-Joy 1012
Ooh Pretty Baby	Sportsmen	1955	Key 503
Ooh Rocking Daddy	Moonglows	1954	Chance 1156
Ooh Sha-La	Rhythm Jesters	1962	Lectra 501
Ooh! She Flew	Avalons	1956	Groove 0141
Ooh, Shucks	Five Stars (Detroit)	1957	Mark-X 7006
Ooh Wah	Montclairs, Mel Williams & the	1955	Rage 101
Ooh Wee Baby	Chants, Little Jerry & the	1960	Ace 606
Ooh Wee Baby	Duvals (New York)	1956	Rainbow 335/Riviera 990 (56)
Ooh Wee Baby	Five Crowns	1955	Riviera 990/Rainbow 335 (56)
Ooh Wee Baby	Majors (Philadelphia)	1963	Imperial 66009
Ooh, What A Guy	Hi-Fashions	1958	Paris 524
Ooh Yeah Baby	Flips, Kip Tyler & the	1958	Challenge 59008
Ooh-Diga-Gow	Young, Cecil (& quartette)	1954	King
Ooh-La-La	Echotones, Skip & the	1959	DR 1001/Warwick 634 (60)
Ooh-La-La	Hollywood Flames	1954	Lucky 006/Decca 29284 (55)/ Hollywood 104
Ooh-Ow	Four Buddies	1953	Savoy 888
Ooh-Poo-Pah-Do	Prophets, Ronnie Dio & the	1962	Atlantic 2145
Ooh-Wee, Pretty Baby	Rockin' Dukes (with Joe Hudson)	1957	Excello 2112
Ookey-Ook	Penguins	1955	Dootone 353
Oo-Kook-A-Boo	Tip Tops	1963	Parkway 868
Oo-La-La	Five Lords	1960	D.S. 2078
Oo-La-La-Limbo	Juniors, Danny & the	1962	Guyden 2076
Oom Baby!	Gross Sisters	1959	Checker 932
Oo-Ma-Liddi	Jackaels, J. J. Jackson & the	1959	Storm 502/Prelude 502 (59)

SONG	GROUP	YEAR	LABEL
Oom-Pah Polka	Poni-Tails	1959	ABC 10027
Oongawa	Zirkons, Johnny Parker & the	NA	C T 302
Ooo Sometimes	Shondelles	1963	King 5755
Ooo Wee	Pebbles	1955	Middle-Tone 2002
Oooh Ouch Stop!			
(Teacher, You're Hurting Me)	Harvey (Harvey Fuqua with the Moonglows)	1959	Chess 1749
Ooooo! Ooooo!	Cocoas	1955	Chesterfield 364
Oo-Oo-Wee	Viscounts	1959	Vega 1003
Ooo-Wee	Searchers	1958	Class 223
Oop Boopy Oop	Meadowlarks, Don Julian & the	1956	Dootone 394/Original Sound 004 (58)
Oop Dee Doo	Rovers, Helen Foster & the	1952	Republic 7013
Oop Shoop	Buzzards, Big John & the	1954	Okeh 7045
Oop Shoop	Hamilton Sisters	1954	Columbia 40319
Oop Shoop	Queens, Shirley Gunter & the	1954	Flair 1050
Oops	Tabs	1959	Noble 720
Oops I'm Sorry	Voice Masters	1959	Anna 101
Oops Oh Lawdy	Nobles (Connecticut)	1958	Tee Gee 101/Cupid 1002 (58)
Oops, There Goes Another Year	Mates, Marci & the	1963	Big Top 3136
Oop-Shoobie-Doop Bam-A-Lam	Fabulous Four	1962	Melic 4114
O-O-Wah	Montclairs, Mel Williams & the	1954	Decca 29370
O-O-Wah	Twilighters, Buddy Milton & the	1954	RPM 419
Oo-Wee	Interludes	1958	RCA 7281
Oo-Wee, Baby	Harptones	1955, 1957	Bruce 128/Rama 221
Oo-Wee Baby	Ivy-Tones	1958	Red Top 105
Oo-Wee Mr. Jeff	Hobson, Emmett & group	1953	Central 1001
Oo-Wee Oh Me Oh My	Ad Libs	1965	Blue Cat 119
Oowee, Oowee, Oowee, Oowee	West Winds	1964	Kapp 588
Oowee Wow	Reflections	1964	Golden World 15
Oo-Wee-Baby	Keynotes, Bill Allen & the	1957	Eldorado 505
Op	Honeycones	1958	Ember 1036
Opelia	Turn Ons, Tim Tam & the	1966	Palmer 5002
Open Arms	Jones, Vivian & group	1962	Twirl 1017
Open House	Chariots	1964	RSVP 1105
Open House In Your Heart	Novairs, Carl Bell & the	1958	Laurie 3014
Open House Party	Kokomos (with the Four Seasons)	1962	Josie 906
Open Sesame	Five Keys	1957	Capitol (unreleased)
Open The Door	Keynotes	NA	Index
Open The Door	Rockets	1953	Atlantic 988
Open The Door Baby	Upstarts	1954	Apollo 468
Open The Door (I Forgot My Key)	Royal Teens	1958	ABC 9955
Open The Door, Richard	Smith, Melvin (with the Night Riders)	1958	Cameo 135
Open Up The Back Door	Midnighters	1956	Federal 12260
Open Up Your Eyes	Peanuts, M&M & the	1964	Money 101
Open Up Your Heart	Bishops	1961	Lute 6010
Open Up Your Heart	Hi Tones, Charles Andrea & the	1961	Tori Ltd. T-2X
Open Up Your Heart	Ka-Rillons	1964	Laurie 3244
Open Up Your Heart	Lanes	1956	Gee 1023
Open Your Eyes	Raye, Jean & group	1962	Whip 275
Open Your Eyes	Seminoles	1961	Go-Gee 287
Open Your Heart	Distants	1960	Warwick 577
Opera Vs. The Blues	Utopians	1963	Imperial 5921
Operator	Hearts, Lee Andrews & the (as Lee Andrews)	1963	Parkway 866
Opportunity	Jewels (female)	1964	Dimension 1034
Orange Peel	Rock-Fellers	1959	Valor 2004
Ordinary Guy	Emblems, Patty & the	1964	Herald 590
Oriental Baby	Tellers, Artie Banks & the	1961	Imperial 5788
Oriental, The	Original Three Friends, Joey & the	1963	Chevron 500
Orphan Boy	Pixies 3	1964	Mercury 72231
Orphan Boy	Voice Masters, Ty Hunter & the	1960	Anna 1114
Os-Ca-Lu-Ski-O	Larks (North Carolina)	1954	Lloyds 114
Other Night, The	Five Dots	1954	Dot 1204
Other Way Around, The	Heathens	NA	Vibra 104
Others Like I, The	Four Students, Lil McKenzie & the	1955	Groove 0113
Our Anniversary	Fiestas	1959	Old Town 1069

SONG	GROUP	YEAR	LABEL
Our Anniversary	Five Satins	1957	Ember 1025
Our Anniversary	Laurels	1995	Swing Club 028
Our Anniversary	Limelites, Shep & the	1962	Hull 748
Our Anniversary	Yesterday's News	1979	U.G.H.A. 06
Our Cha-Lypso Of Love	Don Juans, Marsha Renay & the	1960	Hi-Q 5017
Our Day Is Here	Skyliners, Jimmy Beaumont & the	1976	Drive 6520
Our Day Will Come	Earls	NA	Woodbury LP 104
Our Day Will Come	Fireflies	1962	Taurus LP 1002
Our Drummer Can't	Azaleas	1963	Romulus 3001
Our First Kiss	Aquatones	1958	Fargo 1003
Our Future	Yachtsmen	1961	Har-Glo 420
Our Last Goodbye	Concords (Brooklyn)	1961	Gramercy 304
Our Love	Arcades	1960	Julia 1100
Our Love	Foxettes, Lady Fox & the	1962	Don-El 114
Our Love	Jones, Davey & group	1959	Marlin 6062
Our Love	Meadowlarks, Don Julian & the	1988	Classic Artists 101
Our Love	Page Boys	NA	Camelot 114
Our Love	Pixies 3	1963	Mercury 72130
Our Love	Relf, Bobby (with the Laurels)	1956	Cash 1019
Our Love	Rivieras	1959	Coed 513
Our Love Can Never Be	Margilators, Buddy Bennett & the	1959	Blue Moon 412
Our Love Is Beautiful	Mello-Kings	1960	Herald 548
Our Love Is Dying	Swallows (Maryland)	1953	King 4612
Our Love Is Forever	Five Satins	1957	Ember 1014
Our Love Is Here To Stay	Sharps	1957	Lamp 2007
Our Love Is Our Affair	Goldentones	1956	Rainbow 351
Our Love Is Over	Raindrops, Tony & the	1962	Chesapeake 609
Our Love Is So True	Catalinas, Phil & the	1960	Olimpic
Our Love Is True	Del Rays	1958	Cord 101
Our Love Song	Adorables	NA	N/A
Our Love Song	Thor-Ables	1962	Titanic 1001
Our Love Wasn't Meant To Be	Concords (Brooklyn)	1962	Herald 576
Our Love Will Be	Aladdins	1963	Witch 111
Our Love Will Grow	Symphonics	1963	Tru-Lite 116
Our Love Will Last	Skyliners	1961	Colpix 613
Our Love Will Never Be The Same	Modern Red Caps	1965	Lawn 254
Our Love Will Never End	Avons	1956	Hull 717
Our Love's Forever Blessed	Hayes, Linda & group	1955	Recorded In Hollywood 1032/ Decca 29644 (55)
Our Miss Brooks	Goofers	1956	Coral 61664
Our Own Little World	Flips, Little Joey & the	1960	Joy 243
Our Parents Talked It Over	Innocents, Kathy Young & the	1961	Indigo 121
Our Romance	King, Clyde & group	1957	Specialty 605
Our Romance Is Gone	Robins	1950	Savoy 738
Our School Days	Monitors	1957	Specialty 595
Our Song	Imperials, Little Anthony & the	1965	DCP 1136/Veep 1243 (66)
Our Song	Treasures, Bonnie & the	1965	Phi-Dan 5005
Our Song	Volumes	1963	Jubilee 5454
Our Songs Of Love	Allures	1986	Starlight 48
Our Songs Of Love	Dunn, Leona & group	1965	Hallmark 500
Our Songs Of Love	Love Notes (Wilshire)	1963	Wilshire 200
Our Star	Du-Kanes	1964	HSH 501
Our Summer Song	Jaguars	1988	Classic Artists 106
Our Theme	Squires (Chan)	1961	Chan 102/MGM 13044 (61)
Our Wedding Day	Gibralters, Jimmy Barnes & the	1960	Savoy 1581
Our Wedding Day	Off Keys	1962	Rowe 003/Technicord 1001 (62)
Our Wedding Day	Shells	1963	Josie 912
Our Winter Love	Hi-Lites (King)	1963	King 5730
Our Winter Love	Sinceres	1963	Epic 9583
Our Wonderful Love	Accents (Brooklyn)	1962	Jive 888/Vee Jay 484 (62)
Our Wonderful Love	Reactions	1965	Mutual 509
Our Young Love	Original Jaguars	NA	Val-Vo 110
Ours	Rock-Fellers	1959	Valor 2004
Out In Colorado	Belmonts, Dion & the	1957	Mohawk 105
Out In Colorado	Timberlanes, Dino & the	1957	Mohawk 105/Jubilee 5294 (58)

SONG	GROUP	YEAR	LABEL
Out In The Cold Again	Crests	1961	Coed (unreleased)
Out In The Cold Again	Dovells	1961	Parkway 827 (first pressing)
Out In The Cold Again	Earls	NA	Woodbury LP 104
Out In The Cold Again	Ravens(with Dinah Washington)	1951	Columbia 39408
Out In The Cold Again	Teenagers, Frankie Lymon & the	1957	Gee 1036
Out Love Is A Vow	Levee Songsters	1959	Karen 1004/Relic 515 (64)
Out Of A Dream	Ravens	1946, 1949	King 4234/National 9064
Out Of A Dream	Three Clouds	1948	
Out Of A Million Girls	Creators, George Davis & the	1963	Phillips
Out Of A Million Girls	Davis, George & group	1962	Philips 40082
Out Of A Million Girls	Jaynells	1984	N/A
Out Of My Heart	Nutmegs	1965	Relic 1006
Out Of My Life	Expressions	1964	Federal 12533
Out Of My Mind	Evans, Jerry (with the Off Keys)	1962	Bubble 1333
Out Of My Mind	Platters	1958	Mercury 71289
Out Of My Mind	Renditions, Billy De Marco & the	1960	Up 113
Out Of My Mind	Twilighters (Bronx, N.Y.)	1968	Vanco 204
Out Of Sight	Halos, Cammy Carol & the	1961	Elmor 302
Out Of Sight, Out Of Mind	Bon-Aires	1976	Flamingo 1001
Out Of Sight, Out Of Mind	Del-Chords, Donnie & the	1963	Taurus LP 1000
Out Of Sight, Out Of Mind	Ecstasies	1990	Clifton 87
Out Of Sight, Out Of Mind	Essex	1963	Roulette 4530
Out Of Sight, Out Of Mind	Fantastic Five Keys	1962	Capitol 4828
Out Of Sight Out Of Mind	Five Jades (Bronx, N.Y.)	1972	Kelway 103
Out Of Sight, Out Of Mind	Five Keys	1956, 1961	Capitol 3502/Seg-Way 1008
Out Of Sight, Out Of Mind	Shields, Johnny & group	1963	Armour 4466
Out Of Sight Out Of Mind	Subway Serenade	1980	Clifton 53
Out Of Sight, Out Of Mind	Sunglows, Sunny & the	1964	Tear Drop 3027
Out Of Sight Out Of Mind	Vocalaires	1962	Herald (unreleased)
Out Of Sight, Out Of Mind (acappella)	Five Keys	1973	Bim Bam Boom 116
Out Of The Blue	Groves	NA	Riff 104
Out Of The Mist	Pheasants	1963	Throne 802
Out Of The Picture	Reflections	1965	Golden World 24
Out Of The Picture	Robins	1955	Whippet 200
Out Of This World	Chiffons	1966	Laurie 3350
Out Of This World	Earls	1975 (1954)	Gem 227
Out Of This World	Four Sparks	1958	ABC 9906
Out Of Your Heart	Viscounts, Sammy Hagen & the	1957	Capitol 3772
Out To Lunch	Page Boys	1959	Tel 1007
Outside My Window	Fleetwoods	1960	Dolton 15
Outside Of Paradise	Four Gems	1972	Broadcast 4/Broadcast 1001
Outside The Chapel Door	Treckles	1959	Gone 5078
Outside World, The	Drifters (1959-forward)	1965	Atlantic 2292
Over A Cup Of Coffee	Castelles	1954	Grand 109
Over Again	Channels, Earl Lewis & the	1973	Channel 1004
Over And Over	Hargro, Charles & group	1959	DAB 101
Over And Over	Harris, Thurston (with the Sharps)	1958	Aladdin 3430
Over And Over	Satellites, Bobby Day & the	1958	Class 229/Trip 29
Over And Over Again	Buccaneers	1954	Tiffany 1308
Over And Over Again	Moonglows	1956	Chess 1646
Over Easy	Themes, Lanny Hunt & the	1964	Sure Star 5001
Over My Room	Down Beats	1965	Down Beat 1029
Over Someone Else's Shoulder	Harris, Thurston (with the Sharps)	1958	Aladdin 3435
Over The Hump	Quails (Harvey Fuqua)	1962	Harvey 120
Over The Mountain	Johnnie & Joe	1988	Ambient Sound
Over The Ocean	Flints	1958	Petite 101
Over The Rainbow	Admirations (featuring Joseph Lorello)	1974	Kelway 108
Over The Rainbow	Aztecs, Billy Thorpe & the	1965	GNP Crescendo 340
Over The Rainbow	Baysiders	1960	Everest 19366
Over The Rainbow	Blue Belles, Patti LaBelle & the	1965	Atlantic 2318
Over The Rainbow	Buddies, Little Butchie Saunders & his	1959	Angle Tone 535
Over The Rainbow	Castelles	1954	Grand 118
Over The Rainbow	Chanters, Bud Johnson & the	1958	DeLuxe 6177
Over The Rainbow	Checkers	1954	King 4719
Over The Rainbow	Darchaes, Nicky Addeo & the	1964	Selsom 104

SONG	GROUP	YEAR	LABEL
Over The Rainbow	Deja-Vu	1984	Starlight 22
Over The Rainbow	Dell Vikings	1973	Blue Sky 104
Over The Rainbow	Delrons	1961	Forum 700
Over The Rainbow	Demensions	1960, 1966	Mohawk 116/Coral 65559
Over The Rainbow	Dominoes	1955	King 1502
Over The Rainbow	Echoes	1957	Specialty 601
Over The Rainbow	Emjays	1959	Paris 538
Over The Rainbow	Five Boroughs	1991	Mona 31866
Over The Rainbow	Five Fashions	1965	Catamount 103
Over The Rainbow	Guys, Little Sammy Rozzi & the	NA	Pelham 722/Jaclyn 1161
Over The Rainbow	Hamiltons, Alexander & the	1966	Warner Bros. 5844
Over The Rainbow	Hi-Liters	1958	Hico 2433/Zircon 1006
Over The Rainbow	Image	1982	Clifton 68
Over The Rainbow	Imperials, Little Anthony & the	1959	End LP 303/End EP 204 (59)
Over The Rainbow	Kac-Ties	1963	Kape 702
Over The Rainbow	Lytations	1964	Times Square 107
Over The Rainbow	Marcels	1975	Monogram 113
Over The Rainbow	Monarchs	1962	Reegal 512
Over The Rainbow	Mondellos, Yul McClay & the	1957	Rhythm 105
Over The Rainbow	Mustangs	1965	Vest 8005
Over The Rainbow	Mystics	NA	Collectables LP 5043
Over The Rainbow	Original Checkers	1962	King 5592
Over The Rainbow	Portraits	1968	Sidewalk 935
Over The Rainbow	Regents	NA	Unreleased
Over The Rainbow	Remainders	NA	Vico 1
Over The Rainbow	Ricquettes, Danny Skeene & the	NA	Valex 105/106
Over The Rainbow	Satisfiers	1957	Coral 61788
Over The Rainbow	Tones, Little Sammy & the	1962	Pelham 722/Jaclyn 1161 (62)
Over The Rainbow	Vibrations	1962	Checker 1002
Over The Rainbow (acappella)	Young Ones	1965	Times Square 104
Over The Summer Vacation	Empires	1961	Lake 711
Over The Wall	Invictas	1958	Pix 1101
Over The Weekend	Classics (Brooklyn)	1966	Josie 939
Over The Weekend	Crests (Tymes)	1963	Cameo 256
Over The Weekend	Essentials, Billy & the	1962	Jamie 1239
Over The Weekend	Maestro, Johnny & the Tymes	1963	Cameo 256
Over The Weekend	Playboys	1958	Martinique 101/Cameo 142 (58)
Over The Weekend	Spi-Dells	NA	Tyme 200/Tyme 263
Over There (Stands My Baby)	Bobbettes	1962	Jubilee 5427
Over Yonder	Legends	1963	Falco 305
Over You	Capreez	1956	Sound 126/Sound 149 (65)
Ow	Admirals (with Cathy Ryan)	1955	King 4792
Ow Wow Oo Wee	Midnighters	1958	Federal 12339
Ow' You're So Fine	Gems (Broadcast)	1973, 1975	Broadcast 995 (unreleased)/ Drexel 900 (unreleased)
Owee-Nellie	Love Letters	1957	Acme 714
Owl Sees You, The	Showmen	NA	Unreleased
Ozeta	Magnificents	1958	Vee Jay 281

P

SONG	GROUP	YEAR	LABEL
P. S. I Love You	Angels (New Jersey)	1960	Astro AS202-1
P. S., I Love You	Platters	1964	Mercury 72305
P.B. Baby	Pleasers, Wilbur Whitfield & the	1957	Aladdin 3381
P.S. I Love You	Classics (Brooklyn)	1963	Musicnote 118
P.S. I Love You	Four Vagabonds	1953	Lloyds 102
P.S. I Love You	Hearts, Lee Andrews & the (as Lee Andrews)	1961	Swan 4087
P.S. I Love You	Starlets	1960	Astro 202/203
P.T.A., The	Coasters	1963	Atco 6251
Pa And Billie	Strangers	1962	Checker 1010
Pa Pa Ooh Mau Mau	Del-Tinos	1964	Sonic 1451
Pa-Cha	Pagents	1964	Era 3134
Pachuko Hop	Runaways	1962	Moonglow 202
Pack Your Bags And Go	Little Coolbreezers	1956	Ebony 1015
Packing Up My Memories	Stylettes	1964	Cameo 337
Page From The Future	Rhythmettes	1958	Brunswick 55097

SONG	GROUP	YEAR	LABEL
Page Of My Scrapbook	Five Playboys	1957	Fee Bee 213/Dot 15605 (57)
Page One	Bluenotes	1957	Colonial 434
Pages Of My Heart	Five Playboys	1958	Fee Bee 213
Pain In My Heart	Darchaes	1983	Nobell 7001
Pain In My Heart	Dells	1957	Vee Jay 258
Pains In My Heart	Enchantments	1963	Ritz 17003
Pains In My Heart	Innocents	1961	Indigo 132
Pains Of Love	White, Floyd & group	1958	Tee Vee 302
Paint A Sky For Me	Crows, Viola Watkins & the	1951	
Paint Me A Pretty Picture	Impossibles	1964	Reprise 0305
Painted Picture	Spaniels	1955	Vee Jay 154 (second pressing)
Pair Of Eyes	Georgettes	1960	Fleet 1111/United Artists 237 (60)
Pajama Party	Sugar Buns	1959	Warner Bros. 5046
Pajama Party	Teenagers, Frankie Lymon & the	1957	Roulette LP 25021
Pajama Song, The	Serenades	1957	Chief 7002
Pal Of Mine	Orioles, Sonny Til & the	1951	Jubilee 5055
Pal That I Loved Stole The Gal That I Loved, The	Three Beaus And A Peep	1954	Columbia 40344
Pal, The	Arcades	1960	Julia 1100
Palladium	Execs	1958	Fargo 1055
Pamela Jean	Tune Weavers	1957	Casa Grande 4038
Pancakes	Four Lords	1978	Crystal Ball 124
Pancho's Villa	Exceptions	1963	Pro 1/Cameo 378 (65)
Pandora	Fydells	1959	Camelia 100
Panic	Charms, Otis Williams & the	1961	King 5527
Panic Button	Po Boys, Edgar Allen & the	1962	Rust 5053
Panic Stricken	Jayes	1958	Arc 4443
Papa	Earls	1966	Mr. G. 801
Papa	Untouchables	1962	Liberty 55423
Papa Did The Chicken	Little Sammy & group	1956	Shade 1002
Papa Shame	Happytones	1963	Colpix 693
Papa Was A Rolling Stone	Yesterday's News	NA	Starlight 1
Papa-Oom-Mow-Mow	Rivingtons	1962, 1973	Liberty 55427/Wand 11253 (63)
Papa's Side Of The Bed	Angels (New Jersey)	1974	Polydor 14222
Papa's Yellow Tie	V-Eights	1960	Vibro 4005/ABC 10201 (61)
Pa-Pa-Ya, Baby	Jumpin' Jacks, Danny Lamego & the	1954	Bruce 115
Paper Boy	Twilights, Tony Richards & the	1960	Colpix 178
Paper Castles	Teenagers, Frankie Lymon & the	1957	Gee 1032
Paper Crown	Crests	1959	Coed 521
Paper Doll	Tyce, Napoleon & group	1960	Norwood 105
Paper Roses	Echoes	1965	Ascot 2188
Paper Route Baby	Sweet Teens, Faith Taylor & the	1960	Bea & Baby 105
Pappa Knew	Nornetts	1964	Wand 153
Para Siempre	Hollywood Teeners, Jimmy Norman & the	1960	Fun 102
Paradiddle	Centurys	1960	Veltone 104
Paradise	Chimes, Lenny & the	1962	Tag 450
Paradise	Invaders	1963	El Toro 503
Paradise For Two	Hall, Betty & group	1963	Ember 1096
Paradise For Two	Jordan, Lou (with the Chaperones)	1962	Josie 888
Paradise Hill	Embers	1953	Ember 101/Herald 410 (53)
Paradise Hill	Escorts (Essex)	1954	Essex 383
Paradise Hill	Flamingo, Johnny & female group	1958	Specialty 640
Paradise Hill	Harris, Thurston (with the Sharps)	1959	Aladdin 3456
Paradise Is Where He Is	Manselles	1965	Diamond 172
Paradise On Earth	Five Satins	1963	Times Square 21/Times Square 94 (64)
Paradise Princess	Dukes, Billy Duke & the	1956	Teen 110
Pardners	Casuals	NA	Black Hawk 500
Pardon Me	Cezannes (featuring Cerressa)	1963	Markay 108
Pardon Me	Charms, Otis Williams & his	1957, 1961	DeLuxe 6105/King 5527
Pardon Me	Runaways	1961	Lavender 003
Pardon My Heart	Clusters	1958	Tee Gee 102/End 1115 (62)
Pardon My Tears	Moroccos	1955	United 188
Parents Keep-A Preachin'	Nite-Liters	1960	Sudden 101
Paris After Dark	Nomads	1958	Balboa 006/Josie 851 (58)
Park Your Love	Five Notes	1956	Chess 1614

SONG	GROUP	YEAR	LABEL
Parking Field 4	Keytones	1961	Chelsea 1002
Parking Meter	Coquettes, Mike Burnette & the	1959	Imperial 5610
Part Of Everything	Cupcakes, Cookie & the	1961	Mercury 71748
Part Of Me	Lamplighters	1953	Federal 12149
Part Of Me	Sensations	1961	Argo 5391
Part Of Our Love (acappella)	Apparitions	1975	Relic LP 103
Part Of You	Scott Brothers	1959	Skyline 502
Part Time Love	Falcons (Detroit)	1986	Relic LP 8006
Part Time Sweetheart	Jones, Jimmy (with the Pretenders)	1961	Port 70040
Part Time Sweetheart	Pretenders	1955	Whirlin' Disc 106/Port 70040 (61)
Parting	Pharoahs	19??	
Partners For Life	Midnighters	1956	Federal 12251
Partners Paradise	Four Beaus	1959	Todd 1028
Party '66	G-Clefs	1966	Loma 2034
Party Across The Hall	Sensations, Yvonne Baker & the	1962	Argo 5420
Party At Lesters	Bandmasters, Lou Rall & the	1964	Way Out (no number)
Party Boys	Parliaments	1959	Apt 25036
Party Doll	Beltones	1961	Decca 31288
Party Doll	Crests	1960	Coed LP 901
Party Doll	Royal Dukes, Don Ellis & the	1960	Bee 201
Party For Two	Cadillacs	1954	Unreleased
Party For Two	Limelites, Shep & the	1965	Hull 770
Party Ice	Playboys	1959	Dolton 8
Party Lights	Spinners, Claudine Clark & the	1962	Chancellor 1113
Party Line	Lovers	1961	Keller 101
Party Line	Wilder Brothers	1959	Leeds 781
Party People	Chips	1965	Tollie 9042
Party Season	Page, Joey & group	1961	Roulette 4373
Party Starts At Nine, The	Videls	NA	Magic Carpet LP 1005
Party Time	Caliphs	1973	Vintage 1008
Party Time	Corsells	1964	Hudson 8104
Party Time	Crowns	1962	Chordette 1001
Party Time	McElroy, Sollie & female group	NA	Ja-Wes 101
Party Time	Pieces Of Eight	1967	A&M 907
Party Time	Ray-O-Vacs	1956, 1957	Kaiser 384/Atco 6085
Party Time	Tamaras, Lee Durell & the	1960	Music City 836
Party's Over, The	Fiestas	1963	Old Town 1140
Pass It Along	Bon-Bons	1955	London International 1585
Pass It On	Preeteens	1959	J&S 1756
Pass The Gin	Meadowlarks	1954	RPM 406
Passing By	Versatiles	1958	Atlantic 2004
Passing Time	Cookies	1956	Atlantic 1084/Atlantic 2079 (60)
Passion	East-Men, Hal Jaxon & Watsie Lumbard & the	NA	Glow 100
Path In The Wilderness	Elegants, Vito Piccone with the	1963	IPG 1016
Path Of Broken Hearts	Five Crystals	1958	Music City 821/Delcro 827
Patience	Bey Sisters	1956	Jaguar 3016
Patiently	Scotties	1959	Scottie 1305
Patricia	Lyrics	1984	
Patricia	Rhythm Masters	1956	Flip 314
Patricia	Tides	1962	Mercury 72045
Patricia	Youngtones	1958	X-Tra 110/Times Square 13 (63)
Patti	Averones, Bob & the	1964	Brent 7054
Patti's Prayer	Blue Belles, Patti LaBelle & the	1966	Atlantic 2333
Patty	Long, Bobby & his Cherrios	1958	Arrow 727
Patty	Tritones, Terry & the	NA	Kaybee
Patty Ann	Holidays	1962	Track 101
Patty Cake, The	Bradley, Mamie & group	1958	Sue 702
Patty Patty	Equalos	1959	Mad 1296
Paul Loves Betty	Perryman, Paul & group	1959	Duke 305
Paul Revere	Furness Brothers	1952	MGM 11356
Paula Is Mine	Tones	1962	Elmar 6001
Pauline	Dell-Rays	1958	Boptown 102
Paul's Love	Sweeties	1961	End 1110
Pay Day	Da-Prees	1963	Twist 70913

SONG	GROUP	YEAR	LABEL
Pay Me Some Attention	Champions	1956	Chart 620
Payday	Elegants	1959	Apt 25029
Payin' (For The Wrong I've Done)	Lovejoys	1964	Tiger 105/Red Bird 003 (64)
Peace And Contentment	Clicks	1955	Josie 780
Peace And Love	Five Keys	1956	Capitol 3455
Peace Of Mind	Blue Moons	NA	Jaguar 1001
Peace Of Mind	Five Scripts	1963	Long Fiber 201
Peace Of Mind	Continentals (Brooklyn)	NA	Relic LP 5036
Peace Of Mind	Drifters (1959-forward)	1973	Steeltown 671
Peace Of Mind	Dubs, Richard Blandon & the	1987	Starlight 51
Peace Of Mind	Fabulous Marcels	1975	St. Clair 13711
Peace Of Mind	Five Scripts	1963	Long Fiber 201
Peace Of Mind	Four Dots (Pittsburgh)	1956	Bullseye 104
Peace Of Mind	Marcels (as the Fabulous Marcels)	1975	St. Clair 13711/Owl 324
Peace Of Mind	Penguins	1956	Wing 90076
Peace Of Mind	Royal Five	1968	Arctic 160
Peace Of Mind	Spaniels	1974	Canterbury EP101
Peace Of Mind	Spydels	1962	Assault 1860
Peace Of Mind	Visions, Connie McGill & the	1963	Triode 115
Peace Of Mind	Young Lords	1970	Kelway 100
Peace Of Mind (acappella)	Notations	1975	Relic LP 109
Peace Of Mind (acappella)	Spirals	1975	Relic LP 108
Peaches	Escapades	1964	Glow 87896
Peanut Brittle	Actors	1962	Laurie 3135
Peanut Butter	Marathons	1961	Arvee 5027/5389/Chess 1790
Peanut Butter Song	Angels, Gabriel & the	1963	Swan 4133
Peanut Man	Tones, W. Williams & the	NA	Kennedy 5146
Peanuts	Catalinas	1960	Up
Peanuts	Keens, Rick & the	1961	Austin 313/Le Cam 721 (61)/ Smash 1705 (61)
Peanuts	Thrillers, Little Joe & the	1957, 1963	Okeh 7088/Reprise 20142
Peanuts And Popcorn	Thrillers, Little Joe & the	1964	Enjoy 2011
Peanuts (La Cacahuta)	Sunglows, Sunny & the	1965	Sunglow 107/Disco Grande 1021
Pearl	Schoolboys (Leslie Martin with the Cadillacs)	1957	Okeh 7090
Pearl Of My Heart	Arlin, Bob & group	1960	Olympia 823/824
Pearlie Mae	Jewels (Los Angeles)	1959	Antler 1102
Pecan Mambo	Fuller, Walter & group	1954	Kicks 4
Pedal Pushin' Papa	Dominoes	1952	Federal 12114
Peddler Of Dreams	Fi-Tones	1973	Relic LP 5010
Peddler Of Dreams	Thorne, Roscoe (with the Caverliers)	1953	Atlas 1033
Pee Wee	Valrays	1963	Parkway 880
Peek, Peek-A-Boo	Ermines	1955	Loma 701
Peek-A-Boo	Cadillacs	1958	Jo-Z 846 (first pressing)/ Josie 846 (58) (second pressing)
Peek-A-Boo	Elbert, Donnie & group	1958	DeLuxe 6161
Peek-A-Boo Love	Volchords	1961	Regatta 2004
Peek-A-Boo Mary Lou	Richards, Ricky & group	1961	Wye 1011
Peeper, The	Delegates	1965	Aura 88120
Peepin' Through The Window	Cymbals, Lee Williams & the	1965	Carnival 527
Peewee's Boogie	Jive Bombers	1952	Citation 1161
Peg O' My Heart	Trophies	1962	Challenge 9149
Peg Of My Heart	Candles, Rochell & the	1961	Swingin' 640
Peggy	Heralds	1968	Tamborine 2
Peggy	Hollywood Flames	1954	Lucky 006/Decca 29284 (55)/ Hollywood 104
Peggy Darling	Impalas (Brooklyn)	1959	Cub 9053
Peggy Sue	Upbeats, Ray Allen & the	1962	Blast 204
Peggy's Party	Saints, Danny & the	1959	Warner Bros. 5134
Pen In Hand	Remainders	NA	Vico 1
Pen Pal	Gaytunes	1958	Joyce 106
Pen Pal	Maidens, Sir Joe & the	1962	Lenox 5563
Penalty Of Love	Velvetones	1959	D 1049/Glad
Penalty, The	Rookies	1959	Donna 1313
Pencil Song	Diamonds	1960	Mercury 71633
Penetration	Pyramids (Best)	1963	Best 102/Best 13002 (64)

SONG	GROUP	YEAR	LABEL
Pennies For A Beggar	Majestics (Florida)	1960	Knight 105
Pennies From Heaven	Clovers	1959	United Artists LP 3033
Pennies From Heaven	Dreamers, Hal Hedges & the	1963	ABC 10406
Pennies From Heaven	Five Fashions	1964	Catamount 102
Pennies From Heaven	Four Tops	1962	Riverside 4534
Pennies From Heaven	Matadors	1958	Sue 700
Pennies From Heaven	Metronomes (Harold Sonny Wright)	1960	Wynne EP/Wynne LP 706 (60)
Pennies From Heaven	Skyliners	1960	Calico 117/Original Sound 36 (63)
Pennies From Heaven (acappella)	Citadels	1975	Relic LP 103
Pennies From Heaven (acappella)	Pretenders	1975	Relic LP 101
Penny	Dimensions	1966	Panorama 25/HBR 1477 (66)/ Hanna Barbera 477 (66)
Penny	Mello-Kings	1961	Herald 561
Penny Arcade	Moonglows, Bobby Lester & the	1962	Chess 1811
Penny In A Wishing Well	Teasers, Sammy & the	1958	Airport 101
Penny Loafers	Plushtones	1960	Plush 601
Penny Whistle Band	Tokens (Brooklyn)	1974	Atco 7009
People Are Funny	Accents (featuring Sandi)	NA	Gazzari 90391
People Are Talking	Gray, Maureen & group	1962	Landa 692
People Are Talking (Slow Version)	Heartbeats	1956	Hull 716/Gee 1061 (61)
People Call Me Little Boy	Travelers, Roger & the	1961	
People From Another World	Jive Five	1961	Beltone 1014/Relic 1030 (78)
People Gonna Talk	Don-Tels	1963	Witch 119
People Say	Flints	1959	Okeh 7126
People Say	Vibrations	1961, 1977	Checker LP 2978
People Sure Act Funny	Webs	1966	MGM 13602
People Will Say We're In Love	Spaniels	1959	Vee Jay 342
People Will Talk	Singing Doves, Cliff Butler & the	1953	States 123
Pepe La Phew	Resonics	1963	Unity 101
Pepper-Hot Baby	Belvederes	1955	Baton 217
Peppermint	Chantiers	1964	DJB 112
Peppermint Jerk	Peppermints	1965	RSVP 1112
Peppermint Stick	Adventurers	1961	Columbia
Peppermint Stick	Elchords, Butchie Saunders & the	1957	Good 544/Musictone 1107 (59)
Peppermint Stick	Valentinos	1982	Crystal Ball 147
Peppermint Twist	Starlighters, Joey Dee & the	1962	Roulette 4401
Peppermint Twist	Twisters, Joey & the	1961	Dual 502
Peppermint Twist, The	Jumpin' Jacks, Danny Peppermint & the	1961	Carlton 565
Peppi	Starbells, Terry Star & the	1963	New-Art 1008
Perdelia	Continental Five	1959	Nu Kat 10132
Perfect Crime, The	Nomads	1958	Balboa 006/Josie 851 (58)
Perfect Example, The	Clean Cut Clan, Dan & the	1962	Accent 1116
Perfect Love	Ascots	1962	Ace 650
Perfect Love	Barons (Dart)	1963	Dart 134
Perfect Night	Hume, Don & group	1963	Felsted 8679
Perfect Night For Love	Chaps	1960	Brent 7016
Perfect Woman	Runarounds	1966	Capitol 5644
Perfidia	Ellis, Lorraine (with the Crows)	1954	Gee 1/Bullseye 100 (55)
Perfidia	Goofers	1959	Tiara 6127
Perfidia	Matadors	1963	Colpix 698
Periwinkle Blue	Four Cheers	1958	End 1034
Peruvian Wedding Song	Chantels	1987	Murray Hill LP 000385
Pete The Mongoose	Cashmeres, Dale & the	1961	Matt 161
Peter Cottontail	Taffys	1963	Pageant 608
Peter Peter	Royal Kings	1961	Forlin 502/Candlelight 410
Peter, Peter, Pumpkin Eater	Troupers	1959, 1974	Red Top 118
Peter's Gun	Four Sounds	1961	Tuff 1
Petticoat Baby	Four Fellows (Brooklyn - Glory)	1956	Glory 241
Phantom Stage Coach	Ravens	1950	National 9131
Phantom, The	Cronies, Herb & the	1960	Personality 700
Philadelphia Girl	Students (Philadelphia)	1992	Clifton 103
Phillie, The	Peanuts, M&M & the	1964	Money 107
Philly Dog	Larks (Don Julian)	1965	Money 122
Philly Jerk	Meadowlarks, Don Julian & the	1965	Jerk 100
Philly Stomp	Joey, Guy & group	1961	Coed 563

SONG	GROUP	YEAR	LABEL
Phoebe	Cool Gents, Deroy Green & the	NA	Unreleased
Phone Booth On The Highway	Crests	1965	Apt 25075
Phony Baloney	Four Bars	1960	Time 4
Phyllis	Meadows, Larry & group	1959	Strato-Lite 969
Phyllis	Stenotones, Billy James & the	1961	Rust 5038
Phyllis Beloved	Desires	1962	Dasa 102
Physical Fitness	First Platoon	1963	SPQR 3303
Physical Fitness Blues	Tabbys	1963	Metro 2
Piano Player Play A Tune	Ellis, Lorraine (with the Crows)	1954	Gee 1/Bullseye 100 (55)
Piccadilly	Jaguars	1958	Ebb 129
Pick It Up	Chessmen	1962	Amy 841
Pick Up	Galleons	1959	Vita 184
Pick Up And Deliver	Chuck-A-Lucks	1961	Warner Bros. 5198
Pickin' On The Wrong Chicken	Five Stars (Detroit)	1958	Note 10011/Hunt 318 (58)/ ABC 9911 (58)
Pickin' Petals	Avons	1960	Mercury 71618
Pickin' Up The Pieces Of My Heart	Pictures, C.L. & the	1963	Dunes 2021
Picture In My Wallet	Oxfords, Darrell & the	1959	Roulette 4174
Picture Of An Angel	Crystalaires	NA	Magic Carpet EP 512
Picture Of An Angel	Four Graduates	1963	Rust 5062
Picture Of Love	Continentals (Brooklyn)	1956	Whirlin' Disc 105/Port 70024 (59)
Picture Of Love	El Sierros	1964	Times Square 36/Relic 527 (65)
Picture Of Love	Endings	1975	Barrier 102
Picture Of Love	Laurels	1959	ABC 10048
Picture Of My Baby	Uniques	1960	Peacock 1695
Picture On The Wall	Kool Gents	1963	Bethlehem 3061
Picture, The	McDonald, Ken & group	1958	Prep 128
Picture, The	Universals (Philadelphia)	1958	Cora-Lee 501
Pied Piper	Cupcakes	1965	Diamond 177
Piel Canela	Cinnamon Skin	1959	Checker 917
Pigeon	Dynamics	1959	Delta 1002
Pigeon	Gum Drops	1957	King 5051
Pigtails And Blue Jeans	Carbo, Leonard & group	1958	Vee Jay 291
Pigtails Eyes Are Blue	Premiers (Connecticut)	1960	Fury 1029
Pile Driver	Gleams	1963	Kapp 565
Pillow Wet With Tears	Individuals	1964	Chase 1300
Pimples And Braces	Fallen Angels	NA	Eceip 1004
Pina Colada	Four Mints	1959	NRC 037
Ping Pong	Glowtones	1957	East West 101/Atlantic 1156 (57)
Ping Pong	Tangiers (Strand)	1961	Strand 25039
Ping Pong Baby	Voxpoppers	1958	Mercury 71315
Pink Champagne	Continentals (Vandan)	1962	Vandan 8453
Pink Champagne	Tyrones	1957	Mercury 71104
Pink Dominoes	Crescents, Chiyo & the	1963	Break Out 4/Era 3116 (63)
Pink Lips	Caravelles	1961	Star Maker 1925
Pink Panther, The	Tads	1956	Liberty Bell 9010/Dot 15518 (56)
Pinocchio	Crystalaires	NA	Mickey B Juke Box Review 101
Pistol Packin' Mama	Dell Vikings	1960	Alpine 66
Pistol Packin' Mama	Hurricanes	1955	King 4817
Pistol Packin' Mama	Knightsmen	1961	Bocaldun 1006
Pistol Packin' Mama	Powell, Sandy & group	1960	Herald 557/Impala 211
Pistol Packing Mama	Lovers, Pete Peter & the	1960	Derby 1030
Pitter Patter	Blue Belles	1962	Newtown 5006 (1st printing)
Pitter Patter	Five Fleets	1961	Seville 112
Pitter Patter	Four Sportsmen	1961	Sunnybrook 4
Pitter Patter Boom Boom	Jaye Sisters	1958	Atlantic 1171
Pitter Patter Heart	Seniors	1960	Kent 342
Pittery Pat	Hubcaps, Holt Davey & the	1958	United Artists 110X
Pittsburgh Twist And Freeze	Saints, Orlie & the	1961	Band Box 253
Pity Me	Satin Angels	1985	Relic 8004
Pizza Pie	Rob-Roys, Norman Fox & the	1958	Hammer 544/Capitol 4128 (59)
Place	Beechwoods	1963	Smash 1843
Place I Know	Fabulous Twilights, Nathaniel Mayer & the	1963	Fortune 562
Plain Old Love	Jones, Jimmy (with the Pretenders)	1960	Roulette 4232
Plain Old Love	Pretenders, Jimmy Jones & the	1956	Rama 210/Roulette 4322 (60)

SONG	GROUP	YEAR	LABEL
Plan For Love	Flamingos	1953	Chance 1149
Plan, The	Trains	1964	Swan 4196
Planet Rock	Royal Teens	1957	Power 215/ABC 9882 (58)
Planters Cafe	Parisians	1959	Bullseye 1028
Play A Love Song	Jaguars	1989	Classic Artists 113
Play A Sad Song	Daniels, Dotty & group	1963	Amy 885
Play Boy	Lyres	1953	J&G 101
Play By The Rules Of Love	Cavaliers	1958	Apt 25004
Play It Again	Four Stars	1961	Bamboo 512
Play It Cool	Rey, Tony & group	1959	King Bee 101
Play It Cool	Spaniels	1954	Vee Jay 116
Play The Game Fair	Shields	1958	Tender 521/Dot 15940 (58)
Play Those Oldies Mr. D.J.	Sophomores, Anthony & the	1963	Mercury 72103
Playboy	Expressions	1965	Reprise 0360
Playboy	Fairlanes	1961	Continental 1001
Playboy	Fidelitones	1961	Marlo 1518
Playboy	Playboys, Gene Vito & the	1964	Blast 214
Playboy	Shadows, Dave & the	1964	Fenton 942
Playboy	Veltones	1959	Coy 101/Kapp 268 (59)
Playboy (acappella)	Nutmegs	NA	Unreleased
Playboy (Don't You Play In School)	Diablos	1963	Fortune 551
Playboy (Don't You Play In School)	Nite Sounds	1962	Fortune 551
	Melvin Davis with the Diablos & the		
Playboy Lover	King Krooners	1958	Unreleased
Playgirl	Four Winds	1964	Dery 1002/Felsted 8703 (64)
Playgirl	Young Sisters	1961	Twirl 2008
Playing A Game Of Love	Five Discs	1979	Crystal Ball 136
Playing For Keeps	Cineramas	1960	Rhapsody 71984
Playing For Keeps	Love, Darlene & group	1963	Philles 111
Playing Hard To Get	Juniors, Danny & the	1959	ABC 10052
Playing Hide And Seek	Ly-Dells	1964	Southern Sound 122
Playing Me For A Fool	Wilson, Faye & group	1957	Hip 401
Playing Possum	Downbeats	1960	Wilco 16
Playing The Field	Caruso, Dick & group	1959	MGM 12827
Playing The Field	Counts, Frankie Brent & the	1958	Vik 0322
Playmate Of The Year	Sunsets	1963	Challenge 9198
Playmates	Regents	1965	Blue Cat 110
Plaything	Pleasers, Wilbur Whitfield & the	1957	Aladdin 3396
Plaything	Pleasures	1964	RSVP 1102
Playthings	Shirelles, Shirley & the	1969	Bell 787
Plea In The Moonlight	Gaytunes	1958	Joyce 106
Plea Of Love	Gay Notes	1958	Zynn 504
Plea, The	Chantels	1957	End 1001
Plea, The	Jesters	1958	Winley 225
Plea, The	Tangiers (Los Angeles)	1962	A-J 905
Pleadin' Heart	Whips	1954	Flair 1025
Pleading	Willis, Robert (Chick)	1959	Bay-Tone 104
Pleading Blues	Swallows (Maryland)	1953	King 4656
Pleading For Your Love	Four Dots, Jerry Stone & the	1959	Freedom 44005
	(with Eddie Cochran & Jewel Akens)		
Pleading From My Heart To You	Casanovas	1989	Relic LP 5081
Pleading No More	Shells	1958	Johnson 106/Juanita 106 (58)
Pleading To You	Five Owls	1955	Vulcan 1025
Please	Coins	1955	Model 2001
Please	Revels	1960	Andie 5077
Please	Wanderers	1959	Cub 9023
Please	Zodiacs, Maurice Williams & the	1961	Herald 565
Please Accept My Love	Wilson, Jimmy & group	1959	Goldband 1074
Please Answer	Heartbreakers (Bronx, N.Y.)	1964	Linda 114
Please Baby	Cardinals	1954	Atlantic 1025
Please Baby	Curry, James (with the Jayhawks)	1956	Flash 110
Please, Baby	Five Willows	1953	Pee Dee 290
Please Baby Be Mine	Individuals (with the Merceedees)	1962	Gold Seal 1000
Please Baby Please	Monograms	1957	Saga 1000
Please Baby Please	Realistics	1970	De-Lite 528

SONG	GROUP	YEAR	LABEL
Please Baby Please	Swallows (Maryland)	1952	King 4579
Please Baby, Please	Tune Tones	1958	Herald 524
Please, Baby, Please	Vice-Roys	1955	Aladdin 3273
Please Baby Please (Come On Back To Me)	Jive Five	NA	United Artists 936
Please Be Fair	La Rells	1961	Robbee 109
Please Be Fair	Maresca, Ernie (with the Del Satins)	1963	Seville 129
Please Be Good To Me	Debs, Ty Robin & the	1960	Rex 1010
Please Be Honest With Me	Browns, Barbara & the	1964	Stax 158
Please Be Mine	Casanovas	1957	Apollo 519
Please Be Mine	Classic IV	1962	Twist 1003/1004
Please Be Mine	Consorts	1961	Cousins 1004/Apt 25066 (62)
Please Be Mine	Four-Evers	1964	Smash 1887 (first pressing)
Please Be Mine	Knockouts	1960	Shad 5018
Please Be Mine	Rhythm Jesters	1962	Lectra 501
Please Be Mine	Sweet Teens, Faith Taylor & the	1960	Bea & Baby 104
Please Be Mine	Teenagers, Frankie Lymon & the	1956	Gee 1002
Please Be Mine	Vels	1957	Trebco 16/Trebco 702 (57)
Please Be Mine	Wayne, James & female group	1957	Peacock 1672
Please Be Mine (acappella)	Four Clefs	1966	B-J 1000
Please Be My Boyfriend	Shirelles	1960	Scepter 1207
Please Be My Girl	Fabulous Earthquakes	1960	Meridian 1518
Please Be My Girlfriend	Dahills	1976	Clifton 13/14
Please Be My Girlfriend	Spotlighters	1958	Aladdin 3436
Please Be My Guy	Crystaliers, Cleo & the	1957, 1976	Johnson 103/Cindy 3003 (57)
Please Be My Love	Boyfriends, Janis & Her	1958	RCA 7318
Please Be My Love	Casanovas	1955	Apollo 477
Please Be My Love	Mendell, Johnny & group	1962	Jamie 1214
Please Be My Love	Ross, Stefan & group	1960	
Please Be My Love	Spirals	1961	Smash 1719
Please Be My Love Tonight	Charades	1963	Ava 154
Please Be My Love Tonight	Saxons	1957	Our
Please Be Satisfied	Suedes	1959	Dart 117
Please Believe I Love You	Hi-Lites	1959	Reno 1030
Please Believe In Me	Charms, Otis Williams & the	1954	DeLuxe 6034
Please Believe In Me	Twilights, Tony Richards & the	1960	Colpix 178
Please Believe Me	Browne, Doris (with the Capris)	1953	Gotham 290
Please Believe Me	Capris (Philadelphia)	NA	Collectables LP 5000
Please Believe Me	Elegants	1958	Apt 25017
Please Believe Me	Mayfield, Percy & group	1957	Specialty 607
Please Believe Me	Ravens	Between 1947 & 1950	National (unreleased)
Please Believe Me	Team Mates	1965	Soft 104/Paula 220 (65)
Please Big Mama	Gray, Rudy & group	1955	Capitol 3149
Please Bring Yourself Back Home	Ramblers (Baltimore)	1954	MGM 11850
Please Buy My Record	Lee, Addie & group	1958	End 1018
Please Call	Chimes (Tennessee)	1957	Arrow 724
Please Change Your Mind	Gems (Recorte)	1958	Recorte 407
Please Come Back	Acorns	1959	Unart 2015
Please Come Back	Daylighters, Betty Everett & the	1960	C.J. 611
Please Come Back	Echoes	1953	Rockin' (unreleased)
Please Come Back	Emeralds, Bobby Woods & the	1961	Rumble 348
Please Come Back	Fi-Dels	1958	Bardo 529
Please Come Back	Majorettes	1963	Troy 1000
Please Come Back	Metrotones (with the Little Walkin' Willie Quartet)	1957	Reserve 116
Please Come Back	Mon-Clairs	1962	Joey 6101
Please Come Back	Twisters	1961	Sunset 501
Please Come Back	V-8s	1959	Most 711/713
Please Come Back Home	Flamingos	1955	Checker 821
Please Come Back Home	Orientals	1958	Kayo 927
Please Come Back To Me	Alma-Keys	1962, 1980	Kiski 2056
Please Come Back To Me	Avons	1958	Hull 728
Please Come Back To Me	Intervals	1959	Ad 103
Please Come Back To Me	Rhythm Tones	1959	Vest 828
Please Come Back To Me	Sparrows Quartette	1973	Del Tone 3001

SONG	GROUP	YEAR	LABEL
Please Come Back To Me	Stereos	1961	Cub 9095
Please Come Back To Me	Swann, Claudia (with Buddy Griffin & group)	1954	Chess 1586
Please Come Home	Cheaters	NA	JBJ
Please Come Home	Dolls	1959	Okeh 7122
Please Come Home	Embers, Joe D'Ambra & the	1960	Mercury 71725
Please Come Home	Five Embers	1954	Gem 224
Please Come Home	Quarter Notes	1957	Dot 15685
Please Come Home	Twilighters (Bronx, N.Y.)	1960	Super 1003
Please Come Home For Christmas	Saints	1984	Angela 104
Please Come On To Me	Clovers	1958	Poplar 110/Poplar 139 (59)
Please Consider	Gainors	1960	Mercury 71569
Please Daddy	McNeil, Angele & group	1957	Felsted 8503
Please Dear	Quin-Tones (Pennsylvania)	1958	Red Top 108/Hunt 321 (58)
Please Don't	Lyrics, Ike Perry & the	1979	King Tut 181
Please Don't Ask Me	Four Gents	1961	Nite Owl 50
Please Don't Be Angry With Me	Dimples	1964	Cameo 325
Please Don't Be Mad	Rydell, Bobby & group	1959	Cameo 160
Please Don't Be Mad At Me	Visuals	1963, 1981	Poplar 121
Please Don't Call Me Fool	Furness Brothers, Al Berry & the	1957, 1964	Prep 107/Melmar 115
Please Don't Cheat On Me	Roomates	1963	Philips 40153/Philips 40161 (63)
Please Don't Cheat On Me	Sinceres	1961	Richie 545
Please Don't Come Crying	Blackwells	1959	G&G 126
Please Don't Crush My Dreams	Emerals	1958, 1967	Triple X 100/101/Times Square 111
Please Don't Cry	Wonders	1962	Bamboo 523
Please Don't Deprive Me Of Love	Four Fellows (Brooklyn - Glory)	1956	Glory 242
Please Don't Ever Leave Me Baby	Emblems, Patty & the	1967	Kapp 850
Please Don't Freeze	Brown, Ruth & Rhythmakers	1955	Atlantic 1036
Please Don't Go	Bumble Bees	NA	Relic LP 5043
Please Don't Go	Centuries	1985	Relic LP 5053
Please Don't Go	Chanters	19??	
Please Don't Go	Cordells	1958	Bullseye 1017
Please Don't Go	Gailtones	1958	Decca 30726
Please Don't Go	Ozells	1963	Cub 9126
Please Don't Go	Thrillers, Little Joe & the	1960	Okeh 7136
Please Don't Go	Tonettes	1962	Volt 101
Please Don't Go (Back To Baltimore)	Acey, Johnny & group	1960	Fire 1015
Please Don't Hurt Me	Byrd, Bobby & group	1955	Sage & Sand 203
Please Don't Kiss Me Again	Charmettes	1963	Kapp 547
Please Don't Leave	Miller Sisters	1956	Hull 718
Please Don't Leave Me	Anderson, Bubba & group	1962	Ace 662
Please Don't Leave Me	Cardinals	1951	Atlantic 938
Please Don't Leave Me	Clefs	1954	Peacock 1643
Please Don't Leave Me	Crowns, Arthur Lee Maye & the	1955	RPM 438
Please Don't Leave Me	Czars Of Rhythm	1965	De-Voice 2501
Please Don't Leave Me	Dreamers (Mercury)	1952	Mercury 70019
Please Don't Leave Me	Four Lovers	1956	RCA 6519
Please Don't Leave Me	Lawrence Brothers, Bill Lawrence & the	1960	Bertram International 227
Please Don't Leave Me	Parrots	1953	Parrot 758/Checker 772 (54)
Please Don't Leave Me	Vocaltones	1989	Relic LP 5082
Please Don't Leave Me Dear	Falcons (Detroit)	1985	Relic LP 8005
Please Don't Leave Me Now	Royal-Aires	1957	Gallo 110
Please Don't Leave Me This Way	Lyrics, Leo Valentine & the	1962	Skylight 201
Please Don't Leave, Please Don't Go	Valentines	1960	King 5338
Please Don't Let Me Go	Velvateens	NA	Velvet 1001
Please Don't Let Me Know	Covay, Don & group	1964	Rosemart 802
Please Don't Love Him	Knickerbockers	1966	Challenge 59348
Please Don't Make Me Cry	Chevrons	1962	Sara 6462
Please Don't Say Goodbye	Delphis, Tony & the	NA	New Group 6001
Please Don't Say Goodbye	Townsmen (New York - Columbia)	1964	Columbia 43207
Please Don't Say No	Dominoes	1959	Liberty 55181
Please Don't Say No	Majestics (Detroit)	1958	NRC 502
Please Don't Say No To Me	Bell Hops	1956	Tin Pan Alley 153
Please Don't Say We're Through	Debonaires (Golden World)	1964	Golden World 17/26
Please Don't Stay Away Too Long	U.S. Four	1962	Heritage 110
Please Don't Take Away The Girl I Love	Sheiks	1960	Amy 807

SONG	GROUP	YEAR	LABEL
Please Don't Talk About Me	Bay City 5, Luigi Martini & the	1954	Jaguar 3001
Please Don't Talk About Me	Rock-A-Tones	NA	Judytone 369
Please Don't Tease	Crescents	1985	Relic LP 5053
Please Don't Tease	Spaniels	1956	Vee Jay 229
Please Don't Tell 'Em	Blue Dots	1957	Ace 526
Please Don't Tell Her	Cordell, Richie & group	1962	Rori 707
Please Don't Tell Me Now	Dean & Jean (with the Del Satins)	1964	Rust 5075
Please Don't Wake Me	Cinderellas	1964	Dimension 1026
Please Forgive Me	Coraltones	1956	Speck
Please Forgive Me	Emblems	1959	Topic 8570
Please Forgive Me	Playboys	1959	Martinique 400
Please Give Me A Chance	Starr, Bobby & group	1959	Radio 120
Please (Give Me A Little Love)	Martino, Lou & group	1964	Columbia 43126
Please Give Me One More Chance	Serenaders, Gene Mumford & the	1956	Whiz 1500
Please Give My Heart A Break	Orioles, Sonny Til & the	1949	Jubilee 5002
Please Go	Imperials, Little Anthony & the	1964	DCP 1104/Veep 1240 (66)
Please Go Away	Bees, Honey & the	1959	Pentagon 500
Please Have Mercy	Platters, Linda Hayes & the	1955	King 4773
Please Hear My Plea	Rochells	NA	Spacey 202
Please Help	Dukays	1962	Vee Jay 442
Please Holy Father	Velveteens	1961	Stark 12591
Please Hurry Home	Swans (Cameo)	1964	Cameo 302
Please Jan	Ideals	1959	Stars Of Hollywood 1001
Please Keep The Beatles In England	Minute Men	1964	Argo 5469
Please Kiss This Letter	Solitaires	1957	Old Town 1034/Argo 5316 (58)
Please Leave Me	En-Solids, Drake & the	NA	Alteen 8652
Please Let Her	Casinos	1962	S&G 301
Please Let Her Know	Duprees	1964	Coed 591
Please Let It Be	Bumble Bees	NA	Relic LP 5043
Please Let It Be Me	Fashions	1962	Elmor 301
Please Let It Be Me	Orlons	1962	Cameo 211
Please Let Me Be	Cruisers	1961	Pharaoh 128
Please Let Me Be The One	Collegians	1956	Groove 0163
Please Let Me Know	Darlings	1963	Mercury 72185
Please Let Me Know	Five Pearls	1954	Aladdin 3265
Please Let Me Know	Overtones	1966	Ajax 173
Please Let Me Love You	Jesters	1957	Winley 221
Please Let Me Love You	Ripples	1960	Bond 1479
Please Let Me Love You (acappella)	Five Chancells	1965	Fellatio 103/Dawn 302
Please Lie To Me	Reminiscents	1963	Cleopatra 104
Please Listen To Me	Zip, Danny & group	1964	MGM 13254
Please Love A Fool	Meadowlarks, Don Julian & the	1956	Dootone 394/Original Sound 004 (58)
Please Love Me	Aladdins	1962	Witch 109
Please Love Me	Cameos (Flagship)	1959	Flagship 115
Please Love Me	Marylanders	1952	Jubilee 5091
Please Love Me Baby	Five Jets	1954	DeLuxe 6071
Please Love Me Forever	Roomates, Cathy Jean & the	1960	Valmor 007
Please Love Me Forever	Sedates	1958	MRB 171/20th Century 1011 (59)/ Port 70004 (59)/20th Century 1212 (61)
Please Love Me Now	Northern Lights	1960	Patt 059
Please Make Up Your Mind	Kentones	1958	Siroc 202
Please Mary Lou	Rockin' Chairs	1959	Recorte 404
Please Mister Moon	Buzz-Off Boys Quintet	1978	Clifton 28
Please Mr. Cupid	Gay Poppers	1961	Fire 1039
Please Mr. D.J.	Caine, Gladys & group	1963	Togo 602
Please Mr. D.J.	Miller Sisters	1960	Miller 1143
Please Mr. Disc Jockey	Debonaires, Dickie & the	1965, 1982	Valli 302
Please Mr. Disc Jockey	Sensations	1956	Atco 6067
Please, Mr. Johnson	Cadillacs	1959	Josie 861
Please Mr. Scientist	Redwoods	1962	Epic 9505
Please Mr. Sun	Clovermen, Tippie & the	1962	Stenton 7001
Please, Mr. Sun	Embers	1960	Dot 16162
Please Mr. Sun	Innocents	1961	Indigo 111
Please Pass The Biscuits	Parks, Gino	1957	Fortune 839X

SONG	GROUP	YEAR	LABEL
Please Play My Song	Four Fellows (Brooklyn - Glory)	1956	Glory 244
Please, Please	Eagles	1954	Mercury 70391
Please Please	Scholars	NA	Ruby-Ray 2
Please, Please Baby	Curios, Bobby Brown & the	1959	Vaden 109
Please, Please, Baby	Five Hearts (Los Angeles)	1954	Flair 1026
Please, Please Darling	Dew Drops, Henry Clement & the	1961	Zynn 503
Please, Please Forgive Me	Serenaders (Detroit)	1954	DeLuxe 6022
Please Please Me	Fireflies	1962	Taurus LP 1002
Please, Please, Please	Five Royales	1960	Home Of The Blues 112
Please, Please, Please	Moreland, Prentice & group	1959	Edsel 778
Please, Please, Please	Night Riders, Johnny Fairchild & the	1959	Ace 565
Please Please Please	Olympics	1969	Warner Bros. 7369
Please Pretty Baby	Fabulous Koolcats, Ruben Siggers & the	1957	Spinks 600
Please Remember My Heart	Five Bells	1971	Stolper 100
Please Remember My Heart	Solitaires	1954, 1958	Old Town 1006/1007/1059
Please Remember My Love	Storytellers	1990	Classic Artists 118
Please Return	Jewels (Los Angeles)	1955	Imperial 5362
Please Ring My Phone	Starlettes	1958	Checker 895
Please Say	Magic Moments	1999	Magic Moments 100
Please Say I'm Wrong	Hollywood Four Flames	1951	Unique 015
Please Say It Isn't So	Decades	1980	Avenue D 1
Please Say It Isn't So	Swinging Hearts	1960	Lucky Four 1011/Diamond 162 (64)
Please Say It Isn't So (acappella)	Sintells	1975	Relic LP 105
Please Say You Do	Victorians	1956	Selma 1002
Please Say You Love Me	Crowns, Arthur Lee Maye & the	1955	RPM 420 (unreleased)
Please (Say You Love Me)	Meadowlarks, Don Julian & the	1958	Original Sound 03
Please Say You Love Me	Sunglows	NA	Carrib 1025
Please Say You Want Me	Averones, Bob & the	1964	Brent 7054
Please Say You Want Me	Carvells	1978	Clifton 30
Please Say You Want Me	Cleftones	1976	Robin Hood 133
Please Say You Want Me	Cleftones (featuring Pat Spann)	1961	Gee LP 705
Please Say You Want Me	Del-Chords, Donnie & the	1963	Taurus LP 1000
Please Say You Want Me	Fourteen Karat Soul	1980	Catamount 738
Please Say You Want Me	Imperials, Little Anthony & the	1960	End 1086
Please Say You Want Me	Matadors	1963	Lee 5466
Please Say You Want Me	Monels	1989	Starlight 66
Please Say You Want Me	Renowns, Richie & the	1963	Streke 247
Please Say You Want Me	Schoolboys	1956	Okeh 7076
Please Say You Want Me	Tokens (Brooklyn)	1966	B.T. Puppy 525
Please Say You Want Me Too	Royal Jesters	1965	Jox 029
Please Say You'll Be Mine	Sunbeams	1957	Acme 109
Please Say You'll Be True	Vel-Tones	1960	Vel 9178
Please Say You'll Love Me	Jillettes	1962	Amazon 711
Please Say You're Mine	Echoes	1953	Rockin' 523
Please Say You're Mine	Savoys, Jimmy Jones & the	1955	Savoy 1186
Please Send Me Someone	Moonglows	1972	All Platinum 109
Please Send Me Someone To Love	Moonglows	1957	Chess 1661
Please Sing My Blues Tonight	Orioles, Sonny Til & the	1955	Jubilee 5221
Please Squeeze	Dovers, Miriam Grate & the	1955	Apollo 472
Please Stay	Delvons	1967	J.D.F. 760
Please Stay	Drifters (1959-forward)	1961	Atlantic 2105
Please Stay Away	Crystalettes	1962	Crystalette 752
Please Surrender	Eldaros	1958	Vesta 101/102
Please Take A Chance	Four Lovers	1959	Decca 30994
Please Take A Chance On Me	Angels, Hannibal & the	1960	Pan World 517
Please Take A Chance On Me	Arabians	1964	Le Mans 001
Please Take Me Back	Blenders (New York)	1953	MGM 11531
Please Take My Love	Delights	1961	Nite 1034
Please Take My Ring	Sportsmen	1959	A 103
Please Talk To Me	Del Tones	1961	USA 711
Please Talk To Me	Thrillers (Detroit)	1954	Herald 432
Please Tell It To Me	Four Bells	1953	Gem 207/Crystal 102
Please Tell Me	Dreamers, Richard Berry & the	1963	Crown LP 5371
Please Tell Me	Flairs, Richard Berry & the	1955	Flair 1064
Please Tell me	Fleetones	1961	Bandera 2511

SONG	GROUP	YEAR	LABEL
Please Tell Me	Paradons	1960	Milestone 2005
Please Tell Me	Roomates, Cathy Jean & the	1962	Valmor 016
Please Tell Me	Tiffanys	1964	MRS 777/Atlantic 2240
Please Tell Me Now	Flames	1950	Selective 113
Please Tell Me So	Cherokees (Philadelphia)	1954	Grand 110
Please Tell Me When	Gems (Broadcast)	1973	Broadcast 995 (unreleased)
Please Tell Me Why	Vibra Tones	1961	ABC 10218
Please Tell Me Why	Vibrations, Evelyn Dell & the	1961	ABC 10218
Please Tell Me You're Mine	Twilighters (Baltimore)	1953	Marshall 702
Please Tell The Angels	Teenchords, Lewis Lymon & the	1957, 1984	Fury 1003
Please The Crowd	Dubs, Richard Blandon & the	1990	Starlight 51
Please Think Of Me	Cooke, L.C. & group	1959	Checker 925
Please Try To Love Me	Red Hots, Johnny Hansley & the	1959	Kip 402
(Please Try) To Understand Me	Belltones (Olimpic)	1962	Olimpic 1068/Itzy 1 (62)
Please Understand	Twilighters, Buddy Milton & the	1954	RPM 418/Cadet
Please Wait For Me	Elrods, Ronnie Speeks & the	1961	King 5548
Please Wait, My Love	Valiants (Los Angeles)	1958, 1995	Keen 4026/Andex 4026 (59)
Please Won't You Call Me	Sonnets	1956	Herald 477
Please Write	Tokens (Brooklyn)	1963	Laurie 3180
Please Write Me A Letter	C-Larks	1956	Nova 106
Please Write Me A Letter	Darlin, Chris & group	1961	Dore 578
Please Write While I'm Away	G-Clefs	1956	Pilgrim 720
Pleasin' You Pleases Me	Lincolns	1957	Atlas 1100
Pleasing	Amaker, Donald & group	1959	Raines 418
Pleasing You	Del Roys	1961	Carol 4113
Pleasure Is All Mine, The	Emerson, Billy The Kid & female group	1957	Vee Jay 247
Pleasure Me	Five Emeralds	1954	S-R-C 107
Pleasure Of Love, The	Tiffanys (male)	1962	Swan 4104
Pleasure's All Mine, The	Ecstasies	1991	Ronnie 207
Pledge Of A Fool	Barons (Epic)	1963	Epic 9586/Epic 10093 (66)
Pledge Of Love	Arvettes	1966	Ideal 100
Pledge Of Love	Blue Jays (Los Angeles)	1956	Dig EP 777
Pledge Of Love	Copeland, Ken	1956	Atlantic
Pledge Of Love	Lee, Curtis (with the Halos)	1961	Dunes 2003
Pledge Of Love	Penguins	1957	Atlantic 1132
Pledging My Love	Belvin, Jesse & group	1958	RCA 7387
Pledging My Love	Desires, Rosko & the	1963	Domain 1021
Pledging My Love	Echelons	1992	Clifton 97
Pledging My Love	Ovations (Starlight)	1986	Starlight 45
Pledging My Love	Paramounts	1985	Avenue D 10
Pledging My Love	Thunderbirds	1955	DeLuxe 6075
Plenty Of Love	Creations	1967	Globe 1000
Plumb Crazy	Accents, Jim Murphy & the	1957	Rev 3508
Pluto	Popcorns	1963	Vee Jay 537
Po' Mary	Capistranos, John Littleton & the (with James Brown)	1958	Duke 179
Pocahontas	Camelots	1963	Ember 1108
Pocket Full Of Money	Williams, Little Cheryl & group	1962	Kapp 500X
Poco Loco	Capri Sisters	1961	Warwick 673
Poesia En Movim Lento	Latin Lads, Julito & the	1963	Rico-Vox 27
Point Of View	Powers, Wayne & group	1958	Phillips International 3523
Poison Ivy	Cinders	1965	Ric 156
Poison Ivy	Coasters	1959	Atco 6146
Poison Ivy	Consuls, Little Caesar & the	1965	Mala 512
Polly	Four Deuces	1959	Everest 19311
Polly Molly	Five Masks	1958	Jan 101
Polly Want A Cracker	Five Knights, Tommy Taylor & the	1961	Minit 636
Pollyanna	Corey, John (with the Four Seasons)	1961	Vee Jay 466
Pony	Hi-Lites (Jet)	1961	Jet 501
Pony Dance	Miller Sisters	1960	Miller 1141
Pony Express	Juniors, Danny & the	1961	Swan 4068
Pony Express Riders	Highbrows, Shadoe & the	1961	Gem 102
Pony In Dixie	Crystals (Brooklyn)	1961	Regalia 17
Pony Party	Secrets, Carlo & the	1962	Throne 801
Pony Race	Dolphins	1962	Tip Top 2003/Gemini 501 (62)

SONG	GROUP	YEAR	LABEL
Pony Rock, The	Penguins	1962	Sun State 101
Pony Tail	Temptations (New Jersey)	1958	Savoy (unreleased)
Pony Tail	Voxpoppers	1958	Mercury 71315
Pony Tails	Jays, Armonda & the	1959	Apollo 540
Pony, The	Flares	NA	London (England) LP 8034
Pool Gal	Chaparrals (featuring Tooter Boatman)	1958	Rebel 108
Poopsie	Montclairs	1965	Sunburst 115
Poor Amigos Rock	Elektras	1960	End 1082
Poor Baby	Clovers	1965	Port 3004
Poor Bonnie	Colbert, Bertha & female group	1962	Roulette 4435
Poor Boy Needs A Preacher	Untouchables	1960	Madison 128
Poor Boys Dream	Twinkle Tones, Jimmie Hombs & the	1959	Jack Bee 1001
Poor Butterfly	Ebon-Knights	1958	Stepheny 1817
Poor Folk	Terrell, Clyde & group	1959	Excello 2151
Poor Girl	Corvets, Arthur & the	1964	Na-R-Co 203
Poor Humpty Dumpty	Emblems	1962	Bay Front 107
Poor Little Boy	Dells	1965	Vee Jay 712
Poor Little Dancing Girl	Hurricanes	1955	King 4817
Poor Little Doggie	Scholars	1956	Dot 15519
Poor Little Fool	Dodgers	1958	Skyway 119
Poor Little Girl	Fleetwoods	1961	Dolton 45
Poor Little Girl	Taylortones	1961	Star Maker 1926
Poor Little Me	Four Bars	1962	Dayco 2500
Poor Little Puppet	Carroll, Cathy (with the Earls)	1962	Warner Bros. 5284
Poor Little Puppet	Senators	1958	Golden Crest 514
Poor Little Sad Eyed Sue	Sundowners, Big Jim & the	1962	Chip 1008
Poor Man	Tokens (Brooklyn)	1968	Warner Bros. 7169
Poor Mans Roses	Friday Knights	1960	Strand 25019
Poor Man's Son	Reflections	1965	Golden World 20
Poor Me	Emmets	1959	Addison 15002
Poor Me	Jokers, Jivin' Gene & the	1961	Mercury 71751
Poor Orphan Boy	Dukes, Keith Alexander & the	1962	Gemini 901
Poor Rock 'N' Roll	Nobles (Connecticut)	1957	Klik 305/Times Square 1 (62)/ Lost Nite 153
Poor Town	Cavaliers, Little Bernie & the	NA	Ascot 2183
Poor Willie	Parliaments	1959	Apt 25036
Pop Your Corn	Rivingtons	1969	RCA 74-0301
Pop Your Finger	Miller Sisters	1961	Glodis 1003
Popcorn	Keens, Rick & the	1961	Smash 1722
Popcorn	Pipes, Rudy Harvey & the	1959	Capri 103
Popcorn Party	Four Winds	1965	Sherluck 1027
Popcorn Willie	Five Crowns	1955	Caravan 15609/Trans-World 717 (56)
Popcorn Willie	Marquis	1956	Rainbow 358
Popeye	Dreams	1963	Talent 1004
Popeye	Enchantments	1962	Romac 1001
Popeye	Meadowlarks, Don Julian & the	1962	Dynamite 1112
Popeye Once More	Romans, Little Caesar & the	1961	Del-Fi 4177
Popeye The Sailor Man	Gaylads	1961	Audan 120
Poppa Loves Momma	Cues	1991	Capitol (unreleased) (recorded 1955)
Poppin' The Whip	Midnighters, Hank Ballard & the	1965	King 5996
Popsicle	Todds	1961	Todd 1076
Pork And Beans	Solotones	1955	Excello 2060
Pork Chop Boogie	Jive Bombers	1952	Citation 1160
Pork Chops	Alamos	1957	Hi-Q 5030
Pork Chops	Dorsets	1961	Asnes 101
Portia	Masquerades	NA	Unreleased
Portrait Of Love	Devotions	1994	Avenue D 22
Portrait Of Love	Jaynells	1984	N/A
Portrait Of My Love	Tokens (Brooklyn)	1967	Warner Bros. 5900
Posse, The	Spaniels	1960, 1974	Vee Jay LP 1024
Possessive Love	Pretenders	1956	Rama 198
Possibility	Crowns	1963	Old Town 1171
Pots And Pans	Presidents	1962	Mercury 72016
Pounding	Crowns, Arthur Lee Maye & the	1958	Cash 1065
Pounding Of My Heart, The	Revolvers	1994	JL 101

SONG	GROUP	YEAR	LABEL
Pour The Corn	Whalers, Hal Paige & the	1957	Fury 1002/Checker 873 (57)
Pow! You're In Love	Falcons (Detroit)	1961	United Artists 289
Power Of A Prayer	Bystanders	1957	Demon 1502
Power Of Love	Quintones (Chicago)	1961	Lee 1113
Power Of Love, The	Ambassadors	1962	Bon 001/Reel 117 (62)
Power Of Love, The	Saxons	NA	Jim Dandy 1002
Practical Joker	Blue Jays (Roulette)	1959	Roulette 4169
Pray For Me	Four Kings, Ray Agee & the	1960	Check 102/Plaid 105
Pray For Me	Four Pharaohs	1957	Ransom 100
Pray Tell Me	Belgians	1964	Teek 4824-3/4824-4
Prayee	Chantels	1958	End 1026
Prayer	Halos, Carl Spencer & the	1959	Southside 1002
Prayer	Spencer, Carl & group	1962	Southside 1007
Prayer Of Love	Chessmen	1959	Golden Crest 2661
Prayer Of Love	Melotones	1962	Lee Tone 700
Prayer Of Love	Universals (Philadelphia)	1960	Southern 101
Prayer To An Angel	Mystics	1982	Ambient Sound 02871
Prayer To An Angel	Overons	1958	Unreleased
Prayer To The Moon	Curtis, Tex & group	1954	Gee 9
Praying For A Miracle	Angelones	NA	Relic LP 5044
Praying For A Miracle	Dreamtones	1959	Express 501
Praying For A Miracle	Syncapates	1963	Times Square 7
Praying For You	Dodds, Billy & group	1962	Prime 2601
Preacher Man	Sonics	1962	Amco 001
Preachin'	Spotlighters	1958	Aladdin 3441
Precious Lilly	Bailey, Herb & group	1964	Movin' 126
Precious Love	Cookies	1955	Atlantic 1061
Precious Love	Wheels, Midge Olinde & the	1962	Viking 1011
Precious Memories	Romeos	NA	Mark II 101
Precious Moments	Fabulous Four	1961	Chancellor 1068
Precious One	Cardinals, Bobby Gregory & the	1959	Kip 403
Precious One	Ricardo, Ricky & group	NA	Taylor 801
Prelude To Love	Danleers	1959	Mercury 71401
Present Of Love	Jays, Armonda & the	1959	Apollo 540
Pretend	Holidays	1961	Robbee 103
Pretend	Jades, Bobby Klint & the	1959	Christy 117
Pretend You're Still Mine	Sheppards (Chicago - Okeh)	1963	Okeh 7173
Pretending	Elgins (A-B-S)	1961	A-B-S 113
Prettiest Girl In School, The	Tempos	1957	Kapp 199
Prettiest Girl In The World	Victorials	1956	Imperial 5398
Pretty	Bishops (with the Mellow-Tones)	1961	Bridges 1105
Pretty Baby	Bachelors (Washington, D.C.)	1953	Aladdin 3210
Pretty Baby	Cupids	1964	Times Square 1
Pretty Baby	Dodgers	1957	Skyway 117
Pretty Baby	Euniques	1961	620 1003
Pretty Baby	Falcons, Jack Richards & the	1958	Dawn 233
Pretty Baby	Five Satins	1957	Ember 1025/Ember LP 100/ Ember EP 104
Pretty Baby	Olympics	1966	Mirwood LP 7003
Pretty Baby	Primettes	1961	Lu Pine 120
Pretty Baby	Taylor, Bobby & group	1962	Barbara 62640
Pretty Baby, Baby	Gazelles	1956	Gotham 315
Pretty Baby Blues	Cardinals	1951	Atlantic 952
Pretty Baby, What's Your Name?	Mellows, Lillian Leach & the	1955	Jay-Dee 797
Pretty Betty Jean	Nightwinds, Frank & Jack & the	1958	Felsted 8539
Pretty Brown Eyes	Dreamers, Richard Berry & the	1963	Crown LP 5371
Pretty Brown Eyes	Starlites, Kenny Esquire & the	1957	Ember 1011
Pretty Darling	Velvet Sounds	NA	Cosmopolitan 105/106
Pretty Evey (Evelyn)	Cadets, Aaron Collins & the	1957	Modern 1019
Pretty Eyes	Mann, Gloria & group	1955	Sound 114
Pretty Eyes	Packards	1956	Decca (unreleased)
Pretty Face	Cashman, Terry & group	1966	Boom 60005
Pretty Face	Chords	1959	Metro 20015
Pretty Face	Hi-Lites (Connecticut)	1962, 1976	Dandee LP 206/Monogram 121
Pretty Face	Inadequates	1959	Capitol 4232

SONG	GROUP	YEAR	LABEL
Pretty, Fickle Woman	Foster Brothers	1960	B&F 1333
Pretty Girl	Dusters	1957	ABC 9886
Pretty Girl	Fidelitones	1958	Aladdin 3442
Pretty Girl	Fireside Singers	1963	Herald 582
Pretty Girl	Golden Bells	1959	Sure 1002
Pretty Girl	Mohawks, Popcorn & his	1960	Northern
Pretty Girl	Roosters	1962	Epic 9487/Felsted 8642 (62)
Pretty Girl	V-8s	1959	Most 711/713
Pretty Girls Everywhere	Fellows, Eugene Church & the	1958	Class 235
Pretty Huggin' Baby	Quails	1955	DeLuxe 6085
Pretty Knees	El Venos	1958	Amp 3 (unreleased)
Pretty Little Angel	Belairs, Barry Petricoin & the	1958	Al-Stan 103
Pretty Little Angel	Crests	1958	Coed 501
Pretty Little Angel Eyes	Lee, Curtis (with the Halos)	1961	Dunes 2007
Pretty Little Dolly	Robins	1958	Knight 2001
Pretty Little Girl	Chevells	NA	Justice 1004
Pretty Little Girl	Chimes (Los Angeles - Specialty)	1956	Specialty 574
Pretty Little Girl	Dreamlovers	1963	Columbia 42842
Pretty Little Girl	El Sierros	1964	Times Square 101
Pretty Little Girl	Goodfellows	1958	Sun-Nel 0535
Pretty Little Girl	King Krooners	1958	Unreleased
Pretty Little Girl	Monarchs	1956	Neil 101/Melba 101 (56)
Pretty Little Girl	Shells	1958	End 1022/Gone 5103 (61)
Pretty Little Girl	Sheppards (Chicago - United)	1956	United (unreleased)
Pretty Little Girl	Starlites, Eddie & the	1959	Scepter 1202
Pretty Little Girl Next Door	Twisters	1960	Apt 25045
Pretty Little Hula Girl	Jokers	1960	Danco 117
Pretty Little Mama	Hinton, Joe & group	1959	Back Beat 526
Pretty Little Mama	Hit-Makers	1959	Beat 526
Pretty Little Nashville Girl	Catalinas	1963	20th Fox 299
Pretty Little Pearly	Click-Clacks	1958	Apt 25010
Pretty Little Pet	Classmates	1960	Marquee 102
Pretty Little Pretty	Hollywood Saxons	1975	Action Pac 2023 EP
Pretty Little Pretty	Senders	1958	Entra 711/Kent
Pretty Little Rita	Mendell, Johnny & group	1962	Jamie 1214
Pretty Little Thing	Carousels	1961	Gone 5118 (first pressing)
Pretty Little Thing	Five Arrows, Gloria Valdez, the Paul Bascomb Orch. & the	1955	Parrot 816
Pretty Little Thing	Interpreters	1967	A-Bet 9425
Pretty Little Things Called Girls	Charms, Otis Williams & the	1959	DeLuxe 6181
Pretty Little Things Called Girls	Dell Vikings	1958	Mercury 71345
Pretty Mama	Inspirations (Philadelphia)	1989	Relic LP 5080
Pretty Nola	Deans	NA	Tin Pan Alley 319
Pretty One	Savoys (Raynard)	NA	Raynard RS 10019
Pretty Patti	Lavenders, Robin Lee & the	1960	Circle Dot 103
Pretty Plaid Skirt	Night Riders, Mel Smith & the	1959	Sue 713
Pretty Please	Kinglets	1959	Bobbin 104
Pretty Please	Twiggs, Mal Hogan & the	1954	Blaze 108
Pretty Pretty Eyes	Quarter Notes	1963	Guyden 2083
Pretty, Pretty Girl (The New Beat)	Timetones	1961	Atco 6201 (Times Square Productions)/Relic 539 (65)
Pretty, Pretty Rain	Orioles, Sonny Til & the	1983	Murray Hill LP M61277
Pretty Statue	Price, Del & group	1975	Kelway 113
Pretty Thing	Solitaires	1961	Old Town 1096
Pretty Ways	Temptashuns	1964	Federal 12530
Pretty Wild	Sh-Booms	1955	Cat 117
Pretzel, The	Sweet Sick Teens	1961	RCA 7940
Price Of Love, The	Sensations	1962	River 228
Priceless	Hurricanes	1957	King 5042
Pride And Joy	Twilighters (Atlanta)	1957	Ebb 117
Pride's No Match For Love	Blue Belles, Patti LaBelle & the	1969	Atlantic 2629
Prima Vera	Gemtones, Eddie Woods & the	1953	Gem 204
Prince Charming	Laurie, Linda & group	1960	Rust 5022
Prince Of Players, The	Hi-Notes, Tommy Frederick & the	1958	Carlton 450
Prince Or Pauper	Cues	1956	Capitol 3582

SONG	GROUP	YEAR	LABEL
Princess	Brothers, Little Toni & the	1960	Top Rank 2090
Princess	Winters, David & group	1959	Addison 15004
Priscilla	Dimples, Eddie Cooley & the	1956, 1960	Royal Roost 621/Roulette 4272
Prison Break	Paramours	1961	Smash 1701
Prison Of Love	Jones, Hillard & group	1962	Cortland 101
Prisoner Of Love	Fabulous Four	1961	Chancellor 1085
Prisoner To You	Moore, Sonny & group	1958	Old Town 1063
Prisoner's Song, The	Cameron, Ken & group	1961	Zynn 500
Private Eye	Olympics	1959	Arvee 562
Private Party	Nightingales	1961	Ray Star 784
Private Property	Q Tones, Don Q & the	NA	Bullet 330
Prize, The	Sherry Sisters	NA	N/A
Problem Child	Melody Masters	1957	Renown 107
Professor Loco	Locos	1958	20th Fox 102
Progress	Spencer, Carl & group	1965	Rust 5104
Promenade	Melody Mates	1961	Nix 100
Promise	Blue Chips	1962	Groove 0006
Promise Her Anything	Stratfords	NA	Universal Artists 1215
Promise Love	Belltones (Philadelphia)	1954	Grand 102
Promise Me	Tempos (Four Eldorados)	1958	Rhythm 121
Promise Me A Rose	Carmelettes	1959	Alpine 53
Promise Of Love	Montgomerys	1963	Amy 883
Promise That You'll Wait	Shantons, Skip Jackson & the	1969	Dot-Mar 324
Promise, The	Dreamers (Fairmount)	1963	Fairmount 612
Promise, The	Swans (Parkway)	1963	Parkway 881
Promise To Be True	Blakely, Cornel & group	1957	Fulton 2543
Promises	Charmers, Janice Christian & Johnny & the	1964	Swan 4174
Promises	Elegants	1963	Limelight 3013
Promises	La Mar, Tony & group	1960	Duco 5001
Promises	Reed, Johnny & group	1958	Major 100
Promises, Promises, Promises	Penguins	1955	Mercury 70703
Proud Of You	Dawn Quartet	1973	Vintage 1010
Proud Of You	Four Dolls	1957	Capitol 3766
Proud Of You	Orioles, Sonny Til & the	1952	Jubilee 5076
Prove Every Word You Say	Jive Five	1964	Sketch 219/United Artists 807 (64)
Prove It	Evans, Kay & group	1961	Whip 274
Prove It Tonight	Duponts	1957	Royal Roost 627
Prowler, The	Idols	1958	RCA 7339
Psychology	Dandevilles	1959	Forte 314
Pt. 2	Cadillacs	1972	Polydor 14031
Pu Pu Pa Doo	Gay Notes	1955	Drexel 905
Public Lover No. 1	Vendors	1963	MGM 13133
Public Opinion	Thrillers, Little Joe & the	1960	Okeh 7140/Epic 9431 (61)
Public Transportation	La Rells	1961	Robbee 114
Pucker Up	Four Lovers	1957	Epic 9255
Pucker Your Lips	Blue Notes, Harold Melvin & the	1961	20th Century 1213
Pucker Your Lips	Tycoon	1985	Starlight 28
Puddin' And Tain	Relations	1971	Lebby 7966
Puddin' 'N Tain' (Ask Me Again, I'll Tell You The Same)	Alley Cats	1962	Philles 108
Puddin' Pie	Lockettes	1958	Flip 334
Puddin' Pie	Smith, Wendell & group	1959	United Artists 166
Puddin' Tain	Splendors	1962	Jano 004
Puddles Of Tears	Blue Chips	1961	RCA 7923
Pull, Mon, Pull	Dimples, Eddie Cooley & the	1957	Royal Roost 628
Pulling String	Randle, Johnny & female group	1961	Jayree 2205
Pulling Time	Don Juans, Andre Williams & the	1956	Fortune 824
Pulsebeat	Buddies	1964	Swan 4170
Punch Your Nose	Empires	1962	Epic 9527
Punctuation	Carnations, Cosmo & the	1963	Laurie 3163
Punkanilla	Quarter Notes	1958	RCA 7327
Puppet, The	Corals	1962	Cheer 1001
Puppy Love	Ebb Tides, Nino & the	1958	Recorte 405
Puppy Love	King Bees	1957	Flip 323
Puppy Love	Rogues	1956	Old Town 304

SONG	GROUP	YEAR	LABEL
Puppy Love	Sweethearts	1963	H-III 116
Puppy Love	Tops, Little Jimmy Rivers & the	1961	Len 1011/Swan 4091 (61)/ V-Tone 102 (61)
Pure Love	Lee, Curtis (with the Halos)	1960	Warrior 1555
Purple Shadows	Ebb Tides, Nino & the	1958	Recorte 408
Purple Stew	Masters, Thurston Harris & the	1958	Aladdin 3440
Push A Little Button	Kingsmen, Johnny Knight & the	1963	Chance (N.Y.) 568
Push A Little Harder	Avons	1963	Groove 0022
Push, Kick And Shout	Gents, Little Freddie & the	1965	Showcase 402
Push, Shake, Kick And Shout	Laddins	1963	Angie 1003/Bardell 776 (63)
Push, The	Silhouettes	1962	Imperial 5899
Pushbutton Automobile	Medallions, Vernon Green & the	1956	Dootone 400
Push-Em Up	Monterays (Dominion)	1964	Dominion 1019/Ultima 704
Pushing Up Daisies	Stylers	1963	Gordy 7018
Put A Nickel In The Jukebox	Five Hollywood Blue Jays	1952	Recorded In Hollywood 162
Put Her Down	Invictors	1963	TPE 8223
Put That Tear Back	Gleams, Berlin Perry & the	1959	Ribbon 6902
Put The Hurt On You	Continentals, Billy John & the	1962	N-Joy 1014
Put This Ring On Your Finger	Five Pennies	NA	Herald (unreleased)
Put Your Arms Around Me	Pastels (Chicago)	1956	United 196
Put Your House In Order	Diamonds	1956	Mercury 70983
Put Your Trust In Me	Cavaliers	1962	Gum 1002
Put Yourself In My Place	Elgins (V.I.P)	1965	V.I.P. 25029
Put Yourself In My Place	Harmonaires, Billy Ford & the	1961	Slate 3065
Puzzling Love	Lovettes	1959	Knight 2010
Pygmy	Delegates	1965	Aura 88120
Pygmy	Kingsmen	1962	Shelly 164
Pyramid	Links	1958	Brunswick 55081

Q

SONG	GROUP	YEAR	LABEL
Quando, Quando, Quando	Drifters (1959-forward)	1965	Atlantic LP 8113
Quarrel, The	Newlyweds	1961	Homogenized Soul 601
Quarter To Four Stomp	Stompers	1962	Landa 684
Quarter To Three	Rainbows, Randy & the	1966	Mike 4004
Quarter To Three	Revivals	1989	Sultra 101
Quarter To Twelve	Robins	1958	Knight 2001
Que La Bozena	Poni-Tails	1957	Point 8
Que Sera Sera	Shirelles	1966	Scepter 12150
Queen Bee	Orbits	NA	Space 1116
Queen Bee	Five Secrets	1957	Decca 30350 (first pressing, second is by the Secrets)
Queen Of All The Girls	Blue Crystals	1959	Mercury 71455
Queen Of Angels	Orients	1964	Laurie 3232
Queen Of Fools	Deccors, Marie & the	1962	Cub 9115
Queen Of Hearts	Sheppards (Chicago - Constellation)	1964, 1974	Constellation LP 4/ Collectables LP 5078
Queen Of Love	Mint Juleps	NA	Herald (unreleased)
Queen Of My Heart	Star Lites, Junior & the	NA	Mex Melody 121
Queen Of Rock And Roll	Weber, Lewis & group	1959	Scottie 1304
Queen Of Swing	Labradors	1958	Chief 7009
Queen Of The Hop	Little Ernie & group	1963	Summit 0008
Queen, The	Rip Chords	1963	Columbia 42921
Queen Without A King	Four Duchesses	1957	Chief 7014
Queenie Bee	Rodans	1959	Vest 825
Question	Webs	1963	Guyden 2090
Question Mark Twist, The	Careless Five	1962	Careful 1010
Quickie Wedding	Meadowlarks, Don Julian & the	1988	Classic Artists 101
Quicksand	Dorn, Jerry (with the Hurricanes)	1957	King 5029
Quicksand	Watts, Maymie & group	1955	Groove 0103
Quien Sabe (Who Knows, Who Knows)	Secrets	1960	Columbia 41861
Quiet	Baby Dolls	1959	Warner Bros. 5086
Quiet As It's Kept	Hearts, Lee Andrews & the	1966, 1968	RCA 8929/Lost Nite 1005
Quiet Night	Wanderers	1960	Panama 3900
Quiet Now	Melvettes	NA	Tela-Star 110
Quiet One, The	Caslons	1961	Seeco 6078

SONG	GROUP	YEAR	LABEL
Quiet Please	Charms, Otis Williams & the	1954	DeLuxe 6050
Quiet Riot	Good Guys, Doug Robertson & the	1964	Jerden 729
Quiet Village	Five Glow Tones	1959	Jax 101
Quit My Job	Marchan, Bobby (with the Clowns)	1960	Ace 595
Quit Pulling My Woman	El Capris	1960	Ring-O 308
Quit Pushin'	Quails, Bill Robinson & the	1954	DeLuxe 6030
Quit While You're Ahead	Chordells	1963	Tiger 601
Quiver, The	Cavaliers	1962	Gum 1004

R

SONG	GROUP	YEAR	LABEL
Ra Cha Cha	Radiants	1958	Wizz 713
Rabbit On A Log	Hunters	1953	Flair 1017
Race Of A Man	Robins, Maggie Hathaway & the	1950	Recorded In Hollywood 112
Rack'Em Back	Toppers, Bobby Mitchell & the	1953	Imperial 5236
Rag Doll	Chellows	1966	Hlt 134
Rag Doll	Destinaires	1965	Old Timer 609
Rag Mop	Four Kings	1958	Stomper Time 1163
Rag Mop	Spinners (California)	1959	Warner Bros. 5084
Ragged And Hungry	Empires, Lightning Junior & the	1955	Harlem 2334
Rags	Romeos	1954	Apollo 466
Rags To Riches	Accents (Brooklyn)	1963	Sultan 5500
Rags To Riches	Dominoes	1953	King 1280
Rags To Riches	English, Scott (with the Accents)	1963	Sultan 5500
Rags To Riches	Rays, Hal Miller & the	1958	Cameo 133
Rags To Riches	Rubber Biscuits	1986	Starlight 35
Rags To Riches	Sunglows, Sunny & the	1963	Tear Drop 3022/Sunglow 111
Raiders From Outer Space	Raiders	1958	Atco 6125
Railroad Song, The	Fiestas	1962	Old Town 1122
Railroad Song, The	Startime Kids	1959	Okeh 7111
Rain	Clippers	1957	Fox 961
Rain	Dells	1984, 1985	Solid Smoke LP 8029/ Charly LP 1055 (85)
Rain	Demolyrs	1964	U.W.R. 900/Jason 45-7
Rain	Four Clippers	1957	Fox 960/961
Rain	Jive Five	1963	Beltone 2034
Rain	Raindrops	1959	Capitol 4136
Rain Don't Fall	Magicians	1965	Columbia 43435
Rain Down Kisses	Harptones	1960	Coed 540
Rain Down Tears	Midnighters, Hank Ballard & the	1959	King 5215
Rain In My Eyes	Continentals, Michael & the	1965	Audio Fidelity 139
Rain Or Shine	El Tempos, Big Mike Gordon & the	1955	Savoy 1152
Rain Rain	Tingles	1961	Era 3040
Rain Rain Go Away	Elegants	1958	Hull (unreleased)
Rain Starts To Fall, The	Parakeets Quintet (New Jersey)	1956	Atlas 1068/Angletone 1068
Rain, The	Marquees	1956	Grand 141
Rainbow	Emotions	1963	20th Fox 452
Rainbow	Fleetwoods	1964	Dolton 310
Rainbow Of Love	Cherokees (Philadelphia)	1954	Grand 106
Rainbow Of Love	Prince, Rod & group	1961	Comet 2140
Rainbow Of Love	Superbs	1961	Heritage 103
Rainbow On The River	Platters	1960	Mercury LP 20481/ Mercury LP 60160 (60)
Rainbow Valley	Shirelles	1962	Scepter LP 502
Rainbow's End	Dolphins	1961	Empress 102
Rainbow's End	Nomads	1963	Josie 905
Raindrop	Viscounts	1957	Mercury 71073
Raindrops	Angorians	1964	Tishman 9078
Raindrops	Inspirations (Philadelphia)	1956	Apollo 494
Raindrops	Kartunes	1958	MGM 12598
Raindrops	Plushtones	1960	Plush 601
Raindrops	Vernalls	1958	Rulu 6753
Raindrops, Memories And Tears	Superbs	1964	Dore 715
Rainin' In My Heart	Olympics	1964	Loma 2010
Raining In My Heart	Bachelors (Washington, D.C.)	NA	Royal Roost (unreleased)
Raining In My Heart	Five Satins	1962	Chancellor 1110

SONG	GROUP	YEAR	LABEL
Raining In My Heart	Hurricanes	1956	King 4898
Raining Teardrops	Demures	1963	Brunswick 55284
Rainy Day Bells	Globetrotters	1970	Kirshner 5008/Collectables LP 7000
Rainy Day Bells	Rob-Roys, Norman Fox & the	1988	Back Beat 500
Rainy Day Lovin'	Counts, Tommy Burk & the	1964	H.I.P. 101
Rainy Days In New York	Infernos	1980	BAB 127
Rainy Night	Genells	1963	Dewey 101
Rainy Sunday	Crescendos (Nasco)	1958	Nasco 6021
Raisin' A Ruckus	Meadowlarks	1951	Imperial 5146
Raisin' Sugar Cane	Untouchables	1961	Madison 147
Rakin' And Scrapin'	Four Pals, Dean Beard & the	1957	Atlantic 1137
Rama Lama	Tip Tops	1965	Kapp 726
Rama Lama Ding Dong	Bear Cats	NA	Bravo EP 70-2
Rama Lama Ding Dong	Edsels	1961	Dub 2843/Twin 600 (61)/ Winley 700/Musictone1144 (64)
Rambling	Ramblers (Addit)	1960	Addit 1257
Ram-Bunk-Shus	Rendezvous	NA	Paradise 1017
Ramona	Blue Diamonds	1960	London 1954
Randy The Snow Shoe Rabbit	Robinson, Faith & group	1960	Dolphin
Rang Dang Do Lally	Outcasts, Mac Boswell & the	1960	Wonder 117
Rang Tang Ding Dong (I Am The Japanese Sandman)	Cellos	1957	Apollo 510
Ranga Lang Lang	Montells	1963	Golden Crest 582
Rat Race	Camelots	1965	Relic 530
Rat Race	Drifters (1959-forward)	1963	Atlantic 2191
Rat Race	Jewels (Los Angeles)	1962	Imperial 5897
Rat, The	Starlarks	1964	Astra 100
Rat-A-Tat	Colts, Jackie Kelso & the	1955	Vita 114
Rattle My Bones	Delairs	1956	Rainbow 348
Rattle Snake Shake	Roberts, Lou & group	1966	Genie 102
Rattlesnake Roll	Mello-Tones	1957	Gee 1040
Rave On	Revlons, Tino & the	1965	Dearborn 525
Raven, The	Impollos	1958	Felsted 8520
Raven's Blues, The	Ravens	NA	Mercury (unreleased)
Raw Deal	Meteors, Junior Thompson with the	1956	Meteor 5029
Ray Pearl	Jivers	1956	Aladdin 3347
Razzamatazz	Omegas	1959	Chord 1305
Re Bop-De-Boom	Four Blues	1950	Apollo 1145
Reach Our Goal	Rivingtons	1967	Baton Master 202
Reaching For A Rainbow	Velvetones	NA	Vanda 0001
Reaching For A Star	Platters	1962	Mercury 71921
Read The Book Of Love	Davis, Hal Sonny & group	1960	Del-Fi 4146
Readin' Ritin' Rithmetic' & Rock 'n' Roll	Five Encores	1955	Rama 185
Reading The Book Of Love	Monotones	1960	Hull 735
Ready For Your Love	Limelites, Shep & the	1961	Hull 742/1009/Roulette 102
Ready For Your Love	Tears Of Joy	1986	Starlight 47
Ready, Willing And Able	Raytones	1958	Cash 1059
Real Gone Baby	Velvatones	1957	Meteor 5042
Real Gone Mama	Moonglows	1954	Chance 1152/Vee Jay 423 (62)
Real Good Lovin'	Mohawks, Popcorn & the	1962	Motown 1019
Real Good Lovin' Man	Flairs	19??	
Real Humdinger	Five Pearls	1954	Aladdin 3265
Real Love	Jaye Sisters	1958	Atlantic 1190
Real Love And Affection	Crackerjacks, O. Jay Oliver & the	1958	Coed 500
Real Meaning Of Christmas, The	Ebb Tides, Nino & the	1958	Recorte 408
Real Pretty Mama	Meadowlarks, Don Julian & the	1954	RPM 399
Real Thing, The	Chiffons	1965	Laurie 3301
Real Thing, The	Five Royales	1959	King 5162
Real Thing, The	Spiders	1954	Imperial 5305
Real (This Is Real)	Romans, Frankie Valle & the	1959	Cindy 3012
Real True Love	Diamonds	1960	Mercury 71586
Real True Love	Ovations (New Jersey)	1961	Epic 9470
Reality	Elgins, De Jan & the	1960	Lessie 99
Realize	Three Chuckles	1955	X 0150
Really	Four Tops, Carolyn Hayes & the	1956	Chateau 2001

SONG	GROUP	YEAR	LABEL
Really	Scooters	1957	Dawn 224
Really I Do	Triangles	1964	Fifo 107
Really Need Your Love	Marcels	1961	Colpix 624
Really Paradise	Higgins, Ben (with the Five Satins)	1962	Jamie 1217
Really Really Baby	Garnets, Buel Moore & the	1957	Vita 174
Really, Really, Really, Really, Really, Really Love	Dolls, Spongy & the	1966	Bridgeview 7001
Really Rockin'	Epsilons	1969	Stax 0021
Really Wish You Were Here	Keynotes	1956	Apollo 493
Really-O Truly-O	Five Keys	1958	Capitol 4092
Reap What You Sow	Chimes, Gene Moore & the	1955	Combo 63
Reap What You Sow	Daylighters	1959	Key Hole 107
Reason For Love	Davi (with the Spidels)	1962	Stark 110
Reason, The	Chanels	1958	Deb 500
Reason To Love	Wyatt, Don & group	1961	Brent 7026
Reason Why I Love Him, The	School Girls	1962	Express 712
Reason (Why I Love You), The	Passions	1961	Unique 79X/79XX/Fantastic 79
Rebel	Cupids, Sandy & the	1963	Charter 2
Rebel Beat	Ebb Tones	1961	Bee 301
Recess	Altecs	1961	Felsted 8618
Recess	Fascinators (Brooklyn)	1995 (1959)	Capitol (unreleased)
Recess In Heaven	Ebb Tones, Don Grissom & the	1956	Million $ 2011
Recess In Heaven	Five Boroughs	1991	Mona 31866
Recess In Heaven	Four Gabriels	1948	World 2505
Recipe For Going Steady	Sherwoods	1963	Mercury 72042
Record Hop Blues	Quarter Notes	1959	Whizz 715
Records, Records, Records	Four Sportsmen	1962	Sunnybrook 6
Red And Yellow Polka Dots	Satellites	NA	Arc 149
Red Dog	Jacks & Jills	1958	MGM 12671
Red Headed Woman	Worley-Birds, Wayne Worley & the	1961	Brent 7024
Red Hot	Five Scamps	1954	Okeh 7049
Red Hot	Royal Jokers	1961	Big Top 3064
Red Hot Love (Oo This Love)	Charms, Otis Williams & his	1958	DeLuxe 6165
Red Hot Momma	Marvellos	1958	Marvello 5005
Red Hots And Chili Mac	Moroccos	1955	United 193/B&F 193 (60)
Red Light	Accents (California)	1959	Jubilee 5353
Red Light	Dandies	1959	Peach 726
Red Light	Robinson, Mike & group	1961	Vibro 4000
Red Light Bandit	Premiers (Los Angeles)	1960	Dore 547
Red Lips	Rock-A-Fellas	1958	ABC 9923
Red Lips	Village Voices	1961	Topix 6000
Red Red Robin	Camerons	1977	Crystal Ball 112
Red Red Robin	Mystics	1959	Unreleased
Red Roses Will Never Fade	Satellites, Bobby Long & the	1964	Vegas 555-2
Red Ruby	Dupree, Nelson & group	1960	Palm 201
Red Sails In The Sunset	Balladeers	1992	Clifton 96
Red Sails In The Sunset	Cleftones	1962	Gee LP 707
Red Sails In The Sunset	Five Keys	1952, 1971	Aladdin 3127
Red Sails In The Sunset	Jarmels	1962	Laurie 3124
Red Sails In The Sunset	Platters	1960	Mercury 71656/Mercury 10038 (60)
Red Sails In The Sunset	Premiers (Los Angeles)	1957	Dig 141 (unreleased)/ Relic LP 5052 (85)
Red Sails In The Sunset	Spaniels	1959	Charly LP 1114 (86)
Red Sails In The Sunset	Three Chuckles	1956	Vik LP 1067
Red Tape	Chavelles	1956	Vita 127
Red Tape	Chevelles	1973	Relic LP 5007
Red Wine	Five Chords	1961	Cuca 1031
Red Wing	Carnations	1960	Fraternity 863
Redheaded Woman With Green Velvet Eyes	Clef Dwellers	1958	Singular 713
Re-Entry	Starfires	1963	Sonic 7163
Reflections In The Water	Platters	1960	Mercury LP 20481/ Mercury LP 60160 (60)
Reflections Of You	Teens, Barbara Jean & the	1962	Allison
Refreshing	Holidays	1959	Pam 111

SONG	GROUP	YEAR	LABEL
Refrigerator	Rivieras	1961	Coed 551
Regina	Ray-Vons	1964	Laurie 3248
Regretting	Vibra-Tones, Sabby Lewis & the	1956	ABC 9687
Rejected Love	Convincers	1962	Movin' 100
Release My Heart	Redtops, Eddie Dugosh & the	1958	Award 116
Relief	Del Satins	1965	B.T. Puppy 514
Relief Check	Freeloaders, Bobby Sue & the	1955	Harlem 2335
Remember	Aladdins	1955	Aladdin 3275
Remember	Chesterfields	1953	Chess (unreleased)
Remember	Darts, Sherman & the	1957	Fury 1014
Remember	Del Satins	1961	Win 702
Remember	Explorers, Dennis & the	1961	Coral 62295
Remember	Four Fellows (Brooklyn - Nestor)	1955	Nestor 27
Remember	Hesitations, Don Sweet & the	1964	D-Town 383
Remember	Velours	1958	Onyx 520/Orbit 9001 (58)/ Cub 9001 (58)
Remember Baby	Limelites, Shep & the	1963	Hull 756
Remember Last Summer	Four Winds	1964	Swing 100
Remember Lori	Casanovas, Little Romeo & the	1965	Ascot 2192
Remember Me	Barrett, Richard & group	1958	MGM 12616
Remember Me	Five Satins	1963	Warner Bros. 5367
Remember Me	Millionaires, Rocky & the	1963	Orchestra 102
Remember Me	Tangiers (Los Angeles)	1956	Decca 29971
Remember Me Baby	Earls	1965	Old Town 1181/1182
Remember Me, Baby	Essentials, Billy & the	1965	Cameo 344
Remember Me (I'm The One Who Loves You)	Diablos	1984	Fortune LP 8020
Remember Me To My Darling	Swensons	1956	X-Tra 100
Remember Rita	Barons (Epic)	1964	Epic 9747
Remember Sherrie	Fabulous El Dorados	1987	Delano 1099
Remember That	Miller Sisters	1960	Miller 1140
Remember That Crazy Rock	Satisfiers	1958	Coral 61945
Remember That Crazy Rock 'N Roll Tune	Shepherd Sisters	1957	Melba 108
Remember The Day	Admirations (featuring Joseph Lorello)	NA	Mercury (unreleased)
Remember The Night	Atlantics	1962	Linda 107
Remember The Night	Del-Larks	1958, 1992	East West 116
Remember The Night	Newtones	1959	Baton 260
Remember The Nite	Loungers	1958	Herald 534
Remember Then	Earls	1962, 1971	Old Town 1130
Remember Then	Zircons	1965	Old Timer 606
Remember (Walking In The Sand)	Rainbows, Randy & the	1982	Ambient Sound 451
Remember When	Earls	1978	
Remember When	Platters	1959	Mercury 71467
Remember When?	Cherokees (Philadelphia)	1954	Grand 110
Remember (You're My Girl)	Mystics, Gene Fisher & the	1962	Plateau 101
Remembering	Ovations (Queens, N.Y.)	1964	Josie 916
Reminiscences	Belmonts	1968	Dot 17173
Rendezvous	Carousels	1959	Jaguar 3029/Spry 121 (59)
Rendezvous	Rays	1958	Cameo 128
Rendezvous With You	Street-Tones, Patty & the	1979	U.G.H.A. 09
Rent Man	Silhouettes	1962	Junior 993
Rented Tuxedo	Rocky Fellers	1965	Warner Bros. 5613
Repeat After Me	Delvets	1961	End 1106
Repetition	Blendairs	1958	Tin Pan Alley 252
Reputation	Imperials, Little Anthony & the	1965	DCP 1128/Veep 1242 (66)
Request Of A Fool	Downbeats	1962	Tamla 54056
Resolutions	Essentials, Billy & the	1981	Crystal Ball 145
Respectable	Chants	1961	Tru Eko 3567/UWR 4243 (61)/ MGM 13008 (61)
Respectable	Chants, Jimmy Soul & the	1963	20th Fox 413
Respectable	Fourmost	1963	Atco 6285
Rest Of My Life (acappella), The	Kac-Ties	1975	Relic LP 108
Restless	Ultratones	1960	San Tana 101
Restless Breed	Skipper, Buddy & group	1968	Smash 2173
Restless Days, Sleepless Nights	Dells	1983	Charly LP 1056

SONG	GROUP	YEAR	LABEL
Restless Love	Twiliters	1961	Sara
Restless Lover	Collegiates	1959	Capo 001
Retreat	Fabulous Dinos	1964	Saber 1009
Retribution Blues, The	Blue Notes, Todd Randall & the	1957	Josie 823
Return	Zodiacs, Maurice Williams & the	NA	Sea-Horn 503
Return My Heart	Classmates	1956	Dot 15460
Return Of Big Boy Pete	Olympics	1962	Duo Disc 105
Return Of The Watusi	Olympics	1962	Duo Disc 105
Return To Me	Values	1962	Invicta 1002
Return To Me (acappella)	Foretells	1965	Catamount 109
Return To Sender	Things To Come	1993	Clifton 108
Revenge	Corona, Larry & group	1956	Fortune 523
Revenge	Foster Brothers	1960	B&F 1333
Revenue Man	Cap-Tans	1962	Design LP DLP704
Reverie	Premiers (Clock)	1961	Clock 1042
Revolution	Seventeens, Robby John & the	1959	Del-Fi 4115
Rhythm	Laurels	1985	Nobletown 821
Rhythm And Blues	Titans	1957	Vita 148
Rhythm And Blues	Vitamins	1972	Vita 101
Rhythm Marie	Faithfuls, Philip & the	1964	Goldwax 109
Rhythm Train	Zippers	1963	Long Fiber 202
Rich Boy Poor Boy	Knockouts	1960	Shad 5018
Rich Girl	Van Dykes	1965, 1967	Green Sea 101/Co-Op 515
Rich Woman	Creoles, Lil Millet & His	1956	Specialty 565
Rich Woman	Geoles, Lil Millet & the	1955	Specialty 565
Richard Pry, Private Eye	Spinners (California)	1959	End 1045
Richie, Come On Down	Domineers	1960	Roulette 4245
Rickety Rickshaw Man	Charms, Otis Williams & the	1960	King 5332
Rickety Rock	Jewels (Los Angeles)	1956	Imperial 5377
Rickety Tickety Melody	Collegians	1954	Cat 110
Rickey-Do, Rickey-Do	Ramblers (Baltimore)	1955	MGM 55006
Ricky	Coquettes, Mike Burnette & the	1959	Imperial 5610
Ricky's Blues	Ravens	1949	National 9065
Ricochet	Dunhills	1961	Royal 110
Riddle Riddle Mar Randy O	Philettes	1964	Hudson 8105
Riddle, The	Cadets	1963	Crown LP 5370
Riddle, The	Tokens (Brooklyn)	1962	RCA 8018
Ride	Metronomes	1953	Specialty 462 (unreleased)
Ride Along	Cosytones	1956	Melba
Ride Along	Tempo-Tones	1957	Acme 713
Ride Away	Revlons	1963	Times Square 15
Ride Eddie Ride	Swallows (Maryland)	1991	Starbound 511
Ride, Helen, Ride	Hollywood Flames	1954	Lucky 001
Ride In My 225	Fortune Bravos, Spider Turner & the	1963	Fortune 570
Ride In My Oldsmobile	Rockets	NA	Atlantic (unreleased)
Ride Jimmy Ride	Five Thrills	1990	Relic LP 5087
Ride, Jockey, Ride	Lamplighters	1954	Federal 12182
Ride My Pony	Mystics	NA	Ren-Vell 320
Ride Of Paul Revere, The	Terracetones	1958	Apt 25016
Ride On	Clefs	1952	Chess 1521
Ride On	Empires	1959	
Ride On	Tramps	1959	Arvee 548
Ride On, Little Girl	Royal Jokers	1956	Atco 6077
Ride, Ride, Ride	Smoothies	1960	Decca 31159
Riders In The Sky	Four Flares	1958	Edison International 402
Ridin' And Rockin'	Hornets	1981	P-Vine Special LP 9036
Ridin' Herd	Zeppa, Ben (with the Four Jacks)	1958	Hush 1000
Ridin' Hood	Coasters	1962	Atco 6219
Riding High	Ray-O-Vacs	1954	Josie 763
Riding On A Train	Commodores	1955	Dot 15372
Riff Rock	Homesteaders	1958	End 1017
Rigetty Tick	Rivals (Darryl)	1957	Darryl 722
(Right) After School	Dame, Freddy & group	1962	Nic Nac 331
Right Around The Corner	Collegians	1961	Winley 263
Right Around The Corner	Five Royales	1956	King 4869

SONG	GROUP	YEAR	LABEL
Right By Her Side	Profiles	1965	Gait 1444
Right From The Git Go	Cleftones	1964	Ware 6001
Right Kind Of Lovin', The	Cadillacs, Ray Brewster & the	1963	Arctic 101
Right Now	Five Vets	1956	All Star 713
Right Now	Four Students, Zilla Mays & the	1955	Groove 0127
Right Now	Roses, Don & His	1958	Dot 15755
Right Now	Uniques	1957	Peacock 1677
Right Time For Love	Dreamers (ABC)	1956	ABC 9746
Right Time, The	Cavaliers	1962	Gum 1004
Right Time, The	Evergreens, Dante & the	1960	Madison 130
Right To Love	Four Steps Of Rhythm, Bill Johnson & the	1959	Talos 402
Right To Love, The	Blue Jays (Venice, Calif.)	1962	Milestone 2012
Right To Love, The	Hamilton, Roy (with the Cues)	1957	Epic 9257
Right Way, The	Adams, Richie & group	1961	Beltone 1001
Ring A Ding Ding	Tides	1961	Dore 611
Ring A Ling A Ding	Jesters, Richie Thompson & the	1961	Diamond 103
Ring Around My Finger	Charms, Tiny Topsy & the	1957	Federal 12309
Ring Around Your Neck	Rialtos, Bobby Hollister & the	1961	Pike 5910
Ring Chimes	Cadets	1957	Modern 1026
Ring Chimes	I. V. Leaguers	1957	Porter 1003/1004/Dot 15677 (58)
Ring Dang Doo Ting A Ling	Bell Hops	1958	Barb 100
Ring Dong	Elads	NA	Unreleased
Ring Of Love	Duprees	1968	Heritage 804
Ring Of Love	Starfires	1960	Pama 115
Ring Of Stars	Catalinas	1960	Rita 107/Rita 1006 (60)
Ring Rang Roe	Unbelievables	1965	Era 3155
Ring Telephone	Jackals, J. J. Jackson & the	1963	Everest 2012
Ring, The	Four Sounds	1961	Tuff 1
Ring The Telephone	West, Eastin & group	1963	Everest 2028
Ring Those Bells	Inspirations (Rondak)	1961	Rondak 9787
Ring Ting-A-Ling	Dials	1960	Norgolde 105/Hilltop 2010
Ringa Ding	Delicates	1959	Unart 2024
Ring-A-Ling	Carlo (Carlo Mastrangelo) (with the Tremonts)	1964	Laurie 3227
Ring-A-Ling-A-Ling	Midnighters	1955	Federal 12210
Ring-A-Ting-A-Ling	Crystals (Brooklyn)	1967	Michelle 4113
Ringing In A Brand New Year	Dominoes	1953	King 1281
Ringo	Starlets	1964	Siana 717
Rink-A-Din-Ki-Do	Edsels	1959	Roulette 4151
Rinky Tinky Rhythm	So-And-Sos, Anita & the	1961	RCA 7974
Riot	Apollo Brothers	1960	Cleveland 108/Locket 108 (60)
Riot In Cell Block #9	Coasters	1958	Atco LP 101
Riot In Cell Block #9	Crew, Ron & Joe & the	1959	Strand 25001
Riot In Cell Block #9	Robins (Richard Berry)	1954	Spark 103
Riot In Cell Block #9	Rumblers	1964	Downey 119
Riot In Room 3C	Knockouts	1959	Shad 5013
Rip Van Ronnie	Street Corner Society	1979	Clifton 35
Rip Van Winkle	Adventurers	1959	Capitol 4292
Rip Van Winkle	Devotions	1961	Delta 1001/Roulette 4406 (61)/ Roulette 4541 (64)
Rip Van Winkle	Mr. Bassman	1963	Graphic Arts 1000
Rip Van Winkle	Nutmegs	1962	Herald 574
Rippling Waters	Aristocrats, Tony Smith & His	NA	Mad 1006
Rise And Shine	Contenders	1964	Chattahoochee 656
Rising Sun, The	Ravens	1959	Top Rank 2003
Rising Tide, The	Midnighters, Hank Ballard & the	1962	King 5713
Rita	Fabulous Four	1963	Fortune LP 8017
Rita	Four Dots (Pittsburgh)	1956	Bullseye 103
Rita	Latars	1975	Monogram 100
Rita	Monterays (Brooklyn)	1960	Prince 5060
Rita My Teenage Bride	Genotones	NA	WGW 3003
Ritha Mae	Elgins (Congress)	1964	Congress 214
Rival Blues	Rivals (New Jersey)	1950	Apollo 1166
River Of Tears	Executives	1963	Explosive 3821/Mink 5004
River Of Tears	Flamingos	1959	End (unreleased)

SONG	GROUP	YEAR	LABEL
River Path	Imperials, Little Anthony & the	1959	End 1047
River, The	Lisi, Ricky (with the Concords)	1963	Roulette 4511
River Wide	Rocky Fellers, Leroy & the	1961	Cameo 194
Rivers In The Sky	Four Triumphs	1958	Mira 2050
Roach, The	Sweethearts, Gene & Wendell with the	1961	Ray Star 777
Roaches	Court Jesters	1961	Blast 201/Blast 208 (63)
Roach's Rock	Temptations (New Jersey)	1958	King 5118
Road I'm On, The	DiMucci, Dion (with the Del Satins)	1964	Columbia 42977
Road Man	Bowties, Cirino & the	NA	Royal Roost (unreleased)
Road Of Blues	Phaetons	1963	Sahara 102
Road Of Romance	Neons	1957	Tetra 4449
Road To Happiness	Beavers	1958	Capitol 4015
Roadrunner	Emeralds (St. Louis)	1961	Toy 7734
Roamin' Candle	Sparks	1957	Decca 30509
Roamin' Heart	Chell-Mars	1963	Jamie 1266
Roamin' Romeo	Stereos, Dave & the	1961	Pennant 1001
Roasted Peanuts	Milestones	1961	Swingin' 649
Robe Of Calvary	Orioles, Sonny Til & the	1953	Jubilee 5134
Robin Red Breast	Sparks	1958	Arwin 114
Robin, The	Holidays	1957	Melba 112
Rochelle	Rocco, Lenny & group	1961	Delsey 301
R-O-C-K	Four Jacks	1956	Gateway 1136
Rock & Roll	Turbo Jets, Cliff Davis & the	1959	Federal 12366
Rock & Roll Cha Cha	Shepherd Sisters	1954	Capitol 2706/Melba 101 (56)
Rock & Roll Holiday	Tabs	1959	Noble 719/Gardena 110 (60)
Rock & Roll Show	Hollywood Saxons	1965	Relic 1011
Rock & Roll's Good For The Soul	Four Counts	1958	Cham 003
Rock A Bye Blues	Five Dreamers, Eddie Banks & the	1956	Josie 804
Rock A Little Bit	Vi-Kings	1960	Del-Mann 545
Rock And Cry	McPhatter, Clyde (with the Cookies & the Cues)	1957	Atlantic 1158
Rock And Ree-Ah-Zole	Bobbettes	1958	Atlantic 1181
Rock And Roll Age	Four J's	1958	United Artists 125
Rock And Roll Baby	Chorals	1956	Decca 29914
Rock And Roll Baby	Excels, Bill Daniels & the	1955	X
Rock And Roll Baby	Four Temptations	1958	ABC 9920
Rock And Roll Blues	Torkays, Little Denny & the	NA	Perri 1
Rock And Roll Boogie	Clouds	1956	Cobra 5001
Rock And Roll Boogie	Croom Brothers	1958	Vee Jay 283
Rock And Roll Daddy	Daddy-O's, Joey Castle & the	1959	Headline 1008
Rock And Roll Heaven	Flares	1961	Press 2800
Rock And Roll Indian Dance	Buddies, Little Butchie Saunders & his	1956	Herald 485
Rock And Roll Is Here To Stay	Juniors, Danny & the	1957, 1968	ABC 9888/Lub 252
Rock And Roll Lullabye (acappella)	Belmonts	1972	Buddah LP 5123
Rock And Roll March	Flamingos	1958	Decca 30687
Rock And Roll Molly	Five Jades (Cleveland)	1958	Duke 188
Rock And Roll Nursery Rhymes	Nobletones	1973	Vintage 1014
Rock And Roll Show	Saxons	1958	Contender 1313
Rock And Roll Tango	Clovers	1959	United Artists 174
Rock And Roll Tango, The	Mitchell, Billy & group	1957	Poplar 105
Rock And Roll Uprising	Adventurers	1961	Columbia 42227
Rock And Roll Wedding	Midnighters	1955	Federal 12240
Rock And Rolly	Seniors	1960	ESV 1016
Rock Around	Enchanters (Bald Eagle)	1958	Bald Eagle 3001
Rock Around The Christmas Tree	Gypsies	1955	Groove 0129
Rock At The Hop	Dusters	1958	Cupid 5003
Rock Boom Boom	Thunderbirds	1955	G.G. 518
Rock Bottom	Flairs	1963	Crown LP 5356
Rock Bottom	Rams, Arthur Lee Maye & the	1955	Flair 1066
Rock Granny Roll	Midnighters	1956	Federal 12260
Rock In Your Head	Woods, Cora & group	1955	Federal 12223
Rock It, Davy, Rock It	Jaguars	1956, 1958	Aardell 0003/R-Dell 45
Rock Junction	Midnighters, Hank Ballard & the	1961	King 5449
Rock Lilly Rock	Corsairs	1957	Hy-Tone 110
Rock, Little Francis	Five Willows	1953	Allen 1000

SONG	GROUP	YEAR	LABEL
Rock Love	Harmonaires, Elaine Gay & the	1955	DeLuxe 2029
Rock Me All Night Long	Ravens	1952	Mercury 70060
Rock Me Baby	Travelers	1959	MGM 928
Rock Me Gently	Tides	1959	Dore 529
Rock Me, Mama	Sentimentals	1958	Mint 803
Rock Me, Squeeze Me	Nutmegs	1955	Herald 459
Rock Me The Blues	Jades, Bobby Klint & the	1959	Christy 109
Rock, Moan And Cry	Playboys	1954	Cat 108
Rock My Baby	Mel-O-Dots	1989	Relic LP 5077
Rock My Heart	Four Of A Kind	1956	Melba 110
Rock 'n' Roll Cha Cha	Eternals	1959	Hollywood 68/Musictone 1111 (61)
Rock 'N' Roll Cha Cha (acappella)	Enchantments	1966	Relic LP 103
Rock 'N' Roll Drive-In	Flairs, Fatso Theus & the	1956	Aladdin 3324
Rock 'N' Roll Forever	Monitors	1957	Specialty 622
Rock 'n' Roll Is Here To Stay	Cadillacs	1960	Unreleased
Rock N' Roll Mama	Larados	1957	Unreleased
Rock 'N Roll 'N Rock 'N Roll	Lexons	1958	Lexington 100
Rock 'N' Roll Revival	Five Discs	1972	Laurie 3601
Rock N' Roll Ruby	Skyliners	NA	Double AA 1045
Rock 'N Roll Sal	Rockin' Kings, Ronnie & the	1958	RCA 7248
Rock 'N Roll Tragedy	Chestnuts	NA	Night Train 906
Rock 'n' Rollin' 'n' Rhythm 'n' Blues-n'	Heartbeats	1955	Hull 711
Rock 'n' Roll's for Me	El Dorados	1956	Vee Jay 180
Rock On	Lopez, Trini & group	1959	King 5187
Rock, Plymouth Rock	Dominoes	1957	Decca 30199
Rock, Pretty Baby	Bowties, Cirino & the (with Ivy Schulman)	1956	Royal Roost 624
Rock Pretty Baby	Capris (Philadelphia)	1958, 1963	Lifetime 610/Candlelite 422
Rock Pretty Baby	Moniques	1963	Centaur 105
Rock Rhythm And Blues	Charmers	1957	Silhouette 522
Rock Ridges	Castells	1968	Laurie 3444
Rock Rock Rock	Blue Jays (Venice, Calif.)	1961, 1962, 1963	Milestone 2010/2012/2021
Rock Rock Rock	Moonglows	1958	Chess LP 1425
Rock Rock Rock A Bye Baby	Big Boys	1964	Melmar 113
Rock, Rock, Rock (This Dance Is Crazy)	Pharaohs, Richard Berry & the	1957	Flip 327
Rock, Roll And Rhythm	Swing Teens, Wayne McGinnis & the	1956	Meteor 5035
Rock The House	Jolly Jacks	1963	Landa 707
Rock Tick Tock	Offbeats, Jimmy Dee & the	1959	TNT 161
Rock To The Music	Rhythm Jesters	1956	Rama 213
Rock To The Philadelphia	Steadies	1958	Josie 837
Rock With Me Baby	Deans, Barry & the	1960	Zirkon 1001
Rock With Me Marie	Five Gents	1958	Crest 516
Rocka Locka	Five Wings	1959	King 5199/King 4781 (55) (as the Five Wings)
Rocka Rolla Rock	Savoys, Sonny Brooks & the	1956	Tip Top 1007
Rock-A-Baby Rock	Raindrops	1959	Capitol 4136
Rock-A-Bayou-Baby	Moonlighters	1958	Tara 102
Rockabilly	Four Jacks	1956	Gateway 1213
Rock-A-Billy Yodeler	Three Pals, Johnny Cardell & the	1957	Rama 227
Rock-A-Bock	Eldaros	1958	Vesta 101/102
Rock-A-Bop	Sparkles, Lorelei Lynn & the	1959	Award 128
Rock-A-Bye	Deb-Tones	1958	RCA 7384
Rock-A-Bye	Four Hues	1956	Crown 159
Rockabye Baby	Tonettes	1989	Relic LP 5081
Rock-A-Bye Baby	Fiestas	1963	Old Town 1148
Rock-A-Bye Baby Rock	Swallows (Maryland)	1958	Federal 12328
Rock-A-Bye Boogie	Rock-A-Bops, Jeannie Dell, Johnnie B & the	1960	Josie 878
Rock-A-Bye Girl	Van Dykes	1967	Co-Op 516
Rockalick Baby	Dewtones	1954	States (unreleased)
Rock-A-Locka	Five Wings	1955	King 4781/King 5199
Rocka-Mow-Mow	Dinks	1966	Sully 925
Rock-A-My Soul	Four Closures	1958	Specialty 643
Rockateen	Satellites	1959	Cupid 5004/ABC 10038 (59)
Rocket Of Love	El Reyes	1965	Ideal 94706
Rocket Ride	Davies, Johnny Greco & the	1963	Pageant 602
Rocket Roll	Click-Clacks	1958	Algonquin 715/Apt 25032 (59)

SONG	GROUP	YEAR	LABEL
Rocket Ship	Medallions, Vernon Green & the	1959	Dooto 454
Rocket To The Moon	Reflections	1962	Crossroads 402
Rocket To The Moon	Welch, Lenny & group	1958	Decca 30637
Rockin'	Robbins	1951	Modern 807
Rockin'	Robins	1951	Modern 20-807
Rockin'	Strikes	1957	Imperial 5446
Rockin' And Rollin'	Winners	1956	Rainbow 331
Rockin' And Strollin'	Bel-Aires (Chicago)	1958	Decca 30631
Rockin' Around The Christmas Tree	Crosstones	NA	Clifton EP 511
Rockin' Around The Mountain	Corvettes	1959	Arco 104
Rockin' At Midnight	Darts, Sherman & the	1957	Fury 1014
Rockin' At Midnight	Five Thrills	1990	Relic LP 8020
Rockin' At The Bandstand	Royal Holidays	1959	Herald 536
Rockin' At The Drive In	Beavers	1958	Capitol 3956
Rockin' At The Record Hop	Ravens	NA	Jubilee (unreleased)
Rockin' Beat	Chromatics, Bob Williams & the	1955	Blend 1006
Rockin' Blues	Beau-Marks	1961	Time 1032
Rockin' Chair	Five Cats	1955	RCA 6012
Rockin' Chair	Goldtones, Bill Bryan & the	1962	Pike 5913
Rockin' Chair Boogie	Rockin' Chairs	1959	Recorte 402
Rockin' Chair Song	Jeromes	1961	Dar 300
Rockin' Daddy-O	Heartbreakers (Washington, D.C.)	1952	RCA 4662
Rockin' Horse	Prisonaires	1976	Sun 516
Rockin' Horse	Sapphires, Howie & the	1959	Okeh 7112
Rockin' Horses	Apollos	1960	Mercury 71614
Rockin' In The Jungle	Cap-Tans	1962	Hawkeye 0430
Rockin' In The Jungle	Eternals	1959	Hollywood 68/Musictone 1111 (61)
Rockin' In The Knees	Honeycones	1958	Ember 1042
Rockin' In The Rocket Room	Larks (North Carolina)	1954	Lloyds 108
Rockin' MacDonald	Isley Brothers	1959	Mark-X 8000
Rockin' Man	Serenaders (Detroit)	1974 (1952)	Roadhouse 1018
Rockin' Mary	Treys, Wes Griffin & the	1959	Bella 17
Rockin' Mule	Twilighters (Bronx, N.Y.)	1961	Ricki 907
Rockin' 'n' Rollin' With Santa Claus	Hepsters	1955	Ronel 107
Rockin' Nellie	Dales	1960	Crest 1069
Rockin' Old Man	Charmaines	1961	Fraternity 873
Rockin' On The Farm	Raindrops	1958	Spin-It 106
Rockin' On The Moon	Rock And Rollers, Deacon & the	1959	Nau-Voo 804
Rockin' Pretty Baby	Gypsies	1956	Groove 0137
Rockin' Robin	Satellites, Bobby Day & the	1958	Class 229/Trip 29
Rockin' Rudolph	Uniques	1963	Demand 2936
Rockin' Santa Claus	Bella Tones, Eulis Mason & the	1959	Bella 20
Rockin' Santa Claus	Martels, Eulis Mason & the	1959	Bella 20
Rockin' Santa Claus	Moods	1959	Sarg 184
Rockin' Satellite	Three Honeydrops	1957	Music City 814
Rockin' Shoes	Ivies, Ezra & the	1959	United Artists 165
Rockin' Strings	Arcs, J. Lambert & the	1958	K&C 100
Rockin', Swingin' Man	Larktones	1958	ABC 9909
Rockin' The Boogie	Majors (Felsted)	1957	Felsted 8501
Rockin' The Tease	Revelaires	1960	Crystalette 737
Rockin' The Tease	Talents	1961	Skylark 106
Rockin' Time	Collegians	NA	N/A
Rockin' With Joe	Valiants, Norman Sands & the	1960	Warwick 598
Rockin' With Rosie	Flips	NA	Arctic 102
Rockin' Yodel	Champs	NA	Chatam 350
Rockin' Yodel	Mystics	NA	Chatam 350/351
Rockin' Zombie	Crewnecks	1959	Rhapsody 71961
Rocking And Crying Blues	Five Keys	1971 (1953)	Aladdin 3182
Rocking Chair	Gold Tones, Bill Bryan & the	1962	Pike 5913
Rocking Chair Baby	Peppers	1954	Chess 1577
Rocking Good Feeling	Bond, Dave & group	1961	Khoury's 723
Rocking Jimmy	Rhythm Cadets	1957	Vesta 501/502
Rocking Too Much	Starlighters	1957	Lamp 2014
Rock'n Baby	Fretts	1959	Blue Moon 414
Rock'n Cha Cha	Deltones	1958	Roulette 4081

SONG	GROUP	YEAR	LABEL
Rock'n Roll Mr. Oriole	Cues	1988	Capitol (unreleased) (recorded 1956)
Rock'n Roll'n Cowboy	Youngsters	1956	Empire 104
Rocks In My Pillow	Royal Jokers	1956	Atco 6062
Rockville, U.S.A.	Turks	1959	Class 256
Rocky Piano	Dukes, Billy Duke & the	1956	Teen 112
Rocky Road	Scholars	1956	Dot 15498
Roll Back The Rug (And Twist)	Miller Sisters, Jeannie & the	1962	Hull 750
Roll 'Em Pete	Zeniths	NA	Chess/Checker (unreleased)
Roll On	Ardells (Johnny Maestro)	1961	Marco 102
Roll On	Futuretones	1959	Tress 1/2
Roll On	Lamplighters	1955	Federal 12212
Roll Over Beethoven	Dovells	1970	Event 3310
Roll Over Beethoven	Four Chaps	1956	Rama 199
Roll Over Beethoven	Velaires	1961	Jamie 1198
Roll, Roll, Pretty Baby	Swallows (Maryland)	1952	King 4515
Roll, The	Nite Sounds	1962	Fortune 552
Roller	Burgess, Dewayne & group	NA	Branley 103
Roller Coaster	Carver, Bobby & group	1962	Coral 62337
Roller Motion	Halos, Johnny Angel & the	1962	Felsted 8659
Rollin'	Striders	1954	Derby 857
Rollin' Home	Charms, Otis Williams & his	1956	DeLuxe 6092
Rollin' Stone	Cadets	1955, 1975	Modern 960/Relic 1032
Rollin' Stone	Du Droppers	1955	Groove EP EGA-5
Rollin' Stone	Marigolds	1955	Excello 2057
Rollin' Tears	Caldwell, Joe & group	1959	Esta 100
Rolling On	Upsetters	1960	Gee 1055
Rolling River	Holidays	1953	King 1217
Rolling Stone	Avons	1963	Groove 0033
Rolling Stone	Blazers, Rodney & the	1960	Dore 572
Roly Poly	Volumes	NA	Chex
Roma Rocka-Rolla	Click-Clacks	1958	Apt 25010
Roman, The	Larks (Don Julian)	1964	Money 112
Romance	Blue Beards	1958	Guide 1002
Romance In The Dark	Diamonds (Harold Sonny Wright)	1953	Atlantic 1017
Romance In The Dark	Ricks, Jimmy & female group	1964	Atlantic 2246
Romance In The Dark	Sensations	1958	Atco 6115
Romance In The Park	Heard, Lonnie (with the Halos)	1961	Arliss 1008
Romance In The Spring	Five Candlelights (actually the Five Roses)	NA	Candlelight 431
Romance In The Spring	Five Roses	1959, 1975	Nu Kat 100/101/Clifton 11
Romanita	Falcons (Detroit)	1958	Kudo 661
Romantic Memories	Gaylarks	1955	Music City 793
Rome Wasn't Built In A Day	Taylor, Johnny & group	1962	Sar 131
Romeo	Cadillacs	1959	Josie 866
Romeo	Castells	1961	Era 3038
Romeo	Cutups	1962	Music Makers 301
Romeo	Velours	1957	Onyx 508/Relic 502 (64)
Romeo And Juliet	Starlets	1960	Astro 204
Romeo Rodriguez	Sweethearts, Valentine & the	1963	Big Top 3147
Rondevous	Montels	1961	Kink 9365
Ronnie	G-Notes	1958	Tender 510/Jackpot 48000 (59)
Ronnie	Playground	1983	Clifton 72
Ronnie I Jingle	Infernos	NA	Clifton EP 502
Ronnie I Pizza Pie	Street Corner Society	1979	Clifton 35
Ronnie Is My Lover	Delicates	1959	Unart 2017
Room Full Of Tears	Drifters (1959-forward)	1961	Atlantic 2127
Room In Your Heart	Pips	1961	Huntom 2510/Vee Jay 386 (61)/ Fury 1050 (61)
Rooster	Ravens	1948	National 9062/Mercury 70505 (54)/ Savoy 1540 (54)
Rooster, The	Angels, Gabriel & the	1961	Amy 823
Rootie Tootie	Berry Kids	1957	MGM 12496
Rope Of Sand	Gunter, Cornell & group	1962	Warner Bros. 5266
Rosa	Belairs	NA	Relic LP 5029
Rosabel	Magic Notes	1962	
Rosalie	Jewels, Johnny Torrance with the	1954	R&B 1306

SONG	GROUP	YEAR	LABEL
Rosanna	Capreez	1956	Sound 126/Sound 149 (65)
Roscoe James McClain	Tymes	1963	Parkway 871A (first pressing)
Rose Ann (acappella)	Rajahs	1973	Klik 1019
Rose Anna	Cheertones	1961	ABC 10277
Rose Marie	Jets, Buck Rogers & the	1959	Montel 2002
Rose Mary	Five Satins	1956	Standord 100
Rose Of Tangier	Four Kings	1955	Fortune 517
Roseann	Crescents	1957	N/A
Roseanne Of Charing Cross	Hollywood Flames	195?	Unreleased
Rosebud	Continentals, Lenny & the	1963	Tribute 125
Rosemarie	Five Chimes	1955	Betta 2011
Rosemarie	Shepherd, Johnnie & group	1964	ABC 10548
Rose-Marie	Capitols, Mickey Toliver & the	1957	Cindy 3002
Rosemarie (acappella)	Five Jades (Bronx, N.Y.)	1965	Your Choice 1011
Rosemary	Vine, Marty & group	1961	Mastermade 101
Roses	Five Discs	1959	Dwain 6072/Dwain 803 (59)/Mello Mood 1002 (64)/Downstairs 1001
Roses Are Blooming	Silva-Tones	1957	Monarch 5281/Argo 5281 (57)
Roses Are Red	Oxfords, Darrell & the	1959	Roulette 4174
Roses Never Fade	Jacks & Jills	1956	Empire 101
Roses Never Fade	Williams, Mel (with the Montclairs)	1955	Decca 29499
Roses Of Picardy	Platters	1954	Federal 12181
Rosetta	Ebonaires	1988	Relic LP 5076
Rosetta	Five Keys	1960	King 5330
Rosie Lee	Mello-Tones	1957	Fascination 1001/Gee 1037 (57)
Rosie Lee	Tune Drops	1957	Gone 5003
Rosie's Blues	Whips	1958	Dore 502
Rosina	Futures, Vic Fontaine & the	NA	Adam & Eve LP 504
Rough Ridin'	Ravens	1953	Mercury 70119
Round And Round	Notes	1956	MGM 12338
Round And Round	Rogers, Pauline & group	1956	Atco 6071
Round And Round	Sundowners	1965	Coed 603
'Round Goes My Heart	Solitaires	1959	Old Town 1066
Round In Circles	Marchand, Donny & group	1960	Craft 3000
Round the Rocket	Cap-Tans	1963	Sabu 103
Roundabout	Jaguars	1959	Epic 9308
Route 16	Diablos (featuring Nolan Strong)	1955	Fortune 514
Route 66	Blue Stars	1998	Clifton CD (recorded in 1986)
Route 66	Hi-Liters	1955	Wen-Dee 1927
Route 66	Underbeats	1964	Garret 4004
Rovin' Kind	Maresca, Ernie (with the Del Satins)	1963	Seville 129
Row Boat	Catalinas	1960	Up
Row Boat	Inventions	1960	Up 111
Row, Row, Row	Bobbettes	1963	Diamond 133
Row Row Your Boat	Ends	1960	Vin 1029
Row The Boat Ashore	Platters	1964	Mercury 72242
Row Your Boat	Chanters (New York)	1958, 1963	DeLuxe 6166/6200
Row Your Boat	Retrospect	NA	Collage
Rowdy Mae	Caldwell, Joe & group	1959	Esta 100
Rowdy Mae	Epics	1961	Bandera 2512
Rowdy Mae Is Back In Town Again	Caldwell, Joe & group	NA	M-C-I
Roxanna	Quailtones, Sax Kari & the	1955	Josie 779
Royal Queen	Williams, Clarence & group	1962	Chancellor 1118
Royal Twist	Royal Teens	1962	Allnew 1415/Jubilee 5418 (62)
Royal Whirl	Royaltones, Ruth McFadden & the	1960	Goldisc 3017
Rubber Biscuit	Chips	1956	Josie 803/Jozie 803 (56)
Rubber Dolly	Allan, Johnny (with the Krazy Kats)	1962	Viking 1016
Ruby Baby	DiMucci, Dion (with the Del Satins)	1963	Columbia 42662
Ruby Baby	Drifters (Pre-1959)	1956	Atlantic 1089
Ruby Baby	Four Mints	1957	Decca 30465
Ruby Baby	Rendezvous	NA	Paradise 1017
Ruby Baby	Stuart, Glen & chorus	1960	Abel 235
Ruby Baby	Temptations, Cody Brennan & the	1961	Swan 4089
Ruby Has Gone	Diatones	1960	Bandera 2509

SONG	GROUP	YEAR	LABEL
Ruby Lee	Five Arcades (Dave Antrell overdubbed)	1973. 1985	Sacto 103 (phony label; rec. 1973)/ Antrell 103
Ruby My Love	Dreamers, Donnie & the	1961	Decca 31312
Ruby Red, Baby Blue	Fleetwoods	1964	Dolton 93
Ruby, Ruby	Littlefield, Little Willie (with the Mondellos)	1957	Rhythm 108/Bullseye 1005 (57)/ Argyle
Ruby Ruby	Porto, Billy & group	1957	Mercury 71205
Rudolph The Red Nosed Reindeer	Street-Tones, Patty & the	1981	Clifton 66
Rudolph The Red-Nosed Reindeer	Cadillacs	1956	Josie 807
Rudolph The Red-Nosed Reindeer	Melodeers	1960	Studio 9908
Rudolph The Red-Nosed Reindeer	Prancers	1959	Guaranteed 204
Rudy Vadoo	Continentals, Joey & the	1965	Claridge 304
Rufus	Blue Notes	1961	Accent 1069
Rules Of Love	Carrol, Eddie & group	1961	Guyden 2046
Rum Jamaica Rum	Cadets, Aaron Collins & the	1957	Modern 1019
Rumba	Paramounts	1987	Relic LP 5069
Rumblin' Tumblin' Baby	Emeralds (St. Louis)	1960	Bobbin 121
Rumors	Brightones	1964	Warner Bros. 5472
Run	Candy Girls	1964	Rotate 5001
Run Along	Four Students, Lil McKenzie & the	1955	Groove 0113
Run Along Baby	Premiers (New York)	1957	RCA 6958/Coast 102
Run And Tell	Marsh, Billy & group	1956	Arrow 716
Run Around, The	Four Jokers	1958	Sue 703
Run Betty Run	Van Dykes	1958	Decca 30654
Run Fast	Unique Teens	1957	Dynamic 110/Relic 518 (64)
Run For Your Love	Lynn, Gloria (with the Wheels)	1957	Premium 412
Run Like The Wind	Arrows	1960	Cupid 105
Run Little Girl	Thrillers, Little Joe & the	1960	Okeh 7140/Epic 9431 (61)
Run Little Linda	Innocents, Ral Donner & the	1963	Reprise 20192
Run Manny Run	Jets, Ronnie Grett & the	1955	Capitol 3174
Run My Heart	Counts, Bobby Comstock & the	1963	Lawn 224
Run, Pretty Baby	Goldentones	1955	Jay-Dee 806/Beacon 560 (55)
Run Pretty Baby	Regals	1954	Aladdin 3266
Run Red Run	Coasters	1959	Atco 6153
Run Rose	Miranda, Billy & group	1960	Checker 957
Run, Run, Little Joe	Gladiolas	1957	Excello 2110
Run Run Run	Corrente, Sal & group	1966	Roulette 4673
Run, Run, Run	Douglas, Ronnie & group	1961	Everest 19413
Run, Run, Run	Sparks	1957	Hull 723
Run Run Run	Vance, Sammy & group	1958	Ebb 134
Run Run Senorita	Wanderers	1962	United Artists 570
Run Sinner Run	Stereos	1962	Robins Nest 1588
Run Steven Run	Dreamettes	1965	United Artists 921
Run To Me	Concords (Neal Scott)	1962	Comet 2151
Run To Me, Baby	Downbeats	1956	Sarg 173
Run To The Movies	Legends	1963	Capitol 5014
Run Uncle John Run	Upstarts, Jerry McCain & the	1956	Excello 2081
Run While It's Dark	Platters '65 (featuring Linda Hayes)	1965	Entree 107
Runaround	Candy Girls	1964	Rotate 5005
Runaround	Chuckles	1961	ABC 10276
Runaround	Consorts	NA	Clifton EP 501
Runaround	Dubs	NA	
Runaround	Fireflies	1966	Taurus 376
Runaround	Fleetwoods	1960	Dolton 22
Runaround	Orioles, Sonny Til & the	1954	Jubilee 5172
Runaround	Ovations (Hawk)	1964	Hawk 153
Runaround	Regents	1961	Gee 1071
Runaround	Three Chuckles	1954, 1961, 1966	Boulevard 100/X 0066 (54)/ ABC 10276/Cloud 507
Run-A-Round	Capri Sisters	1958	Dot 15851
Runaround Baby	Kodaks	1960	Fury 1020
Runaround Girl	Portraits	1968	Sidewalk 935
Runaround Lou	Del-Rays	1961 1963	Tammy 1020

SONG	GROUP	YEAR	LABEL
Runaround Ronnie	Canaries	1964	Dimension 1047
Runaround Sue	DiMucci, Dion (with the Del Satins)	1961	Laurie 3110/Monument (No #)
Runaround Sue	Good Guys, Doug Robertson & the	1965	Jerden 767
Runaway	Consuls	1959	Abel 222
Runaway Girl	DiMucci, Dion (with the Del Satins)	1961	Laurie 3110
Runaway Lover	Embers, Gene Pitney & the	1990	Relic LP 5085
Runaways	Cyclones, Wayne Brooks & the	1961	Warwick 629
Runch Happy	Gems (Vergelle)	1961	Vergelle 711
Runk Bunk	Harris, Thurston (with the Sharps)	1959	Aladdin 3452
Runnin'	Jewels (Los Angeles)	1954	R&B 1301
Runnin'	Lighters, Mary Hylor & Billy Rolle & the	NA	El-Lor 1058
Runnin' Around	D'Accords	1961	Don-El 110
Runnin' Around Town	Myron, Mitch & group	1960	Bay-Tone 109
Running After You	Boptones	NA	Ember (unreleased)
Running Around	Zodiacs, Maurice Williams & the	NA	Sphere Sound LP 7007
Running Around Town	Twilights, Teddy & the	1962	Swan 4115
Running Away From Love	Fortunes	1962	DRA 320
Running To You	Mello-Kings	1959	Herald 536

S

SONG	GROUP	YEAR	LABEL
'S O.K., 'S Alright	Goofers	1959	Tiara 6123
S' Cadillac	Squires (California)	1976	Relic LP 5007
S' Why Hard	Royal Drifters	1959	Teen 506
S.O.S.	Packards	1956	Decca (unreleased)
S.R. Blues	Coins	1954	Gee 11
Sabby	Uniques	1959	Gone 5074
Saccharin Sally	Tu-Tones	1959	Lin 5021
Sack And Chemise Gang Fight	Emberglows	1961	Dore 591
Sack Dress	Beavers	1958	Capitol 3956
Sack Dresses	Sad Sacks	1958	Imperial 5517
Sackbut, The Psaltery And The Dulcimer, The	Collegians	1954	Cat 110
Sacred	Castells	1961	Era 3048
Sacroiliac Swing	Drifters	1954	Crown 108
Sad And Blue	Monorails	1976	Broadcast 1136
Sad And Lonely	Lamplighters	1955	Federal (unreleased)
Sad And Lonely	Pagents	1964	Era 3134
Sad And Lonesome	Belvin, Jesse & group	1957	Modern 1020
Sad Avenue	Chancellors	1959	Capacity 61023
Sad Day	Jewels (Los Angeles)	1953	Imperial 5230
Sad Eyes	Echoes	1961	Seg-Way 106
Sad Feeling	Flairs, James Stallcup & the	1961	Le Cam 724
Sad Fool	Rollettes, Googie Rene & the	1956	Class 201
Sad Girl	Continentals, Joey & the	1965	Laurie 3294
Sad Girl	Denims	1965	Columbia 43367
Sad Girl	Gallahads	1960	Beechwood 3000/Starla 15
Sad Girl	Juniors, Danny & the	1964	Mercury 72240
Sad Girl	Showstoppers, Curtis & the	1964	Travis 039
Sad Life	Lamplighters, Jimmy Witherspoon & the	1953	Federal 12156
Sad Little Boy	Concepts	1964	ABC 10526
Sad Little Boy	Fraternity Brothers	1960	Date 1528
Sad Love Affair	Continentals (Red Top)	1959	Red Top 121
Sad River	Platters	1960	Mercury 71656/Mercury 10038 (60)
Sad Sad Boy	Dreamlovers	1963	Columbia 42698
Sad Sad Boy	Larks (Don Julian)	1965	Money 115
Sad, Sad Day	Superbs	1964	Dore 722
Sad, Sad Girl And Boy	Impressions	1963	ABC 10431
Sad, Sad Hours	Moroccos	1957	United 207
Sad Sad Memories	Tempos	1967	Canterbury 504
Sad Sad Song	Exotics	1964	Coral 62399
Sad Saturday	Rays	1964	Amy 900
Sad Song	Channels	1963	Enjoy 2001
Sad Story	Peacocks, Junior Ryder & the	1954	Duke 119
Saddest Hour	Belltones, Ronnie Dove & the	1962	Jalo 1406
Saddle Up	Largos	1961	Starmaker/Dot 16292 (62)

SONG	GROUP	YEAR	LABEL
Sadie Mae	Moroccans, Sammy Fitzhugh & the	1958	
Sadie My Lady	Drifters (1959-forward)	1960	Atlantic LP 8041
Safari	Catalinas	1963	20th Fox 299
Safari	El Capris	1960	Ring-O 308
Safronia Ida B. Brown	Five Hollywood Blue Jays	1952	Recorded In Hollywood 162
Sahara	Cotillions	1962	Alley 1003
Sail Away	Carousels	1965	Autumn 13
Sail Away	De Ville Sisters, Rueben Grundy & the	1958	Spry 110
Sailor Boy	Chiffons	1964	Laurie 3262
Sailor Boy	Dootones	1962	Dooto 471
Sailor Boy	Stags	1958	M&S 502
Sails	Little Dippers	1964	Dot 16602
Sake Wa Duke	Scotchtones	1960	Rustone 1402
Saki Laki Waki	Viscounts	1959	Vega 103/Vega 1003 (unreleased)
Sales Talk	Banners	1960	MGM 12862
Sallie Mae	Dusters	1956	Arc 3000
Sally	Hi-Fis	1960	Mark 148/Devere 006
Sally Ann	Riptides	1966	Sidewalk 904
Sally Bad	Utopias	1963	Fortune 568
Sally Goodheart	Wanderers	1961	Cub 9089
Sally Green	Jesters	1960	Winley 242
Sally Lou	Emeralds (St. Louis)	1954	Kicks 3/Allied 10002/10003 (58)
Sally Put Your Red Dress On	Overtones	1966	Ajax 174
Sally, Sally	Rivals (Treyco)	1963	Treyco 401
Sally, The Cosmetic Queen	Notemakers	1976	Monogram 118
Sally Walker	Counts	1955	Dot 1265
Sally's Got A Sister	Perks, Bill Pinky & the	1958	Phillips International 3524
Saloogy	Tokens (Brooklyn)	1967	B.T. Puppy 552
Salt Mine	Sevilles	1961	JC 118
Salty	Raiders, Tony Castle & the	1961	Gone 5099
Salty Dog	Lamplighters	1954	Federal 12182
Salty Sam	Marvellos	1962	Exodus 6214/Reprise 20008 (62)
Salute To Johnny Ace	Rovers	1955	Music City 780
Sam (The 8th Of May)	Embraceables	1962	Dover 4100
Same As Before	Barnes, Othea & group	1963	ABC 10434
Same Identical Thing, The	Gillettes	1964	J&S 1391
Same Ol' Thing	Shells	1965	Genie 100/101
Same Old Story, The	Champions	1956	Chart 620
Same Old Thing, The	Olympics	1967	Mirwood 5529
Same Old Valarie	Vipers	NA	Duchess 102
Same Sweet Wonderful One, The	Ricks, Jimmy (Rickateers)	NA	Jubilee (unreleased)
Same Time Same Place	McQuinn, Kevin & group	1962	Diamond 109
Same Way, The	Four Sparks	1958	Cleff-Tone 152
Sample Kiss	Clusters, Gus Coletti & the	1957	Tin Pan Alley 207
Sam's Back	Royal Jokers	1960	Metro 20032
San Antonio Rose	Four Lovers	1957	RCA LP 1317
San Juan	Delrons, Reperata & the	1969	Kapp 2010
Sand And The Sea, The	Duprees	1964	Coed 587
Sand Dune	Desires, Julie & the	1964	Laurie 3266
Sandman	Bobbettes	1964	Diamond 156
Sandman Of Love	Watkins, Billy & group	1954	Allied 10000
Sandra	Volumes	1963	Jubilee 5446
Sandra Baby	Gleems	1963	Parkway 893
Sands Of Gold	Holidays	1958	Brunswick 55084
Sandstorm	Sportsmen	1959	A 104
Sandy	Anteaters, Chuck Harrod & the	1959	Champion 1013
Sandy	Capri, Tony & group	1961	Liban 1001
Sandy	Colonairs	1957	Ember 1017
Sandy	Count Downs, Chuck Hix & the	1959	Verve 10169
Sandy	Dawn	1967	Laurie 3417
Sandy	DiMucci, Dion (with the Del Satins)	1963	Laurie 3153
Sandy	Joseph, Mike & group	1962	Lucky Four 1017
Sandy Went Away	Impalas (Brooklyn)	1959	Cub 9033
Santa	Teen Dreams, Debbie & the	1962	Vernon 101
Santa Claus Boogie	Voices	1955	Cash 1016

SONG	GROUP	YEAR	LABEL
Santa Claus Boogie Song	Swans (St. Louis)	1955	Ballad 1007
Santa Claus Is Coming	Midnighters, Hank Ballard & the	1963	King 5729
Santa Claus Is Coming To Town	Harmony Grits	1959	End 1063
Santa Claus Is Coming To Town	Shantons, Skip Jackson & the	1960	Jay-Mar 181/Dot-Mar (69)
Santa Claus Parade	Little Angels	1961	Warwick 672
Santa Done Got Hip	Marquees	1959	Warner Bros. 5127
Santa Fe	Don Clairs, Harold Perkins & the	1958	Amp-3 1001/1002
Santa Lucie	Five Cats	1954	RCA 5885
Santa Margarita	Belmonts, Dion & the	1957	Mohawk 106
Santa Santa	Rocky Fellers	1962	Scepter 1245
Santa, Teach Me To Dance	Darnels, Debbie & the	1962	Vernon 101
Santa Town, U.S.A.	Crisis, Lonnie & the	1961	Universal 103/Times Square 25 (63)/ Relic 532 (65)
Santa's Got A Coupe De Ville	Four Imperials	1959	Twirl 2005
Santa's On This Way	Ad Libs	1988	Johnnie Boy 1
Sapphire	Larados, Danny Zella & the	1957	Dial 100
Sapphire	Oliver, Big Danny & group	1958	Trend 012X/Kapp 941
Sassafras	Mello-Kings	1957	Herald 507
Sassy	Rogers, Frantic Johnny & group	1958	Cindy 3010
Sassy Fran	Juniors, Danny & the	1958	ABC 9978
Sassy Sue	Pacers	1963	Coral 62398
Sat It	Freeloaders, Little Prince & the	1973	M&M 1263
Satchelmouth Baby	Cap-Tans	1950	DC 8048
Satellite Dan	Countdowns	1962	Rori 706
Satellite Love	Randolph, Lil & group	1958	Chock Full Of Hits 103
Satin Doll	Romaines, Romaine Brown & His	1957	Decca 30399
Satin Shoes	Upbeats	1959	Joy 229
Satisfied	Bel-Larks	1963	Ransom 5001
Satisfied	Cashmeres (Brooklyn)	1960	Lake 705/Relic 1005 (65)
Satisfied	Casualairs	1959	Mona Lee 136
Satisfied	Chateaus	1958	Warner Bros. 5023
Satisfied	Jades, McMillin Brothers & the	1959	Christy 120
Satisfied	Shells, Roy Jones & the	1960	Swirl 101
Satisfy Me	Baker, Joan	1964	Diamond 164
Saturday Hop	Coronados	1961	Peerless 5134
Saturday Night	Blazers, Jimmy Feagans & the	1961	Howard 501
Saturday Night At The Movies	Drifters (1959-forward)	1964	Atlantic 2260
Saturday Night Daddy	Little Esther (with the Robins)	1952	Federal 12100
Saturday Night Fish Fry	Blue Dots	1957	Ace 526
Saturday Night Fish Fry	Coasters	1966	Atco 6407
Saturday Night Function	Four Dots, Deke Watson & the	1952	Castle 2006
Saturday Romance	Pageants	1962	Du-Well 101/Arlen 731 (62)
Save	Escorts, Felix & the	1962	Jag 685
Save A Chance	Castells	NA	Black Gold 306
Save A Dream	Videls	NA	Magic Carpet LP 1005
Save A Little Monkey	Corsairs	1963	Tuff 375
Save All Your Love For Me	Blue Dots	1954	DeLuxe 6061
Save Her Doctor	Boyd, Eddie (with His Chess Men)	1957	J.O.B. 1114
Save Her For Me	Love, Frankie	1962	La Rosa 101
Save It	Madara, Johnny & group	1962	Landa 687
Save It For Me	Cliches	NA	Wes Mar 1020
Save Me From This Misery	Distants, Richard Street & the	1961	Thelma/Harmon 1002 (62)
Save Me, Save Me	New Group, Otis Williams & his	1956	DeLuxe 6090
Save Me Some Kisses	Tenderfoots	1955	Federal 12219
Save The Last Dance For Me	Binders	NA	Sara 7772/Ankh 7772
Save The Last Dance For Me	Drifters (1959-forward)	1960	Atlantic 2071
Save The Last Dance For Me	Fabulous Persians	1974	Bobby-O 3123
Save This Fallen Heart	Four Friends	1957	Fee Bee 225
Save Your Love For Me	Dee, Ricky (with the Embers)	1960	Palette 5068
Savin' My Love	Triangles	1960	Herald 549
Saving My Love For You	Mad Lads, Little Becky Cook & the	1961	CBM 504
Saxophone Pete	Marionettes, Chris Allen & the	1959	Hollywood 1908
Saxophone Rag	Cuff Links	1957	Dootone 422
Say A Prayer	Apollos	1961	Galaxy 708
Say A Prayer	Satellites, Joe Potito & the	1957	Safari 1003

SONG	GROUP	YEAR	LABEL
Say A Prayer For Me	De Bonairs	1956	Ping 1001
Say A Prayer For Me	Nash, Marvin & group	NA	Pharoah 1001
Say Always	Keystoners	1984	Starbound 502
Say Another Word	Twilighters, Buddy Milton & the	1954	RPM 418/Cadet
Say Didd-I-Lee Hey (Gonna See My Baby)	Douglas, Ronnie & group	1965	Epic 9843
Say Goodbye To Angelina	Drifters (1959-forward)	1974	Bell 1339
Say Hello To An Angel	Collegiates	1960	Campus 10
Say Hey	Marquees	1958	Len 100
Say Hey	Night Riders, Doc Starkes & the	1954	Apollo 460
Say Hey Baby	Dreamtones	1957	Mercury 71222
Say Hey Girl	Sultans	1961	Knowles 105
Say Hey Hey	Clouds	NA	Vons 1000
Say Hey Pretty Baby	Fidelitones	1961	Marlo 1518
Say Hey Pretty Baby	Teeners, Lulu Reed & the	1962	Federal 12477
Say Hey, Willie Mays	Singing Wanderers	1954	Decca 29230
Say It	Five Royales	1957	King 5082
Say It	Tip Tops, Tiny Tip & the	1962	Chess 1822
Say It Isn't So	Cymbals, Lee Williams & the	1968	N/A
Say It Isn't So	Furness Brothers	1964	Melmar 116
Say It Isn't So	Masters, Johnny (Johnny Maestro with the Crests)	1960	Coed 527
Say It To My Face	Royals Five	NA	Tyler 200
Say It Was A Dream	Bradford, Chuck & group	1961	Fire 505
Say Mama	Legends	1962	Ermine 39
Say Mama	Royal Lancers, Paul Stefan & the	1963	Citation 5003
Say Man	Top Notes	1960	Atlantic 2080
Say No More	Nolan, Miss Frankie (with Nino & the Ebbtides)	1961, 1963	Madison 151/Mr. Peeke 123
Say Something Nice To Me	Mack, Lonnie & female group	1964	Fraternity 920
Say Sweet Things	Bohemians	1962	Chex 1007
Say That You Care	McCline, Charles & group	1964	Larry-O 101
Say That You Care	Plaids, Willie Logan & the	1964	Jerry-O 103
Say That You Care	Rock-Its, Dale Wright & the	1957	Fraternity 792
Say That You Love Me	Del-Chords	1960	Jin 126
Say That You Love Me	Impressions	1962	Vee Jay 424/Vee Jay 621 (64)
Say The Word	Down Beats	NA	Dawn 4531
Say The Word	Starnotes	1962	Caper 101
Say There	Wonders	1963	Colpix 699
Say Those Words Of Love	Temptones (Daryl Hall)	1967	Arctic 136
Say What	Cyclones	1961	Festival 25003
Say What You Mean	Fashions, Frankie & the	1994	Avenue D 21
Say Yeah	Imperials, Little Anthony & the	1961	End 1091
Say Yeah	Joylets	1963	ABC 10403
Say Yeah	Willows, Tony Middleton & the	1958	Gone 5015
Say Yeah	Zodiacs, Maurice Williams & the	1959	Selwyn 5121
Say Yes	L'Cap-Tans	1959	Savoy 1567/D.C. 0416 (59)
Say Yes	Satellites, Bobby Day & the	1959	Class 245
Say Yes Baby	Matadors	NA	Chavis 103
Say You Care	Melodeers, Tony Thomas & the	1955	Capri 777
Say You Love Me	Clouds	1990	Relic LP 5088
Say You Love Me	Kids, Billy & the	NA	Julian 104
Say You Love Me	Relations	1963	Zells 712
Say You Love Me	Schooners, Smokey Armen & the	1958	Peek-A-Boo 102
Say You Love Me	Tops, Little Jimmy Rivers & the	1961	Len 1011/Swan 4091 (61)/ V-Tone 102 (61)
Say You Will Be Mine	Chapman, Grady (with the Suedes)	1958	Knight 2003
Say You'll Be Mine	Aquatones	1958	Fargo 1002
Say You'll Be Mine	Covacs	NA	Herald (unreleased)
Say You'll Be Mine	Ecuadors	1959	Argo 5353
Say You'll Be Mine	Gladiolas	1958	Excello 2136
Say You'll Be Mine	Majors (Big Three)	NA	Big Three 403
Say You'll Be Mine	Sonics	1987	Relic LP 8011
Say You'll Be Mine	Vows	1963	Tamara 760 (same # used twice)/ Sta-Set 402 (63)

SONG	GROUP	YEAR	LABEL
Say You're Mine	Blen-Dells	1962	Bella 608
Say You're Mine	G-Notes	1959	Form 102
Say You're Mine	Jokers	1961	Grace 510
Say You're Mine	Savoys (New York)	1956	Savoy 1188
Say You're Mine	Tides	1961	Dore 579
Sayonara	Squires (Flair)	1954	Flair 1030
Scandal	Sugar Tones	1954	Benida 5021
Scandalous	Interludes	1959	Valley 1005
Scarlet Angel	Ledo, Les & group	1960	Shell 721
Scarlet Angel	Styles	1961	Serene 1501
Scarlet Hour	Rivieras	NA	Coed LP only
Scarlet Ribbons	Concords (Brooklyn)	1962	Gramercy 305
Scary Harry	Stylists (Maryland)	1960	Sage 317
Scheming	Burt, Wanda (with the Crescendos)	1961	Music City 840
Scheming	Griffins	1955	Mercury 70650
Scheming	Senators	1959	Bristol 1916
Scheming	Warblers	1973	Baron 106
Schoen-A, Schoen-A	Shepherd Sisters	1961	Big Top 3066
School Bells	Nobles, Nicky & the	1958	Gone 5039/End 1098 (61)/Times Square 37 (64)/Relic 544 (66)
School Bells Are Ringing	Dials	1960	Hilltop 2010
School Bells To Chapel Bells	Styles	1964	Josie 920
School Blues	Rich, Dave & group	1959	RCA 7141
School Boy	McFadden, Ruth (with the Harptones)	1956	Old Town 1030
School Boy Blues	King, Buzzy & group	1959	Top Rank 2027
School Boy Blues	Toppers, Bobby Mitchell & the	1954	Imperial 5282
School Boy Romance	Juniors, Danny & the	1957	ABC 9888
School Day	Initials, Angelo & the	1964	Congress 207
School Day Blues	Jammers, Johnny & the	1960	Dart 131
School Day Crush	Nobles, Nicky & the	1958	Gone 5039/End 1098 (61)/Times Square 37 (64)/Relic 544 (66)
School Days	Echoes, Allan Roberts & the	1960	Spotlight 101
School Days	Egyptian Kings	NA	Nanc (unreleased) (Rec. 1961)
School Days	Gliders	1962	Southern Sound 103
School Days Will Be Over	Tangiers (Los Angeles)	1958	Class 224
School Girl	Crescendos (Nasco)	1958	Nasco 6009
School Girl	El Pollos	1957	Neptune 1001
School Girl	Five Royales	1954	King 4762
School Girl	Harptones	1985	Murray Hill LP 000083
School Girl	Ramblers (Almont)	1964	Almont 313
School Girl	Valentines, Little Tom & the	1961	Mr. Big 222
School Girl Blues	Robins	1950	Recorded In Hollywood 150
School Girl's Crush	Brooktones	1958	Coed 507
School Is Cool	Arabians	NA	Mary Jane 1006
School Is Out	Beau-Marks	1961	Rust 5035
School Is Over	Adrian, Lee (with the Chaperones)	1962	SMC 1386
School Is Over	Clif-Tones	1976	Clifton 15
School Is Over	Crystalaires	1990	Crystal Ball 158
School Kid	Mason, Little Billy (with the Rhythm Jesters)	1957	Gee 1042
School Letter	Charmettes	1959	Federal 12345
School Of Rock And Roll	Rebels, Gene Summers & the	1958	Jan
School Prom	Fortune Tellers	1961	Sheryl 340
School Rock	Gems (Pat)	1961	Pat 101
School Rock	Montagues	1995	Early Bird 002
Schoolgirl	Hawks	1970	Imperial LP 94003 (rec. 1955)
Schoolhouse Rock	Nobles, Nicky & the	1958	End 1021
School's All Over	Adorables	1964	Golden World 10
School's Beginning	Schoolboys, Bob Hamilton & the	1986	Relic LP 8008
School's Out	Jaye Sisters	1958	Atlantic 1190
Schooner Blues	Schooners	1958	Ember 1041
Scoochie Scoochie	Cues	1954	Lamp 8007
Scooter Town	Del-Rays, Dave T. & the	1959	Carousel 213
Scorpion	Carnations, Cosmo & the	1961	Tilt 780
Scotch 'N' Soda	Royaltones, Ruth McFadden & the	1961	Goldisc 3028
Scotch, The	Mandels	1961	Lilly 502

SONG	GROUP	YEAR	LABEL
Scotch, The	Olympics	1962	Arvee 5056
Scratch	Bel-Aires, Little D & the	1962	Raft 604
Scratch	Camelots	1962	Comet 930
Scratch My Back	Echoes, Sonny Roberts & the	1958	Swan 4013
Scratch My Name Off The Mail Box	Shells	1963	Johnson 125
Scratchin'	Fleas	1961	Challenge 9115
Scratchin'	Twilighters (Bronx, N.Y.)	1960	Chess 1803
Screamin' At Dracula's Ball	Duponts	1958	Roulette 4060
Scribbling On The Wall	Gallant, Billy (with the Roulettes)	1961	Dee Dee 501
Scrunchy	Links	1958	Brunswick 55081
Scuba Duba	Four Del-Aires, Lucy Ann Grassi & the	1964	Volcanic 1002
Sea Cruise	Revivals	1989	Sultra 101
Sea Of Glass	Dominoes	1959	Liberty LP 3056
Sea Of Love	Phillips, Phil (with the Twilights)	1959	Khoury's 711/Mercury 71465 (59)
Sea Of Love	Songettes	1959	Decca 30945
Sea Tides	Orbits (Lani Zee)	1961	Seeco 6074
Seal It With A Kiss	Turn Ons, Tim Tam & the	1966	Palmer 5003
Sealed With A Kiss	Celestials, Bobby Gee & the	1960	XYZ 611
Seaport At Sunset	Chancellors	1958	XYZ 105
Search For Love	Zodiacs, Johnny Ballad & the	1959	Wildcat 0017
Search Is Over, The	Blossoms	1962	Challenge 9138
Search Is Over, The	Colos, David Dayton & the	1955	Lomar 704
Search Is Over, The	Imaginations	1961	Music Makers 103
Search My Heart	Ramblers (Baltimore)	1953	Jax 319
Search, The	Nobles, Nicky & the	1963	Times Square 33
Searchin'	Coasters	1957	Atco 6087
Searchin'	Nu-Trons	NA	Eldee 85
Searchin'	Romans, Little Caesar & the	1961	Del-Fi LP 1218
Searchin' 75	Coasters Two Plus Two	1975	Chelan 2000
Searchin' For My Love	Nobells	1962	Mar 101
Searchin' In Vain	Medwick, Joe & group	1959	Duke 311
Searching	Renaults, Bobby Colquitt & the	1961	Colt 621/CJ 621
Searching	Romeos	NA	Mark II 103
Searching	Tamaneers	NA	Bramley 102
Searching for A New Love	Belmonts	1961	Sabrina 501
Searching For A New Love	Majestics (Detroit)	1961	Pixie 6901/Jordan 123 (61)/Nu-Tone 123 (61)
Searching For A New Love	Sandmen	1965	Blue Jay 5002
Searching For Love	Barons (New Orleans)	1955	Imperial 5370
Searching For Love	Devilles	1960	Jerden 107
Searching For Love	Ravens	1947	National 9038
Searching For Love	Starlights, Bill Perry & the	NA	Premium 101
Searching For My Baby	Camelots	1963	Ember 1108
Searching For Olive Oil	SeÒors	1962	Sue 756
Searching For You	Jamies	1958	Epic 9281
Second Fiddle	Rays	1957	Argo 1074/Chess 1678 (57)
Second Hand Heart	Cashmeres (Philadelphia)	1955	Mercury 70679
Second Hand Love	Jamecos, Diana Tyler & Nat Brown with the	1965	Jameco 2004
Second Hand Love	Royale Cita Chorus	1956	Rama 204
Second Time Around, The	Autumns, Joel & the	1979	BAB 128
Seconds	Dreamers (Dream)	1958	Dream 101
Seconds Of Soul	Durhams	1965	Relic 1018
Secret	Charms, Otis Williams & the	1958	DeLuxe 6178
Secret Agents	Olympics	1965, 1966	Mirwood 5504/5513
Secret Heart	Kingsmen, Johnny Knight & the	1963	Chance (N.Y.) 568
Secret Love	Cyclones, Wayne Brooks & the	1961	Warwick 629
Secret Love	Headliners, George Goodman & the	1965	Val 5
Secret Love	Moonglows	1954	Chance 1152/Vee Jay 423 (62)
Secret Love	Orioles, Sonny Til & the	1954, 1962	Jubilee 5137/Charlie Parker 211
Secret Love	Royaltones, Ruth McFadden & the	1960	Goldisc 3011
Secret Love	Subway Serenade	NA	Clifton EP 504
Secret Love (acappella)	Vibraharps	1975	Relic LP 108
Secret Lover	Royal Teentones, Bobby Sands & the	1959	Nugget 1003
Secret, The	Charms, Otis Williams & the	1961	King 5558
Secret, The	Gainors	1958	Cameo 151

SONG	GROUP	YEAR	LABEL
Secret World (Of Tears)	Visions	1962	Big Top 3119
See About Me	Playboys, Caleb & the	1963	Olimpic 4575
See Here Pretty Baby	Magichords	NA	Tri-Tone 1002
See Me Once Again	Creels	1959	Judd 1005
See Saw	Moonglows	1956, 1964	Chess 1629/Lana 133
See See Rider	Chanaclairs	1955	Coleman 1056
See See Rider	Orioles, Sonny Til & the	1952	Jubilee 5092
See Them Laugh	Four Young Men	1961	Crest 1076
See What Tomorrow Brings	Blake, Cicero & group	1963	Success 107
See What You Done?	Emeralds, Luther Bond & the	1954	Savoy 1124
See You In September	Murals	1959	Climax 110
See You In September	Quotations	1962	Verve 10261
See You In September	Tempos	1959	Climax 102
See You In The Morning	Hollywood Argyles	1961	Finer Arts 1002
See You In The Morning	Regals	1960	Lavender 1452
See You Next Year	Cleftones	1957	Gee 1038
See You Next Year	Five Secrets	1957	Decca 30350 (first pressing, second is by the Secrets)
Seeing Is Believing	Bermudas	1964	Era 3133
Seems Like Only Yesterday	Dynamics	1960	Decca 31046/Decca 31450 (62)
Seems Like Only Yesterday	Meadowbrooks	1965	Catamount 106
Seesaw	Royal Tones	1959	Jubilee 5362
See-Saw	Valiants (Los Angeles)	1961	Fairlane 21007
Self Pity	Boss Men	1964	Score 1003
Selfish	Bachelors (Palace)	1955	Palace 140
Seminole	Crusaders	1962	D.K.R.
Send Back My Love	Holidays	1963	Galaxy 714
Send For Me If You Need Me	Ravens	1948	National 9042
Send Her Away	Innocents, Kathy Young & the	1962	Indigo 147
Send Her Back	Runarounds	1964	Felsted 8704
Send Her To Me	Chance, Wayne & group	1964	Whirlybird 2006
Send Him To Me	Uniques	1963	Roulette 4528
Send It	Hondas	1962	Eden 4
Send Me	Mellotones, Doug Williams & the	1959	Hy-Tone 125
Send Me A Picture Baby	Starlarks	1957	Elm 001/Ember 1013 (57)
Send Me Flowers	Six Teens	1956	Flip 317
Send Me Someone To Love	Celtics	1957	Al Jacks 2
Send Me Someone To Love Who Will Love Me	Upfronts	1961	Lummtone 107
Send Me Something	Tangents	1960	Fresh 1
Send My Love	Hi-Lites, Ronnie & the	1962	Joy 265
Send My Records C.O.D.	Four Rivers, Little Lynn & the	1962	Music City 845
Sending This Letter	Tunemasters	1957	Mark-X 7002
Sending You This Letter	Tunemasters, Willie Wilson & Arlene Smith & the	1958	End 1011
Senior Stroll	Double Daters	1958	Carlton 457
Senorita	Belvin, Jesse & group	1957, 1958	Modern 1013/Kent 326
Senorita	Caronators	1960	Clock 1045
Senorita (acappella)	Uniques	1975	Relic LP 105
Senorita I Love You	Impressions	1959, 1962	Abner 1025/Vee Jay 424/621 (64)
Senorita Lolita	Five Satins	1958	Ember 1038
Sent Up	Falcons (Detroit)	1957	Silhouette 521
Sentence Of Love	Bombers	1956	Orpheus 1105
Sentence, The	Dovers	1961	New Horizon 501
Sentimental Baby	Baritones	1958	Dore 501
Sentimental Heart	Checkers	1959	Federal 12355
Sentimental Heart	Sheiks	1955	Federal 12237/Federal 12355 (59)
Sentimental Heaven	Dorn, Jerry (with the Hurricanes)	1956	King 4932
Sentimental Journey	Bey Sisters	1956	Jaguar 3018/Flip 328 (57)
Sentimental Journey	Cordials	1960	Cordial 1001
Sentimental Journey	Efics (with Harvey Connell)	1961	Fraternity 891
Sentimental Journey	Platters	1963	Mercury LP 20759/ Mercury LP 60759 (63)
Sentimental Journey	Starlites	1960	Queen 5000
Sentimental Memory	Silvertones	1960	Silver Slipper 1000

SONG	GROUP	YEAR	LABEL
Sentimental Reasons	Belvin, Jesse & group	1958	Kent 326
Sentimental Reasons	Emberglows	1962	Amazon 1005
Sentimental Reasons (acappella)	Chessmen	1975	Relic LP 102
September In The Rain	Duprees	1962	Coed LP 905
September In The Rain	Royal Jokers	1957	Hi-Q 5004
September Song	Belmonts, Dion & the	1960	Laurie LP 2006
September Song	Chordells	1959	Jaro 77005
September Song	Del Chords	1962	Midas 09
September Song	Dominoes	1957	Decca 30514
September Song	Flamingos	1964	Constellation LP 3
September Song	Ravens	1948, 1954	Mercury 70240
Serenade	Nobles (Sollie McElroy)	1962	Stacy 926
Serenade	Sophomores, Anthony & the	1966	Jamie 1330
Serenade In Blue	Rivieras	NA	Post LP 2000
Serenade Of The Bells	Stardust	1982	Clifton 71
Serenade Of The Bells	Vibrations	1961	Checker LP 2978
Serenade Of The Bells	Wrens	1955	Rama 174
Serenades	Nobels	1960	
Seriously In Love	Ashley, John & group	1960	Silver 1002
Servant Of Love	Indigos	1958, 1977	Cornel 3001
Serve Another Round	Five Keys	1955, 1971 (1953)	Aladdin 3158/3167A (unreleased)/3312
Service With A Smile	Kuf-Linx	1958	Challenge 59004
Session, The	Del Rios	1958	Big 613
Session, The	Vanguards, Buddy Gibson & the	1959	Swingin' 615
Set A Wedding Day	Four Students, Oscar Black & Sue Allen with the	1955	Groove 0130
Set Me Free (My Darling)	Desires	1960	Hull 733
Set My Heart Free	Crowns, Arthur Lee Maye & the	1954	Modern 944
Settle Down	Ives, Jimmy & group	1961	Comet 2141
Settle Down	Rocking Rebels, Ray Fournia & the	NA	Diamond Disk 101
Settle Me Down	Caslons	1962	Amy 836
Seven Day Fool	Starlites	1965	Sphere Sound 705
Seven Days	Bennett, Chuck & group	1962	Bonnie 101
Seven Days	McPhatter, Clyde & female group	1955	Atlantic 1081
Seven Days	Ricquettes, Danny Skeene & the	NA	Valex 105/106
Seven Days A Week	Anastasia & group	1961	Stasi 1001
Seven Days A Week	Demensions	1961	Coral 62293/Coral 65611 (67)
Seven Days In September	Snaps, Ginger Davis & the	1965	MGM 13413
Seven Lonely Days	Crows	1953	Rama 3
Seven Lonely Days	Four Imperials	1959	Twirl 2005
Seven Lonely Days	Teddy Bears	1959	Imperial 5594
Seven Lonely Nights	Ardells (Johnny Maestro)	1963	Selma 4001
Seven Minutes In Heaven	Poni-Tails	1958	ABC 9969
Seven Minutes Till Four	Travelers	1962	Don Ray 5965
Seven Piece Bathing Suit	Silvertones	1964	Sweet 16
Seven Steps To An Angel	Jives, Bobby Taylor with Charlie & the	1961	Hour 102
Seven Teens, The	Jokers, Johnny & the	1980	Clifton 46
Seven Times Heaven	Flares, Paul Ballenger & the	1958	Reed 711
Seven Wonders Of The World	Bop Shop	1972	Kelway 105
Seven Wonders Of The World	Escorts (Brooklyn)	1962	Coral 62302
Seven Wonders Of The World	Keytones	1957	Old Town 1041 (second pressing)
7-L	Three Graces	1960	Golden Crest 534
Seventeen	Creations	1962	Patti-Jo 1703
Seventeen Guys On A Blanket At The Beach	Initials, Angelo & the	1964	Congress 219
Seventeen Steps	Fairlanes	1959	Lucky Seven 102
Seven-Up Jingles	Autumns	1980	Clifton 52
Sexy	Coasters	1958	Unreleased
Sexy Ways	Midnighters	1954	Federal 12185
Sha Pobo Baby	Starlites, Jackie & the	1962	Mascot 130
Sha-Ba-Da-Ba-Doo	Jac-O-Lacs	1955	Tampa 103
Shabby Little Hut	Reflections	1965	Golden World 19
Sha-Bee-Dah-Ah Ding	Four Vanns	1956	Vik 0246
Sha-Boom Bang	Decades, Brother Zee & the	1962	Ramco 3725

SONG	GROUP	YEAR	LABEL
Shack, Pack And Stack Your Blues Away	Five Wings, Billy Nelson & the	1956	Savoy 1183
Shack, The	Arabians	1960	Jam 3738/Twin Star 1018 (60)
Shaddy Daddy Dip Dip	Edsels	1962	Capitol 4836
Shades Of Blue	Shirelles	1966	Scepter 12162
Shades Of Summer	Sherwoods	1961	Johnson 121
Shadow	Dawns, Billy Horton & the	1964	Lawn 241
Shadow Knows, The	Coasters	1958	Atco 6126
Shadows	Five Satins	1959	Ember 1056
Shadows	Safaris	1960	Eldo 110
Shadows Of Love	Pearls	1956	Atco 6057
Shadows Of Love	Stardusters, Bobby Chandler & His	1957	O.J. 1005
Shadows On The Very Last Row	Cleftones	1960	Roulette 4302
Shadrach Meshack And Abednego	Wanderers	1959	Cub 9023
Shadrack	Larks (North Carolina)	1952	Apollo 1189
Shaggin'	Adventurers	1959	Mecca 11
Shaggin'	Red Hots, Johnny Hansley & the	1959	Kip 402
Shaggy Dog	Velaires, Danny & the	1967	Brent 7072
Shake	Runaways	1978	Crystal Ball 125
Shake A Hand	Four Lovers	1957	RCA 6812
Shake Baby	Caravelles	1962	Joey 301
Shake 'Em Up	Feathers	1954	Aladdin 3267
Shake 'Em Up And Let 'Em Roll	Coasters	1968	Unreleased
Shake It Easy	Coleman, Lenny (with Nino & the Ebbtides)	1965	Laurie 3290
Shake It For Me	Underbeats	1966	Soma 1458
Shake It Up	Royals, Fay Simmons & the	1960	Jordan 122
Shake It Up Mambo	Platters	1954	Federal 12198
Shake, Pretty Baby, Shake	Curtis, Tex & group	1954	Gee 9
Shake, Shake	Blue Tones	1957	King 5088
Shake Shake Sherry	Edsels	1962	Capitol 4675
Shake Shake Sherry	Redwoods	1961	Epic 9447
Shake, Shimmy And Stroll	Flares	NA	London (England) LP 8034
Shake That Thing	Rainbows	19??	
Shake, The	Five Jets	1964	Jewel 739
Shake, The	Shakers, Buddy Sharpe & the	NA	Rumble
Shake The Dice	Barons (New Orleans)	NA	Imperial (unreleased)
Shake The Town	Counts	1958	Mercury 71318
Shake Till I'm Shook	Students, Beverly Wright & the	1956	Groove 0153
Shake-A-Link	Five Chances	1955	Blue Lake 115
Shakey Mae	Beatnicks	1960	Key-Lock 913
Shakey Mae	Midnighters, Hank Ballard & the	1962	King 5693
Shakin' All Over	Pirates, Johnny Kidd & the	1960	Apt 25040
Shakin' Fit	Pyramids (Detroit)	1963	Vee Jay 489
Shakin' Inside	Three Queens	1960	J.O.B. 1122
Shaky Bird, The	Rivingtons	1963	Liberty 55585
Sha-La-La	Prophets	1963	Jairick 201
Sha-La-La	Shirelles	1964	Scepter 1267
Shall I Tell Him You're Not Here	Mates, Marci & the	1962	Big Top 3116
Shalom	Four Coachmen	1960	Adonis 106/Stellar 712 (60)/ Dot 16297 (61)
Sham Rock	Royal Teens	1958	ABC 9918
Shame, Shame, Shame	Co-Ops	1959	Versailles 100
Shame Shame Shame	Escos	1963	Federal 12493
Sham-Rock	Tempos	1959	Hi-Q 100
Shang Lang A Ding Dong	Charades	1958	United Artists 132
Shang Shang	Creations	1961	Jamie 1197
Shanga Langa Ding Dong	Cameos (Flagship)	1959	Flagship 115
Shang-Dang-Do	Cytones, Johnny Duraine & the	1961	Dore 624
Shangri-La	Parakeets	1961	Jubilee 5407
Shape You Left Me In, The	Chants, Little Jerry & the	1960	Ace 606
Share	Teenagers, Frankie Lymon & the	1956	Gee 1022
Share (live)	Brooklyn Connection	1982	50th U.G.H.A. Show Commemoration 45
Share Me	Eccentrics	1964	Applause 1008
Share My Love	Calendars, Shell Dupont & the	1965	Tribune 1001

SONG	GROUP	YEAR	LABEL
Share Your Love	Eko's, Penny & the	1958	Argo 5295
Sharin'	Rainbows, Randy & the	1964	Rust 5091
Sharin' Lockers	Planets	1959	Nu-Clear 7422
Shark In The Park	Corvets	1960	20th Fox 223
Sharon	Premiers, Ronnie & the	1961	Highland 1014
Sharon Lee	Nu-Tones	1961	Cha Cha 716
Shasta	Corvettes	1959	Arco 104
Shattered Dreams	Youngsters	1956	Empire 104
Sha-Wa-Wa	Angels (Philadelphia)	1956	Irma 105
Sh-Boom	Cardinals	1963	Rose 835
Sh-Boom	Chords	1954	Cat 104 (first pressing)
Sh-Boom	Crowns, Arthur Lee Maye & the	1957	Dig 149 (unreleased)
Sh-Boom	Jayos, Johnny Otis & the	1957	Dig LP 104
Sh-Boom	Popular Five	1967	Rae-Cox 1001
Sh-Boom	Sh-Booms	1961	Atco 6213
She	Chiffons, Ginger & the	1962	Groove 0003
She Belongs To Me	Impalas (Brooklyn)	19??	Unreleased
She Blew A Good Thing	Poets	NA	Symbol 214
She Blew My Mind	Channels, Earl Lewis & the	1971	Rare Bird 5017
She Boodle Dee, Boodle Dee	Moroccos, Lillian Brooks & the	1956	King 4934
She Can	Coasters	1968	Date 1607
She Can't Be Real	Accents, Danny & the	1965	Valli 307
She Can't Stop Dancing	Magics	1963	Debra 1003
She Can't Stop Dancing	Palisades	1963	Debra 1003
She Comes And Goes	Tokens (Brooklyn)	1967	Warner Bros. 5900
She Couldn't Be Found	Toppers, Bobby Mitchell & the	1954	Imperial 5309
She Did	Ascots	1962	Bethlehem 3046
She Didn't Even Say Hello	Impacs	1964	King 5891
She Didn't Notice Me	Hawkins, Sam & group	1959	Gone 5054
She Doesn't Care	Galaboochies	NA	Staff 108
She Doesn't Know	Viscount V	NA	Lavette 5009
She Done Me Wrong	Whips	1954	Flair 1025
She Don't Deserve You	Honey Bees	1964	Smash 1939
She Don't Know	James, Jimmy & group	1963	Coed 583
She Don't Run Around	El Dorados	1981	Charly LP 1022
She Don't Wanna (Dance No More)	Romans, Little Caesar & the	1961	Del-Fi 4158
She Don't Want Me No More	Supremes (Bronx, N.Y.)	1956	Old Town 1024 (first pressing)
She Drives Me Crazy	Hearts (Bronx, N.Y.)	1956	Baton 228
She Fell In Love	Revellons, Ria & the	1964	RSVP 1110
She Gives Me Fever	Premiers (Connecticut)	1961	Rust 5032
She Gives Me Love	Romancers	1966	Linda 123
She Goes Oonka Chicka	Premiers (Los Angeles)	1961	Dore 614
She Got Everything	Mystics	1964	Constellation 138/Safice 333
She Had Me Reelin'	Knight, Sonny & group	1962	Original Sound 18
She Has	F. J. Babies	1961	Apt 25068
She Has Gone	Cutups	1962	Jim 852
She Is Mine	Blue Notes, Harold Melvin & the	1960	Lost 105
She Is Mine	Tycoon	1985	Starlight 28
She Is My Baby	Heartbreakers (Bronx, N.Y.)	1964	Linda 114
She Is My Dream	Tads	1958	Rev 3513
She Is The Girl For Me	Fabulous Fabuliers	1959	Angle Tone 539
She Is The Girl For Me	Fi-Tones	1959	Angle Tone 53
She Is Your Girl	Pageants	1965	Groove 0056
She Keeps Me Wondering	Spiders	1954	Imperial 5318
She Kissed Me	Butlers, Frankie Beverly & the	1967	Fairmount 1012
She Laughed At Me	Matches	NA	Jaguar 712
She Left Me	Midnights	1954	Music City 762
She Lets Her Hair Down	Tokens (Brooklyn)	1969	Buddah 151
She Loves To Dance	Flairs	1955	Flair 1067
She Loves To Dance	Jarmels	1961	Laurie 3085
She Loves To Rock	Flairs, Cornel Gunter & the	1956	ABC 9698
She Makes Me Wanna Dance	Rocky Fellers	1963	Scepter 1263
She Must Be From A Different Planet	Fanados	1957	Carter 2050
She Needs A Guy	Twilighters (Bronx, N.Y.)	1960	Chess 1803
She Needs To Be Loved	Blasers	1956	United 191

SONG	GROUP	YEAR	LABEL
She Never Talked To Me That Way	Drifters (1959-forward)	1961	Atlantic (unreleased)
She Only Wants To Do Her Own Thing	Belmonts	1968	Dot 17173
She Rides With Me	Continentals, Joey & the	1965	Claridge 304
She Rocks	Cardinals	1952	Atlantic 972
She Said That She Loved Me	Four J's	1964	Jamie 1267
She Say	Treetoppers	1953	Bell 107
She Say (Oom Dooby Doom)	Diamonds	1959	Mercury 71404
She, She, Little Sheila	Darnells	1962	Sara 1055
She Still Loves Me	Capris (Philadelphia)	NA	Collectables LP 5000
She Thinks I Still Care	Rip Chords	1963	Columbia 42812
She Told A Lie	Counts, Tommy Burk & the	1964	Rich Rose 1003
She Told Me Lies	Marvellos	1962	Exodus 6214/Reprise 20008 (62)
She Took His Love Away	Young Sisters	1963	Mala 467
She Took My Oldsmobile	Romancers	1966	Linda 124
She Tried To Kiss Me	Butlers	1964	Liberty Bell 1024
She Waits For Him	Duprees	1965	Columbia 43464
(She Wants) Candy And Flowers	Tyrones	1956	Wing 90072
She Wants To Mambo	Chanters (California)	1954	RPM 415
She Wants To Rock	Flairs	1953	Flair 1012
She Was Love	Thorpe, Lionel (Chords)	1960	Roulette
She Was My First Love	Night Rockers, Freddie Hall & the	1959	CJ 610
She Was Never Mine (To Lose)	Cascades	1964	Charter 1018
She Wasn't Meant For Me	Shells	1959	Roulette 4156
She Wears My Ring	Revelaires	1965	Decca 31830
She Wears My Ring	Wanderers	1961	Cub 9099
She Went That-A-Way	Bell Notes	1959	Time 1010
She Went That-A-Way	Neptunes	1958	Payson 101/102
She Wobbles (All Night Long)	Four Hits & A Miss	1962	Flamingo
She Won't Go Steady	Boardwalkers, Ronnie & the	1961	Rex 103
She Won't Hang Up	Jokers, Willie & the	1962	Viking 1007
She Won't Say Yes	Counts	1954	Dot 1210
She Wouldn't Quit	New Invictas	1962	Hale 500
Shedding Teardrops	Paramounts	1963	Ember 1099
Shedding Tears For You	Medallions, Vernon Green & the	1956	Dootone 400
Sheik Of Araby	Colts	1959	Antler 4003/4007
Sheik Of Araby	Rebels, Jimmy & the	1959	Roulette 4201
Sheila	Four Checkers	1959	Ace 129
Sheila Baby	Crystal, Lou & group	1962	SFAZ 1001
She'll Break Your Heart	Hi Tensions, Leon Peels & the	1964	Whirlybird 2005
She'll Come To Me	Revlons	1962	Capitol 4739
She'll Never Know	Rhythm Jesters, Bob Davis & the	1957	Rama 224
She'll Stand Up For You	Mellow Drops	NA	Imperial (unreleased)
She'll Understand	Neptunes	1960	Checker 967
Shelly	Velons	1963	Blast 216
Shelly My Love	Crowns, Terry & the	1977	Harvey 103
Sheree	Derringers	1961	Capitol 4532
Sherlock Jones	Five Shades	1961	MGM 13035
Sherry	Cavaliers, Jerry Cox & the	1959	Frantic 751
Sherry	Glitters	1962	You 6
Sherry	Ly-Dells	1978	Clifton LP 2002
Sherry	Sheppards (Chicago - United)	1956	United 198/B&F 198 (56)
Sherry	Valets	1959	Vulcan/Jon 4219 (59)
Sherry	Zeu Review, Ziggy & the	NA	Zeu 5011
Sherry My Love	Fascinators, Glin Littleton & the	NA	Lake 1003
She's A Bad Motorcycle	Crestones	1964	Markie 117
She's A Fat Girl	Rock-A-Bouts	1959	Chancellor 1030
She's A Fine Chick	Quarter Notes, Neil Darrow & the	1959	Whizz 717
She's A Flirt	Four Jokers	1962	Amy 832
She's A Flirt	Jewels (Los Angeles)	1956	RPM 474
She's A Good One	Larks (North Carolina)	1974	Broadcast 1002
She's A Heartbreaker	Chandeliers	1962	Sue 761
She's A Heartbreaker	Ramblers (Larkwood)	1963	Larkwood 1104
She's A Loser	Buddies	1959	Tiara 6121
She's A Tease	Teasers, Bobby & the	1960	Fleetwood 1012
She's A Troublemaker	Majors (Philadelphia)	1962	Imperial 5879

SONG	GROUP	YEAR	LABEL
She's A Yum Yum	Coasters	1966	Atco 6407
She's All Mine Alone	Crests	1965	Apt 25075
She's All Right	Hawks	1954	Imperial 5281
She's All Right With Me	Moonglows	1977	Monogram 128
She's Allright	Five Knights	1959	Tau 104
She's An Angel	Dahills	1978	Crystal Ball 107
She's Back	Vails	1960	Belmont 4004
She's Boss	Dimensions	1966	Panorama 25/HBR 1477 (66)/ Hanna Barbera 477 (66)
She's Coming Home	Chanteers	1962	Mercury 71979
She's Everybody's Darling	Torkays, Little Denny & the	NA	Perri 2
She's Fine	Hi-Lites, Roy Smith & the	1959, 1961	Nu Tone 1182
She's Fine-She's Mine	Rickateers, Jimmy Ricks & the	1956	Josie 796
She's Forgotten You	Cleftones	1964	Ware 6001
She's Funny That Way	Goldentones	1956	Rainbow 351
She's Going Away	Hill, Grant & group	1959	Topaz 1300
She's Gone	Blend Tones	1961	Chic-Car 100/Don-El 106 (61)/ Imperial 5758 (61)
She's Gone	Bob-Wheels	1963	Tarx 1008
She's Gone	Carians	1961	Indigo 136
She's Gone	Chordliners, Mike & the	1989	Crystal Ball 154
She's Gone	Cleftones	1960	Roulette 4302
She's Gone	Del Royals	1960	Minit 610
She's Gone	Gainors	1960	Mercury 71569
She's Gone	Heartbreakers (Bronx, N.Y.)	1975	Broadcast 99
She's Gone	Metronomes, Gene Moore & the	1953	Specialty 472
She's Gone	Moonglows	1955	Chess 1589
She's Gone	Star Drifts	1962	Goldisc G3
She's Gone, Gone	Penguins	1956	Mercury 70799
She's Gone (With The Wind)	Five Satins	1961, 1974	Candlelite 411
She's Gone (With The Wind)	Scarlets, Fred Parris & the	1958, 1961	Klik 7905/Candlelite 411 (74)
She's Gonna Be Right	Impollos	1958	Felsted 8520
She's Got Everything	Essex	1963	Roulette 4530
She's Got His Nose Wide Open	Lyrics, Ike Perry & the	1965	Bee 95/Bee 1875
She's Got It	Camerons	1960	Cousins (unreleased)
She's Got Something	Hollywood Four Flames	1952	Recorded In Hollywood 164
She's Got Soul	Midnighters, Hank Ballard & the	1964	King 5901
She's Got The Blues	Travelers	1963	Princess 52/Vault 911
She's Got To Go	Ravens	1953	Okeh 6888
She's Gotta Grin	Velvets (New York)	1953	Red Robin 120
She's Just An Angel	Dells	1979, 1984	Solid Smoke LP 8029
She's Just My Style	Clintonian Cubs (Jimmy Castor)	1960	My Brother's 7/508
She's Lost You	Zephyrs	1965	Rotate 5006
She's Mine	American Beetles	1964	BYP 1001
She's Mine	Belairs, Mike & the	1963	Cobra 6666
She's Mine	Chants	1964	Interphon 7703
She's Mine	Corvettes, Little Sonny & the	1986	Relic LP 8008
She's Mine	Dandoliers	1956	States 160/B&F 160
She's Mine	Earthmen	NA	Tropical 123
She's Mine	Fiestas	1961	Old Town 1111
She's Mine	Guytones	1957	DeLuxe 6152
She's Mine	Monarchs, Chuck Mills & the	1959	Band Box 221
She's Mine	Pentagons	1961	Jamie 1201
She's Mine	Rivals (Puff)	1962	Puff 3912
She's Mine	Tears	1961	Astronaut 501
She's Mine	Three G's	1960	Columbia 41868
She's Mine	Zodiacs, Maurice Williams & the	1959	Cole 101
She's Mine All Mine	King Crooners	1959	Hart 1002
She's Mine, All Mine	Royal Jokers	1956	Atco 6077
She's Mine Not Yours	Rockers, Rockin' Bradley & the	1958	Hull 729
She's My Angel	Ovations (Starlight)	1986	Starlight 43
She's My Angel	Rainbows, Randy & the	1963	Rust 5073
She's My Baby	Banks, Otis & group	1957	Bow 304
She's My Baby	Capri, Mike & group	NA	Cecil 4450
She's My Baby	Emotions	1965	Calla 122

SONG	GROUP	YEAR	LABEL
She's My Baby	Five Knights	1963	Bumps 1504
She's My Baby	Five Playboys	1959	Fee Bee 232/Petite 504
She's My Baby	Hornets	1964	V.I.P. 25004
She's My Baby	Redcoats, Steve Alaimo & the	1959	Marlin 6067
She's My Connection	Cadillacs	NA	Roulette 4654
She's My Everything	Wrens	1955	Rama 175
She's My Girl	Capris (New York)	1982	Ambient Sound LP FZ-37714
She's My Girl	Coastliners	1960	Back Beat 566
She's My Girl	Federals	1957	Fury 1009
She's My Girl	Jive Five	1963	Beltone 2034
She's My Girl	Motifs	NA	Baton 23112
She's My Heart's Desire	Falcons (Detroit)	1986	Relic LP 8006
She's My Heart's Desire	Ohio Untouchables	1962	Lu Pine 1009/Lu Pine 109 (62)
She's My Lollipop	Gainors	1959	Mercury 71466
She's Neat	Rock-Its, Dale Wright & the	1957	Fraternity 792
She's Not Coming Home	Excellents	1961	Unreleased
She's Not Coming Home	Videls	1960	Tic Tac Toe 5005/JDS 5005 (60)
She's Not Yours	Silvertones, Ronnie Rice & the	1964	Limelight 3029
She's Real Cool	Mello-Kings	1958, 1961	Herald 518/567
She's Right With Me	Tune Tones	1959	Herald 539
She's So Fine	Cleftones	1958	Roulette 4094
She's So Fine	Fabulous Tears, Little Dooley & the	1965	Baylor 101
She's So Wonderful	Del Amos	1959	Nikko 703
She's Sugar Sweet	Hudson, Eddie & group	1958	Excello 2135
She's Sumpin' Else	Key, Troyce & group	1959	Warner Bros. 5070
She's Swinging	Casual Teens	1958	Felsted 8529
She's The Most	Five Keys	1956	Capitol 3392
She's The One	Chartbusters	1964	Mutual 502
She's The One	Laddins	1960	Isle 801
She's The One	Links	1958	Teenage 1009
She's The One	Medallions	1960	Dooto 456 EP
She's The One	Midnighters	1954	Federal 12195
She's The One	Midnighters, Hank Ballard & the	1962	King 5703
She's The One For Me	Aquatones	1958	Fargo 1001
She's The Only Girl	Four Uniques	1962	Adam 9004
She's Too Tall For Love	Warblers	1974	Outhouse 102
She's Wrong For You Baby	Four Jewels	1964	Tec 3007
Shhh, I'm Watching The Movies	Shirelles	1965	Scepter 1296
Shifting Sands	Nutmegs	1965, 1973	Relic 1006
Shifting Sands	Rajahs	1957	Klik 7805
Shilly Dilly	Flamingos	1956	Checker 846
Shim Sham	Chips, Billy Bobbs & the	1958	Edison International 400/Edison International 416 (59)
Shim Sham Shufflin' Jive	Arrows, Joe Lyons & the	1959	Hit Maker 600
Shimmies And The Shakes	Dukes (California)	1956	Imperial 5401
Shimmy And Stomp	Flares	1961	Press 2808
Shimmy Baby	Starliters, Joey Dee & the	1960	Scepter 1210
Shimmy Gully	Mohawks, Popcorn & the	1960	Motown 1002
Shimmy Like Kate	Olympics	1960	Arvee 5006
Shimmy Sham	Egyptians, King Pharaoh & the	1961	Federal 12413
Shimmy, Shimmy	Impacs	1964	King 5863
Shimmy Shimmy (Cha Cha Cha)	Darts, Herb Price & the	1959	Tempus 1506
(Shimmy, Shimmy) Ko Ko Wop	El Capris	1956	Bullseye 102/Argyle 1010 (61)
Shimmy, Shimmy, Ko-Ko-Bop	Imperials, Little Anthony & the	1959	End 1060
Shimmy Shimmy Shake	Medallions, Vernon Green & the	1962	Pan World 71
Shimmy, Shimmy, Shimmy, Shimmy	Everglades, Jerry Hayward & the	1962	Symbol 916
Shimmy Stomp	Squires (Robway)	NA	Robway 1
Shindig	Rock-A-Fellas, Eddie Bell & the	1958	Coed 505
Shine 'Em On	Wheelers	1960	Cenco 107
Shine 'Em Shake 'Em! Roll 'Em! Let The Dice Decide	Holidays	1954	King 1246
Shine On Harvest Moon	Platters	1963	Mercury LP 20759/ Mercury LP 60759 (63)
Shining Armor	Versalettes	1963	Witch 116
Shining Star	Broken Hearts	1962	Diamond 123

SONG	GROUP	YEAR	LABEL
Shining Star	Chaperones	1962	Josie 885
Shining Star	Dedications	1963, 1981	C&A 506
Shining Star (acappella)	Young Ones	1975	Relic LP 102/Relic LP 5079 (89)
Shinny Up Your Own Side	Castells	1964	Warner Bros. 5445
Shiny Colors	Shirelles	1967	Scepter 12192
Ship Of Love	Lyres	1953	J&G 101
Ship Of Love	Nutmegs	1955	Herald 459
Shipwreck	Twilights	1967	Parkway 128
Shirley	Clark, Jimmy & group	1964	Diamond 157
Shirley	Empires	1955	Wing 90023
Shirley	Heartspinners, Dino & the	NA	Pyramid 164
Shirley	Mello Kings	1950	Imperial 5105
Shirley	Playboys, John Fred & the	1962	Montel 998
Shirley	Promineers	1957	Budget
Shirley	Rainbows	1956	Pilgrim 711/Argyle 1012 (62)
Shirley	Schoolboys	1956	Okeh 7076
Shirley	Sharks	1975	Broadcast 1128
Shirley	Sharks Quintet	NA	Broadway
Shirley	Vitells	1962	Decca 31362
Shirley Ann	Chancers	1958	Dot 15870
Shirley Shirley	Edwards, Joey & group	1960	Lilly 501
Shirley's Tuff	K-Doe, Ernie & group	1961	Ember 1075
Shivers And Shakes	Fascinators (Los Angeles)	1958	Dooto 441
Sho' Know A Lot About Love	Hollywood Argyles	1960	Lute 5905
Sho Nuf M.F.	Dukays	1964	Jerry-O 106
Shock	Holland, Bryant & group	1958	Kudo 667
Shock-A-Doo	Cadillacs	1956	Josie 807
Shombalor	Ravels, Sheriff & the	1959	Vee Jay 306
Shoo Be Do Wah	Shades Of Brown	1982	Clifton EP 505
Shoo Bee Doo	Videos	1972	Bim Bam Boom 101
Shoo Do Be Do	Blue Jays (Los Angeles)	1956	Dig EP 780
Shoo Doo Be Doo	Moonglows	1964	Lana 134
Shoo Doo Be Doo (My Lovin' Baby)	Moonglows	1954	Checker 806
	(Moonlighters, Bobby Lester & the)		
Shoo Doo De Doo	Debs	1955	Bruce 129
Shoo Fly Pie	Genies	1963	Lennox 5562
Shoo-be Shoo-be do	Checkmates	1962	Regency 26
Shoo-Bee-Doo-Bee Cha Cha Cha	Videos	1959	Casino 105
Shook My Head	Five Keys	1955	Capitol (unreleased)
Shoom Ba Boom	Creators	1963	Philips 40060
Shooma Dom Dom	Shells	1959	End 1050
Shoop	Desires	1958	Herald (unreleased)
Shoop Shoop	Gladiolas	1958	Excello 2136
Shoopy Pop-A-Doo	Fluorescents	1959, 1963	Hanover 4520/Candelite 420 (59)
Shoo-Shoo	Tune Blenders	1954	Federal 12201
Shop Around	Velvet Five	1973	Nostalgia 102
Shoplifting Molly	Mohawks	1964	Mutual 504
Shoppin' And Hoppin'	Majestics (Florida)	1962	Chex 1000
Shoppin' For Clothes	Coasters	1960	Atco 6178
Shoppin' 'Round For Love	Teenettes, Betty Jayne & the	1961	Net 101
Short Daddy	Demens	1957	Teenage 1007
Short Line	Royaltones, Ruth McFadden & the	1960	Goldisc 3004
Short Short Twist	Royal Teens	1962	Allnew 1415/Jubilee 5418 (62)
Short Short'nin'	Prancers	1959	Guaranteed 204
Short Shorts	Four Winds	1957	Decor 175
Short Shorts	Royal Teens	1957	Power 215/ABC 9882 (58)
Short Skirts	Sh-Booms	1960	Atlantic 2074
Shortcut To A Heartache	Four Nuggets	1963	Songbird 204
Shortnin' Bread	Bell Notes	1960	Madison 136
Shortnin' Bread	Blisters	1963	Liberty 55577
Shortnin' Bread	Customs, Dave &	1965	Dac 500
Shortnin' Bread	Emeralds, Paul Chaplain & His	1960	Harper 100
Shortnin' Bread	Playboys	NA	Catalina 1069
Shorty The Pimp	Larks, Don Julian & the	1965	Jerk 202
Shorty's Got To Go	Impressions	1958	Bandera 2504/Port 70031 (60)

SONG	GROUP	YEAR	LABEL
Shot Gun Wedding	Higgins, Chuck & group	1954	Kicks 6
Shotgun	Playboys	1959	Rik 572
Should I	Twinkletones, Rocky Storm & the	1958	Josie 847
Should I Call	Redcoats, Steve Alaimo & the	1959	Marlin 6067
Should I Cry	Concords (Brooklyn)	1964	Epic 9697
Should I Ever Love Again	Del-Reys	1960	Delreco 500
Should I Ever Love Again	Matadors	1963	Lee 5466
Should I Ever Love Again	Ridgley, Tommy & group	1961	Ric 978
Should I Keep On Waiting	Crystals (Brooklyn)	1967	Michelle 4113
Should I Love You So Much?	Emeralds, Luther Bond & the	1960	Showboat 1505
Should Pretending End	Williams, Eddie & group	1964	Corsair 402
Shouldn't I	Blend-Aires	1978	Story Untold 501
Shouldn't I	Covacs	NA	Herald (unreleased)
Shouldn't I Know	Cardinals	1951	Atlantic 938
Shouldn't I?	Orients	1964	Laurie 3232
Shout	DiMucci, Dion (with the Del Satins)	1964	Laurie 3240
Shout (acappella)	Five Jades (Bronx, N.Y.)	1975	Relic LP 108
Shout It Out	Flamingos	1963	End (unreleased)
Shout Mama	Hughes, Fred & group	1965	Minasa 709
Shout Mama Linda	Cymbals	1962	Amazon 709
Shout My Name	Twilights, Tony Richards & the	1961	Colpix 199
Shout! Shout! (Knock Yourself Out)	Maresca, Ernie (with the Del Satins)	1962	Seville 117
Shoutin' Twist	Teen Tones	1961	Tri Disc 102
Show Is All Over, The	Cardinals	1956	Atlantic (unreleased)
Show Me	Davis, Hal Sonny & group	1962	Gardena 125
Show Me	Foster Brothers	1958	Mercury 71360
Show Me A Man	Starlets, Jenny Lee & the	1962	Congress 107
Show Me The Merengue	Hearts, Lee Andrews & the	1956	Gotham 318
Show Me The Rose	Atomics, Dennis Brown & the	1957	Atomic 57-101
Show Me The Way	Five Notes	1956	Chess 1614
Show Me The Way	Neville, Aaron & group	1960	Minit 618
Show Me The Way	Three Chimes	1964	Crossway 444
Show Me The Way To Go Home	Pirates, Black Beard & the	1958	Ad 101
Show Me The Way To Your Heart	Culmer, Little Iris (with the Majestics)	1956	Marlin 803
Show Must Go On, The	Reveres	1963	Jubilee 5463
Show Them You Can Dance	Pageants	1955	Beacon 559
Show You How To Make Love To Me	Headhunters, Cannibal & the	1965	Rampart 642
Show Your Love	Teenettes, Betty Jayne & the	1961	Carellen 101
Shrimp Boats	Orioles, Sonny Til & the	1952	Jubilee 5074
Shrimp Boats Are Coming	Blue Notes	1961	Gamut 100
Shrine Of St. Cecilia, The	Bon-Aires	1964	Rust 5097
Shrine Of St. Cecilia, The	Five Discs	1978	Crystal Ball 120
Shrine Of St. Cecilia, The	Harptones	1957	Rama 221
Shrine Of St. Cecilia, The	Infernos	NA	Clifton EP 502
Shrine of St. Cecilia, The	Royals	1953	Federal 12121
Shrine Of The Echo	Singleton, Bebo (with the Notes)	1959, 1960	Stentor 101
Shrine, The	Palisades	1960	Leader 806
Shtiggy Boom	Houston, Joe & group	1955	RPM 426
Shtiggy Boom	Nuggets	1955	Capitol 3052
Shtiggy Boom	Patti Anne	1955	Aladdin 3280
	(Patti Anne Mesner with the Flames)		
Shubby Dubby Doo	Shamans	1959	Kayham 1/2
Shuck, The	Freeman, Ernie	1956	Cash 1019
Shuffle In The Gravel	Young Jessie & group	1957	Atco 6101
Shuffle, The	Temps, Bobby & the	1963	ABC 10428
Shufflin'	Sharps	1957	Aladdin 3401
Shut Down	Tokens (Brooklyn)	NA	RCA LP 2886
Shut The Door, Baby	Jumpin' Jaguars	1956	Decca 29938
Shut Your Mouth	Eboniers	1959	Port 70013
Shy Boy	Boy Friends	1961	Glasser 1000
Shy Girl	Dells	1964	Vee Jay 595
Shy Girl	Expressions, Johnny & the	1966	Josie 955
Shy Guy	Charmers	1963	Laurie 3173
Shy Guy	Crystalettes	1962	Crystalette 752
Shy Guy	Mac, Bobby & group	1962	Vended 104

SONG	GROUP	YEAR	LABEL
Shy One	Impossibles, Linda Carr & the	1961	Ray Star 779
Si Senor	Miller Sisters	1965	Yorktown 75
Siam	Rhythm Four, Joe Therrien & the	1961	Sentinel 8906
Siam Sam	Val-Tones	1955	DeLuxe 6084
Sick Sick Sick	Boy Friends, Terry Corin & the	1960	Colony 110
Sick Sick Sick	Goofers	1955	Coral 61545
Sick, Sick, Sick	Wilder Brothers	1959	Leeds 781
Sick Song	Funny Bunnies	1960	Dore 542
Sick Spell	La Dolls	1985	Relic LP 8004
Side Street	Intervals	1958	Ad 104/Apt 25019 (58)
Side Wind, The	Lyrics, William Wigfall & the	1963	Goldwax 105/ABC 10560 (64)
Sidewalk Rock & Roll	Jokers, J.W. & the	1959	Simpson 1130
Sidewalks Of New York	Desires	NA	Hull (unreleased)
Sie Tu (It's You, It's You)	Gum Drops	1959	Coral 62102
Sign From Above (acappella), The	Gents, Vic & the	1964	Dorana 1170
Sign Of Happiness, The	Expressions	1961	Arliss 1012
Signal, The	Tri-Tones, Al Barkle & the	1957	Vita 171
Silence	Barons (Imperial)	1964	Imperial 66057
Silent Grief	Solitaires	1993	Old Town 1992
Silent Night	Ecstasies	1979	Clifton 40
Silent Night	Ravens	1948	National 9059
Silent Night	Tycoon	1985	Starlight 27
Silent Tears	Hayden Sisters	1961	Tilt 784
Silently	Gallahads	1958	Vik 0332
Silhouettes	Crests	1960	Coed LP 901
Silhouettes	Diamonds	1957	Mercury 71197
Silhouettes	Parisians	1959, 1961	Bullseye 1028/Argyle 1006
Silhouettes	Rays	1957	XYZ 102/Cameo 117 (57)
Silhouettes-You Cheated You Lied	Exodus	1963	Wand 11248
Silly Affair	Trem-Los	1961	Nolta 350
Silly And Sappy	Fi-Tones	1956	Atlas 1055
Silly And Sappy	Parakeets, Vic Donna & the	1957	Atlas 1071
Silly Chili	Twisters, Joey & the	1961	Dual 502
Silly Dilly	Hornets, Don Ray & the	1959	Hornet 501
Silly Dilly	Pentagons	1958	Specialty 644
Silly Girl	Cook, Gene & group	NA	Jarrell 101
Silly Girl	Miller Sisters	1963	Roulette 4491
Silly Grin	Trends	1959	Scope 102
Silly Heart	Ravens	NA	Mercury (unreleased)
Silly Little Boy	Ramblers (Almont)	1964	Almont 315
Silly Milly	Devotions	1958	Cub 9020
Silly Willie	Jaybirds, Bobby Darin & the	1956	Decca 29922
Silly Willy	El Vireos	1959	Revello 1002
Silver	Emeralds (St. Louis)	1961	Toy 7734
Silver Dollar	Darvell, Barry & group	1961	Atlantic 2128
Silver Lining	Starlites	1960	Fury 1045
Silver Medal	Classmen	1963	Gateway 712
Silver Star	Charms, Otis Williams & the	1960	King 5332
Silver Star	Velvet Sounds	NA	Cosmopolitan 100/101
Silver Starlight	Rays	1960	XYZ 608
Silver Waters	Five Satins	1974	Relic LP 5024
Silvery Moon	Euniques	1980	Jason Scott 6
Silvery Moon	Uniques	1962	Lucky Four 1024
Simon Says	Ravens	1956	Argo (unreleased)
Simple Simon	Aladdins	1963	Witch 111
Simple Simon	Quarter Tones, Chip & the	1964	Carlton 604
Simple Things	Curtiss, Jimmy & group	1960	United Artists 215
Simply Because	Clifford, Buzz (with the Teenagers)	1962	Columbia 41979
Simply Say Goodbye	Four Buddies	1951	Savoy 823
Sin	Four Buddies	1951	Savoy 817
Since I Don't Have You	Lopez, Trini & group	1959	King 5187
Since I Don't Have You	Round Robins	1953	Bell 108
Since I Don't Have You	Skyliners	1959	Calico 103/104/Original Sound 35 (63)
Since I Fell For You	Buckeyes	1957	DeLuxe 6110
Since I Fell For You	Filets Of Sole	1968	Savoy 1630

SONG	GROUP	YEAR	LABEL
Since I Fell For You	Gems (Illinois)	1954	Drexel 902
Since I Fell For You	Halos	1965	Congress 249
Since I Fell For You	Harptones	1954	Bruce 113
Since I Fell For You	Love Notes (Massachusetts)	1954	Riviera 975
Since I Fell For You	Persuasions	1971	Reprise 0977
Since I Fell For You	Sharptones	1955	Post 2009
Since I Fell For You	Skyliners	1963	Atco 6270/Motown 1046 (63)
Since I Fell For You	Spaniels	1956	Vee Jay 202
Since I Fell For You	Vibrations	1963	Checker 1038
Since I Fell For You	Logan, Dorothy (with the Gems)	1954	Drexel 902
Since I Fell For You & Rockin' Robin	Diablos	1984	Fortune LP 8020
Since I Fell For You (acappella)	Apparitions	1975	Relic LP 108
Since I First Met You	Robins	1957	Whippet 203
Since I Last Saw You	Lidos	1957	Band Box 359
Since I Lost You	Simmons, Little Maxine & group	NA	Varbee 117
Since I Made You Cary	Rivieras	1959	Coed 522
Since I Met You	Deltones	1961	Dayhill 1002
Since I Met You	Hosea, Don & group	1961	Sun 368
Since I Met You Baby	Fender, Freddy & group	1959	Duncan 1004
Since I've Been Away	Martells	1965	Atco 6336
Since I've Been Going With Him	Pillows, Penny Baker & the	1964	Witch 123
Since I've Lost You	Now & Then	1981	Clifton 65
Since Love's Been Knockin'	Crosstones	NA	Clifton EP 510
Since My Baby's Been Gone	Supremes, Ruth McFadden & the	1956	Old Town 1017
Since We Fell In Love	Cleftones	1957, 1976	Robin Hood 132/Roulette LP 25021
Since You	Hightower, Donna (with the Jacks)	1955	RPM 439
Since You Been Gone	Counts, Bobby Comstock & the	1964	Lawn 229
Since You Came	Nic Nacks	1963	Ovation 6201
Since You Came Into My Life	El Dorados	1971	Paula 347
Since You Left My World	Centurians	1959	Tiger 1001
Since You Went Away	Fascinations	1972	A&G 101
Since You Went Away	Tassells	1963	Goldisc G11
Since You Went Away To School	Roses, Don & His	1958	Dot 15755
Since Your Love Has Grown Cold	Cupcakes, Shelton Dunaway & the	1961	Khoury's 727
Since You're Gone	Diablos, Nolan Strong & the	1960	Fortune 536
Since You're Gone	Jesters	1960	Shimmy 1054
Since You've Been Away	Swallows (Maryland)	1951, 1986	King 4466/Starbound 506
Since You've Been Gone	Dreamers, Richard Berry & the	1956	Flip 319/Flip 354 (61)
Since You've Been Gone	Fabulons (with the Tikis)	1966	Tower 259
Since You've Been Gone	Heartbreakers (Bronx, N.Y.)	1962	Markay 106
Since You've Been Gone	McPhatter, Clyde (with the Cookies & the Cues)	1959	Atlantic 2028
Since You've Been Gone (acappella)	Velvet Angels	1964	Medieval 207
Since You've Gone Away	Medalions	1960	Card 1
Sincere	Pyramids	NA	Kllk (unreleased)
Sincerely	Blue Emotions	1982	Ambient Sound 03409
Sincerely	Blue Jays (Los Angeles)	1956	Dig EP 777
Sincerely	Crowns, Arthur Lee Maye & the	1957	Dig 149 (unreleased)
Sincerely	Durhams	1965	Relic 1018
Sincerely	Emery's	1977	Clifton 18
Sincerely	Jacks, Julie Jordan & the	NA	Rush 1003
Sincerely	Jayos, Johnny Otis & the	1957	Dig LP 104
Sincerely	Mission Bells	1965	London 9760
Sincerely	Moonglows	1954, 1964	Chess 1581/Lana 130
Sincerely	Platters	1964	Mercury 72305
Sincerely	Raiders, Tony Castle & the	1961	Gone 5105
Sincerely	Rhythmaires (with Gayle Lark)	NA	Tops EP 252
Sincerely	Sinceres	1964	Columbia 43110
Sincerely	Tokens (Brooklyn)	1961	RCA 7925
Sincerely	Vibra Tones	1961	ABC 10218
Sincerely	Vibrations, Evelyn Dell & the	1961	ABC 10218
Sincerely (acappella)	Zircons	1964	Siamese 403/Old Timer 603 (64)
Sincerely 72	Moonglows	1971, 1972	Big P 101/RCA 74-0759
Sincerely With All My Heart	Deckers	1958	Yeadon 101
Sindy	Squires (California)	1955	Mambo 105/Vita 105 (60)

SONG	GROUP	YEAR	LABEL
Sindy	Tenderfoots	1955	Federal 12228
Sing A Silly Sing Song	Mellow Larks	1957	Argo 5285
Sing A Song Of Sixpence	Corvairs	1960	Cub 9065
Sing All The Day	Manhattans	1962	Capitol 4730
Sing Along	Playboys	1959	Martinique 400
(Sing Along) I Still Love Him	Joys	1964	Valiant 6042
Sing To Me	Griffins	1955	Mercury 70558
Singing Bells	Off Keys	1962	Rowe 003/Technicord 1001 (62)
Singing Waters	Cashmeres (Brooklyn)	1961	Laurie 3088
Singing Waters	Truetones	1961	Felsted 8625
Single And Free	Empires, Eddie Friend & the	1959	Colpix 112
Sinner Man	Celtics, Bobby Lanz & the	NA	Bridges 2204
Sinner, The	Flamingos	1962	End LP 316
Sinner's Prayer	Midnighters	1953	Federal 12169
Sioux City Sioux	Ebonaires	1988	Relic LP 5076
Sippin' A Cup Of Coffee	Ordells	NA	Dionn 505
Sippin' Soda	Shells	1958	End 1022/Gone 5103 (61)
Sipping A Cup Of Coffee	Hearts, Lee Andrews & the	1981	Gotham 323
Sister Lucy	Toppers, Bobby Mitchell & the	1954	Imperial 5270
Sister Of The Girl I Once Loved	Ultratones	1962	Cary 2001
Sister Sookey	Earls	1978	
Sister Sookey	Turbans (Philadelphia)	1956	Herald 469
Sister Sookey Comes Home	Limelighters	1957	Gilco 213
Sit And Cry	Grand Prees	1963	Candi 1020
Sit And Hold My Hand	Masters, Rick & the	1992	Clifton 104
Sit And Hold My Hand	Swallows (Maryland)	1986	Starbound 503
Sit By The Fire	Willows	1964	Heidi 107
Sit Down Girl	Zircons	1967	Heigh Ho 608/609
Sit, Hope And Cry	Warner, Merrill & group	NA	Travel 505
Sit Right Down And Cry	Twilighters (Bronx, N.Y.)	1960	Super 1003
Sittin'	Playthings	1958	Liberty 55147
Sittin' Alphabetically	Hammel Jr., Karl & group	1961	Arliss 1011
Sittin' And Cryin'	Sunsets	1959	Rae-Cox 102
Sittin' By The River	Marylanders	1952	Jubilee 5079
Sittin' Here Wondering	Marylanders	1972	Roadhouse 1003
Sittin' In A Corner	Twiliters	1956, 1961	Groove 0154
Sittin' On The Porch	Five Peaks	1987	Jay-R 100
Sittin' On Top Of The World	Mar, Jerry & group	1957	Amp-3 131
Sittin' On Your Doorstep	Corsairs	1962	Tuff 1818/Chess 1818
Sittin' With My Baby	Royal Teens	1957	Astra 1012/Power 113
Sitting By My Window	Five Tinos	1955	Sun 222
Sitting Here	Tyce, Napoleon & group	1960	Norwood 105
Sitting In The Moonlight	G-Clefs	1962	Terrace 7510
Six Button Benny	Nite Riders, Doc Starkes & the	1958	Swan 4003
Six Days A Week	Kinglets	1956	Calvert 101
Six Foot Hole	Emeralds, Luther Bond & the	1959	Federal 12368
Six Gun	Marquis	1959	Class 251
6 Months, 3 Weeks, 2 Days, 1 Hour	Sharps	1957	Tag 2200/Chess 1690 (58)
Six Months, Three Weeks, Two Days, One Hour	Lamplighters	1958	Tag 2200/Chess 1690
Six Nights A Week	Crests	1959	Coed 509
Six Nights A Week	Splendors	1982	Clifton 69
Six O'Clock In The Morning	Five Royales	1955	Apollo 467
Six Pack	Revels	1959	Swingin' 620
Six Pretty Girls	Ekhoes, Con Pierson & the	1964	LeMans 007
Six Questions	Turbans (Philadelphia)	1961	Imperial 5807
Sixteen	Count Downs, Chuck Hix & the	1959	Verve 10169
Sixteen Candles	Crests	1958	Coed 506
Sixteen Candles	Passions	1963	Diamond 146
Sixteen Candles	Sirs	1968	Charay 33
Sixteen Tons	Chirps, Marvin & the	1958	Tip Top 202
Sixteen Tons	Platters	1973	Wing LP MGW 12112
Sixty Minute Man	Dominoes	1951, 1960	Federal 12022
Sixty Minute Man	Ecstasies	1979	U.G.H.A. 04
Sixty Minute Man	Four Sportsmen	1962	Sunnybrook 5

SONG	GROUP	YEAR	LABEL
60 Minute Man	Untouchables	1960	Madison 139
$64,000 Question , The	Tuggle, Bobby & group	1955	Checker 823
Sixty-Nine (69)	Arondies	NA	Sherry 69
Ska Light, Ska Bright	Fleetwoods	1964	Dolton 97
Skate, The	Larks (Don Julian)	1965	Money 127
Skating In The Blue Light	Charmettes	1958	Hi 2003
Skid Row	Jewels (Los Angeles)	NA	Imperial (unreleased)
Skiddily Doo	Five Chanels	1958	Deb 500
Skier Jones	Faces	1965	Regina 1326
Skinny Jimmy	Dillard, Varetta (with the Four Students)	1956	Groove 0159
Skinny Minnie	Expressions	1965	Guyden 2122
Skinny Minnie	Sprouts	1957	RCA 7172
Skinny Woman Story, The	Five Birds, Willie Headen & the	1957	Authentic 410/Dootone 410
Skip, The	Del-Prados	1962	Lucky Four 1021
Skippin' And Jumpin'	Flints	1959	Okeh 7126
Skippity Doo	Five Satins	1959	First 104
Skitter, Skatter	Metrotones	1957	Reserve 116
	(with the Little Walkin' Willie Quartet)		
Skitter Skatter Pitter Patter	Raytones, Rudy Rae Moore & the	1957	Ball 0500
Skokian	Escorts, Del & the	1960	Symbol 913
Sky, The	Lancers	1965	Vee Jay 654
Skylark	Blue Flames	1954	Grand 113
Skylark	Clovers	1951	Atlantic 934
Skylark	Fleetwoods	1960	Dolton BLP 2002/BST 8002
Skylark	Four Fellows	1980	U.G.H.A. 15
	(Brooklyn - same group as on Glory)		
Sky's The Limit, The	Duprees	1969, 1975	Heritage 808/RCA 10407
Sky's The Limit, The	Italian Asphalt And Pavement Company	1970	Colossus 110
Slauson Shuffle	Meadowlarks, Don Julian & the	1962	Dynamite 1114
Slave Girl	Diamonds	1960	Mercury 71633
Slave To Love	Walker, Charles (with the Daffodils)	1959	Champion 1014
Sleep And Dream	Keystoners	1961	Riff 202
Sleep Beauty Sleep	Noblemen	1963	USA 1215
Sleep Tight	Kid, The & group	NA	Rumble 1347
Sleep Tight	Pastels (Pastel)	1964	Pastel 506
Sleep Walk	Del-Larks, Sammy & the	1961	Stop 101
Sleep With A Dream	Five Johnson Brothers	1958	Fulton 2455/Carrie 012
Sleepless Nights	Corvans	1959	Cabot 131
Sleepless Nights	Originals	1959	Jackpot 48012
Sleepy Cowboy	Five Sharps	1952, 1972	Jubilee 5104/Bim Bam Boom 103
Sleepy Head Mama	Casanovas	1955	Apollo 483
Sleepy Hollow	Carnations	1960	Terry Tone 199
Sleepy Lagoon	Platters	1960	Mercury 71563
Sleepy Little Cowboy	Deep River Boys	1953	Beacon 104
Sleepy Time Girl	Dimensionals, Donnie Baker with the	1953	Rainbow 219
Sleepytime Rock	Jumpers, Jay Nelson & the	1959	Excello 2149
Slide My Baby Slide	Metro-Chords	1961	Admiral 300
Slide On By	Empires	1963	Candi 1033
Slide, Slide, Slide	Five Ramblers	1963	Lummtone 111
Slide, The	Blendtones	1963	Success 105
Slide, The	Lavenders	1961	C.R. 103
Slide, The	Schoolboys	1958, 1972	Juanita 103
Slide-Cha-Lypso	LP's, Denny & the	1958	Rock-It 001
Slight Case Of Love	Five Fleets	1958	Felsted 8522
Slim Little Annie	Genos	1959	Sundance 202
Slime, The	Coasters	1962	Atco 6234
Slippin' And Slidin'	Citations	1962	Sara 3301/Epic 9603 (63)
Slippin' And Slidin'	Cleftones	1963	Unreleased
Slippin' And Slidin'	Green, Barbara & group	1963	Atco 6250
Slippin' Through Your Fingers	Chartbusters	1964	Mutual 502
Slipping Away	Monterays (Brooklyn)	1956	Saturn 1005
Slipping Into Darkness	Reunion	NA	Starlight 18
Slipping Out	Starlighters	1957	Lamp 2014
Slip-Slop	Harris, Thurston (with the Sharps)	1959	Aladdin 3456
Sloo Foot Soo	Seniors	1958	Excello 2130

SONG	GROUP	YEAR	LABEL
Sloop And Slide	Midnighters, Hank Ballard & the	1965	King 6018
Sloop It Out	Invaders	1963	El Toro 503
Slop Stroll Walk	Moonglows	1958	Chess (unreleased)
Slop, The	Olympics	1960	Arvee 595
Slop Time	Shirelles	1958	Decca 30669
Sloppin'	Gems, Pearl Woods & the	1962	Wall 552
Sloppy Drunk	Spaniels	1953	Vee Jay (unreleased)
Sloppy Jalopy	Dunes	1961	Madison 156
Slow Burn	Five Stars, Dottie Ferguson & the	1957	Kernel 003/Mercury 71129
Slow, But Sure	Vectors	1958	Standord 700
Slow But Sure	Victors	1958	N/A
Slow Dance	Hornets	1958	Rev 3515
Slow Dance	Kelly, Karol & group	1962	Joy 272
Slow Dance	Revivals	1991	Avenue D 17
Slow Down	Forevers	1958	Apt 25022
Slow Down	Mac, Lou (with the Palms)	1955	Blue Lake 114
Slow Down	Moonglows	1955	Chess 1598
Slow Down	Ron-Dells	1963	Arlen 723
Slow Down	Tennyson, Bill & group	1958	Pet 805
Slow Down Your Life	Dunham, Jackie & group	1961	Imperial 5768
Slow Locomotion	Four Buddies	1965	Philips 40122
Slow Pokey Joe	Satellites, Bobby Day & the	1962	Rendezvous 175
Slow Rock	Verity, Lady Jane &	1959	Palette 5031
Slowly But Surely	Sparks	1975	Broadcast 1121
Slowly Losing My Mind	Wright, Willie (with the Sparklers)	1960	Federal 12372
Slummer The Slum, The	Five Royales	1958	King 5153
Smack Dab In The Middle	Cadets	NA	Modern LP 1215
Smack Dab In The Middle	Du Droppers	1955	Groove EP EGA-5
Smack Dab In The Middle	Jacks	1955	RPM 428 (first pressing)
Small Fry	Davis, Billy & group	1960	R-Dell 118
Small Town Girl	Rounders, Jimmy Tig & the	1963	Spar 779
Small Town Gossip	Counts, Cosmo & the	1963	Sound Stage 7 2504
Smart Too Late	Intimates	1964	Epic 9743
Smashed	V-Notes	1958	Volk 102
Smile	Kac-Ties	1962	Trans Atlas 695/Kape 502 (63)
Smile	Mello-Larks, Vince Massey & the	1953	Herald 414
Smile	Pretenders	1961	Power-Martin 1001/Relic 1004 (65)
Smile	Travelers, Roger & the	1978	Crystal Ball 128
Smile	Victors, Little Man & the	1964	Roulette 4576
Smile A Little Smile For Me	Royal Teens	1969	Musicor 139
Smile (Baby)	Relations	1963	Kape 504
Smile, Just Smile	Nortones	1959	Warner Bros. 5115
Smile Through My Tears	Majestics (MGM)	1966	MGM 13488
Smoke From Your Cigarette	Belmonts	1961	Surprise 1000/Sabrina 500 (61)
Smoke From Your Cigarette	Drake Sisters	1964	Chattahoochee 649
Smoke From Your Cigarette	Fabulons	1960	Ember 1069
Smoke From Your Cigarette	Mellows, Lillian Leach & the	1955	Jay-Dee 797
Smoke Gets In Your Eyes	Barrett, Richard & group	1958	MGM 12616
Smoke Gets In Your Eyes	Crescents	1963	Arlen 743
Smoke Gets In Your Eyes	Platters	1958	Mercury 71383/Mercury 10001 (58)
Smoke Gets In Your Eyes (acappella)	Five Delights	1960	A Cappella - Best of the Bronx (98)
Smoke Signals	Tides	1959	Dore 546
Smoke! Smoke! Smoke!	Whirlaways	1958	Crest 1051
Smokey Joe	Jewels (female)	1964	Dimension 1048
Smokey Joes	Harris, Thurston (with the Sharps)	1958	Aladdin 3428
Smokey Joe's Cafe	Robins	1955	Spark 122/Atco 6059 (56)
Smokey The Bear	Decades, Brother Zee & the	1962	Ramco 3725
Smokie Joe's	Jewels (female)	1966	King 6068
Smoky Places	Corsairs	1961	Tuff 1808/Chess 1808 (61)
Smooch Me	Diamonds	1955	Coral 61577
Smoochie, Poochie	Viscounts, Sammy Hagen & the	1957	Capitol 3772
Smoochin' In The Sewer	Empalas	1958	Mark V 501
Smootchie	Lamplighters	1953	Federal 12166
Smooth, Slow And Easy	Drivers	1956	DeLuxe 6094
Smoothie	Tune Drops	1959	Gone 5072

SONG	GROUP	YEAR	LABEL
Snacky Poo	Del-Mars	1964	Mercury 72244
Snake And The Bookworm	Coasters	1960	Atco 6178
Snake In The Grass	Boy Friends	1961	Glasser 1000
Snake, The	Five Shillings	1958	Decca 30722
Snaky Poo	Ring-A-Dings	1962	Infinity 014
Snap Crackle & Pop	Nitecaps	NA	Detour LP 33-010
Snap, Crackle & Pop	Supremes (Ohio)	1958	Mark 129
Snap, Crackle And Pop	Alley Cats	1957	Whippet 209
Snap, Crackle, Pop	Kelloggs	1969	Laurie 3476
Snap Dragon	Saints	1958	Prescott 1570
Snap Jack	Bowties, Cirino & the	1956	Royal Roost 622
Snap Your Fingers	Sinceres	1964	Columbia 43110
Snatchin' Back	Bees	1954	Imperial 5314
Sneakin' Around	Lapels	1960	Melker 103/Dot 16129 (60)
Sneakin' Around	Sherwoods	1961	Johnson 121
Sneaky Alligator	Diamonds	1959	Mercury 71468
Sneaky Alligator	Ellis Brothers	1958	ABC 9954
Sneaky Alligator	La Rells	1962	Liberty 55430
Sneaky Blues	Lapels	1960	Melker 103/Dot 16129 (60)
Snoopin' And Accusin'	Tick Tocks, Bobby Marchan & the	1960	Fire 1014
Snooty Friends	Carians	1961	Indigo 136
Snooty Poo	Three Coquettes	1960	Hope 1002
Snorin'	Sparrows, Little Jimmy & the	1958	Val-Ue 101
Snow Dreams	Three Dots	1960	Rich 1003
Snow Queen	Rhythmettes	1960	Coral 62186
Snow Train	Jamies	1958	Epic 9299/Epic 9565 (63)
Snow White	Blazers, Rodney & the	1961	Dore 588
Snow White	Devotions	1964	Roulette 4580
Snow White And The Three Stooges	Blue Belles	1961	20th Fox 249
Snow White Winter	Sensationals	1960	Candix 306
Snowball	Robins	1958	Whippet 212
Snowbound	Dell Vikings	1957	Mercury 71241
Snowflakes And Teardrops	Angels (New Jersey)	1964	Smash 1870
Snowtime	Echelons	1991	BAB 132
Snuggle Bunny	Viscounts, Sammy Hagen & the	1958	Capitol 3885
So Afraid	Tantones	1957	Lamp 2008
So All Alone	Flames	1956	Aladdin 3349
So All Alone	Moonlighters, Bobby Lester & the	1954	Checker 806
So Bad	Calvaes, Oscar Boyd & the	1959	Checker 928
So Bad	Carthays	1961	Tag 446
So Bad	Medallions, Vernon Green & the	1988	Classic Artists 103
So Be It	Charms, Otis Williams & the	1960	King 5389
So Blue	Debonaires, Bob & the	1961	Debonair
So Blue	Jades	1958	Time 1002
So Blue	Vibrations	1960	Bet 001/Checker 954 (60)
So Can I	Charms, Otis Williams & the	1961	King 5455
So Close	Visions	1961	Brunswick 55206
So Close To An Angel	Desires	NA	Hull (unreleased)
So Dearly	Thunderbirds, Ron Holden & the	1961	Donna 1338
So Deep	Monterays (Brooklyn)	1959	Impala 213
So Deep Within	Spaniels	1960, 1979	Vee Jay LP 1024
So Disappointed With Love	Volumes, Lacille Watkins & the	1954	Jaguar 3006
So Doggone Lonely	Satellites, Sonny King & the	1955	Nocturne 1003/1004
So Don't Go	Sensational	1958	Mida 109
So Far Away	Blue Chords	NA	Reverb 6745
So Far Away	Candles, Rochell & the	1961	Swingin' 634
So Far Away	Hi Tensions, Leon Peels & the	1960	Audio 201/K&G 101
So Far Away	Pastels (Washington, D.C.)	1958	Argo 5314
So Far Away From Home	Knight Lites, Gary & the	1965	Bell 643
So Fine	Aquatones	1958	Fargo 1002
So Fine	Chancellors	1965	Soma 1435
So Fine	Checkers	1959	Federal 12355
So Fine	Classics, Mike Sabeh & the	NA	Empress 1001
So Fine	Dynamics	1963	Dynamic 1002/Reprise 20183 (63)
So Fine	Edgewoods	1968	Epic 10275

SONG	GROUP	YEAR	LABEL
So Fine	Fiestas	1959, 1971	Old Town 1062/Vigor 712/ Cotillion 4417
So Fine	Hollywood Argyles	1960	Lute 6002
So Fine	Santells	1964	Courier 115
So Fine	Sheiks	1955	Federal 12237/Federal 1281 (59)
So Fine	Sheppards (Chicago - Owl)	1974	Owl 330
So Fine	Zodiacs, Maurice Williams & the	1965	Sphere Sound 707
So Fine (acappella)	Shells	1966	Candlelite LP 1000
So Fine, So Fine, So Fine	Paradons	1960	Warner Bros. 5186
So Glad	Ambers	1960	Todd 1042
So Glad	Eager, Johnny & group	1959	End 1054
So Glad	Five Keys	1954	Capitol (unreleased)
So Glad	Heart-Throbs	1957	Aladdin 3394/Lamp 2010 (57)
So Glad	Sapphires	1958	RCA 7357
So Glad I'm Crying	Robins, Mike Robin & the	NA	Clarity 105
So Good	Harmonizers, Premo & the	NA	Doctor Bird
So Good	Hollywood Flames	1959, 1988	Ebb 158/Specialty LP 2166
So Good	Playboys	1956	Tetra 4447
So Good	Shades	NA	Klik
So Good	Versatones	NA	N/A
So Good, So Fine, You're Mine	Harptones (with Harriet Toni Williams)	1957	Gee 1045
So Good To Me	Raytones, Rudy Ray Moore & the	1958	Cash 1060
So Good To Me (You've Been)	Dippers, Georgie Torrence & the	1960	King 5376
So Goodbye	Olympics	1963	Tri Disc 112
So Happy	Six Teens	1960	Flip 350
So Hard To Get Along	Lyrics, William Wigfall & the	1963	Goldwax 105/ABC 10560 (64)
So Hard To Laugh, So Easy To Cry	Escorts (RCA)	1957	RCA 6963
So Hard To Laugh, So Easy To Cry	Titans	1957	Vita 148
So Hard To Take	Raging Storms	1962	Trans Atlas 691
So Help Me	Five Willows	1954	Herald 442
So Help Me I Love You	Nuggets	1954	Capitol 2989
So High	Sensationals, Jimmy Jones & the	1965	Savoy 4234
(So How Come) No One Loves You	Omegas	1960	Decca 31094
So I Can Forget	Majestics (Florida)	1962	Chex 1000
So I Guess	Tidal Waves	NA	Strafford 6503
So In Love	Classics (Brooklyn)	1959	Dart 1015/Musictone 1114 (63)
So In Love	Echotones	1959	Dart 1009
So In Love	Latons	1962	Port 70030
So In Love	Re-Vels	1956	Teen 122
So In Love	Sunliners	1962	Hercules 184
So In Love	Tymes	1963	Parkway 871A (first pressing)
So In Love With You	Aristocats	1958	Sue 714
So In Need For Love	Eskridge, Murrie & group	1961	Apex 7764
So In Need For Love	Sheppards (Chicago - Apex)	NA	Collectables LP 5078
So (It's Over)	Marveltones	1952	Regent 194
So Jealous	Bees	NA	Finch 506
So Left Alone	Hayden, Gil & group	1961	V-Tone 219
So Little Time	Duprees	1964	Coed 595
So Little Time	Neptunes	1960	Checker 967
So Little Time	Vibrations	1960, 1977	Checker 967
So Live	Vanguards	1954	Derby 854
So Lonely	Computones	1978	U.G.H.A. 3
So Lonely	Del-Chords, Donnie & the	1961	Taurus 352/Epic 9495 (62)
So Lonely	Fabulous Pearl Devines	1959	Alco 101
So Lonely	Wilco, Roger & group	1961	Milestone 2007
So Lonely, Baby	Five Stars (Detroit)	1957	Blue Boys Kingdom 106
So Lonesome	Five Echoes	1954	Sabre 105
So Long	Corvets	1960	Laurel 1012
So Long	El Rays (Willie Dixon)	1954	Checker (unreleased)
So Long	Gallahads	1961	Nite Owl 20
So Long	Jelly Beans	1964	Red Bird 10-003
So Long	Little David & group	1963	Savoy 1617
So Long	Perkins, Al & group	1966	Jive 1003
So Long	Pipes	1958	Jacy 001
So Long	Three Chuckles	1955	X 0134

SONG	GROUP	YEAR	LABEL
So Long Baby	Hearts (Bronx, N.Y.)	1957	J&S 1660
So Long Baby	Satellites, Bobby Day & the	1957	Class 207
So Long, Daddy	Souvenirs	1957	Dooto 412
So Long Darling	Laddins	1959	Grey Cliff (unreleased)
So Long, Farewell, Bye-Bye	Aladdins	1956	Aladdin 3314
(So Long) Gee, I Hate To See You Go	Diablos	1984	Fortune LP 8020
So Long, Goodbye	Sugar Lumps, Sugar Boy & the	1963	Peacock 1925
So Long Love	Dukes (California)	1954	Specialty
So Long, Lover's Island	Blue Jays (Venice, Calif.)	1987	Relic LP 5064
So Long, My Darling	Barons (New Orleans)	1954	Imperial 5283
So Long My Darling	Famous Flames	1960	Harlem 114
So Long My Darling	Flames	1960	Harlem 114
So Long, My Sailor	Debelaires	1962	Lectra 502
So Long So Long	Dynamo, Skinny & group	1956	Excello 2097
So Long Young Girl	Five Thrills	1990	Relic LP 5087
So Lost	Owls	NA	Arden 1000
So Loved Am I	Johnson, Jesse & group	1958	Symbol 901
So Loved Am I	Royal Lancers, Ronnie Premiere & the	1961	Sara 1020
So Many Days	Vonns	1963	King 5793
So Many Have Told You	Duprees	1964	Coed 593
So Many Reasons Why	Sheppard, Buddy & group	1959	Play Me 3517
So Many Sleepless Nights	Sierras (Four Sierras)	1962	Knox 102
So Many Tears	Downbeats	1958	Peacock 1679
So Many Tears Ago	Squires (Gee)	1962	Gee 1082
So Many Times	Epics	1960	Dante 3004
So Many Women	Williams, Bobby & group	1960	Swingin' 619
So Much	Enchanters (Vargo)	1964	Vargo 10
So Much	Imperials, Little Anthony & the	1958	End 1036
So Much	Orioles, Sonny Til & the	1949	Jubilee 5016
So Much	Salutations, Vito & the	1978	Crystal Ball 104
So Much	Starfires	1961	Bargain 5001
So Much In Love	Chiffons	1970	Buddah 171
So Much In Love	Laurels	1985	R.A.M. 501012
So Much In Love	Metropolitans	1958	Junior 395
So Much In Love	Tymes	1963	Parkway 871C (second pressing)
So Much In Love With You	Upfronts	NA	Unreleased
So Much Younger	Wanderers, Dion & the	1966	Columbia 43692
So Near	Matadors	1962	Jamie 1226
So Near And Yet So Far	Cues	1955	Groove (unreleased) (recorded 1955)
So Near And Yet So Far	Four Students	1955	Groove 0110
So Near And Yet So Far	Imperials, Little Anthony & the	1959, 1960	End 1053/1086
So Nice	Angels (New Jersey)	1968	RCA 9681
So Nice	Blazers (with Dave Baby Cortez)	1961	Winley 1001
So Nice	Fiestas	1960	Old Town 1090
So Real	Chantels	1987	Murray Hill LP 000385
So Sad	Ramblers (Trumpet)	1963	Trumpet 102
So Shy	Flannels	1956	Tampa 121
So Shy	Leen Teens	1959	Imperial 5593
So Shy	Sensational	1958	Mida 106
So Sick	Clark, Lucky & group	1961	Chess 1782
So Sincere	Sporttones	1959	Munich 101
So So Long (Good Goodbye)	Knight, Bob	1961	Taurus 100
So Soon	Woodside Sisters & Harptones	1954	X
So Strange	Five Dollars	1956	Fortune 826
So Strange	Jesters	1957	Winley 218
So Strange	Lovetones	1974	Barrier 100
So Strange	Mellows, Lillian Leach & the	1989	Relic LP 5080
So Sweet Of You	Johnson, Bill	1957	Baton 239
So Tenderly	Darrells	1961	Lyco 1003
So Tenderly	Mystics	1959	Laurie 3038
So Tenderly	Valor, Tony & group	1963	Musictone 1119
So There	Four Shades Of Rhythm	1952	Chance 1126
So They Say	Tempo-Tones, Nancy Lee & the	1957	Acme 711
So This Is Love	Castells	1962	Era 3073
So Tired	Carbo, Leonard & group	1958	Vee Jay 291

SONG	GROUP	YEAR	LABEL
So Tired	Chavis Brothers	1962	Clock 1025
So Tired	Embers, Gene Pitney & the	1990	Relic LP 5085
So Tough	Casuals	1958	Back Beat 503 (first pressing, second is by Original Casuals)
So Tough	Cuff Links	1958	Dooto 433
So Tough	Kuf-Linx	1958	Challenge 1013/Challenge 59002 (58)
So Tough	Original Casuals	1958	Back Beat 503 (second pressing, first is by Casuals)
So Tough	Wombats, Gary & the	1963	Regina 297
So Unimportant	Harrison, Lee & group	1958	Judd 1003
So Unimportant	Kounts, Lee Harrison & the	1958	Pearl 717
So Unnecessary	Sounds	1955	Modern 975
So Very Much	Four Deans	1992 (1958)	Park Ave. 7
So Weak	Sequins, Jessie & the	1959	Boxer 201/Profile 4008 (59)
So What	Minor Chords	1986	Relic LP 8008
So What	Taylor, Carmen & group	1957	King 5085
So Why	Bop Chords	1957	Holiday 2608
So Will I	Cadets	1956	Modern 969
So Will I	Four Fellows, Bette McLaurin & the	1955	Glory 233
So Wonderful	Wonderlettes	NA	Baja 4506
So Wonderful (My Love)	Salutations, Vito & the	1966	Red Boy 1001/Sandbag 103
So Worried	Five Hollywood Blue Jays	1951	Recorded In Hollywood 185
So Wrong	Barin, Pete (with the Belmonts)	1962	Sabina 504
So Wrong	Jacks	1956, 1975	RPM 454/Relic 1031
So You And I Can Climb	Cleftones	1976	Robin Hood 133
So You Want To Rock	Majestics (Detroit)	1959	Faro 592
So You Will Know	Paragons	1958, 1960	Winley 228/240/Times Square 9
So Young	Clovers	1957	Atlantic 1139
So Young	Destineers	1962	RCA 8049
So Young	Dialtones	1963	Lawn 203
So Young	Giants, Little Guy & the	1961	Lawn 103
So Young	Nitecaps, Clyde Stacy & the	1957	Candlelight 1015
So Young	Poets	NA	Symbol 216
So Young And So In Love	Wheels	1958, 1996	Time 1003
So Young And So Pretty	Four Vanns	1956	Vik 0246
So Young, So Fine	Fallen Angels	1965	Tollie 9049
So Young, So Sweet	Marvels (Washington, D.C.)	1958	Laurie 3016
So Young, So Warm, So Beautiful	Cavaliers	1963	Music World 101
So Young, So Warm, So Wonderful	Planetts	1963	Goldisc G7
Soap 'N Water	Terrans, Rene Harris & the	1963	Graham 801
Sobbin'	Blue Angels	1959	Palette 5038
Society Girl	Sheppards (Chicago - Apex)	1960	Apex 7759
Sock Hop	Flares	NA	London (England) LP 8034
Sock Hop	Sharptones	1959	Ace 133
Soda Pop	Jan Raye Quartet, Lily Ann & the	NA	Baton 221
Soda Pop	Moonglows	1958	Chess 1689
(Soda Pop) Jukebox Rock	Emerals	1958, 1967	Triple X 100/101/Times Square 111
Soda Shop	Blenders (Aladdin)	1959	Aladdin 3449
Soft	Embers, Pete Bennett & the	1961	Sunset 1002
Soft And Pretty	Counts, Cosmo & the	1963	Sound Stage 7 2520
Soft And Sweet	Continentals (Brooklyn)	1956	Whirlin' Disc 105/Port 70024 (59)
Soft And Sweet	Selections	1958	Antone 101/Mona Lee 129
Soft Is The Breeze	Dardenelles	NA	Playgirl 501
Soft Lips	Dynamics, Johnny Christmas & the	1959	P.D.Q. 5002
Soft Pillow	Blue Notes, Joe Weaver & his	1953	DeLuxe 6006
Soft Shadows	Monotones	1959	Argo 5321
Soft Shadows	Orchids	1961	Wall 549
Soft Silk	Hurricanes	19??	
Soft Summer Breeze	Diamonds	1956	Mercury 70934
Soft Summer Breeze	Romaines, Romaine Brown & His	1956	Decca 30054
Soft, Sweet And Really Fine	Five Dukes Of Rhythm	1954	Rendezvous 812/Fortune 812 (54)
Soft Touch	Davis, George & group	1962	Philips 40082
Soft Wind	Diplomats, Dino & the	1961	Vida 0102/0103
Softie	Quintones (Chicago)	1962	Phillips International 3586
Softly	Smoothies	1960	Decca 31105

SONG	GROUP	YEAR	LABEL
Softly And Tenderly	Prisonaires	1953	Sun 189
Softly In The Night	Cookies	1963	Dimension 1008
Soldier Baby (Of Mine)	Carmen, Jerry & group	1962	Cameo 355
Soldier Boy	Echoes	NA	4 Hits EP 11
Soldier Boy	Five Echoes	1956	Vee Jay 190
Soldier Boy	Four Fellows (Brooklyn - Glory)	1955	Glory 234
Soldier Boy	Marie, Elena & group	1962	Gee Bee 01
Soldier Boy	Shirelles	1962, 1965	Scepter 1228/12123
Soldier Boy	Taylor, Bert & group	1955	Essex 396
Soldier Boy	Williams, Mel & group	1955	Federal 12236
Soldier Boy, I'm Sorry	Montells	1963	Golden Crest 582
Soldier Boy (live)	Four Fellows (Brooklyn - same group as on Glory)	1980 (1956)	U.G.H.A. 15
Soldier In Korea	Five Vultures	1973	Roadhouse 1006
Soldier Of Fortune	Drifters (Pre-1959)	1956	Atlantic 1101
Soldier Of Fortune	Safaris	1961	Eldo 113
Solid Rock	Royaltones, El Pauling & the	1960	Federal 12383
Solid Sender	Satintones	1960	Tamla 54024
Solitaire	Embers	1961	Empress 101
Solitaire	Five Fashions	1965	Catamount 103
Solitaire	Harborside	1991	Clifton 93
Solitude	Carousels	1960	G&C 201
Solitude	Dominoes	1958	Liberty 55126
Solitude	Ravens	1959	Top Rank 2003
Solitude	Riff-Tones, Riff Ruffin & the	1957	Ball 0501
Solitude	Satisfiers	1957	Coral 61788
Solitude	Three Chuckles	1956	Vik LP 1067
Some Day	Dapps, Johnnie Mae Matthews & the	1960	Northern 3729
Some Day	Spellbounds, Johnny Adams & the	1963	Watch 6333
Some Enchanted Evening	Castells	1963, 1968	Era 3107/United Artists 50324
Some Happy Day	Bohemians	1962	Chex 1007
Some Kind Of Blue	Cleftones	1961	Gee 1080
Some Kind Of Nut	Juniors, Danny & the	1961, 1962	Swan 4084/4092
Some Kind Of Wonderful	Drifters (1959-forward)	1961	Atlantic 2096
Some Of These Days	Classmates	1962	Radar 3962
Some Of These Days	Oro, Emmy & group	1962	Chelsea 1005
Some Of These Nights	Top Hands, Joe Dee & His	1962	Pat Riccio 1107
Some Of Your Lovin'	Honey Bees	1965	Fontana 1505
Some Other Fellow	Casual Three	1956	Luniverse 109
Some Other Guy	Ervin, Frankie (with the Shields)	1960	Hart 1691-52
Some Other Spring	Powell Quintet	1951	Decca 48206
Some People Sleep	Tokens (Brooklyn)	1968, 1970	Warner Bros. 7255/Buddah 159
Some People Think	Capris (New York)	1961	Old Town 1099
Some Saturday	Students (Philadelphia)	1992	Clifton 103
Some Tears Fall Dry	Chantels	1963	Ludix 106
Somebody	Duponts	1957	Royal Roost 627
Somebody Bad Stole De Wedding Bell	Bobbettes	1963	Diamond 142
Somebody Changed The Lock	Empires, Lightning Junior & the	1955	Harlem 2334
Somebody Else	Day Brothers	1960	Chancellor 1059
Somebody Else Is Taking My Place	Jumpin' Jacks, Danny Peppermint & the	1961	Carlton 565
Somebody Else Took Her Home	Travellers, Frankie Valley & the (featuring Frankie Valli)	1954	Mercury 70381
Somebody Else's Fool	Five Bars	1957	Money 224
Somebody Else's Sweetheart	Wanderers	1961	Cub 9099
Somebody Goofed	Dubs	1973	Johnson 098 (recorded in 1957)
Somebody Help Me	Casuals	1957	Nu-Sound 801/Dot 15557 (57)
Somebody Help Me	Delighters, Donald & the	1963	Cortland 112
Somebody Mentioned Your Name	Juniors, Jimmy Castor & the	1957	Atomic 100
Somebody New Dancin' With You	Drifters (1959-forward)	1961	Atlantic 2127
Somebody Nobody Wants	DiMucci, Dion (with the Del Satins)	1961	Laurie 3101
Somebody Really Loves You	Victones	1959	Front Page 2302
Somebody Really Mine	James, Jesse (with the Royal Aces)	1961	Musicor 1008
Somebody Said (I'd Cry Someday)	Monarchs, Porgy & the	1963	Mala 462
Somebody Show Me	Emerson, Billy The Kid & female group	1957	Vee Jay 247
Somebody Somewhere	Allison, Gene & group	1956	Calvert 106/Decca 30185 (56)

SONG	GROUP	YEAR	LABEL
Somebody, Somewhere	Chapters, Helen Foster & the	1953	Republic 7037
Somebody Tell Me	Arabians	1961	Carrie 1516
Somebody To Love	Darin, Bobby & group	1960	Atco 6179
Somebody To Love	Sandmen	1955	Okeh 7052
Somebody Work On My Baby's Mind (The Seven Sisters)	Du Droppers	1953	RCA 5425
Somebody's Been Plowing My Mule	Romeos	1989	Relic LP 5078
Somebody's Got My Baby	Go Boys	NA	Robbins
Somebody's In Love	Cosmic Rays	1960	Saturn 222
Somebody's Lyin	Blenders (New York)	1956	RCA
Somebody's Lyin'	Millionaires	1955	Davis 441
Someday	Casuals	1963	Moonbeam 71613
Someday	Linnettes	1960	Palette 5112
Someday	Pyramids (California)	1955	Hollywood 1047/C Note 1206 (56)
Someday	Ravens	1949	National 9085
Someday	Rubies	1955	Verne 103
Someday	Temptations (Goldisc)	1960	Goldisc 3001
Someday	Veltones	1959	Satellite 100/Mercury 71526 (59)
Someday	Zodiacs, Maurice Williams & the	1961	Herald 563
Someday (I Know, I Know)	Taylor, Ted & group	1960	Top Rank 3001
Someday I'll Be The One	Maroons	1962	Queen 24012
Someday (I'll Fall In Love)	Ebb Tides, Nino & the	1961	Marco 105
Someday My Love Will Come My Way	Chanteclairs	1954	Dot 1227
Someday She'll Come Along	Downbeats	1959	Peacock 1689
Someday She'll Come My Way	Velvets	NA	
Someday She'll Love Me	Initials, Angelo & the	1964	Congress 229
Someday, Someday	Four Seasons, Gigi Parker & the	1962	Coral 62314
Someday Someway	Flamingos	1953	Chance 1133
Someday Someway	Initials, Angelo & the	1973	Vintage 1006
Someday Somewhere	Dukes (California)	1956	Imperial 5385 (unreleased)
Someday Sweetheart	Five Keys	1954	Aladdin 3228
Someday We'll Meet Again	Royals (Muskateers)	1954	Venus 103
Someday We'll Meet Again	Scooters	1957	Dawn 224
Someday (When I'm Gone)	Santos, Larry (with the Four Seasons)	1964	Atlantic 2250
Someday You Will Pay	Miller Sisters	1956	Flip 504
Someday You'll Be My Girl	Beginners	1964	Dot 16629
Someday You'll Be My Girl	London, Ralph & group	1964	Coed 588
Someday You'll Pay	Lovers, Little Louie & the	1962	Viscount 102
Someday You'll Want Me	Original Charmers	1972	Blue Sky 102
Someday You'll Want Me To Want You	Diablos	NA	Fortune LP 8010
Someday You'll Want Me To Want You	Drifters (Pre-1959)	1954	Atlantic 1043
Someday You'll Want Me To Want You	Jeeters, Ron Willis & the	1960	Ace 588
Somehow	Ballads (Connecticut)	1960	Ron-Cris 1003
Somehow I Can't Forget	Juniors, Danny & the	1959	ABC 10004
Someone	Contrails	1965	Reuben 711/Diamond 213 (66)
Someone	Dynamics	1958	Impala 501/Seeco 6008 (59)
Someone	Echoes	1957	Specialty 601
Someone	Honey-Do's	1961	Sue 746
Someone	Lovers	1966	Gate 501/Philips 40353 (66)
Someone	Metros	NA	Ra-Sel
Someone	Whirlwinds, Joe Welden & the	1959	Khoury's 714
Someone For Everybody	Avons	1960	Hull LP 1000
Someone For Everyone	Moonglows	1977	Monogram 128
Someone For Me	Little Beats	1957	Mercury 71155
Someone For Me	Thrillers, Little Joe & the	NA	Peanuts 85211
Someone For Me	Upstarts, Don Dell & the	1962	East Coast 105/106
Someone Greater Than I	Dominoes	1957	Liberty 55111
Someone In Love	Kids From Cleveland	1957	Whippet 204
Someone In Love	Signatures	1957	Whippet 210/Gen Norman 210X (57)
Someone Like Joe	Mellomen, Kitty White & the	1955	Century 711
Someone Like You	Casuals, Gary & the	1962	Vandan 609
Someone Like You	Fascinations	1963	ABC 10387
Someone Like You	Montereys (Nestor)	1956	Nestor 15/Teenage 1001 (56)
Someone Like You	Royals	1953	Federal 12160
Someone Like You	Tricks	1959	Jane 108

SONG	GROUP	YEAR	LABEL
Someone Loves You, Joe	Singing Belles	1960	Madison 126
Someone Made You For Me	Five Royales	1955	King 4830
Someone New	Keens, Rick & the	1964	Le Cam 113/Tollie 9016 (64)
Someone Should Have Told Me	Miflin Triplets	1958	Ember 1045
Someone, Somewhere (Help Me)	Nutmegs	1960	Tel 1014
Someone Special	Four Jewels	1963	Start 638 (same # used twice)
Someone Stole My			
Baby While Doing The Twist	Hart, Rocky (with the Passions)	1961	Glo 216
Someone To Call Me Darling	Dells	1979, 1984, 1985	Solid Smoke LP 8029
Someone To Call My Own	Ecuadors	1961	Miracle 7
Someone To Care	Blends	1960	Casa Grande 5037
Someone To Care	Fabulous Blends	1960	Casa Grande 3037
Someone To Care	Sundowners	1960	Fargo 1051
Someone To Love	Dedications	1964	Ramarca 602
Someone To Love	Innocents, Kathy Young & the	1961	Indigo 115
Someone To Love	Ravens, Billy & the	NA	Sahara 108
Someone To Love	Sharps, T. Phillips & the	1960	Firefly 332
Someone To Love	Vidaltones	1961	Josie 900
Someone To Love Me	Emeralds, Luther Bond & the	1960	Showboat 1505
Someone To Show Me The Way	Four Sounds	1961	Federal 12421
Someone To Watch Over Me	Escorts, Del & the	1961	Rome 103
Someone To Watch Over Me	Flamingos	1975	Ronze 115
Someone To Watch Over Me	Martino, Lou & group	1964	Columbia 43126
Someone To Watch Over Me	Precisions	1962	Golden Crest 571
Someone To Watch Over Me	Roommates (Roomates)	NA	Canadian American (unreleased)
Someone Touched Me	Mercurys	1959	Madison 119
Someone Up There	Chryslers, Little Nate & the	1959	Johnson 318
Someone Up There	Shells, Little Nate & the	1977	Clifton 21
Someone You Can Trust	Sultans	1963	Guyden 2079
Someone's Gonna Cry	Five Cats	1955	RCA 6181
Someone's In The Kitchen With Dinah	Charades	1964	Skylark 502
Somethin' Baby	Dazzlers	1958	Lee 100
Somethin' Else	Trophies	NA	Nork 79907
Something	Battery Park	1973	Vintage 1001
Something About My Baby	Johnson, Arthur & group	1959	Wanger 190
Something About You Boy	Dovells	1970	Event 3310
Something About You Darling	Dolphins, Doc & the	NA	Dino 2
Something Awful	Five Blue Notes	1964	Onda 888
Something Blue	Fabulous Enchanters	1961	Finer Arts 1007
Something Cool	Academics	1958	Elmont 1001/1002
Something Else	Carousels	1964	Guyden 2102
Something Happened	Sparks	1958	Arwin 114
Something Happens	Friends, Dante & his	1961	Imperial 5798
Something Happens To Me	Belvin, Jesse & group	1960	RCA 7675
Something Has Changed Him	Escorts (Brooklyn)	1963	Coral 62372
Something I Want To Tell You	Expressions, Johnny & the	1965	Josie 946
Something Is Wrong	Daylighters	1959	Domino 904
Something Made Me Stop	Swinging Hearts	1960	Lucky Four 1011/Diamond 162 (64)
Something Old Something New	Russ, Lonnie & group	1962	4-J 501
Something On Your Mind	Rey, Tony & group	1959	KingBee 101
Something Special	Gay Notes	1959	Vim 501
Something Tells Me	Drifters (1959-forward)	1972	Bell 1269
Something Tells Me I'm In Love	Carmelettes	1960	Alpine 61
Something To Remember You By	Gentlemen	1954	Apollo 464
Something To Remember You By	Teardrops, Honey & the	1959	Val 202
Something Wild	Corvairs	1961	Crown 004
Something Wrong	Rhythm Tones	1959	Vest 828
Something You've Got Baby	Royal Robins	1964	ABC 10542
Something's Got A Hold On Me	Wagner, Cliff & group	1964	Jolum 2509
Sometime Lately	Darts	1978	Magnet-United Artists LP 850G
Sometime, Somewhere	Lincolns	1961	Bud 113
Sometimes	Bachelors (MGM)	1958	MGM 12668
Sometimes	Bowery Boys	1985	N/A
Sometimes	Dovells	1972	Verve 10701
Sometimes	Four Townsmen	1963	Artflow 145

SONG	GROUP	YEAR	LABEL
Sometimes	Juniors, Danny & the	1968	Lub 252
Sometimes I Feel	Apollos	1961	Galaxy 707
Sometimes I Get Lonely	Cotillions	1963	ABC 10413
Sometimes I Wonder	Ascots	1965	Mir-A-Don 1001
Sometimes I Wonder	Drifters (1959-forward)	1962	Atlantic 2151
Sometimes I Wonder	Heartbeats	1958	Roulette 4091
Sometimes I'm Happy	Jo-Vals	1964	Laurie 3229
Sometimes I'm Happy	Melodeers, Tony Thomas & the	1955	Capri 777
Sometimes Little Girl	Vells, Little Butchie & the	1959	Angletone 535
Sometimes (When I'm All Alone)	Da-Prees	1963	Twist 70913
Sometimes When I'm All Alone	Juniors, Danny & the	1957	Singular 711 (57)/ABC 9871 (57)
Someway Somehow	Bailey, Herb & group	1964	Movin' 126
Somewhere	Escorts, Goldie & the	1962	Coral 62336
Somewhere	Jaynes, Lonnie Jay & the	1963	Arlen 724
Somewhere	Knight, Bob	1962	Josie 899
Somewhere	Sparks Of Rhythm	1989	Relic LP 5080
Somewhere	Teenagers (Frankie Lymon)	1964	Columbia 43094
Somewhere	Things To Come	1993	Clifton 107
Somewhere	Tymes	1963	Parkway 891
Somewhere	Uniques	1957	Peacock 1677
(Somewhere) A Voice Is Calling	Five Satins	1961, 1974	Candlelite 411
Somewhere Down The Line	Scott, Jimmy & group	1958	King 5104
Somewhere In Life	Mar-Vels	1961	Tammy 1016
Somewhere In Love (You'll Find Your Love)	Marvels (Bishop)	1960	Bishop 1002
Somewhere In My Heart	Ebonaires	1959	Lena 1001
Somewhere In This World	Gaylarks	1957	Music City 812
Somewhere Over The Rainbow	Delchords, David Campanella & the	1959, 1962	Kane 25593
Somewhere Over The Rainbow	Dell Vikings	1957	Luniverse 106
Somewhere Over The Rainbow	Moroccos	1955	United 193/B&F 193 (60)
Somewhere, Somebody Cares	Quails, Bill Robinson & the	1954	DeLuxe 6057
Somewhere Somehow	Calvert, Duane & group	1964	D.M.D. 102
Somewhere, Somehow, Sweetheart	Knickerbockers	1953	It's A Natural 3000
Somewhere, Sometime, Someday	Cavaliers	1955	Decca 29556
Somewhere, Sometime, Someday	Honeytones	1955	Mercury 70557
Somewhere, Somewhere	Foretells	1966	Catamount 113
Somewhere There Is Someone	Tempo-Tones	1957	Acme 718
Somewhere There's A Girl	Tokens (Brooklyn)	1963	
Somewhere There's A Rainbow	Pharaohs	1960	Flip 352
Son Of Raunchy	Hi-Fives	1964	Bell 634
Song For The Lonely	Platters	1962	Mercury 71904
Song In My Heart	Dubs	1958	Gone 5034/Mark-X 8008 (60)
Song Is Ended, The	Jones Boys	1954	S&G 5007
Song Of A Lover, The	Vals	1962	Unique Laboratories (no #)
Song Of India	Twigs, Sonny Woods & the	1954	Hollywood 1015
Song Of Love	Mellomoods	1954	Recorded In Hollywood 399
Song Of Love	Velveteers	1961	Caprice 101
Song Of Old	Sheiks	1959	Jamie 1147
Song Of Songs	Barons (Whitehall)	1959	Whitehall 30008
Song Of The Dreamer	Roomates	NA	Relic LP 5041
Song Of The Nairobi Trio	Fortune Tellers	1961	Music Makers 105
Songs We Used To Sing, The	Drifters (1959-forward)	1973	Bell 45,387
Son-In-Law	Co-Eds	1961	Challenge 9109
Sonny Boy	Berets	1973	Night Train 904
Sonotone Bounce	Sonotones	1954	Bruce 105
Sonya's Place	Belairs, Lee Bantell & the	NA	Coral 61735
Soom	Clusters	NA	Unreleased
Soon I Will Be Done	Pipes	1962	Carlton 575
Soon You'll Be Leaving Me	Roulettes	1964	United Artists 718
Sooner Or Later	Four-Evers	1961	Josie 901
Sooner Or Later	Team Mates	1959	Le Cam 701
Sophia	Charades	1962	Northridge 1002
Sorcerer's Apprentice	Dell Vikings	1963	ABC 10425
Sore Feet	Montclairs	1965	Sunburst 115
Sorrento	Dials	1960	Hilltop 2009

SONG	GROUP	YEAR	LABEL
Sorrow Valley	Mellotones, Doug Williams & the	1959	Hy-Tone 122
Sorrowful Heart	Flames, Patti Anne Mesner & the	1953	Aladdin 3198/7-11 2109 (unreleased)
Sorry	Chessmen	1964	G-Clef 707
Sorry	Clefs	1973	Baron 104
Sorry	Escorts (New Jersey)	1956	Premium 407
Sorry	Evans, Donna & group	1962	Cheer 1003
Sorry	Huskies, Kenny Kole & the	1958	Klik 8205
Sorry	Tams	1960	Swan 4055
Sorry But I'm Gonna Have To Pass	Coasters	1958	Atco 6126
Sorry Daddy	Sweethearts	1961	Ray Star 778
(Sorry I Just Had To) Li'l Darlin'	Eloise Trio	NA	Carib 1032
Sorry I Lied	Reasons, Ria & the	1964	Amy 888
Sorry (I Ran All The Way Home)	Impalas (Brooklyn)	1959	Cub 9022
Sorry Sorry	Teenage Moonlighters	1960	Mark 134
Sorry, Sorry (I Ran All The Way Home)	Tags, Johnny Newton & the	1959	Bell 114
Soul	Valtairs	1964	Selsom 101
Soul Ain't You Thrilled	Orientals	NA	New Dawn 413
Soul Dinner	Jets (Arrow)	1963	Arrow 100
Soul Fool	Down Beats	1965	Down Beat
Soul Jerk	Larks (North Carolina)	1964	Money 110
Soul Of A Soldier	Chantels	1966	Verve 10387
Soul Pad	Coasters	1967	Date 1552
Soul Sloopy	Dynamics	NA	Top Ten 100
Soul St.	Fabulous Fidels	1962	Jaa Dee 106
Sound And The Fury, The	Platters	1959	Mercury 71427
Sound Of Heartbreak (acappella)	Count Five	1975	Relic LP 105
Sound Of Love	Embers	1953	Ember 101/Herald 410 (53)
Sound Of Music Makes Me Want To Dance, The	Emblems, Patty & the	1964	Herald 593
Sound Of Summer, The	Fabulous Four	1961	Chancellor 1078
Sound Of The Sun	Ran-Dells	1963	Chairman 4407
Sound Of The Wind	Dunhills	1961	Royal 110
Sound Of Your Voice, The	Ebbtides, David Ford & the	1956	Specialty 588
Sound Of Your Voice, The	Penguins	1956	Unreleased
Sound, The	Originals, Rachael & the	1962	Night Star 010
Sound, The	Unitones	1959	Candy 005
Soup	Impacts	1959	Watts 5599
Soup Line	Chordones, Leon Tarver & The	1954	Checker (unreleased)
Soupin' Up Your Motor	Laurie, Linda & group	1960	Rust 5022
South Of The Border	Solitaires	1954	Old Town 1006/1007
South Pacific Twist	Rocky Fellers	1962	Parkway 836
South Sea Island	Quintones (Chicago)	1957	Park 57-111/57-112
Southern California	Shamans	1959	Kayham 3/4
Southern Love	Hawks, Ronnie Hawkins & the	1959	Roulette 4209
Southern Train	DiMucci, Dion (with the Del Satins)	1969	Columbia 44719
Souvenirs	Drifters (1959-forward)	1960	Atlantic LP 8041
Souvenirs Of Summertime	Rays	1958	XYZ 2001
Space Girl	Earthboys	1958	Capitol 4067
Space Hop	Astra-Lites	1962	Tribute 101
Space Men	Velvetones	1959	D 1072
Space Ship	Missiles	1960	Novel 200
Space Walk	Bel-Aires (Arc)	1959	Arc 4451
Spang-A-Lang	Alley Cats	1956	Whippet 202
Spanish Boy	Rubies	1964	Vee Jay 596
Spanish Harlem	Dominions	NA	Graves 1091
Spanish Harlem	Revelations	NA	N/A
Spanish Lace	Di Sentri, Turner	1961	Topix 6001
Spanish Lace	Drifters (1959-forward)	1964	Atlantic 2260
Spanish Love	Swinging Hearts	1961	620 1002/NRM 1002 (61)
Spanish Love Song	Magic Tones	1957	Howfum 101
Spanish Moon	Travelers	1963	Princess 52/Vault 911
Spanish Nights	Five Counts	1962	Brent 7034
Spare Time	Ginger (with the Safaris)	1961	Titan 1717
Spark Plug	Four Teens	1958	Challenge 59021
Sparkle And Shine	Four Couquettes	1961	Capitol 4534

SONG	GROUP	YEAR	LABEL
Sparkle And Shine	Innocents, Kathy Young & the	NA	Indigo EP 1001
SPCLG (Society For The Prevention Of Cruelty To Little Girls)	Society Girls	1963	Vee Jay 524
Speak For Yourself	Tune Drops	1957	Gone 5003
Speak Low	Elegants	1960	United Artists 230
Speak Now	Four Bars	1964	Flying Hawk 1501
Speak Softly And Carry A Big Horn	Quotations	1963	Liberty 55527
Speak To Me Of Love	Cosytones	1956	Melba
Speak To Me Of Love	Del Capris	1963	Almont 304
Speak With Your Eyes	Five Crowns (with Jan Andre)	1955	Emerald 2007
Speak Words Of Love	Fiats	1964	Universal 5003
Speaking Of Love	Coanjos	1961	Dapt 208
Speaking Of You	Premiers (Odex)	NA	Odex 1711
Special Day, The	Hi-Tones	1960	Candix 307
Special Delivery	Markeys	1958	Gone 5028
Special Delivery	Shondelles	1962	King 5705
Special Love	Lee, Curtis (with the Halos)	1960	Dunes 2001
Special Occasions	Heartbreakers (MGM)	1963	MGM 13129
Speechless	Catalinas	1958	Back Beat 513
Speed King	Du Droppers	1954	Groove 0001
Speed Limit	Twisters	1959	Felco 103
Speedilac	Versatiles, Sonny Day & the	1958	Checker 886
Speedin'	Medallions	1955	Dootone 364
Speedo Is Back	Cadillacs	1958	Josie 836
Speedoo	Cadillacs	1955, 1964	Josie 785/Lana 118
Speedoo	Commodores	1956	Dot 15439
Speedoo (acappella)	Uniques	1975	Relic LP 105
Speedoo's Back In Town	Coasters	1964	Atco 6287
Speedy	Bobbettes	1957	Atlantic 1159
Speedy	Casinos	1959	Maske 803
Spellbound	Dappers (Star-X)	1958	Star-X 505
Spellbound By The Moon	Enchanters (Spellbound)	1956	Stardust 102
Spider And The Fly	Tellers, Artie Banks & the	1961	Imperial 5788
Spider, The	Marveliers	NA	Joanie 4439
Spiders, The	Demires	1959	Lunar 519
Spin The Wheel	Scholars	1956	Dot 15498
Spinnin'	Earls	1954	Gem 221/Crystal 100
Spinning	Hollywood Saxons, Stan Beverly & the	1958	Entra 711
Spinning	Senders	1958	Entra 711/Kent
Spinning, Spinning, Spinning	Macs, Terry & the	1956	ABC 9721
Spiral	Elegants	1961	United Artists 295
Spiral (acappella)	Semesters	1975	Relic LP 104
Spitfire	Spitfires, Tony Carmen & the	1959	Abel 224
Splashing	Shades	1959	Scottie 1309
Split	Tokens (Brooklyn)	1966	B.T. Puppy 524
Split A Kiss	Interludes	1959	Star-Hi 103
Split Personality	Resonics	1963	Unity 101
Spongie	Midnighters, Hank Ballard & the	1961	King 5449
Spooksville	Nutrends	1963	Lawn 216
Spooky Spider	Buddies	1961	Swan 4073
Spoonful	DiMucci, Dion (with the Del Satins)	1965	Columbia 43293
Spoonful	Superbs	1965	Dore 753
Sposin'	Ebonaires	1988	Relic LP 5076
Spring	Royal Jokers	1957	Hi-Q 5004
Spring Fever	Velvets (Texas)	1961	Monument 441/Monument 515
Springer, The	Dells	1957	Vee Jay 274
Springtime	Envoys	1977	Crystal Ball 110
Spunky Onions	Legends, Billy Davis & the	1960	Peacock 1694
Sputnik Dance	Ecuadors	1958	RCA EP 4286
Sputnik (Satellite Girl)	Four Ekkos, Jerry Engler & the	1957	Brunswick 55037
Sputnik 3	Garnets, Buel Moore & the	1957	Vita 174
Sputnik II	Tri-Tones, Al Barkle & the	1957	Vita 173
Spy, The	Destinaires	1965	Old Timer 614
Squat And Squirm	Blenders (Chicago)	1963	Witch 117
Squat With Me Baby	Candles, Rochell & the	1961	Swingin' 640

SONG	GROUP	YEAR	LABEL
Squeeze	Three D's	NA	Square 502
Squeeze Me	Aristocrats	1962	Home Of The Blues 237
Squeeze Me	Gales	1960	Winn 916
Squeeze Me, Baby	Crystals (New York)	1954	Luna 100/101/Luna 5001 (54)
Squidgy Bod	Wombats, Gary & the	1963	Regina 291
St. Lou	Night Riders	1959	Sue 719
St. Louis Blues	Dominoes	1956, 1957	Decca EP 2549/Decca LP 7885 (57)/ Decca LP 8621 (57)
St. Therese Of The Roses	Dominoes	1956	Decca 29933
Stagger	Madisons	1965	Jomada 601/Jumaca 601
Stairsteps To Heaven	Cashmeres (Brooklyn)	1959	ACA 1216/1217
Stairsteps To Heaven	Lyrics, Ike Perry & the	1958	Bridge 110
Stairway To Love	Poka-Dotts	1954	Modern 945
Stamps Baby Stamps	Ebb Tides, Nino & the	1962	Mr. Peacock 117
Stand Behind Me	Dreamtones	1958, 1975, 1996	Klik 8505/Sold 501 (75)
Stand By Me	BQE	1988	Starlight 60
Stand By Me	Decades	1980	Avenue D 2
Stand By Me	Paramounts	1982	Avenue D 7
Stand By Me	Price, Del & group	1975	Kelway 113
Stand By Me	Yesterday's News	1981	Clifton 60
Stand By Me (acappella)	Five Sharks	1964	Old Timer 605
Stand In Line	Spaniels	1970	North American 002
Stand There Mountain	Castells	1962	Era 3083
Stand There Mountain	Planets	1957	Era 1038
Stand There, Mountain	Williams, Mel & group	1957	Dig 140
Standin' Right There	Feathers	1955	Aladdin 3277
Standing Alone	Nobles (Timbers)	1958	ABC 9984
Standing Alone	Temptations (New Jersey)	1958	King 5118
Standing At The Altar	Deltairs	1958	Ivy 105
Standing On Guard	Falcons (Big Wheel)	1966	Big Wheel 1967
Standing On The Highway	Barons, Walter Miller & the	1956	Meteor 5037
Standing On The Mountain	Pastel Keys, Ronnie Gill & the	1958	Rip 108/Rio 129/Expiditus 500
Stanwyck Theme	Jays	1961	Barry 103
Star	Lovetones, Raymond Pope & the	1962	Squalor 1313
Star Above	Consorts	1977	Crystal Ball 111
Star Bright	Trentons	1962	Shepherd 2204
Star Crossed Lovers	Mystics	1961	Laurie 3086
Star Of Love	Ebbtides	1964	Duane 1022
Star Of Love	Lovenotes	1954	Unreleased
Star Of Love	Moonbeams, Jeanne Sterling & the (with Johnny Otis)	1957	Capitol 3802
Star Of Paradise	Itels	1961	Magnifico 101
Star Of Wonder	Baker, Charlie & group	1959	Liberty 55226
Starbright	Four Cal-Quettes	1961	Capitol 4574
Stardust	Dominoes	1957	Liberty 55071
Stardust	Four Blades	1956	Gateway 1174
Stardust	Jive Bombers	1959	Savoy 1560
Stardust	Myers, James Quintet	198?	
Stardust	Persuasions	1970	Catamount 1957
Stardust	Skyliners	1961	Unreleased
Stardust In Her Eyes	Big Five	1960	Shad 5019
Starlight	Angel, Johnny & group	1958	Power 250
Starlight	Fortunes	1955	Checker (unreleased)
Starlight	Moonglows	1955	Chess 1605
Starlight	Preludes Five	1961	Pik 231
Starlight	Stringbeans	1964	Gina 7001
Starlight And Moonbeams	Headliners, George Goodman & the	1965	Val 6
Starlight And You	Nite Riders	1958	Teen 116
Starlight Starbright	Chapman, Grady (with the Suedes)	1958	Knight 2003
Starlight, Starbright	Emeralds, Luther Bond & the	1954	Savoy 1131
Starlight Tonight	Inspirators	1958	Old Town 1053/Old Town LP
Starlit Night	Emotions	1963	Laurie 3167
Starry Eyes	Four Trumpets, Susie & the	1962	United Artists 471
Starry Eyes	Rainsford, Billy & group	NA	Hermitage 803
Starry Eyes	Velvetones	1963	Ascot 2126

SONG	GROUP	YEAR	LABEL
Stars	Eccentrics	1964	Applause 1008
Stars	Randell, Rick & group	1962	United Artists 448
Stars Are In The Sky	Sparks Of Rhythm	1955	Apollo 481
Stars Are Out Tonight, The	Teardrops	1954	Josie 766/Port 70019 (60)
Stars Fell (acappella)	Chessmen	1965	Relic 1017
Stars In My Eyes	Sharptones, Billy Sharp & the	1958	Kudo 668
Stars In The Blue What Should I Do	Dee Cals	1959	Co-Ed 1960/Mayhams 1960 (61)
Stars In The Skies	Chanters (New York)	1958	DeLuxe 6166
Stars In The Sky	Capris (New York)	NA	Collectables LP 5016
Stars In The Sky	Channels, Earl Lewis & the	1956	Whirlin' Disc 102/Port 70017 (60)
Stars In The Sky	Dreamers, Denny & the	NA	N/A
Stars In The Sky	Heartbeats	1956	Rama (unreleased)
Stars Of Wonder	Velvetones	1959	Deb 1008
Stars, The	Allures	1986	Starlight 48
Stars, The	Bop Shop	NA	Horizon Ent. Ltd.
Stars, The	Ocapellos	1965	General 107/Checker 1144 (66)
Stars Tonight, The	Catalinas	1973	Jayne 812
Stars Will Remember	Holidays	1960	Andie 5019
Stars Will Remember, The	Buccaneers	1953	Rama 21
Stars Will Remember, The	Idols	1961	Galaxie 77
Stars Will Remember, The	Pizani, Frank (with the Highlights)	1959	Afton 617
Start Lovin' Me	Ray-O-Vacs	1952	Jubilee 5098
Start The Fire	Jayhawks	1957	Eastman 792
Starting From Tonight	Midnighters, Henry Booth & the	1960	DeLuxe 6190
Starting From Tonight	Royals	1952	Federal 12077
Station Hurt	Cheerios, Bobby Long & the	1963	Cub 9120
Stay	Challengers	1962	Tri-Phi 1012
Stay	Monarchs, Porgy & the	1963	Mala 462
Stay	Rainbows	1956	Pilgrim 711/Argyle 1012 (62)
Stay	Shadows	1953	Decca 28765
Stay	Thrillers, Little Joe & the	1960	Okeh 7136
Stay	Zodiacs, Maurice Williams & the	1960, 1967	Herald 552/Dee-Su 318
Stay A Little Longer	Ecuadors	1958	RCA EP 4286
Stay As You Are	Channels, Earl Lewis & the	1957	Gone 5012
Stay At Home Sue	Del Satins, Linda Laurie with the	1962	Rust 5042
Stay Away From Joe	Olympics	1960	Arvee LP A-423
Stay Away From My Baby	Midnighters, Hank Ballard & the	1964	King 5901
Stay Awhile	Clovers	1959	United Artists 180
Stay By Me	Eager, Johnny & group	1959	End 1054
Stay By My Side	Midnighters	1958	Federal 12317
Stay Clear Of Love	Delvons	1967	J.D.F. 760
Stay Here	Royal Jokers	1955	Atco 6052
Stay In My Corner	Dells	1965	Vee Jay 674
Stay In My Heart	Rivieras	1960	Coed 542
Stay Mine	Falcons (Flip)	1954	Flip 301
Stay On My J.O.B.	Four Bars	1962	Dayco 2500
Stay Put	Sanders, Will & group	1961	Regatta 2003
Stay Where You Are	Olympics	1961	Arvee 6501/Everest
Stay With Me	Exploits, Bobby Maxwell & the	1959	Fargo 1009
Stay With Me	Marquees, Terry Brown & the	1960	Jo-Ann 128
Stay With Me	Williams, Mel & group	1957	Capitol EP 940
Stay With Me, Always	Vel-Aires, Donald Woods & the	1955	Flip 309
Stayin' Up Late	Devlin, Johnny & group	1962	Coral 62335
Steady Cha Cha	Pizani, Frank (with the Highlights)	1959	Afton 617
Steady Freddy	Sands, Jeri Lynn & group	1959	Arcade 153
Steady Girl	Essentials, Little Billy & the	1962	Landa 691/Jamie 1229 (62)
Steady Guy	Seventeens	1958	Golden Crest 503
Steady Kind, The	Persians	1963	Pageant 601
Steady Love	Nichol, Joey & group	1958	ABC 9951
Steady Man	Gallahads	1958	Vik 0316
Steady Vows	Fortunes	1959	Top Rank 2019
Steal Away	Drifters (1959-forward)	1969	Atlantic 2624
Steal Away	Sheppards (Chicago - Bunky)	1969	Bunky 7764
Steal Away (With Your Baby)	Limelites, Shep & the	1963	Hull 759
Steamboat	Drifters (Pre-1959)	1955	Atlantic 1078

SONG	GROUP	YEAR	LABEL
Steamboat	Webs	1963	Guyden 2090
Stella	Renaults	1959	Warner Bros. 5094
Stella's Got A Fella	Fireflies	1959	Ribbon 6901
Step By Step	Crests	1960	Coed 525
Step By Step	Four Hollidays	1963	Markie 109
Step By Step	Vikings, Erik & the	1965	Karate 503
Step Right Up	Monterays (Brooklyn)	1963	Astra 1018/Blast 219
Step Up	Anthony, Paul & group	NA	Metro International 1003
Step Up And Go	Triangles	1962	Fargo 1023
Steppin' Out	Flairs, Cornel Gunter & the	1956	ABC 9740
Steppin' Stones	Mystics	NA	Olympia 2131
Steppin' Stones	Vendors	1963	MGM 13133
Stepping Stone	Falcons (RCA)	1957	RCA 7076
Steps Of Love	King Krooners	NA	Unreleased
Stereo Freeze	Stereos	1967	Cadet 5577
Stereophonic	El Venos	1960	Calico (unreleased)
Steve Allen	Emperors	1964	Olimpic 245
Stewball	Coasters	1960	Atco 6168
Stewed Tomatoes	Joylets	1963	ABC 10403
Stick By Me (And I'll Stick By You)	Limelites, Shep & the	1963	Hull 757
Stick With Her	Gunga Dins	NA	Busy-B 2
Stick With Me Baby	Paragons	1957	Winley 220
Sticks And Stones	Velaires	1961	Jamie 1203
Sticky	Accents, Ron Peterson & the	1965	Jerden 728
Stiki De Boom Boom	Castells	1961	Era 3064
Still Burning In My Heart	Drifters (1959-forward)	1968	Atlantic 2471
Still I Forgive You	Johnson, Kripp & group	1959	Mercury 71486
Still In Love	Quintones, Jimmy Witherspoon & the	1956	Atco 6084
Still In Love With You	Chevrons	1962	Sara 6462
Still In Love With You	Tu-Tones	1959	Lin 5021
Still In Your Teens	Poni-Tails	1957	Marc 1001
Still Love You Baby	Tabs	1958	Nasco 6016
Still Miss You So	Delcos	1963	Sound Stage 7 2515
Still Thinking Of You	Three Chuckles	1955	X 0162
Still Waiting	Elegants	1958	Hull LP 1002
Still You Left Me Baby	Cadillacs	1962	Jubilee LP 5009
Stinger, The	Runaways	1962	Moonglow 202
Stingy Little Thing	Midnighters	1954	Federal 12202
Stolen Angel	Renegades	1961	Dorset 5007
Stolen Angel	Scott Brothers	1960	Ribbon 6905
Stolen Angel	Tonettes	1963	Volt 104
Stolen Hours	Arvettes	1966	Ideal 100
Stolen Love	Flamingos	1959	Checker LP 3005/Chess LP 1433 (59)
Stolen Love	Four Bel-Aires, Larry Lee & the	1959	M-Z 006
Stolen Love	Larks (North Carolina)	1952	Apollo 1190
Stomp, The	Citations	1964	Mercury 72286
Stomp, The	Electras	1962	Infinity 016
Stomp, The	Olympics	1961	Arvee 5044
Stompin' Everywhere	Dovells	1963	Parkway 867
Stompin' Round The Christmas Tree	Stompers	1961	Gone 5120
Stompin' Sh-Boom	Dories	1962	Dore 629
Stone Broke	Arrogants	1962	Vanessa 200
Stoned	Tides	1959	Dore 529
Stool Pigeon	Inspirations (Al-Brite)	1960	Al-Brite 1650/1651/Sparkle 102 (60)/ Gone 5097 (60)
Stool Pigeon Baby	Lewis, Billy & group	1956	Flo-Lou 101
Stop	Candies	1963	Fleetwood 7003
Stop	Tic Tocs	1957	Rush 1042
Stop! . . . You're Sending Me	Dominoes	NA	Jubilee (unreleased)
Stop By My House	Parker, Bobby & group	1960	Amanda 1001
Stop Crying	Four Fellows (Brooklyn - Tri-Boro)	1953	Tri-Boro 101
Stop Crying	Nobles (Connecticut)	1958	Tee Gee 101/Cupid 1002 (58)
Stop Driving Me Crazy	Calendars, Shell Dupont & the	1965	Tribune 1001
Stop Foolin' Around	Four Jacks, Shirley Haven & the	1952	Federal 12092
Stop It Little Girl	Octobers	1963	Chairman 4402

SONG	GROUP	YEAR	LABEL
Stop It! Quit It!	Four Bars	1954	Josie 768
Stop Jibing, Baby	Vibes	1954	After Hours 105/Chariot 105 (54)
Stop Leading Me On	Precisions	1963	Debra 1001
Stop Look And Listen	Chiffons	1966	Laurie 3357
Stop Look And Listen	Chimes (Limelight)	1957	Limelight 3002
Stop, Look And Listen	Parktowns	1960	Impala 214/Thor 3258
Stop, Look And Listen (For The Heart You Save)	Three Moods	1955	Sarg 124
Stop, Look And Love Me	Williams, Fletcher & group	1957	Bullseye 1001
Stop Me	Shirelles	1958	Decca 30761
Stop Monkeyin' Aroun'	Dovells	1963	Parkway 889
Stop On Red, Go On Green	Envoys, Bill Tally & the	1959	Canadian American 104
Stop Playing Ping Pong (With My Heart)	Six Teens	1957	Flip 329
Stop Pretending	Clovers, Buddy Bailey & the	1963	Porwin 1001
Stop Right Now	Vibrations	1961	Checker 987
Stop Shovin' Me Around	Delicates	1965	Challenge 59304
Stop That Wedding	Gold Bugs	1965	Coral 62453
Stop The Clock	Stidham, Arbee & group	1953	Chess (unreleased)
Stop The Clock	Wailers	1954	Columbia 40288
Stop The Music	Shirelles	1962	Scepter 1237
Stop The Wedding	Charmettes	1965	World Artists 1053
Stop The World	Bon-Aires	1956	King 4975
Stop Torturing Me!	Vibes	1954	After Hours 105/Chariot 105 (54)
Stop What You're Doing	Five Keys	1973	Landmark 101
Stop What You're Doing	La Roc, Dal & group	1961	Arteen 1010
Stop What You're Doing	Viscaynes	1961	Tropo 101
Stop Your Crying	Five Keys	1961	King 5496
Stop Your Crying	Stringbeans	1964	Gina 7001
Stop Your Hittin' On Me	Four Buddies	NA	Savoy 959 (unreleased)
Stop, You're Knocking Me Out	Jaye Sisters	1958	Atlantic 2000
Storehouse Of His Love	Brooklyn Allstars	1974	Jewell 236
Storm	Riffs	1978	Crystal Ball 130
Storm (So Blue), The	Vitones	1989	Relic LP 5079
Storm (So Blue) (acappella), The	Vi-Tones	1964	Times Square 105
Storm, The	Amorettes, Armond Adams & the	1964	Fortune 572
Storm Tossed Sea Of Love	Dahlias	1957	Big H 612
Storm Warning	Volcanos	NA	Arctic 106
Stormy	Corsairs	1963	Tuff 1847/Chess 1847 (63)
Stormy	Four-Evers	1965	Constellation 151
Stormy	Prophets	1956	Atco 6078
Stormy Dreams	Chessmen	1962	Amy 841
Stormy Weather	Catalinas	1963	Million 77
Stormy Weather	Chantones	1961	Capitol 4661
Stormy Weather	Connotations, Joel & the	1979	Clifton 33
Stormy Weather	Counts, Tommy Burk & the	1962	Nat 101/Smash 1821 (63)
Stormy Weather	Earls	1976	Rome 111/Power-Martin 1005 (76)
Stormy Weather	Five Bars	1957	Money 224
Stormy Weather	Five Sharps	1952, 1964, 1972	Jubilee 5104/5478/Bim Bam Boom 103
Stormy Weather	Five Shits	1970	Chance 1163
Stormy Weather	Four Casts	1964	Atlantic 2228
Stormy Weather	Four Sierras (Sierras)	1963	Mail Call 2333/2334
Stormy Weather	Leaders	1955	Glory 235
Stormy Weather	Ly-Dells	NA	Clifton LP 2002
Stormy Weather	Orchids, Dick Bardi & the	NA	Maestro 409/410
Stormy Weather	Spaniels	1958	Vee Jay 290
Stormy Weather (acappella)	Zircons	1964	Siamese 403/Old Timer 603 (64)
Stomy Weather (Short & Long Versions)	Five Sharks	1964	Times Square 35/Relic 525 (65)
Story Blues	Four Buddies	1952	Savoy 845
Story Book Of Love, The	Superbs	1964	Dore 704
Story In My Heart	Valor, Tony & group	1963	Musictone 1119
Story Of A Fool, The	Blue Belles	1953	Atlantic 987
Story Of A Love Gone Cold	Gentlemen	1955	Apollo
Story Of An Evergreen Tree	Kenjolairs	1962	A&M 704
Story Of Bonnie, The	Count Victors	1961	Rust 5034
Story Of Daddy Cool, The	Blue Sky Boys	1973	Blue Sky 107

SONG	GROUP	YEAR	LABEL
Story Of Jack And Jill, The	Crowns, Danny & the	1963	Mercury 72096
Story Of Love	Desires	1962	Seville 118
Story Of Love	Five Keys	1955	Aladdin 3312
Story Of Love	Joyettes	1956	Onyx 502
Story Of Love, The	Angel, Johnny & group	1958	Power 250
Story Of Love, The	Starlighters	1960	End
Story Of Love, The	Treasurers	1961	Crown 005
Story Of My Heart, The	Mascots	1960	King 5377
Story Of My Life	Illusions	1964	Little Debbie 105
Story Of My Love	Carlo (Carlo Mastrangelo) (with the Tremonts)	1963	Laurie 3175
Story Of Our Love	Revlons, Tino & the	1960	Mark 154
Story, The	Cinders	1964	Original Sound 43
Story, The	Ervin, Frankie & group	1959	Rendezvous 112
Story, The	Georgettes	1963	Troy 1001
Story, The	I. V. Leaguers	1957	Porter 1003/1004/Dot 15677 (58
Story To You (acappella)	Rajahs	1973	Klik 1020
Story Untold	Baker, Bill (Satins)	1998	Clifton CD 3014 (recorded in 1983)
Story Untold	Du Droppers	1955	Groove EP EGA-5
Story Untold	Nutmegs	1955	Herald 452
Story Untold '72	Nutmegs	1972	Baby Grand 800
Story-Book Love	Lile, Bobby & group	1963	Marsh 204
Straight From The Grapevine	Cameos, Londie & the	1963	ABC 10508
Straightaway	Chancellors	1962	Brent 7031
Straightaway	Ebbtides	1962	Monument 520
Stranded In The Jungle	Apostles	1966	A-Square 401
Stranded In The Jungle	Cadets	1956, 1975	Modern 994/Relic 1032
Stranded In The Jungle	Gadabouts	1956	Mercury 70898
Stranded In The Jungle	Jayhawks	1956	Flash 109
Stranded In The Jungle	Vibrations	1960	Checker 982
Stranded Love	Kingsmen	1956	Neil 102
Strange Are The Ways Of Love	Fingerpoppers, Ronny Williams & the	1960	Ultra Sonic 111
Strange As It May Seem	Gaynotes	1958	Aladdin 3424
Strange As It Seems	Four Dots, Deke Watson & the	1952	Castle 2006
Strange As It Seems	Lovers	1961	Keller 101
Strange As It Seems	Quintones (Gee)	1956	Gee 1009
Strange Dreams	Robin, Richie	1960	Gone 5083
Strange Feelings	Four Winds	1964	Swing 100
Strange Girl	Showmen	NA	Unreleased
Strange Is Love	Marquis	1959	Class 251
Strange Lady	Codas, Charles Gully & the	1963	C.J. 641
Strange Land	Del Roys	1959	Sparkell 102
Strange Land Blues	Flames	1952	Spin 101
Strange Little Girl	V.I.P.s	1961	Congress 211
Strange Love	Crescendos (Scarlet)	1960	Scarlet 4007
Strange Love	Crests	1958	Coed (unreleased)
Strange Love	Delicates	1961	Roulette 4387
Strange Love	Native Boys	1956	Combo 113
Strange Love Affair	Dootones	1962	Dooto 470
Strange Oh Strange	Horizons	1964	Regina 1321
Strange Strange Feeling	Chiffons	1965, 1968, 1970	Laurie 3275//B.T. Puppy 558/ Buddah 171
Strange World	Majestics (Detroit)	1963	Linda 111
Strange World	Rhythm Heirs	1959	Yucca 105
Stranger	Renegades, Patty McCoy & the	1962	Counsel 116
Stranger	Tides	1961	Warwick 653
Stranger In My Arms	Carlo (Carlo Mastrangelo) (with the Tremonts)	1964	Laurie 3227
Stranger In My Arms	Cookies	1962	Dimension 1002
Stranger In Paradise	Galens	1964	Challenge 59253
Stranger On The Shore	Drifters (1959-forward)	1962	Atlantic 2143
Stranger, The	Four Lovers	1957	RCA 6812
Stranger, The	Marathons	1959	Sabrina 334/JC 101 (59)
Strangers	Platters	1963	Mercury 72129
Strangers Away	Valtairs	1964	Selsom 101

SONG	GROUP	YEAR	LABEL
Strawberry Man	Temptashuns	1964	Federal 12530
Strawberry Peak	Jewels (Monogram)	1976	Monogram 117
Strawberry Stomp	Birdies, Robert Byrd & His	1956	Spark 501/Jamie 1039 (57)
Street Corner	Wizards	1982	
Street Corner Serenade	Memory	1981	Avenue D 5
Street Corner Symphony (acappella)	Belmonts	1972	Buddah LP 5123
Street Dance	Twisters	1961	Campus 125
Street Lights	Nunn, Bobby	1953	Federal 12122
	(with the Robins & Little Esther)		
Street Of Loneliness	Hi-Fidelities	1957	Hi-Q 5000
Street Of Love	Pets, Jerry Warren & the	1959	Arwin 118
Street Of Memories	Tyrones	1957	Mercury 71104
Street Of Sorrow	Blue Dots	1954	DeLuxe 6055
Street Of Sorrow	Canadian Meteors, Buddy Burke & the	1957	Bullseye 1002
Street Scene	Elgins (California)	1965	Valiant 712
Street Scene	RPMs	1963	Port 70032
Street, The	Tunisians, Terry & the	1963	Seville 131
Streetlite Serenade	Echelons	1992	Clifton 97
Streets Of Love	Videls	1960	Kapp 361
Stretch, The	Contours	1961	Motown 1012
Strictly Polynesian	Dolphins, Davey Jones & the	1961	Audicon 117
Strike It Rich	Rockafellas	1963	SCA 18003/Southern Sound 112
String Along	Del Vikings	1958	Mercury LP 30353
String Around My Heart	Cleftones	1956	Gee 1025
String Band Hop	Corvettes	1958	ABC 9891
String-A-Long	Majors, Jesse Powell & the	1958	Josie 845
Stroll, The	Diamonds	1957	Mercury 71242
Stroll, The	Flares	NA	London (England) LP 8034
Strollin'	Hornets	1958	Rev 3515
Strollin' At Clifton Music	House Rockers	1973	
Strollin' Baby	Hearts, Lee Andrews & the	NA	Collectables LP 5003
Strollin' On The Beach	Hollywood Flames	1958	Ebb 144
Strollin' Time	Centurys	1960	Veltone 104
Strollin' With My Baby	Tempos	1958	Kapp 213
Strolling After Dark	Shades	1959	Scottie 1309
Strolling Through The Park	Creations	1961	Pine Crest 101
Strong Love	Iridescents	1963	Hudson 8102
Struggler, The	Drifters (1959-forward)	1973	Steeltown 671
Strut And Stroll	Yachtsmen	1961	Har-Glo 420
Strut Time	Varnells	1961	Arnold 1003
Stubborn Heart	Sheppards (Chicago - Mirwood)	1966	Mirwood 5534
Stuck On You	Carroll, Yvonne & group	1963	Domain 1018
Study Hall	Omegas	1960	Decca 31094
Stumble And Fall	Love, Darlene & group	1964, 1976	Philles 123/Warner-Spector 0410
Stupid	Mathews Brothers	1963	ABC 10473
Stupid Heart	Goode, Ray & group	1959	Vel-Tone 25
Stupidity	Van Dykes	1962	Atlantic 2161
Stuttering	Avalons	1957	Unreleased
Submarine Race, The	Visuals	1962	Poplar 115
Submarine Race Watching	Escorts, Goldie & the	1962	Coral 62336
Submarine Races	Hillsiders, Bobby Angel & the	1962	Astra 300
Such A Fool	Eagles	1954	Mercury 70464
Such A Fool	Ervin, Frankie & group	1962	Indigo 138
Such A Fool	Royal Reveros	NA	Jump Up 114
Such A Fool For You	Diplomats, Dino & the	1961	Vida 0102/0103
Such A Fool Was I	Dippers, Georgie Torrence & the	1961	Epic 9453
Such A Good Night For Dreaming	Four-Evers	1962, 1980	Columbia 42303/Jason Scott 4
Such A Long Way	Belmonts, Dion & the	1961	Laurie 3080
Such A Love	Sensations	1956	Atco 6083
Such A Lovin'	Sundowners	1960	Fargo 1051
Such A Night	Drifters (Pre-1959)	1954	Atlantic 1019
Such A Night	Four Lovers	1957	RCA LP 1317
Such A Night	Paul, Bunny (with the Harptones)	1954	Essex 352
Such A Night	Willows	1964	Heidi 107
Such Is Love	Boogie Ramblers	1957	Goldband 1030

SONG	GROUP	YEAR	LABEL
Such Lovin'	Dubs	1957	Gone 5011/Musictone 1141 (61)
Suddenly	Avalons	1987	Relic LP 5072
Suddenly	Giant, Jimmy & group	1960	Vee Jay 345
Suddenly	Keynotes	1955	Apollo 478
Suddenly	Sorrows, Nicky De Matteo & the	1960	Guyden 2024
Suddenly In Love	Six Teens	1960	Flip 351
Suddenly There Were Tears	Chappies	NA	Chelton 750
Suddenly There's A Valley	Drifters (1959-forward)	1960	Atlantic 2087
Suddenly There's A Valley	Streetcorner Serenade	1989	Starlight 70
Suddenly We're Strangers	Mates, Marci & the	1963	Big Top 3136
Suddenly You Want To Dance	Four Troys	1959	Freedom 44013
Suffer	Blue Belles, Patti LaBelle & the	1970	Atlantic 2712
Suffer So	Passionettes	1958	Unreleased
Sugah Woogah	Three Playmates	1958	Savoy 1528
Sugar	Chic-Chocs	1961	Broadway 103
Sugar	Five Satins	1957	Ember LP 100/Ember EP 101
Sugar Baby	Jacks	1956	RPM 458/Victory
Sugar Baby	Kapers, Paul London & the	1962	Check Mate 1006
Sugar Baby	Orioles, Sonny Til & the	1957	Abner 1016/Vee Jay 244 (57)
Sugar Baby	Teardrops	1958	Rendezvous 102
Sugar Baby	Treys	1959	Bella 16
Sugar Beat	Playgirls	1960	RCA 7719
Sugar Bird	Whalers, Hal Paige & the	1957	J&S 1601
Sugar Boy	Charmettes	1965	World Artists 1053
Sugar Cake	Roomates, Cathy Jean & the	1961, 1962	Valmor 009/016
Sugar Candy	Miller Sisters	1957	Onyx 507
Sugar Cane	Rubies	1964	Enith International 720
Sugar Coated Candy Kisses	Donettes, Don Eddy & the	1960	Rona 1002
Sugar Cookie	Bey Sisters	1956	Jaguar 3018/Flip 328 (57)
Sugar Daddy	Satintones	1960	Motown 1000
Sugar Diabetes	Five Dreamers, Eddie Banks & the	1956	Josie 804
Sugar Doll	Belvin, Jesse (with the Feathers)	1958	Aladdin 3431
Sugar Doll	Five Pyramids	1975	Nile 101
Sugar Doll	Sharptones, Jesse Belvin & the	1958	Aladdin 3431
Sugar G	Tru-Tones, Terry Clement & the	1959	Rocko 517
Sugar Girl	Rocco, Lenny & group	1961	Delsey 301
Sugar Hill	Todds	1961	Todd 1076
Sugar Lips	Five Chances	1956	States 156
Sugar Love	Little Beavers, Johnny Briscoe & the	1971	Atlantic 2822
Sugar Lump	Owens, Buddy & group	1964	Tec 3003
Sugar Lump	Playboys	1958	United Artists 124
Sugar Lump	Prophets	1955	Go-Lish
Sugar Mama	Orbits	1957	Argo (unreleased)
Sugar Man Song, The	Ricks, Jimmy & group	1957	Paris 504
Sugar Sugar	Avalons	1956	Groove 0174
Sugar, Sugar	Cadillacs	1957	Josie 812
Sugar Sweet	Arcados	1963	Fam 502
Sugar Ways	Tenderfoots	1955	Federal 12228
Sugaree	Five Jets	1964	Jewel 739
Sugaree	Midnighters, Hank Ballard & the	1959	King 5215
Sugaree	Sonics	1962	Jamie 1235
Suicide	Ivy Three	1961	Shell 306
Sukey, Sukey, Sukey	Spiders	1955	Imperial 5344
Sukiyaki Rocki	Lincolns	1961	Bud 113
Suki-Yaki-Rocki	Quarter Notes	1959	Whizz 715
Summer	Impacts	1964	Anderson 104
Summer	Pawns	NA	Baystate 1267
Summer Day	Tymes	1964	Parkway LP 7032
Summer Days	Sweethearts	1963	Hi-Ill 117
Summer In New York	Five Satins	1971	RCA 74-0478
Summer In The Mountains	Double Daters	1958	Dot 15780
Summer Is Here	Pals	1958	Turf 1000/1001/Guyden 2019 (59)
Summer Is Through	Harper, Chuck & group	1962	Felsted 8658
Summer Job	Serenaders (Hanover)	1958	Hanover 4507
Summer Love	Altones	1961	Archer 104

SONG	GROUP	YEAR	LABEL
Summer Love	Blue Notes	1959, 1960	Brooke 111 (first pressing)/119
Summer Love	Strollers	1960	20th Fox 226
Summer Love	Valentines	1954	Old Town 1009
Summer Love	Velons	1968	BJM 6568
Summer Love	Wonders	1961	Chesapeake 604
Summer Night	Chimes (Brooklyn)	1960	Tag 444/Music Note 1101
Summer Night	Computones	1978	U.G.H.A. 1
Summer Night Love	Gates	1959	Peach 716
Summer Nights	Safaris	1960	Eldo 105
Summer Nights (acappella)	Semesters	1975	Relic LP 104
Summer Reverie	Ping Pongs	1960	United Artists 236
Summer Romance	Melodears	1958	Gone 5033
Summer School	Casualtones	1963	Success 102
Summer School	Originals	1962	Diamond 116
Summer Souvenir	Alamos, Sammy Houston & the	1960	Cleveland 104
Summer Souvenirs	Hammel Jr., Karl & group	1961	Arliss 1007
Summer Steady	Ramadas	1963	Philips 40117
Summer Sun	Envoys, Bill Tally & the	1959	Canadian American 104
Summer Sunrise	Five Masqueraders, Seaphus Scott & the	1958	Joyce 303
Summer Thoughts	Delrons, Reperata & the	1965	World Artists 1075
Summer Vacation	Four Esquires	1956	Pilgrim 717
Summer's Comin'	Dawson, Ronnie & group	1960	Swan 4054
Summer's Coming	Twilights, Tony Richards & the	1961	Colpix 199
Summer's Coming In	Epics	1961	Bandera 2512
Summer's Gonna Be A Ball	Laurels	1982	Alexis 6873
Summer's Here	Chateaus	1963	Coral 62364
Summer's Here At Last	Prizes	1964	Parkway 917
Summer's Love	Barrett, Richard & group	1963	Crackerjack 4012
Summer's Love	Bee, Richie	1961	Gone 5060
	(Richard Barrett with the Chantels)		
Summer's Over	Healeys, Tom Austin & his	1963	Old Town 1147
Summer's Over	Wombats, Gary & the	1963	Regina 291
Summertime	Belmonts	1965	United Artists 809
Summertime	Belvin, Jesse & group	1957	Modern 1025
Summertime	Blazers, Rodney & the	1960	Kampus 100
Summertime	Careless Five	NA	Vitose 101
Summertime	Chantels	1961	Carlton 569
Summertime	Chipettes, Chip Allan & the	1963	Corsican 100
Summertime	Dell Vikings	1957	Mercury LP 20314/
			Mercury EP 3363 (57)
Summertime	Drifters	1953	Rama 22
Summertime	Duprees, Willis Sanders & the	1961	Regatta 2000
Summertime	Holidays	1966	Relic 542
Summertime	Marcels	1961	Colpix 196
Summertime	Ravens	1947	National 9035
Summertime	Regents	1961	Gee LP 706
Summertime	Slades	1959	Domino 1000
Summertime	Belmonts	1964	Sabina 521
Summertime Angel	Intentions	1963, 1980	Jamie 1253
Summertime Blues	All Nighters	1964	GMA 1
Summertime Blues	Apolloes	1964	Look 001
Summertime Blues	Aztecs, Billy Thorpe & the	1965	GNP Crescendo 346
Summertime Blues	Legends	1963	Capitol 5014
Summertime Blues	Regents	NA	Peoria 0008
Summertime Goodbyes	Quotations	1962	Verve 10261
Summertime Is Gone	Wil-Ettes	1962	Jamie 1234
Summertime Is Near	Persianettes, Timmy & the	1963	Olympia 101
Summertime Is Time For Love	Statens	1961	Mark-X 8011
Summertime Love	Donato, Mike & group	NA	PM 0101
Summertime Nights	Happytones	1963	Colpix 693
Summertime, Summertime	Jamies	1958	Epic 9281
Summertime Sweetheart	Pinard, Henry & the Three D's	NA	Lowell 212
Summertime With You	Young Lions	1959	United Artists 177
Sum'pin Else	Twilights	1962	Twilight 1028
Sun Don't Shine (Everyday), The	Saints	NA	Kent 480

SONG	GROUP	YEAR	LABEL
Sun Glasses	Shades	1958	Big Top 3003
Sun Shines Once Again, The	Sugar Tones	1951	Okeh 6814
Sun Showers	Petites	1960	Columbia 41662
Sun, The	Dell Vikings	1960	Alpine 66
Sun, The	Fourteen Karat Soul	1979	Catamount 120
Sun, The	Persuasions	1978	King Tut 171
Sun Will Rise, The	Teenettes, Betty Jayne & the	1961	Carellen 101
Sunday In May	Cavaliers	1959	Apt 25031/ABC
Sunday Kind Of Love	Bees, Honey & the	1968	Arctic 158
Sunday Kind Of Love	Camelots	1963	AAnko 1004
Sunday Kind Of Love	Clusters	NA	Unreleased
Sunday Kind Of Love	El Sierros	1963	Yussels 7702
Sunday Kind Of Love	Emery's	1977	Clifton 19
Sunday Kind Of Love	Excellents	1964	Bobby 601/Old Timer 601 (64)
Sunday Kind Of Love	Five Boroughs	1988	Avenue D 15
Sunday Kind Of Love	Gothics	1959	Dynamic 101
Sunday Kind Of Love	High Seas	1960	D-M-G 1001/D-M-G 4000
Sunday Kind Of Love	Highlanders	1957	Ray's 36
Sunday Kind Of Love	Hollywood Saxons	Mid to late 1950s	(Early 1980s on EP; originally unreleased)
Sunday Kind Of Love	Kings, Bobby Hall & the	1953, 1973	Jax 320
Sunday Kind Of Love	Lambert, Rudy (with the Lyrics)	1958	Rhythm 128
Sunday Kind Of Love	Marcels		Cycle 2001 (unreleased)/ Colpix LP 416
Sunday Kind Of Love	Persians	1962	RTO 100
Sunday Kind Of Love	Rapid-Tones, Willie Winfield & the	1962	Rapid 101
Sunday Kind Of Love	Regents	1961	Gee LP 706/Forum Circle LP
Sunday Kind Of Love	Roommates (Roomates)	1962	Cameo 233
Sunday Kind Of Love	Sentimentals	1957	Mint 802
Sunday Kind Of Love	Statics, Lynn & the	NA	Mantis 101
Sunday Kind Of Love	Themes	NA	Ideal
Sunday Kind Of Love	Winters, David & group	1959	Addison 15004
Sunday Kind Of Love (acappella)	Five Shadows	1965	Mellomood 011/012
Sunday Kind Of Love (acappella)	Timetones	1963	Times Square 26/Relic 5466
Sundown	Frederick, Tommy & group	1960	Coral 62170
Sunny	Counts, Bobby Comstock & the	1963	Lawn 217
Sunny Side Of The Street	Bees	1954	Imperial (unreleased)
Sunnyside Of The Street	Shallows	1986	Starlight 49
Sun's Message, The	Butlers	1964	Liberty Bell 1024
Sunset	Harptones	1963	KT 201
Sunset	Serenaders (Detroit)	1974	Roadhouse 1022
Sunset	Shonnie & group	1954	TNT 113
Sunset To Sunrise	Duprees	1990	Rhino CD R2 71004
Sunshine	Buddies, Carl Ell & the	1959	Combo 154
Sunshine	Fabulous Echoes	1965	Diamond 187
Sunshine	Ivies	1958	Ivy 110/Brunswick 55112 (58)
Sunshine	Lamplighters	1955	Federal (unreleased)
Sunshine And Rain	Dukes, Skip Arne & the	1964	Little Fort 8688/Dot 16627 (64)
Sunshine Of Our Love	Flairs, Etta James & the	1959	Kent 304
Suntan Tattoo	Valiants, Sandy Vale & the	1959	Decca 30941
Super Chick	Rock-A-Fellas, Eddie Bell & the	1959	Coed 517
Super Hawk	Deltas, Jay & the	1964	Warner Bros. 5404
Super Soul	Tip Tops	1965	Kapp 726
Superman Lover	Marglows, Andy & the	1963	Liberty 55627
Sure As The Flowers	Endings	1980	Clifton 41
Sure As The Flowers	Hi-Tones	1961	Seg-Way 105
Sure As You're Born	Storm, Billy (with the Storms)	1960	Atlantic 2076
Sure Clue For The Blues	Four Jacks (with Cora Williams & Shirley Haven)	1952	Federal 12079
Sure Enough	Cardinals	1974	Atlantic EP/Bim Bam Boom EP 1000 (74)
Sure Fire	Orioles, Sonny Til & the	1955	Jubilee (unreleased)
Sure Is Lonesome Downtown	Fleetwoods	1963	Dolton 74
Sure Of Love	Chantels	1958	End 1026
Surely	Keynotes	NA	Apollo LP 1000/Relic LP 5072 (1000)

SONG	GROUP	YEAR	LABEL
Surely	Zodiacs, Maurice Williams & the	1966	Dee-Su 309
Surely Will	Ravens	NA	Argo (unreleased)
Surf 'N' Stomp	Charades	1964	Impact 2
Surf Train	Fairlanes	1963	Reprise 20213
Surf Twist	Cotillions	1962	Alley 1003
Surfer Boy	Catalinas	1966	Ric 164
Surfer Street	Allisons	1963	Tip 1011
Surfer's Memories	Fashions	1963	Felsted 8689
Surfin' '69	Ebb Tides, Nino & the	1969	R&R
Surfin' Back To School	Fashions	1963	Felsted 8689
Surfin' East Coast	Dolphins	1966	Yorkshire 125
Surfin' Here We Go	Tru Tones	NA	Tree
Surfin' In The Sunset	Zircons	1963	Bagdad 1007
Surfin' Santa	Ramblers (Almont)	1964	Almont 315
Surfin' Shark	Rhoades, Darryl & group	1976	Wonder 1976-1
Surfin' The Summer Away	Beachcombers	1964	Diamond 168
Surfin' Wild	Deltas, Jim Waller & the	1962	Arvee 5072
Surfing At Makaha	Mar-Vels	1964	IN 102
Surfside	Chants	1968	Checker 1209
Surfside	Notables	1963	Big Top 3141
Surleen	Prisonaires	1976	Sun 519
Surprise	Contenders	1966	Java 102
Surprise	Magnets	1955	Groove 0058
Surprise	Valiants (Los Angeles)	1959	Shar-Dee 703
Surrender	Four Sportsmen	1960	Sunnybrook 1
Surrender	Kings (Baltimore)	1959	Jay-Wing 5805
Surrender My Love	Charmettes	1962	Marlin 16001
Surrender To Love	Castelles, George Grant & the	1991	Classic Artists 126
Surrender Your Heart	Love Notes (Massachusetts)	1953	Imperial 5254
Susan Ann	Teen Tones	1960	Deb 132
Susie	Four Labels	1958	Gralow 5524
Susie	Keynotes, Gene Anderson & the	NA	Top Ten 252
Susie Baby	Counts, Bobby Comstock & the	1963	Lawn 210
Susie Jane	Thunderbirds, Ron Holden & the	1960	Donna 1324
Susie Jones	Nortones	1959	Warner Bros. 5065
Susie-Q	Osburn, Bobby & group	1964	Arlen 747
Suspicious Of You, Baby	Dolls	1958	Kangaroo 101
Suzanne	Belvederes	1958	Dot 15852
Suzanne	Cheaters	1965	Wax 213
Suzie	Berry Kids	NA	Soo 12
Swamp Legend	Four Coachmen	1960	Adonis 106/Stellar 712 (60)/ Dot 16297 (61)
Swamp Water	Chantels	1963	Ludix 101
Swanee	Copas	1979	U.G.H.A. 10
Swanee River Fling	Lonely Ones	1960	Rendezvous 125
Swanee River Rock	Chimes (Jay-Tee)	NA	Jay-Tee 1000
Swanee River Rock	Red Tops	NA	Sky 703/RCA 7144
Sway, The	Concepts (with the Emanons)	NA	J&J 3000
Sway, The	Emanons (Brooklyn) (with the Concepts)	NA	J&J 3000
Swayback	Invincibles	1959	Chess 1727
Sweeney's Twist	Corvairs, Billy Martin & the	NA	Monitor 1402
Sweet & Lovely	Hi-Lites	1959	Reno 1030
Sweet And Heavenly Melody	Broadways	1967	MGM 13592
Sweet And Lovely	Cleftones	1963	Unreleased
Sweet And Lovely	Davis, Hal Sonny & group	1959	Alden 1301
Sweet And Lovely	Flamingos	1960	End LP 307
Sweet And Lovely	Teenagers (Frankie Lymon)	1964	Columbia 43094
Sweet And Lovely	Tritones	1955	Grand 126/Jamie 1035 (57)
Sweet Angel	Commodores	1957	Challenge 1004
Sweet Annie	Dales	1960	Crest 1069
Sweet Annie Laurie	Twisters, Sammy Turner & the	1958	Big Top 3007
Sweet As A Flower	Dovers	1959	Davis 465
Sweet As An Angel	Jiving Juniors	1961	Asnes 103
Sweet Baby	Fascinators (Detroit)	1959	Your Copy 1135
Sweet Baby	Jets, Ronnie Grett & the	1955	Capitol 3174

SONG	GROUP	YEAR	LABEL
Sweet Breeze	Phantoms, Vernon Green & the	1956	Specialty 581
Sweet Chariot	Keytones	1963	Chelsea 1013
Sweet Cucumber	Blue Notes, Little Bill & the	1960	Topaz 1302
Sweet Daddy	Storey Sisters	1958	Cameo 126/Peak 5001
Sweet Diane Cha Cha	Suburbans	1959	Port 70011
Sweet Dreams	Crescendos (Los Angeles)	1956, 1959	Atlantic 1109/2014
Sweet Dreams	McLain, Tommy & group	NA	MSL 197
Sweet Dreams	Precisions	1963	Debra 1001
Sweet Dreams	Timberlanes	1958	Dragon 101
Sweet Georgia Brown	Blue Jays (Laurie)	1959	Laurie 3037
Sweet Georgia Brown	Chantones	1961	Capitol 4661
Sweet Georgia Brown	Coasters	1957	Atco 6104
Sweet Girl	Four Intruders	1979	King Tut 179
Sweet Girl	Squires (California)	1955	Vita 113
Sweet Juanita	Kappas	1959	Wonder 112
Sweet Kind Of Loneliness	Darlettes	1965	Mira 203
Sweet Laurie, Fair Laurie	Tokens (Brooklyn)	1962	Unreleased
Sweet Lies	Chaparrals (featuring Tooter Boatman)	1958	Rebel 108
Sweet Lies	Glasers, Tompall & the	1958	Robbins 1006
Sweet Lips	Embers	1954	Columbia 40287
Sweet Lips	Twilighters (Bronx, N.Y.)	1964	Roulette 4546/Paloma 100
Sweet Little Angel	Royal Jokers	1958	Fortune 840
Sweet Little Baby	Darts	1958	Dot 15752
Sweet Little Baby Of Mine	Five Hi Lighters	1959	Cannon 580488
Sweet Little Girl	Peachettes, Lynn Taylor & the	1960	Clock 1033/Hawk 2001
Sweet Little Girl	Sunliners	1962	Hercules 182
Sweet Little Jane	Downbeats	NA	Hampshire 1002
Sweet Little Surfing Girl	Palisades, Frank Gonzales & the	1961	FG 1001
Sweet Little Thing	Satellites, Bobby Day & the	1958	Class 220
Sweet Little Thing (Called Love)	Caribbeans, George Torrence & the	1958	Galliant 1003
Sweet Loretta	Maharajahs	1958	Flip 335
Sweet Lorraine	Mellows, Lillian Leach & the	1956	Celeste 3004
Sweet Lorraine	Upbeats, Ray Allen & the	1961	Sinclair 1004
Sweet Love	Moontars, Don Deal & the	1958	Era 1070
Sweet Love	Penguins	1958	Dooto 432
Sweet Love Of Mine	Boys Next Door	1956	Vik 0207
Sweet Lovin'	Creations	NA	Tan
Sweet Lovin'	Visuals	1959	Poplar 117
Sweet Lovin' Daddy-O	Teardrops	1952	Sampson 634
Sweet Lovin' Maryann	Fi-Tones, Carl Thomas & the	1959	Stroll 101/O Gee 1004 (59)
Sweet Lucy	Incas	1977	Monogram 127
Sweet Lulu	Love Notes (Massachusetts)	1954	Riviera 970/Rainbow 266 (54)
Sweet Mama Do Right	Midnighters	1956	Federal 12251
Sweet Man	Starr, Bobby & group	1959	Radio 120
Sweet Memories	Hustlers, Carl Burnett & the	1965	Carmax 102
Sweet Names	Counts	1956	Note 20000
Sweet One	A Moment's Pleasure	1986	Starlight 39
Sweet One	Majestics (with the Nightwinds)	1959	Sioux 91459/20th Century 171 (59)/ Foxie 7004 (59)
Sweet Pauline	Blue Jays (Venice, Calif.)	1972	Roadhouse 113472
Sweet Pea	Gee-Tones	1956	Gee 1013 (unreleased)
Sweet Pea	Howard, Gregory (with the Cadillacs)	1963	Kapp 536
Sweet Peach	Titans	1957	Specialty 614
Sweet Peas And Bronc Busters	Fabulous Playboys	1959	Contour 004
Sweet Promises	Spinner, Alice & group	NA	Hugo 11722
Sweet Rockin' Mama	Hi-Tombs	NA	Cannon 832
Sweet Rocking Mama	Daylighters	1960	C.J. 614
Sweet Shop	Stevens, Randy & group	1959	Loma 301
Sweet Side Of A Soulful Woman	Clovers	1968	Josie 997
Sweet Sixteen	Belairs, Lee Bantell & the	1956	Coral 61605
Sweet Sixteen	Colts	1956, 1962	Vita 121/Plaza 505
Sweet Sixteen	Platters	NA	Mercury EP 3353
Sweet Sixteen	Relatives	1961	Colpix 481/Colpix 601 (61)
Sweet Sixteen	Sounds	1956	Modern 981
Sweet Sixteen	Tropicals	NA	Specialty

SONG	GROUP	YEAR	LABEL
Sweet Sixteen	Velours	1960	Goldisc 3012
Sweet Slumber	Four Buddies	1951	Savoy 779
Sweet Slumber	Rovers	1974	Vintage 1018
Sweet Slumber	Sabres	1965	Jameco 2002
Sweet Slumber	Vibrations	1961	Checker LP 2978
Sweet Sue	Blend Aires	1977	Arcade 104
Sweet Sue	Raye, Jan	1955	Baton 213
Sweet Sue	Starliters	1955	Combo 73
Sweet Sue (It's You)	Crows	1955	Rama 50
Sweet Sue Mambo	Blue Flames	1954	Grand 108
Sweet Sugar You	Pharaohs, Richard Berry & the	1957	Flip 327
Sweet Sweet Baby	DiMucci, Dion (with the Del Satins)	1965	Columbia 43213
Sweet, Sweet Memory	Ambers, Joey & the	1960	Big Top 3052
Sweet Sweet William	Moroccos, Lillian Brooks & the	1956	King 4956
Sweet Sweetheart	Sharps	1957	Jamie 1040/Vik 0264 (57)/VDJ 6
Sweet Talk	Accents (featuring Sandi)	1965	Challenge 9294
Sweet Talk	Charmers	1963	Laurie 3203
Sweet Talk	Counts, Bobby Comstock & the	1959	Blaze 349
Sweet Talk	Knockout Mays	1960	Cos-De 1003
Sweet Talk	Playboys	1959	Imperial 5586
Sweet Talk	Youngsters	1958	Apt 25021
Sweet Talkin' Guy	Chiffons	1966	Laurie 3340
Sweet Thing	Corvettes	NA	Oak 4429/4430
Sweet Thing	Ding Dongs	1960	Eldo 109
Sweet Thing	Nitecaps	1956	Groove 0147
Sweet Thing	Rams	1955	Flair 1066
Sweet Thing	Three G's	1958	Columbia 41256
Sweet Tooth For My Baby	Four Buddies	1952	Savoy 866
Sweet Was The Wine	Harmony	1980	Starlight 7
Sweet Was The Wine	Impressions, Jerry Butler & the	1958	Vee Jay 280/Falcon 1013 (58)/ Abner 1013 (58)/Vee Jay 396 (61)
Sweet Was The Wine	Keystoners	1992	Starbound 516
Sweet Was The Wine	Marcels	1975	Monogram 113
Sweet Water	Stereos	1961	Cub 9103
Sweet Words Of Love	Underbeats	1964	Bangar 00632
Sweeter	Daylighters	1964	Tip Top 2010
Sweeter Than	Emery's	1977	Clifton 18
Sweeter Than	Young Ones	1964	Times Square 36/Relic 527 (65)
Sweeter Than Wine	Fabulous Fanatics	1961	T-Bird 201
Sweeter Than Words	Moonglows	1958	Chess 1701
Sweetest Angel	Condors	1962	Hunter 2503/2504
Sweetest Darlin'	Imperials, Stacy Henry & the	1961	Flippin' 108
Sweetest One	Crests	1957, 1961, 1963	Joyce 103/Musictone 1106 (62)
Sweetest One	Shells	1961, 1963	Johnson 112/Josie LP 4001
Sweetest One	Vilons	1973	Vintage 1011
Sweetest Thing This Side Of Heaven, The	Bartley, Chris & group	1967	Vando 101
Sweetheart	Catalinas	1961	20th Fox 286
Sweetheart	Five Keys	1972	Roadhouse 1003
Sweetheart Darling	Savoys, Sonny Brooks & the	1956	Tip Top 1008
Sweetheart Of Mine	Valentines	1986	Murray Hill LP 000202
Sweetheart Of Senior High	Four Young Men	1961	Crest 1083
Sweetheart Of The Prom	Notes, Reed Harper & the	1958	Vik 0328/Smart 1001 (58)
Sweetheart Please Don't Go	Cosmo (with the Carnations)	1962	Tilt 789
Sweetheart Please Don't Go	Gladiolas	1957	Excello 2101
Sweetheart Song, The	Raindrops	1961	Imperial 5785
Sweetheart, Sweetheart	Sweethearts	1968	Como 451
Sweethearts On Parade	Dominoes	1955	Jubilee 5213
Sweetie Pie	Allen, Charlie & group	1961	Portrait 107
Sweetie Pie	Petites	1958	Spinning 6005
Sweetness	Castelles	1953	Grand 101
Sweetpea's In Love	Stereos	1959	Gibraltar 105
Sweetpea's In Love	Sterios	1966	Ideal 110
Sweets For My Sweet	Del Satins	1965	B.T. Puppy 509
Sweets For My Sweet	Drifters (1959-forward)	1961	Atlantic 2117

SONG	GROUP	YEAR	LABEL
Sweets For My Sweet	Good Guys, Doug Robertson & the	1964	Jerden 729
Swim	Casinos	1963	Itzy 404/Olimpic 251 (65)
Swim	Falcons (Detroit)	1962	Lu Pine 103/Lu Pine 1003
Swim Swim Swim	Brightones	1964	Warner Bros. 5472
Swim, The	Butterflys	1964	Red Bird 10-009
Swimmin' U.S.A.	Huff, Chauncey & group	1964	Fantasy 587
Swimming Around The World	Mints	1958	Airport 103
Swing	Tokens (Brooklyn)	1964	B.T. Puppy 500/Music Makers 110
Swing Low	Victory Five	1958	Terp 101
Swing Pretty Mama	Flairs	1959	Antler 4005
Swing Swang	School Belles	1959	Hanover 4526
Swingin' At Chariot	Sophomores, Anthony & the	1963	Mercury 72168
Swingin' Partner	Four Kings, Ray Agee & the	1960	Check 102/Plaid 105
Swingin' Platoon, The	Tune Drops, Malcolm Dodds & the	1958	Decca 30653
Swingin' Shepherd Blues, The	Honeydreamers, Kirk Stuart & the	1958	Josie 832
Swingin' Soiree	Dolphins	1963	Laurie 3202
Swingin' Street	Prophets, Ronnie Dio & the	1963	Lawn 218
Swingin' Stroll	Del-Sharps, Sonny Ace & the	1958	TNT 153
Swingin' Summer	Check Mates	NA	Arvee 5037
Swingin' Teens	Dells	1961	Vee Jay 376
Swingin' Wedding	Visions	1962	Big Top 3119
Swinging Affair	Harmony Kings, Clyde Tillis & the	1958	Cash 1064
Swinging Little Chickie	Belltones (Olimpic)	1962	Olimpic 1068/Itzy 1 (62)
Swinging On A Star	Belmonts, Dion & the	1960	Laurie LP 2006
Swinging Smitty, The	Corvettes	1961	Sheraton 201
Swinging Thing, The	McCracklin, Jimmy & group	1958	Peacock 1683
Swinging Week-End	Crusaders	1963	Dooto 472
Swish Fish	Showmen	1963	Minit 662
Switch, The	Ambassadors	1956	Air 5065
Switch, The	Pleasers, Bobbie Please & the	1959	Jamie 1118
Switch-A-Roo, The	Midnighters, Hank Ballard & the	1961	King 5510
Switchie Witchie Titchie	Midnighters	1955	Federal 12220
Sylvia	Kilts, Charlie Jester & the	1961	Le Cam 722
Sylvia	Ravens	NA	National (unreleased)
Sylvia	Team Mates	1960	Le Cam 709
Sylvie Sleepin'	Tokens (Brooklyn)	1965	B.T. Puppy 507
Symbol Of Heaven	Tigers, Little Julian Herrera & the	1957	Dig 137
Symbol Of Love	G-Clefs	1957	Paris 502
Symbol Of Love	Majestics (Vintage)	1973	Vintage 1002
Symbol Of Love	Royale Cita Chorus	1956	Rama 204
Symbol Of Love	Titones	1959, 1960	Scepter 1206/Wand 105
Sympathy	Cadillacs	1955	Josie 773
Sympathy	Crescents	1985	Relic LP 5053
Sympathy	Sensations	1956	Atco 6056
Symphony	Marglows, Andy & the	1963	Liberty 55570
Symptoms Of Love	Carousels	1961	ABC 10233
Syracuse, The	Escorts, Felix & the	1962	Jag 685

T

SONG	GROUP	YEAR	LABEL
T Town	Zodiacs, Maurice Williams & the	1959	Cole 100
T. V. Baby	Suburbans	1956	Baton 227
T. V. Gal	Keystoners	1961	Riff 202
T.V. Commercial	Zirkons, Johnny Parker & the	NA	C T 302
T.V. Mix Up	Clouds	1959	Round 1008
Ta Ta Song, The	Shamrocks, Little Henry & the	1961	Kent 398
Tabarin	Hollywood Four Flames (Four Flames)	1951	Unique 009/Fidelity 3001
Tabarin	Tangiers (Los Angeles)	1955	Decca 29603
Tafu	Senators	1959	Bristol 1916
Tag Along	Belmonts, Dion & the	1957	Mohawk 107
Tag Along	DiMucci, Dion (with the Del Satins)	1963	Laurie 3187
Tag Along	Teenettes, Betty Jayne & the	1961	Carellen 107
Tail Light	Viscounts, Sammy Hagen & the	1958	Capitol 3885
Taint It The Truth	K-Doe, Ernie & group	1960	Minit 614
T'ain't Nothin' To Me	Coasters	1964	Atco 6287
Take A Break	Rendezvous	1961	Rust 5041

SONG	GROUP	YEAR	LABEL
Take A Chance	Charades	1964	Original Sound 47
Take A Chance	Indexes, John Golden & the	1961	Douglas 101
Take A Chance	Valadiers	1961	Miracle 6
Take A Chance On Love	Kids, Billy & the	1961	Lute 6016/Lute 312
Take A Chance On Love	Pyramids, Doug & Freddy & the	1961	Finer Arts 1001
Take A Gamble On Me	Continentals (New York - Key)	1956	Key 517
Take A Giant Step	Drakes	1955	States (unreleased)
Take A Giant Step	Profiles	1962	Goldie 1103
Take A Hike	Hi Larks	1959	Beat 0050
Take A Little	Rockets, Herb Kenny & the	1953	MGM 11397
Take A Look	Arnells	1963	Roulette 4519
Take A Look	Destineers	1962	RCA 8049
Take A Look Around You	Delrons, Reperata & the	1965	RCA 8721
(Take A Look At My Guy) The Greatest Lover	Shepherd Sisters	1963	Atlantic 2195
Take A Ride	Veltones	1959	Jin 107
Take A Walk	Counts, Bobby Comstock & the	1963	Lawn 210
Take All Of Me	Five Royales	1952	Apollo 443
Take All Of Me	Paradons	1960	Warner Bros. 5186
Take All The Kisses	Cones, Connie & the	1960	Roulette 4313
Take Another Look At Me	Tiffanys	1966	Josie 952
Take Back My Ring	Gallahads	1957	Vik 0291
Take Everything But You	Carter Rays, Eddie Carter & the	1954	Grand 107 (first pressing)
Take Five	Five Stars (Detroit)	1956	Atco 6065
Take It Back	Class-Notes	1958	Hamilton 50011
Take It Easy, Baby	Lovetones	1956	Plus 108
Take It Easy Casanova	Rubies	1961	District 301
Take It From A Fool	Dreamlovers	1960	Len 1006
Take It Like A Man	Visions, Connie McGill & the	1964	Edge 502
Take It Or Leave It	Barbarians (with Vito Piccone & the Elegants)	1965	Laurie 3308
Take It Or Leave It	Satisfactions	1964	Smash
Take Life Easy	Arrogants	1962	Vanessa 200
Take Me	Arabians	1960	Magnificent 114
Take Me	Citations	1959	University 101
Take Me	Youngsters	1961	Candix 313
Take Me And Make Me Yours	Nutmegs	1973	Night Train 905
Take Me As I Am	Chantels	1965	TCF-Arrawak 123
Take Me As I Am	Demens	1957	Teenage 1006
Take Me As I Am	Duprees	1962, 1963	Coed 569/580
Take Me As I Am	Notemakers	1976	Monogram 118
Take Me As I Am	Spi-Dells	NA	Tyme 200/Tyme 263
Take Me Back	Calvanes	1991	Classic Artists 127
Take Me Back	Imperials, Little Anthony & the	1965	DCP 1136/Veep 1243 (66)
Take Me Back	Marcels	1973	Baron 109
Take Me Back	Marcels, Bob Jeffries & the	1958	Jody 123
Take Me Back	Shanteers	1962	Rori 708
Take Me Back Again	Volcanos	1965	Harthon 146
Take Me Back, Baby	Four Fellows (Brooklyn - Glory)	1955	Glory 234
Take Me Back, Baby	Quails	1963	American 1023
Take Me Back Lover	Carpenter, Freddie & group	1958	East West 112
Take Me Back, Take Me Back	Platters	1954	Federal 12204
Take Me Back To Heaven	Dominoes	1955	Jubilee 5213
Take Me For A Little While	Blue Belles, Patti LaBelle & the	1966	Atlantic 2373
Take Me In Your Arms	Five Knights	1959	Tau 104
Take Me In Your Arms	Platters	NA	Mercury EP 3345
Take Me Out Of Your Heart	Four Hues	1956	Crown 159
Take Me To Paradise	Romancers	1959	Marquee 701
Take Me With You	Powell, Tiny & group	1964	Wax 101/Wax 14
Take Me With You Baby	Five Royales	1961	Home Of The Blues 232
Take My Hand	Centurys	1959	Fortune 533
Take My Hand	Echoes	1988	Relic LP 5076
Take My Heart	Crescendos (Berkeley)	1957, 1960	Music City 831/Gone 5100 (61)
Take My Heart	Illusions	1966	Columbia 43700
Take My Heart	Paramounts	1959	Combo 156

SONG	GROUP	YEAR	LABEL
Take My Heart	Premiers, Julie Stevens & the	1957	Dig 129
Take My Heart	Romancers	1966	Linda 123
Take My Heart	Slades	1961	Domino 906
Take My Heart	Stevens, Julie (with the Premiers)	1957	Dig 129
Take My Love	Corvells	1962	ABC 10324
Take My Love	Demensions	NA	Coral LP 57430
Take My Love	Gallahads	1956	Jubilee 5259
Take My Love	Three G's	1960	Columbia 41868
Take My Love Along With You	Tabs	1963	Wand 139
Take My Name And Number	Randell, Rick & group	1962	United Artists 448
Take One Step	Melvettes	NA	Tela-Star 110
Take That	Thrillers (Detroit)	NA	Herald (unreleased)
Take That Step	Three G's	1960	Columbia 41584
Take The Freeway	Dynamics	NA	Corsican 651
Take The Key (And Open Up My Heart)	Pharaohs, Richard Berry & the	1956	Flip 318
Take This Heart	Phillips, Phil (with the Twilights)	1959	Mercury 71531
Take This Hurt Off Me	Covay, Don & group	1964	Rosemart 802
Take This Love I've Got	Falcons (Detroit)	1963	Atlantic 2179
Take Time	Parkway	1990	BAB 131
Take You Back Again	Jovations	1963	Taurus 362
Takes Two To Make A Home	Voices	1955	Cash 1015
Taking A Chance On You	Embers, Willis Sanders & the	1957	Juno 213/Jvpiter 213 (57)
Taking Care Of Business	Trippers	1967	Ruby-Doo 5
Talk About Him, Girlie	Hearts (Bronx, N.Y.)	1955	Baton 211
Talk About My Woman	Five Royales	1962	Vee Jay 431
Talk About The Girl	Pirates, Terry & the	1958	Valli 100/Chess 1695 (58)
Talk About The Weather	Gems (Illinois)	1954	Drexel 901
(Talk About) True Love	Flamingos	1962	End 1124
Talk Is Cheap	Ex-Cels Five	1964	Enith 722
Talk Is Cheap	Shepherd Sisters	1963	Atlantic 2195
Talk It Over	Marktones	1957	Ember 1022
Talk It Over	Rocketeers	1956	Modern 999
Talk That Talk	Du Droppers	1955	Groove 0104
Talk That Talk	Vibrations	1961	Checker (unreleased)
Talk To An Angel	Lovetones	1956	Plus 108
Talk To Audrey	Hollywood Playboys	1960	Sure 105
Talk To Me	Avons	1967	A-Bet 9419
Talk To Me	Meter-Tones	1959	Jax 1002
Talk To Me	Spydels, John Dow & the	1962	Assault 1866
Talk To Me	Sunglows, Sunny & the	1963	Tear Drop 3014/Sunglow 110
Talk To Me Baby	Night Riders	1960	Sue 731
Talk To The Angels	Josie, Lou & group	1961	Rendezvous 143
Talk While You Walk	Enchanters (Musitron)	1961	Musitron 1072
Talkin' 'Bout My Friends	Reed, A. C. & group	NA	Nike 2002
Talkin' 'Bout My Girl	Reflections	1964	Golden World 15
Talkin' Trash	Marathons	1961	Arvee 5027
Talking About My Baby	Impressions	1964	ABC 10511
Talking About My Baby	Pictures, C.L. & the	1964	Kirk 639/Monument 854 (64)
Talking About My Love	Dares, Joey Daye & the	1961	Fortune 868
Talking To My Heart	Revels	1959	Norgolde 103 (first pressing)
Talking To My Heart (acappella)	Vibraharps	1975	Relic LP 109
Talking To Myself	Charms, Otis Williams & his	1957	DeLuxe 6137
Talking To Myself	Lydells	1959	Pam 103/Parkway 897 (64)
Tall Cool One	Wailers	1959	
Tall Lanky Papa	Four Sounds	1957	Celeste 3010
Tall Len	Blue Jays (Venice, Calif.)	1962	Milestone 2014
Tallahassee Lassie	Juniors, Danny & the	NA	Singular LP 569
Tally Wally	Little Nat (with the Shells)	1961	Pik 242
Tammy	Citizens	1961	Laurie 3107
Tam-O-Shanter	Royal Jacks	1962	Amy 865
Tangerock	Chantones	1960	Top Rank 2066
Tangier	Strollers	1963	Jubilee 5449
Tango Moon	Hornets	1957	Flash 125
Tango Of Love	Passions	1958	Dore 505
Tanya	Downbeats, O. S. Grant & the	1956	Sarg 200

SONG	GROUP	YEAR	LABEL
Tap Tap Daisy	Montclairs	1967	United International 1007
Tapun Tapun	Sharps	1987	Relic LP 5069
Tara's Theme	Raiders, Tony Castle & the	1961	Gone 5105
Tarnished Angel	Fortunes	1958	Decca 30541
Tarzan	Tillman, Lee	1962	Sonora 211
Tarzan's Date	Chuck-A-Lucks	1961	Jubilee 5415
Taste Of A Tear, The	Kings, Johnny & the	1961	Warwick 658
Tastee Freeze	Five Echoes	1955	Vee Jay 156
Tasty Kisses	Chantels	1957	Unreleased
Tasty Kisses	Tunemasters	1990	Mark-X 7010
Tattle Tale Blues	Christopher, Rod & group	1962	Tru-Lite 111
Tattletale	Monotones	1961	Hull 741
Tattoo	Double Dates	1959	Luck 103
Taxi Cab	Smith, Shad & group	1962	Smash 1765
Te Na Na	Williams, Dicky & group	1960	Vin 1021
Tea For Two	Ravens	NA	National (unreleased)
Teach Me	Fabulous Three, Gorgeous George & the	1962	Hale 501
Teach Me How	Chiffons	1967	Laurie 3423
Teach Me How To Dance	Moniques	1962	Benn-X 58
Teach Me How To Limbo	Majestics (Detroit)	1962	Chex 1009
Teach Me How To Shimmy	Coasters	1962	Atco 6219
Teach Me How To Twist	Limelites, Shep & the	1962	Hull 751
Teach Me Mama	Crayons	1963	Counsel 121
Teach Me Tonight	Bobbettes	1961	End 1093
Teach Me Tonight	Five Dipps	1955	Original 1005
Teach Me Tonight	Rivingtons	1967	Baton Master 202
Teacher Crush	Casals	1961	Seville 105
Teacher Don't Keep Me In	Martells	1959	Nasco 6026
Teacher, The	Falcons (Detroit)	1960	United Artists 229
Teachin' And Preachin'	Royal Kings	1952	Specialty 444
Teamwork	Pipes	1962	Carlton 575
Tear After Tear	Blue Belles, Patti LaBelle & the	1962	Newtown 5007
Tear Drops	Five Palms (Palms)	1957	States 163
Teardrop Eyes	Dukes (California)	1956	Imperial 5401
Teardrop Eyes	Fascinators (Los Angeles)	1958	Dooto 441
Teardrop Motel	Goofers	1956	Coral 61650
Teardrop Sea	Tonettes	1963	Volt 104
Teardrops	Castells	1964	Warner Bros. 5421
Teardrops	Dedications	1970	White Whale
Teardrops	Hearts, Lee Andrews & the	1957	Grand 156/Main Line 105 (57)/ Argo 1000 (57)/Chess 1675 (57)
Teardrops	Hurricanes, Bob Gaye & the	1954	Audivox 109
Teardrops	Ko Kos	NA	Gilt-Edge
Teardrops	Markeets	1957	Melatone 1005
Teardrops	Palms	1957	United 208
Teardrops	Rochells	NA	Spacey 202
Teardrops	Rockets, Bill Bodaford & the	1958	Back Beat 507
Teardrops	Tri-Tones	1964	Miss Julie 6501
Teardrops	Valaquons	1964	Laguna 102
Teardrops	Vestee, Russ & group	1962	Amy 833
Teardrops (acappella)	Destinaires	1965	Old Timer 609
Teardrops Are Falling	Checkers	1959	King 5199/King 4781 (55) (as the Five Wings)
Teardrops Are Falling	Five Wings	1955	King 4781/King 5199
Teardrops Are Falling	Gifts, Little Natalie & Henry & the	1963	Roulette 4540
Teardrops Are Falling	Persians	1961	Goldisc G1/Goldisc 1004 (63)
Teardrops Fell	Scarlets	1976	Robin Hood 134
Teardrops Follow Me	Del Satins	1962	Laurie 3132
Teardrops Follow Me	Del-Capris	1966	Catamount 115
Teardrops Follow Me	Devotions	1972	Kape 701
Teardrops Follow Me	Platinums	1979	J&M 122648
Teardrops From My Eyes	Four Guys	1963	Stride 5001
Teardrops In My Eyes	Five Keys	1953	Aladdin 3204
Teardrops In The Night	Arabians	1960	Magnificent 114
Teardrops On A Letter	Colbert, Bertha & female group	1962	Roulette 4435

SONG	GROUP	YEAR	LABEL
Teardrops On My Letter	Ringo, Eddie & group	1960	Twin Star 1016
Teardrops On My Pillow	Orioles, Sonny Til & the	1953	Jubilee 5108
Teardrops On Your Letter	Midnighters, Hank Ballard & the	1959	King 5171/Federal 12345 (59)
Tears	Fleas	1961	Challenge 9115
Tears	Keyavas, Harry & the	1963	IPG 1011
Tears	Native Boys	1956	Combo 115
Tears	Newports	1964	Guyden 2116
Tears	Persuaders	1959	Winley 235/Relic 1002 (65)
Tears And Dreams	Monograms	1960	Safire 102
Tears And Dreams	Whooping Cranes	NA	El Rey 1000
Tears And Pain	Three Chimes	1964	Crossway 444
Tears And Wine	Brown, Juanita	1953	Sun 182
Tears Are Falling	Blue Jays (Venice, Calif.)	1961	Milestone 2009
Tears Are Just For Fools	Starlites, Kenny Esquire & the	1957	Ember 1021
Tears Began To Flow	Spiders	1954	Imperial 5280
Tears Bring Heartaches	Standards	1963	Debro 3178/Roulette 4487 (63)
Tears Came Rolling Down, The	Hollywood Saxons, Stan Beverly & the	1963	Entra 1214
Tears Fall	Vanguards	NA	Regency 743
Tears Fell From My Eyes	Tellers	1960	Fire 1038
Tears From A Broken Heart	Devotions	1964	Roulette 4556
Tears From An Angels Eyes	Chimes (House of Beauty)	1959	House Of Beauty 3
Tears From My Eyes	Lexingtons, Joey & the	1963	Dunes 2029
Tears From My Heart	Harris, Thurston (with the Sharps)	1958	Aladdin 3435
Tears Had Fallen	Williams, Eddie & group	1964	Corsair 402
Tears In My Eyes	Amber, Kenny & group	NA	Zenette
Tears In My Eyes	Baltineers	1956	Teenage 1002
Tears In My Eyes	Capris (New York)	1961	Old Town 1103
Tears In My Eyes	Dreamers (Philadelphia)	1955	Grand 131
Tears In My Eyes	Empires, Eddie Friend & the	1959	Colpix 112
Tears In My Eyes	Fascinations	1963	ABC 10443
Tears In My Eyes	Hamber, Kenny & group	1963	Spar 101
Tears In My Eyes	Magic Tones	1957	Howfum 101
Tears In My Eyes	Monograms	1975	Monogram 106
Tears In My Eyes	New Yorkers (Fred Parris)	1961	Wall 548
Tears In My Eyes	Roman, Nat & group	1964	Sahara 103
Tears In My Eyes	Tru-Tones	1957	Chart 634
Tears In My Eyes	Willows	1964	Heidi 103
Tears In My Eyes (acappella)	Universals (Philadelphia)	1973	Relic LP 5006
Tears In My Heart	Impacs	1963	Parkway 865
Tears In Your Eyes	Chords	1958	Casino 451
Tears Keep Tumbling Down	Flames	1953	7-11 2108 (unreleased)
Tears Of Happiness	Charms, Otis Williams & his	1959	DeLuxe 6185
Tears Of Joy	Five Royales	1957, 1963	King 5032/5756
Tears Of Love	Little Miss Peggy & group	1960	Goldband 1109
Tears Of Love	Persians	1962	RSVP 114
Tears Of Love	Quailtones, Sax Kari & the	1955	Josie 779
Tears Of Remember	Taylor, Bert & group	1955	Essex 396
Tears Of Sorrow	Primettes	1961	Lu Pine 120
Tears On My Pillow	Chimes (Los Angeles - Specialty)	1955	Specialty 555
Tears On My Pillow	Corlettes	NA	Pace/Nita 711
Tears On My Pillow	Cymbols, Little Sonny Knight & the	NA	New Teenage 5001
Tears On My Pillow	El Dorados	1957	Vee Jay 250
Tears On My Pillow	Imperials	1958	End 1027 (first pressing, second is by Little Anthony & the Imperials)
Tears On My Pillow	Paris, Bobby & group	1966	Cameo 396
Tears On My Pillow	Town, Julie & group	1958	Bell
Tears On My Pillow	Viceroys	1964	Bethlehem 3088
Tears On My Pillow	Vilons	1973	Vintage 1011
Tears, Tears, Tears	Fabulous Playboys	1960	Apollo 760
Tears Tears Tears	Metronomes	1962	Challenge 9157
Tears Will Fall	Crests	1963	Selma 4000
Tease Me	Richards, Norm & group	1959	Imperial 5567
Teasin'	Castaways	1954	Excello 2038
Teasin' Heart	Wheels	1956	Premium 408
Teasin' Me	Shirelles	1967	Scepter 12178

SONG	GROUP	YEAR	LABEL
Teasing Me	Mel-O-Aires, Rudy Jackson & the	1957	Imperial 5425
Teddy	Bobbettes	1963, 1965	Diamond 133/189
Teddy Bear	Dubs, The Cleveland Still	1986	Clifton 77
Tee Vee	Fascinators (King)	1958	King 5119
Teen Age Baby	Moonbeems	1955	Sapphire 1052/Sapphire 1003 (58)/ Checker 912 (59)
Teen Age Fool	Four Imperials	1958	Chant 101
Teen Age Gossip	Majestics (Detroit)	1960	Contour 501
Teen Age Idol	Peppermints	1959	House Of Beauty 1
Teen Age Machine Age	Travelers	1958	Andex 4006
Teen Age Rock	Gadabouts	1955	Wing 90043
Teen Age World	Young Champions	1985	Nobletown 822
Teen Angel	Belmonts, Dion & the	1958	Laurie 3013
Teen Angel	Manis, Georgie & group	1958	Eclaire 105
Teen Baby	Accents, Gary Trexler & the	1957	Rev 3507
Teen Billy Baby	Sprouts	1957	RCA 7080/Spangle 2002 (57)
Teen Blues	Dynamos	1961	Press 101
Teen Bride	Coachmen	1960	Iona 1004
Teen Heart	Sparks, Nathan Ray & the	1958	Rocko 510
Teen Hoppers Ball	Peacocks	1958	4 Star 1718
Teen Life Swag	Goodtimers, Don Covay & the	1962	Columbia 42197
Teen Prayer	Velveteens	1961	Stark 101
Teen Talk	Three Cheers	1959	Glory 291
Teen Town Hop	Philharmonics	1958	Future 2200
Teenage Angel	Tri-Tones, Al Barkle & the	1957	Vita 171
Teen-Age Ball	Boleros, Carmen Taylor & the	1956	Apollo 489
Teen-Age Beauty	Candy Canes, Jimmy James & the	1958	Columbia 41192
Teenage Bells	Loungers	1991	Park Ave. 5
Teenage Bells	Secrets	1991	Park Ave. 5
Teenage Bill Of Rights	Seventeens, Robby John & the	1959	Del-Fi 4115
Teenage Blues	Caruso, Dick & group	1959	MGM 12827
Teenage Blues	Cupids, Carlo & the	1959	Parker 501/Judd 1007 (59)
Teenage Blues	Dante's Infernos	1957	Lido 507
Teenage Blues	Four Chickadees	1956	Checker 849
Teenage Blues	Spinners, Claudine Clark & the	1958	Herald 521
Teenage Broken Heart	Red Coats	NA	Kikko 610
Teen-Age Caravan	Medallionaires	1958	Mercury 71309
Teenage Chant	Highschool Chanters	1959	Fashion 001
Teenage Cinderella	Blazers, Rodney & the	1960	Dore 572/Kampus 100
Teenage Clementine	Belmonts, Dion & the	1957	Mohawk 106
Teenage Creature	Kingsmen	1959	Frantic 107
Teenage Dream	Ramadas	1963	Philips 40097
Teenage Girl	Sharps	1958	Win 702
Teen-Age Guy And Gal	Counts	1958	Mercury 71318
Teenage Hall Of Fame	Aztecs	1964	Card 901
Teen-Age Heart	Nu-Tones	1959	Spin Time 1001
Teenage Hop	Ravons	1958	Arrow 734
Teenage Idol	Delmonicos	1961	Aku 6139
Teen-Age Idol	Ravons	1959	Davis 464
Teenage Island	Milky Ways	1960	Liberty 55255
Teenage Jamboree	Dusters	1958	Glory 287
Teenage Jamboree	Johnson, Dave & group	1960	Apt 25054
Teen-Age Jive	Chris-Tones, Tommy Christy & the	1958	Scot 19999
Teenage Josephine	Golden Nuggets	1959	Futura 2-1691
Teenage Joy	Royal Teentones, Bobby Sands & the	1959	Nugget 1003
Teenage Kids	Hippies	1963	Parkway 863
Teenage Kids	Stereos	1959	Mink 022/Parkway 863
Teenage Love	Chaperones, Maria Mae & the	1961	Phantom 986
Teenage Love	Desires	NA	Unreleased
Teenage Love	Dreamers, Donnie & the	1961	Whale 505
Teenage Love	Hardin-Aires	1956	
Teenage Love	Orbits, Bobby & the	1959	Seeco 6030
Teenage Love	Scott Brothers	196?	

SONG	GROUP	YEAR	LABEL
Teenage Love	Teenagers, Frankie Lymon & the	1957	Gee 1032
Teenage Love	Universals (Philadelphia)	1957	Mark-X 7004
Teenage Love Affair	Chatters	1959	Viking 1001
Teen-Age Lover	Nitebeats	1959	Peach 718
Teenage Mambo	Gaylarks	1956	Music City 805
Teenage Memory	Bachelors (MGM)	1958	MGM 12668
Teenage Neighbor	Four Dates	1958	Chancellor 1027
Teenage Night Theme	Terrytones	1960	Wye 1003
	(with Claire Charles & Gayle Fortune)		
Teenage Paradise	Volumes	1963	Jubilee 5446
Teen-Age Partner	Superphonics	1961	Lindy 102
Teenage Plea	Collegiates	1960	RD Globe 009
Teenage Prayer	Creschendos	1960	Music City 839
Teenage Promise	Six Teens	1956	Flip 315
Teenage Rock	Classmates, Ronnie Jones & the	1957, 1963	End 1002/1125
Teenage Rock	Four Pips, Pop & the	1959	Mercedes 5001
Teenage Rock	Tru-Tones, Terry Clement & the	1959	Rocko 517
Teenage Romance	Crowns, Terry & the	1977	Harvey 103
Teen-Age Romeo	Perryman, Paul & group	1959	Duke 305
Teenage Rose	Decades	1980	Avenue D 2
Teenage Rose	Parakeets, Vic Donna & the	1957	Atlas 1071
Teenage Style	Runaways	NA	Teensound 1924
Teenage Sweetheart	Champs	NA	Chatam 350
Teenage Sweetheart	Mystics	NA	Chatam 350/351
Teenage Talk	Macree, Vincent & group	1957	Gametime 103
Teenage Tangle	Echoes, Jerry Starr & the	1959	Ron 321
Teenage Tears	Ly-Dells	1961	Master 111
Teenage Triangle	Baker, Bill & group	1962	Musicnote 119
Teenage Twister	Classmates	1963	Radar 2624
Teenage Vows Of Love	Dreamers (Yonkers, N.Y.)	1960	Goldisc 3015
Teenage Wedding	Fascinators (Brooklyn)	1995 (1959)	Capitol (unreleased)
Teenage Wedding Song	Chantiers, Rodney Baker & the	1961	Jan Ell 8
Teenage Wonderland	Four Mints	1958	NRC 003
Teenage Years	Bell Hops	1958	Barb 101/102
Teenager	De Vaurs	1956	D-Tone A-3
Teenager Susan	Youngsters	1958	Apt 25021
Teenagers Are Really Hep	Montagues	1995	Early Bird 002
Teenagers Dream	Lam, Tommy & group	1962	R 303
Teenagers Dream	Valentinos	1998	Clifton CD
Teenager's Dream	Deltars, Pearl & the	1961	Fury 1048
Teenager's Dream	Kodaks	1957	Fury 1007
Teenager's Dream (acappella)	Versailles	1957	Harlequin 401
Teenager's Letter Of Promises	Five Joys,	1961	Pink Clouds 333
	Juanita Rogers & Lynn Hollings & Mr. J's		
Teenager's Life	Visions	1960	Elgey 1003/Lost Nite 102 (61)
Teenager's Love	Delatones	1960	TNT 9028
Teenager's Love Letter	Rogers, Juanita (with the Five Joys)	1961	Pink Clouds 333
Teenager's Love Song	Pharaohs, Ricky & the	1956	Class 202
Teenagers Past	Moods	1959, 1960	Sarg 184/185
Teenager's Waltz	Rollers	1961	Liberty 55357
Teenie	Olenn, Johnny (with the Blockbusters)	1959	Personality 1002
Teenie, Teenie, Teenager	Sentimentals	1957	Mint 801/Checker 875
Teenie Weenie Bikini	Upbeats	1959	Joy 229
Teenie Weenie Little Bit	Collegians	1961	Winley 263
Teens	Ideals	1961	Paso 6402/Dusty Disc
Teeter Totter	Drivers	1960	Lin 1002
Teeter Totter Love	Marcels	1961, 1963	Colpix 196/694
Teeth & Tongue Will Get You Hung	Five Keys	NA	Detour LP 33-010
Tee-U-Eee	Little Four Quartet	NA	Southern 122
Telegram	Kelley, Charles (with the 3 Of Us Trio)	1958	York 3332
Telegram, The	Medallions	1955	Dootone 357
Telegraph	Dots, Tiny Dee & the	1963	Success 104
Telephone	Crystalaires	1990	Magic Carpet EP 512
Telephone Game	Spinners, Claudine Clark & the	1962	Chancellor 1124
Telephone Is Ringing, The	Rainbows	19??	

SONG	GROUP	YEAR	LABEL
Tell Daddy Baby	Renaults, Bobby Colquitt & the	1961	Colt 621/CJ 621
Tell Gina	Elgins (Bronx)	1963	Dot 16563
Tell Her	Destinations	1966	Cameo 422
Tell Her	Riffs	1964	Jamie 1296
Tell Her	Shadows	1953	Decca 48307
Tell Her	Sinceres	1966	Taurus 377
Tell Her	Velvets (New York)	1954	Red Robin 127/Pilgrim 710
Tell Her For Me	Johnson, Ernie & group	1961	Asnes 104
Tell Her I Love Her	Romancers	1965	Linda 119
Tell Her If I Could	Castells	1964	Warner Bros. 5486
Tell Her Now	Visions	1965	Co-Ed 598
Tell Her That I Love Her (acappella)	Five Jades (Bronx, N.Y.)	1975	Relic LP 107
Tell Her You Love Her	Carnegies, Alphonso Jones & the	1963	Brunswick 55230
Tell Him	Drew-Vels, Patti Drew & the	1963	Capitol 5055
Tell Him	Gainors	1961	Tally-Ho 105
Tell Him	Miller Sisters	1963	Riverside 4535
Tell Him Again	Elites	1960	Hi-Lite 106
Tell Him No	Jackson Brothers	1954	Atlantic 1034/Atco 6139 (59)
Tell It Like It Is	Cherlos	1956	Ultra D'Or 8
Tell It Like It Is	Nomads	1963	Josie 905
Tell It To Me Baby	Four Kings, Willie Mitchell & the	1958	Stomper Time 1160
Tell It To The Judge	Monotones	1959	Argo 5339
Tell Me	Accents (featuring Sandi)	1965	Challenge 9294
Tell Me	Arabians	NA	Mary Jane 1006
Tell Me	Bandits	NA	Jerden 773
Tell Me	Blends	1960	Talent 110/Skylark 108 (61)
Tell Me	Bond, Dave & group	1961	Khoury's 723
Tell Me	Crystals, Jesse & the	NA	Geno 12348
Tell Me	Daylighters	1966	Smash 2040
Tell Me	Fairlanes	1964	Radiant 101
Tell Me	Five C's	1954	United 172
Tell Me	Five Speeds	1959	Wiggie 131
Tell Me	Fortunes	1962	DRA 320
Tell Me	Four Kings, Sue Tornay & the	1961	Dore 594
Tell Me	Gassers	1956	Cash 1035
Tell Me	Gliders, Glen Pace & the	1960	ABC 10091
Tell Me	Heartbeats	1956	Rama (unreleased)
Tell Me	Idols	1961	Galaxie 77
Tell Me	Lovers	1958, 1963	Aladdin 3419/Lamp 2018 (58)/ Imperial 5960
Tell Me	Marcels	1963, 1977	Extra Play LP 10101
Tell Me	Master-Tones	1954	Bruce 111
Tell Me	Nutmegs	1972	Baby Grand 800
Tell Me	Rhythm Four, Joe Therrien & the	1961	Sentinel 8906
Tell Me	Sensation-Ivies	1961	Willow 23003
Tell Me	Sharmettes	1962	King 5686
Tell Me	Skyliners	1962	Viscount 104
Tell Me	Tantones	1957	Lamp 2008
Tell Me	Thomas, Jerry & group	1958	Khoury's 708
Tell Me	Three Chuckles	1956	X 0194/Vik 0194 (56)
Tell Me	Vows	1965	V.I.P. 25016
Tell Me	Wonders, Tony Allen & the	1958	Forward 601/Tampa 157 (58)
Tell Me (Are You Really Mine)	Playboys	1954	Cat 108
Tell Me Baby	Blazers, Rodney & the	1961	Dore 588
Tell Me Baby	Channels, Earl Lewis & the	1978	King Tut 173
Tell Me, Baby	Five Echos	1955	Vee Jay 129
Tell Me Baby	Honeycones	1959	Ember 1049
Tell Me, Baby	Hurricanes	1956	King 4898
Tell Me Baby	Idols, Little Joe Bonner & the	1955	B&S 1570
Tell Me Baby	Orbits	NA	Dooto 601
Tell Me Baby	Sounds	1959	Sarg 181
Tell Me, Darling	Gaylarks	1955	Music City 792
Tell Me Dear	Five Satins	1960	Ember 1070
Tell Me How Long	Flamingos	1960	End LP 307
Tell Me (How Was I To Know)	Guytones	1958	DeLuxe 6169

SONG	GROUP	YEAR	LABEL
Tell Me If You Know	Teen-Kings	1959	Bee 1115
Tell Me I'm The One For You	Dell Vikings	1957	Fee Bee 227
Tell Me Little Darling	Chestnuts, Bill Baker & the	1959	Elgin 007/008
Tell Me Little Girl	Spices	1958	Carlton 480
Tell Me Love	Dariens	NA	Carlson International 0027
Tell Me, Love	Teenchords, Lewis Lymon & the	1957	End 1007/Fury 1007 (57)
Tell Me My Darling	Miracletones	1958	Jam 5803
Tell Me My Love	Teenangels	1963	Sun 388
Tell Me Not To Go	Martin, Kenny & group	1959	Federal 12350
Tell Me Now	Accents (California)	1963	Mercury 72154
Tell Me Now	Bachelors, Dean Barlow & the	1955	Earl 102
Tell Me Now	Dolls	1958	Kangaroo 101
Tell Me Now	Four Jokers	1954	MGM 11815
Tell Me Now	New Group, Otis Williams & his	1955	DeLuxe 6088
Tell Me Now	Tingles	1961	Era 3040
Tell Me One More Time	Raves	1959	Swade 104
Tell Me, Pretty Baby	Empires	1955	Wing 90050
Tell Me Pretty Baby	Everglades	NA	Brenne 502
Tell Me Pretty Baby	Jades	1959	Christy 111
Tell Me Right Now	Careless Five	NA	Vitose 101
Tell Me So	Devilles	1959	Orbit 540
Tell Me So	Elbert, Donnie & group	1957	DeLuxe 6143
Tell Me So	Orioles, Sonny Til & the	1949, 1959	Jubilee 5005/5363
Tell Me Tell Me	George, Sunny & group	1958	MGM 12697
Tell Me, Tell Me Baby	Five Hearts	NA	Unreleased
Tell Me That You Love Me	Lewis, James & group	1958	Arrow 730
Tell Me That You Love Me	Three D's	1956	Pilgrim 719
Tell Me The Truth	Clips, Larry Birdsong & the	1956	Calvert 104
Tell Me, Thrill Me	Chanters (California)	1954	RPM 415
Tell Me To Go	Superiors	1965	Verve 10370
Tell Me Today	Cadillacs, Speedo & the	1960	Josie 876
Tell Me Today	Chipettes, Chip Allan & the	1963	Corsican 100
Tell Me What Is Wrong	Lincoln's Quintett	1958	Angle Tone 522
Tell Me (What's On Your Mind)	Accents (featuring Sandi)	1964	Commerce 5012/Challenge 1112 (64)/Challenge 59254 (64)
Tell Me What's On Your Mind	Blendors	1961	Decca 31284
Tell Me Who	Foster Brothers	1957	El-Bee 161
Tell Me Who	Members, Wayne Marshall & the	1965	
Tell Me Why	Allumns	1978	Crystal Ball 118
Tell Me Why	Ardees, Phil Alan & the	NA	Ko Co Bo 1010
Tell Me Why	Armen, Mickey & group	1958	Peek-A-Boo 1001
Tell Me Why	Belairs	1958	X-Tra 113/Times Square 23 (63)/Relic 536 (65)
Tell Me Why	Belmonts	1961	Surprise 1000/Sabrina 500 (61)
Tell Me Why	Blues Busters	1962	Capitol 4895
Tell Me Why	Con Chords, Bob Brady & the	1966	Chariot 100
Tell Me Why	Dukes (California)	1956	Imperial 5385 (unreleased)
Tell Me Why	Dwellers	1963	Howard 503
Tell Me Why	Falcons (Cash)	1955	Cash 1002
Tell Me Why	Five Chances	1957	Federal 12303
Tell Me Why	Four Bel-Aires	1958	X-Tra 113
Tell Me Why	Knight, Marie & group	1956	Wing 90069
Tell Me Why	Montereys, Dean Barlow & the	1957	Onyx 517
Tell Me Why	Paramounts	1982	Avenue D7
Tell Me Why	Phantoms, Vernon Green & the	1956	Specialty unreleased
Tell Me Why	Rob-Roys, Norman Fox & the	1957	Back Beat 501
Tell Me Why	Rockers	1956	Carter 3029
Tell Me Why	Sunbeams	1955	Herald 451
Tell Me Why	Swallows (Maryland)	1952	King 4515
Tell Me Why	Toppers (Stacy)	1962	Stacy 927
Tell Me Why	Walcoes	1959	Drum 011
Tell Me Why (That's What I Want To Know)	Barnes, Johnny & group	1961	Flippin' 105
Tell Me (Will You Ever Be Mine)	Cubans (Davie Little Caesar Johnson)	1958	Flash 133
Tell Me Yes	Corals	1962	Cheer 1001

SONG	GROUP	YEAR	LABEL
Tell Me You Care	Five Royales	1959	King 5237
Tell Me You Care	Lamplighters	1953	Federal 12176
Tell Me You Care	Nitelites, Nickie & the	1959	Brunswick 55155
Tell Me You Love Me	Five Chancellors	1957	Port 5000
Tell Me You Love Me	Five Keys	NA	Popular Request 2001
Tell Me You Love Me	Flairs	1953	Flair 1019
Tell Me You Love Me	Gaytunes	1996	Joyce (unreleased)/Relic CD 7118
Tell Me You Love Me	Hollywood Bluejays	1953	Recorded In Hollywood 396
Tell Me You Love Me	Keynotes	1989	Relic LP 5080
Tell Me You're Mine	Five Hollywood Blue Jays	1952	Recorded In Hollywood 396
Tell Me You're Mine	Five Jets	1954	DeLuxe 6058
Tell Me You're Mine	Flairs	1963	Crown LP 5356
Tell Me You're Mine	Velveteers	1956	Spitfire 15
Tell Me You're Mine	Visions	1961	Big Top 3092
Tell My Baby	Sparrows	1953	Jay-Dee 783
Tell Tale Friends	Riffs	1965	Old Town 1179
Tell The Angels	Uniques	1958	End 1012
Tell The Truth	Diamonds	1960	Mercury 71586
Tell The Truth	Five Royales	1958	King 5141
Tell The Truth	Legends	1962	Jamie 1228
Tell The Truth	Nightriders	1956	Sound 128
Tell The World	Concords, Tony Colton & the	1963	Roulette 4475
Tell The World	Dells	1955	Vee Jay 134
Tell The World	Platters	1954, 1955	Federal 12188/12250
Tell The World I Do	Ebb Tides, Nino & the	1959	Recorte 409
Tell Them	Midnighters	1954	Federal 12202
Tell Them About It	Marcels	1962	Colpix (unreleased)
Tell Them All About It	Marcels	1977	Pop N' Rock LP
Tell This Lonely Heart Goodbye	Shadows	1961	Dottie 1006
Tell Ya What	Five Hearts (Music City)	1960	Music City 833
Teller Of Fortune	Dootones	1955	Dootone 366
Tell-Tale Kisses	Dolphins	1960	Shad 5020
Temptation	Drifters (1959-forward)	1965	Atlantic LP 8113
Temptation	Legends	1962	Ermine 45
Temptation	Platters	NA	Mercury EP 3345
Temptation	Temptations (New Jersey)	1958	Savoy (unreleased)
Temptation Of My Heart	Valiants, Billy Storm & the	1969, 1995	Famous LP 504
Temptations	Temptations (Parkway)	1959	Parkway 803
Tempting	Moonglows	1954	Chess 1581
Ten Cats Down	Miller Sisters	1956	Sun 255
Ten Commandments	Brooklyn Allstars	1974	Jewell 236
Ten Commandments Of Love, The	Five Diamonds	1955	Treat 501
Ten Commandments Of Love, The	Five Fashions	1964	Catamount 102
Ten Commandments Of Love, The	Moonglows	1964, 1976	Lana 135
Ten Commandments Of Love, The	Moonglows, Harvey & the	1958	Chess 1705
Ten Commandments Of Love, The	Neville Brothers	NA	N/A
Ten Commandments Of Love, The	Romans, Little Caesar & the	1961	Del-Fi 4170
Ten Commandments Of Love (acappella), The	Shadows	1975	Relic LP 102
Ten Days In Jail	Robins	1953	RCA 5489
10 Days With Brenda	Prophets, Ronnie Dio & the	1967	Parkway 143
Ten Lonely Guys	Broken Hearts	1962	Diamond 123
Ten Miles From Nowhere	Citations	1963	Vangee 301/Fraternity 910 (63)/ Fraternity 992 (67)
Ten Million Tears	Di Sentri, Turner	1961	Topix 6001
Ten Minutes To Midnight	Quarter Notes	1957	DeLuxe 6129
Ten Pairs Of Shoes	Cleftones	1957	Gee 1038
Ten Past Midnight	Du Droppers	1953	Unreleased
Ten Questions	Renaults	1963	Chicory 160
Ten Steps To Love	Electras	1961	Infinity 012/Constellation
Ten Steps To Love	Freedoms	1964	Constellation 105
Ten Times Blue	Fleetwoods	1964	Dolton 97
Ten Ways	First Platoon	1963	SPQR 3303
Tenants' Blues, The	Impossibles	1961	RMP 508
Tend To Business	Rivingtons	1966	Columbia 43581

SONG	GROUP	YEAR	LABEL
Tender Beloved	McGee, Al & group	1961	Donna 1348
Tender Darling	Val-Tones	1955	DeLuxe 6084
Tender Love	Chandeliers	1973	Relic LP 5012
Tender Love	King Bees	1959	Noble 715
Tender Love	Pageants	NA	Club
Tender Love	Peacocks	1958	Noble 711
Tender Passion	Diablos	1984	Fortune LP 8016
Tender Touch	Pharaos	1960	Donna 1327
Tender Words	Blue Belles, Patti LaBelle & the	1966	Atlantic 2390
Tender Years	Beau-Marks	1962	Rust 5050
Tender Years	Keens, Rick & the	1962	Le Cam 958/Jamie 1219
Tenderly	Dominoes	1954	King 1342
Tenderly	Flamingos	1960	End LP 308
Tenderly	Henderson, Floyd & group	1959	Triangle 51315
Tennessee	Todds	1961	Todd 1064
Tennessee Rock And Roll	Goofers	1956	Coral 61650
Tennessee Slim	Spiders	1960	Imperial 5714
Tennessee Waltz	Counts, Bobby Comstock & the	1959	Blaze 349
Tennessee Waltz	Gleams, Berlin Perry & the	1959	Ribbon 6902
Terry	Chimes, Leigh Bell & the	1961	Rust 5031
Test Of Love	Coeds, Johnny Maestro with the	1961	Coed 552
Texas	Bachelors, Dean Barlow & the	1955	Excel 106
Texas Stomp	Little, Horace & group	1962	Ascot 2102
Thank Heaven	Baker, Bill & Group	1960	Vim
Thank Heaven For Little Girls	Mason, Peter & group	1960	Lawn 105
Thank The Lord, Thank The Lord	Orioles, Sonny Til & the	1954	Jubilee 5154
Thank You	Encores	1957	Bow 302
Thank You And Goodnight	Angels (New Jersey)	1963	Smash 1854
Thank You And Goodnight	Swisher, Debra & group	1966	Boom 60001
Thank You Baby	Shirelles	1964	Scepter 1278
Thank You Mister Ballard (For Creating The Twist)	Escos	1961	Federal 12445
Thank You Mister Moon	Marionettes, Chris Allen & the	1959	Hollywood 1908
Thank You Mother	Arabians, Edward Hamilton & the	NA	Mary Jane 1007/1008
Thank You Mr. Moon	Blue Sonnets	1963	Columbia 42793
Thank You Pretty Lady	Autumns	1981	BAB 128
Thanks For The Memories	Covinas	NA	Hilton 3751
Thanks, Mr. Dee-Jay	Baby Dolls	1961	Maske 701
That Ain't All	Rexettes, Larry & the	NA	Zorro 420
That American Dance	Belmonts	1961	Sabina 502
That Angel Is You	Jumpin' Tones	1964	Raven 8005
That Background Sound	Holidays, Buddy Sheppard & the	1963	Sabina 510
That Big Old Moon	Canadian Meteors, Buddy Burke & the	1957	Bullseye 1002
That Boy Is Messin' Up My Mind	Orchids	1964	Columbia 42913
That Boy John	Raindrops	1963	Jubilee 5466
That Boy Of Mine	Sparkels	1964	Old Town 1160
That Certain Kind	Statens	1961	Mark-X 8011
That Certain One	Fydells	1959	Camelia 100
That Comes With Love	Chevrons	1959	Brent 7000
That Crazy Feeling	Rogers, Kenneth & group	1958	Carlton 454
That Crazy Little House	Lamarr, Gene (with the Blue Flames)	1958	Spry 113
That Crazy Little House On The Hill	Blue Flames	1961	Spry 113
That Day	Rockers, Rick Randle & the	1958	Arc 4445
That Day Will Never Come	Parktowns	1961	Crimson 1006
That Dubonnet Wine	Mellomoods	1954	Recorded In Hollywood 399
That Feeling	Bradford Boys	1955	Rainbow 307
That Girl	Parliaments, Freddie & the	1959	Twirl 1003
That Girl	Reactions	1965	Mutual 509
That Girl Of Mine	Citations	1965	MGM 13373
That Girl Of Mine	Persians	1963	Sir Rah 501
That House On The Hill	Midnighters	1955	Federal 12240
That I Love	Aztecs, Billy Thorpe & the	1965	GNP Crescendo 340
That Is Rock 'n' Roll	Baker, Bill (Satins)	1998	Clifton CD 3014 (recorded in 1983)
That Is Rock 'n' Roll	Coasters	1959	Atco 6141
That Is Why (I Love You)	Javalons	1961	Tru-Eko 6901/Pip 6902

SONG	GROUP	YEAR	LABEL
That Kiss You Gave Me	Four Fellows (Brooklyn - Nestor)	1955	Nestor 27
That Lady Of Mine	Infernos	1980	BAB 126
That Lil' Ole Lovemaker Me	Imperials, Little Anthony & the	1963	Roulette 4379
That Little Girl Was Mine	Embers, Larry Lee & the	1990	Relic LP 5085
That Long Lost Baby	Hudson, Eddie & group	1958	Excello 2135
That Look In Your Eye	Jackaels, J. J. Jackson & the	1959	Storm 501
That Look In Your Eye	Strollers	1960	Dart 1017
That Love Affair	Five Delights	1959	Abel 228
That Love Is You	Flamingos	1957, 1958	Decca (unreleased)/End 1035
That Love Was Magic	Street Corner Symphony	1975	Bang 722
That Low Down Move	Midnighters, Hank Ballard & the	1963	King 5719
That Lucky Old Sun	Adorations	1971	Dreamtone 200
That Lucky Old Sun	Catalinas	1979	Crystal Ball 135
That Lucky Old Sun	Delights	1962	Golden Crest 574
That Lucky Old Sun	Ecstasies	1962	Amy 853
That Lucky Old Sun	Fabulous Marcels	1975	St. Clair 13711
That Lucky Old Sun	Floridians	1961	ABC 10185
That Lucky Old Sun	Lullabies, Tommy Tucker & the	1975	N/A
That Lucky Old Sun	Romancers	1961	Palette 5085
That Lucky Old Sun	Tangents	1960	Fresh 2274
That Lucky Old Sun	Velvets (Texas)	1961	Monument 435
That Man Paul	Four Young Men	1961	Dore 621
That My Man	Skylighters	NA	Emjay 6152
That Night	Packards	1956	Decca (unreleased)
That Old Black Magic	Attitudes	1967	Times Square 110
That Old Black Magic	Marcels	1963	Colpix 683
That Old Black Magic	Nacks, Nicky & the	1962	Barry 108
That Old Black Magic	Robins	1957	Whippet 203
That Old Black Magic	Tymes	1964	Parkway LP 7032
That Old Feeling	Del-Chords, Donnie & the	1963	Taurus 361
That Old Feeling	Lambert, Rudy (with the Lyrics)	1958	Rhythm 128
That Old Feeling	York, Patti (with the Sentimentals)	1958	Mint 806
That Old Gang Of Mine	Ravens	1951	Okeh 6825
That Other Guy	Little Ellen & group	1961	Smash 1724
That Same Old Feeling	Volumes	1966	Impact 1017
That Same Old Song	Fabulous Dinos	1962	Musicor 1025
That Thing Called A Girl	Four Coachmen	1960	Adonis A-102
That Was Me	Fiestas	1959	Old Town 1074
That Was My Girl	Pebbles	1965	Eiffel 2085
That Was The Time	Five Discs	1962	Cheer 1000
That Was Yesterday	Lawrence, Bernie & group	1961	United Artists 388
That' What You Are	Hawks	1954	Imperial 5317
That Woman	Midnighters	1953, 1955	Federal 12177/12230
That Wonderful Secret Of Love	Six Teens	1960	Flip 350
That Would Be So Good	Preludes	1962	Octavia 8008
That You Love Me	Impressions	1960	Abner 1034
That'll Be The Day	Ravens	1957	Argo 5276/Checker 871
That'll Get It	Imps	1961	Do-Ra-Mi 1414
That'll Make It Nice	Manhattans, Eli Price & the	1959	Dooto 445
That's A Bad Thing To Know	Bobbettes	1971	Mayhew 712297/712298
That's A Plenty	Rhythmettes	1958	Brunswick 55050
That's A Promise	Bryant, Helen & group	1961	Fury 1042
That's A Teenage Girl	Dale, Alan & group	1961	Sinclair 1003
That's A Teen-Age Love	Teen-Kings	1959	Bee 1115
That's All	Casanovas	1955	Apollo 471
That's All	Conservatives	1968	Ebonic Sound 6569
That's All	Ebb-Tones	1956	Crest 1016
That's All	Mystics	NA	Jenny Lynn 101
That's All	Pacesetters	1962	Wink 1008
That's All I Ask Of You	Angels (New Jersey)	1962	Caprice 112
(That's) All I Need	Cadillacs	1956	Josie 805
That's All I Need	Du Droppers	1955	Groove EP EGA-5
That's All I Need	Sandmen, Lincoln Chase & the	1955	Columbia 40475
That's All I Need	Turner, Ike & group	1959	Sue 722
That's All I Need To Know	Cooke, Sam & group	1958	Specialty 627

SONG	GROUP	YEAR	LABEL
That's All I Want	Extremes (with Bobby Sanders)	1962	Paro 733
That's All I Want	Satellites, Bobby Day & the	1959	Class 245
That's All I Want From You	Artis, Ray & group	1961	A 111
That's All I Want From You	Darnell, Larry & group	1955	Savoy 1151
That's All I Want From You	Silva-Tones	1957	Monarch 5281/Argo 5281 (57)
That's All I Want From You	Trophies	1962	Challenge 9170
That's All I Want To Do	Hi-Tones	1958	Skyline 701
That's All I Want To Do	Hitones, Leonard Wayne & the	1964	Andre 701
That's All I Want Tonight	Paramours	1962	Moonglow 214
That's All I'll Ever Need	Townsmen (Louie Lymon)	1963	PJ 1340/1341
That's All I'm Asking Of You	Rainbeaus	1960	World Pacific 810
That's All It Took	Blue Jays (Venice, Calif.)	1987	Relic LP 5064
That's All Over Baby	Pentagons	1986	True Gems LP
That's All Right	Classmates, Dwain Louis & the	NA	Carole 611
That's All Right	Invictors	1963	TPE 8221
That's All Right	Velons	1968	BJM 6569
That's All Right	Vendors	1963	Victorio 128
That's All She Left Me	Crescents	1965	Watch 1902
That's All, That's All, That's All	Dappers (New York)	1956	Groove 0156
That's Alright	Egyptians	1962	Danae 1002
That's Alright	Silks, Charles McCullough & the	1962	Dooto 465
That's Alright With Me	Montels	1956	Universal 101
That's Bad	Dynamics	1963	Emjay 1928
That's Bad	Metronomes, Gene Moore & the	1953	Specialty 472
That's Enough	Spiders	1955	Imperial 5331
That's Enough For Me	McPhatter, Clyde (with the Cookies & the Cues)	1958	Atlantic 1170
That's How I Feel	Bop Shop	NA	Horizon Ent. Ltd.
That's How I Feel	Students (Ohio)	1958	Note 10019/Checker 1004 (62)
That's How I Feel	Valentines	1960	King 5433
That's How I Feel About You	Taylor, Andrew & group	1961	Gone 5109
That's How I Feel (acappella)	Royal Counts	1972	Catamount 1958
That's How I Go For You	Butler, Cliff & group	1958	Nasco 6010
That's How I Need You	Belmonts, Dion & the	1962	Laurie LP 2016/Ace LP 155
That's How It Goes	Breakaways	1964	Cameo 323
That's How It Goes	Jesters	1961	Winley 248
That's How Little Girls Get Boys	Casanovas, Little Romeo & the	1965	Ascot 2192
That's How Love Goes	Capris (New York)	1982	Ambient Sound LP FZ-37714
That's How Much I Need You	Penguins	1957	Dooto 428
That's How We'll Be	Kartels, Wilbert Lombard & the	1957	Deb 1002
That's It	Chums, Mary Eustace & the	NA	Apt 25009
That's It	Royals	1953	Federal 12160
That's It Man	Valentines	1960	King 5338
That's Life	Escos	1963	Federal 12493
That's Life	Mellards	1956	Ballad 1016
That's Life (That's Tough)	Angels, Gabriel & the	1959, 1962	Casino 107/Swan 4118 (62)/Itzy 7 (62)
That's Love	Rob-Roys, Norman Fox & the	1988	Back Beat 500
That's Love	True Tones	1965	Soulville/Josie 950 (65)/Josie 1003 (69)
That's Love	Uniques	1959	World Pacific 808
That's Me	Starlings	1959	World Pacific 809
That's My Baby	Ballads (Klik)	1972	Klik 1021
That's My Baby	Five Echoes	1971	Sabre 111
That's My Baby	Suns	1964	Times Square 32/Relic 541 (65)
That's My Baby (acappella)	Universals (Philadelphia)	1973	Relic LP 5006
That's My Business	Sharell, Jerry & group	1961	Alanna 560
That's My Desire	Alaimo, Chuck	1957	MGM 12449
That's My Desire	Belmonts, Dion & the	1960	Laurie 3044
That's My Desire	Butanes	1961	Enrica 1007
That's My Desire	Channels, Earl Lewis & the	1957	Gone 5012
That's My Desire	Chessmen	1965	Relic 1017
That's My Desire	Del-Mars	1963	ABC 10426
That's My Desire	Emery's	1977	Clifton 17
That's My Desire	Exotics	1961	Coral 62268
That's My Desire	Flamingos	1953	Chance 1140
That's My Desire	Golden Arrow Quartet	NA	Continental 6048

SONG	GROUP	YEAR	LABEL
That's My Desire	Sensations, Yvonne Baker & the	1962	Argo 5412
That's My Desire	Spiders	1957	Imperial 5423
That's My Desire	Sunny Lads	1959	Jax 103
That's My Desire	Tren-Dells	1965	Boss 9921
That's My Desire (acappella)	Five Jades (Bronx, N.Y.)	1975	Relic LP 107
That's My Girl	Elgins, De Jan & the	1960, 1967	Lessie 99/Times Square 112
That's My Girl	Heartspinners, Dino & the	1972, 1976	Bim Bam Boom 108/Barrier 103
That's My Girl	Marcel, Vic & group	1963	Don-But 17349
That's My Girl	Subway Serenade	1980	Clifton 53
That's My Kind Of Love	Anastasia & group	1960	Laurie 3066
That's Right	Bell Notes	1959	Time 1013
That's Right	Five Keys	1956	Capitol 3502
That's The Game To Play	Idols	1958	Redd-E 1017
That's The Girl I Married	Sha-Weez, Big Boy Myles & the	1955	Specialty 564
That's The Kind Of Love	Mystics	1964	Teako 370
That's The Way	Capri, Tony & group	1961	Liban 1005
That's The Way	Casinos	1964	Terry 116/Airtown 886
That's The Way	Classics (Brooklyn)	1961	Dart 1038/Mercury 71829 (61)
That's The Way	Contenders	1963	Saxony 1001
That's The Way	Matadors, Tommy Liss & the	1993	Saxony 1001
That's The Way	Values	1962	Invicta 1002
That's The Way I Feel	Marquees, Terry Brown & the	1960	Jo-Ann 128
That's The Way I Feel	Mascots	1960	King 5435
That's The Way I Feel	Tornados	1956	Chess (unreleased)
That's The Way I Like It	Queens, Shirley Gunter & the	1955	Flair 1070
That's The Way I Want To Go	Hillsiders, Bobby Angel & the	1961	Rhum 101
That's The Way It Goes	Ecstasies	1979	U.G.H.A. 05
That's The Way It Goes	Five Dollars	1960	Fortune 854
That's The Way It Goes	Five Jades (Bronx, N.Y.)	1984	Clifton 73
That's The Way It Goes	Harptones	1956. 1974	Rama 203
That's The Way It Goes	Manhattan Transfer	1984	Atlantic 89594
That's The Way It Goes (acappella)	Five Jades (Bronx, N.Y.)	1975	Relic LP 107
That's The Way It'll Be	Glenwoods	1960	Jubilee 5402
That's The Way It's Gonna Be	Shields	1958	Tender 513/Dot 15805 (58)
That's The Way It's Got To Be	Emeralds (St. Louis)	1959	Bobbin 107
That's The Way The Cookie Crumbles	Nortones	1959	Warner Bros. 5065
That's The Way To My Heart	Valiants (Los Angeles)	1959	N/A
That's The Way To Win My Heart	Spiders	1956	Imperial 5405
That's The Way We Love	Paramours	1961	Smash 1701
That's Tough	Fabulous Winds, Joe Boot & the	1958	Celestial 111
That's What Boys Are Made For	Bees, Honey & the	NA	Bell 217
That's What He Said	Monograms	1960	Safire 102
That's What I Aim To Do	Falcons (Detroit)	1960	Flick 008
That's What I Call A Good Time	Five Spenders	1960	Versatile 113
That's What I Call A Good Time	Regents	1960	Kayo 101
That's What I Call Love	Mondellos	1957	Rhythm 106
That's What I Call Love	Mondellos, Rudy Lambert & the	1958	Rhythm 114
That's What I Like	Allen Trio	1955	Original 1005
That's What I Like	Snap Shots	1963	Federal 12496
That's What I Want	R-Dells	1962	Gone 5128
That's What I Will Be	Clovers, Buddy Bailey & the	1963	Porwin 1004
That's What I'm Gonna Do	Crowns, Arthur Lee Maye & the	1985	Relic LP 5052
That's What It's Like	Jokers, Jivin' Gene & the	1961	Mercury 71751
That's What Love Can Do	Velons	1968	BJM 6569
That's What Makes Her Boss	Hustlers	1965	Fascination 6570
(That's What Sends Men To The) Bowery	Delrons, Reperata & the	1969	Kapp 989
That's What The Good Book Says	Robbins	1951	Modern 807
That's What They Put Erasers On Pencils For	Four Jewels	1964	Checker 1069
That's What They Say	Quintones, Pat Foster & the	1960	Lee 1114
That's What They Want	Upstarts, Jerry McCain & the	1956	Excello 2068
That's What You Do To Me	Laddins	1962, 1974	Groove 4-5/Relic LP 5018
That's What You Do To Me	Tempos	1957	Kapp 178
That's What You Gotta Do	Sensations	1963	Junior 1005

SONG	GROUP	YEAR	LABEL
That's What You Mean To Me	Ross, Johnny & group	1958	Corvette
That's What You Think	Pemberton, Jimmy (with the Chantels)	1959	End 1059/Mark-X 8002 (59)
That's What You're Doing To Me	Capris (Philadelphia)	1954	Gotham 7304/ 20th Century 7304 (57)
That's What You're Doing To Me	Diablos	1984	Fortune LP 8016
That's What You're Doing To Me	Dominoes	1951	Federal 12059
That's What You're Doing To Me	Five Keys	1961	King 5446
That's What You're Doing To Me	Renowns, Richie & the	1963	Streke 247
That's What You've Gotta Do	Sensations	1963	Junior 988/Tollie 9009 (64)
That's What's Happening	Pictures, C.L. & the	1963	Dunes 2023
That's When I Fell In Love	Five Sounds	1960	Baritone 940/941
That's When the Good Lord Will Smile	Orioles, Sonny Til & the	1955	Jubilee 5189
That's When You Know You're Growing Old	Dominoes	1961	King 5463
That's When Your Heartaches Began	Buddies, Billy Bunn & the	1952	RCA 4657
That's When Your Heartaches Begin	Masquerades	NA	Unreleased
That's Where I Belong	Crystals (Metro)	1959	Metro 20026
That's Where The Difference Lies	Stevens, Jimmy (with the Safaris)	1963	Valiant 6033
That's Why	Cadillacs	1960	Josie 883
That's Why I Cry	Castaleers	1960	Planet 44/Donna 1349 (61)
That's Why I Dream	Keystoners	1984	Starbound 502
That's Why I Dream	Sensational	1958	Mida 106
That's Why I Love You	Flamingos	1960	End 1085
That's Why I Love You	Magic Touch	1990	Starlight 73
That's Why I Love You	Romancers	1966	Linda 124
That's Why (I Love You So)	Del Vikings	1958	Mercury LP 30353
That's Why I Pray	Four Fellows (Brooklyn - Ad Lib)	1962	Ad Lib 0208
That's Why I'm Crying	Ivy League	1965	Cameo 365
That's Why You're Happy	Chantels	1963	Ludix 106
That's You, That's Me	Petty, Eddie ¡Princeî & group	1957	Guest 1003
That's Your Mistake	Charms, Otis Williams & the	1956	DeLuxe 6091
(The Sun Will) Shine Again	Adelphis	1958	Rim 2022
Thelesa	Hollywood Saxons	1975	Action Pac 2023 EP
Them Of American Beetles	American Beetles	1964	BYP 1001
Them There Eyes	Chic-Chocs	1961	Broadway 103
Them There Eyes	Keystoners	1992	Starbound 516
Them There Eyes	Teenchords, Lewis Lymon & the	1958	Juanita 101
Theme For A Broken Heart	Immortals	1961	Laurie 3099
Theme From Sleeping Moondog	Pageants	1961	Paxley 753
Then	Aladdins	1962	Prism 6001
Then He Kissed Me	Crystals (Brooklyn)	1963	Philles 115
Then He Starts To Cry	Accents (featuring Sandi)	1964	Charter 1017
Then I Got Everything	Pirates, Johnny Kidd & the	1963	Capitol 5065
Then I Know	Vondells	1964	Marvello 5005
Then I Walked Away	Belmonts	1965	United Artists 904
Then I'll Be Home	Chants	1964	Interphon 7703
Then I'll Be Tired Of You	DiMucci, Dion (with the Del Satins)	1963	Laurie 3225
Then I'll Be Tired Of You	Holidays	1961	Robbee 107
Then I'll Know	Lee, Curtis (with the Halos)	1960, 1961	Dunes 801/2003
Then I'll Know	Pictures, C.L. & the	1963	Cadette 8005
Then I'll Still Love You	Sierras	1963	Cham 101/Dot 16569 (63)
Then (I'll Stop Loving You)	Embers, Jeff Milner & the	1959	Dale 114
Then You Can Tell Me Goodbye	Emery's	1977	Clifton 19
Then You Can Tell Me Goodbye	Stormy Weather	1976	Catamount 133
There Ain't No Bears In The Forest	Four Deals	1950	Capitol 1313
There Ain't No Use Beggin'	Robins	1950	Savoy 738
There Are So Many Ways	Hearts (Bronx, N.Y.)	1956	J&S 1002/1003
There But For Her Go I	Capri Sisters	1960	ABC 10158
There Comes A Time	Kestrels	1960	Laurie 3053
There Comes A Time	Persianettes, Timmy & the	1963	Olympia 100
There Goes A Fool	Gay-Tunes	1974	Broadcast 1100
There Goes (A Pretty Girl)	Enchanters (Detroit)	1957, 1967	Coral 61832/65610
There Goes A Young Love	Crawford, Peter & group	1961	Sandy
There Goes My Baby	Drifters (1959-forward)	1959	Atlantic 2025
There Goes My Baby (acappella)	Chessmen	1975	Relic LP 106

SONG	GROUP	YEAR	LABEL
There Goes My First Love	Drifters (1959-forward)	1975	Bell (UK) 1433
There Goes My Girl	Five Chancellors	1957	Port 5000
There Goes My Heart	Roomates	1961	Valmor LP 78/Valmor LP 789 (62)/ Relic LP 5041
There Goes My Heart Again	Holidays, Tony & the	1959	ABC 10029/ABC 10295 (62)
There Goes My Heart To You	Cardinals	1955	Atlantic 1079
There Goes My Love	Bop Shop	1998	Clifton CD (recorded in 1989)
There Goes My Love	Fantastics	1959	RCA 7572
There Goes My Love	Oasis	1979	Story Untold 502
There Goes That Train	Genies	1960	Warwick 573
There Goes That Train	Watts, Maymie & group	1955	Groove 0103
There Goes The Boy	Lydells	1959	Pam 103/Parkway 897 (64)
There Goes The Girl I Love	Creations	1956	Lido 501/Tip Top 501 (56)
There Goes The Train	Trebelaires	1955	Nestor 16
There He Goes	Deltairs	1973	Vintage 1005
There He Goes	Deltears	NA	Ray-Born 132/133
There He Is At My Door	Vells	1962	Mel-O-Dy 103
There I Go	Dell Vikings	1958/1973	Mercury LP 30353/Luniverse 114
There I Go Again	Desires	1962	Smash 1763
There In The Moonlight	Decals	1975	Monogram 103
There In The Night	El Dorados	1956	Vee Jay 211
There Is A Beauty	Spindles, Frankie & the	1968	Roc-Ker 575
There Is A Boy	Gray, Maureen & group	1961	Chancellor 1100
There Is A Girl	Larks (Philadelphia)	1961	Sheryl 338
There Is A Great Big Moon	Sliders	1961	Chevron 012/Chevron 750
There Is Love	Hodges, Charles (with the Fi-Tones)	1965	Alto 2016
There Is Love	Johnny (with the Kids)	1962	Luck 101
There Is Love In You	Prisonaires	1954	Sun 207
There Is No Greater Love	Wanderers	1962	Cub 9109/MGM 13082 (62)
There Is No Love At All	Hearts (Bronx, N.Y.)	1957	J&S 4571/4572
There Is No Love For Me	Barnes, Johnny & group	1961	Flippin' 105
There Is No Right Way To Do Me Wrong	Miller Sisters	1955	Sun 230
There Is Nothin' Like A Dame	Impalas (20th C. Fox)	1963, 1982	20th Fox 428
There Is Something On Your Mind	Hollywood Flames	1959	Ebb 158
There Is Time	Heartbreakers (Washington, D.C.)	1952	RCA 4869
There! I've Said It Again	Gardner, Don & group	1957	DeLuxe 6155
There Must Be A Reason	Brooktones	1958	Coed 502
There Must Be A Reason	Five Flames	1959	Federal 12348
There Must Be A Way	Cabarettes	1963	Saxony 1002
There Once Was A Time	Laddins	1961	Theatre 111
There Ought To Be A Law (Against Breaking A Heart)	Five Keys	1953	Aladdin 3175
There Oughta Be A Law	Charmanes, Yolanda & the	NA	Smash 1777
There She Goes	Bell Tones	1959	Clock 71889/Mercury 71889 (61)
There She Goes	Belltones (Mercury)	1961	Mercury 71889
There She Goes	Cleftones	1961	Gee 1079
There She Goes (She's Walking)	Paramours	1962	Moonglow 214
There Stands My Love	Tune Weavers	1958	Casa Grande 4040
There Stands The Glass	Shadows	1958	Delta 1509
There They Go	Delfonics	1962	Fling 727
There They Go	Delmonicos	1963	Aku 6318
There Was A Party	Epps, Arthur & group	1961	Spark 900
There Was A Time (acappella)	Count Five	1975	Relic LP 103
There Were Others	Stylers	1954	Kicks 2
There Will Always Be	Darchaes, Ray & the	1962	Buzzy 202
There Will Come A Day	Jades	1964	Port 70042
There Will Come A Time	Five Scalders	1956	Drummond 3000/Sugarhill 3000 (56)
There You Go	McPhatter, Clyde (with the Drifters)	1959	Atlantic 2038
There'll Always Be A Christmas	Regals	1954	MGM 11869
There'll Be No Goodbye	Five Delights	1958	Newport 7002/Unart 2003 (58)
There'll Be No Next Time	Visions	1961	Brunswick 55206
There'll Be No One Else But You	Embers	1954	Columbia 40287
There'll Be No Sorrow	Quin-Tones (Pennsylvania)	1958	Hunt 322 (58)
There'll Come A Time	Vails	1960	Belmont 4004

SONG	GROUP	YEAR	LABEL
There's A Boat Leaving Soon For New York	Skylarks	1957	Verve 10082
There's A Boy	Terry, Maureen & group	1964	Maria 102
There's A Dance Goin' On	Willows	1961	Four Star 1753
There's A Fool Born Every Day	Five Superiors	1962	Garpax 44170
There's A Girl	Cruisers	1958, 1981	Zebra 119
There's A Girl	Dovells	1966	MGM 13628
There's A Girl	Meadowlarks, Don Julian & the	1959	Original Sound 12
There's A Girl Down The Way	Notations, Augie Rios & the	1963	Shelley 181
There's A Girl Down The Way	Overtones	1967	Ajax 175
There's A Girl In My Heart	Semitones, Ron Ricky & the	NA	Semitone 1
There's A Little Bit Of Heaven	Unbelievables	1965	Era 3155
There's A Long Long Trail	Aquatones	1959	Fargo 1015
There's A Love	Del Rios	1962	Stax 125
There's A Love	Gentrys	1967	MGM 13690
There's A Moon Out Again	Capris (New York)	1982	Ambient Sound 02697
There's A Moon Out Tonight	Capris (New York)	1958	Planet 1010/1011/Old Town 1094 (60)/ Lost Nite 101 (60)/Trommers 101 (60)
There's A Moon Out Tonight	Streetcorner Serenade	1989	Starlight 65
There's A Reason	Dandevilles	1959	Guyden 2014
There's A Rumor	Cashmeres (Philadelphia)	1955	Mercury 70679
There's A Small Hotel	Baby Dolls	NA	Parnaso 227
There's A Time And Place For Everything	Santells	1964	Courier 103
There's A Wall Between Us	Embraceables	1962	Dover 4100
There's Always Something There To Remind Me	Blue Belles, Patti LaBelle & the	1966	Atlantic 2390
There's Been A Change	King Krooners	1958	Unreleased
There's Going To Be A Way	Royal Knights	NA	Radio City 1001
There's Going To Be An Angel	Creators	1961	Time 1038
There's Lots More	Gari, Frank & group	1961	Crusade 1024
There's No Forgetting You	Chantels	1965	TCF-Arrawak 123
There's No Forgetting You	Pearls	NA	Astor 1005
There's No Moon Out Tonight	Themes	1964	Stork 001
There's No One But You	Orioles, Sonny Til & the	1953	Jubilee 5134
There's No One But You	Strollers	1961	Carlton 546
There's No One For Me	Bee Jay & group	1961	Clock 1743
There's No One Like My Love	Gems (Pat)	1961	Pat 101
There's No Other (Like My Baby)	Crystals (Brooklyn)	1961	Philles 100
There's No Return From Love	Lawson Boys, Teddy Lawson & the	1957	Mansfield 611/612
There's No Tomorrow	Clovers	1957	Atlantic 1152
There's No Tomorrow	Five C's	1981	P-Vine Special LP 9036
There's No Use Pretending	Ravens	1951	Rendition 5001
There's No You	Ravens	1948	King 4260
There's No You	Sensations	NA	N/A
There's Nothing Like A Woman In Love	Ravens	1949	National 9073
There's Our Song Again	Chantels	1961	End 1105
There's Rain In My Eyes	Robins	1950	Savoy 752
There's So Much About My Baby (That I Love)	Christain, Diane & group	1963	Smash 1862
There's Somebody Over There	Five Royales	1963	Todd 1088
There's Something About You	Zephyrs	1965	Rotate 5006
There's Something In Your Eyes, Eloise	Blue Notes, Todd Randall & the	1956	Josie 800/Port 70021
There's Something On Your Mind	Jolly Jacks	1963	Landa 707
Theresa	Del Capris	1963	Almont 304
Theresa	Demensions	1960	Mohawk 123
Theresa	Littlefield, Little Willie & female group	1958	Rhythm 124
Theresa	Treble Chords	1959	Decca 31015
These Are Love	Santells	1964	Courier 115
These Are The Little Things	Three G's	1958	Columbia 41292
These Are The Things I Love	Paragons	1961	Tap 504
These Are The Things I Love	Strangers	1964	Warner Bros. 5438
These Are The Things That Matter	Carterays, Eddie Carter & the	1954	Sound 105
These Are The Things We'll Share	Marveleers	1955	Dot 15320
These Blues	Hawks	1955	Post 2004

SONG	GROUP	YEAR	LABEL
These Empty Arms	Vocalaires	1962	Herald 573
These Foolish Things	Companions	1963	Arlen 722/Gina 722
These Foolish Things	Dials	1962	Philips 40040
These Foolish Things	Five Keys	1953	Aladdin 3190
These Foolish Things	Five Satins	1960	Cub 9077
These Foolish Things	Masquerades	NA	Unreleased
These Foolish Things	Starfires	1961	D&H 200
These Foolish Things	Three Chuckles	1956	Vik LP 1067
These Foolish Things Remind Me Of You	Dominoes	1953	Federal 12129
These Foolish Things Remind Me Of You	Duprees	1962	Coed LP 905
These Four Letters	El Pollos	1958	Studio 999
These Golden Rings	Jive Five	1962	Beltone 2029/Relic 1029 (77)
These Hearts Were Mine	Four Winds	1958	Hide-A-Way 101
These Kissable Lips	Daffodils	1955	CJ 100
These Lonely Nights	El Capris	1958	Hi-Q 5006
These Oldies But Goodies Remind Me Of You	Romans, Little Caesar & the	1961	Del-Fi 4158
These Red Roses	Masquerades	1960	Formal 1011/1012
These Things Are True	Agee, Ray & group	1962	Marjan 001
These Things I Miss	Dreamers (New York - Jubilee)	1951	Jubilee 5053
These Three Words	Spaniels	1959	Vee Jay 328
These Were Our Songs	Bernard, Rod & group	1966	Arbee 105
These Will Be The Good Old Days	Dreamlovers	1964	Cameo 326
These Young Girls	Midnighters, Hank Ballard & the	1964	King 5884
They Call Me A Dreamer	Starlites, Kenny Esquire & the	1957	Ember 1011
They Call Me A Fool	Churchill, Savannah & group	1956	Argo 5251
They Call Me Crazy	Southwinds	1958	Fury 1017
They Call Me Fool	Calvanes	1955	Dooto EP 205
They Can Dream	Modern Red Caps	1963	Rowax 801
They Didn't Believe Me	All Americans, Joey Rogers & the	1958	Nu-Clear (no number)
They Don't Know	Five Royales	1961	Vee Jay 412/Home Of The Blues 234
They Don't Say	Melodears	1959	Gone 5040
They Go Ape	Cherubs	1960	Dore 545
They Go Ape	Dories	1960	Dore 556
They Laughed At Me	Starlites, Jackie & the	1957	Fire & Fury 1000
They Lied	Brochures	1961	Apollo 757
They Said It Couldn't Be Done	Duprees	1965	Columbia 43336
They Said It Couldn't Happen	Sugar Tones	1951	Onyx 2008
They Say	Impacts	1959	Watts 5600/RCA 7609 (59)
They Say	Keynotes	1954	Dot 15225
They Say	Rainbows	1957	Rama 209/Hamilton 143
They Say	Thunderbirds, Johnny & the	1959	Clover 1001
They Say It's Wonderful	Imperials, Little Anthony & the	1961	End LP 311
They Talk Too Much	Electrons	1964	Laguna 103
They Talk Too Much	Sweethearts	1963	H-III 116
They Tell Me	Chapters, Helen Foster & the	1953	Republic 7037
They Tell Me It's Summer	Fleetwoods	1962	Dolton 62
They Tried	Velvets (New York)	1953	Red Robin 120
They Turned The Party Out Down At Bessie's House	Rocketeers	1958	M.J.C. 501
They Wake Me	Gum Drops	1959	Coral 62138
They Wanna Fight	Anteaters, Chuck Harrod & the	1959	Champion 1013
They'll Call Me Away	G-Clefs	1962	Terrace 7507
They'll Never Be	Chaps	1959	Matador 1814
They're Always Laughing At Me	El Capris	1958	Paris 525
They're Dancing Now	Sequins	1962	Terrace 7511
They're Rockin' Down The Street	Fabulous Clovers	1961	Winley 265
Thief, The	Shells	1959	Roulette 4156
Thing, The	Deckers	1958	Yeadon 1041
Thing-A-Ma-Jig	Delacardos	1960	United Artists 276
Things Ain't Right	Upstarts, Jerry McCain & the	1956	Excello 2081
Things Are Changing	Blossoms	1965	EEOC-8472
Things Are Going To Break Up	Page Boys	NA	Camelot 114
Things Don't Happen That Way	Twiliters, Ron Holden & the	1962	Baronet 3
Things I Do For You, The	Anglos, Linda Martell & the	1962	Fire 512

SONG	GROUP	YEAR	LABEL
Things I Love, The	Duprees	1963	Coed 584
Things I Love, The	Fidelitys	1958	Baton 252
Things I Might Have Been, The	Oliver, Johnny & group	1956	MGM 12319
Things I Want To Hear (Pretty Words), The	Shirelles	1961	Scepter 1227
Things I'd Like To Do	Counts, Cosmo & the	1963	Sound Stage 7 2504
Things She Used To Do, The	Quails	1955	DeLuxe 6085
Things That Made Me Laugh	Olympics	1969	Jubilee 5674
Things We Can't Forget	Fiestas	1959	
Things We Did Last Summer, The	Ivorytones	1960	Norwood 101
Things You Do To Me, The	Symbols	1967	Laurie 3401
Things You Do To Me, The	Vows	1963	Tamara 760 (same # used twice)
Think	Five Royales	1957	King 5053
Think	Universals (Murray Hill)	1985	Murray Hill LP 000083
Think Again	Strangers	1955	King 4821
Think And Cry	Tune Weavers	NA	Casa Grande (unreleased)
Think Back	Mandells	NA	Trans World 821
Think Before You Say Goodbye	Hayden, Gil & group	1961	V-Tone 219
Think Of Poor Me	Gems, Pearl Woods & the	1962	Wall 551
Think Of Tomorrow	Four Students, Oscar Black & Sue Allen with the	1955	Groove 0130
Think Right	Resonics	1964	Lucky Token 108
Think Smart	Fiestas	1964	Old Town 1178
Think Sweet Thoughts	Evergreens, Dante & the	1961	Madison 154
Think Twice	Four Ekkos	1959	Label 2022
Think You're Smart	Clocks & Classmen	1958	Mail Call 1011
Thinkin' And Thinkin'	Ebonaires	1959	Colonial 117
Thinkin' (Maybe She's Changed Her Ways)	Corsairs	1961	Tuff 1808/Chess 1808 (61)
Thinking	Tune Timers	1955	Okeh 7081
Thinking, Hoping And Wishing	Gallant, Billy (with the Roulettes)	1961, 1962	Dee Dee 501/Goldisc G6
Thinking Of You	Jaguars	1959	Original Sound 06/ Original Sound 20 (62)
Thinking Of You	Mason, Little Billy (with the Rhythm Jesters)	1957	Rama 223
Thinking Of You	Silvertones	1962	Joey 302
Thinking Of You	Wanderers	1957	Onyx 518
Third Window From The Right	Barlow, Dean & group	1961	Lescay 3004
Thirteen	Castle Sisters	1960	Roulette 4220
Thirty Days	Hearts, Buddy & the	1964	Landa 701
Thirty Days	Idols	1958	RCA 7339
Thirty Days	McPhatter, Clyde & female group	1956	Atlantic 1106
Thirty Minutes To Go	Antennas	1962	United (unreleased)
Thirty Second Lover	Five Royales	1957	King 5032
Thirty-Nine - Twenty-One - Forty Shape	Showmen	1963	Minit
31 Flavors	Shirelles	1963	Scepter 1260
This Big Wide World	Belltones, Ronnie Baker & the	1963	Jell 200
This Broken Heart	Sonics (New York - Harvard)	1959	Harvard 801/Harvard 922 (59)/ Checker 922 (59)
This Can't Be Love	Tune Weavers	1960	Casa Grande 3038
This Can't Be The End	Cardinals	1952	Atlantic (unreleased)
This Can't Be True	Holman, Eddie & group	1965	Parkway 960
This Can't Go On	Marvells	NA	Yorsey
This Could Be The Night	Velours	1957, 1984	Onyx 515/Relic 516 (64)
This Could Be The Start Of Something Big	Metronomes	1962	Riverside 4523
This Could Be The Start Of Something Good	Temptones (Daryl Hall)	1967	Arctic 136
This Couldn't Be Me	Sweethearts	1966	Kent 442
This Day	Falcons (Detroit)	1956	Mercury 70940
This Day Is Ours	Lalarettes, La La & the	1963	Elpeco 2922
This Doesn't Seem Real	June Voices, Jimmy Von Carl & the	1959	Flick 002
This Empty Heart (My Love Has Gone)	Jacks	1955, 1960	RPM 444/Kent 344
This Feeling	Sequins, Janice Rado & the	1961	Edsel 782
This Feeling	Zodiacs, Maurice Williams & the	1967	Dee-Su 304
This Girl Of Mine	Fidelitys	1960	Sir 276

SONG	GROUP	YEAR	LABEL
This Girl Of Mine	Juniors, Jimmy Castor & the	1957	Atomic 100
This Heart Of Mine	Daylighters	1961	Nike 1011/Astra 1001 (65)
This Heart Of Mine	Dell Vikings	1963	Crown LP 5368
This Heart Of Mine	Falcons (Detroit)	1958, 1959	Kudo 661/Chess 1743 (59)/ Anna 1110 (60)
This Heart Of Mine	Hollywood Flames	1988	Specialty LP 2166
This Heart Of Mine	Turks	1956	Bally 1017
This Heart Of Mine	Williams, Curley & group	1956	Modern 1004
This I Declare	Treney, Joey & group	1961	Magenta 05
This I Do Believe	Harris, Dimples & group	1956	Crest 1013
This I Feel	Lavenders	1964	Dot 16584
This I Give To You	Page Boys	1957	Prep 117
This I Know	Coachmen Five	NA	Janson 100
This I Know	Limelites, Shep & the	1961	Hull 740
This I Know	Thrillers, Little Joe & the	1956	Okeh 7075
This I Know, Little Girl	Thrillers, Little Joe & the	1965	Uptown 715
This I Promise	Five Keys	1957	Capitol 3738
This I Swear	Dreamers (Dream)	NA	Dream 1223
This I Swear	Dubs	1963	Josie 911
This I Swear	El-Rich Trio	1966	Elco SK-1
This I Swear	Holidays	1966	Relic 542
This I Swear	Skyliners	1959, 1963	Calico 106/Original Sound 37
This I'll Do My Darling	Orioles, Sonny Til & the	1951	Jubilee (unreleased)
This Is A Lovely Way To Spend An Evening	Spaniels	1958	Vee Jay LP 1002
This Is A Miracle	Don Juans, Little Eddie & the	1955	Fortune 836
This Is A Miracle	Montclairs, Floyd Smith with the	1961	Fortune 540
This Is A Perfect Moment	Gainors	1961	Tally-Ho 102
This Is All I Ask	Epitomes, Buford Busbee & the	1959	Dee Dee 101
This Is Goodbye	Bel-Aires, Donald Woods & the	1955	Flip 304
This Is Goodbye	Capris (Fable)	1959	Fable 665
This Is Goodbye	Romancers	1956	Dootone 404
This Is It	Starnotes	1962	Caper 101
This Is Love	Fortunes	1964	Yucca 168/170/Bishop 1005
This Is Love	Guytones	1958	DeLuxe 6159
This Is Love	Paradons	1960	Tuffest 102
This Is Love	Phantones	1958	Code 707
This Is Love	Trend-Tones	1959	Superb 100
This Is Magic	Ballads (Tina)	1964	Tina 102
This Is My Last Affair	Four Jacks, Mac Burney & the	1955	Aladdin 3274
This Is My Love	Beachcombers	1964	Diamond 168
This Is My Love	Chestnuts	1958	Aladdin 3444
This Is My Love	Creations, Bobby Richardson & the	1961	Ember 1076
This Is My Love	Emjays	1959	Greenwich 411
This Is My Love	Passions	1960	Audicon 105
This Is My Love (acappella)	Durhams	1975	Relic LP 103
This Is My Plea	Celebritys	1956	Caroline 2301
This Is My Prayer	Fleetwoods	1964	Dolton 98
This Is My Song	Four Intruders	1961	Gowen 1404
This Is My Story	Dinos	NA	Van 03265
This Is My Story	Four Lovers	1957	RCA LP 1317
This Is My Story	Jewels (Federal)	1963	Federal 12541
This Is My Story	Sa-Shays	1961	Zen 110
This Is My Story	Spotlighters	1958	Aladdin 3441
This Is My Story	Turbans (Philadelphia)	1962	Imperial 5828
This Is My Wedding Day	Computones	1979	Clifton 32
This Is My Wedding Day	Fantastics	1960	RCA 7664
This Is Our Day	Dolls	1965	Maltese 100
This Is Our First Date	Richettes	1962	Apt 25069
This Is Our Night	Creations	1962	Mel-o-Dy 101
This Is Our Night	Toledos	1961	Down 2003/End 1094 (61)
This Is Our Wedding Day	Four Chevelles	1957	Band Box 357/Delft 357 (64)
This Is Paradise	Rituals	1959	Arwin 127
This Is Really Real	Earthquakes & Rhythm Kings	1960	Fortune 538
This Is Something Else	Five Keys	1959	King 5305

SONG	GROUP	YEAR	LABEL
This Is The End	Fabulons	1963	Benson Ritco 100/Benson 100 (63)
This Is The End	Isley Brothers	1958	Cindy 3009
This Is The End	Popsicles	1958	Knight 2002
This Is The End	Twisters	1961	Sunset 501
This Is The End	Willows	1956	Club 1014/Michelle 501
This Is The End Of Love	Klixs	1958	Music City 817
This Is The Life	Tick Tocks, Bobby Marchan & the	1960	Fire 1014
This Is The Moment	Revalons	1958	Pet 802
This Is The Night	Kool Gents	1956	Vee Jay 173
This Is The Night	Roman, Nat & group	1964	Sahara 103
This Is The Night	Tamblyn, Larry (with the Standells)	1965	Faro 612
This Is The Night	Valiants (Los Angeles)	1957, 1961	Keen 34004/82120
This Is The Night	Vocaleers	1960	Old Town 1089
This Is The Night For Love	Flairs	1954	Flair 1044
This Is The Nite	Palisades	1962	Medieval 205
This Is The Nite	Rose, Andy (with the Thorns)	1961	Coral 62271
This Is The Nite For Love	Crowns, Arthur Lee Maye & the	1956	Dig 124
This Is The Real Thing	Dawn Quartet	1974	Decatur 3001
This Is The Real Thing Now	Dawn Quartet	1952	Decatur 3001
This Is The Same	Harvey Sisters	1962	Newtime 512
This Is The Time	Caronators	1960	Clock 1049
This Is The Way	Tangerines	1961	Wildcat 603
This Is What I Ask	Dukes, Billy Duke & the	1956	Sound 130
This Is What I Was Made For	Mystics	NA	Ren-Vell 320
This Is Where I See Her	Fleetwoods	1964	Dolton 315
This Is Why	Continentals (Owl)	1974	Owl 331
This Is Why I Love You	Martin, Benny & group	1960	Astro 109
This Is Your Life	Crystals, Claudia & the	1961	Dore 601
This Land Is Your Land	Blue Jeans, Bob B. Soxx & the	1963	Philles LP 4002
This Letter To You	Gallahads, Jimmy Pipkin & the	1962	Donna 1361
This Letter To You	Monograms	1975	Monogram 105
This Little Boy Of Mine	Uniques	1963	Roulette 4528
This Little Girl	DiMucci, Dion (with the Del Satins)	1963	Columbia 42776
This Little Girl	Edwards, Joey & group	1960	Lilly 501
This Little Light Of Mine	Peebles, Robert & group	1959	Jax 132
This Little Love Of Mine	Counts, Bobby Comstock & the	1963	Lawn 219
This Little Man Of Mine	Golden Tones, Marie Reynaud & the	1958	Goldband 1049
This Lonely Boy	Limelighters	1957	Gilco 213
This Love	Joy-Tones	1964	Coed 600
This Love	Moonglows	1958	Chess 1701
This Love Is True Love	Humphries, Teddy & group	1958	King 5151
This Love Of Mine	Cari, Eddie & group	1963	Mermaid 104
This Love Of Mine	Dominoes	1965	Ro-Zan 10001
This Love Of Mine	Imperials, Little Anthony & the	1961	End LP 311
This Love Of Mine	Quotations	1962	Verve 10252
This Love Of Ours	Delrons	1961	Forum 700
This Love Of Ours	Dynamics	1963	Emjay 1935
This Love Of Ours	Five Discs	1980	Crystal Ball 141
This Love Was Real	Showcases	1964	Galaxy 732
This Love Will Last Forever	Calhoun, Millie & group	1965	Lo Lace 708
This Lovely Night	Alteers	1964	G-Clef 705
This Magic Moment	Drifters (1959-forward)	1960	Atlantic 2050
This Magic Moment (acappella)	Majestics, Little Joe & the	1975	Relic LP 105
This Makes Me Mad	Charters	1963	Merry-Go-Round 103
This May Be Your Life	Four Guys	1955	Wing 90036
This Misery	Showmen	NA	Unreleased
This Moment	Cashmeres (Rubbertown)	NA	Rubbertown 103
This Must Be Love	Stereos, Dave & the	1961	Pennant 1001
This Must Be Paradise	Debonaires (Elmont)	1958	Elmont 1004
This Must Be Paradise	Meadowlarks, Don Julian & the	1955	Dootone 372
This Must Be The Place	Bowties, Cirino & the	1956	Royal Roost 619
This My Love	Neptunes	1961	RCA 7931
This Nearly Was Mine	Gardner, Don & group	1957	DeLuxe 6133
This Night Is Our Night	Satins, Sunny & the	1978	Crystal Ball 122
This Old Heart	Monarchs	1962	Jam 104

SONG	GROUP	YEAR	LABEL
This Old Heartache	Ascots	1965	M.B.S. 106
This Old Love Of Mine	Overtones	1961	Slate 3072
This Ole Body	Accents (California)	1956	Accent 1037
This Ole Love Of Mine	Magnificents	1984	Solid Smoke LP 8030
This Paradise	Bel-Aires, Donald Woods & the	1955	Flip 303 (first pressing, second is by Vel-Aires)
This Restless Heart	Revlons	1961	Rae-Cox 105
This Road	Cotillions	1962	Ascot 2105
This Should Go On Forever	Downbeats, Gene Terry & the	1959	Savoy 1559
This Silver Ring	Blue Sky Boys	1974	Blue Sky 108
This Silver Ring	Castelles	1954	Grand 103
This Song Is Number One	Initials, Angelo & the	1964	Congress 207
This Spring	Passionettes	1958	Herald (unreleased)
This Thing Called Love	Alley Cats	1956	Whippet 202
This Thing Called Love	Danleers	1964	Lemans 008
This Thing Called Love	Invictors	1962	TPE 8217
This Thing Called Love	Webs	1967	Popside 4593
This Time	G-Clefs	1966	Veep 1226
This Time	Royal Lancers, Paul Stefan & the	1963	Hi Mar HM-501
This Time	Sentimentals	1972	Mint 808
This Time For Christmas	Detroit Jr. & group	1961	Foxy 002
This Time I'm Gonna Cry	Edwards, Sonny & group	1963	Cavetone 508
This Time I'm Losing You	Regan, Tommy (with the Marcels)	1964	Colpix 725
This Time It's Real	Flairs (Jenell & Ricky)	19??	
This Time Last Year	Depippo Sisters	1964	Magnifico 104
This Time Next Summer	Gigi & group	1961	Seg-Way 1010
This Time Next Year	Demensions	1964	Coral 62432
This To Me Is Love	Dubs	1961, 1975	End 1108/Clifton 5
This Year's Mister New	Videls	1961	Kapp 405
This-A-Way	Hepsters	1956	Ronel 110
Those Dreamy Eyes	Royal Jesters	1960	Harlem 105
Those Golden Bells	Tenderfoots	1955	Federal 12225
Those Golden Oldies	Edgewoods	1968	Epic 10275
Those Lonely, Lonely Feelings	Midnighters, Hank Ballard & the	1963	King 5798
Those Love Me Blues	Fabulous Koolcats, Ruben Siggers & the	1957	Spinks 600
Those Magic Words	Nichols, Ann (Bluebirds)	1950	
Those Oldies But Goodies Are Dedicated To You	Knight, Sonny & group	1962	Original Sound 18
Those Oldies But Goodies (Remind Me Of You)	Ebb Tides, Nino & the	1961	Madison 162
Those Oldies But Goodies (Remind Me Of You)	Romans, Little Caesar & the	1961	Del-Fi 4158
Those Precious Love Letters	Young Ones	1963	Yussels 7701
Those Pretty Brown Eyes	Hull, Terry (with the Starfires)	NA	Staff 103
Those Three Little Words	Delcos	1962	Ebony 01/02/Showcase 2501 (63)/ Sound Stage 7 2501 (63)
Those Wedding Bells	Rommels	1960	Trend 4104
Thought Of Losing You, The	Five Delights	1959	Abel 228
Thought Of You Darling, The	Four Naturals	1959, 1977	Red Top 125/Arcade 1004
Three Bells, The	Tokens (Brooklyn)	1966	B.T. Puppy 516
Three Blind Mice	Portraits	1963	Tri-Disc 109
Three Charms	Notes, Reed Harper & the	1960	Luck 105
Three Chartreuse Buzzards Sittin' On The Fence	Sidewinders, Jim Harris & the	1966	Fabar 15564
Three Coins In The Fountain	Dominoes	1954	King 1364
Three Coins In The Fountain	Iridescents	1963	Hudson 8102
Three Coins In The Fountain	Skyliners	1962	Cameo 215
Three Coins In The Fountain (acappella)	Young Ones	1963	Yussels 7704
Three Cool Cats	Coasters	1959	Atco 6132
Three Deuces And Twin Pipes	Melodeers	1962	Shelley 161
Three Dips Of Ice Cream	Chiffons	1969	Laurie 3497
Three Friends (Two Lovers)	Turbans (Philadelphia)	1961	Roulette 4326
Three Hearts	Goldtones, Bill Bryan & the	1962	Pike 5915
Three Kinds Of People	Vocaltones	1956	Apollo 492
Three Kisses Past Midnight	Original Casuals	1958	Back Beat 514

SONG	GROUP	YEAR	LABEL
Three Little Fishes	Clifford, Buzz (with the Teenagers)	1962	Columbia 41979
Three Little Fishes	Empires	1962	Colpix 680
Three Little Fishes	Kookie Beavers	1960	Gone 5086
Three Little Fishes	Talents	1961	Twink 1215
Three Little Letters	El Pollos	1958	Neptune (unreleased)
Three Little Lovers	Santos, Larry (with the Tones)	1959	Baton 265
Three Little Monkeys	Ly-Dells	1964	Southern Sound 122
Three Love Letters Ago	Sherwoods	1960	V-Tone 506
Three Months Of Rain	Vi-Counts	1960	Ace 587
Three O'Clock In The Morning	Ebonaires (with the Maxwell Davis Orch.)	1953	Aladdin 3211
Three O'Clock Rock	Capitols	1959	Triumph 601
Three O'Clock Rock	Five Reasons	1958	Cub 9006
Three On A Date	Four Dolls	1957	Capitol 3766
Three Precious Words	Edsels	1961	Tammy 1014/Ember 1078 (61)
Three Reasons Why	El Dorados	1957	Vee Jay 263
Three Roads	Toppers (ABC)	1956	ABC 9759
Three Roses	Singing Wanderers	1954	Decca 29298
Three Roses	Starfires	1958	Decca 30730
Three Signs Of Love	Counts, Bobby & the	NA	Count 6985
Three Sixty	Inspirators	1955	Treat 502
Three Speed Girl	Royal Notes	1958	Kelit 7032
Three Stars	Teen Tones	1959	Crest 1057
Three Steps From The Altar	Limelites, Shep & the	1961	Hull 747
Three Steps To Go	Starlites, Eddie & the	1972	Bim Bam Boom 102
Three Steps To The Altar	Limelites, Shep & the	1961	Roulette 102
Three Steps To The Phone	Terrytones	1961	Wye 1010
	(with Claire Charles & Gayle Fortune)		
Three Sundays	Marveltones	1952	Regent 196
Three Tears In A Bucket	Crests	1962	Trans Atlas 696
Three Teens	Bon Bons	1956	Columbia 40800
Three Thirty Three	Drifters (1959-forward)	1971	Atco LP 375
Three Time Loser	Dukes (California)	1956	Imperial 5408
Three Time Mama	Tilters	NA	Chess (unreleased)
Three Window Coupe	Rip Chords	1964	Columbia 43035
Three Wishes	Harptones	1956	Rama 203
Three Wishes	Sonnetts	1958	Checker 884
Three Years	Offbeats, Harold L & the	1961	Happy Hearts 124
Three Young Rebs From Georgia	Satellites, Bobby Day & the	1959	Class 257
Thrill	Expressions	1963	Smash 1848
Thrill Is Gone, The	Five Owls	1974	Owl 327
Thrill Is Gone, The	Four Students, Tommy Brown & the	1956	Groove 0143
Thrill Me	Mello-Kings	NA	Relic LP 5035
Thrill Me	Moonglows	1976	Chess LP 701
Thrill Me Baby	Five Notes, Henry Pierce & the	1952	Specialty 461
Thrill Me Night And Day	Meadowlarks, Don Julian & the	1955	Dootone EP 103/Dootone EP 203
Thrill Me So	Cadillacs, Bobby Ray & the	1961	Mercury 71738
Thrill Of Love	Solitaires	1957	Old Town 1044
Thrill Of Romance	Gay Tunes	1953	Timely 1002
Thrill Upon A Hill	Broken Hearts	NA	Rosina 147
Thrills And Heartaches	Jay, Lori & group	1956	Rim 2016
Through A Long And Sleepless Night	Chances	1964	Roulette 4549
Through Eternity (acappella)	Creations	1975	Relic LP 109
Through My Tears	Reid, Matthew (with the Four Seasons)	1962	ABC 10305
Through The Years	Montereys, Dean Barlow & the	1957	Onyx 513/Relic 511 (64)
Through The Years (acappella)	Five Delights	1960	A Cappella - Best of the Bronx (98)
Throw Stones	Stratfords	1964	O'Dell 114
Throwaway Song	Del Satins	1965	B.T. Puppy 514
Thrust, The	Emblems, Eddie Carl & the	1962	Oh My 1001
Thum-A-Lum-A	Top Hits	1961	Norman 504
Thumb Print	Popsicles	1958	Knight 2002
Thumbin' A Ride	Coasters	1961	Atco 6186
Thumpin'	Cobras (Philadelphia)	1964	Monogram 519
Thunderbird	Casual-Aires	1958	Brunswick 55064
Thunderbird	Del-Brooks	1958	Kid 101
Thunderbird	Five Blue Notes	1959	Onda 108

SONG	GROUP	YEAR	LABEL
Thunderbird	Quantrils, Freddie & the	1964	Karem
Thunderbird	Whalers, Hal Paige & the	1957	J&S 1601
Thunderbird Baby	Paramounts	1959	Combo 156
Thunderbolt	Twisters, Sammy Turner & the	1958	Big Top 3007
Tic Tac Toe	Stereos	1962	Columbia 42626
Tic Toc	Reflections	1962	Tigre 602
Tick Tick Tock	Continentals, Teddy & the	1961, 1962	Richie 1001/Pik 235 (61)/Rago 201
Tick Tock	Catalinas	1967	Scepter 12188
Tick Tock	Cordell, Richie & group	1962	Rori 707
Tick Tock	Innocents	1960	Trans World 7001
Tick Tock A-Woo	Turbans (Philadelphia)	1955	Money 209
Tick-A-Tick-A-Tock	Harbor Lites (with Jay Black)	1960	Mala 422
Tick-Tock	Bel-Aires (Crown)	1954	Crown 126
Tic-Toc	Four Knights	1962	Triode 104
Tide Has Turned, The	Mark IVs	1962	Barry 105
Tie Me Surfer Board Down, Sport	Travelers	1963	Gass 1000
Tiger (Everybody Wants To Be A)	Rocky Fellers	1964	Warner Bros. 5440
Tiger Lil	Naturals, Jack Bailey & the	1959	Ford 113
Tiger Lily	Five Keys	1957	Capitol 3660
Tiger's Wide Awake, The	Romeos	1962	Amy 840
Tight Shoes	Four Beaus	1959	Todd 1028
Tight Skirt And Sweater	Versatones	1958	All Star 501/Fenway 7001 (60)/ Atlantic 2211 (63)
Tight Skirts And Crazy Sweaters	Cap-Tans	1960	Anna 1122
Tight Sweater	Marathons	1961	Arvee 5038
Tighten Up	Continentals, Teddy & the	1961	Richie 445
Tighten Up Your Own Thing	Bobbettes	1972	Mayhew 712237
Til	Angels (New Jersey)	1961	Caprice 107
Til I Fell In Love	Dar-Letts	1964	Shell 101
'Til I Hear From You	Monarchs	1962	Jam 104
'Til I Return	Masters	1958	Len 103
Til I Say Well Done	Kings (New Orleans)	1954	Specialty 497
Til I Waltz Again With You	Twiliters	1961	Flippin' 106
Til Kingdom Come	Dominoes	1957	Decca 30199
'Til The 13th Month	Lions	1961	Mark IV 104
Til The End Of Time	Teen Five	1963	Times Square 4/ Times Square 98 (64)
Til There Were None	Mello-Kings	1961	Herald 561
Til You Were Gone	Excels	1961	R.S.V.P. 111
Till	Tokens (Brooklyn)	1968	Warner Bros. 7169
Till Dawn And Tomorrow	Five Bills	1953	Brunswick 84004
Till Eternity	Winn, Ricky & group	NA	Campbell 1001
Till I Come Home To You	Impulse, Dee & group	1961	
Till I Heard It From You	Dialtones	1960	Goldisc 3005/Goldisc 3020 (61)
Till I Met Sweet You	McKinnon, Preston & group	1960	Sharp 104
Till I Waltz Again With You	Five Bills	1953	Brunswick 84002
Till My Baby Comes Home	Rhythmettes	1958	Brunswick 55050
Till My Baby Comes Home	Shirelles	1966	Scepter 12150
Till The Day I Die	Gems (Illinois)	1957	Drexel 915
Till The End	Five Satins	1961	United Artists 368
Till The End Of Our Days	Chaperones, Maria Mae & the	1961	Phantom 986
Till The End Of The Dance	Plaids	1958	Nasco 6011
Till The End Of Time	El Rays	1963	M.M. 104/Wolf 104
Till The End Of Time	Flames, Allan & the	1960	Colonial 7006/Campbell 225-1
Till The End Of Time	Nobles (Timbers)	1958	ABC 9984
Till The End Of Time (acappella)	Teen 5	1964	Times Square 4/ Times Square 98 (64)
Till The Sun Stops Shining	Twiggs, Mal Hogan & the	1954	Blaze 108
Till The Wee, Wee Morning	Romaines	1954	Groove 0035
Till Then	Classics (Brooklyn)	1963	Musicnote 1116
Till Then	Orioles, Sonny Til & the	1953	Jubilee 5107
Till Then	Vocal-Teens	1972	Downstairs 1000
Till Tomorrow	Rainbows	1962	Gramo 5508
Till We Meet Again	Prestos	1955	Mercury 70747
Till You	Kings (Baltimore)	1958	RCA 7419

SONG	GROUP	YEAR	LABEL
Till You Bring Your Love Back	Accents (California)	1962	Joker 200
Till You Come Back To Me	Casuals	1957	Dot 15671
Till You'll Be Mine	Teddy Bears	1959	Dore 520
Tilly, Take Your Time	Chestnuts	NA	
Timberlands	Mascots	1962	Mermaid 107
Time	Basics	NA	Lavender 2002
Time	C-Larks	1956	Nova 106
Time	Dreamlovers	1961	V-Tone 229
Time	Echoes	1959	Andex 22102
Time	Innocents	1959	Andex 22012/Indigo 141 (62)
Time	Intentions	1965	Uptown 710
Time	Sparks, Milton (with the Delroys)	1957	Apollo 514
Time	Upstarts, Don Dell & the	1961	East Coast 101/102
Time & Time Again	Field Brothers	1958	Carlton 475
Time After Time	Centuries	1985	Relic LP 5053
Time After Time	Co-Eds	1961	Sheryl 337
Time After Time	Consorts	1961	Cousins 1004/Apt 25066 (62)
Time After Time	Go-Togethers	1963	Coast 100
Time After Time	Keytones	1962	Chess 1821
Time After Time	Meadowbrooks	1965	Catamount 106
Time After Time	Moonglows	1964	Lana 130
Time After Time	Paragons	1963	Music Clef 3001/3002
Time After Time	Van Delles	1962	Bolo 731
Time After Time	Vibrations	1961, 1977	Checker LP 2978
Time After Time (acappella)	Four Clefs	1966	B-J 1000
Time After Time (acappella)	Holidays	1975	Relic LP 102
Time Alone Will Tell	Rookies, Joe Perkins & the	1957	King 5005
Time And Again	Nutones	1963	Dart 135
Time And Again	Velvets (Texas)	1961	Monument 435
Time And Tide	Platters	NA	Mercury EP 3355
Time And Time Again	Fi Dells	1961	India 5822
Time And Time Again	Four Cousins, Bill Murray & the	1955	20th Century 75020
Time Bomb	Anastasia & group	1960	Laurie 3066
Time For Dreams	Nicholls, Dave (with the Coins)	1961	Sparton 1062
Time For Love	Antones, Joey Pfarr & the	1957	Black Crest 107
Time For Love	Four Jewels	1964	Checker 1069
Time For Love, The	Incas	1977	Monogram 126
Time Has Come, The	Bel-Airs Five	1964	USA 764
Time In My Heart For You	Wanderers, Dion & the	1966	Columbia 43483
Time Is A-Passin'	Ravens	NA	Mercury (unreleased)
Time Is Here, The	Solitaires	1963	Old Town 1139
Time Is Marching On	Ravens	1951	Mercury 8257
Time Is Moving On	Encores	1954	Look 105/Ronnex 1003 (54)/ Hollywood 1034 (55)
Time Is Near (Rosie), The	Originals, Rosie & the	1961	Brunswick 55213
Time Is Passing	Rodans	1959	Vest 825
Time Is Running Out On Our Love	Cleftones	1961	Gee LP 705
Time Is Tough	Matadors, Tommy Liss & the	1963, 1997	Saxony 1005
Time Machine	Evergreens, Dante & the	1960	Madison 135
Time Makes You Change	Dells	1957	Vee Jay 258
Time Marches On	Pendulums	1962	May 109
Time Out	Four Imperials	1959	Dial 101
Time Out For Love	Five Fortunes	1958	Ransom 103
Time Out For Tears	Embers, Willis Sanders & the	1959	Coral 62146
Time Runs Out	Kidds, Morry Williams & the	1960, 1974	Luck 102
Time Stood Still	Shades	NA	Klik
Time Takes Care Of Everything	Ravens	1950	National 9101
Time, The	Darnels, Debbie & the	1961	Vernon 100
Time, The	Del Pris	1961	Varbee 2003
Time, The	Five Satins	1960	Ember 1066
Time, The	Teen Dreams, Debbie & the	1961	Vernon 100
Time To Dream My Love Is Real	Holidays, Buddy Sheppard & the	1962	Sabina 506
Time To Rock	Five Teenbeats	1960	Big Top 3062
Time To Say Goodbye	Elegant IV	1965	Mercury 72516
Time Waits	Corsairs	1961	Smash 1715

SONG	GROUP	YEAR	LABEL
Time Was	Flamingos	1961	End 1092
Time Was	Honey Dreamers	1959	Dot 15925
Time Will Allow	Five Playboys	1958	Mercury 71269
Time Will Bring A Change	Paramounts	1964	Magnum 722
Time Will Tell	Majors (Philadelphia)	1962	Imperial 5855
Time Will Tell	Storytellers	1963	Dimension 1014/Ramarca 501 (63)
Time Will Tell	Teenettes, Betty Jayne & the	1961	Mona Lee 139
Time, The (long version)	Five Satins	1987	Standord 7107 (rec. Ember 1960)
Times	Carbo, Chuck (with the Spiders)	1957	Imperial 5479
Times And Places	Fairmounts	1962	Planet 53
Times Are Changing	Creations	1967	Globe 102
Times Are Getting Harder	Five Knights	1961	Minit 626
Times Change	Uniques	1963	Dot 16533/Demand 2940
Times Have Changed	Angels (with Sonny Gordon)	1954	Grand 115
Times Is Tough	Cabarettes	1963	Saxony 1002
Time's Run Out	Pop Overs	NA	Toppette 1020
Time's Running Out	James, Jimmy & group	1963	Coed 583
Times Sho' Gettin' Rough	Quintones (Chicago)	1962	Phillips International 3586
Times Square Stomp	Summits	1973	Clifton 1
Times Two, I Love You	Three Chuckles	1955	X 0162
Times We've Wasted, The	Elgins (Congress)	1964	Congress 214
Timmy Boy	Persianettes, Timmy & the	1963	Olympia 100
Tina	Five Kings	1966	Yvette 101
Tina	Raindrops, Tony & the	1962	Crosley 340
Tina	Rondels	1963	Shalimar 104/Dot 17323 (70)
Tina	Spaniels	1958	Vee Jay 278
Tina	Tokens (Brooklyn)	1961	RCA 7954
Ting A Ling	Lovenotes	1953	Family Library EP 1040
Ting Aling Ting Toy	Demensions, Lenny Dell & the	1964	Coral 62444
Ting Tang Tagalu	McCain, Jerry & group	1965	Continental 777
Ting-A-Ling	Clovers	1952	Atlantic 969
Ting-A-Ling	Nobles (Connecticut)	1957	Klik 305/Times Square 1 (62)/ Lost Nite 153
Ting-A-Ling	Poka-Dotts	1954	Modern 945
Ting-A-Ling-Ling	Sweethearts	1961	Ray Star 778
Tiny Cloud	Elegants	1961	ABC 10219
Tip Toe	Three Dots	1959	Buzz 104
Tip Toe Through The Tulips With Me	Foxes	1963	ABC 10446
Tippin'	Topps	1954	Red Robin 126
Tippin' In	Larks (North Carolina)	1954	Lloyds 110
Tippi-Tippi-Wang-Wang	Kashmirs	1958	Wonder 104
Tippity Top	Rays	1955	Chess 1613
Tired Of Being A Little Boy	Triotones	1959	Intrastate 43
Tired Of Me	Skyliners	1959	Calico LP 3000
Tired Of Waiting	Apostles	1966	A-Square 401
Tired Of Work	Spencer, Carl & group	1962	Southside 1007
Tired Of You	Gentlemen	1954	Apollo 464
Tired Of Your Rock & Rolling	Velours	1959	Cub 9029
Tired Of Your Sexy Ways	Four Jacks, Mac Burney & the	1955	Aladdin 3274
Tired Out	Belvederes	NA	Rhapsody 5163
'Tis A Pity	Triangles	1960	Herald 549
'Tis Night	Laurels	1955	X 0143
To A Soldier Boy	Tassels	1959	Madison 117/Amy 946 (66)
To A Young Lover	Tassels	1959	Madison 121
To Be	La Chords	1962	Gay 629
To Be A Part Of You	Click-Ettes	1960	Dice 92/93
To Be Alone	Parliaments	1961	U.S.A. 719
To Be Alone	Worley-Birds, Wayne Worley & the	1961	Brent 7024
To Be Fair	Five Discs	1980	Crystal Ball 141
To Be In Love With You	Shantons	1959	Jay-Mar 242
To Be Loved	Imaginations	1991	Collectables CD 5726
To Be Loved	Pretenders, James Moore & the	1964	Tishman 905
To Be Loved (Forever)	Capris (New York)	1982	Ambient Sound LP FZ-37714
To Be Loved (Forever)	Pentagons	1960	Fleet Int'l 100/Donna 1337 (61)
To Be Mine	Criterions, Tygh & the	1963	Flite 101

SONG	GROUP	YEAR	LABEL
To Be My Love	Travelers, Roger & the	1978	Crystal Ball 128
To Be Or Not To Be	Co-Eds	1961	Sheryl 337
To Be Or Not To Be	Jesters	1959	Spry 118
To Be With You	Belmonts	1965	United Artists 966
To Be With You	Highlights	1957	Bally 1027
To Be With You	Kays	NA	Choice 3757
To Be With You	Orioles, Sonny Til & the	1948	Jubilee 5001
To Be Without You	Debonairs	1960	Winter 502
To Be Young	Sequins	1959	Cameo 161
To Cry	Expressions	1963	Parkway 892
To Each His Own	Bell Notes	1960	Madison 136
To Each His Own	Clovers	1959	United Artists LP 3033
To Each His Own	Dominoes	1957	Decca 30420
To Each His Own	Five Keys	1957	Capitol LP 828/Capitol EP 1-828 (57)
To Each His Own	Platters	1960	Mercury 71697
To Each His Own	Royal Drifters	1959	Teen 508
To Each His Own	Three Chuckles	1956	Vik LP 1067/Vik EP 192
To Each His Own	Tymes	1964	Parkway 908
To Each His Own	Young, Bobby (with Rick & the Masters)	1968	Guyden 2087
To Find An Angel Like You	Shondelles, Rickey Leigh & the	1963	Savoy 1620
To Have A Little Girl	Kingtones	1962	Kitoco/Drummond 105 (65)
To Have And To Hold	Playboy Band, John Fred & His	1962	Montel 2001
To Hold Your Love	King Cobras	1959	Irvanne 117
To Keep Our Love	Penguins, Cleve Duncan & the	1961	Eldo 119
To Keep Our Love	Radiants, Cleve Duncan & the	1959	Dooto 451
To Keep Your Love	Chanticleers	1958	Lyric 103
To Know Him Is To Love Him	Darlings	1963	Dore 663
To Know Him Is To Love Him	Teddy Bears	1958	Dore 503
To Live Again	El Capris	1957	Fee Bee 216
To Live My Life Again	Smith, Arlene & group	1963	End 1120
To Live The Life Of A Lie	Flasher Brothers	1952	Aladdin 3156
To Love Again	Tempos	1984	Rhythm 129
To Love In Vain	Twilighters (Bronx, N.Y.)	1961	Fraternity 889
To Love Or Not To Love	Four Winds	1964	Chattahoochee 655
To Make A Long Story Short	Decades	1980	Avenue D 3
To Make A Long Story Short	Starlites, Eddie & the	1959	Scepter 1202
To Make A Long Story Short (acappella)	Young Ones	1975	Relic LP 102
To Make A Long Story Shorter	Five Bars	1963	Bullet 1009
To Make You Mine	Redjacks	1958	Apt 25006/Oklahoma 5005
To Me	Holidays	NA	Willjer 6002
To Me	Nobles (Timbers)	1959	ABC 10012
To Me You're A Song	Upbeats	1959	Joy 233
To Our Love	Counts	1955	Dot 1275
To Prove My Love	Dove, Diane & group	1959	NRC 018
To Reconcile	Darlettes	NA	Taffi 100
To The Aisle	Admirations (featuring Joseph Lorello)	1962	Mercury 71883
To The Aisle	Baker, Bill & group	1962	Audicon 118/Musictone 1108 (62)
To The Aisle	Five Satins	1957, 1961	Ember 1019/Musictone 1108
To The Aisle	Hi-Lites (Connecticut)	1962	Dandee LP 206
To The Aisle	Roomates	1961	Valmor LP 78/Valmor LP 789 (62)/ Relic LP 5041
To The Aisle	Winstons	1957	Cinemascope 8705
To The Aisle (acappella)	Quotations	1975	Relic LP 105
To The Church	Classinettes	1962	Markay 107
To The Party	Bay Bops	1958	Coral 62004
To The School House	Rock-A-Fellas, Eddie Bell & the	1959	Coed 517
To The Winner Goes The Prize	G-Clefs	1964	Regina 1314
To Think We're Only Friends	Winners	1952	Derby 802
To Win The Race	Citations	1967	Ballad 101
To You	Wright, Rubin & group	1959	Lancer 101
To You, My Darling	Jumpers, Jay Nelson & the	1959	Excello 2165
Toast, The	Presidents	1962	Mercury 72016
Toast To Lovers	Monotones	1962, 1974	Hull LP 1002
Today	Eternals	1961	Warwick 611
Today I Met The Boy I'm Gonna Marry	Love, Darlene & group	1963	Philles 111

SONG	GROUP	YEAR	LABEL
Today Is Your Birthday	Enchanters (Queens, N.Y.)	1952	Jubilee 5072 (52)
Today Is Your Birthday	Sugar Tones	1951, 1952	Onyx 2007/Okeh 6877
Today My Love Has Gone Away	Belmonts	1965	United Artists 904
Today, Tomorrow, Forever	Bachelors (National)	1958	National 115
Today, Tomorrow, Forevermore	Cardinals	1955	Atlantic (unreleased)
Today's The Day	Gray, Maureen & group	1961	Chancellor 1082
Together	Berry, Richard (with the Flairs)	1956	Flair 1075
Together	Down Beats	NA	Dawn 4531
Together	Dreamers, Richard Berry & the	1955	Flair 1075
Together	Dreamlovers	1963	Swan 4167/Casino 1308 (63)/ Swan 5619
Together	Flames	1953	7-11 2107
Together	Ideals	1961	Paso 6401/Dusty Disc
Together	Nutrends	1963	Lawn 216
Together	Ravens	1948	King 4260
Together	Teenagers, Frankie Lymon & the	1986	Murray Hill LP 000148
Together	Tycoon	1985	Starlight 31
Together	Woods, Sonny & group	NA	Lu Pine
Together Again	Hearts, Lee Andrews & the	1962	Gowen 1403
Together Again	Holmes, Eddie & group	1958	Eagle 1000
Together At Last	Dippers, Georgie Torrence & the	1965	Duo-Disc 117
Together Forever	Rivieras	1958	Algonquin 718 (first pressing, second is by the Ravenaires)
Together Just We Two	Dell-Fi's, Leon Peterson & the	1960	Kable 437
Togetherness	Midnighters, Hank Ballard & the	1965	King 6031
Toki-Roll, Toki-Rock	Jumping Jacks	1956	Capitol 3496
Tokyo Girl	Crystalaires	1995	Crystal Ball 163
Told By The Stars	I. V. Leaguers	1959	Nau-Voo 803
Told The Sunshine	Cheerettes	1956	Vita 143/Vita 145 (56)
Tom Boy	Arrogants	1960	Big A 12184/12185
Tom Foolery	Monotones	1958	Argo 5301
Tomboy	Concords (Neal Scott)	1962	Comet 2151
Tomboy	Highbrows, Shadoe & the	1961	Gem 102
Tommy	Chicklettes, Angie & the	1965	Apt 25080
Tommy	Clickettes, Angie & the	1959	Apt 25080
Tommy	Delrons, Reperata & the	1965	World Artists 1051
Tommy	Gales	1963	Debra 1002
Tommy's Girl	Visions	1962	Mercury 72188
Tomorrow	Decoys (Belairs)	1964	Times Square 9/ Times Square 96 (64)
Tomorrow	Marvells	1962	Finer Arts 2026
Tomorrow	Shirelles	1960	Scepter 1211 (first pressing)
Tomorrow	Skyliners	1959	Calico 106
Tomorrow	Spindles, Frankie & the	1968	Roc-Ker 575
Tomorrow	Starfires	1959	Decca 30916
Tomorrow	Webs	1967	Popside 4593
Tomorrow And Always	Satintones	1961	Motown 1006 (first pressing)
Tomorrow Is On Your Side	Whispers	NA	N/A
Tomorrow My Love	Candy Girls	1964	Rotate 5001
Tomorrow Never Comes	Carlton, Chick & group	1962	Imperial 5873
Tomorrow Night	Four Mints	1959	NRC 037
Tomorrow Night	Lifesavers, Lucien Farrar & the	1957	Jupiter 2
Tomorrow Night	Popular Five	1967	Rae-Cox 1001
Tomorrow Night	Serenaders (Detroit)	1952	J.V.B. 2001
Tomorrow We'll Be Married	Knight, Bob	1964	Goal 4/Jubilee
Tomorrow Will Come	Classics, Lou Christie & the	1963	Alcar 208
Tomorrow Won't Bring The Rain	DiMucci, Dion (with the Wanderers)	1965	Columbia 43423
Tomorrow's Memories	Imaginations	1991	Collectables CD 5726
Tom-Tom	Tunisians, Terry & the	1963	Seville 131
Tongue Twister	Continentals (Davis)	1959	Davis 466
Toni My Love	Five Satins	1959	Ember 1056
Tonight	Carlos Brothers	1959	Del-Fi 4112
Tonight	Drifters (1959-forward)	1965	Atlantic LP 8113
Tonight	Ebb Tides, Nino & the	1961	Madison 151
Tonight	Fireflies	1967	Taurus 380

SONG	GROUP	YEAR	LABEL
Tonight	Little Dippers	1960	University 6053/6054
Tonight	Love Notes (New York)	1957	Holiday 2605
Tonight	Mar-Vells	NA	Harlem 1002
Tonight	Metrotones	1955	Columbia 40420
Tonight	Premiers (Mink)	1959	Mink 021/Parkway 807 (60)
Tonight	Pretenders	1957	Holiday 2610
Tonight	Supremes (Bronx, N.Y.)	1956	Old Town 1024 (first pressing)
Tonight	Tune Drops, Malcolm Dodds & the	1957	End 1010
Tonight And Forever	Whirlers	1957	Whirlin' Disc 108/Port 70025 (60)
Tonight At The Prom	Shirelles	1961	Scepter LP 501
Tonight Could Be The Night	BQE	1988	Starlight 61
Tonight (Could Be The Night)	Earls	1977	Woodbury 101
Tonight (Could Be The Night)	Run-A-Rounds	NA	Unreleased
Tonight (Could Be The Night)	Velvets (Texas)	1961	Monument 441/Monument 515
Tonight I Fell In Love	Tokens (Brooklyn)	1961	Warwick 615
Tonight I Met An Angel	Chiffons	1963	Laurie 3224
Tonight I Met An Angel	Parlettes	1963	Jubilee 5467
Tonight I Met An Angel	Tokens (Brooklyn)	1963	RCA 8148
Tonight I'm Gonna Dream	Chiffons	1965	Laurie 3318
Tonight I'm So In Love	Capris (New York)	1982	Ambient Sound LP FZ-37714
Tonight Is Another Night	Martineques	1962	Danceland 777/Roulette 4423 (62)
Tonight Kathleen	Valentines	1954	Old Town 1009
Tonight Kiss Your Baby Goodbye	Avons	1963	Groove 0039
Tonight Must Live On	Dawn Quartet	1974	Firefly 330
Tonight Must Live On	Five Sounds, Russ Riley & the	1957, 1977	Aljon 115/Arcade 1005
Tonight My Heart She Is Crying	Temptations, Neil Stevens & the	1961	Goldisc 3019
Tonight My Love	Lynn, Bobby & group	1961	CR 102
Tonight Tonight	Barries	1963	Ember 1101
Tonight Tonight	BQE	1988	Starlight 58
Tonight Tonight	Essex	1964	Roulette 4591
Tonight, Tonight	Mello-Kings	1957	Herald 502 (second pressing, first is by Mellotones)
Tonight Tonight	Tokens (Brooklyn)	NA	RCA LP 3685
Tonight Was Like A Dream	Street Singers	1956	Tuxedo 899
Tonight We Love	Four Directions	1965	Coral 68456
Tonight We Wail	Lyndon, Frank (with the Regents)	NA	Jab 1004
Tonight You Belong To Me	Tonettes	1956	Modern 997
Tonight You're Gonna Fall In Love With Me	Shirelles	1964	Scepter 1264
Tonight's My Night To Cry	Smith, Wendell & group	1959	United Artists 166
Tonight's The Night	Chiffons	1960	Big Deal 6003/Zircon 1012
Tonight's The Night	Monitors	1955	Aladdin 3309
Tonight's The Night	Shirelles	1960	Scepter 1208
Tonight's The Night	Teenagers (Joe Negroni/Kenny Bobo)	1960	End 1071
Tonite I Fell In Love (acappella)	Citadels	1975	Relic LP 103
Tonite Oh Tonite	Collegians	1961	Winley 261
Tony, My Darling	Charmers	1954	Central 1006
Too Bad	Daychords, Roxy & the	1962	Don-El 120
Too Bad	Honeytones	1955	Mercury 70557
Too Big For Her Bikini	Granahan, Gerry (with the Wildwoods)	1961	Caprice 108
Too Cool	Hitmakers	1959	Angletone 1104
Too Far To Turn Around	Creators	1962	Dore 635/Lummtone
Too Far To Turn Around	Upfronts	1960	Lummtone 104
Too Fat	Rockets, Little Freddy & the	1957	Chief 33
Too Good To Be True	Academics	1957	Ancho 101/Relic 510 (64)
Too Good To Be True	Casinos	1964	Terry 116/Airtown 886
Too Hot To Handle	Blue Notes (with Joe Loco & Quintette)	1953	Rama 25
Too Hurt To Cry, Too Much In Love To Say Goodbye	Darnells	1963	Gordy 7024
Too Late	Chromatics, Augie Austin & the	1958	Brunswick 55080
Too Late	Chromatics, Eddie Singleton & the	1958	Amasco 3701
Too Late	Dreams	1962	Smash 1748
Too Late	Five Keys	1951	Aladdin 3085
Too Late	Moonglows	1957	Chess 1681
Too Late	Pastimes	1986	Starlight 36

SONG	GROUP	YEAR	LABEL
Too Late	Vals	1964	Ascot 2163
Too Late For Tears	Boyce, Tommy & group	1962	RCA 8074
Too Late For Tears	Lassiter, Art & group	1956	Ballad 1024
Too Late For Tears	Wheeler, Art & group	1962	Swingin' 642
Too Late I Learned	Anders, Bernie & group	1955	King 4833
Too Late I Learned	Gayles	1955	King 4860
Too Late I Learned	O.W. & His New Group	1956	DeLuxe 6091
Too Late To Forgive	Delltones, J. Jay & the	1963	Cobra 5555
Too Late To Love	Blue Diamonds; Don & the	1961	Skylark 113
Too Late To Say You're Sorry	Love, Darlene & group	1966	Reprise 534
Too Late To Worry	Jesters, Richie Thompson & the	1961	Diamond 103
Too Long	Beasley, Billy & group	NA	Dee Cal 500
Too Long Without Some Loving	Clovers	1968	Josie 992
Too Many Girls	Misters	1959	Chante 1002/Decca 31026 (59)
Too Many Loves	Rocket-Tones	1963	3-Sons Records 928
Too Many Memories	Chancellors	1956	Unique 341
Too Many Memories	Passions	1961	Unique 79X/79XX/Fantastic 79
Too Many Miles	Dell Vikings	1963	ABC 10425
Too Much	Aire-Dales, Rocky Roberts & the	1965	Brunswick 55357
Too Much	Four Jacks	1956	Gateway 1204
Too Much Ain't Enough	Beltones, L. Farr & the	1964	N-Joy 1001
Too Much Competition	Baum, Allen (with the Larks)	1954	Red Robin 124
Too Much Lovin'	Five Royales	1953	Apollo 448
Too Much Of a Good Thing	Shirelles	1967	Scepter 12192
Too Much Of A Little Bit	Five Royales	1951	Apollo 434
Too Much True Lovin'	Charmettes	1962	Markay 101
Too Old To Cry	Class-Aires	NA, 1982	Honey Bee 1
Too Poor To Love	Capris (Philadelphia)	1955	Gotham 7306
Too Proud To Cry	Castro, Vince (with the Tonettes)	1958	Apt 25025
Too Proud To Let You Know	Relations	1963	Kape 703/Demand 501/ Davy Jones 664
Too Shy	Realistics	1970	De-Lite 528
Too Soon	Caribbeans, George Torrence & the	1958	Galliant 1003
Too Soon	Ravens	1952	
Too Soon To Know	Flamingos	1962	End LP 316
Too Young	Classics (Brooklyn)	1964	Musictone 6131
Too Young	Cunningham, Dale & female group	1958	Cash 1067
Too Young	Dodd, Cally & group	1959	Calico 110
Too Young	Echoes, Tommy Vann & the	1966	Academy 118
Too Young	Emblems	1962	Bay Front 108
Too Young	Four Uniques	1961	Adam 9002
Too Young	Hi-Lites, Ronnie & the	1965	ABC 10685
Too Young	Joy, Arlene & group	1962	Rendezvous 185
Too Young	Regal, Mike & group	1963	Kapp 506
Too Young	Revivals	NA	N/A
Too Young	Sebastian & group	1959	Mr. Maestro 801/Take 2 2002 (59)
Too Young	Serenaders, Larry Lee & the	1990	Relic LP 5085
Too Young	Squeaks, Bobby Knotts & the	1961	Gee Clef 077
Too Young	Teenchords, Lewis Lymon & the	1957	End 1003
Too Young	Travelers	1961	World Wide 8511
Too Young Or Too Old	Bell Notes	1960	Autograph 204
Too Young To Be Blue	Four Jacks, Bill Erwin & the	1960	Pel 501/Fairlane 21020 (62)
Too Young To Date	Delicates	1960	United Artists 228
Too Young To Fall In Love	Teenettes	1958	Josie 830
Too Young To Know	Ravenetts	1959	Moon 103
Too Young To Love	Taylortones	NA	C&T 0001
Too Young To Start	Village Voices	1961	Topix 6000
Too Young To Wed	Sheppard, Shane (with the Limelites)	1959	Apt 25038
Toodaloo Kangaroo	Four Ekkos	1958	RIP 12558
Took A Chance (I Took A Chance)	Javalons	1961	Tru-Eko 6901/Pip 6902
Toom Toom (Is A Little Boy)	Delrons, Reperata & the	1968	Mala 589
Tootin' Tutor	Titans	1959	Class 244
Tootles	Dots, Lenny Capello & the	1960	Ric 960
Tootsie Roll	Dominoes	1954	Federal 12178
Tootsie Roll	Pee Wees	1958	Josie 838

SONG	GROUP	YEAR	LABEL
Tootsie Wootsie	Jones, Davey & group	1959	Glades 601
Top Down Time	Dantes	1964	Rotate 5008
Top Down Time	Rockaways	1964	Red Bird 10-005
Topless Bathing Suit	Dolphins, Doc & the	NA	Dino 2
Torch Is Out, The	Hitmakers, Linda Lou & the	1965	Lama 7786
Tore Up Over You	Escorts (RCA)	1957	RCA 6834
Tore Up Over You	Midnighters	1956	Federal 12270
Tormented	Belvederes	NA	Count
Tormented	Heart Beats Quintet	1955	Network 71200/Candlelite 437 (72)/ Candlelite 1135 (76)
Tossin' And Turnin'	Laddins	1974	Relic LP 5018
Tossin' And Turnin'	Lewis, Bobby & female group	1961	Beltone 1002
Tossing And Turning	Ivy League	1965	Cameo 377
Touch Me	Counts	1961	Sunset 502
Touch Me	Jack, Johnny & group	1962	Gone 5132
Touch Of Love	Enchanters (Orbit)	1959	Orbit 532/Bamboo 513 (61)
Touch Of You, The	O'Henry, Lenny (with the Four Seasons)	1961	ABC 10272
Touchdown	Young Ideas	1959	Swan 4044
Tough Cat	Ferros	1958	Hi-Q 5008
Tough Chick	Rockbusters	1959	Cadence 1371
Tough Enough	Bees	NA	Finch 506
Tough Enough	Jayos, Johnny Otis & the	1957	Dig 131
Tough Love	Daylighters	1960	C.J. 614
Tough Mama	Nitecaps	1956	Groove 0147
Touring	Sunglows, Sunny & the	1959	Sunglow 104/Okeh 7143 (62)
Town Sensation	Satin Angels	1985	Relic 8004
Toy Bell	Bees	1954	Imperial 5314
Toy Boy	Hall Brothers	1962	Four Star 1760
Toy Telephone	Dimples	1958	Era 1079/Era 3079 (62)
Tra La La La La	Viriations	1968	Amy 11006
Track That Cat	Bonnie Sisters	1956	Rainbow 333
Tracks Of My Tears (acappella)	Knick-Knacks	1975	Relic LP 108
Tracy (All I Have Is Yours)	Atlantics, Barry White & the	1963	Faro 613
Tradewinds Tradewinds	Nobles, Aki Aleong & the	1961	Reprise 20021
Traffic Jam	Aztecs	1964	Card 901
Tragedy	Fleetwoods	1961	Dolton 40
Tragedy	Wayne, Thomas (DeLons)	1959	Fraternity
Tragedy Of Love	Dories	1959	Dore 528
Tragic	Sheppards (Chicago - Apex)	1961, 1962	Apex 7762/Vee Jay 441
Trail Blazer	Adventurers	1959	Capitol 4292
Train	Go-Togethers	1963	Coast 100
Train Keep Rolling On	Du Droppers	1953	Unreleased
Train Of Love	Entros, Gloria Fowler & the	1965	Cee Jay 654
Train Of Love	Wonders, Tony Allen & the	1959	Jamie 1143
Train Of Memphis	Darlings	1963	Dore 663
Train Of No Return	Blue Knights, Steve Colt & the	1962	Fleetwood 4550
Train, The	Belgianettes	1963	Okeh 7172
Train, The	Magnetics	1962	Allrite 620
Train Whistle Blues	Montereys (Nestor)	1956	Nestor 15/Teenage 1001 (56)
Trains, Cars, Boats	Climbers	1957	J&S 1658
Trakey-Doo, The	Twilighters, Tony Allen & the	1962	Bethlehem 3004
Tra-La-La	Majors (Philadelphia)	1963	Imperial 5936
Trampoline Queen	Teamates, Tandi & the	1960	Ember 1068
Trance	Topics, Billy Dixon & the	1960, 1961	Topix 6002/6008
Trans Zistor	Ideals	1962	Fargo 1024
Transfusion	Four Jokers	1956	Diamond 3004
Transylvania Mist	Del-Chords, Donnie & the	1963	Taurus 361
Trap Of Love, The	Premiers (Los Angeles)	1957	Fortune 527
Trapped	Emeralds (St. Louis)	1960	Yale 232
Trapped, Lost, Gone	Five Keys	1954	Capitol (unreleased)
Traveled	Diante, Denny & group	1964	Holiday 1211
Traveler	Travelers	1962	Don Ray 5965
Travelin'	Dawns	1959	Catalina 1000
Travelin'	Spotlites	1959	Catalina 1001
Traveling All Alone	Dixieaires	1954	Harlem

SONG	GROUP	YEAR	LABEL
Traveling Lady	Hi Tensions	NA	Milestone
Traveling Man	Derbys	1962	Savoy 1609
Traveling Man	Fireflies	1962	Taurus LP 1002
Traveling Salesman	Resolutions	1962	Valentine 1001
Traveling Stranger	Ambitions	1962	Cross 1005
Traveling Stranger	Copas	1979	U.G.H.A. 11
Traveling Stranger	Destinaires	1964	Old Timer 64
Traveling Stranger	Imperials, Little Anthony & the	1961	End 1091
Traveling Stranger	Jive Chords	1974	Vintage 1017
Traveling Stranger	Johnson, Bill	1957	Baton 239
Traveling Stranger (acappella)	Kooltones	1975	Relic LP 101
Treasure In My Heart	Ambers, Joey & the	1960	Big Top 3052
Treasure Of Love	Reflections, Howie Butler & the	1960	Gaity 6017
Treat Her Nice	Gifts, Young Henry Ford & the	1964	Roulette 4552
Treat Him Tender, Maureen (Now That Ringo Belongs To You)	Chicklettes, Angie & the	1965	Apt 25080
Treat Me Like You Want To Be Treated	Majestics (Florida)	1962	Chex 1004
Treat Me Right	Lovenotes	NA	Joyce (unreleased)
Treat Me So Good	Lamar, Chris & group	1963	Don-El 121
Treat You Right	Sevilles	1964	Galaxy 717
Treatment For The Cure	Johnson 3 Plus 1	1969	Tangerine 1013
Tree In The Meadow	Carnations	1952	Derby 789
Tree In The Meadow	Pearls	1956	Onyx 506/Relic 519 (64)
Tree Of Love	Elites	1963	ABC 10460
Tree Top Len	Blue Jays (Venice, Calif.)	1961	Milestone 2009
Trees	Baysiders	1960	Everest 19386
Trees	Fortunes	1958	Decca 30688
Trees	Platters	1961	Mercury 71791
Trees	Spaniels	1959	Vee Jay 310
Tremble	Embers, Larry Lee & the	1990	Relic LP 5085
Tremble	Esquires, Lord Luther & the	1960	Music City 833
Tremble	Galaxies	1961	Dot 16212
Tremblin'	Green, Birdie & group	1962	End 1117
Trembling Hand	Royal Demons	1961	Pek 8101
Tres Chic	Sheiks	1959	Jamie 1132
Tres Suspiros	Star Lites, Junior & the	NA	Mex Melody 121
Trial Of My Love, The	Court Jesters	1961	Blast 201/Blast 208 (63)
Triangle	Rays	1958	Cameo 128
Triangle Love	Shantons	1959	Jay-Mar 165
Triangle Love	Sonics	1959	Nocturne 110/RKO Unique 411 (59)
Trick Knees	Cuff Links	1958	Dooto 434
Trickle Trickle	Endings	1976	Barrier 104
Trickle Trickle	Manhattan Transfer	1980	Atlantic 3772
Trickle Trickle	Reality	1978	U.G.H.A. 02
Trickle Trickle	Videos	1958	Main Line 106/Casino 102 (58)
Tricky Tricky	Hi-Fi-Dels	1961	Atlantic 2121
Tried And Tasted	Jumping Jacks	1957	ABC 9859
Trojan's Walls	Trojans	1961	Zynn 1006
Trouble	Agents	NA	Liberty Bell 3260
Trouble	Fleetwoods	1961	Dolton 49
Trouble	Robins	NA	Push 764
Trouble And Misery	Belvin, Jesse & group	1955	Money 208
Trouble Child	Mason, Barbara (with the Larks)	1964	Crusader 114/Arctic (65)
Trouble In Mind	Ricks, Jimmy & female group	1964	Atlantic 2246
Trouble In Mind	Seminoles	NA	Hi-Lite 87568
Trouble In My Life	Cupcakes, Cookie & the	1964	Lyric 1020/Paula 230 (65)
Trouble In My Soul	Belles	1961	Choice 18
Trouble In Paradise	Crests	1960	Coed 531
Trouble In Paradise	Trutones	NA	N/A
Trouble In The Candy Shop	Morrocos, Little Joe & the	1959	Bumble Bee 500
Trouble Is You, The	Newports	1965	Laurie 3327
Trouble I've Had	Hearts (with Clarence Ashe)	1964	J&S 1466
Trouble I've Seen	Volumes	1966	Impact 1017
Trouble On My Mind	Savage, Al & group	1957	Herald 505
Trouble Trouble	El Dorados	1981	Charly LP 1022

SONG	GROUP	YEAR	LABEL
Trouble, Trouble	Tuxedos	1960	Forte 1414
Trouble With Love, The	Fourteen Karat Soul	1980	Catamount 738
Troubled Heart	De Villes	1960	Dixie 1108
Troubled Times	Wilson, Sonny & group	1961	Plaza 1
Troubles	Jackson Brothers	1959	Candy 002
Troubles	Millionaires, Benny Curtis & the	1961	Bridges 1102
Troubles	Pastel Six	1963	
Troubles	Rogers, Lee & group	1962	Mah's 000.9
Troubles Don't Last	Kings (Baltimore)	1959	RCA 7544
Troubles Not At End	Cupids	1956	Chan 107
Troubles Of My Own	Four Jacks, Shirley Haven & the	1952	Federal 12092
Troubles, Troubles	Tuxedos	1960	Forte 1414
Truck And Trailer	Flares	1961	Press 2802
Trudy	Carallons, Lonnie & the	1959	Mohawk 111
Trudy	Cleftones	1958	Roulette 4094
Trudy	Lidos	1957	Band Box 359
True	Santos, Larry (with the Four Seasons)	1964	Atlantic 2250
True Blue	James, Bobby & group	NA	Lant 66009
True Blue Lou	Three Belles	1955	Jubilee 5219
True By You	Tic Tocs	1957	Rush 1042
True Confession	Michels, Ginny & group	1962	Mala 446
True Deep Love	Premiers (Los Angeles)	1960	Dore 547
True, Fine Mama	Little Richard & group	1958	Specialty 633
True Fine Mama	Showmen	1962	Minit 654
True Fine Mama	Tigers, Little Julian Herrera & the	1957	Starla 6
True Love	Classmen	1963	Gateway 712
True Love	Coralites	NA	Carib 1008
True Love	Dell Vikings	1956	Fee Bee 210
True Love	Ermines	1955	Loma 701
True Love	Scarlets	1955	Red Robin 135
True Love	Seminoles	1961	Go-Gee 287
True Love Affair	Elegants	1959	Apt 25029
True Love At First Sight	Jack, Johnny & group	1964	Lawn 226
True Love Came My Way	Shalons	1977	Ronnie 203
True Love Can Be	Thunderbirds, Ron Holden & the	1960	Donna 1328
True Love Gone	Counts, Tommy Burk & the	1962	Nat 101/Smash 1821 (63)
True Love Gone	Enchanters (Detroit)	1963	Coral 62373
True Love Gone (Come On Home)	Enchanters (Detroit)	1956	Mercer 992/Coral 61756 (57)
True Love Is A Treasure	Versalettes	1963	Witch 116
True Love (Is Hard To Find)	Kid, The & group	NA	Rumble 1347
True Love Is Hard To Find	Mandells	1966	Jubilee 5519
True Love Is Hard To Find	Myron, Mitch & group	1960	Bay-Tone 109
True Love Is Hard To Find	Rivieras	1958, 1959	Coed 503/513
True Love, True Love	Cupids	1962	UWR 4241/4242
True Love, True Love	Royals, Ronnie Bennett & the	1960	Jin 143
True Love, True Love (If You Cry)	Derringers	1961	Capitol 4532
True Love Was Born (With Our Last Goodbye)	Sherwoods	1963	Dot 16540
True Lover	Campbell, Charlotte & group	1959	Wanger 194
True Lover	Platters	1961	Mercury 71749
True Lover Girl	Watts, Jimmy Mack &	1960	Gee 1056
True Lovers	Four Chaps	1962	Co & Ce 231 (65)
True Romance	Grandisons	1962	RCA 8159
True Story	Classic IV	1962	Algonquin 1651
True True Love	Corvairs	1962	Comet 2145
True True Love	Dares, Joey Daye & the	1961	Fortune 868
True You Don't Love Me	Spiders	1961	Imperial LP 9140
Truly	Crowns, Arthur Lee Maye & the	1955	RPM 424
Truly	Dinning Sisters	1955	Essex 392
Truly	Snaps, Ginger Davis & the	1961	Tore 1008
Truly (acappella)	Spaniels	NA	Unreleased
Truly Do	Fleetwoods	1960	Dolton 22
Truly, I Love You Truly	Mellos, Terri Corin & the	NA	Rider 108
Truly, Truly	Laurels	1955	X 0143
Truly Yours	Scarlets	1960	Fury 1036

SONG	GROUP	YEAR	LABEL
Trust In God	Mellotones, Doug Williams & the	1959	Hy-Tone 125
Trust In Love	Del Royals	1960	Destiny 101
Trust In Me	Foster Brothers	1959	Profile 4004
Trust In Me	Four Brothers And A Cousin	1954	Jaguar 3003
Trust In Me	Notes	1956	MGM 12338
Trust In Me	Orioles, Sonny Til & the	1952	Jubilee 5074
Trust In Me	Van Loan Quartet, The Joe	1954	Carver 1402
Trust In Our Love	Perry, Tony & group	1957	Ember 1015
Trust Me	Cunningham, Dale & female group	1958	Cash 1067
Trust Me	Swallows (Maryland)	1953	King 4656
Trustin' In You	Blue Belles, Patti LaBelle & the	1970	Atlantic 2712
Trusting In You	Madison Brothers	1960	Cedargrove 314/Apt 25050 (60)
Truth About Youth, The	Velvet Keys	1958	King 5109
Truth Hurts, The	Birds, Bobby Byrd & the	1956	Cash 1031
Truth Hurts, The	Danleers	1964	Lemans 004
Truthfully	Deep River Boys	1951	Beacon 9143
Truthfully	Laurels	1986	R.A.M. 706005
Try	Miller Brothers	1958	Mercury 71293
Try	Zodiacs, Maurice Williams & the	NA	Plus 4401
Try A Little Love	Enchanted Five	1961	CVS 1002
Try And Get Me	Blenders, Earl Curry & the	1956	R&B 1313
Try And Try Again	Wayne, Art & group	1961	Xavier 8890
Try Baby Try	Vogues	1958	Dot 15859
Try It One More Time	Fiestas	1963	Old Town 1140
Try It, You Won't Forget It	Emblems, Patty & the	1966	Kapp 791
Try Love (One More Time)	Sparkels	1964	Old Town 1160
Try Me	Crests	1966	Parkway 987
Try Me And You'll See	Belles, Glorius Wilson & the	1956	Fairbanks 2002
Try Me One More Time	Diablos, Nolan Strong & the	1956	Fortune 522
Try Me One More Time	Four Bars	1962, 1963	Dayco 101/Shelley 180
Try My Arms	Blue Chips	1959	Wren 302
Try My Love	Fashions	1961	Ember 1084
Try My Love	Showmen, Toni & the	1965	Ten Star 103
Try My Lovin' On You	Clovers	1968	Josie 997
Try The Impossible	Hearts, Lee Andrews & the	1958	Casino 452/United Artists 123 (58)
Try The Impossible	Rainbows, Randy & the	1982	Ambient Sound 02872
Try To Care	Spears, Frankie Ervin & the	1961	Don 202
Try To Realize	Intervals	1958	Irma 820
Try To Remember	Swallows (Maryland)	1991	Starbound 511
Try To Remember	Vann, Joey & group	1965	Coed 606
Try To Understand	Five Pennies, Big Miller & the	1955	Savoy 1181
Try, Try Again	Laddins	1962	Groove 4-5
Try Try Baby	McPhatter, Clyde	1959	Atlantic 2028
	(with the Cookies & the Cues)		
Tryin' To Get To You	Astronauts	1961	Palladium 610
Tryin' To Get To You	Eagles	1954	Mercury 70391
Tryin' To Hold My Gal	Checkers	1955	King 4764
Trying	Fabulons	1963	Jo-Dee 1001
Trying	Five Bob-O-Links	1952	Okeh
Trying	Paramounts	1960	Carlton 524
Trying	Saxons	1958	Tampa 139
Trying To Get Back Home	Meteors	1963	Beltone 2041
Trying To Get To You	Imperial Wonders	1969	Black Prince 317
Trying To Make It	Leopards, Lee & the	1962	Gordy 7002/Laurie 3197 (63)
Trying To Please	Upstarts, Jerry McCain & the	1957	Excello 2103
Tsetse Fly	Five Sequins, Gary Haines & the	1961	Kapp 383
Tucson	Neons	1961	Waldon 1001
Tuff-A-Nuff	Fireflies	1963	Hamilton 50036
Tug Of War	Chordials	1964	Big Top 513
Tumblin' Down	Duotones	NA	Harlequin 611026
Tunnel Of Love	Embers, Ricky Dee & the	1962	Newtown 5001
Tunnel Of Love	Mobley, John & group	1962	Town & Country 6601
Turkey Hop, The	Robins (with Johnny Otis)	1950	Savoy 732
Turn Around	Contours, Texas Red & the	1957	Bullseye 1009
Turn Around Girl	Neptunes	1963	Gem 100

SONG	GROUP	YEAR	LABEL
Turn Around Shoes	Highlights	1958	Bally 1044
Turn Her Down	Candles, Rochell & the	1962	Challenge 9158
Turn Her Down	Cupons, Materlyn & the	1964	Impact 28
Turn Him Down	Charades	1963	Ava 154
Turn Him Down	Lord, Emmett & group	1962	Liberty 55491
Turn It On	Globeliters	1964	Guyden 2119
Turn Me Loose	Lamplighters	1953	Federal 12149
Turn Me Loose	Roomates, Cathy Jean & the	1961	Valmor LP 78/Valmor LP 789 (62)
Turn Me Loose	Royal Robins	1963	ABC 10504
Turn Me On	Frazier, Ray & group	1955	Excel 111
Turn On Me	Moonrays, Ray Frazier & the	1956	Excel 111
Turn Out The Lights	Spaniels, Pookie Hudson & the	1962	Parkway 839
Turn The Key	Garnets, Lord Luther & the	1958	Frantic 107
Turn The Page	Twisters	1960	Capitol 4451
Turn To Me	Isley Brothers	1959	RCA 7537
Turn To Me	Jays	1961	Barry 103
Turnaround	Haff-Tones	1961	Twilight 001
Turning To Stone	Gladiators	1958	Donnie 701
Turtle	Fabulous Uptones	1962	Tulip 100
Turtle Dove	Dee, Larry & group	1961	Lagree 703
Turtle Dovin'	Coasters	1956	Atco 6064
Turtle Dovin'	Midnight Riders, Kasandrea & the	1959	Imperial 5638
Turtle Dovin'	School Belles	1958	Dot 15801
Tutti Frutti	Jesters	1961	Winley 248
Tutti Frutti (Pop-Pi)	Baby Dolls	1958	RCA 7296
TV Cowboys	Majestics (Detroit)	1959	Faro 592
Twangin' Marie	Accidentals	1962	Beau Monde 1633
Tweeda	Altecs	NA	Cloister 6201
Tweedle De Dum Dum	Chips, Billy Bobbs & the	1958	Edison International 400/Edison International 416 (59)
Tweedle Dee	Crests	1978	King Tut 172
Tweedley Dee	Revels	1959	Norgolde 104
Tweet-Tweet	Knockouts	1964	Tribute 201
Twelfth Of Never, The	Tassells	1963	Goldisc G11
Twelfth Of Never, The	Tymes	1964	Parkway 933
Twelve Feet High	Hondas	1962	Eden 4
Twelve Months Of The Year	Harvey (Harvey Fuqua with the Moonglows)	1959	Chess 1725
Twentieth Century Rock And Roll	Shirelles	1964	Scepter 1264
Twenty Four Hours	Daye, Billie with male group	1961	Bliss 1002
Twenty Four Hours	Edsels	1961	Tammy 1027
Twenty Four Sad Hours	Lamplighters	1955	Federal (unreleased)
Twenty Minutes (Before The Hour)	Valentines	1956	Rama 201
Twenty One	Blair, Ronnie & group	1961	Crest 1084
Twenty Second Day	Diamonds	1959	Mercury 10017/Mercury 71505 (59)
24 Hours	Nitecaps	1961	Vandan 3587
24 Hours	Pyramids, Dave White & the	1960	Pink 705
24 Hours A Day	Davis, Eunice & group	1954	DeLuxe 6068
24 Hours A Day	Four Fellows, Cathy Ryan & the	1955	King 1495
24 Hours A Day	Gillettes	1964	J&S 1391
Twenty-Nine Ways	Dixon, Willie & group	1956	Checker 851
Twenty-One	Goofers	1955	Coral 61545
21	Shirelles	1961	Scepter 1223
21	Spiders	1954	Imperial 5318
22 Del Rio Avenue	Accents (California)	1959	Jubilee 5353
22 Years Of Love	Channels, Earl Lewis & the	1978	King Tut 175
Twilight	Paragons	1958	Winley 227
Twilight (acappella)	Majestics (Relic)	1975	Relic LP 105
Twilight Time	Aztecs, Billy Thorpe & the	1965	GNP Crescendo 359
Twilight Time	Platters	1958	Mercury 30075
Twine And Slide	Superbs	1965	Dore 731
Twinkle	Cuff Links	1957	Dootone 414
Twins	Kingtones	1964	Derry 101
Twirl, The	Madison Brothers, Farris Hill & the	1962	V-Tone 231
Twirl, The	Von Gayels	1960, 1963	Dore 544/USA 1221
Twist	Olympics	1962	Arvee 5051

SONG	GROUP	YEAR	LABEL
Twist And Shout	Fireflies	1962	Taurus LP 1002
Twist And Shout	Majors (Philadelphia)	1964	Imperial LP 9222
Twist And Shout	Top Notes	1961	Atlantic 2115
Twist Around The Clock	Cole, Clay (with the Capris)	1961	Imperial 5804
Twist In School	Travelers	1961	World Wide 8511
Twist Like This	Clearwater, Eddie & group	1962	Federal 12446
Twist Mary Sue	Sabers, J. & the	1962	Vavrey 1003
Twist Me Henry	McKnight, June & group	1962	Jeannie 1225
Twist That Twist	Sheiks	1961	Le Grand 1016
Twist, The	Checker, Chubby (with the Dreamlovers)	1960	Parkway 811
Twist, The	Flares	NA	London (England) LP 8034
Twist, The	Midnighters, Hank Ballard & the	1959	King 5171/Federal 12345 (59)
Twista Twistin'	Kodaks	1961	Wink 1004
Twist-A-Taste	Fourmost	1962	Lu Pine 105
Twistin' All Night	Counts	1961	Sunset 502
Twistin' All Night Long	Juniors, Danny & the	1962	Top Rank 604/Swan 4092
Twistin' And Kissin'	Hi-Lites, Ronnie & the	1962	Joy 260
Twistin' Around	Four Uniques	1962	Adam 9004
Twistin' At The Pool	Charmers, Prince Charles & the	1962	Class 301
Twistin' England	Juniors, Danny & the	1962	Top Rank 604
Twistin' Fever	Marcels	1962	Colpix 629
Twistin' Irene	Dinos	1962	Fox 101
Twistin' Marie	Caravelles	1962	Joey 6208
Twistin' Pneumonia	Genies	1960	Warwick 607
Twistin' Pony	Hi-Lites (Twist Time)	1962	Twist Time 12
Twistin' Susie Q	Joy, Arlene & group	1962	Rendezvous 185
Twistin' Time	Hi-Lites (Twist Time)	1962	Twist Time 12
Twistin' Town	Echoes	1961	Hi Tide 106/Felsted 8614 (61)
Twistin' Train	Flips, Mario & the	1961	Decca 31252
Twistin' U.S.A.	Juniors, Danny & the	1960	Swan 4060
Twisting Home	Lollipops, Little Bob & the	1962	Decca 31412
Twisting On Bandstand	Sprouts	1960	Mercury 71727
Twisting Saturday Night	Clicks	1963	Rush 2004
Twisting With Crazee Babee	Zeroes	1963	Ty-Tex 105
Two Broken Hearts	Del Satins	1964	Mala 475
Two Brothers	Barnette, Billy & group	1961	Parkway 826
Two By Four	Little Dippers	1959	University 210
Two Cars	Tokens (Brooklyn)	1964	RCA 8309
Two Crazy Scientists	Orbits	NA	Dooto 601
Two Different Worlds	Duprees	1969	Heritage 811
Two Different Worlds	Five Satins	1974	Kirshner 4252
Two Different Worlds	Sentimentals	1960	Coral 62172
Two Face	Renaults	1963	Chicory 160
Two For The Blues	Five Grands	1958	Brunswick 55059
Two Friends	Knight, Bob	1963	Jubilee 5451
Two Guys From Trinidad	Rocky Fellers	1963	Scepter 1271
Two Hearts	Charms, Otis Williams & the	1954, 1961	DeLuxe 6065/King 5558
Two Hearts	Doodlers	1955	RCA 6074
Two Hearts Are Better Than One	Dubs	1961	Unreleased
Two Hearts Are Better Than One	Paragons	1957	Winley 223
Two Hearts Fall In Love	Connotations	1962, 1978	Technichord 1000/1001
Two Hearts Make A Romance	Gifts, Young Henry Ford & the	1964	Roulette 4552
Two Hearts Make One Love	Wisdoms	1959	Gaity 169
Two Hearts On A Window Pane	Wanderers	1958	Cub 9019
Two Hearts Together	Sparrows, Little Jimmy & the	1958	Val-Ue 101
Two In Love (With Only One Heart)	Royaltones, Ruth McFadden & the	1956	Old Town 1020
Two Innocent Loves	Romeos	1958	Felsted 8528
Two Kinds Of People	Clark, Lucky & group	1961	Chess 1782
Two Kinds Of People (acappella)	Chessmen	1975	Relic LP 101
Two Kinds Of People In The World	Heartspinners, Dino & the	1972	Bim Bam Boom 112
Two Left Feet	Carlton, Chick & group	1962	Imperial 5925
Two Lips	El Torros	1961	Duke 333
Two Little Bees	Hollywood Flames	1988	Specialty LP 2166
Two Little Monkeys	Revels	1960	Andie 5077
Two Lovers	Castells	1968	United Artists 50324

SONG	GROUP	YEAR	LABEL
Two Lovers	Voicemasters	1960	Frisco 15235
Two Lovers In Love	Steadies	1959	Tad 0711
Two Lovers Make One Fool	Serenaders (New Jersey)	1963	Riverside 4549
Two Loves	Blenders (Aladdin)	1959	Aladdin 3449
Two Loves Have I	Colonials	1956	Gee 1007
Two Loves Have I	Colonials, Bill Bass Gordon & the	1954	Gee 12
Two Loves Have I	Commodores	1956	Dot 15461
Two Loves Have I	Diamonds (Harold Sonny Wright)	1953	Atlantic 1003
Two Loving Hearts	Chantels	1959	Unreleased
Two Loving Hearts	Sheppard, Shane (with the Limelites)	1959, 1960	Apt 25038/25039
Two More Days	Mint, Little Eddie & group	1959	Memo 17921
219 Train	Moonglows	1954	Chance 1161
Two O'Clock Express	Adventurers	1959	Mecca 11
Two Party Line	Orioles, Sonny Til & the	1948	Jubilee (unreleased)
Two People In Love	Blue Nighthawks, Irvin Rucker & the	NA	Duplex
Two People In The World	Imperials	1958	End 1027 (first pressing, second is by Little Anthony & the Imperials)
Two People In The World	Marcels	1975	Monogram 115
Two People In The World	Pyramids	NA	Klik (unreleased)
Two Purple Shadows	Majestics (Vintage)	1973	Vintage 1002
Two Sides Of Love	Victones	1959	Front Page 2302
Two Skeletons On A Roof	Buddies	1956	Decca 29840
Two Steps Downstairs In The Basement	Rocky Fellers	1965	Warner Bros. 5613
Two Strangers	Impacs	1964	King 5851
Two Strangers	Marigolds	1955	Excello 2061
Two Strangers	Prisonaires	1976	Sun 517
Two Straws In The Wind	Classmates	1956	Dot 15464
Two Stupid Feet	Tabs	1962	Wand 130
Two Things I Love	Cardinals	1955	Atlantic 1067
Two Things I Love	Gadabouts	1955	Wing 90008
Two Things I Love	Voices	1955	Cash 1011
Two Time Loser	Darlings	1963	Mercury 72185
Two Times Two	Chimes, Lenny & the	1964	Vee Jay 605
Two Timing Love	Lions	1960	Rendezvous 116
Two Ton Feather	Wanderers, Dion & the	1966	Columbia 43692
2 Won't Do	Cherlos	1956	Ultra D'Or 8
Two-Time Heart	Bombers	1956	Orpheus 1105

U

SONG	GROUP	YEAR	LABEL
U.G.H.A.	Memories	1980	U.G.H.A. 14
U.G.H.A.	Ribitones	1980	U.G.H.A. 14
Ubangi Baby	Antennas	1962	United (unreleased)
Ubangi Stomp	Jives, Bobby Taylor with Charlie & the	1961	Hour 102
Ubangi Stomp	Velaires	1962	Jamie 1211
Uggaboo	Four Jokers	1962	Amy 832
Ugly Duckling	Escorts, Don Crawford & the	1959	Scepter 1201
Ugly Duckling	Fortunes	1961	Queen 24010
Ugly Face	Pearls	1959	On The Square 320
Ugly George	Nite Riders, Melvin Smith & the	1962	Chime 101
Ugly Girl	Dinks	1966	Sully 925
Ugly Pills (You're Takin')	English, Scott (with the Accents)	1962	Joker 777
Uh Huh	Four Wheels	1992	Park Ave. 6 (rec. 1961)
Uh Huh Huh	Hosea, Don & group	1961	Sun 368
Uh Oh	Trammell, Bobby Lee & group	1958	Radio 102/Fabor 127 (64)
Uh Uh	Romans	1958	MMI 1238
Uh Uh Baby	Blue Flames	1954	Grand 108
Uh, Uh, Baby	Dell Vikings	1956	Fee Bee 210
Uh-Huh	Four Joes	1957	Darl 1005
Uh-Huh	Gaynels	1959	Okeh 7114
Uh-Huh	Premiers (Bond)	1958	Bond 5803/5804
Uh-Oh	Imps	1961	Do-Ra-Mi 1414
Uh-Oh	Tonettes	1958	Doe 103
Uh-Uh-Baby	Rockets, Dick Holler & His	1958	Ace 540
Um Bow Wow	Bobbettes	1958	Atlantic 1194

SONG	GROUP	YEAR	LABEL
Um-Ba-Pa	Demilles	1964	Laurie 3230
Umgowa	Raves, Jimmy Ricks & the	1962	Festival 25004
Unbelievable	Cytations, Chris & the	1963	Catamount 100
Unbelievable	Duprees	1964	Coed 593
Unbelievable	Five Hearts (Philadelphia)	1959	Arcade 107
Unbelievable	Regents	1962	KC 116
Unbelievable	Reunited	1980	Clifton 50
Unbelievable Love	Upbeats	1959	Joy 233
Unbeliever, The	Rickateers, Jimmy Ricks & the	1956	Josie 796
Unchain My Heart	Harper, Thelma, & group	1962	Jell 191
Unchained Melody	Blackwells	1960	Jamie 1157
Unchained Melody	Blue Belles, Patti LaBelle & the	1966	Atlantic 2408
Unchained Melody	Catalinas	1961	20th Fox 286
Unchained Melody	Coralites	NA	Carib 1008
Unchained Melody	Diplomats	1964	Arock 1000
Unchained Melody	Five Discs	1978	Crystal Ball 120
Unchained Melody	Honey Boys	1974	Boogie Music 1
Unchained Melody	Imaginations	1991	Collectables CD 5726
Unchained Melody	Players, Leroy Lovett & the	1955	Atlantic 1058
Unchained Melody	Salutations, Vito & the	1963, 1978	Herald 583/Crystal Ball 104
Unchained Melody	Satellites, Bobby Day & the	1959	Class 257
Unchained Melody (acappella)	Five Jades (Bronx, N.Y.)	1975	Relic LP 107
Unchained Melody (acappella)	Fleetwoods	1959	Dolton BLP 2001/BST 8001
Unchangeable Heart	Diplomats, Debbie & the	1958	Stepheny 1826
Uncle Ben's Concentrated Blueberry Jam	Casual Crescendos	1963	MRC 12001
Uncle Henry's Basement	Jesters	1961	Winley 252
Uncle Sam	Magnificent Four	1961	Whale 506/Blast 210 (63)
Uncle Sam	Sherwoods	1960	V-Tone 506
Uncle Sam (acappella)	Chevieres	1975	Relic LP 109
Uncle Sam Needs You	Biscaynes	1961	VPM 1006
Uncle Sam Needs You	Viceroys	1961	Little Star 107/Smash 1716 (61)
Uncle Sam's Man	Elgins (California)	1961	Flip 353
Unconditional Surrender	Chuck-A-Lucks	1961	Jubilee 5415
Unconditional Surrender	Rosebuds	1957	Gee 1033
Undecided	Imperials, Little Anthony & the	1961	End LP 311
Undecided	One, Bobby & group	1959	NRC 021
Undecided	Satellites, Bobby Day & the	1962	Rendezvous 175
Undecided Now	Hi-Lighters	1956	Celeste 3005
Under A Blanket Of Blue	Cardinals	1954	Atlantic 1025
Under Hawaiian Skies	Chapelaires	1961	Hac 102
Under Stars Of Love	Carlos Brothers	1959	Cascade-Drop LP 1008
Under Ten Flags	Tempos	1959	Paris 550
Under The Boardwalk	Drifters (1959-forward)	1964	Atlantic 2237
Under The Boardwalk	Echelons	1992	Clifton 102
Under The Boardwalk	Memory	1981	Avenue D 6
Under The Boardwalk	Revivals	1987	DCA 100/Clifton 84 (89)
Under The Bridges Of Paris	Notables	1958	Big Top 3001
Under The Moon Of Love	Lee, Curtis (with the Halos)	1961	Dunes 2008
Under The Stars	Starfires	1962	Duel 518
Under The Stars Of Love	Shadows	1958	Del-Fi 4109
Under The Tropical Sky	Style Kings	1959	Sotoplay 0011
Under The Willow	Dreams	1954	Savoy 1140
Under Your Spell	Cellos	1957	Apollo 515
Under Your Spell	Paramounts	1964	Magnum 722
Under Your Window	Stories, Smitty & the	1961	Elf 102
Understand	Dell Vikings, Buddy Carle & the	NA	Eedee 3501/Star 223
Understanding Love	Sentimentals	1959	Coral 62100
Undertaker	Walker, Sonny	1973	Baron 100
Undivided Attention	Shades	1958	Big Top 3003
Unemployed	Tradewinds, Rudy & the	1962	Angle Tone 543
Unemployment	Moonglows, Harvey & the	1959	Chess 1738
Unemployment Insurance	Redwoods	1961	Epic 9473
Unfaithful	Quinns	1965	Relic 1012
Unfaithful One	Allan, Johnny (with the Krazy Kats)	1962	Viking 1016

SONG	GROUP	YEAR	LABEL
Unfaithful One	Four Ekkos, Jerry Engler & the	1957	Brunswick 55037
Unfinished Fifth	Rocky Fellers, Leroy & the	1961	Cameo 194
Unfinished Rock, The	Aristocrats, Murray Schaff & the	1955	Josie 788
Unforgotten Love	Five Bops	1959	Hamilton 50023
Ungaua	Kingpins	1958	United Artists 111
Unhappy And Blue	Majestics (Florida)	1962	Chex 1004
Union Hall	Montels	1956, 1963	Universal 101/Times Square 10/ Richie 2
United	Charms, Otis Williams & his	1957	DeLuxe 6138
United	Flamingo, Johnny & group	1959	Malynn 101
United	Jive Five	1964	Sketch 219/United Artists 807 (64)
United	Love Notes (New York)	1957	Holiday 2605
United In Harmony	Fashions, Frankie & the	1994	Crystal Ball 162
Universal Twist	Penguins, Cleve Duncan & the	1961	Eldo 119
Unknown Love	Martineques	1962	Danceland 777/Roulette 4423 (62)
Unless You Let Me	Washington, Roger & group	1964	Beacon 563
Unless You Mean It	Stereos	1962	Cub 9106
Unloved, Unwanted Me	DiMucci, Dion (with the Del Satins)	1965	Columbia 43213
Unlucky	Shirelles	1961	Scepter LP 501
Unlucky	Yeomans	1964	Heidi 113
Unlucky Me	Videls	NA	Magic Carpet LP 1005
Unseen	Medallions, Vernon Green & the	1957	Dooto 425
Unspoken Love	Tune Drops, Malcolm Dodds & the	1957	End 1010
Untie Me	Tams	1962	Arlen 711
Until	Viceroys	1963	Bolo 750
Until I Die	Fawns	1958	Apt 15035/Apt 25015 (58)
Until I Die	Midnighters	1953, 1954	Federal 12169
Until I Fell For You	Van Loan Quartet, The Joe	1954	Carver 1402
Until I Know	Knight, Alan & group	1960	Tide 007
Until Next Year	Catalinas	1973	Jayne 177
Until Now	Rhythmasters	NA	Bennett 401
Until The 13th Chime	Barons (Dart)	1963	Dart 134
Until The Day I Die	Halos, Cammy Carol & the	1961	Elmor 302
Until The Day I Die	Marquees	1960	Warner Bros. 5139
Until The Day I Die	Tears	1956	Dig 112
Until The End Of Time	Browne, Doris (with the Capris)	1953	Gotham 296
Until The Next Time	Galaxies	1960	Capitol 4427
Until The Real Thing Comes Along	Buddies, Billy Bunn & the	1952	RCA 4657
Until The Real Thing Comes Along	Dominoes	1954	Federal 12162
Until The Real Thing Comes Along	Ecstasies	1991	Ronnie 207
Until The Real Thing Comes Along	Harptones	1972, 1976	Roulette LP 114/ Murray Hill LP 001098 (88)
Until The Real Thing Comes Along	Hearts (Bronx, N.Y.)	1955	Baton 215
Until The Real Thing Comes Along	Ravens	1948	National 9042
Until The Real Thing Comes Along	Stone, Lawrence & group	1957	Dig 130
Until Then	Classmates	1960	Marquee 102
Until Then	Cupcakes, Cookie & the	1959, 1963	Judd 1015/Lyric 1004/1012
Until Then	Pentagons	1962	Jamie 1210/Caldwell 411 (62)
Until We Meet Again	Echoes, Frankie & the	1958	Savoy 1544
Until We Two Are One	Relations	1963	Kape 504
Until You	Delmonicos	1964	Musictone 6122
Until You Come Home I'll Walk Alone	Miller Sisters	1967	GMC 10006
Until You Return	Starlighters	1956	Sun Coast 1001
Until You Say We're Through	Bonnevilles	1959	Capri 102
Until You're In My Arms	Raytones	1958	Cash 1059
Until You're Mine	Miller Sisters	1955	Herald 455/Herald 527 (58)
Untrue	Crows	1954	Rama 29
Untrue	Meadowlarks, Don Julian & the	1957	Dooto LP 224
Untrue Love	Bobbettes	1960	Atlantic 2069
Unwanted Love	Dappers (New York)	1956	Groove 0156
Unwelcome Guest	Young Hearts	1961	Infinity 006
Unwind Yourself	Midnighters, Hank Ballard & the	1967	King 6119
Unwritten Law	Lee, Jerry & group	1961	Rendezvous 147
Up All Night	Five Dreams	1957	Mercury 71150

SONG	GROUP	YEAR	LABEL
Up In The Streets Of Harlem	Drifters (1959-forward)	1966	Atlantic 2336
Up Jumped The Devil	Drifters (1959-forward)	1967	Atlantic 2426
Up On The Bridge	Chiffons	1968	Laurie 3460
Up On The Mountain	Fallen Angels	1965	Tollie 9049
Up On The Mountain	Magnificents	1956, 1960	Vee Jay 183/Vee Jay 367
Up On The Roof	Del-Capris	1966	Amber 854
Up On The Roof	Drifters (1959-forward)	1962	Atlantic 2162
Up On The Roof	Five Sharks	1986	Starlight 34
Up Till Now	Rogers, Pauline & group	1955	Atco 6050
Up To The Rooftop	Velvet Satins	1965	General American 006
Up, Up And Away	Daybreakers	1958	Lamp 2016/Aladdin 3434 (58)
Up, Up And Away	Jokers, Jivin' Gene & the	1959	Jin 109/Jin 7331
Upon The Mountain	Original Magnificenes, Jimmy Higgins & the	1961	
Upside Down	Chancellors	1962	Brent 7031
Uptown	Crystals (Brooklyn)	1962	Philles 102
Uptown	Sunglows, Sunny & the	1961	Lynn 511
Uptown-Downtown	Hi-Lites, Ronnie & the	1963	Win 252
Uranium	Commodores	1955	Dot 15372
Ursula's Blues	Reed, Ursula (with the Solitaires)	1954	Old Town 1001
U-T, The	Marvels, Harry M & the	1961	ABC 10243
U-Turn Baby	Four Of A Kind	1961	Rex 104

V

SONG	GROUP	YEAR	LABEL
Va Va Voom	Bellatones	1959	Bella 21
Va Va Voom	Martells	1961	Cessna 477/Bella 45 (61)/ Relic 517 (64)
Vacation Days Are Over	Argyles	1959	Brent 7004
Vacation In The Mountains	Cox, Herbie (with the Cleftones)	1958	Rama 233
Vacation Time	Chapelaires, Joni Kay & the	1965	Gateway 746
Vacation Time	Cutouts, Brian Brent & the	1963	Penny 2201
Vacation Time	Madara, Johnny & group	1961	Bamboo 511
Vacation Time	Tams	1961	Heritage 101
Vadunt-Un-Va-Da Song	Ramblers (Baltimore)	1954	MGM 11850
Vagabond	Classics (Brooklyn)	1971	Sire 353
Vagabond	Profits	1971	Sire 353
Valarie	Madisons	1965	Twin Hit 2865
Valarie	Shaynes	1961	Pee Vee 5000
Valarie	Starlites	1960, 1963	Fury 1034
Valencia	Jumping Jacks	1956	Capitol 3496
Valentine	Statens	1978	Crystal Ball 115
Valentino	Vondells	1964	Marvello 5003
Valerie	Attributes	1979	U.G.H.A. 12
Valerie	Del Rios	1963	Rust 5066
Valerie	El Sierros	1964	Times Square 29/Relic 534 (65)
Valerie	Hi-Lites, Ronnie & the	1962	Raven 8000
Valerie	Leopards	1963	Leopard 5006
Valerie	Litterbugs	1963	Okeh 7164
Valerie	Madisons	1965	Twin Hit 2865
Valerie	Mark III	1961	ABC 10280/BRB 100
Valerie	Mello-Harps	1955	Do-Re-Mi 203
Valerie	Mello-Kings	1958	Herald 518
Valerie	Premiers (New York)	1957	Gone 5009
Valerie (acappella)	Apparitions	1975	Relic LP 109
Valerie Jo	Triotones	1959	Intrastate 43
Valley High	School Belles	1962	Crest 1104
Valley Of Love	Chavelles	1956	Vita 127
Valley Of Love	Five Keys	1960	King 5398
Valley Of Love	Showmen	1963	Airecords 334
Valley Of Love	Tams	1960	Swan 4055
Valley Of Love (Fast & Slow Versions)	Chevelles	1973	Relic LP 5007
Valley Of Lovers	Native Boys	1956	Combo 119
Valley Of Tears	Destinations	1961	Fortune 864
Valley Of Tears	Four Imperials	1959	Dial 101
Valley Of Tears	Shamans	1959	Kayham 1/2
Valley Of Tears	Turbans (Philadelphia)	1957	Herald 495

SONG	GROUP	YEAR	LABEL
Vangie	Prodigals	1958	Falcon 1015/Abner 1015 (58)
Vanishing American	Diamonds	1962	Mercury 71956
Vanishing Angel	Preludes	1958	Acme 730/Cub 9005 (58)
Vararie (misspelled)	Starlites	NA	Everlast 5027
Vault Of Memories	Persians	1961	Goldisc G1/Goldisc 1004 (63)
Vaya Con Dios	Clovers	1959	United Artists LP 3033
Vaya Con Dios	Drifters (1959-forward)	1964	Atlantic 2216
Vegetable Song, The	Four Blues	1950	Apollo 1145
Velma	Valiants (New York)	1958	Speck 1001
Velvet Waters	Dolphins, Davey Jones & the	1961	Audicon 116
Vengeance (Will Be Mine)	Matadors	1958	Sue 700
Venus	Dreamers, Danny & the	1960	Dream 7
Venus	Squires (California)	1956, 1976	Vita 128
Venus In Blue Jeans	Bruno, Bruce & group	1962	Roulette 4427
Venus My Love	Blue Jays (Venice, Calif.)	1962	Milestone 2014
Verdict, The	Five Keys	1955	Capitol 3127
Verdie Mae	Phillips, Phil (with the Twilights)	1959	Mercury 71531
Very Best Luck In The World, The	Ebonaires	1956	Money 220
Very End, The	Casualtones	1963	Success 102
Very First Tear	Crystalaires	NA	Mickey B Juke Box Review 101
Very Merry Christmas	Holidays	1960	Monument 431
Very Precious Oldies	Five Satins	1973	Kirshner 4251
Very Truly Yours	Evergreens	1955	Chart 605
Very Young, The	Raye, Jean & group	1961	Whip 275
Vicki	Uptowners	1964	Le Cam 126
Vicki Lee	Untouchables	1960	Madison 134
Vickie	Five Shades	1965	Veep 1208
Vickie Sue	Ebbs	1959	Dore 521
Vicky	Endells	1963	Heigh Ho 604/605
Vicky	Statlers	1962	Little Star 108
Victory	Embers, Gene Pitney & the	1990	Relic LP 5085
Viddley Biddley Baby	Schooners	1958	Ember 1041
View From My Window	Tymes	1963	Parkway 891
Village Of Love	Diablos, Nolan Strong & the	1964	Fortune 563
Village Of Love	Fabulous Twilights, Nathaniel Mayer & the	1962	Fortune 545/United Artists 449 (62)/ Fortune 563 (63)
Village Of Love	Halos	1962	Trans Atlas 690
Village Of Love	Thomas, Vic (with the Four-Evers)	1964	Philips 40228
Vilma's Jump-Up	Comets, Lynn Tiatt & the	NA	Pussycat 1
Vines Of Love, The	Del Rios	1958	Big 613
Vip-A-Dip	Mint Juleps	1956	Herald 481
Vippity Vop	Honey Boys	1956	Modern 980
Vision In The Night	Silhouettes	19??	
Vision Of Love	Explorers	1960	Coral 62147
Vision Of Love	Savoys (New Jersey)	1980	Catamount 778
Vision Of You	Honeycones	1958	Ember 1036
Vision Of You, The	Castells	1961	Era 3064
Vision, The	Key-Noters	1959	Swan 4048
Visiting Day	Charmers	1962	Terrace 7512
Vito's House	Reflections	1966	ABC 10794
Viva Ju Juy	Platters	1963	Mercury 72194
Voice Of A Fool, The	Cymbals	1963	Dot 16472
Voice Of An Angel, The	Mifflin Triplets	NA	Ember (unreleased)
Voice Of Love, The	Sparks, Milton & group	1958	Vulcan/Hunt 320 (58)
Voice Of The Bayous	Accents (California)	1956	Accent 1036
Voice Of The Drums	Futuretones, Jim Holiday & the	1958	4 Star 1720
Voice, The	Five Satins	1973	Night Train 901
Voice, The	Scarlets, Fred Parris & the	1958, 1961	Klik 7905/Candlelite 411 (74)
Voice Within, The	Maytones, Percy Mayfield & the	1954	Specialty 544
Voices Of Love	Kings & Queens	1957	Everlast 5003
Volare	Belvin, Jesse & group	1958	RCA 7310
Volcano	Flames	1953	7-11 2109 (unreleased)
Volcano	Jets (7-11)	1953	7-11 2101/2102
Voo Doo Dolly	Invictas & Hollywood Rebels with Jimmie Hombs	1959	Jack Bee 1004

SONG	GROUP	YEAR	LABEL
Voo Doo Hurt	Mar-Vels	1961	Tammy 1016
Voodoo	Chippendales	1960	Rust 5023
Voodoo	Combinations	NA	Carrie 010
Voodoo	Ivies	1959	Roulette 4183
Voodoo Doll	Interiors	1961	Worthy 1008
Voodoo Eyes	Silhouettes	1958	Ember 1037
Voodoo Man	Shades	1963	Times Square 16/ Times Square 93 (64)
Voodoo Man, The	Dell Vikings	1958	Mercury 71266/Mercury LP 30353
Voodoo Man, The	Kings Five	1959	Trophy 9
Voo-Vee-Ah-Bee	Platters	1954, 1955	Federal 12198/Power 7012
Vow, The	Cadillacs	1959	Unreleased
Vow, The	Capes	NA	Chat 5005
Vow, The	Flamingos	1956	Checker 846
Vow, The	Pearls	19??	
Vow, The	Philadelphians	1962	Cameo 216
Vow, The (acappella)	Concepts	1966	Catamount 112
Vowels Of Love	Poets	1958	Pull 129/Flash 129 (58)
Vows Of Love, The	Paragons	1958	Winley 227
Voyage	Chessmen	1964	G-Clef 707
Voyager, The	Belmonts	1976	Strawberry 106
Vut Vut	Imperials, Little Anthony & the	1961	Carlton 566

W

SONG	GROUP	YEAR	LABEL
Wabble Loo	Chromatics, Sherry Washington & the	1956	Million 2016
Wacky Wacky	Cardigans	1959	Mercury 71349
Wadda Doo, The	Turbans (Philadelphia)	1957	Herald 510
Waddle, The	Cavaliers, Little Bernie & the	1962	Jove 100
Waddle, The	Dukes, Don Barber & the	1960	Thunderbird 105
Waddle, The	Jay Cees	1962	Enjoy 1004
Waddle, The	Slades	1958	Domino 500
Waddle, The	Tangents	1960	United Artists 201
Waddle, The	Tangiers (Los Angeles)	1962	A-J 905
Waddle, Waddle	Bracelets	1962	Congress 104
Wa-Do-Wa	Nutmegs	1964	Times Square 103
Wagon Wheels	Blue Notes, Todd Randall & the	1957	Josie 823
Wagon Wheels	Hollywood Flames	1957	Cash 1042
Wagon Wheels	Ravens	1951	Rendition 5001
Wah-Bop-Sh-Wah	Twilighters (Atlanta)	1955	Specialty 548
Wah-Wahini	Rip Chords	1964	Columbia 43093
Wailin' Little Mama	Counts	1955	Dot 1235
Wait	Charms, Otis Williams & the	1960	King 5421
Wait A Little Longer	Sputniks	1958	Class 222
Wait A Little Longer Son	Imaginations	1962	Ballad 500
Wait A Minute	Coasters	1961	Atco 6186
Wait A Minute	Ivy League	1965	Cameo 343
Wait A Minute	Mosquitos	1964	Herald 587
Wait A Minute	Turn Ons, Tim Tam & the	1966	Palmer 5002
Wait A Minute Baby	Charms, Otis Williams & the	1960	King 5372
Wait A Minute, Baby	Enchanters (Detroit)	1956	Mercer 992/Coral 61756 (57)
Wait A Minute Baby	Magic-Tones	1974	Broadcast 1101
Wait Eternally	Carroll, Eddie & group	1962	Santo 504
Wait For Me	Berry, Richard (with the Dreamers)	1956	RPM 477
Wait For Me	Chandler, Lenny & group	1963	Laurie 3158
Wait For Me	Day Brothers	1962	Firebird 103
Wait For Me	Dreamers, Richard Berry & the	1963	Crown LP 5371
Wait For Me	Embers	1960	Dot 16101
Wait For Me	Inconquerables	1964	Flodavieur 803
Wait For Me	Margilators	1959	Blue Moon 409
Wait For Me	Montclairs	1965	Sunburst 106
Wait For Me	Three Dolls, Larry Stevens & the	1960	Epic 9358
Wait For Me	Versatones	1957	RCA 6917
Wait For Me Baby	Top Notes	1962	Festival 1021
Wait For My Gal	Silvertones	1964	Sweet 16

SONG	GROUP	YEAR	LABEL
Wait 'Round The Corner	Lovejoys, Leola & the	1964	Tiger 101
Wait 'Til My Bobby Gets Home	Love, Darlene & group	1963, 1974	Philles 114/Warner-Spector 0401
Wait 'Til Tomorrow	Dells	1964	Vee Jay 615
Wait Up	Cameos (New Jersey)	1960	Dean 504/Johnson 108 (60)
Wait Up Baby	Duals	1957	Fury 1013
Wait, Wait, Wait	Del Rios	1959	Neptune 108
Waited So Long	Houston, David & group	1958	NRC 005
Waited So Long	Mascots	1974	Rumble 4197
Waitin' Around For You	Counts	1954	Dot 1226
Waitin' For My Date	School Belles	1958	Dot 15746
Waitin' On The Right Guy	Four Bars	1964	Falew 108
Waitin' (The Pitty Pat Song)	Emjays	1959	Greenwich 411
Waiting	Dodds, Billy & group	1962	Prime 2601
Waiting	Four Chanels, Virgil & the	1959	Deb 508
Waiting	Gems (Recorte)	1958	Recorte 407
Waiting	Midnighters, Hank Ballard & the	1960	King 5312
Waiting	Orioles, Sonny Til & the	1952	Jubilee 5082
Waiting	Page Boys	1957	Prep 117
Waiting	Rivingtons	1963	Liberty 55528
Waiting At The Station	Cap-Tans	1951	Gotham 268
Waiting For My Baby	Fortes	1964	Current 103
Waiting For You	Falcons (Detroit)	1960	United Artists 229
Waiting For You	Passions	1990	Crystal Ball 157
Waiting For You	Trueleers	1963	Checker 1026
Waiting For Your Call	Fi-Tones	1956	Atlas 1056
Waiting For Your Love	Phantones	1959	Bale 105
Waiting In The Chapel	Gay Notes	1958	Zynn 504
Waiting In The Schoolroom	Nite Riders	1958	Teen 120
Waiting (To Take You Home)	Hi-Lites, Skippy & the	1962	Elmor/Stream-Lite 1027
Waiting, Wanting	Five Bills	1953	Brunswick 84004
Wake Me, Shake Me	Coasters	1960	Atco 6168
Wake Up	Bey Sisters	1956	Jaguar 3016
Wake Up	Elegants	1965	Laurie 3298
Wake Up	Fi-Tones	1958	Angle Tone 525
Wake Up Baby	Wanderers, Dion & the	1966	Columbia 43483
Wake Up In The Morning	Contenders	NA	Whitney Sound 1929
Walk	Daffodils	1955	CJ 101
Walk A Little Faster	Restless Hearts, Fred Parris & the	1965	Checker 1108
Walk About	Ron-Dels (Delbert McClinton)	1965	Brownfield 18/Smash 1986 (65)
Walk Alone	Muffins	1963	Planet 59
Walk Along	Five Wings, Billy Nelson & the	1956	Savoy 1183
Walk Away	Revieras	1964	Victoria 103
Walk Beside Him	Gay Charmers	1959	Savoy 1561
Walk Beside Me	Suburbans	1963	Shelley 184
Walk Beside Me	Vibraharps	1956	Beech 713
Walk Don't Run	Fireflies	1962	Taurus LP 1002
Walk In The Garden	Sensationals, Jimmy Jones & the	1959	Savoy 4116
Walk In With Love	Echoes, Allan Roberts & the	1960	Spotlight 101
Walk Me Home	Spinners, Claudine Clark & the	1963	Chancellor 1130
Walk On	Miller Sisters	1962	Rayna 5004
Walk On By	Belmonts	1963	Sabina 513
Walk On By	Rogers, Lee & group	1962	Mah's 000.9
Walk On The Wild Side	Prime	NA	Clifton EP 506
Walk On With The Duke	Chandler, Gene (with the Dukays)	1962	Vee Jay 440
Walk On With Your Nose Up	Danderliers	1967	Midas 9004
Walk Right In	Berry, Richard & group	1960	Warner Bros. 5164
Walk Softly	Mello-Kings	1962	Lescay 3009
Walk Softly Away	Starglows	1963	Atco 6272
Walk, Talk And Kiss	Webtones	1958	MGM 12724
Walk That Walk	Sheiks	1955	Cat 116
Walk Through The Darkness	Perry, Charles & group	1962	Melic 4119
Walk With Me	Blendaires, Bobby Carle & the	1958	Decca 30605
Walk With The Wind	Fidelitys	1959	Sir 274
Walkie Talkie Baby	Levee Songsters	1959	Karen 1004/Relic 515 (64)
Walkie Talkie Baby	Teentones	1958	Rego 1004

SONG	GROUP	YEAR	LABEL
Walkin'	Dalton, Danny & group	1959	Teen 505
Walkin'	Salutations, Vito & the	1965	Apt 25079
Walkin'	Sheppards (Chicago - Okeh)	1963	Okeh 7173
Walkin'	Squires (Herald)	1963	Herald 580
Walkin' After Midnight	Charms, Otis Williams & his	1957	DeLuxe 6115
Walkin' Along	Solitaires	1957	Old Town 1034/Argo 5316 (58)
Walkin' Along	Trem-Los	1961	Nolta 350
Walkin' An' Talkin'	Five Stars (New York)	1954	Show Time 1102
Walkin' And Talkin'	Feathers	1955	Show Time
Walkin' And Talkin'	Midnighters, Hank Ballard & the	1963	King 5746
Walkin' And Talkin'	Solitaires	1957	Old Town 1049
Walkin' And Talkin' Blues	King Toppers	1956, 1957	Josie 811
Walkin' By The School	Guys	1965	Original Sound 56
Walkin' Down Broadway	Penguins	1955	Mercury 70654
Walkin' Down The Track	Pilgrims	1956	Baton 235
Walkin' Girl	Valiants (Los Angeles)	1957, 1959, 1961	Keen 34007/82120/Ensign 4035
Walkin' In The Garden	Belvederes	1959	Jopz 1771
Walkin' In The Rain	Execs	1958	Fargo 1055
Walkin' My Baby	Vocaltones	1957	Cindy 3004
Walkin' My Baby Back Home	Revolvers	1994	JL 101
Walkin' My Blues Away	Dreamers (Mercury)	1952	Mercury 70019
Walkin' My Blues Away	Ravens	1953	Mercury 70213
Walkin' Shoes	Three Friends	1961	Cal Gold 169
Walkin' The Dog	Trophies	NA	Nork 79907
Walkin' The Stroll	Diamonds	1959	Mercury 71534
Walkin' Through A Cemetery	Spinners, Claudine Clark & the	1962	Chancellor 1124
Walkin' Through The Jungle	Five Cashmeres	1962	Golden Leaf 108
Walkin' Together	Morris, Pete & group	1957	End 1006
Walkin' With Love	Top Notes	1960	Atlantic 2066
Walkin' With My Baby	Tops	1957	Singular 712
Walkin' With My Baby	Vocal-Tones	1957, 1973	Juanita 100
Walking All Alone	Jades	1959	Nau-Voo 807
Walking Alone	Four Dukes	1976	Sun (unreleased)
Walking Alone	Tic Tocs	1957	Back Beat 502
Walking Along	Diamonds	1958	Mercury 71366
Walking Along	Four Kings	1958	Stomper Time 1163
Walking Along	Innocents	1961	Indigo LP 503
Walking Along	Jades	NA	Prism 1924
Walking Along	Stereos	NA	Unreleased
Walking And Crying	Four Jacks, Mac Burney & the	1956	Hollywood 1058
Walking Around In Circles	Spiders	1961	Imperial LP 9140
Walking At Your Will	Four Kings, Willie Mitchell & the	1958	Stomper Time 1160
Walking Boy	Illusions	1964	Little Debbie 105
Walking By The River	Orioles, Sonny Til & the	1983	Murray Hill LP M61277
Walking Down Main Street	Charmaines	1996	Saxony 2005
Walking Down The Aisle	Cupcakes, Little Alfred with the	1964, 1965	Lyric 1016/Jewel 744 (65)
Walking Down The Aisle	Little Alfred & group	1962	Lyric 1016
Walking Down The Hall	Ramadas	1964	New World 2000
Walking Down The Street	Videls	1964	Fargo 1062
Walking From School	Starlites, Jackie & the	1963	Mascot 131
Walking In Different Circles	Prophets, Ronnie Dio & the	1967	Parkway 143
Walking In The Rain	Delrons, Reperata & the	1970	Kapp 2050
Walking In The Rain	Kac-Ties	1962	Trans Atlas 695/Kape 502 (63)
Walking In The Rain	Platinums	1980	J & M 649
Walking In The Rain (acappella)	Islanders	1975	Relic LP 104
Walking My Baby Back Home	Chalets	1982	L.I.R.R.A. 1000
Walking My Baby Back Home	Flamingos	1964	Times Square 102
Walking My Baby Back Home	Hi-Lites (Connecticut)	1961	Record Fair 500
Walking My Baby Back Home	Overtones, Penny & the	1958	N/A
Walking On	Royal Playboys	1961	Imperial 5782
Walking On Air	Downbeats,	1959	Goldband 1083
	Beth Murphy with Gene Terry & the		
Walking Out The Back Door	Del-Tones	1959	Ro-Ann 1001
Walking Sad	Pharaohs	1957	Fascination 001/Skylor 101
Walking The Dog	Laurels	1995	Swing Club 028

SONG	GROUP	YEAR	LABEL
Walking The Dog	Nitecaps	1966	Vandan 4733
Walking The Streets Alone	Love Letters	1957	Acme 714
Walking Through Dreamland	Chantels, Richard Barrett & the	1959	Gone 5056
Walking Through The Jungle	Raiders	1958	Brunswick 55090
Walking To School With My Love	Trinities, Kayo & the	1960	Souvenir 1004
Walking With My Love	Frazier, Ray & group	1956	Excel 111
Walking With My New Love	Chevelles, G.W. & the	1968	Flaming Arrow 37
Walking You To School	Rockin R's	1960	Stepheny 1842
Wallflower	Adventurers	NA	Columbia LP 8547
Wallflower	Vibrations	1960	Checker 969
Wallflower, The	Peaches, Etta James with the	1954	Modern 947
Wallop, The	Tabs	1962	Wand 130
Walter	Kittens	1963	Don-El 122
Waltz, The	Carterays, Gloria Mann & the	1954	Sound 102
Wanda	Dupree, Lebron & group	1959	Spann 411
Wanda	Heartbreakers (Washington, D.C.)	1951	RCA 4327
Wanda	Meteors, Jimmy Dee & the	1961	Pixie 7411
Wanderer, The	DiMucci, Dion (with the Del Satins)	1961	Laurie 3115
Wanderer, The	Foreign Intrigue	1972	E.M. 1001
Wanderin'	Barons (Bellaire)	1963	Bellaire 103
Wandering	Viscounts	1963	Star-Fax
Wandering Heart	Bonnie Sisters	1956	Rainbow 333
Wang Dang Dula	Delighters, Donald Jenkins & the	1963	Cortland 109
Wanna Dance	Pizani, Frank (with the Highlights)	1959	Afton 616
Wanna Go Home	Monarchs	1955	Wing 90040
Wanna Lee	Vocal-Tones	1957, 1973	Juanita 100
Wanna Make Him Mine	Emeralds (Jubilee)	1964	Jubilee 5474
Want Me	Penguins	1959	Dooto LP 242/Dooto EP 241
Want To Be Happy	Corvets	1965	Soma 1425
Want You	Havens	1963	Poplar 123
Want You To Know	Kiddieos, Jay Bryant & the	NA	Alfa 201
Want Your Lovin'	Bobbies	1964	Crusader 115
Wanted	Dream Girls, Bobbie Smith & the	1961	Big Top 3085
Wanted	Orioles, Sonny Til & the	1983	Murray Hill LP M61277
Wanted (A Solid Gold Cadillac)	Aquatones	1960	Fargo 1016
Wanted Dead Or Alive	Spydels	1961	MZ 103/MZ 009
War Hoss Mash	Daylighters	1963	Checker 1051
Warm	Dynamics, Ray Murray & the	1963	Fleetwood 7005
Warm	Skyliners	1959	Calico LP 3000
Warm Is The Sun	Gladiators, Bruno & the	1962	Vault 901
Warm Love	Lloyd, Jackie (with the Harbor Lights)	1960	Heros 342
Warm, Soft And Lovely	Click-Ettes	1960	Dice 94/95
Warm Spot	Cues	1991	Capitol (unreleased) (recorded 1956)
Warm Summer Nights	Stimulators	NA	Sound-A-Riffic
Warm Your Heart	Drifters (Pre-1959)	1954	Atlantic 1029
Warm Your Heart	Top Notes	1960	Atlantic 2080
Warmth Of The Sun, The	Lancers	1965	Vee Jay 654
Warning Voice, The	Maestro, Johnny & group	1961	Coed 549
Was I Dreaming	Dreamtones	1957	Mercury 71222
Was It A Dream	Sixteens	1964	Regency 626
Was It A Dream Of Mine?	Six Teens	1957	Flip 322
Was It a Dream?	Royal Teens	1960	Capitol 4335
Was It All Right	Unforgettables	1961	Colpix 192
Was It Meant To Be This Way	Zircons	1967	Heigh Ho 645/646
Was Judy There	Ivy Three	1960	Shell 720
Was That The Right Thing To Do	Glory Tones	1957	Epic 9243
Washboard	Poor Boys, King Richard & the	1961	Apollo 1203
Washed My Heart Of Love	Classmates	1956	Silhouette 509/510
Wasted	Dynamics	1959	Dynamic 1001
Wasted Words	Goldtones, Bill Bryan & the	1962	Pike 5913
Wasting Time	Magnetics	NA	JV 2501
Watch Dog	Charms, Otis Williams & his	1959	DeLuxe 6183
Watch My Smoke	4 Most, Lincoln Chase & the	1956	Dawn 217
Watch On	Blue Flamers	1954	Excello 2026
Watch Out	Crowns (with Larry Chance)	1963	Old Town 1171

SONG	GROUP	YEAR	LABEL
Watch What You Do	Charmers	1963	Co-Rec 101
Watch What.....	Midnighters, Hank Ballard & the	1964	King 5963
Watch Your Mouth	Key, Troyce & group	1959	Warner Bros. 5035
Watch Your Step	Thornton Sisters	1964	Bobsan 1000
Watcha Bet	Escos	1961	Federal 12430
Watcha Gonna Do	Expressions, Billy Harner & the	1964	Lawn 239
Watcha Know New?	Unique Teens	1957	Dynamic 110/Relic 518 (64)
Watching The Moon	Dell Vikings (with Charles Jackson)	1959, 1973	Petite 503/Bim Bam Boom 113
Watching The Rainbow	Unisons, George Jackson & the	1961	Lescay 3006
Watching Willie Wobble	Chex, Tex & the	1963	Newtown 5010
Watching You	Crystals (Bronx)	1959	Cub 9064
Water Boy	Ravens	1956	Argo 5261
Watermelon	Countdowns	1961	Image 5002
Watermelon Man	Five Counts	1962	Brent 7034
Waterproof	Scamps	1955	Peacock 1655
Waterproof Eyes	Topsy, Tiny (with the Five Chances)	1958	Federal 12315
Water-Water	Twilighters (Bronx, N.Y.)	1957	J.V.B. 83
Watts	Chanters, Brother Woodman & the	1955	Combo 78
Watusi	Pharaohs, Ricky & the	1956	Class 202
Watusi One More Time	Shondelles	1963	King 5755
Watusi, The	Vibrations	1960	Checker 969
Watusi With Lucy	Dovells	1964	Parkway 925
Watusi Wobble	Profiles	1962	Goldie 1103
Watussi Wussi Wo	Tenderfoots	1955	Federal 12214
Wa-Wabble, The	Debelaires	1962	Lectra 502
Way Beyond Today	Tymes	1964	Parkway LP 7032
Way Beyond Tomorrow	Prospects	1989	Starlight 69
Way Down Low	Symphonics	1963	Tru-Lite 116
Way Down Yonder In New Orleans	Love, Jimmy & group	1963	Violet 1052
Way I Feel, The	Drifters (Pre-1959)	1953	Atlantic 1006
Way I Feel, The	Montels	1961	Kink 9365
Way I See It, The	Royaltones, El Pauling & the	1960	Lute 5801
Way I Want You, The	Blends	1960	Talent 110/Skylark 108 (61)
Way In The Middle Of A Dream	Nite Riders, Doc Starkes & the	1958	Teen 114
Way In The Night	Cymbals	1963	Dot 16472
Way It Used To Be, The	Kids, Billy & the	1961	Lute 6016/Lute 312
Way Love Goes, The	Mack, Dell (with the Golden Gate Quartet)	1958	Goldband 1064
Way Love Should Be, The	Nutmegs	1963	Times Square 14/Relic 533 (65)
Way Over There	Royal Counts	1972	Catamount 1958
Way Over Yonder	Dippers, Georgie Torrence & the	1961	Epic 9453
Way The Ball Bounces, The	Ebon-Knights	1958	Stepheny 1817
Way To My Heart	Starlets, Hal Davis & the	1959	Kelley 105
Way To My Heart, The	Storm, Billy & group	1958	Barbary Coast 1001
Way Up	Dates, Lincoln Fig & the	1958	Worthy 1006
Way Up In The Sky	Starlites	1963	Fury 1034/Everlast 5027
Way You Carry On, The	Five Orleans	1957	Ebb 125
Way You Carry On, The	Roulettes	1957	Ebb 124
Way You Do The Things You Do (acappella), The	Shells	1966	Candlelite LP 1000
Way You Dog Me Around, The	Diablos (featuring Nolan Strong)	1955, 1980	Fortune 518/574
Way You Gotta Swing Today, The	Clef Dwellers	1958	Singular 713
Way You Look Tonight, The	Classics (Brooklyn)	NA	Bed-Stuy 222
Way You Look Tonight, The	Davis, Hal Sonny & female group	1959	Kelley 105
Way You Look Tonight, The	Dellrays	NA	Lavette 1007
Way You Look Tonight, The	Jaguars	1956,1959,1961,1965	R-Dell 11/Baronet 1/ Original Sound 59
Way You Look Tonight, The	Jarmels	1961	Laurie 3098
Way You Look Tonight, The	Latin Lads	1987	Ronnie 206
Way You Look Tonight, The	Lonely Guys	1957	Caddy 117
Way You Look Tonight, The	Maestro, Johnny & group	1961	Coed 557
Way You Look Tonight, The	Rays, Rich & the	1956	Richloy 101
Way You Look Tonight, The	Starlets, Hal Davis & the	1959	Kelley 105
Way You'll Always Be, The	Moonbeems	NA	Sapphire (unreleased)
Ways Of Love, The	Johnson, Stella & male group	1960	Vin 1022
Ways Of Romance (acappella)	Chessmen	1965	Relic 1016

SONG	GROUP	YEAR	LABEL
Wayward Wanderer, The	Original Cadillacs	1964	Josie 915
Wayward Wind	Counts, Bobby Comstock & the	1960	Mohawk 124
Wayward Wind, The	Centennials	1961	Dot 16180
We Ain't Gonna Ride No More	Arrows	1973	Baron 102
We All Warned You	Peppermints	1965	RSVP 1112
We Are Like One	Five Masters	1959	Bumble Bee 502
We Are Together	Four Bars	1964	Flying Hawk 1501
We Belong To Each Other	Janettes	1962	Goldie 1102
We Belong Together	Belmonts, Dion & the	1961	Laurie 3080
We Belong Together	Channels, Earl Lewis & the	1972	Channel 1001
We Belong Together	Essex	1963	Roulette LP 25234
We Belong Together	Five Hungry Men	1964	Melmar 122
We Belong Together	Love Notes, Honey Love & the	1965	Cameo 380
We Belong Together	Missiles	1960	Novel 200
We Belong Together	New Silhouettes	1967	Jamie 1333
We Belong Together	Pageants	1961	Paxley 753
We Belong Together	Paramounts	1985	Avenue D 10
We Belong Together	Prime	NA	Clifton EP 506
We Belong Together	Raye, Cal & group	1965	Providence 412
We Belong Together	Rhythm Rockers	1960	Satin 921
We Belong Together	Romans, Little Caesar & the	1977	Essar 7803
We Belong Together	Santos, Larry (with the Tones)	1959	Baton 265
We Belong Together	Videls	1963	Musicnote 117
We Belong Together	Webs	1968	Verve 10610
We Better Slow Down	Castells	1967	Solomon 1351
We Build A Nest	Actuals	1976	Candlelite 438/Ronnie 200
We Can Live Off Love	Babettes	1963	Hope
We Can Try It Again	Spina, Vic & group	NA	VM
We Could Find Happiness	Wanderers	1953	Savoy 1109
We Dance	Escos	1960	Federal 12380
We Danced In The Moonlight	Five Stars (New York)	1955	Treat 505
We Dream	Falcons, Jack Richards & the	1958	Dawn 233
We Fell In Love	Avons	1960	Mercury 71618
We Fell In Love	Enchantones	1962	Poplar 116
We Five Boys (acappella)	Five C's	NA	Standord (unreleased)
We Go Together	Casuals	NA	Black Hawk 500
We Go Together	High Seas	1960	D-M-G 1001/D-M-G 4000
We Go Together	Moonglows	1956, 1964, 1972	Chess 1619/Lana 134/ All Platinum 109
We Go Together	Olympics	1966	Mirwood LP 7003
We Go Together	Royal Jesters	1962	Jester 104
We Go Together (Pretty Baby)	Olympics	1965	Mirwood 5504
We Got It	Sparkles	1963	Poplar 119
We Got Soul	Juniors, Danny & the	1962	Swan 4113
We Got Together	Boys Next Door	1956	Rainbow 349
We Gotta Sing	Drifters (1959-forward)	1965	Atlantic 2310
We Had A Quarrel	Merri Men, Robin Hood & his	1961	Delsey 303
We Have Love	Cobanas, Roy Hines & the	NA	Solitaire 1001
We Haven't A Moment To Lose	Royal, Billy Joe & group	1961	Fairlane 21009
We Kiss In The Shadows	Luvs	1963	Stallion 1002
We Knew	Storm, Billy & group	NA	Famous LP 501
We Knew	Valiants, Billy Storm & the	1959	Ensign 4035
We Know	Ballads (Tina)	1964	Tina 102
We Like Birdland	Satellites	1960	Palace 102
We Like Crew Cuts	Debs	1958	Josie 833
We Like Girls	Scott Brothers	196?	
We Loved	Robins	1961	Gone 5101
We Made A Vow	Corvells	1957	Lido 509/Tip Top 509 (57)
We Made A Vow	Savoys, Jimmy Jones & the	NA	Savoy (unreleased)
We Made Romance	Celebritys	1956	Caroline 2302
We Make Mistakes	Enchanters (Sharp)	1960	Sharp 105
We Mean More To Each Other	Centurians	1959	Tiger 1001
We Met At A Dance	Castle-Tones	1960, 1974	Fire Fly 321/Rift 504
We Met At A Dance	Hi-Tones, Johnny Wyatt & the	1959	Big Time 1927
We Met At The Altar	Romancers	1959	Marquee 701

SONG	GROUP	YEAR	LABEL
We Met In Catalina	Four Jokers	1959	Crystalette 730
We Must Carry On	Lords, Yvette & the	1964	Yvette 103
We' Raise A Ruckus Tonight	Ravens	1955	Jubilee 5203
We Really Love Each Other	Lumpkin, Henry & group	1961	Motown 1005
We Sing For Fun	Sparrows Quartette	1975	Jet 3021
We Teenagers (Know What We Want)	Emanons (Brooklyn)	1958	Winley 226/ABC 9913 (58)
We Three	Clefs	1952	Chess 1521
We Three	Dell Vikings	1964	Gateway 743
We Three	Dubs	1973	Candlelite 438
We Three	Rhythm Rockers	NA	Emperor 112
We Three	Sentimentals	1959	Coral 62100
We Three	Sharps	1958	Win 702
We Too	Belvederes	1955	Baton 217
We Two	Trains	1964	Swan 4196
We Walk Down The Aisle	Lighters, Mary Hylor & Billy Rolle & the	NA	El-Lor 1058
We Walked In The Moonlight	Modern Red Caps	1965	Penntown
We Want To Rock	Swallows (Maryland)	1958	Federal 12328
We Went Away	Belmonts, Dion & the	1957	Mohawk 107
We Were Made For Each Other	Flamingos	1959	End (unreleased)
We Were Meant For Each Other	C-Notes	1959	Arc 4447
We Were Meant To Be	Sensations	1963, 1964	Junior 1002/1021
We Will Walk Together	Satisfactions	1962	Chesapeake 610
We Won't Tell	Teardrops	1958	Josie 856
Weak In My Knees	Med-Tones, Johnny Daril & the	1959	Vita 188
Wear My Class Ring On A Ribbon	Bel-Aires, Eddy Bell & the	1961	Mercury 71763
Wear My Ring	Creators (with the Alamos)	1957	Hi-Q 5021
Wear My Ring	Uptones	1964	Watts 1080
Wear My Ring	Uptones	1963	Watts 1080/Magnum 714 (63)
Weary Blues	Dominos, Don & the	1962	Cuca 1109
Weather Forecast	Delrons, Reperata & the	1968	Mala 12016
Web Of Lies	Larson, Key & group	1961	Lawn 106
Web, The	Emeralds (St. Louis)	1960	Yale 232
Wedding	Bailey, Don & group	1962	USA 723
Wedding Bells	Five Bell Aires, John Hall & the	1990	Relic LP 5085
Wedding Bells	Heartbeats	1957	Rama 222
Wedding Bells	Hits, Tiny Tim & the	1958	Roulette 4123
Wedding Bells	Individuals	1964	Chase 1300
Wedding Bells	Loungers	1958	Herald (unreleased)
Wedding Bells	Loungers	1991	Park Ave. 5
Wedding Bells	Paragons	1960	Musicraft 1102/Musictone 1102 (62)
Wedding Bells	Secrets	1991	Park Ave. 5
Wedding Bells	Senators	1962	Winn 1917
Wedding Bells	Sentimentals	1957	Mint 802
Wedding Bells	Sequins	1958	Del-Fi 4107
Wedding Bells	Street-Tones, Patty & the	1979	Clifton 37
Wedding Bells	Timberlanes	1958	Dragon 101
Wedding Bells	Victorians	1956	Selma 1002
Wedding Bells Are Ringing	Toppers, Bobby Mitchell & the	1954	Imperial 5295
Wedding Bells (Are Ringing In My Ears)	Angels (with Sonny Gordon)	1954	Grand 115
Wedding Bells Are Ringing In My Ears	Blue Sky Boys	1973	Blue Sky 107
Wedding Bells Gonna Ring	Gates	1959	Peach 716
Wedding Bells (Just For You And Me)	Kittens, Terri & the	1961	Imperial 5728
Wedding Bells, Oh Wedding Bells	Swans, Paul Lewis & the	1955	Fortune 813
Wedding Bells, The	Five Pennies	1978	King Tut 176
Wedding Bells Will Ring	Revlons, Tino & the	1963	Pip 4000
Wedding Day	Dells	1958	Vee Jay 300
Wedding Day	Hornets, Lester Johnson & the	1962	
Wedding Song	Fabulaires	1963	Chelsea 103
Wedding Song (If You Say I Do)	Hi Tensions	NA	Milestone
Wedding, The	Bell Tones	1955	Rama 170
Wedding, The	Bishops (with the Mellow-Tones)	1961	Bridges 1105
Wedding, The	Creations	1962	Meridian 7550
Wedding, The	Harris, Billy & group	1959	Plaid 101
Wedding, The	Solitaires	1955	Old Town 1014
Wedding, The	Stick Legs & The Butchering Persians	1962	Hard Times 3002

SONG	GROUP	YEAR	LABEL
Wedding, The	Valiants (New York)	1958	Speck 1001
Wee Small Hours	Duvals, Phil Johnson & the	1958	Kelit 7034
Wee, Wee Baby	Five Thrills	1954	Parrot 800
Weejee Walk	Rivingtons	1964	Liberty 55671
Week Is Over, The	Impressions, Joey & the	NA	Cagg 101
Weekend Blues	Bachelors, Dean Barlow & the	1951	International 777
Week-End Lover	Teamates, Tandi & the	1960	Ember 1068
Weekend Man	Five Dollars	1979, 1979	Fortune LP 8016/Skylark 561
Weekend Man	Spriggs, Walter & group	1955	Blue Lake 109
Weep No More	Tyrants, Terry & the	1961	Kent 399
Weep No More	Valleyites, Nathan McKinney & the	1964	Rayco 526
Weep, Weep, Weep	Parrots	1953	Parrot 758/Checker 772 (54)
Weeping Eyes	Vistas, Little Victor & the	1962	Rendezvous 183
Weeping River	Tokens (Brooklyn)	1962	RCA 7991
Weeping Willow	Five Satins	1956	Ember 1008
Weeping Willow	Lam, Tommy & group	1962	R 303
Weeping Willow Blues	Dominoes	1951	Federal 12039
Weight Broke The Wagon Down	Romaines	1954	Groove (unreleased)
Weird	Four Jays	1958	MGM 12687
Welcome Back To My Heart	Utopias	1963	Fortune 568
Welcome Home	Charms, Otis Williams & the	1959, 1966	DeLuxe 6181/Okeh 7248
Welcome Home	Dreamlovers	1961	Heritage 104
Welcome Home	First Ward Dukes	1977	Clifton 20
Welcome Home	Flamingos	1974	Ronze 111
Welcome Home Baby	Shirelles	1962	Scepter 1234
Welcome Me	Scott Brothers	1963	Comet 2161
Welcome Me Home	Fabulous Four	1962	Melic 4114
Welcome To My Heart	Bouquets	1965	Blue Cat 115
Welfare Blues	Dell Vikings	1977	Fee Bee 173
Well	Olympics	1958	Demon 1508
Well Alright	Vestee, Russ & group	1962	Amy 833
We'll Always Have Each Other	Rogers, Kenneth & group	1958	Carlton 454
Well Baby	Darts	1958	Apt 25023
We'll Be Together	Spy-Dels	1962	Crackerjack 4001
Well Darling	Legends	1963	Falco 305
Well Done Baby	Spartones	1972	Vintage 1000
We'll Have A Chance	Originals, Rosie & the	1961	Brunswick 55205/Highland 1031 (61)
Well Honey	Bua, Gene & group	1958	Safari 1007/ABC 9928 (58)
Well I Told You	Chantels	1961	Carlton 564
Well, I'm Glad	Knight, Bob	1961	Laurel 1025
Well It's Alright	Impossibles	1959, 1960	RMP 1030/501
Well It's Alright	Jo-Vals	1964	Grove 105
Well, I've Got News	Fabulous Twilights, Nathaniel Mayer & the	1962	Fortune 550
Well, Little Baby	Five Dots	1955	Note 10003
We'll Make It Someday	Williams, Colly & group	1963	Poplar 118
We'll Never Meet Again	Midnighters	1955	Federal 12243
Well Now	Wonders	1957	Reserve 122
Well Of Loneliness, The	Hustlers, Richard Ward & the	1964	Downey 121
Well Oh Well	Charms, Otis Williams & his	1957	DeLuxe 6149
We'll Reach Heaven Together	Quotations	1962	Verve 10252
We'll Still Be Together	Cameos (Pittsburgh)	1960, 1985	Matador 1808
We'll Wait	Debonaires (New York)	1960	Gee 1054
Wendy, Wendy, Went Away	Graduates	1960	Malvern 500
Went To Chinatown	Q's, Bruce Clark & the	1964	Hull 762
We're All In This Together	Dovells	NA	Paramount 0134
We're Getting Married	Whispers	1955	Gotham 312
We're Goin' To The Hop	Samuels, Clarence & group	1959	Apt 25028
We're Going Steady	Newtones	1965	Relic 1010
We're Going Steady (You Belong To Me)	Starlets, Danetta & the	1962	Okeh 7155
We're Gonna Get Married	Royal Robins, Patricia Conley & the	1962	Aldo 504
We're Gonna Have A Good Time	Elgins (Congress)	1964	Congress 225
We're Gonna Have A Rockin' Party	Winchell, Danny (with Nino & the Ebbtides)	1959	Recorte 410
We're Gonna Have Some Fun	Heartbreakers (Washington, D.C.)	1952	Roadhouse 1012
We're Gonna Hold The Night	Delrons, Reperata & the	1969	Kapp 2010
We're Gonna Love	Johnson Quartet, Bill	1955	Jubilee 5211

SONG	GROUP	YEAR	LABEL
We're Gonna Party	Portraits	1963	Tri-Disc 109
We're Gonna Rock	Five Dollars, Jim Sands with the	1958	Hi-Q 5010
We're Gonna Rock Tonight	Three Chuckles	1956	Vik 0244
We're In Love	Creations	1962	Penny 9022/Take Ten 1501 (63)
We're In Love	Crystalettes	1963	Crystalette 755
We're In Love	Dappers (Star-X)	1958	Star-X 505
We're In Love	Ebonaires	1959	Colonial 117
We're In Love	Spydells	1960	Addit 1220
We're In Love	Strangers	1959	Christy 107/108
We're In Our Teens	Petite Teens	1959	Brunswick 55119
We're Just Friends Now	Levons	1963	Columbia 42798
We're Lovers	Gladiolas	1974	Owl 326
We're Lovers	Zodiacs, Maurice Williams & the	1974	Relic LP 5017/Collectables LP 5021
We're Not Getting Along (Like We Used To)	Keynotes	1959	Top Rank 2005
We're Old Enough	Creations, Johnny Angel & the	1959	Jamie 1134
We're Only Young Once	Raphael, Johnny & group	1958	Aladdin 3409
We're Still Holding Hands	Three Chuckles	1956	X 0216/Vik 0216 (56)
We're Strollin'	Royals, Richie & the	1962	Golden Crest 573/Rello 3
We're Strolling	Strollers	1958	Warner 1018
We're Supposed To Be Through	Orioles, Sonny Til & the	1950	Jubilee 5031
We're Through	Meadows, Larry & group	1959	Strato-Lite 969
Were You Ever Mine To Lose	Lancers	1953	Trend 63
Were You There	Dominoes	1959	Liberty LP 3056
Were You There?	Danleers	1964	Smash 1872
Were-Wolf	Kac-Ties	1963	Shelley 163/Kape 503 (63)
Western Movies	Olympics	1958, 1966	Demon 1508/Mirwood 5523
Western Union	Swinging Reeds, Don Reed & the	1958	United 215
Westside Boy, Eastside Girl	Fabulous Fidels	1962	Jaa Dee 106
We've Believed In Love	Team Mates	1962	Philips 40029
We've Got Love On Our Side	Skyliners	1978	Tortoise Int'l 11343
We've Got Something	Tropics, Eddie & the	1965	Josie 930
Whadaya Want	Charms, Otis Williams & the	1955	DeLuxe 6080
Whadaya Want	Robins	1955	Spark 110
Whadaya Want?	Debs	1955	Bruce 129
What A Crazy Feeling	Eagles	1955	Mercury 70524
What A Difference A Day Makes	Moonglows	1964	Lana 131
What A Dolly	Bel Raves, Lou Berry & the	1959	Dreem 1001
What A Fool	La Roc, Dal & group	1961	Arteen 1010
What A Fool	Prisonaires	1976	Sun 516
What A Guy	Raindrops	1963	Jubilee 5444
What A Kiss That Was	West Winds	1964	Enith International 1269
What A Lie	Chips	1961	Ember 1077
What A Love This Is	Revlons	1962	Toy 101
What A Man Can Do	Bluenotes, Harold Melvin & the	1966	Arctic 135
What A Nice Way To Turn Seventeen	Crystals (Brooklyn)	1962	Philles 102
What A Night	Chippendales	1959	Andie 5013
What A Night For Love	Notations	1958, 1980	Wonder 100
What A Night (What A Morning)	Christmas, Connie & group	1962	Checker 1015
What A Pity	Maldoneers (with the Deltairs)	1973	Vintage 1015
What A Pretty You'd Be	Hi-Lites, Ronnie & the	1982 (1962)	UGHA 16 (previously unreleased - Joy)
What A Scene	Four-Evers	1966	Red Bird 10-078
What A Shape I'm In	Naturals	1958	Beacon 462
What A Surprise	Embers	1961	Empress 108
What A Surprise	Maestro, Johnny & group	1961	Coed 549
What A Sweet Thing That Was	Shirelles	1961	Scepter 1220
What A Weekend	Travelers	1960	ABC 10119
What A Wonderful Love	Baby Dolls	1961	Maske 701
What About Frank Clement	Prisonaires	1978	Charly CR 30148
What About Love	Romancers	1962	Palette 5095
What About Me	Castanets, Yolanda & the	1961	Tandem 7002
What About Me	Daylighters	1966	Smash 2040
What About Me	Leopards, Lee & the	1964	Fortune 867
What About Me	Players	1963	Tarx 1007

SONG	GROUP	YEAR	LABEL
What About The Mountain	Marvells	1961	Finer Arts 2019
What About Tonight	Blenders (New York)	1950	Decca 48183
What About Us	Coasters	1959	Atco 6153
What Am I	Duvals (Illinois)	1963	Boss 2117/Red Rocket 471 (63)
What Am I Goin' To Do?	Fi-Tones	1958	Angle Tone 530
What Am I Gonna Do	Classmates	1955	King 1487
What Am I Gonna Do With You	Intentions	NA	Black Pearl 100
What Am I Gonna Do With You, Baby	Chiffons	1965	Laurie 3275
What Am I Guilty Of	Cymbals, Lee Williams & the	NA	Rapda
What Am I Livin' For	Velaires, Danny & the	1967	Brent 7072
What Am I To Do? (The Letter)	Quin-Tones (Pennsylvania)	1958	Hunt 322 (58)
What Am I To Do?	Rockers	1956	Federal 12267
What Are Boys Made Of	Percells	1963	ABC 10401
What Are You Doing	Chanters	NA	SSP
What Are You Doing New Years Eve	Tune Weavers, Margo Sylvia & the	1988	Classic Artists 107
What Are You Doing New Year's Eve	Evergreens, Dante & the	1960	Madison 143
What Are You Doing New Year's Eve	Four Sevilles	1985	Starlight 30
What Are You Doing New Year's Eve	Orioles, Sonny Til & the	1949, 1962, 1964	Jubilee 5017/ Charlie Parker 214/Lana 109
What Are You Doing New Year's Eve	Subway Serenade	1981	Avenue D 4
What Are You Doing New Year's Eve?	Dominoes	1965	King 6016
What Are You Doing Tonight?	Florescents	1963	Bethlehem 3079
What Are You Going To Do?	Moonglows	1957	Unreleased
What Are You Gonna Be	Calendars	1974	Relic LP 5019
What Are You Gonna Be	Callenders	1959	Cyclone 5012
What Are You Gonna Be	Remaining Few	1991	Clifton 94
What Brought Us Together	Wizards	1982	C&J 22651
What Brought Us Together?	Edsels	1960	Tammy 1010
What Can I Do	Gay Charmers	1959	Grand 2001/Swan 4032 (59)
What Can I Do	Martells	1965	Atco 6336
What Can I Do?	Kings (New Orleans)	1954	Specialty 497
What Can I Do?	Sophomores (Massachusetts)	1957	Chord 1302/Epic 9259 (57)
What Can I Say	Ray-O-Vacs	1952	Jubilee 5098
What Can I Tell Her Now	Bells	1955	Rama 166
What Can It Be	Alvans	1961	May 102
What Can It Be	Astors	1963	Stax 139
What Can The Matter Be?	Quadrells	1956	Whirlin' Disc 103
What Can You Do With A Broken Heart	Echoes, Tommy Vann & the	1966	Academy 123
What Cha Gonna Do	A Moment's Pleasure	1986	Starlight 42
What Could Be Better	Dee-Vines	1958	Brunswick 55095
What Could Be More Beautiful	Ravens	NA	Mercury (unreleased)
What Could Have Been Can't Be	King Bees	1959	Noble 715
What Could It Be	Persuaders	1959	Winley 235/Relic 1002 (65)
What Did Daddy Do	Limelites, Shep & the	1962	Hull 751
What Did He Say	Pirates, Terry & the	1958	Valli 100/Chess 1695 (58)
What Did I Do	Clefs	1954	Peacock (unreleased)
What Did I Do	Deckers, Lynn Christie & the	1957	Nar 225
What Did I Do	Imperials, Little Anthony & the	1959	End LP 303/End EP 204 (59)
What Did I Do	Royals	1952	Federal 12113
What Did I Do	Stardust	1982	Clifton
What Did I Do	Sweethearts	1963	Brunswick 55240
What Did I Do That Was Wrong	Cleftones	1957	Gee 1041
What Did I Do Wrong	Fireflies	1959	Ribbon 6904
What Did I Do Wrong	Scholars	1956	Cue 7927
What Did I Do Wrong (acappella)	Kac-Ties	1975	Relic LP 108
What Did I Do Wrong?	Relations	1963	Kape 703
What Did I Do?	Essex, Anita Humes & the	1964	Roulette 4542
What Did She Do Wrong	Blades, Carol (with the Harptones)	1957	Gee 1029
What Did She Say?	Solitaires	1955	Old Town 1012
What Did She Use	Bon-Aires	1977	Flamingo 1002
(What Did That Genie Mean When He Said) Ali Coochie	Diablos, Nolan Strong & the	1963	Fortune 569
What Difference Does It Make?	Queens, Shirley Gunter & the	1955	Flair 1065
What Do I Do	Wanderers	1975	Savoy 1099 (unreleased)
What Do I Mean To You	Rosebuds, Rosemary & the	1963	Larkwood 1101

SONG	GROUP	YEAR	LABEL
What Do I Say (When I'm Close To You)	Orbits, Bobby & the	1959	Seeco 6030
What Do Little Girls Dream Of?	Castells	1963	Era 3107
What Do They Know	Johnson, Stella & male group	1960	Vin 1022
What Do We Prove?	Dells	1964	Vee Jay 595
What Do You Do	Checkmates	1962	Regency 26
What Do You Do (Fast Ver.)	Channels, Earl Lewis & the	NA	Collectables LP 5012
What Do You Do?			
(To Make Me Love You So)	Topps	1954	Red Robin 126
What Do You Do When	Comic Books	1962	Cuca 6494
What Do You Do?	Channels, Earl Lewis & the	1956	Whirlin' Disc 107/Port 70023 (60)
What Do You Know About Heartaches	Jivers	1959	RCA 7478
What Do You Know About Love	Carr, Wynonie & group	1957	Specialty 600
What Do You Know About That	Charms, Otis Williams & the	1953	DeLuxe 6014
What Do You Mean To Me	Davis, Hal Sonny & group	1961	Wizard 101/Vee Jay 387 (61)
What Do You Want If			
You Don't Want Love?	Flares	1960	Felsted 8607
What Do You Want To Make			
Those Eyes At Me For?	Checkmates, Emil Ford & the	1959	Andie 5018/Cub 9063 (60)
What Do You Want With Me	Bad Boys	1964	Herald 592
What Does A Girl Do	Shirelles	1963	Scepter 1259
What Does It Matter	Platters	1959	Mercury 71538
What Does That Dream Mean	Goofers	1955	Coral 61480
What Does The Future Hold	King Krooners	NA	Unreleased
What For	Deans, Dolly & the	NA	Thornett 1008
What Goes On	Five Keys	1956	Capitol 3318
What Good Am I Without You	Indigos	1965	Cor 6581/Verve Folkways 5002
What Good Are My Dreams?	Mello-Harps	1956	Tin Pan Alley 157/158
What Good Is Graduation	Graduates	1959	Corsican 0058
What Good Is Money	Star Fires	1962	Haral 7777/7778
What Happened To Saturday	Mistics	1964	Kirk 636
What Happened To You	Orioles, Sonny Til & the	NA	Collectables LP 5014
What Happened To Your Halo?	Thrillers, Little Joe & the	1958	Okeh 7099
What Has Happened To You	Precisions, Tommy Genova & the	1962	Bella 606
What Have I Done Wrong	Dewdrops, Little Henry & the	1957	
What Have I Done?	Titans	1960	Fidelity 3016
What Have I Got To Dream About	Tune Timers	1955	Okeh 7081
What Have I Got To Lose	McDonald, Ken & group	1957	DeLuxe 6121
What Have You Been Doin'?	Majors (Philadelphia)	1963	Imperial 5936
What Have You Got	Blenders (Chicago)	1962	Cortland 103
What Have You Got	Jones, Hillard & group	1962	Cortland 101
What I Don't Know Won't Hurt Me	Essex	1963	Roulette 4515
What I Gotta Do	Starlets, Jenny Lee & the	1962	Congress 107
What I Want	Deltas, Jim Waller & the	1961	Trac 502
What I Wouldn't Do	Gordon, Roscoe & group	1961	Vee Jay 385
What I'd Do For Your Love	Sheiks	1961	Le Grand 1013
What If You	Emeralds, Luther Bond & the	1954	Savoy 1124
What In The World	Majors (Philadelphia)	1963	Imperial 5914
What In The World Can I Do	Hep Cats	1961	Del-Fi 4159
What In The World's Come Over You?	Dovells	1964	Parkway 925
What Is A Dream	Collegiates	1960	Campus 10
What Is A Tear	Charmettes	1963	Kapp 547
What Is A Teen-Ager's Prayer?	Moroccos	1956	United 204/B&F 1347
What Is A Young Girl Made Of	Cadets, Kenny & the	1960	Randy 422
What Is Love	Fi-Dells	1961	Imperial 5780
What Is Love	Pyramids (Detroit)	1963	Vee Jay 489
What Is Love	Superiors	1961	Fal 301
What Is Love	Sweethearts	1963	Hi-III 117
What Is There Left For Me	Alston, Henry & group	1959	Skyline 551
What Is This Dream (I Have)	Faces	1965	Regina 1326
What Is This Thing Called Love	Clovers	1959	United Artists LP 3033
What Is This Thing Called Love	Sounds, Lee & the	1959	Lido 600
What Is Your Decision	Harptones	1956	Andrea 100
What Is Your Secret	Harptones	1988	Murray Hill LP 001098
What Is Your Technique	Elrods, Ronnie Speeks & the	1961	King 5548

SONG	GROUP	YEAR	LABEL
What Kind Of Day Has It Been	Cotillions	1962	Ascot 2105
What Kind Of Fool	Drifters (1959-forward)	1965	Atlantic LP 8113
What Kind Of Fool Am I	Our Gang	NA	Starlight 4
What Kind Of Fool Am I?	Cordials	1962	Felsted 8653
What Kind Of Fool Am I?	Vilons	1961	Lake 713
What Kind Of Fool (Do You Think I Am)	Harptones	1960	Warwick 551
What Kind Of Girl (Do You Think I Am)	Charmaines	1961	Fraternity 880
What Kind Of Man Is This?	Combo-Nettes, Jane Porter & the	1956	Combo 118
What Love Can Do	Ascots	1956	J&S 1628/1629
What Love Can Do	Avons	1959	Hull 731
What Love Has Joined Together	Royal Jesters	1962	Jester 102
What Made Maggie Run?	Dell Vikings	1956, 1957	Fee Bee 210/Dot 15571 (56)
What Made You Change Your Mind	Midnighters	1957	Federal 12305
What Made You Change Your Mind	Monarchs	1964	Sound Stage 7 2516
What Made You Change Your Mind	Vibrations	1961	Checker 990
What Made You Forget	Overtones, Penny & the	1958	Rim 2021
What Makes A Man Fool Around?	Ebb-Tones	1956	Crest 1024
What Makes Little Girls Cry	Diante, Denny & group	1964	Holiday 1211
What Makes Little Girls Cry	Premiers (Los Angeles)	1961	Dore 614
What Makes Little Girls Cry	Shepherd Sisters	1963	Atlantic 2176
What Makes Little Girls Cry	Victorians	1963	Liberty 55574
What Makes Love	Blossoms	1963	Okeh 7162
What Makes Me Feel This Way?	Sultans	1954	Duke 135
What Makes Me Love You	Preeteens	1959	J&S 1756
What Makes The World Go Round	Vidletts	1963	Herald 594
What Makes You Do The Things That You Do?	Wrens	1955	Rama 184
What Makes You Think You're In Love	Williams, Dicky & group	1960	Vin 1021
What More Can I Ask	Powell, Austin (with the James Quintet)	1952	Atlantic 968
What More Can I Ask For	Star-Tels	NA	Lamarr 1000
What More Do You Want	Ivy League	1965	Cameo 343
What More Is There To Say	Diadems	1961	Lavere 187
What Now My Love	Jesters	1986	Starlight 41
What Sin	Scott, Jimmy & group	1957	King 5086
What The Next Day May Bring	Hi-Lites, Ronnie & the	1963	Win 250/Reo
What' This Fussin'	Swing Masters, Angel & the	1959	DC 0420
What Time Is It	Jive Five	1962	Beltone 2024/Relic 1028 (76)
What Time Is It	Natural Facts	NA	Lucky Lou 813
What Time Is It?	Four Havens	1965	Veep 1214
What To Do	Angels (New Jersey)	1967	RCA 9129
What To Do	Drifters (1959-forward)	1962	Atlantic 2143
What To Do	Falcons (Detroit)	1986	Relic LP 8006
What To Do	Ohio Untouchables	1962	Lu Pine 1009/Lu Pine 109 (62)
What Was The Cause Of It All	Hi-Tones	1961	Eon 101
What Will I Do	Classic IV	1962	Algonquin 1651
What Will I Do (If You Go Away)	Avons	1958	Hull 728
What Will I Do (Without You)	Classic IV	1962	Twist 1001
What Will I Gain?	Sharps	1957	Aladdin 3401
What Will I Tell My Heart	Harptones	1961	Companion 103
What Will I Tell My Heart?	Balladiers	1952	Aladdin 3123
What Will Mother Say	Sweethearts	1963	Brunswick 55255
What Will The Outcome Be	Modernistics, Al Lewis & the	1959	Music City 829
What Would I Do	Monotones	1964	Hickory 1250
What Would I Do	Superiors	1965	Verve 10370
What Would I Do Without You	Harbor Lites (with Jay Black)	1960	Jaro 77020
What Would You Do	Beau-Jives	1962	Shepherd 2202
What Would You Do	Dingoes	1957	Dallas 2001
What Would You Do	Precisions	NA	Wild 903
What Would You Do	Silhouettes	1958	Ace 552/Junior 396 (58)
What Would You Do If There Wasn't Any Rock 'N' Roll	Monotones	1986	Murray Hill LP 000180
What Would You Do To Me	Flairs, Richard Berry & the	1955	Flair 1055
What Would You Say?	Chances	1964	Roulette 4549
What You Bet	Cadillacs	1961	Smash 1712
What You Do To Me	Berry, Richard (with the Flairs)	1955	Flair 1055

SONG	GROUP	YEAR	LABEL
What You Do To Me	Velours	1957	Onyx 508/Relic 502 (64)
What You Don't Know	Burrage, Harold & group	1959	Vee Jay 318
What You Gonna Do	Thunderbirds, Chris Farlow & the	1965	General American 718
What You Have Done To Me	Del Vikings	1958	Mercury LP 30353
What You Say Baby	Dells	1957	Vee Jay 274
Whatcha Bet	Pitter Pats	1967	Instant 3284
Whatcha Gonna Do	Corvairs	1961	Clock 1037
What'cha Gonna Do	Drifters (Pre-1959)	1955	Atlantic 1055
What'Cha Gonna Do	Four Mints	1956	Choctaw 8002/Imperial 5432 (57)
What'Cha Gonna Do	Kuf-Linx	1958	Challenge 1013/ Challenge 59002 (58)
What'Cha Gonna Do About It	Aztecs, Billy Thorpe & the	1965	GNP Crescendo 346
Whatcha Gonna Do (acappella)	Five Delights	1960	A Cappella - Best of the Bronx (98)
What'Cha Gonna Do 'Bout It	Royal Jesters	1965	Jox 029
What'Cha Gotta Lose	Dell Vikings	1957	Mercury 71180
Whatcha Know New	Valentinos	1982	Clifton 70
Whatchamacallit, The	Crystals, Sam Hawkins & the	1959	Gone 5042
What'd I Say	Cousins	1961	Chancellor 1074
What'd I Say	Halos	1961	7 Arts 720
What'd I Say	Olympics	1962	Arvee 5073
Whatever Happened To Baby Jane?	Charmers	1962	Terrace 7512
Whatever Happened To Our Love	Avons	1963	Groove 0039
Whatever Happened To Our Love	Charlettes	1963	Angie 1002
Whatever Happened To You	Carroll, W.L.	1955	Baton 213
Whatever Happens	Tempos	1959	Climax 105
Whatever Hurts You	Shades Of Brown	1982	Clifton EP 505
Whatever You Desire	Walker, Wayne & group	1957	Columbia 40905
Whatever You're Doin'	Du Droppers	1953	RCA 5425
What'll I Do	Boardwalkers, Ronnie & the	1961	Rex 103
What'll I Do	Fleetwoods	1963	Dolton 86
What'll You Do Next	Prisonaires	1954	Sun 207
What'll You Do?	Master-Tones	1954	Bruce 111
What's A Matter Baby	Royal Demons	1958	Rhythm 5004
What's A Personality	Jades, Jerry Coulston & the	1959	Christy 119
What's Buggin' You, Baby?	El Dorados	1955	Vee Jay 147
What's Happening, Baby?	Runaways	NA	Hitt 2001
What's Her Name?	Vibes	1958	Allied 10006
What's In An Angel's Eyes	Shells	1960	Johnson 104 (reissue)
What's In The Heart	Five Royales	1962	ABC 10368
What's Mine Is Yours	Shirelles	1962	Scepter LP 502
What's New, What's New	Hi-Fives	1958	Decca 30744
What's New With You	Arrows, Joe Lyons & the	1956	Hollywood 1065
What's Next	Dolls	1965	Maltese 100
What's On Your Mind	Knockouts	1964	Tribute 201
What's On Your Mind	Teenagers, Joey & the	1961	Columbia 42054
What's On Your Mind?	Four Bars	1960, 1963	Cadillac 2006/Shelley 180
What's That	Five Royales	1954	Apollo 458
What's That Thing Called Love	Dwellers	1959	Oasis 101
What's The Matter	El Torros	1960	Duke 321
What's The Matter	Larks (North Carolina)	1988	Relic LP 8014
What's The Matter, Baby	Madison Brothers	1960	Cedargrove 314/Apt 25050 (60)
What's The Matter For You?	Cellos	1958	Apollo 524
What's The Matter With Grownups	Craftsmen	1962	Warwick 678
What's The Matter With Me	Cordials	1962	Bethlehem 3019
What's The Matter With Me	Four Buddies	1952	Savoy 866
What's The Matter With Me?	Fabulous Gardenias	1961, 1962	Liz 1004/Fairlane 21019 (62)
What's The Matter With You, Sam	Ideals	1961	Paso 6401/Dusty Disc
What's The Name Of The Game	Sheppards (Chicago - Sharp)	1961	Sharp 6039
What's The Secret Of Your Success	Coasters	1957	Atco 6104
What's The Use	Marvels, Harry M & the	1961	ABC 10243
What's The World Comin' To	Wonders	1961	Manco 1024
What's This I Hear	Gates, David & group	1960	Mala 413
What's This I See?	Midnighters, Hank Ballard & the	1961	King 5491
What's To Become Of Me	Chessmen	1962	AMC 101/Don-Dee 101 (62)/ Mercury 72559 (65)

SONG	GROUP	YEAR	LABEL
What's To Become Of Me	Honey Bees	1956	Imperial 5416
What's Wrong	Avalons	NA	Collectables LP 5037
What's Wrong With Me	Dynamics	1959	Arc 4453
What's Wrong With Me?	Kings, Chet Reni & the	NA	Georgie 101
What's Wrong With Ringo	Bon-Bons	1964	Coral 62402
What's Your Name	Cliches	1959	Maar C 1530
What's Your Name	Dukes, Don Barber & the	1960	Thunderbird 105
What's Your Name	Four Sevilles	1980	Starlight 3
What's Your Name	Imaginations	1991	Collectables CD 5726
What's Your Name	Midnighters, Hank Ballard & the	1964	King 5931
What's Your Name	Monorays	1958	Nasco 6020
What's Your Name	Mr. Lee (with the Cherokees)	1960	Winter 501
What's Your Name	Noblemen 4	NA	Recap 291
What's Your Name	Top Overs	NA	N/A
What's Your Name Dear	Ebb Tides	1957	Teen 121
Whatsoever We Do	Midnighters	1955	Federal 12224
Wheel Baby Wheel	Five Dukes, Bennie Woods & the	1955	Atlas 1040
Wheel Of Fortune	Cardinals	1952	Atlantic 958
Wheel Of Fortune	Four Flames, Bobby Day & the	1952	Specialty 423
Wheel Of Love	Wig Twisters	1957	A-Ron 1001
Wheel Of Love, The	Classics (Karen)	NA	Karen
Wheel Of Love, The	Pearls	1957	Onyx 516/Relic 522 (64)
Wheelin' And Dealin'	Allen, Charlie & group	1961	Portrait 107
Wheelin' And Dealin'	Four Kings And A Queen	1952	United (unreleased)
Wheelin' And Dealin'	Reflections	1965	Golden World 22
Wheelin' And Dealin'	Dandleers	1958	Amp-3 2115 (first pressing, second is by the Danleers)
Wheels Of Love	Allen, Anisteen (with the Cues)	1955	Capitol 3048
Wheels Of Love	Demires	1959	Lunar 519
When	Corwins	NA	Gilmar 222
When	Dedications	1963	Sultan 4003/Spokane 4003 (63)
When	English, Scott (with the Accents)	1962	Joker 777
When	Flamingos	1955	Checker 815
When	Jivetones	NA	Apt (unreleased)
When A Boy Loves A Girl	Vows	1963	Tamara 760 (same # used twice)/ Sta-Set 402 (63)
When A Girl Gives Her Heart To A Boy	Daye, Billie with male group	1961	Bliss 1002
When A Girl Really Loves You	Mission Bells	1965	London 9760
When A Man Cries	Nite Riders	1958	Teen 120
When Are You Coming Home	Hamilton, Gil & group	1962	Vee Jay 479
When Boy Meets Girl	Four Kittens, Fat Man Matthews & the	1952	Imperial 5211
When Came The Fall	Hollyhawks	1963	Jubilee 5441
When Day Is Done	Scott, Jimmy & group	1957	King 5086
When Did You Leave Heaven?	Four Bars	1954	Republic 7101
When Gabriel Blows His Horn	Robins, Maggie Hathaway & the	1951	Recorded In Hollywood 121
When I Asked My Love	Lovetones	1962	Love-Tone 101
When I Become A Man	Innocents	1961	Indigo 132
When I Call On You	Clark, Dee (with the Kool Gents)	1958	Abner 1019
When I Call On You	Kool Gents	1974	Broadcast 1102
When I Come Home	Dell Vikings	1957	Dot 15636/Mercury 71198 (57)
When I Dream	Paramounts	1963	Centaur 103
When I Fall In Love	Connotations	1980	Clifton 51
When I Fall In Love	Esquires	1962	Meridian 6283
When I Fall In Love	Flamingos	1960	End 1079
When I Fall In Love	Imperial Wonders	1969	Black Prince 317
When I Fall In Love	Latin Lads	1987	Ronnie 206
When I Fall In Love	Savoys (New Jersey)	1965	Catamount 104
When I Fall In Love	Seniors	1961	Decca 31244
When I Fall In Love	Skyliners	1959	Calico LP 3000
When I Fall In Love	Trickels	1959	Gone 5078/Power 250 (59)
When I Fall In Love (acappella)	Citadels	1975	Relic LP 102
When I Fall In Love (acappella)	Five Jades (Bronx, N.Y.)	1975	Relic LP 107
When I Fall In Love (acappella)	Historians, Barbaroso & the	1957	Jade 110
When I Fell In Love (acappella)	Notations	1975	Relic LP 105
When I Find My Love	Four Sounds	1961	Federal 12421

SONG	GROUP	YEAR	LABEL
When I First Fall In Love	Crewnecks	1959	Rhapsody 71961
When I Found You	Heartbeats	1957	Gee 1043
When I Get Like This	Five Royales	1955	King 4806
(When) I Get Scared	Lovelites	NA	Phi-Dan 5008
When I Go To Sleep At Night	Chiffons	NA	Collectables LP 5042
When I Go To Sleep At Night	Tokens (Brooklyn)	1961	RCA 7896
When I Grow Older	Butlers	1963	Guyden 2081
When I Grow Too Old To Dream	Mellow Drops	1954	Imperial 5324
When I Grow Too Old To Dream	Sandmen	1955	Okeh 7052
When I Kneel Down To Pray	Magic Tones	1953	King 4665
When I Lay Me Down To Sleep	Crane, Lor & group	1961	Radiant 1512
When I Leave These Prison Walls	Larks (North Carolina)	1951	Apollo 1180
When I Look Around	Selectones, Jay Jay & the	1962	Guest 6201/6202
When I Look At You	Encores	1953	Checker 760
When I Meet A Girl Like You	Pageboys	1963	Seville 135
When I Meet A Girl Like You	Playboys	1963	Seville 135
When I Met You	Amato, Jerry & group	NA	Tacit 109
When I Met You	Crickets, Dean Barlow & the	1953	Jay-Dee 777
When I Met You	Native Boys	1956	Combo 115
When I Met You	Valets	1958	Jon 4025
When I Need You	Midnighters, Hank Ballard & the	1962	King 5677
When I Needed You Most	Four Bells	1954	Bell 5047
When I Return	Turbans (Philadelphia)	1955	Money 211
When I See Elephants Fly	Five Crows	1986	Ronnie 205
When I See You	Frontiers	1967	MGM 13722
When I Stop Loving You	Jackson, George (with the Jive Five)	NA	Double R 248
When I Walk With My Angel	Vespers	1963	Swan 4156
When I Was Single	Jive Five	1961	Beltone 1006/Relic 1026 (75)
When I Woke Up This Morning	Bop Chords	1957	Holiday 2603
When I Woke Up This Morning	Mello-Moods	1953	Prestige 856
When I Woke Up This Morning	Oasis	1978	Arcade 105
When I Woke Up This Morning (acappella)	Citadels	1975	Relic LP 102
When I'm Blue	Shells	NA	Conlo 879
When I'm Gone	Headen, Willie & D. Williams Orch.	1954	Dootone 345
When I'm In Your Arms	Four Naturals	1959	Red Top 119
When I'm Lonely	Capri, John (with the Fabulous Four)	1959	Bomarc 306
When I'm Walkin' With My Baby	Blendors	1961	Decca 31284
When I'm With You	Centuries	1985	Relic LP 5053
When I'm With You	Chants	1960	Nite Owl 40
When I'm With You	Chips	1980	Clifton 54
When I'm With You	Copas	1967	Catamount 118
When I'm With You	Four Thoughts	1964	Womar 103
When I'm With You	Laurels	1986	R.A.M. 706005
When I'm With You	Moonglows	1956, 1972	Chess 1629/RCA 74-0839
When I'm With You Again	Four Saints	1970	Era 701
When In Love (Do As Lovers Do)	Gee-Tones	1956	Gee 1013 (unreleased)
When In Love (Do As Lovers Do)	Howard, Gregory (with the Cadillacs)	1963	Kapp 536
When In The World	Montalvo, Lenny (with the Crystal Chords)	1958	3-D 373
When Irish Eyes Are Smiling	Dominoes	1957	Decca LP 8621
When It's Over	Co-Eds	1961	Cha Cha 715/Checker 996 (61)
When It's Summer Again	Three G's	1959	Columbia 41383
When Johnny Comes Marching Home	Blue Belles	1962	Newtown 5009
When Love Comes Knocking	Five Discs	1961	Yale 240
When Love Is Young	Mello-Tones	1958	Key 5804
When Love Slips Away	Fashions	1968	20th Fox
When Love Was Born	Casinos	1962	S&G 301
When My Baby Is Gone	Candles, Rochell & the	1960	Swingin' 623
When My Baby Was Born	Dewtones	1954	States (unreleased)
When My Baby Was Born	Four Chimes	1954	United (unreleased)
When My Baby Went Away	Lexingtons	1960	Everest 19369
When My Heart Does All The Talking	Impalas, Speedo & the	1960	Cub 9066
When My Little Girl Is Smiling	Drifters (1959-forward)	1962	Atlantic 2134
When My Little Girl Is Smiling	Motions, Ron & the	NA	Red Bug 0006
When My Lover Comes Home	Sensations, Yvonne Baker & the	1963	Argo 5446

SONG	GROUP	YEAR	LABEL
When My Sugar	Quin-Tones (Pennsylvania)	NA	Vo 5172
When My Teen-Age Days Are Over	Cute-Teens	1959	Aladdin 3458
When My Teenage Days Are Through	Miamians	1958	Amp-3 1006
When Nobody Loves You	Hawkins, Sam & group	1959	Gone 5054
When Paw Was Courtin' Maw	Five Keys	1960	King LP 688
When Peter Walked On Water	Shadows, Jan Strickland & the	1954	Hub
When School Starts Again	Chimes (Reserve)	1957	Reserve 120
When She Wants Good Lovin' My Baby Comes To Me	Coasters	1957	Atco 6098
When She Was My Girl	Lords	1987	Starlight 52
When Sin Stops	Nighthawks	1958	Hamilton 50006
When Someone Loves You	Labradors	1958	Chief 7009
When Summer Gets Back	Flints	1962	Hart 100
When Summer Is Through	Chiffons	1964	Laurie 3262
When The Bells Stop Ringing	Blair, Sandy & group	1963	Bobby 111
When The Boy's Happy	Four Pennies	1963	Rust 5070
When The Boys Talk About The Girls	Shirelles	1966	Scepter 12162
When The Lights Are Low	Shufflers, Jay & the	1962	Crackerjack 4010
When The Lights Go On Again	Comets, Herb Kenny & the	1952	Federal 12083
When The Lights Go On Again	Mellows, Lillian Leach & the	NA	Celeste 3009
When The Music Ends	Four Epics	1962	Heritage 109
When The One You Love Loves You	Gray, Wilhemina & group	1957	MGM 12500
When The Red, Red Robin Comes Bob, Bob, Bobbin' Along	Belmonts, Dion & the	1960	Laurie LP 2006
When The Red Red Robin Comes Bob, Bob Bobbin' Along	Excellents	1963	Mermaid 106
When The Reign Of Love Begins	Ivyliers	1957	Donna A-3
When The Saints Come Marching In	Dynamics	1957	Cindy 3005
When The Saints Go Marching In	Dominoes	1957	Decca 30514
When The Saints Go Twistin' In	Juniors, Danny & the	NA	Singular LP 569
When The Saints Twist	Saints, Ricky & the	1962	7 Teen 101
When The School Bells Ring	Magnets	1958	RCA 7391
When The Summer Is Through	Tokens (Brooklyn)	1961	RCA 7925
When The Sun Goes Down	Jamies	1958	Epic 9299/Epic 9565 (63)
When The Sun Has Begun To Shine	Titans, Don & Dewey & the	1957	Specialty 617
When The Swallows Come Back To Capistrano	Dominoes	1951	Federal 1209
When The Swallows Come Back To Capistrano	Five Satins	1995	X-Bat 1000
When The Swallows Come Back To Capistrano	Satellites, Bobby Day & the	1957	Class 211
When The Swallows Come Back To Capistrano	Swallows (Maryland)	1986	Starbound 503
When The Swallows Come Back To Capistrano	Wildwoods	1960	Caprice 101/102
When They Ask About You	Jades	1963	Dore 687
When True Love Is Gone	Martin, Sonny & group	1959	Rocko 518
When Two People	Storytellers	1963	Dimension 1014/Ramarca 501 (63)
When Was The Last Time	Keys, Rudy West & the	1989	Classic Artists 112
When We Dance	Marveliers	1960	Cougar 1868
When We Get Married	Carvells	1978	Clifton 30
When We Get Married	Dreamlovers	1961	Heritage 102
When We Get Married	Gang, Teddy Field & the	NA	Vita 184
When We Get Married	Persians	1962	RTO 100
When We Get Married (acappella)	Addictions	1972	Kelway 102
When We Get Married (acappella)	Islanders	1975	Relic LP 108
When We Get The Word	Edwards, Jack & group	1963	Michelle 508
When We Get The Word	King, Mabel (with the Harptones)	1963	Amy 874
When We Get The Word	Relations	1963	Club
When We Get Together	Charms, Otis Williams & the	1955, 1961	DeLuxe 6087/King 5682
When We Were So In Love (acappella)	Chessmen	1975	Relic LP 106
When We Were Young	Binders	NA	Sara 7771
When We Were Young	Five Playboys	1957	Fee Bee 213/Dot 15605 (57)
When We're Alone	Del Rays	1958	Future 2203
When We're Apart	Epiks	1965	Process 146

SONG	GROUP	YEAR	LABEL
When We're Together	Trinidads	1959	Formal 1006
When Will I Be Loved	Monotones	1965	Hickory 1306
When Will I Fall In Love	Seniors	1960	Decca 31112
When Will I Know	Blades, Carol (with the Harptones)	1957	Gee 1029
When Will My Troubles End	Five Keys	NA	Detour LP 33-010
When Will The Lights Shine For Me	Solitaires	1958	
When You Are In Love	Premiers (Los Angeles)	1957	Fortune 527
When You Are Mine	Honeytones, Gene Worth & the	NA	Ace 118
When You Ask About Love	Fabulous Futuras	NA	Okon (no #)
When You Come Back To Me	Clovers	1950	Rainbow 11-122
When You Come Back To Me	Re-Vels	1958	Chess 1708
When You Come Back To Me	Striders, Savannah Churchill & the	1951	Regal 3309/Derby 468
When You Dance	Copas	1979	U.G.H.A. 10
When You Dance	Delcos	NA	Monument
When You Dance	Emotions	NA	Unreleased
When You Dance	Impalas (Five Discs)	1966	Red Boy 113/Steady 044
When You Dance	Madison, Glen & group	1962	Ebony 105/Monument
When You Dance	Paramounts	1961	Dot 16201
When You Dance	Rios, Augie & group	1964	Shelley 186
When You Dance	Storm, Billy (with the Storms)	1961	Atlantic 2098
When You Dance	Turbans (Philadelphia)	1955, 1961	Herald 458/Parkway 820
When You Dance (acappella)	Barons (Relic)	1975	Relic LP 101
When You Dance (acappella)	Five Jades (Bronx, N.Y.)	1975	Relic LP 109
When You Find Love Slipping Away	Identities	NA	Together 1410
When You Kiss Me	Upfronts	1961	Lummtone 106
When You Love	Singing Doves, Cliff Butler & the	1953	States 123
When You Love	Stars	1959	Vega 001
When You Loved Me	Tempos	1965	Ascot 2167
When You Said Goodbye	Citadels	1962	Monogram 501
(When You Said) Let's Get Married	Persians	1963	Goldisc G17/Music World 102 (63)
When You See Me Hurt	Show Stoppers	1961	Brent 7021
When You Tell Me Baby	Higgs & Wilson & group	1960	Time 1028
When You Touch Me	Omegas	1959	Decca 31008
When You Walked Out	Arcados	1963	Fam 502
When You Walked Through The Door	Five Royales	1956	King 4869
When You Were Sweet 16	Arrows	1960	Cupid 105
When You Wish Upon A Star	Belmonts, Dion & the	1960	Laurie 3052
When You Wish Upon A Star	Connotations	1980	Clifton 51
When You Wish Upon A Star	Crescents	1963	Hamilton 50033
When You Wish Upon A Star	Imperials, Little Anthony & the	1959	End 1039
When You Wish Upon A Star	Keys	1965	Jam 501
When You Wish Upon a Star	Standards	1969	Amos 134
When You Wish Upon A Star	Stingrays	1964	Crazytown 101/102
When You Wore A Tulip	Platters	1960	Mercury LP 20589/ Mercury LP 60254 (60)
When Your Hair Has Turned To Silver	Jive Bombers	1957	Savoy 1508
When Your Hair Has Turned To Silver	Musical Notes, Bill Johnson & the	1954	Tru-Blue 414
When Your Love Comes Along	Five Satins	1959	First 104
When Your Lover Has Gone	Romaines, Romaine Brown & His	1957	Decca 30399
When You're A Long Long Way Away From Home	Orioles, Sonny Til & the	1951	Jubilee 5057
When You're Alone	Daps	1956	Marterry 5249
When You're Alone	Del-Chords, Donnie & the	1961	Taurus 352/Epic 9495 (62)
When You're Asleep	Dell Vikings	1972	Scepter 12367
When You're Dancin'	Wagner, Cliff & group	1964	Jolum 2509
When You're Dancin' With Me	Swingin' Bears, Bernadette & the	1961	Beach 1001
When You're Gone	Five Keys	1971 (1953)	Aladdin 3175A (unreleased)
When You're Home	Regals	1954	MGM 11869
When You're Hurt	Morris, Pete & group	1957	End 1006
When You're In Love	Corvettes	1959	
When You're Near	Larks (North Carolina)	1954	Lloyds 111
When You're Not Around	Orioles, Sonny Til & the	1952	Jubilee 5071
When You're out Of School	Barries	1964	Di-Nan 101
When You're Smiling	Serenaders, Gene Mumford & the	1956	Whiz 1500
When You're Smiling (acappella)	Velvet Angels	1972	Relic LP 5004

SONG	GROUP	YEAR	LABEL
(When You're Young And) Only Seventeen	Flamingos	1962	End LP 316
Whenever A Teenager Cries	Delrons, Reperata & the	1964	World Artists 1036
Whenever I Get Lonely	Contenders	1963	Saxony 1001
Whenever I Get Lonely	Matadors, Tommy Liss & the	1993	Saxony 1001
Whenever I Look At You	Cap-Tans	1963	Sabu 103
Whenever I'm Without You	Dynamics	NA	Top Ten 927
Whenever You Need Me	Jones, Jimmy & group	1959	Epic 9339
Where	Platters	1959	Mercury 71502/Mercury 10018 (59)
Where All Lovers Meet	Invictors	1963	TPE 8221
Where All Lovers Meet	Vendors	1963	Victorio 128
Where Are You	Blue Belles	1963	Nicetown 5020
Where Are You	De Vaurs	1959	Moon 105/Red Fox 104
Where Are You	Duprees	1964	Coed 591
Where Are You	El-Deens	1959	Federal 12356
Where Are You	Four Bel-Aires	1958, 1976	X-Tra 113
Where Are You	Impacts	1966	Brunswick 55393
Where Are You	Jackson, Dimples & group	1960	Gardena 114
Where Are You	Magnetics	1962	Allrite 620
Where Are You	Montclairs, Eddie Carol & the	1958	Rulu 6098
Where Are You	Woods, Cora & group	1955	Federal 12229
(Where Are You) Now That I Need You	Goodtimers, Don Covay & the	1962	Columbia 42197
Where Are You? (Now That I Need You)	Mello-Moods	1951	Red Robin 105
Where Are You Tonight	Cheerios	1961	Infinity 11/Golden Oldies 1 (61)
Where Are You Tonight	Reunion	1990	Clifton 91
Where Are You?	Belairs	1958	X-Tra 113/Times Square 23 (63)/ Relic 536 (65)
Where Are You?	Deltars, Pearl & the	NA	Unreleased
Where Are You?	Infatuators	1961	Destiny 504/Vee Jay 395 (61)
Where Are You?	Minors	1957	Celeste 3007/Mello 554
Where Can I Go	English, Scott (with the Accents)	1963	Sultan 5500
Where Can I Go Without You	Parkway	1992	Clifton 99
Where Can She Be	Accents	NA	N/A
Where Did Caledonia Go?	Five Stars (New York)	1954	Show Time 1102
Where Did My Baby Go	Jokers, Johnny & the	1962	Beltone 2028
Where Did My Dreamboat Go	Campbell, Charlotte & group	1959	Wanger 194
Where Did My Woman Go	Martells	1959	Nasco 6026
Where Did The Bums Go	Dodgers	1958	Skyway 118
Where Did You Go 'Out', What Did You Do 'Nothing'	Serenaders (Hanover)	1958	Hanover 4514
Where Do I Go From Here	Swallows (Maryland)	1952	King 4579
Where Do We Go From Here	Dubs	1972	Clifton 2
Where Do We Go From Here	Jive Five	1982	Ambient Sound LP 801
Where Has My Lover Gone	Anderson, Bubba & group	1962	Ace 662
Where Have They Gone	Skyliners, Jimmy Beaumont & the	1974	Capitol 3979
Where Have You Been	Cashmeres (Brooklyn)	1961	Josie 894
Where Have You Been	Fabulous Dinos	1962	Musicor 1025
Where I Came In	T-Birds, Don Mikkelsen & the	1959	Deck 600
Where I Fell In Love	Capris (New York)	1961	Old Town 1099
Where I Want To Be	Gainors	1961	Tally-Ho 102
Where In The World	Fidelitys	1960	Sir 276
Where Is He	Click-Ettes	1960	Guyden 2043
Where Is Love?	Danleers	1964	Smash 1895
Where Is My Love	Colonials	NA	Senate 1003
Where Is My Love	Episodes	1965	Four Seasons 1014
Where Is My Love	Watkins, Billy & group	1961	Chess 1786
Where Is My Love Tonight	Angels (New Jersey)	1960	Astro AS202-1
Where Is She	Standards, Larry & the	1962	Laurie 3119
Where Is The Boy Tonight	Charmaines	1962, 1996	Dot 16351
Where Is The Party	Expressions, Johnny & the	1965	Josie 946
Where Lovers Go	Jaguars	1964	Faro 618
Where Mary Go	Flamingos	1958	Decca 30687
Where Now, Little Heart	Dominoes	1953	Federal 12139
Where Or When	Belmonts, Dion & the	1960	Laurie 3044
Where Or When	Flamingos	1959	End LP 304

SONG	GROUP	YEAR	LABEL
Where Or When	Groups In Choir	1966	
Where Or When	Three Chuckles	1956	Vik LP 1067
Where The Candlelight Glows	Fireflies	1958	Roulette 4098
Where There' A Will	Zircons	1967	Heigh Ho 607
Where There Is Love	Darchaes, Nicky Addeo & the	1964	Melody 1417
Where There's A Will	Fantastics	1961	Impresario 124
Where There's A Will	Riffs	1978	Crystal Ball 130
Where There's A Will	Sparkles	1963	Poplar 119
Where There's A Will (There's A Way)	Velours	1957	Onyx 512/Gone 5092 (60)/ Relic 504 (64)
Where Was I	Statens	1978	Crystal Ball 127
Where Were You	Downbeats, Beth Murphy with Gene Terry & the	1959	Goldband 1083
Where Were You	Wheels	1958, 1996	Time 1003
Where Were You Last Night	Chiffons, Ginger & the	1962	Groove 0003
Where Will You Be	Accents (California)	1956	Accent 1036
Where Will You Be	Imperials, Little Anthony & the	1962	Newtime 503
Where Would I Be Without You	Regal Dewey	1977	Milennium 603
Where You Are	Four Tops	1962	Riverside 4534
Where You Belong	Boyd, Eddie (with His Chess Men)	1959	Keyhole 114
Where You Belong	Shy Guys	1966	Palmer 5008
Where You Goin', Little Boy	Zippers, Zip & the	1963	Pageant 607
Where You Live	Flairs, Cornel Gunter & the	NA	Rap 007
Where You Used To Be	Redwoods	1962	Epic 9505
Where'd Ja Go	Frederick, Tommy & group	1960	Coral 62170
Where'd She Go	Rockets	NA	Atlantic (unreleased)
Where'll I Be Tomorrow Night	Satisfiers	1956	Coral 61727
Where's Carolyn Tonight	Paramounts	1963	Centaur 103
Where's My Baby	Picadilly Pipers	1956	Chart 615
Where's My Girl	Belvin, Jesse (with the Feathers)	1955	Specialty 559
Where's My Love	Creations, Johnny Angel & the	1959	Jamie 1134
Where's My True Love	Incidentals	1961	Gar-Lo 1000
Where's The Boy	Charmers	1965	Louis 6806
Where's The Fire?	Robins	1957	Whippet 208
Where's The Joy In Nature Boy	Holland, Bryant & group	1958	Kudo 667
Wherever You Are	Bradford, Chuck & group	1962	Fire 511
Wherever You Are	Del Knights	1961	Chancellor 1075
Wherever You Are	Dubs, Richard Blandon & the	1990	Starlight 51
Wherever You Are	Hallmarks, Rickie & the	1963	Amy 877
Wherever You Go	Casuals, Skip Mahoney & the	1976	Abet
Whether To Resist	Sundials	1962	Guyden 2065
Which One Will It Be	Val-Aires	1959	Willette 114/Coral 62119 (59)/ Coral 62177 (59)
Which Way Did My Heart Go	Storey Sisters	1958	Baton 255
Which Way Did She Go	Majors (Philadelphia)	1963	Imperial 5991
Which Way Did She Go	Silhouettes	1956, 1962	Grand 142/Imperial 5899
Which Way Should I Turn	Midnighters, Hank Ballard & the	1967	King 6131
Which Witch Doctor	Vogues	1958	Dot 15798
Whiffenpoof Song, The	Ravens	1951	National 9148
While	Corsairs	1962	Tuff 1830/Chess 1830 (62)
While I Dream	Tokens (with Neil Sedaka)	1958	Melba 104
While I'm Away	Blue Notes, Todd Randall & the	1962	3 Sons 103
While I'm Away	Valadiers	1962	Gordy 7003
While I'm Happy	Mondellos, Yul McClay & the	NA	N/A
While Our Hearts Are Young	Federals	1957	Fury 1005
While Waiting In The Chapel	Everglades	1963	BPV 112577
While Walking	Del-Airs	1960	MBS 001
While Walking	Fabulaires	1957	East West 103/Main Line 103 (58)
While Walking	Raindrops, Tony & the	1962	Chesapeake 609
While We Were Dancing	Blue Stars	1998	Clifton CD (recorded in 1986)
While We Were Dancing	Dreamlovers	1961	Heritage 107
Whip It On	Moontunes, Smiley Moon & the	1967	Star 601
Whip It On Me	Impalas (Bunky)	1969	Bunky 7762
Whip It To Me Baby	Billie & Lillie (with the Thunderbirds)	1963	ABC 10421
Whip, The	Masquerades	1961	Boyd 1027

SONG	GROUP	YEAR	LABEL
Whiplash	Shells	NA	Conlo 879
Whippety Whirl	Five Keys	1957	Capitol 3861
Whirl-A-Round	Remarkables	1964	Chase 1600
Whirlwind	Charms, Otis Williams & his	1956	DeLuxe 6097
Whirlwind	Truetones	1958	Monument 4501
Whirlwind, The	G-Clefs	1966	Loma 2048/Veep 2048
Whisper	Concepts	1961	Apache 1515/Musictone 1109 (61)
Whisper	Jokers	1961	
Whisper	Nuggets	1973	Vintage 1003
Whisper	Rayber Voices, Marv Johnson & the	1959	United Artists 160/Tamla 101 (59)
Whisper	Spotlighters	1958	Aladdin 3436
Whisper It	Continentals (Hunter)	NA	Hunter 3503
Whisper Of The Wind	Daylighters	1963, 1964	Tip Top 2007/Tollie 9028
Whisper (Softly)	Avons	1963	Astra 1023
Whisper (Softly)	Avons (with the Miller Sisters)	1961	Hull 744
Whisper Your Love	Sunbeams, Donna Rae & the	1959	Satellite 103
Whispering Bells	Big Edsel Band	1978	Clifton 27
Whispering Bells	Dell Vikings	1957, 1980	Fee Bee 214/Dot 15592/ Lightning 9013/Collectables 1252
Whispering Bells	Four Jacks	1956	Big 4 Hits EP 213
Whispering Bells	Teers, Lancelo & the	NA	Promenade 12
Whispering Blues	Debonaires (Atlanta)	1957	Herald 509
Whispering Blues	Five Debonaires	19??	Herald 509
Whispering Campaign	Temples	1958	Date 1004
Whispering Grass	Platters	1960	Mercury LP 20589/ Mercury LP 60254 (60)
Whispering Heart	Empires	1956	Whirlin' Disc 104
Whispering Sorrows	Nutmegs	1955	Herald 466
Whispering Stars	Flamingos	1959	Checker 915
Whispering Winds	Crowns, Arthur Lee Maye & the	1957	Dig 133
Whispering Winds	Four Brothers And A Cousin	1954	Jaguar 3005
Whispering Wings	Shells	1959	End 1050
Whispering Words Of Love	Fideltones	1960	Poop Deck 101
Whistle, My Love	Moonglows	1953	Chance 1147
Whistle, My Love	Pips	1958	Brunswick 55048
Whistle Stop Blues	Four Brothers And A Cousin	1954	Jaguar 3003
Whistlin' Man, The	Jones Boys, Jimmy Jones & the	1957	Arrow 717
Whistlin' Willie	Five Encores	1955	Rama 180
Whistling At The Boys	School Belles	1961	Buena Vista 378
Whistling Bells	School Belles	1961	Buena Vista 378
White Buck Shoes	Continentals (Red Top)	1959	Red Top 121
White Bucks	Mon-Vales	1958	Pen Joy 501
White Bucks	Shy-Tones	1961	Spot 14/15
White Bucks	Velvets, Ronnie Price & the	NA	Carousel 1001
White Buckskin Sneakers And Checkerboard Socks	Bell Notes	1959	Time 1017
White Cadillac	Donna Lou & group	1963	Lomar 703
White Christmas	Diablos	NA	Fortune LP 8010
White Christmas	Drifters (Pre-1959)	1954	Atlantic 1048
White Christmas	Ecstasies	1979	Clifton 40
White Christmas	Four Lovers	1957	RCA LP 1317
White Christmas	Highlighters	1950	Apollo 1141
White Christmas	Love, Darlene & group	1964	Philles EP X-EP
White Christmas	Meadowlarks, Don Julian & the	1988	Classic Artists 105
White Christmas	Precisions	NA	Rayna 1001
White Christmas	Ravens	1948	National 9059
White Christmas	Saints	1984	Angela 103
White Christmas	Statues	1960	Liberty 55292
White Christmas	Subway Serenade	1981	Avenue D 4
White Christmas	Tycoon	1985	Starlight 27
White Cliffs Of Dover	Blue Jays (Checker)	1953	Checker 782
White Cliffs Of Dover	Blue Jeans, Bob B. Soxx & the	1963	Philles LP 4002
White Cliffs Of Dover	Checkers	1954, 1960	King 4675/Federal 12375
White Cliffs Of Dover	English, Scott (with the Accents)	1960	Dot 16099
White Cliffs Of Dover	Epics	1964	Mercury 72283

SONG	GROUP	YEAR	LABEL
White Cliffs Of Dover	Excellents	1961	Unreleased
White Cliffs Of Dover	Five Keys	1971 (1953)	Aladdin 3175A (unreleased)
White Cliffs Of Dover	Five Willows	1953	Allen 1003
White Cliffs Of Dover	Mystics	1960	Laurie 3058
White Cliffs Of Dover	Pelicans	1954	Parrot 793
White Cliffs Of Dover	Robins	1961	Lavender 001
White Cliffs Of Dover	Versatiles	1962	Peacock 1910
White Cliffs Of Dover (acappella)	Nacks, Nicky & the	1975	Relic LP 104
White Cliffs Of Dover, The	Dell Vikings	1973	Luniverse 113
White Cliffs Of Dover, The	Hearts, Lee Andrews & the	1954	Rainbow 256
White Cliffs Of Dover, The	Pharaohs	1958	
White Gardenia	Cadillacs	1962	Capitol 4825
White Levis	Majorettes	1963	Troy 1000
White Port Lemon Juice	Bel-Aires, Donald Woods & the	1955	Flip 304
White Rose	Travelers	1961	Decca 31282
White Sailor Hat	Interludes	1960	Valley 107
White Silk Gloves	Hollywood Producers	1966	Parkway 993
White Silver Sands	Three Dots	1960	Rich 1003
Who	Huskies, Kenny Kole & the	1958	Klik 8205
Who	Keynotes	1954	Dot 15225
Who Am I	Chuck-A-Lucks	1958	Lin 5010
Who Am I Without Your Love	Royal Premiers	1962	Toy 103
Who Are You Foolin' Now	Buccaneers	1958	Crystalette 718
Who Are You Kissing	Day, Dawn & Dusk	1956	Josie 794
Who Are You?	Orbits	1957	Argo 5286
Who Baby Who	Chargers (Jesse Belvin)	NA	N/A
Who Baby Who	Starlights, Jimmy Witherspoon & the	1957	RCA 6977
Who But A Fool	Bell Hops, Buddy White & the	NA	The Wheeler Dealers 501
Who Can Be True	Five Crowns	1952	Rainbow 184
Who Can Explain	Teenagers, Frankie Lymon & the	1956	Gee 1018
Who Can I Turn To	Cap-Tans	1951	Coral 65071
Who Can I Turn To	Drifters (1959-forward)	1965	Atlantic LP 8113
Who Can I Turn To	Modernistics	1965	Pioneer 7315
Who Can It Be	Splendors	1959	Taurus 102
Who Can Say	Four Holidays	1959	United Artists 163 (unreleased)
Who Can She Be	Devotions	1976	Robin Hood 137
Who Cares	Del Satins	1963	Columbia 42802
Who Cares About Love	Nobletones	1958, 1973	C&M 182/Times Square 18 (63)
Who Cares?	Fortunes	1958	Decca 30541
Who Could It Be	Fabulous Four	1964	Brass 314
Who Created Love	Varnells	1961	Arnold 1003
Who Dat	Commodores	1959	Brunswick 55126
Who Do You Know In Heaven	Five Keys	1957	Capitol LP 828/Capitol EP 1-828 (57)
Who Do You Love?	Skyliners	1966	Jubilee 5512
Who Do You Think You Are	Fascinators (Brooklyn)	1959	Capitol 4137
Who Do You Think You Are?	Heartspinners, Dino & the	NA	Robin Hood 142
Who Do You Think You Are?	Remaining Few	1991	Clifton 94
Who Does He Cry To	Chevrons	1964	Kiski 2065
Who Does She Think She Is	Keynoters	1975	Vanguard 9093
Who Is Eddie	Reardon, Eddie (with the Three Friends)	1958	Brunswick 55062
Who Is The Girl	Rivileers, Gene Pearson & the	1957	Baton 241/Dark 241
Who Kicked The Light Plug Out Of The Socket	Petites	1958	Spinning 6005
Who Knows	Holidays	1959	Wonder 115
Who Knows Better Than I?	Chestnuts	1957	Standord 100/Eldorado 511
Who Knows, Do You?	Swallows (Maryland)	1958	Federal 12333
Who Knows The Secret	Twin Tones	1958	RCA 7235
Who Knows, Who Cares	Holidays	1960	Andie 5019
Who Knows?	Charms, Otis Williams & the	1954, 1959	DeLuxe 6062/6186
Who' Lovin' You	Reality	1980	Bey 130
Who Me	Jet Streams	1958	Decca 30743
Who, Me?	Mandells	1961	Smart 323/Chess 1794 (61)
Who Needs Love	Ovations (Queens, N.Y.)	1964	Josie 916
Who Needs You	Paris, Bobby & group	1963	Chattahoochee 631
Who Put The Bomp	Gilman, Tony & group	NA	J&S 1391

SONG	GROUP	YEAR	LABEL
Who Put The Bomp (In The Bomp, Bomp, Bomp)	Mann, Barry (with the Edsels)	1961	ABC 10237
Who Said I Said That	Commodores	1956	Dot 15461
Who Said You Wasn't Mine (acappella)	Delstars	1964	Mellomood 1004/Relic 1014 (65)
Who Says There Ain't No Santa Claus?	Thunderbirds, Ron Holden & the	1960	Donna 1331
Who Sent This Love Note	Lady Bugs	1962	Legrand 1033
Who Shot The Hole In My Sombrero	Challengers	1962	Tri-Phi 1015/Challenge 1105 (62)
Who Showed My Baby How To Love	Darnell, Larry & group	1955	Savoy 1151
Who Slammed The Door	Little Caesar & group	1958	RCA 7270
Who Stole The Cookies	Quinns	1965	Relic 1012
Who Told The Sandman	Limelites, Shep & the	1962	Hull 748
Who Told You	Tides	1961	620 1007
Who Took My Girl	Velvetones	1959	Deb 1008
Who Walks In When I Walk Out	Larks (North Carolina)	1954	Lloyds 111
Who Was The Fool	Monarchs, Chuck Mills & the	1959	Band Box 221
Who, What, When, Where And Why?	Royal Jacks	1959	Studio 9903
Who, When And Why	Poni-Tails	1960	ABC 10114
Who Will Be The First One	Marquees	1959	Warner Bros. 5072
Who Will Be The One?	Del Royals	1960	Minit 610
Who (Will It Be Today)	Blue Rays	1964	Philips 40186
Who Will You Hurt	Spinners, Claudine Clark & the	1963	Chancellor 1130
Who Would Have Thought	Cupcakes, Shelton Dunaway & the	1959	Khoury's 715
Who Would Have Thought	Dudes	1961	Keith 6501
Who Would Have Thought It	Deltairs	1958	Felsted 8525
Who Ya Gonna Kiss	Pearls, Speedo & the	1959	Josie 865
Who You Gonna Run To	Honeybirds	1964	Coral 62414
Whoa!	Honey Bears	1955	Spark 111
Whoa Baby, That's All	Mark IVs	1962	Barry 105
Whoever You Are	Chantels	1958, 1960	End 1015/1069
Whoever You Are	Deltairs	1973	Vintage 1005
Whoever You Are	Deltears	NA	Ray-Born 132/133
Whoever You Are	Earls	1976	Rome 114
Whoever You Are	Terry, Maureen & group	1964	Maria 102
Whole Lot Imagination	Robins	1960	Arvee 5001
Whole Lot Of Love	Rovers	1955	Music City 792
Whole Lot Of Lovin' To Do	Catalinas	1963	Million 77
Whole Lotta Love	Dominos, Don & the	1962	Cuca 1109
Whole Lotta Shakin' Goin' On	Commodores	1956	Dot 15439
Whole Wide World	Angels, Little Bobby Bell & the	1957	Demon 1501
Whole Wide World	Ovations (New Jersey)	1960	Andie 5017
Who'll Be The Fool	Ravens	1953	Mercury 70119
Who'll Be The Fool From Now On	Marshall Brothers	1951	Savoy 825
Who'll Take My Place	Velvet Sounds	NA	Cosmopolitan 105/106
Whomp, Whomp!	Starlighters	1956	Sun Coast 1001
Whoop-A-Lala	Four Dolls	1958	Capitol 3895
Whoopee (Love's A Wonderful Thing)	Allen, Mimi & group	1961	Three Speed 711
Whoo-Wee, Baby	Five C's	1954	United 172
Whop	Squires (Los Angeles)	1953	Combo 35
Who's Been Fooling You?	Sha-Weez, Big Boy Myles & the	1955	Specialty 564
Who's Been Loving You?	D'Accords	1961	Don-El 110
Who's Been Riding My Mule	Nobles (Chicago)	1958	Sapphire 1051
Who's Fooling Who	Chromatics, Bob Williams & the (with the Tornados)	1955	Blend 1005
Who's Gonna Hold Your Hand	Dalton, Danny & group	1959	Teen 505
Who's Gonna Know	Seniors	1959	Tampa 163
Who's Gonna Pick Up The Pieces	Harlems, Little D & the	1963	Josie 914
Who's Gonna Take You To The Prom	Classmates	1956	Dot 15460
Who's Laughing Who's Crying	Chalets	1961	Tru-Lite 1001/Dart 1026 (61)/ Musicnote 1115 (61)
Who's Laughing, Who's Crying	Classics (Brooklyn)	1964	Musictone 6131
Who's Lovin' You?	Supremes (Detroit)	1961	Tamla 54045
Who's Our Pet, Annette	Friends, Junior & His	1960	ABC 10089
Who's Sorry Now	Ravens	NA	National (unreleased)
Who's That Girl	Sir Nites, T.L. Clemons & the	1960	Combo 168

SONG	GROUP	YEAR	LABEL
Who's That Knockin'	Genies	1959	Shad 5002
Who's That Knockin'	Yesterday's Today	NA	Starlight 2
Who's That Knocking	Catalinas	1979	Crystal Ball 135
Whose Baby Are You	Thrills, George Zimmerman & the	1956	Jab 103
Whose Heart Are You Breakin' Now	Chimes (Brooklyn)	1963	Metro 1/Laurie 3211 (63)
Whose Little Girl Are You	Falcons (Detroit)	1985	Relic LP 8005
Whose Love But Yours	Quills	1959	Casino 106
Why	Acey, Johnny & group	1960	Fire 1015
Why	A-Tones, Roger & the	1961	Nike 002
Why	Ballin, Roger & group	1960	Nike 002
Why	Belmonts	1964	Sabina 519
Why	Challengers	1963	Explosive 3621-10
Why	Chessmen	1959	Safari 1011
Why	C-Notes, Ron Jones & the	1962	Mobie 3419
Why	Coronados	1961	Peerless 5134
Why	Cues	1956	Capitol 3582
Why	Dove, Diane & group	1959	NRC 018
Why	Executives (2) (aka Challengers)	1963	Revenge 5003/Explosive 3621 (63)
Why	Fascinations	1961	Paxley 750/Dore 593 (61)
Why	Five Emprees	1965	Freeport 1002
Why	Five Royales	1960	King 5357
Why	Four Duchesses	1957	Chief 7019
Why	Freelancers, Dan Williams & the	NA	Beth 20/Freelance 20
Why	Mad Lads	1962	Mark Fi 1934
Why	Newmarks	1963	Chattahoochee 627
Why	Travelers	1958	Andex 4006
Why	Volumes	1964	Old Town 1154
Why Am I A Fool	Casinos	1960	Casino 111
Why Am I A Fool For You	Jarmels	NA	Collectables LP 5044
Why Am I So Shy	Three Pennies	1964	B.T. Puppy 501
Why Am I So Shy?	Chiffons	1963	Laurie 3166/3179
Why Are The Nights So Cold	Riffs	1964, 1965	Sunny 22/Old Town 1179
Why Are We Apart	Midnighters	1955	Federal 12220
Why Are We Apart	Santells	1964	Courier 103
Why Are You Crying	Fabulous Enchanters	1961	Finer Arts 1007
Why Are You Tearing Us Apart	Larktones	1960	Riki 140
Why At A Time Like This	Four Buddies	1951	Savoy 789
Why Baby	Hitchhikers, Chuck Thomas & the	1957	Band Box 360
Why, Baby, Why	Ballards, Billy Brown & the	1963	El Tone 439
Why Be A Fool	Five Playboys	1958	Mercury 71269
Why Be A Fool	Nobles, Nicky & the	1963	Times Square 33
Why Can't I Be Loved?	Rockaways, Alicia & the	1956	Epic 9191
Why Can't I Find You	El-Deens	1959	Federal 12347
Why Can't I Have You	Fourmost	1962	Lu Pine 105
Why Can't I Have You	Heralds	1954	Herald (unreleased)
Why Can't I Have You	Mighty Dukes	1952	Duke 104
Why Can't I Make Him Like You	Baby Dolls	1961	Hollywood 1111
Why Can't I Stop Loving You	Hi Fi's	1965	Cameo 349
Why Can't They Understand	Davis Brothers	1965	Guyden 2120
Why Can't This Be So	Romans	1956	Haven 111
Why Can't You	Wrens	1991	Classic Artists 131
Why Can't You Be True	Vernalls	1958	Rulu 6753
Why Can't You Love Me	Four Xs	1960	Lost 20/103
Why Can't You Treat Me Right	Sequins	1956	Red Robin 140
Why Darling Why	Travelers	1953	Okeh 6959
Why Did He Leave	Del-Airs	1962	Arrawak 1003
Why Did I Cry	Electronaires, Chuck Ranado & the	1959	Count 507
Why Did I Cry	Jillettes	1963	Philips 40140
Why Did I Fall In Love	Jacks	1956	RPM 458
Why Did It End?	Spears, Frankie Ervin & the	1961	Don 202
Why Did My Baby Put Me Down	Washington, Baby & group	1959	Neptune 104
Why Did She Go?	Magnificents	1956	Vee Jay 183
Why Did She Leave	Aztecs, Jose & the	1976	Monogram 122
Why Did She Leave Me	Aztecs, Jose & the	1955	Roadhouse LP
Why Did Summer Have To End	Baker, Bill & group	1962	Musicnote 119

SONG	GROUP	YEAR	LABEL
Why Did This Happen	Nutones, Terry Daly & the	1958	Mark 122
Why Did You Do It	Angels, Little Betty & the	1961	Savoy 1603
Why Did You Do It	Four Bars	1960	Time 4
Why Did You Do It	Mellos, Terri Corin & the	NA	Rider 108
Why Did You Fall For Me	Limelites, Shep & the	1964	Hull 767
Why Did You Go	Aladdin, Johnny (with the Passions)	1960	Chip 1001
Why Did You Go	Bobby-Pins	1963	Mercury 72193
Why Did You Go	Orioles, Sonny Til & the	1983	Murray Hill LP M61277
Why Did You Go	Pageants	1960	Goldisc 3013
Why Did You Go	Ravens	NA	Mercury (unreleased)
Why Did You Go	Sprouts	1960	Mercury 71727
Why Did You Go Away	Crowns, Henry Strogin & the	1960, 1963	Dynamic 1002/Ball 1015
Why Did You Go?	Pyramids (Connecticut)	1957	Davis 457
Why Did You Have To Go	Daylighters, Betty Everett & the	1960	C.J. 611
Why Did You Laugh	Excellents	1963	Blast 207
Why Did You Leave	Sparks	1959	Decca 30974
Why Did You Leave Me	Dell-Os, John Shaw & the	1958	U-C 5002/U-C 1031
Why Did You Leave Me	Honeymoons, Denny Dale & the	1966	Soma 1447
Why Did You Leave Me	Ravens	1952	Mercury 5800
Why Did You Leave Me	Sensational	1958	U-C 5002/U-C 1031
Why Did You Leave Me Alone	Taylor, Carmen & group	1957	King 5085
Why Did You Leave Me?	Imperials (Detroit)	1953	Derby 858
Why Did You Leave Me?	Originals, Rosie & the	1961	Highland 1025
Why Did You Leave Me?	Ravons	1962	Yucca 142
Why Did You Leave Me?	Seniors	1958	Excello 2130
Why Did You Leave Me?	Sparrows	1953	Jay-Dee 783
Why Did You Let Me Love You	Dawns	1959	Climax 104
Why Did You Lie	Spencer Sisters	1955	Aladdin 3285
Why Did You Make Me Cry (acappella)	Horizons	1975	Relic LP 103
Why Did You Put Me On	Classmen	1964	JR 5006
Why Did You?	Turks	1956	Bally 1017
Why Didn't I Go	Curls	1959	Everest 19319
Why Didn't I Listen To Mother	Bentleys	1965	Smash 1988
Why Didn't I Listen To Mother	Vampires	1964	Carroll 104
Why Didn't You Tell Me Girl	Colonials	NA	Senate 1003
Why Do Fools Fall In Love	Catalinas	1973	Jayne 175
Why Do Fools Fall In Love	Diamonds	1956	Mercury 70790
Why Do Fools Fall In Love	Fabulous Four	1961	Chancellor 1078
Why Do Fools Fall In Love	Fat Boys, Freddie & the	NA	Fat Man 101
Why Do Fools Fall In Love	Four Jacks, Ben Joe Zeppa & the	1956	Gilmar 278
Why Do Fools Fall In Love	Fourmost	1966	Capitol 5591
Why Do Fools Fall In Love	Gallahads	1961	Rendezvous 153
Why Do Fools Fall In Love	Holman, Eddie & group	1966	Parkway 157
Why Do Fools Fall In Love	Little Beavers, Johnny Briscoe & the	1971	Atlantic 2822
Why Do Fools Fall In Love	Nunn, Dolly & group	NA	Worthmore EP 183
Why Do Fools Fall In Love	Teenagers, Frankie Lymon & the	1956	Gee 1002
Why Do Fools Fall In Love	Teeners	1956	Budget
Why Do Fools Fall In Love	Zeppa, Ben (with the Four Jacks)	1956	Tops 278
Why Do I	Hearts, Lee Andrews & the	1958	United Artists 136
Why Do I Cry	Capris (New York)	1961	Old Town 1103
Why Do I Cry	Electronaires, Chuck Ranado & the	1959	Count 508
Why Do I Cry	Lullabies, Lisa & the	1964	Coed 589
Why Do I Do These Foolish Things	Magicians	1966	Villa 704
Why Do I Dream?	Saucers	1959	Felco 104
Why Do I Go To School?	Six Teens	1959	Flip 346
Why Do I Love Her	Gents	1961	Liberty 55332
Why Do I Love You	Dusters	1956	Hudson 4
Why Do I Love You	Flairs	19??	
Why Do I Love You	Spiders	NA	Imperial (unreleased)
Why Do I Love You So (Baby Don't Go)	Chordones, Leon Tarver & The	1954	Checker (unreleased)
Why Do I Love You, Why Do I Care	Playboys	1957	Mercury 71228
Why Do I Wait?	Quails, Bill Robinson & the	1954	DeLuxe 6059
Why Do I?	Carpets	1956	Federal 12257
Why Do Kids Grow Up?	Rainbows, Randy & the	1963	Rust 5073
Why Do Little Girls Hurt Little Boys	Shondelles, Rickey Leigh & the	1963	Savoy 1620

SONG	GROUP	YEAR	LABEL
Why Do Lovers Break Each Others Hearts	Blue Jeans, Bob B. Soxx & the	1963	Philles 110
Why Do Lovers Break Each Other's Hearts	Big Edsel Band	1980	Clifton 48
Why Do We Have To Say Goodnight	Dahills	1964	Musicor 1041
Why Do You Care	Dabettes, Karen Caple & the	1962	Advance 3933
Why Do You Cry	Charts	1957	Everlast 5002/Lost Nite 180 (81)
Why Do You Cry	Inquisitors, Little Isadore & the	1995	Early Bird 5001
Why Do You Do Me	Capri, Tony & group	1961	Liban 1001
Why Do You Do Me Like You Do	Cleftones	1957	Gee 1031
Why Do You Do Me Like You Do	Quotations	1974	Downstairs 1003
Why Do You Do Me Like You Do (acappella)	Quotations	1975	Relic LP 104
Why Do You Do Me Wrong	Daylighters	1961	Nike 10011/Dot 16326 (62)/ Tip Top 2001 (62)
Why Do You Go	Flints	1962	Hart 100
Why Do You Go Away	Crowns, Henry Strogin & the	1957	Ball 1015
Why Do You Have To Go	Caprisians	1961	Lavender 004
Why Do You Have To Go	Delcos	NA	Monument
Why Do You Have To Go	Madison, Glen & group	1962	Ebony 105/Monument
Why Do You Have To Go (acappella)	Delstars	1964	Mellomood 1004/Relic 1014 (65)
Why Do You Have To Go?	Dells	1957	Vee Jay 236
Why Do You Have To Go?	Paramounts	1961	Dot 16175
Why Do You Hurt Me Darling	Gay Charmers	1959	Savoy 1561
Why Do You Hurt The One Who Loves You	Bees, Honey & the	NA	Arctic 141
Why Do You Look At Me	Medallions	1962	Reo 8693/Lenox 5556 (62)
Why Do You Look The Other Way	Rays	1959	XYZ 600
Why Do You Love Another	Down Beats	NA	Dawn 1031
Why Do You Make Me Cry	Cubs	1956	Savoy 1502
Why Do You Make Me Cry	Microgrooves	1990	Crystal Ball 160
Why Do You Pretend	Overons	1958	Unreleased
Why Do You Treat Me This Way	Belvederes	1962	Poplar 114
Why Do You Treat Me This Way	Four Bars	1955	Josie 783
Why Do You Treat Me This Way	Voxpoppers	1958	Poplar 112
Why Does A Woman Cry	Hi-Tones, Bob Jaxon & the	1955	Cadence 1264
Why Does Everybody	Classmen	1964	JR 5006
Why Does It Have To Be Her	Sensational	1958	U-C 5002/U-C 1031
Why Does It Have To Be Me	Charmers	1954	Central 1002
Why Doesn't She Notice Me	Spartans, Jimmy & the	1960	Satellite 106
Why Don't I	Heartbreakers (Washington, D.C.)	1952	RCA 4662
Why Don't They Understand	Naturals	1964	Chattahoochee 633
Why Don't We Do This More Often	Misters	1959	Chante 1002/Decca 31026 (59)
Why Don't You Answer?	Maharajahs	1958	Flip 332
Why Don't You Be Nice	Day Dreams, Tony & the	1958	Planet 1008/1009
Why Don't You Believe Me	Diadems	1963	Star 514
Why Don't You Believe Me	Duprees	1963	Coed 584
Why Don't You Believe Me	Five Crowns	1953	Rainbow 202
Why Don't You Believe Me	Shantons, Skip Brown & the	1959	Pam 112
Why Don't You Believe Me	Swinging Reeds, Don Reed & the	1958	United 215
Why Don't You Believe Me?	Jaguars	1956	Aardell 0006
Why Don't You Believe?	Rockers	1956	Federal 12273
Why Don't You Come Home	McKnight, June & group	1962	Jeanne 1225
Why Don't You Come On Home	Reed, Lula (with the Teeners)	1955	King 4811
Why Don't You Dance	Spaniels	1956	Vee Jay 189
Why Don't You Do Right	Bees	1954	Imperial (unreleased)
Why Don't You Do Right?	El Tempos, Mike Gordon & the	1954	Cat 101
Why Don't You Do Right?	Serenaders (Detroit)	1952	J.V.B. 2001
Why Don't You Go	Ervin, Frankie & female group	1959	Guyden 2010
Why Don't You Love Me	Davies, Johnny Greco & the	1963	Pageant 602
(Why Don't You) Love Me	Delteens (with the Orbits)	1961	Fortune 541
Why Don't You Love Me Now, Now, Now	Browne, Doris (with the Capris)	1953	Gotham 296
Why Don't You Stay A Little Longer	Fashions	1963	Amy 884
Why Don't You Stop?	Lyrics (San Francisco)	1958	Vee Jay 285

SONG	GROUP	YEAR	LABEL
Why Don't You Write	Velons	1968	BJM 6568
Why Don't You Write Me	Barries	1962	Vernon 102
Why Don't You Write Me	Cardinals	1963	Rose 835
Why Don't You Write Me	Dedications	1962, 1983	Card 335/336/Card 2001 (62)
Why Don't You Write Me	Five Ivories	1962	Sparta 001
Why Don't You Write Me	Jacks	1955, 1960, 1975	RPM 428 (first pressing)/Kent 344/ Victory/Relic 1031
Why Don't You Write Me	Latinaires, Little Joe & the	1970	White Whale 304
Why Don't You Write Me	Sinceres, Johnny H & the	1963	El Zarape 122
Why Don't You Write Me	Tempos	1964	U.S.A. 810
Why Don't You Write Me?	Feathers	1954, 1963	Show Time 1105/Candlelight 427
Why Don't You Write Me?	Philharmonics	1958	Future 2200
Why Don't You?	Marigolds	1955	Excello 2057
Why Feel This Way About You	Magichords	NA	Tri-Tone 1002
Why Fool Yourself	Williams, Bernie & group	1955	Imperial 5360
Why Go On Pretending?	Four Haven Knights	1957, 1973	Atlas 1092/Angletone 1092 (73)
Why (I Want To Know)	Parisians	1962	Pova 1003/1004
Why In The World	Night Owls, Tony Allen & the	1960	Crown LP 5231
Why Is It	Schaefer, Freddy & group	1962	King 5621
Why Is Love So Bad	Chimes (Brooklyn)	1986	Freedom 223
Why I've Got To Know	Four Bars, Betty Wilson & the	1962	Dayco 4564
Why Johnny Why	Blazers (Johnny Moore's)	1955	Hollywood 1031
Why Keep Me Dreaming	Clairmonts	1957	Apollo 517
Why Keep Me Dreaming	Claremonts	1963	Apollo 751
Why Make A Fool Out Of Me	Marshall Brothers	1952	Savoy 833
Why Must I Cry	Bowman, Priscilla & group	1959	Abner 1033
Why Must I Cry	Noble, Beverly & group	1959	Sparrow 100
Why Must I Cry	Swans (St. Louis)	1961	Reveille 1002/Dot 16210 (61)
Why Must I Wonder?	Emeralds (St. Louis)	1954	Kicks 3/Allied 10002/10003 (58)
Why Must It Be	Jokers, Johnny & the	1959	Harvard 804
Why Must We Go To School?	Nutmegs	1963	Times Square 22/Relic 535 (65)
Why Must You Cry	Magicians	1966	Villa 706
Why Must You Go?	Griffins	1956	Mercury 70913
Why My Darling Why	Rhythm Kings	1951	Apollo 1181
Why Not Give Me Your Heart?	LP's, Denny & the	1958	Rock-It 001
Why Oh Baby Why	Companions	1959	Brook's 100/Federal 12397 (60)
Why Oh Why	Catalinas	NA	Wonder 14
Why Oh Why	Charmettes	1962	Tri Disc 103
Why Oh Why	Click-Ettes	1960	Dice 94/95
Why Oh Why	Cliques	1956	Modern 967 (unreleased)
Why, Oh Why	Fantasys	1960	Guyden 2029
Why Oh Why	Five Echoes	1971	Sabre 111
Why Oh Why	Five Jets	1973	Broadcast 999
Why Oh Why	Five Keys	1954	Aladdin 3263
Why Oh Why	Hearts, Eugene Ball with the	1957	Melatone 1001
Why Oh Why	Passionettes	1958	Unreleased
Why Oh Why	Teasers, Jimmy Brinkley & the	1957	Note 10002
Why Oh Why?	Hawks	1955	Post 2004
Why? Oh, Why?	Jubilites	1953	R.&B. 1046 (Newark, NJ)
Why, Oh, Why?	Jumpin' Jacks	1953	Lloyds 101
Why? Oh, Why?	Kings, Bobby Hall & the	1953, 1973	Jax 314
Why, Oh-H?	Rovers	1954	Music City 750/Capitol 3078 (55)
Why Pretend	Frontiers	1961	King 5481
Why Should I	Flips	1955	Sapphire 1052
Why Should I Cry	Manhattans	1963	Big Mack 3911
Why Should I Cry	Richardson, Rudi & group	1957	Sun 271
Why Should I Dance	Sheiks	1961	Le Grand 1013
Why Should I Love You	Harptones	1954	Bruce 109
Why Should I Suffer	Squires (Herald)	1963	Herald 580
Why Should We Break Up	Sonnets	1956	Herald 477
Why Should We Keep On Pretending	Hi Timers	1959	Sonic 1502
Why Should You Taunt Me?	Skyliners	NA	Doc 496
Why Start	Reid, Matthew (with the Four Seasons)	1961	ABC 10259
Why Treat Me This Way?	El Pollos	1957	Neptune 1001
Why Walk Alone	Treney, Joey & group	1961	Magenta 05

SONG	GROUP	YEAR	LABEL
Why Was I Ever Born	Blue Notes, Little Bill & the	1960	Topaz 1302
Why Wasn't I Told	Caston, Bobby & group	1957	Atlas 1103
Why, Why	Cadillacs	1959	Jubilee LP 1089
Why, Why	Darnels, Debbie & the	1961	Vernon 100
Why Why	Teen Dreams, Debbie & the	1961	Vernon 100
Why Why Why	Cavaliers	1959	Apt 25031/ABC
Why Why Why	Escorts, Don Crawford & the	1959	Scepter 1201
Why, Why, Why	Markays, Doug Sahm & the	1961	Harlem 107/Swingin' 625 (61)
Why Why Why	Pitt, Eugene & group	1966	Veep 1229
Why, Why Won't You Believe Me	Limelites, Shep & the	1963	Hull 761
Why Will You Break My Heart	Dolphins	1962	Tip Top 2005
Why Won't You Change Your Ways For Me	Fortes	1964	Current 103
Why?	Chanters, Brother Woodman & the	1955	Combo 78
Why?	Gypsies	1957	Atlas 1073/Angletone 1073 (57)
Why?	Impalas, Bobby Byrd & the	1958	Corvet 1017
Why?	Queens, Shirley Gunter & the	1955	Flair 1060
Why?	Valentines	1955	Rama 196
Why?	Voices	1955	Cash 1011
Wh-y-y Leave Me This Way-ay-ay	Gay Tunes	1953	Timely 1002
Why-Yi-Yi	Foster Brothers	1959	Profile 4004
Wibble, The	Embers, Ray Allen & the	1961	Sinclair 1002
Wicked Ruby	Larados, Danny Zella & the	1959	Fox 10056
Wicked Ruby	Zell Rocks, Danny Zella & His	1959	Fox 10057
Wide Hoop Skirts	Nutmegs	1963	Times Square 14/Relic 533 (65)
Wiggie Waggie Woo	Cadets	1957	Modern 1017
Wiggie Waggie Woo	Jacks	1957	RPM LP 3006/Crown LP 5021 (57)
Wiggle	Four Feathers, Gene Forrest & the	1954	Aladdin 3224
Wiggle, The	Invictors	1962	TPE 8217
Wiggle, The	Tangents	1960	United Artists 201
Wiggle Wiggle	Accents (featuring Robert Draper Jr.)	1958	Brunswick 55100
Wiggle Wiggle	Chestnuts	1958	Aladdin 3444
Wild Baby	Sentimentals, Vickie Evans & the	NA	Playfare 601
Wild Bird	Jiv-A-Tones	NA	Fraternity 823
Wild Bird	Viscounts, Sammy Hagen & the	1957	Capitol 3818
Wild Cherry	Chandeliers	1958	Angle Tone (unreleased)
Wild Child	Bell Notes	1960	Madison 141
Wild Christening Party	Teen Kings	1962	Rago 201
Wild Eyes And Tender Lips	Poni-Tails	1957	ABC 9846
Wild Female, The	Teenagers (Joe Negroni)	1981	Crystal Ball LP 142
Wild For Her	Sophomores, Anthony & the	1966	ABC 10770
Wild Hog	Twilights, James Carter & the	1956	Tuxedo 917
Wild Hog Baby	Twilights, James Carter & the	1959	Tuxedo 932
Wild Ideas	Romans	1958	MMI 1238
Wild Leaves	Planets	1957	Era 1049
Wild Little Willie	Hesitations, Don Sweet & the	1964	D-Town 383
Wild Love	Aliens	NA	Stilt 66801
Wild Love	Daddy-O's, Joey Castle & the	1959	Headline 1008
Wild Love	Jumpers, Jay Nelson & the	1959	Excello 2165
Wild Man	Three G's	1958	Columbia 41175
Wild Man Walk	Ebonettes	1958	Ebb 147
Wild, Man, Wild	Chromatics	1956	Crest 1011
Wild One	Coasters	1964	Atco 6321
Wild One	Epics	1962	
Wild One	Renowns	1961	Everest 19396
Wild Side Of My Baby	Diablos	1984	Fortune LP 8016
Wild Weekend	Barons	1963	Mohawk 902
Wildflower	Triumphs, Tico & the	1962	Amy 845
Wildsville	Loreleis	1955	Spotlight 390
Wildwood Days	Dovells	1963	Parkway 867
Wilhemina	Ervin, Frankie & group	1959	Contender 1316
Will	Imaginations, Darlene Day & the	1961	Music Makers 106
Will I (acappella)	Memories	1964	Times Square 11/ Times Square 95 (64)
Will I Ever Find My Baby	Four Ekkos, Bernie Campbell & the	1961	Fine 26571

SONG	GROUP	YEAR	LABEL
Will I Ever Know	Highlights	1957	Bally 1027
Will I Ever Make It	Duchesses	1960	Chief 7023
Will Love Ever Come My Way	Continentals, Joey & the	1965	Komet 1001
Will My Heart Stand A Chance	Five Keys	1971 (1953)	Aladdin 3182A (unreleased)
Will Power	Cookies	1963	Dimension 1012
Will She Know	Serenaders (Detroit)	1953	Red Robin 115
Will She Return	Versatones	1963	Richie 4081
Will She Think Of Me	Flamingo, Johnny & female group	1958	Specialty 640
Will There Ever Be A Girl	London, Lloyd (with the Yachtsmen)	1959	Destiny 530
Will We Meet Again	Tabs	1958	Nasco 6016
Will Ya William	Monorails	1961	Lute 6017
Will You	Five Keys	1960	King LP 692
Will You	Hinton, Joe & group	1959	Back Beat 526
Will You	Hit-Makers	1959	Beat 526
Will You Be Mine	Crowns, Arthur Lee Maye & the	1958	Cash 1063/Imperial 5790 (61)
Will You Be Mine	Penguins	1957	Mercury 71033
Will You Be Mine	Swallows (Maryland)	1951, 1986	King 4458/Starbound 507
Will You Be Mine	Swans (Parrot)	1981	Parrot (unreleased)/Relic LP 5088 (90)
Will You Be Mine	Upbeats	1958	Prep 131
Will You Be My Guy	Entros, Gloria Fowler & the	1965	Cee Jay 654
Will You Be My Love	Four J's	1963	4-J 506
Will You Be True?	Vocaleers	1954	Red Robin 125
Will You Dream	Skarlettones	1959	Ember 1053
Will You Ever Say You're Mine	Mello-Maids	1956	Baton 231
Will You Go Steady	Knight Lites, Gary & the	1959	Prima 1016
Will You Love Me In Heaven	Delvets	1961	End 1107
Will You Love Me Still	Belmonts, Dion & the	1962	Laurie LP 2016/Ace LP 155
Will You Love Me Tomorrow	Castle Sisters	1960	Roulette 4220
Will You Love Me Tomorrow	Classmates	1962	Stacy 935
Will You Love Me Tomorrow?	Larados	NA	Madog 801
Will You Marry Me	Kartunes	1958	MGM 12598
Will You Miss Me	Shells	1975	Monogram 108
Will You Or Won't You	Four Chaps	1962	Co & Ce 231 (65)
Will You Remember When You Are Far A-Way	Dominoes	1956	Decca 30043
Will You Still Love Me Tomorrow	Escorts, Charlie McCoy & the	1964	Monument 842
Will You Still Love Me Tomorrow	Shirelles	1960	Scepter 1211 (second pressing)
Will You Still Love Me Tomorrow?	Chiffons	NA	Collectables LP 5042
(Will You, Won't You, Can't You) Don't You Wanna Be Mine?	Eagles	1954	Mercury 70464
Willa-Bea	Ambassadors	1954	Timely 1001
Willette	Centuries	1985	Relic LP 5053
Willette	Dell Vikings	1957	Fee Bee 221/Dot 15673 (58)
Willie Jones	Elliots, Andre & the	1962	Barry 106
Willie Jones Got Married	Elliots, Andre & the	1962	Barry 106
Willie The Weeper	Kartunes	1958	MGM 12680
Willie's Dream	Vibra-Tones	1962	Candi 1025
Willingly	Four Kings	1956	Fraternity 752
Willingly	Knight, Bob	1964	Goal 4/Jubilee
Will-O-The-Wisp	Satisfiers	1958	Coral 61945
Willow Blues	Five Scalders	1956	Drummond 3001
Willow Tree	Prinder, Shad	1962	Infinity 009
Willow Weep For Me	Barons (Spartan)	1961	Spartan 400
Willow Wept, The	Heartbreakers (Bronx, N.Y.)	1963	Atco 6258
Willy, The	Rivingtons	1964	Vee Jay 677
Wilted Rose Bud	Interludes	1962	King 5633
Wim O Weh	Mystics	1959	Unreleased
Win Or Lose	Four Stars	1954	King 1382
Win Yourself A Lover	Dials	1961	Hilltop 219
Win Yourself A Lover	Parliaments, Sammy & the	1960	Arnold 1001
Wind	Classics (Brooklyn)	1971	Sire 353
Wind	Pages	1958	Eagle 1005/Don Tan 0001
Wind	Profits	1971	Sir 353
Wind And The Rain, The	Madisons	1964	Lawn 240
Wind, The	Calveys	1961	Comma 84349/Comma 445

SONG	GROUP	YEAR	LABEL
Wind, The	Diablos (featuring Nolan Strong)	1954	Fortune 511
Wind, The	Five Elgins	1977	Ronnie 204
Wind, The	Heartspinners, Dino & the	1981	Starlight 13
Wind, The	Jesters	1960	Winley 242
Wind, The	Jewels (Los Angeles)	1959	Antler 1102
Wind, The	Prophets	1971	Sire 353
Wind (acappella), The	Traditions	1965	Fellatio 102
Window Eyes	Hearts, Lee Andrews & the	1981	Gotham 324
Window Lady	Cadillacs	1955	Josie 778
Window Of Dreams	Four Saints	1970	Era 701
Window Of Love	Three Dots	1959	Buzz 104
Window Shopping On Girls Avenue	Valaquons	1965	Tangerine 951
Window's Eyes	Four Buddies	1951	Savoy 823
Winds, The	Zodiacs, Maurice Williams & the	1965	Sphere Sound 707
Windstorm	Cravers	1958	Chock Full Of Hits 109
Windy And Warm	Travelers	1963	Yellow Sand 2
Windy City Special	Hi-Fives	1960	Bingo 1006
Wine	Daffodils	1955	CJ 100
W-I-N-E	Hollywood Four Flames (Four Flames)	1951	Fidelity 3001/Unique 003
Wine Wine Wine	Nitecaps	1960, 1966	Vandan 4733/7491
Wine, Women And Gold	Porter, Jake (with the Buzzards)	1955	Combo 91
Wine Woogie	Men From Mars, Marvin Phillips & the	NA	Specialty 445
Wings Of An Angel	Bosstones	1959	Boss 401/V-Tone 208 (60)
Wings Of An Angel	Goldtones	1961	YRS 1001
Wings Of An Angel, The	Dennis, Bradford & group	NA	Canadian 1600
Wini Brown	Dukes (California)	1956	Imperial 5415
Winner Take All	Allumns	1978	Crystal Ball 118
Winner Take All	Platters	1956	Mercury 70819
Winner, The	Cuff Links	1957	Dootone 413
Wino O	Ray-O-Vacs	1956	Kaiser 389
Winos On Parade	Mello-Tones, Marga Benitez & the	1954	Decca 48318
Winter Blue	Cupcakes	1965	Diamond 177
Winter Blues	Love, Darlene & group	1965	Philles 125X
Winter Dream	Wombats, Gary & the	1963	Regina 297
Winter Time	Escorts, Bobby Chandler & the	1958	O.J. 1012
Winter Wonderland	Blue Notes, Harold Melvin & the	1960	Val-Ue 215
Winter Wonderland	Bluenotes (4)	1960	Valve 115
Winter Wonderland	Love, Darlene & group	1964	Philles 125
Winter's Romance	Embers, Larry Lee & the	1990	Relic LP 5085
Wintertime	Four Coachmen	1960	Adonis A-102
Wintertime	Ran-Dells	1964	RSVP 1104
Wipe Out	Dischords	1963	Bonneville
Wipe The Tears From Your Eyes	Golden Tones, Sticks Herman & the	1958	Goldband 1056
Wipe The Tears From Your Eyes	Vets	1961	Swami 551/552
Wisdom Of A Fool	Dubs	1963	Josie 911
Wisdom Of A Fool	Five Keys	1956	Capitol 3597
Wisdom Of A Fool	Royal Jesters	1962	Jester 102
Wise Guy	Fun-Atics	1962	Versailles 100
Wise Old Owl	Del Roys	1959	Sparkell 102
Wise Up And Be Smart	Devons	1969	Mr. G 825
Wisest Man In Town, The	Techniques	1958	Roulette 4097
Wish For An Angel	Kingsmen	1961	Musictone 102
Wish I Could Be There	Silhouettes	1956	Grand 142
Wish I Could Change My Mind	Intervals	1962	Class 304
Wish I Didn't Love You So	Clips	1954	Republic 7102
Wish I Didn't Love You So	Waters, Larry & group	1956	Dig 121
Wish I Had My Baby	Emanons (New York)	1956	Josie 801
Wish I Had My Baby	Five Satins	1957	Ember 1019
Wish I Was Back In School	Goldenrods	1959	Vee Jay 307
Wish It Could Be Me	Saber, Johnny (with the Passions)	1960	Adonis 103
Wish It Were Me	Platters	1959	Mercury 71502/Mercury 10018 (59)
Wish She Was Mine	Crests (with Johnny Maestro)	1957	Joyce 105/Times Square 2 (62)
Wish She Was Mine	Vilons	1972	Bim Bam Boom 104
Wish She Were Mine	Nuggets	1973	Vintage 1003
Wish That You Were Here	Casual Crescendos	1963	MRC 12001

SONG	GROUP	YEAR	LABEL
Wish You Were Here With Me	Fawns	1967	Capacity 105
Wished I Was Home	Ebb Tides, Nino & the	1961	Mr. Peacock 102
Wishes	Metrics	1964	Chadwick 101
Wishful Dreaming	Genos	1959	Sundance 202
Wishful Thinking	Gunter, Cornel & group	1964	Challenge
Wishful Thinking	Imperials, Little Anthony & the	1959	End 1039
Wishful Thinking	Saints, Lola & the	1984	N/A
Wishin'	Sugar Tones	1952	Okeh 6877
Wishin' Well	Chanteurs	1961	La Salle 501
Wishing	Tokens (Brooklyn)	1962	RCA 8114
Wishing	Tracers, Walt Perry & the	1962	Three Rivers
Wishing All The Time	Lanham, Richard (with the Tempo-Tones)	1956	Acme 722
Wishing For You	Swallows (Maryland)	1951	King 4466
Wishing For Your Love	Clovers	1958	Atlantic 1175
Wishing For Your Love	Voxpoppers	1958	Amp-3 1004/Mercury 71282 (58)
Wishing Is For Fools	Melodeers	1960	Studio 9908
Wishing Ring	Duprees	1964	Coed 596
Wishing Ring	Five Satins	1960	Ember 1070
Wishing Star	Castle Sisters	1962	Terrace 7506
Wishing Star	Crenshaws	1961	Warner Bros. EP 5505
Wishing Star	Fidelitys	1960	Sir 277
Wishing Star	Newports	1978	Image 501
Wishing Star	Originals, Tony Allen & the	1960	Original Sound 10
Wishing Time	Cari, Eddie & group	1963	Mermaid 104
Wishing Well	Blue Chips	1962	Sparta 001
Wishing Well	Cadillacs	1954	Josie 769
Wishing Well	Dorn, Jerry (with the Hurricanes)	1956	King 4932
Wishing Well	Ivories	1962	Darla (no number)
Wishing Well	Statues, Gary Miles & the	1960	Liberty 55279
Wishing You Were Mine	Epics	1962	Eric 7001
Witchcraft	Spiders	1955, 1961	Imperial 5366/5739
Witchcraft In The Air	Lavette, Betty & group	1964	LuPine 123
Witches Brew	Hood, Darla (with the Rocketeers)	1957	Encino 1007/Acama 122 (60)
Witchy Woman	Stormy Weather	1988	Starlight 63
With A Broken Heart	Five Keys	1951	Aladdin 3085
With A Feeling	Esquires	1963	Argo 5435
With A Girl Like You	Matadors, Frankie & the	NA	Peerless 9012
With A Tear In My Heart	Harmonaires, Eddie Elders & the	1957	Vita 176
With All My Heart	Belvin, Andy & group	NA	Cal State 3200
With All My Heart	Billboards	1961	Vistone 2023
With All My Heart	Carmacks	1960	Autograph 205
With All My Heart	Co-Eds	1959	Dwain 802
With All My Heart	Five Scamps	1954	Okeh 7049
With All My Heart	Green, Janice & group	1958	Nasco 6013
With All My Heart	Lee, Curtis (with the Halos)	1960	Warrior 1555
With All My Heart	Lovers	1962	MC B-003
With All My Heart	Savoys, Jimmy Jones & the	1955	Savoy 1186
With All My Heart	Tymes	1964	Parkway 919
With All My Heart And Soul	Flashes, Jess Davis & the	1959	Bob-O-Link 100/101
With All My Heart And Soul	Kents	1958	Argo 5299
With All My Heart And Soul	Skyliners	1985	Relic LP 5053
With All My Love	Cap-Tans	1950, 1953	Dot 15114
With All My Love	Dynamics, Ray Murray & the	1960	Arbo 222
With All My Love	Five Keys	1958	Capitol 3948
With All Your Heart	Five Royales	1955	Apollo 467
With Each Step A Tear	Trickels	1959	Gone 5078/Power 250 (59)
With Hope In My Heart	Jades, Joe Beilin & the	1960	Christy 122
With Love	Angels (New Jersey)	1967	RCA 9404
With These Hands	Five Willows	1953	Allen 1003
With These Hands	Wonders	1962	Bamboo 523
With These Rings	Keynotes	1959	Top Rank 2005
With These Words	Roman, Nip & group	1957	Flash 121
With This Pen	Blue Notes, Todd Randall & the	1957	Josie 814
With This Ring	Sweet Teens	1957	Gee 1030
With This Ring	Tri-Tones, Al Barkle & the	1957	Vita 173

SONG	GROUP	YEAR	LABEL
With This Ring	Wallace, Jerry (with the Jewels)	1958	Challenge 59013
With You	Four Fellows, Cathy Ryan & the	1955	King 1495
With You	Monterays (Brooklyn)	1956	Saturn 1002
With You	Royal Teens	1960	Capitol 4402
With You	Saints	1957	Cue 7934
With Your Girl	Catalinas	1958	Glory 285
With Your Love To Guide Me	Resonics	NA	Lil-Larry 1005
Within My Heart	Five Royales	1960	King 5357
Without A Cause	Heartbreakers (Bronx, N.Y.)	1957	Vik 0261
Without A Friend	Agee, Ray & female group	1955	R&B 1311
Without A Friend	Strangers	1955	King 4821
Without A Girl	Monterays (Brooklyn)	1959	Impala 213
Without A Song	Checkers	1954	King 4675
Without A Song	Flamingos	1958	End (unreleased)
Without A Song	Humphries, Teddy & group	1958	King 5151
Without A Song	Larks (North Carolina)	1971	Dreamtone 201 (unreleased)
Without A Song	Persuasions	1971	Reprise 0977
Without A Song	Ravens	1953	Mercury 70213
Without A Word	Peanuts, M&M & the	1965	Money 111
Without A Word Of Complaint	Shirelles	1962	Scepter LP 502
Without Her Heart	Halos, Johnny Angel & the	1961	Felsted 8633
Without His Love	Flamingos	1963	End LP 316
Without Love	Barrons	NA	Guest Star LP 1481
Without Love	Mistics	1963	Capri 631
Without Love, Love, Love	Raindrops	1959	Hamilton 50021
Without Love (There Is Nothing)	McPhatter, Clyde (with the Cues)	1956	Atlantic 1117
Without Me	Counts, Tommy Burk & the	1965	Southern Artists 2026
Without Romance	Tornados, Aaron McNeil & the	1960	C.J. 615
Without Success	Individuals	1959	Sparrow 101
Without Warning	Darrells	1961	Lyco 1003
Without Warning	Devilles	1960	Dixie 1108
Without You	Curtiss, Jimmy & group	1960	United Artists 215
Without You	Earls	1961	Rome 101
Without You	Echoes	1960	Edco 100
Without You	Goldtones	1962	YRS 1002
Without You	Norvells	NA	Janis 6366
Without You	Samuels, Clarence & group	1959	Apt 25028
Without You	Sandetts	1960	Smokey 109
Without You Baby	Larks, Irma & the	NA	Priority 322
Without You To Love	Riley, Pat & group	1957	Tin Pan Alley 175
Without Your Love	Clusters, Gus Coletti & the	1957	Tin Pan Alley 206
Without Your Love	Five Jades (Cleveland)	1958	Duke 188
Without Your Love	Jay Birds, Vinnie Monte & the	1956	Josie 793
Without Your Love	Nobles, Aki Aleong & the	1961	Reprise 20021
Without Your Love	Pentagons	1986	True Gems LP
Without Your Love	Treble Chords	NA	Decca (unreleased)
Wizard Of Love	Ly-Dells	1961	Master 251
Wo! Wo! Wo!	Ivorytones	1960	Unidap 448
Wobble	Orioles, Sonny Til & the	1962	Charlie Parker 211
Wobble Party	Blazers (with Dave Baby Cortez)	1961	Winley 1001
Wobble Shank	Chestnuts	1960	Coral 62176
Wobble, The	Darlettes, Diane & the	1962	Dunes 2016
Wobble, The	Harptones	NA	Diplomat LP 2311
Wobble, The	Lee, Curtis (with the Halos)	1962	Dunes 2015
Wobble, The	Onions, Tommy Sena & the	NA	Valmont 905
Wobble, The	Val-Monts, Tommy Sena & the	1962	Valmont 905
Wobble With Me Baby	Rubies	1953	TNT 101/KT
Wobble Wobble	Matadors	1966	Forbes 230/Chartmaker 404
Wob-Ding-A-Ling	Big 5	1958	Junior 5000
Woe Is Me	Blue Jays (Venice, Calif.)	1987	Relic LP 5064
Woe Is Me	Cadillacs	1956	Josie 798
Woe Is Me	Composers	1963	Ampen 221
Woe, Woe	Sparks	1967	Cub 9151
Woe Woe Baby	Personalities	1957	Safari 1002
Woe-Oh Baby	Rockenettes, Donald Simpson & the	1958	Major 1002

SONG	GROUP	YEAR	LABEL
Woh Woh Yea Yea	Dynamos	1961	Cub 9096
Wo-Ho-La-Tee-Da	Zebulons	1960	Cub 9069
Woke Up In The Morning	Creations	1961	Pine Crest 101
Woke Up This Morning	Dell Vikings	1957	Fee Bee 221/Dot 15673 (58)
Woke Up This Morning	Four Tops	1956	Chess (unreleased)
Woke Up This Morning	Hi-Lites (Jet)	1961	Jet 502
Woke Up This Morning	Uniques	NA	Dapper 4401
Woke Up This Morning (acappella)	Five Delights	1960	A Cappella - Best of the Bronx (98)
Wolf	Four Mints	1958	NRC 011
Wolf Call	Tads	1958	Rev 3513
Woman In Love	Four Jacks	1956	Gateway 1151
Woman In My Life	English, Scott (with the Accents)	1972	Janus 192
Woman Is A Funny Thing	Kings, Albert Washington & the	NA	Fraternity 982
Woman Is A Man's Best Friend	Twilights, Teddy & the	1962	Swan 4102
Woman Trouble	Hepcats, Daisy Mae & the	1956	Gotham 317
Woman Was Made For Love	Thrillers (Detroit)	NA	Herald (unreleased)
Woman, Woman, Woman	Sparks Of Rhythm	1955	Apollo 479
Wombie Zombie	Teardrops, Billy Taylor & the	1959	Felco 101
Women	Drivers	1956	DeLuxe 6094
Women	Jesters, Lendon Smith with the	1956	Meteor 5030
Women	Lord, Emmett & group	1962	Liberty 55491
Women & Cadillacs	Night Riders, Doc Starkes & the	1954	Apollo 460
Women About To Make Me Go Crazy	Five Royales	1955	King 4819
Women And Whiskey	Roamers, Wilbert Harrison & the	1954	Savoy 1149
Womp	Del Pris	1961	Varbee 2003
Wonder	Three G's	1958	Columbia 41292
Wonder Boy	Heralds	1968	Tamborine 2
Wonder Of Love, The	Hollidays	1958	Prep 136
Wonder Of Love, The	Newports	1961	Kent 380
Wonder Of The World	Keytones	1957	Old Town 1041 (first pressing)
Wonder Where My Baby's Gone	Clovers	1952	Atlantic 969
Wonder Where Your Love Has Gone	Five Royales	1959, 1964	King 5237/5892
Wonder Why	Five Satins	1974	Relic LP 5024
Wonder Why	Solitaires	1954	Old Town 1000
Wonder Why	Castelles	1954	Grand 103
Wonderful	Blue Belles, Patti LaBelle & the	1968	Atlantic 2548
Wonderful Girl	Belmonts, Dion & the	1960	Laurie 3052
Wonderful Girl	Caribbeans	1963	Amy 871
Wonderful Girl	Chestnuts, Bill Baker & the	1959	Elgin 013/014
Wonderful Girl	Five Satins	1956	Ember 1008
Wonderful Girl	Intentions	1964	Melron 5014
Wonderful Girl	Shallows	1986	Starlight 49
Wonderful Is His Name	Belles	1962	Choice 29
Wonderful Love	Falcons (Detroit)	1960	United Artists 255
Wonderful Love	Sharmettes	1962	King 5656
Wonderful Loveable You	Teddy Bears	1959	Dore 520
Wonderful, Marvelous	Tremaines	1959	Kane 007/008/V-Tone 507 (60)
Wonderful One	Hi-Jacks	1956	ABC 9742
Wonderful One	Smith, Shad & group	1962	Smash 1765
Wonderful Time	Top Notes	1960	Atlantic 2066
Wonderful Tonight	Reunion	1987	Clifton 79
Wonderful! Wonderful!	Tymes	1963	Parkway 884
Wonderful World	Twigs, Sonny Woods & the	1954	Hollywood 1026
Wonderful World Of Children, The	Corby, Doug & group	1963	Vault 922
Wonderful You	Beau Belles	1958	Arrow 729
Wonderful You	Coastliners	1960	Back Beat 554
Wondering	Twilighters (Baltimore)	1953	Marshall 702
Wondering About Your Love	Dials	1960	Hilltop 2009
Wondering Why	Celtics	NA	Coronado 133
Wondering Why	Hi-Tones, Johnny Wyatt & the	1959	Big Time 1927
Wonderland	Carribians	1961, 1974	Brooks 2000/2001/Johnson
Wonderland Of Love	Tymes	1964	Parkway 908
Wonders Of Love	Continentals, Morris Rogers & the	NA	Delta 601
Wondrous	Roberts, Dave & group	1958	PL 14
Won't Have To Cry Anymore	Rhythmaires, Jessie Lee with the	1958	Mida 110

SONG	GROUP	YEAR	LABEL
Won't Someone Tell Me Why?	Sweet Teens, Faith Taylor & the	1959	Federal 12334
Won't You	Ambrose, Kenny & group	1959	Willett 109
Won't You Be My Friend	Platters '65 (featuring Linda Hayes)	1965	Entree 107
Won't You Believe	Prodigals	1958	Falcon 1015/Abner 1015 (58)
Won't You Call Me	Choralettes	1964	Fargo 1063
Won't You Come Home, Baby?	Topps	1954	Red Robin 131
Won't You Come In	Little Coolbreezers	1956	Ebony 1015
Won't You Give Me A Chance	Cupids, Darwin & the	1960	Jerden 9
Won't You Give Me A Chance	Three Chuckles	1956	Vik 0244
Won't You Give Your Love To Me	Pledges	1959	Hamilton 50028
Won't You Let Me Know	King Crooners	1959	Excello 2168
Won't You Let Me Share My Love	Zeniths	NA	Chess/Checker (unreleased)
Won't You Love Me	Fads, Buddy & the	1958	Morocco 1001
Won't You Marry Me	Vibes	1987	Relic LP 8011
Won't You Please	Superlatives	NA	Dynamics 1012
Won't You Tell Me	Debonaires (New York)	1956	Gee 1008
Won't You Tell Me, My Heart?	Chestnuts, Bill Baker & the	1959	Elgin 007/008
Woo, The	Demons, Bobby & the	1960	MCI 1028
Woo Woo Pretty Girl	Indigos	1958, 1977	Cornel 3001
Woo Woo Train	Elegants	1980	Crystal Ball 139
Woo Woo Train	Inquisitors, Little Isadore & the	1995	Early Bird 5000
Woo Woo Train	Valentines	1955	Rama 196
Woodchuck Song	Impalas (Brooklyn)	19??	Unreleased
Woody Surfer, The	Quadrells, Alan & the	1961	Goldisc G14
Wooly Wooly Willie	Catalinas	1960	Rita 107/Rita 1006 (60)
Woomai	Diamonds	1961	Mercury 71818
Words	Regents	1966	Penthouse 502
Words Can't Explain	Alteers	1961	Laurie 3097
Words Of Love	Diamonds	1957	Mercury 71128
Words Of Wisdom	Terracetones	1958	Apt 25016
Words Written On Water	Avons	1963	Groove 0033
Work It Out	Charmers	1963	Laurie 3203
Work It Out	Fabulous Twilights, Nathaniel Mayer & the	1962	Fortune 550
Work Out	Washington, Baby & group	1959	Neptune 107
Work Out Fine	Starfires	1965	Triumph 61
Work Out With Your Pretty Girl	Technics, Tony & the	1962	Chex 1010
Work Song, The	Deltas	1962	Philips 40023
Work With Me Annie	Channels, Earl Lewis & the	1973	Channel 1003
Work With Me Annie	Midnighters	1953, 1954	Federal 12169
Work With Me Annie	Romans, Little Caesar & the	1961	Del-Fi LP 1218
Work Work	Leverett, Chico (with the Satintones)	1963	Bethlehem 3062
Workin' For My Baby	Dubs	1956	Unreleased
Workin' Hard	Olympics	1960	Arvee 5006
Workin' Man	Pennants	1961	World 102
Workin' Man's Song	Falcons (Detroit)	1961	United Artists 289
Working At The Factory	Four Casts	1964	Atlantic 2228
Working For My Baby	Scaletones	1956	
Working Hard	Sevilles	1961	JC 120
Working On A Groovy Thing	Kelway Quintet	1972	Kelway 104
Workout	Embers, Ricky Dee & the	1962	Newtown 5001
Workout	Sophomores, Anthony & the	1966, 1967	Jamie 1330
World Is A Beautiful Place, The	Five Discs	1958	Emge 1004/Vik 0327 (58)/ Rust 5027 (63)
World Is Changing, The	Drifters	1954	Crown 108
World Is Full Of Wonderful Things, The	Tokens (Brooklyn)	1968	Warner Bros. 7255
World Is Waiting For The Sunrise, The	Dominoes	1960	ABC 10128
World Is Waiting For The Sunrise, The	Larks (North Carolina)	1954	Lloyds 112
World Of Confusion	Coronados	1958	United Artists 135
World Of Love	Rogues	1956	Old Town 300
World Of Make Believe, The	Discords, Eddie Corner & the	1960	Smoke 101
World's Biggest Fool	Delmonicos	1964	Musictone 6122
World's Fair U.S.A.	Del Cades	1964	United Sound Associates 175
World's Greatest Lover	Dee-Vines	1960	Lano 2001/Relic 514 (64)
World's Greatest Sinner	Ferns, Baby Ray & the	1963	Donna 1378
Worm, The	Jokers	1962	Viking 1009

SONG	GROUP	YEAR	LABEL
Worried About You Baby	Devotions	1958	Cub 9020
Worried Over You	Velvetones	1959	D 1072
Worryin' Kind	Regents	1966	Penthouse 502
Worst That Could Happen, The	Belmonts	1969	Dot 17257
Worth Waiting For	Douglas, Ronnie & group	1965	Epic 9843
Worthless And Lowdown	Knight, Sonny & group	1957	Dot 15542
Would I Be Crying	Flamingos	1956	Checker 853
Would I Be Crying	Tycoon	1986	Starlight 33
Would I Do It Over	Ultimations	NA	Marvlus 6020
Would I Love You	Cardinals	1977	Robin Hood 154
Would I Love You	Scott Brothers	196?	
Would I Love You
(Love You, Love You)	Orioles, Sonny Til & the	1951	Jubilee 5057
Would I Still Be Loving You	Tides	1961	Warwick 653
Would I Still Be The
One In Your Heart	Blenders	1950	Decca 48158
Would It Hurt You	Venetians, Nick Marco & the	1960	Dwain 813
Would You Be Mine	Prospects	1989	Starlight 69
Would You Believe It	Catalina 6	1962	Flagship 126
Would You Believe Me?	Ravens	1947	National 9034
Would You, Could You	Tornados, Stanley Mitchell & the	1956	Chess 1649
Would You Do The Same To Me	Candlelighters	1957	
Would You Rather	Lyrics, Kenneth Churchill & the	1958	Joyce 304
Would You Still Be Mine	Emblems	1962	Bay Front 107
Would You Still Be
The One In My Heart	Orioles, Sonny Til & the	1950	Jubilee 5018
Wouldn't Be Going Steady	Roulettes	1959	Scepter 1204
Wouldn't Be The Same	Sensationals	1961	Candix 319
Wouldn't It Be Nice	Shades	1962	Joey 6206
Wounded Heart	Royal Teens	1959	Mighty 112
Wow Baby	Ellis Brothers	1958	ABC 9954
Wow Baby Sitter	Earthquakes, Tino Cairo with the	1957	Hi-Q 5020
Wow Wow Baby	Searchers	1958	Class 223
Wow Wow Mary Mary	Belvederes	1958	Trend 2595
Wow Wow Wee (He's The Boy For Me)	Angels (New Jersey)	1964	Smash 1870
Wow Wow Wow	Young, George & group	1957	Chord 1301
Wowie	Madhattans	1957	Atlantic 1142
Wow-Wow Baby	Montclairs, Eddie Carol & the	1958	Rulu 6098
W-P-L-J	Blue Notes, Todd Randall & the	1962	3 Sons 103
W-P-L-J	Four Deuces	1955	Music City 790
Wrangler Stretch, The	Pirouettes	1964	Diamond 165
Wrap It Up	Normanaires	1953	MGM 11622
Wrap It Up	Robins (Richard Berry)	1954	Spark 103
Wrap It Up And Save	Sunbeams	1956	Dot 1280
Wrap My Heart In Velvet	Reptiles, Johnny Cole & the	1961	Radiant 1503
Wrap Your Troubles In Dreams	Dynamics	1961	Lavere 186
Wrap Your Troubles In Dreams
(And Dream Your Troubles Away)	Classics (Brooklyn)	1963	Musicnote 118
Wrapped In Green Made For A Teen	Gates	1959	Peach 628
Wrapped, Tangled And Tied	Ravons	1958	Arrow 734
Wrapped Too Tight	Del Knights	1961	Chancellor 1075
Wrapped Up In A Dream	Candlettes	1963	Rhonda 1001
Wrapped Up In A Dream	Clovers	1961	Winley 255
Wrapped Up In A Dream	Five Keys	1960	King LP 692
Wrecking My Life	Shallows	1961	Rae-Cox 108
Wreckless	Wrens	1986	Rama (unreleased)
Write A Letter	Blue Jays (Los Angeles)	1961	Blujay 1002
Write A Song About Me	Flares, Cookie Jackson & the	1961	Press 2814
Write And Tell Me Why	Orioles, Sonny Til & the	1953, 1963	Jubilee 5127/Charlie Parker 216
Write Me	George, Terry & group	1961	Comet 2144
Write Me	Remarkables	1964	Chase 1600
Write Me	Terry, George & group	1965	Sphere Sound 711
Write Me A Letter	Blends, Glenn Wells & the	1960	Jin 122
Write Me A Letter	Blossoms	1961	Challenge 9122

SONG	GROUP	YEAR	LABEL
Write Me A Letter	Carlo (Carlo Mastrangelo) (with the Tremonts)	1963	Laurie 3151
Write Me A Letter	Ravens	1947, 1951	National 9035/Okeh 6843
Write Me A Love Letter	Capitols	1959	Triumph 601
Write Me Baby	Metrotones	1955	Columbia 40486
Write Me One Sweet Letter	Ravens	1952	Mercury 70060
Write My Name	Pyramids, Dave White & the	1960	Pink 705
Writing This Letter	Fairlanes	1961	Continental 1001
Written In The Stars	Blends, Glenn Wells & the	1960	Jin 133/United Artists 244 (60)
Written In The Stars	Four Jokers	1958	Sue 703
Written In The Stars	Highlanders, Sandra & the	1961	Highland 1015
Written In The Stars	Lovettes	1959	Knight 2010
Written In The Stars	Wilson, Steve & group	1961	Pamela 205
Written On The Wall	King, Clydie & group	1957	Specialty 605
Wrong About You	Impalos	1961	United Artists 327
Wrong Again	Powell, Austin (with the James Quintet)	1952	Atlantic 968
Wrong Door, The	Jackson Brothers	1952	Arrow 1003
Wrong Door, The	Magic Notes	1957	Era 1035
Wrong Girl, The	Showmen	1962	Minit 643
Wrong Number	Four Chaps	1956	Rama 199
Wrong Party Again, The	Singing Wanderers	1954	Decca 29298
Wrong Yo Yo	Suedes, Rosie Stevens & the	1960	Spinning 6011
Wyatt Earp	Marquees	1957	Okeh 7096
Wykiup	Tunesters	1959	Tiara 6129

X

SONG	GROUP	YEAR	LABEL
X Equals Kiss	Three Graces	1959	Golden Crest 515
X Plus Y Equals Z	Threeteens	1958	Rev 3522/Todd 1021 (59)
Xmas In My Heart	Starlites	1962	Goldband 1151
Xmas Party	De Havilons, Eddie & the	1962	Peacock 1920
Xmas Will Soon Be Here	Laurels, John Gaudet & the	1961	Mary Glen 1001

Y

SONG	GROUP	YEAR	LABEL
Ya Got That Lovin' Touch	Twiliters, Ron Holden & the	1962	Baronet 3
Ya Gotta Take A Chance	Bonnets	1963	Unical 3010
Ya Ya	Gee, Frankie & group	1975	Claridge 410
Ya Ya	Revlons	1964	Parkway 107
Ya Ya	Shepherd Sisters	1962	United Artists 456
Ya Ya	Videls	1964	Fargo 1062
Ya Ya Twist	Dee, Joey & the Starliters	1961	Monument (No #)
Yaba Dab Ah Doo	Ramblers (Impact)	1961	Impact 10
Yacka Hoom Boom	Savoys (Combo)	1955	Combo 75
Yackety Yak	Esquires	1956	Meteor 5022
Yadi Yadi Revisited	Rivingtons	1966	Columbia 43772
Yadi-Yadi-Yum-Dum	Rivingtons	1966	Columbia 43772
Yakety Yak	Coasters	1958	Atco 6116
Yakety Yak	Glasers, Tompall & the	1958	Robbins 1006
Yakity Yak	Markeys	1958	RCA 7256
Yea Yea	Rockin' Kids	1958	Dot 15749
Yea, Yea, Baby	Original Cadillacs, Earl Carroll & the	1958	Josie 829
Yea, Yea, Yea	Dupree, Lebron & group	1959	Spann 411
Yea, Yea, Yea, Yea, Yea, Yea	Tyrants, Terry & the	1961	Kent 399
Yea-Boo	Holidays, Dick Holler & the	1962	Comet 2152
Yeah Baby	Evergreens, Dante & the	1960	Madison 143
(Yeah, Baby) It's Because Of You	Diablos, Nolan Strong & the	1963	Fortune 556
Yeah, He's Got It	Creators (New Jersey)	1963	Philips 40058
Yeah Little Girl	Reed, John & group	NA	Fore 611
Yeah Since You Went Away	Five Fabulous Demons	1963	King 5761
Yeah Yeah	Corvairs	1960	Cub 9065
Year Round Love	Tyrones	1956	Mercury 70939
Year That Gave Me You, The	Remarkables, Reggie & the	1962	Musicor 1030
Yearning	Five Keys	1971 (1953)	Aladdin 3182A (unreleased)
Yearning For You	Starfires	1958	Bernice 201
Years Of Tears	Rivingtons	1964	Vee Jay 649
Yea-Yea (I Was Blind)	Chordells	1963	Tiger 601

SONG	GROUP	YEAR	LABEL
Yella Shoes	Four Deuces	1959	Everest 19311
Yellow Hand	El Torros	1957	Duke 175
Yellow Mellow Hardtop	Bystanders	1957	Demon 1502
Yellow Moon	Biscaynes	1961	VPM 1006
Yellow Moon	Dollars, Little Eddie & the	1959	Fortune 845
Yellow Moon	Viscaynes	1961	VPM 1006
Yen Yet Song, The	Friends, Gary Cane & His	1960	Shell 719
Yes	Cap-Tans	1950, 1951	DC 8048/Gotham 268
Yes Daddy	Three Dolls, La Ronda Succeed & the	1961	Magnificent 111
Yes Darling I'll Be Around	Beltones	1961	Decca 31288
Yes I Do	Contenders	1959	Blue Sky 105
Yes I Do	Duvals (La Salle)	1961	La Salle 502
Yes I Do	Relations	NA	Club
Yes I Do	Tabbys	1959	Time 1008
Yes I Know	Ladybirds	1964	Lawn 231
Yes I Love You	Candies	1962	Ember 1092
Yes I Love You Baby	Diadems	1963	Star 514
Yes I Love You Baby	Dynamics	NA	Top Ten 100
Yes I Need Someone	Escos	1961	Federal 12445
Yes I Will	Velvetones	1962	Ascot 2117
Yes Indeed	Orioles, Sonny Til & the	1952	Jubilee (unreleased)
Yes, It Was Me	Velaires	1965	Hi-Mar 9173
Yes It's All Right	Ascots	1965	Mir-A-Don 1002
Yes It's True	Tuxedos	1960	Forte 1414
Yes, It's You	Clovers	1953	Atlantic 989
Yes It's You	Clovers	1960	United Artists 263
Yes Master	Whips	1958	Dore 502
Yes My Baby	Scamps	1955	Peacock 1655
Yes My Baby Please	Capris	NA	Collectables LP 5000
Yes, My Baby Please	Capris (Philadelphia)	1956	20th Century 1201
Yes My Love	Regals	1960	Lavender 1452
Yes My Love	Roomates	NA	Relic LP 5041
Yes, Oh Baby Yes	Laddins	1959	Grey Cliff 721
Yes, Oh Yes	Hi-Fashions	1958	Paris 524
Yes Or No	Twilighters, Tony & the	1960, 1977	Red Top 127
Yes, She's My Baby	Magnificents	1984	Solid Smoke LP 8030
Yes Sir	Cues	1991	Capitol (unreleased) (recorded 1956)
Yes Sir, That's My Baby	Clovers	1950	Rainbow 11-122
Yes Sir, That's My Baby	Essentials, Billy & the	1963	Mercury 72210
Yes Sir, That's My Baby	Five Keys	1952	Aladdin 3118
Yes Sir, That's My Baby	Gayles	1956	Media 1021
Yes Sir, That's My Baby	Hushabyes, Hale & the	1964	Apogee 104/Reprise 0299
Yes Sir, That's My Baby	Mastertones, Elaine Taylor & the	1960	Band Box 233
Yes Sir, That's My Baby	Merry Men, Steve Douglas & his	1962	Philles 104
Yes Sir, That's My Baby	Pirates, Johnny Kidd & the	1960	Apt 25040
Yes Sir, That's My Baby	Sensations	1956	Atco 6056
Yes, Siree	Marktones	1958	Ember 1030
Yes! That's Love	Themes	1959	Excello 2152
Yes They Do	Hollywood Flames	1961	Chess 1787
Yes, Yes	Accents, Jackie Allen & the	1955	Accent 1031
Yes Yes Yes	Cashmeres (Philadelphia)	1954	Mercury 70501
Yes You Are	Twilighters (Bronx, N.Y.)	1960	Spin 0001
Yes, You Made It That Way	Valentines	1962	Bethlehem 3055
Yes You May	Teen Tones	1959	Decca 30895
Yes, You're Mine	Vocaleers	1976	Relic LP 5094
Yesterday And You	La Rays	1963	Arlen 517
Yesterday Standing By	These Gents	NA	Western World 55102
Yesterdays	Four Shades Of Rhythm	1952	Chance 1126
Yesterday's Dreams	Dolphins, Dougie & the	1959	Angle Tone 542
Yesterday's Memories	Mellows, Lillian Leach & the	1955	Jay-Dee 807
Yibby-Yah	Caprisians	1960	Indigo 109
Yo' Good Lovin'	Five Fleets	1958	Felsted 8522
Yo Me Pregunto	Concepts	1966	Catamount 112
Yo Me Pregunto	Valrays	1963	Parkway

SONG	GROUP	YEAR	LABEL
Yo Te Amo	Five Knights	1959	Specialty 675
Yo Te Quiero (I Love You)	Channels, Earl Lewis & the	1978	King Tut 175
Yo Yo	Chancellors	1965	Soma 1421
Yo Yo	Four Flickers	1959	Lee 1002
Yo Yo Girl	Debonaires, Dickie & the	1965, 1982	Valli 302
Yodee Yakee	Drifters (Pre-1959)	1957	Atlantic 1161
Yodelin' Mad	Equalos	1959	Mad 1296
Yogi	Ivy Three	1960	Shell 720
Yok Yok Yok	Altecs	NA	Cloister 6201
Yokel (He Went To Town), The	Lions	1960	Imperial 5678
Yoko Hoko Homa	Peppers	1958	Jane 105
Yolanda	Pictures, C.L. & the	1965	Monument 888
Yon We Go	Flares	1961	Press 2807
You	Apollos, Paul Stefen & the	1962	Cite 5008
You	Aquatones	1958	Fargo 1001
You	Dominoes	1960	ABC 10156
You	Duponts	1955	Winley 212/Savoy 1552 (58)
You	Ebonaires	1988	Relic LP 5076
You	Frontiers	1967	MGM 13722
You	Imperials, Little Anthony & the	1958	Savoy 1552
You	Initials, Angelo & the	1959	Dee 1001/Sherry 667
You	Jive Five	NA	United Artists 50107
You	Lyrics (Hy-Tone)	1958	Hy-Tone 111
You	Savoys (New York)	1956	Savoy 1188
You	Teenagers, Frankie Lymon & the	1986	Murray Hill LP 000148
You	Williams, Bobby & group	1958	Deck 142
You	Willows (Dotty Martin)	1960	Warwick 524
Y-O-U	Darchaes	1980	Clifton 56
You & I	Imaginations	1991	Collectables CD 5726
You Actin' Funny Honey	Dee Jays, Chico Shepherd & the	1954	After Hours 101
You Ain't Movin' Me	Hayes, Linda (with the Flairs)	1956	Antler 4000
You Ain't No Hippie	Hueys	1968	Instant 3289
You Ain't Ready	Flamingos	1953	Chance 1149
You Ain't Right	Nobles (Sollie McElroy)	1962	Stacy 926
You Ain't Sayin' Nothin'	Satellites	1958	Class 234/Malynn 234 (58)
You Ain't Seen Nothing Yet	Bobbettes	1965	Diamond 181
You Ain't So Such A Much	Thrillettes, Bette Renne & the	1964	Lawn 246
You Ain't Too Cool	Strangers	1960	Maske 101
You Alone	Lanes	1956	Gee 1023
You And I	Bossmen	1966	Lucky Eleven 231
You And I	Capri, Bobby & group	1963	Johnson 124
You And I	Originals	1962	Diamond 116
You And I	Rip Chords	1958	MMI 1236
You And I	Savoys (Bella)	1959	Bella 18
You And I	Skylarks	1951	Decca 48241
You And I	Velvet Satins, Bobby Capri & the	1963	Johnson 124
You And I Can Climb	Cleftones	1961	Gee LP 705
You And Me	Hummingbirds	1962	Cannon 4600
You And Me	Supremes (Ohio)	NA	Grog 500
You And Me	Tokens (Brooklyn)	1972	Bell 190
You And Me	Unknowns	1957	Shield 7101/X-Tra 102 (57)
You And Me Baby	Five Stars, Dottie Ferguson & the	1957	Kernel 003/Mercury 71129
You And Only You	Angelettes	1957	Josie 813
You And Only You	Orlando, Tony & group	1959	Milo 101
You And Only You	Ping Pongs	1964	G-Note
You And You Alone	Valets	1959	Vulcan/Jon 4219 (59)
You And Your Fellow	Lyrics (San Francisco)	1961	Fernwood 129/Fleetwood 233 (61)
You And Your Lies	Possessions	1964	Britton 1003/Parkway 930 (64)
You And Yours	Composers	1963	Era 3118
You Are	Cadillacs	1956	Josie 792
You Are	Capris (New York)	1982	Ambient Sound LP FZ-37714
You Are	Crescents	1985	Relic LP 5053
You Are	Diablos, Nolan Strong & the	1955	Fortune 519
You Are	Executive Four	1966	Lumar 202
You Are	Off Keys, Jerry Evans & the	1962	Rowe 002

SONG	GROUP	YEAR	LABEL
You Are	Packards	1956	Decca (unreleased)
You Are	Vibes	1958	Allied 10006
You Are An Angel	Pipes	1956	Dootone 401
You Are Free, I'm Alone	Blackwells	1959	Jamie 1141
You Are Invited	Del Vikings	1973	Broadcast 1123
You Are Irresistible	Medallions	1962	Reo 8693/Lenox 5556 (62)
You Are Laughing	Knockout Mays	1960	Cos-De 1003
You Are Love	Five Satins	1973	Kirshner 4251
You Are Mine	Supremes, Billy the Kid & the	1958	Bernice 202
You Are My Angel	Rollins, Bird & group	1958	Vanguard 35003
You Are My Darling	Creations	1956	Lido 501/Tip Top 501 (56)
You Are My First Love	Orioles, Sonny Til & the	1951	Jubilee 5051
You Are My Heart	Taylor, Bobby & group	1962	Barbara 62640
You Are My Inspiration	Creations	1962	Mel-o-Dy 101
You Are My Love	Marx	1959	Chante 1002/Dahlia 1002
You Are My Love	Royal Notes	1958	Kelit 7034
You Are My Love (You)	Teen Kings	NA	Relic LP 5033
You Are My Only	Five Dreams	1957	Mercury 71150
You Are My Only Love	Cardinals	1953	Atlantic 995
You Are My Only Love	Five Fortunes	1958	Ransom 103
You Are My Only Love	Intervals	1962	Class
You Are My Only Love	Romans	1958	Juno 013/014
You Are My Queen	Casanovas	1958	Apollo 523
You Are My Sunshine	Don Juans, Andre Williams & the (with Gino Purifoy)	1956	Fortune 831/Epic 9196 (56)
You Are My Sunshine	Don Juans, Andre Williams & the (with Gino Purifoy)	1956	Fortune 834
You Are My Sunshine	Marcels	1961	Colpix 606
You Are My Sunshine	Mason, Little Billy (with the Rhythm Jesters)	1957	Rama 223
You Are My Sunshine	Moreland, Prentice & group	1962	Challenge 9154
You Are My Sunshine	Pharaohs, Richard Berry & the	1957, 1962	Flip 321/360
You Are My Sunshine	Planets	1964	Roulette 4551
You Are My Sunshine	Rebels, Jimmy & the	1959	Roulette 4201
You Are My Sunshine	Sonics	1987	Relic LP 8011
You Are My Sunshine	Thunderbirds, Johnny & the	1959	Clover 1001
You Are My Sunshine	Ward, Lee (with the Cymbals)	1961	Gait 407
You Are My Sunshine	Zircons	1964	Cool Sound 1030
You Are My Sweetheart	Bobbettes	1959	Atlantic 2027
You Are So Beautiful	Five Notes	1955	Jen D 4185/Josie 784 (55)
You Are So Close To Me	Avons	1958	Hull 726
You Are Sweeter Than Wine	Valiants (Los Angeles)	1962	Imperial 5843
You Are The First One	Jacks	1963	Crown LP 5372
You Are The First One	Rockets	1956	Modern 992
You Are The One	Antones	1956	Black Crest 106
You Are The One	Hamilton Sisters	1956	King 4892
You Are The One	Starlets	1961	Pam 1003
You Are The One	Teardrops, Honey & the	1959	Val 202
You Are The Only One	Blasers, Eddie Foster & the	1961	Lyons 108
You Are The Only One	Falcons, Candy Rivers & the	1954	Flip 302
You Are The Only One	Wynnewoods	1959	Wynne 108
You Are To Blame	Cadillacs	1961	Smash 1712
You Are Too Beautiful	Platters	NA	Mercury EP 3353
You Are Welcome To My Heart	Lovers	1962	MC B-003
You Aren't The Only One	Classmates	1957	Dot 15589
You Asked Me To Be Yours	Tymes	1964	Parkway LP 7032
You Baby You	Cleftones	1956	Gee 1000
You Baby You	Diamonds	1956	Mercury 70790
You Baby You	Excellents	1962	Blast 205
You Baby You	Zircons	1965	Old Timer 606
You Beat Me To The Punch	Love-Tones, Mary Wells & the	1962	Motown 1032
You Been Torturing Me	Four Young Men	1961	Crest 1076
You Belong To Her	Browns, Barbara & the	1964	Stax 150
You Belong To Me	Cadets	1957	Modern 1017
You Belong To Me	Duprees	1962	Coed 569

SONG	GROUP	YEAR	LABEL
You Belong To Me	Five Discs	1980	Crystal Ball LP
You Belong To Me	Four-Evers	1962, 1980	Columbia 42303/Jason Scott 4
You Belong To Me	Jacks	1957	RPM LP 3006/Crown LP 5021 (57)
You Belong To Me	Lullabyes	1961	Embassy 204
You Belong To Me	Lyrics, Ike Perry & the	1979	King Tut 180
You Belong To Me	Orioles, Sonny Til & the	1952	Jubilee 5102
You Belong To Me	Ping Pongs	1962	Marco 107
You Belong To Me	Rovers, Helen Foster & the	1952	Republic 7013
You Belong To Me	Sharks	1976	Broadcast 1132
You Belong To Me	Sneakers	NA	Delta 1868
You Belong To Me	Street Corner Society	1979	U.G.H.A. 8
You Belong To My Heart	Emeralds (Pittsburgh)	1957	ABC 9889
You Belong To My Heart	Flamingos	1960	End LP 307
You Belong To My Heart	Four Mints	1958	NRC 011
You Belong To My Heart	Valtones	1956	Gee 1004
You Better Be A Good Girl Now	Swans (Swan)	1963	Swan 4151
You Better Believe	Gay Poppers	1959	Savoy 1573
You Better Believe	Limelites, Shep & the	1965	Hull 770
You Better Dig It	Four Steps Of Rhythm, Bill Johnson & the	1959	Talos 402
You Better Go Now	Bees, Honey & the	NA	Arctic 141
You Better Keep Runnin'	Gari, Frank & group	1961	Crusade 1024
You Better Know It	Expressions	1964	Federal 12533
You Better Make It	Twiliters	1964	Paloma 100
You Better Mind	Cap-Tans, Bethea & the	1963	Sabu 501
You Better Move On	Blue Belles, Patti LaBelle & the	1964	Rainbow 1900
You Better Move On	Bracelets	1964	20th Century Fox 539
You Better Move On	Counts, Tommy Burk & the	1964	Atco 6340
You Better Move On	Prodigals	NA	Acadian 1000
You Better Not Do That	Belmonts, Dion & the	1959	Laurie LP 1002/Laurie LP 2002 (60)/ Collectables LP 5025
You Better Stay Home	Society Girls	1963	Vee Jay 524
You Better Stop It	Lovelites	1961	Bandera 2515
You Blew Out The Candles	Crests	NA	Coral 62403
You Broke My Happy Heart	Eldees	1963	Dynamics 1013
You Broke My Heart	Clicks	1955	Josie (unreleased)
You Broke My Heart	Demens	1957	Teenage 1006
You Broke My Heart	Dickson, Richie & group	1962	Class 308
You Broke My Heart	Ermines	1956	Loma 703
You Broke My Heart	Gleams	1962	Kip 236/237
You Broke My Heart	Kidds	1955	Post 2003
You Broke My Heart	Rainbows	19??	
You Broke My Heart	Rosebuds, Richie Dixon & the	1963	Class 308
You Broke My Heart	Rosettes	1961	Herald 562
You Broke Our Hearts	Avalons	1958	Dice 90/91
You Broke The Only Heart	Five Keys	1961	King 5446
You Broke The Rules Of Love	Five Keys	1956	Capitol 3318
You Bug Me Baby	Marathons	1962	Arvee 5048
You Call Everybody Darling	Gondoliers, Johnny Adams & the	1959	Ric 957
You Call Me Angel	Massey, Barbara & group	1961	Imperial 5786
You Came Along	Royal Jokers	1963	Fortune 560
You Came To Me	Allures	1985	Starlight 26
You Came To Me	Blue Sky Boys	1971	Blue Sky 100
You Came To Me	Channels, Earl Lewis & the	1978	King Tut 173
You Came To Me	Duvals (New York)	1956	Rainbow 335/Riviera 990 (56)
You Came To Me	Five Crowns	1955	Riviera 990/Rainbow 335 (56)
You Can Be My Honey	Lyrics, Ike Perry & the	1960	Cowtown 801
You Can Call	Delmonicos	1963	Aku 6318
You Can Come	Carousels	1961	Gone 5118 (first pressing)
You Can Count On Me	Avalons	1959, 1972	Casino 108
You Can Count On Me	Channels	1965	Groove 0061
You Can Count On Me	Five Satins	1964	Roulette 4563
You Can Count On Me	Flaming Embers	1961	Fortune 869
You Can Count On Me	McGee, Al & group	1961	Aries 7-10-2
(You Can) Count On That	Big Town Girls, Shirley Matthews & the	1963	Atlantic 2210
You Can Depend On Me	Darchaes, Nicky Addeo & the	1964	Melody 1417

SONG	GROUP	YEAR	LABEL
You Can Depend On Me	Platters	NA	Mercury EP 3345
You Can Depend On Me	Sabres	1955	Bullseye 101
You Can Fall In Love	Ardells (Johnny Maestro)	1963	Selma 4001
You Can Fall In Love	Redcoats, Steve Alaimo & the	1959	Dade 1805
You Can Get Him-Frankenstein	Castle Kings	1961	Atlantic 2107
You Can Have Any Boy	Juliana & group	1961	RCA 7906
You Can Lump It	Seminoles	1962	Mid Town 101
You Can Make It If You Try	Allison, Gene & group	1957	Vee Jay 256
You Can Run	Notations	1965	Relic 1019
You Can Shake A Tail Feather	Casuals, Harold & the	1959	Scotty 628
You Can Take My Girl	Knockouts	1961	MGM 13010
You Can Tell	Delfonics	1962	Fling 727
You Can Tell Me	Miller Sisters	1955	Sun 230
You Can Tell That This Is Christmas	Lovetones	1962	Love-Tone 101
You Can't Be Sure Of Anything	Lance, Herb (with the Classics)	1957	DeLuxe 6150
You Can't Be Trusted	Trinkets	1958	Imperial 5497
You Can't Believe In Love	Cordials	1965	Liberty 55784
You Can't Change A Boy's Mind	Delrons, Reperata & the	1968	Mala 12016
You Can't Compare With My Baby	Monte, Vince & group	1962	Jubilee 5428
You Can't Even Be My Friend	Escorts (RCA)	1963	RCA 8228
You Can't Fool Me Baby	Hollywood Playboys	1961	Rita 118
You Can't Get Away From Love	Blue Notes	1959	Brooke 111 (second pressing)
You Can't Get Away From Me	Emblems, Patty & the	1964	Herald 595
You Can't Get Kissed	Carnations, Cosmo & the	1961	Tilt 787
You Can't Go It Alone	Backus, Gus & group	1958	Carlton
You Can't Hurt Me Anymore	Bradford, Chuck & group	1962	Fire 511
You Can't Imagine	Zee, Ginny & group	1961	Atco 6218
You Can't Judge A Book By The Cover	Mack, Dell (with the Golden Gate Quartet)	1958	Goldband 1064
You Can't Keep A Good Man Down	Dominoes	1953	Federal 12139
You Can't Keep A Good Man Down	Midnighters, Hank Ballard & the	1969	King LP 1052
You Can't Keep Love	Mellards, Fred Green & the	1955	Ballad 1012
You Can't Love Them All	Drifters (1959-forward)	1966	Atlantic 2336
You Can't Make Me Cry	Cyclones, Bob Williams & the	1958	Trophy 503
You Can't Play Games	Precisions	1960	Strand 25038
You Can't Run Away	Del Royals	1960	Destiny 101
You Can't Run Away From Me	Wanderers	1963	United Artists 648
You Can't Run Away From Yourself	Dovells	1963	Parkway 861
You Can't Sit Down	Dovells	1963	Parkway 867
You Can't Sit Still	Sequins	1963	Ascot 2140
You Can't Stay Here (Step It Up And Go)	Concords, Pearl Reaves & the	1955	Harlem 2332
You Can't Tie A Good Girl Down	Crystals (Brooklyn)	1965	United Artists 927
You Can't Trust A Woman	Four Clippers	1957	Fox 960/961
You Captured My Heart	Sultans	1951	Jubilee 5054
You Changed My Mind	Indexes, John Golden & the (with Blanton McFarlin)	1961	Douglas 101
You Cheated	Daytrippers	NA	AMM 005
You Cheated	Dell Vikings	1958	Mercury 71345
You Cheated	Kittens, Terri & the	1961	Imperial 5728
You Cheated	Noble, Beverly & group	1959	Sparrow 100
You Cheated	Shields	1958	Tender 513/Dot 15805 (58)
You Cheated	Slades	1958	Domino 500
You Conquered Me	McCline, Charles & group	1964	Larry-O 101
You Conquered Me	Plaids, Willie Logan & the	1964	Jerry-O 103
You Could Be My Girl Friend	Fiestas	1960	Old Town 1090
You Could Be My Love	Five Crowns	1952	Old Town 790
You Crack Me Up	Baker, Charlie & group	1959	Liberty 55226
You Crack Me Up	Marvels (Mun Rab)	1959	Mun Rab 1008
You Crack Me Up	Viceroys, Jimmy Norman & the	1963	Little Star 121
You Did	Four Jokers	1956	Diamond 3004
You Did Me Wrong	Buccaneers	1953	Rama 24
You Did Me Wrong	Downbeats, O. S. Grant & the	1956	Sarg 200
You Didn't Answer My Letter	Initials, Angelo & the	1973	Vintage 1006
You Didn't Care	Larados	NA	Madog 801
You Didn't Have To Laugh	Hi-Tones	1958	Skyline 701

SONG	GROUP	YEAR	LABEL
You Didn't Have To Tell Me	Four Guys	1959	Kent 311
You Didn't Learn It Home	Five Royales	1955	King 4770
You Didn't Learn That In School	Majestics, Kirk Taylor & the	1959	Bandera 2507
You Didn't Sign Your Letter With Love	Four Blades	1963	Alert 422
You Didn't Tell The Truth	Celebrities	1959	Boss 502
You Didn't Think I Would	Miller Sisters	1956	Flip 504
You Didn't Want My Love	Nic Nacs, Mickey Champion & the	1950	RPM 313/316/342
You Do Something To Me	Avalons	1959, 1972	Casino 108
You Do Something To Me	Bachelors, T. La Mar & the	1963	Five-Four 5440
You Do Something To Me	Classmates	1957	Dot 15589
You Do Something To Me	Ecstasies	1984	Clifton EP 508
You Do The Dreaming	Blenders (New York)	1951	Decca 48244
You Done Me Wrong	Bouquets, Tootie & the	1963	Parkway 887
You Done Me Wrong	Rocking Rebels, Ray Fournia & the	NA	Diamond Disk 101
You Done Me Wrong	Star Fires	1966	Laurie 3332
You Don't Believe A Word I Say	Jarmels	NA	Collectables LP 5044
You Don't Bug Me	Nutones, Terry Daly & the	1958	Mark 122
You Don't Care Anymore	Five Orleans	1957	Ebb 125
You Don't Care Anymore	Roulettes	1957	Ebb 124
You Don't Have To Cry	Lollipops, Little Bob & the	1962	Decca 31412
You Don't Have To Cry Any More	Binders	NA	Sara 7772/Ankh 7772
You Don't Have To Drop A Heart To Break It	Ravens	1950	Columbia 39070
You Don't Have To Explain	Macs, Terry & the	1956	ABC 9721
You Don't Have To Go	Fender, Freddy & group	1964	Norco 108
You Don't Have To Laugh	Hitones, Leonard Wayne & the	1964	Andre 701
You Don't Have To Say You Love Me	Roomates, Cathy Jean & the	1991	Cure 91-02801
You Don't Know	Five Dreamers	1957	Port 5001
You Don't Know	Glitters	NA	Rubaiyat 413
You Don't Know	Medallions, Vernon Green & the	1973	Dootone 479
You Don't Know Baby	Pacettes	1963	Regina 1306
You Don't Know Me	Four Fellows (Brooklyn - Glory)	1956	Glory 248
You Don't Know My Mind	Five Dollars, Jim Sands with the	1958	Hi-Q 5010
You Don't Know (What I've Been Through)	Fortunes	1963	Cub 9123
You Don't Love Me	Dominoes, Joe Taylor & the	NA	HMF 2002
You Don't Love Me	Escorts, Del & the	1960	Symbol 913
You Don't Love Me	Reflections	NA	Went 001
You Don't Love Me	Revlons	1980	Crystal Ball 138
You Don't Love Me	Starlets	1965	Tower 144
You Don't Love Me Anymore	Blue Flames	1961	Spry 113
You Don't Love Me Anymore	Lamarr, Gene (with the Blue Flames)	1958	Spry 113
You Don't Love Me Anymore	Passions	1960	Audicon 112
You Don't Love Me Anymore	Pastels (Washington, D.C.)	1958	Argo 5297
You Don't Love Me No More	Upstarts, Jerry McCain & the	1956	Excello 2079
You Don't Love Me (True)	Spiders	1961	Imperial 5739
You Don't Mean Me, Right?	Four Kings	1954	Fortune 811
You Don't Mean No Good To Me	Jelly Beans	1965	Eskee 001
You Don't Move Me	Spaniels	1954	Vee Jay 107
You Don't Say	Platters	1961	Mercury 71847
You Don't Seem To Realize	Dynamics	1961	Douglas 200
You Don't Understand	Moontunes, Smiley Moon & the	1967	Star 601
You Don't Understand	Romancers	1958	Bay-Tone 101
You Don't Want Me	Corvets	1965	Soma 1425
You Don't Want Me	Lockettes	1958	Flip 334
You Don't Want My Love	Shirelles	1961	Scepter LP 501
You Drive Me Crazy	Demens, Ray Scott & the	NA	Satellite 104
You Excite Me	Mello-Tones, Nat Williams & the	1959	Aries 1014
You Fascinate Me	Phillipairs	1957	Salem 1014
You Fool	Five Dollars	1957	Fortune 833
You Fool	Jan Raye Quartet, Lily Ann & the	NA	Baton 221
You Fool Again	Sugar Tones	1951	Okeh 6814
You Foolish Thing	Ravens	1951	Columbia 39198
You Foolish Thing	Ecstasies	1990	Clifton 87
You For Me	Hollyhocks	1957	Nasco 6001

SONG	GROUP	YEAR	LABEL
You For Me To Love	Jones, Jimmy & group	1959	Epic 9339
You Forgot How To Love	Blue Belles, Patti LaBelle & the	1965	Atlantic 2311
You Found Yourself Another Fool	Elgins (California)	1965	Valiant 712
You Gambled	Slades	1958	Domino 800
You Gave Me A True Love	Sunglows, Sunny & the	1964	Tear Drop 3034
You Gave Me Love	Tamaras, Lee Durell & the	1960	Music City 836
You Gave Me Peace Of Mind	Carnations	1954	Music City 736
You Gave Me Peace Of Mind	Spaniels	1956	Vee Jay 229
You Gave Me Somebody To Love	Dreamlovers	1965, 1966	Warner Bros. 5619/Mercury 72630
You Gave To Me	Hearts, Lee Andrews & the (as Lee Andrews)	1961	Swan 4076
You Give Me So Much	Naturals	1958	Beacon 462
You Give Your Love To Me	Jive Bombers	1959	Savoy 1560
You Good-Looking Woman	Clovers	1957	Atlantic 1129
You Got It Baby	Volumes	1967	Inferno 2001
You Got Love	Sa-Shays	1961	Alfi 1/Zen 101
You Got Me Baby	Deans	1963	Dean 1928/Star Maker 1928 (63)
You Got Me Bugged	Pacers	1963	Coral 62398
You Got Me Crying	Vibes	NA	Rayna 103
You Got Me Goin'	Innocents	1961	Indigo 128
You Got Me Goin'	Sultans	1961	Tilt 782
You Got Me Uptight	Gay Poppers	1961	Fire 1039
You Got Soul	Four Vibes	1962	Swa-Ray 1001
You Got That Way	Fourmost	1964	Atco 6317
You Got To Be Sincere	Marcels	1963	Colpix 694
You Got To Give	El Tempos, Mike Gordon & the	1954	Cat 101
You Got To Live For Yourself	Fourmosts, Bobby Moore & the	1964	Fantasy 585
You Got To Look Up	Drapers	1962	Gee 1081
You Got To Pay Your Dues	Drifters (1959-forward)	1970	Atlantic 2746
You Got To Reap What You Sow	Miller Sisters	1961	Glodis 1003
You Got To Steal	Flairs, Cornel Gunter & the	NA	Rap 007
You Got To Tell Me	Rivieras, Bobby Meyer & the	1964	Lawn 238/Casino 103
You Got What I Like	Raindrops	1964	Jubilee 5475
You Got What It Takes	Channels, Earl Lewis & the	1972	Channel 1002
You Got Your Magnet On Me Baby	Elgins (California)	1963	Lummtone 110
You Gotta Be Alone To Cry	Twilights, Teddy & the	1962	Swan 4115
You Gotta Change Your Ways	Silvertones	1960	Silver Slipper 1000
You Gotta Dance	Counts, Cosmo & the	1963	Sound Stage 7 2520
You Gotta Go	Kinglets	1956	Calvert 101
You Gotta Go Baby	Five Blue Notes	1954	Sabre 108
You Gotta Know	Knight, Bob	1961	Laurel 1023
You Gotta Love Me Baby	Federals	1957	Fury/Relic 7063-CD
You Gotta Rock And Roll	Sultans, Bob Oakes & the	1956	Regent 7502
You Gotta Tell Me	Downbeats	1962	Dynamite 243/Diamond 243
(You Grow) Sweeter As The Years Go By	Dominoes	1958	Liberty 55126
You Had Time	Heartbreakers (Bronx, N.Y.)	1963	Atco 6258
You Have Come Back	Jaguars	1976	Monogram 124
You Have Everything	Metaphors	NA	Rad (no #)
You Have No Heart	Crescents	1957	Joyce 102
You Have No Secrets	Crescents	1957	N/A
You Have No Time To Lose	Four Pennies (male)	1964	Brunswick 55304
You Haven't The Right	Catalinas	1967	Scepter 12188
You Hear	Lamplighters	1954	Federal 12192
You Hold The Strings To My Heart	Emeralds (Pel)	1962	Pel 3836
You Hurt Me	Channels	1963	Hit Record 700
You Hurt Me	Ervin, Frankie & group	1960	Rendezvous 126
You Hurt Me Inside	Parktowns	1960, 1961	Impala 214/Thor 3258/ Crimson 1006
You Hurt Me So	Marksmen	1957	Starday 320/Mercury 71139
You I Adore	Youngtones	1958, 1963	X-Tra 104/Candlelite 417
You In Disguise	Antell, Pete & group	1963	Cameo 264
You Inspire Me	Class-Notes	1958	Dot 15786
You Insulted Me	Calendars, Roberta Watson & the	1963	Corsican 111
You Just Don't Know	Broadways	1967	MGM 13592

SONG	GROUP	YEAR	LABEL
You Just Said You Love Me	Daisies	1964	Roulette 4571
You Just Say The Word	Magnets	1955	Groove 0058
You Just Say The Word	Street Dreams	1986	Starlight 44
You Just Won't Treat Me Right	Joytones	1956	Rama 191
You Just You	Criterions	1959	Cecelia 1208/Laurie 3305 (65)
You Just You	Midnighters, Hank Ballard & the	1965	King 5996
You Keep Me Guessin'	Hi-Lites, Ronnie & the	1963	Win 251
You Keep Telling Me	Starlites, Jackie & the	1962	Mascot 130
You Killed The Love	Lavette, Betty & group	1964	LuPine 123
You Know	Chelmars	NA	N/A
You Know	Del-Mars	1963	ABC 10426
You Know	Electras	1962	Lola 100/Cee Jam 100
You Know	Kool Gents	1956	Vee Jay 207
You Know	Little Linda & group	1961	Coral 62286
You Know	Rockin' Kings, Ronnie & the	1958	RCA 7248
You Know Baby	Melo-Aires	1958	Nasco 6019
You Know Baby	R-Dells	1960	Dade 1806
You Know Baby	Swingtones	1958	Rhythm 1
You Know Darling	Del Rios, Jimmy Hurt & the	1959	Do-Re-Mi 1401
You Know I Can't Refuse	Five Dollars	1956	Fortune 826
You Know I Care	Charms, Otis Williams & the	1961	King 5497
You Know I Do	Taylor, Ted & group	1960	Top Rank 3001
You Know I Go For You	Coolbreezers	1957, 1974	ABC 9865/Roadhouse 1019
You Know I Know	Five Royales	1952	Apollo 441
You Know I Love You	Jammers, Johnny & the	1960	Dart 131
You Know I Miss You	Emanons (Brooklyn)	NA	GGS 443
You Know I Need You	Spidels	1962	Chavis 1035
You Know I Wanna Love You	Young, George & group	1957	Chord 1301
You Know I'll Miss You	West Winds	1964	Enith International 1269
You Know Me	Kent, Al & group	1959	Wizzard 100
You Know My Heart Is Yours (acappella)	Chessmen	1975	Relic LP 106
You Know What I Would Do	Jive Five	1962	Beltone 3001
You Know! You Know! (I Love You)	Bachelors (Washington, D.C.)	1957	Poplar 101
You Know You're Doing Me Wrong	Harptones	1955	Paradise 101
You Know You're Mine	Tangerines	1964	Gina 7002
You Laff Too Much	Foxes, Johnny Fox & the	1962	Newtime 507
You Left Me	Gaytunes	1957	Joyce 101
You Left Me	Laurels	1960	Spring 1112
You Left Me	Swallows (Maryland)	1952	King 4525
You Left Me	Valiant Trio	1965	EV
You Left Me Blue	Four Buddies	NA	Savoy 955 (unreleased)
You Left Me Forsaken	Stereos	1962	Robins Nest 101
You Left Me Here To Cry Alone	Golden Tones	1960	Hush 102
You Left Me Lonely	Volumes, Lacille Watkins & the	1954	Jaguar 3006
You Left My Heart	Five Scripts	1965	Script 103
You Left Your Happiness	Sheiks, Eddie Williams & the	NA	Coronado 112
You Lied	Electras	1961	Infinity 012/Constellation
You Lied	Freedoms	1964	Constellation 105
You Lied	Runarounds	1967	MGM 13763
You Lied	Sweet Marquees	1961	Apache 1516
You Lied	Tabs, Joanie Taylor & the	1961	Herald 568
You Lied	Three Chuckles	1966	Cloud 507
You Lied And I Cried	Little Ernie & group	1963	Summit 0008
You Lied To Me	Re-Vels	1956	Sound 129
You Little Nothin'	Legends	1961	Magenta 02
You Look Good To Me	El Torros	1958	Duke 194
You Look Like A Flower	Caiton, Richard & group	1964	GNP Crescendo 327
You Look So Good	Pharaohs, Richard Berry & the	1958, 1962	Flip 331/360
You Lost The Game Of Love	Cleftones	1990	CAR 121
You Love Me Only In Your Dreams	Dale, Bobby & group	1961	De Rose 8469
You Made A Boo Boo	Lovelarks, Steve Kass & the	1957	Class 10
You Made A Fool Of Me	Collegians, Jackie Roy & the	1953	Okeh 6970
You Made A Fool Of Me	Sensations	1963	Junior 988/Tollie 9009 (64)
You Made A Fool Out Of Me	Cruisers	1959	Coda 3005
You Made A Fool Out Of Me	Sensations	1963	Junior 1005

SONG	GROUP	YEAR	LABEL
You Made A Promise	Miller Sisters	1957	Acme 717
You Made Me A Prisoner Of Love	Five Stars, Gary Roberts & the	NA	Sterling 681
You Made Me Blue	Larados, Danny Zella & the	1957, 1959	Dial 100
You Made Me Cry	Arlington, Bruce & group	1964	King 5918
You Made Me Cry	Kings, Bobby Hall & the	1953	Jax 316
You Made Me Cry	Moonlighters, Billy & the	1978	Crystal Ball 101
You Made Me Cry	Platters	1955	Federal 12244
You Made Me Cry	Sonics (New York - Harvard)	1959	Harvard 801/Harvard 922 (59)/ Checker 922 (59)
You Made Me Darling	Dreamers (Blue Star)	1960	Blue Star 8001
You Made Me Love You	Flips, Mario & the	1961	Decca 31252
You Made Me Love You	Sensations	1957	Atco 6090
You Made Me Love You (Satisfied With My Love)	Sha-Weez	1953	Aladdin (unreleased)
You Make Me Feel Like A Penny Waitin' For Change	Jones Boys	1954	S&G 5007
You Make Me Feel So Good	Chips	1960	Satellite 105
You Make Me Feel So Good	Gentrys	1967	MGM 13690
You Make Me Happy	Dodgers	1955	Aladdin 3259
You Make Me Wanna Cry	Parliaments	1960	Flipp 100/101
You Make Me Want To Rock And Roll	Ebb Tides, Nino & the	1958	Recorte 405
You Make My Heart Sing	El Dorados	1970	Torrid 100
You May Not Be An Angel	Royal Lancers, Ronnie Premiere & the	1961	Sara 1020
You May Not Know	Hurricanes	1956	King 4947
You May Not Know	Nitecaps	1956	Groove 0158
You May Not Love Me	Blue Notes, Harold Melvin & the	1962	Landa 703
You May Say Yes	El Torros	1961	Duke 333
You, Me And The Sea	Flamingos	1960	End 1065
You Mean Everything To Me	Fleetwoods	1959	Dolton 5
You Mean Everything To Me	Four Buddies, Rudy Greene & the	1956	Club 51 103
You Mean Everything To Me	Gents, Larry & the	1965	Delaware 1711
You Mean Everything To Me	Spades	1957	Domino 200/100/Liberty 55118 (58)
You Mean So Much To Me	Clark, Doreeta & Madison Brothers	19??	
You Mean So Much To Me	Elites	1960	Hi-Lite 106
You Met A Fool	Four Jacks	1952	Federal 12075
You Might As Well Tell The Truth	Marcels	NA	Colpix (unreleased)
You Mostest Girl	Trammell, Bobby Lee & group	1958	Radio 102/Fabor 127 (64)
You Move Me	Hubcaps, Holt Davey & the	1958	United Artists 110X
You Move Me, Babe	DiMucci, Dion (with the Wanderers)	1965	Columbia 43423
You Move Me Baby	Rivingtons	1964	Vee Jay 634/A.R.E. American 100 (64)
You Must Be An Angel	Five Satins	1960	Ember LP 401
You Must Be An Angel	Gainors	1958	Red Top 110/Cameo 156 (59)
You Must Be Blind	Revelaires	1965	Decca 31830
You Must Be True	El Venos	1957	Vik 0305
You Must Believe	Persuasions	1973	Reprise 0977
You Must Come In	Hi-Lighters	1958	Hanover 4506
You Must Know	Knickerbockers	1953	It's A Natural 3000
You Must Know I Love You	Falcons (Detroit)	1960	Flick 008
You Must Pay	Team Mates	1966	ABC 10760
You Must Try	Guides	1959	Guyden 2023 (second pressing, first is by the Swallows)
You Must Try	Slades	1959	Domino 1000
You Must Try	Swallows (California)	1959	Guyden 2023 (first pressing, second is by the Guides)
You Name It	Furness Brothers	1960	Future 1002
You Name It	Patios, Billy & the	1961	Lite 9002
You Name It	Tidal Waves	NA	Strafford 6503
You Need A Love	Players	1963	Tarx 1007
You Need Love	Counts, Danny & the	NA	Coronado 136
You Need Love	Johnson, Ernie & group	1961	Asnes 104
You Need To Fall In Love	Ray, Little Jimmy & group	1959	Galliant 1001
You Never Cared	Monterays (Planet)	1957	Planet 57
You Never Cared For Me	Orioles, Sonny Til & the	1952	Jubilee 5076

SONG	GROUP	YEAR	LABEL
You Never Had It So Good	Checkers	1954	King 4673
You Never Had It So Good	Four-Evers	1966	Red Bird 10-078
You Never Heard A Word I Said	Rockets, Herb Kenny & the	1952	MGM 11332
You Never Knew	Four Kings	1954	Jax 323
You Never Knew	Kings (Baltimore)	1954	Harlem 2322
You Never Loved Me	Endings	1974	Barrier 101
You Never Loved Me	Monotones	1957	Mascot 124/Argo 5290 (58)
You Never Loved Me (acappella)	Islanders	1975	Relic LP 105
You Never Realized	Impollos, Johnny Inman & the	1958	Aladdin 3426
You Never Shoulda Gone Away	Cinderellas	1959	Decca 30925
You Only Came Back To Hurt Me	Glory Tones	1957	Epic 9243
You Or Me Has Got To Go	Hearts (Bronx, N.Y.)	1956	J&S 425/426
You Ought To Be Ashamed	Dudes	1961	Keith 6501
You Ought To Be Ashamed	Squires (California)	1956	Vita 117
You Ought To Belong To Me	Sweet Tymes	1967	Epic 10227
You Painted Pictures	Spaniels	1955	Vee Jay 154 (first pressing)
You Picked Me	Soldier Boys	1962	Scepter 1230
You Played Me A Fool	Storytellers (with Timmy Lymon)	1959	Stack 500
You Played The Game	Hornets	1981	P-Vine Special LP 9036
You Played The Part	Spiders	NA	Imperial (unreleased)
You Pretty Fool	Webs	1966	MGM 13602
You Promise	Candies, Ace Kennedy & the	1960	XYZ 609
You Promised Me Great Things	Jive Five	NA	United Artists 50107
You Promised Me Love	Channels, Earl Lewis & the	1990	Classic Artists 124
You Put A Spell On Me	Volumes	NA	Chex
You Put One Over On Me	Starlites, Jackie & the	1957	Fire & Fury 1000
You Ran Away From My Heart	Clicks	1963	Rush 2004
You Ran Away With My Heart	Five Crowns	1954	Rainbow 281
You Ran Away With My Heart	Majors (Brooklyn)	1951	Derby 779
You Runaround	Rome, Billy & group	1961	Sultan 5501
You Said	Raiders	1958	Mercury 71395
You Said Goodbye	Reflections	1981	Adam &.Eve 1
You Said Goodbye	Teddy Bears	1959	Imperial 5581
You Said That You Loved Me	Montereys (Major)	1959	Major 1009
You Said You Loved Me	Channels, Earl Lewis & the	1971 (1956)	Channel 1000
You Said You Loved Me	Orchids	1955	Parrot 819
You Said You're Leaving Me	Mixers	1958	Bold 101
You Say	Carallons, Lonnie & the	1960	Mohawk 112
You Say	Douglas, Ronnie & group	1961	Everest 19413
You Say	R-Dells	1960	Dade 1806
You Say You Beat Me To The Punch	Offbeats, Jimmy Dee & the	1963	Cutie 1400
You Say You Love Me	Dell Vikings	1957, 1973	Fee Bee 218/Dot 15636/ Bim Bam Boom 113
You Say You Love Me	Hearts (Bronx, N.Y.)	1957	J&S 1660
You Send Me	Belvin, Jesse & group	1957	Modern 1025
You Send Me	Gunter, Cornel (with the Ermines)	1957	Dot 15654
You Send Me	Sunglows, Sunny & the	1964	Tear Drop 3040
You Send Me (acappella)	Five Delights	1960	A Cappella - Best of the Bronx (98)
You Shake Me Up	Frontiers	1962	King 5609
You Shocked Me	Topsy, Tiny (with the Five Chances)	1958	Federal 12315
You Short Changed Me	Diamonds	1961	Mercury 71782
You Should Be Glad	Customs, Dave &	1965	Dac 501
You Should Care For Me	Flairs	1953	Flair 1019
You Should Have Loved Her More	Nighthawks, B. Guitar & the	1958	Decca 30634
You Should Have Told Me	Angels (New Jersey)	1962	Caprice 118
You Should Have Told Me	Imperials (Detroit)	1952	Savoy 1104/Buzzy 1 (62)
You Should Have Told Me	New Yorkers	1964	Tac-Ful 101
You Should Have Told Me	Royal Knights	NA	Radio City 1001
You Should Have Told Me	Three Chuckles	1955	X 0134
You Shouldn't	Satellites, Sonny King & the	1955	Nocturne 1003/1004
You Shouldn't Have Said That	Flips	1956	Chess (unreleased)
You Shouldn't Oughta Don It	Night Owls	1957	NRC 015
You Should've Been There	Fleetwoods	1963	Dolton 74
You Show Me The Way	Czars Of Rhythm	1965	De-Voice 2501
You Speak Of Love	Swinging Hearts	1964	Magic Touch 2001

SONG	GROUP	YEAR	LABEL
You Started It	Snowmen	1964	Herald 597 (second pressing, first is by the Concords)
You Started It	Stagehands	1964	T.A. 101
You Still Got Time	Jets (Arrow)	1963	Arrow 100
You Stole My Heart	C & C Boys	1962	Duke 358
You Stole My Heart	Four Sounds	1957	Celeste 3013
You Stole My Heart Away	Everglades, Jerry Hayward & the	1962	Symbol 916
You Sure Look Good To Me	Robins	1949	Score 4010
You Sweet Girl	Four Fellows (Brooklyn - Glory)	1956	Glory 248
You Sweet Little Thing	Five Stars (Detroit)	1957	Kernel 319574/Dot 15579 (57)
You Talk Too Much	All Nighters	1964	GMA 1
You Talk Too Much	Boys Next Door	1956	Vik 0207
You Talk Too Much	Laddins	1974	Relic LP 5018
You Tease Me	Knight, Bob	1961	Taurus 100
You Tell Me	Stylers	1957	Golden Crest 1181/1182
You Think You're Smart	Bluenotes, James Easterling & the	NA	Reno 133
You Thrill Me So	Caverliers Quartet	1954	Atlas 1031
You Tickle Me, Baby	Royal Jokers	1955, 1963	Atco 6052/Fortune 560
You Told Another Lie	Shields	1961	Continental 4072
You Told Another Lie	Youngsters, Little Pete & the	1962, 1963	Lesley 1925
You Told Everyone But Me	Four Duchesses	1957	Chief 7019
You Told Me	Tiaras	1963	Valiant 6027
You Told Me So	Starlites, Eddie & the	1973	Vintage 1004
You Took Advantage Of A Good Thing	Emblems, Patty & the	1964	Herald 593
You Took Advantage Of Love	Five Arcades, S. J. & the	1985	Antrell 103
You Took Advantage Of Me	Blackwells	1961	Jamie 1199
You Took My Heart	Counts, Tommy Burk & the	1964	Rich Rose 1003
You Took My Heart By Surprise	Four Guys	1959	Kent 311
You Took My Love	Cellos	1957	Apollo 510
You Took My Love	Jive Bombers	1957	Savoy 1515
You Took My Love Too Fast	Nunn, Bobby (with the Robins & Little Esther)	1953	Federal 12122
You Took My Loving	Griffin, Jimmy & female group	1954	Dot 15223
You Took The Joy Out Of Spring	Crests	1960	Coed (unreleased)
You Took Your Love From Me	Dee Jays	1962	Sonata 1100
You Touch Me	Lullabyes	1964	Dimension 1039
You Trimmed My Christmas Tree	Blenders, Baby Jane & the	1963	Witch 112
You Turn Me On Boy	Honey Bees	1965	Fontana 1505
You Upset Me Baby	Arabians	1964	Le Mans 001
You Used To Be	Luvs	1963	Stallion 1002
You Walked Away	Chesterfields	1962	Onyx 40083
You Walked Away With My Heart	York, Patti (with the Sentimentals)	1958	Mint 806
You Walked In	Swallows (Maryland)	1952	King 4533
You Want Too Much Too Soon	Impalas (Brooklyn)	19??	Unreleased
You Wanted Fun	Robins	1958	Whippet 212
You Went Away	Four Kings, Sue Tornay & the	1961	Dore 594
You Went Back On Your Word	McPhatter, Clyde (with the Cookies & the Cues)	1959	Atlantic 2038
You Were Always On My Mind	Reunion	1990	Clifton 91
You Were An Angel To Me	Spydels, John Dow & the	1962	Assault 1866
You Were Made To Love	Four Of A Kind	1958	Cameo 154
You Were Meant For Me	El Tones, Jo Ann Boswell & the	1955	Chief 800
You Were Meant To Be	Belvin, Andy & group	NA	Cal State 3200
You Were Mine	Fireflies	1959	Ribbon 6901
You Were Mine	Five Keys	1959	King 5276
You Were Mine	Russell, Bobby & group	1965	Monument 899
You Were Mine	West Rudy & female group	1959	King 5276
You Were Mine (For Awhile)	Fireflies	1962	Taurus 355
You Were My Baby	Quarter Tones, Chip & the	1964	Carlton 604
You Were My First Affair	Original Four Aces	1954	Big Town 112/Big Town 118 (55)
You Were My Love	Emeralds, Luther Bond & the	1954	Savoy 1131
You Were Sent Down From Heaven	Lamplighters	1956	Federal 12255
You Were There	Emotions	1990	Crystal Ball 155
You Were Untrue	Flairs	1954	Flair 1041
You Were Waiting For Me	King Toppers	1956, 1957	Josie 811

SONG	GROUP	YEAR	LABEL
You Weren't Home	Hearts	1956	J&S 1180/1181
You Weren't There	Rose, Andy (with the Thorns)	1961	Coral 62284
You Will Always Find Me True	Dawn Quartet	1974	Firefly 330
You Will Fill My Eyes No More	Blue Belles, Patti LaBelle & the	1964	Parkway 913
You Win Again	Five Crowns	1952	Rainbow (unreleased)/ Dynamic Group Sounds CD (99)
You Win Again	Romancers	1973	Vintage 1013
You Won My Heart	Greenwood, Paul (with the Four Bel-Aires)	19??	Arc
You Won't Be Satisfied	Deltairs	1958	Felsted 8525
You Won't Be Satisfied	Escorts (Essex)	1954	Essex 372
You Won't Be Satisfied	Vel-Aires, Donald Woods & the	NA	Flip
You Won't Be True	El Venos	1964	RCA 8303
You Won't Be True To Your Heart	Cardinals	1955	Atlantic (unreleased)
You Won't Even Know Her Name	Starlets	1965	Tower 115
You Won't Let Me Go	Four Dots (Washington, D.C.)	1951	Dot 1043
You Won't Let Me Go	Guytones	1957	DeLuxe 6144
You Won't Like It	Ideals	1958	Cool 108
You Won't Remember Me	Royal Dukes, Don Ellis & the	1959	Bee 1114
You Worry Me	Enchanters (Vargo)	1964	Vargo 10
You Wouldn't Tell	Hearts (Bronx, N.Y.)	1957	J&S 1657
You Yakity Yak Too Much	Flippers	1955	Flip 305
You You My Love	Jo-Vals	1964	Laurie 3229
You You You	Flamettes	1961	Laurie 3109
You You You	Hearts, Lee Andrews & the (as Lee Andrews)	1965	V.I.P. 1601
You'd Be Crying Too	Matadors	1963	Keith 6504
You'd Be Mine	Diamonds	1960	Mercury 71734
You'd Better Come Home	Five Fabulous Demons	1963	King 5761
You'd Better Run	Little Boys Blue, Bonnie & the	1960	Nikko 611
You'll Always Be Mine	Creations	1962	Patti-Jo 1703
You'll Always Be My Sweetheart	Cap-Tans	1950	DC 8054
You'll Always Have Someone	Embers, Billy Scandlin & the	1959	Viking 1002
You'll Always Remain	Universals (V-Tone)	1962	V-Tone 236
You'll Be Coming Home Soon	Beck, Carlton & group	1963	Troy 100
You'll Be Coming Home Soon	Shields	1960	Falcon 100/ Transcontinental 1013 (60)
You'll Be Mine	Thunderbirds, Rudy Grayzell & the	1959	Award 130
You'll Be Mine Someday	Tamblyn, Larry (with the Standells)	1964	Linda 112
You'll Be My Baby	Gates, David & group	1960	Mala 413
You'll Be Sorry	Flames, Farrell & the	1961	Fransil 14
You'll Be Sorry	Limelites, Shep & the	1961	Hull 742/Hull 1009
You'll Be Sorry Someday	Valadiers	1963	Gordy 7013
You'll Be The Last	Fi-Tones	1958	Angle Tone 525
You'll Be There	McPhatter, Clyde (with the Cookies & the Cues)	1957	Atlantic 1158
You'll Be There	Mistics	1964	Kirk 636
You'll Break Two Hearts	Elites	1963	ABC 10460
You'll Come Back	Douglas, Ronnie & group	1961	Everest 19425
You'll Feel It Too	Counts, Tommy Burk & the	1962	Nat 100
You'll Find Love	Davis, Hal Sonny & group	1960	MJC 104
You'll Go First	Stylettes	1965	Cameo 353
You'll Have Everything	Sugarmints	1957	Brunswick 55042
You'll Need Me Some Day	McHugh, Richie & group	1963	Raewood 587
You'll Never Be Mine Again	Belairs	1955	GG 521
You'll Never Be Mine Again	Blenders (New York)	1953	Jay-Dee 780
You'll Never Belong To Me	Dubs	1960	ABC 10100
You'll Never Cherish A Love So True (Til You Lose It)	Vells	1962	Mel-O-Dy 103
You'll Never Get Away	Holidays	1956	King 1520
You'll Never Get To Heaven	Angels (New Jersey)	1967	RCA 9246
You'll Never Know	Chantels	1962	Carlton LP 144
You'll Never Know	Classics (Brooklyn)	1965	Stork 2
You'll Never Know	Dee, Fern & group	1958	Ember 1035
You'll Never Know	Demensions	1963	Coral 62359
You'll Never Know	Gordon, Roscoe & group	1960	Duke 320
You'll Never Know	Mondellos	1984	Rhythm 118

SONG	GROUP	YEAR	LABEL
You'll Never Know	Platters	1962	Mercury 71904
You'll Never Know	Quentins	1960	Andie 5014
You'll Never Know	Romancers	1961	Celebrity 701/Beacon 701
You'll Never Never Know	Platters	1956	Mercury 70948
You'll Never See The Forest	Legends	1962	Jamie 1228
You'll Never Walk Alone	Blue Belles, Patti LaBelle & the	1963	Nicetown 5020/Parkway 896 (63)
You'll Never Walk Alone	Flamingos	1960	End LP 308
You'll Never Walk Alone	Imaginations	1991	Collectables CD 5726
You'll Never Walk Alone	Imperials (Detroit)	1953	Gem 212/Great Lakes 1212 (54)
You'll Never Walk Alone	Originals	1990	Starlight 72
You'll Pay	Harps, Little David (Baughan) & the	1955	Savoy 1178
You'll Reap What You Sow	Chateaus	1959	Warner Bros. 5071
You'll Remain Forever	Charms, Otis Williams & his	1958	DeLuxe 6174
You'll Wonder Where	Jumpin' Jaguars	1956	Decca 29973
Young And Beautiful	Christie, Charles (with the Crystals)	1966	HBR 473
Young And In Love	Crescendos (Nasco)	1958	Nasco 6021
Young And In Love	Shaw, Ricky & group	1962	President 822
Young And Innocent	Del Reys	1960	Columbia 41784
Young And Lively	Essex	1964	Roulette LP 24246
Young And Pretty Bride	Vann, Teddy & group	1960	Roulette 4300
Young At Heart	Demensions	1962	Coral 62323
Young At Heart	Essentials, Billy & the	1963	Mercury 72127
Young Blood	Coasters	1957	Atco 6087
Young Blood	Coasters Two Plus Two	1975	Chelan 2000
Young Blood	Fabulous Four	1964	Brass 316
Young Boy	Green, Barbara & group	1964	Vivid 105/Hamilton 50027
Young Boy	Softones	1957	Cee Bee 1062
Young Boy's Love	Martin, Jerry & group	1962	R 507
Young, Broke And In Love	Mason, Little Billy (with the Rhythm Jesters)	1957	Gee 1042
Young Dove's Calling	Couplings	1958	Josie 831
Young Dreamer	Guytones	1958	DeLuxe 6163
Young Dreams	Galens	1966	Challenge 59402
Young Generation	Sandpipers	1966	Kismet 394
Young Girl	Flames	1950	Selective 113
Young Girl	Hollywood Four Flames	1952	Recorded In Hollywood 165 (first pressing)
Young Girl	Jokers, Ty Stewart & the	1961	Amy 828
Young Girl	Peacocks, Johnny Otis & the	1955	Peacock 1625
Young Girl To Calypso	Gypsies	1957	Atlas 1073/Angletone 1073 (57)
Young Girls	Topps	NA	Red Robin (unreleased)
Young Girls, Young Girls	Encores	1953	Checker 760
Young Heartaches	Zeppa, Ben (with the Four Jacks)	1958	Hush 1000
Young Hearts	Four Counts	1958	Dart 1014
Young Hearts	Velvet, Jimmy & group	1965	Velvet Tone 102
Young In Years	Diamonds	1959	Mercury 10017/Mercury 71505 (59)
Young Lady	Midnighters	1960	King LP 700
Young Lady	Rock-A-Tones	NA	Judytone 369
Young Love	Crests	1959	Coed (unreleased)
Young Love Is An Old Story	Metros, Eddie Joy & the	1959	Dart 1008
Young Love Swings The World	Playgirls	1959	RCA 7546
Young Lover	Impressions, Jerry Butler & the	1976	Vee Jay LP 1075
Young Man's Fancy	Charlie & Don & group	1962	Duel 513
Young Queen Chunka Bo Bo	Del-Mingos	1963	Lomar 702
Young Wings Can Fly	Windsong	NA	
Young Years, The	Elegants	1963	Limelight 3013
Younger Than You	Premiers (Nu-Phi)	1959	Nu-Phi 429/Nu-Phi 701
Your Baby's Back	Downbeats	1962	Tamla 54056
Your Best Friend	Drifters (1959-forward)	1969	Atlantic 2624
Your Big Brown Eyes	Counts, Bobby Comstock & the	1963	Jubilee 5396
Your Big Mistake	Delrons, Reperata & the	1964	Laurie 3252
Your Book Of Love	Dell Vikings	1957	Mercury 71241
Your Boyfriend's Back	Counts, Bobby Comstock & the	1963	Lawn 219
Your Candy Kisses	Sweet Teens, Faith Taylor & the	1959	Federal 12334
Your Cash Ain't Nothin' But Trash	Buzzards, Big John & the	1954	Okeh 7045

SONG	GROUP	YEAR	LABEL
Your Cash Ain't Nothin' But Trash	Clovers	1954	Atlantic 1035
Your Change Of Heart	Fabulous Splendors	1960	O-Gee 105
Your Cheatin' Heart	Demensions	1962	Coral 62323
Your Cheatin' Heart	Orbits, Bobby & the	1962	Gone 5126
Your Cheatin' Heart	Pearls	1957	Onyx 510/Relic 520 (64)
Your Cotton Pickin' Heart	Bobolinks	1958	Key 573
Your Cute Little Ways	Jay Birds, Vinnie Monte & the	1956	Josie 793
Your Decision	Four Jokers	1959	Crystalette 730
Your Dog Hates Me	Five Splendors	1960	Stroll 106
Your Drivers License, Please	Pleasers, Bobbie Please & the	1961	Era 3044
Your Face	Honeycones	1959	Ember 1049
Your Face	Sabres	1958	Liberty 55128
Your First Love	Five Letters	1958	Ivy 102
Your Foolish Ways	Runaways	NA	Alamo 105
Your Golden Teardrops	Fabulous Valients	1962	Holiday 61005
Your Gonna Miss Me	Kings, Albert Washington & the	1964	Vim 10990
Your Good Lovin'	Pentagons	1986	True Gems LP
Your Graduation Means Goodbye	Cardigans	1958	Mercury 71251
Your Guardian Angel	Como, Nicky (with the Del Satins)	NA	Tang 1231
Your Hair's Too Long	Juniors, Danny & the	1961	Swan 4084
Your Happiest Years	Delicates	1960	United Artists 210
Your Happiness In Mine	Boyfriends, Wini Brown & the	1952	Mercury 5870
Your Heart Is So Blind	Cadillacs	1959	Unreleased
Your Heart's Bigger Than Mine	Guytones	1958	DeLuxe 6169
Your Initials	Four Graduates	1978	Crystal Ball 119
Your Kind Of Love	Reflections	1965	Golden World 29
Your Kind Of Love	Romaines	1954	Groove 0035
Your Kinda Love	Thrillettes, Bette Renne & the	1964	Lawn 246
Your Kiss	Premiers (Los Angeles)	1957	Dig 141 (unreleased)/ Relic LP 5052 (85)
Your Last Chance	Dovells	1962	Parkway 845
Your Last Chance	Teenchords, Lewis Lymon & the	1957	End 1003
Your Last Goodbye	Fresandos	1958	Star-X 501
Your Letter	Wright, Willie (with the Sparklers)	1960	Federal 12372
Your Life Begins (At Sweet Sixteen)	Majors (Philadelphia)	1963	Imperial 5991
Your Life Is Gone	Delrons, Reperata & the	1971	Laurie 3589
Your Line Is Busy	Thunderbirds, Ron Holden & the	1960	Donna 1331
Your Little Guy	Flamingos	1964	Checker 1084
Your Love	Arribins, Duke Savage & the	1959	Argo 5346
Your Love	Co-Ops	1959	Versailles 100
Your Love	Crickets, Dean Barlow & the	1954	Jay-Dee 785
Your Love	Danleers	1959	Mercury 71441
Your Love	Hollywood Flames	1957	Unreleased
Your Love	Jogettes	1962	Mar 102
Your Love	Kappas	1959	Wonder 112
Your Love	Mighty Jupiters	1958	Warner 1020
Your Love	Olympics	1959	Demon 1514
Your Love	Persians	1955	Capitol 3230
Your Love	Silhouettes	1962	Junior 993
Your Love	Superiors, Tony LaMar & the	1965	Go Go 1000
Your Love	Tramps	1959	Arvee 570
Your Love	Tycoon	1986	Starlight 33
Your Love (acappella)	Dovers	1988	Relic LP 5075
Your Love (acappella)	Velvet Angels	1972	Relic LP 5004
Your Love Captured Me	Regents	1961	Gee LP 706
Your Love Comes Shinin' Through	Triangle	1970	Paramount 0055
Your Love For Me	Domino, Bobby & group	1961	Donna 1339
Your Love Has Gone Away	Drapers	1962	Gee 1081
Your Love (Has Got A Hole In It)	Sheppards (Chicago - Bunky)	1969	Bunky 7766
Your Love Has Got Me Down	Blenders (Chicago)	1966	Mar-V-Lous 6010
Your Love Is A Good Love	Harptones	1961	Cub 9097
Your Love (Is All I Need)	Miracles, Carl Hogan & the	1957	Fury 1001
Your Love Is Just Plain	Incas	1976	Monogram 125
Your Love Is My Love	Ambrose, Kenny & group	1959	Willett 109
Your Love Is Wonderful	Fayettes, Hattie Littles & the	1962	Gordy 7007

SONG	GROUP	YEAR	LABEL
Your Love Reminds Me	Gunter, Gloria & group	1959	Arch 1610
Your Lovely Ways	Elgins (California)	1964	Lummtone 113
Your Lover Man	Fleetones	1961	Bandera 2511
Your Lover Man	Jewels (Los Angeles)	1962	Imperial 5897
Your Lovey Dovey Ways	Dream Girls, Bobbie Smith & the	1962	Big Top 3129
Your Lovin' Kisses	Vowels	NA	Lebam 157
Your Lovin' Moves Me	Clips	1954	Republic 7102
Your Magic Touch	Naturals, Jack Bailey & the	1959	Ford 113
Your Mama Said No	Diaz, Vickie & group	1960	Del-Fi 4149
Your Memory	Five Satins	1960	Cub 9071
Your Mommy Lied To Your Daddy	Del-Cords	1960	Impala 215/Genius 401 (63)
Your Name And Mine	Acorns	1959	Unart 2015
Your Name Shall Be Remembered	Laurels, John Gaudet & the	1961	Mary Glen 1001
Your Only Boy	Hamilton, Judd & group	1963	Dolton 80
Your Only Love	Five Royales	1959	King 5162
Your Other Love	Flamingos	1960	End 1081
Your Picture	King, Buzzy & group	1959	Top Rank 2027
Your Picture On The Wall	Barnes, Othea & group	1963	ABC 10434
Your Precious Love	Halos	1962	Warwick LP 2046
Your Precious Love	Taylor, Sammy & group	1964	Enjoy 2028
Your Promise To Be Mine	Drifters (Pre-1959)	1956	Atlantic 1089
Your Promise To Me	Hurricanes	1956	King 4926
Your Promise To Me Mine	Tycoon	1985	Starlight 31
Your Reason	Tads	1956	Liberty Bell 9010/Dot 15518 (56)
Your Red Wagon (You Can Push It Or Pull It)	Marcels	1964	Kyra
Your Skies Of Blue	Tune Weavers	1962	Checker 1007
Your Souvenirs	Embers, Willis Sanders & the	1957	Juno 213/Jvpiter 213 (57)
Your Star	El Capris	1957	Fee Bee 216
Your Sweet Love	Charms, Otis Williams & the	1966	Okeh 7261
Your Sweet Love	Kings (Baltimore)	1959	RCA 7544
Your Teardrops	Five Keys	1951	Aladdin (unreleased)
Your Teeth And Tongue Will Get You Hung	Five Keys	1973	Owl 321
Your Teeth And Your Tongue	Five Keys	1960	King LP 688
Your Tender Lips	Blue Notes	1961	Accent 1069
Your Tender Lips	Catalinas	1964	Original Sound 48
Your Tender Lips	Clovers	1956	Atlantic 1094
Your Tender Lips	Syncapates	1963	Times Square 7
Your Tender Touch	Raytones, Rudy Ray Moore & the	1958	Ball 0504
Your Time Is Gonna Come	Highlighters, Walter Webb & the	1970	Chess 2091
Your Time's Up	Hawketts	1955	Chess 1591
Your Troubles Will Be My Troubles	Metro-Liners	1976	Catamount 132
Your True Love	Romans, Caesar & the	NA	Hi-Note 602
Your True Love Is Standing Here	Burt, Wanda (with the Crescendos)	1961	Music City 840
Your Turn To Cry	Keens, Rick & the	1962	Le Cam 958/Jamie 1219 (62)
Your Very First Love	Allures	1987	Starlight 50
Your Very First Love	Dubs	1963, 1964	Wilshire 201/Lana 116
Your Voice	Tune Drops, Malcolm Dodds & the	1958	Decca 30653
Your Way	Blue Stars	1977	Arcade 103
Your Way	Camelots	1963, 1973	AAnko 1001/Dream 1001
Your Way	Five Discs	1991	0-0-1
Your Way	Heartbeats	1956	Hull 716/Gee 1061 (61)
Your Way	Newports	1979	Crystal Ball 134
Your Way	Pixies 3	1964	Mercury 72357
Your Way	Salutations, Vito & the	1962	Kram 1202/Kram 5002
Your Way	Zip Codes	1988	Clifton 83
Your Way (acappella)	Delstars	1975	Relic LP 102
Your Way (acappella)	Rob-Roys, Norman Fox & the	19??	
Your Way (acappella)	Zircons	1963	Mellomood 1000/Relic 1008 (65)
Your Wedding Day	Pentagons	1986	True Gems LP
Your Wild Heart	Poni-Tails	1957	Point 8
Your Yah Yah Is Gone	Tren-Teens	1964	Carnival 501
You're A Better Man Than I	Emotions	NA	Johnson 746/South Park 1000
You're A Big Girl Now	Bell Notes	1959	Time 1015

SONG	GROUP	YEAR	LABEL
You're a Drag	Runarounds	1966	Capitol 5644
You're A Fallen Angel	Emeralds (Pel)	1962	Pel 3836
You're A Gas	Four Pennies (male)	1964	Brunswick 55304
You're A Habit	Uptowners	1964	Le Cam 126
You're A Square	Three Friends	1961	Imperial 5773
You're a Square	Tramps	1959	Arvee 548
You're A Star	Jeanettes, Gene & the	1963	Fortune 565
You're À Stranger	Virgos	1965	Pioneer 6621
You're A Sweetheart	Crescents	1985	Relic LP 5053
You're All I Live For	Four Vibes	1962	Swa-Ray 1001
You're All I Need To Get By	Angels (New Jersey)	1974	Polydor 14222
You're All I See	Playboys	1959	ABC 10070
You're All I Want For Christmas	Keystoners	1991	Starbound 514
You're All right Baby	Williams, Mel (with the Montclairs)	1955	Decca EP 2400
You're Always In My Dreams	Ravens	1951	Columbia 39194
You're An Angel	Continentals (New York - Rama)	1956	Rama 190
You're An Angel	Kit Kats	1965	Lawn 249
You're An Angel	Miracles (Cash)	1955	Cash 1008
You're An Angel	Penguins	1960	Dooto EP 456
You're An Angel (With The Devil In Your Eyes)	Youngsters	1956	Empire 107
You're Back With Me	Solitaires	1956	Old Town 1026 (first pressing)
You're Blue	Corvets, Arthur & the	1959	Moon 100
You're Breaking My Heart	Daylighters	1959	Bea & Baby 103
You're Cheating On Me	Destinaires	1965	Old Timer 614
You're Closer To My Heart Than My Shadow	Blue Dots	1958	NRC 504
You're Closer To My Heart Than My Shadow	Blue Dots, Eward Harris & the	NA	NRC 504
You're Crying	Nutmegs	1964	Times Square 103
You're Crying (acappella)	Rajahs	1973	Klik 1019
You're Cute	Parliaments	1963	Symbol 917
You're Daddy's Little Girl	Travelers, Roger & the	1961	Ember 1079
You're Driving Me Crazy	Emeralds (Venus)	1959	Venus 1003
You're Driving Me Crazy	Gentlemen	1955	Apollo
You're Driving Me Crazy	Johnson, Budd (Voices Five)	1959	
You're Driving Me Crazy	Panics	1959	ABC 10072
You're Driving Me Crazy	Voices Five, Budd Johnson & the	1959	Stereo Craft 111A
You're Driving Me Mad	Cleftones	1956	Gee 1011
You're Everthin'	Valentines	1963	Lee 5465
You're Every Beat Of My Heart	Diablos, Nolan Strong & the	1963	Fortune 556
You're Everything	Classics (Brooklyn)	1960	Top Rank 2061
You're Everything	Hi Timers	1959	Sonic 1502
You're Everything To Me	Classics Four, Bob Gerardi & the	1960	Recorte 441
You're Everything To Me	Orchids	1955	Parrot 815
You're Everything To Me	Rogers, Pauline & group	1955	Atco 6050
You're Far From Home	Belgianetts	1963	USA 731
You're Fine But Not My Kind	Robins	1950	Savoy 762
You're For Me	Five Keys	1958	Capitol 3948
You're For Me	McPhatter, Clyde & group	1960	Mercury 71692
You're For Me (And I'm For You)	Escorts, Del & the	1961	Taurus 350
You're Free To Go	Dubs	1962	Gone 5138
You're Going To Miss Me (When I'm Gone)	Bradford, Chuck & group	1961	Fire 505
You're Gone	Incas	1977	Monogram 127
You're Gone	Mellows, Lillian Leach & the	1974	Celeste 3008
You're Gone	Orioles, Sonny Til & the	1950	Jubilee 5028
You're Gone	Perkins, Roy & group	1955	Meladee 112
You're Gone	Shanteers	1962	Rori 708
You're Gone	Star Steppers	1960	Amy 801
You're Gonna Be My Girl	El Venos	1990	Park Ave. 1
You're Gonna Be Sorry	Angelenos, Camille Brown & the	1961	Peepers 2825
You're Gonna Be Sorry	Fascinations	1963	ABC 10443
You're Gonna Be Sorry	Nitecaps	NA	Detour LP 33-010
You're Gonna Cry	Blue Jays (Venice, Calif.)	1961	Milestone 2008

SONG	GROUP	YEAR	LABEL
You're Gonna Cry	Spaniels	1957	Vee Jay 257
You're Gonna Find Out	Reflections	1966	ABC 10822
You're Gonna Grieve When I Leave	Jayes	1958	Arc 4443
You're Gonna Lose Her	Prominents	1965	Lummtone 116
You're Gonna Lose Your Gal	Larks (North Carolina)	1954	Lloyds 115
You're Gonna Lose Your Gal	Ravens	1950	
You're Gonna Miss Me	Del Mates, John Steele & the	1965	Wand 194
You're Gonna Need Me	Harris, Thurston (with the Sharps)	1958	Aladdin 3430
You're Gonna Need My Help Someday	Harptones	1985	Murray Hill LP 000083
You're Gonna Pay	Neevets	1964	Reon 1303
You're Gonna Pay	Rivingtons	1967	Quan 1379
You're Good For Me	Idols	1958	Redd-E 1017
You're Heavenly	Saigons	1955	Dootone 375
You're In Love	Five Vets	1956	Allstar 713/Bruce
You're In Love	Royal-Aires	1957	Gallo 110
You're In Love	Sunny Lads	1959	Jax 103
You're In Love With Someone Else	Four Jacks	1952	MGM 11179-A
You're In Real Good Hands	Midnighters, Hank Ballard & the	1967	King 6119
You're Invited To A Party	Victorians	1963	Liberty 55656
You're Jealous	Jokers, Jivin' Gene & the	1960	Mercury 71561
You're Just A Little Too Young	Four Gents	1961	Nite Owl 50
You're Just An Angel	Five Pastels	1962	Dome 249
You're Just Fooling Yourself	Blue Belles, Patti LaBelle & the	1964	Rainbow 1900
You're Just Fooling Yourself	Bracelets	1964	20th Century Fox 539
You're Just Too Pretty For Me	Curtis, Eddie Tex & group	1956	Dot 15505
You're Late Miss Kate	Offbeats, Jimmy Dee & the	1958	Dot 15721
You're Laughing At Me	Exploits, Bobby Maxwell & the	1959	Fargo 1009
You're Laughing At Me	Val-Chords	1957	Gametime 104
You're Laughing Cause I'm Crying	Reed, Ursula (with the Solitaires)	1954	Old Town 1001
You're Laughing 'Cause I'm Crying	Toppers (Brooklyn)	1954	Jubilee 5136
You're Like a Mystery	Belmonts	1966	United Artists 5007
You're Lonesome Now	Fairlanes, Charles Perrywell & the	1962	Tic Toc 104
You're Lookin' At My Guy	West Winds	1964	Kapp 588
You're Lookin' Good	Clark, Dee (with the Kool Gents)	1957	Falcon 1002/Vee Jay 355 (60)
You're Making A Mistake	Platters	1958	Mercury 71320
You're Mine	Aristocats, Bobby Blue & the	1958	N/A
You're Mine	Cheaters	1964	Raynard 1056
You're Mine	Crickets, Dean Barlow & the	1953	MGM 11428
You're Mine	DiMucci, Dion (with the Del Satins)	1963	Columbia 42852
You're Mine	Dominoes	1960	ABC 10128
You're Mine	Falcons (Detroit)	1959	Unart 2022
You're Mine	Flamingo, Johnny & group	1962	
You're Mine	Flamingos	1962	End LP 316
You're Mine	Four Sevilles	1980	Starlight 6
You're Mine	Love Notes (Family Library of Music)	1953	Family Library Of Music EP 1040
You're Mine	Quails	1963	American 1024
You're Mine	Queens, Shirley Gunter & the	1955	Flair 1060
You're Mine	Rinky-Dinks (with Bobby Darin)	1958	Atco 6128
You're Mine	Sentimentals	1958	Mint 805
You're Mine Again	Capris (Philadelphia)	NA	Collectables LP 5000
You're Mine Already	Du Droppers	1955	Groove 0120
You're Mine Forever	Excels	1957	Central 2601
You're Mine Tonight	Blends, Glenn Wells & the	1960	Jin 133/United Artists 244 (60)
You're More Than A Number In My Little Red Book	Drifters (1959-forward)	1976	Arista (UK) 78
You're My Baby	Allison, Gene & group	1956	Calvert 106/Decca 30185 (56)
You're My Baby	Reflections	1965	Golden World 19
You're My Baby	Vacels	1965	Kama Sutra 200
You're My Boyfriend	Six Teens	19??	
You're My Christmas Present	Skyliners, Jimmy Beaumont & the	1989	Classic Artists 123
You're My Desire	Ecuadors	1961	Miracle 7
You're My Dream	Castaleers	1959	Felsted 8585
You're My Dream Girl	Oberle, Scott & group	1964	Lawn 216
You're My First Love	Coeds (with the Tokens)	1964	Swing 101

SONG	GROUP	YEAR	LABEL
You're My Girl	Castro, Vince (with the Tonettes)	1958, 1960	Doe 102/Apt 25007/2507
You're My Girl	Hot Rods, Doug Connell & the	1959	Alton 600
You're My Girl	Spartans, Jimmy & the	1960	Satellite 106
You're My Girl	Tokens (Brooklyn)	1964	B.T. Puppy 504
You're My Hollywood Star	Teardrops	1959	Josie 862
You're My Ideal	Terrytones, Claire Charles & the	1961	Wye 1002
You're My Inspiration	Five Crowns	1952	Rainbow 179
You're My Love	Diablos, Nolan Strong & the	1963	Fortune 553
You're My Love	Jumpin' Tones	NA	Unreleased
You're My Lover	Sharmeers	1958, 1974	Red Top 109
You're My Lovin' Baby	Raye, Cal & group	1966	Super 101
You're My Teenage Baby	Berry Kids	1957	MGM 12496
You're Never Gonna Find	Halos	1965	Congress 249
You're Never Satisfied	Innocents, Kathy Young & the	1963	Reprise 20125
You're Never Too Young	Delongs	NA	Art Flow 3906
You're No Barking Dog	Nutones	1955	Hollywood Star 798
You're No Good	Down Beats	1965	Down Beat 1030
You're No Good	Dragonaires, Byron Lee & the	NA	Bra 503
You're No Good	Monorays	1965	20th Fox 594
You're Nobody Till Somebody Loves You	Ebonaires (with the Maxwell Davis Orch.)	1953	Aladdin 3212
(You're Not Good Looking- But) You're Presentable	Diablos, Nolan Strong & the	1963	Fortune 569
You're Not in Love With Me	Cadillacs	1959	Unreleased
You're Not In Love With Me	Pearls	19??	
You're Not Too Young	Silks, Charles McCullough & the	1962	Dooto 465
You're Not Welcome	Hollywood Producers	1966	Parkway 993
You're Not Welcome (Anymore)	Davis, Jan & group	1963	Rendezvous 214
You're Nothing But A Girl	Tokens (Brooklyn)	NA	RCA LP 3685
You're On My Mind	Chips	1961	Venice 101/Strand 25027 (61)
You're On My Mind	Cues	1956	Capitol 3310
You're On My Mind	Falcons (Detroit)	1965	Lu Pine 003
You're On Top	Untouchables	1961	Liberty 55335
You're On Top, Girl	Empires	1963	Candi 1033
You're Only Seventeen	Cleeshays, Danny Tyrell & the	1958	Eastman 784
You're Only Young Once	Fabulous Four (with Fabian)	1961	Chancellor 1079
You're Part Of Me	Four Buddies	1952	Savoy 845
You're Playing With Me	Davis, Hal Sonny & group	1960	Del-Fi 4146
You're Ruinin' My Gladness	Royaltones, El Pauling & the	1960	Lute 5801
You're Running Out Of Kisses	Foote, Chuck & group	1961	Soncraft 401
You're Saying Goodnight	Juliana & group	1961	RCA 7906
You're Seventeen	Paramounts	1961	Dot 16201
You're So Close	Etiquettes, Little Nat & the	1961	Clock 2001
You're So Fine	Downbeats	1959	Peacock 1689
You're So Fine	Essentials, Billy & the	1981	Crystal Ball 145
You're So Fine	Falcons (Detroit)	1959	Flick 001/Unart 2013 (59)/ United Artists 2013X (59)/ United Artists 420 (62)
You're So Fine	Four-Evers	NA	Magic Carpet LP 1004
You're So Good To Me	Swisher, Debra & group	1966	Boom 60001
You're So Hard To Say Goodnight To	Hideaways	1963	Duel 521
You're So Necessary To Me	Heartbreakers (Washington, D.C.)	1951	RCA 4508
You're So Nice To Be Near	Loreleis	1955	Spotlight 390
You're So Popular	Empires	1961	Lake 711
You're So Unfaithful	Five Daps	1958	Brax 207/208
You're Still In My Heart	Dells	1984	Solid Smoke LP 8029/ Charly LP 1055 (85)
You're Still In My Heart	Four Fellows, Miss Toni Banks & the	1957	Glory 263
You're Still My Baby	Angels (with Sonny Gordon)	1955	Grand 121
You're Still My Baby	Wade, Earl & group	1961	Seville 111
You're Sweeter Than Wine	Wigs	1964	Golden Crest 592
You're Taking A Long Time Coming Back	Hearts, Lee Andrews & the	1966	RCA 8929
You're The Answer To My Prayer	Roamers, Varetta Dillard & the	1955	Savoy 1160
You're The Apple Of My Eye	Four Lovers	1956	RCA 6518

SONG	GROUP	YEAR	LABEL
You're The Beating Of My Heart	Falcons (Savoy)	1953	Savoy 893
You're The Best For Me	Hypnotics	1959	Warkee 905
You're The Cause Of It	Angels (New Jersey)	1967	RCA 9404
You're The Dream	Marvellos	1955	Theron 117
You're The Girl	Pharaohs, Richard Berry & the	1958	Flip 331
You're The Girl For Me	Monterays (Brooklyn)	1958	Rose 109
You're The Guy	Arketts, Argie & the	1961	Ronnie (no number)
You're The One	Down Beats	NA	Dawn 1031
You're The One	Five Keys, Rudy West & the	1961	Seg-Way 1008
You're The One	Goofers	1954	Coral 61305
You're The One	Gum Drops	1958	Decca 30584
You're The One	Mohawks, Popcorn & his	1960	Northern
You're The One	Royal Masters	1962	Guyden 2078
You're The One	Spiders	1953, 1959, 1960	Imperial 5265/5618 /5714
You're The One	Starfires	1961	Bargain 5001
You're The One	Symbols, Marty & the	1963	Graphic Arts 1000
You're The One For Me	Three Honeydrops	1957	Music City 814
You're The One I Care For	Upbeats	1959	Joy 227
You're The One I Love	Federals	1957	Fury 1005
You're The One To Blame	Starlighters	1959	End 1049
You're The Only Girl	Overtones	1967	Ajax
You're The Only Girl, Dolores	Diablos, Nolan Strong & the	1955	Fortune 519
You're The Only One	Nomads	1959	Northern 503
You're The Only One For Me	Hayes, Linda & group	1955	Recorded In Hollywood 1032/ Decca 29644 (55)
You're The Only One For Me	Strollers	1957	Zebra 22
You're The Prettiest One	Classics (Los Angeles)	1959	Crest 1063
You're The Reason	Charts	1957	Everlast 5006/Lost Nite 186 (81)
You're The Reason	Continentals	NA	N/A
You're The Reason	Four Young Men, Bobby Edwards & the	1961	Crest 1075
You're The Right One	Lancers	1963	Lawn 205
You're The Right One	Whirlwinds, Kenny Beau & the	1959	PL 1015
You're Tired Of Love	Gems (Illinois)	1954	Drexel 904
You're To Blame	Fascinators (Brooklyn)	1962	Trans Atlas 688
You're To Blame	Impalos	1961	United Artists 327
You're Too Fast	Calendars	1961	Coed 564
You're Too Young	Octaves	1958	Val 1001
You're Too Young	Sinceres	1960	Jordan 117
You're Too Young For Me	Dreams, Johnny & the	1961	Richie 457
You're Welcome	Dubs	1975	Clifton 5
You're Welcome Back	Sham-Ettes	1967	MGM 13798
You're Welcome To My Heart	Chantels	1966	Verve 10387
You're With It	Classics, Lou Christie & the	1963	Alcar 208
You're Wrong	Du Droppers	1954	Groove (unreleased)
Yours	Dell Vikings	1957, 1973	Luniverse 110/Mercury LP 20314/Mercury EP 3363
Yours	Duprees	1963	Coed LP 906
Yours	Flamingos	1959	End 1055
Yours	Hurricanes	1956	King 4867
Yours	Lourdes	1960	Mercury 71655
Yours Alone	Dell Tones	1953	Brunswick 84015
Yours Alone	Laurels, Bobby Relf & the	1955	Flair 1063
Yours Forever	Dominoes	1952	Federal 12106
Yours Is My Heart Alone	Ex-Tones, Mr. X & the	NA	H.O.B. 1000
Yours To Command	Personalities	1957	Safari 1002
Yours To Possess	Four Pals	1959	Roulette 4127
Yours Truly	Kokomos (with the Four Seasons)	1962	Gone 5134
You've Been Away Too Long	Four Embers	1963	Smash 1846
You've Been Away Too Long	Gypsies	1955	Groove 0129
You've Been Cheatin' On Me	Angloes, Julie Gibson & the	1962	Herald 575
You've Been Cheating	Ko Kos	1957	Combo 141
You've Been Crying	C-Quins	1962	Ditto 501/Chess 1815 (62)
You've Been Fooling Around	Checkers	1954	King 4719
You've Been Going Steady Too Long	Creslyns	1963	Beltone 2036
You've Been Gone	Fabulous Pearl Devines	1959	Alco 101

SONG	GROUP	YEAR	LABEL
You've Been Gone So Long	Cubans (Davie Little Caesar Johnson)	1958	Flash 133
You've Been Good To Everybody	Du Droppers	1954	Unreleased
You've Been Leading Me On	Steinways	1966	Oliver 2002
You've Been Torturing Me	Hollywood Argyles	1961	Paxley 752
You've Been Untrue	Delfonics	1963	Cameo 272
You've Broken My Heart	Velveteens, Terri & the	1962	Kerwood 711
You've Changed	Fourmost	1966	Capitol 5738
You've Changed	Platters	NA	Mercury EP 3343
You've Chosen Me	Moonglows	1971, 1972	Big P 101/RCA 74-0839
You've Discovered Love	Dubs	1961	Unreleased
You've Done It Again	Live Wires, Andy & the	1960	Applause 1249
You've Gone	Mellows, Lillian Lee & the	1956	Candlelight 1011
You've Got A Bull	Whalers, Moby Dick & the	NA	Forest 2009
You've Got A Great Love	Chanteurs	1963	Vee Jay 519 (63)
You've Got Me Losing My Mind	Five Arrows, Gloria Valdez, the Paul Bascomb Orch. & the	1955	Parrot 816
You've Got Me On A String	Markeys	1956	20th Century 1210
You've Got The Magic Touch	Platters	1956	Mercury 70819
You've Got To Live For Yourself	Blue Dots	1954	DeLuxe 6052
You've Got To Rock And Roll	Sunbeams	1957	Acme 109
You've Got What It Takes	Belltones, Ronnie Baker & the	1962	Jell 188
You've Got What It Takes	Satellites, Bobby Long & the	1964	Vegas 700
You've Got Your Troubles	Drifters (1959-forward)	1973	Bell 45,320
You've Lied	Bachelors (Washington, D.C.)	1956	Royal Roost 620
You've Sinned	Solitaires	1956	Old Town 1026 (first pressing)
Yo-Yo Girl	Portraits	1961	RCA 7900
Yoyo Yo Yoyo	Romans, Little Caesar & the	1961	Del-Fi 4177
Yuletide Love	Chanaclairs	1955	Coleman 1056
Yum Yum	Don Juans	1956	Jaguar 3020
Yum Yum	La Salles	1958	Back Beat 515
Yum Yum	Lamplighters	1954	Federal 12197
Yum Yum	Martin, Kenny & group	1958	Federal 12330
Yum Yum	Swinging Earls	1959	Vega 1001
Yum Yum Yum	Cinderellas	1959	Decca 30830
Yum Yummy	Pearls	1956	Atco 6057
Yum-mee, Yum-mee	Four Counts	1958	Josie 840/Go 103
Yuz-A-Ma-Tuz	Pearls	1957	Onyx 511/Relic 521 (64)
Yvonne	Parakeets Quintet, Leroy Williams & the	1956	Atlas 1069
Yvonne	Searchers	1961	Mac 351
Yvonne	Taylor, Adam & group	NA	N/A
Yvonne	Tigers, Al Tigro & the	NA	Cuppy 112

Z

SONG	GROUP	YEAR	LABEL
Zaki Sue	Smith, Melvin (with the Night Riders)	1958	Cameo 135
Zanzee	Hi-Lites (Okeh)	1954	Okeh 7046
Zebra Shoot	Dantes	1964	Courtney 713
Zenda	Keynotes	1955	Apollo 478
Zig Zag	Counts, Bobby Comstock & the	1959	Triumph 602
Zig Zag	Del-Rays, Detroit Jr. & the	1964	C.J. 636
Zig Zag	Diamond, Ronnie & group	1958	Imperial 5554
Ziggus	Five Keys	1959	King 5251
Zimba Lulu	Rays	1959	XYZ 600
Zindy Lou	Chimes (Los Angeles - Specialty)	1955	Specialty 555
Zindy Lou	Devotions	1964	Roulette 4580
Zindy Lou	Mariners	1955	Cadence 1278
Zing Went The Strings Of My Heart	Angels, Gabriel & the	1961	Amy 823
Zing Went The Strings Of My Heart	BQE	1988	Starlight 58
Zing Went The Strings Of My Heart	Chapters, Reuben & the	1979	Surfside 3
Zing Went The Strings Of My Heart	Coasters	1958	Atco 6116
Zing! Went The Strings Of My Heart	Demensions	1960, 1966	Mohawk 120/Coral 65559
Zing! Went The Strings Of My Heart	Furys	1963	Mach IV 112
Zing! Went The Strings Of My Heart	Rubies	1962	TNT 101
Zing! Went The Strings Of My Heart	Satintones	1961	Motown 1020
Zing Went The Strings Of My Heart	Skyliners	1959	Calico LP 3000

SONG	GROUP	YEAR	LABEL
Zing Went The Strings Of My Heart (acappella)	Spaniels	NA	Unreleased
Zing Zang Zoo	G-Clefs	1957	Paris 506
Zing Zing Zing	Dells	1955	Vee Jay 166
Zing Zong	Pitch Pikes	1957	Mercury 71099
Zinga Zingo	Commodores, Darrell Glenn & the	1957	RPM 488
Zip Boom	Supremes (Bronx, N.Y.)	1985	Murray Hill LP 000083
Zip Zip	Diamonds	1957	Mercury 71165
Zip Zip	Jivetones	NA	Apt (unreleased)
Zip-A-Dee Doo Dah	Blue Jeans, Bob B. Soxx & the	1962	Philles 107
Zippety Zip	Empires	1957	Amp-3 132
Zippety Zippety Zoom	Pearls	1956	Onyx 503/Relic 513 (64)
Zippety Zum (I'm In Love)	Chordcats	1954	Cat 109
Zola	Tic Tocs	1957	Back Beat 502
Zombi	Monotones	1958	Argo 5301
Zombie Lou	Johnson Brothers	1959	Valor 2006
Zoom	Cadillacs	1956	Josie 792
Zoom	Connotations, Joel & the	1979	Clifton 33
Zoom	Crescents	1985	Relic LP 5053
Zoom	Cuff Links	1958	Dooto 438
Zoom!	Heartspinners, Dino & the	NA	Robin Hood 141
Zoom	Starlighters	1960	Hi-Q 5016
Zoom	Unique Echos	1961	Southern Sound 108
Zoom (acappella)	Historians, Barbaroso & the	1957	Jade 110
Zoom Boom Zing	Cadillacs	1959	Jubilee LP 1089
Zoom Zoom Zoom	Collegians	1957	Winley 224
Zoom Zoom Zoom	Craftys	1962	Elmor 310
Zoom Zoom Zoom	Dreamlovers	1961	Heritage 107
Zoom Zoom Zoom	Enchords	1961	Laurie 3089
Zoom Zoom Zoom	Hi-Lites (Connecticut)	1962	Dandee LP 206
Zoom Zoom Zoom	Reminiscents	1963	Day 1000
Zoom Zoom Zoom	Schaefer, Freddy & group	1962	King 5621
Zoomy	Bobbettes	1958	Atlantic 1181
Zoop	Charts	1957	Everlast 5001/Everlast 5026 (63)/ Lost Nite 173 (81)
Zoop	Hi-Lites (Connecticut)	1962, 1976	Dandee LP 206/Monogram 122
Zoop	Krantztones	1980	Crystal Ball 140
Zoop Bop (acappella)	Delstars	1964	Mellomood 1001
Zoop Zoop (Darling I Love You)	Keynotes	NA	Apollo LP 1000/ Relic LP 5072 (1000)
Zorro	Silks, Charles McCullough & the	1961	Dooto 462
Zu Zu	Bonnevilles	1960	Munich 103/Barry 104 (62)
Zup Zup (Ooh You Dance So Nice)	Keynotes	1956	Apollo 498
Zu-Zu	Five Discs	1991	0-0-1
Zyzzle	Ping Pongs	1960	United Artists 236

United In Group Harmony Association
Hall of Fame

1991: Cadillacs, Clovers, Harptones, Heartbeats, Orioles, Ravens, Shep & The Limelites, Frankie Lymon & The Teenagers
Honorary Inductees: Delta Rhythm Boys

1992: Channels, Five Keys, Flamingos, Moonglows, Solitaires, Spaniels
Honorary Inductees: Ink Spots

1993: Cardinals, Dominoes, Pre '59 Drifters, Dubs, Larks
Honorary Inductees: Mills Brothers

1994: Dells, Jive Five, Nutmegs, Platters, Swallows
Honorary Inductees: Deep River Boys, Golden Gate Quartet

1995: Chantels, Five Satins, Lee Andrews & Hearts, Mellows, Robins
Honorary Inductees: Swan Silvertones, Dixie Hummingbirds

1996: Castelles, Chords, Dell Vikings, El Dorados, Jesters, Vocaleers
Honorary Inductees: Harmonizing Four

1997: Diablos, Little Anthony & The Imperials, Paragons, Valentines, Velours
Honorary Inductees: Four Vagabonds, Hollywood Flames

1998: Cleftones, Crows, Four Fellows, Penguins, Wrens
Honorary Inductees: Four Buddies, Jubalaires

1999: Dean Barlow & The Crickets, Five Royales, Jacks/Cadets. Mello-Moods, Spiders
Honorary Inductees: Fairfield Four, Four Knights

2000: Calvanes, Crests, Royals/Midnighters, Turbans, Wanderers
Honorary Inductees: Rivileers, Four Tunes

2001: Otis Williams & The Charms, Hurricanes, Johnny Bragg & The Prisonaires

2002: Charioteers, Fi-Tones, Red Caps, Strangers

2003: Cats & The Fiddle, Chanters, Pearl McKinnon & The Kodaks, Schoolboys, Shells, Louis Lymon & The Teenchords

RANK	SONG	GROUP	YEAR	LABEL
1	Golden Teardrops	Flamingos	1953	Chance
2	My Reverie	Larks	1951	Apollo
3	Crazy For You	Heartbeats	1955	Hull
4	A Sunday Kind Of Love	Harptones	1953	Bruce
5	It's Too Soon To Know	Orioles	1948	It's A Natural
6	Share	Teenagers	1956	Gee
7	Most Of All	Moonglows	1955	Chess
8	Wind, The	Diablos	1954	Fortune
9	I'll Never Tell	Harptones	1953	Bruce
10	Closer You Are, The	Channels	1956	Whirlin' Disc
11	Earth Angel	Penguins	1954	Dootone
12	You Gave Me Peace Of Mind	Spaniels	1956	Vee Jay
13	In The Still of the Night	Five Satins	1956	Standord
14	Your Way	Heartbeats	1956	Hull
15	My Saddest Hour	Five Keys	1953	Aladdin
16	A Thousand Miles Away	Heartbeats	1956	Hull
17	Gloria	Cadillacs	1954	Josie
18	Tell Me	Mastertones	1954	Bruce
19	Life Is But A Dream	Harptones	1955	Paradise
20	Please Remember My Heart	Solitaires	1954	Old Town
21	That's The Way It Goes	Harptones	1956	Rama
22	Can't Help Loving That Girl Of Mine	Hide-A-Ways	1956	Ronni
23	Can I Come Over Tonight	Velours	1957	Onyx
24	Sincerely	Moonglows	1954	Chess
25	Could This Be Magic	Dubs	1957	Gone
26	My Vow To You	Students	1958	Note
27	Deserie	Charts	1957	Everlast
28	What'cha Gonna Do	Drifters	1955	Atlantic
29	Dream Of A Lifetime	Flamingos	1954	Parrot
30	My Memories Of You	Harptones	1954	Bruce
31	Teardrops	Hearts, Lee Andrews & the	1957	Argo
32	I Only Have Eyes For You	Flamingos	1959	End
33	Tormented	Heartbeats	1955	Network
34	My Hero	Blue Notes	1960	Val-Ue
35	Shouldn't I Know	Cardinals	1951	Atlantic
36	Dearest	Swallows	1951	King
37	A Kiss And A Rose	Orioles	1949	Jubilee
38	Crying In The Chapel	Orioles	1953	Jubilee
39	Story Untold	Nutmegs	1955	Herald
40	Lilacs In The Rain	Ravens	1951	National
41	Red Sails In The Sunset	Five Keys	1952	Aladdin
42	Secret Love	Moonglows	1954	Chance
43	That's My Desire	Belmonts, Dion & the	1960	Laurie
44	Only The Angels Know	Esquires	1957	Hi-Po
45	Since I Don't Have You	Skyliners	1959	Calico
46	Let's Make Up	Spaniels	1954	Vee Jay
47	Don't Ask Me To Be Lonely	Dubs	1957	Johnson
48	Island Of Love	Sheppards	1959	Apex
49	Night's Curtains	Checkers	1952	King
50	I'll Be Home	Flamingos	1955	Checker
51	Little Did I Dream	Twilighters	1955	MGM
52	Lost Love	Superiors	1957	Atco
53	My Girl Awaits Me	Castelles	1953	Grand
54	God Only Knows	Capris	1954	Gotham
55	You Belong To Me	Duprees	1962	Coed
56	Come Go With Me	Dell Vikings	1956	Fee Bee
57	Oh What A Night	Dells	1956	Vee Jay
58	This Is My Love	Passions	1960	Audicon
59	Tree In The Meadow	Pearls	1956	Onyx

RANK	SONG	GROUP	YEAR	LABEL
60	Wind, The	Jesters	1960	Winley
61	At My Front Door	El Dorados	1955	Vee-Jay
62	Dear Lord	Continentals	1956	Whirlin' Disc
63	I Won't Be The Fool Anymore	Heartbeats	1957	Rama
64	I'm So Young	Students	1958	Note
65	That's My Desire	Channels	1957	Gone
66	These Foolish Things Remind Me Of You	Dominoes	1953	Federal
67	Lovers Never Say Goodbye	Flamingos	1958	End
68	A Simple Prayer	Ravens	1956	Argo
69	Why Don't You Write Me	Jacks	1955	RPM
70	Beat Of Our Hearts, The	Five Blue Notes	1954	Sabre
71	Blue Velvet	Clovers	1955	Atlantic
72	I Was Wrong	Charmers	1954	Timely
73	When I'm With You	Moonglows	1956	Chess
74	I Wonder Why	Belmonts, Dion & the	1958	Laurie
75	Your Promise To Be Mine	Drifters	1956	Atlantic
76	At Night	Orioles	1950	Jubilee
77	My Heart's Desire	Avalons	1958	Unart
78	My True Story	Jive Five	1961	Beltone
79	One Summer Night	Danleers	1958	AMP 3
80	Tears On My Pillow	Imperials, Little Anthony & the	1958	End
81	Angels Sang, The	Solitaires	1956	Old Town
82	Do Something For Me	Dominoes	1950	Federal
83	Moonlight Cocktails	Rivieras	1960	Coed
84	Please Say You Want Me	Schoolboys	1956	Okeh
85	Wonder Why	Solitaires	1954	Old Town
86	Are You Sorry	Whispers	1955	Gotham
87	Chapel Bells	Fascinators	1958	Capitol
88	Eternally	Swallows	1951	King
89	I Was Such A Fool	Flamingos	1959	End
90	Way You Look Tonight, The	Jaguars	1956	Aardell
91	Maybe	Chantels	1957	End
92	Beside You	Swallows	1952	King
93	Doll Face	Vibranaires	1954	After Hours
94	I Don't Stand A Ghost Of A Chance	Solitaires	1955	Old Town
95	A Kiss From Your Lips	Flamingos	1956	Checker
96	My Love Will Never Die	Channels	1958	Fury
97	Why Do Fools Fall in Love	Teenagers	1956	Gee
98	Close Your Eyes	Five Keys	1955	Capitol
99	Gleam In Your Eyes, The	Channels	1956	Whirlin' Disc
100	Maybe You'll Be There	Hearts, Lee Andrews & the	1954	Rainbow